The Cult of the Goddess Pattini

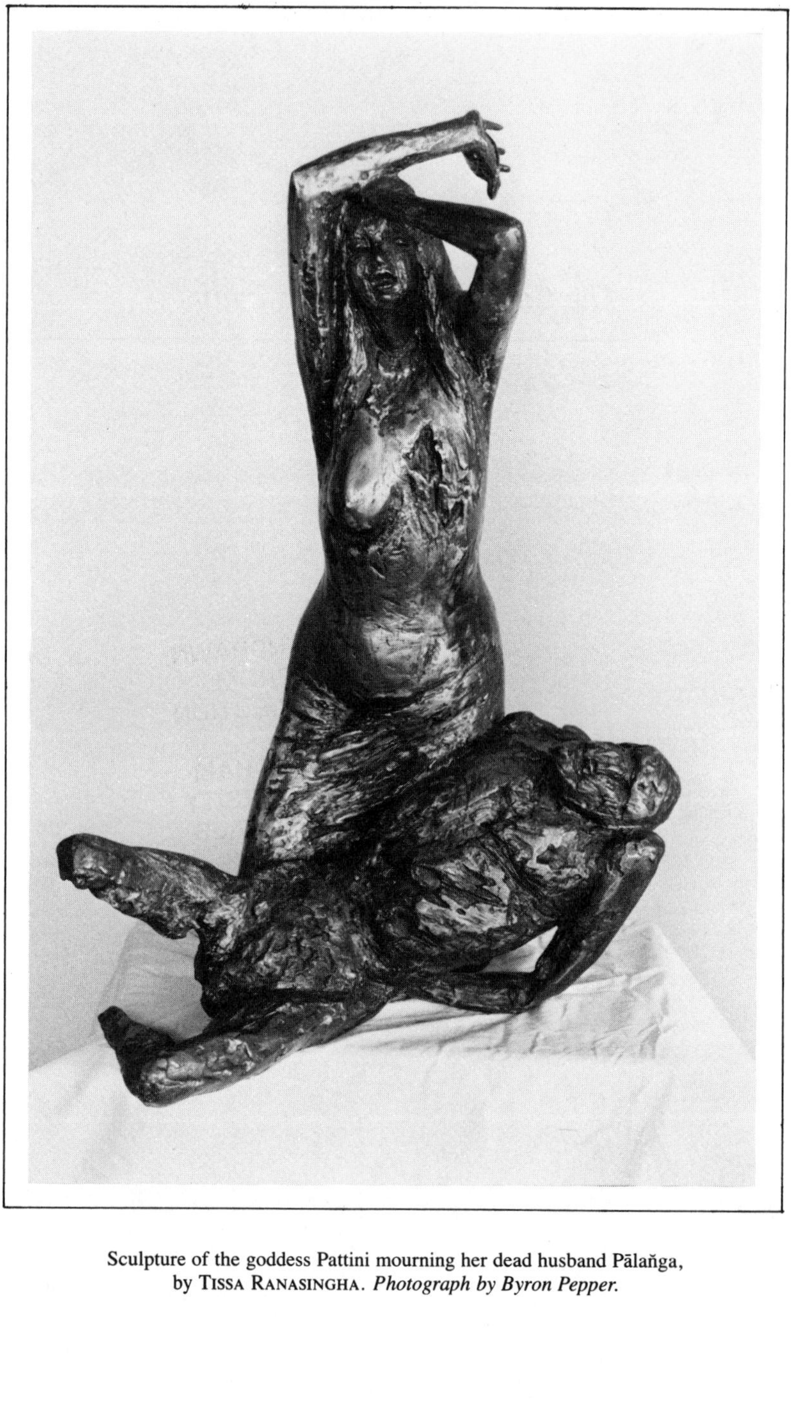

Sculpture of the goddess Pattini mourning her dead husband Pālaňga,
by Tissa Ranasingha. *Photograph by Byron Pepper.*

Gananath
Obeyesekere

The Cult of the Goddess Pattini

The University of Chicago Press

Chicago and London

GANANATH OBEYESEKERE is chairman of the Department of Anthropology at Princeton University. He is the author of *Medusa's Hair*, also published by the University of Chicago Press.

The University of Chicago Press, Chicago 60637
The University of Chicago Press, Ltd., London

Printed in the United States of America
91 90 89 88 87 86 85 84 5 4 3 2 1

Library of Congress Cataloging in Publication Data
Obeyesekere, Gananath.
The cult of the goddess Pattini.

Bibliography: p.
Includes index.
1. Pattini (Hindu deity)—Cult. 2. Pattini (Buddhist deity)—Cult. I. Title.
BL1225.P34023 1984 294.5'51 83-5884
ISBN 0-226-61602-9

For E. F. C. (Lyn) Ludowyk

a gift, long promised

The University of Chicago Press gratefully acknowledges subventions from the National Science Foundation and the Wenner-Gren Foundation for Anthropological Research in partial support of the costs of production of this volume.

Contents

Preface

Completing this manuscript was something of an exorcism. The cult of the goddess Pattini was my first piece of field research, undertaken immediately after I graduated from the University of Sri Lanka in 1955. As an undergraduate at Peradeniya I, like many others of my generation, wondered about my social and personal identity. I had left my own village in early childhood and then lived in Colombo and Kandy. Though I did go back to my village during school vacations, I was really never a part of its social existence. Moreover, my village was a considerably acculturated one, characteristic of parts of the Western and Southern provinces. Inspired by a romantic quest for the really real, I used to wander during university weekends and vacations into remote villages in the North Central Province to collect folk songs and myths. I felt increasingly drawn toward understanding village culture, thereby hoping (futilely, I soon learned) to abolish my own alienation.

After I graduated from the University of Sri Lanka I decided to pursue seriously my interest in Sinhala culture. Inevitably this led me into anthropology. Fortunately for me, I knew nothing of contemporary anthropology and had not heard of people like Radcliffe-Brown, who dominated the field at that time; Malinowski I knew only from his essay on Trobriand language use in Ogden and Richards's *Meaning of Meaning*. As a literature major I had my anthropological education from such unlikely people as T. S. Eliot and W. B. Yeats and via them Frazer, Harrison, and the British anthropological classicists. Fortunately, did I say? Yes, for I had no idea that one was expected to do fieldwork by living in a village for at least a year to study its society and culture in context. I decided that I would study a single cult in a very large area, ignoring local context. Though later on I did much conventional fieldwork, I have grown increasingly sympathetic to the strategy I adopted in my naive years.

Lyn Ludowyk, my teacher, knew of my interests and encouraged me in my quest. He urged me to apply for a Fulbright fellowship to study in the United States and also urged some of his friends to make cash donations for my fieldwork. I gratefully acknowledge the help rendered to a struggling scholar by these people: Sir Ernest Fernando, Mr. H. W. Amarasuriya, H. V. Perera, Q.C., N. E. Weerasooriya, Q.C., Dr. M. V. P. Pieris, and Mrs. K. Mututantri. Ludowyk also found me a job as an unpaid subwarden of one of the residence halls in Peradeniya, which gave me a place to live and eat (whenever I was there). Now I was ready for fieldwork.

I initially thought of studying the Väddas, quite brashly, in their full area spread. An authority on the subject whom I consulted was shocked at the idea: there was no more to know about the Väddas since the Seligmanns had written the final definitive account! Ludowyk then suggested that I study some of the famous low-country exorcistic and other rituals, including the colorful *gammaḍuva* ceremony for the goddess Pattini. Taking his hint, I witnessed a beautiful performance by R. K. D. Yahonis-Pattini, the priest (*kapurāla*) of Rabalīya, who later became my close friend. This was enough; I was hooked on Pattini. I wanted to study the cult wherever it was found, particularly since my early inquiries indicated its impending demise. Armed with a huge Webcor tape recorder, a twelve-volt car battery, and an antediluvian converter (all on loan), I traversed every inch of Buddhist ground in ancient buses and old military trucks graciously left by the British to service remote villages of the island—an anthropological Don Quixote, tilting at who-knows-what. Occasionally T. L. Green, then professor of education at the University of Sri Lanka (Colombo) and a genial companion, took me in his car to watch the Pattini rituals he photographed. Unhappily, Green lost most of his photographs in Sierra Leone. Fortunately Howard Wriggins and his wife Sally, young researchers in Sri Lanka at the time, were present at one of these ceremonies and have preserved some color slides of the crucial ritual of the death of the goddess's consort and his subsequent resurrection by her in the role of *mater dolorosa*. Recently I persuaded the pupils of my friend Yahonis, now deceased, to perform this ritual so I could take some pictures, and they willingly complied. It should be noted, though, that the ritual is moribund, and the last time they had participated in it was when their teacher had performed it more than twenty years before.

I used some of my Pattini data for a master's thesis at the University of Washington in 1958 and later wrote an occasional paper on the subject. The material, however, remained largely untouched. In 1964 Edmund Leach suggested I write up this material, but, though I sometimes went to see Pattini ceremonies when invited by my priest friends, it was not until 1968 that I had the time and motivation to look up my old data. In this year I received a grant from the Foundation's Fund for Research in Psychiatry to study healing rituals. Since the Pattini cult was, among other things, involved in communal healing, I now had an opportunity to get back to fieldwork, studying Pattini rituals as well as exorcistic and healing rituals for individuals in village and urban areas. I now was fully immersed in fieldwork and could soon recite chunks of ritual texts from memory. I was pleased when occasionally one of my priest friends would say, "Now, sir, did you think we did it right?"

All the analytical material except the last two chapters in this book was written in substantially its present form before 1971. As a native speaker of the language, I was able to analyze the voluminous texts of the Pattini cult without actually translating them. The laborious work of translation from tape recordings and written texts took a great deal of time and effort and was completed (in the midst of other work and other commitments) only in 1978. The task of translation received one major setback. As everyone knows, any anthropologist worth his salt must lose his field notes at least once. In 1971 I resigned from the University of Sri Lanka at Peradeniya to join the University of California at San Diego. I carried some of my precious field notes and tape recordings with me on the plane. In San Diego I put some of them in a cardboard box with a note that said "Pattini research," not knowing that a box on the floor with a note scribbled on it meant something else to the university janitor—"throw it away." I lost these, but fortunately I had duplicates of much of the material, and I reconstructed other data during subsequent summer visits to Sri Lanka. Still, some of the psychological interview material was irretrievably lost, and I had no heart to repeat my interviews.

This manuscript was completed in 1978. I have therefore not been able to systematically use some interesting recent research on Indian religion. I especially regret not being able to use Sudhir Kakar's *The Inner World* (1978) in part 5 of this book. I decided to leave these chapters as they were written, since the reader will realize how closely our interpretations of Hindu personality and culture agree, though we argue from different vantage points. Any differences in interpretation should be the subject of future debate and research.

My Pattini research spans the whole of my anthropological career. During this period I have been in debt to many institutions and persons for many things—their generosity, kindness, and help. The following organizations generously supported this research: the Wenner-Gren Foundation for Anthropological Research, the Foundation's Fund for Research in Psychiatry, the Academic Senate of the University of California at San Diego, and most recently the University Committee on Research in the Humanities and Social Sciences of Princeton University. It is not possible to list the names of all the many individuals who helped me in various ways, but I must express my affection and gratitude to my major informants, priests of the Pattini cult: R. K. D. Yahonis (deceased), P. D. Herman Appuhamy (Podi Mahatmaya, deceased), A. Y. Amarasekera, Dharmasiri Rajapakse, Robert de Silva, and Patinayake Pattini Mahatmaya of Ūrubokka. Several colleagues and friends helped me in numerous ways: Sarath Amunugama, Therese Argoud, Sugathapala de Silva, Richard Gombrich, Ian Goonetilleke, Ratna Handurukanda, David McAlpin, Punchi Bandara Meegaskumbura, the late G. C. Mendis, S. R. Perimbanayagam, S. G. Samarasingha, H. L. Seneviratne, Sudharshan Seneviratne, David Shulman, G. P. U. Somaratne, Melford E. Spiro, Amaradasa Virasingha, and Hemapala Wijayawardhana. I record my debt to those Indian scholars who assisted me in my Kerala studies, among them Chummar Choondal, V. T. Induchudan, Gopala Krishnan, Y. Subbarayalu, V. I. Subramonian, Rajan Thomas, and Susan Visvanathan. I must express my gratitude to those friends who helped me in my fieldwork on the east coast of Sri Lanka and in the translation of Tamil texts from that area: Charmaine Alexander, E. Balasundaram, Valentine Daniel, Nadaraja Dharmalingam, K. Kailasapathy, Pandit V. Kandiah, N. Shanmugalingam, and A. S. Rasaratnam. I owe a special debt to Richard Gombrich and Wendy O'Flaherty, who patiently read an enormously long manuscript for the University of Chicago Press and made many important suggestions for revision, and also to my wife Ranjini and to Ernestine McHugh, both of whom read the whole manuscript and, incorporating the suggestions of the Press reviewers, helped me produce this book in its present form. I must especially acknowledge the help rendered by P. B. G. Hevawasam, who assisted me with the translation of old texts that are no longer sung in contemporary rituals, and H. K. J. R. Bandara, who accompanied me on several field trips. And who can forget those who helped to type this manuscript in its various revisions: K. Kumaraswamy, Nandini Gunawardene, Kae Knight, Joyce Krause, June Wilkins, and Padma Karunatilleke, who typed the final version. Last but not least, I am grateful to Lita Osmundsen, who constantly urged me to finish this book. And so, "May they all achieve Nirvāṇa."

Part One

Introduction

Part 1 of this book deals with the sociocultural and historical background of the Pattini cult in Sri Lanka, the dominant village cult in the Western, Southern, and Sabaragamuva provinces. Since 1956 I have studied collective rituals (*gammaḍuva*s) held under the auspices of the goddess through the length and breadth of this region. In particular I have focused on the ritual performances of the following "traditions":

1. Rabalīya (Western Province, Pasdun Kōrale)
2. Heyiaṅtuḍuva (Western Province near Colombo)
3. Ūrubokka (Southern Province, Moravak Kōrale)
4. Sīnigama (Southern Province, near Hikkaḍuva)
5. Mātara (Southern Province)
6. Ratnapura (Sabaragamuva Province)

Through the years I got to know intimately the priests (*kapurāla*s) from the villages and towns listed above. I use the term "tradition" to describe their repertoire of ritual knowledge.

In this work I only briefly refer to the Pattini cult in the Kandy district and other parts of the central highlands. The ritual traditions there are very different from those in the Western, Southern, and Sabaragamuva provinces. The textual tradition of the thirty-five songbooks common to the latter area and the beautiful ritual dramas practiced there are not found in the highlands. I therefore do not deal with the highland traditions at any length, though I may describe them in later publications.

The central shrine of the goddess Pattini is in Navagamuva, near Ruvanvälla in the present-day Sabaragamuva Province. Traditionally Navagamuva was part of Māyāraṭa, along with much of the Western Province (see map, page 00). Today this shrine is an adjunct of a major Buddhist monastery. It is very likely that this monastery was established in recent times by monks occupying the premises of the popular pilgrimage center of the goddess. The rituals and dramas performed in the six traditions mentioned earlier are also performed at Navagamuva during the annual festivities of the shrine. The only special ritual performed at Navagamuva and rarely in village traditions is "water cutting," the significance of which I examine in chapter 1. Moreover, the annual festival at Navagamuva has been thoroughly commercialized in recent times and converted into a large fairground with merry-go-rounds and Ferris wheels. Along with this commercialization, there has been a decline in the integrity of the festival's ritual traditions. Nowadays many persons, mostly women, come to Navagamuva to ask the goddess to vindicate and legitimize their possession, to help transform it from demonic to divine, and to obtain the gift of prophecy—*mukhavaran*, or "mouth boon"—from the goddess. This quest is a radical departure from tradition, and I do not discuss it here.

The culture of the Western, Southern, and Sabaragamuva provinces has been poorly understood by scholars. To better appreciate the significance of this region I shall, in chapter 1, look at Sri Lankan history and culture from a new angle. I shall then describe the nature of the ritual traditions of the Pattini cult and, in chapter 2, present the operative religious pantheon of this vast region.

1

Introducing the Pattini Cult

The goddess Pattini is one of the most popular deities among the Buddhists of Sri Lanka and the Hindus of the east coast of the island. Her life is also the theme of one of the greatest poems in Tamil literature, the *Cilappatikāram*, probably composed during the period A.D. 500–800. This book deals with the cult of this goddess in South India and Sri Lanka. The cult has died out in South India or has been assimilated into the Kālī cult, the Draupadī cult, or other cults of the Indian mother goddess. Thus the analysis of the cult in South India must perforce be an ethnohistorical one.

In this work I am interested not only in the history of the cult but also in its institutionalization. The goddess is an object of worship, and worship must be seen in its sociocultural context.

The worship of the goddess Pattini was most popular in the coastal regions of the Western and Southern provinces and in the Province of Sabaragamuva, which lies in the interior of Sri Lanka adjacent to these two provinces (see map 1). She is also propitiated in the Kandyan region, particularly in and around the main cities of the old Kandyan kingdom—that is, Kandy itself, Mātalē, Haňguraňketa, and Badulla. The goddess is constantly referred to in ritual texts as Pattini of Navagamuva because her main shrine is in a village of that name. This main shrine is a tiny, unimposing structure totally overshadowed by the Buddhist temple that had since been built on the same premises.

The priest of the Pattini cult is known as the *kapurāla*. This term is generally used all over Sri Lanka for any priest propitiating the gods (*dēva*) of the pantheon. In the area under discussion these *kapurāla*s were generally priests of the Pattini cult. To distinguish them from priests of other cults they were sometimes called Pattini Rāla ("Sir Pattini"), or Pattini Mahatmaya ("Mr. Pattini"), Pattini Hāmi ("Sir Pattini or Lady Pattini") or simply Pattini. These priests were found practically everywhere in this region. Some of them had small village shrines, but most *kapurāla*s had no separate shrines. They had at best a separate room, or a special area in their domestic dwelling, where they kept the sacred insignia.

There were two major ritual expressions of the Pattini cult in this region. The most important ceremony performed by the Pattini priests was the *gammaḍuva*, or "hall in the village" (*gam*, "village"; *maḍuva* "shed," "hall"), a cycle of rituals performed as an annual postharvest thanksgiving by a village or village cluster. Sometimes a *gammaḍuva*

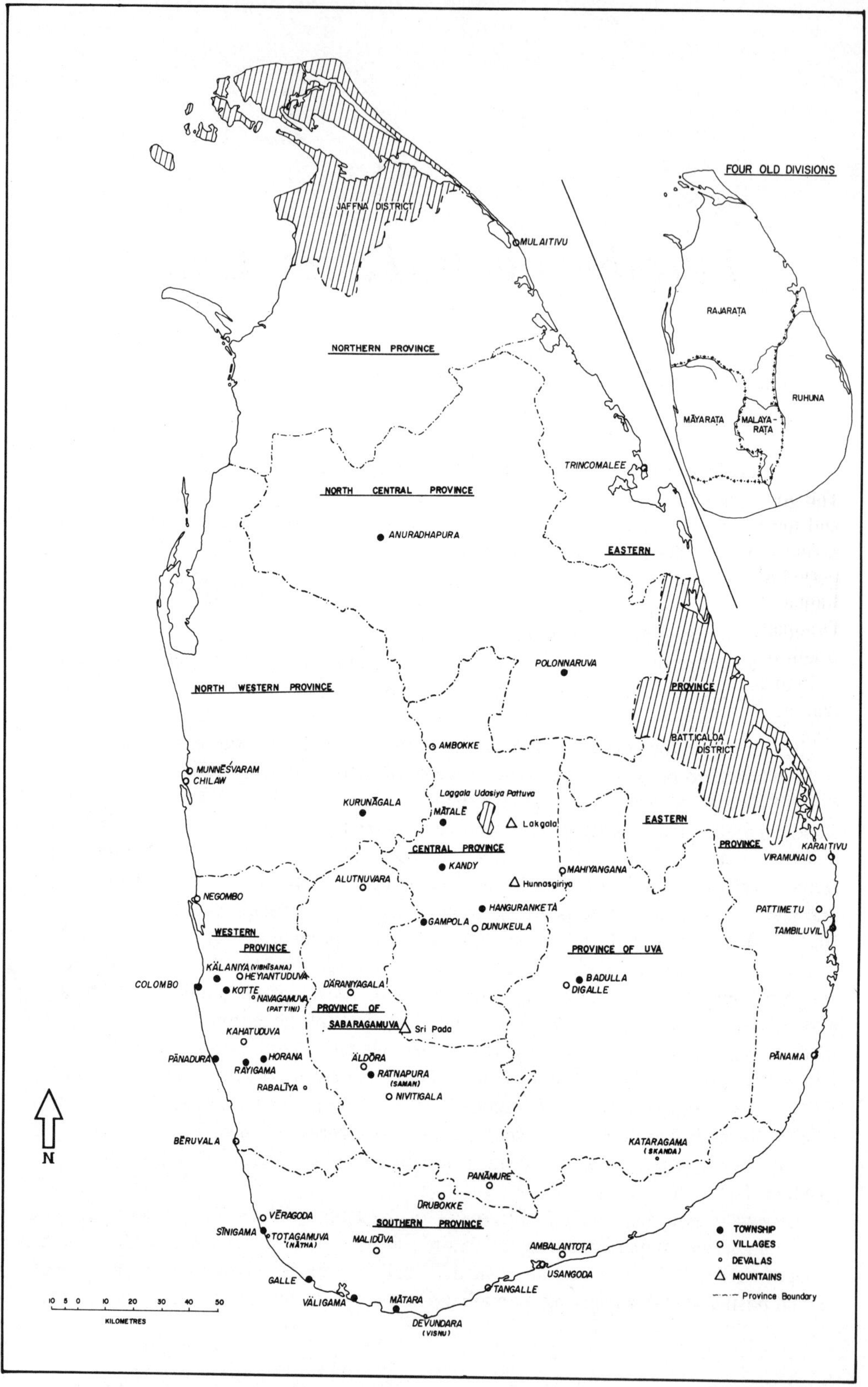
FOUR OLD DIVISIONS
RAJARAṬA
RUHUNA
MĀYARAṬA
MALAYA-RAṬA
JAFFNA DISTRICT
MULAITIVU
NORTHERN PROVINCE
TRINCOMALEE
NORTH CENTRAL PROVINCE
ANURADHAPURA
EASTERN
PROVINCE
POLONNARUVA
NORTH WESTERN PROVINCE
BATTICALOA DISTRICT
AMBOKKE
MUNNĒŚVARAM
CHILAW
Laggala Udasiya Pattuva
KURUNĀGALA
MĀTALĒ
Lakgala
EASTERN
CENTRAL PROVINCE
PROVINCE
KARAITIVU
VIRAMUNAI
KANDY
MAHIYANGANA
ALUTNUVARA
Hunnasgiriya
NEGOMBO
HANGURANKETA
PATTIMETU
GAMPOLA
DUNUKEULA
TAMBILUVIL
WESTERN
PROVINCE
PROVINCE OF UVA
KÄLANIYA (VIBHĪSANA)
HEYIANTUDUVA
COLOMBO
KOTTE
DÄRANIYAGALA
BADULLA
DIGALLE
NAVAGAMUVA (PATTINI)
PROVINCE OF SABARAGAMUVA
Sri Pada
KAHATUDUVA
PĀNADURA
HORANA
RAYIGAMA
ÄLDŌRA
RATNAPURA (SAMAN)
PĀNAMA
RABALĪYA
NIVITIGALA
N
BĒRUVALA
KATARAGAMA (SKANDA)
PANĀMURE
ŪRUBOKKE
VĒRAGODA
SOUTHERN PROVINCE
SĪNIGAMA
TOTAGAMUVA (NĀTHA)
MALIDŪVA
AMBALANTOṬA
USANGODA
GALLE
TANGALLE
VÄLIGAMA
MĀTARA
DEVUNDARA (VISNU)
10 5 0 10 20 30 40 50
KILOMETRES
TOWNSHIP
VILLAGES
DEVALAS
MOUNTAINS
Province Boundary

may be performed when the village is confronted by drought and disease. Smaller, emended versions of the *gammaḍuva* may be performed for individuals or families. Though the term *gammaḍuva* refers to postharvest communal rituals in general, in this region the *gammaḍuva* was associated with the Pattini cult. Elsewhere the *gammaḍuva* may be held under the auspices of other deities. For comparative purposes I also studied the *gammaḍuva* performed in some of the remote areas of the Central Province. Here Pattini had only a formal role; the major operative cult was that of Doḷaha Deviyo, a collectivity of twelve regional gods.

The other important ritual for Pattini was the *aṅkeḷiya* ("horn game"). Unlike the Pattini rituals of the *gammaḍuva*, the *aṅkeḷiya*, at least traditionally, was found almost throughout Sri Lanka—everywhere, in fact, except in much of the North-Central Province and in the Northern Province, which is dominated by orthodox shaivites. In the *gammaḍuva* the major role is played by the priests, who perform the rituals and religious services on behalf of the community. The village is essentially a congregation participating in a service conducted by ritual specialists. By contrast, it is the body of the (male) population that is directly involved in the *aṅkeḷiya*; it is a ritual game in honor of the goddess in which the congregation, or selected members thereof, may participate directly, unmediated by a ritual specialist. During the period of the study *aṅkeḷiya* had practically died out in many parts of Sri Lanka. It is described in detail in part 4 of this book.

The Region in Historical Perspective

The Western, Southern, and Sabaragamuva Provinces

This study focuses primarily on the ritual performances of six traditions in the Sinhala "low country" and in Sabaragamuva: those of Rabalīya, Ḣeyiaṅtuḍuva, Mātara, Sīnigama, Ūrubokka, and Ratnapura (see map, p. 4). The Pattini cult was most popular not in the Kandyan regions but in the Western, Southern, and Sabaragamuva provinces and in the east-coast littoral from Batticaloa to Pānama in the South. The whole coastal belt from Colombo down south and then east up to Pānama constituted the Sinhala Buddhist areas of the Pattini cult; north of Pānama on the east coast were the Tamil Hindu areas, which also propitiated the deity. However, the Sinhala Buddhist (Pānama) and Tamil Hindu areas of the east coast have striking similarities in their rituals and myths that merit separate treatment. By contrast, the Western and Southern provinces (the low country) have a cultural unity. They were also subject to foreign and colonial influences beginning in 1505, the date of the Portuguese arrival. They are areas of high population concentration, economic advancement, and learning. The Buddhist revival movements of the nineteenth century took place in this region. Sabaragamuva Province lies next to these two provinces and was for a long time subject to influences stemming from them. Furthermore, Sabaragamuva was not easily subjected to the rule of the Kandyan king. Ähälēpola, its chief, sided with the British and led the revolt against the last king of Kandy. All the central shrines for the major guardian deities of Sri Lanka are in these three provinces: Viṣṇu at Devundara, Skanda at Kataragama, Nātha at Toṭagamuva, Vibhīṣaṇa at Kälaṇiya, Saman at Ratnapura, and Pattini at Navagamuva. The cultural and social importance of this region was not new, since some of the greatest literary figures of the fifteenth and sixteenth centuries like Śrī Rāhula and Vīdāgama came from here. The literature of the Kōṭṭe period

(1410–1544) and the Mātara period (1750–1850) was all produced here; there was nothing resembling it elsewhere in the nation. Thus the contemporary cultural advancement of the region is a tradition continuing from the past.

The significance of this area has often been misconceived, largely owing to a misunderstanding of historical process. Many scholars think the "true" cultural traditions of Sri Lanka are represented in the Kandyan kingdom, an error arising from the fact that Kandy was the last kingdom to fall to the British in 1815, so that Sinhala Buddhist civilization was concentrated there. In Kandy too was the palace of the tooth relic, the holy of holies in Sri Lanka, lending further weight to the claim that there lay the center of a Sinhala Buddhist civilization.

Nothing could be further from the truth. That the Western and Southern provinces are the most acculturated and least Sinhala Buddhist regions of the country is as much an exaggeration as the view that the Kandyan region was the reverse. Certainly this view is not held by the people in the Western and Southern provinces, who hold themselves to be ultra-Sinhala and Buddhistic. It is also not borne out by a critical examination of Sinhala history. Let me therefore present a reorientation to the history of this region.

The ancient centers of classical Sinhala civilization were in the northern dry zone of the present North Central Province. The earliest center of this civilization was Anurādhapura; later, as a result of attacks from South Indian invaders, it was moved to Polonnaruva. Under Parākramabāhu I (1153–86) Polonnaruva became one of the great cities of South Asia, but its glory was short-lived. The great hydraulic networks of the dry zone were vulnerable to the attacks of invaders. One of the most dreaded of these was Māgha of Kāliṅga, who in 1214 invaded Sri Lanka with a huge mercenary army and devastated the Rajaraṭa (the royal country). Thus the thirteenth century saw the movement to the southwest, first Daṁbadeṇiya, then Yāpahuva, then Gampola, and finally Kōṭṭe in the Western Province in the fifteenth century. When the Portuguese landed in 1505 Kōṭṭe was the capital of the Sinhala kings. The king of Kōṭṭe had nominal suzerainty over the whole island but effective control over only the west and southwest.

The king of Kōṭṭe, Vijayabāhu (1513–21), was murdered by his three sons, who divided the kingdom among themselves. The eldest, Bhuvanekabāhu, ruled from Kōṭṭe, while Māyādunne ruled from the principality of Sītāvaka and his brother from Rayigama. After the latter's death Rayigama was annexed by Māyādunne. Bhuvanekabāhu's son, Dharmapāla, became a Catholic and ceded his kingdom to the Portuguese. Then the locus of kingship and Sinhala nationalism moved to Sītāvaka under the intrepid leadership of Māyādunne's son Rājasiṃha I (1581–93). It should be noted that the effective territories of the kings of Kōṭṭe and Sītāvaka were all in the present Western, Southern, and (to a lesser extent) Sabaragamuva provinces. These kings claimed to be, and were accepted as, heirs to the ancient and continuing tradition of Sinhala kingship.

Where does Kandy come into all this? Kandy was founded by Sēnāsammata Vikramabāhu (1474–1511), who broke away from the Kōṭṭe dynasty. The title Sēnāsammata ("elected by the army") suggests that he may originally have been an army commander. The internal troubles of Kōṭṭe and Sītāvaka, and later the external conflicts of Māyādunne and Rājasiṃha with the Portuguese, helped preserve the integrity of the Kandyan kingdom. This dynasty came to an end when Konappu Baṇḍāra, a Sinhala mercenary in charge of a Portuguese expeditionary force to Kandy, proclaimed himself its king. He routed his erstwhile allies the Portuguese and ascended the throne as Vimala Dharṁa Sūriya I (1591–1604) after marrying the daughter of the previous king. In 1593, Rājasiṃha I of Sitāvaka died, and his extensive kingdom broke up. Some of it was annexed by the Portuguese and the rest by the king of Kandy. After this the king of Kandy became the sole heir to Sinhala kingship.

From the seventeenth century on most of the Western, Southern, and Sabaragamuva provinces was under the nominal control of foreign powers: the Portuguese, Dutch, and British. Effective control of these regions was highly variable and was probably confined to a narrow coastal belt until 1815, when the British annexed Kandy and soon established full control over the island. Until then most Sinhala people looked to Kandy as the seat of Sinhala sovereignty and considered its king their sovereign in reality. This was not a fiction; in 1761 the king of Kandy granted land to the famous monastery at Mulkirigala in the South in what was formally Dutch territory.

The greatest of the Kandyan kings was Rājasiṃha II (1635–87). With the death of his grandson in 1739 the old dynasty of Sinhala kings came to an end. A youth from Madurai, the brother of the queen, inherited the throne. This event is erroneously interpreted by historians as a case of matrilineal inheritance, which it clearly was not. It was more likely one of political strategy; the line of kingship from now onward was with the Nāyakkars of Madurai. The court became highly Hinduized, and a Nāyakkar Hindu elite began to dominate the cultural and political life of Kandy. One should remember, however, that the Nāyakkar kings became Buddhists, and some were patrons of Sinhala Buddhist learning and culture.

Let us now compare the Western and Southern provinces with the Kandyan provinces for continuity of Sinhala Buddhist cultural values. A superficial look at Sinhala history may lead to the view that with the collapse of the classical civilization and the movement to the southwest there was a discontinuity in Sinhala Buddhist civilization, but this was certainly not the case. In classical times the three major divisions of the kingdom were Rajaraṭa (or Pihiṭi raṭa), the center of civilization in the North Central Province; Ruhuna, in the very south, which was extended at times to the Kalu Gaṅga in the Western Province; and Māyāraṭa, which constituted much of the modern Western Province. The fourth region, Malayaraṭa, was forested and desolate hill country and was practically ignored in ancient classification.

Ruhuṇa was not an outpost; it also was the center of a large and prosperous hydraulic civilization, particularly its dry southeastern zone. The prince of Ruhuṇa was sometimes the heir apparent to the throne. Furthermore, when the Rajaraṭa was under attack by South Indian invaders, Ruhuṇa became the center of resistance and the rallying ground for Sinhala forces. Thus three of Sri Lanka's great kings mounted their attack against the Tamils from Ruhuṇa: Duṭugämuṇu (161–137 B.C.), Valagambā (89–77 B.C.), and Vijayabāhu I (A.D. 1055–1110). Another striking feature about Ruhuna was that it was never devastated by South Indian invasions and could thereby preserve a great deal of cultural identity and continuity. This does not mean there were no serious setbacks to Ruhuṇa civilization. The traditional center of Ruhuṇa civilization was the southeastern section of the island, the southern dry zone that duplicated the hydraulic civilization of the North. In later times the locus of Ruhuṇa civilization also moved farther west. Thus the movement to the western wet zone was true not only of the Rajaraṭa, but also of Ruhuṇa. This other factor has not been recognized by scholars, who have dealt with "the collapse of the Rajaraṭa civilization in Ceylon and the drift to the south-west" (Roberts 1971). The common explanation for the drift to the southwest is that it was due to the collapse of the complicated administrative machinery of the hydraulic civilization of the Rajaraṭa (Murphey 1957) or to the forced uprooting of the traditional peasantry from these areas by Māgha (Paranavitana 1960a). More recently Indrapala's view of the occupation of the northern peninsula by an independent and hostile Tamil ruler (Indrapala 1971, pp. 236–62) has gained currency.

None of these explanations seems plausible, though they were perhaps ancillary factors. Indrapala himself says that the Rajaraṭa suffered serious setbacks before Māgha, yet managed to recover. A post-Māgha recovery is a realistic possibility. However, I find Indrapala's own argument equally implausible. If there was a hostile Hindu kingdom in Jaffna, there was all the more reason to reestablish Rajaraṭa, since campaigns could be better conducted from there than from the southwest. That the region had transplanted immigrants from Kerala and Tamil Nāṭu had never been an insurmountable problem, since such patterns of immigration were a common feature of Sri Lankan history. There were many mechanisms for integrating South Indian settlers into the Sinhala social structure (see chap. 8). The major cause for the decline of *both* Rajaraṭa and Ruhuṇa has to be sought elsewhere—in the most powerful of social motivations, the economic imperative.

The collapse of the northern dry zone civilization after Māgha was at best a necessary condition for the abandonment of Rajaraṭa, but it was not a sufficient one. There is no doubt that the invasion of Māgha was socially disastrous and demoralizing for the Sinhalas, but the viability of the civilizations that were established later in the south and west indicates that the kings could have staged a comeback had they wanted to do so. But there was a lure that prevented them and impelled them to the western coast—trade. By the thirteenth century the ports of the Western and Southern provinces from Väligama in the southeast to Colombo, and perhaps even farther north to Chilaw and Kalpiṭiya, had come into prominence, particularly with the advent of Arab traders. It is the control of the lucrative source of income that produced a movement to the wet zone from *both directions*, from Rajaraṭa as well as Ruhuṇa.

The Māyāraṭa consisting of the present-day Western Province, parts of Sabaragamuva, and the North-Western Province was in classical times known as Dakkhiṇadēśa ("southern district"). This region was not as important a civilization as Ruhuṇa, but it was not an isolated wilderness. It was almost totally neglected by the Mahāvaṃsa chronicles, more so than the Ruhuṇa civilization. Furthermore, its geography and its excessive rainfall did not permit the development of a hydraulic civilization on the classical model. The lush tropical environment also perhaps accounted for the virtual absence of monumental archaeological remains.

The province comes into prominence only after the eleventh century A.D., probably with the development of foreign trade. Nevertheless it was not terra incognita. Kälaṇiya with its temple was obviously an important city even in the time of Duṭugämuṇu. Geiger states that from the sixth century onward Dakkhiṇadēśa (i.e., southern region or Māyāraṭa) became for many centuries the regular domain of the heir to the throne. "This was, no doubt, a great advantage for the cultural development of the region" (Geiger 1960, p. 10). Thus my overall argument: the movement to the southwest after the thirteenth century did not imply any real discontinuity in Sinhala civilization, as many historians claim. It simply meant that the old Dakkhiṇadēśa took on a new prominence: after the thirteenth century the capitals of the Sinhala kings were established there, and it was there that the Sinhala Buddhist civilization continued to flourish. The actual shift from Daṁbadeṇiya to Yāpahuva and then to Kōṭṭe was due to the economic factors discussed earlier.

The central highlands of Kandy are another story. Geiger describes the situation well: "According to the Mahāvaṃsa, Malaya was still a wilderness in the 12th century. It was difficult to penetrate owing to the mountains and danger from wild animals and was shut off from intercourse with other men being traversed only by footpaths. . . . Malaya therefore was often the refuge of criminals" (Geiger 1960, p. 3). Mātalē, now part of the Central Province, was really the southern extremity of the northern kingdom. The core of the later Kandyan kingdom—the Kande uḍa pas raṭa—was probably totally outside the pale of the Sinhala Buddhist civilization. This, as well as a large part of Sabaragamuva, probably consisted of isolated villages and tribal groups of Väddas. In other words, the court culture that was initially brought to Kandy was from Kōṭṭe, an external influence. When Kandyan sovereignty passed to the Nāyakkar kings there developed a powerful South Indian Hindu cultural influence in the court and capital. Thus Kandyan civilization was not an old continuing tradition; it was a relatively new phenomenon with a heavy overlay of later South Indian influence. For example, the part of the *Cūlavaṃsa* compiled in Kandyan times in the reign of Śrī Vijaya Rājasiṃha (1739–47) mentions the sixteen great places of pilgrimage, but not one of these was in the Kandyan kingdom (*Cūlavaṃsa* 1929, 2:284–5).

The Central Province: Kandyan Kingdom

Kandy, the capital of the Kandyan kingdom (1474–1815) is here; today's Central Province is the region that was directly influenced by Kandyan civilization. The institutionalization of the Pattini cult here is more problematic than elsewhere. On the formal level the goddess, here as elsewhere, is viewed as one of the major deities in the pantheon. She is central to the official state cultus of the Kandyan kingdom. In the city of Kandy there are four shrines dedicated to Viṣṇu, Nātha, Skanda (Kataragama), and Pattini, collectively known as the *hatara dēvāle* ("the four shrines"), situated around the great palace of the tooth relic (*daḷadā māligāva*). The deities of the four shrines were paraded annually at the great state procession of the relic. Thus it is clear that the goddess Pattini was one of the patron deities of the Kandyan kingdom, and her worship was part of the official state cultus. There were several other important shrines to Pattini in the regions ritually connected to the central shrine in Kandy. Most important of these are the Pattini shrines in Haṅguraṅketa and in Aṅbokka near Mātalē. There were also several other minor shrines, most of them in the area around Mātalē and Badulla. It should be noted that both Mātalē and Haṅguraṅketa were important cities of the Kandyan kingdom.

On the level of village worship, however, the picture is radically different. Here Pattini is formally recognized as a major deity, but village thanksgiving rituals are directed to local and regional deities. Two such ceremonies were operative in the Kandyan area. First, the *kohom̆bā kaṅkāriya*, where a collectivity of deities, Kohom̆bā Deviyo, (also known as *yakku*) and the Doḷaha Deviyo (Twelve Gods) were propitiated. Second, the *gammaḍuva* where the Doḷaha Deviyo were propitiated, as in the Haṅguraṅketa region. Sometimes the Doḷaha Deviyo were propitiated in a ritual known as *aḍukku*, as in the Laggala area. Thus it seems that the goddess Pattini was part of the state cultus; she was *formally* propitiated elsewhere. But the operative folk religion was the cult of local and regional deities, especially the Doḷaha Deviyo. Here Pattini's position was taken by Kiri

Amma ("milk mother"), one of the Doḷaha Deviyo. However, it should be noted that the *aṅkeḷiya* ritual for Pattini was traditionally held everywhere in the Central Province. It is very likely that this was a ritual older than the Pattini cult that was later incorporated into it.

In the Pattini shrines noted earlier several types of ritual activities take place:

1. In the central Pattini shrine at Kandy nowadays daily services to the goddess are performed by the priests. It is likely that traditionally these services were held on Wednesdays and Saturdays known as *kemmura* days, which are specially allocated for the propitiation of deities. Villagers in the outlying regions may also visit this shrine for the fulfillment of vows. This is also true of the shrine at Haňguraṅketa. In both places Pattini is paraded in the annual state procession following the three major male gods of the pantheon, thus: Nātha, Viṣṇu, Kataragama, and finally Pattini.

2. In the minor shrines there are no daily rituals. I am familiar with three shrines in the Mātalē district: Uḍupihilla, Paḍuviṭa, and Aṅbokka. These shrines are officially open once a year, during the annual festival of the shrine. Otherwise the temple doors are opened when an individual wants to make a vow (*bāra*) or offer a special *pūjā* to the goddess. Aṅbokka is the largest of the three shrines and is linked to the central complex in Kandy through its lay trustee, the Basnāyaka Nilame, who represents Aṅbokka in the annual parade of the palace of the tooth relic. The annual rituals of Aṅbokka are also highly elaborate, modeled on the processional and ritual events in the major Pattini shrine in Kandy.

The Priest of the Pattini Cult

Kapurāla is the general term employed for priests of the *dēva* cults. The *kapurāla* stands opposed to the *bhikkhu*, the Buddhist monk. *Kapurāla*s are laymen vis-à-vis Buddhism, inasmuch as the gods are also viewed as part of the larger Buddhist lay order. The relationship between monk and *kapurāla* has been described elsewhere (Yalman 1964). Here it is enough to state that the monk in theory, and almost always in practice, never participates in or even witnesses performances of the *dēva* (and demonic) cults. The only exception to this is where a Pattini ritual (*gammaḍuva*) may be performed in a Buddhist temple, as in Navagamuva, Palātoṭa, and Kahatuḍuva. Navagamuva is the central shrine of the goddess Pattini, but a Buddhist temple subsequently was built in the shrine premises. I suspect that the same is true in Palātoṭa. Kahatuḍuva is the village of Yahōnis, one of the most respected *kapurāla*s in the region. The *gammaḍuva* ritual within the temple was his innovation. This is not heretical, since Pattini is par excellence a virtuous Buddhist deity, though the idea of "secular" (from the Buddhist viewpoint) music and dancing within the temple premises is unusual for the Sinhala low country.

The term *kapurāla* is exclusively used for the *dēva* priest in the culture area under consideration. The priest of the demon cults is known as *kaṭṭaḍirāla*. The *kapurāla* is recruited from the *goyigama* (farmer) caste, and on the western seaboard from the castes dominant in that region, the *salāgama* (cinnamon peelers) and *karāva* (fishermen). Yet outside this culture area the *kapurāla* role may be less specialized, so that in Laggala (a remote region in the Central Province) a *kapurāla* is the priest of both *dēva* and demon cults. The term *ädura* (teacher) is also used for both classes of priest; and in some areas the term *anumätirāla* is used. However, in the low country the term *kapurāla* almost invariably referred to the priest of the Pattini cult. There were *kapurāla*s of other cults like that of Maṅgara, but they were relatively few. Almost all priests of the cult today are males, though I know of two *kapuamma*, or Pattiniamma (*amma*, "mother"), in Uḍupihilla near Mātalē (in 1958) and in Kurunāgala. In the low country I witnessed one ritual in 1956 where the *kapurāla* had his young daughter dance in the *gammaḍuva*. There is, however, considerable historical evidence from the nineteenth century that there were female Pattinis in the Sinhala low country, particularly in the Western Province (Pieris 1914, p. 467).

I believe these female Pattini priests had a subsidiary role in the rituals, either as dancers or, more likely, as attendants of the goddess. For example, even today in the procession of the palace of the tooth relic in Kandy the insignia of the goddess Pattini are carried in a palanquin attended by four females carrying fly whisks; in Kataragama female attendants serve Valli Amma, Skanda's mistress. The role of priestess was analogous to that of assistant or junior *kapurāla* in the present-day *gammaḍuva* ceremonies. The crucial ritual act of carrying the sacred anklets of the deity on the head of the priest has always been the duty of the chief *kapurāla*, or a senior *kapurāla*, who must be male.

There are religious and psychological reasons for excluding females from the priestly role. The goddess Pattini is a female, but unlike a human female she is devoid of polluting attributes. Given the cultural view of females as ritually inferior and liable to regular menstrual impurity, it would be inappropriate for them to handle the sacred insignia of the goddess. Sociologically, Pattini worship is male oriented; women are excluded from some of the most important rituals. Furthermore, there are also good psychological reasons, I shall show later, for the strong male orientation of the Pattini cult.

All the senior *kapurāla*s in the six ritual traditions studied here are themselves members of priestly families. In addition, practically all the senior *kapurāla*s I know in this region are closely related by blood or marriage to other senior *kapurāla*s. In general a novice is connected to several priestly families through a network of kinship and affinal ties. Priestly families tend to contract marriages among themselves. However, there is no clear-cut pattern when we deal with junior and assistant *kapurāla*s: they are invariably recruited from "outside." The reason is simple: not one of the senior *kapurāla*s I interviewed has sons or nephews in training; all are either employed in government or business or are in college or high school. Not one *kapurāla* felt that the priest role was desirable for his sons or nephews. In the generation of their fathers the village *kapurāla* was a high-status position; in the generation of their sons white-collar employment is the ideal. Thus, recent recruitment to the *kapurāla* role has had to be from the low-status members of the village community.

Although recruitment was traditionally from priestly families, it was by no means strictly hereditary. In theory recruitment was open; in fact, it was open only to close kinsmen. However, strict hereditary entitlement did not obtain; the choice of a son or nephew was often based on ability, lack of alternative employment, a strong affective relationship between priest and prospective novice, or other situational factors. In general, a son "chosen" by his father is apprenticed not to his father, but to a mother's brother, actual or classificatory, a distant kinsman, or even an outsider. This is due to the formal relationship between father and son that inhibits learning, as against the intimate one between mother's brother and sister's son, a characteristic feature of the society.

In general novices start their training in early adolescence by assisting a senior *kapu-*

rāla. During his apprenticeship a novice learns the ritual techniques and the ritual songs and singing styles. Dancing ability is not a role requirement. I know of senior *kapurāla*s who officiate in the rituals but do not dance or even sing the ritual songs. It is possible to have professional dancers and singers for these tasks, though it is considered desirable for a *kapurāla* to possess all these skills. In addition, a novice may be apprenticed to an accomplished dancer to be trained in low-country dance styles. Sometimes the dance teacher may himself be a professional *kapurāla*, or he may be a professional dancer from the drummer or *olī* (dancer) caste. Drumming is left to members of the drummer caste, since it is a caste-associated activity of "inferior" status.

The crucial event in the life of the novice is the installation ceremony. Everywhere the event that converts the novice into a *kapurāla* is the placing of the anklets on his head by the chief or senior *kapurāla*. This act legitimates him in the *kapurāla* role and entitles him to practice his profession without fear of *vas* (ritual danger). Sometimes the chief *kapurāla* simply places the sacred anklets on the head of the novice during a *gammaḍuva* ceremony. An account of an installation of a Pattini priest written by Johnston in 1802 is only slightly more elaborate (Pieris 1950, p. 698). Often, however, a special *gammaḍuva* ceremony known as *kalaeliya* ("debut," "installation") may be held for the novice. In Mātara the novice is given a printed certificate by the chief *kapurāla* of the Devundara Viṣṇu *dēvāle*.

In 1956 some senior *kapurāla*s had their own shrines. These were of two types. The most common shrine was a little building on the premises of the priest's own house. Other priests were affiliated with famous Pattini shrines, like the central shrine at Navagamuva, or lesser-known ones like the Pattini shrine at Ratnapura. The general features of such shrines or *dēvāle*s are the same everywhere irrespective of the deity propitiated. Bell describes them well:

> The main building of a dēvālē consists of the dig-gē, or ante room; māligāva or sanctum in which the insignia are kept, with an upper room occasionally called uḍumahalgē. Food for the dēvālē is cooked in the mulutengē, or kitchen, and there is generally a gabaḍāgē or storeroom and the riṭṭāgē, or halting place, for the sacred abarana during procession. Sometimes as at Alutnuvara, all these rooms are under one range, but ordinarily the mulutengē and gabaḍāgē of the smaller dēvālēs are detached compartments. At all dēvālēs of any importance there is a circular procession path (vīdiya: piṭa-maga), and sometimes two, outer and inner. (Bell 1892, p. 19)

Occasionally (e.g., Heyiaṅtuḍuva) a Pattini shrine was affiliated with a Buddhist temple. In two cases the priest was affiliated with a shrine of another deity. Thus, the *kapurāla* of Sīnigama was the incumbent of the shrine for Devol Deviyo there; and Amarasekera of Hittäṭiya (Mātara) was affiliated with the Viṣṇu shrine at Devundara. Yet both were primarily priests of the Pattini cult. While some senior *kapurāla*s had shrines of some sort, there were many who did not. Most *kapurāla*s had no separate shrine at all. The *kapurāla* at Ūrubokka was typical of these priests. He stored his ritual paraphernalia in a box in his attic and brought it out when his services were required. My interviews with senior *kapurāla*s suggest that this practice was the dominant pattern before the twentieth century. The implication is that there were more priestly traditions than indicated by the number of shrines in the region.[1]

1. There is no systematic survey of shrines or *dēvāle*s for this region, though a tentative distribution could be mapped from old administrative reports and gazetteers. For example, H. C. P. Bell's *Report on the Kegalle*

I shall use the term "traditional *kapurāla*" to designate those priests who participate in the established religion of the Pattini cult, to distinguish them from recent *kapurāla*s who have emerged all over urban Sri Lanka. These new priests, whom I have discussed elsewhere, do not practice the rituals of the *gammaḍuva* (Obeyesekere 1978); they have little knowledge of the old rituals and myths. Their knowledge is derived from inspiration, through mediumistic possession by deities, including Pattini. When I commenced my research in 1956 there were only a few of the new *kapurāla*s around: today they are ubiquitous in urban Sri Lanka and are fast displacing the traditional priests of the Pattini cult.

In this work the term "chief *kapurāla*" refers to the priest who, in any specific ceremony, carries the holy insignia, the anklets of the goddess; senior *kapurāla*s are all priests who are entitled to carry the insignia, while assistant *kapurāla*s are priests in training, or junior priests not yet formally installed. In any ritual there may be more than one senior *kapurāla*, but one acts as chief.

The *Kapurāla*: Priest or Shaman?

The formal distinction that anthropologists often make between the statuses of shaman and priest does not obtain in Sinhala classification. The general term everywhere for priest of the *dēva* cults is *kapurāla*. However, the *kapurāla* role as it is performed in some parts of the country may involve mediumistic possession. Thus, the Seligmanns describe the Vädda *kapurāla*s as shamans. In some parts of the country—in Hañguranketa and Laggala, for example—possession, trance, and mediumship are desirable and viewed as essential for the *kapurāla* role. In collective rituals in Hañguranketa and Laggala the *kapurāla* goes into a trance state in which he utters prophecies to individuals who consult him and predicts what the coming year holds for the group. By contrast in the low country, as well as in the main Pattini shrines in the area around Kandy, possession trance is not a cult requirement. I have come across only one case of public prophecy in the *gammaḍuva*. Possession trance is viewed as a valued attribute of a *kaṭṭaḍirāla*, the priest of the demon cults, since often his cult requires possession. But senior *kapurāla*s of the Pattini cult look askance at possession trance. Indeed, there is one ritual sequence (the Vāhala dance, pp. 138–39) in the *gammaḍuva* where a trancelike experience is involved. This sequence is not performed by the chief *kapurāla* but is invariably given over to a younger member of the team.

Sinhala culture everywhere has a clear theory of demon possession. Demons can possess individuals, who then may go into "trance"; such individuals may be cured by a priest who exorcises the spirit by performing a shaman role. In the Sinhala low country it is difficult to extend this theory to the higher gods, given Sinhala Buddhist cultural beliefs. Gods are pure beings; they could not reside in the impure human body. Furthermore, the cultural theory is that these major gods are future Buddhas; thus possession by such noble spiritual beings would be tantamount to heresy. Hence the inescapable conclusion: the more "Buddhist" the area the less likely it is to have a theory of possession by divine beings. Consequently it is less likely in the three provinces under discussion for the *kapurāla* to perform the shaman role. This is confirmed by the information supplied to

---

District of the Province of Sabaragamuva has recorded the distribution of *dēvāle*s for a single district. Bell says that most of the *dēvāle*s in this region are Pattini shrines; there are two or three for Kataragama, one for Nātha, one for Saman, and one for the regional deity of the area, Dēvatā Baṇḍāra at Alutnuvara, plus diverse small shrines for minor deities like Kande Deviyo (Bell 1892, p. 18).

Johnston by *kapurālas* and Buddhist monks in Pānadura, Western Province, in 1802. A senior *kapurāla* from the Pānadura Pattini *dēvāle* stated that a good *kapurāla* will not become possessed. Possession occurs, he said, only in inferior shrines known as *alli*. A similar view was expressed by a Buddhist monk, Rēvata Terunnānse of Patahavatta: "The inspiring of the Cappoas is entirely an imposture for none of the Cappoas in Candy became inspired . . . it is strictly prohibited by the King of Candy" (Quoted in Pieris 1950, p. 698).

By contrast, in Vädda country the operative pantheon consists of deified ancestors, who are significantly called *yakku*, the Sinhala plural for demons. In Haňguraṅketa and Laggala as well as in other remote parts of the country the major gods are only formally propitiated; the operative pantheon consists of deities whose attributes are compounded of both the demonic and the divine. Shamanic possession by these local deities is therefore possible and desirable according to cultural theory. Yet even in these areas no traditional *kapurāla* ever claims to be possessed by the great national deities, namely, Viṣṇu, Skanda, Pattini, Nātha, or Saman.

There is one standard ritual in the *gammaḍuva* where an idea similar to possession prevails. This is the crucial episode when the *kapurāla* wears female clothes and carries the insignia of the deity. During this event the *kapurāla*'s body may sometimes tremble. This trembling of the body is different from the vigorous head and trunk shaking characteristic of shamanic possession elsewhere. These physical differences have cultural meaning: the body tremors are due to the contact with the sacred insignia that contain the essence (*diṣṭi*) of the goddess. The priest is infused with this essence, resulting in a change in his physical and ritual condition. This state is known as *ākarṣaṇa*: magnetism. Possession is "*āveśa*," "*ārūḍha*," being "mounted," or "alighted on"; there the human being is the vehicle for the deity. *Ākarṣaṇa* is a "charge" that "electrifies" or "magnetizes" the body. The priest is ritually transformed and qualified to act as the instrument of the goddess. In all of my research I knew of only one senior *kapurāla* in our region who acted as if possessed, that is, with violent body shaking. But even he maintained the theory of *ākarṣaṇa* and denied *ārūḍha*, or possession.

Impurity and Pollution

The *kapurāla* officiates in services for the *dēvas*, who in Sinhala belief (derived from Hindu sources) are viewed as pure beings. The goddess Pattini is par excellence the exemplar of purity, chastity, and virginity. Thus the *kapurāla*, although a member of village society, is expected to adopt a style of life different from that of ordinary Sinhala Buddhist villagers. His model is based on the Hindu concept of purity. All *kapurālas* assert that they must lead a life of purity, which they all recognize entails a vegetarian diet, abstinence from alcohol, and rigid avoidance of pollution. In reality, however, only a few traditional *kapurālas* have ever subscribed to this dietary ideal. Here is a situation where the ideal has to be accommodated to the practical realities of Sinhala Buddhist village society, which has never had a tradition of vegetarianism. In contemporary village life all types of meat are eaten, including beef, though traditionally beef was considered a base food and was probably not consumed. Thus, among the senior and junior *kapuralās* of the six traditions (numbering well over thirty) only one (the chief of the Rabalīya tradition) was a teetotaler and vegetarian. Everyone recognized that during the period of the ceremony all persons—villagers and priests—should abstain from sexual intercourse, meat eating, and alcohol. In reality it is likely that ordinary villagers were more given to these observances than the priests. Most priests drank alcohol during the ceremony; it helped them perform the strenuous dances, they claimed. The only person to avoid alcohol was the priest who had to carry the insignia of the deity. Very often the organizers of the *gammaḍuva* did not cook anything but vegetarian foods, but on rare occasions even this was ignored, and fresh and dried fish was served to participants and priests, though never to the gods. The prohibition on intercourse is a technicality easily observed, since these rituals rarely last more than thirty-six hours, during which time the priests are actively participating in the rituals. The chief priest is expected to, and probably does, abstain from intercourse for a longer period—generally twenty-four hours before the ceremony.

The contradiction between ideal and reality is resolved by a neat "theory" (one might say) common to the whole region. This theory is that some meats, but not all, are *piḷi* (revulsive, stale). These are beef, as well as those substances that end in the suffix *ran*: thus: *mōran* (shark), *tōran* (Cybium quattatum), *ūran* (pig), *kiňduran* (a mythical bird), and "all such food ending in *ran*," said one *kapurāla*. In fact, no one could give a coherent list of these foods; and except for beef (and sometimes pork) *kapurāla*s would eat every kind of meat and fish outside the ritual context. Even the ending *ran* is hardly justified in Sinhala usage for these animals, except as a plural form. The cultural theory of *ran* is practically a rationalization, in the psychological sense, to justify a widespread laxity in dietary ideals.

Pollution theory in Sri Lanka has obviously had to adapt itself to the ethos of Sinhala Buddhist village society. In this culture certain foods are impure, or *piḷi*, but not polluting, or *kili*. This distinction, inappropriate for Hindu culture, is relevant for Sri Lanka. *Piḷi* has several meanings pertaining to staleness, impurity, and revulsiveness. Thus *piḷikul* means "full of *piḷi*" and also means "revulsive"; all stale foods are *piḷi*. I render these several meanings of *piḷi* as "impure." Impurity is less serious than pollution, so that eating impure foods does not require any purificatory act as does eating *pañcagavya* in Hindu India. Impure foods do not contaminate or pollute. *Kili* by contrast is viewed seriously, and in Sinhala society it especially refers to the pollution attendant on birth, puberty, menstruation, and death. Here the classic Hindu pattern obtains, though the dread associated with these sources of defilement is much less than in Hindu India. This is clearly reflected in the very formal and superficial purificatory rites practiced by polluted persons. However, one prohibition is strictly observed: polluted (*kili*) persons cannot interact with the *dēva*s. Thus a man who has eaten meat may visit a *dēva* shrine, but not a man whose wife is menstruating.

The most widely accepted view regarding the duration of *kili* is as follows: *mās killa* (menstruation) for three days till the woman bathes; *malvara killa* (menarche) for fourteen days; *vädun killa* (childbirth) for thirty days; *maraṇa killa* (death) for ninety days. During this period those who have been in contact with pollution cannot participate in *dēva* rituals. Pollution from menses applies only to members of the immediate family; from menarche or childbirth it applies to the wider family circle. Death, however, is a different problem, since it affects all who participate in the funeral rituals. Thus if a death occurs a *gammaḍuva* cannot be held in the village till the stipulated period is over; that is, until the remembrance ceremonies for the dead man have been performed, three months after death. In a small homogeneous, kin-based hamlet, a *gammaḍuva* may be postponed owing to childbirth and menarche pollution, for the obvious reason that the community is often the equivalent of the larger family circle of the polluted person. Everyone seriously believes that interaction with a *dēva* while polluted may result in *vas*, a condition of ritual danger that renders the individual susceptible to illness, accident, and disaster (*piripata*) in general.

Personality and Priesthood

Since the *kapurāla* in general neither practices a shaman role nor endorses a theory of divine possession or mediumship, role recruitment does not require the special experience of classic shamanism, that is, a prior traumatic illness and its later control—moving from being controlled by spirits to being a "master of spirits." This mark of divine grace, however, is not tabooed, as long as "ecstasy" is not interpreted as "possession." Indeed, it may be useful for at least one sequence in the *gammaḍuva* where the assistant *kapurāla* is inspired by the spirit of Däḍimuṇḍa-Vāhala (see p. 138). It may also help authenticate the experience of handling the divine insignia, but here the possession must be highly controlled and modulated so as not to suggest possession by the goddess. In parts of the Western and Sabaragamuva provinces there is a ritual sequence known as *kurāla* where the *kapurāla* or his assistant, possessed by the Sanni demons, climbs to a high platform in a trance state. This sequence is not intrinsic to the *gammaḍuva*, but it does require ability to go into trance. Here the "trance propensity" may be useful. In most sequences, except those involving demonic or semidivine agents, trance is achieved not so much through a psychological propensity, as in classic shamanism, as through inhalation of resin (*dummala*) and vigorous head shaking to the beat of drums.

The dilemma of achieving trance via resin and head shaking or through a psychological gift is basic to Sinhala ritual specialists, in all parts of the country, even in those areas and cults where shaman role performance is essential. It is also basic, I believe, to all societies where shaman role recruitment is both open, that is, based on "talent," and closed, based on hereditary or loose situational factors. In Sri Lanka, outside our culture area, both modes are important and both types of priests are found. The man who has a shamanic illness experience may in fact sometimes be recruited to the *kapurāla* position. But since hereditary or kin-based mechanisms also operate, a *kapurāla* may be recruited on kin-based situational criteria, since the position carries high prestige and, till very recently, considerable financial reward. In the low country *kapurāla* families marry among themselves, thus forming a loose kin corporation controlling the "status market." In that case a prior illness-possession experience is not a prerequisite for recruitment, since, in order to keep the position within the corporation, kin criteria rather than experiential criteria are considered crucial. However, since the novice is chosen from a list of possible candidates, special aptitude or talent may come into recruitment choice. This, however, is neither universal nor uniform, as I shall presently demonstrate.

Personality and Priesthood: The Case of X

This case study will deal with "X," one of the senior *kapurāla*s in my sample. The condensed genealogy given below (fig. 1) will help illustrate some of the sociological problems discussed earlier, as well as providing necessary background for a discussion of the relationship between personality and the priest role.

The genealogy clearly illustrates the kind of kin corporation that controls the *kapurāla* positions. Such kin corporations also appear in the genealogies of the other senior *ka-*

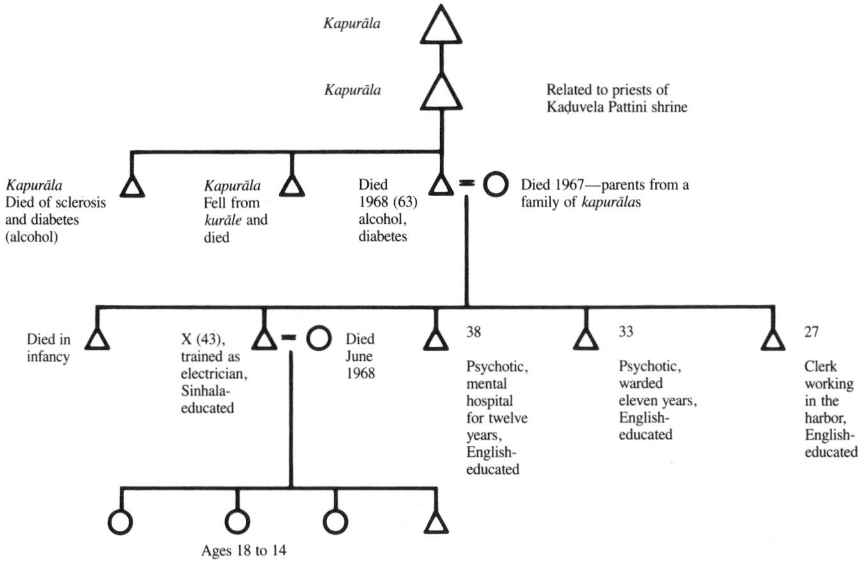

Fig. 1. Segment of the genealogy of X.

purālas, but there the affinal networks are even more important. This genealogy shows that in generation four all the sons except X, the eldest, have been educated for white-collar jobs. X himself does not wish his son to become a *kapurāla*. Note also in generation three that X's own father and his father's brother died of diabetes, exacerbated by excessive consumption of alcohol. None of these *kapurāla*s were vegetarians, either. Clearly, we are dealing with priests of the traditional mold!

I chose the case of X because he is the only one in my sample of senior *kapurāla*s who had a prior mystical experience of shaking, if not possession. X's father was a very influential and wealthy *kapurāla*. He wanted his children educated for modern jobs. His eldest living son, X, was trained as an apprentice electrician, and the younger children went to English high schools that would qualify them for white-collar jobs. When X was eighteen his father was admitted to an expensive private hospital with a severe diabetic condition. During this period X had several dreams in which the god Skanda (Kataragama) and the goddess Pattini "threatened" him to make him take up his father's job.

In the first dream Kataragama hit him with a cane and revealed himself in his divine form. He wore white and said: "Go thou [as if to an inferior] and take charge of the shrine [*dēvāle*]." But X resisted and refused to comply. In the second dream, several weeks later, Pattini herself visited him. She said, "Think of me as a mother and accept what I say. Go take charge of the *dēvāle*." "Again I refused," said X. A couple of weeks later Kataragama appeared again and pushed him out of bed (a standard warning adopted by this deity). "I shouted in fear. My mother came out and said, 'What's the matter, son?' I told her, but again I did not pay heed to the gods' warning." A few days later both X and his mother were drastically threatened by the deity. The mother was told X would be killed, and X was told once again: "Go take charge of the *dēvāle* or I'll kill you." X's mother was frightened and visited her husband in the hospital and told him of these portents. The father told his wife to do whatever she felt was right, but he personally did not want any of his sons to carry on his profession.

The mother made a vow that if the father got well and came back she would do whatever the gods expected of them. Thus, when the old *kapurāla* came back he formally taught his son the "letters," as a guru teaches the first letters of the alphabet to a child at an auspicious time. In this case the father asked his son to read some verses from the Pattini texts.

When X started to memorize the texts the goddess appeared once again and asked him to go to the central shrine of the god Dēvatā Baṇḍāra or Däḍimuṇḍa, the conqueror of demons, at Alutnuvara. He went there with a Buddhist monk. As he approached the shrine he felt as if he was trembling. The *kapurāla* of the temple then made him *pissu* ("mad," i.e., shaking). "He made me face the god, and after that I cannot remember anything." But apparently he had danced there for two hours in trance. The god gave him the power (*balaya*) to last for fifty-seven years. "Thereafter whenever I am in trouble the goddess appears to me in my dreams and befriends me."

X's father taught him, a novice of eighteen, the ritual techniques. He memorized the texts himself and learned dancing from a drummer-caste guru who used to dance in his father's performances. He went with his father as his assistant for six months. One day the father took him inside the *dēvāle* and placed the sacred anklets on his head. He was now a qualified priest. A few years later, when X was twenty-three, his father retired and X became the chief *kapurāla*. When we met X in 1956 he was a fully established and respected *kapurāla*.

The case of X illustrates several features of traditional recruitment. Clearly X had aptitude; witness his dreams, which I treat as projections of his own innermost wishes. Thus was it traditionally also; the person selected from a list of possible candidates often had to have a special aptitude or talent. The dream visitations were not unusual; others have had them also. What was unusual for my sample of priests was the trance state, which few experienced in this manner. X controls this state for religious purposes so that he utters prophecies in *gammaḍuva* rituals, which is unusual for this cultural area. He also climbs the *kurāla* in this state and does not have to rely on resin or head shaking to achieve trance. However, X never interprets this as possession but considers it *ākarṣaṇa balaya*, "power of divine magnetism" given by the goddess. X says that this magnetism of the goddess increases his *rāga* ("passion," especially sexual passion).

Since the trance propensity was not a prerequisite for priestly recruitment, I shall not analyze it here. Rather, I shall deal with a more common psychological feature of the priestly role, focusing once again on X and his genealogy. I refer specifically to the *kapurāla*'s taking on the role of the mother goddess in the most crucial sequences of the *gammaḍuva* ritual, namely, the carrying of the sacred insignia and the rituals that follow and in the *marā ipäddīma* (see pp. 245–71), where the life of the goddess and the death and resurrection of her consort are enacted.

The problem can be stated thus: the *kapurāla* acts the role of deity. Though he denies possession by her, he is nevertheless imbued with a magnetism derived from contact with her insignia. The question is whether a special type of personality is attracted by the role, as for instance with the transvestite shamans of the Chukchi, who are considered some of the group's most feared and powerful religious specialists (Bogoras 1907). One part of this question can easily be answered. Since the role carries high prestige and since recruitment is based on kin factors, there are some *kapurālas* who show no special psychological propensity such as transvestism. Yet the problem is more complex, since there is a larger list of potential recruits and novice *kapurālas* often volunteer for the job. Admittedly, there could be other motivations like the economic or prestige incentive, but psychological factors may be operative when voluntarism is present in role recruitment. It is this problem that I shall now discuss.

Between 1956 and 1961 I saw X perform several *gammaḍuvas*. Before taking up the anklets the priest must dress up as Pattini. Some priests do it without much ado, but consider X in his boudoir, from my notes taken in 1956.

P.M.
11:30 Anoints his body with oil and massages it.
11:40 Washes his body.
12:00 Shaves his face.
A.M.
12:05 Powders his face and ties black cloth over his head, simulating the female hair "bun" or knot at the back of the head.
12:20 Puts on blouse and female underwear.
12:40 Puts on ornaments: bracelets, earrings, necklace, talisman, plus a butterfly-shaped hair ornament pinned on the hair knot (bun).
12:50 Makeup. Puts cold cream on his face. Powders his face and arms.
12:55 Lipstick (unheard of except among elite ladies in Colombo).
1:00 String of flowers on head.
1:10 More hair ornaments.
1:15 Puts on sari.
1:20 Admires himself before mirror, before final touch-up.
1:25 Applies *tilaka* (beauty spot) on forehead. Wears gloves (no Sinhala lady ever wears them, but I suspect this model is derived from pictures of Queen Victoria and other imperial ladies).
1:27 Rouge, beauty spots on cheeks.
1:30 Long necklace.
1:32 Garland of jasmine flowers. Takes handkerchief in one hand and fan in the other. Dressing is complete and "he" is now ready to perform the ritual of *salam̆ba sāntiya*, that is, blessing the audience with the goddess's divine anklets.

Some priests dress up in about half an hour, but X's elaborate toilet, performed with such loving care, takes two hours. The end product is a veritable role transformation: psychologically, if not theologically, the priest has identified himself with the goddess.

I do not have enough clinical data to substantiate whether priests such as X were homosexuals, bisexuals (latent or otherwise), or transvestites. However, three of the six chief *kapurālas* I know well had serious psychological problems before becoming priests, or as a consequence of identification with the mother goddess, or both. These three were also the most famous and highly respected of the chief *kapurālas*, largely owing to the public conception of their "sincerity," which in turn was due to their convincing performance in the goddess role. Y, an extremely influential *kapurāla*, was married but had no children: indirect questioning strongly suggested to me that he was psychogenically impotent. He considered his inability to have children a professional hazard, since the mother goddess herself is, paradoxically, barren. Furthermore, he thought that members of his family tradition should not carry the insignia on the head, since several of his ancestors had died as a result. He therefore carried them on his shoulder. Z, another influential *kapurāla*, was an old bachelor who, so far as I could gather, had no heterosexual life.

I assume that identification with the mother goddess would be encouraged by an infantile identification of the *kapurāla* with his own mother. Furthermore, this could be one important motive for adopting the priestly role. In a later chapter I shall discuss what characteristics of the social structure promote maternal role identification. Here I shall focus on special conditions in the social situation of the prospective *kapurāla* that *may* result in a strong infantile identification with the mother. The discussion will also show how a popular *kapurāla* may in fact produce a son who has psychological characteristics requisite for role identification with both mother and goddess.

The problem is fundamentally simple. The mother-child bond in Sri Lanka as well as in the neighboring subcontinent is strong. Moreover, certain factors may strengthen this bond, in particular the absence of the father. Take the cases of X and Y. Both priests had fathers who were themselves powerful and popular *kapurālas*. The more popular the *kapurāla* the more he is away from home, giving little attention to his son. This pushes the son even closer to the loving mother, intensifying an already close relationship. Idiosyncratic factors may further strengthen the bond. X's genealogy clearly shows one such factor at work. His eldest brother died in early infancy; X was the second son. Given the death of the first child, it is likely that the mother would have focused a great deal of care and attention on X. Furthermore, this attention could have been prolonged, since the third child was not born until five years later, giving X undivided maternal attention and feeding his primary narcissism (a conspicuous trait of the adult X).

Thus far I have discussed an important sociological factor fostering a female identity, compounded by an idiosyncratic factor specific to X's family situation. X's life history, however, was extremely complicated, warranting further discussion.

In the period 1958–61 X was in full form as one of the most respected *kapurālas* in his region, proudly carrying on his father's profession. When I met him in 1973 he had left his village; his wife was dead and his children were in orphanages. He was, in my estimation, clinically paranoid and full of inner rage. The paranoia could not be expressed and contained within the religious idiom as happens in some cases (Obeyesekere 1970). He said that in his dreams the gods told him repeatedly that his enemies would be punished. But he also feared and hated his friends, relations, and even a Buddhist monk who befriended him. He was suspicious of my field assistant, who was, he imagined, a son of a *kapurāla*. Everyone was out to get him, and he in turn would one day destroy them all (with the help of the gods).

Several other obsessions emerged from my conversation with him. He represented in extremis the Sinhala preoccupation with status. He talked constantly, in a highly narcissistic manner, of his own glory, his high status, his enormous dislike for poor and low-status persons. He felt that rich women were in love with him and that one of them would eventually marry him. However, the most powerful theme was his hatred of his dead father and idealization of his mother. He talked openly about this in the most violent language. His father was a cad, a dog: "May his grave be struck by lightning." "He let me down, his eldest son. He will not even be born as a bird in his next birth; he'll continue in *saṃsāra* as an animal, for ever and ever in rebirths." Such hostile conceptions have special enormity in Sinhala Buddhist culture—they virtually deny the father any hope of salvation.

"My father will be doomed for ever . . . but my mother, may she achieve Buddahood! Why should I need a father? My mother is all I want."

Outside of X's paranoid obsessions he could talk rationally about his profession and the events of his life. His memory of the ritual texts was still good in spite of his having given up performing the *gammaḍuva* ritual for the past four years. It was therefore possible to piece together the events that culminated in his psychosis.

X's father not only was regularly absent from home, he was both an alcoholic and a womanizer. He kept several mistresses in the village, in itself nothing unusual for a man of high status, but he also mistreated his wife, often beating her. X's oedipal rage is thoroughly expectable in these circumstances. What was striking in X's family is that two younger siblings, both English-educated and destined for white-collar jobs, ended up at ages eighteen and nineteen in the mental hospital at Aṅgoḍa, near Colombo, where they are still confined. X told me they suffered from *kalakirīma*, "disgust with life," that is, depression. This was probably based on the psychiatrists' diagnoses: however, it is striking that X interpreted his siblings' illness as due to psychological causes, specifically his father's behavior and treatment of his mother. "Father was almost never at home; he was busy with his work and with other women. This is the cause of my brothers' illness, they didn't want to eat even, *kalakirīma*. They all took mother's side when she was beaten."

What was striking in these cases is that the siblings' psychoses appeared in late adolescence, almost at the same age when X experienced the visions that culminated in *his* becoming a novice *kapurāla*. The conclusion is irresistible. In X's case, rage for the father was channeled and expressed in a supernatural idiom: his visions of a powerful authority figure like Skanda permitted him, at a time when his father was critically ill, to usurp the latter's position and dedicate himself to the service of a loving mother, the goddess Pattini. This was made possible because X did not attend English schools; he was trained for a low-status blue-collar job (electrician) and was still rooted in his village culture. His brothers were in a radically different position. They went to English schools; the vocation of *kapurāla* was simply unthinkable for them. Thus when they faced a severe mental crisis in late adolescence there was no symbolic way they could express their rage against their father for his mistreatment and betrayal of their mother and their love and pity for her. Their rage had to be internalized, which probably was a major factor in their psychotic depression. But X could act out his inner conflicts, however pressing, through his public role as a priest of the Pattini cult.

But not for long. In 1967 his mother died and the following year his wife; his father's death followed in the same year. These personal calamities were followed by others, but the details are not clear, since they are so rooted in X's complicated personal problems. X claims that his father gave away much of his property to his mistresses, but what was unbearable was that he gave his house, where X lived, to X's youngest brother, a clerk in the Harbor Department. X claims that his brother encouraged his wife to sleep with his father in order to secure his property. It was difficult to verify any of this, except that X left his paternal village and found a job in a Buddhist temple in Colombo as the resident *kapurāla* of several small *dēva* shrines there. As far as he was concerned he had totally renounced his village and his profession, though some of his close relations in the village (whom I met) were anxious to get him back and reestablish the annual festival of the Pattini shrine in the village. Older informants believed that neglecting this shrine would bring calamity on them all.

My interpretation of these subsequent events, admittedly speculative, is somewhat different. X became a novice at age nineteen when his father was very sick and no longer an efficient practitioner of the cult. Soon he usurped his father's role and was considered as good as his father or even better. X lived in his father's house with him, but the father had practically retired. However, he kept his mistresses in the village and mistreated his wife, exacerbating the others' problems. Siblings 2 and 3 had become psychotic, but sibling 4 was married and had a good job. The time when X became a novice was also the time when his father began to retire; at this time sibling 4 was only three years old. The father was at home more, no longer the absent father. Being more often there, he could give greater love to sibling 4 than to the others, which resulted in a more positive father-son relationship. Furthermore, siblings 2 and 3, for whom X's father had high aspirations, later became depressives, whereas sibling 4 had a good steady job, gratifying at long last the father's aspirations for his sons. Thus he gave his property to the youngest and had his revenge on the oldest son who had usurped his place and forced him into retirement. When he was deprived of his wife, mother, land, and property, X's psychological needs—long held under control—reemerged in his now flagrant paranoid behavior. Rejection of village and profession was the final rejection of the hated father.

The Decline of the Traditional *Kapurāla*

Traditionally the *kapurāla* was a part-time priest who also cultivated his fields. A popular *kapurāla*, however, had very little time for farming. His profession gave him a reasonable income, so that the senior *kapurāla*s in five of the six traditions (not Ratnapura) were economically well off, if not rich. One owned a car. This affluence was, I suspect, due to the economic conditions of the early twentieth century. Famous Pattini priests, like village physicians and government bureaucrats, had access to scarce cash resources that permitted them to invest in land. But in the post-Independence period economic conditions changed radically and the *kapurāla* profession was no longer lucrative; monetary remuneration simply did not keep pace with inflation and the rising standard of living. Furthermore, it was virtually impossible for a single family, or even a village, to muster the resources required for a large-scale *gammaḍuva*. In 1956, when I started my research, almost all the senior *kapurāla*s in the six traditions were busy professionals. It was easy to witness their *gammaḍuva* performances. In 1971 the most influential priest (Yahōnis Pattini) was dead; the others hardly ever performed large-scale *gammaḍuva* rituals, which in 1975 were almost impossible to witness.

The Textual Tradition

My characterization of the *kapurāla* as priest receives reinforcement when we look at the doctrinal and textual traditions of this region. One of the classic definitions of priest as against shaman or magician is that the former has little scope for idiosyncratic manipulation of the public pantheon. As Weber pointed out, the priest's distinguishing quality is his "professional equipment of special knowledge, fixed doctrine, and vocational qualifications which brings him into contrast with sorcerers, prophets, and other types of religious functionaries who exert their influence by personal gifts (charisma) made manifest in miracle and revelation" (Weber 1963, p. 29). The textual traditions of the Pattini cult are embodied in a compendium known as *pantis kōlmura*, "thirty-five ritual texts," or "thirty-five songbooks." All traditions in this region have the thirty-five ritual texts as the basis of their cult. These texts, translated in part 2 of this work, contain most of the ritual prescriptions and instructions pertaining to the cult.

The thirty-five ritual texts are a unique body of material among the ritual traditions of Sri Lanka. (I of course exclude Buddhism and astrology, the two great traditions.) The demon cults have similar (*kōlmura*) texts, but none so well organized, detailed, consistent, and relatively free of textual variation. When we look at other cults of the gods the contrast is striking. There are many shrines for the other major gods of the pantheon, but at best there may be one or two traditional ritual texts for Viṣṇu, Skanda, and Saman, while no texts are extant for Vibhīṣaṇa and Nātha. Outside the culture area under consideration similar textual traditions prevail for other communal cults. In the four *kōralēs* and parts of the Kandyan region (Uḍunuvara, Yaṭinuvara, and Hārispattuva) the ritual cycle was known as *kohom̆bā kan̆kāriya* (the ritual performance of Kohom̆bā deities). This and the *gammaḍuva* in Han̆guran̆keta and other parts of Kandy and Ūva deal with the well-known local collectivity of gods known as Doḷaha Deviyo (the Twelve Gods). But even here there is nothing showing such elaboration of style, skill in versification, and poetic grandeur as the thirty-five ritual texts. Moreover, none of the above traditions focus so many texts exclusively on a single major deity, in this case Pattini. We can legitimately speak of the low-country *gammaḍuva* as an institutionalization of the Pattini cult. Although other gods are also propitiated, the focus of the texts and rituals is on Pattini; the main altar erected in the *gammaḍuva* is also for her; she is the presiding deity of the ceremony. In this regard note again that it is only in relation to the Pattini cult that the priest is given a specific extra designation, Sir Pattini (Pattini rāla).

The predominance of the Pattini cult in this region is seen once again in relation to other cults. For example, the central shrine for Viṣṇu is at Devundara in the southern tip of Sri Lanka, a flourishing shrine in the eighth century. A graphic account of this shrine and its destruction by the Portuguese in 1588 is given by de Couto:

> The temple itself was vast in size, all the roofs being domed and richly carved; round it were several very handsome chapels and over the principal gateway was a tall tower entirely roofed with copper, gilt in various parts. Within was a large square with verandahs and terraces with a handsome gate on each side, while all around were planted sweet-smelling flowers which were used during the processions. We burst in the gates and proceeded to destroy the idols of which there were more than a thousand of different figures of clay and wood and copper, mostly gilded. We destroyed the domes and colonnades and sacked the stores where we found a vast accumulation of ivory, fine cloths, coffee, pepper, sandalwood, jewels, precious stones and all the fittings of the temple, which we plundered as we desired and set the rest on fire. As the greatest affront that could be offered to the place we slaughtered within some cows, this being a stain which could not be purified without the most elaborate ceremonies. We also burnt a magnificent wooden car built like a tower of seven stories and beautifully painted and gilt—a magnificent vehicle in which they were accustomed to convey the chief idol around the city." (Quoted in Powell 1973, p. 27; see also Pieris 1913, p. 241)

The references to an elaborate temple and to the chariot indicate that Hindu-type rituals were conducted here. Paranavitana believed that this Viṣṇu temple was dominated by

Brahmans pushed out of India by the Muslim invasions (Paranavitana 1953, pp. 2–3). But after its destruction control of the temple fell into the hands of traditional Sinhala *kapurālas*. Thus today the striking feature of the annual festival of the Viṣṇu temple is not so much Viṣṇu rituals but a highly elaborate *gammaḍuva* performed there. The folk cult has displaced the Hindu Brahman-influenced cultus. Similarly, in southwestern Sri Lanka at Sīnigama there is the famous temple of Devol Deviyo. But the priest in charge of this temple is a Pattini priest, and the annual celebrations once again enact the ritual texts of the *gammaḍuva*. Clearly the dominant folk cult has set its stamp on the other cults of the region, lesser and major.

Though all practitioners are conscious of the thirty-five ritual texts, the number thirty-five is an ideal and not a reality for today's priests, since many of the texts are moribund. There is, however, a text known as *kavi bäňdīma* or *pot bäňdīma* (tying of the books) or *pada bäňdi paṭuna* (i.e., "chapter titles," in Sabaragamuva) that lists thirty-five, though not all traditions have the exact list. However, what is impressive is that, given the large region under consideration, there is considerable consensus on this tradition of ritual texts. Moreover, the most important texts dealing with Pattini are uniform in the region. Most texts have the same titles, but some of the verses may differ though the substance and content are the same. Differences in versification are completely overshadowed by the striking similarities in the verses of the major texts. It would be tedious to enumerate these differences, though I will make some attempt to show the more important differences in part 2 of this work.

It is necessary to understand in some detail the nature of the traditions embodied in the thirty-five ritual texts if the reader is to comprehend the later description and analysis of the cult. I shall present in table 1 (p. 28) four versions of the thirty-five texts; one each from the Mātara and Rabalīya traditions and two from Hugh Nevill's collection of palm-leaf manuscripts in the London Museum (Nevill 1954, 1955). The Mātara version is in verse, and I have put the text titles down in the order they appear there. The Rabalīya version was given to me by the chief *kapurāla* Yahōnis (now deceased). I have versions from Sīnigama and Ratnapura that I have omitted. Nevill was one of those great British administrators who arrived in Sri Lanka in 1865, and during his tenure he collected an enormous number of palm-leaf manuscripts. With the aid of Sinhala scholars, Nevill gave a brief summary and description of each manuscript, which I shall use here. The Nevill manuscripts are important because they were collected about one hundred years ago and hence reflect a much older collection than mine, which come from ritual practitioners of today. Their texts are copied down on paper from older palm-leaf manuscripts; some possess these originals, but they are in a state of decay. Moreover, ongoing practitioners must adapt older texts to suit present realities. Hence comparing the four versions of the thirty-five ritual texts provides fascinating insights into how texts are formed and transformed through a long historical period. The reader should note that I have arbitrarily selected the Mātara tradition of these ritual texts as the ideal type and then noted whether or not these Mātara texts are present in the other three traditions.

A look at the four versions in toto shows us that they deal with three interrelated traditions. The main body of texts, and those operative in contemporary ritual, deals with the myths relating to Pattini. A second body of mythic material deals with the king of Soḷī (Cōḷa), generally identified with the Cōḷa king Karikāla. Corpus 1 and corpus 2 are linked by the king of Soḷī, who is a crucial figure in both. The major locus of these two mythic traditions is the three great kingdoms of South India, Cēra, Cōḷa, and Pāṇḍya, with their regions, ports, rivers and towns. The third corpus of myth deals with the exploits of King Gajabāhu, a Sinhala culture hero. The Gajabāhu myths are connected only vaguely with Soḷī-Karikāla and peripherally with the Pattini corpus. Before we can draw any conclusions from these data I must present a brief summary of the three corpora. They will be discussed at greater length later.

The Pattini corpus deals with the prior lives of the goddess, and it is cast entirely in a Buddhist mold. The Buddha of our age, Gautama, achieved perfection through *pāramitās*, great deeds performed in earlier births under the dispensation of previous Buddhas. So does Pattini in a lesser key. Myths deal with her offering alms to previous Buddhas, and by "the power of her deeds" she aspires to future Buddhahood herself. Other myths deal with her previous miraculous or *opapātika* births, births unrelated to human procreation and conception, the most famous being her birth from a blue lotus. Eventually she meditates as a saint on Añdungiri Peak (Sanskrit *añjanakūṭa*, "black collyrium mountain"), aspiring to enlightenment. Here Sakra, the Buddhist king of the gods, accosts her and implores her to be born on earth once again to end the famine in the kingdom of the good king of Soḷī and quell the prowess of the evil king of Pāṇḍi—arrogant, tyrannical, possessed of a third eye like Śiva, and aspiring to be a god on earth. Pattini agrees and is conceived in a golden mango in the orchard of the Pāṇḍi king. No one can bring down this miraculous mango, but one old man, Sakra himself in disguise, agrees to do so. He shoots an arrow that hits the mango; its juice falls on the king's middle eye and obliterates it. Frightened, the king places the mango in a golden casket and floats it down the Kāvēri River. It reaches the port of Kāvēri (*kāvēri paṭuna*) where two merchant princes are bathing. One of them takes the casket home, and lo! after seven days a beautiful child emerges. She grows up and is married in childhood to Pālañga, alias Kōvalaṉ, the son of the other merchant prince. From here on the events are similar to those in books 1 and 2 of the great South Indian Tamil epic, the *Cilappatikāram*. However, according to my versions, Pattini and Pālañga do not consummate their marriage. He falls in love with a beautiful courtesan, Mādēvi (Tamil, Mātavi), and squanders his wealth on her. Destitute, he comes back to Pattini, who gives him her precious gem-studded anklet. They set off to Madurai, the city of Pāṇḍi, to seek their fortunes. After many adventures they reach the outskirts of Madurai. Pālañga goes to the city alone; he is betrayed by a goldsmith to whom he tries to sell the anklet. The goldsmith tells the king that Pālañga is the thief who stole the Pāṇḍi queen's own anklet. Pālañga is tortured and executed without trial. Pattini comes in search of him and resurrects him. She then accosts the king of Pāṇḍi, and destroys him and the city by tearing out her left breast and throwing it. Flames overcome the city. The lament of Pattini constitutes some of the finest poetry in Sinhala ritual tradition.

After her apotheosis Pattini appeared in a dream to Sēraman (literally, king of Cēra), who was afflicted by an incurable headache. Learned Brahmans asked him to come to Sri Lanka and construct a *maḍuva* (hall) and propitiate the goddess. Viśvakarma, the divine architect, built this hall, and various rituals were held that cured the king's head disease. This hall and its rituals are the prototype of the present *gammaḍuva*. In the Sinhala traditions this text, known as *maḍupuraya* ("hall city"), is one of the first to be sung.

The second mythic corpus dealing with the king of Soḷī (Karikāla) is never enacted in Sinhala ritual today. It is for all purposes defunct; nevertheless, it is crucial for ethnohistorical analysis. In the Pattini corpus, the three kings of South India are impersonal, unnamed mythic beings simply known as the king of Soḷī, Pāṇḍi, and Sēraman. Soḷī is good, Pāṇḍi is evil, and Sēraman introduced the cult to Sri Lanka. In Corpus 2 the king of Soḷī is explicitly identified with Karikāla, the great king of South Indian history and legend. He still remains the good king. His birth is described, and so is his great achievement in bunding the river Kāvēri for peaceful agricultural purposes. The completion of this project is celebrated by water sports (*diyakeḷi katāva* in our texts).

Corpus 3 is of an entirely different character in that it deals with Gajabāhu, a king in Sri Lankan history and, more important, a culture hero of mythology. Gajabāhu learns that twelve thousand Sinhala prisoners were captured in his father's reign to work as slaves in constructing the bund of the Kāvēri by the king of Soḷī (whose name is never mentioned). (Corpus 2, however, never refers to Sinhala slaves: the bund was built with the aid of a willing citizenry.) Gajabāhu, infuriated, crosses over to India by splitting the ocean with his mace (*yagadāya*), accompanied by Nīla-mahā-yōdaya ("the great blue giant warrior"). He frightens the Soḷī king by his prowess, recovers the Sinhala prisoners, and brings back twelve thousand Tamil prisoners as compensation. In addition, he brings back the insignia of the goddess Pattini. Some texts (not the ones listed above) refer to his having built the central shrine of Pattini at Navagamuva. Another text in Nevill manuscript 727 describes how he installed a sandalwood image of the goddess, but this text is not related in any way to his other grandiose exploits. One text known as *aṅkoṭa haṭana* deals with the treacherous Sinhala peasant who helped the Soḷī king capture Sinhala prisoners.

Now we are in a position to examine, in a preliminary way, the significance of these three corpora of myth. Here I shall assume what I will demonstrate in detail later, namely that the Pattini cult diffused from South India to Sri Lanka. The setting of mythic corpora 1 and 2, the introduction of the cult by Sēraman (king of Cēra), suggests this. However, there is little logical, episodic, or substantive connection between corpus 1 (Pattini) and corpus 2 (Karikāla). Nevertheless it is possible that the Pattini and Karikāla traditions were introduced together with the Pattini cult as a totality from South India. Differing mythic traditions can exist within a larger ceremonial cycle. Even in today's *gammaḍuva* there are other traditions, ritual and mythic, that have nothing to do with the thirty-five ritual texts (*pantis kōlmura*). The reason is simple: these myths are sung in collective group rituals (like postharvest ceremonies) having many gods and many goals. These goals can be met by different mythic and ritual performances. I shall show later that the Karikāla myths and ritual dramas had a clear function in ancient South Indian society. When they diffused to Sri Lanka, these enactments may have continued, but as Karikāla was not a known hero some of these functions became moribund or were displaced to other heroes of Sinhala mythology.

The Gajabāhu corpus (3) presents a different picture entirely. Here is a truly Sinhala culture hero, already credited with deeds of cultural significance for Sinhala people. The Gajabāhu mythology is clearly of indigenous origin, whereas Karikāla is not. It therefore seems equally clear that the Gajabāhu corpus was incorporated into the compendium of thirty-five texts after the diffusion of the Pattini cult (including corpus 2) into Sri Lanka. Furthermore, the Soḷī king in the Gajabāhu myths is different from Karikāla of corpus 2. The former is a bad (not evil) king, frightened out of his wits by Gajabāhu; the latter is a warrior and an upright hero. Gajabāhu would obviously be more appealing to Sinhalas than Karikāla. Gajabāhu gets incorporated into the compendium in various ways, not all consistent. He brought the insignia of the goddess from Cōḷa; he built the central shrine at Navagamuva; he made a sandalwood image of the deity and housed it; and so forth. Important as his myths are in Sinhala culture history, his link with the Pattini cult is tenuous. Hence Gajabāhu of corpus 3 is rarely mentioned in the texts of corpora 1 and 2 in the four traditions listed below (table 1).

The foregoing conclusions can be substantiated by comparing the four traditions in table 1. The following twelve texts are found in all four traditions without substantive difference and overlap, namely, *maḍupuraya* (origin of the *gammaḍuva* by Sēraman) *dan kaṭina* (offerings of robes to monks by Pattini), *patasa* and *soḷīpura sāgataya* (two texts on the conflict between Soḷī and Pāṇḍi, resulting in the drought in Soḷī, which Pattini later must end), *pattini päṭuma* (aspirations to be a chaste woman, a Pattini), *aṁba vidamana* (shooting of the mango, which destroyed Pāṇḍi's might and resulted in Pattini's conception), *valinaḍa* and *kannuran katāva* (journeying toward Madurai by Pattini and her consort), *marā ipäddīma* (killing of Pālaṅga and his resurrection by Pattini), *kī vitti* or *vitti hata* (Pattini moralizing on justice), *sat pattini katāva* (praise songs of Pattini in her seven manifestations), *vädi pūjāva* (offerings by Väddas to Pattini). These texts, one can presume, are the popular as well as the important ones: they are all part of corpus 1 except *patasa* and *soḷīpura sāgataya*. These latter texts are formally part of corpus 2 (on Soḷī and Pāṇḍi), but they are crucially linked to the Pattini tradition. In addition, all four traditions have several texts (1, 4, 4, 3, respectively), on the Mādēvi episode, also part of corpus 1.

The crucial texts in corpus 2 dealing with a named King Karikāla are four in number: 12, 13, 14, and 15 of the Mātara tradition. These texts are never enacted and rarely sung today; their content is often reinterpreted. Nevertheless, their historical importance is clear from the prominence given them at least in the past in the four traditions: 4, 1, 4, and 2 texts. The Gajabāhu corpus has only three texts: *aṅkoṭa haṭana* (conflict of the short horn), *gajabā katāva* (story of Gajabāhu), and *ganaruva* (pure image of Pattini), the last only in Nevill 727. These texts are represented in the four traditions thus: 0, 2, 1, 1. Of these, only *ganaruva* (Nevill 724 and 727) deals with Gajabāhu's building a temple for Pattini and installing a red sandalwood image of the goddess there. By contrast, all four have reference to Sēraman, who instituted the *gammaḍuva*. I will deal with the conflict between these two traditions later.

Let us now see how the four traditions of the thirty-five ritual texts reflect the problems discussed earlier, paying special attention to two of the operative traditions, Mātara and Rabalīya. The reader should bear in mind that the dominant operative tradition consists of corpus 1 (on Pattini); the Karikāla corpus 2 was probably important till recent times, and corpus 3 on Gajabāhu is a popular Sinhala one, but not properly integrated into the Pattini corpus and not part of the texts (corpora 1 and 2) introduced from South India. Now when we look at the Mātara tradition of its present practitioners *aṅkoṭa haṭana* (conflict of the short horn) and *gajabā katāva* (Gajabāhu story) (corpus 2) are absent. This is also true of Nevill manuscript 724, which he says is derived from the Devundara (Dondra) temple near Mātara. I have a text from the Ratnapura tradition: this list also makes no reference to Gajabāhu, corpus 3. Both Mātara and Nevill 724 from the same region have corpus 2 (but Ratnapura does not). We can therefore assume that the "southern" tradition ideally has maintained, to a large extent, the integrity of the original. However, the Karikāla text (corpus 2) is formally enumerated as part of the Mātara tradition, but it is neither sung nor

Table 1
Four Traditions of Pantis Kōlmura

Mātara (Texts Consecutively Numbered)	Rabalīya	Nevill Manuscript 724	Nevill Manuscript 727
	(Texts Not Consecutively Numbered)		
1. *Yahan sähäli*: altar songs	No. 1 present	Absent	Absent
2. *Visituru katāva*: description story (description of Sri Lanka)	No. 2 present but different interpretation. Short account of Pattini's previous births.	Absent	No. 1 present (no. 2 listed below)
3. *Maḍupuraya*: hall city. (origin of the *gammaḍuva*)	No. 3 present	No. 1 present	No. 3 present
4. *Pahan gäm̆bura*: lights on the deep (Pattini offers lights, in honor of Buddha on Nērañjanā river and prays for future Buddhahood)	No. 4 present	Absent	Absent
5. *Dan kaṭina*: offerings of robes (to monks by Pattini, also in a previous birth)	No. 5 present	No. 2 present	No. 4 present
6. *Amārasaya*: taste of ambrosia (description of Pāṇḍi king and his city)	No. 6 present	No. 3 listed below	No. 5 present as *pāṇḍi upata*: (birth of Pāṇḍi)
7. *Patasa*: tank (artificial lake built by Pāṇḍi king with corvée labor)	No. 7 present	No. 4 present	No. 6 present
8. *Soḷīpura sāgataya*: famine in the city of Soḷī (as a result of Pāṇḍi's curse)	No. 8 present	No. 5 present	No. 7 present
9. *Pattini pätuma*: aspiring to be Pattini (a chaste one, by meditating on Am̆dungiri Peak)	No. 9 present	No. 6 present	No. 8 present
10. *Am̆ba vidamana*: shooting of the mango	No. 10 present	No. 7 present	No. 9 present (no. 10, see below)
11. *Vanē visituru kavi*: songs of the description of the forest (i.e., the Himalayan forest)	Absent	No. 8 present	No. 11 present
12. *Kāvēri gam̆ga diyahelīma*; directing of the waters of the Kāvēri (from the skies)	Absent	No. 9 present	No. 12 present as *gam̆ga heli soḷīupata*: (dropping of river and birth of Soḷī)
13. *Rajakulaka kavitāla upata*: origin of song styles of royal dynasty (should read birth of Karikāla of royal dynasty)	Absent	No. 10 present	Absent
14. *Gam̆ga bän̆dīma*: bunding of the river (Kāvēri by	Absent	No. 11 present	Absent

Table 1 (continued)

Mātara (Texts Consecutively Numbered)	Rabalīya	Nevill Manuscript 724	Nevill Manuscript 727
	(Texts Not Consecutively Numbered)		
Karikāla with the help of citizens)			
15. *Diyakeḷi katāva*: story of the water sports (to celebrate completion of Kāvēri project)	No. 11 present, but a different interpretation. Two merchants bathing in the Kāvēri pick up the casket containing the mango	No. 12 present	No. 13 present
16. *Vaňda pavu sā kōvilpēunu raňga*: the sins of barrenness and how she dedicated herself to a *kōvila* (reference to Pālaňga's mother, who was barren)	No. 12 present as *kōvilpēvū katāva* (different interpretation. Pattini stops at a *kōvila* on her way to Madurai).	No. 11 present	Absent
17. *Dun avavāda*: advice given (on the occasion of the marriage of Pattini and Pālaňga)	Absent (no. 13 listed below)	No. 17 present (see also no. 16 listed below)	Nos. 15–18 listed below
18. *Ruvan naḷuva*: beauty of Pattini	No. 14 present	Absent (no. 18 listed below)	Absent
19. *Tapasa*: the hermit life (Pālaňga's father and mother decide to renounce the world)	Absent	No. 19 present	No. 19 present
20. *Mādēvi rāňgun dūkeḷi katāva* (the dance of Mādēvi and the story of the dice game)	Absent (no. 15 listed below)	No. 20 present but Nevill separates *dūkeḷi* and *rāňgun* as two texts. They should be one in order to make thirty-five.	No. 20 present
21. *Kāvēri paṭuna hära giya valinaḍa*: leaving the port of Kāvēri on foot	No. 16 present as *gaman vayinaḍaya*: journey into the Vayinad (Wynad)	No. 21 present as *valibādaya*: combinations of *valinaḍa* and *bādāvaliya* (omens) both found in 21 of Mātara	No. 21 present
22. *Kannuran katāva*: story of *kannuran* (a city or region, full of rivers and forest traversed by Pattini and Pālaňga on route to Madurai)	No. 17 present	No. 22 present	No. 22 present
23. *Vellimaḍama*: rest house of *velli* (where Pattini encounters the demoness of disease and quells her)	No. 18 present	Absent (no. 23 listed below)	Absent (no. 23 listed below)
24. *Pālaňga vada koṭā pālaňga mārīma*: Pālaňga tortured and killed	Absent	No. 24 present	No. 24 present

Table 1 (continued)

Mātara (Texts Consecutively Numbered)	Rabalīya	Nevill Manuscript 724	Nevill Manuscript 727
	(Texts Not Consecutively Numbered)		
25. *Marā ipäddīma*: killing and resurrection (Pattini resurrects Pālaňga)	No. 19 present	No. 25 present	No. 25 present
Kī vitti: Events narrated	*Events narrated:*		
26. Event 1	No. 20, *käṭakirilli vitti*: narrative of the paddy bird	No. 26 present	No. 26 present
27. Event 2	No. 21, *kaṭussa vitti*: narrative of the lizard	No. 27 present	No. 27 present
28. Event 3	No. 22, *darakäṭiyā vitti*: narrative of woodcutter	No. 28 present	No. 28 present
29. Event 4	No. 23, *eladena vitti*: narrative of the cow	No. 29 present	No. 29 present
30. Event 5	No. 24, *hāvā vitti*: narrative of the hare	No. 30 present	No. 30 present
31. Event 6	No. 25, *siňhayā vitti*: narrative of the lion	No. 31 present	No. 31 present
32. Event 7	No. 26, *pālaňga-pattini vitti*: narrative of Pālaňga and Pattini	No. 32 narrative of the dove	No. 32 narrative of the dove
33. *Sat pattini katāva*: story of (praises of) the Seven Pattini	No. 27 present	No. 33 present	No. 33 present
34. *Vädi pūjāva*: offerings by Väddas (to Pattini after she destroyed Madurai)	No. 28 present	No. 34 present	No. 34 present
35. *Mevan pahana*: probably the text for "house cooling"	Absent, instead no. 29, *kāvēri paṭuna*: port of Kāvēri (where the golden mango floats)	Absent, instead no. 35, *ganaruva*: pure image (of Pattini in sandalwood by Gajabāhu)	Absent, instead no. 35, *ganaruva*
	No. 30, *mādēvi katāva*: the story of Mādēvi		
	No. 31, *miṇibändu katāva*: tying of the gem necklace	No. 18, *miṇiruvan naḷuva*: description of gem and gold (necklace)	
	No. 32, *pāṇḍi naḷuva*: description of Pāṇḍi's city	No. 3, *pāṇḍi naḷuva*	
	No. 33, *diya bedīma*: parting of the waters by Pattini		
	No. 34, *aňkoṭa haṭana*: conflict of the short horn		
	No. 35, *Gajabā katāva*: story of Gajabāhu		No. 2, *gajabā*
		No. 14, *turaňgun näguma*: getting on horseback	No. 16, *senḍu keḷiya*: game of dice

Table 1 (continued)

Mātara	Rabalīya	Nevill Manuscript 724	Nevill Manuscript 727
(Texts Consecutively Numbered)	(Texts Not Consecutively Numbered)		
		No. 15, *pandu keḷiya*: ball game	
	No. 13, *maṅgala katā*: marriage proposal (Mātara 17)	No. 16, *vivā katā*: marriage proposal. Mātara 17 is split into two texts, 16 and 17; 16 is probably 17 of Rabalīya.	
	No. 15, *vēsamäḍīma*: taming of the courtesan	No. 23, *vēsamäḍīma*: taming of the courtesan	
			No. 10, *Laṅkāvistara*: description of Laṅka (elaboration of Mātara 2, and of 1 in this tradition)
			No. 11, *taraṅga katāva*: competition talk, probably riddles uttered during marriage ceremonies; in this case, Pattini-Pālaṅga nuptials.
			No. 16, *valalu katāva*: story of bracelets (content unknown)
			No. 17, *salaṁba puvata*: story of anklets; probably *salaṁba sāntiya*, anklet blessings, (see pages
			No. 23, *vesaṅga äňḍīma*: courtesan weeps (lament of Mādēvi)

enacted in any of the dozen rituals I have seen in the area. I was told that it was sung, but not enacted, by the "earlier generations" of *kapurālas*, but the Karikāla corpus has within recent times become totally defunct in the region.

Let us now consider the other operative tradition of Rabalīya. Here the reverse is true: the alien Karikāla corpus is not part of the thirty-five texts, but corpus 3 is included. This is also true of the Heyiaṁtuḍuva list in my possession. But though these texts are mentioned, neither tradition enacts or sings them. Here the matter is more complex. Rabalīya priests assured me of Gajabāhu enactments (ritual dramas) they had witnessed in childhood. Furthermore, Gajabāhu myths (not dramas) are sung at "water-cutting" rituals, which are rare in this tradition and performed only at annual rituals in well-known shrines. Water cutting is also practiced in the annual festival at Pattini shrines in the Kandyan area, and here Gajabāhu myths are often sung in association with this rite. Thus a tentative conclusion, to be substantiated at length later, is that Gajabāhu myths were historically more popular outside our area, especially in the Kandyan regions, and were associated with water-cutting rituals. It is likely that the Gajabāhu myths were incorporated only much later into the compendium of thirty-five texts in Rabalīya and elsewhere. It is probably an attempt to supplant the alien Karikāla tradition or to give a more patriotic focus to the thirty-five ritual texts.

Nevill manuscript 727 and my Ratnapura text present interesting contrasts. Nevill 727 has both corpora 2 and 3. It is difficult to say where the manuscript is from: the dialect is unfamiliar to me, and the text headings are different from all other traditions. Though the text titles are different, their substantive content is identifiable and could be matched with others as I have done in table 1. The Ratnapura compendium (not presented in the table) is the other extreme: neither corpus 2 nor corpus 3 is included. It has totally rationalized the thirty-five texts to be synonymous with the operative Pattini traditions (corpus 1). Here the reason is simple: Gajabāhu mythology was never popular in Ratnapura (and in the larger Sabaragamuva Province), and the bulk of South Indian Karikāla corpus is as remote as can be for this interior region.

Thus there is a clear tendency in the traditions we are dealing with. The number thirty-five is maintained, but when corpora 2 and 3 are eliminated or partly omitted or emended their place is taken by extra Pattini texts from corpus 1 or by casuistric subdivisions of extant Pattini texts to fit the number thirty-five. I suspect that thirty-five was the original number when these texts were introduced from South India, and this original thirty-five had texts relevant to South India but irrelevant to Sri Lanka. Thus there were probably more corpus 2 texts than are now extant, and perhaps also Pattini texts (corpus 1) that were contextually specific to a South Indian ethos. These then are eliminated and other "relevant" texts take their place to form thirty-five. This is what I think has happened to the text known as *vittihata*, the seven events, or *kī vitti* "events narrated" (no. 26 in the Mātara tradition). The *pantis kōlmura* relates *vittihata* as one text: yet in any *count* they are listed as seven. Present-day *kapurāla*s as well as Nevill make the same point. It seems quite unlikely that these seven events—themselves not very significant and never separately listed in the compendium—would have been originally calculated in this manner. They were probably used to fill a void left by texts that had become defunct owing to their lack of cultural relevance.

The splitting of texts to make up the number thirty-five can be easily seen by examining table 1. The "Pālaňga tortured and killed" text 24 of Mātara and of Nevill 727 and 724 is separate from *marā ipäddīma* (killing and resurrection of Pālaňga). In Rabalīya they are both part of the latter, the *marā ipäddīma*. The Mātara tradition has a text on Mādēvi's dance (no. 20) that also deals with Pālaňga's falling in love with her and giving her a necklace. This is split into two in Rabalīya (nos. 30 and 31). Rabalīya also has an important text on the story of Mādēvi, which is included in other Mādēvi texts in the other three traditions.

More significant than textual splitting to maintain the integrity of the number thirty-five is another process whereby old, defunct, or irrelevant texts are infused with relevant content. The old text title remains or is slightly altered, yet the content is totally different. Thus Mātara has a text (no. 14) known as *gaňga bäňdīma* (bunding of the river), also known in other traditions as *diya bäňdīma* (bunding of the waters) that deals with Karikāla's raising the banks of the river Kāvēri. Rabalīya, however, ignores most of corpus 2, from which this comes: it substitutes *diya bedīma*, "parting the waters," which deals with a minor incident in the life of Pattini, elsewhere incorporated into other texts. Mātara, as well as Nevill 727 and 724, has corpus 2 *diya keḷi katāva* (nos. 15, 12, 13, respectively) dealing with the water sports to celebrate the completion of the dam. The title is maintained in Rabalīya, but the content has changed. According to Rabalīya this text refers to the discovery of the golden mango by the merchant princes as they were sporting in the river.

The dominant tradition is corpus 1, focused on Pattini herself, and everything else is subordinated to this tradition. Yet the Pattini corpus itself was introduced from South India. There is also evidence that the Sinhala texts were translations or adaptations from these South Indian texts, in which case there would inevitably be elements inappropriate to the Sinhala situation. One such text is *tapasa*, which deals with the departure of Kōvalaṉ's parents to a hermitage. Kōvalaṉ's parents are rarely mentioned in other texts or in Sinhala folklore. *Tapasa*, as I will show later, was an important text in South India: it is ignored in Sri Lankan performances. There is another text that should be entitled *karikāla upata*, "the birth of Karikāla." Since these Karikāla myths have become moribund, only two traditions mention it. Mātara text 13 refers to it as *rajakulaka kavitāla upata*: "the origin of song titles of royal dynasty," and Nevill 724, text 10, simply records it as *kavitāla upata*: "origin of song styles." Thus Karikāla, the king, becomes *kavitāla*, "song styles." The examination of the actual text, however, shows that it deals with Karikāla, not with song styles. Thus the Mātara version *should have* read: *rajakulaka karikāla upata*: "the birth of Karikāla of royal dynasty."

There are also minor details of South Indian significance that are omitted or amended in the local versions of the thirty-five ritual texts. Let me give one example that beautifully illustrates this feature. Mātara has a text known as "leaving the port of Kāvēri for *valinaḍa* (no. 21); Rabalīya calls it *gaman vayinaḍaya* (journey of *vayinaḍaya*) (no. 16); Nevill 727 has changed it into *vali bādaya* (no. 21); *vali* is the first part of *valinaḍa* or *vayinaḍa*, and *bādaya* is part of the same text known as *bādāvaliya*, "garland of bad omens." All these texts deal with Pattini's leaving *kāvēri paṭuna* (port of Kāvēri) and journeying to Madurai. But what does the text title mean? The term *valinaḍa* makes little sense in Sinhala, though it means "journey along the path" (to Madurai) in Tamil. The Tamil tradition of the east coast of Sri Lanka has this text title. Since the Tamil *valinaḍa* made little sense in Sinhala, it was converted to *gaman vayinaḍa*, journey into the Vayinad (Wynad), a province in ancient Kērala. It is of course possible that Vayinad was the term originally used in the South Indian texts and was later corrupted into *valinaḍa* in both the Tamil east coast and Sinhala areas. Either way, this text illustrates how titles are amended to suit local cultural conditions.

The Ritual Institutionalization of the Pattini Cult

Numerology, as I have shown, gives coherence and a sense of continuity to a ritual tradition. It gives the practitioners of the cult, dispersed over a wide geographical area, a sense of belonging to a single tradition. This promotes communication so that a chief *kapurāla* from a remote Sabaragamuva shrine (let us say Aruggoḍa) can summon a more knowledgeable and famous *kapurāla* like Patināyaka from Ūrubokka in Moravak Kōrale, Southern Province. The practice of some famous *kapurāla*s ranges over a large area. Nevertheless, when a famous *kapurāla* is invited to another province he often performs only the key ritual sequences; others are left to the local priests. This is because each region, or area, has its own ritual procedures and its own local deities, and these may be unfamiliar to the outside priest. In other words, the thirty-five texts are the doctrine of the Pattini cult; their institutionalization at the local level is another matter, which I shall now investigate.

The Pattini texts of corpus 1 are institutionalized in the contemporary *gammaḍuva*. But not all texts of corpus 1 are relevant; some are omitted, and others are "sung" minus rituals or dramatic enactments. There was traditionally (up till the mid twentieth century) a group of persons known as "singers" (*gī kiyana äya*) who, like the hymnologi of the Attis cult, sang texts of the *pantis kōlmura*, generally those that were ritually inoperative or could not be performed owing to lack of time. I saw one such group in Malidūva (Mātara tradition) in 1956; they sang some of the texts of the *pantis kōlmura* to the accompaniment of a small drum, the *uḍäkki*. These singers are nonexistent today.[2]

Since the *gammaḍuva* is generally a collective ritual performed as a postharvest ceremony of first fruits or during critical times like drought or pestilence, it is something more than the institutionalization of the thirty-five ritual texts (*pantis kōlmura*). The major and minor gods of the pantheon are summoned and propitiated under the aegis of Pattini. Demons, those malicious beings who are universally feared, are also placated. Rituals that have little or no substantive connection with the Pattini cult are also performed, since they have purposes crucial to communal welfare. Some rituals (like the "coconut game" and "horn game" to be discussed later) are often performed independently of or in conjunction with the *gammaḍuva*, generally in times of drought or disease. In all likelihood these rituals were originally independent of the Pattini corpus but were later integrated, some more thoroughly than others, with the Pattini mythology. They are rarely mentioned in any extant version of the ritual texts. The *gammaḍuva*, then, is not synonymous with the Pattini cult. It is, rather, an assembly of the deities, who are propitiated by the villagers. The major focus of these collective rituals is on Pattini. In an anthropological study context is critical to understanding religion; thus in analyzing the Pattini cult we are also analyzing its ritual context and institutionalization in the ceremonial cycle of the *gammaḍuva*.

The *gammaḍuva* is organized by a village or a cluster of villagers, generally under the leadership of the village headman, but in old times it was organized under the *gamarāla*, the head of a dominant kin group who acted as tax collector for the king. I shall not describe the details of local organization here, except to state that all the items required for the ceremony—from rice to coconuts to cash payments for the priests—are provided by the village. In recent times, owing to economic scarcity, it has become customary for wealthy patrons to bear most of the costs. Traditionally most households had special trees and specially demarcated areas of their rice fields (*balāpu vī*) reserved for the gods for this purpose.

Let us say that a village that did not have a routine annual *gammaḍuva* is struck by

2. The tradition of singers is still reflected in some low-country village names like *gī kiyana kanda*, "the mountain where songs are sung." There is also a Pattini ceremony known as *gī maḍuva*, "song hall." In this ceremony there are no ritual dramas or other enactments. The main focus is on the recital of texts by, presumably, the hymnologi, or *gī kiyana äya*.

disease or drought. The villagers then decide to hold a *gammaḍuva*. The initial preliminary act is to plant a post known as *kapa*. This can be done very simply, or elaborately with a procession and music. In general the *kapurāla* carries the insignia of the goddess and goes round the boundary (*sīmā*) of the village or group of villages. This is known as *sīmā allagannava*: literally, "holding onto (deciding) the boundary." Four altars made of banana bark and creamy coconut leaves (*gok*) roofed over with branches or thatch are constructed at the four corners of the village. These altars are known as *mal päla*, "huts for placing flowers," owing to their leaf roofs. In Heyiaṅtuḍuva these are for Gambāra Deviyo, the protector of villages, also known as Hūniyan. This custom, I think, is recent, for most other traditions propitiate only with flowers and incense the major gods at the *mal päla*, generally four out of the following: Viṣṇu, Saman, Nātha, Skanda (Kataragama), Vibhīṣaṇa, and Pattini. The numerology is once again maintained. After preliminary invocations for the four gods, the *kapa* is planted (in Heyiaṅtuḍuva, four *kapa*s). A milk tree, that is, a tree yielding milky sap, generally jackfruit—is planted in a central spot by the Pattini priest at an auspicious time. While this is planted four or five of the important *āturas* ("congregation cum patient") hold it, in an act of vicarious participation on behalf of the village. Songs about the *kapa* post (see pp. 101–3, 188–92) are sung, while the drums beat the *magul* (*maṅgala*, "festival") note. Thereafter the milk tree is decorated with *gok* streamers and hung with "five bunches" of palms; *tämbili* (yellow drinking coconut), *bōdili* (tiny green coconut), *nävisi* (ordinary coconut), *lēntäri* (tiny areca nut, *Areca concinna*), *dōtalu* (small areca nut, *Luxococcus rupicola*). This *kapa* is also known as the *äpakanuva*, "bail post": it is a vow that a *gammaḍuva* will be held within a specified period of time, so that the village will be rid of present danger. Where annual *gammaḍuvas* are performed the planting of the *kapa* post is a simple affair.

The *gammaḍuva* proper is a "release from bail": *äpa nidahas kirīma*. By this act the village—its *sīmā*, or boundary—is protected for a specified period of time (*kālasīmā*), generally one to three or four years, depending on the traditions of the locality.

There are three important categories of persons involved in the *gammaḍuva*.

The Ritual Specialists

Most important are the *kapurāla*s and their assistants, who are generally from the highest caste in this region, the *goyigama* ("farmer") caste. In the coastal areas there may be priests of the *karāva* (fishermen) or the *salāgama* (cinnamon peelers) caste. Unlike Brahmans, these persons will perform at most low-caste villages, provided the food is cooked in the right manner (see below).

Other ritual specialists are the drummers, who come from the drummer (*beravā*) caste, and the washermen (*radāva*), who provide the pure white cloths necessary for any ritual. Blacksmiths and potters are now only peripherally involved: the former supply the new knives necessary for cutting the *kapa* post and such, and the latter provide fresh pots used for the ritual and for cooking the food of the gods. Nowadays people may buy these items from the market.

Village Organizers and Assistants

Vaṭṭāṇḍi are those villagers who assist the ritual team in various ways; they are especially important in the "horn game" (*aṅkeḷiya*). The term is sometimes used for all lay assistants at a ritual. Among them there is the *maḍupurayā*, "the man of the hall city," who helps the specialists within the sacred area of the hall where the ritual activities take place. The *koṭṭōruva* (literally, "pillowcase man," a menial who carries things in a pillowcase) is the man (often the same as the *maḍupurayā*) who often acts as a butt for humor and ribald comment during ritual dramas. The most important are those *vaṭṭānḍi* who work in the specially constructed kitchen (*multängē*); they are known as *multänrāla* ("officer of the kitchen"). They cook the vegetarian meals for the gods and prepare the oil necessary for the lamps. They always wear mouth masks (*mukha vaḍam*) while cooking. The fire is also never blown by mouth (as in ordinary kitchens) but is fanned by a winnowing fan (*kulla*). In other parts of the country (e.g., Hañgurañketa) men dressed as women (representing the goddess Kiri Amma) pound and husk the rice, but never in this region.

The "Congregation-Patient," or *Ātura*

The villagers who participate in the ritual as members of the congregation are called *ātura*s. The term *ātura* is used exclusively to refer to the sick person in demon exorcism rituals. In the *gammaḍuva* the whole village participates in the ceremony as a congregation; they are individually and collectively both congregation and patient. As a congregation they propitiate the *dēva*s in collective worship; as patients they seek redress and cure from *dōsa*, or "troubles," both illnesses and other misfortunes. In this work I shall use the terms "audience," "congregation," or "patient" as the context warrants; or I shall use the indigenous term *ātura*, which combines all these meanings. The notion of *ātura* who is both patient and congregation takes us straightaway to the medical meaning of the Pattini cult as embodied in the *gammaḍuva*.

In sum, the Pattini cult and the larger cult of *dēva*s propitiated in the *gammaḍuva* is a religion in the strict Durkheimian sense. It has a body of beliefs (doctrine and myth), a set of associated rituals, a priesthood and other ritual specialists, and "a moral community" of believers or a church (Durkheim 1915, p. 45). In its this-worldly, practical, and medical orientation it is radically different from the basic "other worldly" orientation of Theravāda Buddhism; yet it is integrated into Buddhism and suffused with a Buddhist ethos that makes it vastly different, on the ideological and soteriological plane, from the Hindu worship of *deva*s.

Practitioners say that a *gammaḍuva* can be organized on the basis of twenty-four hours, three days, or seven days. The standard *gammaḍuva* lasts about twenty-four hours. In some traditions—Rabalīya—there is an initial evening ceremony at which the *maḍuva*, or hall, is consecrated; this is followed the next day by a full-scale *gammaḍuva*, giving the illusion of an elaborate, lengthy ceremony. The three-day or seven-day *gammaḍuva* may have been a reality in the past, when most of the thirty-five ritual texts were enacted, but it is a fiction today. However, this fiction might be maintained if the *gammaḍuva* is associated with other festivities. Thus if a *gammaḍuva* is held in a shrine (or Buddhist temple) there may be other ritual activities, such as fulfillment of "vows" (*bāra*), worship of the goddess at her shrine, and daily processions through the *sīmā*, or limits of the village, culminating in the *gammaḍuva* on the final night. On the village level the *gammaḍuva* is sometimes performed jointly with the *aṅkeḷiya* ("horn game") and *polkeḷiya* ("coconut game"), which then extends the festivities to three, seven, or even fifteen days. Till very recent times the *gammaḍuva* consecration and main ceremony were followed by a *pēḷi-*

yāma ("going in file"), a procession through the village, which then gives a "three-day" *gammaḍuva.*

The physical structure of the *gammaḍuva* is related to its etymology: a "hall" or "shed" constructed in a specially consecrated area of the village. Some practitioners, both in this region and elsewhere, hold the view that the shed should be constructed on a harvested field; but this, like other ideal customs, is almost never put into practice. In this regard we are faced with a typical feature of Sinhala Buddhist ritual action. The concern with symbolic space, so crucial in many Hindu festivals, is an ideal rarely put into practice. As practitioners of a this-worldly cult, *kapurālas* are pragmatists and easily adapt or change rules to suit situations. However, other symbolic features such as the cosmological symbolism of the *gammaḍuva* are maintained but, as I shall show in chapter 2, adapted to a Sinhala Buddhist context.

Let me present the Rabalīya version of the *gammaḍuva* spatial layout, since I think it approximates the ideal. The crucial feature of spatial orientation here is very simple: the altar(s) for the four gods, who formally head the pantheon, must be so constructed that the priest faces east while propitiating them. Propitiation of Pattini, the presiding deity of the *gammaḍuva*, must be done facing north; so is it for Dēvatā Baṇḍāra, whereas Devol must be propitiated facing west. But—and here's the rub—all these things can be changed with the "god's permission." Thus the most common layout at Rabalīya, in the ceremonies I have witnessed, is depicted in figure 2. Note that most of the ideal is put into practice except that Dēvatā Baṇḍāra worship requires the priest to face south: but on other occasions I have seen the Dēvatā Baṇḍāra altar in the ideal position. In Rabalīya the propitiation of demons is outside the sacred *sīmā* (boundary) of the *gammaḍuva*. A similar theory is held in other traditions, but all affirm that these rules can be changed, and in fact they often are. The layout of the Heyiantuḍuva tradition is as shown in figure 3.

Part of the lack of spatial focus is due to the overlay of competing traditions of orientation. In classical Buddhism there is the concept of the Guardian Deities of the Four Quarters, rendered in Sinhala as Hatara Varan Deviyo (Gods of the Four Warrants). They are oriented as in figure 4. But if the ancient scheme is followed, Pattini worship is, for example, oriented toward Vaiśravaṇa (or Kuvera), who lives in the north with his demon hosts! Overlaying this ancient pattern is a later one, perhaps derived from Hinduism, where north and east are propitious while south and west are inauspicious, which is also the model followed in Thailand (Davis 1974, p. 14), but with greater scrupulousness.

The Deities of the Pattini Cult

The *gammaḍuva*, as I have noted, represents the institutionalization of the Pattini cult in the villages of the Sinhala low country. The *pantis kōlmura*, the compendium of thirty-five texts, is only partly institutionalized, for reasons noted earlier. Basically the problem of institutionalization pertains to the larger issue of religious *syncretism*: the introduced cult and textual corpus must be accommodated and integrated into the preexisting beliefs of the people, and, of course, into beliefs that are introduced even later. The *gammaḍuva* itself is a communal rite widely dispersed in Sri Lanka, and in some areas it has very little to do with the Pattini cult. The presumption is strong, then, that Pattini would have dis-

Pattini altar
(*toraṇa*)

Magul kapa (post)	*Bisō kapa* (post)
Altar for the major gods and for Buddha prayers	Altar for placing anklets (and for "other dieties," e.g., Twelve Gods, Hūniyan, Kurumbara)
Devol Deviyo	Tree of the torch of time (areca nut tree)
	Dēvatā Baṇḍāra

Stand for demons

Fig. 2. Layout of the Rabalīya *gammaḍuva*.

placed a traditional indigenous deity or deities, and that some of the preexisting deities continue to be propitiated there, since they (presumably) have important ritual functions to perform for the common weal. Cults introduced into the *gammaḍuva* after the Pattini cult were also accommodated and account for the contemporary situation. These problems will be handled in detail in part 2; here I shall briefly introduce the various categories of deities propitiated in the *gammaḍuva*.

The Concept of the Four Gods (Hatara Deviyo) and Four Shrines (*Hatara Dēvāle*)

Numerology is crucial here also in giving coherence and unity to tradition. The four gods in the low country nowadays are generally Viṣṇu, Nātha, Saman, and Kataragama (Skanda). But the list is not standard, since Vibhīṣaṇa and Pattini may also be included. Pattini, however, is most often treated as a separate deity in the low country, though not in Kandy. In the Rabalīya tradition the invocation to the four guardian gods sometimes actually lists five, including Vibhīṣaṇa. Historically Vibhīṣaṇa is an older deity associated with the *Rāmāyana* as Rāvaṇa's younger brother who sided with Rāmā. His seat is Kälaṇiya, also an ancient place of Buddhist worship. I suspect that a relative latecomer, Kataragama, became popular and tended to usurp Vibhīṣaṇa's place.

The four gods, in the low country, are also called Hatara Varan Deviyo. In doctrinal Buddhism the latter were the four guardians of the universe; they are formally propitiated today, but their significance, except for Vaiṣravaṇa (Vessamuni) or Kuvera, lord of the north and overlord of demons, is minimal. Hence the term designating them is often given to the four gods, specifically as guardians of Sri Lanka, and more generally the universe. The four shrines are the abodes of the four gods, generally situated in the capital of the Sinhala kings. Kōṭṭe, for example, had this concept, and in Kandy the four shrines were for the following four gods: Nātha, Viṣṇu, Kataragama, and Pattini. Their location in the capital had political significance: they were guardians of the secular realm and protectors of Buddhism and were crucial for the rituals performed at the center. Their role in Kandy is described by Seneviratne in detail (Seneviratne 1978).

The Lesser Gods

The great gods mentioned earlier constitute the head of the pantheon; they are part of the operative pantheon in this region, whereas in the interior of Kandy and Ūva they are

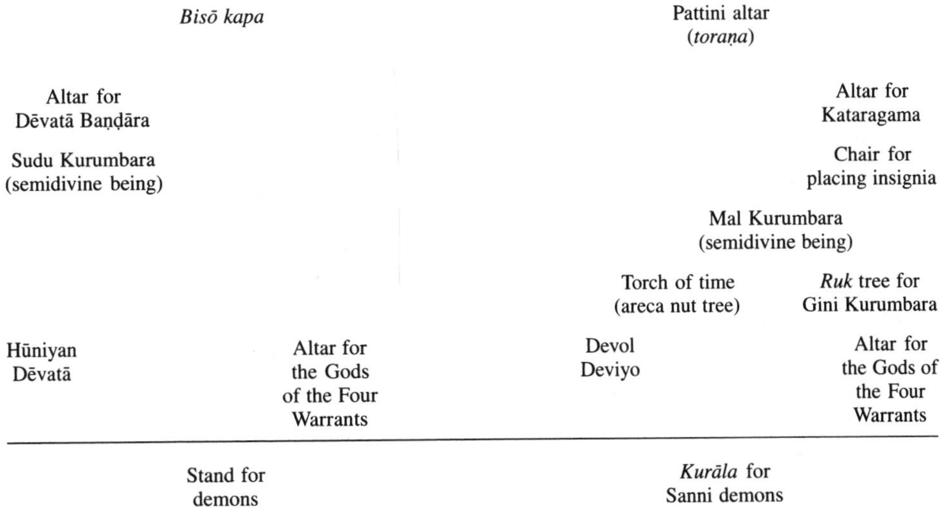

Fig. 3. Layout of the Heyiaṅtuḍuva *gammaḍuva*.

only formally invoked. Their central shrines are here. Below them in status are lesser gods, molded on the image of the four gods. These lesser gods have regional importance; their antecedents will be discussed later. Most important of these is Dēvatā Baṇḍāra, also known as Däḍimuṇḍa, and as "the god of Alutnuvara," from his central shrine in Alutnuvara (literally, "new city") near Māvanälla on the Kandy road. Then there is Devol Deviyo, a collectivity of seven gods, associated with fire walking, whose main shrine is in Sīnigama on the southwest coast. One classification system, no longer popular, groups Dēvatā Baṇḍāra, Devol, and Pattini as a unit: *tunbāge deviyo*; "deities of the three divisions." But this earlier classification has little operative significance today, since Pattini is clearly in the first category of greater deities. However, it may indicate that she once may not have had this preeminence, particularly when the cult was first introduced. This suggestion is reinforced by the fact that Pattini is occasionally referred to in texts as Alut Pattini Deviyo, "the new goddess Pattini." Other lesser gods propitiated are Maṅgara and Kiri Amma ("milk mother"), both important deities in the cults of the interior and part of the pantheon of the Twelve Gods (Doḷaha Deviyo). In parts of the low country, a vague cluster of deities known as Doḷaha Deviyo are also propitiated, but they are different from the collectivity mentioned earlier. Other lesser gods have purely local significance, such as Alut Deviyo in Moravak Kōrale, Basnāhira Deviyo ("western god") in Mātara, and so forth.

Deities of Intermediate Status

Also propitiated in the rituals of the *gammaḍuva* are deities whose status is indefinite or intermediate between divinity and demons. Some of them are deities who are rising up (or moving down) in the hierarchy of the pantheon. The most important among them is Hūniyan, the deity of sorcery, also known as Gambāra Deviyo, "the god in charge of villages." Sometimes demons like Kurumbara are also addressed as *dēvatā*, intermediate between god and demon.

(*Yakṣas*, demons)
headed by Vaiṣravaṇa (Kuvera)

W
Virūpākṣa
(*nāgas*)

E
Dhrtarāṣṭra
(*gandharvas*)

S
Virūḍha
(*kumbhānḍas* and *prētas*)

Fig. 4. Orientation of the Gods of the Four Warrants.

Demons and Evil Spirits

Three demons or classes of demons are propitiated in the three watches of the night. They are the Sanni demons, a cluster of eighteen, who cause various forms of serious physical illness (see Obeyesekere 1969a for a discussion of their role); Mahasōna, the great demon of the graveyard, and Kurumbara, a set of demons who are attendants of Devol Deviyo, the god of fire. In addition there are other demons; some are mentioned in the texts but not propitiated. Offerings are sometimes made to *pretas*, evil ancestral spirits. All altars to demons and evil spirits are in theory, and often in practice, constructed outside the sacred precincts of the hall where the gods reside.

Planetary Deities

In addition, the texts refer to various other classes of supernatural beings like the planetary deities (*graha*) and to the sun, moon, and various beings who are not very important today in the behavioral universe of the villagers. Their significance will be assessed in part 2 where the texts are presented.

The Pattini Cult as a Medical System

I noted earlier that the villagers assembled for worship before their deities are both "congregation and patient," represented in Sinhala by the key word *ātura*. The *ātura*s solicit the aid of the deity because of their *dōsa*, another key word in the medical lexicon of popular culture, derived from Sanskrit *doṣa* and meaning "faults." In Sanskrit the original meaning of "faults" has been superseded by its very specific medical meaning in classic Āyurveda. Here *doṣa* means "faults of the organism," that is, the three humors that constitute the human body (Sanskrit *tri doṣa*, which in Sinhala is rendered as *tun dos*). Thus in Sinhala the term *dōsa* has two meanings: as "humors" in the sense used in classic Āyurveda, which is also the dominant tradition of physical medicine in Sri Lanka, and the more ancient meaning as "faults," which I shall presently show has a broader, less specific meaning than physical illness. The integration of the various meanings into a conceptual system is crucial to understanding the Pattini cult and the rituals associated with it.

I have dealt elsewhere with Āyurvedic medicine in Sri Lanka (Obeyesekere 1969b, 1976). Here I shall deal with it insofar as it helps us to understand the theory of *dōsa* on which the Pattini cult as a system of medicine rests.

According to Āyurvedic theory the universe consists of several constituent elements known as *bhūta*. (The term *bhūta* denotes on the one hand "demons," and on the other the "elements.") There are various classifications of the *bhūta*s. According to some, these *bhūta*s are "space" or "emptiness" (*ākāśa*), "wind" or "air" (*vāyu*), "water" (*āp*), "earth" (*pṛthvī*), "fire" (*tejas*), and, according to some texts, "thought" or "consciousness" (*cetanā* or *viññana*). As constituent elements of the universe they are also manifest in the human body. Three of these *bhūta*s are especially important; the element of wind (*vāta*, *vāyu*) manifests itself in the human body as *vāta* (air, breath); fire appears in the form of bile (*pitta*), and water is present as phlegm (*kapha* or *śleṣman*) (Filliozat 1964, pp. 23–25). These three "humors" are called the *tri dhātu*s ("the three elements"), or more popularly the *tri doṣa* ("the three troubles"). Symptoms are caused by the upsetting ("excitement," "anger") of the homeostasis of the three humors (*sannipāta*). The treatment of illness is also based on humoral nosology. Once the excited *doṣa* has been detected, the treatment is to prescribe a medicine that can counteract this *doṣa* so as to restore the normal homeostasis of the humors. If, for example, bile (*pitta*), or the element of fire, has been excited, then it has to be opposed by the foods that produce phlegm (*śleṣman*), the element of water. Elaborate classifications of food and medical ingredients in terms of their humoral properties are found in the Āyurveda, generally in terms of binary oppositions (for more details see Obeyesekere 1976).

The Āyurvedic theory of the three humors and the whole elaborate system of physical medicine, physiology, and anatomy ultimately rest on a metamedical basis, that is, on the theory of *bhūta*s, an "atomic" theory that explains the constituent structure of the universe. Āyurvedic physicians in Sri Lanka and India deal with a highly sophisticated theory of physical medicine derived from the Sanskrit, often empirical, practical, observational, and sometimes experimental in nature. Ritual medicine, as in the Pattini cult, rests on the same metamedical base of the five *bhūta*s, but it is given further conceptual extension that removes the medical theory from that of physical medicine to religious and supernatural ideology and curing. Let me demonstrate this in relation to some of the rituals described in part 2 of this work.

Fire Trampling and Water Cutting: Metamedical Meaning

The elements or *bhūta*s that govern the organism in their humoral forms or *doṣa* must also logically govern the outer environment. In terms of the traditional peasant environment, the two crucial elements are fire, or heat, and water. Excess of fire in the outer environment leads to drought, which destroys crops, depletes water resources, and brings the threat of famine to the group. Moreover, outer heat affects the body, thus producing an excess of the bilious humor (*pitta*) and thereby causing "heaty" illnesses like smallpox, chicken pox, measles, and other infectious diseases which cannot easily be cured by traditional Āyurvedic medication. Excess of water in the outer environment may also cause flood and crop damage; on the level of body functioning it can produce (in monsoon periods) diseases of phlegm like coughs, colds, and fevers owing to excess water in the body (Obeyesekere 1969b, 1976).

If Āyurvedic practitioners of physical medicine deal with the prophylaxis and cure of physiological malfunction, ritual specialists deal with the malfunctions caused by fire and water in the outer environment. The attempt to control the elements of the universe is best seen in the water cutting (*diya käpīma*) and fire walking (*gini pägīma*) performed in the Pattini rituals described in this book. The water cutting ceremony is performed soon after the fire walking ritual, or it may be performed as an independent rite. In this ritual the priest goes in procession to a special place at a river or stream or a well that symbolically represents a waterway. He cuts the water in two with a sword and collects some in a pot, which is then deposited in a temple or shrine and kept there until the following year. The rituals are conducted in great secrecy, the waterway generally being screened off with a curtain of white cloth. I interpret this ritual as an attempt to control the element of water. The idea of keeping the water in the temple is to magically ensure a constant supply for the community during the year. It would be inauspicious for the water level in the vessel to change in any way.

Fire trampling is the other side of the coin: here the attempt is to control the element of fire. The priest, acting on behalf of the community, walks barefoot over the coals, extinguishes them by trampling them underfoot, and thereby brings under control, magically, a turbulent element in nature. Let us see whether this interpretation is borne out by the traditional fire trampling ritual performed in the *gammaḍuva* (see pp. 139–55 for a complete description).

The fire is made with a branch of the *milla* tree (*Vitex attissima*) about six to twelve feet long, cut into short lengths. This is burned in a small area of about four feet square in the middle of the dancing floor. After the coals have practically died out the priest, in the traditions of the Western Province, faces the "fire" wearing a red shawl. He asks the gods to cool the fire; some practitioners lustrate the fire with charmed water and utter a magic formula known as *gini sisila mantra*: "the fire cooling charm."

Then the priest circumambulates the fire with a water pot (*kalaya*) in his hand, sprinkling a line of water around the fire. He pours some water on his toes, and an attendant incenses his feet. The fire is practically dead by now. The *kapurāla* tramples it and turns round and round in it till it is fully extinguished. He then sits on the upturned water pot and worships the goddess Pattini in her altar. He now sings songs on Devol Deviyo and lustrates the audience with water, singing songs from mythology that describe the gods' extinguishing a prototypic fire in ancient (mythic) times.

> The gods assembled high above
> And from the sky sent flowers of rain
> Like the gushing waters of a maddened river
> That's how Madurā's fire was cooled.

In the *gammaḍuva* traditions of the Western Province it is the priest who tramples the fire: the audience is passive. In the Southern Province, members of the audience walk the fire after the priest has trampled it and doused it completely with water from the pot. In other words, the priest controls the fire, and the audience walks over it after it has been "cooled." In all of these rituals the fire/water opposition is dominant in the symbolism.

The purely formal and symbolic nature of fire-trampling comes out even more clearly in the Sabaragamuva traditions. Here also the ritual is called *gini pägīma*, fire trampling, but live coals are never used. Instead, after the ritual drama of Devol Deviyo has been enacted, four dancers dance for a few minutes with torches. They then place the torches on the dancing floor in the four directions, with the flaming ends facing inward. An actor representing Devol Deviyo wants to know what these flames are, and one of the dancers replies:

> this is a mountain of fire . . . some time back, it was not like this, it was very large, reaching to the skies, these blind *dōsa* that are like flames . . . it has become less and less, and today it is the size of these torches, these *dōsa* . . . you must destroy.

The god agrees to do so, repeating often the phrase "flames that are the *dōsa*." He sings songs recounting how the god made the fire "cool" (*sisil*) and extinguishes the "fire" (torches), which by now has died out. Here the essentially symbolic nature of the fire is clear: the flames are *dōsa*, which is the Sinhala word for "humor." The torches placed in the four directions represent fire as an element of the universe and its constituent structure.

The Goddess of Heat: The Rituals of the East Coast Hindus and Buddhists

According to the peasant ideology of both Sinhala Buddhists and Tamil Hindus of this region, an increase in the element of fire is due to the anger of the superior deities. The anger of the deity is due to "sins" committed by the human population. The very failure to propitiate the deities causes ritual danger and the anger of the deities, which in turn result in excess of fire. Thus the relevant deity has to be propitiated annually to ensure the "common weal."

According to Sri Lanka's east coast Tamils and the Buddhists of Pānama who have been influenced by them, the deity that causes fire in the universe is the goddess Pattini. It is her anger that causes fire, drought, and pestilence; hence she must be propitiated annually. The original fire and drought in the human world were caused by the anger of the goddess. She burned the city of Madurai in mythic times, destroying evil people but sparing the good. The gods in heaven pleaded with her, and she agreed to stop the fire and the attendant famine and pestilence. This was done by a rain that fell from heaven. The human community in turn thanked the goddess by boiling milk in new pots. Thus here also, according to the myth, fire was opposed by water and the depletion of fertility (famine) by milk.

The contemporary rituals for Pattini attempt to control the disturbed elements through ritual technology. Among the Tamil Hindus and Sinhala Buddhists of the east coast the propitiation of Pattini occurs once every year, about May; for the rest of the year the temple doors are closed. When the doors are ceremonially opened the goddess is exposed to public view. According to local belief there is an immediate increase in temperature; the element of fire has temporarily increased. Human beings have to be careful; they abstain from "heaty" foods, and avoid pollution. After about a week the priests start singing the sacred texts that recount the myths of Pattini. This part of the ceremony is known as *kulirtti*, or cooling. By relating the mythic history of the cooling of the goddess's anger the human community is spared drought (fire) and assured adequate water for the coming year. Furthermore, their bodies are cooled, so that pestilence owing to excess of heat is controlled. Both are ensured by the blessings of the deity being propitiated. At the end of these rituals the human community partakes of foods consecrated to the goddess. These are all cooling ritual foods, the most important being rice cooked in milk. All the participants, furthermore, drink the sacred water in which is dipped the anklet, the central symbol of the goddess. This sacred water magically cools the body, so that the humor of *pitta*, or heat, is controlled and infectious diseases are prevented. Among the Sinhalas and Tamils of Pānama (east coast) there is an additional rite of "cooling." The villagers go in procession from the temple to the sea. After an invocation and an offering (*maṭai*) to the goddess, they literally jump into the water and "cool" themselves. After this act they return to the village to resume the mundane activities that have been suspended during the period of the ceremony. A related ritual is that of "house cooling," to be described later (pp. 180–85).

The Larger Concept of *Dōsa*, "Faults"

I stated that the Sinhala people use *dōsa* in its older etymological meaning of "faults" or, to be more exact, "misfortune." It is impossible to prove whether the present meaning of *dōsa* is identical with the ancient Indian meaning before its incorporation into Sanskrit medicine "as faults of the organism." However, it is certainly possible to prove, beyond any doubt, that some of the ritual techniques of healing in the present *gammaḍuva* are derived from folk traditions going as far back as the Atharvaveda. Since the Atharvaveda is itself a compilation of preexisting Indian magical and curing techniques, the present techniques must perforce send taproots into the very dim prehistory of the Indian subcontinent.

The term *dōsa* for misfortune is probably the most common term used in the *gammaḍuva* rituals, constantly appearing and reappearing as leitmotiv in the texts I have translated. The major function of the rituals and the gods is to banish *dōsa*, or the misfortunes of the congregation as patients (*ātura*s). What then is *dōsa*?

Dōsa is a general term that embraces a large class of misfortunes that beset people as a result of their human condition. Ever since Evans-Pritchard's pioneering work on the Azande, anthropologists have shown time and again the need for human beings to explain "misfortune" in religious terms. Sinhala people not only do this but also have a technical term to designate misfortune—*dōsa*.

All ritual specialists, and the texts they narrate, clearly distinguish *dōsa* from *tri doṣa* or *tun dōsa*, the "three humors" of physical medicine. Some ritual specialists resolve the complication by making a distinction between two broad types: *amanuṣya dōsa*, "the *dōsa* caused by nonhumans," and *svābhāvika dōsa*, "the natural *dōsa*." Other specialists make a distinction between *ätul pantiyē dōsa*, "the internal class of *dōsa*," and *piṭa pantiyē dōsa*, "the external class of *dōsa*." All these classifications involve one basic distinction: there are those diseases caused by natural factors, ultimately traceable to the anger (*kōpavīma*) of the three humors, and those caused by nonnatural agents. The former can be cured by the Āyurvedic physician or surgeon; the latter are cured by various types of ritual specialists.

Amanuṣya dōsa or *piṭa pantiyē dōsa* are those misfortunes caused by a punitive noncorporeal being. These misfortunes or *dōsa* form a class wider than illness—for example, family discontent, drought, or famine. Their causes may include the wrath of a *dēva*, envy or assault by a demon, bad planetary constellations, fright from evil spirits, and so on. Thus *piṭa pantiyē dōsa* refer to a wide variety of misfortunes caused by various types of spirits, for the most varied of reasons. They do not spring from within the organism as a result of physical or physiological causes; they are caused by spirits external to the individual. However, when a person is afflicted with an external *dōsa* there will result in turn an excitement of the internal humors. To sum up, *ätul pantiyē dōsa* are caused by physical or physiological factors clinically manifested in the excitement of the humors (*tun dōsa*); *piṭa pantiyē dōsa* are caused by "nonhuman beings" (*amanuṣya*) that, when they affect humans, are also clinically manifest in humoral disequilibrium. External agents may, however, cause *dōsa* (misfortune) in the outer physical environment of man, as I have noted. When this happens there is a disturbance of the constituent elements of the universe, or *bhūta*. When *dōsa* caused by external agents results in the upsetting of the three humors of the organism (*tun dōsa*), physical remedy is ancillary at best to the main treatment, which must perforce be ritual curing.

The Classification of *Dōsa*

Piṭa pantiyē dōsa or *amanuṣya dōsa* are further classified into various types; nosology must be based on the type of external agency ("spirit") causing the misfortune. It must be reiterated that these agencies can cause *dōsa* for either the individual or the larger group (the community, family, or married couple) and that illness is only one form that *piṭa pantiyē dōsa* takes. The following (by no means exhaustive) account gives the various types of *dōsa* in relation to the agencies that cause them.

Deviyannē dōsa (*dōsa* caused by gods): under this class are many subtypes of *dōsa*, all caused by the wrath of the gods (*deviyo*) of the Sinhala Buddhist pantheon. *Avol dōsa* is a form of sorcery where the gods, rather than the demons, are invoked to bring death, ill health, disruption of family life, loss of property, or such, to one's enemy. The technique is by ritual cursing, specially by the utterance of *vas kavi* (literally, "poison songs"). These songs are constructed according to certain astrological calculations and sung before an altar of a god (generally Skanda), sometimes by Buddhist monks. The victim of the sorcerer's malice will be struck with *avol dōsa*. *Divi dōsa* (*divi*, "oath") results from perjury, owing to the gods' annoyance when they are falsely invoked. *Devol dōsa* may sometimes be used as a synonym for the larger class of *deviyannē dōsa*, or more specifically to designate *dōsa* caused by a powerful deity, Devol Deviyo. People will be afflicted with *devol dōsa* when they have been ritually cursed by an enemy at a temple of Devol Deviyo. The most common form of *dōsa* caused by the gods is where individuals have failed to fulfill vows (*bāra*) or *äpa* (literally, "bail") to the gods. The technique of *bāra* is very simple: a vow is made to a god (generally by tying a few coins, *pañḍuru*, in a piece of cloth) to the effect that if the deity removes a source of affliction, or answers a prayer or wish, the individual will perform a *pūjā* (ritual) in his honor or show his gratitude in some other specified way. Till the vow is fulfilled the individual is on bail (*äpa*) to the deity. If the individual fails to fulfill the *bāra* he will be struck with *deviyannē dōsa*. The whole community may be struck with *deviyannē dōsa* if the members have failed to perform the requisite communal rituals for the gods that constitute a kind of *bāra* or *äpa*, or if they have led sinful lives. When the individual is struck with *deviyannē dōsa* it is generally manifested in personal illness or in loss of property and wealth. If the family is afflicted with it, the members may experience similar calamities, or family and kinship dissension may arise. If the community is struck with *deviyannē dōsa* it may be manifested in the destruction of the external environment through drought (the drying up of the element of water) or in devastation of crops, animal life, and the human environment through group illness or through pestilence, plagues, and infectious diseases in general. Rituals like the *gammaḍuva* are performed by the *kapurāla* to banish the effects of *deviyannē dōsa* and to prevent its recurrence.

Graha dōsa: these are the misfortunes attendant on *graha apala* (unlucky planetary influence). A person's *graha* is irrevocably determined at birth: each individual is born under the auspices of a particular planet. Right through his life-span his fortunes are determined to a great extent by his stars. The *dōsa* that come from planets are the most difficult to eradicate, and hence all types of misfortunes that are generally inexplicable or cannot be eliminated by the normal ritual means are classed as *graha dōsa*. The typical ritual performed for those suffering from *graha dōsa* is *bali*. The *bali* ritual cannot "cure" *graha apala*, since this is generally irremediable, but it can minimize or at least ward off bad planetary influences. Owing to this the *bali* ritual is also known as a *sāntiya*, or ritual of "blessing." The specialist who performs the *bali sāntiya* is known as *bali ädura*. Though the banishment of *graha dōsa* is done by a different specialist, the *gammaḍuva* also attempts to banish the effects of bad planetary influence in a more general way.

Yakṣa dōsa: these are *dōsa* caused by demons (*yakṣa*, *yakku*). Each demon has his favorite *dōsa*. For example, the demon Kalu Kumāraya ("the Black Prince") afflicts women (generally young ones) with illness—headaches, hysterical fits, nightmares. Mahasōna ("the great demon of the grave") causes fright and is, along with Hūniyan Yakā, the agent that brings about the *dōsa* that comes from most types of sorcery (*hūniyama*, *koḍivina*, *vina*). *Yakṣa dōsa* almost never afflicts the community as a whole: generally it is the individual who is struck with it, or the family (as may be in the case of sorcery). The type of ritual used to cure an individual or family afflicted with *yakṣa dōsa* would depend on the diagnosis of the nature of the *dōsa* by a *kaṭṭaḍirāla* ("demon priest"), a seer (*pēna kiyanna*), or an astrologer (*sāstrakāraya*). The general term for these curing rites is *yak tovil* ("demon rituals"). As with *graha dōsa*, there may be individuals who cannot afford rituals to banish *yakṣa dōsa* or who may be unaware that they are afflicted by it. The *gammaḍuva* as a communal ritual helps deal with this class of *dōsa* as well as the other *dōsa* described below.

Preta dōsa: these are *dōsa* caused by inferior spirits, or *preta*s. *Preta*s, according to orthodox Buddhist texts, are the most inferior type of spirit. They epitomize the Buddhist notion of *taṇhā*, attachment or craving for the world. They are ugly creatures with distended stomachs, immensely greedy yet unable to eat owing to their needle-thin throats. They are generally ancestors whose greed for what they have left behind has caused them to be born in the domestic household as inferior spirits. These beings possess individuals and cause poltergeist phenomena. Possessing almost the same attributes as *preta*s are the *mala yakku*, ancestors or kinsmen recently dead. However, *mala yakku*, unlike *preta*s, are capable of doing good, for generally they have been reborn in their present state as a result of excessive love (attachment, *taṇhā*) for living kinsmen. But both *preta*s and *mala yakku* can be used by sorcerers to cause family misfortune. All rituals designed to banish *preta*s and *mala yakku* involve one central rite—the capture and incarceration ("binding," *bandanaya*) of the spirit. The binding of the *preta* is considered a sinful act and has unfavorable karmic effects (*karma dōsa*) on the priest performing the ritual.

Vas dōsa: *vas* is an impersonal magical force that is unleashed as a result of certain actions. When a person is struck with *vas dōsa* ("ritual danger"), it is most often manifested in illness. The effect of *vas dōsa* is immediate and automatic, and it may have several causes: (*a*) A person may violate a taboo, as, for example, if someone under pollution (*kili*) participates in a ritual for the gods. (*b*) If a person, even inadvertently, omits or incorrectly performs a ritual, he thereby offends the deities. (*c*) Witchcraft—evil eye (*äsvaha*), evil mouth (*kaṭa vaha*), evil thoughts (*hō vaha*)—all exude *vas*. Failure to fulfill a *bāra* or vow, and the utterance of *vas kavi* mentioned earlier, may also cause *vas*: in these instances *vas* forms a special subtype of *deviyannē dōsa*. Minor charms and rituals are effective for curing *vas* caused by witchcraft. For more serious types of *vas* a ritual for Garā Yakā, who acts as a remover of *vas*, may be necessary. Many large-scale rituals including the *gammaḍuva* often conclude with a ritual for Garā, known as the *garā näṭuma* ("the dance of Garā"). The idea is that Garā will remove any *vas* the participants may have contracted as a result of inadvertent taboo violation or incorrect performance of the ritual.

Karma Dōsa: Misfortunes from Karma

The several causation theories of *dōsa* are conceptually interrelated, a "smaller" theory of disease causation generally "contained" in a larger, and the more concrete contained in the more abstract. Ritual specialists agree that *dōsa*, whether arising out of physical causes or through the agency of spirits, is subsumed under two larger "laws" of causation. First, all *dōsa* arises because of bad planetary influences that can be detected by reading the horoscope. Second, these irrevocable planetary movements are indicators of a person's karma, that is, his good or bad actions in previous births. Thus planets merely chart a person's karma (see Obeyesekere 1966).

How can the theory of supernatural incursions be related to all this? The view is that when a person's *kāla*, or time (i.e., astrological "time") is bad the demons can easily inflict *dōsa*. Gods can also cause *dōsa* because of the bad karma of the individual or group; they are also instruments of karma, rewarding people or punishing them with *dōsa*. They are ineffectual if a person's karma as manifest in his horoscope is good; however, the theory of karma is such that no one can have an entirely good karma (Obeyesekere 1966). Hence, anyone can be afflicted with *dōsa* by supernatural beings. Thus, the *immediate* cause of all illness and misfortunes may be physiological or due to the action of external spirits; the *ultimate* cause is simply the bad karma of the person or groups concerned. In fact, the deities are themselves products of karma—the gods as superior beings have been born in their present state owing to their accumulated good karma, whereas inferior beings are products of bad karma; the general rule is that the lesser the status of the deity, the greater the load of his bad karma, or *karma dōsa*. There are certain logical inconsistencies in this conceptual scheme; for example, how is it that these *dōsa* can be cured if they are determinants of karma and of irrevocable planetary actions (*graha dōsa*)? These inconsistencies are useful in explaining failure to cure *dōsa* through the various therapeutic procedures.

The Cure and Extirpation of *Dōsa*

One of the major goals of the *gammaḍuva* is the cure, control, prophylaxis, or extirpation of *dōsa*. In part 2 and the sections that follow I will show in detail how this is effected. In this section, however, I shall briefly mention one type of ritual technique practiced in the *gammaḍuva*, and in demon exorcistic rituals also, that illustrates the long historical continuity of this tradition of ritual healing. I refer to a magical technique known as *sirasapāda*, ("head-to-foot verse") constantly sung in Pattini rituals.

Sirasapāda literally means *sirasa*, "head," and *pāda*, "feet." *Sirasapāda* verses are sung in every *gammaḍuva*; as many as eight or nine of these *sirasapāda*s can be sung in the course of one ceremony. The purpose of the *sirasapāda* is to magically banish the *dōsa* that lurks in the various parts of the human body from the head down to the feet. The magical technique underlying *sirasapāda* is *satyakkriyā*, or "the power of truth." According to Hindu and Buddhist views, truth has power—as, for example, the magical powers of *rishi*s and *arhat*s because of their knowledge of religious truths. In the *sirasapāda* various incidents from the life of the Buddha or his previous lives (*jātaka*) are recounted, and by the power of the truth contained therein the *dōsa* is banished. Sometimes *sirasapāda* verses recount incidents from the life of various gods like Viṣṇu or Pattini; in these cases they are known as Viṣṇu *sirasapāda* or Pattini *sirasapāda*. Two verses from a long *sirasapāda* will illustrate this:

> The ten million virtues of the Buddha
> Are eighty-four thousand;
> By the power of that fact
> Out go the *dōsa* of the head.

(The virtues of the Buddha are embodied in the *dharma skandha*s or articles of the doctrine, which are viewed by some traditions as eighty-four thousand in number.)

> With the desire of becoming a Buddha
> The king went into the forest and gave a gift;
> By the power of that virtuous act
> Released are the diseases of the palms.

(Reference is to the *Vessantara Jātaka*, in which the future Buddha, born as King Vessantara, gave away his wife and children.)

It is clear that the tradition of *sirasapāda* goes back at least to the Vedic period, though we have no information regarding its diffusion to Sri Lanka. The Vedic literature has several references to the *sirasapāda* type of cures. An example: hymn 10, verse 163, of the Ṛg Veda consists of a charm for chasing *yakṣma* or consumption from all parts of the body. This hymn is enlarged in book 2, hymn 33, of the Atharvaveda, which I quote.

1. From both thy nostrils, from both eyes, from both thine ears, and from thy chin. Forth from thy brain and tongue I root consumption seated in thy head.
2. Forth from the neck and from the nape, from dorsal vertebrae and spine, from arms and shoulder-blades I root consumption seated in thine arms.
3. Forth from thy heart and from thy lungs, from thy gall-bladder and thy sides, from kidneys, spleen, and liver thy consumption we eradicate.
4. From bowels and intestines, from the rectum and the belly, I extirpate thy consumption, from flanks, navel and mesentery.
5. Forth from thy thighs and from thy knees, heels and the foreparts of thy feet, forth from thy loins and hips I draw consumption settled in thy loins.
6. Forth from thy marrows and thy bones, forth from thy tendons and thy veins, I banish thy consumption, from thy hands, thy fingers, and thy nails.

7. In every member, every hair, in every joint wherein it lies, we with the exorcising spell of Kāśyapa drive far away consumption settled in thy skin. (Griffith 1895, 1:76; see also Bloomfield 1897, book 2, p. 44, verse 32)

In general one could say that with the development of Sanskrit (Āyurvedic) medicine in the post–Ṛg Vedic period, many diseases of physical origin were dealt with by Āyurvedic therapy. However, some illnesses (like smallpox) and other misfortunes continued to be cured by ritual medicine, in communal rituals for the gods, where the audience is both patient and congregation (worshiper).

The Audience as Congregation

The audience of villagers assembled in the *gammaḍuva* is a congregation, constituted of a moral community or church, engaged in service, not only of a pragmatic curative kind, but also of an expressive and emotional nature. The deities assembled in the *gammaḍuva*, particularly the goddess Pattini, true enough, do not serve the otherworldly goals of the worshiper, which are the province of Buddhist worship: the Buddha, the Dhamma (doctrines), and the Saṅgha (the order of monks). However, I think it is a mistake (which I am guilty of in earlier papers) to equate the contrast "this-worldly : otherworldly" goals with "pragmatic" or "material : ideal interests." Buddhist otherworldly goals, as Spiro has shown, can have pragmatic material interests associated with them (Spiro 1966). Similarly, the this-worldly goals of the *dēva* cults are not inimical to the ideal interests and the emotional needs of the worshiper. However, as far as Sri Lanka is concerned the gods are *in general* providers of material needs. The goddess Pattini, however, fulfills other needs also; she is an idealized mother figure who serves crucial emotional needs of the congregation. The rituals for the goddess are not simply a series of curing rites: they are religious services conducted by the priests of the cult. The analysis of these needs will be discussed in part 4 of this work.

2

The Assembly of the Gods

In the previous chapter I noted that the goddess Pattini is part of a highly complex polytheistic pantheon and that her cultural significance cannot be understood in isolation from the rest of the pantheon. In the *gammaḍuva* Pattini occupies a presidential status: her altar is given prime place in the layout of the ceremony, and the central rituals and myths sung there pertain to the events of her life. That the goddess occupies a presidential status in the *gammaḍuva* does not mean that her status in the *pantheon* is superior to that of the other deities. Sociologically and psychologically viewed, her cult was traditionally second only to the worship of the Buddha, but her status in the hierarchy of supernaturals was below that of many of the male deities. She is given prime place in the *gammaḍuva* because her role there is paramount.

Man's relation to the gods is everywhere characterized by subordination and dependence. The gods are powerful and superior beings who can do things for their dependent humans. In annual communal rites man expresses his thanks for the gods who have helped them in their "toil and moil." In the *gammaḍuva* all the gods who have a say in men's affairs are invoked and propitiated. It is the appropriate time and place for the village as a community to come together and offer thanksgiving to the gods in common worship.

The *gammaḍuva* as a place brings us to the initial meaning of that term. *Gam* means "village" or "hamlet," and *maḍuva* means "shed." The term therefore refers to the physical structure erected in the village for propitiating the deities. Other collective Pattini ceremonies are known as *pūnā maḍuva*, *aṅ maḍuva*, *gī maḍuva*, and so forth, and have again the term *maḍuva* as a constant feature. Thus *maḍuva* is the physical structure, the thatched cadjan shed where the rituals for the gods are performed. People gather outside the *maḍuva* to offer thanks to the gods and to witness the rituals performed inside.

It is also something more. A Sinhala villager may say "I am going to witness the *gammaḍuva*" or simply *maḍuva* ([*gam*] *maḍu balanna yanava*). Thus, *gammaḍuva* designates the rituals going on within the physical area of the shed. These rituals are viewed as a *pūjā* for the gods and also as a spectacle (*pāḷi*, *peḷapāḷi*) to please their minds. The dances and spectacles offered to them are also a kind of *pūjā*, as the Sinhala term *keḷi puda* (a pūjā of a dance) illustrates. Insofar as spectacles, dances, and games are offered to the gods, the *gammaḍuva* is also a stage, or *rañga maṇḍala*. *Rañga* means "dance," and the Sanskrit word *maṇḍala* here means "hall." It is also known as *maṇḍapa*, a decorated hall, and quite appropriately so, for the shed or *maḍuva* is in fact decorated and transformed into a *maṇḍala* or *maṇḍapa*, a hall where the gods, like royalty, are offered performances that please them.

The term *maṇḍala*, however, has another meaning in both Sanskrit and Sinhala, an esoteric meaning not readily apparent to the worshipers. In ancient Hinduism the term *maṇḍala* originally meant a circle "drawn on the ground to mark out a protected space in which the operator can safely attract or repel invisible forces" (Renou 1962, p. 93). This is the *sīmā* (boundary) of the *gammaḍuva*. *Maṇḍala* also has other meanings: it is the orbit or circle of divine influence. Thus the dance hall is a *maṇḍala*, where the gods are invisibly present, and constitutes the circle of their influence (*anuhas*). When the priests ask the gods to descend into the *raṅga maṇḍala* from their heavenly abodes, the latter meaning of *maṇḍala* becomes the operative one.

The *gammaḍuva* is, then, a shed, a hall, a dance arena, a *maṇḍala* of divine influence. It is an assembly of people (*gama*, village); it is also an assembly of the gods. This is explicitly recognized by the priests, who constantly refer to the *gammaḍuva* as a *dēva sabhāva* (*sabhā*, or assembly of the *dēvas*). The priests invite (*ārādhanā*) the gods to be present in the *sabhā*, the hall or *maṇḍapa*, which is now the physical structure for holding an assembly, again based on the idea of the assembly halls of the kings. The gods in their heavenly abodes are also viewed collectively as a *sabhāva*, where they meet for consultations and decisions, like the king's council (*rāja sabhāva*) or village council (*gam sabhāva*). The gods in heaven are now reassembled on earth in the *sabhā* (assembly), which thereby becomes their sphere (*maṇḍala*) of immediate influence.

It is the priests, acting on behalf of the community, who invite the gods up in heaven to come down to earth. The hall (*maḍuva*) is sometimes referred to in the texts as the "world" or "earth" or "Sri Lanka," which it is from the gods' point of view. The gods come down to earth; the particular human community is for them simply a part of a larger humanity in Sri Lanka and beyond that the whole world. The human participants may see their own community as unique and particular; from the god's point of view they are but devotees like those in other communities elsewhere. Though the *gammaḍuva* is erected physically within the village boundary, it is an impersonal area, clearly demarcated and consecrated as a special place. Humans assemble *outside* the sacred area; the gods remain within it. In other words, the gods are universal deities who, when they enter the *maḍuva*, or hall, also enter the earth, the world, or the island of Sri Lanka, which is their larger area of authority, jurisdiction, or sway.

The gods are present on earth in the hall, but in what form? Obviously they are invisible, yet they are present in an almost physical sense. Not only are they present in a particular community, but they may be present if invoked in other communities and shrines at the same time. They must be in this place and that, in the then and the now. They therefore obviously cannot be present *in person*; rather, they are there in *essence*. How can the gods' essence be manifest in a variety of places at one time? The Indian theory, on which the Sinhala concept is based, tells us that the essence of the supernatural being is manifest in his sight (*diṣṭi*, from the Sanskrit *driṣṭi*), or look (*bälma*). The gods are present in their *looks*; when the gods look upon the altars constructed for them, they are also present in essence in those altars. Thus, *bälma* or *diṣṭi* can be glossed as "look cum essence." This meaning is even more clear in the cultural theory of divine or demonic possession and mediumship: it is the essence of the deity, representing the deity himself, that is present within the possessed individual, or medium.

The importance of the idea of the *diṣṭi* of the god as constituting his essence comes out clearly in the Hindu and Buddhist consecration of images. The image comes to "life" only when the eyes are laid on in a ritual hedged with many taboos (Gombrich 1966). The various implements, arms, and other sacra of the deities found in Hindu temples represent the god only insofar as they have been imbued with the essence of the god through his *diṣṭi*. In the *gammaḍuva* the anklets of the goddess are brought from the priests' own shrine to the hall and ceremonially placed in the altar of the *toraṇa*. Such objects become sacra because they contain the *diṣṭi* of the deity.

Thus the gods reside in the *maṇḍala* or hall in special altars (*mal yahan*, "flower couch") designed for them. From the notion that the hall is also a residence of the gods, a place where they assemble, there flows another set of rich symbolic associations: the hall is a city of the gods. The hall (*maḍuva*) is sometimes explicitly called *pura*, "city." This idea comes out clearly in the first text sung in the *gammaḍuva*, known as *maḍupuraya* (*maḍu*, "hall"; *puraya*, "city"). The attendant who looks after the arrangement of the hall is known as *maḍupurayā*, "the man [in charge] of the *maḍupuraya*." This symbol of the *maḍuva* as a city of the gods is crucial to understanding the significance of the physical structures therein. In the ritual texts the *toraṇa* (ceremonial arch) where the anklets of the goddess are sequestered is sometimes called *vimāna* and at other times a palace (*toran māligāva*). A *vimāna* is the term used in Buddhist doctrine and mythology for an abode where supernatural beings of all types reside. The particular *vimāna* wherein reside the powerful gods of the Sinhala Buddhist pantheon is a "city," that is, a royal city containing the king's palace and its immediate surroundings, which is one of the traditional meanings of the term *pura*. The symbolism of the divine city is further expressed in the names given to the altars. Altars to gods are called *mal yahan*, "flower couch," or *asna*, "superior seat" or "throne." The gods are like royalty, lying comfortably on couches and seats or thrones in the "city," much like Indian and Sinhala royalty witnessing the "shows" offered to them. The terms are in fact derived from royal idiom. The everyday secular terms are *äňda* for bed or couch and *puṭuva* for seat or chair. When an offering has to be kept in a neutral place before being placed in an altar, it is placed in an ordinary chair known as *mal bulat puṭuva*, "flower and betel chair."

The symbolism is further spelled out in reference to the altar of the demons. Demon altars are never referred to as "couches" or "seats," but are called *vīdiya*, "street." This usage makes sense only in reference to the cosmological conceptions outlined previously. In an article on Sinhala ritual Halverson retains the meaning of *vīdiya* as "street," but for him it is a "street" connecting heaven to earth, based this time on Jungian ideas (Halverson 1971). But the "street" as an abode of demons makes complete sense in relation to our preceding discussion: the demons are the denizens of the periphery of the "city," that is, the streets. The image is again that of the traditional city, with its central area of the palace and the streets where the various castes and guilds reside. According to this imagery the gods live in their palatial abodes and lie on their couches witnessing shows, while the inferior demons reside in the outer area, the "streets." This idea is given spatial expression also: the altars ("streets") of the demons are constructed outside the sacred area (*sīmā*) of the *maḍuva* where the gods reside. Thus the *maḍuva* beautifully illustrates the overdetermined nature of ritual symbols and the multiple meanings contained in the vehicle of the symbol.

The Interaction of the Three Worlds

The ritual texts constantly refer to the three worlds, a notion found in Buddhist texts as the world of material form (*rūpa*), the world of sense desire (*kāma*), and the world of no form (*arūpa*). As reinterpreted in Sinhala popular tradition, the three worlds are those of humans, demons, and gods, presided over by the lord of the three worlds, the Buddha. The three worlds are not geographically differentiated; on the contrary, their denizens are found in varied cosmographic settings. Hence the notion of the three worlds is strictly a logical ordering or classification of beings living in diversely situated "worlds."

The ritual arena is a meeting place of the three worlds, where humans interact with gods and demons. It is a difficult interaction, for the gods are awesome beings, demanding respect and attention, and demons are altogether malevolent and vicious. The difficult nature of the interaction is eased by several mechanisms. First, sociologically speaking, the interaction is controlled by the priests acting on behalf of the community. Second, psychologically speaking, humor and sometimes disrespect directed to these supernaturals help relieve the tensions involved—as I shall show later—by creating a joking relationship. Third, a system of interdictions, prohibitions, and injunctions helps put human beings in a proper frame of mind and body to interact with supernaturals, particularly the gods of the pantheon.

Ritual interdictions and prescriptions make sociological sense only in relation to this interaction situation. I avoid using the term "taboo" since it has connotations of irrationality, whereas ritual interdictions and prescriptions are perfectly expectable and rational in relation to the interaction between man and his gods. The crux of the issue is the purity of the gods. Insofar as they are pure beings living in a transmundane sacred sphere, the worshiper must perforce recognize this in his relations with them. If they are to come down to earth they must be invited into a *sacred* area commensurate with their status as pure beings. Thus a special area in the village must be demarcated as sacred; it is purified, and consecration rituals (*maḍu pē*) make it a fit abode for the gods.

Moreover, the gods must be insulated from all sources of pollution and impurity, for, as is well known, according to South Asian beliefs pollution can affect and contaminate purity, but purity does not change pollution (Stevenson 1954). If the gods are brought into contact with impure, particularly polluting, sources, the individual as well as the community will be struck with *vas* (ritual danger)—generally illness. Thus the degree of purity that an individual maintains during the course of the ceremony must depend on the closeness of his relationship with the gods. The priests, *vaṭṭānḍi*, and other attendants, especially those who do the cooking, must be particularly careful to observe the norms of purity.

It should be noted that not only man but the demons also interact with the gods. These demons are propitiated during the three watches of the night. In rituals of demon exorcism performed in Sinhala villages, demons are deliberately offered impure foods—like meat—and burnt offerings (*puluṭu*), but offering these foods becomes difficult in the *gammaḍuva*. Here rituals for the demons are also performed within the sacred arena, so that the demons may listen and heed the commands of their overlords, the gods, and desist from harming the human community. Thus, though the demons are *normally* given impure foods, such foods cannot be brought into the sacred area of the *gammaḍuva* where the gods reside. Some priests resolve the problem by giving rice and vegetable curries to the demons in the tray (*taṭṭu*) that is brought into the arena. But after the ritual is over the offering (*pidēni*) is taken to the demon altar (*vīdiya*) outside the sacred area. Here sometimes meat and burnt offerings may be given to the demons. Thus the principle that the gods should not be brought in touch with impurity is maintained.

The Gods as Kings

I said earlier that the arena is a heavenly city, constructed on the model of the royal city. This is an interesting inversion of the Southeast Asian model of the royal city as a replica of the heavenly city (Heine-Geldern 1942). Both processes are operative: for example, the Sri Lankan kingdom of Kandy was in part based on the cosmic model, and the cosmic model is based on the kingly one. Feedback through historical time perhaps accounts for one being the model of the other and vice versa. One difference has to be noted, though: the arena as a heavenly city is not a replica of the royal city, since such a duplication is impossible given the temporary, makeshift nature of the *gammaḍuva*. Nevertheless, the operative model is the royal one, adapted to the special circumstances of a polytheistic pantheon and the context of local worship. Let us further explore the isomorphism of the divine world and the kingly one.

Gods are explicitly referred to as kings: *rajjuruvō* ("king"), *divya rāja* ("divine king"), *rājōttamayāṇan vahansē* ("noble-royal-lord"), *sakviti* (*cakravartin*, "world ruler"), and so forth. Even the goddess Pattini is a "king," a *rāja*, though a female one.

Kings are not all of equal status and power, and neither are the gods. South Asian peoples are familiar with many kings, subkings (also known as *rāja*), and rulers of provinces. In the operative pantheon of the Sinhalas the great divine kings are the Gods of the Four Warrants—Viṣṇu, Saman, Vibhīṣaṇa, Kataragama, and other major gods like Pattini and Nātha. There are major and minor gods, as there are similar rulers in the secular realm.

Gods, like kings, have areas of jurisdiction and divine authority over people within a physical area or territory. The king of the realm is viewed as a *cakravartin*—world ruler—not in reality, but as his title, betokening a legitimate aspiration. The king also incorporates a code of conduct and concepts of righteousness of a world ruler—the *dasa rāja dharma*, or ten royal virtues, mentioned in Buddhist texts. He is the ruler of the realm, and he delegates his authority to subkings and governors. *Sīmā* is the crucial word here: it designates both territory over which the king has control and also the limits of his authority and jurisdiction. The idea of the king as overlord of his realm, who has delegated his authority to subkings or governors, is translated in respect to the organization of the pantheon. But the translation is not as clear-cut as in the secular realm, for the simple reason that the major gods of the pantheon have similar, if not strictly equal, status. Their areas of jurisdiction must therefore necessarily overlap, which of course poses no real problem in the divine realm, as it would in the secular. Thus the authority structure of the pantheon uses the *idiom* of South Asian feudalism, but it is not a *replica* of the structure of feudalism.

The problem of translation is especially apparent in relation to the major gods propitiated in the *gammaḍuva*. All these gods have similar attributes, rights, and jurisdiction. They are all defenders of the Buddhist faith and protectors of the *sāsana* (the Buddhist church). While they are universal gods in theory, they have clear and undisputed jurisdiction over Sri Lanka and are therefore protectors and divine overlords of the secular realm.

There are also differences in the powers and attributes of these gods, but their broad jurisdiction is identical, a situation that obviously cannot exist in secular kingship. The problem is resolved in the following way: while these major gods have identical universal jurisdiction over Sri Lanka (and the world), they also have areas of special jurisdiction where their power and authority are especially manifest. The idea has its parallel in Sinhala kingship, where the king is ruler of the whole realm but his area of power may be particularly manifest in the region or province where his palace is situated. In the case of the gods, the palace is the shrine. A shrine may be found anywhere, in accordance with the notion of universal sway, but there is also a main shrine of the deity, and the region surrounding that shrine is his special *sīmā*, or territory. Thus Skanda has his shrine in Kataragama, and Viṣṇu has his in Devundara; practically the whole of the contemporary Western and Southern provinces are shared by these two deities. Villagers in these regions could point out the exact boundaries (*sīmā*) of these gods' territories (*dēsa*). Farther north is Sabaragamuva Province, whose presiding deity is the god Saman. These boundaries are not immutable: as the importance and popularity of the deity decline, his territory too shrinks, and he may even be forgotten or rendered irrelevant.

By contrast, minor gods are like governors of provinces having smaller territorial authority within a larger realm. Yet when they become popular they begin to expand their territory and share the attributes of the higher gods, as I shall show in my analyses later on.

Related to *sīmā* are other notions: *pirisa* ("following") or *pirivara* ("retinue") and *däkum* (literally, "seeing," i.e., "paying court"). Briefly stated, the South Asian notions of power relate to control not only of territory, but also of people. A feudal lord's following consists of his tenants, and every man has his following in his kinsmen (*nā̆ pirisa*). The strength of a person's *pirisa* is an index of his status. A man's following may be scattered, but it is mobilized on special occasions like rites of passage, which helps vindicate his public status. In Sinhala culture there are standard occasions where a man's following pays him court or homage. This is known as *däkum*, from the well-known Sanskrit word *darśana*. The Sinhala New Year is an occasion for the tenant to pay *däkum* to his lord, the son to the father, the junior kinsmen to the senior, the low in status to the high. In the realm of kingship, *däkum* is the occasion where the rulers of the provinces pay court to the king. The larger population also may pay homage to the king at annual processional events like the parade of the tooth relic, where the rulers of the divine as well as secular realm appear (*däkum*) before the public (Obeyesekere 1967, pp. 213–26).

In the divine realm the lesser gods constitute a retinue of the major gods: they are viewed as ministers of the king or as subkings. The demons are a part of their larger following; they are like servants of the gods and are under individual direct command of some of the lesser gods. As servants they perforce are at the beck and call of the gods. They are nevertheless wayward beings who must be brought under control and constantly reminded of the gods' commands. The god who is preeminently in charge of demons is Dēvatā Baṇḍāra, who appears with the stick (*daṇḍa*) in hand, a symbol of his authority over the demons. I shall show later that Dēvatā Baṇḍāra's specialized role as lord of the demons was shared by other gods at other times. All gods, nevertheless, in a general and formal sense, have authority over demons, while some (like Dēvatā Baṇḍāra) have this as a major specialized role. The priests invite the demons into the arena and compel them to obey the orders of the gods or remind them of their promises to the gods to desist from harming humans. The demons, as servants, are brought before their masters, the gods, and made to obey their commands (*aṇa*).

The human congregation is like the citizenry of the nation. The *gammaḍuva* is, among other things, a yearly occasion where citizens come to pay their homage and pay court (*däkum*) to the gods. As is appropriate for such occasions, the gods are feasted with spectacles and processional events. I suggest that the ceremonies of first fruits, which occur in many cultures, are translated into the idiom of courtly culture in Sri Lanka. The service to the gods is called *tēvaya*, or *tēvāva*, which is also the term used to describe royal service. The two services are by no means identical, yet some of the services are common to both; as for example, the spectacle of the umbrella, the symbol of sovereignty of the *cakravartin*. These kinds of similarities will be highlighted later when I describe the rituals in part 2.

The Buddha as World Ruler

The Buddha's status in the hierarchy of gods and demons is crucial to understanding the nature of the pantheon. His supreme and superordinate status is unequivocal. Both in behavior and in the ritual texts, in fact in every context of Sinhala culture, this attitude is absolutely clear. The Sinhalas are Buddhists, and the Buddha, the Dhamma, and the Saṅgha are the most important focuses of religious worship. The priests of the Pattini cult are lay Buddhists, as indeed are the gods themselves in Buddhist thinking. The gods are a category of laymen who are followers of the Buddha and, like humans, are in need of salvation. This idea, I shall show, has relevance to the attitude of human beings toward the gods, and vice versa, as well as in that of the gods toward the Buddha.

The role of the Buddha in Sinhala religious thinking is double. In the first place, the Buddha is the enlightened one, the founder and teacher of the Dhamma. He is, in Sinhala conception, the exemplar of all that is spiritual and nonmaterial. He is no longer alive, having achieved final release, or Nirvāṇa, and therefore cannot have any intercessionary role in the affairs of the world, unlike a conventional deity. The order he founded, the Buddhist monkhood, or Saṅgha, carries on this same "fiction," so that monks, barring a few exceptions, do not participate actively in the rituals to the gods.

Whereas the monks stay aloof from the rituals to gods, the Buddha is centrally involved in them. He is viewed as a kind of deity and a "wheel turning world ruler"—the *cakravartin*. All rituals to the gods—in the *gammaḍuva* and elsewhere—must commence with the priest formally seeking permission (*avasara*) from the Buddha, the Dhamma, and Saṅgha; a formal recognition of the supremacy of the Buddhist scheme vis-à-vis the gods and the worldly interests they represent. The Buddha, however, is involved in the pantheon in a less formal and more direct manner. The mythology of the gods sung in the *gammaḍuva* makes constant references to the Buddha. An analysis of these myths yields the following conclusions:

1. The power that the gods possess is subordinate to the power and authority of the Buddha.

2. The power of the gods is exercised under the aegis of the Buddha's authority. The Buddha is the ultimate source and repository of the power they exercise.

3. The gods are Buddhist laymen, though of superior status and closer to salvation than ordinary mortals. As Buddhist beings, they exercise their authority in a *rational* manner, that is by punishing evil and rewarding good and implementing Buddhist ethics and morality. Their control of the evil demons springs from their righteous and rational outlook.

This notion of power is crystallized in the crucial concept of *varan*, again derived from South Asian kingship. In Hinduism, particularly in the mythology of Śiva, scholars have translated this concept as "boon." Thus in Hinduism gods often give boons in an irrational manner, that is, not directed toward social or ethical ends (O'Flaherty 1973, pp. 293–302). In Sinhala Buddhism this is not the case, and the same word could best be translated as "warrant" or "permission." The term is derived from the ideology of kingship. The king as the supreme lord of the soil (*bhūpati*) delegates his authority to others. Subkings and governors of provinces have a warrant or *varan*; they in turn delegate their authority to lesser officials, and so down the line to village headmen. The warrant to exercise authority, or *varan*, is often enshrined in a letter of authority, or *sannasa*. These ideas are transferred to the organization of the pantheon, so that in some ritual dramas the deity may actually read out the letter of authority he received from the Buddha (Obeyesekere 1969a; see also pp. 309–12).

The concept of *varan* in the pantheon implies then a devolution of authority from its source in the Buddha and the rational direction of that authority toward a just, ethically founded order. This authority may be directly given by the Buddha in his own lifetime, or it may be delegated to others by those gods who originally obtained it from the Buddha. The mythology of the major gods is linked with the Buddha mythology in this manner. The most clear-cut examples are Sakra, the guardian of the universal Buddhist church, and Viṣṇu, the protector of the church in Sri Lanka. An indirect instance is the goddess Pattini, who offered alms to a previous Buddha and by virtue of that good deed was born as a hermit in Am̆dungiri, meditating on future Buddhahood. She thus obtains *vivaraṇa* (permission) from previous Buddhas. The term *vivaraṇa* is generally used of the Buddha himself, who obtained permission to achieve Buddhahood from previous Buddhas. Its transference to Pattini mythology indicates the strongly Buddhist nature of this divinity. Later on, in Am̆dungiri, she is accosted by Sakra (whose *varan* comes direct from the Buddha), who gives her *varan* to come down to earth, blind the middle eye of the Pāṇḍi king, and restore rightness and order in the human world.

Very often when a minor deity is moving up to a major position in the pantheon, his mythology is directly linked to the Buddha. Thus Däḍimuṇḍa, or Dēvatā Baṇḍāra, a regional deity not mentioned in ancient sources, became in later mythology a god who stood by the Buddha when he was attacked by the demon hosts of Māra. The Buddha gave him *varan* over demons. This poses a further problem of organization, since according to ancient Buddhist conceptions Vaiṣravaṇa (Vessamuni), the god of the northern quarter, had this *varan* over demons. To resolve this, Dēvatā Baṇḍāra is converted into a *yuvaraja* (subking) of Vaiṣravaṇa, and he is portrayed this way in the *gammaḍuva* texts. Thus Vaiṣravaṇa can continue his traditional role as the overlord of demons.

If the gods are kings and derive their authority from the Buddha, then the latter must surely be the king of them all, which in Indian thinking is *cakravartin*, or world ruler. Although the gods have this as *a title*, they are no more *cakravartin* in reality than is any

South Asian king. It is the Buddha who clearly is one. The term *devātideva*, the god of gods, given as an honorific to the Buddha in the *suttas*, is actualized in the folk adaptation of Buddhism. Thus the Buddha has two roles in Sinhala Buddhism. The dominant operative one is the Buddha as supreme world renouncer, uninvolved in the mundane world. The other, which is operative only in the pantheon, is the polar opposite role of world ruler (*cakravartin*). Buddhists in Sri Lanka recognize this implicitly when they refer to the Buddha in two ways: as *budu hāmuduruvo* "Lord Buddha," the enlightened one, which is his role vis-à-vis man, and as *Budu rajāṇan vahansē*, "the noble Buddha king," which is his role vis-à-vis another segment of the Buddhist lay population, the gods and by extension also man, since both gods and men, in Buddhist thinking, are of the same larger logical class of karma-bound beings involved in *saṃsāra*.[1]

The idea of Buddha as world ruler seems, on the surface, heterodox. According to a famous Buddhist text, the *Mahāpadāna Sutta*, the Buddha was born with the thirty-two marks of the "great man" (*mahā puruṣa*). Astrologers predicted that he would become *either* a Buddha *or* a world ruler. The mythology of his renunciation when he leaves the royal life to take up the homeless one symbolizes his choice of the former. Its ongoing historic and contemporary significance is clear. This myth is enacted in the *upasampadā* ritual when a novice becomes a full-fledged monk (Seneviratne 1973). Yet the *cakravartin* role is an inevitable development; its starting point must surely be in the attempt to incorporate the contemporary gods of Buddha's time into the Buddhist fold. As I said earlier, these gods were viewed in the early Buddhist *suttas* as a category of laymen themselves in need of religious instruction. They listen to the Buddha's sermons, and the Buddha discourses with them. The upshot of including the gods in this manner is to put the Buddha above them. The capacity of the Buddha to interact with the gods is not a heterodox notion, since in Indian thinking in general a great man or saint has supernormal (but not necessarily divine or supernatural) abilities that can give him these powers. But if this line of thinking is carried into the popular tradition that perceives gods as having power and as being kings, it is inevitable that the Buddha should end up king of them all, the final source of divine authority and power. These conceptions developed early in the history of Buddhism, as Reynolds points out in an important essay, so that "the historical life of the founder and the royal mythology and symbolism are thoroughly fused" (Reynolds 1972, p. 16). The process of this transformation should be clear from the preceding discussion.

The germ of the *cakravartin* idea as it appeared in the *suttas*, and its more elaborate treatment in later texts, did not involve a doctrinal contradiction. As Reynolds says, even the doctrine, the Dhamma, was viewed as *cakravartin*, which is absurd from a literal and commonsense point of view. Reynolds also says that in "their efforts to express the meaning of the Dhamma, as in their attempts to convey the meaning of the person of the

1. The distinction between the roles of world renouncer and world conqueror comes out clearly in relation to the buildings that house Buddha images. The village temple is called *vihāra*, but the central shrine in Kandy that houses the tooth relic is a *māligāva*, or palace. The reason is clear: the worshipers at a *vihāra* are human beings, whereas in Kandy this is not the case. In Kandy the tooth relic (representing the Buddha himself) is paraded in the annual procession along with the guardian gods of the realm and also, at least traditionally, with the king and officers of the realm. The ordinary citizens were spectators witnessing a "cultural performance." Given this role of the Buddha as overlord of the guardian gods and of the king himself, it is highly appropriate that he resides in a palace or *māligāva* rather than a temple or *vihāra* (for details, see Seneviratne 1978).

founder, the early Buddhist turned to the symbolism and images of sovereignty" (Reynolds 1972, p. 17). The problem, however, is more complex in the *later* development of this idea in Sinhala Buddhism, as is evident in the *gammaḍuva* and other ritual traditions of Sri Lanka. According to orthodox doctrinal conceptions, the power to alter events cannot lie with the gods, but rather resides within man himself in his good and bad actions over the course of his many births and rebirths (i.e., in his karma). In the Sinhala ritual traditions man asks the gods to help him, which must subvert the karmic law and produce a doctrinally heterodox notion. Furthermore, the idea that the Buddha is a god involved in the affairs of the world is totally undoctrinal. These complications are handled in the following way: First, the idea that the gods have power to alter karma remains, for the very idea of propitiating the gods is a means of escaping from the harsh inevitability of the doctrinal law of karma. Yet there is a partial attempt to meet the doctrinal issue in the idea that the powers of the gods *ultimately* derive from the founder himself. Second, the Buddha is spared from being a conventional intercessionary god through the Sinhala view that he allocated these powers while he was alive, that is, before his death and final release (*parinibbāṇa*). Thus the idea that the Buddha is no longer alive and active is maintained. However, gods who received the original *varan* are active in the world in maintaining a Buddhist social and moral order. The Buddha as *cakravartin* is pitched in the past tense, never the present, as far as the ideology governing the pantheon is concerned.

The Integration of the Pantheon

It is evident from the preceding discussion that, although the pantheon is constituted from several historical sources, it is not a thing of shreds and patches. The Pattini cult is a coherent tradition with a common body of thirty-five texts, the *pantis kōlmura*. The priests of the Pattini cult were primarily responsible for the continuity of that tradition and its modification under changed sociohistorical circumstances. These priests were not as specialized as the Buddhist monks and did not produce a systematic or speculative theology. Nevertheless, the textual compendium is not an ad hoc collection of texts; the texts and the mythic traditions they represent are an orderly system of beliefs. In these texts there are attempts to integrate diverse mythological traditions into a coherent framework, or into several frameworks. Let me show how this is accomplished.

There is an attempt to see the cult of the gods (*dēva*) as a system of worship that exists within the larger belief system of the Sinhalas. Thus the texts sometimes refer to the *dēva sāsana*, the church of the *dēva*s, in contrast to the Buddha *sāsana*. The *kapurāla*s are priests of the *dēva sāsana* as monks are of the Buddha *sāsana*, and as *kaṭṭaḍirāla*s are exorcists of the demon cults. The distinction between *kapurāla* and *kaṭṭaḍirāla* is very clear in the Southern, Western, and Sabaragamuva provinces, but not elsewhere in Sri Lanka. The *dēva sāsana* is part of the larger Buddha *sāsana*; inferior and subordinate to the latter. It is from the perspective of *dēva* worship and its authority structure that the Buddha is seen as a *cakravartin*.

While the Buddha's status is thus redefined in terms of his role vis-à-vis the pantheon, the nature of the gods is also redefined and brought into line with the supreme status of the Buddha. That is, while the Buddha is made into a kind of god, the god is also made into a kind of Buddha. This is inherently possible within the Buddhist tradition, which postulates previous and future Buddhas. Thus all the major and most of the minor gods are seen as aspirants to future Buddhahood, that is, as bodhisattvas. The technique simply converts foreign Hindu and folk deities into Buddhist ones, much as the Buddha is converted into an avatar of Viṣṇu according to some Hindu belief systems. Moreover, the gods as bodhisattvas are made to fit in with the larger tradition of Theravāda Buddhism. They are not savior gods who have deliberately postponed their own salvation to save the world as in Mahāyāna. Rather, they are strictly *aspiring* to become Buddhas—some closer to their goal than others, the next in line being Nātha, who is viewed as the very next Buddha Maitreya, followed by the other pious, benevolent gods Saman and Viṣṇu. If gods aspire to Buddhahood they must do good. Thus, the more benevolent the god, the closer he is to Buddhahood; and the closer he is to Buddhahood the more "remote" he becomes, like the Buddha himself, having progressively little to say in the affairs of the world. Hence Saman and sometimes Viṣṇu are perceived by Sinhala Buddhists as *sōvahan* (Pāli *sotāpanna*, i.e., in the first stage of Nirvāṇa), while Kataragama, who is closely involved in affairs of the world, still has a long way to go.

The redefinition of these gods as bodhisattvas has several implications.

1. The bodhisattva status of the god annuls his linkage with the prior Hindu or folk tradition. Thus previously Hindu gods like Viṣṇu and Skanda cease to be purveyors of salvation in the Sinhala Buddhist tradition. Salvation continues to depend on life lived in accordance with the Dhamma rather than on the intercession of a god. Gods help men cope with the problems of the mundane world; they have no say whatever in man's salvation.

2. As aspirants to future Buddhahood, the gods must perforce acquire good karma, or merit, to speed up the achievement of their goal. The help that gods give man is expressed in the Buddhist idiom of merit making. For example, the goddess Pattini is meditating for future Buddhahood when Sakra asks her to be reborn in the human world to alleviate the suffering in the kingdom of Soḷī. She will eventually become a Buddha after, of course, being reborn for the last time as a male, since according to the popular tradition a female cannot become a Buddha. Man's gratitude to the gods comes out in the custom of *deviyanṭa pindīma*: giving merit to the gods. *Pindīma*, or merit giving, has two meanings. The gods do good and earn merit; and we humans are grateful and acknowledge those meritorious actions, much like a beggar who, on receipt of goods or money, says "may you acquire merit." The meritorious act of the giver is enhanced by the gratitude of the receiver: the motives of giver and receiver are matched. Thus, *pindīma* means "thanksgiving," and the *gammaḍuva* is full of references to this custom.

3. Man too can help the gods to speed up their Buddha aspiration. Here the popular Buddhist notion of merit transfer is utilized. Man transfers to the gods the merit *he* has acquired by doing good, which then enhances *their* store of merit and brings them closer to salvation. There are constant references to this idea in the invocations of the *gammaḍuva*. The relationship between man and the gods, like social relationships in general, is one of true reciprocity. The gods help man obtain the goods of the world and alleviate human suffering; man then helps the gods in their salvation quest by transferring merit to them. The upshot of all of these ideas is the view that man as well as his gods is karma-bound, in the Buddhist sense, and all belong to a larger Buddhist conception of life, *saṃsāra*. *Saṃsāra* embraces the whole of existence—not simply human existence, but that of all beings. Gods are a category of beings who, by the good they have done, have achieved

their high status; they are embodiments of Buddhist values, just as demons represent devalued opposites like hate (*krodha*), greed (*lobha*), and attachment (*taṇhā*).

The integration of alien deities into a Buddhist scheme is not unique to the *dēva* cult but permeates all of Sinhala culture. Some aspects of this integration are in fact specific to the *dēva* cult and more narrowly to the Pattini cult itself, indicating a specific orientation of the *dēva* cult in relation to other cults like that of demons and planetary deities. All cults are translated into a Buddhist ethos in the manner sketched earlier, but the specific details of that translation reflect the orientation of the cult in question and of its priests. Let me give several examples of those specifics.

1. In the *dēva* cult, the demons obtain *varan* from the gods, who have in turn obtained it from the Buddha. This reflects the specific integration of the demons into an orderly scheme of things from the point of view of the *dēva* cult. However, in rituals performed by the priests of the demon cult, some demons *directly* obtain *varan* from the Buddha. There is also an attempt to link some of the demonic mythology to events in the life of the Buddha (Obeyesekere 1969a).

2. In the demon cult the demon Mahasōna has a mythological history that has nothing to do with the *dēva* cult (Wirz 1954, pp. 28–30). This mythology is also the one popularly accepted by the people. Yet in the *dēva* cult Mahasōna is born out of the flames that emerged from Basma the *asura*, thus linking him clearly to the *dēva* cult (p. 142) and Skanda worship. Along with Mahasōna are also born other demons like Gini Kurumbara, who have practically no role in the demon cult but are important in the *dēva* cult as attendants of the god Devol. Thus you may have within the larger culture a contradictory mythology, but little contradiction exists when things are viewed from the perspective of a particular cult. Ordinary people may accept one or both versions. However, everyone is agreed on the *general* issue that the gods as bodhisattvas are superior to the demons and can command them, and that all supernaturals are involved in *saṃsāra* and are bound by the karmic law.

The Nature of the Deities

The gods, like humans and other species, have a general nature common to all, and specific attributes and histories differentiate them from one another. All deities—gods as well as demons—have their natures and attributes defined in relation to the Buddha, the superdeity who heads the pantheon. The Buddha, as I have noted, is completely benevolent; the gods who are future Buddhas must also be benevolent. The Buddha no longer exercises power: the gods to whom he has delegated power through warrants (*varan*) exercise it in the furtherance of the Buddhist *sāsana* and the Buddhists of Sri Lanka. The ends of power must be just, righteous, and ethical. The gods help man; but men must also be good Buddhist laymen living up to the injunctions of Buddhist morality. This idea is formally recognized in the custom where the *kapurāla*, before eating the evening meal, recites the five precepts along with his assistants and the congregation. Buddhist gods may be punitive, but it is a *rational* punitiveness that punishes evil and rewards good. Some of the gods like Dēvatā Baṇḍāra mercilessly beat demons, but this is to make them submissive and to prevent them from harming human beings. To sum up some major attributes: gods are benevolent, but also powerful; they are rational deities, acting to bring about moral order in the world.

The texts refer to several terms that are coordinate with the general terms "power" and "benevolence."

balaya: power	*karuṇā*: benevolence
aṇasaka: command, renown	*met*: compassion (*maitriya*, *mettā*)
vikrama: valor, heroism	*pihiṭa*: help
mahima: might	
kīrti: renown, fame	

An exercise of power due to spiritual virtues, that is, a combination of power with benevolence, is *ānubhāva*, "spiritual influence." The result of these attributes is the gods' capacity to help people: *rakinava*, "to protect," and *pihiṭavenava*, "to help," "to succor." It is interesting that the terms in the second column above are from doctrinal Buddhism, particularly the key terms *karuṇā* and *maitriya*. The terms in the first column are from the ideology of kingship. However, some key Buddhist doctrinal terms associated with *karuṇā* and *maitriya* are absent from the list: *muditā* ("tenderness") and *upekkhā* ("equanimity"). I suspect that this is because the gods are involved in the world, and equanimity in particular is a value involving detachment from the world. *Muditā*, "tenderness," is also not possible for the king-gods, who have to punish and mete out justice, whereas compassion and benevolence (at least as these ideas are adapted in popular usage) may entail a rational or righteous punitiveness. Gods as kings cannot have tender minds, nor can they look on the world with equanimity.

The gods have certain physical attributes that are also related to the notions of royal power and spiritual benevolence. They are attractive and handsome and are "pure"—that is, pollution free—pollution being associated with bodily processes from which they are to a large extent exempt. However, the most crucial attribute is *teda*, from the Sanskrit word *tejas*. The Sinhala term has connotations of power, but also physical connotations of "shining," "spreading of glory," "splendor." *Teda* is like Wordsworth's idea of "trailing clouds of glory," the physical emanation of light, an outer manifestation of the qualities of power and benevolence. *Teda* is both physical and spiritual power as well, in its manifestations in the outer appearance of the gods as full of light, shine, and splendor. The prototypic meaning of *teda* is from the Buddha mythology where Buddha defeated the hosts of Māra (Death) by his spiritual power coming from *tapas* (ascetic self-control); there he emitted rays of various colors that kept the evil forces at bay. The gods likewise control evil demons, and likewise they exude glory—both aspects of their *teda*.

The demons, in contrast to the gods, are irrational beings that inflict harm without just cause or principle, upset the moral order by their wickedness, and make humans suffer. The vagaries of fortune that contradict a rational conception of order are often explained in terms of demonic intervention. Gods are kings: kings have powers, but they cannot always anticipate disruptions of the secular order by crime and violence. Thus king-gods cannot stop demons from causing harm; they can admonish them, punish them if they do evil, and control them. But wickedness and evil cannot be stopped. The demons have power, but they are not benevolent. In the gods power is associated with positive physical and moral qualities; in the demons power is a negative force. Demons are ugly, low (*nīca*), impure. Their outstanding characteristic is cruelty. The *gammaḍuva* texts do not give detailed accounts of demons, but practitioners of the demon cults, as well as the public, have fairly elaborate conceptions of them. I shall not discuss these here except to say that, if the gods represent Buddhist virtues of *karuṇā* and *maitriya*, the demons represent their polar opposites: attachment (*taṇhā*), greed (*lobha*), hate (*krodha*), enmity (*vaira*), and so forth. The demons are embodiments of bad and evil qualities devalued by the Buddhists. The gods must control the demons to prevent disruption of the social order and the physical health of people.

Deference and Propitiation

The gods are kings, but superior to their earthly counterparts. The latter are *bhūpāla*, lords of the soil or earth, whereas the former are *lōkapāla*, rulers of the worlds. They are addressed as noble (*utum*) and exalted (*sah̆da*). Though qualitatively different, kings and gods fall into the same class: sovereigns. The attitude of the worshiper to both king-gods and god-kings is similar, subject of course to the constraints of time and place. For example, when a citizen confronts the king, he has to undergo a ceremony of abject propitiation involving prostration. This is rarely practiced among Sinhala Buddhists toward their gods and was not done in any of the *gammaḍuva* rituals I have seen. Again one must see the deference behavior of people toward their gods in relation to the Buddha. One bends low or kneels before the Buddha, and one may sometimes briefly place one's hand on the floor, but falling on the floor is not required and is rarely practiced. There is evidence in the *gammaḍuva* (see chap. 7) that the extreme forms of prostration given the king were resented by the Sinhala people. The deference behavior accorded the Buddha is, of course, set by the Buddhist monks, not the priests of the *dēva* cult. But since the *dēva* cult takes its place in relation to the former, its modes of deference cannot surpass those accorded the Buddha, for that would upset the whole status hierarchy and order of precedence in the pantheon. It is no accident that Sinhala Buddhists perceived the abject prostrations that developed in the courts in later times, particularly in the Kandyan period, as not quite "right" and not quite Buddhist.

In the *gammaḍuva*, constant references are made to the Buddha, the Dhamma, and the Saṅgha. The gods are inferior to these Three Jewels (*tun ruvan*), and deference behavior to the gods is concomitantly lower than that accorded the Buddha (and the monks). No kneeling is practiced; people worship the gods with hands on foreheads, either standing, squatting, or seated on the floor on mats. In accordance with the status of gods as pure beings and future Buddhas, they are offered only pure foods, flowers, soft incense, lights, and a vegetarian diet. By contrast, demons are never "worshiped": they are not offered flowers, except red flowers and hibiscus, which traditionally were used to garland criminals taken to execution.

Concomitant with their respective status is a language distinction that is consistently maintained in respect to gods and demons.

1. Language of invitation: gods are invited as *vaḍinna*, a term used for social superiors, which perhaps could be translated "respectfully arrive," whereas demons are invited with *varennē*, "come" as used toward social inferiors.
2. Gods are given *puda* (from *pūjā*), demons are placated with *doḷa*, an inferior oblation signifying "craving."
3. Gods reside in a *mal yahana* ("flower couch") or *asna* ("throne"), demons in a *vīdiya* ("street").

4. The term *pē* is used for "consecration," "dedication," or "sacralization" regarding the gods; *käpa* is used regarding demons.

These language distinctions are subject to one change: the words used regarding the gods can be used for demons when the priest wants to flatter and cajole them, but the words used in demon propitiation can never be used regarding the gods. Thus demons can be flattered with a *puda* (from the Sanskrit, *pūjā*) but never can a *doḷa* be used for the gods. Following the same logic, the term *puda* cannot be used in respect to an offering given to the Buddha; the Buddha offering is a *pūjā*, the high-sounding Sanskrit term.[2] But, though the Buddha cannot be offered *puda*, the gods can be offered a *pūjā*. A *pūjā* for demons is unthinkable.

The preceding discussion has dealt with the general character and attributes of the deities: gods and demons. While the deities share generic traits, they are also individual beings with attributes that differentiate them from one another. These differences pertain to the myths that deal with the origin and life of the deities, and some of the personal qualities, character traits, virtues, or weaknesses that are unique to particular gods. Alternatively, some of the generic traits discussed earlier may be emphasized in one god and deemphasized in another.

God and demon have both categorical and individual significance. These differences are important in respect to the individual's relationship with the deity, since what he expects must perforce be related to the god's character and nature. It would be out of character, for example, for a Catholic to ask the Lord to find him a job or cure his wife's migraine headache; such petty demands fall within the purview of a saint. So it is with the supernaturals in the Sinhala Buddhist pantheon.

The Internal Dynamics of the Pantheon

Four gods—Viṣṇu, Saman, Vibhīṣaṇa, and Kataragama—are classed as the Gods of the Four Warrants and are propitiated in that order. Other gods of similar status are Nātha and Pattini. While all of them have similar attributes, they have different mythological histories. Their attributes, however, are not evenly distributed. Viṣṇu, Saman, and Nātha are more benevolent than punitive, closer to the Buddha and sharing some of his character. Nātha is the very next Buddha, Maitreya; Viṣṇu is in charge of the *sāsana* in Sri Lanka; and Saman is overlord of the Samanala Peak where lies the sacred footprint of the Buddha. Now we can formulate the cultural principles that govern change in the pantheon.

PRINCIPLE A: *Wherever the Buddhist virtues of compassion (*maitriya*) and benevolence (*karuṇā*) increase in the character of a god, there is a concomitant decrease in his punitiveness, however righteous it may be.*

PRINCIPLE B: *The more benevolent and compassionate the god, the more remote he becomes in relation to the worshiper.*

Let me elaborate on these principles. I noted earlier the popular view that Viṣṇu and Saman are on the first stage to Nirvāṇa as a result of the good they have done. Nātha is

2. I must qualify this, however. It is possible to say in Sinhala *Buduṇṭa mal pudanava*, where *pudanava* is a verb, but it is never used as a noun. This is because *pūjā karanava* is an awkward utterance in Sinhala.

even closer to salvation as the next Buddha. Once a deity is defined in this manner he is brought in line with the Buddha and the *arhat*s, who, of course, would not practice punishment of any sort. These gods are *not* Buddhas; they do punish, but the latter role diminishes in proportion to the increase in benevolence. Furthermore, benevolent gods tend to be idealized, so that one does not typically ask them for material benefits. As a result the god becomes progressively "remote."

These changes do not, of course, imply that external socioeconomic conditions are not important in fostering changes in the pantheon. Indeed, such conditions account for some gods' going out of vogue, without any reference to the principles mentioned earlier. Alternatively, external changes may be rationalized or justified in terms of these cultural principles, or both processes may occur simultaneously. Take the case of Nātha, whom people have practically ceased to propitiate in Sri Lanka today. In the *gammaḍuva* he is offered flowers and incense; but in the plaint (*kannalavva*) uttered by the priest his name is omitted. Yet in the time of the Kandyan kings he was viewed not only as the next Buddha, but also as the god who legitimated the sovereignty of the Kandyan kings. When Kandy fell to the British and kingship was abolished, the god fell into disfavor. Here at least the sudden fall of the deity seems related to external political events rather than to his benevolence. But in *explaining* his lack of involvement in the mundane world people will emphasize his benevolence, his Buddhist virtues.

That there has been an erosion of the functions of Viṣṇu and Saman is apparent when we examine their mythology. In myth, both deities had fought and subjugated the demons; they are depicted as punishing and beating them. Yet the current view of these gods deemphasizes that aspect. In the *gammaḍuva* the god who subjugates demons is Dēvatā Baṇḍāra: his prowess is enacted in the Vāhala dance. Dēvatā Baṇḍāra once was a minor deity but is fast becoming a major one. Among the major gods Kataragama is least associated with the Buddhist virtues; indeed, some priests refer to him as heretic (*mityā dṛṣṭiyek*). No myths link him with the Buddha. Nevertheless, most people view him as a future Buddha, but with a long way yet to go. He is supposed to have obtained *varan* from the Buddha, yet no myths have developed on these lines. Mythology, as well as current belief, associates him as a vanquisher of *asura*s (titans). He is more punitive, less benevolent, and more involved in the world. More and more people look to him for material welfare and help. In other words, among the major deities, Kataragama has become the most popular and is most involved in helping people. I cannot examine the causes for the rise of this deity here, except to emphasize his more world-involved nature. His worldliness emerges in his sexual behavior also. He has a wife and a mistress (Valli Amma). By contrast, Viṣṇu, who had a consort in Hindu belief, is single in the contemporary Buddhist tradition. So are the other gods; they all share the Buddhist ascetic view of sexual abstinence. When adopted into the Buddhist tradition, the old Hindu gods tend to lose their female counterparts, or *śakti*.

When we examine the history of the cult of some of the Buddhist gods, we notice that their past is not so different from Kataragama's. Viṣṇu and Saman in particular were viewed as vanquishers of demons; they had warlike roles, very much like that of Kataragama. They also had spouses or consorts and had more to do with the world than they do today. If so, there are internal reasons for the change in the attitude of the worshiper irrespective of the external factors of change in the politicoeconomic domain. That is, when a deity begins to grant favors and help man, man expresses his gratitude by offering merit and thanks to the deity, which hastens the deity's salvation. The public, in other words, sees him as an increasingly meritorious deity doing good by helping people. As this occurs through time, the dimension of benevolence increases, and punitiveness and world involvement decrease in accordance with principles A and B. This can be rephrased another way. The popularity of the deity results in his idealization, which, in the context of Buddhist culture, will be expressed in terms of increasing benevolence and compassion and nonpunitiveness. Nātha's sudden fall was largely due to external factors, though perhaps the fact that he was already defined as next Buddha made it easier.[3] Here I am suggesting an internal cultural dialectic occurring very slowly through time: the very popularity of a deity as a god granting favors will, in the long run, render him otiose. The very rise of the deity is also paradoxically the cause of his "fall." Thus we have principle C.

PRINCIPLE C: *The more favors the deity grants the worshiper the more he is viewed as benevolent and compassionate; the more benevolent he is, the less involved he becomes in the affairs of the world, which makes him progressively otiose.*

When these processes occur, deities from the bottom of the pantheon may move up. When we examine the minor deities we note at once their involvement in the world and their immediacy to the worshiper. Their mythology is sung in great detail, and they come alive in the ritual dramas. Take the case of Dēvatā Baṇḍāra or Däḍimuṇḍa, who acts out his role as the intrepid vanquisher of the demons in the Vāhala dance (see pp. 138–39). Devol Deviyo, another important deity among the minor gods, walks the fire and extinguishes it in one ritual drama. He is helped by his demonic servants, known as Gini Kurumbara.

When we examine the mythology of these two gods we are also struck that, while they are for the most part viewed as gods, they are also on occasion referred to as demons (see pp. 85–89). In the case of Dēvatā Baṇḍāra, his pedigree shows that his father was the demon Pūrṇaka, which, in the context of South Asian ideas of procreation, must taint him as demonic. In the case of Devol Deviyo, the texts refer to both Devol Deviyo and Devol Yakku (demons). Sometimes the impression created is that they are the same; at other times they seem to be different beings. Informants are, however, agreed on the divine status of Dēvatā Baṇḍāra; but Devol Deviyo, according to some informants, is a combination of demon and god. According to Wirz, he has a demonic as well as a divine aspect (Wirz 1954, pp. 140–43); others say that the Devol Yakku (demons) are attendants of the Devol Deviyo (gods). Their status is clearly ambiguous; but there are sufficient grounds for assuming that these were demons who were later converted into gods. Alternatively, they were beings who were composites of both demon and god, known as *dēvatās*. The deities of the operative pantheons in isolated areas outside the culture area under consideration often have this character (see pp. 285–93). Sometimes a *dēvatā* is simply a demon on his way up the pantheon's hierarchy. If so, we can formulate a fourth cultural principle governing the pantheon.

PRINCIPLE D: *When major gods become further removed, others move up to take their places, the movement generally being from demonic to divine status.*

It must not, however, be assumed that this is the only process occurring. It can be shown that a major Hindu god like Kataragama can be adopted by the Sinhalas and in-

3. It is possible that Nātha was already becoming otiose when the British captured Kandy. It is otherwise difficult to explain his dramatic loss of public favor and his near obsolescence today.

cluded in the pantheon without having to graduate from a demonic or semidivine status. But the latter is the dominant pattern, though not the only one. If we examine the mythic history of the major gods, Vibhīṣaṇa clearly was a demon at one time, being the brother of Rāvaṇa, the demon king of the *Rāmāyaṇa*. The same probably is true of the god Saman, who, according to Paranavitana (1958), was originally Yama, the god of the underworld; Yama, in popular conception, is a demonic being.

The question we must now ask is, Why do demons get converted into gods, and how does this occur? The cultural ideology of Buddhism permits the status change. Unlike Christianity, Buddhism has no concept of eternal damnation: only the most inferior and sinful of demonic beings, the *preta*s, come close to this notion. In general, beings are born as demons owing to their karma, and as demons they continue to acquire bad karma through their evil actions. But this life course is not irrevocable, since they may have done good in their past births that at some point may bear fruit and cause a change in status. Or demons, like other beings, may exercise their own volition and simply desist from doing evil and become converted to Buddhism. Cases of demons being converted into good Buddhist laymen (*upāsaka*) are found in both the popular and the doctrinal traditions. In a culture that does not have an ideology of karma and rebirth, the apotheosis of the demon may be difficult to justify, but not in the Hindu Buddhist religious traditions.

The experiential factor is also important. Unlike that of gods, the presence of demons is constantly validated by experience. It is true that in Sri Lanka, as elsewhere, individuals may have mystical communications with the gods. But these are not common, unlike experiences with demons. People are afraid to be out alone in the dark or in lonely places because of demons, and, though they may not have seen them, most people have felt anxiety at the possibility of meeting them. More important, people have seen others possessed by demons and have witnessed the rituals of exorcism to banish them. Periodically someone in the village is frightened or struck by a demon. Sorcery is generally practiced with demonic aid. Thus the demonic experience is existentially real. Demons are involved in the world; they are attracted by flesh, death, sex, blood; they are born out of violence.

We must note that the demon's rise in status is due to conditions in the upper hierarchy of the pantheon. When gods become more remote, others must perforce take their place—dictated, of course, by the needs of humans. The immediately visible deities are the minor gods and the demons. These beings are already there—available for promotion, so to speak—obviating the need to invent new gods. Consider the case of demons. They are known, felt presences. Like the gods, they have power that has immediacy and relevance for many people. Their power, unlike that of the gods, is directed toward evil, but if it could be harnessed for good then surely its effects must be as profound for good as it was previously in the sphere of evil. There is strong motivation for people to convert powerful agents who do bad into powerful agents who do good. The cultural theory provides a way of accomplishing this. Human beings, in fact, can prevent demonic activity and cure persons afflicted by them by a variety of techniques: through propitiation with offerings, intercession of the gods, magic and talismans, or a combination of these techniques. If, for example, demons will desist from doing harm when we propitiate them, then they may perhaps be influenced to do us good; if the gods can compel the demons to refrain from evil, they can surely compel them to do good.

I have elucidated the cultural logic underlying the rise of the deity, which is entirely an internal dialectic of change. Explaining why a specific deity is chosen rather than another requires a consideration of external factors in the socioeconomic and political domains that is outside the purview of this chapter. I shall also not discuss the exact way a deity rises in the pantheon, but rather will examine the cultural mechanisms that ease the movement from one status to another.

The first major mechanism in divine mobility can be formulated as principle E.

PRINCIPLE E: *When a particular demon ascends through the pantheon's hierarchy, his identity is often split into two, a divine one and a demonic one, the latter progressively decreasing in importance as the importance of the former increases.*

PRINCIPLE F: *If the deity ascending through the hierarchy is already a composite of demon and god or dēvatā, then the divine aspect is enhanced as the demonic declines.*

To illustrate this principle, let us consider a case where the status of the deity does not seem, at first glance, to be in doubt. In the *gammaḍuva*, three classes of demons are propitiated in the three watches of the night: Mahasōna, the Sanni demons, and the Kurumbara (see pp. 109, 135, 155). Take the Kurumbara demons, who are viewed as servants of the Devol Deviyo and walked the fire and danced on it with the god(s). In the dawn watch ritual the Kurumbara are unequivocally demons; yet elsewhere they are addressed as "god." In the plaint (*kannalavva*) given on page 155 these demons are addressed in the singular as "the noble divine king Gini Kurumbara," and elsewhere merit is offered to him, thus:

> That god whose power is like a fire
> Whose body shines like fiery colors
> That god arrives with fiery rays
> O Gini Kurumbara god accept the merit we give you.

Since the dawn oblation to the Kurumbara demons is an integral part of the structure of the *gammaḍuva*, we must assume that the demonic is the older as well as the more important identity of the Kurumbara. In the myths of Devol Deviyo they are also clearly demons (see pp. 150–51). The references to the *god* known as Gini (fire) Kurumbara are found in only a few places; if these are deleted the ritual is in no way affected. Indeed, some ritual traditions do not mention Kurumbara as a god. Another Kurumbara demon who is sometimes deified is Mal ("flower") Kurumbara. Though Mal Kurumbara receives even less prominence than the god Gini Kurumbara, he is clearly deified by some fire walkers of Kataragama I have interviewed. These fire walkers state that Gini (fire) Kurumbara is a demon, but Mal (flower) Kurumbara is a god! These uncertainties of identity indicate the indeterminant status of the deity as he splits his identity in the process of upward mobility. The apotheosis of Kurumbara is due, I think, to his association with fire walking. Some performers assert that it is Kurumbara who quells the fire rather than Devol Deviyo. Any demon(s) who could do such a mighty thing could surely be a potent force for good, according to the previous discussion. If Kurumbara is a demon who can quell the fire, then the priests who do the fire walking must solicit his aid. The demon is converted to a personal guardian of the priests. But the moment a demon appears as guardian or protector he can no longer, according to Sinhala Buddhist conceptions, be a demon, since by definition demons are totally malevolent. He is on the way to becoming a god. The popularity of Kurumbara has increased recently owing to the increased popularity of the elaborate and spectacular fire walking rituals in Kataragama within the past decade. The fire walkers, interestingly enough, treat their deity as a servant of Kataragama (Skanda), since their fire walking rituals are under his auspices, rather than those of Devol Deviyo as in the traditional *gammaḍuva*.

This mechanism of splitting can be seen in respect to deities who are generally outside the *gammaḍuva* traditions.

Kaḍavara: In Sinhala exorcistic rites the Kaḍavara are a group of demons. They are also viewed as demons and placated by some practitioners of the *gammaḍuva*—for example, in the Heyiaṅtuḍuva tradition. In the Sinhala myths of the low country, Kaḍavara are servants of Kataragama, so that songs refer to Kataragama as accompanied "by the retinue of beautiful Tamil Kaḍavara hosts" (*nalla demala kaḍavara maha golla pirivarā*). Among fire walkers, the Kaḍavara are sometimes viewed once again as a single god.

Kalu Kumāraya: In the Sinhala low country one of the most feared demons is Kalu Kumāraya (the Black Prince). A dark demonic lover, he afflicts women with illness. He has a crucial place in the rituals and traditions of the demon cults. In parts of the up-country he has a double status: as demon and as god. One shrine in Haňguraňketa propitiates him in both roles: inside the shrine as a god, outside as a demon.

Now we can go back to the two important regional gods discussed earlier: Devol Deviyo and Däḍimuṇḍa, alias Dēvatā Baṇḍāra. We noted that there are references to Devol Deviyo (god) and Devol Yakku (demons). In this case the demons have ceased to be important and may eventually disappear in normal circumstances, since the divine status here is paramount.

In Dēvatā Baṇḍāra's case, the occasional reference to him in the texts as demon is probably a *survival* reflecting his past status as either demon or semidivine being. His status has risen recently and he is, as far as worshipers are concerned, unequivocally a god.

I noted earlier that the deity who has recently been elevated from demonic to divine status still retains some of his demonic character: his status is intermediate and shares both qualities. This intermediate status is often conceptualized as *dēvatā*, as I stated earlier.

PRINCIPLE G: *A deity moving up through the supernatural hierarchy possesses at a certain stage an anomalous status composite of demon and god, which is often conceptualized as* dēvatā.

The term *dēvatā* in the Buddhist doctrinal texts simply meant deity. As the term is used in Sinhala Buddhism, it refers primarily to animistic deities of trees (*vṛkṣa dēvatā*), as on page 140, where reference is made to the *dēvatā* of the *milla* tree used for fire walking. The *dēvatā*s of trees have only limited significance in Sinhala village life. When people are out in the forest, on pilgrimages or journeys, they inevitably break branches and hang them on trees that such *dēvatā*s inhabit. Sometimes the term *dēvatā* is used as an honorific for a demon: for example, the demon Sanni, because he was of royal parentage, is called *dēvatā*. The tree *dēvatā* has the characteristics of both demon and god: he can cause harm if he is disturbed or annoyed, but he is not truly evil. However, in the context of Sinhala culture, the most important use of the term *dēvatā* is to describe the intermediate status between god and demon. Thus informants would say that Kurumbara is not *really* a god; he is a *dēvatā*. Kalu Kumāraya is often addressed as *dēvatā*. This does not imply that every supernatural being who is addressed as *dēvatā* was at one time unequivocally a demon. In Sinhala culture deified ancestors can have composite attributes, as in the Baṇḍāra cult of the Kandyans (see pp. 286–89), in which case principle F alone applies.

The ideal typical case of a *dēvatā* is the deity Hūniyan Dēvatā. Hūniyan is not a deity of the *gammaḍuva* as such, but he is the personal guardian deity of some of the priests of the cult. The word *hūniyan* means sorcery; and in exorcistic rituals of countersorcery Hūniyan is a demon (Hūniyan Yakā). Hūniyan has within recent times come into prominence, especially as a personal guardian. The mechanism here is like the transformation of Kurumbara: the demon in charge of sorcery is enlisted to *protect* the individual from sorcery, which thereby causes a status change. But Hūniyan is generally addressed as *dēvatā*. In Hūniyan's case the theory is that he is a single deity: during the waning (*ava*) of the moon he is a demon, in the waxing (*pura*) he is a *dēvatā*. The two identities are not yet fully separated; they are twin aspects of a single larger identity. But eventually, according to principle F, they *must* separate, particularly if the divine aspects of the deity gradually predominate. This, in fact, seems to be happening today. However, in Hūniyan's case there is a linguistic obstacle that prevents the separation of his dual identity: it would be grossly anomalous to call this deity Hūniyan *Deviyo*, which means "sorcery god," a contradiction in contemporary Sinhala language use. But this is being fast overcome by giving an alias to the deity. He is also known as Gambāra Deviyo, the god in charge of villages. The use of the new label is fascinating. Hūniyan, as I noted, is a *personal* guardian deity; Gambāra Deviyo is a *category* term used to designate gods who protect *villages*, the *grāma dēvatās* found in the literature. Contemporary Indian villages still have *grāma dēvatās*, but in Sri Lanka they are scarcely mentioned, their place being usurped by the great regional and national gods. Here we have a case where the near defunct category term "village guardian god" is resurrected as an alias to Hūniyan, "an individual's guardian god," largely to resolve the language discrepancy that arises from labeling a sorcery deity as a god. I suspect that as the importance of Hūniyan increases, as is certainly happening in urban Sri Lanka, the term Hūniyan Dēvatā will wither away, leaving the alias Gambāra Deviyo as the predominant term in the set, eventually displacing the earlier identity completely. Alternatively, the term *hūniyan* (sorcery) must lose its pejorative connotation if it is going to designate a god. We might now note the general principle here.

PRINCIPLE H: *When an inferior deity passes into divine status, he may retain some pejorative identity in his name, which is initially resolved by giving him an alias or a prefix that qualifies his former pejorative name; or he may be given a totally new name.*

We can illustrate this in respect to Dēvatā Baṇḍāra, who has three aliases—Alutnuvara Deviyo (the god of Alutnuvara where the main shrine of this god is situated), Vāhala Deviyo, and Däḍimuṇḍa. I will demonstrate in chapter 6 that the title Alutnuvara Deviyo, by which he is increasingly being referred to, was given to him last (see pp. 317–21). Initially he was Dēvatā Baṇḍāra, God of the Four Kōrales; subsequently he was given the title Däḍimuṇḍa. According to mythology Dēvatā Baṇḍāra got the latter title when he, alone among the gods, stood by the Buddha when the latter was being assailed by the hosts of Māra (pp. 210–12). Before that he was called Vāhala ("palace god"), since he was the guardian of the Viṣṇu shrine, which was at one time in Alutnuvara and later was transferred to Kandy. His earliest designation, Dēvatā Baṇḍāra, indicates a being of semi-divine status. It should be noted that humans also change their names to hide their caste or ethnic identity.

Part Two

Introduction

In this section I shall present detailed descriptions of the rituals of the *gammaḍuva* traditions and translations of texts. In chapter 1 I noted that the six traditions discussed there possessed a set of thirty-five ritual texts known as the *pantis kōlmura*. However, not all these texts are sung or enacted in present-day rituals, and there are many rituals and texts in the contemporary *gammaḍuva* that are not found in the corpus of thirty-five texts. In chapters 3 and 4 I shall describe in detail a full-scale *gammaḍuva* from the Rabalīya tradition. I shall note any important differences between this tradition and the five other traditions. There are many minor differences I must omit for lack of space. These differences pertain to the following:

1. There are differences in the timing of the rituals in all of these traditions, and even within a single tradition, depending on the scale of the festival.

2. Several traditions propitiate minor local and regional deities (such as those of the Baṇḍāra cult) that I do not describe because they would detract from the more important rituals.

I regret, however, that I have decided to exclude one major ritual practiced occasionally in the *gammaḍuva*. This is the *pūnā* ritual, where the misfortunes (*dōsa*) of the audience are magically collected into a pot known as the *pūnāva* and deposited in a stream or river. I omit this important ritual because its myths and traditions have nothing to do with the Pattini cult but are linked with an older stratum of mythology, the Vijaya legends. I believe the *pūnā* is an older ritual later incorporated into the Pattini cult. In any case the *pūnā* ritual is generally performed when the *gammaḍuva* is held for a family rather than for a village; the title of the ceremony is also changed from *gammaḍuva* ("village hall") to *pūnā maḍuva* ("a *pūnā* hall"). Gunasekera has an excellent description of a *pūnā* ritual (Gunasekera 1953, pp. 63–75), and my own account of it will appear in Obeyesekere (1983).

In chapter 5 I present a series of myths pertaining to the goddess Pattini from the corpus of thirty-five texts. Some of these myths are enacted in ritual dramas and are central to the Pattini cult, especially the drama of the killing of the consort and his resurrection by the goddess. Some of these myths are sung in *gammaḍuva* rituals, others have gone out of vogue. But they are all important insofar as they deal with the life of the goddess, and therefore I have included them here. Moribund texts that do not deal with the life of the goddess (corpora 2 and 3 on pp. 25–27) are examined in part 3 of this book. In chapter 6 I shall try to unscramble the various traditions that constitute the present-day *gammaḍuva* and present a "stratification" of the myths and rituals it contains.

I have used three major sources in my translations of texts. The most important source is my actual tape recordings of the rituals in situ. Where these tape recordings are unclear I have used my second source, namely handwritten palm-leaf manuscripts in the possession of the priests (*kapurālas*). The third source is Hevawasam's 1974 edition of the thirty-five ritual texts. Since this edition is available to any reader who wishes to consult the original Sinhala, I have used it whenever Hevawasam's texts agree substantially with the texts of the priests. This obviates the need for the reader to accept many of my translations on faith. It should be borne in mind that most material in chapters 3 and 4 is from actual field recordings of the rituals, while chapter 5 relies heavily on Hevawasam (1974).

Many problems are involved in translating Sinhala ritual texts into English, and I deal with them in the body of this work. Here let me mention problems of transliteration. Sinhala terms are sometimes close to their Sanskrit originals, and this poses a problem of whether they should be transliterated in their Sinhala or Sanskrit (or sometimes Pāli) form. I did not devise any rules on this matter but made my own judgments as I thought fit. An even greater difficulty lies with the Tamil and Malayalam terms that appear in part 6 of this book. The Sinhala as well as the South Indian traditions deal with substantively similar mythic material. Yet the same personal and place names may be differently written and pronounced. Thus Mādēvi in Sinhala is Mātavi in Tamil. In these cases I have generally retained the uniqueness of each language tradition. But sometimes even this is hard to do without confusing the reader. For example, the Sinhala texts refer to the king of Pāṇḍi; in Malayalam texts he is referred to as Pānṭi. In this and similar situations I continue to use the Sinhala term. Place names, too, can cause problems. For example, Madurai (the city in South India) is Madurā or Madurāpura in Sinhala. In translating Sinhala texts I use "Madurā," but when I refer to the city in my analysis or commentary I use "Madurai." Here again purists may object, since strictly speaking it should be rendered "Maturai"!

In transliterating Sinhala and Sanskrit, and Tamil and Malayalam terms, I have used the conventions accepted by scholars of these languages. However, I have occasionally omitted minor diacritical distinctions, and in several instances I have preferred popular English renderings of terms (e.g., Madurai, Pandya) to strictly phonetic ones. In every instance I had in mind a reading public who may not be familiar with the niceties of the several language traditions encompassed in this work and who may be confused by overscrupulous transliterations.

3

The Consecration (Pē) of the Gammaḍuva

The *kapurālas*, *vaṭṭānḍi*, assistants, and other helpers assemble on the morning of the consecration to construct the altars and prepare the ingredients and ritual objects needed for the *gammaḍuva*. The day chosen could be almost any day, with one reservation: astrologically unpropitious days are avoided, as are the Buddhist holy days, or *pōya* days. The latter rule illustrates the incompatibility of the two types of worship: *dēva* worship, being a form of lay activity, from the superior Buddhist viewpoint, cannot be performed on a *pōya* day, the full-moon *pōya* being especially taboo. In a society where "rules" are often ignored or violated with the flimsiest rationalizations, the interdiction forbidding rituals for gods on full-moon days is steadfastly followed.

The consecration rituals commence soon after the priests have eaten their evening meal, or *pē bat*, "consecrated rice." This meal, almost always vegetarian, is specially prepared for the priests. It commences with the utterance of the Buddhist five precepts, recited by the chief *kapurāla* and repeated by the whole assembly. The significance of this act is very clear: the audience affirms itself as a Buddhist congregation and formally recognizes the supremacy of this great tradition. Thereafter the meal is eaten.

All personnel nowadays generally sit at the same table or mat; the high-caste *kapurālas* as well as the low-caste drummers and even occasionally the member of the washerman caste who supplies the white cloths for the ceremony. The latter, since they are not direct participants in the rituals, normally eat separately earlier. As a form of courtesy, the chief *kapurāla* often sees to it that the low-caste drummers are served first, then the high-caste *kapurālas*.

The consecration rituals can be performed on the evening of the main festivities or on the preceding evening. In the description given here the consecration occurs the evening before, since this was probably the traditional arrangement. In order for sacred beings to reside in the village or a household compound, which are profane environments, a special area must be marked out and converted into a sacred area. This is done through rites of sanctification or consecration (*pē kirīma*), which are prerequisite to the commencement of the main event.

The special area is practically bare for the consecration ceremonies. The only construction that is absolutely essential is the *toraṇa*, or pandal or ceremonial arch, for the goddess Pattini and several stools or chairs that could hold trays or *taṭṭu* containing offerings for other deities. Figure 5 gives a fairly typical layout of the sacred area on the night of the consecration. The preliminary rites performed on the night of the consecration are similar to those performed at the start of the main ceremony. In both the gods are invited to the sacred area and are asked to present themselves invisibly in the special "thrones," or *asnas*, constructed for them. The procedure in the consecration rituals is highly abbreviated, however, since not all the altars have yet been constructed. The ritual texts also are not sung in full here. Nevertheless, since the ritual procedure is basically the same I shall quote the ritual texts in full but shall note, whenever relevant, that the full text is sung only during the invitation to the gods at the main ceremony. This will obviate the need to describe the same set of rites twice.

Hakgeḍi Pūjāva: Conch Offering

The consecration (*pē*) rituals start about 9:00 P.M. The *kapurāla* and his assistants (about four) are dressed in white. The ornaments of the deity (*ābharaṇa*) have already been placed in the altar to the guardian gods. These ornaments are never exposed to public view but are covered with a red cloth over which is placed a rosary (*nāguna väla*) with 108 beads, a magical number coming down from at least the time of the Atharvaveda. The chief *kapurāla* approaches the main altar, *mal yahana* or "flower couch" (altar 1 in fig. 5), which is for the guardians of the four quarters (Hatara Varan Deviyo), and the major gods of the pantheon, and the three refuges—the Buddha, the Dhamma, and the Saṅgha. The *kapurāla* blows a conch three times before this altar, while the drummers beat the auspicious festival note (*magul bera*). Conch and festival drum proclaim the commencement of an auspicious act, in this case the *gammaḍuva*. They also indicate ritual service or *tēvāva* for the gods; they are also symbols of auspiciousness (*magul*, *maṅgala*). The *kapurāla* then leaves the conch under the red cloth and dances a step (*pada*) in an act of obeisance. These acts herald the commencement of the *gammaḍuva* rituals.

Pahan Pūjāva: Offering of Lights

The lights are offered on behalf of the gods, or in their honor (*deviyannē namaṭa*). Before the actual lighting of the lamps the *kapurāla* invites (*ārādhanā*) the deities into the ritual arena by his songs (text 1). They are asked respectfully to reside in their "flower thrones" (*mal asna*), or "flower couches" (*mal yahana*), which I also translate as "altar." Here as elsewhere in the ritual proceedings the second *kapurāla* may sing alternate stanzas; or one or more of the assistants may do so or may act as a chorus. The songs are interspersed, as always, with dances. Meanwhile an attendant wearing a mouth mask enters from one end of the *maḍuva* ("hall") under a white canopy held by four people. He wears a white "turban" on his head, and on it he has a container (*kolapata*) of coconut oil. The attendant stands within the *sīmā* ("limits") of the hall but well outside the dancing area. The *kapurāla* and his assistants dance before the altars singing praises of the gods and asking their permission (*avasara*). After a few minutes the attendant advances into the dancing area. The chief *kapurāla* takes the oil container reverently in both hands, places it against his forehead, and dances before altar 1 (for the four gods), then before the others. The

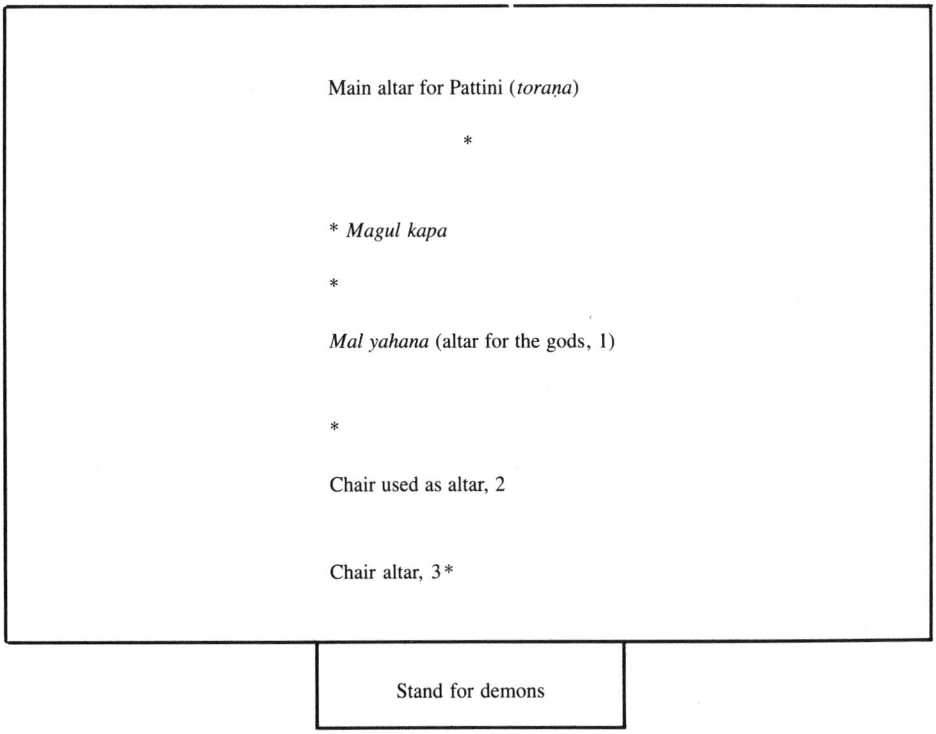

Fig. 5. Layout of the sacred area of the *gammaḍuva* on the night of the consecration.

attendant incenses the altar; then the *kapurāla* holds the oil container for incensing. He pours oil into the small clay lamps on altar 1, then moves to the *toraṇa* and finally to altars 2 and 3, while assistants light the lamps. He then summons the chief *ātura* ("patient," i.e., the chief householder or chief organizer of the *maḍuva*), who holds the oil container. Holding a ritual object here as elsewhere indicates vicarious participation, in this case by the villager on behalf of his community (or household). The *kapurāla* utters a standard formula: the *äpa* or bail made by the village is being fulfilled (*oppu*). This offering of lights will bring prosperity to all assembled here. At the conclusion of this short formula the *ātura* pours oil into the already lighted lamps. This formula is summarized below.

> In the name of the noble, royal four gods presiding over the four *dēvāle*s, the gods of the *tunbāge* [Pattini, Devol, and Dēvatā Baṇḍāra or Vāhala], and *mahābāge* gods [the major gods of the pantheon, including the four mentioned earlier]; and . . . the sacred goddess Pattini, and in the name of all royal gods residing in all the *kōvil* and *dēvāle*s; holding these beings in high esteem, on behalf of our village [or family if the ceremony is not for the community] . . . we are fulfilling [*oppu*] a *pūjā* of lamps in their honor, . . . we will obtain the protection of the gods in whose honor this *pūjā* is held . . . may they banish all the *apala* [bad planetary effects] and the darkness of *dōsa*, and dangers, and may we obtain *magul* ["auspicious"] happiness, and help [*pihiṭa*] and protection [*ārakṣāva*] from these noble gods . . . think like this, and ask all the others also to touch the oil container.

Daḷumura Pūjāva: Offering of Betel Leaves

Daḷumura pūjāva commences about twenty minutes after the lighting of lamps. *Daḷumura* is the ritual term for *bulat*, or betel leaves, but the ritual also involves the offering of flowers and dedicated coins or *pan̆ḍuru* ("gifts"). The significance of betel leaves in Sinhala culture needs explaining. Formal and respectful greeting, generally from an inferior to a superior, is done with betel leaves. A sheaf of betel leaves is also given as an invitation (e.g., to a wedding). If the stems point toward the giver, the invitation or announcement is an inauspicious one (a funeral), indicated by inversion of the propitious routine. The *gammaḍuva* is an auspicious *magul* (*maṅgala*) event, and hence the gods are invited respectfully and deferentially with betel leaves.

An assistant brings a *vaṭṭi* ("cane tray") containing flowers, betel leaves, and rose water into the arena. The chief *kapurāla* lustrates the flowers and betel leaves with rose water. He holds the tray of flowers in one hand and faces altar 1 while an assistant or an attendant incenses it. The *kapurāla* dances with the tray in one hand, then repeats the performance at the "chair" altars. He sings and lays betel leaves, areca flowers, and other flowers on altar 1, followed by offerings on the "chair" altars (text 2). He asks Kataragama to *vaḍinna* ("reside") in his throne (*asna*). Then he comes to the *toraṇa* and sings songs on Devol Deviyo, who is also called Malala Devol of Malaladēsa (Malabar). He also asks the Divi Yakku (leopard demons) to come from Māyā Kōvila (temple of illusion). Other deities invoked are Pattini, Vibhīṣaṇa, Däḍimuṇḍa, Nātha, Saman, Siriyā Dēvi (the goddess Śrī), Amarāpati (a female deity, one of the Kiri Amma), who comes along with Doḷaha Deviyo (the Twelve Gods), and the various planets. The *kapurāla* lights incense powder, camphor, and incense sticks (*han̆dun kūru*). He then lays betel leaves and flowers at the *toraṇa* and the other altars. He goes outside the *sīmā* and asks the Divi Yakku demons to reside in the outside stand where their offering is placed. He comes back to the arena, invokes Hatara Varan Deviyo (the Gods of the Four Warrants), transfers merit (*pin anumōdan kirīma*) to them and to the other gods, and asks them to protect the audience. He ends with the conventional *āvaḍārakṣāyubōvēvā*—"may your years of life increase, may you be protected [by the gods], and may you have long life."

Transfer of merit to the gods is a standard act in Sinhala culture. The idea is simple: the gods help people, and as a result they (the gods) earn merit that in turn advances their chances of salvation and brings them closer to their goal of Buddhahood. Thus people help the gods to achieve merit. As noted in chapter 2, *pin* ("merit") in the ritual context has the meaning of "thanksgiving": we pray that the gods earn merit for the good they have done, and will do, for us. Also, all formal acts of worship and offerings are themselves intrinsically merit producing. Thus the merit we earn by these acts is transferred to the gods. Offering the coconut flower symbolizes and seals that act of merit giving to the gods. Text 2 of the *daḷumura pūjāva* is sung in full both on the consecration night and on the evening of the main ceremony.

Magul Kapa Hiṭavīma: Planting of the Festival Bough

About 9:30 P.M. the chief *kapurāla* holds in his hand a water pot (*pän kotale*, *kenḍiya*) and lustrates the *magul kapa*, or festival bough, which is on the right side of the *toraṇa*.

He then faces the altar for the Gods of the Four Warrants (altar 1) with the water pot in his right hand. He sprays the "festival bough" (*magul kapa*). Then he utters a long plaint (*kannalavva*) to the gods of the pantheon (text 3), after which he comes over to where the chief *ātura*s are assembled and blesses them with a long-drawn-out "*āyubovēvā*," "may you live long." This is over at 10:00 P.M.

Soon after the lustration of the festival bough and the uttering of the plaint, the ritual planting of the bough commences. This is one of the most important rituals in the *gam-maḍuva* and rounds off the ceremony of consecration.

A *kapa* is a post; very often the trunk of an areca tree is used. Though the *kapa* used in the origin myth measured seven *riyan* (ten and a half feet), no measurement is prescribed for the post used nowadays. Generally a post about five to six feet tall is chosen. It is decorated with *gok* leaves so as to make a bulge at the top and placed near the arena till it is used. When the time for its use arrives, it is brought into the middle of the arena and placed on a chair covered with white cloth. The *kapurāla* starts the ceremony by sprinkling some water from the water pot. The number of songs sung and incantations uttered depends, as usual, on the scale of the ceremony. Generally the chief householder or organizer (*ātura*) is asked to face the *kapa*, clasping his hands in worship while the *kapurāla*, with the water pot in his hand, invokes the blessings of the various gods and asks them to banish disease and bring prosperity and happiness to the village (or household). The *kapurāla* then dips a sprig of areca in the water and sprays the *ātura* and afterward pours some water into his cupped hands for him to drink. Sometimes the ritual begins with a conventional chant and a short sketch of the origin myth of the *kapa*.

A typical ritual starts about 10:00 P.M. when an assistant dances with an areca flower in his hand before altar 1. Then he dances with a water pot, spraying the altars with the areca sprig dipped into the water pot in the following order: altar 1, altar 2, *toraṇa*, and altar 3. He then dances with a censer (*aňguru kabala*) and incenses the altars in the same order. Sometimes this is performed with drums but no songs; at other times the *kapurāla* may sing various songs on the *kapa* (text 5). Several assistants may join in the dancing and singing.

About 10:35 P.M. the *kapurāla* dances in the arena with a lighted torch in hand, singing "head-to-foot verses" (*sirasapāda*). He is joined in the singing by others in the team. He lowers the torch often, conferring blessings on the audience. Then the song entitled the "birth of the *maḍuva*" (text 4) is sung.

The assistant sprays the festival bough with water when reference is made in the songs to the original anointing of the prototypic *kapa*. Meanwhile, others dig a hole on the right of the *toraṇa* and next to the main altar for the four gods for planting the *kapa*. The chief *kapurāla* asks the chief householder or villager (*ātura*) to bring a betel leaf and a coin (*paňḍuru*). The *kapurāla* holds the *kapa* upright while the *ātura* places the betel leaf against the *kapa* and holds the *kapa* firmly. The chief *kapurāla* then makes a short invocation in which he says that the ritual is to fulfil an *äpa* ("bail") and that this *ātura* has fulfilled it on behalf of all the others. The *ātura* places the coin and betel leaf in the hole and, with the assistance of others, plants the *kapa*. Then others hang two green coconuts, several yellow drinking coconuts, and areca flowers on the *kapa*. Twelve torches (for the Twelve Gods) are also planted around the base of the *kapa* on betel leaves. Then incense sticks are planted and the *kapa* is incensed by an attendant.

The texts of the festival bough come from various, even contradictory sources, but the symbolic significance of the *kapa* is not affected by the conflicting myths associated with it. A *kapa*, or post, is planted in many rituals and festivities in South Asia and is derived from Hindu ritual. Thus in Hindu weddings there is a similar "wedding post." In the *gammaḍuva* the *kapa* signifies the following:

1. A vow or act of commitment. The *kapa* planted before any festival is an act of "bail," a promise that a festival will be held within a specified time. Thus all major festivals in Sri Lanka are preceded by a "*kapa*-planting ritual."

2. In the *gammaḍuva*, the *kapa* that is planted is a *magul* ("festival") and a *bisō* ("queen") *kapa*. The festival bough is a commemorative act, releasing the community from the vow or bail.

3. *Bisō* ("queen") and *magul* ("festival," "auspicious") posts may in all likelihood have originated in a different manner from that stated in the myths. In Thailand, for example, there are two posts in every house with almost identical designations, the auspicious post and the lady post, the former on the auspicious east side of the sleeping area and the latter on the inauspicious west side (Davis 1974, p. 13). These widespread symbols may have once been operative in Sinhala house construction and have been transferred to the construction of the hall. Thus *bisō kapa* ideally should be on the west and *magul kapa* on the east side of the hall. These ideals are no longer operative in Sinhala ritual. Nowadays the *magul kapa* is planted on the right of the *toraṇa* and *bisō kapa* on the left (but these can also be reversed).

4. As it is currently employed in the *gammaḍuva*, and in Sinhala ritual generally, the *kapa* is a symbol of auspiciousness. Mythologically it recreates the *kapruka* (*kalpa vṛkṣa*), the wish-fulfilling tree of Buddhist and Hindu mythology. The meaning of the planting of the *kapa*, then, has further symbolic significance: may the wishes of the congregation for long life, health, wealth, and prosperity be realized by the planting of the *kapa*.

5. Further evidence that the *kapa* is the symbolic recreation of the "wish-fulfilling tree" comes out in the rituals. Nine types of precious things are placed (only ideally) at the bottom of the *kapa*; also, the bare post is later decorated with bunches of coconuts and such, representing a fertile tree with many types of fruit. The *kapa* is surmounted by a decoration of *gok* leaves; this decoration represents the "full pot," an ancient Buddhist symbol of fertility.

6. The idea of the *kapruka* (Sinhala for *kalpa vṛkṣa*) is given symbolic meaning in other rites in Sri Lanka. For example, peasants would sometimes ceremonially tie a large white cloth at the base of a Buddhist *dāgäba* and call this a *kapruka*, "wish-fulfilling tree." There is, however, no tree or post; yet the *dāgäba* has been symbolically converted into a *kapruka* by the tying of the white cloth. Since the act of worshiping the *dāgäba* is meritorious, peasants utter a wish (*prārthanā*) that they may, *in their next lives*, realize their hopes for a good life. The contrast with the *kapa* of the *gammaḍuva* is clear: there the wishes pertain to one's present mundane existence. In the Buddhist act, as is to be expected, it relates to one's future existence.

Planting of the Torch of Time (*Kāla Pandama*) for Viṣṇu

As soon as the *kapa* is planted the *kapurāla* gives the torch he held in his hand to the chief *ātura*, who fixes it on the *kapa*. This is the torch of time for Viṣṇu. While the torch is being fixed on the *kapa* the *kapurāla* utters a *yādinna* (invocation) to Viṣṇu (text 6).

Theoretically the torch of time should be planted in a special post known as the "tree of the torch of time" (*kāla pandam gaha*), which is planted in the opposite end of the hall from the *toraṇa*, but this post has not yet been constructed. The present torch for Viṣṇu represents time past; on the main night a torch for Kataragama (time present) and later one for Dēvatā Baṇḍāra (time future) are also planted. (For the classical Hindu view of Viṣṇu as Time (*kāla*) see the *Viṣṇu Purāṇa*, edited by Wilson [1961], p. 11.)

Ritual Texts

Texts of the *Pahan Pūjāva*: Offering of Lights

Text 1 Songs for the Gods

The first songs are for the Gods of the Four Warrants (Hatara Varan Deviyo). These gods in classical Buddhist mythology were the guardian gods of the four quarters: Dhrtarāṣṭra, Virūḍha, Virūpākṣa, and Vaiṣravaṇa. In Sinhala ritual there is another set of four gods with the same label, who are guardian gods of Sri Lanka. In general the latter are the four gods who are most often referred to by that term. In the Rabalīya tradition they are Viṣṇu, Saman, Vibhīṣaṇa, and Kataragama, but in other areas Nātha or Pattini may be substituted for Saman or Vibhīṣaṇa or both. Practitioners are aware of the distinction between the four guardian gods of the universe and these guardians of Sri Lanka. Both types of guardian gods are worshiped at altar 1.

Songs on the Four Guardian Gods

1. He is known throughout the world as the noble [*utum*] Viṣṇu
   He surveys the three world systems [*sakvaḷa*] with his divine eye
   He extinguishes [*nivā*] the suffering and calamities [*uvaduru*] that beset all beings
   O noble god Viṣṇu I ceremonially escort you [*väḍamavanava*] into this arena.

Väḍamavanava is a term meaning "escort," "invite," or "come," but is confined to high-status persons such as divinity, royalty, and monks. I translate it here as "ceremonially escort you"; a related word, *vaḍinava*, I shall simply translate as "invite," "reside," "enter," or "come," depending on context.

2. His genealogy [*vaṃsa*] is known the world over as Viṣṇu
   Of noble dynasty [*vaṃsa*] he obtained warrant [*varan*] to fight the *asura*s ["titans"]
   Of noble dynasty he destroyed the demons to protect the human world
   O Viṣṇu of noble birth I humbly invite you here.

Vaṃsa can mean "dynasty," "genealogy," "caste," or "birth," but it always refers to high status. Note that Viṣṇu, as I stated in chapter 2, was viewed at one time as a destroyer of demons. He is now totally benevolent and saintly.

3. He can banish the suffering that has occurred here
   We place our hands on our heads in worship and implore you

These beings here assembled, free them [from suffering] and protect them
Kataragama, mighty [*teda*] one come and reside [*vaḍinna*] here.

Teda, used to describe the gods, is from the Sanskrit *tejas*. It has the meaning of "glory," "might," "shining," "splendor," or "fiery energy." Sometimes Sinhala texts use the Sanskrit word *tejas* in order to sound more formal and impressive.

4. Kataragama has given alms and has acquired merit from previous births
   There is no one to match him on this earth
   [Banish] all types of *dōsa* [troubles] of humans living in this world
   O Kataragama, chief of the army [of gods], give us victory.

The last line indicates the Sanskritic view of Kataragama or Skanda as Mahāsena, head of the divine army.

5. With pearl umbrella unfurled he rides his golden peacock
   And constantly makes wishes [*prārthanā*] for future Buddhahood
   I, your servant [*gäti*], sing songs [in your praise] on this occasion
   How we worship Prince Skanda the *sura*.

"Wishes" is an inadequate translation of *prārthanā*, which means "a wish associated with an act of merit," or a "will to achieve a Buddhist goal." *Sura* is the Vedic term for "god," as against *asura* ("titan").

6. Like soft dew fallen on a paddy field
   Or heavenly ambrosia rained [upon the world]
   Wipe out the fear of *nāga*s ["snake beings"] and evil spirits [*pisas*]
   And free us from disease every day of our lives.

Pisas is from the Sanskrit *piśāca*, a type of evil spirit in early Buddhism.

7. Concentrate on the name of the glorious [*teda*] Kataragama
   Wear a white cloth and wash the head
   Lay pure lights, lamps, and betel leaves
   People [*danō*] worship him with bowed heads.

Line 2 gives instructions to the ritual specialists regarding purity.

8. Pick a coconut and make oil from it
   Carefully pick fresh flowers
   Go early and arrange the altars [couches]
   Perform this *yāga* ["ritual"] now and you'll derive good.

9. O gods who bring us blessings; whose minds permeate the three worlds
   For certain you will achieve future Buddhahood
   With happy heart we have worshiped you all
   You will acquire merit, so give us your blessings, protect these *ātura*s ["patients"].

Note here what I stated in chapter 2; gods are viewed as future Buddhas, or bodhisattvas. Line 4, *ātura* is patient cum congregation.

10. Your divine eyes scan the world in four directions
    No demons are permitted to remain [by them] even by chance
    O mighty Kataragama, O Saman-Boksäl
    O Gods of the Four Warrants come and reside [*vaḍinava*] in this arena.

The god Saman is referred to as Saman-Boksäl, or simply Boksäl. The etymology of *boksäl* is unclear. Paranavitana says it is derived from *bhoga-śālin*, "abounding in wealth and prosperity" (Paranavitana 1958, p. 38). My texts indicate that it is a honorific given to other gods also.

Songs on the Goddess Pattini

11. Long ago she listened to Buddha's sermons hoping thereby to achieve Nirvāṇa
    On her behalf the god Sakra looked on [the world's suffering] with his thousand eyes
    She saw [then] the wrongs done by the three-eyed Pāṇḍi king
    Is there any other divine being but you? O Pattini come [*vaḍinna*] to this human world.

Note the importance of Pattini in village worship, as indicated by the phrase "Is there any other divine being but you?" (or "There is no divine being but you"). The phrase does not indicate any tendency toward monotheism; rather, it is a compliment, or praise given to the goddess. "Deviyo" in Sinhala can mean either god or goddess; hence I have translated it here as "divine being."

12. The god Sakra saw the goddess Pattini residing in Aňdungiri
    The god Sakra came there for food, feigned hunger, and demanded alms
    "I am intent on Nirvāṇa, [so how can I] give you alms?"
    At this Sakra-king commanded her to wipe out Pāṇḍi's eye.

This as well as the previous verse shows that Pattini is a very Buddhist type of deity, intent on Nirvāṇa.

13. First [she was] born from the *siṅguräl* plant of the god Oṃ.
    From the flower, from the tear of the cobra, from the shoulder shawl [*uramāla*], from lightning,
    She said *namō* ["hail"], worshiped the Buddha, and obtained permission [*vivaraṇa*] from him
    Come quickly Pattini, mother, lady, to the golden flower throne [*mal asna*].

Line 1 is obscure. The god Oṃ is probably Śiva. *Siṅguräl* is a plant from which Umayaṅganā, Śiva's consort, created a prince who later became Gaṇeśa, according to some myths; see Parker 1909, p. 156.

14. O mighty goddess Uramāla Pattini, born from the jeweled shawl worn over the shoulder
    I speak to you O lovely goddess Pattini born from the shoulder [shawl]
    O Pattini born from the flower and Pattini of the fire
    At all times protect all beings O Pattini of Navagamuva.

The Sinhala term *upata*, here and elsewhere, literally means "birth." It also means "origin," and in some cases may simply mean "of." Thus Pattini is literally born of a flower in a previous birth, but she is the goddess *of* the fire. She wears a shawl and hence is *of* (born of) the shawl.

15. With a retinue of the Twelve [Gods] and also with twelve forms [births]
Perfect [*siddha*] Pattini, lady, who destroyed by fire the city of King Pāṇḍi
Pure Pattini, lady, forgive us errors we have [inadvertently] committed
By the power of the Twelve Pattini give auspicious blessings to these *ātura*s.

Siddha is a Sanskrit word meaning "perfected"; it often refers to a pure group of supernatural beings. It could also mean "endowed with supernatural faculties." Pattini is referred to as *siddha*, since she is the perfect wife and a pure being and also endowed with the power to perform miracles. She is sometimes known as Twelve Pattini, since she arrives with the Twelve Gods, or because she has twelve incarnations, according to some accounts. The retinue of Twelve Gods will be discussed later.

16. The god Sakra many *yodun* tall came to the *asura* palace
The force of his thousand eyes hit the *asura*s
The Thousand-Eyed visited the goddess at Aňdungiri Peak
Having come from Aňdungiri. . . .

Reference here to Sakra as Indra of the Vedas and the conqueror of *asura*s. Indra has a thousand eyes. *Yodun* is from the Sanskrit *yojana*, a distance of about seven miles.

17. Lady Pattini O goddess shining over the world like the full moon
We remember you and give you offerings of dances [*keḷi pudak*]
If these people have done wrongs [*varada*] be patient, O lady full of merit
Lady, mighty Pattini, joyously take the offerings given in this hall.

18. On the day the blessed hair relic was brought ceremonially
The gods participated in worship in Nirvāṇa city
That day God Viskam created [a *stūpa* to hold it]
That was the day the goddess Pattini arrived in the human world.

This song is repeated later in *dēvābharaṇa väḍamavīma*, verse 1, page 120. Pattini is constantly linked with Buddhist myth, and she is born in the human world, in one of her rebirths, on the day the Buddha's hair relic was deposited in heaven. Viskam is Viśvakarma, the divine architect.

19. The goddess descends from wind and cloud and sky
She looks at the sorrows in Sri Lanka with her divine eyes
She takes the anklet and carries it on her shoulder
Arrive [*vaḍinna*] O Pattini of wind and cloud and flower.

20. We invite her who was conceived in the holy [*sīla*] golden mango
She who gave the anklet to her husband and told him its worth
With the anklet she broke the prowess [*oda*, "pride"] of the Pāṇḍi king
O Pattini who resurrected the dead body, come and reside here.

Pattini is often referred to as one "who resurrected the dead body," suggesting the crucial nature for Sinhala mythology of the act of resurrecting her husband.

21. That day she went to the Velli rest house [*maḍama*]
    She subjugated the demoness who lived there
    By the power of the chastity and morality she zealously guards
    Listen and come this day into this hall [*maḍuva*] O mighty Pattini.

Reference here is to Pattini's quelling the demoness of pestilence, Vaduru Mādēvi, at the Velli (silver) rest house, on her way to Madurai in search of her husband.

22. Pure Pattini the goddess enters [*vaḍinava*] this human world
    She prevents calamities [*uvaduru*] from striking us
    She, who is here now, and in charge of the Buddha's church [*sāsana*]
    Pure goddess Pattini come and be present in this dancing area.

All the major gods in the pantheon are viewed as guardians of the Buddhist church.

23. Seven times was the Seven Pattini born
    In seven places and on seven days
    With compassion [*met*] and kindness [*karuṇā*] protect us mortals
    O Seven Goddess Pattini come into your flower throne [*mal asna*].

Most of the songs quoted above are omitted on the night of consecration but recited in full at the commencement of the main ceremony. The Rabalīya tradition has several other songs on Pattini explicitly sung at the consecration, but most of them have the same thematic content as those translated above. I will, however, translate two of these special verses below.

24. At the time of our Muni Kakusaňda lived a princess zealously observing the precepts
    The merit from having offered [Kakusaňda] a golden mango
    By that great merit [*kusala*] she became a saintly Pattini
    O goddess by the power of that merit come into this dance arena.

The reference here is to Pattini's giving an alms offering to a previous Buddha Kakusaňda. Pattini, like the Buddha himself, acquires her perfection through acts of morality in previous existences. This event is described in one of the later texts (see chap. 5, p. 225). The mango offering is an explanation, in karmic terms, of how she came to be born in a mango in her final rebirth on earth.

25. Born of the pure dynasty of the sun
    O Kaṇṇaki, a goddess of the three worlds
    Residing on the mountain top, meditating on the Buddhist doctrine [*dhamma*]
    Banish suffering with your kindness, and protect these *āturas* [congregation].

South Indian kings often trace their ancestry to the sun or moon. Pattini's ancestral connection with the solar dynasty not only is an honorific but also is relevant to her role as the goddess of heat. The concept of the three worlds in popular Sinhala Buddhism refers to the worlds of men, of demons in the underworld or demonic world, and of gods. The doctrinal interpretation of three worlds is the world of material form (*rūpa*), the world of sense desire (*kāma*), and *arūpa* (the world of no form; see Ariyapala 1956, p. 225). The doctrinal meanings have been anthropomorphically concretized here. Thus the material form is the human world, the world of sense desire is the demon world, and the world of no form is the divine world.

Songs on Däḍimuṇḍa Deviyo, Alias Dēvatā Baṇḍāra, Alias Vāhala

26. Decorate the couch [altar] and hang curtains red and blue
    Place on it ointment of musk [*kasturi*], sweet dewy water [rose water], and sandlewood scent
    Look! the flower stands [*mal päl*] are glowing with lights
    Here comes Dēvatā Baṇḍāra, of proud dynasty.

27. The body feels crushed, headaches appear and general lassitude
    Back and spine aches, no desire for food
    So lazy one gets, there's no time even for *pūjā*s
    Let me explain: these are diseases of Vāsala Dēvatā.

Vāsala or *Vāhala* is palace or temple gate or entrance; *dēvatā* is a minor deity. Thus Vāsala Dēvatā is a deity guarding the entrance to a palace or temple. *Vāsala* can also mean palace, as in the stanza below. Dēvatā Baṇḍāra was called Vāsala because he was at one time the guardian of the Viṣṇu shrine at Alutnuvara (see pp. 317–21).

28. Wearing white clothes he takes his stick [*sōlu*] in hand
    With his *irdhi* power he travels into every country and comes back to his palace [*vāsala*]
    In those countries he chases *dēvata*s and beats them
    O Lord, possessor of might [*teda*], cure us of karmic diseases.

Irdhi (Sanskrit *ṛddhi*) is the magical power to travel through the air, characteristic of both gods and saints. Karmic diseases are those caused by sins in previous births, rather than by natural causes.

29. In the heavenly city of Tusita aspiring to be Buddha
    [He thought] in whose care shall I place the human world
    Däḍimuṇḍa got that blessing [*karuṇāva*, literally, "kindness"]
    That god was given charge of the human world.

The Buddha, when he was in Tusita heaven awaiting rebirth as Siddhārtha, the Buddha to be, decided to give Däḍimuṇḍa charge of the world. This charge is given to the other major gods also.

30. From the time of the auspicious *kalpa* [in which a Buddha appears]
    From the time he obtained *varan* [warrant] from Rāma the Sura
    From the time the Buddha saw him with his divine eye
    From those times was he named Däḍimuṇḍa.

This part of the mythology of the god probably dates from the time he was associated with Viṣṇu (i.e., Rāma the Sura) at Alutnuvara. Elsewhere in Sinhala myth the god was given the name Däḍimuṇḍa (the fearless) because he stood by the Buddha when the latter was resisting the attacks of Māra, the Buddhist personification of lust, evil, and death.

31. Happily he surveys the world with his divine eyes
See him arrive with yak-tail [*cāmara*] fans in his two hands
You protector of the three worlds
O Dēvatā Baṇḍāra, god, be present here.

I assume Dēvatā Baṇḍāra carries two yak tails to fan the Buddha and attend him.

32. With moral intentions [*sīla guṇen*] he comes down to our earth
In order to help beings to cross *saṃsāra*
To placate the demons who are in his charge
Shouldn't we make vows to Däḍimuṇḍa the Sura?

Sīla is Buddhist morality; the gods here are moral beings. Gods help people to cross *saṃsāra*; that is, the Buddhist notion of existence and reexistence, by making them do good.

33. He takes in his hand the cane woven in gold
He shows its power by beating the demons
He helps all beings living in the three worlds to cross *saṃsāra*
O Dēvatā Baṇḍāra, who has earned great merit, arrive here.

34. With the gold- and jewel-encrusted cane in his hand
He chases *the other demons* and beats them
He helps us and banishes sudden dangers that face us
Come soon, come O Dēvatā Baṇḍāra.

"The other demons"; a clear case of survival, indicating that this god was once viewed as a demon.

35. He sees the port [*toṭamuna*] of Pānadura
He takes up his weapons, he anoints himself with sandalwood paste
O proud Vāsala god!
Protect these folk [*ātura*] like a lamp's effulgence.

Däḍimuṇḍa is again referred to as a guardian god of a palace or temple. In addition to being the guardian of the Viṣṇu shrine he is sometimes viewed as guardian of the Buddhist *dāgäba* and has a shrine at its entrance. Perhaps this comes from his role as defender and protector of the Buddha himself during the Māra struggle.

36. Make a throne [*asna*] for Upulvan the Sura
Bring flowers and make him a scented couch [*yahana*]
Light lamps and give the right offerings
Playfully, O Däḍimuṇḍa, visit us here.

Line 1 is very important. It may refer to the god Upulvan (lotus-hued), whom Paranavitana thinks was later transformed into the Hindu Viṣṇu. However, this does not make much sense. It clearly refers to Dēvatā Baṇḍāra (Däḍimuṇḍa) himself, in which case Upulvan is a term used in reference to more than one deity. For a resolution of this problem see chapter 6 (pp. 312–20).

Songs on Devol Deviyo and His Retinue

Most of these songs are sung on the night of the main ceremony.

37. They left their rice fields, their crops, and the fruit trees they had cultivated
Then with their retinue and following of kinsmen [*nǟ pirisa*]
They carefully packed [the ship] with goods
Sing ritual songs [*kavi kōlmura*] about the Devol gods.

38. There were none others like these seafarers [*marakkala*]
These seafarers lived in the port of Kuḍḍhuppura
They had [their] seven queens and a retinue of traders
There were no other queens like them in the city.

Line 3 is not clear. The Sinhala reads: *bisō satak näva veḷaňdō pirivara*. *Marakkala* are seafaring merchants.

39. There were no others [like them] in that city
They flourished, lacking neither money nor wealth
Rice and betel they had in plenty
Leisurely they spent their easeful days.

"Rice and betel leaves": idiomatic phrase meaning "bread and butter."

40. They talked with their ladies
And decked them in ornaments sixty-four
Then they collected goods for selling
The merchant ladies wept [on being left behind].

The merchants leave their "queens" behind and go abroad.

41. One of the merchants knew how to steer [i.e., knew the routes]
They built a trading vessel at the port
They thought: "let's build a ship and travel abroad. . . ."

42. O gods who please me always
When we are with them our minds are clear
In order to reach the Sinhala land
They unfurled the sails in midocean.

Lines 1 and 2 are not clear to me. Perhaps they refer to the merchants who prayed to their gods before departure.

43. Cautiously they neared Horavala
They were shown the way in their dreams
That was the day they planted the *sōlu* stick
That day they said: "May no being ever suffer."

This text omits several narrative sequences concerning the journey of the Devol god(s). Other texts, sung later, give more details. Briefly, their ship is destroyed by monsoon winds, and they try to land in Sri Lanka, but the major gods prevent them. Ultimately Pattini permits them to land in Sīnigama, on the southwest coast, where the central shrine of this deity is situated. From Sīnigama they go to Vēragoḍa, where they plant their stick (*sōlu*, "cane"). This stick miraculously grows into the large tree seen today in the premises of the Devol Deviyo shrine at Vēragoḍa. The last line simply refers to the role of the god as alleviating suffering and material want. Devol is viewed as singular, or as a collectivity of seven gods.

44. Expeditiously they built the *kōvila* at Sīnigama
Every day it shines forth with great beauty
Decked as it is with red and blue cloths
People worship it with hands on their heads.

45. Having come to the shade of Sīnigama
He shows the power of his command constantly
He settled there the god Vāsala
Place *pañḍuru* ["coins"] and worship his sacred feet.

Line 3 is not clear. The chief *kapurāla* glosses it as "Devol Deviyo" invited the god Vāsala (i.e., Dēvatā Baṇḍāra) to the shrine. In other traditions (Ratnapura) Vāsala is sometimes identified as one of the Devol gods. However, the *vāsala* role (i.e., guardian of the palace or temple) could be taken by any of the minor gods—for example, Devol as a guardian of a Pattini shrine and Dēvatā Baṇḍāra as the guardian of the former Viṣṇu shrine at Alutnuvara.

46. Invoking the name of the sacred Devol god
Who asks for dance offerings and *pañḍuru* ["dedicated coins"]
In a mighty stone raft
That's how they landed at Sīnigama.

Concluding Song for the Guardian Gods

47. They see in four directions with their divine eyes
They permit not the demons to stay around
O Kataragama, Boksäl-Saman mighty gods!
O Gods of the Four Warrants come and reside in this arena.

Texts of the *Daḷumura Pūjāva*: Offering of Betel Leaves

Text 2 Songs for the Gods of the Four Warrants

1. He performs acts of kindness and helps all beings
He has obtained warrant [*varan*] from previous births to accept lakhs of dance offerings
Beautifully blue colored, he rides a *guruḷu* [eagle] vehicle
Respectfully reside in this throne [*asna*] and kindly accept these offerings.

The reference here is to Viṣṇu.

2. Like wind and lightning he [immediately] helps people and is kind [to them]
With his wise [all-seeing] eyes he sees us and is kind to us all
That his command may last in this world, he accepts meritorious offerings of processions [*perahära*]
We invite you to this flower throne, god Saman, and make us prosper.

3. It is awesome the way he banishes the darkness [of *dōsa*, "misfortunes"]
   O chief *dēvatā* of cloud, water, air, and river
   He resides in the lower Toṭagamuva temple [*vihāra*] and is kind to all beings
   O god Nātha respectfully reside in this flower couch and bring us plenty.

Line 2: it is rare for a major god to be addressed as *dēvatā*; I suspect this is due to the constraints of the rhyme scheme of this verse. Toṭagamuva is a famous Buddhist *vihāra*; Nātha's shrine there is "lower," not spatially but structurally, in relation to the Buddha temple.

4. You obtained permission [*vivaraṇa*, from the Buddha] to establish your command and do good
   By that permission [*vivaraṇa*] your divine eyes rest on the Kälaṇiya temple
   The folk here have offered you scents of flowers and light
   O god Vibhīṣaṇa respectfully reside in this flower throne and bring us plenty.

Normally gods obtain warrant or *varan* from the Buddha. *Vivaraṇa* has a similar meaning, but it is a term from Buddha mythology. The Buddha himself has obtained *vivaraṇa* from all the previous Buddhas, according to popular Buddhism. Here Vibhīṣaṇa is viewed as obtaining *vivaraṇa* rather than *varan*, perhaps because he is in charge of Kälaṇiya, the spot consecrated by the Buddha himself. The other deity who has obtained *vivaraṇa* rather than *varan* is Pattini herself.

5. By his powers of *irdhi*, he rides often over Sri Lanka on his peacock
   His eyes survey the four corners of the [milky] ocean and he accepts our offerings
   Your divine eyes survey the four quarters, you perform acts of kindness to all beings
   O god Kataragama respectfully reside in this flower throne and bring us plenty.

Both direct or indirect reference to a deity (he, you) is characteristic of ritual songs.

Songs on Pattini

6. O goddess who having renounced sensual pleasures resides at Aňdungiri Peak
   You caused god Sakra's seat to get warm
   O goddess who cooked *älvī* rice and gave alms to Sakra-king
   O Pattini Dēvi patiently accept the betel leaves on this flower couch [altar].

7. With the deep sounds of the anklet a hundred pestilences [*vaduru*] are banished
   She wandered from place to place, then saw her murdered husband with her divine eye
   By the power [of the act] of muddying the rock and sowing *älvī* rice
   O goddess Pattini reside in this flower throne and may you achieve Buddhahood.

Stanzas 8 and 9 refer to the Pattini mythology, which is described in great detail on pages 225–38.

8. She guarded from ancient times her fidelity, virtue, and morality
She went to the divine world and prayed for future Buddhahood
With devotion we raise our hands above our heads in worship
To the beautiful goddess Orumāla Pattini.

Orumāla: informants gloss this as "of the boat," since Pattini was "born of the boat" (*oru*) according to the ritual text *am̆ba vidamana*. It is possible that the word is derived from the Tamil *orumā*, "peerless."

9. She resides on An̆dungiri Peak adhering to moral precepts
She blinded the eye of the Pāṇḍi king on Sakra's orders
O goddess Orumāla Pattini full of power and glory [*teda*]
Accept this rightful offering of betel given by us this day.

10. She went to Pāṇḍi city in search of her husband
How she threw the anklet at the Pāṇḍi king!
Its rays spread wide and destroyed that city
O Pattini Dēvi come, respectfully reside in this flower throne.

11. O beautiful goddess who from times of old resides in Navagamuva
By the power [of the act] of punishing the Tamil gods
O unblemished [*nimala*] Pattini accept the offerings before you here
We worship you in all directions our hands upon our heads.

Pattini as a goddess punishing alien Tamil gods is a piece of Sinhala patriotism. It is not found in extant mythology except perhaps for her quelling the demoness of pestilence at Velli (Velliya) rest house.

12. That you may look down upon us from the heavenly city of Tusita
That you may accept offerings of betel [*daḷumura*] given this occasion
That you may now banish misfortunes [*dōsa*] of these *ātura*s
We have made a seat for you O goddess to reside on.

Line 1 shows that Pattini is now in Tusita heaven awaiting to be born as a future Buddha. Bodhisattvas, before being born as Buddhas on earth, reside in Tusita.

Songs on Däḍimuṇḍa and Devol Deviyo

13. He emerged from the ashes of the cruel *sura* Basma destroyed [by Viṣṇu]
On that occasion was born the powerful and good Dēvatā Baṇḍāra
O hard Dēvatā Baṇḍāra, who crushed *yaka*s and *rākṣa*s [demons]
Come down for this service [*tēvaya*] of betel.

In fact it was not Dēvatā Baṇḍāra but Devol who was born out of the ashes of Basma the *asura*. There is a tendency in these texts to relate the origin of many deities to that event. In this case it contradicts the conventional mythology of Dēvatā Baṇḍāra recited elsewhere in the *gammaḍuva*. Note also that this song refers to *sura* Basma. In fact it should be *asura*, but adding *a* would introduce an extra syllable and upset the rhyme scheme and rhythm. Hence *sura* is used instead of *asura*, giving a totally opposite meaning! *Asura* could also mean "divinity" in early Sanskrit, but Sinhala priests and laymen could not possibly have been aware of this meaning or of its semantic equivalence with *sura*.

14. His greatness and might radiates the world over
Cane [*sōlu*] in hand he beats the demons on their bleeding backs
O radiant Vāsala Dēvatā Baṇḍāra kindly listen
Rest your divine eyes kindly on this offering of betel.

15. He has the Buddha's permission and he accepts dance offerings from mortals
Full of glory [*teda*], and of heroic warrior prowess
O powerful Däḍimuṇḍa Vāhala god, O prince scented with sandal!
Kindly accept fragrant betel leaves placed on this couch.

Stanzas 14 and 15: *s* and *h* are often interchangeable in Sinhala. Thus Vāhala = Vāsala.

16. Taking along with them a ship full [of goods]
They left the country [*dēsa*] of Malala
O Malala god who resides in the port of Sīnigama
Descend onto this dance area, O god Devol of Malala.

Devol is clearly identified as a god from Malabar or Malala *dēsa*. Malala Devol is asked to come down (*bäsa*). *Bäsa* is a peremptory command and is generally used for demons, which indicates that Devol is a kind of demon. In stanza 19 below Devol's body shakes—another demonic attribute of this god.

17. With joy we offer him scents and dewy water
He listens to our songs, verse by verse, and sees our dances
To banish the illnesses and suffering of those who give offerings,
O mighty and fearsome [*gambhīra*] Devol, respectfully reside on this couch.

18. With bow in hand he prepares [to attack demons]
He chases evil spirits [*pisas*] and demons and batters them
He is pleased with the flowers and betel we have given him
There! the mighty god Devol is approaching his couch.

19. He decks himself with ornaments and his red apparel
His whiskers [*kāňgul*] on both sides are shining
His body shakes with the sound of *davul* and *bera* drums and bells [*gigiri*]
O god Devol come, accept the offerings of betel.

Songs on Gini Kurumbara and Hūniyan

20. Construct a stand with a fork [*katira*]
Then play drums and dance and sing
For with warlike fire torches [*gini pandam*] in his hands
Comes the mighty and handsome Gini Kurumbara.

I discussed the rise of these minor deities like Gini Kurumbara and Hūniyan in chapter 2. The inferior, almost demonic, status of Gini Kurumbara is evident from the nature of his altar. His is not a throne (*asna*) or couch (*yahana*) but a stand with a fork on top to hold offerings (*katira*).

21. Offspring of the great King Paňḍuvas
He sits on the cobra vehicle, after being consecrated [*pē*]

Grant me the favors that I ask of you
O Sūniyan Dēvatā please accept merit from me.

Hūniyan or Sūniyan as offspring of King Paňḍuvas of Sinhala mythology is not part of the current or popular mythology of Hūniyan, which traces him to India (Orissa). Here is an attempt to link an alien god with an indigenous mythic tradition. This is not very successful because in current mythology he is in general viewed as Oḍḍi Kumāraya, that is, Prince of Orissa. Alternatively Hūniyan may have been an older indigenous deity linked with the mythology of King Paňḍuvas and later identified with Hūniyan from South India.

22. You hold the cane [*sōlu*] in order to plant it in Sri Lanka
Your appearance delights the mortals who see you
It is my time to perform this ritual [*yāgaya*] well
O god who is in charge of the country, come into this flower throne.

Line 3: "it is my time": Hūniyan is the personal guardian of the priest, rather than of the group. Note that unlike Kurumbara he is given a superior altar.

23. By the power of your fruitful merit [*pin sāre*] you aspire to Nirvāṇa
You often help [*pihiṭa*] the mortals living in *saṃsāra*
I, your servant, vowed to serve you, give you betel leaves and merit
Look, god Gambāra is coming into the flower seat.

As seen in chapter 2, Hūniyan is also known as Gambāra, "he who is in charge of villages."

Verses of Merit Giving to the Gods

24. By the truth of our refuge in the Transmundane Lord, and the refuge of the Dhamma
By the permission of Saman and Vibhīṣaṇa
By the warrant of Pattini born of a mango
Let us recite the praise of "merit giving to the gods."

"Transmundane Lord"; the Sinhala *lovuturu muni*, from the Pāli *lokuttara*, "transmundane."

25. We give offerings to the noble gods everywhere present
They accept the offerings [*puda*] given to them by mortals
The mighty gods: Kataragama, Saman-Boksäl
O Gods of the Four Warrants accept the merit we give you.

26. With delight your servants [*gäti*] decorate your couch
They consecrate [*pē*] themselves by washing their heads and incensing
They deck your seats and offer merit [*pin*] to the god
O god Viṣṇu accept the merit of coconut flower offerings.

27. He resides on the top of Saman Peak
His command [*aṇasaka*] spreads through many leagues
Forgive us for wrongs which you may see us doing
O god Saman accept the merit of coconut flower offerings.

28. In this country he has many shrines [*kōvil*] built for him
We worship this god, wherever we go, whatever trip we undertake
Worship the god who is kind and full of knowledge
O god Gaṇa [Gaṇeśa] accept the merit of coconut flower offerings.

29. He rides loftily on his peacock vehicle
His gaze embraces the brim of the [milky] ocean
This priest [*ädura*] gives you offerings of coconut flowers
O god Kadirāsana [Kataragama] accept the merit of coconut flower offerings.

30. Enthusiastically we give offerings to the goddess
We blow hollow horns and flutes [*horaṇǟ*]
We sound the five instruments and the conch
O recent [*alut*, "new"] goddess Pattini accept our merit.

Pattini is called "new goddess"; a survival from the period in which she was seen as new or recent.

31. O Pattini goddess of Madurā
Her command spreads over the whole world
Today this priest [*ädura*] gives you merit of coconut flower offerings
O goddess Amarāpati accept the merit we give you.

Amarāpati is an old indigenous deity, one of the seven Kiri Amma, whose significance is discussed in chapter 6. This verse suggests that Amarāpati and Pattini are identified as one goddess.

32. Prepare offerings of dances in this place
He loves to eat sweetmeats and tasty foods
He banishes the troubles [*dōsa*] caused by fierce, horrifying [*ruduru*] demons
O god Dēvatā Baṇḍāra accept the merit of coconut flower offerings.

33. A mighty god in charge of the palace [*vāsala*]
His command over this country [*dēsa*] will last forever
Prepare pure coconut flowers [for offerings]
O Vāsala god accept the merit of coconut flower offerings.

34. Seven rafts they built and landed in this city [of Sīnigama]
He [they] demarcated an area for [building] a shrine [*dēvāle*] worth a city
Prepare sweet-smelling flowers for offerings
We give you merit, forgive us wrongs [unknowingly] committed by us.

35. That god whose prowess is like a fire
Whose body shines like fiery colors
That god arrives with fiery rays
O Gini Kurumbara god accept the merit we give you.

Note that Gini Kurumbara is treated as a god in this stanza, as against stanza 20 above.

36. In the village square we perform rituals [*pūjā*]
We create separate "seats" for the gods

We worship the gods and give them merit
O gods of the three worlds accept the merit of coconut flower offerings

37. O gods who reside in the earth and sky
We worship you with our hands on our heads
The sun and moon gods, recent friends of ours
And the Twelve Gods accept the merit of coconut flower offerings.

Sun and moon are "recent friends," that is, "recently" incorporated into the Sinhala pantheon, but how recently I do not know. The songs indicate that the act of merit transfer is sealed with "coconut flower offerings." Sometimes coconut flowers are used but most often areca flowers, which are considered prettier, are substituted.

Texts of the Planting of the Festival Bough

Text 3 The *Kannalavva*, or Plaint, Chanted by the Chief *Kapurāla*

These plaints are exceptionally long, and I have omitted many sentences from each. However, the translation gives much of the detail and the "feel" of these chants.

May you live long [for] five thousand years, five thousand years, five thousand years, till the end of a *kalpa* ["age," i.e., one day of Brahma].

May you become a Buddha. While the earth and sky and sun and moon last, while the *sāsana* of the Buddha and the *sāsana* of the *dēva*s last, for a whole *kalpa* lasting a long period of time, may you live long [*āyubōvēvā*] and may you achieve Buddhahood,

O Sahampati the great [Mahā] Brahma, noble king possessed of great spiritual power [*ānubhāva*], who looks upon this Isle of Sri Lanka with divine kindness and listens to us—

Listen with divine kindness to the exhortations [*ārādhanā*, "invitation"] made in your name, O Sakra, chief of the world of gods, listen with divine kindness to the requests made in your name—

O Śrī Viṣṇu possessed of great spiritual powers, protector of Sri Lanka and the *sāsana* of the Buddha who listens [to us] and benevolently looks on us, O great king, with divine kindness listen to the requests we make in your name ———. In addition listen reverend sir who was born as offspring of King Dasaratha [as Rāma] born from the virgin womb of your divine mother, listen [to the troubles] in this isle of Sri Lanka, you who reside in a heavenly abode [*vimāna*] on the top of Sudharśana Peak, close to the Milky Ocean, O great Viṣṇu, noblest king listen ———. Reverend sir you [who existed] from the very birth of the *kalpa*s ["ages"], at a time when the rising waters reached the Brahma world, when the gods assembled in the Sura world said, "Who could create a flat earth on these waters? then O Nārāyaṇa, Śrī Viṣṇu, noble divine Lord, you took a Pūrṇaka [demonic?] guise and dived into the waters as a boar [*varāha*], if it be true then [that you raised the earth], O lord possessed of glory [*teda*] and influence [*ānubhāva*], you who were born into this age [*kalpa*] with resplendent blue-colored body, and with great beauty, with four arms and a bow and also wearing numberless divine ornaments, and responsible for the *sāsana* of the Buddha that will last for five thousand years, complete in ten manifestations [*dasa avatāra*], subjugator of an endless number of *yakṣa*s and *rākṣa*s [demons], who rides the *guruḷu* [eagle] vehicle toward Vaikunṭha Peak, O Viṣṇu most noble king listen to the pleas made by your servant [*gäti*], accept our merit and protect us because of this merit we give you—

And next, O Śrī Sumana Saman, whose looks fall on the wilderness of the Samanaḷa Peak, the heavenly abode of the golden "red coconut trees" [*tämbili*], on Divāguhā, on the Sabaragamuva *dēvāle*, on the Deraṇiyāgala and Boltumbe *dēvāle*s, and on the *dēvāle*s at Horaguṇa, Nivitigala, and Vīdiyagoḍa, whose looks fall on the procession at Äsaḷa [July] [at the *dēvāle* of Ratnapura] on the golden sword and golden bow, and on the elephant tusker vehicle—who with goodness, looks with kindness on Sri Lanka, on the throne [of the Sinhala kings], on the pearl umbrella [symbol of kingship] and whose kind looks fall on the Samanaḷa wilderness, O Śrī Sumana, in whose name we make our request, listen and accept merit from us, and because of this merit, protect us—

In the name of Vibhīṣaṇa, noble divine king, conqueror of the *asura*s whose kind looks fall on the great Kälaṇiya temple [*vihāra*], listen to the announcement of our requests—accept our merit and protect us—

O Gaṇa Deviyo [Gaṇeśa], divine king, divine listener, chief of Ruhuṇa country, bringer of all knowledge and intelligence, we plead in your name, and also in your name, O god Skanda, divine king, listen to the announcement of our requests, and also you, who were created by the divine noble King Viṣṇu when the *asura* Basma was burned into ashes, you created of six faces, twelve eyes, twelve hands, who climbed the golden peacock and landed in Devundara [Devinuvara or Dondra in south Sri Lanka], crossed the river Valavē, the river Kiri [milk river] the river Mäṇik [gem river] and reached the seven hills of Kataragama where you made a palace and a hut of reeds; you have a retinue of seven sets of Väddas [aboriginal hunters], you married Valli, a heavenly being—. You spread your looks with divine kindness on the great Kataragama *dēvāle*, the minor Kataragama *dēvāle* [at Koṭabōve], the shrine for Gaṇa Deviyo, the *kōvil* of Valli mater [*mātā*], whose look falls on the top of Swear Rock [*divurungala*] on Väḍahiṭi Kanda, Sella Kataragama, the noble Kiri Vehera, the Däḍimuṇḍa *dēvāle* (at Kiri Vehera), the reverend *bodhi* tree, the seven mountains and three villages [of Kataragama], the Devundara *dēvāle*, the *kōvila* in the middle of the sea [Sīnigama?] and the whole island of Sri Lanka, and on the throne, the pearl umbrella, the herd of milk cattle and herd of deer [belonging to the king?]; you who look with divine kindness on all these and on the human world three times a day with divine compassion, O Kataragama possessor of great spiritual influence [*ānubhāva*], divine, noble king listen to the pleas made in your name, and accept merit, and protect us for merit given.

And also, perfect [*siddha*] goddess Seven Pattini whose kindness and look falls on Navagamuva, Mädagoḍa, Palugasvāsala, and our original shrine at Rabalīya, on specially designated *kōvil*, on the anklets seventy-nine [or seven times nine], look and listen with divine kindness to the pleas made by us in your name—

And, furthermore, goddess born in the human world from the leaf of a *kaduru* [*Tabernaemontana dichotoma*] tree, from a *mī* tree [*Bassia longifolia*], from the *demaṭa* flower [*Gmelina asiatica*], from the *tämbili* [red coconut] flower, from the essence of sandalwood, from the column of smoke that rose up to the sky, from a drop of dew, from the shoulder of Īśvara, and from his thigh, from the light of *mäṇik* [gems], from the golden mango, thus born ninety-nine times including the birth from the tear that fell from the eye of Mahākāla the king of Nāgas, you who then went to Aňdungiri to observe *tapas* [meditation, austerities], O pure Pattini divine being, listen with divine kindness to the requests made by us in your name, listen kindly, accept our merit, and protect us by the merit you have accepted from us—

Also, in the name of Śrī Dēvatā Baṇḍāra, noble divine king of Alutnuvara and also in the name of Devol and their retinue, and of the noble divine king Gini Kurumbara, and Hūniyan who is in charge of villages [*gambāra*] and the Seven Irdhi Queens, and the Seven Kiri Amma ["milk mothers"] who also have *irdhi* [*ṛddhi*], I, your servant, have exhorted you [all you divine beings mentioned in this plaint] on behalf of all these villagers who believe in you so that they may never see or hear of pestilence and plagues and disease, and calamities [*upadrava*], give them divine protection, save them from *avol* [ritual cursing] and *devol* [curses at Devol shrines], from the evil looks [*diṣṭi*] of *dēvatā*s, from bad times—

And also save them from the dangers, diseases, and sudden calamities that may result from divine anger and wrath [*udahasa*], from the looks [*diṣṭi*] of *dēvatā*s, from bodily error [pollution]—

And also [save us] from the misfortune that may have already struck us from the nine planets, Ravi [sun], Candra [moon], Kuja [Mars], Buda [Mercury], Guru [Jupiter], Kivi [Venus], Säni [Saturn], Rāhu [Dragon's head], Kētu [Dragon's tail] obtain for us royal success, and also protect us and help us to thrive in the fields we hereafter cultivate, in journeys we make, in our trades, in our jobs and professions—When you do these things O lords, it brings you merit in your future births and renown in your present existence.

We plead thus that in the future you would obtain for these people, who have praised your names and worshiped you, the wisdom of Gaṇa Deviyo [Gaṇeśa] on their heads, the blessings of Sarasvatī to be in their mouths, and also to create Śrī Kāntā's gaze in their houses and fields and gardens, and obtain for them years of long life from Mahā Brahma, the great divine noble king, and then [you may] worship the sacred feet of the Buddha. Once, twice, thrice, O reverend lords give us your kindness and your forgiveness. For a long period of time may you live, for five thousand years, for the duration of a *kalpa*, you may live long!

The *kapurāla* makes references to the name of the village or the household at various points in the plaint.

Commentary on Text 3: The *Kannalavva*, or Plaint

1. This text starts with Brahma Sahampati, a deity important in doctrinal Buddhism but not in contemporary practice. Soon after his enlightenment the Buddha was undecided whether to opt for his own personal salvation or to proclaim the doctrine to the world, "for the welfare of the many." On this occasion Brahma Sahampati pleaded with the Buddha to proclaim his message for the salvation of mankind. It is clear from this text that on the popular level Brahma Sahampati is equated with the Hindu creator god Mahá Brahma. But in the popular, as in the doctrinal, tradition, he is no longer the powerful creator, but a higher type of Buddhist layman and a protector of Buddhism. Both he and Sakra are only formally invoked in Sinhala rituals.

2. Viṣṇu is the de facto head of the current Sinhala Buddhist pantheon. The plaint shows a basic familiarity with his Hindu background, as boar apparition and as Rāma. The concept of the ten avatars, however, is known, but nowhere in the *gammaḍuva* texts are they individually listed. Some of the mythological references are vague or false. Viṣṇu as *varāha*, or boar, is viewed as a Pūrṇaka apparition. Pūrṇaka is a demon in Buddhist Jātaka mythology, and I have glossed it as "demon." Sudharśana is referred to here as Viṣṇu's

mountain, whereas it should be Viṣṇu's discus or one of the outer peaks of the mythic Meru mountain, or Indra's city. However, the *guruḷu* vehicle is firmly incorporated into the current version of Viṣṇu among the Buddhists.

3. Saman is also called Śrī Sumana and is popularly identified as Lakṣmaṇa, younger brother of Rāma. For the history of the Saman cult, see Paranavitana 1958.

4. Gaṇeśa is called "chief of Ruhuṇa raṭa." In fact, he is not an important deity in Ruhuṇa, or in the low country and Sabaragamuva. The chief of Ruhuṇa is Kataragama (Skanda), but since Gaṇeśa is Kataragama's elder brother, he also becomes "chief of Ruhuṇa" through his kin connection to Kataragama.

5. Kataragama: according to the operative myth, Skanda or Kataragama was created by Viṣṇu in his female form (see pp. 113–14). The Kataragama mythology and the places associated with it (Swear Rock, etc.) will be dealt with later in this work.

6. Pattini is often called *siddha*, a class of perfected beings in Hinduism and Jainism. The term is rarely used in Buddhism. The many births of Pattini have little significance. The conventional number is seven or twelve.

7. The Seven Irdhi (*ṛddhi*) queens are a group of semidivine beings placated in a ritual for barren women known as the *raṭa yäkuma*. They are also known as *riddhi bisavu*.

8. The distinction between the operative pantheon and the actual pantheon comes out clearly in the *kannalavva*, or plaint, uttered by the chief priest. Several principles seem to operate here:

a. Gods who are important in status like Brahmā Sahampati and Sakra are given formal recognition and importance. They are invoked at the beginning of the plaint.

b. Gods who are important in the actual operative religion are given greater importance by the length of the invocation.

c. Minor but operatively important gods appear at the conclusion: they are also given brief mention, and in this respect are like the major but inoperative deities. Their operative importance is diminished by their lower status.

d. Even the operative gods are not *equally* operative. Thus Nātha is never mentioned in the invocation; Gaṇeśa and Vibhīṣaṇa are only briefly mentioned. The indication is that these gods are fast becoming inoperative (Vibhīṣaṇa and Nātha). Gaṇeśa is there by virtue of being the elder brother of Kataragama.

As is evident from the description of the ritual, many songs are sung at the *magul kapa*, or festival bough ritual. The most important text is the origin myth of the *gammaḍuva*, which is sung at the conclusion of the *magul kapa* ritual. The other texts sung often mention events in the same myth, and hence it is not necessary to quote them. Also the *sirasapāda* (head-to-foot verse sung here) is standard and appears in other sections of the ceremony. It will be quoted later. I shall invert the order of the ritual and present the text of the origin myth first, then quote those parts of the other texts that either fill in gaps in the myth or present additional or contradictory detail.

Text 4 *Maḍupuraya*: Hall and City, or *Maḍu Upata*: Birth of the *Maḍuva* (Hall)

Sasiri bara me siri laka!
[Heavy with prosperity, this Sri Lanka]
Sēraman the king was
Born into this world
One day alone in the forest

He heard a Sambar cry
And wanted to eat its flesh.
His mind was agitated
He summoned his ministers
With beat of drums
They surrounded the forest.
That day in the whole forest
They failed to find the [wounded] Sambar
Who's escaped into another forest.
The Sambar suffered greatly
And died in that forest.
He was reborn as a frog
And went to the king's pond
Awaiting the king's arrival.
In a blue lotus [*mānel*] flower
He hid waiting
The king had a sudden thought
To go to the lotus pond
He picked a blue lotus
And inhaled its fragrance.
The frog jumped into his head
And clutched at his brain
Then Sēraman the king
Had this terrible headache.
He went into the palace
And reclined on his couch
He sent messengers to where
Physicians could be found.
When they were summoned
They came with medicines
They examined very carefully
The great king's head
But his headache grew worse
He couldn't eat sweetmeats,
He could bear it no longer
So he performed a demon exorcism
Gave sacrifices and held rituals
For the nine planetary gods.
Then the great king
Spent a lakh in money
For performing a good *nasna*
But no progress at all.
Then, for this good reason
On Mount Kailāsa, the seat of Sakra [*paṇḍuvāsana*]
Which senses joy and suffering grew warm
Sakra said, "Alas! who is suffering now?"

He looked with his divine eyes
On this misfortune in the human world.
And in order to banish the disease
Of Sēraman the great king
Afflicted with a headache
[Sakra caused] Pattini the goddess to appear
To the king in a dream.

Her hair like a peacock's
Her forehead like the sickle moon
Her eyebrows like rainbows
Her nose, curved like a goad
Her two lips like tender *nā* leaves [*Mesua ferrea*]
Her fingers like beautiful buds
Her shoulders a decorative arch [*toraṇa*]
Her bosom like golden plates
Her neck like that of a water pot [*kalageḍi*]
Her waist the narrow curve of a bow [*dunumiṭa*]
Her thighs smooth like banana trunks
Her shanks like the *dunukē* flower [*Pandanus foetidus*]
Her feet like a flower
Her nails like a parrot's beak.
"A beautiful maiden
With a veil over her head
And shawl over the shoulder
And anklet in her hands
Tinkling bells on her feet
Saw I approach"
He told his ministers.
To perform a ceremony
For the king's head disease.
God Viśvakarma came
And decided to build a hall
Measuring sixty *riyan* long
Thirty *riyan* wide
Fifteen *riyan* high
With bricks and plaster he built it
And sprayed white sand.
A seven-tiered altar
Decorated in gold.
To decorate the pot of prosperity [*pun kalasa*]
He needed a lucky flower
He went to Sakra's palace
And obtained a golden coconut flower [*ran tämbili*]
And offered it to the king
And made the king offer a golden coin [*pañḍuru*]

After that day's ceremony.
Sēraman the king's
Headache was cured
To perpetuate it among humans
To spread it among humans
Aṅ maḍu, gī maḍu
Vahal maḍu, mal yahan
Pahan maḍu, devol maḍu
The Twelve Gods being assembled
Together with Viṣṇu
Together with Saman
Together with Kataragama
Together with Vibhīṣaṇa
Together with pure Pattini
Together with god Vāhala
Together with Devol Deviyo
Together with Doḷaha Deviyo
They have assembled in this hall here
Among these good *ātura*s.
They performed a hall *then*
Income and money increased
Crops and trees increased
Cattle and other herds multiplied.

For these good *ātura*s here
The cattle in their herds
The money in the box
For their fields, plots, crops of rice
Their pretty little children
That they may be disciplined
For bringing prosperity and plenty
Āvaḍā balavaḍā
Yasavaḍā, siri vaḍā
Siri säpata vädivädī
Epasvā säpatvī, dinēmatu dinēvā
Āyurakṣāvanna āyubōvēvā

Commentary on Text 4: "The Birth of the Hall"

1. Clarification of terms

a. *Nasna* (line 46) is a technique employed in Ayurvedic medicine for clearing the nasal passages to get rid of noxious humors congealed inside the head.

b. The goddess appears in the king's dream wearing a *moṭṭäkkili*, or veil, and an *osariya*, or shawl (lines 74–75). These are standard features of the goddess's attire and are worn by the priests when they impersonate the goddess. For a discussion of the historical significance of this attire see chapter 14 (pp. 538–39).

c. *Riyan* (lines 84–87) is a Sinhala measure roughly equivalent to eighteen inches.

d. This text mentions various types of rituals over which Pattini presides. They are *aṅ maḍu*, a hall where the *aṅkeḷiya* ritual is held; *gī maḍu*, an amended version of the *gammaḍuva* where the songs from the Pattini texts are sung, without the ritual dramas; *vahal maḍu*, where the emphasis is on rituals for the god Dēvatā Baṇḍāra; *mal yahan*, a minor ritual where the deities are propitiated at their altars (*mal yahan*, "flower couches"); *pahan maḍu* ("hall of lights"), also an amended version of the *gammaḍuva*; and *devol maḍu*, a version of the *gammaḍuva* for an individual, generally someone afflicted with divine misfortune or retribution.

2. *Maḍu upata* is an important text that describes the origin of the prototypic *gammaḍuva*. All five ritual traditions I studied have this text, as well as other texts with the same substantive content. A clear distinction should be made between the origin of the hall and the origin of the central Pattini shrine at Navagamuva. The latter, according to some traditions, was built by King Gajabāhu, whereas the protagonist of the former myth is Sēraman, king of Cēra (Kerala). The myth explains how the original *gammaḍuva* came to be held—to cure the king's headache that resulted from a frog's clutching his brain! I find it hard to interpret this myth; the notion of karmic effect, however, is clearly brought out. The king commits an evil act; he mortally wounds a sambar; this animal dies bearing hatred against the king and causing his affliction. I think this belongs to a class of myths that have emerged from dreams or from the unconscious and are later given conscious cognitive organization and plot structure. My guess is that the symbolism of kissing the *mānel* (blue lotus) flower originated as an indirect representation of an incestuous wish regarding the mother, since lotuses are female symbols in South Asian culture. Moreover, Pattini was born out of a *mānel* flower in one of her births. The headache of Sēraman is the suffering and guilt caused by this primal wish and can be alleviated only through propitiation of the mother goddess. Sēraman's headache is the prototypic motive for holding the original *gammaḍuva*; the consequence of holding the *gammaḍuva* is prosperity, fertility, and the general weal.

The present ritual is the reenactment of the prototypic event. The phrase "then and now" appears often in these rituals: "then" refers to the prototypic effects (prosperity, etc.); "now" refers to the hope that the *present* performance will produce the same effects.

The myth is a charter for the present *gammaḍuva*. Sēraman (king of Cēra) was probably associated with the origin myth of the Pattini rituals in South India (possibly in Kerala).

In the Sinhala myth he is also responsible for the first *gammaḍuva* held in Ruvanvälla. In the *Cilappatikāram*, Sēraman does not appear; instead a specific king of Cēra, Ceṅkuṭṭuvaṉ, takes his place. Ceṅkuṭṭuvaṉ is also associated with an "origin myth"; he builds the first temple for Pattini in Vañci, his capital, according to the *Cilappatikāram*. Like Sēraman of our text, he also sees a vision of Pattini (Dikshitar 1939, p. 33).

3. Mount Kailāsa is in fact the abode of Śiva in Hindu mythology. Here it is viewed as Sakra's abode. In Sinhala myth there is a tendency for Sakra to absorb elements from Śiva mythology. Kailāsa could easily be assimilated into Paṇḍukambalaśayilāsana, Sakra's seat.

4. The concluding formula is a standard ending to invocations in Sinhala ritual. It can be translated thus:

May your life-span increase, and your power,
Your beauty and prosperity increase,
May you have great happiness, may you enjoy daily triumphs,
Protected be your life-span, may you live long.

Text 5 Miscellaneous Songs from the *Magul Kapa* Ritual

The first set of songs sung in the ritual of the festival bough refer to another tradition of myth associated with the *kapa*. Let me quote a few of these songs.

The noble jewel of the Buddha
The refuge of the Dhamma he taught
And the jewel of the Saṅgha
With *śraddhā* [piety] we worship these Three Refuges.

We first worship the Buddha
Second the transmundane Dhamma
Third the jewel of the great Saṅgha
We must at first worship these Three Refuges.

At the time of Duṭugämuṇu
Was constructed the Four Dēvāle
At that time the *kapa*
Was cut and planted at dawn.

In order to perpetuate it on earth
Duṭugämuṇu the king arrived
At Kataragama city and that day
Planted with joy the *kapa*.

The reference is to the great Sinhala king Duṭugämuṇu (161–137 B.C.) who constructed four (seven in some accounts) temples at Kataragama in gratitude to the god Skanda, who helped him defeat the Tamils. The *kapa* he planted commemorates his victory: hence *magul* ("auspicious," "victorious") *kapa*, say our informants. Informants say that this *kapa* is different from the one planted to cure King Sēraman's disease. The rest of this text consists of twenty-one short stanzas and sixteen long stanzas. They do not elaborate the Duṭugämuṇu myth. Instead, it is an instructional text dealing with the manner of cutting the *kapa* in the forest, decorating it, its dimensions and the type of priests who should cut it. It concludes with the banishment of disease (*rōga*) by the power of the *magul kapa*. I quote a few stanzas:

Thus having cut the *kapa*
Giving prime place to the Twelve Gods
Arrange the *āturas* in two lines
And thus bless them with the *kapa*.

Line 2 indicates that the Twelve Gods were important at one time than they are now.

Cut it at a length of seven *riyan*
Shave it and make it eight sided

Dig a hole one *riyan* in depth
Bathe the *kapa* with a pot of water.

"Eight sided": to represent the eight directions.

Cut the *magul kapa* in the midst of the forest
Beat drums and the sounds of the five instruments
If you do these tasks in a propitious [*magul*] manner
You will have *magul säpa* ["auspicious happiness"] as long as sun and moon last.

Shout *āvaḍā* and banish the *divi dōsa* [effects of perjury]
Strain perfumed water and bathe the *kapa* with it
With full heart plant the *kapa*
Bind five bunches [of fruit from palms] and tie them on the *kapa*.

Other instructions, which are not observed in the actual ritual, states that nine types of precious things (*navaratna*) should be buried under the *kapa*.

Another set of songs sung while the *kapa* is being planted give further information on the origin myth. These songs also state that Sēraman was from Soḷī raṭa. Sēraman literally means "king of Cēra," which is not Cōḷa (Soḷī). The significance of this "mistake" will be discussed in chapter 15 (pp. 554–55).

These songs state that King Sēraman saw a beautiful apparition in a dream and consulted a Brahman from Benares, who interpreted the dream as a vision of the goddess Pattini. The king and his ministers then went to Sri Lanka to perform the ritual. The *kapurāla* explains this event in his address to the audience: "Pattini is a Buddhist goddess and the ritual had to be performed in Sri Lanka since Buddhism had died out in India." The original *kapa* was from a sandalwood tree from the venue of the prototypic *gammaḍuva*. The songs also refer to a special seat (*asna*) for the Twelve Gods.

There are two major myths of the *kapa* in the Rabalīya tradition, coming from different sources. One is the *magul kapa* (festival bough) planted on the night of the consecration and the other the *bisō kapa* (queen post) planted on the main night. Some ritual traditions state that *bisō* and *magul kapa* are the same; both were planted on the occasion of the original prototypic *gammaḍuva* of Sēraman. In Rabalīya there is real confusion. The *kapa* that is planted on the consecration night is clearly associated with the Sēraman myth that is sung there: it was planted on the prototypic occasion. But there is another set of songs that state that the *kapa* was planted by the great Sinhala king and hero Duṭugämuṇu, who to commemorate his victory over the Tamils built the shrine for Skanda at Kataragama and also the shrines for the other three major gods. A *kapa* was planted on this occasion, and this was the *magul kapa* (festival post).

According to other accounts, Sēraman's queen (*bisō*) had a pregnancy longing that was fulfilled by Brahmans who performed the ritual of *salu sälma* ("fanning with Pattini's shawl") to satisfy her. This was part of the original *gammaḍuva* rituals. By this account it was Sēraman's queen who planted the *kapa* in the special pavilion (*pāya*) built for her. Hence the *kapa* is also called *bisō pāya* (queen's pavilion). The songs that deal with this theme are as follows:

When Sēraman the king was present in ancient Sri Lanka
His chief queen was afflicted with a pregnancy longing

[They obtained] a red shawl sixteen *riyan* long
And asked Brahmans to perform a *yāga* of shawl fanning for her.

The Brahmans performed shawl fanning for the queen.
For the king, other queens and their children
For the four ministers, courtiers, and their ladies
All were fanned by Brahmans in old times.

It is clear that Rabalīya tries to combine two traditions of *kapa*: one from the Duṭugämuṇu-Skanda mythology and the other from the Pattini tradition, the former derived from the planting of the *kapa* at the Skanda shrine at Kataragama to herald the annual festival for that deity. I think the Pattini *kapa* is the older tradition, since references to Duṭugämuṇu's association with Kataragama occurs only in very late literary accounts. None of the well-known chronicles, either Pāli or Sinhala, mention it.

Texts of the Ritual of the Torch of Time

Text 6 *Yādinna*, or Invocation to Viṣṇu

I have cut up this *yādinna* into verse paragraphs for the convenience of the reader.

Heavy with prosperity, this blessed Sri Lanka!
The birth of god Viṣṇu in old times [I recount]
Whose blessings spread wide
Whose glory o'erspreads the earth
Like the moon shining o'er the world.

Fathered by King Sundara
Of Candrāvati his queen
From her womb rose a craving
[That her son to be born]
Would with filaments of flowers
Placed on his blessed hands
[Worship the Buddha]
And wage war against Māra
And thereby obtain warrant [from the Buddha].

By that queen's wish
Ten months elapsed
And she felt birth pains
On the full moon of Poson [June]
Under the sign of Aquarius [*kumbha*]
And the *dasā* [period] of Saturn [*senasuru*].
Then the Brahman named Jyoti
Served him with gold milk [*ran kiri*]
And named him Great Viṣṇu [Mahā Viṣṇu]
And then with gold ornaments
He decked the god.

Jyoti śāstra is astrology; the Brahman Jyoti is the very founder of astrological science. Gold milk refers to the Sinhala custom where a piece of gold is rubbed into breast milk and the "gold milk" is then gently spread on the infant's lips. The idea is to ensure a life of good fortune.

Full seven years went by
Till the Māra war was won.
And then our Muni with pleasure
Named him Glorious Viṣṇu [*teda* Viṣṇu]
In charge of Sri Lanka.

The details of how Viṣṇu defended the Buddha during the Māra war are not mentioned. But the presumption is that Viṣṇu obtained *varan* from the Buddha on this occasion. This idea of obtaining *varan* during the Māra war is no longer associated with Viṣṇu, but rather with Dēvatā Baṇḍāra.

He was asked to measure
The earth in three steps,
And take charge of it
But he couldn't complete it
And was given the title Aḍa Viṣṇu [half-Viṣṇu].
On the third occasion
At the city of Viśālā
He banished the demons
And was named Mulu Viṣṇu [complete Viṣṇu]
On the fourth occasion
He was named Śrī Viṣṇu
And on the fifth occasion
He was given the title Mahā Viṣṇu.
[Taking the forms of ten avatars
Obtaining *varan* ten times
To protect the Buddha *sāsana*].

The last three lines are not actually sung in my tape-recorded versions but are found in a written text from the Sīnigama tradition. I quote them because they clearly show the attempt to give Buddhist meaning and significance to the Hindu idea of the ten avatars of Viṣṇu.

As instructed [by the Buddha]
We give you merit O king
All of us who live in Sri Lanka
By offering you a torch of time.
From the suffering that has befallen us
Help us cross over to the other shore!
We'll take an emerald[s]
And place it above.

The last two lines are somewhat obscure to me. They could refer to offering an emerald to a Viṣṇu image, or more likely refer to an emerald on a well-known Viṣṇu image. In this case the lines mean: "Help us since we have given you an emerald for your head." The use of the present tense is not unusual: the offering given in the past is now being given (vicariously) in the present. It reflects our good intentions. Perhaps the reference is to the old Viṣṇu image in Devundara before it was plundered by the Portuguese in 1588. Śrī Rāhula writing in the fifteenth century refers to two rubies that adorned the ears of the deity; and Ibn Battuta noted earlier that two large gems (probably alexandrite) encased in the eyes of the deity glistened in the night. If there were gems in the eyes and the ears of the statue it was likely there was also one in the forehead.

As the goddess Pattini wished
You created a stone raft
For Prince Devol to land
At the shrine of Sīnigama.
You gave him warrant to land there.
In a *guruḷu* [eagle] vehicle
The king of the gods was invited (to Sīnigama).
From that day it's been told to us
To give prime place to Viṣṇu
And secondarily to the god Devol
To allocate special [coconut] trees from the orchard
And make oil from them and
Make a torch of time
And offer merit to the god as instructed.
Today also to this god, we give
The merit from this [torch] offering.

The myths of Devol Deviyo sung in the *gammaḍuva* state that Sakra or in some versions Maṇimekhalā, goddess of the sea, created the stone raft on which Devol landed in Sri Lanka. These myths also state that Pattini gave Devol warrant to land in Sīnigama. Here, however, Viṣṇu, in accordance with Pattini's wishes, created the stone raft and also gave *varan* to Devol. The necessity of linking Viṣṇu and Devol is, I think, due to the offering of the torch. Devol is the god of fire and must be in some sense associated with it.

O god Mahā Viṣṇu
I sing about your goodness
Listen with your divine ear
And see with your divine eye
Come down into this dance arena [*rañga maṇḍala*]
And for the *āturas* here
Ninety-eight types of *rōga* [diseases]
And ninety-nine *vyādhi* [pains] banish
And the two hundred and three dangers
Banish forever.
May you live long—may your beauty increase. . . .

Commentary on Text 6: The Invocation to Viṣṇu

I shall defer the analysis of this ritual for later on when it is again performed in honor of Kataragama at the main ceremony. The text, however, is a very important one and illustrates some of the processes depicted in chapter 2 whereby Hindu gods are converted into Buddhist gods. The present invocation (*yādinna*) omits many details in the Buddhist Viṣṇu mythology, but it is still useful for our analysis.

Compare this text with the plaint for Viṣṇu on page 93. In the latter several elements of Viṣṇu mythology from the Hindu tradition are recounted, but very summarily, and sometimes erroneously. Here Viṣṇu is incorporated into a Buddhist framework.

1. His birth as offspring of King Sundara and Queen Candrāvati is a Sinhala invention. Queen Candrāvati has an unusual pregnancy craving that her son should worship the Buddha with tender filaments of flowers and help him in his battle against the army of Māra. Viṣṇu is born on the full moon of Poson, a Buddhist holiday in Sri Lanka, commemorating the introduction of Buddhism to the Island by Mahinda. Thus Viṣṇu's birth is given Sinhala Buddhist legitimacy.

2. Viṣṇu is linked with a key episode in Buddha mythology. Viṣṇu's defense of the Buddha during the Māra war is not spelled out in detail here, but it was obviously well known in the past. The fifteenth-century poems clearly refer to Viṣṇu's defending the Buddha in the Māra war (see pp. 318–19).

3. Viṣṇu gets warrant or *varan* (that crucial term) from the Buddha during the Māra war, though the actual event is not described in this text. Viṣṇu has a specific warrant to protect Sri Lanka.

4. In Hindu mythology Viṣṇu has ten manifestations. Most of these are unfamiliar to the Buddhists. Here an attempt is made to retranslate the ten forms into a Buddhist idiom. The Buddha gives five names or titles to Viṣṇu. I suspect that other texts would have ten titles, but most of these titles are devoid of mythological significance and hence omitted in recital. But it *is* significant that these titles are given to Viṣṇu by the Buddha.

5. One of the titles given by the Buddha to Viṣṇu is Aḍa Viṣṇu, or half- or incomplete Viṣṇu, a title hardly becoming to this very important Hindu deity. It was given when he took three steps across the universe. This famous Vedic myth is given a Buddhist interpretation. The Buddha asked Viṣṇu to take three steps and thereby show his control over the world, but Viṣṇu failed. Thus he is Aḍa Viṣṇu or half-Viṣṇu. The Buddhists have symbolically cut Viṣṇu down to size when they incorporated him into their pantheon. Viṣṇu is then given a chance to be whole or complete: this is when he banished the demons of disease from Viśālā, thereby performing an exemplary Buddhist deed. Here Viṣṇu is linked to the Buddhist mythology of the *Ratana Sutta*. According to Buddhist tradition the Buddha recited that text to dispel a pestilence that ravaged the city of Viśālā.

6. In the three lines from the Sīnigama tradition the concept of the ten avatars is related to the notion of a warrant (*varan*) given by the Buddha to Viṣṇu ten times to protect the Buddhist church (*sāsana*). These warrants are obviously the titles given to Viṣṇu in our text.

4

The Main Ceremony

Bisō Kapa Hiṭavīma: Planting of the *Bisō Kapa*

In the Rabalīya tradition the main ceremony starts with the *bisō kapa*, meaning literally "the bough, or *kapa*, of the queen."[1] In those traditions that do not require consecration the night before, the main ceremony must begin with the lighting of the lamps, the offerings of light, incense, flowers, and betel to the gods rather than with the *bisō kapa*. In several traditions—Mātara, Ūrubokka, Heyiaṅtuḍuva—there is no separate ritual known as *magul kapa*; only the *bisō kapa* is known. The *magul kapa* is performed by those traditions (Rabalīya, Sīnigama) that have a prior consecration ceremony.

The planting of the *bisō kapa* is a simple ritual. In the origin myth a sandalwood post was used for the *kapa*, but now it is a trunk of a banana tree, about four feet high, the outer bark nicely peeled so that the *kapa* shows a shiny cream color. The head of the *kapa* is decorated with tender coconut (*gok*) leaves forming a bulge on top in the shape of the full pot symbolizing fertility. Coconut and areca flowers are stuck on the *kapa*.

Sometimes the *bisō kapa* ritual starts with a brief lecture by the *kapurāla*. This kind of expository lecture can occur at any point in the ceremony, depending on time and circumstance. I quote this speech from one of the rituals I witnessed. Here the *kapurāla* explains the significance of the *bisō kapa* and tries to reconcile conflicting mythic traditions that his audience may be aware of. Only relevant portions of the speech will be translated here. The rest will be summarized.

> *Kapurāla*: Respectfully, ladies and gentlemen, I beg permission from this audience. Today to banish the darkness of the *dōsa* that has befallen these *ātura*s [congregation] we have given prime place to the Gods of the Four Warrants who have their residence in the Four Dēvāles and whose gaze falls thereon; we also have given recognition to the Gods of the Three Divisions [*tunbāge*, i.e., Pattini, Devol, Dēvatā Baṇḍāra] who have their looks [*bälma*] in the great original place of Rabalīya.
>
> [He goes on to say:] This *dēva pūjā* was originally performed in the Island of Lanka in times of yore in honor of the gods, who desire merit from us. Since Bud-

1. Another meaning of *bisō* is "anointed," from the Sanskrit *abhiṣeka*. However, this meaning is not consonant with the origin myth of *bisō kapa* (pp. 188–92).

> dhism was declining in India at that time, King Sēraman and his followers had to come to Sri Lanka where the immortal doctrine of the Buddha flourished. The *dēva pūjā* was held according to the dream of King Sēraman's queen. Earlier remedies had failed to cure the king's illness. In this dream she saw a lady the Brahman astrologers said was Pattini. They told the king of his past karma that caused the illness and said that to cure this illness he must give prime place to the Three Jewels and offer lights to the Three Refuges. Then this merit must be transferred [*anumōdan*] to the gods who rule the universe—these being the *alpē śākya* gods [the gods of the lower category] and *mahē śākya* gods [of the higher category]—and also to those beings who reside in rivers, hills, and dales. And since the picture of the divine lady Pattini appeared in the dream she must be given a chief place in this ceremony. Thus the king had to come to Sri Lanka from Soḷīpura. He sailed his ship and landed at Vattala-toṭa. From there he went to Kälaṇiya and worshiped the *vihāra* there; then he rested at Attanagalla, and from there he went to Ruvanvälla. Since this was a good place to hold the ceremony a hall was constructed facing north, with separate altars [*yahana*] and arches [*toraṇa*] for the Gods of the Four Warrants, and also a separate altar for the Three Jewels. For that ceremony the queen brought with her an "invitation post" [*ārādhanā kaṇuvak*] for the gods, with the wish [*prārthanā*] that by the ritual [*yāga*] for the Gods of the Four Warrants the king's illness would be cured. This post was beautified by carpenters and brought in procession to the hall. The king and queen and their followers were blessed with this by the Brahmans. By the magnetism [*ākarṣaṇa*] of this *bisō kapa* the king's headache was cured and the *dosā* destroyed. That day the *bisō kapa* was made of sandalwood; today we cannot do as our kings of old did. Today we make it out of a banana trunk and tender coconut leaves. That day they sang the first book of the thirty-five ritual texts [*pantis kōlmura*], which deals with the manner in which the *bisō kapa* was brought into the arena. This is what we'll sing here now. [Actually this text, "the origin of the hall" (text 4) was sung the previous evening.]
>
> The Brahmans who came to Sri Lanka to perform the ritual [*yāga*] for King Sēraman went back to Soḷīpura with King Gajabāhu. Why? Because the Soḷī king had taken the goddess Pattini's ornaments and the bowl relic of the Buddha and also twelve thousand Sinhala prisoners. Gajabāhu brought these back as well as twelve thousand extra persons as compensation. The anklets of the goddess Pattini were in the possession of the Pāṇḍi king's daughter, Amarāpati. She accompanied Gajabāhu to Sri Lanka and personally carried the anklets to Ruvanvälla, where the first *gammaḍuva* was held.

After this speech the *kapa* is placed on a chair covered with a white cloth. Dancers dance round the *kapa* to the beat of drums while the two *kapurāla*s sing the praises of the *kapa* (text 7, 6:30 P.M.). One dancer takes the *kapa* in his hand and dances with it. Then he leaves it on the chair and dances with a water pot, and after this with an areca sprig that he afterward places on top of the *kapa*. He then incenses the *kapa* and the various altars. Now a thin torch is lit and stuck at the end of the *kapa*, and the dancer once more takes the *kapa* and dances. He waves it before the audience in blessing, making a graceful downward movement at the correct point in the songs.

While the dancing is progressing a hole is dug on the side (left or right) of the main altar, a few feet away from it. When the dance is over the *kapa* is brought near this hole. The chief *kapurāla* sings songs that end with the word *mangalam* ("festival joy"). Then the chief *kapurāla* utters a *kannalavva* (plaint), imploring the gods to banish *dōsa* and disease. This is almost identical with the plaint uttered at the *magul kapa* ritual (text 3). The chant ends with *tīnduyi nivāraṇayi* ("it is consummated")—the chief householder or organizer (*ātura*) puts some betel leaves and gifts of coins (*pañḍuru*) into the hole. He holds the *kapa* in the hole while someone else puts back the earth and tramples it to hold the *kapa* in place. *Pähiňdun*—a bag containing paddy, two coconuts, and a few bananas—is placed on the ground near the *kapa*.

Though the songs state that five types of "bunches" (of fruit) should be hung on the *bisō kapa*, this is not generally practiced in this tradition. It is done elsewhere.

Sändā Samayama: Evening Demon Time

After the *bisō kapa* ritual there is a brief interval, then the ritual of the *sändā samayama* starts.

According to traditional Sinhala belief, no longer operative, each day consists of sixty hours (*päya*). The night is divided into three watches, each consisting of ten Sinhala hours (*päya*). The first watch is *pera yāma*, roughly from 6:00 P.M. to 10:00 P.M.; middle watch, or *mäda yāma*, 10:00 P.M. to 2:00 A.M.; and *aluyama*, or dawn watch, from 2:00 A.M. to 6:00 A.M. These beliefs on *yāma* are important even today. Demons are active at crucial points of these watches; hence they are called *samayama* times, or demon times. A demon that may inflict injury at this time may simply be called *samayama*. According to the Rabalīya tradition, and the others also, the evening *samayama* is for the demons of the Devol group (*devol samayamē yakku*), especially Mahasōna, the middle is for the Sanni demons, and the dawn is for Kurumbara, also a member of the Devol troop. The content of these traditions is not found among the demon exorcists in the same cultural area. Nevertheless, they also have the concept of *yāma* and of *samayan* times. *Iramudun samayama* (midday demon time), which is not observed in the *gammaḍuva*, is an important part of the division of the day (midday) in some rituals of demon exorcism.

The ritual involves offerings (*doḷa*) for the demons in a tray, or *pidēni taṭṭu*, made of banana bark, placed on a small stool facing the altar of Dēvatā Baṇḍara, who has special control over demons. The chief *ātura* ("patient"), or the chief organizers of the ceremony, sits on a mat facing the chair containing the demon offering. A dancer faces the chair and dances first with an areca sprig, then with a pot of water in the other hand. He dips the areca sprig in the water pot and lustrates the offering for demons (*pidēni*), the Dēvatā Baṇḍāra altar, and some of the other altars. Then he incenses the altars. Thereafter he takes a lighted torch and throws resin at it while dancing, so that flames burst impressively in the night air. This is to clear the arena of various evil spirits before inviting the evening demons. This is followed by a dance with a torch in each hand. Other dancers may join in, and all of them go round and round in a circle in the middle of the arena, demarcating the area of control where the demons must reside. Occasionally the two lighted ends of the torches are brought together and placed crossways across the chest, indicating obeisance to the gods. This is over at 7:00 P.M., with shouts of *āvaḍā* ("may your life-span increase"). Meanwhile some of the dancers take pots in their hands and dance with them. Each dancer plants a thin torch in his pot, and they place a pot on the head of each of the *ātura*s, who already have over their heads tricolored cloths falling well below their shoulders. Text 8 is sung by the dancers while they perform these actions. This is over about 7:10 P.M.

The chief *kapurāla* utters a *kannalavva* (plaint), facing the *ātura*s with the pots on their heads. The first part of the *kannalavva* is uttered by the chief *kapurāla* and is a variation of the standard one quoted earlier. He invokes the protection of the Gods of the Four Warrants and the other major deities. He asks the *ātura*s to say "*tīnduyi nivāraṇayi*" ("it is done, consummated") three times at the conclusion of the plaint, indicating that all types of misfortunes (*dōsa*) and dangers (*antarā*) will leave them by the blessings of these deities.

The second plaint is uttered by the senior *kapurāla*. He says that the foremost place has been given to the Gods of the Four Warrants, the gods of the Three Divisions (Pattini, Dēvatā Baṇḍāra, Devol), and the gods of the Twelve Divisions (the Doḷaha Deviyo, or Twelve Gods), and an oblation has been given to demons at this *samayama* time. These oblations have been made *käpa* (dedicated) on behalf of their bodies, their five *skandha*s ("constituent aggregates," according to Buddhism). If there be any demons who would attack or harm these *ātura*s while they eat, walk, drink, bathe, go on journeys, or such, they must now accept this oblation and leave the bodies of these patients by the command of the great King Vaiṣravaṇa, or Vessamuni. By the dedication of this oblation, "one, two, and three," all the misfortunes (*dōsa*) are *tīnduyi nivāraṇayi*. (The *ātura*s repeat the last phrase, meaning "it is done, consummated.")

After this the *kapurāla*s sing *sirasapāda*s or head-to-foot verses, to banish *dōsa* from various parts of the body (text 9). Meanwhile an assistant takes the pots and places them in the stand for demons outside the limits of the hall. The two *kapurāla*s continue singing, inviting the demons to come, presumably to partake of the *doḷa* offered to them in their stand outside the sacred area. As they sing they look up invitingly and beckon them to come down (text 10). The pot contains the rice offering (*bat doḷa*) for the demons—rice plus a curry of seven vegetables (*hat mālu*). The oblation on the chair also has a pot of rice with two cupped leaves (*goṭu*) containing *aňdun* (collyrium, actually soot), sandalwood paste, milk, and *rīri* (blood, actually simulated blood made with turmeric). They are also given shampoo (*nānu*) and flowers for their baths and personal adornment. In contrast to exorcistic rituals, no meat or fish is given to the demons, since it would violate the norms of purity that should prevail in the sacred area. The oblation given to demons is called *doḷa*, which literally means "craving," or *bili*, "sacrifices," in contrast to the *pūjā* offered to the gods and the Buddha. The term *pidēni* is also used to designate the offerings to the demons and the tray that contains the offerings.

Saňgaḷa Pē Kirīma: Consecration of the Priest's Robe

After the demons have been invoked the performers eat their evening consecrated meal (*pē bata*). Then the more formal part of the main ceremony begins, when the chief *kapurāla* wears his white ceremonial outfit, the *saňgaḷa*.

The *saňgaḷa* (or *haňgaḷa* in Kandyan areas) is a white cloth eighteen feet long and thirty inches wide that the *kapurāla* wears during the major part of the ceremony. It is generally provided by the washerman; sometimes a new cloth is given by the organizers of the ritual. Most *kapurāla*s wear this during the whole ritual, except during the "killing and resurrection" ritual (*marā ipäddīma*) and the ritual of blessings with the anklet (*salam̆ba sāntiya*), for which they wear female clothes. It should be noted that the word *san̆gaḷa* is also used to designate the yellow double robe or *sivura* of the fully ordained (*upasampadā*) Buddhist monk.

The consecration of the robe begins soon after the evening meal, about 8:10 P.M. The robe is made into a bundle and covered with another white cloth and placed on a chair in front of the *toraṇa* (arch). Also on the chair are a mat and a set of bells (*gejji*) for the legs. An assistant incenses the robe while singing parts of text 11. He then takes the robe and dances with it, and he continues to sing with the other assistants joining in. The songs end with the conventional *āyubōvēvā* ("may you live long"). Then another assistant lays the mat on the floor; the robe is placed on this mat. An assistant sits on the mat and removes the white cloth covering the robe and also the coins (*pan̆ḍuru*) tied to the white cloth. The drummer and assistants gather round the mat and "admire" the robe. Then they start "making" it—that is, setting the ruffles. After this they help the chief *kapurāla* put it on, a process that takes about twenty minutes.

The text sung during this ritual (text 11) is not an important one in content, and I shall only quote excerpts from it. In Buddhist parlance the term *san̆gaḷa* is synonymous with *sivura*, or the robe of the monk. I do not know whether the term was taken over from Buddhism to the *dēva* cults or if it happened the other way around. However, the two kinds of robes are related to the two kinds of ritual roles. The ideal otherworldly orientation of the Buddhist monk is reflected in the patched yellow robe, which in theory should be made of rags. Much of the monk's robe (ideally) relates to his involvement in processes of death and decay (polluting activities). This involves the food he begs for, the robe he wears, and many other aspects of his life. Nowadays these associations are related to the monk's conventional public roles—they are symbols without the psychological and social significance of doctrinal Buddhism. By contrast, the *kapurāla* has to interact with gods who are pure: his *san̆gaḷa* is a consecrated *white* cloth, symbolic of purity.

Pahan Pūjāva: Offering of Lights for the Gods

The chief *kapurāla* has donned his white robe and is now ready for the crucial part of the ceremony, the invitation for the gods to be present in the hall in essence. He invites them (*ārādhanā*) initially by consecrating the altars with the lighting of lamps and secondarily by offering them betel leaves and flowers (*daḷumura pūjāva*).

The ritual songs inviting the deities are identical with those sung in the similar rite performed on the night of the consecration of the hall (text 1). However, on the night of the consecration (*maḍu pē*) only some of the altars have been constructed, and the gods are not individually invited to separate altars. I shall describe here the order in which the deities are invited, since it indicates an order of precedence.

At 8:45 P.M. the chief *kapurāla* has donned the *san̆gaḷa*, and he, his second, and the other assistants are assembled near the altar for the Gods of the Four Warrants. Outside the boundary (*sīmā*), an attendant wearing a mouth mask holds an oil container on his head; he advances under a canopy into the sacred area to the beat of drums. The chief *kapurāla* faces the altar of the Gods of the Four Warrants and blows the conch three times. He dances before the altar and sings songs inviting Viṣṇu, and subsequently the other three gods, exactly as in the consecration ritual. The chief *kapurāla* takes the oil container and pours oil into the two lamps at the two ends of the altar, while the attendant leaves the arena. Then he incenses the altar, after which he lights the lamp on the right side of the altar. Then one of the organizers (*āturas*) light the left lamp. Next he dances special steps (*pattini pada*, "Pattini steps") before the goddess's altar (*toraṇa*) and sings songs in her praise (9:00 P.M.). The oil bearer advances once again. The chief *kapurāla* now holds the oil container and dances with it before the Pattini altar, occasionally raising the container to his forehead in obeisance. Then he goes up to the altar of Doḷaha Deviyo (the Twelve Gods) and pays them similar obeisance. Then he lights the right-hand lamp of the Pattini altar (*toraṇa*) while a member from the congregation (*ātura*) lights the left. After this three others (*āturas*) on their own light the lamps in the Doḷaha Deviyo altar (indicating, perhaps, that these gods are not as important as the others). He then incenses the altars.

A similar procedure is followed in respect to the next deity, Dēvatā Baṇḍāra. Here also the chief *kapurāla* lights the right lamp while an *ātura* lights the left. After this Devol Deviyo is treated in the same manner. Thus in the Rabalīya tradition the basic order of precedence is very clear: (1) the Gods of the Four Warrants and Nātha, (2) Pattini, (3) Doḷaha Deviyo, (4) Dēvatā Baṇḍāra alias Vāhala alias Däḍimuṇḍa, (5) Devol Deviyo. Furthermore, the *kapurāla* lights the propitious right side of each altar while the congregation light the left.

At 9:25 P.M. the chief *kapurāla* comes to the altar with a pot of turmeric water (*kahadiyara*). He holds this pot before the altar of Dēvatā Baṇḍāra and silently mutters a mantra (charm). Then he takes a bag full of resin from an attendant, which he also charms. An assistant meanwhile places a new water pot with coconut flowers stuck in its mouth on the altar of Dēvatā Baṇḍāra. The chief then takes the stick (*daṇḍa*) of the god from his altar and dances with it, after which he lays the stick back on the altar and worships the deity (9:30). He then takes a flaming torch (as always, from an attendant) in his right hand and goes clockwise (toward the right) around the arena in front of the various altars. Then he engages in a dialogue with the drummer, the gist of which is obtaining permission (*avasara*) from the Three Jewels, the gods who are in control of the universe (*lōkapālaka*; note word), and finally from the audience. He says that such permission is necessary because "the hand may go wrong and the mouth may go wrong." "Thus if there is some accidental fault on our part you must forgive us." After this he dances with the torch before the altar of Dēvatā Baṇḍāra and throws resin into the torch, creating spectacular masses of flame in the air. Thereafter he throws resin in the direction of the altar of the Gods of the Four Warrants; then, standing at the far end of the arena, he throws flames of resin at the Pattini altar at the other end.

Why is such great prominence given to Dēvatā Baṇḍāra at this time? He is the controller of demons, and the arena has to be cleared of evil spirits before the gods can be invited in the *daḷumura pūjāva* to follow soon. Demons are cleared away with *kahadiyara* (turmeric water), a cleansing fluid, and resin, an inferior, acrid incense generally used for demons. Gods by contrast are offered a superior water, sandalwood-milk-water (*haňdun kiri pän*), sweet incense (*kaṭṭakumañjal*), and camphor (*kapuru*).

Kāla Pandama: The Torch of Time

The torch of time is now planted on behalf of god Kataragama. The time is 10:00 P.M., and the chief *kapurāla* summons the important villagers (*āturas*; or the members of the family, as the case may be) to sit on a mat on the arena floor. He then explains to them the significance of the *kāla pandama*. He says that they have just offered a *pūjā* of lights to the "divine king/gods who control the universe" (*lōkapālaka divya rajāṇan vahansēlā*). Their divine eyes (*dēva bälma*) have fallen here. They are the gods of the Four Warrants and Pattini, Vāsala–Dēvatā Baṇḍāra, and the seven Devol gods. At the conclusion of this *pūjā* he will offer another offering of lights, *pahan pūjā*, known as the *kāla pandam pūjava* (torch of time). This *kāla pandama* is for those sections of time known as past, present, and future, so that untimely (*akāla*) disasters will not strike this family (or village), and so that this congregation (*āturas*) will obtain succor (*pihiṭa*) from the god Kataragama. Then with a torch in one hand and a betel leaf in the other he sings *set kiyaman* (verses of blessings) on Kataragama (text 12). As he sings he periodically blesses each *ātura* by placing the betel leaf against the *ātura*'s head. After this he tells the drummer that these *āturas* and their kinsmen will have a happy and prosperous time, a long life. Now all the *āturas* and others around touch the torch, which an assistant takes and plants on the tree of time. After this the chief *kapurāla* and his second sing *set* (blessing) songs recounting events in the life of the Buddha. I have not translated this text since it is similar to others. Often an invocation (*yādinna*) for Kataragama is sung, very similar in style to the Viṣṇu invocation sung at the torch of time ritual of the previous night (text 6). I have not translated this either, since it has the standard content of all Kataragama songs sung earlier (e.g., text 1, stanzas 3–10).

The torch of time, according to informants, is meant to avert "bad times." It is planted in honor of three gods: Viṣṇu, time past; Kataragama, time present; and Dēvatā Baṇḍāra, time future. The ritual actions of the priests are a kind of symbolic behavior that the actors are not conscious of. Viṣṇu is the head of the pantheon, but he is a benign god; he belongs to the time past. In fact, in the past he was less benign and more involved in the affairs of man, as we saw in chapter 2. Kataragama is today widely propitiated for overcoming current problems: he belongs to "time present," the operative here and now. But according to the karmic logic spelled out in chapter 2 his rise must eventually result in his downfall; when this happens a lesser god like Dēvatā Baṇḍāra must take his place. This is in fact what is happening now. Thus Dēvatā Baṇḍāra represents "time future."

On occasion, during the performance of the ritual of the torch of time, the chief *kapurāla* will give a short lecture on the birth of the god Kataragama or Skanda. This important myth also deals with the origins of Devol Deviyo, the Kurumbara, and other demons. I quote it below.

> The Myth of the Birth of Kumumbara, Devol Deviyo, and Skanda (Kataragama)
>
> The *asura* named Basma was learning arts and science [*śilpa śāstra*] from Īśvara. He fell in love with Umayaṅganā [Pārvatī], wife of Īśvara, and secretly thought of seducing her. Īśvara, because of Pārvatī's intercession, had reluctantly given him a boon, a secret mantra known as the "essence of fire spell" [*gina sāra dähäna*], the power to convert everything he touched to fire and ash. Basma decided to

touch Īśvara and burn him up, but when the Īśvara saw him coming, he ran away. This was the time when Mahā Viṣṇu with divine kindness was looking at Sri Lanka. He saw that Basma was trying to seduce his sister Umā. Viṣṇu then took on the guise of an even more beautiful woman and, creating a golden swing, appeared in Basma's path, swinging and singing love songs.

Basma was infatuated by "her" and asked her who she was. "Can't you see I am a female," Viṣṇu said.

Basma: Are you married?
Viṣṇu: No
Basma: Are you willing to marry me?
Viṣṇu: Yes, but I can't trust men. Therefore, place your hand on your head and swear that you'll be faithful to me and never leave me.

Basma the *asura* was so infatuated that he forgot his hand was charmed. He touched his head and swore fidelity to the beautiful woman and thus was consumed into ashes. Out of these ashes arose Devol Deviyo and Gini Kurumbara.

Īśvara meanwhile saw no sign of Basma, so he came back from hiding. He saw instead the same beautiful woman on the swing. He also was infatuated and wanted to marry her. But the woman asked him: "Are you married?" He said "Yes." "Then I can't marry you. Go tell Umayaṅganā that there is a beautiful woman on a swing, singing love songs, and ask her whether you may bring her as your chief queen [*mahēsi*]."

Īśvara went to his palace and asked Umayaṅganā's permission to bring home the beautiful woman as his queen [*mahēsi*]. "Yes, go bring her," said Umayaṅganā.

But when Īśvara came back, the beautiful woman was pregnant. She said, "I can't marry you now since I am pregnant. So ask Umayaṅganā's permission to bring home a pregnant woman." Īśvara went back, and once again Umā agreed. But when he returned this time the woman had had a child and was once again pregnant. She said: "This also cannot be done, you have to ask your wife's permission to bring home a pregnant woman with a child."

This happened six times. Meanwhile the eldest child was big enough to walk, and he was away picking flowers. When Īśvara came for the seventh time he thought that this was a wonder, a miraculous creation, not normal birth. So Īśvara brought Umā to see the woman. Viṣṇu saw them come and shed his female guise. He awaited their arrival with six of the children, since the eldest was away picking flowers. Īśvara's wife saw the child and said, "*Ane*, my brother has a heap of children" [*kanda*, "heap," "mountain," "lot of"]. She embraced the children together saying, "*is kandak*" ["a mountain of heads"]. Thus Skanda [i.e., Is-kanda] was born with six faces and twelve arms. The eldest brother escaped this transformation. He was named Aiyanāyaka, "eldest brother," "chief brother."[2]

Toran Yāgaya: Ritual of the Ceremonial Archway

The ritual of the *toraṇa* starts about 10:45 P.M. with the second *kapurāla* invoking the Three Jewels. Then with all the assistants and drummers he faces the Pattini altar and

2. For a South Indian version of this myth, see Shulman (1980, p. 309). In this version it is Aiyaṉār alone who is born out of the (sexual) union of Viṣṇu as female and Śiva. The Sinhala myth is their own invention, I

utters *stotra*, thanksgiving verses or verses of praise, followed by *sanna*, an exposition. The verses of praise are supposed to be in Sanskrit couplets, or *śloka*, but this is not so in reality.

Stotra (thanks) are highly formalized verse or prose texts generally recited as a thanksgiving to the Three Jewels or the higher gods. In some *stotra*s practically every word is in formal, stylized Pāli or Sanskrit generally unintelligible to the audience, though the gist is clear. Sometimes high Sinhala may be used, but always the language is stately and uttered in solemn, sonorous tones. The *sanna* is an elucidation of the *stotra* in less formal, but nevertheless "good" Sinhala. It is almost impossible to render the feel of these *stotra*s in an English translation, and I shall not attempt to do so. The impact on the audience is clear: the *stotra*s are diacritically separable from the other utterances in the ritual. The remote, stately language helps place the Three Jewels praised in a category apart from other classes of sacred entities.

Facing the altar of the *toraṇa*, the *kapurāla* says: "Respectfully, ladies and gentlemen, I seek your permission to speak. We are performing here today a festival [*maṅgalya*] of the gods, in honor of the Goddess Pattini together with the Gods of the Four Warrants. For this purpose the congregation (*ātura*) here have constructed a tall *toraṇa*. We shall recount here today the origin of that *yāga*."

Then he utters the line:

> *Utum budu ruvanē* [noble jewel of the Buddha].

The drummer says:

> *Lova desu dahamsaraṇē* [the refuge of the Dhamma preached for the world].

And an assistant:

> *Samaga saṅga ruvanē* [together with the jewel of the monk order].

And all together:

> *Sadā vaňdimuva me tun saraṇē* [with devotion let us worship these Three Refuges].

Then the *kapurāla* repeats separately each line of the stanza above, followed by an exposition (*sanna*) of it. The "exposition" is in reality a further elaboration of the line, a *varṇanāva*, or praise. This is grand rhetoric deliberately based on classical conventions, which elevates the subject matter of the text. After praising each of the Three Jewels, the *kapurāla* pays homage or obeisance to each.

Then *namaskāra*, or homage, is paid to the Gods of the Four Warrants of the classical tradition and to other classes of divine agents, all constituting a *samūhaya*, or collectivity of divinities. The *toraṇa* should be worthy of these divinities and reflect their beauty and power (text 13). By their blessings (*set*) may diseases—listed below—be banished, he says.

> By their good influence . . . the diseases of blood and bile, *olmāda* ["madness," from Sanskrit *unmāda*], *apasmāra* [epilepsy], *kuṣṭha* [eczema], and other bodily

suspect. The folk etymology of Skanda as "Is" *plus* "Kanda" cannot be justified in Tamil. In the Tamil myth Viṣṇu as female (Mōhinī) has intercourse with Śiva; this would be much too indecorous for the Sri Lankan Viṣṇu.

> [*kāyika*] diseases, and mental diseases [*mānasika rōga*] like sorrow and fear, and lurking dangers caused by *bhūtas* [demons] and mean spirits [*pisas*], and *dōsa* of the evil eye and evil mouth, and *dōsa* from cursing [*avol*], and *devol dōsa* from swearing false oaths, and the *dōsa* that comes from great wealth [envy of others], and *dōsa* that comes from pricking pins, and discomforts [due to bad omens] that come from seeing certain animals such as dogs and birds such as crows, and all types of dangers and illnesses . . . such as the sun that has seen the dark or the fire that has sighted butter . . . may they all vanish and may the heat be calmed by cool waters . . . and may you achieve great wealth and prosperity.

Then the *kapurāla* and his assistants dance in front of the *toraṇa* while singing the songs of the *toraṇa* (*toran kavi*) (text 14). After this he removes the white curtain (*kaḍaturāva*) covering the *toraṇa* altar and uses it to bless the chief *ātura*. The bundle of divine ornaments covered in red cloth is now exposed to view. He then dances with the others in a circle, the shawl over his shoulders. Now text 14, dealing with the way the *toraṇa* is built, is sung. As he sings the *kapurāla* points out the relevant parts of the *toraṇa* mentioned in the text. After this he puts the white shawl away in the altar.

The ritual of the *toraṇa* is important for demonstrating the existence of "survivals," or items that have little cultural or social structural significance in contemporary society. Comparing this performance with others in different areas of Sri Lanka shows that the ritual of the *toraṇa* arch or *toran yāgaya* consists of two textual traditions, an ancient one and a more recent one. The ancient part I have somewhat arbitrarily designated as text 14b (verses 6–20). This text is identical with that sung in the collective rituals of Haňguraňketa and Laggala, where Pattini is *not* given prime place. It is also sung in exorcistic rituals of the same culture area as the *gammaḍuva*. This text has no reference to persons and places; it could quite easily be attached to other texts. The rest of the ritual text deals with the Pattini story and refers to the origin of the *toraṇa* in the prototypic *gammaḍuva*. Yet how could we decide by comparing these two texts that one is older than the other and is a survival from the past?

1. Text 14b has a pan-Sinhala distribution and is sung even in the most remote areas of the country. This text, for example, is sung in exorcistic rituals of the Western and Southern provinces, but not the other texts 13, 14a, and 14c of the *gammaḍuva*, since exorcistic rituals have their own origin myth of the *toraṇa*. Thus while text 14b is common to many Sinhala ritual traditions, the other texts are variable. We can reasonably infer that the pan-Sinhala text 14b is the older one.

2. Consider the style of text 14b. It is in extremely simple stanzas; often each line is the same as the others except for one word, as if they were designed for easy memorization. In isolated regions of Haňguraňketa and Laggala most ritual songs have this simple style, as befits a nonliterate oral tradition. Moreover, the songs are sung line by line by the *kapurāla*; each line is repeated by his assistants or novices in training. By contrast in the *gammaḍuva* tradition of our culture area, the *kapurālas* depend exclusively on memorizing written texts. In our version of the *toran yāgaya*, texts 13, 14a, and 14c have a more complex rhyme structure than is found in the remoter areas. Thus one can assume that the simpler text is the older one; the other texts show the influence of a high literary tradition that, as I shall show later, developed after the fifteenth century in our culture area.

3. Text 14b contains fascinating information on ancient Sinhala social structure. It refers to four *kulas*, or "castes"—*raja* (royal), *bamuṇu* (Brahman), *veḷaňda* (trader), and

govi (farmer). This is probably the Sinhala version of the Indian *varṇa* scheme except that royalty is superior to Brahman (as it always was in Buddhist Sri Lanka). Also, *vaiśya* and *śūdra* in the Indian scheme denoted a very large number of castes, whereas the Sinhala classification mentions two very specific ones. But it is likely that the Sinhala scheme recognized only the socially important castes: the lower castes were all *hīnajātiyo* ("lower kind") according to the *Saddharmaratnāvaliya*, a thirteenth-century Sinhala text. This text mentions *raja*, *brāhmaṇa*, *vyāparayō* (traders), *govi*, and *hīnajātiyo*. It is not surprising that the *hīnajātiyo* are excluded from the fourfold classification of the *toraṇa* ritual in a society with farmers numerically dominant, then and now. *Hīnajātiyo* is a residual category, structurally but not substantively analagous to the "untouchables" or *mleccha*, those outside the Hindu *varṇa* scheme and outside Hindu society.

This Sinhala fourfold classification has little behavioral significance, at least since the fall of Kandy in 1815. Since then there have been no castes of royalty, Brahmans, and even merchants. Brahmans have always been small groups attached to the courts. It is also likely that there were no separate castes of merchants in Buddhist Sri Lanka after the fifteenth century; merchants tended to be assimilated into the *goyigama* (farmer) caste. We do know, however, that this fourfold scheme had significance in the heyday of Sinhala civilization, before its "decline" in the thirteenth century. A thirteenth-century source recounts the existing ceremony of royal coronation, which requires participation by four groups: *kṣatriya* (royalty), *brahman*, *seṭṭhi* (merchant), and *gahapati* (householder) (Geiger 1960, p. 116). The last, however, is glossed in other thirteenth-century texts as *govi* (farmer). *Pūjāvaliya*, a thirteenth-century text, also mentions a fourfold division: *raja* (royal), *siṭu* (merchant nobility), *bamuṇu* (Brahman), and *veḷaňda* (merchant), but in another place the higher class of merchants (*siṭu*) is dropped and *govi* (farmer) is substituted (Ariyapala 1956, p. 288). It seems feasible to infer that the fourfold classification of my texts refers to conditions even before the thirteenth century in Sri Lanka. When Sinhala civilizations moved to the south and west in the fourteenth and fifteenth centuries this scheme gradually lost its relevance. Yet as a system of classification it has survived into contemporary Sinhala ritual, largely perhaps through oral tradition.

Daḷumura Pūjāva: Offering of Betel Leaves

I shall only briefly describe this ritual, since it is basically the same as the one performed the night before at the consecration rites, except that the gods are individually offered betel leaves and flowers, especially coconut flowers. *Daḷumura Pūjāva* is a formal invitation to the gods to "reside" in their altars and is based on a secular custom of the same sort, as I noted earlier. Since the songs have been recorded earlier (text 2), I shall merely list the order in which the deities are "invited" to their respective altars. (*a*) the gods of the Four Warrants in the following order: Viṣṇu, Saman, Vibhīṣaṇa, Kataragama; (*b*) the goddess Pattini; (*c*) Dēvatā Baṇḍāra alias Vāhala alias Däḍimuṇḍa; (*d*) Devol Deviyo and attendants.

Several minor deities such as Bhairava, the Twelve Gods, and the planetary deities are also invited to the altars. These deities are often ignored in the consecration rituals (text 2) but are generally mentioned in the main ceremony. The Twelve Gods are especially interesting, for, although there is a special altar for them, they are not propitiated there. That altar is used for other deities like Kurumbara and Hūniyan (text 2, stanzas 20–23, pp. 90–91). The three stanzas quoted below are sung by the priests in the middle of the arena.

1. We have skillfully decorated the couch and have offered many flowers
   Humbly we utter a plaint and invite you here
   Purify [*pē*] this altar O victorious lord along with your divine hosts
   God Bhairava, lord of the eight quarters, come on to this flower couch

2. Perfumed with sandalwood scent and bathed in dewy water
   The endless ranks of divine beings have cast their eyes on these offerings
   Mindful are we of the gods' command and great influence
   The Twelve Gods, accompanied by Amarāpati, have come on to this couch.

3. Climb the mountain and apply sandal paste on the pinnacle there
   Bathe in flowing water, in dew, and apply the scent of sandal
   With kindness listen to the plaints uttered by your servants, bending low
   Sun, Moon, Mars, Mercury, Jupiter, Venus, and Saturn have come on to this couch.

Line 1 in stanza 3 probably asks the planets to purify themselves and pay homage to either the mountain of the sacred footprint (Śrī Pāda) or some *dāgäba* (*stūpa*) on a mountaintop.

The ritual starts about 11:00 P.M. and is generally over at 11:20 P.M.

Devābharaṇa Väḍamavīma: Divine Ornaments Ceremonially Brought Forth

We now have the formal ceremonial entry into the arena of the *kapurāla* with the ornaments of the goddess. Actually the ornaments (anklets) have been brought into the arena and laid in the *toraṇa* arch, but it was not a ceremonial, official act. Now comes the public, official act of bringing in the ornaments. For this purpose the anklets of the deity in their casket are placed on a chair covered with white cloth, in front of the altar for the Gods of the Four Warrants. On the chair are also five cloths of different colors; they are theoretically the colors of the five Buddha rays, but in fact any five colors can be used. According to some informants there should be seven cloths; this is very likely the older tradition, and the reduction to five is perhaps an attempt to integrate this older tradition with the Buddhist view of the five main colors of the Buddha halo: blue, yellow, red, white, and crimson. Sometimes two texts are sung when the ornaments are brought from the *toraṇa* to the chair, but often they are omitted, since the ceremonial act of taking the anklets to the altar soon follows. I have quoted one of these texts below (text 15); the other, which describes how the anklets are made, is omitted.

Four attendants wait near the chair at altar 1, holding a canopy, while a washerman waits in readiness to lay the foot cloths (*pāvaḍa*) (11:50 P.M.). The chief *kapurāla* is under the canopy, his feet on the white foot cloth. He wears the white *sañgaḷa* robe, and also a red jacket. With his second he sings various couplets (*śloka*) followed by a *sanna* "exposition" (text 16 below). As he sings he dons the various cloths that are on the chair, putting several layers of the colored cloth over his head so they fall well below the shoulders. This is Pattini's headdress, or *moṭṭäkkili*. He has a red sash over his shoulder: the *osariya*, which is the term for the fold of the sari that women wear over one shoulder. When the shawl is used over the shoulders it is called *uramāla* ("shoulder shawl"). The *moṭṭäkkili* is firmly held in place by a silk strap across the forehead, with jewelry in front to resemble a tiara. The *osariya* and *moṭṭäkkili* are the essential elements of the Pattini dress everywhere in this region.

The singing of the *stotra* and *śloka* go on for fifteen minutes. The *kapurāla* picks up the "yak-tail fan" from the chair and sings songs while waving the fan. Now he is fully dressed. He gives the yak-tail fan to his assistant, who fans Pattini (the *kapurāla* is dressed as Pattini now) from behind, while they both sing songs (text 17 below). Meanwhile the foot cloths are laid by the washerman from the altar of the Gods of the Four Warrants up to the altar (*toraṇa*) of the goddess. The chief *kapurāla* advances very, very slowly on the foot cloth to the blowing of a conch, carrying the ornaments of the goddess covered in red silk cloth over his right shoulder (in other traditions, on the head). The second *kapurāla* fans him; other assistants dance facing him. The canopy is held over him and moves as he advances; an attendant follows behind him with a multicolored umbrella ("the pearl umbrella of royalty") under the canopy. As they advance the second *kapurāla* sings songs asking the various manifestations of Pattini "to be present here." Ultimately the *kapurāla* arrives at the *toraṇa*, deposits the ornaments in the *toraṇa* altar, kneels, and worships the ornaments in a highly stylized manner (12:20 A.M.).

Soon after there is a long interchange between the chief *kapurāla* and the drummer. In brief, this is a challenge by the drummer to the chief *kapurāla* to dance the Pattini *pada*, or the "dance steps of Pattini." According to the dialogue, these dance steps are *stotra*, or thanksgiving for Pattini, which will bring prosperity to the village. The technique is as follows: the drummer beats a difficult beat; it is a challenge for the *kapurāla*, who must follow the rhythm. Each *pada* is more difficult than the last. This goes on for about fifteen minutes. Then the *kapurāla* dances up to the several altars and worships them. He then takes a conch from the *toraṇa* altar and blows it three times. He then blesses the audience, who have lined up, by waving the two ends of the shawl, starting with the chief *ātura*. He suddenly takes off the headdress (*moṭṭäkkili*) and shawl, deposits them in the altar of the *toraṇa*, hangs on the *toraṇa* as if in great stress, his body trembling, then drops to his knees, his hands still grasping the altar. Meanwhile his assistant addresses the audience:

> Here is a kind message for those of you who are assembled here. Today we have *dēva pūjāva* festival where we have given first place to the jewel of the Buddha and the Three Refuges. In this hall city [*maḍupuraya*] built to banish the disease of King Sēraman, in this city, the king and his followers dedicated [*oppu*] *pañḍuru* [coins] to the goddess. This is how it was done.

He takes a red shoulder shawl (*uramāla*) and sings, with his assistants; as he sings he fans the audience, assembled in two lines on the sides of the hall (text 18 below). This text refers to the valuable coins, jewelry, and such, that were offered by royalty during the prototypic *gammaḍuva*. Other texts blessing the audience may also be sung, depending on the time available, but I shall not quote them here. At about 1:00 A.M. the second *kapurāla* reminds the audience to come forward and offer (*oppu*) coins (*pañḍuru*) to the anklets placed in the altar.

Text 15 The Anklets Ceremonially Brought Forth

Text 15 is for bringing the ornaments from the *toraṇa* altar where they had been initially sequestered to the chair near the altar for the Gods of the Four Warrants.

1. On the day the blessed hair relic was brought ceremonially
The gods participated in worship in Nirvāṇa city
That day god Viskam [Viśvakarma] created [a *stūpa* to hold it]
That was also the day goddess Pattini came down to the human world.

2. Amid the winds and clouds of the sky comes the goddess
She looks on suffering in Lanka with her divine eye
She carries the golden anklet on her shoulder
Come O Pattini of wind and rain and of the flower.

3. We invite her who was conceived in the golden mango
She who gave the anklet to her husband and told him its worth
With the anklet she broke the pride of the Pāṇḍi king
O Pattini who resurrected the dead come and reside here.

4. That day she went to the Velli rest house
And subjugated the demoness who lived there
By the power of the chastity and morality she zealously guards
Listen and come this day into this hall O mighty Pattini.

5. The perfect [*siddha*] goddess Pattini arrives in the human world
She prevents dangers from striking us
In charge of the Buddhist church [*sāsana*] she now arrives here
Pure goddess Pattini arrives in the dance arena.

6. We take the anklets used on her tender feet
And make a flawless and beautiful casket to keep them
She who brought back life to the dead body
Surely there's no other divine being like the goddess Pattini.

Note that Pattini, like any Indian woman, wears several anklets. One of these is the special one endowed with miraculous powers.

7. She resides on Aňdungiri Peak
She was born in a mango by the merit of giving alms
O protect the humans who have assembled here
By the influence of the golden mango arrive here O goddess.

8. O Pattini descendant of a righteous dynasty [*vaṃsa*]
Were not luminous gems used in your anklet?
Its clear tinkling [*gigiri*] sounds spread in all directions
The ancestral sins of these people are no more.

9. O goddess Pattini of the glorious rays [or halo]
She wears the *osariya* shawl shining like gems on her shoulder
She holds the glorious, shining anklet in her hand
Come into the flower couch luminous like the moon's rays.

Text 16 *Sat Pattini Kavi*: Songs of Seven Pattini and *Stotra* and *Sanna*: Thanksgiving, Praise, and Exposition

1. The three-eyed powerful god
From his right thigh was she born
She brings about the weal of all
Enter, Śrī Pattini, glorious one.

Sanna: [exposition]
To banish the night, the blind darkness that enveloped this isle, Sri Lanka, like Sūrya, the sun god-king himself, and bounteously endowed with all the divine virtues, [she who was] born on the first occasion from the thigh of Īśvara, O Śrī goddess Pattini, divine exalted lady, today also I plead you to grace this dance hall of the *dēva*s, *sēkvā*.

Sinhala myth is silent regarding Pattini's birth from Īśvara's thigh. This again is probably a survival from the South Indian context of the cult. *Sēkvā* literally means "may you" in high style; thus "may you arrive," "may you grace this dance hall." In this ritual it is used because of its high-sounding connotations.

2. She was born from the womb of the blue lotus [*mānel*]
Endowed with beauty, a blooming divine maiden
O the might of the gem bracelet on your feet!
Arrive, O noble lady, Pattini of the flower.

Endowed with the resplendent five colors, and possessed of qualities pleasing, born for the second time in the womb [*garbha*] of a *mānel* flower, O Pattini, Divine Lady of the Flower, today too grace this divine dance hall and provide us with plenty and prosperity, *sēkvā*.

The flower birth of Pattini is recounted in great detail in the mango shooting (*aṁba vidamana*) myth (text 36, pp. 227–38). Pattini is endowed with five colors, according to the exposition, or *sanna*. These are the colors emanating from the Buddha himself, which again establishes Pattini's Buddhalike nature. The exposition is full of Sanskritized diction, such as *sambhāvayan*, *samalankṛta*, *manōjña*. It is difficult to communicate the flavor of the "high style" in English.

3. Among humans living in Sri Lanka
She banishes darkness and disaster [*piripota*]
She who was born in the tear being shed
Arrive, O Maṇimegha Pattini.

Maṇimegha literally means "gem cloud" or "jeweled cloud," that is, the cloud that brings rain. The mango shooting (*aṁba vidamana*) ritual has a brief reference to Pattini's birth from the "tear" of the *nāga* (cobra deity) king. Pattini is often referred to as Maṇimegha Pattini in the *gammaḍuva* texts, since she was once born in the city of Maṇimegha. This designation is appropriate, since she ended the drought in Madurai with rain, as she does even now in times of drought.

She, like Sūrya, the sun god, who banishes the blind darkness and night that has enveloped this isle of Sri Lanka; endowed is she of all the qualities of a divine lady; O tender Pattini, who was born for the third time from the tear of a *nāga* king, O

Maṇimegha Pattini, realize for this congregation [*ātura*] assembled here today their hopes for prosperity and happiness.

4. Those humans living in Sri Lanka
 She banishes darkness and disaster [*piripata*, Pāli, *paripantha*]
 She was born in the tear being shed
 O Maṇimegha Pattini arrive.

She like Sūrya the sun god who banishes the blind darkness and night that has enveloped this isle of Sri Lanka; endowed is she of all the qualities of a divine lady; O tender Pattini who was born for the third time from the tear of a *nāga* king realize for these *ātura*s assembled here today in this hall their wishes for prosperity and happiness.

The same *śloka* and *sanna* with minor variations are repeated for "effect," in this as well as in some other stanzas.

5. Her body shines with blue and golden hues
 Her clothes are shining like a half-moon
 Love fills the minds of those who behold her
 Enter O goddess Pattini of the flame.

Her blue golden body is like a festive board replete with everything [*cambōjanayak*], O Pattini of the cascades of fire, noble divine lady, with your fire anklet in hand, today also grace this dance hall with your presence, *sēkvā*!

I have translated the term *cambōjanayak* as "festive board," but as far as I know there is no such word. *Cambōjanayak* is a corruption of the Sanskrit *sambhojana*, "eating together." A Sinhalized noun from this could be *sambōjanayak*, "a festive communal meal." The *s* in the word above is converted into *c* or *ch* to make it more high-sounding and more Sanskritic than the original Sanskrit! Pattini of the fire is the opposite of Pattini of the "rain cloud." According to myth, her wrath produced the prototypic fire of Madurai (see pp. 43–45 for a discussion of Pattini as goddess of heat).

6. How she wiped out the Pāṇḍi king's eye
 And was conceived in his pleasure garden!
 And out of the mango there she was born.
 Enter today O Pattini by the power [of that deed].

Her blue and golden body complete with everything like a festive board, O Pattini of the cascades of fire, noble divine lady, with your fire anklet in hand, today also grace this dance hall with your presence, *sēkvā*!

7. The manner in which she wiped out the eye of the Pāṇḍi king,
 Conceived in the pleasure garden
 And born out of the mango there
 Today enter O Pattini by the power [of that deed].

Conceived in the eminent mango in the orchard or pleasure garden of the great Pāṇḍi king in order to create a glory over the inhabitants of the three worlds, O Orumāla Pattini divine lady, born for the fifth time out of a mango, today also grace this dance hall with your presence and realize for these assembled here their wishes for prosperity and happiness, *sēkvā*!

8. Out of compassion for all mankind
And in order to give them relief
Justly, was she born in a dew drop
Come Pattini O tender goddess.

Like Sūrya the sun god who banishes the blind darkness and night that has enveloped this isle of Sri Lanka and endowed with all the qualities of a divinity, O tender goddess born for the sixth time from a dewdrop, bring prosperity and blessings for the *ātura*s assembled here in the dance hall of the *dēva*s.

Pattini's birth from a dewdrop is not spelled out in any of the extant myths.

9. The anklet held aloft in her hand
O golden body born from the boat [*oruva*]
Bring blessings on the *ātura*s here
Come O Pattini Ayirānga.

Ayirānga puzzles me. It is from Ayiranganī (Airanganī), a well-known female name in Sinhala, but I do not know its mythological significance. Perhaps it is derived from the Sanskrit *aira*, "pertaining to food or water." Thus Pattini-Ayiranganī is the giver of prosperity. Alternatively, Airanganī could be a folk derivation from Aryāngani, "noble [aryan] female features."

10. First from the tear of the cobra
From the dewdrop, from the mango
By the power of her journey in the boat
By that power enter O seven Pattini.

The boat is the casket in which the mango was floated downstream by the king of Pāṇḍi.

Arriving seven times, like a golden body, and bearing a golden form, possessed of all the qualities of Ayirānganī, O goddess Pattini, your divine ornaments have been placed on the top of your head, and you have now come into this dance arena, we have invited into this dance arena Pattini of the flower, Pattini of the gem cloud [Maṇimegha], Pattini of the flames, Pattini of the boat garland [*orumāla*], the tender Pattini [of the dewdrop] and Ayirānganī, these seven Pattini divine goddess we have today invited here to cool the ninety-eight diseases [*rōga*], to rid us of ninety-nine *vyādhi* [pains] banish two hundred and three *antarā* [dangers] for a determinate time and to grant us long life and blessings.

If we include Pattini born from Īśvara's thigh (stanza 1) to this list we have seven Pattini, satisfying the numerological criterion. Actually casuistry is required to make the number seven. The Sīnigama text does not even make the attempt; it lists four Pattini, though the text is named "Seven Pattini." Many mother goddesses appear in South India as a collectivity of seven. In Sri Lanka Pattini took the place of Kiri Amma, an ancient local deity who had seven manifestations, as I shall show in chapter 6. Her cult also displaced the indigenous cult of Twelve Gods (Doḷaha Deviyo). Numerology (numbers seven and twelve) helps continuity of tradition.

Text 17 Entry of the Goddess Seven Pattini

1. For the hall that was built [then]
The divine ornaments [*devinan*] were anointed [*nānumura*]
The earth-god-king gave permission
To ceremonially escort it.

The hall the gods enter is also our world—that is, earth—hence the permission of the earth god is required. Generally the earth is represented in the goddess Śrī. However, Sanskrit texts on house construction refer to an earth god variously referred to as Pṛthivī-dhara, Mahīdhara, or Bhūdara. It is this deity that is probably referred to in my text.

2. Today in the dance hall
In order to bring the golden anklet
All the divine king-gods with joy
Give permission for the ceremonial escorting.

3. Falsely accused and killed under the *kohom̆ba* tree
Her husband was brought back to life by her
She chases away illness and suffering
There! the noble Pattini enters the arena.

4. Hold a decorated canopy above
Hold incense of camphor and musk
Blow the conch loudly
As Pattini, exalted one, enters the arena.

5. She placed her feet on the harsh sands
And burn marks appeared on her tender feet
Now we've offered you gifts of coins [*pan̆ḍuru*]
Respectfully enter O Pattini on the foot cloth.

Lines 1 and 2 refer to Pattini's trip to Madurai.

6. Hold lovely canopies above
Make music to please the goddess
Banish the *dōsa* of these *ātura*s
Tread the foot cloths, O goddess Pattini.

7. With the golden anklets in hand
Enter along the foot cloth
Banish the *dōsa* among these humans
And bring the anklets onto the altar.

8. Hold canopies above and curtains alongside
And softly spray sandal and sweet-scented water
The world's mortals worship you thus
Enter the hall O goddess on the foot cloth.

9. Today in this dance hall
Several divine eyes are looking

Into this human world
And thereby banish pestilence [*janapadarōga*].

10. The gods look with their divine eyes
Today at this dance arena
Forgive us wrongs we have done
And fail not to protect this congregation [*ātura*].

11. In order to welcome you from above
I, a human, am down here below
O exalted Orumāla Pattini
Arrive in splendor from above.

12. We have here a large building for a hall
And we have the right scents [of flowers]
Banish [O gods] the *dōsa* that has arisen
Arrive into this hall O army of *suras*!

13. Together you Twelve Gods
Direct your divine eyes on this hall
Fanning twelve shawls
Arrive O Twelve Gods into this hall.

14. From the sun and moon gods
From my teacher and the nobles here
And everybody in this assembly
I crave permission from them all.

15. May you live long—may your work prosper
May illness be banished—May you have happiness by this ritual [*yāga*].

Several stanzas in the conclusion of text 17 cannot be translated because they are obscure or unclear or contain corrupt words.

16. Hold as a sky canopy thirty *riyan* of silk shawls
Open up the pearl umbrella and move under the canopy
Perform the fanning ritual with ornate yak-tail fans on both sides
Sound the five instruments and thus you'll enter the hall.

The canopy on one level of symbolism represents the clouds or sky above, whence the gods arrive. On another level the canopy above and the foot cloths below create a specially demarcated area for the gods, isolated from the mundane world.

17. When the procession arrives in the hall with appropriate music
Sing the songs and your mind will be soothed
God Devol is permitted second place in the thirty-*riyan* arch [*toraṇa*]
Worship him second; then worship the *bisō kapa* of Madura Mā.

Line 3: Devol also has a right to the *toraṇa* arch. The first place is given to Pattini, and third to Dēvatā Baṇḍāra. Together these three are known as the *tunbāge*, "the three divisions." This classification no longer obtains. Line 4: "the *bisō kapa* of Madura Mā" is puzzling. According to informants this is Sēraman's wife. Nevertheless, the *Cilappatikāram*, as well as some Sinhala texts, speaks of Madura Mādēvi as the tutelary goddess of Madurai who calmed Pattini's anger and liberated the city of Madurai from the fire (Dikshitar 1939, p. 269). It therefore makes sense to have a *kapa* for her in collective rituals of the Pattini cult. Since this deity has little significance for Sinhala people, she may have been converted into Sēraman's wife in the *gammaḍuva* traditions. In Ūrubokka traditions there is a separate altar for Madura Mādēvi, but no rituals are performed in her honor. She is viewed as a previous incarnation of Pattini.

18. Raise up the *bisō kapa*, plant it and enclose it
Assemble together singing-priests and *ātura*s
Expeditiously lay a large white cloth on the couch [*yahana*]
For the goddess Pattini, who brings prosperity, arrives in the hall.

19. The eminent priest must offer scents, camphor, musk, and *irivēriya*
And with great devotion offer flowers and lights
Free people of *dōsa* by the gold anklet in its lovely couch
Offer ornaments and thirty-two gold coins by everyone's hand.

Line 1: *irivēriya* is *Plectranthus zeylanicus*. Line 4: "everyone's hand"; the custom of holding an offering and thereby participating in the ritual act.

20. Lovely damsels beautiful of form line up the two sides—
Take the anklet in hand and spread its tinkling sounds
Wear the *osari* shawl on the shoulder and with it banish pestilence
By the power of the Seven Pattini banish all *dōsa*.

Note again the importance of the shoulder shawl in these rituals.

21. By her command I inform this audience
This anklet will be used for sounding today
Ailments and diseases shall be banished from this day on
The gem anklet has arrived in the dance arena.

Text 18 Offerings Made to the Divine Ornaments

1. When the golden anklet was brought into the hall
With joy; the mighty goddess Pattini
First was given coins [*pan̆ḍuru*] by the king
He offered three thousand gold pieces.

2. Then the royal queen took a golden measure [full of coins]
And offered it to the couch with full heart
And the good folk around who witnessed this
Offered coins with good intentions as an example to the world.

3. The good ministers brought handfuls of gold coins
With pleasant thoughts they placed them on the couch
Those assembled who witnessed these pleasant deeds
Poured various ornaments onto the couch.

4. Anklets, bracelets, chains, necklaces and so forth
   Pins, bangles, rings were all brought out
   Golden lime containers and areca-nut cutters
   And offered them with auspicious thoughts.

5. Many gods from above witnessed these happenings
   Dances and songs were uttered to please those present
   Humbly place the hands on the head; gracefully
   Wave the shawl and bring about prosperity and good luck.

6. From now while the sun and moon lasts
   The hundred pestilences won't strike you
   By the coins [*paňḍuru*] offered at the three watches
   Certainly your life is protected forever.

Change in singing style:

7. The Goddess Pattini's glorious anklet is now in the couch on the *toraṇa* arch
   We've offered it sandal, musk, camphor, and dewy water and five fruits,
   Lovely, young twelve-year-old maids line up to receive blessings
   Pattini has arrived, she blesses and banishes the *dōsa* of the congregation
   [*ātura*].

8. Born of the water, and of the blue lotus, *maṅgalam*!
   Then from the dewdrop, the fire and from the mango, *maṅgalam*!
   From the shining boat, the tear of the cobra, and as Pattini, *maṅgalam*!
   By the power of these Seven Pattini, *jayamaṅgalam* for these *ātura*s.

9. By the *jayamaṅgalam* of the offerings of a lamp on the banks of Nērañjanā
   By the *maṅgalam* of having offered jasmine flowers to Konāgama Buddha
   By the *maṅgalam* of a sweet mango given with love to Buddha Konāgama
   By these influences may there be *jayamaṅgalam* for these *ātura*s.

10. *Maṅgalam*, by the twenty-four Teacher Munis, *maṅgalam*
    Maṅgalam, by the blessings of our Muni, *maṅgalam*
    Maṅgalam, by the solace of the arhat monks, *maṅgalam*
    Maṅgalam, by the Three Refuges, may all beings be protected,
    jayamaṅgalam

Line 1: according to some classifications there were twenty-four previous Buddhas; according to others there were twenty-eight. *Maṅgalam* means "festival joy," "prosperity," "happiness," "auspiciousness." *Jaya* is "victory." *Jayamaṅgala* means (1) victorious festival joy and prosperity, or (2) a festival celebrating victory. The prototype victory is that of the Buddha over the forces of Māra. This is celebrated in *jayamaṅgala gāthā*, sung at auspicious occasions. At the conclusion of this recital the congregation offers dedicated coins (*paňḍuru*) to the divine ornaments in the altar.

The Drummers Perform in Honor of Pattini

At 1:20 A.M. the drummers assemble before the *toraṇa*. They utter a *stōtra* and drum the festival note (*magul bera*) and dance before the goddess. This is over at 1:40 A.M.

Telmē: The Dance of the Lights

The *telmē* is a dance in honor of the Doḷaha Deviyo, or Twelve Gods. The term is probably derived from the word *tel* meaning "oil": hence the ritual is an offering of lights to the Twelve Gods, the lights in this case being tapers or *vilakku*. There is not much ritual action here, but the dance is very elaborate and impressive and goes on for more than an hour. The chief *kapurāla* (here as well as in Heyiaṅtuḍuva) does not participate in the ritual, but a senior *kapurāla* dances with six or seven assistants.

The *telmē* tray, or *taṭṭu*, is placed on a decorated stand near the tree of the torch of time (1:40 A.M.). In it are twelve betel leaves, twelve unlit tapers (*vilakku*), and flowers. The dancers go round and round the stand *counterclockwise*, half marching, half dancing. Then a prominent person (*ātura*) lights the one taper and sticks it upright in the tray (*taṭṭu*). One assistant takes the *telmē* tray and carries it to the members of the audience, who touch it and thus vicariously participate in the dedication (*oppu*) of the offering. The others again dance in a circle, *counterclockwise*, while the second *kapurāla* sings text 19*a*, inviting the Twelve Gods to witness the *telmē* dance. The *telmē* tray is put back in its stand, and the assistant lights the other tapers. Now they continue the counterclockwise march-dance, but the tempo of the drums increases, and the dancers imitate a rider on a horse, again befiting the Twelve Gods, who are also kings. The *telmē* stand is brought near the *toraṇa*, and they dance in a circle before the Gods of the Four Warrants; then the *telmē* tray is placed near the altar for the Twelve Gods. At this point the senior *kapurāla* addresses the audience and tells them what the *telmē* is all about.

> Ladies and Gentlemen, at the time when the hall [*maḍuva*] was performed for King Sēraman, the Twelve Kings were not pleased. In order to please them the *telmē* was performed.

After this a smaller number of dancers (generally three), perform rather good dancing while others sing text 19*b* on the Twelve Gods.

Salaṁba Sāntiya or *Devinan Tēvaya Kirīma*: Blessings of the Anklet or Service of the Divine Ornaments

This is a crucial rite where the *kapurāla* blesses the audience by waving the anklets. A washerman lays a foot cloth from the *toraṇa* to the other end of the hall. The villagers line themselves up on both sides of the foot cloth awaiting the blessings of the anklets. The ritual consists of three rounds or *vaṭṭama*. Each round is complete when the *kapurāla* goes past the two lines of assembled people and circles back to the altar.

The ritual starts (3:15 A.M.) with the chief *kapurāla* in front of the altar of the *toraṇa*. He wears his full ritual regalia with robe, jacket, headdress (*moṭṭākkili*), and shawl (*osariya*). The anklets are in their casket covered by a red cloth and have not been yet exposed to public view. There are four torchbearers, one on each side of the *toraṇa* and two behind the *kapurāla*. The chief *kapurāla* puts his head into the altar covering the ornaments so as not to be seen by the public. He (presumably) holds several anklets against the red shawl, then emerges into full view with the anklets and shakes them while an attendant incenses the altar and an assistant blows a loud blast on the conch. He now goes past the audience clockwise waving the anklets and singing the songs of blessing (text 20 below), swinging the anklets forward and back in a semicircular arch. As he goes past the audience the chief *kapurāla* tramples the people's feet (imitating Pattini's trampling of the mud to produce rice in mythic times). He completes one round and comes back to the altar; he holds the altar with both hands, bends his face low, and continues to sing. He ties more anklets of various sizes to each end of the shoulder shawl, turns around and shakes these anklets, then places his elbows on the altar and sings the songs of the second round. Then the conch blows three times and he starts his second round in the identical manner. He then goes on his third round, comes back to the altar, and deposits the anklets back in their receptacle, along with the shoulder shawl.

Now starts another part of the ritual—the shawl fanning rite, or *salu sälma*. The *kapurāla* sings the first few songs of the *salu sälma*, assisted by a junior *kapurāla* (texts 21, 22 below). Then he removes his headdress (*moṭṭäkkili*) and blesses the two lines of assembled people with the shoulder shawl. He holds the red shawl in both hands with about ten inches hanging loose on each side and waves these folds gracefully before the audience. This is over at 3:45 A.M.

Text 20 *Salaṁba Sāntiya*: Blessings of the Anklet

First Round

1. Cut the brush, clear the ground, and sweep correctly
   Sprinkle white sand and smooth the floor
   For the festive arrival of Pattini, beauteous and kind
   Who comes into this city to banish *dōsa*.

Note again that the hall is equated with the city.

2. According to the good customs of old times
   Recite fully in the midst of this assembly
   Utter without error the words [of the text]
   Recite well the verses from "the story of the anklet."

3. Sing the songs of the mighty anklet
   The ancient story of the glorious ornament
   The ankle bracelet worn by the wife Pattini
   By its *gigiri* sound the world's dangers go away.

Gigiri is an onomatopoeic word like "tinkling."

4. There are three anklets in the world of the *nāga*s
   A golden one there is in this human world
   The power of the ankle bracelet shines everywhere
   By its influence disease and suffering have gone away.

5. After worshiping you O virtuous lady Pattini
Humans down here offer you merit
They obtain happiness from the anklet's *gigiri* sound
By this act disease and suffering have departed.

6. O virtuous goddess Pattini, lady and wife
Take the joy-creating anklet in your hand
Descend to earth and banish the woes of humans
Sound the anklet and bring blessings on our land.

7. Wearing her robes like a fluff of cloud
Her hair tied up like a flower
She stands among the audience like a gem in a pinnacle
See how gracefully Pattini has decked herself.

8. By her past merit she will be a future Buddha
By her morality she was born in the golden mango
If wicked people see her they cannot come back
A red and blue gem lies inside the anklet.

I am not sure of the accuracy of lines 2 and 3 in stanza 8 of my translation or of line 1 in stanza 9.

9. Don't hide the anklet, give it to me O goddess
Only the goddess of the earth knows where it is
If you happen to offend the lovely anklet
You'll for certain know the might of the goddess Pattini.

10. Bathe my body with sweet-smelling water
And hold my hands in the smoke of sweet incense
I rub my body with sweet-scented sandal paste
And take the exalted divine ornaments [*devinan*] in my hand.

The person reference in this stanza, as in many other places, is ambiguous. "I" could be "you," but in either case it refers to the priest.

11. The rays of her renown increase
The cruel demons are being sent away
Unfailingly she banishes disease and suffering
The *irdhi* anklet now arrives here.

Irdhi (Sanskrit *ṛddhi*) is the capacity to "levitate"; it is a power generally associated with Buddhist *arhat*s.

12. Holding an anklet in each hand
Under the cover of the *osariya* fold
O Mānāyuru who is good
O King Yā sound the anklet.

Lines 3 and 4 make little sense because the mythological references have no relevance nowadays. Mānāyuru is the "father of Pattini," and King Yā is one of the Twelve Gods and a kinsman of Kōvalaṉ.

13. Alert, behold these happenings
    That fill the world with joy
    Listen all you gentle folk assembled here
    To the sounding of Pattini's anklet.

14. We hold the two hands aloft
    And worship, our hands on our heads
    Today we banish the *dōsa* of the past
    King Yā, sound the anklet.

15. The minds of all beings are full of joy
    She protects the beings of the air
    All the *dōsa* of friendly beings is banished
    O Pattini sound the anklet.

I have translated lines 1–3 of stanza 15 as best as I could. Several unintelligible words were used here for rhyme effect—for example, *dulam̆ba satun*, *salam̆ba satun*, *nilam̆ba satun*.

Second Round

16. Cover the head with the veil [*moṭṭäkkili*] and wear the pure *osari* shawl over the shoulder
    Advance along the assembled line singing songs in their midst
    Banish the disaster [*piripata*] that has befallen them and blow with pure heart the victorious conch
    To banish skin eruptions shake the anklet before the assembled people.

Skin eruption is *kuṣṭha rōga*, which also means eczema.

17. Like the full moon her courage [*vīriya*] shone over the three worlds
    Among the dynasty of heavenly ladies the eminent Pattini appears most beautiful
    Beautiful glorious Pattini, O goddess, foremost among heavenly ladies
    O Pattini of the solar dynasty shake the anklet and bring us happiness.

18. Sprinkle the body with sandal, scents of flowers and dewy water
    For the folk assembled here, with bowed heads, are worshiping the wife Pattini
    Step forward with pomp, trailing the spreading scents of flowers
    And like the beauteous full moon appear before the audience shaking the anklet.

Lines 1, 3 and 4 refer to the *kapurāla* in his role as Pattini.

Third Round

19. With the red silk shawl cover the head and anklets in each hand
    Decked with the sixty-four pleasing ornaments and wearing collyrium [*am̆dun*]
    She muddied the rock by the power of her devotion to the Dhamma
    By the sound of the pearl anklet all diseases are gone.

20. She gave away alms as if dispensing gems and gold
She went up to Sakra, the chief god, and had his permission [*vivaraṇa*]
Is there anyone else in the world who displayed such prowess?
By the sound of the gem anklet all diseases are gone.

21. She quelled the mountains of fire that ravaged Madurā and thus showed her might [*teda bala*]
She destroyed the eye of the great Pāṇḍi king
And showed her prowess by awakening the dead body
By the sound of that mighty anklet all diseases are gone.

22. The golden boat stopped off at the port of Mantonḍun
She was raised by Mānāyuru of the solar dynasty
The goddess Pattini, full of merit, was named after the boat
By the sound of her golden anklet all diseases are gone.

Text 21 *Salu sälma*: Shawl Fanning

Technique: the chief *kapurāla* signs the first part of each line and the second *kapurāla* the next half.

1. Like the *sēsat*'s shade—she sends away the sufferings of all beings
Narrate the events in the pleasant story—and sing everywhere in verse form
Honored [*pūjita*], pure and blessed one—O Pattini lady and *muni*
Any deadly infectious disease here—banish them by your powers.

Sēsat: the sun and moon emblems carried in procession.

2. I bow low before your sacred feet—and place my humble head in worship
Forgive me for any wrongs I've done—O Pattini goddess, may you acquire merit
Wetting the shawl with water transformed into ambrosia—O sovereign who quenched the fires thus
The company of the Twelve Gods have arrived—they'll banish all the *dōsa* of these *āturas*.

3. O you devotees in this assembly—why have you come here patiently wishing?
Because of the power of having sown and offered alms—a fistful of pure *älvī* rice
Come, citizens of the country from the eight directions—to give merit to her who eases your suffering
What a powerful victorious being is this?—O glorious Pattini with the power of airy flight [*irdhi*].

4. She who muddied the rock of Aňdungiri with her feet—and sowed the seed and offered alms
To King Sakra who refused to accept her alms—but swiftly ascended the sky and looked down;

She who was born of the mango in the orchard—in order to wipe out the forehead eye of the king
O goddess Pattini who has reached the peak of attainment—banish the pain caused by illnesses.

5. She went to Aňdungiri Peak to observe the precepts—and god Sakra in the guise of an old Brahman
Said, sister my belly aches with great hunger—and begged her for alms
By the power of having readily offered alms—to King Sakra [in disguise]
All diseases from the head downward—I shall banish by the goddess Pattini's power.

From now onward there is a change in singing style, with the chief *kapurāla* singing the first two lines and his senior *kapurāla* the last two lines of each stanza.

6. If fevers, headaches, pains in the joints, and an excess of phlegm arise
And wounds, cancers, indigestion, madness, and babbling
If excess phlegm in the body causes coughs, colds; also diseases of the three humors
All these disasters [*piripata*] are brushed away by Pattini's shawl.

7. Plague, infectious diseases, chicken pox, smallpox, dysentery, and yaws
Swollen cheeks [mumps?], throat constrictions, goiter, and measles
If all sorts of fears arise from poisonous reptiles and fierce animals [in dreams]
Wipe these disasters away with Pattini's shawl and they will leave you.

8. Wasps and tiny bees [*kana mī*] build their nests and mushrooms appear in the middle of the house
Monitor lizards, miserable rat snakes creep into the house and attack you and wrap themselves around
Hornets and bees build their nests, the sides of the well collapse
These dangerous *dōsa* arising from *vas* are brushed away by Pattini's shawl.

In this stanza only symptoms of *vas* are given, not the underlying cause. However, we know from Sinhala folklore that lizards and snakes copulating ("wrap themselves around") indicate *vas* from thoughts of sibling incest (see my discussion of the Garā ritual, p. 184).

9. Your wife and children, siblings, grandchildren, and younger brothers
If these people were born at a bad time; or if there were menstrual impurities
And troubles from false oaths [*divi dōsa*] coming to you from your parents and ancestors
We eliminate them by waving the Pattini shawl and we bring you blessings.

10. Wood from *kos*, *milla*, *kalumädiriya*, *kaluvara*, *nädun*, *pubbēriya*
And *gasnada* and *sūriya* wood; with these you make windows and doorways
When you make tables, wardrobes, chairs and people talk
The *vas* that comes from these are wiped clean with the shawl.

Somewhat obscure verse. Probably refers to the *vas* that strikes a person who works on wood. Also refers to the evil mouths of people who envy one's good furniture.

11. If ninety-eight *rōga* and ninety-nine *vyādhi* diseases occur
    Whether externally or from within, from phlegm and bile and the three humors
    The thirty-two external dangers that affect the body
    These diseases we banish quite by fanning with Pattini's shawl.

Text 22 *Sirasapāda*: Head-to-Foot Verses

Sometimes a *sirasapāda*, or head-to-foot verse, is sung as part of the *salu sälma*. This text may be omitted or sung elsewhere in the ritual.

1. The renown of the Seven Pattini goddess is known throughout the whole country
   Today also her glorious power shines resplendent over the world and destroys suffering
   If there be *dōsa* from evil magic it is gone and Pattini's blessings realized
   The *dōsa* has descended from the head, forehead, eyes, nose, and mouth.

2. All sorts of sorcery, illusions, magic-dangers that could destroy humans have struck you
   Then curses at Devol shrines, magic signs may have hit you, and demons made to stare at you
   You are free from this *dōsa* when you bear the command of the noble goddess Pattini
   The *dōsa* descends from the ears, neck, shoulders, hands, and out of the fingers.

3. Babbling ceaselessly in a demented state, talking in a crazy manner
   Jabbering meaninglessly and acting as if deaf
   By wearing her merit you are freed from this *dōsa*
   The *dōsa* has descended from the chest, belly, and navel.

4. The body weakens, it is lifeless and heavy and subject to spasms
   Fatigue and breathlessness, nausea, and revulsion for food
   With care wear the merit of the noble Pattini
   The *dōsa* descends from the thighs, knees, shanks, and ankles.

5. If *dōsa* has visited this body it is gone by Pattini's command
   Which dispels sufferings, brings blessings and life to this congregation [*ātura*]
   If there be sorcery and magic they are gone, banished by Pattini's command
   Any remaining *dōsa* departs from the soles of the feet and toenails.

6. In the mango branch of the three-eyed Pāṇḍi king's orchard
   An unseasonal mango grew like a golden water pot
   Some juice from it fell and the king's eye was no more
   By the might of the meritorious Pattini all *dōsa* is gone.

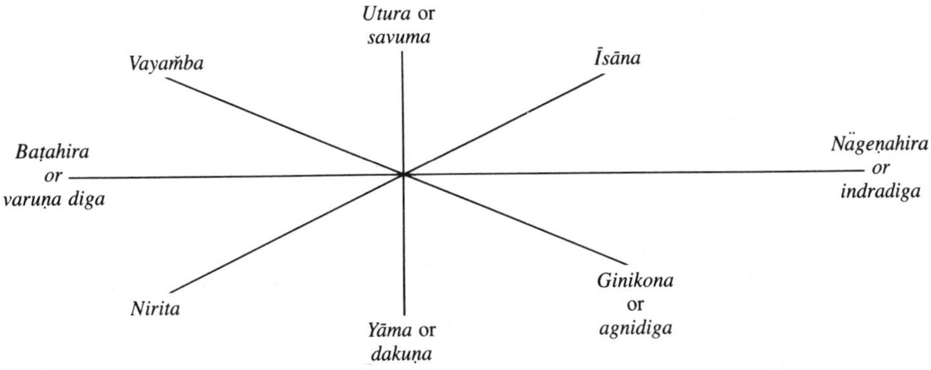

Fig. 6. The eight points of the Sinhala compass, from which the demons approach.

Sanniyakunṭa Mahajāme Pidavilla: Oblation to the Sanni Demons at the Main Watch

The middle watch (*mäda yāma*) is also known as the "main watch" (*mahā yāma*). Technically the offerings to the Sanni demons known as *pidavilla* or *pidēni* must be made between 10:00 P.M. and 2:00 A.M., preferably near midnight, when demons are most active. This rarely can be put into practice, hence the rule is generally violated. This simple ritual starts at 4:00 A.M. when a village leader (*ātura*), on behalf of the community, holds a pot with a lighted taper stuck in it. The pot contains the same offering as in the previous ritual at the evening watch. An assistant dances with torch in hand, going round and round the arena, while the chief *kapurāla* and his second sing songs asking the Sanni demons to arrive. The idea is to dedicate, or *käpa*, the offering—*pidēni*—to the eighteen Sanni demons, so that any dangers from demons will be prevented.

The demons come in from the eight points of the Sinhala compass, as illustrated in figure 6. They are then asked to consume the offerings and depart.

Thereafter the assistant places the pot and the torch in the stand for demons outside the hall limits. On some occasions, if time permits, the *kapurāla* may conclude the proceedings with a standard *kannalavva*, or plaint. He asks the demons to listen to the command of the Gods of the Four Warrants, the Gods of the Three Divisions (Pattini, Devol, Vāhala), and the Twelve Gods and then leave the five *skandhas* (bodily aggregates) of people assembled here. He also asks the demons to remove their *diṣṭi* ("look," "essence") from any afflicted person by the *varan* (warrant) given them by Vaiṣravaṇa-Vessamuni (both names being used hyphenated). In this plaint Sanni is referred to as *dēvatā*.

Text 23 Invitation to the Sanni Demons

1. They reside in the beautiful places of the sky
Their tusks shine like thunderbolts
Cast your eyes on this offering with the speed of titans [*asura*]
From the eastern direction enter here O Sanni.

2. Heed the compassionate, beautiful Muni, Teacher of the Three Worlds
Heed his command that appears on Samanaḷa Peak and Mecca

By the might of Gautama who quelled the demons
From the southeast enter here O Sanni.

Reference in line 2 is to the footprints of the Buddha, which, according to Buddhists, are seen both on Adam's Peak (Samanaḷa) and in the sands of Mecca! Hence Buddha is sometimes referred to as Makkama Muni, Lord of Mecca. See chapter 6 (p. 307) for a discussion of this problem.

3. They have come into this country and exhibited their pride
   And they cause illness without restraint
   By the might of the Buddha's rays and the power of his command
   Enter from the southern direction O powerful Sanni.

4. O demons who cause dreadful apparitions
   You cannot remain here by the power of *pirit*
   But the influence of the power of *pirit*
   Enter from the southwest O Sanni.

"Power of *pirit*" is the power of the word; *pirit* or *pāritta* are Buddhist texts uttered by monks to bring blessings.

5. By the [power of the] refuge of Dīpaṅkara Muni
   By the [power of the] refuge of Kondañña Muni
   Accept these offerings without rage
   Descend from the west to this place O Sanni.

6. The demoness watches the sun and goes into the shade
   She casts her shadow and causes illness
   By the power of Gautama Muni's influence
   From the north enter O Sanni for this offering.

Line 1 is not clear to me. Perhaps it refers to evil female demonesses associated with Sanni.

7. Roaming the countryside with greed
   In the dark they demand oblations
   Heed the power of the Buddha's rays and his mighty influence
   From the northeast enter O powerful Sanni.

8. From the east, southeast, south, and southwest
   From the west, northwest, north
   From the northeastern skies and from the depths below
   Descend briskly O Sanni from the eight directions.

9. He comes from the city of Avaṅka
   He was born from the corpse of his mother
   After ten months elapsed on a Tuesday
   Under the hour of the *rākṣa* [*demon*].

Avaṅka means "uncorrupted" and makes no sense to me; perhaps a mistake for "Avanti," a city mentioned in Buddhist texts.

10. His mother was destroyed the day he was born
    That day he took on the guise of the demon
    With corpses on his hand and in his mouth
    He goes to the city of Viśālā, shrieking.

11. To whatever city he goes he causes diseases
    He eats the corpse he holds in his hand
    Since that day offerings were given to him
    To leave and cause no more suffering and disease.

12. In the time of old sages, a company in a ship
    Listened to our Muni preach the Dhamma
    Our Muni, possessed of twenty-eight virtues, saw this
    And sent Goḷu Sanni, full of bile, away.

I am at a loss to interpret this stanza. Goḷu Sanni (Dumb Sanni) is one of the eighteen Sanni demons.

13. The Ānanda Thero who banishes demons
    Our Muni did not come close to them
    Our Muni arrived at Jetavanārāma
    Vāta Sanni was sent away by Devadatta Thero.

Sinhala myth states that the Buddha arrived with Ānanda, his favorite disciple, to Viśālā to quell the Sanni demons. However, the last line does not make sense unless it refers to some myth where Devadatta, Buddha's archenemy, sent Vāta Sanni to assail the Buddha. *Vāta* diseases are those caused by excess "air."

14. By his looks villages are devastated
    Wherever he goes he kills humans
    Only he who leaves the village can escape
    Dēva Sanni leave the diseases you have caused.

Dēva Sanni: one form of Sanni in the guise of a *dēva*. He generally appears to people in dreams.

15. Accept the food that has been consecrated [*käpa*] to you
    Know the command of the gods in heaven
    Take the *puda* offered here in this divine assembly
    Dēva Sanni leave the disease you have caused.

16. For the eighteen Sanni demons and demonesses
    We have dedicated [*käpa*] eighteen offerings for them
    Also we have offered eighteen *pańḍuru* [coins]
    Leave the diseases you've caused O Eighteen Sanni.

I have written at length elsewhere on the Sanni demons and their incorporation into the Buddhist pantheon (Obeyesekere 1969b). In brief, the mother of Sanni was a queen of the Liccāvis who was accused by the king of infidelity. She was taken to a cemetery and executed, and out of her dead body arose Sanni. He collected eighteen companions, and with them came to Viśālā city, killed his father, and ravaged the country. Sanni was quelled by the Buddha and his disciple Ānanda. The Buddha recited the *Ratana Sutta* on this occasion. Here is a clear case where a later folk belief has been incorporated into the great tradition of Buddhism.

The *Kurāla* for the Sanni Demons: The Heyiaṅtuḍuva Tradition

In the Heyiaṅtuḍuva tradition there is a highly elaborate ritual for the Sanni demons at the main (middle) watch. This is known as the *kurāla* from the structure (altar) thus named. It is performed in most parts of the Sabaragamuva tradition, and the northern parts of the Western Province to the east of Colombo. It is absent in the Southern Province and most parts of the Western Province.

The *kurāla* is a tall areca pole surmounted by a stand (*mässa*) for the *kapurāla* to lie upon (*däpanava*) in a trance. It is planted outside the sacred area. The distance from the ground to the base of the *kurāla* stand is eighteen *riyan* (twenty-six feet). The length from the base of the stand to the top is a further five *riyan*, to make an impressive structure twenty-three *riyan* high. Eighteen rungs (representing the eighteen Sanni demons) are added one *riyan* apart so the *kapurāla* can climb up to the stand. Before the performance an assistant must climb the *kurāla*, incense and consecrate (*käpa*) it, and hang a tray (*taṭṭu*) of offerings from the side of the stand. The offerings consist of the following in portions of eighteen placed in the eighteen *alli*, or *koṭu* (sections), of the tray: cupped leaves (*goṭu*) combining goat (or chicken) blood; rice and seven curries (*hat mālu*); meat and fish (*goḍadiya mas*).

The ritual itself is impressive but brief, lasting about fifteen minutes. The *kapurāla* inhales the smoke of resin and goes into a trance. In this state he climbs the *kurāla* and sways perilously on the top. After that he lies flat on the stand. This is *däpanava*, or *däpavilla*: offering *himself* to the demons. The *däpavilla* comes from exorcistic ritual where the priest offers (*käpa*, i.e., "consecrates and offers") his body to the demons. The idea is to make the demon take the body of the priest instead of the patient (*ātura*); but the priest in fact cannot be taken by the demon, since he is protected by powerful charms (mantras). In the *kurāla* ritual the *kapurāla* sways precariously in trance in the stand, then collapses—that is, he "dies" and offers himself to the demons. Subsequently assistants spray charmed water, and he gets up and climbs down the *kurāla*.

The Sanni demons placated in the *kurāla* are some of the most feared in Sinhala society. They cause serious physical illnesses and psychotic states. Thus they are given special prominence by some *gammaḍuva* traditions. The high *kurāla* tower is a way to approach them as they come down from the eight directions; unimpeded in space, there is a direct confrontation between the demons and the priest as controller of demons. Furthermore, these beings could be offered their favorite foods—blood and meat—in the high stand, away from the pure gods resident in their couches and thrones.

Planting the Torch of Time in Honor of Dēvatā Baṇḍāra and Dressing up as Vāhala (*Vāhala Äňdīma*)

The dressing up as Vāhala commences about 4:10 A.M. Vāhala, as I noted before, is also known as Dēvatā Baṇḍāra or Däḍimuṇḍa in the Rabalīya tradition and most parts of the Western Province. This "dance" is not performed in the Mātara tradition. In Sabaragamuva (and in Sīnigama) Vāhala is viewed as part of the Devol Deviyo troupe and distinct from Dēvatā Baṇḍāra. The chief *kapurāla* does not perform the Vāhala dance but assigns it to the senior *kapurāla* or to one of the assistants.

An assistant is dressed as Vāhala in a red cone-shaped hat (*vāhala toppi*), tight trousers, and a long sleeved jersey. He carries a torch, which he incenses by throwing resin at it. He now recites the invocation (*yādinna*) on the "birth" of Däḍimuṇḍa (text 24). Another assistant takes the torch in Vāhala's hand and plants it on the *kāla pandama* tree—not on top of it, but about six feet from the bottom—then lays *pähiňdun* (rice, banana, and coconut) at the foot of the tree. Then the *kapurāla* pours water on the feet of Vāhala, while another assistant brings a brazier and incenses Vāhala's feet. Meanwhile the *kapurāla* and a few assistants sing the songs of Vāhala (text 25), while Vāhala holds his face close to the brazier, puts resin into it, and deeply and continuously inhales the resinous fumes. He is then blindfolded. Drums beat faster, and he jumps up briskly from his seat and begins the Vāhala dance (4:25 A.M.).

The Vāhala dance is one of the highlights of the *gammaḍuva* and holds great interest for the audience. The dance enacts the "strength" (*vīriya*) or courage of Vāhala, and the dancer demonstrates this by his own capacity for endurance, since it goes on for about an hour and twenty minutes. At the start the blindfolded Vāhala has two areca sprigs in his hands, and he goes round and round the arena in a slow mechanical dance to the monotonously regular beat of the drums. He raises the areca sprigs to his head in a gesture indicating obeisance (to the Four Gods), then brings them as far down as possible. The movement is relaxed to start with, but after some time it becomes limp, as if his hands were acting independently of the rest of his body. The pace of the dance and the movement gradually increase with the increasingly rapid beat of the drums. This goes on for about fifty minutes. The dancer is next given two torches, which he raises in a similar gesture of obeisance so that the two lighted ends meet. He then draws them downward. He constantly incenses the altars with huge amounts of resin that burst into flames in the night air and come perilously close to the awed audience. However, soon he is so exhausted that he just waves the torches limply. His mouth is open, and in some cases his tongue lolls out. The drums beat faster, and Vāhala accelerates his dancing and suddenly collapses (5:45 A.M.). Assistants spray charmed water on him, and he gets up after a few minutes. After some time the *kapurāla* sings more songs on Vāhala, while Vāhala, apparently refreshed, minus his cone-shaped hat, vest, and blindfold, dances round and round in a circle. This dance is known as the *däḍimuṇḍa savudama* (dance of Däḍimuṇḍa).

After the dance an offering of seven vegetables cooked together (*hat mālu*), rice, *kävun* (oil cakes), and bananas is placed in the Vāhala altar for the deity. Then a curtain is drawn across the altar.

There is a short break after the Vāhala dance. At about 6:00 A.M. the *aṁba vidamana* ("shooting of the mango") is performed. This is described in detail elsewhere (see text 36, pp. 227–38, and pp. 490–95).

Fire Trampling Rituals

The actual ritual of fire trampling starts about 8:35 A.M. in the Rabalīya tradition. However, the preparation begins much earlier when people go in procession to cut the *milla* wood for the fire. Let me therefore describe this ritual first.

Milla Käpilla: Cutting the *Milla* Tree (*Vitex attissima*)

The cutting of the *milla* tree occurs about 4:00 P.M. on the afternoon of the main ceremony, but it is not viewed as heralding the commencement of the *gammaḍuva*. It is an independent rite performed for the purpose of collecting wood for the fire walking ritual to be held next morning. Since *milla* trees are not readily available, a group of villagers who have purified themselves go out earlier into the forest, or anyplace where a tree is available, cut a large branch about ten feet long, and plant it within an accessible distance of the hall. The distance varies with the scale of the ceremony, so that if the organizers want a grand procession the *milla* tree can be about half a mile away.

The *kapurāla* is dressed in white: white cloth, short-sleeved white jersey, a white "turban," and a shoulder shawl (*uramāla*)—a large white cloth (*piruvaṭa*)—over his shoulders so the ends fall over the chest on both sides. He dances a few steps (*pada*) in the compound outside the hall, in honor of the assembled gods, then dances with the vessel of turmeric water (*kahadiyara kotale*) and the incense holder (*aňguru kabala*). These preliminaries are sometimes dispensed with in Rabalīya, but are strictly followed in the Heyiaṅtuḍuva tradition.

Then the procession departs to cut the *milla* tree. At the head of the procession is a canopy under which walk two attendants (*koṭṭōruva*). They take with them an ax and a long knife, the censer and the water pot, and *pähiňdun*—that is, a bunch of bananas, a measure of rice, and a coconut. The *kapurāla* walks behind them with a torch in hand followed by two or more drummers and other villagers. In Heyiaṅtuḍuva the *kapurāla* takes with him the *mugura*, or rod, of Devol Deviyo. In Rabalīya betel leaves are placed on a special stand and a torch is lit for Devol Deviyo. The offering of *pähiňdun* is placed at the foot of the tree for the tree deities and for Devol (and later taken back). The *kapurāla*, torch in hand, incenses the stand and the tree and utters an invocation (*yādinna*) while an attendant cuts the "tree" at its base and covers it with a white cloth (*piruvaṭa*) (text 26 below). Then they come back in procession, the *kapurāla* singing songs on the prowess of Devol Deviyo (text 27). The wood is carried on the shoulders of an attendant under the canopy. It is incensed all the way. Back in the arena the *kapurāla* takes the *milla* tree from the attendants and dances with it before the *toraṇa* arch. After this attendants cut the "tree" into smaller pieces and stack them, covered with a white cloth, in a bundle at the back of the altar of the *toraṇa*.

In the Heyiaṅtuḍuva tradition a somewhat different procedure is followed. No *pähiňdun* is taken. Instead seven betel leaves, seven *paňḍurus* (coins), and seven *goṭus* (cupped leaves) of puffed rice are taken in the procession. The attendant places the betel leaves around the tree and the seven coins on top of the leaves and lights seven wicks on the betel leaves. The number seven represents the seven Devol gods. Then the invocation (text 26) is recited. Halfway through the recital the *kapurāla* cuts a piece of the bark of the tree and gives it to the attendant, who keeps it in his white cloth (*piruvaṭa*). This indicates that the tree has been symbolically cut by the *kapurāla*. The others then actually cut it, the length of three measures of the rod or cane stick (*sōlu*) or *mugura* ("rod") of Devol. In this tradition the wood is placed on two sticks projecting out from the back of the special altar for Devol.

Text 26 The Birth of Devol Deviyo

Let us go find a tree
Give an ax to an attendant [*vaṭṭānḍi*]
Hold incense and light lamps
We have measured and cut the tree.

In this prosperous Sri Lanka
Full of greatness and plenty
Listen to the dramatic birth
Of god Devol in ancient times.

The mighty titan Basma
When meditating before Īśvara
Obtained a boon [*varan*] from Īśvara
That when he charmed his hand
Fires should emerge from whatever he touched
He then pursued Īśvara [to kill him].

Then the god [Viṣṇu], lord of the three worlds
That powerful god then
Flew through the air, and
In the guise of a female
Awaited his arrival
He created a swing
And was swinging in it.

The titan [*asura*] seeing her thought
"Such a beautiful divine maiden
I shall not leave her."
He was greedy with lust
Forgetting the power of the charm [*dähäna*]
Impatiently he talked to her
In order to marry her.

Then she said joyfully
Keep your hand on your head
And swear steadfastly
That you will marry me and forsake me never.

"Sister I swear to you
That I will obey your wishes"
He thus made his pledge
And placed his hand on his head.
Instantly fires sprang forth
A huge mountain of fire!
Tearing from that mountain of fire
Prince Devol was born

Bursting forth from the surrounding heat
Was born Mal [flower] Kurumbara.

Bursting forth from the coals
Was born Kalu [black] Kurumbara
From that graveyard also
Emerged the demon Mahasōna
From the cascade of flames
Was born Gini [fire] Kurumbara.

These people talked together
Let us go to the Sinhala country
It's a good country for trading
Thought they and boarded the ships.
Into seven ships they boarded.
They stacked the ships with goods
Gold shawls and silk shawls
Reams of blue cloth
Blue cloths and shoulder shawls
And handkerchiefs they loaded with
And spices of various sorts—
Beaten rice [*habala peti*] and round halvah [*aggalā*]
With all these things
They loaded the seven ships
[And with Mukkarus
And tough rowdy Tamils
And official singers].

On a Friday evening
When the stars were seen
At the right time
Their retinue boarded ships
That swept through the ocean.

Heavy winds swept the seas
Whirlwinds and hurricanes
And thunder and lightning
And the winds increased
Creating mountains of waves.
Then in the middle of the ocean
Were destroyed the seven ships.
Crying aloud in their hard plight
They swam the waves
For seven days they swam
Full of sorrow they complained.

Then Maṇimekhalā, goddess of the sea
Created a stone raft

And floated it [toward them] like a wad of cotton
With delight they climbed aboard this
And came toward the shore.

The goddess Pattini then thought
"These demons coming on a ship
I'll not allow them to land"
She created seven mountains of fire
And sent it across their path.

Then the Devol prince
Extinguished it and destroyed the fire
And got warrant for the *devol bāge* ritual
And obtained dance offerings during it.

From that time at Gintota
Unavaṭuna, Vēragoḍa, Pälǟviya,
Sīnigama, Uḍugampiṭiya
Then also at Lunumōdera village
And at Pānadura temple
The seven villages
Were made into offerings
And given to them
Permanently as theirs.

Now having constructed a hall of lights [*pahan maḍu*]
Decorated it with yellow streamers
And offered songs and poems
And having done no wrong
O mighty god Devol
Listen to my songs in your goodness
Listen with your divine ears
See with your divine eyes
And descend into this dance arena.

Banish away from these *ātura*s
Ninety-eight types of diseases [*rōga*]
Ninety-nine types of *vyādhi* [pains]
And two hundred and three dangers
Send these far far away
Āvaḍā, balavaḍā, yasavaḍā,
Siri säpata väḍiväḍī
Dahas kal rakitvā
Dinēmatudinēvā
Dinē set kerēvā. . . .

Commentary on Text 26: The Birth of Devol Deviyo

The birth of Devol Deviyo is based on an episode from the Skanda Purāna where Basma the *asura* was reluctantly given a boon by Śiva on the pleas of Pārvatī. The birth of Devol from Basma's ashes is, however, a folk invention. Note again that the term used for boon is *varan*. *Varan* in the Hindu context is best translated "boon," since it is given on impulse—it is irrational, going counter to Śiva's own rational judgment. The boon can also lead to disastrous consequences, unlike a warrant or *varan* from the Buddha, which has a rational purpose and leads to socially productive ends. The Buddhist *varan* is the opposite of the Hindu. In the case of the myth of the birth of Devol the Buddhists have retained the Hindu concept of *varan*, but the Devol deities remain alien till they have been given a further *varan* in the Buddhist sense. This is ultimately given by Pattini, an exemplar of Buddhist values.

Skanda's own birth is also related to this myth, though the Sinhala version is different from that in the Skanda Purāna and other Indian versions (see pp. 113–14). The Devol story is an attempt to give legitimacy to Devol Deviyo by linking him to an event in Skanda mythology. Furthermore, as I noted in chapter 2, various demons like Gini Kurumbara and Mal Kurumbara and Mahasōna are also incorporated into a single mythological charter. In the present text Devol Deviyo is seen as a single deity, not a cluster of seven as he is depicted elsewhere. Gini and Mal Kurumbara and Mahasōna are seen as the companions who sailed with him to Sri Lanka.

The Sīnigama text has minor differences. Mahasōna is not mentioned there as arising from the flames; this means that Sīnigama has retained the popular view expressed in the exorcistic cults and in general among Sinhala peasants, that Mahasōna is an older indigenous deity (see Wirz 1954, pp. 28–30, for different myths of Mahasōna). Sīnigama also ignores Mal Kurumbara. The three lines included in brackets are found only in the Sīnigama tradition.

Gini Pāgīma: Trampling the Fire

The fire trampling commences about 8:35 A.M. A small fire, built with the *milla* wood brought in earlier, is lit in the middle of the arena. Two attendants hold a rope made from a white sheet (*piruvaṭa*) in front of the fire. This rope represents the barrier or city gates (*kaḍavata*), and the two attendants are the guards, or *murakārayo*. The *kapurāla*, wearing white with a red shawl in his hand, stands in front of the rope with another assistant. Both the assistant and the *kapurāla*, representing the Devol gods, pull at the rope, but they are not allowed to cross the fire.

Then ensues the conventional dialogue between Devol Deviyo and the guards (the drummer speaks on behalf of the guards). Devol Deviyo speaks in a ridiculous Tamil accent and makes all sorts of verbal errors. For example, the guards say they are acting as guards for Pattini—*Pattini deviyaṇta muraṭa innava*. This is converted into an outrageous verbal error by Devol: *Pattini deviyanṭa hora minihaṭa innava* ("You are the adulterous partner of goddess Pattini").

After much dialogue of this sort the guards tell Devol that he must state his birth and pedigree and obtain *varan* from the gods. Devol now refers to an event in the past births of both Devol and Pattini.

1. At this aeon's beginning when the sage Kakusañda proclaimed the transmundane Dhamma
   Seven princes were born in the womb of a woman of the merchant caste
   Together they decided to offer alms of robes to the Muni
   They prayed [instead] to be born as gods and offered the *kaṭina* [robes] alms.

2. Also in Maṇimekhalā city into the Brahman caste
   Was born a young, lovely, and goodly lass
   She took a honey mango and offered it to the sage with a wish:
   "Let me become a Pattini"; thus she obtained *vivaraṇa* [permission].

"Maṇimekhalā city": in other places Pattini is said to have been once born in Maṇimegha city.

3. The seven princes who heard her wish came up to her
   "At the time you become Pattini may we be born as Devol
   We will come in search of you, wherever you are, sister."
   There they made a pact to jointly obtain offerings from the same hall [*maḍuva*].

The Devol gods now address Pattini (invisibly present behind the barrier) for permission to cross it. Now they sing the songs that recount their attempts to land in various parts of Lanka. They were forbidden to enter by Viṣṇu, Saman, and Kataragama. Ultimately they try to land at Sīnigama, and the goddess Pattini creates seven mountains of fire. These songs (quoted on pp. 152–53) indicate that the barrier also represents the isle of Sri Lanka, and the two guards act on behalf of the gods who refuse them permission to land.

Ultimately Devol asks *varan* from Viṣṇu and Saman to trample the fire.

4. Having worshiped god Viṣṇu with special fervor
   [They] obtained his auspicious *varan* to trample the fire
   They also worshiped god Saman, the giver of blessings
   Whose command radiates throughout the three worlds.

The Devol gods then go to Kataragama and obtain Skanda's warrant. Then they ask Pattini to cool the fire.

5. "I give you unlimited merit to achieve Nirvāṇa
   I worship you, give you merit; hear my plea, you
   Who resides in Tusita listening to sermons and aspiring to Buddhahood
   O mother Pattini cool this fire for us."

6. Pattini with her anklet came to Pāṇḍi city
   By the glory of having cooled the fire that day
   There is no succor for us except your help
   O Pattini goddess cool this fire for us.

After a few more verses of "permission," the barrier is opened and the Devol gods (impersonated by the *kapurāla*) get ready to trample the fire.

Before the actual fire trampling a village leader (*ātura*) takes the red shawl, ties a coin (*paṅḍuru*) in it, and places the shawl on the *kapurāla*'s head. The *kapurāla* then faces the fire. Then with a water pot (*kalaya*) in his hand he circumambulates the fire, sprinkling a line of water around it. Then he puts some water on his toes, and an attendant incenses his feet. The fire is practically dead by now. The *kapurāla* tramples it, turning round and round in it till it is fully extinguished. He then sits on the upturned water pot and worships the goddess Pattini before the *toraṇa* arch at the far end. Then he sings songs on Devol and lustrates the audience with water, singing the well-known stanza from the text *marā ipäddīma* ("killing and resurrection"), which describes the quenching of the flames of Madurai.

The gods assembled high above
And from the sky sent flowers of rain
Like the gushing waters of a maddened river
That's how the fire in Madurā was cooled.

The ritual is over at 9:40 A.M.

Fire Trampling in the Ratnapura Tradition

I shall describe in detail the fire trampling tradition of Sabaragamuva (as practiced in Ratnapura), since it brings out clearly the essentially symbolic nature of walking over coals.

On one level the fire walking ritual is an enactment of the landing of Devol Deviyo on Sri Lanka. The ritual starts with the blowing of the conch, followed by several minutes of preliminary drumming. Then the chief *kapurāla* and three other dancers, dressed in the dancing kit characteristic of Sabaragamuva, worship the goddess's anklets in the *toraṇa* and perform several dances in her honor. Then the ritual proper starts, and now they represent the seven Devol gods. One dancer acts the role of Devol Deviyo (the seven viewed collectively as one). He stands behind the *toraṇa* arch, partially covered by it. The *toraṇa* acts as the barrier in the other traditions. The drummer and the other dancers now accost him. One of the dancers takes the role of the audience-commentator, conventionally taken by the drummer in the ritual traditions of the low country.

Devol: Ah *gala gala gale* . . . [unintelligible gibberish] I have looked toward Mecca, toward Kälaṇiya, toward the Peak of the Sacred Footprint, I look at the whole country and *sitōsē renavā*.

Dancer: What's that, ha ha, what did you say? ha! ha!

Devol: I look at the whole country and *sitōsē renavā* ["I shit with pleasure"].

Dancer: No no, not *sitōsē renavā*, but *Sri Lanka dvīpete enava* ["I come to Sri Lanka"].

Devol: Hey! Hey! what's the miserable sound.

Dancer: No! no, we are offering a *pūjā* of music for our gods [*apē deviyanṭa sabda pūjā karanavā*].

Devol: *Tope deviyanṭa hodda pūjā karanavā* ["You are offering a curry (*hodda*) to the gods"].

This type of verbal error goes on through the entire episode. Devol also feigns a Tamil accent. The dancer admonishes him and says that they are worshiping the Sri Lankan gods. First, he says, there's Śrī Viṣṇu, the Lord. But Devol interprets Śrī Viṣṇu as *kiripusmba* ("smell of milk").

Dancer: Don't talk like that. He is such a good deity.
Devol: I am not afraid. . . . O you mean the noble deity, son of Dasaratha, Rāma, and born of the womb of queen . . . , the noble Śrī Viṣṇu has cast his divine eye here.
Dancer: Yes, that's who I mean.
Devol: Who else is there?
Dancer: There is Sumana.

Devol thinks it's Ḍomina, the village idiot, but again he is corrected.

Dancer: It's Sumana-Saman, the great god-king.
Devol: O you mean the younger brother of the noble god-king Śrī Viṣṇu.

Then he proceeds with a heavily Sanskritized eulogy on Saman, the great god riding his elephant vehicle. In a similar vein he deals with Kataragama, ruler of the Ruhuṇa country, and Däḍimuṇḍa, chief of the district of *satara kōralē*. Däḍimuṇḍa is referred to as commander-in-chief (*senevirat*) and the subking (*yuvaraja*) of demons. (It is interesting that Vibhīṣaṇa is omitted in this list.) Then he praises the god Vāhala, who is an independent deity distinct from Däḍimuṇḍa in Sabaragamuva. The dancer says he is a god in charge of palaces (*vāhala*). Then Devol lists the eight Vāhala gods: Āma Vāhala, Kāma Vāhala, Rōma Vāhala, Kumāra Vāhala, Bhairava Vāhala, Avol Vāhala, Devol Vāhala, Puṣpa Vāhala.

Devol: Who else is there?
Dancer: Why there's Pattini.
Devol: Hikkini? ["sticks from the *hik* tree"].
Dancer: Siddha [perfect] Pattini
Devol: *Redde tuttiri*? ["dress stuck with burrs?"]
Dancer: Don't say that, she is the goddess Pattini of Aldōra *dēvāle*. . . .
Devol: O yes . . . the goddess who resurrected the dead man under the shade of the *kohom̆ba* tree . . . the goddess who quelled the Vaduru Yakini [the demoness of disease] and gave her charge of [these diseases] in the human world. . . .
Dancer: . . . we have these beings here because there's illness around, also diseases of crops and cattle, and we have given gifts of coins [*pan̆ḍuru*] and offerings and invited these gods to come here. . . .

Devol says he likes to *palanna* ("split open") these gods, but the dancer says you can *balanna* ("see") them. (Confusion of *b*'s and *p*'s is very common among Tamils speaking Sinhala.) After many more mistakes of this sort, the dancer tells Devol he can come and look at the gods of Sri Lanka.

Devol: Yes, so we'll come and look at the gods.

Drums beat, and they start singing the songs of Devol. He sings one line and the other dancers in conjunction sing the next. The singing style is closer to the Kandyan than to that of the Western and Southern provinces. While singing text 28 they dance, each with torch in hand.

Text 28 The Landing of Devol Deviyo

1. The merchant princes were born in the city of Kāvēri
   They talked among themselves and build the ships all at once

They tied golden sails on the ships, all at once.
Let us go to Sinhala that beautiful land, for trading.

2. Their faithful followers filled the ships with goods
And hung flags and ensigns on all the ships
These faithful followers blew conches and made *kombu* music
The seven ships set sail on Wednesday morning.

Note that they set sail on Wednesday, not on Friday as in Sīnigama and Rabalīya.

3. The seven merchant princes along with their retinue
Wearing gossamer shawls and golden crowns on their heads
With the beat of *tambōru* and music from flutes
That's how they passed the first day since boarding ship.

Tambōru is a large drum; cf. tambourine.

4. When those wealthy merchant princes boarded ship
They said, "Look how the skies thunder like the sound of guns"
The earth trembled as if in sorrow
Two days passed since the seven ships sailed forth.

5. The ship set sail to foreign lands
"Is there anyone with greater prowess than me?"
The earth goddess shook the earth in sorrow
Three days passed since the ships sailed forth.

6. Inside the ship they sing songs, poems, and *rāga*s
They sound the music of *kombu*, flute, and cymbal
They dance to the sound of the five instruments
In this manner they passed four days on the ocean.

Drums beat loudly, and there is a somewhat faster pace in the singing.

7. O the protection help [*pihiṭa*] given to them by the wondrous gods
They eat and drink plenteously, such delectable food,
No suffering here, they play all the time aboard
For five days they sailed in happiness over the high seas.

8. Perhaps by the power of the pure god Sakra
They encountered no dangers thus far
With full heart they sang songs and *rāga*s
In great comfort the sixth day went by.

9. While one's spirits are high one can sing and dance!
Until the seventh day they met with no sorrow
Soon they were to lose all their wealth by cruel fate [*iraṇama*]
Dolefully they wept on the seventh day on the waters.

10. "The bales of goods were swallowed by the greedy ocean
Only the clothes we were wearing were left for us

Alas that the effects of our previous sins hadn't yet expired
Why O Maṇimekhalā did you not see our suffering?"

11. As if a lush paddy field broke its fence for the cow!
Their *rāgas*, and music and money were all destroyed
Excited they railed loudly over
The noise of the sea, growling like the city of *nāgas* [*nāga paṭuna*].

12. Thus sorrowfully they wept in great pain
They were talking to each other in great fear
Relentlessly a mountain of fire seemed to reach skyward
With hands on their heads they prayed that they be swept ashore.

13. The propitious Maṇimegha [Maṇimekhalā] ruler of the seven seas
Saw with her divine eye the suffering of these seven
Till such time as their birth karma had expired
Seven stone rafts floated toward them.

14. Hastily they clambered aboard the seven rafts
They were famished, their mouths and throats were parched
Ceaselessly they cried aloud in their exhaustion
Then seeing the shore they hurriedly prepared to land.

Drums beat, and the troupe dances briskly in the arena for several minutes. They then place the torches on the arena floor, in the four directions, with the flaming ends facing inward. Then the dialogue recommences between Devol and the dancer. Devol wants to know what these flames are, and the dancer replies:

> This is a mountain of fire . . . some time back it was not like this; it was very large, reaching to the skies, these blind *dōsa* which are like flames . . . but we had planted a *kapa*, and since then it became less and less and today it is the size of these torches, these *dōsa* . . . you must destroy these."

The dancer promises Devol five pieces of gold and five of silver, as well as cattle and a gun for hunting if he will banish these blind *dōsa* that are fires. Devol agrees to send the *dōsa* away from the premises, to the brook and river and then the ocean, and ultimately the mouth of *makara*, the mythical dragon. The phrase "flames that are the *dōsa*" is repeated several times.

Singing and dancing (text 28 continued):

15. The seven bathe playfully in the waters of the pond
It will become cool as if you bathed in a brook
Take virgin *milla* wood from the forest
Give me O Devol warrant to trample the fire.

16. May her fame spread through a thousand world systems [*sakvaḷa*]
"Who sent these mighty beings in secret here
In anger she inquired?"—and may she not incur bad karma—
She created seven mountains of fire reaching unto the skies

17. They charm the fire for the coals to scatter
Like fireworks lit one after the other the coals splutter
They stayed near the flames as if ready for battle
Shaking their ankle bells they jump into the fire.

18. The fire burned not and became cool like the river waters
Proudly they jumped into the fire without fear
Those who saw this from the shore spread afar their renown
That day Pattini gave them the name Devol Devi.

19. They who jumped into the midst of the fire without fear
And crossed over like an arrow shot from a bow
Several lands and villages were officially given to them forever
And they were allowed to receive offerings from the same altar.

At this point the drums beat faster and Devol crosses the "barrier" to trample and extinguish the "fire," which has practically died out by now. He waves the torches and puts them away behind the *toraṇa* arch.

The Myth of Devol Deviyo: Sīnigama Version

The center of Devol Deviyo worship is Sīnigama. The shrine for Devol in Sīnigama is now well out in the ocean, but it very likely was once part of the coast. The Devol shrine is famous in the whole region as a place for ritual cursing (see Obeyesekere 1975a for a description of the sorcery practiced here). A few miles in the interior is Vēragoḍa, where according to myth Devol Deviyo planted his stick, from which grew the enormous tree that is found in the premises of the shrine. There are six lesser-known shrines for Devol on the western and southern coasts: Horavala, Uḍugalpiṭiya, Gintoṭa, Unavaṭuna, Ridīgaldēvale, Lanumōdera.

The Sīnigama shrine is in a region where the *salāgama* caste (originally weavers, later cinnamon peelers from the Malabar coast) are dominant. Nevertheless the *kapurāla* is from the *karāva* (fisher) caste, probably owing to cross-caste marriages in earlier generations. According to him, his family had held this office for many generations. A few years ago the *salāgama* evicted the *karāva kapurāla*, who then moved into a new subsidiary shrine at Ambalangoḍa Mōdera.

The Devol Deviyo myth as stated by the *kapurāla* of Sīnigama is as follows:

> During the time of Kakusaňda Buddha in India there lived in the city of Kālingapura a merchant prince named Bolaňda. To his wife Yasavatī was born a daughter named Padminī and seven sons: Devol Sāmi, Iru räs Sāmi ("lord of the sun's rays"), Saňda räs Sāmi ("moon's rays"), Gini räs Sāmi ("rays of fire"), Teda räs Sāmi ("rays of glory or *tejas*"), Budu räs Sāmi ("Buddha rays"), and Maha Sāmi ("great lord"). Padminī, the daughter, by offering a mango to the Buddha Kakusaňda, was later reborn as Pattini. The seven brothers offered robes to the Buddha and made a wish to become Devol gods. Padminī in her birth as Pattini came to reside at Sīnigama.
>
> The seven brothers were eventually reborn in another part of India (Kuḍḍhuppura). They filled the ship with textiles and other goods and with a large retinue of people decided to go to Sri Lanka. [The rest of the myth is as depicted in the pre-

vious texts: there was a shipwreck, and Sakra asked Maṇimekhalā to create a stone raft, to which they clung. They tried to land in Sri Lanka, but the major gods would not allow it. Desperate, they headed toward Sīnigama and tried to land there. At this point all the gods of the island assembled at Sīnigama and implored Pattini not to permit them to land.]

Then Pattini created seven walls of fire to prevent Devol Sāmi and his retinue from landing. But Devol Sāmi and his brothers jumped into the fire and quelled it. Since they quelled the fire, they were also known as Gini Kurumbara. Devol Sāmi was able to overcome the heat of this fire because Pattini had been his sister and had cooled the fire. This was the beginning of the fire walking ritual in Sri Lanka.

Pattini then gave over her throne to Devol Sāmi and went to reside at Navagamuva [the present central Pattini shrine]. Devol Sāmi performed all sorts of magic and astonished the local people of Sīnigama. He was known as a very powerful man endowed with miraculous powers. He made sugar out of the sands of the beach—hence the name of the village, Sīnigama, or sugar village. Eventually he married a local woman and lived in Vēragoḍa.

Devol Sāmi's son had seen his father come home each day with rice for his evening meal. This surprised the son, since the father never worked in the rice fields. The son followed the father one day and saw him put sea sand in the tucked-up folds of his sarong. When the father came home that day the sand had not been converted to rice. When Devol Sāmi found out that his son had discovered his secret, he twisted his neck and killed him. After Devol Sāmi's death people began to make offerings and worship him as a *dēvatā*. Later on a shrine was built in his honor by King Dapulasena, at the same time as he built the shrine for Viṣṇu at Devundara.

Commentary on the Myth of Devol Deviyo

1. The Sīnigama version of the Devol Deviyo myth adds further legitimacy to Devol and integrates his cult with that of Pattini. The first part of the myth links Devol and Pattini in a previous birth as offspring of Bolaňda, whereas in the main Pattini texts there is no reference to Devol as a sister of Pattini. The myth also tries to show that Gini Kurumbara is simply another name for Devol, which is very unlikely, since soon after the fire, walking ritual there is a separate ritual for the Kurumbara demons. There, as in many other places, the Kurumbara are seen as a separate group of demons. Kurumbara is also a Dravidian name; one can only guess at its origin. It probably is related to a tribe found in many parts of Vayinad (Wynad) in Malabar and Mysore, known as Kurumba in Tamil, which when rendered into Sinhala becomes Kurumbara. The wild Kurumba of Mysore have in fact a tribal division known as *kolli* ("firebrand") who are expert woodsmen, according to Thurston (1909, p. 159). Kolli Kurumba when translated into Sinhala is Gini Kurumbara, the demon associated with fire walking. I do not know how or why a tribal group was apotheosed in this way.

2. The folk etymology of Sīnigama (sugar village) is, I think, incorrect. I interpret "sīni" as "Chinese"; Sīnigama, or "Chinese village," was probably a port of call for early Chinese traders.

Ritual Drama of Devol Deviyo's Entry into Sri Lanka: Ratnapura Tradition

Soon after the fire is trampled the same actors continue to enact the myth of Devol Deviyo's arrival in Sri Lanka. Two attendants and the dancer (once again representing the audience) place themselves before the *toraṇa* arch, where Devol Deviyo confronts them. In the performance described below no physical barrier is used, but in other performances at Sabaragamuva I have seen a rope held by the attendants. Nevertheless, there is an invisible barrier: Devol repeatedly tries to go past the attendants (guards at the city gates) to the *toraṇa*—the *vimāna*, or abode of the great gods of Sri Lanka.

Theoretically this performance should have come before the fire trampling. The reason for its coming after is that this act is followed by *rāmā märīma*, killing of Rāma, which in many places is the comic substitute for the *marā ipäddīma* ritual ("killing and resurrection") many people are afraid to perform. In Ratnapura the chief character in *rāmā märīma* is Guru Hāmi, who is identified with Devol Sāmi (or Hāmi), one of the Devol gods. This is not the case elsewhere, where Guru Hāmi is a different character, also known as Āňḍi Guru. Guru Hāmi or Āňḍi Guru is also the ludicrous hero of the folk play Sokari (Sarachchandra 1966, p. 85). Since Guru Hāmi is identified with Devol Sāmi, the Ratnapura tradition prefaces *rāmā märīma* with a short enactment of the landing of Devol in Sri Lanka. I shall describe this part of the drama here and reserve the latter part on the killing of Rāma for later presentation (chap. 5, pp. 277–82). However, the reader should bear in mind the sequence in the Ratnapura tradition—fire trampling followed by the ritual drama of the landing of Devol in Sri Lanka, then the killing of Rāma.

Devol Deviyo in his dancing kit enters the arena and conducts a dialogue with the dancer. He has a long conversation with the dancer (audience) and speaks like a Tamil. Much of the dialogue is stylistically similar to other ritual dramas, and I shall give only a bare summary. Devol tries to introduce himself to the dancer (i.e., the audience), who says he doesn't know him. He says he lives nearby—just seven times beyond seven seas, in Suddhuppuru (or Kuḍḍhuppuru) a city port. He was born in the womb of merchant Mānāyuru-Marakkāli, seven were born as seven cross-cousins in one womb (*Nodōkin*! "May I never see you in my future births!"—the way the Tamils reckon relationships—says the dancer), and the eldest was a younger sister (*naṅgi*) (a reference to Pattini). He then describes, with many verbal errors, the building of the ship by carpenters from the eighteen provinces (*dēsa*), and the loading of the seven ships. The first ship had onions, shallots, garlic, lentils; in the second were various pins, female ornaments and things, fishhooks; the third ship had salt and the five types of metals; the fourth ship was loaded with various spices (*duru*); the fifth ship had cloth of various types; the sixth ship contained Tamil soldiers from the eighteen provinces. When they were ready to board the seventh ship, one fellow they knew said not to go, since there would be many disasters. Nevertheless they did, and the rest of the experiences of Devol are described—the storm, the stone rafts sent by Maṇimekhalā. They sailed in these rafts till they reached the first port (*toṭa*).

> Devol: Here there was a bad fellow.
> Dancer and others: How do you mean "bad"?
> Devol: When I first looked at him he had the complexion of the *bäbila* flower [yellow]; next the color of the blue skies; next black, and then white . . . every time I look a different color, ten times, ten colors. . . .

The dancer corrects him and says that this was the great god Viṣṇu; then the dancer bursts into a prose paean of praise on Viṣṇu in highly elaborate (*praśasti*) Sanskritized language.

> Devol: What a shame, I couldn't recognize him. Actually he did me a favor once. When the *asura* named Basma was burned to ashes, Gini Kurumbara was born

and god Viṣṇu told us to take Gini Kurumbara in our ship as steersman. O yes, that lord is very good.

Song:

1. The great ocean advanced on them
   The seven ships that swiftly sped were destroyed
   "I will not permit you to land here"
   Śrī Viṣṇu did not permit them ashore.

2. Excitedly they saw land and wanted to disembark
   "I am reluctant to let them enter
   It is wrong to let them in without seeing them"
   The god Saman did not permit them to land.

Drums beat and Devol dances as if advancing, then suddenly confronts the "barrier" and retreats. He had seen a stupid man in white, on the top of a rest house (*ambalama*), performing all sorts of antics. The dancer corrects him and says it is the great god Saman. Devol says his servant Simon told him it was not a fool but he did not believe him. Simon is a new character in the arena; he wears a sarong and is bare bodied like a servant. He is also the *koṭṭōruva*, or pillowcase man. He is also literally Simple Simon, the village fool, who can be ridiculed with impunity. He later appears as Rāma in the ritual drama *rāmā märīma*. Simon is a European personal name popular in some Sinhala villages.

Devol goes on to say that Simon may be correct after all and that this may indeed be the great god Saman, the noble being riding an elephant vehicle. He then follows the dancer's earlier example and bursts into a highfalutin panegyric in praise of Saman. This is followed by the next song:

Hurriedly they try to land ashore
O what effort they take to get there
"Let us no longer show reluctance to land"
Yet god Kataragama did not permit them to come.

Devol: Don't ask me what that fellow looks like. I won't tell you.
Dancer: Why . . . ?
Devol: He looked awful; he had six heads, he had twelve hands, and pointed things and things that look like sticks . . . when I saw him I wanted to spit out, I was so disgusted, he was so ugly.
Dancer: But didn't you ask Simon?
Devol: Yes I did . . . but Simon told me, "uncle, I am sorry to say that the man is a bastard born of six fathers. . . ."

Devol hauls up Simon, but Simon does not talk. Ultimately he recognizes his error and describes how the heads were created according to the Kataragama origin myth. This is followed by the typical panegyric extolling the virtues of Kataragama.

Song:

Having passed the three ports where they had struggled [to enter]
Is there any other port these demons could reach?
The pure goddess Pattini saw them with her divine eye
She did not permit entry, however much they sought.

Devol now describes Pattini insultingly as an ugly woman with her right breast elongated about four *riyan* long and the other only about three and a half inches. "She wore white. . . . She made a fire for us, thinking we were cold. Simon told me that her adulterous lover had torn out her breast and eaten it."

Dancer: [in outraged tones] Oh no, oh no . . . !

But Devol goes on to say that later Simon told him the truth. He then bursts into praise of Pattini, recounting her prowess when she tore out her left breast and burned the city of Pāṇḍi . . . that city is still burning. . . . The dancer then reminds Devol that she also created mountains of fire to prevent Devol and his followers from landing.

Devol: How can she stop us? We can dance on fire, play ball on fire, swim on fire and eat fire . . . do anything with fire. We therefore played on the fire, made it cool [*sisil*] and came ashore. . . .

The dancer then says that since Devol Deviyo successfully quelled the fire he is allowed, by Pattini, to accept offerings, in the same *yahanāva* (altar, "couch") with her.

Devol is strutting up and down the arena and tries to go up to the *toraṇa* arch. When he inquires what it is, the dancer says it is the heavenly abode (*vimāna*) of the gods.

Devol: Your gods have a lot of *telijja* [unfermented toddy].
Dancer: No . . . but they have *tējasa* [glory, power]. They don't tap for toddy.

Then Devol asks him whether they catch crabs from ponds; the dancer replies that his gods look on all the *kōvil* [shrines] with their divine eyes. Devol feigns great impatience and runs up to the dancer, grabs him by his waist, and says: "Tell me, What kind of power do your gods have?"

Dancer: Our gods can do whatever they wish . . . they can convert mountains into plains and plains into mountains; they can cause a living body to die and a dead body to live, if there is any injustice. . . .
Devol: Don't tell me . . . can I bribe them? [He aggressively jumps on the dancer, threatening assault.]
Dancer: No . . . our gods are just and punish wrongs.
Devol: Our gods are not like that. Our gods can turn plains into plains and mountains into mountains, and make the live come alive and the dead they can cause to die. Do your gods help you to clean up the dishes in the evening . . . and bring firewood? [This is an insulting reference to the Brahmanic idea of the husband as a god, yet also someone who helps the woman wash dishes.]
Dancer: No, no . . . our gods aren't that intimate with us.
Devol: Our gods help us . . . your gods are thieves . . . when our ships were destroyed they stole our golden rod [*mugura*] . . . there it is.

Devol now points his hand toward the *toraṇa*, where the rod (a stick) has been placed beforehand. He tries to go up there but he cannot cross the barrier. What has happened is that the *āyudha*, or weapon of Devol, was removed by the divine power (*dēva balaya*) of the Sinhala gods. Thus the *toraṇa* represents the heavenly abodes where Devol's weapon, the rod, is sequestered. Devol then asks the dancer to get it for him, but the latter says he cannot even approach the throne of the gods.

Devol: Shall I break open the *dēvāle* and take it?
Dancer: Yes, try if you can.

Devol runs up in a dance toward the *toraṇa* but comes back frightened.

> Dancer: "See what I said . . . you must make a plaint [*kannalavva*] and plead humbly with the gods. . . . All the great gods are here. . . .
> Devol: O great gods I ask thee [rude address] for my golden rod.

He shakes his head, but the dancer says that's like a lizard, not the right obeisance.

> Dancer: No . . . you should tie a *pañḍuru* [coin] for the gods.

Again he does it badly and addresses the gods in a rude fashion and confuses *paṭa pañḍuru* (coins) with *baṭa pañduru* (bamboo bush).

> Dancer: You *must* worship the gods. . . .
> Devol: When she heard that I was coming to Lanka my mother-in-law gave me such good advice which I cannot but heed. She said don't worship the Buddha, don't worship at *dēvāle*s, don't worship fellows wearing yellow robes, don't respect elders; break open temples and *dēvāle*s, plunder Buddhist shrines, assault monks, scold your elders. . . . If I hear you have disobeyed me, said she, I'll cut off your hand with the ax and hang it on your ear.
> Dancer: Ha! Ha! Ha! What lovely advice from the mother-in-law! . . . But you *must* worship the gods.
> Devol: I'll worship the gods if you say so, but no one here must let my mother-in-law know about it.

The other dancers also agree, and so does Simon. Devol goes up to the *toraṇa* and placing his folded hands on his head respectfully worships the Sinhala deities and takes two "sticks" from the *toraṇa*. He comes back and accosts the dancer.

> Devol: Really, they are good gods. . . . I asked only for one rod [*mugura*], but they said, "Son, take both."

Offering of the Dawn Watch to the Kurumbara Demons

At about 9:50 A.M. an assistant brings a *taṭṭu* (tray) shaped like a boat with a miniature sail containing the offering to the Kurumbara demons and representing the ship in which Devol and Kurumbara sailed to Sri Lanka. The following ingredients are in it: betel leaves, seven curries, rice, and five *goṭu*, or cupped leaves, containing *añdun* (collyrium, in reality soot), sandalwood paste, milk, flowers, and treacle. The chief householder or villager (*ātura*) holds the offering and sings songs asking the Kurumbara demons to accept the offering by the command of King Vessamuni (text 29). After this he utters a plaint to the Kurumbaras (text 30, quoted below).

Text 30 *Kannalavva*, or Plaint to Kurumbara

> May you live for five thousand years, five thousand years O sixty Kurumbara who have obtained the *varan* of divine knowledge, who rose up in the sky [and stayed there] without coming down to earth and thereby showed the miracle of walking [in midair]; in the name of the sixty Kurumbara *dēvatā*s, and also remembering the names of the great divine kings of the Four Warrants who have great influence, here at the early dawn watch of the demons, we have dedicated [*käpa*] this offering to the sixty Kurumbara *dēvatā*s at this dance hall [*rañga mañḍala*] in order to send them away. . . . The oblation [*pidēni*] of the boat sails has been consecrated to the sixty noble Kurumbara *dēvatā*s by these village people, who have been beset by afflic-

tions from various demons such as *yakku*, *preta*, *kumbhāṇḍa*, and *piśāca* and so forth . . . and if there be any Kurumbara *dēvatā*s intent on frightening these people, threatening to drink their blood or scaring them into fits of fainting—if there be such, by this *pidēni* oblation we have given you, sirs, by the power of Vaiṣravaṇa-Vessamuni who had given you *varan* to banish illness from the five aggregates [*skandha*] and also from within people's bodies, by his power and command and also of the great divine kings, it is done-consummated [*tīnduyi nivāraṇayi*]—once, twice, and three times.

The chief *āturas* repeat the phrase three times as they wipe away their *dōsa* by putting their hands on their heads and bringing them downward into the *pidēni* oblation three times.

Doḷaha Peḷapāḷiya: Spectacle to the Twelve Gods

Doḷaha peḷapāḷiya can mean either series (*peḷa*) of dances, spectacles, or ritual items (*pāḷiya*) to the Twelve Gods (Doḷaha Deviyo) or "a series of twelve ritual items." The latter meaning is employed in other Sinhala rituals (e.g., in low-country exorcistic rituals), but the items performed show some variation. In the *gammaḍuva* the reference is to the twelve displays or spectacles performed in honor of the Twelve Gods, or Doḷaha Deviyo. In the preface to the ritual the *kapurāla* mentions a list of items to be performed that includes more than the twelve actually included in the ritual. Following the twelve items there are two others in honor of Doḷaha Deviyo—the *ät bandana* ("capture of the elephant") and the *mī bandana* ("capture of the buffalo").

The ritual commences with one of the *kapurāla*s dancing in the arena with a large multicolored umbrella edged with beads that hang down, representing pearls. Four or five other dancers dance round the *kapurāla* to the beat of the drums. Meanwhile the chief *kapurāla* enters the arena, with the anklets (*halan*) of the goddess Pattini covered in red silk on his right shoulder, and dances around the umbrella. Conventional songs on the various births of Pattini are sung. An *āyubōvēvā* ("may you live long") is uttered at the conclusion of the dance, and the anklets are replaced on the altar. Then the chief *kapurāla* chants the list of the items that constitute the ritual alternately with the senior *kapurāla* (hereafter referred to simply as *kapurāla*.)

Chief *kapurāla*: With prime place given to the *sura*s—we give offerings of dances in this hall.

Kapurāla: To the very same *sura*s, the Twelve Gods who eyed—the dance offering of the *telmē*

According to the customs of ancient times—give coins [*pañḍuru*] as gifts

Also a canopy, foot cloths, pearl umbrella, and a flag—a sun-moon emblem [*sēsat*], fan [*cāmara*], for performing dance items for the god

Sound the *bera* drum, and the *davul* drum—according to the styles set in old times

Davul drums and *tammaṭṭan* drums—the sweet music of the trumpet [*horaṇā*] and curved horn [*kombu*]

The gentle music of the *vīṇā* and flute [*nalāva*]—and the deafening sound of the conch

You must also anoint the head with *nānu*—and comb the dark glossy hair
Trim the beard [*andam keṭīma*]—dedicate and offer [*oppu*] a tusker elephant to the god(s)
And in the name of the god Maṅgara—dedicate and offer a water buffalo
Without error, in the right manner—and bring blessings to us all by performing the *doḷaha peḷapāḷiya*.

In this ritual the "Twelve Gods" are often referred to as Doḷaha Deviňdu, or Doḷaha Devi, which is singular. However, in English translation "Twelve God" makes little sense.

Then follows the typical dialogue between the drummer and the *kapurāla*. The *kapurāla* says he has recited a list of twelve items (actually sixteen); now, he tells the drummer, these have to be separately performed and offered to the Twelve Gods. To start with he will offer a *riyana* (i.e., eighteen inches), an obvious malapropism for *viyana* "canopy." The drummer corrects him.

Kapurāla: Now you say we should *oppu* [dedicate and offer] a canopy spectacle to the god. Teacher [*gurunnānse*], I talk out of turn sometimes, so forgive me.

Uḍuviyan Peḷapāḷiya: Spectacle of the Canopy

Then drums beat and the chief *kapurāla* and the second *kapurāla* sing songs, alternating lines. The second *kapurāla* has a piece of folded cloth about a foot or two long in his hand, and while he sings he dances gracefully in the arena.

Chief *kapurāla*: At the song festival [*gī maḍuva*] of Sēraman the king
Kapurāla: The Twelve Gods were all dutifully present
Prestigious Brahman priests had also arrived
Without fail we'll give an offering of a canopy.

Measure a goodly shawl sixty *riyan* in length
Brahma gave us permission to tie a canopy
We make offerings to the gods in all eight directions
O gods banish all *dōsa* and enter under this canopy.

We give this offering to the noble Twelve Gods
Their command has spread over all the three worlds
Relate the procedure as it prevailed in old times
We bring blessings by performing the canopy spectacle.

The drummer beats a quicker note as the singing stops; the *kapurāla* dances a brisker dance with the cloth in his hands and, uttering the conventional "may you live long," lays the cloth on the altar.

Pāvaḍa Peḷapāḷiya: Spectacle of the Foot Cloth

Kapurāla: . . . Teacher, we have offered a good spectacle of the canopy and the gods say they are pleased, they say it was excellent. What now, teacher?
Drummer: *Pāvaḍa* [foot cloth].
Kapurāla: What *pappaḍaṃ*? I thought that's something one eats?

The drummer scolds the *kapurāla* and tells him that it's a foot cloth that has to be made *oppu* (dedicated and offered) to the deity (i.e., the Twelve Gods).

Chief *kapurāla*: The Seven Queens have picked cotton.
Kapurāla: Seated in one place they spin thread
They make a lovely white cloth, sixty *riyan* long
In this skillful manner they laid the foot cloth.

Seven Queens: In Sinhala mythology these are barren "queens" who offered a cloth to the Buddha Kakusaňda in order to conceive.

Blessing us with long life, the Twelve Gods are arriving
Now we lay the foot cloth and offer it to them
This tradition is given the world from ancient times
The gods are now arriving on the foot cloth.

While singing the *kapurāla* dances with cloth in hand to the beat of drums and occasionally bends down as if laying the cloth on the floor.

We give this offering to the Twelve Gods
All the Twelve Gods are coming to this ritual [*yāga*]
They arrive on the cloth laid on the floor
O Twelve Gods protect these *ātura*s [patients-people].

The drums beat faster, the dance becomes brisker, and then the *kapurāla* lays the cloth on the altar of the *toraṇa*.

Kuḍa Peḷapāḷiya: Spectacle of the Pearl Umbrella

Kapurāla: . . . We have now dedicated and offered the canopy and *pāvaḍa* to the gods, who say they are pleased. When these *ātura*s and gentlemen have laid *pāvaḍa* or hung canopies in their homes, the gods may have been angry. So we pray that the *dōsa* they may have thus acquired be banished with the help of the gods, who are now pleased. . . . What now?
Drummer: *Mutukuḍa* [pearl umbrella].
Kapurāla: *Dumkuḍa*? [snuff?] . . . O you mean a pearl umbrella.

He takes a multicolored umbrella and dances with it while singing.

Chief *kapurāla*: In old times in India, the chief king of the Soḷī
Second *kapurāla*: Had a headache and could not stay in bed.
He sent messages to the Brahmans in Benares
It was from this day that Brahmans performed rituals.

To give offerings in the hall performed by Brahmans that day
They didn't have an umbrella to give to the gods
That day god Viskam [Viśvakarma] from his heavenly abode
Made a pearl umbrella and gave it to the priests.

How the net of pearls hangs from the beautiful umbrella!
The tiny gems hanging from it jingle pleasantly
Together with the twelve spokes they tremble with joy
With this marvelous umbrella the gods assure us blessings.

The drumming, dancing, and culminating "may you live long" follow as before.

Koḍi Peḷapāḷiya: Spectacle of the Flag

Kapurāla: Teacher, the gods say they are pleased with the performance, what now?
Drummer: *Koḍiyak* [flag].
Kapurāla: *Boḍiyak*? [bodice].
Drummer: No, stupid, a *koḍiyak* [flag].
Kapurāla: What's the difference, only a mere consonant, a *boḍiyak* or *koḍiyak*. Perhaps you mean *dadayak* ["wound" instead of *dhajayak* "pennant"]?
Drummer: If so you'll itch; no you fool, a flag.
Kapurāla: Teacher, you've heard me say *boḍiyak*, that's a wrong [*varada*], forgive me. Now let us dedicate and offer [*oppu*] a flag to the Twelve Gods.

While singing the songs quoted below with his chief, the *kapurāla* dances in the arena with a ridiculous tiny paper flag.

In order to banish the headache of the great king of Soḷī
The priests performed a ritual for seven days
Today also, to banish the disasters befallen these *ātura*s
The priests make a pennant and offer it to the gods.

Note here and elsewhere Sēraman (literally, King of Cēra) is referred to as king of Soḷī or Cōḷa.

The priest wears a white cloth sixteen *riyan* long
He makes a great pennant with sixteen "openings"
Perform the ritual as the thirty-two Brahmans did before
O Twelve Gods we beg you witness the spectacle of the pennant.

In the dialogue the ridiculous paper flag is referred to as *koḍi*; this parodies the real flag of the gods, for which the Sanskritized word *dhajaya* ("pennant") is used in the songs. In line 2 the Sinhala phase *soḷos kavul* literally means "sixteen openings." What these are, I do not know.

The pennant was made by the Brahman priest for the ancient song festival
That priest performed spectacles for the Twelve Gods who arrived that day
On this occasion also, enter into this dance arena, O Twelve Gods
Take the offering [*oppu*] of the pennant, and bring us blessing, O great Twelve.

All the while the *kapurāla* is dancing with the ludicrous paper flag in a manner unbecoming in a true flag bearer. Ultimately he lays the flag in the *toraṇa* altar.

Sēsat Peḷapāḷiya: Spectacle of the Sun and Moon Ensign

Kapurāla: Teacher, it is done and the gods say they are pleased, what next?
Drummer: You must dedicate and offer [*oppu*] a sun and moon ensign [*sēsat*] for the gods.
Kapurāla: *Sēsat*? . . . in cash or kind or real estate?

The reference here is to the several meanings of *sēsat*. In Sinhala ritual the *sēsat* refers to the picture of the sun and moon painted on a board (or engraved in silver or brass) attached to a long handle and carried in procession by special bearers. In this ritual a caricature of the real *sēsat* is used—a little wooden one. However the word *sēsat* could also mean "property" or "wealth" or "everything one owns." The two meanings are put to magical use when the *kapurāla* says that by performing the spectacle of the *sēsat* ("ensign"), the *sēsat* ("wealth") of the congregation will increase.

> *Kapurāla*: How do you make a *sēsat*?
> Drummer: Take a board and paint one.
> *Kapurāla*: Yes, let us go make one.

> On the day the Great Being, awaiting Buddhahood, destroyed the Māra hosts
> The earth goddess trembled; and emerging victorious he became the Buddha of this our world;
> With this *sēsat* and *cāmara* [yak-tail fan] our Muni ascended into the sky
> Today, with our great Muni's *sēsat* we banish the *dōsa* of the people and then offer it [to the Twelve Gods].

> When King Sēraman of the rose apple continent [i.e., the Indian subcontinent] came to the dance hall
> Thirty-two serene Brahman priests came into the arena to perform the *sēsat* spectacle
> God Viskam made a *sēsat* and sent it to that ancient hall
> This day too the priests will make a *sēsat* with sandalwood and offer it.

> Get a skilled carpenter to carve designs and make a *sēsat*
> Draw beautifully the sun and moon on each side with various colors
> All those assembled here and the Twelve Gods and Pattini witness the spectacle of the *sēsat*
> End the calamities [*piripata*] of the patients [*ātura*s] by the spectacle of the *sēsat*.

Cāmara Pāḷiya: Spectacle of the Yak-Tail Fan

The *kapurāla* tells the drummer that the gods are pleased, and so what next? "A *cāmara pāḷiya*," says the drummer. "*Semara pēḷiyak*? [a line of yaks?]" "No," says the drummer "a *cāmara* for fanning." "How about a winnowing fan?" After many such misunderstandings the *kapurāla* takes the "fan" and dances in the arena.

A *cāmara*, like the shawl, is used for fanning the gods. About eighteen inches long, it consists of long strands of fiber or thread or hemp attached to a wooden handle. Theoretically the strands are supposed to represent the brush of the (mythical) yak or *semara muvā*, which has a delicate and sensitive tail. The *kapurāla*s say that if the yak gets its tail accidentally entangled in a bush it would rather die than lose it. The *kapurāla* dances with the mock *cāmara* and fans the *toraṇa* and the altar of the four gods while singing. It should be noted that each item has its particular form of dance, imitative action, and drumming style.

> Decorate the altars [couches] of the dance hall; make offerings and serve the gods
> Select a priest of good ancestry from the farmer caste
> Deck him with scent of sandal and bring him to the dance hall
> And [make him] fan the Twelve Gods with the *cāmara*.

> In order to make offerings at the hall of the great Soḷī king
> There was no *semara* brush available anywhere

These gentlemen went to the city of Indra in search of one
And without killing it got a *semara*'s brush for this ritual.

The Twelve Gods are here told a white lie—that the fake *cāmara* is a real one provided by the congregation from Indra's city (Iňdurāpura)!

With handles made of silver we have the *cāmara*
Thus [in old times] the priests banished the *dōsa* in the king's head
The Twelve Gods are arriving to witness the *cāmara*
O Twelve Gods protect and give blessings to this congregation [*ātura*].

Davul Pāḷiya: Spectacle of the *Davul* Drum

Kapurāla: Teacher . . . the gods are pleased and say that the *cāmara pāḷiya* was excellent . . . and the *dōsa* of these noble folk has gone. Is there more to be done?
Drummer: A sound [*nāda*] of the *davul* drum.

After many verbal quibbles (e.g., *davul* and *daval* "daytime"), the *kapurāla* says he will make a *davul* according to the instructions given in ancient songs. As usual the real *davul* is not used. Instead, the *kapurāla* dances with a small areca trunk with skins covering the two hollows.

With skill hollow the trunk of the tree,
Without crumpling it, cover the hollows with a skin,
Tie both sides evenly with the ropes
Make the *davul* drum in this manner.

While singing the *kapurāla* dances, beating the fake *davul* with a stick. It emits a hollow noise, and the audience is greatly amused. The real drummer mocks the "skill" of the other "drummer."

With pleasure take the drumstick in your hand
And firmly holding it beat the drum
Its sound will banish family ills and misfortunes
We make *davul* music and dedicate [*oppu*] it to the gods.

May confusion [*avul*] be banished among the audience
May it please the minds of all assembled here
This offering—we give it in the gods' name
May the sound of the *davul* banish all *dōsa*.

Tammaṭṭan Pāḷiya: Spectacle of the *Tammaṭṭan* Drum

During the interlude, a typical pun is made by the *kapurāla*. As usual, the interlude commences with the *kapurāla*'s statement that the gods are pleased. What then? asks the *kapurāla*. The drummer says "*tammaṭṭan*." Now *tan* could mean "breasts" and *maṭṭan* could mean "smooth"—actually the *tammaṭṭan* resembles two bowls turned upside down. Its resemblance to the breasts is put to a great deal of comic use in the interlude by the *kapurāla*. But the drummer tells him he is not referring to cutting off the breasts and smoothing the chest; the *tammaṭṭan* is something you beat. After more punning and verbal play, the *kapurāla* starts making the *tammaṭṭan*.

Dig out the wood and make it circular
With care weave the leather bands into shape
Tie the beautiful "bowls" of the same size together
Thus with great skill make the *tammaṭṭan*.

He then dances in the arena and beats the fake *tammaṭṭan* as in the earlier episode.

Take a drumstick in each hand
Beat it hard, but don't cause commotion
Make pleasant sounds with the *tammaṭṭan*
Dedicate and offer it to the delightful god.

The *kapurāla* beats the toy drum in such a ridiculous manner as to evoke scathing comments by the drummer.

Pleasing those who are here in the audience,
I am making an offering to god Viskam [Viśvakarma]
There will now be happiness and prosperity in this house,
The sound of the *tammaṭṭan* will send away all *dōsa*.

Horaṇǟ Pāḷiya: Spectacle of the Trumpet

Kapurāla: Teacher, the gods are pleased . . . now by the influence of the gods, the *dōsa* of these *āturas* has gone away, beyond the outer worlds [*piṭa sakvaḷa*]. Now what?
Drummer: A *horaṇǟ* [trumpet].

Much of the same procedure is followed as in the earlier stanzas. A fake *horaṇǟ* made of coconut leaves is used, but in the songs the procedure for making the real *horaṇǟ* is sung. The thin squeaking noise, once again, parodies ritually the sound of the real *horaṇǟ*.

Chief *kapurāla*: Pierce the holes and make lovely "eyes"
In the beautifully shaped bronze.
Kapurāla: Shape a mouthpiece for blowing
Make the *horaṇǟ* in this manner.

Place correctly the *horaṇǟ* in the mouth
With devotion to your teacher press the "keys," one by one
These pleasing sounds of the *horaṇǟ*
Play for the god Sakra.

Without mistakes play well the *horaṇǟ*
To please the ears of those assembled
O gods with your divine eyes who have seen the *horaṇǟ*
May you give us auspicious blessings by the *horaṇǟ* music.

Nalā Pāḷiya: Spectacle of the Flute

Kapurāla: . . . if a blacksmith sees me he'll make a bellows out of me, so nice the sounds I made with that trumpet . . . the gods say they are pleased . . . now a flute, you say, teacher?

The same procedure as before is followed. Again a fake flute made of coconut leaves is used, and there is a similar parody of its music.

Take a [bamboo] stick and shave off the branches
Tie the mouthpiece at the top
Pierce six holes carefully
And make the flute in this fashion.

The people who are assembled here are pleased
By the stanzas we sing to the sound of the flute
Having made elaborate music with this flute
We now perform on it for the pleasure of the god.

The next item should be the *kombu* (curved horn) *pāḷiya*, but this is never performed. The *kombu*, like the *vīṇā*, is well known in South India and probably also was in Sri Lanka at one time, but not today. The next item, the *vīṇā*, however, is performed.

Vīṇā Pāḷiya: Spectacle of the *Vīṇā*

The *vīṇā* is an Indian stringed instrument and is never used in Sinhala ritual, though references in literature suggest that it was used earlier in history. The village audiences are familiar with the word, if not the instrument, from their knowledge of the popular *jātaka* tale of the Buddha in a previous birth as Guttila, the *vīṇā* music teacher. The *kapurāla* parodies the sound of the *vīṇā* by making high-pitched nasal sounds. (In the Ūrubokka tradition the *kapurāla* parodies the *vīṇā* by lightly rubbing one stick on another like a violinist with a bow, which they are familiar with.) During the interlude with the drummer, the *kapurāla* admits he has not seen a *vīṇā*. One of the songs suggests how a *vīṇā* is made, but the instrument described is not the classical *vīṇā* of the Indian orchestra but a folk *vīṇā* made of a coconut shell and used by beggars and minstrels in Sri Lanka. The drummer in fact tells the *kapurāla* that he should use a *pol käṭa* (coconut shell cup) for a *vīṇā*. This leads to some verbal play, since *pol käṭa* is used for drinking toddy in local taverns. Much of the verses sung here does not make sense largely because Sinhala audiences are not familiar with this instrument. However, I shall quote one stanza where the making of the toy *vīṇā* is described.

Bore a coconut shell and fix a handle to it
Take a skin and cover the bowl
Without fail make seven strings
In this manner you make the *vīṇā*.

Saṅka Nāda: The Sound of the Conch

Kapurāla: . . . the gods are pleased and the *dōsa* has vanished. . . . What now?
Drummer: . . . the sound of the conch.

During this interlude the *kapurāla* tells the drummer that by this offering of the conch sounds the *dōsa* caused by *yakṣa*s and *rākṣa*s (demons) will be banished—in the same manner as the god Sakra banished the *yakṣa* hosts by the sound of the victorious conch blown from Sakvaḷa rock. Then songs are sung.

Wearing a shawl on the head, the priests
Shouting "long life" [*āvaḍā*] to the sound of the conch
Blowing the conch again and again and spreading its sound
To send away the *vas dōsa* of the patients [*ātura*s].

Then three loud blasts of the conch are blown to the beat of the drums. Then more drumming, dancing, and "may you live long" (*āyubōvēvā*).

> When god Sakra blows his conch from his diamond throne
> The *yakṣa* and *rākṣa* demons flee in all directions
> The auspicious blessings of the god with the wonderful eyes
> We bring about by the sound of the conch.

"Wonderful eyes": the god Sakra has a thousand eyes.

After this performance the *kapurāla* tells the drummer with mock seriousness that since everything is over he must now go home. But the drummer insists that he stay because there is more to do. At this point the chief *kapurāla* intervenes and addresses the drummer:

> Not so teacher, we must explain what's meant by "being over." The twelve items for the gods who have warrant over the *doḷaha bāge* [the division of the Twelve Gods]—the twelve kings Kalikot, Kulakonta, Sātā, Madirāja, Golusan rāja, Baṇḍāra rāja, Yuva rāja, and so forth—are over. . . . Now there are two more spectacles to perform.

Ät Bandana: Capture of the Elephant

The drummer says that the *ät bandana* should be performed now, which leads the *kapurāla* to say, "Teacher, do you have a frying pan . . . ?" using *badinava*, "to fry," instead of *bañdinava*, "to tie." This is followed by many malapropisms where the *kapurāla* pretends to be an illiterate villager.

The drama has a full-throated robust humor that members of the audience as well as the actors enjoy fully. It commences with the conventional dialogue. The *kapurāla* says it is time to capture a tusker for the Twelve Gods, and he goes out looking for one—singing and dancing and acting out the content of the songs.

> Chief *kapurāla*: In the name of the Twelve Gods immeasurably beautiful
> *Kapurāla*: They aren't satisfied however many such spectacles we provide
> That the Twelve may protect this congregation [*ātura*]
> We'll find a tusker and tie him up for a vow [*pañḍuru*].

The word *pañḍuru* rather than *puda* is used here and elsewhere in this episode. *Pañḍuru* in general refers to coins given as gifts to the drummers or coins that are tied in white cloth indicating a vow to the gods. It could also be translated as "a gift to the gods."

While singing, the *kapurāla* in a dance imitates going into the forest.

> I scan the forests of Puttalam lagoon
> And wander into the wilds where the Väddas dwell, ha! ha! ha!
> I wander everywhere in the wilds of Māgama
> Let me not get lost in the forests where the elephants dwell.
>
> Stumbling at various places in the forest vastness
> What could we do, not a soul in sight?
> Everywhere, I scan, nothing in truth I say,
> At last! an elephant on a tree trunk [*ēdaṇḍa*] o'er the river.

In the interlude that follows the *kapurāla* recapitulates the adventures he has gone through.

Kapurāla: Teacher, an elephant! . . . I was going with my pillowcase man [*koṭṭōruva*]—eating, drinking, shitting, bathing, and doing all sorts of things. . . . Then we reached the Valavē river and the fellow told me, "Stop. I see an elephant." "Where?" I cried. "On the *ēdaṇḍa*," he replied, and sure enough, teacher, there he was on the *ēdaṇḍa* . . . seeing us he scampered away.

Drummer: What did he look like?

Kapurāla: He looked like an elephant!

Drummer: So what?

Kapurāla: Well, he had five legs and when he saw us, he jumped "*jabuk*" into the river, and "*bubuk*" he started bubbling.

Drummer: *Nodōkin*! [May I never see you in future births.] What elephant! . . . an *ibba* [tortoise].

Kapurāla: What *imba* ["kiss," "smell"]—I couldn't even get near him—he stank fearfully.

Drummer: No—I mean the creature you saw was an *ibba*.

Kapurāla: Teacher, then I was mistaken, wasn't I? That was no tusker, but an "apparition of a tortoise" [*kuruma avatāra*]. It was a sign that the *dōsa* of these *ātura*s are disappearing. In the same way as the tortoise dived into the water may the *dōsa* vanish and blessing accrue. So you are asking me to go seek another, eh?

Drums, dancing, and imitative action.

Lo, in the forest, eating the tender leaves of branches,
Shaking his beard, he yelled at us
Holding a son under his belly, it stood there
We saw a tusker, jumping from tree to tree.

Kapurāla: Teacher, just as you asked us, we went searching for an elephant—but before long both of us were thirsty. Ah! teacher, not a drop of water anywhere. . . . I sent him [the attendant] in search of water, while I sat down there and looked up. [He points to the sky.] There I was with my mouth open, teacher, when lo! some water fell . . . *sarrasara*. . . . I was greatly pleased.

Drummer: What? How do you find water up above?

Kapurāla: What? Where else do you find water if not up above? [He feigns great anger.] How the devil did it trickle down then? Trying to make a fool of me, eh?

Drummer: *Nodōkin*! . . . only when it rains.

Kapurāla: When I looked up—say, I hope there isn't anyone from my village in the crowd?—I saw him on the tree whose name one can't utter.

Drummer: The *īriya* tree you mean [*īriya*, a sow].

Kapurāla: Shhh! don't mention it. In the *īriya* tree, there he was, breaking tender leaves and then water fell, *sarrasara*. . . .

Drummer: *Nodōkin*! he pissed, pissed I say.

Kapurāla: [innocently] What! No, surely not. He couldn't have pissed . . . though it did look rather yellow.

Drummer: Ha! Ha! . . .

Kapurāla: So I drank, he drank too. . . . You see the animal had all the characteristics of the elephant, all, all.

Drummer: How?

Kapurāla: His trunk was trailing on the tree, his beard was white as if he had just eaten some curds. Seeing us, he shook the branches shouting *ummmm* . . . *ummmmmm* . . . [he superbly imitates the cry of the monkey.]

Drummer: What elephant! That was a monkey.

Kapurāla: So that was it. That too was an *anda manda dōsa* [mental confusion] a monkey apparition [*avatāra*], a sign that the *dōsa* of these *ātura*s is disappearing. Just as the monkey jumped from tree to tree and vanished, the *dōsa* of these *ātura*s will vanish also, "may you live long."

And so he goes on his search again.

His horns raised high on his head
His ears stuck out like canopy poles
Here and there white spots have appeared
A ferocious, handsome elephant I saw today.

In the interlude the *kapurāla* discloses that he saw some raisins on the road and ate them. Then he saw some tracks "and followed them, and followed them" until he saw tusker carrying a bundle of wood on his head. He is corrected by the drummer, who says he's seen only a deer. The *kapurāla* realizes that this too is a case of mental confusion (*anda manda dōsa*) and a sign that the *dōsa* of the *ātura*s is disappearing. Urged by the drummer, he once more sets forth on his travels.

Drums, dancing.

Chief *kapurāla*: Not a soul in the mountains and hills of that wilderness.
Kapurāla: Tired, worn out in the futile quest for tuskers.
His head red in color he crept along a branch
A dancing tusker I've met at last, today.

In the interlude the *kapurāla* reveals that the tusker he saw had obviously just returned from some foreign land—probably England—after passing his bar exams. For he had seen the tusker wearing a hat, a collar, and also a pen stuck at the back. The drummer disillusions him, saying he has seen a lizard (chameleon).

Kapurāla: As the lizard's tail thins at the end may the *dōsa* and disasters of these *ātura*s thin out and fade away, *āyubōvēvā*.

Once again the search is on. This time they come across a real tusker—an assistant dressed up comically like an elephant and prowling on the far side of the arena.

Drums, dancing.

Chief *kapurāla*: We invoke the Twelve Gods in all good faith.
Kapurāla: We have tied coins [*pañḍuru*] in shrines as offerings
We will tie his four legs tightly
Thus we shall offer a tusker to the gods.

His body and four legs, a large mansion
His beautiful protruding tusks are like banana trunks
Like a storm he breaks trees and vines
Look I see at last a magnificent elephant.

Meanwhile the elephant roars and stamps and shies violently when the *kapurāla* approaches him. Frightened, the *kapurāla* goes dancing up to the drummer, who chides him for his timidity. The *kapurāla* tells the drummer and the audience about his last adventure.

He had traveled as usual in the jungle and had at length come across a phenomenon he considered a hallucination [*avatāra*]—a house that walked. Outside the house, on the ground, steaming sweet balls were scattered, and since the *kapurāla* was hungry he ate them. As the stocks diminished, the house graciously replenished them. The drummer replies by telling him that when he [the *kapurāla*] at last actually saw a *real* elephant he had foolishly mistaken it for a hallucination. He then suggests that the *kapurāla* should capture the elephant. Drums beat and the *kapurāla* dances, sings, and goes after the elephant. The elephant roars, shies, runs around the arena, and commits all sorts of pranks, to the great amusement of the audience. The elephant is finally captured against this background of song, dance, and mime. I shall quote a few stanzas here. The first part of the singing describes the beauty of the elephant and its recalcitrant spirit; the latter stanzas partially illuminate the ritual importance of the drama.

> Like small baskets are the feet of this tusker
> The freckles on his body like *bäbila* flowers
> His tusks are like peeled banana trunks
> O untamed tusker, rare beauty like a snake gem.

"Snake gem" refers to the Sinhala belief that the most expensive gems are found in a rare type of cobra. *Bäbila*: *Sida veronicaefolia*.

Meanwhile the "elephant" in the arena "growls" and stamps impatiently.

> O where come your beautifully rounded feet like baskets?
> O where come your freckles like *bäbila* flowers?
> And where come those tusks like banana trunks?
> O untamed elephant rare like a snake gem.

More fooling around and horseplay, and three more songs describing elephants bathing along the Kalu Gaňga and the Valavē Gaňga and scaring people.

> Beyond the riverbanks are the abodes of elephants
> From the nether bank we see their gleaming tusks
> Let us go capture these elephants
> Look! We have here a freckled tusker elephant.
>
> The tusker is trying to escape, O Kiri Amma
> Let him not take one step away from me!
> Send him from the forest to our herd
> O send him to me, Amarāpati Amma.

Kiri Amma ("milk mother") are seven goddesses worshiped in the more remote parts of the country. Amarāpati Amma ("immortal mother") is one of the Kiri Amma. See chapter 6 for a discussion of this cult and its displacement by the Pattini cult.

> That we may capture the elephant and tame him
> That we may use the goad without ill effects
> That you [O god] may not be angry by wrongs we'd [inadvertently] committed
> We will bathe the elephant and make a vow [*bāra*] to you.

The preceding stanza is an obvious reference to ritual danger or *vas* that may strike elephant tamers and mahouts.

Correctly bathe the elephant and tap his joints
With reddish turmeric water purify his body
Cut his two tusks and offer them to the gods
With this *ät bandana* may the *dōsa* of *ātura*s depart.

The comic ritual action continues. The *kapurāla* mistakes the back of the elephant for its front. Then the elephant is "cleansed," "bathed," and "measured." The joints of the elephant are "tapped," the tusks of the elephant are "rubbed," and then, under the instructions of the drummer, the tusks are cut. Part of the comic effect is that the "elephant" is a known member of the audience who is being made fun of here. I have omitted a great deal of the comedy.

Kapurāla: Well, teacher, the tusks are cut . . . now the *dōsa* of these *ātura*s will be banished . . . the gods say they are pleased with the spectacle. Owing to this good deed may the *ātura*s be blessed with long life. As for us, teacher, we had made a vow to offer the tusks to the gods if we successfully captured a tusker—now the vow has been fulfilled. . . .

After this, the tusker is sent away into the "jungle," and the actors are ready for the next episode.

Kapurāla: Teacher, we have yet another performance. The buffalo and cattle of these *ātura*s may contract certain illnesses like worms, earaches, mumps, and other infectious diseases—now we have to dedicate a *mī bandana* in order to banish these. . . .

Mī Bandana: Capture of the Buffalo

The capture ("tying") of the buffalo follows the same lines as the previous rite, so I shall not go into great detail over it. The comedy of errors follows the earlier pattern. The songs, however, have a rich poetic-comic content—they describe with appropriate imagery and comic overtones the idiosyncrasies of each animal seen. The drama commences with the *kapurāla*'s going in search of a buffalo; soon he thinks he has found one.

Chief *kapurāla*: For the exalted Twelve Gods endowed with great might
Kapurāla: At the end of the *doḷaha peḷapāḷiya* you just witnessed
For the eminent god Maṅgara full of weal
We will look for a buffalo as a vow [*paňḍura*] for him.

His tail curled up and a barb swollen at its end
He stretches out his claws and slowly advances
He was digging the soil under a rock when he saw me
I saw a buffalo excellently suited for this rite.

The *kapurāla* brags to the drummer about his discovery, but the latter points out that he has made an asinine blunder—that it was not a *gonvassa* (young calf) he saw, but a *gōnussa* (scorpion). When the *kapurāla* realizes this, he says, "This too is mental confusion [*anda manda dōsa*]—a *dōsa* emanating from poisonous reptiles—I'll go seek another."

His belly is white, he has a yellowish beard
He draws his long tail along the ground

Seeing a cat on the road he scampers away in fear
I saw a buffalo hiding under a pot.

This time the drummer tells him he has seen a *mīya* (rat) not a *mīma* (buffalo). This too is a case of mental confusion (*anda manda dōsa*), and off he goes in search of another.

He wears a beautiful black coat and flies in the air
With food balanced on his legs he creeps into his house
He chases people and stings 'em with his back end
I saw a buffalo taking pollen from a flower!

This time he has confused *mī mässa* (bee) with *mī vassa* (buffalo calf). This too is an *anda manda dōsa*, and so he goes once more on his quest, this time to offer a real buffalo to the god Maṅgara, he says. At last he sees a real buffalo—an assistant dressed up comically like a buffalo. The singing, dancing, and comedy follow the conventional lines, but I shall quote a few stanzas for illustration.

The horns are beautifully curved and gleam above his ears
He shakes his ears like glossy *divi kaduru* leaves
He shakes his feet as if ready to run
Now the beautiful bull buffalo is in the fields.

Divi kaduru: *Tabernaemontana dichotoma*.

Like a red *dunukē* flower is his face
His ears like two golden cups
Look at his body beautiful like the flowers decorating the *toraṇa*
O god here is your buffalo, lovely like the *nā* flower's filaments.

Dunukē: *Pandanus foetidus*; *nā*: ironwood, *Mesua ferrea*.

The buffalo is there on the farther bank
He steps into the flowing, thunderous stream
He shakes his beautifully curving horns
O god at last he appears to stay.

Along by the fields of Kadirāna
I was walking here and there
Not a soul had been on that road
No buffalo to be seen anywhere.

Kadirāna, or Kadirāva, a village associated with the god Maṅgara's exploits.

Along the Giruvā road in Mātara
I was walking here and there
Not a soul had been on that road
No buffalo to be seen anywhere.

Along the roads by the Koccikaḍe fields
I was walking here and there
By the road near Kiri gat paṭṭiya
Near ocean village he was there.

Kiri gat paṭṭiya: "herd where milk was obtained," probably a name of a village associated with the Maṅgara myth.

Now there are several other songs on Maṅgara.

> Then the god Maṅgara
> Took up the golden noose
> And tied the buffalo with it.
> [The buffalo] then lifted him high on its horns.

This is a reference to the god Maṅgara killed by the buffalo; see pages 296–301 for the myth of Maṅgara.

> With anger it removed the noose
> And joined the rest of the herd
> And shouted in joy
> Now tie the right foot.

The last line is instruction to the assistant to tie the foot of the buffalo in the arena. In the myth god Maṅgara is killed and the buffalo is free; in the ritual the buffalo is captured and tied, a case of ritualistic *lex talionis*.

The *kapurāla* leads the buffalo ignominiously all over the arena while an attendant tries to tie him.

> Tie the bull buffalo and be ready to lead him away
> Deck him as if he were going to the heavenly abodes
> In the name of the glorious god Maṅgara
> We offer this buffalo to him, the god Maṅgara.

This stanza substantiates my view, spelled out in chapter 6, that this ritual and all of the *doḷaha peḷapāḷiya* were for Maṅgara and an indigenous collectivity of deities known as Doḷaha Deviyo (the Twelve Gods). In the *gammaḍuva* tradition this earlier collectivity was replaced by another one—the Twelve Gods (kings) mentioned in the beginning of this section.

After much comic action, the *kapurāla* addresses the drummer thus:

> Now listen, teacher, when the cattle and buffalo of these *ātura*s destroy the fields and enclosures of other people, they are bound to utter curses, such as "may the tiger or viper get you." . . . In order to dispel the darkness of such *dōsa*, we hope to dedicate and offer [*oppu*] a *mī bandana* for the gods. . . .

Once more the comic note is taken up when the *kapurāla* asks the drummer if he has eaten curds made from the milk of a buffalo. The drummer tells him not to be an ass, for how could a male buffalo give milk? The *kapurāla*, undaunted, smacks his lips and replies that he had eaten with great relish a solid substance and an accompanying liquid which the buffalo had obligingly offered him. The drummer informs him that he'd eaten dung and urine, not curds. The *kapurāla* realizes his error and says, "when a bit of dung or urine falls into the milk from the cattle belonging to these *ātura*s, the milk will not curdle. *Dōsa* will befall them . . . may such *dōsa* vanish. . . ." Then the *kapurāla* asks the drummer what the people in the drummer's village do when they capture a buffalo. "We breed them, of course," the drummer replies. The *kapurāla* says he hopes to breed the buffalo he has captured. When the drummer tells him that male buffalo cannot increase, the *kapurāla* points out that one can increase a buffalo in a couple of days by collecting some dung in a bucket, adding water, and leaving it. In a matter of days there will be lots and lots of tiny white creatures. The drummer mocks him by saying that he wasn't speaking of breeding worms. . . . The *kapurāla* realizes again that this too is an *anda manda dōsa*. To remedy this they should take the shawl the "buffalo" is wearing and bring blessing on the audience by fanning them with it. This he performs forthwith, to the beat of the drums.

> This method of bringing blessing on all creatures, [and]
> Banishing all diseases that have befallen them.
> Shining with kindness and compassion
> O gracious Pattini fan them with your shawl.
>
> There was a shawl-fanning ritual here today
> We sang ritual songs and poems
> For our kinsmen and the cattle in their herds
> To protect them we perform the "shawl fanning."

The *doḷaha peḷapāḷiya* is performed with little variation in all of the Western, Southern, and Sabaragamuva provinces. Some of the items like the *kombu*, anointing, and shaving are not performed in the Rabalīya tradition. In the Ūrubokka tradition one *kapurāla* performs the "head anointing" plus another item not even mentioned in the Rabalīya tradition—*lī keḷiya*, or "game of the sticks." Though there are these slight variations within each tradition, the general pattern of the *doḷaha peḷapāḷiya*, like that of the *gammaḍuva* in general, is the same.

Anointing the Head with *Nānumura*

This is the first item in the *doḷaha peḷapāḷiya* to be performed by members of the Ūrubokka tradition. Two attendants (*vaṭṭānḍi*) are seated on a mat in midarena facing the altar. The *kapurāla* dances behind them with a torch in his hand and occasionally waves the torch over their heads in blessing. He then dances with half a lime—slightly burned—in one hand and a *goṭṭa* (cupped leaf) containing ground *mī äta* (seeds of *Bassia longifolia*) in the other and dabs the heads of the helpers with these. Then he dances again, and this time he rubs their heads with coconut milk from another cup (*goṭṭa*), then "combs" their hair comically with an areca sprig. After this he anoints their heads with coconut oil and sandalwood paste, massages their heads thoroughly, and "combs" their hair. No songs are sung while this is being performed. This also is meant to be part of the royal service for the Twelve Gods.

Lī Keḷiya: Stick Game

The *lī keḷiya* is an elaborate dance performed at Sinhala religious processions or *perahära*. Two lines of dancers (often children) face each other, each person hitting his two sticks against those of the person directly facing him, according to a fixed rhythm. Songs are sung also. Nothing so elaborate is performed here, though, the *kapurāla* takes a stick in each hand and hits them together rhythmically, singing conventional ditties in praise of Pattini.

Commentary on *Doḷaha Peḷapāḷiya*

In chapter 6 I shall analyze the historical and cultural significance of the collectivity of Twelve Gods known as Doḷaha Deviyo. Here it is enough to note that, while these gods are given high prominence in the *gammaḍuva*, their names and identities are either vague or unknown to both priests and audience. My view, to be expressed at length later, is that the Twelve Gods of the *gammaḍuva* usurped a well-known collectivity of older gods by the same name. These latter deities are even today worshiped in the more remote parts of Sri Lanka outside our culture area.

The first part of the *doḷaha peḷapāḷiya*, where various items are offered to the gods, is reasonably clear. These gods are both gods and kings. In the service dedicated to them they are offered symbols of both divinity and kingship; the pearl umbrella, for example, is the symbol of sovereignty of the world ruler (*cakravartin*); the sun and moon symbols, as well as the other offerings of sounds (*sabda pūja*), indicate ritual service to both king and divinity. The significance of parodying this royal service in the *doḷaha peḷapāḷiya* will be discussed later.

The two ritual dramas that follow have a rationale or purpose that is not difficult to interpret. The tying of the elephant or buffalo is a vow to the Twelve Gods. The elephant is tied, and its tusks are cut and offered to the gods—that is, the elephant is rendered helpless and symbolically castrated. So with the buffalo. Only after the animal is offered to the god is it released. What, then, is the significance of this act?

In Rabalīya and Mātara as well as in most parts of the Western and Southern provinces forests have been depleted of these animals for more than a hundred years, but in other parts of our culture area this was not true until recently. Thus both the Ratnapura and Ūrubokka traditions had the answer; the priests stated that these rituals were performed for those who trapped elephants and wild buffalo. In Haňguraňketa, outside our culture area also, these two rituals were performed, but their purpose was different: to keep these beasts away from the village and thereby avert damage to their crops. In both cases the underlying idea is to "tame" the animal and render him impotent: in one case to make his capture easy, and in the other to keep him away. In this regard we must note the double significance of the term *bandana*. It means literally to capture or bind; also in Sinhala magic *bandana* means "a charm that could bind a person's will." Thus there are various types of sorcery known as *bandana*, in which the victim is in "bondage" to the sorcerer, bereft of will and rendered impotent.

The two dramas also highlight a form of *dōsa* known as *anda manda dōsa*, "mental confusion," "misapprehension of reality." Ideally *anda manda dōsa* occurs when one is out for a long time in the forest—that is, among hunters and trappers of elephant and buffalo. Then people's vision becomes distorted—they hallucinate, as the protagonist does when he mistakes a tortoise or monkey for an elephant. The terms used in this ritual—*kuruma avatāra* ("apparition of the tortoise") and *hanuma avatāra* ("apparition of the monkey") do not have the Hindu meaning of avatar; here *avatāra* simply means "hallucination."

Before this century *anda manda dōsa* would have been a reality for many people, whose villages were hemmed in by large forests. Many had to cross forests in their travel or to procure forest products. When one loses one's bearing in the forest, one can be stricken with mental confusion, like the protagonist of the ritual. Today, however, both rituals are largely anachronistic, since forests are depleted and elephants and wild buffalo are largely confined to the wildlife reserves. These rituals therefore have only limited meaning and significance in the life of contemporary villagers in the low country. However, in remote parts of the country *anda manda dōsa* is still a reality. Kande Deviyo, an important deity in charge of mountain wildernesses who is placated in parts of the hill country, also banishes the effects of *anda manda dōsa* in the collective rituals performed in those areas.

Nevertheless, practitioners who perform these rituals must attempt to invest them with contemporary relevance. In the Western Province wild elephants and wild buffalo—indeed, forests—are almost never seen, yet the priests of Heyiaṅtuḍuva, Sīnigama, and Rabalīya all say that the buffalo capture will help banish *dōsa* of cattle, particularly tame buffalo. Thus the Rabalīya tradition states that the ritual will help cure diseases of cattle through the intervention of the god Maṅgara. Also, *vas* from people who may have envied your cattle (causing milk to curdle) will be banished. Yet what about elephants, since no villager, then or now, owned tame elephants? Here also the *kapurāla* says that *vas* and *dōsa* of the *āturas* will vanish, like the lizard's tail thinning away or the tortoise jumping in the river.[3]

Garā Näṭuma: The Dance of Garā

Many Sinhala religious ceremonies end in the Garā ritual. Garā is the demon who banishes *vas dōsa*, which includes minor witchcraft from the evil eye, mouth, and tongue as well as ritual danger from inadvertent taboo violation or incorrect performance of ritual (*vas*). Some villages, like Malidūva near Mātara, very often have a procession headed by Garā that goes through the eleven villages associated with its celebrations and banishes *vas* from their boundaries. In the typical *gammaḍuva* Garā removes *vas* from the people assembled by a technique known as *ves pāma*, "shaking his guise."

Ves means "guise" or "mask." The essential features of Garā's guise are a mask with a demonic face, bulging (phallic) eyes, long (phallic) tusks and nose, three cobra hoods over the forehead, the middle hood being prominent and large, and round disks edged with lotus designs for ears, representing *sēsat* (sun and moon symbols). The mask is tied to the performer's face with a cloth: the head is ornamented with fan-shaped yellow coconut leaves representing a diadem or tiara, symbolizing Garā's royal birth. Another essential item of his guise consists of thin bunches of yellow coconut leaves representing his headdress (*moṭṭäkkili*), falling in long strands on each side of his head well below the waist. He holds a set of strands in each hand and waves them before the audience in an act signifying both blessing and wiping out *vas dōsa*. *Ves pāma* refers to the shaking of Garā's guise: his mask and the strands falling over his back.

Sometimes there are two Garā dancers, but one is adequate. Garā has a typical perch known as *ayile* ("swing") constructed outside the sacred area. The *ayile* is constructed with two jackfruit posts (or posts of any milk tree), with a crossbar on which Garā sits. The *ayile* is decorated with areca and coconut flowers and with yellow *gok* streamers and leaves. *Ayile padinava*, or swinging on the *ayile*, is his favorite sport: he holds the two posts and swings the *ayile* forward and back in a dizzy movement.

3. For a description of a ritual game similar to the *ät bandana*, see Emeneau's account in *Ritual Games of the Kotas* (1937).

When the *gammaḍuva* is performed for a family (*devol maḍuva*), Garā performs an extra act: he banishes *vas dōsa* from the house and its immediate precincts. In the *gammaḍuva* proper everything but "the cooling of the house" item is performed. Here also sometimes the house of the chief ātura, the headman or wealthy donor, may be cleansed of *vas*. Traditionally the procedure must have been the same as in Malidūva, where the procession cleanses the villages, or individual households in each village, as in Pānama (see p. 392). The following ritual includes the act of cleansing the house, which is of considerable cultural and historical interest.

Traditionally there was a full-scale ritual for individuals or families afflicted with *vas* known as *garā yäkuma* (see Wirz 1954, pp. 129–30 for a description), often, though not always, performed by a small, inferior caste of dancers known as *olī* in the low country. In the *gammaḍuva* also I was told that *olī*-caste dancers traditionally performed the *garā* ritual, but this no longer was the case. *Olī* were *garā* dancers because their inferior caste status fitted them for the Garā role, Garā being associated with sibling incest. Nowadays assistant *kapurāla*s of high caste perform this dance, but senior priests disdain it.

There is no fixed time for the *garā* dance, though one text mentions early morning and another mentions evening. The performance depends on when the *gammaḍuva* is over: generally in the late morning or early afternoon. I shall describe a typical ritual performed at 11:05 A.M. The first act is putting on the guise: donning the mask and headdress with the help of the attendants. This should ideally be done while the dancer is seated on the swing (*ayile*), but if the sun is hot it may take place in some shady nook. Often while the mask tying is going on a senior *kapurāla* introduces the performance, saying that this act will banish *vas*: *äsvaha* ("evil eye"), *kaṭa vaha* ("evil mouth"), *hō vaha* ("evil thoughts"). To banish *vas* one must make offerings to Dolos Garā (Twelve Garā) and Dolos Giri (Twelve Giri), who live in the *dam̆ba* (rose apple) tree in Jambudvīpa (the rose apple continent, i.e., India). This performance, he says, is to wave the guise (*ves*) in the eight and twelve corners of the house and banish noxious vapors (*visa vāyu*), bring blessings on the house, and send the ashes of all *vas* into the mouth of the mythical dragon, *makara*.

Garā (or sometimes an assistant) sings songs while putting on his mask. The songs typically start with invocations to the Buddha, the Dhamma, and the Saṅgha. Meanwhile the headdress is tied at the appropriate point in the verse. Garā then goes up to Pattini's altar and twirls his headdress there, singing songs. He periodically comes back to the *ayile* and swings on it, at the point where the songs describe this. The songs are sung by him and other assistants. The *ātura*s meanwhile are lined up near the steps of the house: he charges at them, "scaring" them out of their wits, though it is also funny. He then blesses them by twirling his headdress before them from the head down to the feet. (In a village *gammaḍuva* this is done before the whole group.) He then climbs the *ayile* and swings on it, singing songs. Thereafter he engages in a dialogue with the drummer and also often with a senior *kapurāla*. At 10:30 A.M. the *ātura*s go into the house. Let me quote the songs and dialogue up to this moment.

Text 31 Songs on Garā

The songs are introduced, as always, by the invocation to the Three Jewels, which I omit.

1. On the top is a golden diadem; the ears are of *sēsat* [sun and moon emblem] and coconut leaf ornaments

A shawl hangs over from behind the ears.

2. He wears the elephant form; and three forms [of snakes] on the head
   He sets the divine diadem; he now "resides" in this house.

The shawl is part of his guise (*ves*); thus the twirling of the shawl is like the ritual of the waving of the shawl or *salu sälma* (pp. 132–34). "Resides" is *arakgatta*; the term is appropriate for animistic beings (*dēvatā*) who reside in trees and such.

3. Demon thy name is Daḷa and thy wife's name is Giri Dēvi.
   She possesses great beauty; I sing songs inviting you both.

Garā is also called Daḷa, meaning "tusks," or Daḷa Kumāra, "tusk prince," or Daḷa Rāja, "tusk king." I use "thy," "thee," "ye," and "thou" to indicate forms of address as to a social inferior.

4. From a polluted "open cemetery," from a pyre that has been lit
   From your abode [*vimāna*] in the early morn,
   Come O Tusk King to this swing [*ayile*].

"Open cemetery": *amu sohona* literally means "raw cemetery," an area in the forest where corpses are thrown rather than buried.

5. Choose the right spot for the *ayile*, plant jackfruit [*kos*] posts in there
   Wear a headdress [*moṭṭäkkili*] and listen well to these songs and couplets.

6. Brilliant you look with your wide snake hoods; descend ye as the Garā demon
   Garā, handsome and coy [*kōla*], also sucks blood everywhere he goes.

7. Pulse beats, pulse beats, demonic pulse beats on the rocky mountaintop.
   It is time for the demons to approach, so deck this *ayile* beautifully.

Demons have special pulse beats: a demon exorcist would often feel the pulse of a possessed patient to verify his diagnosis. "The rocky mountaintop" probably refers to the mythical Sakvaḷa Rock beyond which demons reside, having been banished there by the Buddha. The demons' pulses would beat faster as they prepare to come down to earth.

8. Demons, we have for you diverse dishes, and *kävun* you so much relish.
   Also many ornaments, so kindly banish the diseases caused by Giri.

Kävun is a ritual food and favorite sweetmeat. It is made with dough put in a pan of hot coconut oil. One takes a thin stick and repeatedly pricks the middle of the lump of dough in a phallic gesture. A protruberance then arises from the dough, called the *buriya*, "navel." Actually the reference is to children's protruding navels, caused by umbilical hernias. The result is a sweetmeat whose form suggests the conjunction of penis and vagina. Giri is not physically represented in the ritual, but she is invisibly present. Some practitioners state that the Garā demons, when they appear as a pair, represent Garā and Giri, but this does not seem correct, since both wear Garā's guise. Garā, however, also wears a veil and a blouse and is, I think, in this ritual, androgynous—a combination of Garā and Giri.

9. Giri causing diseases of Giri; Giri greedy for his tusks
   Bring her to this dance floor with her army of demonesses.

10. Gem-studded diadem on top; the head shines with three snake hoods
    Bulging bull's eyes, red lips, and white Garā's teeth.

11. With brilliant broad snake hoods; come down to earth as demon Garā
    Garā who always sucks blood; comely, handsome gentleman!

12. Staring from each separate eye, vigorously shaking his tusks
    Frightening all beings, comes now the cruel Garā.

13. Rolling his two eyes, frightening all beings
    Uttering thunderous roars, enters Garā before this audience.

Everywhere in the Garā ritual are phallic symbols, perhaps owing to the theme of incest. In most Garā masks the nose and eyes bulge out like penises. The tusks are also phallic objects, hence Giri is greedy for them.

Dialogue between Drummer or Priest and Garā

Since the dialogue between Garā and the drummer (i.e., the audience) is similar to other comic dialogues in the ritual dramas described here, I shall merely refer to a few important sequences.

Garā introduces himself and his lady and their twelve manifestations. He says he came here because he heard the sound of drums. "Then I saw the human world with my kind divine eyes." The lord Kataragama had to have a lady to accompany him to his wedding ceremony with Valli Amma of the Väddas.

Drummer: Then?

Garā: Then the kind noble Kataragama invited the pure divine lady Pattini. "Sister," he said, "You must accompany me to my wedding, it is absolutely necessary." Then I saw that she was at the Velli rest house, but she couldn't proceed to the city of Väddas because it was *piḷikul* [impure], *aiyo*! and so ugly. The Väddas had constructed a wedding hall with sambar legs and deer legs for posts, skin for decorations, and chunks of meat, leagues long, for feasting; there was a boat full of blood for drinking and waters from the sea; it was an impure [*piḷikul*] hall for the wedding. Then Pattini divine lady said, "If I were to go there, there will be disease and pestilence in Vädda land, since I am a pure goddess." She implored me to make the place suitable for her. Then I, Garā, the *dēvatā*, on that occasion took this hall constructed by the Vädda king Ilanke [Tamil word for Lanka], rolled it up into a heap, and put the whole thing in my mouth on one side. I ate it all, and the Väddas scattered away in flight. Then I purified the place, spread white sand, constructed seats for the gods, with canopies above, and then went to the Velli rest house where the goddess Pattini was staying. She said: "For this resourceful thing you have done I can offer something. I had in my charge fifteen torches of which I gave twelve to the Twelve Gods. There are three remaining for you; hold them aloft and bless homes which have become desolate [through *vas*] and also desolate gardens and other places. She tied the three torches into one and gave it to me. By that act I will today twirl this torch around and inside this house and with the help of the Three Jewels and the protective magnetism [*ākarṣaṇa*] of the gods, and the command of my parents and teachers [here the assistant is speaking as himself] I shall bless this house and utter these songs. [For a related account where Garā gobbles up impure foods given by Väddas to Pattini, see *vädi pūjāva*, text 44, pp. 276–77.]

Text 31 Continued: Songs on Garā

14. For the auspicious wedding overflowing with bounteous blessings
    Pattini Dēvi arrives together with the Tusk Prince
    With a mace that shakes the Sakvaḷas
    Pattini arrives for Prince Kanda's [Skanda's] wedding.

15. Dressed beautifully, decked with ornaments and a new waist cloth [*naruva*]
    She tries on a necklace worth a thousand gold pieces
    There will be great dishonor as a result of this wedding
    Invite and bring along Daḷa Rāja, the king.

16. That day the goddess Pattini was all set to depart
    Sister [said Skanda] there is no strategem I know [to stop this calamity]
    She cast her divine eye to see who would help
    Lo! she immediately gave him a *ves* [guise] to arrive.

17. From the time he was born Garā used to dance thus
    A Garā demon arrives and causes illness, among these noble folk
    At the time the lovely cattle are being herded
    Offerings [*doḷa puda*] for the Garā demons are given at eventime.

18. O Giri maid residing in the east
    Descend to earth to the sound of the five instruments
    Giri maid, here is betel, rice, and other food for thee
    O Giri maid, with shaking body, come into this dance hall.

19. Her swanlike hair shines with blue black hue
    A cobra of noble dynasty, coiled around her body
    She causes swellings in the body and in the joints
    Banish O Giri of high birth diseases caused by you.

20. Growling this woman consumes raw flesh
    In death's guise she causes illness through fright
    O Death come descend from the south and take these offerings
    O Death heed our words and enter this dance arena.

21. Decked beautifully in divine garments, scented with sandal
    Wantonly she waits craving for those tusks
    Accept tasty betel and flowers and also a mirror
    Illnesses you caused then, O Giri demoness, send away *now*.

Line 2, note again that the sister-wife of Garā craves for his tusks.

22. She always watches over the ferry where the washerwomen gather
    Carrying a little baby she lovingly cuddles him
    By her side are children lulled by her
    Banish the diseases caused by Giri, the wife-demoness.

One of the most frightening themes in Sinhala folk mythology is of the demoness who carries a child in her arms. She will ask you to hold it for a moment; if you do, you are dead. This vision can be caused by many evil spirits, including Giri.

23. She always watches over the cemeteries
She makes ghostly noises where people offer lamps
Kindly descend from your abodes and take these offerings
O banish the diseases caused by Giri of the graveyard.

In this and the previous verse, and elsewhere in Sinhala ritual, "banish" may refer to asking the deity to banish the disease or asking the priest impersonating the deity to banish the disease. Giri of the graveyard (Sohon Giri) is one of the twelve apparitions of Giri Dēvi.

24. O mischievous one residing in the open cemetery of Paṭṭipola
He scoots off, making ill everyone in sight
On the wide basket, nicely decorated with food offerings
Cast your *diṣṭi* O Garā of the great graveyard.

Garā, as Sohon Garā or Garā of the graveyard, can be a puckish creature. He utters nonsense in this guise. The wide basket suits Garā's greedy appetite. Note that wide baskets with offerings are also given to another species of greedy spirit in Buddhist mythology, the *preta*s.

25. He arrives at sunset where three roads meet
Shakes branches and frightens those on the roads
Possessed of great might like the giant Gōdimbara (Goṭhayimbara)
Come Garā of the graveyard, gaze upon these offerings.

According to Sinhala beliefs demons are typically found at the junction of three roads. Gōḍimbara is a giant who helped King Duṭugämuṇu in his war against Eḷāra, the Tamil invader.

26. The shade of the *daṁba* [rose apple] tree is good to hide and spy upon
He performs demonic activities [*samayan*] in the winds above
Here is a red fowl for you to tear apart
Friend, Garā of the graveyard, accept these offerings.

Actually no red fowl is given, since it is wrong to bring any meat or impure substance into the sacred area of the gods. Even in exorcistic rituals a fowl is rarely killed: instead, the demon is given a feather or a little blood. These symbolic substitutes indicate the influence of Buddhism.

27. To please the mind of the Garā demon
We give him demonic offerings to gobble up
Many spans wide in both length and breadth
Is this broad food basket made of banana bark.

28. Select twelve cloths and put them aside
Wrap twelve torches and light them
Offer to them twelve cups [*goṭu*] of rice
And murmur verses twelve times for *japa*.

The twelve torches are for the twelve apparitions of Garā and Giri. *Japa* is an ancient Vedic technique of repeating mantras or formulas to make it magically effective. *Japa* is very popular among Sinhala magicians.

29. Make rings from the golden *tämbili* coconut
Offer them along with tasty sweetmeats
Without fail fry some hen's eggs
With these offerings you will be lucky.

One standard item in Garā's basket are "rings" nicely carved out of the kernel of the coconut; again vaginal symbols. No eggs are given here, for the reason noted earlier.

30. The *asura* was burnt into ashes [that day]
He was born out of that arrogant ash
Garā of the graveyard along with this appropriate offering
All arose that day from the ashes.

Garā in demonic mythology in Sri Lanka was *not* born out of the *asura* Basma's ashes. But in the tradition of the *gammaḍuva* births of demons are linked to the death of the *asura* Basma, who was consumed into ashes (see pp. 113–14). Thus one of the Garā's apparitions is also integrated into *gammaḍuva* mythology in this manner. Perhaps Sohon Garā is identified with Mahasōna, the demon of the graveyard.

31. Like Anaṅga [Cupid], the *rishi* [*ṛṣi*] born in old times
He also dances always around the worlds [*sakvaḷa*]
He looks down with fiery, fixed, demonic guise
He was given the name Tusk Prince.

Garā is like Anaṅga in respect to his sensuality.

32. Having obtained *varan* he roams among humans
Though not divine he has a great army
He obtains from humans offerings of food
As customary from generation to generation.

33. Ferocious demon of the buffalo herd
The hunter of cattle is on the hunt!
His friends are black buffalo and black Väddas
He roams with twelve others and five hundred attendants.

After the *āturas* go into the house Garā follows them inside and shakes his guise (*ves*) before them. Meanwhile an attendant follows him with a wide basket containing the following items: twelve coins (*pañḍuru*), twelve betel leaves, twelve wicks (for twelve torches), twelve lumps of rice, two bananas, and *kävun* (oil cakes). Some practitioners have *puluṭu* (burned meat or fish), or just soot to represent meat and fish that Garā likes.

Now follows *bhūta kathā* (literally, "demon talk," i.e., "nonsense"). Garā takes a "coconut ring" and thinks it is a *gigiri valalla* ("bracelet") and sings and dances with it. He looks at the "mirror" (i.e., the coconut ring) and says "The devil take it! A demon, a demon!" He simulates fright. "Take a stick and chase it away" (to the audience's great amusement).

Drummer: Not a demon you fool, your own damn face!

Garā: Ah yes, how nice my face looks, so sweet, so good. Look snakes on the top of my head, nose like an anthill, my mouth a cave, lovely. People who see me, hmm, fall in love with me, eh?

Garā is ludicrously narcissistic, a polymorphous perverse creature!

Drums beat, as he again looks at the mirror, holding a banana that he mistakes for a razor. He shaves and then says that the *dōsa* from cutting hair and shaving is no more. He makes vulgar jokes about the *buriya* ("navel," "protruberance") of the *kävun* and attempts to put the banana in the attendant's ears. He eats the sweets, but they stick in his throat. Then there is a sudden shift to seriousness as he faces the audience. He lights the wicks and places them in the basket. An attendant gives him three torches tied into one and lights it. The attendant stands behind him, ready, with the resin container. Garā says:

> Now these *ātura*s, these gentlemen shave their faces, trim their beards and whiskers, and cut the hair of their little ones. Now if this is done at a bad astrological time you may get *vas*, you may go blind or dumb or deaf or have other troubles. If there are such dark *dōsa*, and other *dōsa* we banish them by the influence of the truth of the Buddha's hair being deposited in Siḷumini Sǟya in the Tāvatiṃsa heaven.

Garā then goes through the house systematically, spraying resin into the torch, cleansing the house of the dangers from *vas*, and ends in the back porch. He sings the following song, spraying resin at the appropriate places mentioned in text 32.

Text 32 Songs on the House

1. For the welfare of all she was born in King Pāṇḍi's time
   By the act of having offered robes to Kakusan̆da Muni.
   A *kapa* was planted [for her] for this house at the auspicious time
   The *dōsa* from having planted the *magul kapa* in this house is no more.

The reference is to the *kapa* planted when a house is being built; not the *kapa* of the *gammaḍuva*.

2. The foundations made by communal labor with stones and bricks
   On this was built the *pil pōruva* and windows above
   Many other things have been made for this house
   The *dōsa* from these activities have gone by Viskam's might.

Pil pōruva: the flat bench made of masonry outside village homes for visitors to sit on before being invited into the house. Viskam = Viśvakarma, the divine architect of Hinduism.

3. Long-handled knives, hoes, adzes, and chisels
   Gleaming swords, daggers, and other arms
   Carpenter's tools, knives, scissors, coconut scrapers
   The *dōsa* from making them are banished by Viskam's might.

According to traditional Sinhala belief, no longer very relevant, making steel or iron implements may cause *vas*.

4. *Kap* were planted for this house at an auspicious time
   Crossbars on the walls, a peaked roof on rafters
   Soon from out of the crevices the *dōsa* will emerge in a heap
   And move over to the attic from here.

5. You have placed pillars and crosspoles carefully
 Carefully over them boards to make your attic
 The remaining *dōsa* we banish by collecting them here
 And removing them from the attic to the middle of the house.

6. May the Earth Goddess reside forever in this house
 The goddess who is present in the full pot [*pun kalasa*]
 The *dōsa* from the middle of the house is now gathered
 And from here it has gone to the back porch.

The Earth Goddess is Śrī, Mihikata, or Mahīkāntā. She has been incorporated into Buddhist mythology. When Buddha was attacked by Māra's hosts the Earth Goddess took a pot of water (*pun kalasa*) and cursed Māra. The *pun kalasa* ("full pot") is an old fertility symbol in Buddhist art and sculpture.

7. Seated with a book in his hand
 Sword and trident and a plumb line
 The *dōsa* are collected from the crevices of the back porch [by Viskam's might]
 And from there it goes to the steps outside.

Perhaps lines 1 and 2 refer to Viśvakarma himself.

8. With fire and thunder they [Garā] have arrived here
 With a retinue of twelve they bless the house
 Yet they remain not here, by the power of our Muni's kindness
 From the lower steps the *dōsa* reaches the ground below the eaves.

9. May the lovely glorious Earth Goddess reside here
 Who banishes *dōsa* with a bunch of *ruk* flowers
 The *dōsa* remains not, by the power of goddess Pattini
 The *dōsa* from below the eaves have gone into the backyard.

Ruk: *Alstonia scholaris*.

10. She was born to bring prosperity and long life to all on earth
 That eminent, lofty being we believe in her forever
 And we also listen to the goodness of our blessed Muni
 Go away *dōsa* from the backyard to the grounds beyond.

11. For a moment the *dōsa* strays at the stile
 But by the [goddess's] power that lies at the stile posts
 Gather all the *dōsa* thus far collected
 And dump it in the stream with loud cries.

Garā, however, does not go beyond the area of the steps. He sings these songs while he is there. He sprays flaming resin on the steps and runs round the outside of the house, then goes back into the house incensing furiously while the tempo of the drums increases. Neither Garā nor the priest needs to worry, since the power of the truth will remove the *dōsa* from the house to the outside.

12. From time to time great clouds shall pour forth rain
And swirling currents shall flow beneath the waters
By the command of Kāśyapa and Gautama Buddhas
The *dōsa* flows from the stream into the river.

13. To listen to the sermons of the Buddha and his monks
People patiently waited in lines leagues long
All the *dōsa* in the river have churned up
And Maṇimekhalā took the evil *dōsa* to the ocean.

14. As long as these *āturas* live in *saṃsāra*
May they never suffer from sudden danger
May they always obtain long life and prosperity
The *dōsa* go into Makara's mouth and burn to ashes.

Now the priest has loosened his mask and resumes his role as priest. The singing style changes. Drums beat louder, and there is more incensing with resin as the priest now banishes the dreaded Giri from the house. Here the priest is in his role as controller of demons. He faces the audience and frantically twirls his headdress as if brushing away *dōsa*.

15. Go away demoness, stay not at the doorway or within the house
Go away demoness, not outside either, or on the roadway
Not at streams, brooks, and places where we bathe, go away demoness
Go away, we evoke the power of the many Buddhas.

16. The blessings of the Buddha refuge for the doorway and inside the house
The blessings of the Dhamma refuge for the outside and wherever we go
The blessings of the Saṅgha refuge for this village and for this land
For me and for these *āturas* the blessings of the Three Refuges.

The term *saraṇa* is repeated in each line in two senses: in the classic sense of "refuge" and in the extended meaning that Sinhala people give to that word as "blessings."

17. You give food tasting of ambrosia in men's night dreams
But we will make god Hanuman, leagues tall, beat you.
Depart from the three worlds where the Buddha has resided
By Buddha's power save your life demoness, and depart.

18. Vasavat Māra battling with our Muni threw at him a fiery discus
Like an offering of a foot rug the discus lay at his feet
And then it appeared as a halo like the moon's rings o'er his head
Today demoness I will hit you with that fiery discus.

After the banishment of Giri and the *dōsa* caused by her, a new part of the ritual, short but important, commences. The *kapurāla* is given a new pot full of water; an assistant gives him a coconut flower. The priest dips the coconut flower into the pot and lustrates various parts of the house and the front- and backyards; then, facing the *āturas*, he utters a head-to-foot (*sirasapāda*) blessing, touching their heads with the coconut sprig as he sings. In this typical head-to-foot verse the emphasis is entirely on the virtues of the Buddha and events from his life. I quote one verse:

19. Our Muni-King having become Buddha strolled under the bō tree's shade
    The god Sakra went there and worshiped our Muni-King
    He goes accompanied by a retinue of five hundred *arhats*
    The *dōsa* from the soles of the feet and toenails is going into the full pot.

During the previous episodes the priest has taken the mask off his face and put it loosely over his head, as if to signify that he is unambiguously acting his role as priest. He now goes to the back steps of the house and utters the key stanza from the *marā ipäddīma* ("killing and resurrection").

20. On that occasion the mighty gods saw it all
    They rained showers like flowers from the skies above
    Like a torrent from a maddened river
    Thus was the fire of Madurā put out.

21. Having put out the fire she stayed on in Madurā
    So that a second calamity might not befall that city
    Having put out the flames she blessed all with her kindness
    And Pattini ascended to heaven for the hermit's life.

The priest breaks the pot on the steps of the house. This act signifies the movement of the *dōsa* into Makara's mouth, as well as the more archetypical meaning of cooling. Sometimes more songs are sung on the removal of *vas*, but these merely duplicate the content of earlier utterances.

In Rabalīya the ritual is meant to conclude with the planting of twelve thin torches (*vilakku*) in front of the altar for the Twelve Gods. Actually, eleven are planted on a large piece of banana bark and one is planted on the ground. Yahōnis, the chief *kapurāla*, told me that Garā is one of the Twelve Gods but is inferior to the rest and therefore is given a lower position. However, Garā did not appear in the list of the Twelve Gods he gave me. Sīnigama probably reflects the correct position. Here *thirteen* thin torches are planted before the Garā ritual; twelve for the Twelve Gods and one for Garā on the ground. Nevertheless this act is titled *doḷaha vilakku*: the twelve torches.

Garā is one of the best-known deities in Sinhala mythology, and he is propitiated in most parts of Sri Lanka. Since Garā removes *vas*, he appears at the conclusion of most major Sinhala rituals. He can also be propitiated independently by individuals or families afflicted with *vas*. The standard Garā mask with three snake heads, lotus ears, and phallic eyes and nose is described in the ritual. Sometimes the mask has *one* snake head; then he is called Kīḷa Garā. Whereas Garā removes *vas*, Kīḷa Garā brings blessings (*set*). The former is the better-known conception of Garā.

Garā as he appears in ritual is an androgynous representation of Daḷa Kumāra (Tusk Prince) and his sister Giri Dēvi. Wirz gives the most popular version of this myth (Wirz 1954, pp. 129–30). I shall give a brief outline here.

Garā was the son of a king. At his birth royal astrologers predicted that he would desire his own sister. To avoid this calamity the king sent his son to live away from home with the king's brother. As the prince grew up he was called Daḷa Kumāra, or Tusk Prince, because of his tusklike canines.

The prince's mother gave birth to a beautiful girl named Giri Dēvi, but Daḷa Kumāra was never told about this. The girl grew up and it was decided to give her in marriage. The king's brother was invited, but not Daḷa Kumāra. However, the prince heard about the wedding and went home to attend the nuptials. He demanded to see his sister, and in his rage he smashed everything around him and ate all the food. Ultimately he was shown the princess. Daḷa Kumāra was seized by a deep passion; he carried his sister away to the forest and lived with her there, subsisting on wild foods. One day, when her brother-husband was away, Giri Dēvi ran away and hanged herself from some forest vines.

Daḷa Kumāra was in a rage; he caused great havoc. Even the gods were afraid of him, since he shook the wish-fulfilling tree (*parasatugaha*) under which the gods assembled. (It is this event that is represented in the shaking of the swing [*ayile*] in the ritual.) Ultimately he was shown his sister's corpse; but his rage, fever, and thirst grew worse. Finally the gods pleaded with him to desist from killing and destruction. He was given twelve attendants by the king of demons, Vessamuni.

Garā literally means devour, and Garā is the greedy demon who eats up everything, including polluted substances. Garā's omnivorous appetite has, however, a further dimension: his aberrant sexuality. It is well known that food and sexuality are often linked: in Garā's case his abnormal sexuality and his abnormal appetite. Often the food he eats has sexual connotations: bananas, *kävun*, coconut rings. Garā's manifest ritual role is clear; he is like the washerman in secular life whose caste duty is to dispose of polluted objects. In Garā's case he disposes of *vas*; all those ritual dangers that have occurred as a result of taboo violation, inadvertent irreverence toward deities, and so on. Polluted objects may be cleansed by the washerman, but *vas* is an invisible force that cannot be handled by a human agent. Removing *vas* is a dangerous enterprise, but Garā can do it because he is immune to the effects of pollution. In myth he has committed the archetypal *vas*-producing act—incest—and nothing can pollute him further. Thus he gobbles up the impure foods laid out by Väddas for Skanda's nuptials, as well as the impurities in the human household.

In the ritual the various types of *vas* Garā removes are listed, with one significant exception: sibling incest. This is the central theme of the Garā myth, yet it is nowhere recognized in the Garā ritual. Here we have an important feature of Sinhala ritual: incest fears are very deep, yet latent, never given conscious recognition in ritual. In the Garā myth sibling incestuous wishes or fears are projected onto Garā and seen objectively as the base passion of the demon, whereas subjectively they are a latent concern of the audience. Garā's rage at his sister's marriage is paralleled in the rage Sinhala people often feel when a sister's honor has been sullied. Garā's manifest incest represents the latent incest fears of the congregation. The latent incest wish is again expressed indirectly in traditional Sinhala folklore. Pattini is said to have given *varan* to Garā to desist from causing illness except in houses where copulation of two rat snakes, lizards, or scorpions has been noticed. These are signs of *vas*; what they signify is left unsaid. However, the Garā myth makes the answer clear: copulation of two of the same species or family represents sibling incest. In the Garā rituals what is unstated is as significant as what is said.

The latter part of the Garā ritual is known as *geval nivīma*, "cooling of the house," or "calming" the house. Here two key verses on the cooling of Madurai from the Pattini episode are sung. They have no substantive connection with the Garā myth at all and are sung by the priest qua priest. These verses are sung whenever "cooling" is entailed; in this case to "cool" the heat caused by *vas* and other *dōsa*. More directly the idea is to prevent fires from striking the home and keep the house "cool" for a prescribed period (*sīmā*) of time. The breaking of the full pot signifies the culmination of this act of cooling.

In general only these two verses are sung. However, some versions of the *pantis kōlmura* have a text entitled *mevan pahana* or *gevan pahana*, consisting of about twenty-eight stanzas meant to be sung for the "house cooling" ritual.

Sending the Gods Back to Their Abodes

The last act in the *gammaḍuva* refers back to the first. In the beginning the gods are invited to come into their altars from the *vimāna*, or abodes, where they reside. Now they are requested to leave the hall and go back. These abodes are not the heavens above, but more immediately the major shrines where they "reside." This rite commences with the *kapurāla*'s literally packing up his ritual paraphernalia sequestered in the *toraṇa*. As he is packing up he recites text 33, quoted below, together with the other *kapurāla*s and assistants.

Text 33 *Deviyan Vimangata Kirīma*: The Gods Are Sent Back to Their Abodes

1. He who sees the whole of *saṃsāra* with his divine eyes and is with us here
   Accept the merit we give you with full heart with flowers and offerings
   Banish the *vas dōsa* that has befallen us and protect the *āturas* here
   Śrī Viṣṇu, glorious god, we ceremonially escort you to your *dēvāle*.

2. With the golden bow in hand he resides in the white Samanaḷa Peak
   That day he cleaved the rock in two with his golden arrow
   Now your glory and influence spread over this world
   Now we ceremonially escort you, Sumana-Saman, O glorious god to your *dēvāle*.

In line 1, "white" (*säli*), I assume, means "pure." Line 2: according to Sinhala conceptions, Saman or Sumana is Lakṣmaṇa, the brother of Rāma. In popular lore he cleaved a rock (either Hunnasgiriya or Lakgala in Sri Lanka) with his arrow during the war with Rāvaṇa.

3. Born as the offspring of the great King Paňḍuvas
   Sanctifying [*pēvemin*] himself he rides on his horse vehicle
   Fulfill the wishes I seek from you
   O Hūniyan Dēvatā accept our merit.

The interposition of a verse on Hūniyan seems odd at this point, before some of the other major gods have been invoked. It does point out the importance of Hūniyan as a personal guardian, in this case of the priest. Line 3 clearly recognizes it with the clear reference to "I," that is, the priest. Note that since Hūniyan is not a major god he is not ceremonially escorted to his *dēvalē*. In line 2 *pēvemin* is difficult to translate. Elsewhere I have translated *pē* as "consecrate"; but "consecrate himself" does not make much sense in English, and therefore I have used "sanctifying himself." *Pē* refers to objects or persons being consecrated or sanctified by incense, abstentions, penances, or mantras. In this sense an individual by the right kind of ritual actions can "sanctify" himself.

4. O god who views the continent on the tortoise's back and is now with us here
   Accept the merit from the oil lamps and flowers given to you by humans

Banish all *vas dōsa* that may have occurred and protect all these *ātura*s
We ceremonially escort you O Kataragama mighty god to your *dēvāle*.

Line 1 refers to the Hindu idea that the earth rests on the back of the tortoise swimming in the milk ocean.

5. The perfect goddess born in the city of Tusita [heaven] now resides here
By her moral powers she resides in the Needle Mountain of Tusita
Banish the *vas dōsa* that's arisen here and protect these *ātura*s
Ceremonially we escort you O Seven Pattini glorious goddess to your *dēvāle*.

6. O Dēvatā Baṇḍāra who resides at Alutnuvara and now is with us here
With cane [*sōlu*] in his hand how he batters the demon hosts
Banish illness, *vas dōsa*, and protect the *ātura*s assembled here
Ceremonially we escort you to your *dēvāle*, O god Dēvatā Baṇḍāra.

7. They reached this human world in seven stone rafts
They reside in Vēragoḍa where they planted the *sōlu* stick
Banish all *vas dōsa* that's in this village and protect its *ātura*s
Dēva Devol, O mighty god, we escort you ceremonially to your *dēvāle*.

Devol is plural in line 1 and singular in line 4. The Devol gods in myth land in Sri Lanka, which, as I show in chapter 2, could also mean "the world."

8. O gods who watch over the continent on the tortoise's back and are now here
Accept the merit of lights and flowers given to you by humans
Save them from calamity [*piripota*] and protect these *ātura*s
O glorious Gods of the Four Warrants we ceremonially escort you to your *dēvāle*s.

9. All you gods who reside in the mansions of the *asura*s
All you gods who reside in the mansions of the *nāga*s
All you gods who reside in the mansions of the *guruḷu* birds
Leave these flower couches all you gods.

Line 3 refers to the god who resides in the realm of the *guruḷu* bird, that is, the mythical eagle, Viṣṇu's vehicle. I doubt Sinhala people ever had a conception of such a "world" except, as in this case, as a nice poetic image. Actually lines 1–3 simply mean "all you gods wherever you come from please leave these altars and go back to your abodes."

10. In the flower seat decorated in the northern direction
Resides Vāsala Baṇḍāra full of friendship for us
With friendship accept the offerings we've given you
With a speed of an *asura*, depart, and stay not here.

Nowadays most traditions identify Vāhala or Vāsala with Dēvatā Baṇḍāra. However, a separate stanza for Vāsala suggests once again that this is a category term that could be used as an alias for other gods also. Otherwise there is no reason to list the same god twice in this text.

11. O divine Brahmas numbering thirty-six lakhs
And Sakra, noble king-god who'll rule long over us

Forgive us for wrong words we may have spoken
Thirty-two *koṭi*s of gods please accept our merit.

In Buddhism there are many Brahmas residing in the Brahma heaven. A lakh is 100,000, and a *kōṭi* is a hundred lakhs, or 10,000,000.

12. To the company of gods who reside in the Brahma world
Birds and serpents, all animals, humans and *asura*s
Those beings who reside on earth and water, near and far,
To you all we transfer merit with full heart.

Here we have the beautiful Buddhist conception of merit transfer to all beings, based on the notion of *maitriya*, or universal compassion.

13. The gods Kisiräli-Upulvan and Boksäl
And Saman the preeminent *sura* and the great god Śrī Viṣṇu
The goddesses Śrī Kāntā, Sarasvatī, and Pattini
Īśvara, Nātha, and all gods accept our merit.

Here Kisiräli-Upulvan and Boksäl are listed separately, not identified with Viṣṇu and Saman respectively as they are today. I shall discuss this problem in chapter 6.

14. For the Sun God who shines in the morning
For the Moon God who rises at eventime
And for the Four Gods of the Four Warrants
We worship you and give you merit to achieve Nirvāṇa.

15. Those who live a league or a half away
And those who helped us with these proceedings
To our teachers and our parents
We worship them, give them merit to achieve Nirvāṇa.

16. Twirling his beard, his sooty face like a demon's
With fierce looks, he yells full-throated
He'll banish deadly diseases and *dōsa*
Baṁbura will bring full happiness to this village.

The last stanza clearly illustrates a survival. It is interesting that it refers to Baṁbura, a deity who is never propitiated in the Rabalīya tradition. Yet clearly he was an important deity at one time, otherwise there is no reason for his mention in the last stanza. Comic Baṁbura rituals are, however, performed in the Sīnigama and Mātara traditions. The latter are described later in this work. The significance of Baṁbura is discussed in chapter 6 (pp. 301–6).

After these verses are recited the *kapurāla* takes a water pot and, facing the *toraṇa*, utters a formal Pāli text of merit transfer to the gods, while the audience is seated facing the *toraṇa*, hands clasped in worship. This is followed by a Sinhala formula of merit transfer, which I quote.

> With compassionate thoughts [I pray]: May all you divine beings residing in the seven oceans, in the *asura* world, the *nāga* world, the six celestial worlds [heavens], this slab on earth, the four *dēvalē*s, the mountain of Saman, and that of the Himalayas, the pond of *anōtatta*, the sky and the earth, and all the Brahma realms,

our own world system [*sakvaḷa*], and this isle of Sri Lanka, assemble and accept our merit, and then may you eventually see the King-Muni and realize Nirvāṇa.

The *kapurāla* then collects the coins (*pańḍuru*) that have been placed in the altar and gives them to the drummer and the washerman, both of lower castes. Then he murmurs a secret mantra into the water pot and gives the water to members of the audience to drink.

RITUAL TEXTS

Text of the *Bisō Kapa* Ritual

Text 7 Songs Sung at the *Bisō Kapa* Ritual

1. The noble refuge of the Buddha
   The preeminent refuge of the Dhamma
   Together with the refuge of the Saṅgha
   With devotion we worship these Three Refuges.

2. First worship the Buddha
   Second the Dhamma he preached
   Then the good refuge of the Saṅgha
   First, worship these Three Refuges.

3. The only refuge is the refuge of the Muni
   The only refuge is the refuge of the eternal Dhamma
   The only refuge is the refuge of the Saṅgha
   The refuges we pay homage to are the Three Refuges.

4. By the blessings [*saraṇa*] of the Three Refuges
   By the power of the twenty-eight Munis
   And him who has knowledge and splendor [*teda*]
   Let us worship him with our hands on our heads.

There is an ancient Sinhala tradition embodied in folk ritual of twenty-eight rather than twenty-four previous Buddhas. "Him" in line 3 is the present Buddha, Gautama.

5. Possessed of power and might—Forever in this world
   Pattini possessor of power and glory [*teda*]—We worship your feet with deep love.

6. In the city of Soḷī, in the country of Mala—A disease once grew
   Inside King Sēraman's head—He and his followers crossed over to this country.

Again Mala or Malabar, where Sēraman ruled is viewed as part of Cōḷa (Soḷī).

7. In order to give offerings and *pańḍuru* [coins]—With great devotion to the goddess
   They built a dancing hall—Thus was the *bisō kapa* first planted.

8. According to the old traditions—A priest with great purity

Banishes the *dōsa* afflicting humans—That's why the *bisō kapa* was planted
in old times.

Note tense change: "banishes," indicating the present efficacy of the ritual.

9. May you live long—May your works prosper
May diseases be banished—May this ritual give you happiness.

Thus far there has been no drumming or dancing. The text is recited by the *kapurāla*. But from here onward the chief *kapurāla* and a senior *kapurāla* sing in turn while an assistant dances with the *bisō kapa* to the beat of drums.

10. The goddess Pattini powerful like the sun's rays!
King Sēraman landed in old times
In order to plant the blessed [*saraṇa*] *bisō* in the dancing hall—
The *bisō kapa* was planted according to the ancient rules.

The word *saraṇa* normally means "refuge," but often it can also mean "blessed" in Sinhala usage, as in line 3.

11. Select a pure ritual specialist at the auspicious hour
Encircle a sandalwood tree with yellow streamers [*gok*]
Offer gold coins, sprinkle auspicious water
Cut off the top and bottom and plant it.

12. Hang canopies under which dancers can vigorously play
Make music with the conch and the five kinds of instruments
Bring performers of ritual [*yāga*] in a procession
With the king, subking, and nobles leading it.

13. When you bring in that sandalwood branch with incense and music
Show it to the priests, please their minds and eyes with the sight
Involve Brahmans who know songs and rituals [*yāga*]
Then take it to the house where the king resides.

Reference here to the king's participating in the festival must be at large-scale rituals in cities rather than village rituals. The reference to his house must surely be to the special house constructed for him, as is done today in some large *dēvāle* rituals such as in Kataragama for the lay trustee of the *dēvāle*.

14. Glorious King Sēraman chief of the Malala country
Brought skilled Tamil carpenters with great haste
The shining sandal bough cut into an octagonal shape
And carved with beautiful designs of various styles.

"Tamil" in general means South Indian and could include Telegu or Malayalam speakers.

15. The great King Sēraman, chief of men, whose goodness overspreads [the
world]
Saw the beautiful details of the *kapa*
He decked the dancing hall specially built for this occasion
And ordered joyous music with the five instruments.

16. Hang a thousand curtains and canopies without stinting
Wet the grounds with sandal-milk-water
[The immortal king, without attachment, held incense]
And then bring the *bisō kapa* to the dance hall.

Line 3 refers to Sēraman's action in mythic times.

17. When the glorious [*teda*] King Sēraman had a headache
Powerful Pattini, like dew on a lotus, was nobly seen,
According to the custom of learned Brahman priests
Today too we plant the *bisō kapa* in midarena.

18. To cure the head disease of Sēraman, chief of men
A dancing hall was constructed with great skill
According to ancient instructions given for making the *bisō kapa*
Do not be offended, listen with joy to those instructions.

Many more songs of this sort are sung in the actual ritual. The rhyme structure can be quite complex, as in the preceding verse, with beginning and end rhyme:

narana — *hisē dosē*
harana — *desē yasē*
toraṇa — *desē lesē*
urana — *tosē mesē*

This kind of complexity is a function of greater specialization, literacy and book learning and closeness to Buddhist civilizing influences.

At this point the singing style changes and several long stanzas are sung:

19. With devotion to the goddess Pattini who has vast power over all beings
The Tamil king Sēraman came to Lanka to the place of golden sands
There was built the queen's pavilion auspiciously as [part of] the dance hall
Sing the songs of the lovely *bisō kapa* sung by ancient teachers.

Line 2: "the place of golden sands" is Ruvanvälla, now an important market town near the central shrine of Pattini at Navagamuva.

20. The lawful, great lord, Sēraman of Soḷī country of wide renown
Summoned astrologically wise Brahmans who at an auspicious time
With five scents, flowers, and lights propitiated the deity of the trees
These Brahmans versed in poetry then cut the tree according to his orders.

The reference of course is to propitiating the tree deity by asking him to leave before cutting the tree.

21. Fell a twenty-*riyan* branch and cut it into eight-sided shape
Over it a tall seven-storied dome according to the book of rules
Decorate it with eight-branched vines like crisscrossing ropes bridging coconut trees
Decorate the sandal branch in this manner and plant it at an auspicious time.

22. Under the influence of the immortal planet Guru [Jupiter] on a Sunday morning

With a pure *yoga* and the sign of the sun [*mitiri*]
Take this nobly decorated *bisō kapa* and hang on it bunches of red coconut and palmyra,
And deck with beautiful *dōtalu* and areca: in all five types of bunches and flowers.

Dōtalu: *Luxococcus rupilola*.

23. In life (*saṃsāra*) there is no refuge but the Three Refuges
We worship the Four Gods including Sumana, that noble god and the kingly Kadirā [Kataragama]
Also glorious Pattini whose fame spreads over the four quarters, we worship her
We servants of the gods sing auspicious verses, about "long life" [*āvaḍā*], according to ancient instructions.

24. O lord Uvindu, the *sura* Sumana and Mahasen [Skanda] we praise you in these long stanzas!
The chief of the gods [Sakra] took ambrosia water in his sacred hand and spraying it banished all *dōsa*
Likewise by the influence of glorious Pattini, King Sēraman's head disease was cured that day
The suffering of the king was banished [that day] and prosperity and luck is brought today to these *ātura*s.

Viṣṇu is referred to as "Uvindu" from the Sanskrit *upendra*, "younger brother of Indra." Also note the tense changes in the last line.

25. Pattini has arrived like the sun in your midst in great beauty and has brought us good fortune
In the audience [then] were assembled thousands of Brahmans knowledgeable in ritual [*yāga*]
They said "*āvaḍā*," sprayed water, sang songs of victory among the audience
While these songs were sung the *kapa* was planted and the king's *dōsa* banished.

The audience also would shout "*āvaḍā*" (literally, "may your life span increase!") while this song is sung. "Songs of victory," or *jayamaṅgala gī*: songs on Buddha's victory over Māra.

26. The head disease of the famous and renowned King Sēraman was cured at that time
By the goddess Pattini, full of glory whose lotus feet we worship
Then the *bisō kapa* was planted in front of the *toraṇa* built for dancing
In the same way the congregation [*ātura*] here forever receive luck and prosperity.

27. *Maṅgalam*, by the *maṅgala* blessings that our Lord Buddha gave god Sakra
Maṅgalam, the *maṅgala* blessings from the *pirit* water given to King Vijaya
Maṅgalam, the *maṅgala* blessings he gave to *sura*s, *asura*s, humans, and all beings

Maṅgalam, may the gentlefolk here have forever the *maṅgalam* of victory!
[*jayamaṅgala*]

In addition to this a brief *yādinna* on the origins of the hall is sung, but I have omitted it since it is generally a shorter version of the *maḍu upata*, quoted earlier (pp. 96–99).

(*Maṅgala* is almost impossible to translate; in general it means prosperity, joy, auspiciousness, blessings, happiness. Line 2: according to Sinhala myth, Prince Vijaya, the founder of the Sinhala nation, landed in Sri Lanka on the day the Buddha died. On his arrival there he was met by the god Upulvan (Viṣṇu), who blessed him (*maṅgala*) with *pirit* water—that is, water consecrated by recital of Buddhist texts known as *pārittas*. The last line has *jayamaṅgala*, or *maṅgala* of victory. In Buddhism this refers to the Buddha's triumph over Māra, Death).

Texts of *Sändā Samayana*, or Evening Demon Time

Text 8 Arrival of the Demons

1. Holding a conch that has a demonic sound
   Creating wondrous cascades of fire
   Uttering shouts like peals of thunder
   Come the Devol demons for the *samayama* dance.

2. You are frightened by their *samayama* dance
   You see them like the flaming sun
   Then your body shakes and shivers
   That's how they appear in the *pūnā* dance.

The body shakes: the idea is that the demon is present in the patient who is possessed by him. "*Pūnā* dance": another term for the Devol dance, since that deity is associated with the *pūnā* ritual. For an account of the *pūnā* ritual see Obeyesekere 1983.

3. On *kemmura* days when he is present
   And he wanders during the three *samayan* times
   He causes diseases on such occasions
   Calm these diseases O Devol god.

Devol can be addressed in the singular or the plural. *Kemmura* days are special days when the influence of the deities is especially manifest; generally Wednesdays and Saturdays.

4. Make offerings of sandalwood, scents, and water [*pän*]
   And also rice which has been nicely cooked
   Make torches with cloth and plant them
   Place your hand on their heads and bless them with long life.

Reference in line 4 is to the custom where the *kapurāla* touches the head of the patient while uttering the plaint and subsequently blesses him. Here specifically the reference is to the pots on the heads of select representatives of the congregation (*ātura*).

5. That demons may accept offerings from the human world
   They were scolded and threatened [with being put] in the smokehouse

He beat them with his powerful and stern rod [*mugura*]
We give offerings and dances to the Devol demons.

Line 3 refers either to Dēvatā Baṇḍāra who quelled demons or to the *god* Devol who quells the Devol *demons*.

6. They arrive with Devol in the stone raft
They consume meat and the blood of fowls
Accept these offerings without misgivings
Come down O demons of the *devol samayama*.

Here the reference is clearly to the demons constituting the retinue of Devol Deviyo.

7. They created a chariot to travel on land
And built a ship to journey over the seas
They created two streams of fire in both hands
We dedicate [*käpa*] these offerings to the *devol* demon dance.

The word *käpa* is translated as "dedicate"; Actually *käpa* is some item "dedicated [or consecrated] to demons"; the word is rarely used in reference to the gods.

8. Great lord, powerful one, listen to us
O chief of the twelve *samayama* [demons]
Listen to the songs and mantras I have uttered
Great lord, protect the congregation [*ātura*] here.

Reference is possibly to the god Devol as leader of the demon troop associated with him.

9. During the cremation of the powerful *asura* Basma
The second to be created was Mahasōna
Soon the form of Mahasōna took shape
He obtained *varan* and entered the human world.

The Devol gods (demons) were born from the ashes of Basma, the *asura*; so was Mahasōna, according to *gammaḍuva* tradition.

10. He swings his sword in his hand
He captures an elephant and splits it in two
And sucks its blood like water from a brook
Comes the demon Mahasōna playfully dancing.

11. Mahasōna possessed of the face of a bear
Is seen by people as a fearful apparition
Through the infinite virtues of our Lord Buddha
We cure the illness he causes in this manner [i.e., by apparitions].

12. Grasping corpses in his hand and eating them
Drinking blood of humans, crazed with passions
At the three *samayama* times he screams weirdly
Crazy [*vikāra*] Mahasōna comes down from his abode.

13. Mahasōna whose body is white
Whose face shines at night like a mirror

Sucking the blood of a human in his grasp
Come down here O fearful Mahasōna.

14. Like lightning we see him from afar
We hear him like the peal of thunder
Accept these offerings specially made for you
With the sound of thunder comes the demon, Mahasōna.

15. Mahasōna with a retinue of thirty thousand
He is present in sixty thousand lonely paths
Take the *doḷa* of meat and burnt offerings dedicated [*käpa*] to you
Banish the diseases caused by the thirty thousand and leave this place.

Note that meat and burnt offerings are not given, since it would pollute the arena of the gods.

16. Respectfully arrive for the evening *samayama*
Accept the rice and *doḷa* [oblation] I give you
By the powers of the prince, god Skanda
O evening demons [*sändǟ samayama*] leave the disease and depart.

17. In the evening at the fence gate
At dusk where cattle are corralled
At the brooks and streams and at bathing places
O gathering demons leave the disease and depart.

18. When people come home after worship of gods
And they eat burned foods and meat
O demons who cast their eyes on such things
O demons leave the disease and depart.

The Sinhala belief is that demons are attracted by meat and by burned and fried foods.

19. The evening *samayama* is that of the Devol demons
The middle *samayama* is that of the Sanni demons
The dawn *samayama* is for Kurumbara demons
O *samayama* demons leave the disease and depart.

20. Demons of the three watches [*samayama*] cast their looks [*bälma*]
Take the offerings dedicated to you here
Accept the rice offerings I give you
O demons of the three watches [*samayama*] leave the disease and depart.

21. By the power of the Gods of the Four Warrants
By the power of Kakusaňda and Konāgama Buddhas
By the power of the sun and moon that shine over Lanka
O evening demons leave the disease and depart.

22. By the power of the pure Muni Dīpaṅkara
Leave the diseases that belong to you
By the power of the chaste goddess Pattini
The diseases of evening demons have left this very day.

Divakurumuni, the old Sinhala word for Dīpaṅkara, is used in these texts.

23. I give you rice offerings, I dedicate [*käpa*] offerings to you
And thereby banish the *dōsa* you've caused
I shall invoke the name of the Gods of the Four Warrants
Look! the evening demons have left the diseases and they depart.

Text 9 *Sirasapāda*, or Head-to-Foot Verses

1. Our Muni was born on the day of Mars [Tuesday] at the Vesak full moon
That day he was told he'd be Buddha [by astrologers] from the well-known signs
Then his father worshiped him three times his hands on his forehead
By that influence descend O demons from the head, forehead, and eyes.

Line 2 refers to the famous signs of the great man (*mahā puruṣa*) seen on the Buddha at his birth by the court astrologers.

2. Taking on the guise of an old man he [Buddha] went to Sakvaḷa Rock where demons resided
The demons residing there asked the old man to leave the rock
But it was the demons who couldn't remain there when the Buddha rays spread o'er their faces
By that influence descend O demons from the ears, mouth, and neck.

In popular myth Buddha is often depicted as banishing demons beyond the Sakvaḷa Rock of popular Buddhist mythology.

3. That preeminent bodhisattva with his mother and followers sailed the seas
The winds struck the ship and destroyed it; the followers were cast in the ocean
But he swam for seven days with his mother on his shoulder till he saw land
By that influence descend O demons from the shoulders, elbows, and ten fingers.

The reference here is to a popular noncanonical story of one of the exemplary deeds (*pāramitā*) performed by the Buddha in one of his previous births as a woodcutter. This event is constantly mentioned in the head-to-foot verses of the country's ritual traditions. It is also incorporated in medieval Sinhala texts such as the *Saddharmālaṃkāraya* (1911, pp. 41–42) and in more detail in the *Saddharmāvāda Saṃgrahava* (1909, pp. 22–26). I will present a brief summary of this important myth.

A dweller in one of the Brahma realms (Brahmarāja), who had attained arhatship, rose from his deep meditation and looked upon the world and realized that there had been no Buddha for many eons (*kalpa*), which would be harmful for the world. He then looked out on the world to see which great human being might be capable of achieving this task of Buddhahood and was very pleased when he saw thousands of bodhisattvas fulfilling their *pāramitā*s and striving to attain ultimate Buddhahood. He looked again and saw the Buddha of our time (Siddhārtha) possessed of fine intellect and unfaltering effort, and he instilled in him the wish to become a Buddha. How did this happen?

This was at a time when the bodhisattva was born into a caste of woodcutters. He was solely devoted to his parents and looked after them lovingly. Once his father died he gave all his time and effort to look after his mother. Soon he was indigent, and he persuaded a group of merchants to take him and his mother to Burma where they might earn some wealth. After seven days at sea the ship was destroyed by a storm. Braving the waves that rose to the skies like huge boulders churned up by the wind, the bodhisattva began to swim with his mother upon his back. At this moment the Brahmarāja, mentioned earlier, saw the bodhisattva and thought: here is a great man disregarding love of his own life in order to save his mother who gave him birth, and he braves this boundless ocean and the many dangers from crocodiles(!), sharks, and other sea creatures. Such a strong and resolute person will no doubt be successful in the task of achieving Buddhahood. He then implanted this wish for Buddhahood in the consciousness of the woodcutter.

The Buddha-to-be arrived safely ashore, reached a certain village, and lived there with his mother. He cared for her all his life, and at death he went to heaven and enjoyed heavenly happiness and was later reborn as a son to Queen Śrīmatī and King Brahmadatta of the rose apple continent (India); and on the death of his father he became the king.

4. Our bodhisattva as hermit Sumedha saw Muni Dīpaṅkara and achieved understanding
Having understood he obtained *vivaraṇa* [permission] from Dīpaṅkara to achieve future Buddhahood
Then our Muni worshiped Dīpaṅkara with a handful of jasmine flowers placed against his chest
By that influence descend O demons from the breast, chest, and belly.

All Buddhas-to-be obtain *vivaraṇa* (permission) from previous Buddhas through an exemplary act as gods and demons obtain *varan* (warrant) from the Buddha. The Buddha Gautama was born as Sumedha in the time of Dīpaṅkara Buddha. "While on a visit to Ramma-nagara, he saw people decorating the road for Dīpaṅkara Buddha and undertook to do one portion of the road himself. The Buddha arrived before his work was finished, and Sumedha lay down on a rut for the Buddha to walk over him. He resolved that he too would become a Buddha, and Dīpaṅkara, looking into the future, saw that his wish would come true" (Malalasekera 1938, pp. 1249–56). This was the beginning of Gautama's quest for enlightenment.

5. Our bodhisattva of immeasurable kindness, was once born as Dharmapāla
His royal father caused that prince to be tortured
The mother placed the compassionate Muni-King's head on her lap
By that act O demons fly from your hiding place in the lap and the feet.

The reference here is to Jataka 358 where the Buddha was born as Prince Dhammapāla, son of King Mahapatāpa and Queen Canda. The king, jealous of the mother's love for the son, ordered the son's hands to be cut off. The queen volunteered to give her own hands to the executioner's ax, but to no avail. Similarly the boy's feet and then his head were cut off. The mother placed the head on her lap and died of a broken heart. The evil king was engulfed in flames in the hell of *avīci*. This myth of the castrating father and loving mother is a very popular one, often referred to in *sirasapāda* texts.

6. From previous births, the cruel Devadatta intended to kill the Buddha

To kill the Buddha he sent the drunken elephant Nālāgiri to attack him
The elephant charged him and suddenly bowed his knees at Buddha's feet
By that prowess O demons leave the knees, shanks, and ankles.

Stanza 6 refers to a famous episode from Buddha mythology where Buddha's cousin and archenemy Devadatta tries to kill him by training a drunken elephant to attack him.

Text 10 Invitation to the Demons to Come down and Consume the Offerings

Kapurāla: Demons around the moon, and those above and those on earth, stay not there, descend
Chief *kapurāla*: Do not stay in the *sakvaḷas*, come down [*varennē*]
Those in the outer *sakvaḷas*, stay not there, come down into the dancing hall
Demons who command illness, come down
Those in the *nāga* world, the *asura* world up in the sky, stay not there, come down into this world to dance
Do not linger in *madura* shrines, O demons.

Madura means *vaduru*, "infectious diseases."

Demons who command illness, come down
Come down from the *maṇḍala* of the moon, accept offerings, and we'll fan you
And stay while in these pleasant shades
You apparitions—ha, ha, ha—enter dancing through these golden doors
Step out of riverbanks and come down respectfully
By the influence of the Buddha, the Dhamma, and the Saṅgha leave your abodes [*vimāna*]
You will otherwise melt under the power of our Muni
By the power of the *pirit* uttered by our Muni come O you demons
From the North [*utura*] come into this dancing hall O demons
Den—denna, denā—ha! ha! ha!

Sakvaḷa, from the Sanskrit *cakravāḷa* and Pāli *Cakkavāḷa*, means "world system," of which there are countless ones in Buddhism. In the middle of our world system is Mount Meru, surrounded by seven mountain ranges. The demons have been banished from our world system into the outer world systems. Sinhala mythology also mentions a Sakvaḷa Rock beyond which demons dwell. Demons have to be summoned from these outer regions into this world. The dance arena is seen as a microcosm representing the earth; it is also a *maṇḍala*, an area magically marked out in a circle where they can be controlled by the priests. The demons are addressed as equals or inferiors, *varennē*, unlike *vaḍinna*, the respectful term used for the gods. The demons are also viewed as residing in the north under the headship of Vaiṣravaṇa, the guardian god of the northern quarter.

Text for the Consecration of the Priest's Robe

Text 11 Description of the Robe (*Saňgaḷa*)

1. Of the noble solar dynasty [*diniňdukula*]
Victorious and possessed of great prosperity

In the great city of Kābēri
Sēraman the king lives.

The river Kāvēri and its city are sometimes pronounced Kābēri, which nowadays means Kaffir or Negro.

2. An unknown disease
Arose in the king's head
And the eminent Pattini *dēvi*
Appeared one day in a dream.

3. Wearing shining jeweled ornaments
The divine maiden appeared in the sky.
The king couldn't sense the taste of food
The great king was exhausted.

4. These diseases will be banished by
The glorious goddess Pattini
Give dances and offerings
Thus the king was informed.

5. Measure four times fifteen *riyan*
Construct a hall auspiciously
Invite twelve priests
To perform the auspicious ritual.

6. The *sañgaḷa* given by Sakra
Mind pleasing is this *sañgaḷa*
Unaware of its length and breadth
People hold it and put in the ruffles.

This interesting stanza tries to give a Buddhist pedigree to the vestment of the *kapurāla*. The *sañgaḷa* he wears is related to the prototypic *sañgaḷa* or robe given to the Buddha by the god Sakra. This is an attempt to give a Buddhist validation to his vocation in spite of the different ritual and role association of the two kinds of vestments.

7. In the guise of a priestly guru [*guru ädura*]
Came god Viskam then
He measured its length and breadth
And departed satisfied [that the measurements were right].

8. Thirty-one and sixteen "fingers" [inches] long
Twenty-four and two hundred and fifteen in length
Cut the cloth in this manner
And show how beautifully you wear the *sañgaḷa*.

In verses 7 and 8 the attempt is to link the *sañgaḷa* (and the priest role) to the mythic tradition of the *gammaḍuva*. The god Viśvakarma constructed the prototypic hall; he also measured the robe (*sañgaḷa*) the priest wore on that occasion. There is of course no contradiction between this and the preceding pedigree.

9. Sound the five instruments and please the mind
And decorate [altars] with streamers
Priests get ready to please
The minds of the folk assembled here.

10. The robe [*saňgaḷa*] must be wide enough to cover the body
We set the ruffles in the robe with pleasure
We hold wondrous sweet-smelling incense
The ruffles are set all around to make it nice.

11. The god [Sakra] saw the king's disease with his divine eye
He thereby spread his blessings over the world
The offerings and dances performed here were seen in a dream
The birth [origin] of the robe was recited in Tamil in ancient times.

In line 4 we have the persistent theme that the texts of the *gammaḍuva* were originally recited in Tamil.

Conclusion of the *Saňgaḷa* Songs

12. Without any love for the body—the Buddha came to observe the *sīla* [precepts]
That day he proclaimed for all a garland of gems—this day I shall sing the garland of the Buddha's virtues
The bodhisattva left domestic love—he saw his playful son Rāhula [sleeping]
He asked the trustworthy minister Candana—to get his horse ready.

This and the following stanzas have a very complex rhyme structure: the first words of all the lines rhyme with each other; the middle and end words of each rhyme with each other and with every other middle and end word in the stanza.

13. Born without any of the defilements—blessed with the pleasing auspicious signs
The bodhisattva with joy, sat on his horse regally—riding his horse he reached the river Nērañjanā
Thirty *yodun* he passed in this manner—without fear he spent that night
Thus he rode on his bedecked horse—and he went past thirty *yodun*.

14. Determined to destroy the evil powers—he overcame the daughters of Māra who tempted him
Having overcome them he preached the Dhamma—the gentlefolk here are protected by that prowess
Seated in the beautiful white sands—he gathered his lush hair in his left hand
With his splendid sword he cut off his hair—with his own hands Puradara [Sakra] took it respectfully.

These songs once again show the permeation of the *dēva* cults with a Buddhist ethos; here the *saňgaḷa* rite is concluded with reference to key events in Buddha's life: his birth, his leaving home and crossing the river Nērañjanā; his conflict with Māra's daughters; his renunciation and Sakra's depositing his hair in heaven. In stanza 14 Sakra is referred to as Puradara (Purandara), "the destroyer of cities," which is one of his ancient Vedic appellations.

15. Our Muni arrived in stately manner in the city of Viśālā
And blessed all beings by the Dhamma he preached
Today also may all the *dōsa* of these patients [*āturas*] leave
Like a festival house may they be protected for five thousand years.

The reference here is to the visit of the Buddha to Viśālā at a time when that city was suffering from a pestilence. According to Buddhist commentaries this was the occasion for the recital of the *paritta* text *Ratana Sutta*, which relates the banishment of demons by the power of the word (i.e., the Dhamma). Line 4: five thousand years is the period of duration of Buddha's doctrine on earth.

Text of the Torch of Time for Kataragama

Text 12 Blessings of Kataragama

1. O noble Prince Skanda full of power and glory
Who banishes the dangers that confront us
He sits nobly on his honorable throne
Banish the diseases of the crown of the head.

2. Prince Skanda, possessed of great glory
Riding his peacock vehicle
Send the *dōsa* away
From inside the nose, mouth, and ears.

3. Sir Kadirā, possessed of signs of glory
Who shows his prowess like a peal of thunder
From the base of the head, neck, shoulders
Today banish the *dōsa* arisen there.

Kadirā is from the Tamil for Kataragama.

4. Abandon not us mortals
Banish the *dōsa* of the *pā̄ḷaviya*
The might of his golden noose spreads
Banish the *dōsa* of the two shoulders.

Pā̄ḷaviya: the day after the new or full moon, considered inauspicious. "Golden noose" is one of the weapons of this deity.

Change of singing style:

5. In the comely city of Kadirā
He steps forth under the *sēsat*'s shade
From the ten fingers and nails
The *dōsa* have gone away.

Sēsat, as I noted earlier, is an ensign with sun and moon embossed in banners or on a disk at the end of a long pole. Like the pearl umbrella, it is held as a "sunshade" for royalty and divinity.

6. O divine Prince Skanda
   Riding the tusker, his vehicle
   From the spine and the two breasts
   Send away disasters [*piripata*].

7. The golden plates on your breasts
   Sends away the dangers [*uvaduru*] of the chest
   By the power of your just and mighty kingship [literally, "throne"]
   O Prince Kanda [Skanda] banish all *dōsa*.

8. With wondrous umbrellas, flags, five instruments
   See the prowess of the beautiful god as he steps forth!
   In the belly and in the bowels
   Banish their diseases and ailments.

9. From the relic of the Buddha who saved us
   Was built the glorious Kiri Vehera *stūpa*
   From the waist and the back
   Eliminate and send away the disasters [*piripata*].

Kiri Vehera is the impressive *dāgäba* (*stūpa*, "relic chambers") near the central shrine of the deity of Kataragama.

Change into fast singing style:

10. O golden bodied, noble Kadirā
    The three worlds glow with your splendor
    By the influence of your golden sword
    The thigh's *dōsa* have forever departed.

11. The influence of water cutting and water play
    Lights up the whole human world
    By the power of the water cutting influence
    Gone are the disasters of the shanks.

12. He looks upon us with kindness
    O chief god Kadirā, the glorious
    By the influence of the river Kirinda
    The *dōsa* of the feet have departed.

13. Thus from the head down to the feet
    The diseases aren't any longer there
    Like the waters of the three rivers
    Quench the diseases forever.

"Three rivers": probably a reference to the three sacred rivers of India.

14. The ninety-eight *rōga* have left

And the ninety-nine kinds of *vyādhi* [pains]
Two hundred and three *antarā* (dangers)
Banish, and protect us forever.

15. The hundred and twenty diseases inside the body have gone
And the hundred and ten diseases of the body's exterior
The god has arrived from a hundred directions!
And may you have a hundred and twenty years of life.

Stanzas 14 and 15 mention the standard number of diseases, probably based on an ancient source. *Rōga* are diseases in general. *Vyādhi* nowadays simply means diseases. It is derived from the Sanskrit *vyadh*, "to pierce or wound." One may be able therefore to gloss *vyādhi* as "aches and pains" or as wounds, abscesses, and various types of skin eruptions.

Texts of the *Toraṇ Yāgaya*

Text 13 *Stotra* and *Sanna*, or Praise and Exposition

I shall quote one example of *stotra* and *sanna* to illustrate the convention involved. This is for Brahma Sahampati of Buddhism (the Mahā Brahma of pre-Buddhist Brahmanism); it is also simultaneously a praise for the *toraṇa*.

Stotra: Praise of the *Toraṇa*, Which Is Like Brahma's Beauty and Power

Brahmā sarvāyuru manā nāde—Kanṭha kīnō mahēśvaraṃ
Agnīndō bhūmi sanno—me ran toraṇe lakṣanaṃ.

This is a high-sounding combination of Pāli or Sanskrit, or both, and Sinhala. The last line is straight Sinhala ("the beauty of this golden *toraṇa*") except that the last word, which should read *lakṣaṇa* in Sinhala, is given an ending *ṃ* to make it sound "classical" and thereby profound. It is, however, entirely possible that these *stotra*s were originally composed by persons familiar with Pāli or Sanskrit and later became distorted in the traditions of priests literate only in Sinhala.

Sanna: Exposition

[The *toraṇa* should be] like the ocean of Brahma described earlier, forty-eight leagues [*gavva*, about three and a half miles] in length, having mounds [?] about half a league in width, having a base seven and half leagues high; [the *toraṇa* should be] like the golden jeweled throne of the great Brahma Sahampati [Mahā Brahma Sahampati], king of heaven, who has a life-span of one *kalpa* [aeon], who is accompanied by a retinue of a Brahma army of one hundred thousand, who bears a jeweled crown twelve *yodun* [a *yoduna* is four *gavva*] high, who wears an heavenly shawl sixteen *yodun* long, and who is capable of illuminating ten thousand world systems [*sakvaḷa*] with the rays emanating from one [jeweled] finger. . . .

In these praises it is style as style that matters, not content. The *toraṇa* obviously cannot resemble Brahma's ocean or his person. The total impact of the verse *is* its exaggeration, which is an accepted literary convention. In addition, the highfalutin language and sonorous diction lend the *toraṇa* grandeur and dignity. It is very clear that the traditions of the *gammaḍuva* have been strongly influenced by the literary high culture.

Text 14a Songs on the *Toraṇa*

1. Take permission from the three-eyed guru
Extol the great virtues he possesses
Unfailingly then will blessings fall on us
Day by day may all flourish and prosper.

"Three-eyed guru": This could of course be Śiva, but it could also be Sakra, since some Sinhala traditions give him three eyes. However the appellation guru is appropriate for Śiva.

2. O Sun God possessed of great glory
And Moon God serenely shining
O Pattini Dēvi possessed of great might
Those who believe in you are gathered here.

3. Having journeyed to the mountaintop
She offered alms to a Pacceka Muni
And wished to become a Pattini
By such wishes [*prārthanā*] one's hopes are fulfilled.

Note that "a Pattini" suggests a sacred type like "a Buddha" or "a god." Thus Pattini of our texts is "a Pattini"; there could be others.

4. In ancient times
An illness afflicted
King Sēraman's head
That day, for that purpose a hall was performed.

5. Various ritual items [*pāli*] were performed
For the *toraṇa* then
It comes to us from that time
According to what knowledgeable priests tell us.

Text 14b

6. A golden *toraṇa* for the royal caste
A *toraṇa* of gems for the Brahman caste
A cloth *toraṇa* for the merchant caste
A *ram̆ba toraṇa* for the farmer caste.

I have translated *kula* as caste; it could mean "dynasty" also. *Kula* here is the ancient Sinhala equivalent of the Indian *varṇa*. *Ram̆ba toraṇa*: a *toraṇa* made of banana trunks, with the outer bark peeled off so that the creamy, glistening trunk is displayed. The *toraṇa* of the *gammaḍuva* is largely made of banana trunk and bark.

7. A royal caste must have gold
For the elephant caste it's surely gems

The *vaḍiga* class must have cloth
The *kula* with fields and lands must have a *ram̆ba toraṇa*

Elephant caste members are Brahmans, since they are to the social order what elephants are to the forest. I have translated the Sinhala word *pila* as class; it could also mean a team. *Vaḍiga*: Telegu country where many merchants probably originated.

Change in singing style: also brisk dancing in a circle.

8. What *toraṇa* for the royal caste?
What *toraṇa* for the Brahman caste?
What *toraṇa* for the merchant caste?
What *toraṇa* for the farmer caste?

9. A golden *toraṇa* for the royal caste
A gem *toraṇa* for the Brahman caste
A cloth *toraṇa* for the merchant caste
A *ram̆ba toraṇa* for the farmer caste.

10. How many days [of ritual] for the royal caste?
How many days for the Brahman caste?
How many days for the merchant caste?
How many days for the farmer caste?

11. Nine days for the royal caste
Seven days for the Brahman caste
Five days for the merchant caste
Three days for the farmer caste.

12. What pot for the royal caste?
What pot for the Brahman caste?
What pot for the merchant caste?
What pot for the farmer caste?

13. A golden pot for the royal caste
A pot made of gems for the Brahman caste
A pot made of cloth for the merchant caste
A full pot for the farmer caste.

The pots referred to are ornamental pots decorating the *toraṇa*. The farmer caste has an ordinary clay pot, but "full." All pots here, however, refer to the "full pot" (*pun kalasa*), symbol of plenty.

14. What kind of song for the gold *toraṇa*? Nine days' singing was performed
What kind of song for the Brahman caste? Seven days' singing was performed
What kind of song for the merchant caste? Five days' singing was performed.
What kind of song for the farmer caste? Three days' singing was performed.

15. A gold *toraṇa* for the royal caste: nine days' shawl fanning was performed
A gem *toraṇa* for the Brahman caste: seven days' shawl fanning was performed

A cloth *toraṇa* for the merchant caste: five days' shawl fanning was performed
A banana *toraṇa* for the farmer caste: three days' shawl fanning was performed.

16. Obtain the blessings of the caste god
    Obtain *varan* from the four castes [*kula*]
    And build *toraṇa*s for the four castes
    Respectfully singing these songs.

17. Brahmans possessed of wisdom
    They belong to an ancient caste
    Make a flower with gems
    The gem *toraṇa* of the Brahmans.

18. Heed the ancient caste [*kula*] rules
    And briskly collect a group of people
    Sing the praises of Pattini
    And construct a cloth *toraṇa* for merchants.

19. At an auspicious time
    Perform dances and construct the "openings" [*gäba*]
    Construct "openings" of four kinds
    Thus decorate the *ram̆ba toraṇa* of farmers.

The *gäba* or "womb" in the *toraṇa* refer to the separate sections, or openings, where various ritual objects can be placed.

Text 14c

20. That day she offered alms
    In the name of the great arhat(s)
    She arrives in a pleasing manner
    Pattini arrives from the plains of the sky.

Note tense changes in line 3 and 4 to indicate her arrival in the dance arena.

21. Owing to his past sins
    The king had a head disease—
    The comely Pattini arrived
    They prepared dances and offerings for her.

22. With great devotion the king and his following
    Decorated the dance land
    Like the *vimāna* of a divine city
    For the goddess, in ancient times.

Note again that dance arena is a "land" and the *toraṇa* is the *vimāna*, or abode of the gods.

23. By the [influence of] the *toraṇa*, the *dōsa*
    Will leave like ornaments taken off

For the *ātura*s here
May they be happily protected for five thousand years.

24. For achieving permanent happiness
[As if lustrated with ambrosial waters]
Place the folded hands on high
And worship with your hands on your head.

25. As if Brahma Sahampati had blessed them
All happiness is yours to win
May you live long
May your work prosper
May the *dōsa* be banished
And happiness be yours by this ritual [*yāga*].

Text 14d Further Songs on the *Toraṇa*

1. The royal caste coming from ancient times
The earthly caste [counterpart] of the *cakravartin* Brahma
The royal dance arena is as old as the ocean
The *makara toraṇa* is for the ancient royal caste.

Makara toraṇa: this is the classic design of the *toraṇa* as temple arch surmounted with the mythical dragon, *makara*.

2. Brahmans for what purpose is your knowledge of the four Vedas?
It is to banish the diseases [*rōga*] and suffering of earthly beings
Let us give praise [*āsiri*] for the merit of [Brahmans] helping mortals
The gem *toraṇa* is built for the comely Brahman caste.

3. Take golden shawls and cloth for the merchant *toraṇa*
That lady placed a signet [*pērās*] ring there
Give praise to the lovely Pattini
The *toraṇa* of the merchants must be built of cloth.

Line 2 is not clear to me. Perhaps it should read "as if that lady Pattini had placed her own signet ring there," that is, signifying her presence. Pattini in myth is a member of the merchant caste.

4. That day in King Gajabāhu's time
A *toraṇa* was built for the rightful use of men
Today we save these patients [*ātura*s] from disease and suffering
That day a *raṁba toraṇa* was made for the farmer caste.

Note again the relationship between time past and time present: "that day—today." "That day" in this case refers to Gajabāhu, who is credited with constructing a *toraṇa*. The Gajabāhu reference here seems to contradict the notion that the original *toraṇa* of the *gammaḍuva* was constructed by Sēraman. However, it may also refer to Gajabāhu's constructing a *toraṇa* for the central Pattini shrine at Navagamuva.

5. Construct a seven-tiered *toraṇa* and make openings therein

And on the sides make spires and beauteous paintings
Perform processions in honor of the good Pattini
And take the golden anklet and place it there.

6. Light lamps, give offerings, and coins [*pańḍuru*] to the priest
Here are humans who are worshiping the goddess
Take the anklet and be ready to move
Toward the *āturas*; protect them and obtain merit.

7. Then the goddess Seven Pattini sees with her divine eyes
The people in this country who have arranged dances in her honor
She sees with divine eyes the sufferings of all mortals
With your warrant protect this country [place] for five thousand years.

8. She looks upon the suffering borne by mortals
She takes the golden anklet, with gems inside it, and sounds it
Today I have built a *toraṇa* and I implore you
O goddess Pattini to protect these mortals assembled here.

9. In the name of the noble Pattini, glorious goddess
I have made a *toraṇa* palace according to her wishes
And we play music to please the *toraṇa*
This *toraṇa* we display to the goddess in her honor.

Note again, the *toraṇa* is a palace of the goddess: it is also a gift to the goddess, a palace offered to her by her devotees.

10. At the four corners put in flowers made of yellow coconut leaves
Remember the dragon vehicle [*makara vāhana*] below
Bring beautiful pots to decorate the sides
And build the *makara toraṇa* in this manner.

Several verses containing formal descriptions of the decorations in the *toraṇa* are omitted.

11. That day in Ruvanvälla the people assembled
And constructed a *toraṇa* within the sixty-*riyan* hall
That day musk and camphor were offered
That day a ritual [*yāga*] was performed to banish *dōsa*.

12. At the right height make a throne [*asna*] for the deity
Select red and blue colored flowers
Light lamps and spray the throne with water [*pän*]
The *toraṇa* thus displayed will banish pestilence.

13. In the eight corners are designs of flower petals
Decorate the middle openings with festoons of trailing vines
Play music to please the *toraṇa*
This *toraṇa* we display in honor of the goddess.

The *toraṇa yāgaya* is standard all over the cultural area discussed here, and some of it has a pan-Sinhala application. In Sīnigama there is an extra text in which praise is given to the major gods in the form of *śloka* (Sanskrit couplets) and *sanna* (exposition) in the following order: Nātha, Viṣṇu, Saman, Kataragama, Pattini, Dēvatā Baṇḍāra, and Devol Deviyo. Note that Vibhīṣaṇa is otiose.

Texts of the *Telmē* Ritual

Text 19a Inviting the Twelve Gods to Witness [Eye] the *Telmē*

1. Bow low and worship the Three Jewels
Then Sumana [Saman] and Mahasen [Kataragama]
These mighty beings with devotion
Secondarily give this [dance offering] to the Twelve Gods.

The Twelve Gods are secondary (*devanuven*) to the main ones, hence perhaps the counterclockwise dance. For a further analysis of the cult of the Twelve Gods see chapter 6 (pp. 285–93).

2. Purify the dance area well
Near the couch
Of the foremost Prince Skanda
And decorate [the altar] beautifully.

3. Sandal-milk-water and coconut flowers
And objects necessary for the hair wash [*nānu*]
Keep them decorously on the couch
Offer them to the Twelve Gods with glad heart.

4. Dance with enthusiasm
The *telmē* dance consecrated to them
The Twelve Gods cast their eyes
Their divine eyes on the *telmē* dance.

5. For the *telmē* dance offering
People give *pañḍuru* in good spirit
The Twelve Gods cast their divine eyes
On the *telmē* dance offering.

6. Plant a taper [*vilakku*] above
Make an offering of a gold coin
Purify a priest
And offer thanks to the god.

The god here is Doḷaha Deviyo or the Twelve Gods viewed in the singular as a collectivity.

7. In the name of these patients [*ātura*s]
Make an offering of lights
Light up the fire fence
Banish *dōsa* by the *pañḍuru* given.

"Fire fence": I suppose this refers to the line of torches in the dance.

Text 19b

1. The goddess Pattini, who has warrant, has arrived in her couch [*yahana*]
   That golden chair [*puṭuva*] is beautifully and elaborately decorated
   With proper spirit offer coconut flowers scented like sandal
   And joyously give lights and the smoke from coal and *dummala* [resin].

Line 2 refers to the altar as a phenomenal object (the chair), while line 1 refers to the altar as a symbolic object (couch). Line 4: actually *dummala*, or resin, is not used for the gods except to clear evil spirits around them and to purify the sacred area.

2. Hang canopies above, curtains around, and light torches
   With beautiful body movements to please the mind
   Offer the *telmē* in good spirit in the dance arena
   Ensure today that the Twelve King-Gods will set their eyes here.

3. Preeminent Viṣṇu, Saman, Vibhīṣaṇa, Nātha, and Skanda
   Beautiful Pattini of the fire, Vāsala, and mighty Devol
   O preeminent *suras*, rulers of human beings
   Take the offering of the *telmē* in this fruitful dance hall.

I shall demonstrate in chapter 6 that the Twelve Gods are a set of moribund deities in this culture area. There is therefore a tendency to replace them with the well-known gods of the pantheon.

4. Decorate a seat beautifully for him who arrives first
   Kalikot nānu, you have arrived for the offering of the *telmē*
   Make a brightly colored seat for the first who arrives
   Kalikot, Kulakonta, Sātā have now arrived.

Kalikot: could mean "Calicut"; the other terms are obscure, except Sātā, who is referred to in other texts, along with Yā. See pages 589–90 for a possible identification of Sātā.

5. You priests diligently sanctify [*pē*] the throne [*asna*] for the king
   Worship and listen to the plaints uttered by the worshiping priests
   The minor king [*mada raja*], the subking [*yuvaraja*, "crown prince"] and the two *kaṇḍāraja*
   Today O gods witness with pleasure this *telmē* dance.

I have translated *mada raja* as minor king (or subking) in one sense of *mada*, meaning "little." However *mada* is lust, and *mada raja* can refer to Anaṅga, the Indian Cupid. *Kaṇḍāraja*: Pānama people translated this as *baṇḍāra*, "lord," that is, governor. It could also mean chief (*rāja*) of a regiment (*kaṇḍāyama*).

6. The sacred [*pē*] goddess Pattini appeared in Pāṇḍi city
   That time she performed rites and quelled the flames
   She placed the country in charge of Yā raja and Sulaṁbā raja
   I offer her the *telmē* performed in this auspicious dance arena.

I have translated *pē* as "sacred" instead of "consecrated." Yā raja is a kinsmen of Kōvalaṉ, Pattini's husband; and Sulaṁbā raja is an obscure personage unknown to present-day performers. The verse refers to Pattini's giving over the ravaged city of Madurai to these two kings.

7. Lay coconut flowers removed from their sheaths; light lamps
Offer the *äsala* procession of *telmē*
Mada raja, Yuvaraja, Kalikot come down here
Bring festival joy to this village here

Äsala perahära: *telmē* is viewed as a "procession in Äsala," like that of the annual procession of the palace of the tooth relic. In the latter in Äsala (July) the king and chiefs assemble in public and parade with the gods and the tooth relic.

8. Make blue silk curtains for the couch you have made
The Mada raja and Yuvaraja have cast their looks here
And also the kings, Kalikot, Sātā, Kulakonta
This day continue to make this village prosper.

The significance of the Twelve Gods will be discussed in the ritual known as the spectacle for the Twelve Gods performed later (pp. 156–71) and in my analysis of the stratigraphy of *gammaḍuva* myths and rituals in chapter 6.

Texts on the Torch of Time for Vāhala Alias Däḍimuṇḍa Alias Dēvatā Baṇḍāra Alias Alutnuvara Deviyo

Text 24 Invocation to Däḍimuṇḍa

I have arbitrarily broken up this invocation into verse paragraphs for convenience.

A. Heavy with prosperity this Sri Lanka
The Vāsala god's birth
I shall recite in an invocation.
Lord of the rose apple continent
Born in the middle *maṇḍala*
Possessed of ten avatars
Known as Däḍimuṇḍa
Wearing white shawls
With a golden stick
Held in his hand
A gem-studded gold crown
Worn on his head.
He carries a thousand arrows
And with a thundering sound
He holds the thousand arrows
With the little finger of his right hand
And shoots the thousand arrows
With the little finger of his left hand
Thus his glory and renown
Spread the world over.

B. Our Muni, in order to be Buddha
Arrived expeditiously [under the bo tree]
He threw eight fistfuls of *kusa* grass
And the earth trembled
A diamond throne [*vajrāsana*] miraculously arose
Many *riyan* its height.
This diamond throne having arisen
Settled against the sacred bo tree.
The Buddha resolved thus:
By the power of past merit
I will be victorious in the Māra struggle
And won't leave till I am Buddha.
Seated against the bo tree
On his diamond throne
There he stayed full of joy.

C. The god Sakra with his divine eye
Saw that they [the gods] must attend
The victory festival of the Buddha.
From the sixteen Brahmā worlds
The gods assembled there
The gods of the ten heavens
Also assembled there
And the *nāga* kings of the *nāga* world
And the *asura*s of the *asura* world
And the gods in this, our world.
All these gods assembled
Displaying their power and glory
They awaited with pleasure
For our Muni to become Buddha.

D. But Vasavat who saw all this
Fearing our Muni's Buddhahood
Assembled his huge Māra army
With a force to tilt the earth o'er.
That Vasavat unafraid
Climbed atop his war elephant
He created ten hands [for himself]
Then armed with a discus
He stood on Sakvaḷa Rock
And shouted his *māra* [death] cry
The gods who heard that cry
Ran away in fear
All the gods in fright
With multitudinous cries ran away
Leaving our Muni all alone.

Yet by the power of his ten perfections [*pāramitā*]
He would triumph in the Māra war
And become Buddha of the three worlds.

E. Then thought our Muni
Who stays near me now?
The *dēvatā* named Däḍimuṇḍa
Possessed of ten apparitions
Stayed near him unafraid.
[The Buddha told him]
Those demon hosts haunting this world
Are in your charge now.
He was given a warrant that day
To cast his divine eye upon
The five hundred apparitional forms
And the two thousand small islands
Over the Four Dēvāles
And the twenty-four little shrines [*alli*].
The backs of *dēvatā*s
He infested with worms
And beating them, chased 'em away
He spread his glory, power, and might.
There's no one with your might
None so bold [*däḍi*] in the whole world
For this glorious god
We make a couch
And build a *ram̆ba toraṇa*
Flowers and betel leaves
Incense, musk, and *kuṅkuma*
Offer we in your altar [*yahana*]
And sound the five kinds of music. . . .

Paragraph E ends with the conventional plea asking the god to protect the congregation, banish disease, and bring about prosperity and long life. I have omitted this finale.

Commentary on the Invocation to Däḍimuṇḍa

Paragraph A

In line 1 the god is called Vāsala, or Vāhala, which means palace. In Sīnigama this deity is also called Vāsala; thus he is, or was at one time, viewed as a guardian of a palace. In Ratnapura Vāsala is seen as a different god, one of the Devol Deviyo; it is of course possible for there to be several such guardians. However, in Rabalīya, Heyiaṅtuḍuva, and Mātara the god Vāsala is clearly identified with Dēvatā Baṇḍāra or Däḍimuṇḍa. We can make two reasonable inferences on the basis of our data: That Vāsala was a separate god, distinct from Däḍimuṇḍa, but later identified with him, or that Vāsala was an honorific given to several deities. In this culture area Vāsala Mudali (translated into English as Gate Mudaliyar) was an official of the palace, an honorific highly appropriate to a minor god like Dēvatā Baṇḍāra or Devol Deviyo. In Dēvatā Baṇḍāra's case the designation is highly appropriate because he built a temple (*vāsala*) at Alutnuvara. Furthermore, historically he was not the major god of Alutnuvara (who was Viṣṇu until the mid-seventeenth century) but probably his attendant, like a *vāsala* official, or the guardian of the palace (i.e., temple) of Viṣṇu.

Paragraph B

Here the poem refers to Buddha legend where the Buddha threw seven blades of *kusa* grass that were miraculously transformed into a diamond throne, or *vajrāsana*. *Vajra*, translated as "diamond," also means "thunderbolt," generally Indra's thunderbolt. Both are viewed as hard and perhaps of the same substance.

Paragraph C

This paragraph contains a reference to the Buddha's impending enlightenment, or *budu magul*. *Magul* or *maṅgala* indicates that it is a joyous and auspicious event; it is also known as *jayamaṅgala* (*jaya* meaning "victory") owing to Buddha's triumph over Māra, or death.

Paragraph D

Māra, or death, is personified in Buddhism as Vasavat, a divine being, much like Satan in Christianity (see Ling 1962; Boyd 1975). He is accompanied by a host of demons and female temptresses. The hosts of Māra are *dasa bimbara*, translated as "a force to tilt the earth o'er." Literally *bimbara* is a multitude that if placed on one side of the earth will tilt it; *dasa* is ten; thus "ten times an earth-tilting multitude."

The Buddha's perfections, or *pāramitā*, refer to the ten virtues cultivated by Buddhas through many lifetimes. These virtues are necessary for achieving Buddhahood.

Paragraph E

This paragraph explains why the god is called Däḍimuṇḍa. He is *däḍi*, "fearless," "stern," "firm," since he stood by the Buddha when others fled. However the Sinhala texts do not explain *muṇḍa*. In Sinhala *muṇḍa* means "empty," or it could by extension refer to a shaven head. Perhaps the meaning of Däḍimuṇḍa is like the English "headstrong," like another god Vīramuṇḍa, Muṇḍa the courageous. It is also possible that *muṇḍa* is derived from a Dravidian word whose origin is unknown. There is also the remote possibility that Däḍimuṇḍa and Vīramuṇḍa were originally from eastern India where Muṇḍa languages are spoken. Dowson's dictionary of mythology says that Muṇḍa is the name of a demon slain by Durgā. Hence one appelation of Durgā is Cā-muṇḍa, victorious over Muṇḍa (Dowson 1953, pp. 64–65). It is possible that Däḍimuṇḍa is related to this personage, but the connections, if any, are impossible to determine at this stage of research.

The case for Däḍimuṇḍa as an original Dravidian god receives extra support from references to numerology not found elsewhere in Sinhala mythology. For example, he is in charge of two thousand small islands and twenty-four small shrines or *alli*. The latter is a South Indian (Dravidian) concept only rarely used in Sri Lanka. Some of these "alien" references are changed in the Rabalīya text quoted above but are found intact in the Sīnigama text. For example, Sīnigama texts refer to "five hundred large islands," which is converted into "five hundred apparitional forms" in Rabalīya. Sīnigama also refers to an alien notion in the line "over the two thousand large islands," which is converted in Rabalīya into "over the Four Dēvāles," which does not make much sense.

The significance of the myths of Dēvatā Baṇḍāra for Sinhala culture history will be analyzed in chapter 6. Here it is enough to state that Dēvatā Baṇḍāra has assimilated some of the Viṣṇu mythology, both indigenous or Buddhist Viṣṇu mythology and also Hindu Viṣṇu mythology. For example, he is the defender of the Buddha in the Māra war, a role attributed to Upulvan (or Viṣṇu) in fifteenth-century poetry, and in our Viṣṇu invocation (chap. 3, text 6). He has ten avatars, a part of his taking over Hindu attributes of Viṣṇu. So also is the reference to his being "lord of the rose apple continent," and perhaps being "born in the middle *maṇḍala*."

Text 25 *Däḍimuṇḍa Hālla*, or the Story of Däḍimuṇḍa

Text 25 sung during the Vāhala dance is one of the most popular ritual texts in Sri Lanka, sold in cheap popular editions everywhere as *galakäpū hālla*, or "the story of the hewing of the rock."

The text recited in the Vāhala dance is identical to the printed versions I have seen except that the latter have twenty-eight stanzas whereas only about half that many are actually sung in the *gammaḍuva*. In view of the importance of this text, I have translated the full printed version edited by N. J. Cooray in 1961 and included two stanzas sung in the Rabalīya tradition that are not found in the Cooray edition.

1. The noble sage Siduhat Siddhārtha
And the Dhamma he gave the whole world
And the Saṅgha, these triple gems
I worship, head bowed, with devotion.

2. When the Māra hosts assembled
In ten "earth-tilting hosts" for war
The gods ran away
Far beyond Sakvaḷa Rock.

3. With his back against the bo tree
He sat on his diamond throne [*vidurāsana*]
Even if Māra comes to do battle
I'll move not, till I achieve enlightenment.

4. Vasavat saw him that day
And gathered together his Māra [Death] army
In order to prevent his Buddhahood
[Vasavat] surrounded him with his Māra host.

5. The gods ran away
Leaving the Buddha all alone
Yet a resolute deity stayed on
"I will fight them" he said.

Line 3: the Sinhala word is *däḍi*, which I translate here as "resolute," and elsewhere as "firm," "stern," "bold."

6. Without taking up a weapon
With only his golden cane in his right hand
"I'll beat them and cut them up"
"I will do battle," he told the sage.

7. "I have offered ten kinds of alms
And reared the ten warriors
Patiently look how I wage war"
Thus said the sage to Māra.

Line 1 refers to the various kinds of self-sacrifices performed by the Buddha in previous births; and line 2 is a metaphor for the ten perfections cultivated by him through many lifetimes.

8. Neither in the six worlds of gods
Nor in the *nāga* world, nor the three worlds
There is none to compare
With him who is named Muṇḍa, the stern [*däḍi*].

9. Worshiping the Buddha and obtaining his permission [literally, "forgiveness"]
He went to pay respects to king Vessamuni
Who gave him charge over all demons,
Then he paid homage to Pulvan the *sura*.

10. He [Upulvan] surveyed the world
And told the great *dēvatā* thus:
Descend into Māyāraṭa
To build a city there.

Māyāraṭa is one of the three divisions of ancient Sri Lanka, consisting largely of the present Western Province and parts of Sabaragamuva. The shrine of Dēvatā Baṇḍāra at Alutnuvara was probably on the fringe of Māyāraṭa. "City" in line 4 means "divine city."

11. Conceived in Somavati's womb
And born in nine months and half
He died soon after
In the house which was burned to ashes.

12. The woman's child who was burned
He was seen lying in the ashes
Next morning by the king's ministers
That prince was raised back to life.

Stanzas 11 and 12 are references to Däḍimuṇḍa's unusual birth, probably a previous birth, suddenly included here; a not uncharacteristic feature of Sinhala ritual texts. Actually the text begins with a catalog of events in the life of Däḍimuṇḍa. It starts with his defense of the Buddha and then makes brief references to his birth. The following verses deal with the image (of this god?) washed up on the shore. All these are poetic techniques that give the reader glimpses into the god's prowess as a preliminary to the main thrust of the text, which is a description of one major event in his life—how he broke the rock and built the shrine at Alutnuvara with the aid of demons.

13. In the ocean's midst
Torches shed a vast light
Showing a great sandal log
The waves' force brought it ashore.

14. Two persons got possessed,
Taking the gods image
Near a city in Māya
They placed it in a cave.

The reference here is to the image of Viṣṇu washed ashore near Devundara, which was later enshrined in the great temple for Viṣṇu; see Paranavitana (1953) for details. I shall discuss in chapter 6 the manner in which the Viṣṇu and Dädimuṇḍa myths coalesced. Note, however, that the sandalwood "log" is here identified with the god of Alutnuvara.

15. The king protected it for twenty years
He performed processions in Äsala [in its honor]
Throughout his city and kingdom
He offered it various gifts.

16. Thereafter that noble king
Who showed compassion on the hill country [*uḍa raṭa*]
According to ancient custom
Chose a central site in the Four Kōrales.

The Four Kōrales is where Alutnuvara is situated. Dēvatā Baṇḍāra is the god of the Four Kōrales.

17. Surveying his surroundings
He reached Kirungandeniya
Then along a road
Till he reached a beautiful rock cave.

Kirungandeniya is the village near Alutnuvara Dēvāle. "Beautiful rock cave" in a literal translation should read "golden rock cave." The last line implies, I think, that he deposited the "sandal log" in the cave. The Sinhala reads:

pāraka gosin siṭa
vaḍamakaravan gal guhāvaṭa.

18. In the city of the king
The milk cows yielded blood
What kind of magic is this?
The wise ministers informed [the king].

19. The king saw [a location] in a dream
The ground was cleared of trees and roots
He built a three-story pavilion
Where the [god's] cane was found.

Stanzas 18 and 19 sound enigmatic, since many details familiar to the audience are left unsaid. The king had deposited the "sandal log" (or image) in a cave near Kirungandeniya. But obviously this was not an adequate abode for the god. Hence evil omens appeared—the king's cows yielded blood instead of milk. Thereafter the king dreamed a dream in which he was instructed to build a "city" for the god at the place where the god's cane would be found.

20. A dome of sandalwood
He made and an antechamber [*diggē*] in the center
And six and thirty halls
Then he built the beautiful [Alutnuvara].

Alutnuvara literally means "new city," that is, a new city of the gods, in the same sense that the *gammaḍuva* is a divine city. In chapter 6 I shall show that this new city was built originally for Viṣṇu-Upulvan, and not for Dēvatā Baṇḍāra-Däḍimuṇḍa. Note that even here Dēvatā Baṇḍāra only helped in the construction of the city. It is not said anywhere that this is his "city."

21. The entrance to the *maluva*
Was blocked by a large rock
"We can't break this"
They [the ministers] informed the "chief of *dēvatās*" [*dēvatā suriňdu*].

Maluva is the large compound at the entrance of a sacred shrine. It is possible that the "king" in the earlier stanzas is Dēvatā Baṇḍāra himself.

22. Having listened to the ministers
He saw that the compound was uneven
I will show my power over the demons
Make them break the rock for the *maluva*.

23. Make *kävun* and squares of milk rice
We won't make them small, we'll give you one, even two
This offering will banish the fatigue of the demons
Break down the rock this night itself [O demons].

24. Now the floor was smeared with sandal paste and cow dung
And hung all around with areca nut flowers
Lovely sensual damsels came there
And heaped large amounts of milk rice.

Reference is to the compound floor purified and decorated, and full of milk rice for the demons who were going to break the rock that blocked its entrance.

25. Demons from Bangala, Gavudi and Malala
From Kongani, Jāvaka, and Vaḍiga Dēsa
From Kannaḍi, Kavuḍi, and Vaḍiga land
These demons were brought to Sinhala.

Bangala, Bengal; Gavudi, eastern India; Malala, Malabar; Kongani, Konkani (Goa?); Jāvaka, Java; Vaḍiga, Andhra Pradesh; Kannaḍi, Kannaḍa land; Kavuḍi, Gavuḍi, eastern India.

26. Here are utterly delicious foods for you to eat

Take up your pickaxes and crowbars
And whatever weapons you may need
And totally destroy the rock.

27. Like peals of thunder across the sky
Or the anger of the Earth Goddess
Or the sound of a gun to shake the earth
They broke the rock as if playing ball.

28. Each spoke the language of the country he came from
O Tamil demons whose joyful cries resound!
Some of them exchange blows in anger
These demons who knew not Sinhala.

29. Truly each one broke the rock hard
Sometimes by mistake they fought each other
Those that lost moved aside [in shame]
Others used their shoulders to push aside the rocks.

30. They broke the rock and leveled the ground
They filled streams and ponds and evened the ground
And made decorative arches with the stones
And sought permission [from the god] to leave.

In line 3 the Sinhala word *rälapana* baffles me. I have intuitively translated it as "decorative arches" (*rälipālam*). Line 4: the demons have finished their task, but they are reluctant to leave.

31. "Permit us to stay in this country
And we'll do whatever you say O king
Else we'll not be able to see our god."
Sorrowful they fell and wept at his sacred feet.

The real reason for the demons' reluctance to go is that they are attracted by Sinhala girls, whom they would like to possess.

32. "Their beauty, sensuousness and golden form like sandal
Their prattle like chatter of female parrots
With their hair down and decked with flowers
How can we leave these coy damsels and depart?"

33. "O demons you know not the magic of Sinhalas
We'll bind you with mantras and hold you prisoner
We'll place you on machines and torture you
And put you in the smokehouse to inhale black soot.

34. "Cause not illness in the women you behold
And envy not those around you
Like the waters from a breached tank bund
Go ye all to your own land."

35. People heard he'd smashed the rock and showed his might
They crowded in from province and village
Crowd upon crowd came there to watch
And came there to worship [the god].

36. They wash their hair and brush their teeth
And wear white cloth set with ruffles
They take gifts of betel, areca, and rice
They offer it [to him] and happily depart.

37. People bring along women possessed by demons
With burning feelings in their lower bellies
They come to the compound and whirl around
The demons [within them] seek permission to depart.

Note line 2, which suggests the sexual nature of female demonic possession.

38. Tied to trees they are beaten, till the cane breaks
They stand in the sun with stones on their heads
"Do not deceive, make a sign that you'll leave."
"Without looking back we'll leave this land."

39. [Thorny] kapok posts were planted around the compound
The Devol demons were then invited [to possess the patient]
They had to embrace the posts; then tied to them.
O Devol heed the god's command and leave [the patient].

Stanza 37 refers to possessed women who come to be cured at the Alutnuvara shrine. Stanza 38 shows that these women were beaten (i.e., the demons within them) and made to suffer. Beating women for this purpose is common in Sinhala exorcisms (see Obeyesekere 1975b for a case study). Line 3 of the same stanza refers to the fact that demons make a sign (e.g., breaking the branch of a tree) as they leave the patient's body and the premises. H. C. P. Bell in his *Report on the Kegalle District* (1892), pp. 46–48) has a good description from the late nineteenth century of the large numbers of females who came here to be exorcised. Stanza 39 refers to Devol *demons* who possess women rather than to Devol gods.

40. O the pain inflicted on Pilli and Sūniyan demons
They were brought into *alli* shrines, tied and beaten
With fallen faces, they fell down and worshiped [the god]
Pilli demons depart if you want to escape further tortures.

Alli are small shrines where exorcisms take place. They are no longer extant but were known in the nineteenth century.

The printed text has eight long verses that are not sung in the *gammaḍuva*. I have omitted them here. In the Rabalīya tradition this text concludes with two stanzas that are not found in the printed text.

41. Speak of his command for the whole world to hear

Is there any other *sura* who rules over demons?
He who stayed near the Buddha and did him service
Arrive O glorious divine *sura*.

42. Make a throne [*asna*] for Pulvan the *sura*
Offer flowers and scents on his altar
Light lamps and make the right offerings
Playfully arrive here O Däḍimuṇḍa.

Line 1 refers to Däḍimuṇḍa as Upulvan (Pulvan), a deity generally identified as Viṣṇu. The further identification of Upulvan with Däḍimuṇḍa will be explained in chapter 6.

Text Sung at the Cutting of the *Milla* Tree

Text 27 Songs on Devol Deviyo

1. In old times they left for their desolate journey
They started their voyage for trading purposes
May such suffering never occur again!
Let us sing about the might of the Devol god.

2. They expeditiously built seven ships
And got ready to leave their country and cross the seas
They sighted the good port of Pānadura
And soon they saw the Sambar Rock [Gōnāgala].

Fast singing style:

3. The ship swept past Gintoṭa
They saw Unavaṭuna, a good place to stay
In order to land there on that day
The ship turned around [toward land].

4. The monsoon winds strongly erupted
Frightening waves relentlessly bore on
It was impossible to land ashore
The richly laden ship broke asunder.

5. Ropes, oars, sails all broke loose
They clung to the beautiful boards
They tied various bundles together
And swam looking hither and thither.

6. They swam for seven days in the ocean
Their renown and might will spread over the world!
O great Sāmi possessed of might and rightness
He created a stone raft according to his wish.

A somewhat ambiguous last line. Contradicts other accounts that say the goddess of the sea created the stone raft. However, line 3 has "great Sāmi," which could refer to this goddess, in which case line 4 should have "she" instead of "he." The text from the Devol Deviyo temple at Sīnigama is identical.

7. Like a fluff of cotton floats the stone raft
   What being could have created this!
   By the command of Devol, god of this age [*kalpa*]
   Before long the stone raft reached the shore.

8. The strong winds smashed the seven ships
   Their sin and merit must have had its course that day
   The fires [from the ships] spread over the earth
   Like the shining heavenly abodes of the gods.

This stanza logically should have come earlier.

9. At the *dēvāle* of the strong mighty god
   Accept at this time offerings and *pan̆ḍuru* [coins]
   We blow *kombu* and *horaṇǟ* in your honor
   Vēragoḍa is where the god's *dēvāle* lies.

Verses 7, 8, and 9 are not found in the Sīnigama tradition.
Change in singing style to quick, rapid verse

Go into the forest and cut fresh *milla*
Make a fire and enclose it with curtains
It lights up like cotton wool aflame
Look at the fire's might O Devol demons.

Devol demons come dance in the arena!
And alight on the burning flaming logs
Make cool the fire like the waters of the sea
The Devol troop enters and plays in the fire.

There are many more songs that can be sung here. The Sīnigama tradition has six other songs with emphasis in the cooling of the fire, three of which I quote below. It should be noted that the invocation for Devol (text 26) could be recited here and at other places where Devol is invoked in the hall. The songs above are specially meant for the fire trampling ritual, but they are sung in the *milla käpīma* procession also.

Text 27 Songs on Devol Deviyo (Sīnigama)

1. God Devol, he is arriving in his stone raft
   He accepts dance offerings from all
   They have been given neighboring villages as offerings
   See! Devol god has arrived in the midst of the fire.

2. It will be cool like the waters of the paddy field
   It will become cool as if you have dived and swam in water
   Break virgin wood from the forest and bring it here
   O Devol give us warrant to trample the fire.

3. It will be cool like bathing in an unfamiliar river

With courage unflinching they jump into the middle of the fire
That day they landed and their renown spread wide and far
That day the goddess Pattini named them Devol god.

Notice the last line: "named them Devol god": they are plural and singular.

Text of the Dawn Watch to the Kurumbara Demons

Text 29 Invitation to Kurumbara

1. Basma at one time obtained permission from Viṣṇu
While he was practising *tapas* [austerities]
His hand was consumed by fire by Viṣṇu's great command
Descend O glorious Kurumbara of the fire and take this offering.

Line 1 is puzzling, since myth states that it was Śiva who gave the boon to Basma. Perhaps the "permission" referred to here is where Viṣṇu in the form of Mōhinī asked Basma (gave him permission) to marry "him." See text 26 (pp. 141–43) for details of this myth. Line 4: "Descend" is *bäsa*, a brusque form of address as if to a social inferior. Nevertheless, Kurumbara also has *teda* "glory," "might," largely because he is born of fire.

2. He saw her and asked her to marry her
The lady asked him to swear to leave her never
"I'll never leave you" he swore [and touched his head]
Come descend O glorious Kurumbara of the fire.

In line 1, "her" refers to Viṣṇu in the guise of a female (Mōhinī). See text 26 for details of the Basma myth.

3. "Divine maiden how can I lie in bed alone?
Is there a married person in this city?
I remember the joys of love I experienced before."
Come and take this offering O Kurumbara of the fire.

Lines 1 and 3 are not fully clear to me. I think they refer to Basma the *asura* pining for the love of Śiva's consort, Umā. In line 2 Basma thinks of Śiva, who is Umā's husband.

4. In ancient times that god [Viṣṇu] created a swing
She was walking up and down in great beauty
The *asura* observed her there
Come then O Fire Kurumbara into this dance hall.

This stanza again refers to the Basma myth. "She" in line 2 is Viṣṇu in the guise of Umā, Śiva's consort, out to seduce and destroy Basma. Line 4: "dance hall" is *raňga maṇḍala*, which, as I said earlier, could have the meaning of "orbit of [divine] influence."

The preceding songs on Gini (fire) Kurumbara are called *nurā kavi*, or love poetry. This is because Gini Kurumbara arose from the flames of the lustful *asura* Basma. He is "born of Basma" and is a manifestation of him, sharing his lustful propensities. Fire here represents Basma's consuming passion and has strong erotic connotations. Gini Kurumbara is the major form of Kurumbara. The rest of the stanzas deal with other apparitional forms of this deity.

5. With lust, the noble one looks upon human abodes
His twelve apparitions are seen everywhere
I shall now utter the command of Vessamuni
O Samayan Kurumbara come take this offering.

Line 3: Vessamuni is Vaiṣaravaṇa, the Buddhist guardian of the north and the overlord of demons. Last line: "Samayan" simply means "demon."

6. Caskets are floating in the middle of the seven seas
There are golden necklaces around these seven caskets
Golden flowers are blooming in the seven necklaces
Rāja Kurumbara you are invited to take this offering.

The mythology here eludes me. Perhaps this is an ancient myth of Kurumbara and his coming to Sri Lanka across the oceans. One *gammaḍuva* myth states that he came to Sri Lanka with Devol Deviyo.

The last line contains an interesting linguistic usage. I have translated *väḍa* as "you are invited." Actually *väḍa* is from *vaḍinava*, an invitational form to superiors, such as monks and deities, as we saw earlier. Thus it is appropriate for this form of Kurumbara, who is a *rāja* (king). Nevertheless, this is only an apparitional form of Kurumbara, who is basically a demon. Hence *väḍa*, a brusque form of the more elevated *vaḍinava*, is used.

7. Our bodhisattva as a monkey stepped into the river
And he became a prey of the crocodile
There's a prey for you up this river
O Kurumbara of pestilence come down for this offering.

Lines 1 and 2 refer to *Kapi Jātaka*; see Cowell, 3:218). "Prey": the Sinhala term *godura* in line 3 refers to the offering the priest promises to place upstream—probably an empty promise.

8. With a golden goad in hand
And with a golden yoke
And stopping the bulls at Kiriňdi river
O Gopāla Kurumbara descend and take this offering.

Gopāla is "cowherd." This is one form of Kurumbara.

9. The sixty [Kurumbara] accompanied by a retinue of demons
Going from one country to another
Rightfully I'll give the Buddha's command
O sixty Kurumbara come and get these offerings.

Line 1 shows that Kurumbara is a powerful demon accompanied by a host of other demons.

10. [She] guards the resounding waterways
And haunts the sandbanks raised in midriver
Here's a sacrifice all ready for your play
O Giri Kurumbara of the streams take this offering.

Here Kurumbara is "Giri," a female counterpart of Garā. Probably a female Kurumbara who seduces the unwary like Giri of the Garā myth. See texts 31 and 32.

11. With a jump he ascends the skies
And wanders from region to region
Weren't you born in the region of Kāsi
O Dēsa [region] Kurumbara come and take this offering.

5

The Myths of the Pattini Cycle

The Sinhala myths directly relating to the life of Pattini are strikingly similar to those sung by the east coast Tamils (Hindus) of Sri Lanka, and also to the *Cilappatikāram*. They all are very likely derived from the same tradition of myth and ritual. In the Sinhala areas only two of these myths are enacted: *aṁba vidamana*, or the shooting of the mango," and *marā ipäddīma*, "killing and resurrection." In this chapter I shall present these two enactments in detail and summarize the other important myths of the Pattini cycle. For the most part I shall use Hevawasam's edition of the Pattini myths so that the reader familiar with Sinhala can refer to this edition for more information (Hevawasam 1974).

Text 34 *Pattini Pätuma*: The Wish to Become a Pattini

Pätuma is from the Sanskrit *prārthanā*, a wish associated with the performance of a meritorious act.

A good summary of this text is available in Nevill (1955, p. 150) which I quote below.

> This is one of the Pan-tis-kol-mura collection used at the Dondra temple. The subject is the birth of Pattini as daughter of Tirima Kulangana, queen of Manimega nuwara, and the Situ Bolanda. When she was seven years old, she went to bathe with a thousand maidens, and on her way heard that a merchant of Kalinga was giving Buddhist robes in alms, and she desired herself to give one. There were in those days a thousand Bambas or Brahmans in Manimega nuwara, who received alms from the citizens, as did Kakusanda Budu and his rahats. Pattini then offered in alms one thousand katina robes, and three thousand ordinary robes, herself. At the same time her maidens brought a honey mango as a gift for the priests. As one mango was useless, Pattini planted it, and it grew miraculously and produced ripe fruit, which she offered to Kakusanda Budu and his rahats. She then formed the wish that by the merit of the honey mango alms she might be born in a golden mango, and subdue the pride of a mighty king, becoming greater than gods and men, able to emit flames from her ten fingers, and again to quench those flames with nectar. The merchant from Kalinga prayed that he might become the king of Pandi.
>
> After this, by permission of Kakusanda, and of her parents, she became irddi on the Andun Giri, or Black-rock mountains.

Most of this text deals with the description of Maṇimegha city, the pregnancy longings of Tirimā, or Sirimā, the birth of Pattini, and the description of the magnificent alms of robes, as well as of the miracle mango. The episode of the mango seems to have been influenced by the Buddha legend. According to this legend the Buddha wanted to show (reluctantly) his capacity to perform miracles in order to vanquish the Jainas. He said he would perform a miracle under a mango tree. To prevent this, the Jainas cut all the mango trees. Then the Buddha took a mango seed and planted it: immediately it grew to full size and bore fruit.

The text is a relatively short one, seventy-eight stanzas in Hevawasam's edition. It ends with Pattini's wish to be born from a mango.

69. When the time for offering mangoes arrived
And seeing that the mangoes were ripe
She covered them in cloth at the correct time
And offered them to [Kakusaňda] Buddha.

71. By the merit of the mango I gave
May I be born in a golden mango
Like a great king full of power
By this act of merit.

72. May I be superior to the gods
May I be superior to men
May I be in the foremost caste
And obtain the power of a Pattini.

After obtaining "warrant" from Kakusaňda and from her parents, Pattini (as always) went up to Aňdungiri Peak to meditate.

76. I'll go to Aňdungiri's top
And live there as a hermit
She worshiped her parents
And asked their permission to depart.

78. Kaṇṇaki, with the warrant obtained
From Kakusaňda and her parents
With her retinue like a cluster of stars
She flew by *irdhi* to Aňdungiri Peak.

The significance of this text is that it gives a karmic rationale for Pattini's subsequent birth from a mango in the Pāṇḍi king's orchard. Both Pattini and Pāṇḍi (who was the merchant of Kālinga at the time of Kakusaňda) were implicated in the same karmic web. The text also has a strong Buddhist element, for, unlike other major deities in the Sinhala pantheon, Pattini has practically no roots in Hindi or Brahmanic myth. Like the Buddha, she has been committed to virtue for forty *kalpa*s and will become a Buddha herself.

Text 35 *Pahan Gäm̆bura*: Lights in the Deep

Pahan gäm̆bura has seventy stanzas, many of them extolling the beauty and virtue of Pattini in a previous birth during the lifetime of the Buddha of our age, Gautama. The authorship is attributed to Vīdāgama Maitreya, the great fifteenth-century poet. Vīdāgama, who heard about this story from Pandit Däḍigamuvē Divākara, put it into verse. The poem is extremely well constructed and has many words and phrases that are archaic and difficult to translate, though the gist is clear. The authorship itself is doubtful, but the influence of Vīdāgama's style is also apparent. The poem itself could have been written in the fifteenth century.

The poem is not of much significance for the study of the Pattini cult. It does, however, illustrate the entirely Buddhist nature of the goddess. She is referred to as one who obtained *vivaraṇa* from the Buddha seven times (or from seven previous Buddhas, stanza 13). The poem refers to her exemplary piety and chastity. For example, by the power of her chastity, she once stopped the flow of the sky river (*ahas gaňga*, the mythological Ganges or possibly the Kāvēri, stanza 19). The poem refers to another such act: how, by the power of her piety, she miraculously created lamps from the waters of Nēranjanā and offered these to the Buddha in his honor. The gist of the poem is as follows:

Accompanied by a thousand girl friends, she went up to the river Nērañjanā (Pāli, Nerañjarā). This river is famous in Buddha mythology; when he renounced the world, the Buddha rode his horse Kanthaka, who took one leap across the river. Crossing the river signifies leaving worldly existence for the hermit's life. In the present poem, Pattini is born in Gautama's dispensation: she is associated with his life and mythology. She went to Nērañjanā and created bubbles of water, which then rose in the air. But of these she created thousands of lights (lamps) in honor of the Buddha. The ladies who saw this were delighted and astonished. The gods, including Sakra himself, watched this miracle from above. Sakra gave her flowers from the wish-fulfilling tree (*parasatumal*) and gave her a warrant (*varan*) for her to be born in the human world and receive offerings from people. The concluding stanzas refer to her offering these lamps in honor of the Buddha for seven days. It mentions that she herself rose up into the sky as a result of her piety, and that the gods showered flowers from above. Having lit these lamps, Pattini made a wish to be born as a male in order to achieve eventual Buddahood. (This text also fully incorporates Pattini into a Buddhist ethos.)

Text 36 *Aṁba Vidamana*: The Shooting of the Mango

This text actually describes three "births" of Pattini—from the tear of the *nāga* (cobra deity) king, from the blue lotus, and from the mango in the Pāṇḍi king's orchard. A myth is often enacted in a ritual drama, but ritual drama is not a literal enactment of a myth. In the mango shooting ritual the major enactment focuses on an event that seems peripheral to the myth—Sakra appears onstage and carries on a comic dialogue with the drummer and sundry members of the audience. I give an almost verbatim account of this comic drama later in this book (chap. 12, pp. 490–95). Here I shall present a translation of the text sung in the Rabalīya tradition. In general the procedure is as follows: the *kapurāla* and his assistant sing the first part of the myth up to the appearance of Sakra; Sakra appears onstage and carries out the comic dialogue mentioned earlier; Sakra shoots the mango while the *kapurāla* sings the rest of the narrative. In some traditions the comic ritual drama is enacted first and the myth of the mango shooting is sung at its conclusion.

1. Sit in this assembly and listen with pleasure
To my words: do not be distracted
Some are ignorant of this poem's beauty
But gifted poets truly know.

2. Those who know not the sweetness and beauty of poetry
   Can construct only four slipshod lines
   They cast baleful aspersions on learned priests
   Such mean ones care only for their bellies' sake.

3. Listen how Pattini, glorious and stern, showed her power
   By destroying the arrogance of the Pāṇḍi king
   The story of the mango shooting, in elegant lines
   I relate, heed with attentive ears and eyes.

4. Once a goodly *nāga* king named Navakeḷa
   Stepped into a pond and joyfully sported there
   When a cruel wind drifted him high like a flower
   And placed him on the rock of Mahāmēru.

5. The storm raged furiously for seven days
   By his *tejas* [glory, might] the *nāga* king bore it patiently
   Tears streamed from his eyes, he could not sleep
   Not one day longer could he last, he felt.

6. "Why," thought the good *nāga* king, Navakeḷa
   "Why is it that I am doomed to stay here?"
   His mind was drawn to his tears that rained
   And decided to stay there longer, that *nāga* king.

7. His mind craved for the tears that fell from his eyes
   He stayed there, that *nāga* king, and mused and mused
   He gathered his tears in his wound-up coils
   There he stayed for several days longer.

The psychological symbolism here is interesting: the *nāga* king is attracted (in a sexual sense) to his own tears. The *nāga* is both a supernatural being and also a phallic object. His tears are almost semen; hence his craving for them. The next stanza says that a damsel (Pattini) was born out of his tears (semen). Pattini herself is *dolorosa*, and tears are highly appropriate for her. Moreover, being born in this manner exempts Pattini from childbirth pollution.

8. From the tears that he "protected" thus
   A damsel emerged, never her like in the *nāga* world before
   The *nāga* king was greatly pleased,
   And left that very day for the *nāga* world.

The *nāga* king "protects" the tears he initially craved. The Sinhala term *rakinava* is wider than the English term "protect"; a hen brooding her eggs is described as *rakinava*. This latter meaning is important in the stanza above.

9. This maid came down to the human world for water sports
   Decked with the sixty-four ornaments
   Escorted with a retinue of twice five hundred
   She came down to sport in the waters.

Sixty-four is the classic Indian number for the wiles of women; here it is also used for their attire and ornaments.

10. She sported in the waters for several days
That *nāga* lady, beautiful, like a heavenly maiden
That day a sinful thief stole her clothes
Without any thought of compassion.

11. She sported awhile and stepped onto the bank
And searched for the clothes she wore
But her clothes were taken by a thief
In shame that noble lady jumped into the pond.

Change in singing style and drum music.

12. A Brahman came here for his daily bath
He knew not that a lady lay hiding there
[Through shame] the noble lady was born as a flower
The Brahman thought he would like to pick it.

13. I will pick the flower, thought the Brahman with desire
As an ornament to deck his lovely wife
But as the Brahman reached for the flower
The flower hid in the depths of the pond.

14. With noble thoughts the Brahman observed the [Buddhist] precepts
After observing abstinences for several days,
He told his wife about his plans,
He purified [*pē*] himself and left at the auspicious time.

15. He bowed his head in worship and held out his hands
An infant girl emerged into his cupped hands
Surely it is due to his merit in some distant birth
That she hid in the bottom of the pond that day?

The *nāga* damsel has been transformed into an infant, a sexless being, as a result of her sexual shame.

16. He brought the infant to his wife, the Brahman woman
Who gave her "gold milk" [1] from her oozing paps
Thus was their merit fulfilled that day
She placed the girl on a golden seat.

17. That virgin maid was born in a lovely flower
Was not a renowned Brahman both a father and a mother?
His Brahman woman loved her, as if she herself bore her
'Twas Flower Pattini who was born of the blue lotus?

18. When she had reached her sixteenth year

1. See p. 104 for an explanation of "gold milk."

The Brahman woman told her husband thus:
"Let us give her three portions of gold and gems
And arrange a match for her, O lord."

19. When Pattini pondered over the words [of her parents]
Pain hit her mind with great force
"Am I to be married to a human thing?"
She thought, and sought the hermit's life.

"Human thing," a contemptuous reference to a male. The Sinhala is *naralova ekekuṭa*. The reason is clear: Pattini should never be sullied by sexuality.

20. Angry the exalted Pattini left that place
Without telling anyone, not even thinking about herself
Determined to observe the precepts well, she went
To reside on the top of Aňdungiri Peak.

It is clear that Pattini must retain her virginity, purity, and piety. She is born in extraordinary circumstances, first from the cobra king's tears (phallus and semen) and "protected" by him (like a hen with her eggs). Later in sexual shame she is transformed into a flower, a blue lotus, symbol of her virginity. She is reborn again, as an infant, only after the Brahman abstained from sex and held out his hands. Now when marriage is suggested she *must* perforce leave her adopted parents.

21. Joyously King Sakra in mendicant Brahman guise
Went up to Pattini living on Aňdungiri Peak
"O sister give me some alms," he said
"And may you be born in Tusita heaven."

22. Why old Brahman are you babbling thus?
Why are you here on Aňdungiri's top?
What alms can I give you O noble one?
The Brahman replied with nonsensical words.

23. Then she trampled Aňdungiri with her feet
And lo! she created *rat hāl* [red rice]
"Lord sit down and eat the alms I offer"
And thus she assuaged his hunger.

24. Sakra who saw her glory [*teda*] that day
Before eating her alms instructed her thus
By this act [of mind] you'll go to Pāṇḍi's city
To erase and destroy Pāṇḍi's forehead eye.

25. That day on god Sakra's plea
Gracious Pattini went to Pāṇḍi city
"I shall show the world my mango birth
And thereby give succor to all."

26. Beauteous Pattini, full of glory, thus went
To the orchard of Pāṇḍi, lord of men

Surrounded by a retinue of a thousand mangoes—
A mango grew out of season in that orchard!

27. When you know of Pattini's glory and might
You'll not be surprised at this wondrous fruit
In a tree supreme among other trees
Like the moon among a cluster of stars.

28. Look how it stays there amid the thick foliage!
That wondrous mango, so pleasant to see
Increasingly every day it spread its glorious rays
Like a shimmering golden water pot.

29. The king's servant in his eagerness
Paid full attention to his job
One day at the orchard he received a surprise—
He wanted to investigate it further.

This stanza is not sung by the Rabalīya tradition but is found in Hevawasam's edition as stanza 41. I included it here since it provides a useful piece of information.

30. "A honey mango like this I've never seen
Large, like a spotless water pot"
That proud orchard keeper pondered,
"I've never seen a mango such as this."

31. "As he sits before his subjects from various lands,
The king of Pāṇḍi in his assembly
I'll go present him this miracle mango
And surely I'll obtain high office."

The next thirteen stanzas are not sung in the Rabalīya tradition. They are from Hevawasam's edition. I include them here because I have heard almost identical songs sung in other performances of *aṁba vidamana*. They are not intrinsic to the ritual. In Rabalīya the events described below are summarized in a prose narrative recited by the *kapurāla*.

32. Thinking thus he stood near the tree
"If I throw sticks and stones at it
I am sure it won't ever reach the tree
And I'll only tire myself, I'll fail."

33. He put a rope ring around his feet
To climb the mighty honey mango tree
Unaware of it's divine power he climbed
His hands and feet slipped and down he slid.

34. A fruit has grown here out of season
This is the work of some divine power
Hence I'll not try to bring it down
But I'd better inform the king.

35. The orchard keeper ran to the king
And worshiped the king in his pure seat
He spoke of the miracle in the orchard
After respectfully paying him obeisance.

36. "Sire, such a powerful mango hasn't been seen before
With lovely colors like a heavenly rose apple
It's grown in the orchard amid a large retinue
There'll never be a miracle like this in our age."

37. Possessor of a great eye in the middle of his forehead
The gem of the pure dynasty of the sun!
The king was pleased with the words of the keeper
Yet the king of Pāṇḍi probed him further.

38. "You've come here and bragged a tale
About a mango growing in my orchard
I am not sure you've not invented lies
I've some doubts about your story."

39. "Your glory spreads over the earth
O protector and refuge for the weak.
I've served in the shadow of your feet
Have I ever told you lies before?"

40. Then the mighty king ordered that
His ministers be promptly summoned
"Take with you people tall and short
And bring me back a thousand mangoes."

Presumably the king wants the strange mango as well as a "retinue" of mangoes.

41. They utter boastful shouts and climb the tree
But soon they slip down frightened
They suffer greatly as their chests and bellies bruise
These people went back to the king.

42. "Even though we brought sticks and stones
To throw at the tree, nothing happened
Those mangoes are too mighty for us,
Lord of men, we cannot meet your wish."

43. The assembled ministers were upset by these words
Spoken forcefully before the king
"These mangoes I desire and will pick them somehow"
The great Pāṇḍi king went into his orchard.

There are two versions of what occurred subsequently. Hevawasam's text (1974, p. 141, verses 57–59) describes how the king himself went to the orchard and gazed at the fruit, whose rays blinded his middle eye. Verse 59 describes this well.

44. Like the spreading rays of the sun [the mango shone]
The king in his orchard gazed at the mango
The glorious rays of Pattini spread like the sun
And erased the mighty forehead eye of the king.

Even in Hevawasam's own edition of the Pattini texts there are references to the juice from the mango (shot by Sakra) obliterating the middle eye of the king. This is the version current among contemporary practitioners of the *gammaḍuva*, including Rabalīya. The Rabalīya text also does not refer to the blinding of the Pāṇḍi king. This is simply because the priests are afraid to act this in the drama—for fear they will be struck with *vas* (ritual danger) owing to inadvertent error while performing the ritual. *Vas* may actually cause the actor to go blind. However, the other songs sung in the *gammaḍuva* clearly refer to this event. This and the events that follow are also implicitly referred to in the very next stanza.

45. A great famine crept into Soḷī land!
He who ruled over the world
That proud Pāṇḍi king's eye was destroyed!
O there's none other than Pattini for power and glory

46. In the guise of a Brahman went Sakra
To the top of the peak of Aňdungiri
"I'll get alms from her," he said
That day she performed a miracle.

The preceding verses refer to events in the future and the past, not an unusual feature of ritual poetry. The narrative continuity is deliberately broken, as if to remind the audience of the larger context of the story.

47. The great Pāṇḍi king's retinue
Were tired after shooting at the mango
The king himself felt empty
Look the City Destroyer [Puradara] comes into the king's assembly.

At this point Sakra enters the arena, dancing bells jingling. Meanwhile the singing continues.

48. In his right hand a walking stick
His head of hair a withered cane flower
He looks a hundred years old
Comes the god Sakra to the assembly in filthy guise!

49. A pouch and a fierce bow slung on one shoulder
An arrow held in his left hand
Bent in two head down to the feet
Shivering, as if in deadly fright, he comes.

Now the drama of the god Sakra starts. This has very little to do with the actual myth, but it is crucial to some of my interpretations. Basically it deals with Sakra's antics and his dialogue with the drummer and members of the audience. The text of this comic drama is translated on pages 490–95. After this drama is over the singing is resumed.

50. The soldiers who were around impatiently
Scoffed at him trying to shoot the mango
They tugged at his sooty beard
Fondled his belly and pushed him around.

51. "Your body full of scales and swollen varicose veins
Head and pointed chin stuck with gray hair
Teeth all fallen, sunken jaws like a jackal's
Grandpa, we've not seen your likes before."

52. "Cowardly boys, abject servants of the king
No more will you cause me vexation
If I bring down the mango as I vowed
Which kinsmen of yours will you give me as wife!

The last line is a vulgar insult implying that Sakra is going to sleep with a mother or sister of one of the soldiers.

53. "You can't shoot the mango; it is my right
I am not fooling you, I'll bring it down
Even if the *asura* hosts come, I'll not back down
You'll not see my match in the three worlds.

54. "Bent though I am friends laugh not at me
I am like the City Destroyer, Lord of the Three Worlds
If you bundle up all your bows and your arrows
I'll surely break them as an elephant a banana tree."

55. They heard his speech, his scornful words:
"Sure there's none as clever as you grandpa.
Now draw this bow we've given you
It's one that no one here could draw."

56. Like the great king who frightened the army
That filled the earth, the sky and the plains of Brahmā
He asked, "At what point shall I break the bow?"
Of the soldiers who were in that place.

Line 1 probably refers either to Rāma's feats or even to the Lord Buddha's conquest of Māra's hosts.

57. At this the assembled people replied in unison:
"Split the bow in two in this manner"
"Why shouldn't I split it into three pieces?
Sure there none to equal me, City Destroyer."

58. Angered by the words of the assembled people
He held the arrow, like Kāma's own, in his right hand

Fully drawing the bow held against his shoulder
In great rage he broke the bow into three.

59. The haft broke by the force of his draw
And broken was the pride of the soldiers
Their minds were shattered like bunches of falling coconuts
Or like herbs wilting in the sun.

60. He came like a man wracked with age
And broke the pride of the now-tired soldiers
In order that his fame shall last forever
The Thousand-Eyed showed his might to all.

61. To destroy indolence, to bring prosperity—
This is no lie, it was done for future good—
He showed his greatness in that assembly's midst
By breaking the bow and the soldiers' pride.

62. He proclaimed his goodness to the world
He then got rid of his guise
Spreading his glory over the world
He now took his own handsome form.

63. A *kēsara* lion among elephants[2]
A *garuḍa* eagle among cobras
A cobra king among frogs
That's how he stood among the notables.

64. Thus he showed his power and might
And they were ashamed
He did the good he said he would
The assembly crouched in fear.

The following stanza is found in the Sīnigama tradition:

65. Wearing golden ornaments
Lighting up the world like lightning
A golden bow in his right hand
Sakra whirled it around.

66. Shall I shoot the arrow to fly above?
Or shall I shoot it from down below?
How shall I shoot the mango and bring it down?
How do you [thou] wish it done?

67. "To shoot an upward-bound arrow
Is a feat that'll cause wonder
Yet to shoot straight from down below
That would indeed be good," they said.

2. A *kēsara* is a mythical lion that can terrify even the elephant, king of beasts.

Stanza 67 refers to the manner in which Sakra shoots the arrow—he falls flat on the ground, places the bow on his belly, and shoots "from down below." This mode of shooting is depicted in the ritual drama I witnessed in Beralapanātara (Ūrubokka tradition) in 1956. It is not done in this manner in Rabalīya or Sīnigama. That it is the expected manner is clear from the texts; the sexual symbolism (Sakra fertilizing the mango that produces Pattini) is obvious.

68. With a thunderclap filling the skies
For all to hear
He drew the bow
And shot it like a bolt.

69. Cutting through the [mango's] stalk
It sped thirty *yodun* past villages
And on to Sakra's city
Then fast back to earth.

70. Thunderously piercing the stalk
It went to Sakra's seat[3]
That beautiful mango stalk
It was cut for certain.

71. By the shining Pattini's wish
It came close to the earth
Like a sun shining at dawn
That mango danced in the sky's womb.

72. A wondrous miracle to please the mind!
They held a canopy up above
As the strange mango came to earth
So the whole world may offer it gifts [*pañḍuru*].

73. The king heard his words
He decorated a golden boat
Placed the mango under a cover
And sent it down midriver.

74. The boat was ornately carved
Hastily it was sent down the river
It did not stay there long
But reached Mantundon city.

The rest of the myth is in short four-line stanzas, but it is actually sung onstage very fast, as in "verse paragraphs."

75. The good Mānāyuru with Marakkāli his queen lady,
with their retinue were bathing in the river,

3. Sakra's seat is referred to here as *vajrāsana*: thunderbolt seat.

shining like a jewel they beheld, the boat came
down the river.

76. Mānāyuru who came at dawn, said the boat is mine
while Marakkāli, his queen, said the goods in it
are mine.

77. They went up to the boat, to hold the boat in place,
but as they went, the boat retreated.

78. They entreated the boat to come, held pearls before
it, and lo! the boat came up to them, and stayed.

79. They brought the boat ashore, placed it in a
mind-pleasing chariot, and with their retinue
took it to their palace.

80. With great pleasure they placed it in a golden
room within a larger hall, these two with great
amity.

81. A week passed by, Sakra took the guise of a Brahman.

82. He created a Brahman guise, "my Brahman wife has
a pregnancy craving, a deep craving for a mango,
I've come to inquire if you have one."

83. Impressed by these words, they thought it good,
if the sweet mango were given to him.

84. Then that queen, to give him alms [*dāna*] of a
sweet mango, went into the hall with happy thoughts,
to find the mango.

85. What she saw was a divine princess, worth the whole
world, full of beauty, she saw the infant that day.

86. "Come my husband, stay not there, come here my
beloved lord, look at the golden vessel and the
infant princess in it."

87. In the city of Sāgala they held an auspicious
procession for the birth of the infant; milk
oozed from her breasts, as she wished to nurture
the princess.

88. She was raised from the boat, that lady so lovely,
thus she was named Orumāla Pattini.

89. O Pattini born of the boat, O Orumāla Pattini,
O Pattini born of the mango, O Sirimā Muni Pattini.

90. By these verses spoken, may there be no suffering ever, may prosperity and joy increase, and may all have blessings and long life.

In Sīnigama a *sirasapāda*, or "head-to-foot verse," is sung in honor of Pattini. I have omitted it here since the reader is already familiar with this rite.

Text 37 *Mādēvi Katāva*: The Story of Mādēvi

The first part of this text is a description of Indra in his glory in the heavenly world, sporting in the pond Nandana with an attendance of divine damsels. After his water sports, he went back to his throne. He then asked the divine nymphs to dance before him. Thereupon the goddess Ūruvisi (Urvaśī), who lives with Sakra himself, began to dance and display the beauty of her body. While Ūruvisi was dancing, she fell in love with Kāma (?). For this reason Sakra cursed her to be born in the human world and suffer separation from her (adulterous) lover. Thus Ūruvisi was born as Citrāpati, the leader of the professional dancers (of the Soḷī king's city). After a long period of barrenness, Ūruvisi bore a girl, whom she named Mādēvi.

About a hundred verses deal with the education of Mādēvi and her beauty as a grown woman. She learned the sixty-four techniques of lovemaking, the various divisions of music, and the sixty-four branches of rhetoric. Citrāpati, aware of Mādēvi's beauty, took her to the court of the Soḷī king for her debut as a dancer. The king was infatuated by Mādēvi as she danced before the king and courtiers. After the performance the king presented a precious necklace to Mādēvi and asked her to place it round the neck of someone she would like to live with. Mādēvi, looking around the assembly, saw the handsome Pālaṅga, fell in love with him, and garlanded him with the necklace. She and Pālaṅga lived together in great joy like Umā and Īśvara.

Pālaṅga lived with Mādēvi for many years and squandered his wealth on her. Since Pālaṅga was now a poor man, Mādēvi's mother, Citrāpati, urged her to give him up. Pālaṅga overheard this, and he was full of sorrow. Mādēvi, however, told her mother that she would never leave Pālaṅga. The mother and daughter had a heated argument.

Mādēvi and Pālaṅga then went to sport in the Kāvēri river. Pālaṅga felt that Mādēvi was neglectful of him (or felt she had another lover?) and decided to leave her. Mādēvi was distraught and wept copious tears. She tried various ways to get her lord back. First she consulted a diviner ("light reader"), but she soon realized its futility. Then she sent her pet parrot to Pālaṅga. The parrot told Pālaṅga of Mādēvi's enormous sorrow, but Pālaṅga was unmoved. Finally she sent a maid Vayantimālā with a letter written on a palm leaf (*ola*, "manuscript paper"). But Kōvalaṉ (this name is now used instead of Pālaṅga) was unmoved. He said (stanza 345): "Would one walk on a slimy rock if one is aware it's slippery? Is it possible for one to drink water from a dried-up pond? Can sour curd be reconverted into milk? Can pieces of pottery be put together to make a vessel suitable for water?" All this in spite of Vayantimālā's entreaties and the lure of seeing his daughter, named Maṇimekhalā, born to Mādēvi in his absence. The poem ends with the distraught, anguished Mādēvi pining for Kōvalaṉ.

This poem is remarkably close to the *Cilappatikāram* story, but it provides somewhat different details of Sakra (Indra, in the *Cilappatikāram*) sporting in heaven and Urvaśī's curse.

PLATE 1. Ritual specialists eating the consecrated rice (*pē bat*).

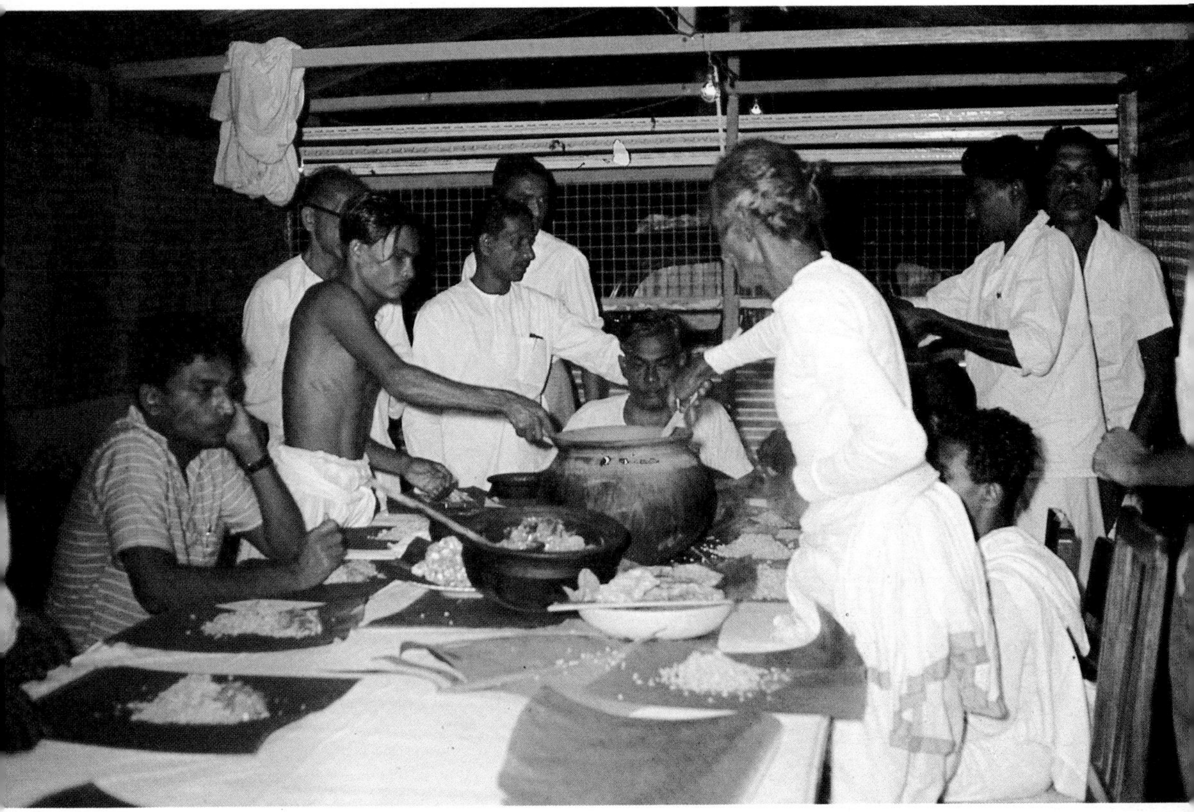

PLATE 2. The *toraṇa*, or ceremonial arch, for the goddess Pattini, made of banana bark and large leaves and ornamented with conventional designs.

PLATE 3. (bottom left) A tall areca-nut tree decorated with streamers representing the tree of the torch of time. In front is a typical altar for the gods, in this case for Dēvatā Baṇḍāra.

PLATE 4. (bottom right) The *magul kapa*, or "auspicious post," decorated with coconut flowers and with lighted tapers at its base. Beside it is an altar with the insignia of the goddess temporarily placed there.

PLATE 5. The priest, dressed as Pattini and wearing several veils, walks under a white canopy carrying the sacred insignia of the goddess covered in red cloth.

PLATE 6. The god Vāhala (Däḍi-muṇḍa) in a trance during the ritual of "dressing up as Vāhala."

PLATE 7. The god Vāhala, collapsed after his trance, is given charmed water.

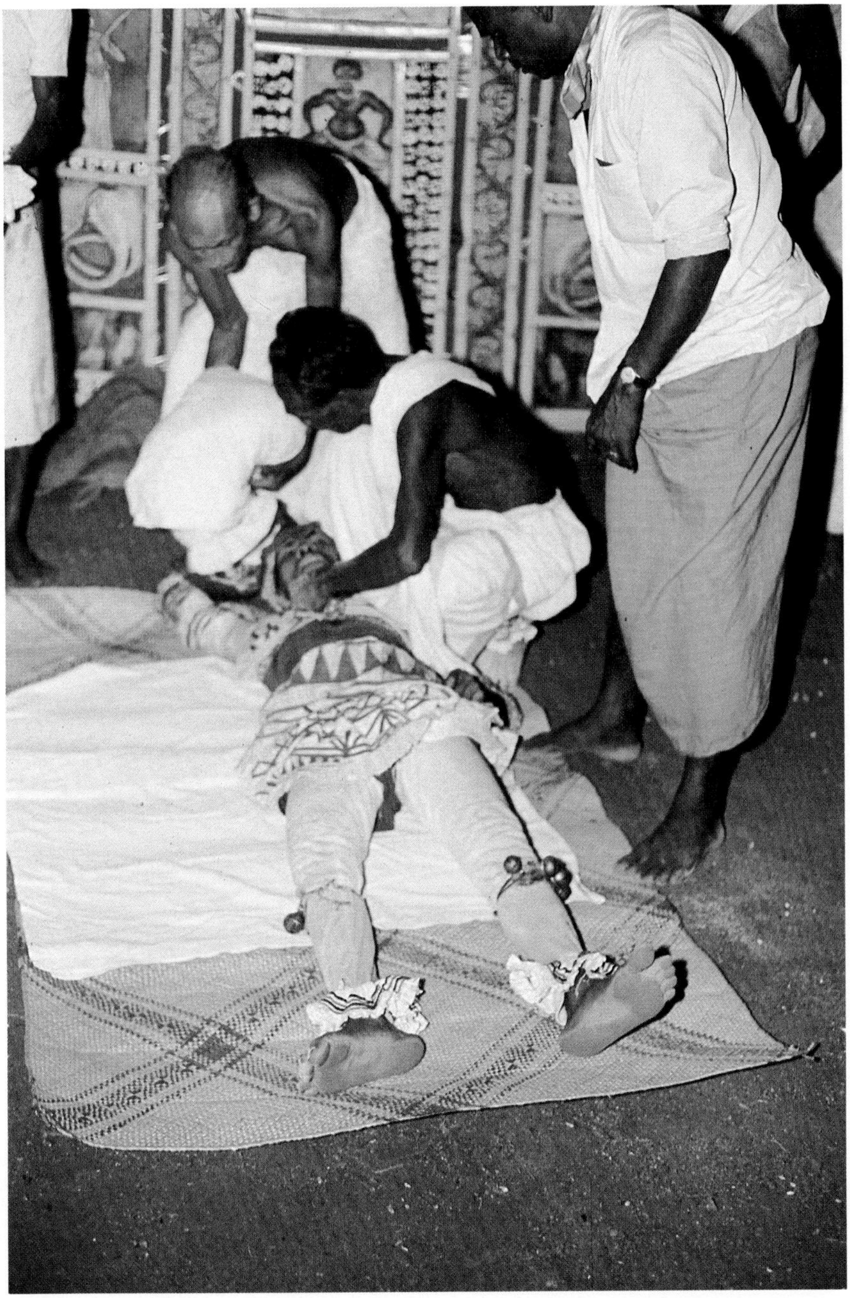

PLATE 8. Bringing in the *milla* wood for fire trampling.

PLATE 9. The god Devol reads the letter of authority permitting him to cross the barrier.

PLATE 10. The god Sakra with his humped front plays pranks with the attendant (*koṭṭōruva*) in the ritual drama of "the shooting of the mango."

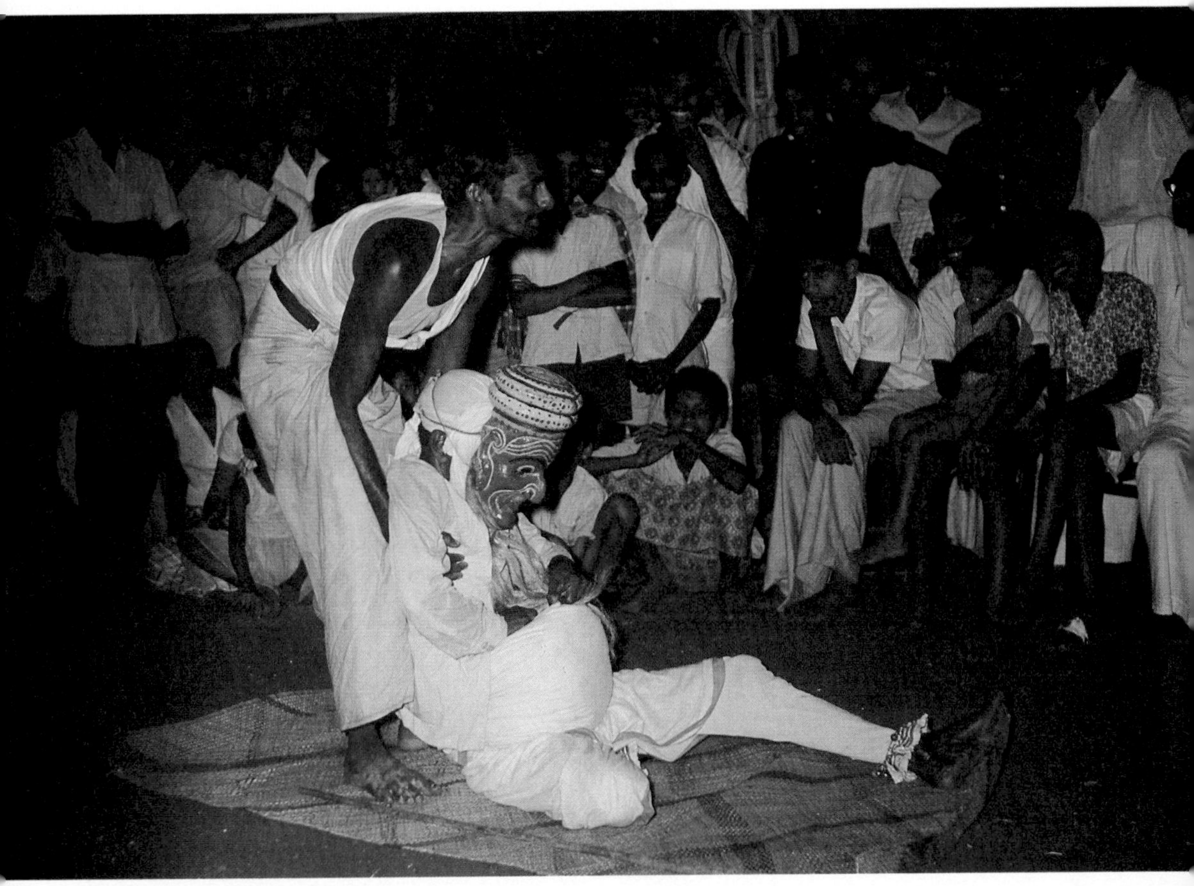

PLATE 11. Baṁbura examining his phallic gun in the ritual drama of "the shooting of the gun."

PLATE 12. (bottom) Baṁbura as the demonic barber in the ritual of "the shaving."

Plate 13. Large wooden horn used in Biyanvila is taken in procession in the *aṅkeḷiya* (horn game).

PLATE 14. Hooking of the horns by experts known as *aṅ vaṭṭāṇḍi* in the *aṅkeḷiya* ritual.

PLATE 15. (bottom) A man sings abusive songs in the *aṅkeḷiya*. In one hand he carries a piece of the broken horn, the castrated penises of his opponents.

PLATE 16. Priests of the Karaitivu temple reading the story of the goddess from a palm leaf manuscript.

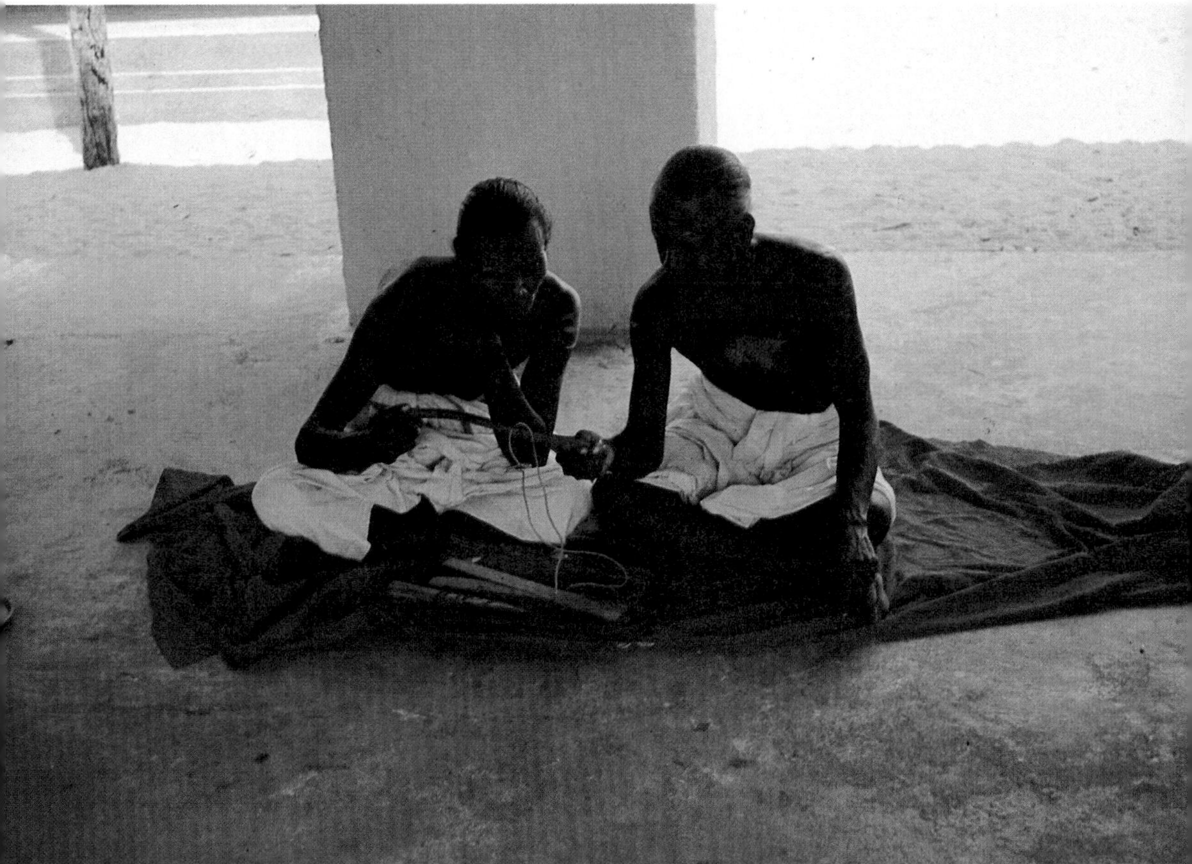

PLATE 17. Death, or Maruva, dressed as a demon and as an executioner, arrives onstage in "the killing and resurrection."

PLATE 18. Maruva drinks Pālaṅga's blood, which is dripping from his sword.

Plate 19. The goddess Pattini with her servant Kālī accosts the ferryman in the ritual drama of "the killing and resurrection."

Plate 20. (bottom left) Schoolchildren inform the goddess Pattini that her husband, Pālañga, lies slain under the *kohom̆ba* tree.

Plate 21. (bottom right) Pattini wails over the corpse of her dead husband, covered with a white shroud, imploring him to awaken.

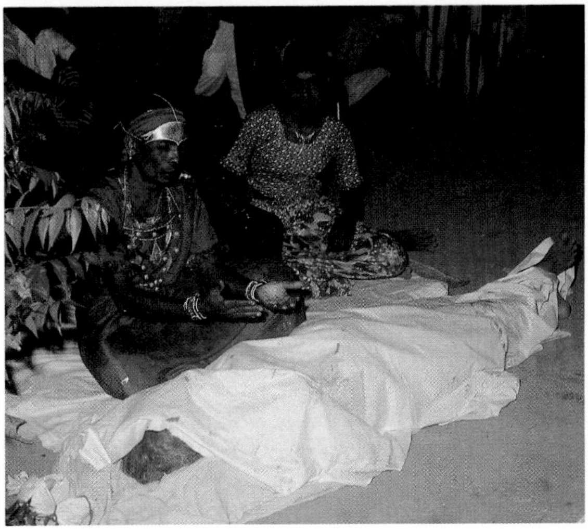

PLATE 22. Guru Hāmi, mat in hand, engages in a comic dialogue with a dancer in the drama of "the killing of Rāma."

PLATE 23. The androgynous demon Garā.

PLATE 24. (bottom) The demon Garā seated on his *ayile*, or swing, admiring himself.

PLATE 25. Carving on stone pillar at Kālī shrine, Koṭuṅkoḷūr. A portion of the secret chamber is visible in the background on the right. *Photograph by Rajan John.*

Text 38 *Turañgun Näguma* and *Sen̩du Ke̩liya*: Mounting the Horse and Playing Dice

This is a short poem of little significance. It is not sung in the *gammaḍuva*. The two texts are listed separately in some traditions of *gammaḍuva*. In Hevawasam's edition both are viewed as one short text of thirty-four verses. *Turañgun näguma* deals with Pālañga (also called Kōvalan in this text) on his horse. His beauty is extolled; the ladies of the city admire him. He then rides to the residence of a courtesan named Kolivara Vēsi ("Kolivara courtesan"). He loses a bet to her and as a consequence is forced to live with her for seven years. Kōvalan̲'s father sends his wet nurse (*kiri mava*) to look for Kōvalan̲. She finds him in the courtesan's house. The wet nurse assaults the courtesan and brings Kōvalan̲ home.

This text seems singularly out of place in the corpus of thirty-five texts, having very little to do with the Pattini-Pālañga-Mādēvi triangle. It is very explicit that the courtesan here is not Mādēvi. If so, does this mean that Kōvalan̲ lived with one courtesan for seven years and then with another for practically the same period? This is most unlikely, particularly since Kolivara Vēsi is not mentioned in any other Pattini text. If so, what is the place of this text in the Pattini corpus?

I consider *sen̩du ke̩liya* a text like that of the killing of Rāma (*rāmā märīma*). The latter is a comic parody of the *marā ipäddīma* ("killing and resurrection"). Since the *marā ippäddīma* is not often performed, owing to fear of *vas* (ritual danger), the *rāmā märīma* (and in some places a comic ritual of the Bam̐bura demons, pp. 495–99) is substituted. I suspect this was true of *mādēvi katāva* (story of Mādēvi) also; the present text is probably a parody of it originally enacted as a substitute comic ritual drama. Hence the protagonist's ritual name, Pālañga, is not used; instead his secular name, Kōvalan̲, is substituted.

Text 39 *Vañda Puvata* and *Kōvil Pēvīma*: The Story of the Barrenness and How She Performed Penances at Shrines

Hevawasam's edition has only the latter text. *Vañda puvata* is simply a preliminary to the latter. None of these texts are important; they are never sung in contemporary ritual. Many practitioners are ignorant of their content, which refer to Pālañga-Kōvalan̲'s parents, who are of little significance in Sinhala mythology.

The basic theme of the two texts is very simple. *Vañda puvata* is the lament of Kōvalan̲'s mother about her barrenness. The text is meant to be a compendium of causes (bad karma in past lives) that produce barrenness in women, barrenness of course being a dreadful thing in South Asia, and India in particular. I have a complete translation of this text, but a few verses give the general feel of this text. My copy is from the Ratnapura tradition.

1. Did I insult my mother ignoring my kinship?
   Did I tie up and kill innocent calves?
   Or did I utter lies numberless?
   Is that why my womb is barren?

2. Did I set fire to Buddhist temples and flower altars?
   Did I steal temple property?
   Did I plunder temple lands?
   Is that why my womb is barren?

3. Did I refuse water to a thirsty man?
   Did I stamp on the ground and drive him away?
   Did I cut up fish live and cook them?
   Is that why my womb is barren?

4. Did I chase away those seeking shelter?
   Did I refuse food to the poor and hungry?
   Did I commit such serious sins?
   Is that why my womb is barren?

My text has thirty-nine verses all in the same vein.

Kovil pēvīma describes how Kōvalan̲'s mother went from one shrine to another making vows and penances and performing *pūjā*s to obtain a child. She went to 108 temples by ship, accompanied by a large retinue of attendants. Ultimately she went to a temple of Īśvara and offered him an image of a bull. She fell prostrate and begged the god to cure her of barrenness. Īśvara granted her wish, and she conceived. The latter part of the text deals with her pregnancy revulsions and cravings. Ultimately she delivered the baby, and when the child was three months old he was taken outside to worship the sun god.

This text is of little significance. It does indicate the affluence of Kōvalan̲'s parents and the social class of merchants and traders they came from. In this sense it is close to the social conditions depicted in the *Cilappatikāram*. Hevawasam's edition has 169 stanzas.

Text 40 *Tapas Gamana*: Leaving for the Hermit's Life

This text is also available in palm-leaf manuscripts and in Hevawasam's edition. It is never sung in any of the rituals I have seen; informants are unaware of its content. It is thoroughly moribund and is a survival only in the purely technical sense that it is available in palm-leaf manuscript versions. I shall present a brief summary of the text, then comment on its significance.

The text deals with the parents of Pālan̆ga (Kōvalan̲), who decide to renounce the world for a hermit's life.

Stanzas 9–11

The city of Kāvēri (Kāvēri paṭuna) of the rose apple continent (India), inhabited by rich merchants, was like a celestial city. In this city there lived a noble merchant called Mahāmatuma ("great gentleman") who often listened to the Dhamma and practiced love toward all beings.

Stanzas 12–14

One day while resting in bed in his heavenly mansion he looked at himself in the mirror and saw one gray hair on his head. He suddenly became aware of the dreadful effects of worldly life and began to think of its impermanence.

Stanzas 15–20

He thought thus. It is futile to live in the world. I enjoy good food, living, and ornamentation, but all of this is impermanent and subject to decay. The death and decay of this body is inevitable; hence what use is all my wealth and splendor if I do not acquire merit before I die?

The life of one who leads a worldly existence, without heeding the Buddha's teachings, is like a drop of dew on a blade of grass (*pokuraṁba*), lasting only till the sun's rays fall on it. Men possessed of power and strength end up by losing them and die in pain. There is no end to suffering if we acquire no merit in the course of our human existence.

Even though one lives for thousands of years and amasses great wealth, one cannot overcome the suffering (i.e., impermanence) of human existence. This can be overcome only by the practice of giving (*dāna*) and the observance of the precepts. These alone can lead us to salvation (*mōkṣa*).

Stanzas 21–22

Mahāmatuma resolved then to leave for the hermit's life. He summoned his spouse and children. He told his spouse that his black hair had turned gray and that his good fortune was a hindrance. He had therefore decided to go forth immediately to the hermit's life.

Stanzas 23–24

The wife feared that her husband would abandon all his wealth and depart at once. She asked him to live in comfort and do meritorious acts like giving alms to beggars.

Stanzas 25–38

In reply Mahāmatuma cited the case of the Buddha himself, who left his home for the homeless life. And of the King Makhādeva (in the *Jātaka*s) who, on seeing a gray hair on his head, donned the robes and abandoned his wealth and possessions. He told his wife, "Though we have great wealth and retinue of followers we cannot take away any of this when we die." He asked his wife to remain and practice virtue and acquire merit.

Stanzas 39–41

Having listened to her husband's words, this lady pondered the transience and suffering entailed by existence. She then wanted to join him in the hermit's life. But Mahāmatuma raised several objections. People will ridicule us, he said, if we jointly renounce the world, for could man and wife live together and yet observe the precepts? He quoted examples of women seducing men from their steadfastness. Even arhats gifted with the power of levitation have lost these powers through seduction by women.

Stanzas 43–46

The wife replied with contrary examples. "Were not there men in the past who attained liberation by practicing the precepts even though they were living with their wives? They prevented body contact by placing a garland between them in bed." She quoted the case of King Vessantara who lived with his wife and children in the forest. Hence, she said, she would like to join him in the forest so that they could practice meditation together.

Stanzas 47–54

Mahāmatuma and his wife together resolved to renounce the world, and before departure they summoned their children (Pālaṅga and his wife Pattini) to give them advice. They exhorted Pālaṅga and Pattini to live in amity; to desist from envying others; to share their happiness with friends and kinsmen; to avoid courtesans; to save their own wealth and not to envy others; to refrain from abusing servants, from taking life, from intoxicants, and from the company of drunkards; to associate with friends and avoid enemies; to be impartial and just as a pair of scales; and above all to have their hearts full of compassion by listening to the Dhamma of the Buddha.

Stanzas 55–64

Having advised Pālaňga in this manner, they prepared to set forth. Mahāmatuma, sensing that his followers would prevent his leaving, waited for dusk. Meanwhile the sun, whose rays had illuminated the whole world, set in the west, as if to show the impermanence of things, and the soothing rays of the moon fell from the east, as if to advise them to observe the virtues, pure as the moon's rays. The couple meditated on these phenomena, and as soon as their followers were asleep, they donned mendicant robes and descended from the upper floor, intent on eventually achieving release. They went past streets of the city, avoiding people who may have prevented them from leaving. Hastily they climbed aboard a ship as if to cross the ocean of existence.

Stanzas 65–74

Pālaňga saw in a dream that a golden vine had embraced a beautiful tree and then it shot up to the blue sky, with a *guruḷu* eagle resting on it. He asked Kaṇṇaki (this name is used in the text) to explain the dream, whereupon she said: "the golden vine represents a noble woman, the blue sky is the ocean, the hawk is a ship; it is certain that our parents are going away by ship, leaving us here." They were filled with such sorrow that they began to cry. They lamented thus: Why did you abandon and leave us? If you wanted to leave us why did you make a vow to have children (reference to *vaňda puvata*, or sins of barrenness, the preceding text). Even the four-footed animals love their offspring. O why did you leave us thus? Is it due to our past sins that our followers did not tell us of your departure?

Stanzas 75–81

Crying thus, they became exhausted. Both of them resolved to get back to their parents. Then the moon reached the crest of the "Morning Rock," dispelling the world's darkness as if to show their parents in the clear light. Pālaňga saw the ship afar and asked Pattini to call it back. Why, he said, did our parents leave us, after bringing us up with love and affection? Then Pattini demonstrated her powers and pleased her husband by calling the ship back to shore.

Stanzas 82–89

The parents were grieved that their children did this, in spite of the advice given earlier. They said that they were going to forested mountains to observe the Dhamma and that their children should not trouble them any longer. Then Pattini and Pālaňga worshiped their parents and took leave of them. They cried. The ship stood still; the ocean looked like a galaxy of lights; it was like a lake full of lotuses fluttering in the breeze. Then like an arrow shot from a bow the ship reached Kāňci. The couple lived like hermits, wearing leopard skins, and ultimately they achieved Nirvāṇa.

Stanzas 91–98

The rest of the poem invokes the Twelve Gods and Madura Mādēvi, the Gods of the Four Warrants, and concludes on a pious note with praises of the Three Jewels and the ultimate wish of achieving Nirvāṇa.

Tapas gamana is of no significance in the current Pattini rituals and mythology, yet it is interesting for historical reasons. In the Indian traditions represented by *Cilappatikāram* and *Maṇimēkalai*, Pattini's parents as well as Kōvalaṉ's were so grief-stricken at the death of their children that they either died of grief or renounced the world.

Cilappatikāram: "Kovalan's father heard what happened to his son and daughter-in-law and also to the righteous monarch of Madura, and became deeply afflicted. He distributed all his wealth in charity, entered the seven Indra-viharas" (i.e., a Buddhist monastery) (Dikshitar 1939, p. 309). His wife died of sorrow. Kaṇṇaki's (Pattini's) father became an Ājīvaka ascetic, practicing penances, while her mother died of grief. Mādēvi (Mātavi) also became a Buddhist nun. In *Maṇimēkalai*, the heroine, Maṇimekhalā or Maṇimēkalai, the daughter of Kōvalaṉ and Mādēvi, sees her grandfather in Vañci (in Kerala) practicing Buddhist meditation.

It is clear that the protagonists of these myths belonged to the heterodox religions—Buddhism, Jainism, and Ājīvakaism. If we assume that the *Maṇimēkalai* and *Cilappatikāram* utilized existing traditions, it seems that the Pattini myths that developed in South India believed that Kōvalaṉ's father became a Buddhist hermit. However, his mother died of sorrow. These myths have inner plausibility, since renunciation often occurs under great personal stress, rather than because of an improbable event like Mahāmatuma's discovery of a single gray hair. The Sinhala tradition seems forced and out of place.

Yet how could we explain the myth's presence in the Sinhala tradition? Logically viewed, the Sinhala myth of *tapas gamana* is out of place. The incident could have occurred either when Pattini and Pālaṅga were married, before his leaving her for Mādēvi, or when they were reconciled later on. The text itself has little significance for the Pattini myth except as a homily on Buddhism. What happened in all probability is that the Indian tradition that Kōvalaṉ's father became a Buddhist hermit was known in Sri Lanka. Yet in the rituals practiced here the culminating event is the resurrection of Pālaṅga by Pattini. To have a ritual text on the renunciation of the world by Kōvalaṉ's father (and others) would be an anticlimax after the drama of the killing and resurrection. Thus Kōvalaṉ's father's renunciation had to come earlier. But what about the *motive* for renouncing the world? This was solved by utilizing a preexistent myth from the Buddhist *Jātaka Tales* (*Makhādeva Jātaka*), where a nobleman renounces the world after seeing a single gray hair on his head (Cowell 1957, 1:30). The substance of the *Jātaka* is retained; the protagonists, however, are different—they are Kōvalaṉ's parents. Note that while the Indian traditions state that only Kōvalaṉ's father became a hermit, this is not possible in the *Jātaka* adaptation, for in the latter both husband and wife leave for the homeless life. Thus Kōvalaṉ's mother cannot die of a broken heart in the Sinhala tradition; she must perforce join her husband in Kāñci, a great center of South Indian Buddhism.

Though *tapas gamana* has little mythological significance in respect to the Pattini corpus, it does illustrate a central feature of Pālaṅga's personality: his lack of autonomy, his dependence on his parents, especially his mother, and also his dependence on his spouse. He is incapable of executive autonomy: his wife must act on his behalf.

Text 41 *Gaman Valinaḍaya*: The Journey on Foot (toward Madurai)

This text is rarely sung in the *gammaḍuva* rituals. In theory it should be sung immediately before *kannuran katāva*, parts of which are sung in the ritual drama of the killing and resurrection.

Gaman valinaḍaya describes the journey undertaken by Pattini and Kōvalaṉ-Pālaňga (accompanied by one other person, possibly Pattini's servant Kālī) to Madurai from their home city of Kāvēri paṭuna. Pālaňga had by then left Mādēvi and was reconciled with Pattini. They hoped to recover their fortunes by selling Pattini's priceless anklet in Madurai. On the road to Madurai they worshiped at the Diya Bäňdi Kōvil ("the shrine near the dam"), then at the Induvara Muni Vihāra. Thereafter they went to a palace (*mahā vāsala*), or possibly a large temple, then rested in a park containing sal trees (*Shorea robusta*).

Pattini was exhausted by her travels. Pālaňga asked her to go home, but Pattini responded that there was no one to see (since Pālaňga was not there). She loved Pālaňga and would not leave him. They resumed their travels and ultimately reached the temple of a female ascetic named Kavunti.

> The two shining with beauty and youth
> Saw her temple and went inside
> There lived Kavunti who warmly greeted them
> She had banished sin and observed the precepts.
>
> (Hevawasam 1974, p. 331, stanza 44)

After resting here, all four (including Kālī and Kavunti) went toward Madurai in the moonlight.

Pattini was once again suffering from fatigue and pain, described in great detail in the text. Kālī massaged her body with oil. Tired though she was, they dared not stay there, since the forest was full of dangerous animals—elephants, mythic creatures like *kaňgavēna* ("unicorn"), tigers, wild boars, bears who would scoop out one's eyes, pythons, and bloodsucking mosquitoes. (The characteristics of each creature are dealt with in a single stanza, and the poetry is of high quality.) The four then reached a madding river, full of rushing waters, huge logs, and debris. There were man-eating crocodiles and sharp-toothed sharks in the water. There was no ferryman, and no way of crossing. Pattini then threw her royal ring on the river. The waters parted, and they walked across. The ring came back and rested in her hand. Thereafter they went to Kannuran city near Madurai, whose king, named Yā, was Pālaňga's kinsman. Pālaňga asked Pattini to tarry while he went to Yā's palace.

Pālaňga stayed in Yā's palace while the latter went with a large retinue, like Sakra himself, to escort Pattini to his city. Pattini saw him arrive without Pālaňga and imagined that he had killed her husband and had come to take her as his mistress (note Pattini's own guilt feelings). She became wrathful and created flames from her ten fingers that burned up much of Yā's retinue and elephants. Yā then convinced Pattini of his good intentions. Then Pattini, that embodiment of goodness, created a pond of ambrosia, wet her shawl with its waters, and resurrected the dead.

Yā's mother, who was with him, was jealous and angry that Pattini did not greet her with kisses. (How could Pattini, a goddess, kiss a mere woman, even though the latter was an elder?) Pattini made the woman immobile, but once the woman repented Pattini released her from this bond. Yā then escorted Pattini to his palace with pomp and ceremony.

This text is much less elaborate than the long and rich account of the trip to Madurai in the *Cilappatikāram*. Yet it shows a remarkable similarity in at least one respect. Canto 10 of the *Cilappatikāram* ("The Sight of the Kingdom") describes in detail Pattini and Kōvalaṉ getting ready to leave Puhar (Kāvēripūmppaṭṭinam) for Madurai. As they leave Puhar they visit the following places:

1. The temple sacred to Maṇivaṇṇan (Viṣṇu), which they circumambulate.
2. A Buddhist monastery, "the Seven Vihāras of Indra."
3. A Jaina temple.
4. A lake and a grove full of different kinds of flowers.
5. The residence of the saint Kavunti.

These five places have their parallels in the Sinhala account, which clearly mentions two of these—the Induvara Muni Vihāra, which most certainly is the Indra Vihāra mentioned in the *Cilappatikāram* (and *Maṇimēkalai* 1928, p. 199), and the residence of Kavunti. Clearly the two traditions are closely related. If the third and the fifth places they visited are identical in the two accounts, then the following identifications are also possible.

Sinhala text	*Cilappatikāram*
Diya Bäňdi Kōvil ("the shrine near the dam")	Maṇivaṇṇan (Viṣṇu) shrine
The palace or large temple (*mahā vāsala*)	Jaina shrine
Park with sal trees	Lake and flower grove

Text 42 *Marā Ipäddīma*: Killing and Resurrection

Introduction

The myth of *marā ipäddīma* is enacted in a ritual drama that deals with the events from the time Pattini and Pālaňga left Kāvēri paṭuna for Madurai till his murder and subsequent resurrection by the goddess. Though the ritual drama is designated *marā ipäddīma* ("killing and resurrection"), it in fact comprises sections of six texts of the ritual corpus, these being *kannuran katāva* ("the story of Kannuran city"), *bādāvaliya* ("the garland of bad omens"), *pālaňga märima* ("killing of Pālaňga"), *marā ipäddīma* ("killing and resurrection"), *vittiya* or *vittihata* ("exemplary stories"), and *vädi pūjāva* ("offerings by Väddas"). The ritual drama is called *marā ipäddīma* owing to the centrality of that text in the events enacted. All these texts except *bādāvaliya* are available in Hevawasam (1974, pp. 326–457). My version of the ritual drama is somewhat different from Hevawasam's, and therefore I quote it in detail.

Before I proceed with the description of the ritual drama of the "killing and resurrection," let me comment on a text that is practically moribund today but was of some significance in the past. This is the *bādāvaliya*, or "garland of bad omens," which helps us to understand some important traditional South Asian beliefs.

Omens have lost much of their significance in contemporary society, though they were crucial in traditional villages. In the present ritual only a few stanzas from the much larger *bādāvaliya* ("garland of bad omens") are sung. In the texts of the Hindus of the east coast of Sri Lanka (see pp. 574–75) there are also constant references to omens, good and bad. I interpret omens as a substitute or functional equivalent for astrology in traditional society. Nowadays astrology has taken the place of omens, so that one determines astrologically propitious and unpropitious times before any significant undertaking. Traditionally this was not possible. It is true that most people in traditional South Asian societies believed in astrology and horoscopes; yet they did not fully act on their beliefs. Astrology requires a notion of *exact* time that was not possible in village society before the availability of the modern clock. It is true that villages had a notion of inauspicious days (e.g., Tuesday, day of Saturn) and auspicious days (e.g., Thursday, day of Jupiter), but more exact calculations (such as the exact time to undertake a journey) were not possible in the villages. Thus astrologers were most often found in courts and urban centers. In the east coast texts Kōvalaṉ consults an astrologer in the schoolhouse (p. 576); at other times he resorts to omens. In the Sinhala texts there is practically no reference to astrologers, except in the courts of kings. Omens were a substitute for astrology in another sense; they constituted an objective index or sign of astrologically good or bad times. This is recognized in verses 37 and 38 of the present text. Here Pālañga sees a crow who ate some of his food, a bad omen; The verse says "he knew what these signs meant"—he was in danger "owing to the effects of bad time." Omens therefore chart astrologically propitious or unpropitious time.

The modern situation is very different. The easy availability of clocks has given an enormous fillip to the belief in astrology; concomitantly, the belief in omens has declined.

The ritual drama is acted dramatically in the early hours of the morning, though it is rarely performed nowadays. I have seen this only three times, twice performed in the Rabalīya tradition in 1956 and the other by the Heyiaṅtuḍuva *kapurāla* in 1960.

The stage setting for the ritual drama is very simple. A little hut representing the *velli ambalama* (Tamil, "silver rest house") made of tender coconut (*gok*) leaves and banana bark is erected on the right side of the arena. Opposite this, hung from the roof of the hall (*maḍuva*) on the left, are a few branches of *kohom̆ba* (margosa) representing the *kohom̆ba* tree under which Pālañga was executed on the orders of the king of Pāṇḍi. A man representing the dead Pālañga lies on a mat. He is totally covered in a white "shroud." From the opposite end of the arena enters the *kapurāla*, impersonating Pattini, dressed up in sari, bangles, and makeup. He is followed by a young assistant dressed in the garment of a domestic servant and carrying a small traveling bag. She is Kālī, servant of Pattini. Pattini stands at the end of the arena hardly moving at all while she sings the first part of the *marā ipäddīma*, known as the *bādāvaliya* ("garland of bad omens"). An assistant *kapurāla* acts as a chorus to Pattini, sometimes singing alternate lines but most often merely drawling the last syllable or two of each line. It is only with the *marā ipäddīma* proper that some form of dramatic enactment takes place. A greater emphasis was given to the dramatic aspects of this ritual at one time, according to the chief *kapurāla*.

1. Gracious Pattini known throughout the world
Gives the young Pālaṅga, her good husband
Her priceless anklet to be sold.
She thrusts the anklet in his hand.

2. He puts the anklet in his pouch and ties it
Its price is truly inestimable.
Studded with gems and stones of two thousand colors
At its base this gem anklet has gold worth eight thousand.[4]

I have omitted several stanzas that describe the value of the anklet, since my tape recording is not clear.

3. As if sensing the death that waits him
The attractive Pālaṅga took the anklet
—A goldsmith had an enmity from a previous birth—
He thought: let me go to the city of Madurā.

4. Her beloved Pālaṅga took the anklet
Full of sorrow at the thought of leaving
—All due to the past enmity of a goldsmith—
He prepared to leave for the city of Madurā.

5. "Your virtues spread like the shimmering moon
O lord full of auspiciousness and charm
What will become of me when you're gone?
Where shall I stay when you aren't here?"

6. "Both of us have come together from our native land
My tears," he said, "prevent me from sleeping
Do not go here and there O gracious Pattini
Stay here while I come back to you."

7. "O lady possessed of bounteous kindness and glory
I shall not sleep, my eyes won't close
Till I return after leaving you today
O King Yā she is in your charge."

8. "You did not listen to my words
With your own hands promise me
To go see the undying, powerful king
And come back to me in haste.

9. "We left the city of Kāvēri where we lived
Bereft of our kinsmen, and in a strange land
They were stricken with sorrow for their children
How hard it was to leave them and go.

4. Gold is measured in terms of *kalan*; each *kalan* is about forty grains.

10. "Blue lotuses opening in the dawn
Auspicious flowers with blue lotus hues
Sal flowers, and golden petals in the dawn
May your journey be as pleasant."

11. Thus Pattini said worshiping his feet
Tears flowed from her eyes, a shower after a drought
"Kind and loving lord be careful
As you go past paths and streets.

12. "If you see someone with goodness and generosity
Give him the anklet and ask for its value
But if you see those cunning goldsmiths
Don't join hands with them, those cobras.

13. "With firm resolve like a single tree I lived
Together unseparated from him till now[5]
Till he comes back from Madurā's kingdom
When will I see him again?

14. "Like people making joyful love constantly
We enjoyed prosperity in one bed together
When you go my breast will be empty
Lord without you how shall I live?"

Lines 1 and 2 of stanza 14 are most unusual. It is very clear that Pattini and Pālaṅga enjoy prosperity and amity but not lovemaking—others may do that, but how could Pattini? Hevawasam's edition (verse 22, p. 356) does not have line 1 but simply refers to their living well. Sinhala tradition may have utilized an Indian source that deals with Pattini and her husband making love, then changed it to suit the Sinhala notions of Pattini's purity. More likely "lying in one bed together" is an idiomatic usage indicating "living in amity together."

15. "My beloved lord, loving and kind
Cannot you see the mountain fire of my pain?
See how I implore you with my cries
Alas, alas, to whom shall I tell my sorrow?"

16. Possessed of dainty feet and eyes and body
Pattini the decorous noble lady then
Gave, with proper thoughts, to Pālaṅga
Cooked rice and vegetables to carry.

17. "O my good lord speaker of loving words
I have come with you to this place
But now you go to a distant land, my lord
How can my breast take this pain?

5. Lines 1 and 2 of stanza 13 presumably refer to Pattini's own fidelity rather than Pālaṅga's.

18. "My eyes a dam holding back a stream of falling water
My shoulders a shade held over my sorrowing breast
My hands a battle stick held aloft
But my mind a firm Meru rock that cannot be cleaved.

19. "A herd that comes down to rest
Is easily captured, my beloved
And owing to the nature of harlots
Ne'er look at them, go your way.

20. "These sayings coming down from old times
Truths handed down in our country
If you care for me listen lord
If you see omens do not make the trip.[6]

21. "Women with empty hands and empty pots
Dumb ones, deaf and blind folk, and lame
It's inauspicious to see these on your journey
Which then will become fruitless.

22. "Red flowers and cruel "torture flowers" if you see[7]
Or come across a snakeskin in your path
If someone confronts you and asks you where you're bound
These are omens listed from old times.

23. "Here's a truth coming from old times
If gecko lizards and woodpeckers screech
Or you see Väddas come from Ruhuṇa direction
You see danger them, they are obstacles [omens].

24. "If you see, in your journey, signs of lizards
Cobras fighting and pigeons and crows
Or deer cross from right to left[8]
Don't take the journey, if you love me lord.

25. "The cries of the peacock, woodpecker, and owl
Cobras, rat snakes, and herds of marsh deer
Foxes, mongooses, and hare, if you see
Don't go, dear lord, it bodes no good.

26. "If the earth in anger trembles
The skies thunder and down comes the rain
If you see these happen
There's no point in your journey.

6. The Sinhala word for a bad omen is *bādā*, which literally means "obstacle" or "hindrance." I translate it here simply as "omens." All these omens are obstacles in Sinhala usage.

7. Hibiscus flowers are called *vada mal*, or "torture flowers," because they were used to garland the executioner as well as those to be executed.

8. Right to left crossings are inauspicious in South Asian thought.

27. "Old men living like paupers
Men with noses cut off, crippled hands and feet
If you see soldiers or thieves with weapons
Take not the trip lest you meet death.

28. "But if you see these beautiful things
Like women nursing infants, saying loving words
It's a good sign to see them on your trip
Wherever you go, it'll be auspicious.

29. "Respected lord possessed of much tenderness
Remember well my loving words"
Then Pattini's husband, full of good qualities
Took his leave by pressing her breasts and kissing them.

Line 4 is a form of leave-taking no longer practiced in Sri Lanka! However, insofar as Pattini is mother and wife this form of leave-taking is singularly appropriate: a combination of nurturance and eroticism.

30. Like the ocean waves bursting on the shore
Tears streamed from Pattini's eyes.
A strange sorrow flamed in her body
As she gave Pālaňga permission to depart.

Note that Pattini, as a goddess, is superior, and she gives him leave to depart. In these poems there is a constant interplay between wife role and goddess role.

31. Exalted Pattini advised him thus
And tied the anklet in his pouch
Then the noble lord of the virtuous Pattini
Got ready to depart.

32. He did not heed the words
Of Pattini filled with reasonableness
Several days the merchant traveled
In spite of seeing bad omens.

33. The sun's rays hid under the tree's shade
Flashing turtles sported in the waters
See the many-plumaged birds bathe—
These he saw in a beautiful lake.

34. He rested himself and got ready to eat
He found lotus leaves to serve as plates
Then Pālaňga sat under a shade
And got ready to eat rice and curries.

Lines 1 and 2 in my tape recording are not clear, and so I have used the equivalent lines in Hevawasam (1974, stanza 35, p. 357).

35. Taking up the packet of rice to eat

He sprinkled water and praised the Buddha
He offered a portion to the gods
The subking then sat down to eat.[9]

36. A crow sat in the sun on a branch
He looked all around and grabbed some of his food
That low sinful creature
Cawed three times loudly crying.

37. The crow now climbed on a branch
With the rice held in its beak
[Pālaňga knew what these signs meant]
Soon the crow flew away.

38. Knowing the danger he was in
Owing to the effects of bad time
He gave some of his own blood to demons
And some rice, and went his way.

Line 3 probably refers to the practice of demon priests or exorcists of giving a drop or two of one's own blood to appease evil spirits.

39. Singing pleasant songs he wound his way
The youth's strength was sapped
The noble one was sorely tired
When he reached Madurā city.

There is a change in singing style from the next stanza on to indicate a shift in the plot of the story.

40. Pālaňga did not tarry for long
With the anklet in hand, in his innocence
[To expiate the bad karma he'd gathered]
Unknowingly reached the goldsmiths' street.

41. His karma from previous births
Now led him to Death himself
Pālaňga, handsome of feature, that day
Wended his way to the goldsmiths' street.

42. The cruel and bloody goldsmith
To prevent Pālaňga from leaving soon
Asked him courteously to be seated
And inquired the price of the anklet.

43. He filled his ears with honeyed words
Then sitting in dignity weighed the anklet
"I'll offer a good price for this, he told him"
And swiftly ran to the king's palace.

9. Pālaňga's father is a merchant-*rāja*, and therefore Pālaňga is a *yuvaraja*, or subking or prince.

44. Pretending to go to a shop nearby
He went to the king's assembly
He clasped his hands, fell down, and moved backward
And spoke to the king of the sun dynasty.

45. He bowed his head and worshiped the king
"I remember the beautiful queen said
That her beautiful anklet was stolen one day
This day I've seen the anklet thief.

46. "If you don't surround him
And hold him prisoner
The thief will soon hear rumors
And hide himself somewhere."

47. The king's crafty wrestlers came
Up to the handsome Pālaṅga
They abused him and beat him
And took him to the palace.

48. A full moon handsome body
And a gold complexion
A blow bent that body in two
Then red eyes and bound hands.

49. "The anklet I repaired
Here's the thief who stole it."
"I haven't even dreamed of theft."
"I've brought the thief that took it."

50. "This thief craved the anklet and stole it
Famished with terrible greed"
Then the goldsmith-sorcerer said:
"It is true, I never tell lies."

51. That sinful goldsmith lied
And destroyed the noble king
"This is the thief," he said
"Hated by gods and men."

52. The hardened wrestlers now
Stood all around him
They grabbed the anklet from him
They dragged him and tied him up.

53. The goldsmith showed his duplicity
He informed the Pāṇḍi king
He brought the wrestlers
"Now bind this wretched man."

54. A large and eager bunch
That day led Pālañga south
Tied up and drawn like an ox
And presented to the king.

55. When Pālañga was there in this wise
And he saw the king of Pāṇḍi
He bowed his head but worshiped not
"Look at this thief's audacity."

56. "Thief, why don't you worship
This honored king of immeasurable goodness
Mind pleasing in his worthiness
The Pāṇḍi king of illimitable preeminence?"

57. "Only to the Buddha and the Saṅgha
My teachers and parents dear
Even though you call me thief
I'll not worship anyone else."

58. The bonds were firm and tight
So death may come for certain
"Look he brags without paying obeisance
Which in itself proves his guilt."

59. "This anklet belongs to Pattini
And not to the Pāṇḍi queen
Listen Pāṇḍi to my words
Else this assembly will be cursed."

60. "Let the queen be summoned
To examine the anklet
Tie up the thief again
Now let's ask the queen."

61. As the king said
The queen was swiftly summoned
Curtains were held around her
And she seated there within.

62. The queen came to the royal house
"Tell us gladly what you know."
She was given the gold anklet
And the thief was shown to her.

63. The queen, stately as a divine maiden,
Took the jeweled anklet in her hand
As she held the fiery anklet
Her hands were sorely burned.

64. "This anklet is not mine
"It belongs to a Pattini with *tejas*
It's one she wears on her foot
Dear lord doubt it not."

The term "a Pattini" suggests once again that Pattini is also used for a class of female supernaturals. The word *tejas* here has the meaning of "fiery energy from the observance of *tapas*" rather than the simple notion of "glory."

65. "O Pāṇḍi king known the world over
This is not my anklet, alas!
If you execute this thief
Our country will be utterly ruined."

The last line refers to the notion that the king's injustice will cause his country to suffer.

66. "Note these words I've spoken
Pay them heed, doubt not
If you now kill the thief
Dire calamity will befall us."

67. "My queen what do you mean?
Didn't we give you your anklet
We've caught the thief with his goods
Queen, is not this your anklet?"

68. "Why did you bring me here?
Is it to display your might
Do not kill the thief
It's wrong O Pāṇḍi king."

69. "When they see the beauty of men
Women will always lie
How then can we believe you?
Women are fickle things."

70. The queen was fair and proper
Her words will last long
"Listen lord to my words
That goldsmith did grave wrong.

71. "Words unkind and untruthful
Were spoken by the goldsmith
They'll cause great confusion, lord
Desist, you'll later regret."

72. At the exalted queen's words
The goldsmith was enraged
He spoke to the Pāṇḍi king
Urging him thus.

The following are examples of female infidelity. Many more cases are listed in Hevawasam's edition.

73. "Passionately in love with a thief
She laid for him a large sheet
This she did though of noble birth
She was a queen, yet she did wrong.

74. "Giving the sword to the thief
And the scabbard to her lord
Haven't you heard this old tale [10]
Of women's wrongs.

75. "Lusting after a dwarf, a woman
Pushed the great bodhisattva from a rock
And greedily collected his head
She was a queen, yet she did wrong.

76. "O renowned Pāṇḍi king
Of pure and noble dynasty
Faultless women did you say?
Haven't you heard them gripe?

77. "Infatuated by his beauty
She now says he's no thief
She knows you'd commit sin
She's a queen yet she does wrong."

78. He listened to the goldsmith's words
And was struck with rage
He brought his elephant out
In order to kill the thief.

79. It was given toddy and liquors
Sharpened tusks and foaming mouth!
See how the goldsmith leads him in
Without others' seeing him!

Line 3 of stanza 79 suggests action taking place in a ritual drama. However, this event is not enacted in the present one.

80. Like a wasp drawn to a scent
He followed it wielding a big goad
He beat it, till it dropped dung all over
Uttering thunderous roars.

81. There was Pālan̄ga tied up
And the elephant some distance away

10. The reference is to the popular *Manamē Jātaka*, in which a princess, infatuated with a Vädda chief, betrays her husband and causes his death.

Then it was set loose
To kill the faultless thief.

82. It stood in front of Pālaňga
And saw him lying there
It let loose blood and dung
Then fell down on the ground.

83. Now the ignorant man in anger
Went again before the king
He tapped the king's pride
"Now send the lowly dogs."

84. When they saw him, that pack
They sniffed, and ran around him
Then came near and kissed his feet
And ran away, that lowly pack.

85. "Why goldsmith won't you speak up
How shall we execute this thief?
In order to kill this thief
Whom shall we summon?"

86. "Tell me where a *maruva* lives"
"He lives somewhere near
A distance of three *gavu*."
"Command him to come here."

I have kept the Sinhala term *maruva*, which has three interrelated meanings as executioner, as death in the abstract, and as the demonic representation of death.

87. With hatred coming from past lives
The goldsmith uttered falsehoods
He appeared before the king
"Tomorrow I'll bring *maruva*."

88. On the day he sent for *maruva*
The *maruva* was away from home.
Though it was height of noon
His wife was lying in bed.

89. While sleeping in her bed
She dreamed a dreadful dream
Her husband came home that day
And she told him her dream.

90. The *maruva*'s wife, a good woman
[Even though she sleeps at noon]
Related to her husband
The dreadful dream she saw.

91. "Lips like flower petals
Wife with golden body
As you lay in bed
What dreadful dream did you see?"

92. "It thundered and poured forth fire
The golden dome collapsed
The palace destroyed by fire
These three things I dreamed.

93. "Thunderbolt's a fire that'll spread
The golden dome a great king
Lightning is a queen
Danger awaits the city of Madurā."

94. Danger lies ahead, he thought.
It's because of this dream
That the great king of Pāṇḍi
Sent messengers to summon him.

95. The *maruva*'s wife, a good woman
Related her dream again
"It's bound to be true now"
She murmured in his ear.

96. He put aside the clothes he wore
He's dressed like a demon from hell
Ash on his body, and a large beard
And red hibiscus crowning his head.

97. Dressed in a showy turban
The curls from his wig falling o'er
With his hell rod in his hand
He was dressed like a creature from hell.

98. In this guise went *maruva*
To see the Pāṇḍi king
He fell prostrate on the floor
Went backward, then faced him.

99. Good man I'll give you gifts and position
Do as I tell you
If you kill this hard thief
Maruva, I'll give you gifts and pay.

100. Then the unjust king
Told *maruva* who worshiped him
"Take away the thief today
Torture him, cut him up, kill him."

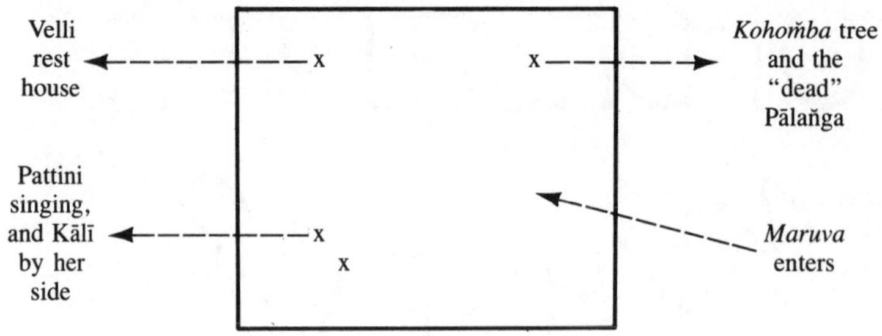

Fig. 7. Arrangement of the actors in the arena during the killing and resurrection of Pālañga.

Now begins the really dramatic part of the ritual. Hitherto the whole drama has been narrated by the *kapurāla*, who is both goddess and narrator. An assistant dressed as *maruva* in a weird garb that resembles a bearskin stalks at the back of the arena, sword in hand. *Maruva* now is the executioner in the Pattini story and the demonic personification of death.

The *kapurāla* changes his style of singing: it is now in the style of a rapid invocation to summon demons in exorcistic rites. Here it has a superb melodramatic effect—the drumbeat too changes, adding to the effect. A short, terse summary of what happened to Pālañga is sung in a few lines. The verses are sung rapidly—a quick, urgent utterance. They are in the present tense, which also helps give a sense of immediacy and directness to the situation.

101. He takes the jeweled, tinkling anklet
Of the glorious Pattini
He quickly goes to the city
Of the noble Pāṇḍi king.

102. He goes into the city
And meets the goldsmith
Who takes the anklet
And gives it to the queen.

103. The great king listens
The beastly smith talks
O the chief queen said
"Tell me the worth of my anklet."

104. "The anklet which was lost
For a very long time
See it with your own eyes"
Said the envious goldsmith.

105. To devise a frame-up
And to destroy a thief in Pāṇḍi
To get money for the anklet
He went to *maruva* to give him a life.

106. Decked in death's guise
The hell rod in his right hand
"I'll take away Pālaṅga
Kill him and drink his blood," he thinks.

Den den dena dena
Den denna denan denadena.

The *maruva* enters the arena, shrieking, hooting, and jumping around the body of Pālaṅga while the *kapurāla* sings:

Maruva here you come
Uttering demon cries
The world stands aghast
A demon now comes to do his dance.

Den den dena dena
Den denna denan denadena.

For about fifteen minutes the *maruva* holds the audience in a spell. He dances, shrieking occasionally and brandishing his sword while the drums pound away furiously. After a while he thrusts his sword at Pālaṅga and "hacks" him—bloodstains appear on Pālaṅga's white garb. More dancing and stalking around, and he then thrusts his sword under Pālaṅga's sarong and draws out his "bowels," dripping blood. It is a fantastic and yet convincing display—some members of the audience for a moment believe the person lying on the arena floor has actually been killed and disemboweled. The bloodstains are liquid dye, and the bowels are rags skillfully rolled up, dipped in dye, and ingeniously hidden inside the *maruva*'s sleeve. Having killed Pālaṅga, the *maruva* leaves the arena. The *kapurāla* continues singing once more. What he now sings is the killing and resurrection ritual (*marā ipäddīma*) proper, at least according to most versions of the "thirty-five songbooks." It is obviously recognized even in this drama as a separate text, though the action continues without interruption. The diacritical marks that set it out are the preliminary invocations to the Three Jewels and a summary of the preceding events, both of which I omit in this translation.

107. "I've been separated from my husband
Yet my love for him is still here"
Crushed by the grief that o'ercame her
Pattini laments in this manner.

108. "My husband went to trade
To the city of Madurā
How far is it to get there
Tell me Kālī-Kōḍi.

109. Then replied Kālī-Kōḍi
Listen graciously Pattini, O goddess
You want the distance to Pāṇḍi city
It is fifty *gavu* from here.

Kālī is of course Pattini's maid carrying her mistress's "suitcase," just like any servant in a Sinhala household. If in Kerala Pattini has been fully incorporated into Kālī, here Kālī, the ferocious mother goddess of Hinduism, is a harmless servant of Pattini. Kālī's transformation is analogous to the early Buddhist transformation of the warlike Indra of the Ṛg Veda to the Buddhist Sakra.

110. "Like the moon and the hare in its center
In harmony we lived together
O my lord exalted server
Why haven't you returned yet?"

Note that Pattini refers to her husband as *väḍakaru*, "servant" or "server." He is both lord (husband) of Pattini and also her servant (in her divine role).

111. "Hasn't he yet sold the anklet?
He's been enticed by another?
Or has he met with disaster?
Why has my lord delayed?"

112. Crows sit on the pillars
Then circle around the house
Presenting a deadly omen
They caw flock upon flock.

113. Cows refuse to give milk
They break loose and scamper
They shiver when tethered
And the young calves moan.

114. The sorrows yet to come
Appeared in deadly signs
Distraught by fear and doubt
Pattini suffers in her grief.

115. Gracious Pattini's great love
Wouldn't leave her breast
Darkness spread over the world
As did her grief.

116. "Unceasingly love shoots his arrows.
The gentle wind feels like fire
The cuckoo's tones sound like a demon's[11]
How can I sleep in a lone bed?

117. "You've left me here one night
Yet it seems a thousand years
That's how I feel his absence
I can't bear it any longer."

11. The *kovul*, or black cuckoo, in Indian and Sri Lankan poetry has a pleasant note, unlike its Western counterpart whose note is "unpleasing to the married ear."

118. Renowned Pattini now sleeps
And in her sleep she dreams
Of Pālaňga, a sword in his hand[12]
It's no sword but his absence.

119. "She prays to the Tender Queens[13]
Permit me to leave today"
"I needn't give you permission
Do as your heart tells you."

120. "O Sun God shining over the earth
Give me leave to go to Pāṇḍi city."
She gets his warrant and approval
She worships all gods and gets their warrant.

121. "To search for my blameless lord
I'll use my full power
How can I be blamed?
Let us go now to Pāṇḍi city."

122. Sesame cakes and *mun* cakes
Round halvah and milk balls
These she puts in a box
Then she summons Kālī.

123. She gives the box to Kālī
They travel thirty *gavu*
"Lady, my feet hurt badly"
"If thou canst not, I'll take the box."

124. "What folly is this, woman?
We can't leave this box behind"
"Lady I'll die of weariness
Let's stop under some shade."

Thus far the *kapurāla* (dressed as Pattini) has merely sung the songs, but now he moves from his stationary position. While singing he slowly walks toward the Velli rest house. Kālī, with her basket, follows him. The second *kapurāla*, who acts as the chorus, brings up the rear. Here another drama awaits them.

125. They reach the Velli rest house
A demoness lives there
From the fields below she comes, mouth open
"Today I'll have my prey" she thought.

While the *kapurāla* sings these lines, an assistant dressed from head to foot in a monstrous garb, teeth bared, shrieks "I'll eat you, I'll eat you." The *kapurāla* continues his song. As he sings the demoness jumps all over the dance floor shrieking and hooting.

12. Apparently the sword in Pālaňga's hand is a bad sign, implying that he will be killed by the sword.
13. "Tender Queens" are probably a group of goddesses who are worshiped as a collectivity.

126. She comes, mouth open wide like the plains of the sky
Teeth bared like the bodies of cobras
"How Kālī shall we escape today?"
"Lady there's nothing I can say.

127. "Except tie me up as a sacrifice
And I'll expiate my sins."
"Shame Kālī, say not so
I'll display the power of *tejas*."

128. She now raises her little finger
Fire bursts from the four directions
Then Pattini comes forth
And again raises her little finger.

The stanza above is not sung in the ritual I witnessed, but it is found in all popular printed texts. I quote it to illustrate Pattini's association with fire as a *bhūta* ("element") of the universe.

129. "I'll strike you with plague from head to foot
Why stand you there? Come into this rest house"
"Lady I cannot raise my feet"
"I order you to come forth here."

130. She loosens her dress and steps back
And "locks" the demoness's mouth and hands
"What ignorant things you do!
What sins you commit by this vagrant life."

131. "Lady how else can I survive"
"Listen to my angry words
Take charge of this human world of mine
Accept processions in Äsala [July]

132. "Accept *pūjās* of horn pulling
Also take my sari drape
Yes, you may take my sari drape
I'll now name you Maduru Māla."

"Sari drape" is the part of the sari that falls over the shoulder, or simply a shawl a woman wears over her shoulder. The shawl used by Pattini to bless audiences is sometimes identified as her drape.

133. "Take charge of my human world
I go to the land my husband went
I may never make the return journey
I will now leave this place."

134. Gracious Pattini now departs
She reaches the cowherds' street
"What city is this," she asks
From a cow girl that accosts her.

135. She leaves this street and moves forward
Cowherders now accost her
"Where are you gong alone dear girl"
"I go in search of my husband."

The following stanzas (136, 137, 138) are well known to the Rabalīya performers, but they were not sung in the present ritual. Since these are also found in all printed versions, I shall quote them here. It seems as if this episode, like others referred to in this text, has been designed for dramatic purposes—as Pattini walks toward Madurai, she would be confronted by two assistants dressed as cowherders onstage. However, it is not enacted any longer. Stanza 139 sung by the Rabalīya performers makes sense only in relation to the ones they have omitted.

136. "We shall give you an earring for your ear
A precious necklace for your shoulders
We shall drape your body in a golden dress
Tinkling bangles to wear in your arms.

137. "Medallions and toe rings for your feet
Silk and gossamer shawls for your waist
We shall hang curtains and canopies about your bed
We shall find a place for you to sleep in this city."

138. "Whatever you say I cannot delay
When I meet my husband, I'll rest in bed
I follow the path my husband took
Though cowherds ask me I cannot stay."

139. She passed their street and goes afar
"See how the cowherds abused me
It's you, lord, who causes all this
But for this you mustn't get bad karma."

140. She comes to the river Kāvēri
Its waters—not produced by rain—rushed forth[14]
"Why ferryman won't you [thou] ply your trade
When a woman like me is waiting."

141. "To whom do you jabber thus, wench
We don't have women like you in this city
We don't ply our boat for the likes of you
Women like you don't ride in our boat."

142. "Brother do not abuse me
If you want a lass go find one
I'll give you money the weight of a lad
Take it, but row me across."

143. "What kind of babble is this, wench

14. According to myth the waters of the Kāvēri were produced not by rain but rather from the upturned water pot of Saint Agastya (see pp. 346–48 for details).

This river is under royal interdict"
"Why is it under interdict, brother?"
"I don't know why, nor do I care."

It is clear that, like the shepherd sequence, this is supposed to be enacted. However, only the barest action takes place in Rabalīya. An ordinary basin is placed on the stage in front of Pattini and Kālī. This represents the "Kāvēri ferry." A "ferryman" with a water-pot appears on stage while the *kapurāla* and his second go on singing.

144. She rails at the earth and the sky
She takes the royal ring in her right hand
"Which god has caused me this pain?
With both hands she throws the gold ring in the river.

At this point Pattini (*kapurāla*) removes a large, ornate ring from her finger and throws it into the "basin" (the river Kāvēri). The "ferryman" leaves the stage.

145. The waters parted in two above
The waters parted in two below
White sands blossomed in between
And the noble Pattini walks over these.

146. "May pestilence strike the ferryman's kind"
The ferryman falls prostrate at her feet
"Did you not see my might"
She calmed his pain and went forth.

147. The parted waters met again
With gunshot sound.
"How lady shall we find the ring?" [Kālī says]
The ring now fell at her feet.

148. The exalted Pattini goes forth from there
She asks people for news of her husband
Swiftly sixty *gavu* pass by
That's how she showed her glory.

Now there is a change in singing style and drumming as the priests sing the "long songs." Changes in singing style often indicate a diacritic shift in the plot or theme of the story.

149. "O lady bird pecking mango and rose apple and holding them in your beak
Kissing your breasts and combing its feathers
O cuckoos making sweet melodious sounds
Quickly say—have you seen my noble lord?

150. "Nibbling the mango with your sharp parrot teeth
Sucking its juice and enjoying its taste
O flock of parrots hopping from branch to branch
If you've seen my noble lord I'll give you merit.

151. "Stepping out of the woods with your tender babes

Coyly nudging, eating sweet fruits
Frolicking in the meadow to please our minds
O herd of deer, say, if you've seen my noble lord."

There is very little dramatic enactment in the preceding narrative except gesticulation by the *kapurāla*, who moves about the arena while singing. But now two children with books in their hands accost the *kapurāla*—they represent children going to school. Pattini has now reached Madurai and, seeing these children, asks them the whereabouts of Pālaňga. The children do not speak any lines—they merely confront the *kapurāla*. As before, it is the *kapurāla* who sings the songs. The *kapurāla*, facing the two children, continues the narrative.

152. They've recited their lessons and worshiped their teacher
With books in hand in the middle of the street
"Good children you'll get great merit
If you show me where his corpse lies."[15]

153. "A handsome noble merchant came to this city
With an anklet. Do you know if he's been killed?" she asked
"Good children you'll get great merit
If you show me where his corpse lies."

154. "We eagerly went to school in the morning
We studied the letters and read our books
Now we are tired and hungry.
Yet we'll show you where he was killed."

155. She gave them sweets and balls of puffed rice
Fed them lovingly, gave them water, and pleased them
She held them close, brushed their hair with her hand
And said: "Come show me where his body lies."

156. They led her past the city streets
And pointed a right hand for Pattini to see
Like a cloud seen from beneath a branch
They asked her to look under the margosa's shade.

As this and the next stanza are being recited the goddess walks toward the corner of the dance floor where Pālaňga is lying.

157. Her dark hair falls over her anguished face
Tears stain her breasts
She goes up to see her husband's corpse
And Pattini weeps in her terrible grief.

The goddess is now near Pālaňga: she bends over him and wails in piteous tones. The "lament songs" that follow are all sung in broken tones, interspersed with sobs. As a result the words are not clear and hence are difficult to translate. I have, however, given

15. The Sinhala *kumaru* may mean "children of noble birth" or "princes." Some texts explicitly identify these children as Pāṇḍi's own offspring.

approximate translations. Many versions of this lament—one of the most popular in Sinhala folk culture—are available. Some are very beautiful. For the present purpose I have chosen to use the Rabalīya text, though I shall also quote a few representative stanzas from a popular version known as *Pattini Hälla*.

158. Pattini the Muni arrived there, alone in her grief
She saw the graceful "lake body" lying on the ground[16]
Like lightning flashing its colors over an evening cloud
Alone in her suffering she embraced her lord's body.

159. The maiden Pattini, compassionate, wears a *tilaka* on her forehead like a flower
She places her head against her lord's red lotus feet
She raises her hands and worships him again and again
She cries and cries in her pain of mind and grief.

160. "Where is that youthful body I created, O sounder of cuckoo notes
O warrior mine whom I fed with milk like the ocean
O my lotus feet, overflowing with love, whom I worship
My own dear lord why has this great pain visited me?"

Note lines 1 and 2, where Pattini looks upon her husband as if he were her own child. This is one kind of projection found in these myths, but not the most important.

161. "Did you rub sandal and rose water on your body only to forsake me
Did you shed all those tears only to go meet Death himself
Lord did you bring the anklet only to give it to the Pāṇḍi king
And did you marry me, lord, only to cause me the heat of grief?

162. "I know why I came here, as clearly as I see my face in a mirror
Where is my pride if I don't bring you back to life
The women of Kāvēri will shame me surely
By the power of my courage put on your robe lord and awake.

163. "The good queen of Pāṇḍi had a hand bracelet
But the goldsmith lied and falsely killed Pālaṅga
My innocent lord, your vital centers destroyed
I'll avenge his death, O how can I be consoled?"

Here is the first reference to the queen's having a hand bracelet. The Sinhala term *salam̆ba* is applicable to both.

164. "My exalted lord came here
But now he's scattered
His life extinguished
This sin must bear fruit."

165. By the arrow of Benares's king

16. "Lake body": perhaps the notion is that at death the body reverts to its original fluid state.

A *kiňdurā* was struck dead
This *kiňdurā*'s woman
Had power to bring him back.

The *kiňdurā* (*kinnara*) is a beautiful mythological creature, half human and half peacock. The reference is to the *Saňda Kiňduru Jātaka* where the bodhisattva was born as a *kiňdurā*; while he was blissfully sporting in the forest with his wife, the king of Benares shot him dead. The female *kiňdurī* wept, and Sakra intervened and brought him back to life.

166. The god Sakra came there
"Please protect my husband," she said
"May not I have that power
I'll show how my power will bear fruit.

167. "Like mercury and gold our minds were bound[17]
O my noble lord, brimming with love
How is it that you've left me now
By this death you've met?

168. "Pale body observe me weep
Wake up and open your eyes
Wake, wake up now my lord
And bring me joy."

I shall quote below a few stanzas found in several of my texts. Some of these are known to the Rabalīya group but were not sung in the rituals I witnessed. The lament of Pattini consists of 177 stanzas in Hevawasam's edition. Naturally only a few are sung in any given ritual.

169. "At one time in a gay city
We enjoyed prosperity together
Now there is no turning back
Alone with sun and bitter wind. . . .

170. "O my beautiful lord
Woe is me my husband dear
How like you this 'happiness' now
My husband lord of love.

171. "Dazed with love and passion
Suffering, I came to this city
You lie on this stretch of sand
Handsome my lord awake.

172. "O downy golden body
In the bosom of the margosa shade
No more shawls to lie on
Blissfully asleep on these cruel sands.

17. Mercury and gold are an Indian alchemical and medicinal combination.

173. "Tears overbrim, fall over
The body burns unceasing
How could I bear it any longer
Renowned my lord awake.

174. "Can't you hear your girl cry
Today O lovely one.
Your beauty drawn with brush erased
Asleep, sprawled on these sands.

175. "I came here in great wrath
I say these words to you
'Look! the power I possess'
My dear husband awake.

176. "Your golden body pales
By my affection waxes
My heart throbs painfully
Lord, I will be revenged.

177. "Husband, sweet of speech
I took the road you walked
Why am I thus meek?
Could I bring you back to life?"

Now there is a change in singing style. Several four-line unrhymed stanzas are sung rapidly, as always to convey a sense of urgency. These verses seem very old and, at least in their style, reflect pre-fifteenth-century tradition. Only a few are sung in the Rabalīya tradition, but Hevawasam's edition has thirty-one stanzas.

178. "In the blazing sun
Without a shade
O Lord you're in the sun
Your corpse is also there.

179. "Have you sown *rat taṇa*
To give to flies and worms?
Why live in a watch hut
If one remains silent?"

These terse lines are metaphoric. *Rat-taṇa* could mean "red cereal," or even "gems." Thus: "Have you sown an expensive cereal/gem only to give the harvest to flies and worms?" Lines 3 and 4: One lives in a watch hut to shout at animals invading the field, not to remain silent.

180. "One lights a fire
Two raise the flames
To quell this fire
Two others pour water."

This and the next verse indicates Pattini's sense of futility and meaninglessness.

181. "When there's a slashed *hēna*[18]
An unslashed *hēna* catches fire
Is it another *hēna*
If you know, lord, tell me?

182. "The rising floodwater
Spreads like an echo
Is there any solace
For my great pain?"

Stanza 182 is an example of the "pathetic fallacy."

183. "Why should you like lime
If you have an orange?
Shouldn't you use unripe lime
If it's needed for a *nasna*?"

Nasna is draining of the sinuses in Sinhala medicine. Unripe limes are used for this purpose. I am not sure of the significance of these lines. Perhaps they mean, "I have to do something bitter, even if I don't like it, because it's necessary for the cure"—her reference to the destruction of Madurai.

184. "It's I who asked you
To go a-trading
I ask you again
Do come back and trade."

Now more conventional, rhymed stanzas are sung but in the same stacatto style.

185. Thus she related the virtues
Of her beloved husband
Crying and sobbing and sobbing
'Twas to Pattini's glory.

186. Her virtue spread o'er the world
Her power germinated
Mount Meru became warm
And warm Sakra's jewel throne.

187. Sakra was living there
In full happiness
When his seat grew warm
He wanted to know why.

188. He created an ambrosia pond
Wetted the shawl with its water

18. *Hēna* (or the Anglicized *chena*) is a forest used for swidden cultivation; it could also mean "swidden cultivation."

Placed his hand on Pālaňga's head
And told him to get up.

It is not clear from the Sinhala whether Sakra or Pattini created the ambrosia pond and resurrected Pālaňga. As sometimes happens in Sinhala, no personal pronoun actually is used in the stanza. Some texts in my possession do not refer to Sakra's entry. Instead, Pattini asks Pālaňga to rise, and the power of her chastity directly makes him awake from the dead. It is possible that Pattini directly awakening her dead husband is an older version of the myth.

189. As if lying in a bed
Deep in cool sleep
By the influence of Pattini
The prince rose joyous.

190. God Sakra then
Pleasantly said:
"To please Pattini
Pālaňga now rise."

191. O the great fatigue she suffered!
The power of her *tejas*!
Bring a singing priest
Utter the "resurrection," and calm the fire.

At this point Pālaňga gets up and moves off the dance floor. Drums beat, and the singing style changes as another part of the myth is unfolded. Much of the action is now over, and the *kapurāla* continues to sing the rest of the text. There are two versions of the subsequent events. Hevawasam's edition describes how the goddess in her wrath went up to the Pāṇḍi king. She proved to the king and queen that her own anklet (or bracelet) was "stolen" by the court peacock, who had swallowed it. The peacock was then brought before the king and made to vomit out the anklet. Pattini took her remaining anklet, which she threw at the city. The city was destroyed. The god Sātā implored her to desist. This text makes no reference to her tearing out her breast. However, in this same text in verse 82, Pattini says she is going to tear her breast and burn Madurai (Hevawasam 1974, p. 379). In some traditions she burned the city of Madurai by tearing out her breast and throwing it into the king's palace. In Rabalīya both traditions are combined: she first threw her anklet, then her breast. Unfortunately my tape recording is not clear enough for a translation of the whole text. I shall summarize part of the text and translate other parts of it.

192. "I shall show the might of my *tejas*
On my good husband's behalf
I shall display my full power
As I am a Pattini for this world."[19]

19. Note the reference to "a Pattini" again in stanza 192. The goddess is "a Pattini for this world" as Gautama is a Buddha for this world.

193. How Pattini showed her might
In this manner, to the world
Its golden sound spread confusion
As she threw the anklet on this slab of earth.

194. The sound of the spreading anklet
Shook the blood of those near and far
The king hid in fear
His blood shook from the mouth below.[20]

195. Grabbing the gold from people
And leading a deceitful life
O cunning goldsmiths
Why do you kill the innocent?

Stanza 195 gives us one sociological reason for the public resentment against goldsmiths. It also generalizes the accusation of murder to all goldsmiths.

196. Ignorant of royal Dhamma
Lacking in foresight
Committing iniquity, not rightness
King what canst thou do now?

There are several stanzas about the failings of the Pāṇḍi king. Pattini insults him by calling him a "lad who does not know merit and sin." He is not a king, but a "lad" among kings of the rose apple continent (India). She scolds him (*banimin*) and insults him (*nindā*). Then she creates a fire outside the palace door and in her wrath sends it inside the palace. She now accosts the king, who insults her again.

197. "What do you want O wife of the anklet thief?
I'll tear off your breast and make you eat it"
"Why do I need my tainted breast any longer?"
She broke it and threw its golden plate.

Perhaps line 3 means that the breast has been polluted by the king's insult.

198. As it struck, the city burst into flame
If you say 'tis false your mouth will smart
Such is the strength of the goddess Pattini
The palace became a mound of ashes.

But Pattini saved the good queen. The fire spread rapidly and consumed all sinners and liars in the city; it struck at the street of goldsmiths, wreaking havoc. But it spared the good—the temples, the abodes of Buddhist monks, houses of Buddhist relics, sermon halls, dwellings of good folk, the houses of merchants and farmers, cowherders, and washermen. Fearing further destruction, however, a deity named Sātā implored Pattini to quell the fury of the fire.

20. "Blood shook": idiomatic, meaning that the king shook with fear.

199. King Sātā, who saw this event, said thus:
"Pattini cause no more suffering"
He implored Pattini with his hands on his forehead
"Cause no more pain and human deaths."

200. Thus King Sātā bowed before her
And asked her to stop the fire soon
"I destroyed the Pāṇḍi king and evil people only
Did you not see, sir, this yourself?"

201. She spoke thus to King Sātā
She said she'd stop the fire
"If you give me tribute of drums
Then I'll end this conflagration."

However, there were no drums or drummers available in the city—so the king's cow was killed and a drum was made from its hide. Pattini was pleased—she placed the remainder of the hide over the corpse of the cow and:

202. So the cow got up at once again
The calf [who suffered from its mother's death]
Could now pull at her udder
With the calf near her, the cow could now give milk.

203. Following the instructions of old teachers
They milked the cow and poured the milk in a pot
They built a *toraṇa* in the right manner
And boiled milk outside for the Sun God.

This is actually performed in the arena—a pot of milk is placed on a three-stone fireplace in front of the main altar and a fire is lit. Rice too is put into the pot, and after a few minutes the pot overflows.

204. Thus they performed it as she'd wished
Sweet-smelling flowers were offered all day
Beautiful leaves of betel were also offered
And milk boiled in front of each household.

205. And so she brought happiness to the world
She created a pond of ambrosia that day
She wetted the end of her shawl with it
Brought blessing on all by fanning.

In stanza 205 it is she, not Sakra, who creates the ambrosia pond.

206. Then the gods assembled in their glory
They showered glorious "rain flowers" from the sky
As if a roaring river was falling
That's how the Madurā fire was quenched.

This stanza is one of the most famous in the whole corpus. Versions of this stanza are sung in many places in the *gammaḍuva* as well as in the *aṅkeḷiya* rituals, generally in the context of the cooling of heat or fire—in the medical and metamedical sense.

207. Having quenched the fire, she stayed for a while there
That a second calamity might not befall this city
She quenched the flames with compassion
And departed then for the Velli rest house.

She gave the kingdom of Madurai in charge of the queen and the commander-in-chief. She then mounted a chariot and went toward the Velli rest house (*ambalama*), and from there the chariot ascended to heaven. The text says she went there to meditate (*devlova tapasaṭa*).

208. She saw the chariot that was sent and was pleased
She prayed for a Buddhahood to come soon
With thoughts of compassion and the observance of precepts
She went away in the chariot that was sent.

Text 43 *Vitti Hata*: The Seven Exemplary Stories

This text is sometimes simply labeled *vittiya*, "exemplary stories." In this text Pattini confronts the king of Pāṇḍi and tells him about his injustice. She relates seven exemplary stories. However, as in all these ritual texts, the preceding events of her life are summarized. This text also shows some remarkable resemblances to the *Cilappatikāram*, again suggesting that both texts derive from a common tradition.

The poem starts with a recital of the events that led to the confrontation between Pattini and the king of Pāṇḍi. Much of this appears in *marā ipäddīma* and other texts. However, verses 43–52 in Hevawasam's edition seem to parallel the account in the *Cilappatikāram*, canto 20, "The Demand for Justice," lines 8–23 (Dikshitar 1939, pp. 246–47). The Sinhala text describes how Pattini arrives at the entrance to Pāṇḍi's palace. The citizens of Madurai have dreams that indicate disaster:

> The royal elephant seemed to be dying and fell down with a crash; the royal sword broke in two; the palace entrance shattered; the royal dome collapsed and fell down; fires engulfed Madurā. (verses 43, 44)

These are paralleled in the prognostications described in the *Cilappatikāram*, though they are not identical.

As in the *Cilappatikāram*, in the Sinhala text Pattini goes up to the palace guard and identifies herself as the wife of the anklet thief. The Sinhala description of Pattini, however, does not appear in the *Cilappatikāram*, for in the Sinhala account she appears wearing a silk veil, or *moṭṭakkili*. In the Sinhala text the king's guard goes up to Pāṇḍi and describes Pattini's beauty in extravagant language. This is not found in the *Cilappatikāram*. However, another event in the *Cilappatikāram* reference (Dikshitar 1939, p. 249, lines 66–70) has its parallel in Sinhala. There Kaṇṇaki confronts the king and says that her anklet contained gems, and the king replies that his wife's contained pearls. "Kannaki then broke open her beautiful anklet, and a gem flew into the king's face." In the Sinhala account Pattini dashes her anklet, which contains gems, on the floor. "The glistening anklet burst open and the gems scattered all over. One of the gems hit against the king's forehead [or cheek] and caused bleeding" (verse 260, Hevawasam 1974, p. 442).

The main focus of the story, however, is on Pattini's narrating exemplary stories for the edification of the king (and of course the audience). These stories deal with two themes—first, the triumph of the weak over the strong, and, second, examples of just and good kingship. It is interesting that the *Cilappatikāram* makes no reference to these in its canto entitled "The Demand for Justice." The next canto, however, has examples of seven women of chastity. It is likely that the "seven exemplary stories" and "seven women of chastity" reflect a tradition of seven stories Pattini related. The kind of stories told probably varied with the cultural tradition involved.

I shall briefly summarize the seven exemplary tales in the present text.

1. Soon after the demise of the Buddha Dīpaṅkara, the bodhisattva was born as a king elephant living in the Himalayas with a retinue of a thousand elephants. A little paddy bird (*käṭakirilla*) who lived in the neighborhood saw the elephants advance toward her. She begged the king elephant to protect the nest that contained her children. The king elephant stood over the nest protecting it while his troop went by. He then informed the bird that an outcaste rogue elephant would soon pass that way and urged her to be on her guard.

The rogue elephant came upon the bird and the nest, but he had no compunction. Ignoring the pleas of the mother bird, he crushed the nest underfoot and killed the little birds. The mother wept in grief and decided to wreak vengeance. She persuaded a female crow to pluck out the elephant's eyes, which soon festered and became infested with maggots. The elephant went blind and wandered around famished and thirsty. The bird then asked a frog to croak loudly near a precipice; the elephant, thinking this sign indicated water, rushed forward and fell to his death.

Pattini related this story to Pāṇḍi and told him further: "The paddy bird who saw the dying elephant went up to him and walked over his body weeping over the death of her children. O king, wait till I show you the power of my vows of chastity which I have observed for fourteen aeons [*kalpa*]."

2. This story is not described in detail. The audience's familiarity with it is assumed. It is about two lizards who to protect their offspring combated a herd of a thousand elephants. How they did it is not stated, but it was probably by creeping into the brain of the (chief?) elephant, or the whole lot of them, through the trunk. (In this section Pattini threatens to destroy Madurai by fire as the lizards destroyed the elephants.)

3. Once the king of Soḷī (Cōḷa) saw a cobra catch a frog as his prey. He gave a portion of his own flesh to the cobra in order to save the frog. (In the conclusion of this story Pattini deliberately contrasts the good king of Soḷī with Pāṇḍi, who "does not have these virtues"—stanza 91.)

4. A lion and a hare lived in the same Himalayan forest. The lion captured the hare and took it to his lair. He played with it before attempting to kill it. The hare then pleaded with the lion to spare its life. The hare told the lion there was another lion in the forest who was his peer. The lion was curious, since he did not believe there was anyone like him. The hare took him to an abandoned well and asked the lion to peep into it. The lion saw his own reflection on the water and, thinking it was the other lion, he jumped into the well to attack him and was drowned.

5. The teacher to the king fell in love with the beautiful wife of Darakäṭiyā ("woodcutter"). He went into Darakäṭiyā's house, usurped his bed, and threw Darakäṭiyā out of the house. Darakäṭiyā took shelter under the eaves. Meanwhile the king of Soḷī went forth in disguise as a palace guard to find out the troubles in his kingdom. He saw Darakäṭiyā and asked him for shelter. Darakäṭiyā told him that one man had driven him out of his house and taken his wife and now another wanted to deprive him of his temporary shelter under the eaves. The king ordered the woodcutter to open the door. He punished the royal teacher and gave the woman back to Darakäṭiyā. Later he invited Darakäṭiyā to the court and rewarded him with many gifts, including a silver ax.

Pattini tells the Pāṇḍi king about Soḷī's goodness and virtue.

> The king of Soḷī, blessed with abundance and prosperity, ruled the kingdom according to the dictates of justice; he comforted the poor by giving them adequate and just wages. O Pāṇḍi king listen to the just king who ruled according to the ten principles of kingship. (Hevawasam 1974, p. 425, stanza 135).

This is followed by a panegyric on the king of Soḷī.

During Soḷī's reign there was peace and unity even among animals. Goats played affectionately with tigers and hares with jackals; mice with cats, frogs with cobras, peacocks with cobras, and so forth. The king's subjects also lived in peace and harmony: there was no crime in villages and marketplaces. The deities were also pleased with the king, who lived according to the ten virtues of a just king, according to the example of King Dharmāsoka (i.e., Asoka). By contrast Pattini accuses the Pāṇḍi king of unjustly killing her husband. She now relates another exemplary event pertaining to the king of Soḷī's justice.

6. A calf was run over and killed by the chariot driven by the son of the king of Soḷī. The mother cow came up to the palace and rang the bell of justice, which had lain still for many years (since there was no injustice in Soḷī land). The cow cried and wailed in grief. The text has many stanzas on the cow's lament, very much like that of Pattini. The king's courtiers tried to cover up for the prince, but the king, in his empathy for the cow, said that justice must prevail. He ordered that his own son be driven over by the chariot and killed, even though he was stricken by grief at the thought of his son's death. The courtiers tried to prevent this act, but to no avail. However, after the prince was killed, Sakra came down to earth and restored him to life. (This story is attributed to many "just" Tamil kings, including the king of Pandya (Pāṇḍi) in the *Cilappatikāram*. The resurrection of the prince by Sakra seems, interestingly, to be a specifically Buddhist invention.)

7. Sakra wanted to test the king's commitment to justice. He asked a deity to assume the form of a dove while he took the guise of a Vädda (aboriginal hunter). When the king of Soḷī was going on his rounds he found a Vädda chasing a dove with his stick, trying to kill it. The dove ran to the king for protection, and the Vädda also went up to him and demanded he surrender the bird. Instead of surrendering it the king wanted to give some of his own flesh to the Vädda. The Vädda agreed. The dove was placed on one side of the scales and some of the king's flesh on the other. The dove's side went down, however much of his own flesh the king placed on his side of the scales. Ultimately the king was practically stripped to the bone, but since the scales still went down, the Vädda decided to spare the bird.

Stanzas 224–29

Some people in the crowd were "snapping their fingers," some clapped their hands, others sang the praises of the king, while some worshiped his feet.

They praised the king thus: "There's never been a better king than you before, who reigns in accordance with *dasa rāja dharma* [the ten virtues of kingship]."

Sakra, seeing the crowd, renounced his guise of Vädda and assumed his real form, illuminating the assembly with his splendor.

The king and the people were delighted at the arrival of Sakra. The ministers threw gems and pearls at his feet.

Thereupon the world of gods on the summit of Mount Meru began to be visible (to ordinary men).

The gods descended to earth and showered much wealth on the assembled people and blessed them.

Clearly Soḷī is the model of the good king who rules the country very much in the tradition of that Buddhist exemplar King Asoka and in accordance with the ten principles of kingship laid down in Buddhist texts. The good king brings about prosperity and protects the common weal, whereas the bad king brings about a wasteland.

Text 44 *Vädi Pūjāva*: An Offering Given by Väddas

Vädi pūjāva is never sung or performed in any of the rituals I have seen, though most senior practitioners are aware of it. The text is, however, an important one, since it clearly illustrates the connection of the Sinhala tradition with that embodied in the *Cilappatikāram*. The first stanza of canto 23 ("The Explanation") states how Madurāpati, the guardian goddess of Madurai, appeared before Pattini and unfolded her husband's past karma that resulted in his present misfortune. Madurāpati appears with "her head decorated with a crescent and her matted locks, *kuvalai* like eyes, white radiant face, with the left half of her body dark blue, and the right half golden, with a golden lotus in her right hand, and a glittering and terrifying sword in her right, with a victorious kalal on her right leg, and a matchless jingling anklet on her left" (Dikshitar 1939, p. 262). The first stanza of *vädi pūjāva* has a much less elaborate description of Madurāpati. But the Sinhala text (Hevawasam 1974, p. 445) describes her as coming down from heaven, wearing a holy anklet, bangles on her feet, matted locks, a lotus in one hand and a diamond weapon in the other. Pattini is also described as blue and gold in text 16 (pp. 122–23). Clearly the Sinhala tradition is related to that of the *Cilappatikāram*.

In Sinhala the goddess is called Madura Mādēvi, which is equivalent to Madurāpati. However, since this deity is of little significance in Sinhala culture, she is identified with Vaduru Mādēvi, the demoness of pestilence who appears in the "killing and resurrection." Moreover, her role here is minimal. In the *Cilappatikāram* she gives an elaborate account of Kōvalaṉ's past karma. In the Sinhala account she merely states that he was born as a merchant prince in the city of Kapila and that his present death is due to the sins he committed then. These sins are not specified; however, "it is not possible even for a Buddha to escape from the consequences of his karma" (Hevawasam 1974, p. 445, verse 4).

Pattini asks Madura Mādēvi whether she will be able to see her husband. As in the

Cilappatikāram, Madura Mādēvi promises to show him to her in his divine form. When she sees her husband, her missing breast will reappear.

The rest of the text deals with the offerings made by Väddas to Pattini. After she destroyed Madurā, the Väddas decided to honor her, since there was no one like her in the three worlds. The king of the Väddas proclaimed to his people that Pattini was on her way to their "city" after setting Madurā on fire. He ordered his people to clean up the "city" by removing sticks and stones, so that they might honor this Buddha-to-be. The Väddas then constructed a hall (*maḍuva*) for performing *pūjās* in her honor. They hung leopard skins as a canopy, and streamers of betel leaves and branches for decorations. The walls also were of leopard and deer skins. They lit lamps and burned incense in her honor. They had skins for carpets and meals prepared with *ūru vī* (literally, "pig rice"—i.e., "polluted," "inferior" rice). Then the Väddas awaited Pattini's arrival. The earth goddess prepared her way by creating hundreds of streets and decorating these streets with festoons and flowers. She also created a golden pot and filled it with water for Pattini to wash herself.

Now Sakra's seat grew warm like ghee (because of the polluting offerings inadvertently given by the Väddas). He summoned Daḷa Kumāra (the demon Garā, who gobbles up impurities). This demon came down to earth carrying an iron rod in one hand and a sword in the other. Pattini saw him and summoned him and gave him a warrant to take the offerings for himself. Daḷa Kumāra went to Vädda land, frightened all the Väddas, and gobbled up everything, the food as well as the physical structures. Pattini then gave Daḷa Kumāra permission to accept various collective rituals on her behalf from the Väddas. Then she witnessed the dances, drumming, and other displays of the Väddas in her honor.

Thereafter, in Sakra's own chariot, driven by Mātali, his charioteer, Pattini ascended to Tusita heaven. There she lives, hoping to see the Buddha Maitreya in the future, and also hoping for Buddhahood for herself, after being born as a male. When she went into heaven she preached a sermon with quiet concentration, while all the gods listened attentively.

This text is different from the one sung in the Garā ritual described on pages 173–85. It is, however, a clear attempt to incorporate Pattini as a deity who is suzerain over the Vädda pantheon. It is also probably a mechanism for incorporating the Väddas into the Sinhala Buddhist ritual system while at the same time affirming their separateness.

Text 45 *Rāmā Märīma*: The Killing of Rāma

Many *kapurālas* believe that the "killing and resurrection" (*marā ipäddīma*) is not performed nowadays because of *vas* that may strike the actors. Instead, a substitute comic drama known as the killing of Rāma is performed. In a ritual I saw in Ratnapura in 1960 the dancer who impersonated Rāma told me of three deaths that resulted from performing the *marā ipäddīma*. The following account of "the killing of Rāma" is from the Sabaragamuva tradition.

The chief *kapurāla* here is also the priest in charge of the Pattini *dēvāle*, an adjunct shrine to that of the Sabaragamuva Mahā Dēvāle, the central shrine of the god Saman at Ratnapura. He does not, however, directly participate in the *rāmā märīma* ritual, or any ritual drama involving humor and obscenity, since this would be beneath his dignity.

Among some practitioners the actual *marā ipäddīma* has gone out of vogue for so long that the Rāma play and the *marā ipäddīma* are viewed as the same, the latter viewed as simply another term for the former. Haramānis, who acted as Rāma in 1974, was not aware of the distinction; but Hīn Nilame, who did it in 1960, knew of the difference. The chief *kapurāla* is of course thoroughly familiar with the thirty-five ritual texts.

In most parts of the Southern and Western provinces the *rāmā mārīma* ritual has nothing to do with the mythology of any of the deities of the *gammaḍuva*. However, in Sabaragamuva an attempt is made to link the Rāma ritual with the Devol Deviyo myth. In Sabaragamuva the ritual drama starts with the entry of Devol Deviyo into Sri Lanka, but this part seems clearly added on, since the main body of the drama, which deals with Guru Hāmi, the trader, and his servant, Rāma, has no reference whatever to Devol Deviyo, which is exactly how it is in the traditions of the Southern and Western provinces. Nevertheless the Sabaragamuva tradition's attempt to integrate the Rāma ritual into the Devol Deviyo tradition is relevant for the study of ritual traditions.

In the performance at Ratnapura, Guru Hāmi, the protagonist of *rāmā mārīma*, is identified as Devol Deviyo. Simon (or Rāma) is his servant.

An attendant brings a mat into the ritual arena. Guru Hāmi says he wants *piduru* ("straw") to sleep on, but the dancer corrects his poor Sinhala and says *pädura* ("mat"). Simon now holds the mat and acts the role of the mat seller. "This is Rs. 1.25," he says, but Guru replies, "I'll give you Rs. 2.50 for it." This kind of dialogue goes on for some time. Guru counts the money and gives it to Simon, who gives him the mat. He complains about the dirty mat and tries to assault Simon and the dancer with it. He asks how a mat is "woven," which is also a pun for "cooking," and then he attempts to cook and eat the mat. He wants to sleep now, and the drummer says "You must put your head on it." Guru puts the mat on his head; then on his shoulders. He snores. The dancer shouts "Guru! Guru! are you asleep?"

> Guru: Yes, I am sleeping with the mat on my back.
> Dancer: Guru, that's no way to sleep, you must be *on* the mat.

I shall skip much of the comedy of errors that follows. Ultimately the dancer tells Guru Hāmi that he must sleep with Rāma. Guru Hāmi now takes the mat and dances with it in the arena, singing the following songs with the dancer:

> Our Muni destroyed the Māra hosts and became the Buddha of the three worlds
> The gods, whose glory shine in the three worlds, worshiped him with joy
> May there be no *dōsa* for the songs that I now sing
> Give me permission to recite the ritual [*yakkama*] of Rāma.
>
> The seven people from abroad landed on these shores
> They unloaded here the goods they had brought
> They erected separate shops and stores
> From far these look like a heavenly city.
>
> In the sands where they unloaded their goods
> They ate and drank heartily seated at table
> They have such pleasing ways when they sell goods
> "There are none like us in the whole world."

They sold their goods to many people
Now here comes someone to buy some cloth
"How much money do you have for buying cloth?"
"I have money to buy one piece of cloth."

Eventually having sold the cloth
They hastily consumed opium and ganja
Intoxicated, they curled up in deep sleep
Rāma who saw this was mightily pleased.

Then Rāma was so greatly pleased
He tied up the goods in a bundle
Bent in two he stealthily crept away
And hid away secretly, in a far, far village.

The events described in the preceding verse are contextualized locally and enacted. Simon now takes the role of a villager buying cloth for his wedding. Guru Hāmi is seated on the mat like a Tamil merchant, and the dancer acts as a friend (and prompter) of Simon. Several events are enacted.

a. Simon wants to buy cloth for his bride. Guru Hāmi wants to give it free to the "new bride, just as a present." Guru Hāmi now is the lascivious Tamil merchant. He asks Simon the path to his house and tells him be sure to clear it and remove those stones that may stub one's toes in the dark. Simon and his friend will have none of it. Ultimately Guru Hāmi measures the cloth, this time parodying the cunning Tamil merchant with his false measures.

b. The first part of the story moves imperceptibly to the next. The goods have been sold, and now Simon takes the role of Rāma, Guru Hāmi's servant. Guru Hāmi having sold his goods wants to go smoke some ganja and asks Rāma to look after the shop. He comes back in an intoxicated state and hiccups. He is now sprawled on the mat. He asks Rāma to massage his legs (a custom that many old Sinhala people much enjoy). Now Guru is asleep, and Rāma runs away.

Dancer: Guru, Guru . . . Rāma has gone, there's no one in the shop.
Guru Hāmi: This can't be, he is lying at my feet.
Dancer: Rāma isn't here, get up . . . when I came here there wasn't anyone . . . what's happened to him? I don't know, I wasn't here.
Guru Hāmi: Rāma . . . O Rāma . . . Rāma my son, where are you [he starts crying].

He struts all over the arena looking for Rāma. He seeks advice from the drummer who says, "you can catch him with magic." Guru Hāmi utters a comic parody of a mantra, but still no Rāma. The dancer says that maybe Guru Hāmi should ask "our gods" for help. The idea is to send a charmed object or *däpa*, in this case a coconut. Guru Hāmi holds it in his hand and dances with it, singing the following songs.

Bearing the command of the Gods of the Four Warrants
He kept aside the charmed coconut
The consecrated coconut he kept for seven days
"Even if he's left the country, I'll get him next morning."

With the permission of the Gods of the Four Warrants
He consecrated the coconut and kept it aside
He obtained a warrant for the charmed coconut to move
"Go search carefully and seek out the thief."

The coconut went forth and fell at Rāma's feet
"You ingrate, I'll teach you a good lesson"
He tied Rāma securely with two strands of rope
"I will torture him and ask him why he ran away."

Guru Hāmi utters a mantra and rolls the coconut on the arena floor, and it rests near Rāma (who has been in the arena physically, though not in terms of the conventions of the play). Guru Hāmi ties up Rāma with a white sheet twisted into a rope. Guru Hāmi weeps when he realizes that his goods have been lost, especially a powerful medicine, a panacea, that his mother-in-law gave him. He simulates beating Rāma, then tries to squeeze his neck. The dancer tells him that just *any* punishment won't do, but only the kinds made out by royal decree. Guru Hāmi now bursts into song, and while singing "assaults" Rāma.

"The shop that contained the shared wealth of the Seven
Look, what a terrible robbery this fellow performed"
He hit him on his sides, rolling him in the mud
"*Aḍe!* Tell me where you hid the goods."

His head was shaved and the nose cut off
He was branded and his body beaten
The marks of the whip left weals and lumps
Thus Rāma was tortured and then killed.

Dancer: Now you have to shave his hair.
Guru Hāmi: You thief, you rogue elephant, see what I'll do to you.

He uses his stick to imitate sharpening the razor, then "shaves" Rāma's hair. Then, under instructions from the dancer, he cuts off Rāma's ears. "Now you must cut off the nose," the drummer tells him. After much tomfoolery about the quality of Rāma's nose, it too is cut off. "Now you have to brand him." Guru Hāmi imitates heating the branding iron (his stick) in the fire, then brands Rāma's body and buttocks. Rāma's limbs are now lopped off one by one, and then he is beaten with a whip, to the sound of drums. "Now you must tear open his bowels . . . everything must be pulled out . . . ," the dancer darkly hints. Guru Hāmi: Don't move, we must perform the "operation" (he uses the English word) correctly.

He hits Rāma below the abdomen with his "knife." Then he goes back a few yards and runs toward Rāma with the "knife" and pulls out, in imitative actions, enormous lengths of bowels. Finally he clearly imitates cutting off Rāma's genitals. He then covers the dead Rāma with a white cloth and ties the four ends of the cloth together.

Guru Hāmi laughs and gloats over the dead body. The dancer tells him: "This is serious, you have murdered someone. No . . . no . . . bribery won't do. . . ." Guru Hāmi says, "He isn't dead . . . Rāma, Rāma, listen . . . listen. . . ." He tries to run away, but he is detained by the dancer and others.

Dancer: . . . no way. You'll have to resurrect him; perhaps you can implore the gods.

Guru Hāmi: O Gods of the Four Warrants: Viṣṇu, Sumana, Skanda, Dädimuṇḍa, Vāhala, Seven Pattini, and Devol, O gods, don't permit Rāma to rise from this death mat!

Naturally this does not make Rāma awake, so Guru Hāmi tries again. He sings:

O Rāma helpmate in my troubles
Look, believe me, Guru's eyes are full of tears
Guru is crying loud and long in his sorrow
Awake, your father's arrived, Rāma awake.

Guru shakes Rāma by the shoulders and tells him, "awake, your father's come," but to no avail.

O Rāma who helped me from the very start
Who gave me ganja and opium lovingly
This Guru is lonely, crying out loud and long,
Awake, your aunt's arrived, O Rāma awake.

The aunt's arrival is also of no use; even the presence of the aunt's daughter (marriageable cross-cousin) is no help. The dancer says, "you must implore the help [*pihiṭa*] of the gods."

In the very beginning of the *kalpa*
In the guise of a boar he tore apart the earth
By the influence of Śrī Viṣṇu
By his command may Rāma's life come back.

Dance and drumming. He asks Rāma to get up by the power of Viṣṇu.

Dancer: The god Viṣṇu is noble and mighty . . . but even he cannot resurrect the dead. So let us try some other god.

Song:

His glory shines [like the sun] over the world systems [*sakvaḷa*]
He burned the arrogant *asura* to ashes
O god Saman whose glory and might overspreads the worlds [*sakvaḷa*]
Today, by your power, bring him back to life.

Guru utters a panegyric on Saman and asks Rāma to awake, but again it is futile, for not even Saman can resurrect the dead.

He who clove the *asura* in two with his lance
And created the peacock and the fowl [vehicles]
By the influence of the god of Kadirāpura [Kataragama]
Recover the life that Death is taking away.

But Skanda is no help, either, powerful though he is.

From above the clouds he fought the Māra hosts
And worshiped the feet of all the famous gods
If the command of the god Däḍimuṇḍa is true
This corpse will arise by that god's influence.

Since Däḍimuṇḍa cannot help, Guru Hāmi seeks the help of Vāhala.

In his hand the cane with the gold handle
Quickly he beats the arrogant demons
If the command of god Vāhala prevails in this land
Quickly make this dead man arise.

Dancer: . . . even god Vāhala can't help you, but there's a deity who in fact resurrected the dead. . . .

Guru Hāmi: You mean the goddess who awoke her husband under the shade of the Kohom̆ba tree.

Song:

She arrives from heaven into this world
She sees with her divine eyes the woes of mortals
By invoking the command of the noble goddess Pattini
Now Rāma open your eyes and awake.

Guru Hāmi praises Pattini and asks Rāma to awake by the power of her glory and might, or *tejas*, and her *ānubhāva* ("influence"). He lifts the white cloth covering Rāma, and he awakes.

6

Mythic Stratigraphy

Any mythological tradition comes from historically diverse sources. A tradition of myth is a composite of preexisting beliefs, beliefs that are newly invented, and those incorporated from other belief systems. An analysis of the sources of a given mythic tradition may help us unravel the processes by which a religious tradition came to be constituted. Anthropologists have been averse to a historical study of myth ever since Radcliffe-Brown castigated the diachronic study of oral tradition as "pseudohistory." However, in a literate culture like Sri Lanka, with historical records going back about two thousand years, it may be possible to relate the tradition of myth and ritual to historical periods or events and thereby to "verify" hypotheses or propositions regarding the former. It may therefore be possible to construct a "speculative history" of a mythic tradition, grounded on historical data. Archaeological interpretation, for example, is a species of speculative history of the type advocated here. In social anthropology or ethnology, speculative history may not give us a coherent chronological account of the development of a mythic tradition, but it can, I shall show, help us elucidate the *processes*, both historical and sociological, by which such a tradition comes into being. For this the data from history are not sufficient; they must be substantiated by data from the mythic tradition itself. In other words, we must devise a method whereby we can unravel the several "strata" of beliefs that constitute a living mythic tradition by first relating it to verifiable historical events, episodes, or periods and then considering the content of the mythic tradition itself for evidence that elucidates historical and sociological process. It is the latter task that I shall attempt in this chapter: in later chapters I shall deal more explicitly with historical chronology.

The method I shall adopt for studying mythic stratigraphy is basically threefold. I shall not attempt to justify in detail these three strategies on a priori grounds, but rather shall assess their actual success in the study of historical process.

1. *Symbolic statements*. Nowhere shall I attempt to resurrect the old-fashioned technique of arbitrarily extracting historical elements from myth. I shall treat myth holistically, as anthropologists have done. Myth is impersonal and symbolic, yet—as anthropologists and psychoanalysts have shown time and again—its symbolism is multilayered and overdetermined, consisting of several levels of meaning. I shall show that historical process is often reflected, or expressed, in symbolic form in both myth and ritual. For example, historical processes such as the displacement of one cult by another, or the diffu-

sion of myth and ritual from one area to another, may be expressed in symbolic form, either as symbolic statements in myth or as symbolic action in ritual.

2. *Survivals*. Anthropologists of the nineteenth century found the doctrine of survivals crucial to their evolutionary view of culture and society; yet it was thoroughly debunked by twentieth-century social anthropology on the grounds that so-called survivals had important functions in the ongoing sociocultural system. I wish to resurrect this concept for the study of mythic stratigraphy and to justify its use.

It is difficult to reject the idea of survivals a priori. In the biological sphere the existence of vestigial or nonfunctional organs is undisputed; furthermore, such survivals help us understand evolutionary process. In paleontology the so-called living fossils, like the duck-billed platypus and the coelacanth, are creatures from the remote past surviving into our own day under special environmental conditions. In the latter cases the question of function is irrelevant to the study of the item as a survival from the past.

I therefore justify the concept of survivals on the following grounds.

A. There may be items from an earlier religious stratum that have little or no function in the ongoing system. Such items may *eventually* disappear. Yet an item that has ceased to have a function does not disappear overnight. In anthropological fieldwork we study a ritual tradition at a certain point in its history; in doing so we are bound to come across survivals from prior periods that have not yet disappeared. In a conservative religious tradition such items may survive even longer. In the Sinhala case many myths and ritual traditions are written down in palm-leaf manuscripts, probably from about the fifteenth century, in almost their present form. Many aspects of the sociocultural system have changed since then, yet it can be shown in this and subsequent chapters that the written traditions have not been drastically altered. Sometimes nonfunctional rituals are not enacted; instead, their mythic content may simply be recited. In other instances the rituals of the *gammaḍuva* refer to various personages who have little bearing on or relevance to contemporary culture. Yet the texts that refer to such beings are still being sung in current rituals, largely because they are respected as part of a continuing tradition that should not be tampered with. In many cultures the continuity of tradition is itself an important value that goes counter to the interests of change and functional relevance.

B. Defining survivals in terms of function is misleading, for it is possible that survivals or vestigal items can survive under special conditions both in nature and in culture, as in my earlier example, where the continuity of tradition itself constitutes a value promoting survivals. Moreover, an item can survive from the past under a different set of cultural conditions or functional supports. We have several examples of this from the *gammaḍuva* tradition, as, for example, the different uses of Bam̆bura Yaka among aboriginal Väddas and Sinhala peasants. Alternatively, an item may continue to survive to the present day with diminished importance or limited functional significance, like the *doḷaha peḷapāḷiya* described earlier (pp. 172–73).

In sum, the notion of survivals is philosophically defensible; it can, I shall show, be put to analytical uses. Furthermore, if one ignores survivals one may strain to interpret an item in synchronic-sociological or functional terms when such an interpretation must necessarily be an ethnohistorical or a diachronic-sociological one.

3. *Comparison*. Comparing a ritual performance with substantively or functionally similar ones in a larger culture-sharing area may be indispensable for the study of mythic stratigraphy. In Sri Lanka the Sinhala-speaking Buddhists belong to a large culture-

sharing area within which regional differences exist. Thus all Sinhala Buddhists share a common set of beliefs pertaining to Buddhism. They also propitiate, or believe in, the major gods of their pantheon; yet regions have their own local deities as well as their own ritual techniques and procedures. Comparing a similar ritual in different parts of the larger culture-sharing area may help us in our study of historical process. A ritual that is a survival in one area may be vitally important in the other, permitting us to make a proposition of the following sort: If two versions of the same ritual, one a survival and the other functional, are performed in different regions of the same culture-sharing area, then the item that is functional represents the historical past of the item that is a survival. Furthermore, comparing items in *space* may on occasion help us understand their devolution through *time*. However, there can be no rule of thumb regarding the technique of comparison: tentative formulations based on comparison must be cross-checked with other kinds of historical and sociological information.

The Mystery of the Missing Deities: The Twelve Gods

In this section I shall apply some of the methodological strategies described earlier, to show how myth and ritual are stratified in the *gammaḍuva*. In the *gammaḍuva* there are constant references to the Twelve Gods, or Doḷaha Deviyo, often worshiped in the singular as a collectivity. They are offered the aesthetically elegant dance of the *telmē* and the rituals of the *doḷaha peḷapāḷiya*, the *ät bandana* (elephant capture), and the *mī bandana* (capture of the buffalo). Yet, though they are given such prominence, they are rarely mentioned by name, and very little mythology is available regarding them. My assumption is that we have observed a ritual at a certain point in history where an older cult is fast becoming moribund and will soon be extinct. The cult of the Twelve Gods is a survival; yet comparative and symbolic analysis can help us understand its prior significance and its lack of contemporary relevance in our region.

I shall compare the situation in our region with other areas in Sri Lanka where the cult of the Twelve Gods is still in vogue. The data are from Hañguranketa, about twenty miles to the south of Kandy, and other regions in Sri Lanka that I am familiar with. In Hañguranketa the collective rituals are also called *gammaḍuva*, but the presiding deity is not Pattini but the Twelve Gods. In addition, I shall use the data on the Twelve Gods supplied by Gombrich for Mīgala, a village twelve miles east of Kandy. While the cult of the Twelve Gods in the *gammaḍuva* is moribund, it is, or was until very recently, an active cult in many parts of Sri Lanka. In most parts of Sinhala Buddhist Sri Lanka, except the North Western and North Central provinces, which I am not familiar with, some of the gods of the Doḷaha Deviyo cult of Hañguranketa are propitiated, even though the concept of the Twelve Gods is not employed.

The cult of the Twelve Gods in Hañguranketa and elsewhere can be understood only in reference to the cult of the Four Gods. As I explained in chapter 2, the Four Gods have always existed in Sri Lanka as guardian deities protecting the secular realm from the four directions. The capital of each kingdom had to have shrines for four guardian gods. The identity of the gods varied through time and place, yet the concept was integral to Sinhala religion right through history. Thus, in the post-eighteenth-century Kandyan kingdom the Four Gods were Nātha, Viṣṇu, Kataragama, and Pattini; in the kingdom of Kōṭṭe of the fifteenth and sixteenth centuries the Four Gods were in all probability Vibhīṣaṇa, Viṣṇu, Saman, and Kataragama; and in the *gammaḍuva* at Rabalīya they are Viṣṇu, Saman, Kataragama, and Vighīṣaṇa. Since the fifteenth century, however, the Four Gods everywhere comprise some combination of the following pan-Sinhala deities: Viṣṇu, Saman, Nātha, Vibhīṣaṇa, Pattini, and Kataragama. In general one of the Four Gods had a role in protecting the sovereignty of the kings, as did Nātha in Kandy and probably Vibhīṣaṇa in the Kōṭṭe-Kälaṇiya kingdoms.

Everywhere in Sri Lanka the Four Gods—the pan-Sinhala deities—are at least formally invoked in collective rituals. In Hañguraṅketa, as in all other "provincial" areas, the operative pantheon consists of the cult of the Twelve Gods, many of whom have demonic attributes. In the collective rituals they are also referred to as *dēvatā*. Some, like Irugal Baṇḍāra and Dēvatā Baṇḍāra, are close to divine status; others, like Kalu Kumāra, are split into both good (divine) and evil (demonic) manifestations, while others, like Gañgē Baṇḍāra, are true *dēvatās*, a composite of divine and demonic attributes. These Twelve Gods are associated with most of the social, economic, and personal needs of the worshiper—hunting, animal husbandry, and rice cultivation, as well as with the cure of individual afflictions such as illnesses from demonic incursions.

In the collective rituals at Hañguraṇketa these gods are given *tēvāva* ("service") similar to the *doḷaha peḷapāḷiya* of our *gammaḍuva*, though some of the symbols of the former are not used—for example, the *cakravartin* symbol of the pearl umbrella. In the service of fanning (*halu vaḍanava*) each god is listed separately in the ritual texts and then ceremonially fanned by the *kapurāla*. I noted eleven deities in one tape-recorded version from Hañguraṅketa in the following order.

1. Irugal Baṇḍāra
2. Piṭīyē Deviňdu
3. Pallebädde Deviňdu
4. Dēvatā Baṇḍāra
5. Alut Deviňdu
6. Kalu Kumāra Devi
7. Kīrti Baṇḍāra
8. Vāsala Deviňdu
9. Kalu Dēvatā Deviňdu
10. Kaḍavara Deviňdu
11. Vanniyē Baṇḍāra Deviňdu

Number 12 is probably Gañgē Baṇḍāra, an important deity in the area. Other deities of the same class referred to in the texts are Mäṇik Baṇḍāra and, most important, Maṅgara Deviyo, and the female deity Kiri Amma worshiped individually or as a collectivity of seven manifestations. Maṅgara Deviyo and Kiri Amma are also worshiped in our culture area, but with diminished significance. They are very important deities in other areas like Laggala, a remote region to the northeast of Kandy (totally removed from our culture area), as well as in the southern dry zone, near Panāmure and Hambegamuva, which is adjacent to our culture area. Maṅgara is associated with cattle; Kiri Amma is often associated with children's diseases. Because of their pan-Sinhala spread, Kiri Amma and Maṅgara are outside many of the formal lists of the Twelve Gods.

In Mīgala, Gombrich (1971a, p. 185) has recorded three lists of Doḷaha Deviyo with considerable overlap. One of Gombrich's lists has twelve deities, but one has fourteen and the other fifteen. In Hañguraṅketa I also noted that in fact there were fifteen deities, and lists from informants showed the kind of variation Gombrich has noted. Thus it is clear that numerology has the same function here as elsewhere in Sri Lanka: the number itself is crucial, but the content shows some variations. Numerology permits continuity in tradition within the context of change and cultural and areal variation. It provides an overall sense of cultural unity within a large geographical area.

The cult of the Twelve Gods is often identified with the so-called Baṇḍāra cult of the Kandyan Sinhala. This term was introduced by Parker, and has been used by Seligmann and many others since then, to designate the worship of deified ancestors among the Kandyans. As Gombrich points out, the term is a misnomer and a "gross oversimplification" (1971a, p. 189). The Seligmanns have described a form of ancestor worship among Väddas known as the cult of the *nā yakku* ("kinsmen-deities"), but the Kandyans have no such cult. The title Baṇḍāra, as Gombrich says, "is a Kandyan naturalization certificate" (1971a, p. 189). However, the term "Baṇḍāra cult" is a useful descriptive label as long as we do not equate it with ancestor worship but confine it to euhemerism characteristic of much of South Asian religion. These euhemeristic deities are viewed as regional chiefs or aristocrats (i.e., Baṇḍāras), rather than as kings or *cakravartins*. The myths of some of these Baṇḍāras have South Indian backgrounds. Almost all of them were humans (but not ancestors) who have been deified after death, which of course is entirely consonant with Buddhist and Hindu theories of karma and rebirth.

The Twelve Gods, then, constitute a cult of regional deities that are part of the operative pantheon in many villages of Buddhist Sri Lanka outside our culture area. Some of them have national status, particularly Maṅgara, Kiri Amma, and more recently Dēvatā Baṇḍāra. Yet when we look at the Rabalīya (and other) *gammaḍuva* traditions we note that the cult of the Twelve Gods there is quite different. According to priests, they were twelve kings who participated in the prototypic *gammaḍuva* of Sēraman. Yet Sarachchandra, in his study of folk drama in this region, has in fact a list of the Twelve Gods that is strikingly similar to the Haṅguraṅketa and Mīgala lists. He writes: "Along with Pattini are invoked a number of gods like Kataragama Deviyo. . . . Vāhala Deviyo, and the Twelve Gods called collectively Dolaha Deviyo. The names of these gods are given in some places as Mänik Devi, Māvatte Devi, Kosgama Devi, Parakāsa Devi, Kumāra Devi, Miriyabädde Devi, Vanni Baṇḍāra, Kalu Baṇḍāra, Bōvala Devi, Mīgahapiṭiyē Devi, Mirisvattē Alut Devi and Kivulēgedera Alut Devi. These gods are regarded by some as attendants of Pattini" (Sarachchandra 1966, pp. 30–31). Here we have a list that duplicates some gods from the earlier lists (Vanni Baṇḍāra, Kalu Kumāra), yet many are indigenous to a local area. Thus Kosgama Devi, Mīgahapiṭiyē Devi, Mirisvattē Alut Devi, Māvattē Devi, and Kivulegēdera Devi are minor gods who have names of villages, some of them from our region. Parakāsa Deviyo is also worshiped in parts of the southern dry zone. Kivulēgedera Devi is almost certainly Kivulēgedera Mohoṭṭāla, who, along with Käppeṭṭipola, was an important leader of the 1818 rebellion against the British. He was captured and executed by the British and subsequently was deified in some parts of the country as Punci Alut Baṇḍāra Deviyo ("the younger new Baṇḍāra god"). There is a painting of this chieftan-deity in the Liṅdamulle Pattini shrine near Badulla (Pieris 1950, p. 421). Their being named after localities indicates that these gods are deified local heroes. The evidence then is clear that the cult of the Twelve Gods existed not only in the Kandyan areas, but also in the culture area I am dealing with. Furthermore, there is an overlap from one region to another; but each region has its own local deities unrepresented in other areas. Thus this cult of the Twelve Gods once constituted a series of overlapping circles covering most parts of the Western, Southern, Sabaragamuva, and Kandyan areas.

Now let us consider the cult of the Twelve Gods as it is expressed in the *gammaḍuva*.

For convenience let me label the Twelve Gods of the *gammaḍuva* as the Twelve Kings, since they are viewed as such. However, the label is my invention, not that of the people. The texts of the *telmē* give a list of nine kings, namely, Kalikot, Kulakonta, Sātā, Mada raja, Yuvaraja, Kaṇḍāraja, Yā raja, Sulaṁbā raja, and Golusan. Nowhere in the *pantis kōlmura* or other texts of the *gammaḍuva* have I seen a fuller list. A few of these names make some sense, such as Yuvaraja (heir apparent), but for the most part they make no sense in Sinhala language or mythology. Yā raja, a kinsman of Pālaṅga (see text 41, pp. 244–45), is obviously an important figure, since he is often mentioned in these texts, but his mythological roots are probably in ancient South Indian tradition. Sātā is either the deity Cāttaṉ, who appears several times in the *Cilappatikāram*, or more likely Cāttaṉ the author of *Maṇimēkalai* (see pp. 589–90). The chief *kapurāla*, however, added three other names to make it twelve—Sēraman himself, Daḷa Kumāra, and Vīramuṇḍa. It is strange that Sēraman should be one of the Twelve Gods that came for his (Sēraman's) own ritual. Daḷa Kumāra (or Garā) and Vīramuṇḍa are never associated with any of the "Twelve Kings" in any text I have seen. Yet these two additions are significant. Vīramuṇḍa is one of the Twelve Gods in some areas in Kandy and is an important deity in the collective rituals known as *kohoṁbā kaṅkāriya* performed in *hatara kōrale* and other areas, and Daḷa Kumāra is also an important deity of the same class (i.e., *dēvatā*). Thus it is possible that these gods were part of the original indigenous class of Twelve Gods before their places were usurped by the Twelve Kings. Regarding Vīramuṇḍa there is little doubt, since he is elsewhere regarded as one of the twelve. For Daḷa Kumāra also we have the evidence of the rite of the *doḷaha vilakku*, or twelve torches (see p. 182). These are twelve torches planted for the Twelve Gods (Kings) of the *gammaḍuva*, yet one torch, at a lower level, is also planted for Daḷa Kumāra, or Garā. This is a symbolic statement meaning that Garā is one of the Twelve Gods, yet inferior to the others. Why? In the other pantheons (e.g., Haṅguraṅketa) there are demonic beings among the Twelve Gods very much like Daḷa Kumāra (e.g., Hūniyan, Kaḍavara, Kalu Kumāra). In such a pantheon he would not be a subordinate being; yet he is clearly so in relation to the superior *kings* who are propitiated as the Twelve Gods in the *gammaḍuva* traditions. The implication of the symbolic statement is relatively clear: Daḷa Kumāra was a deity from a previous pantheon of Twelve Gods. Since he is indispensable for banishing *vas*, he alone is retained in the reconstituted pantheon of the Twelve Kings of the *gammaḍuva*. But in relation to these kings he is clearly inferior; this is recognized in the lower position of the torch planted in his honor.

Let me quote another symbolic statement—a symbolic slip, one might say—in relation to the Twelve Kings. The *kapurāla* gives a list in one place (p. 209) and repeats the list again (p. 164), but with one significant difference: the word Baṇḍāra raja is substituted for Kaṇḍāraja in the second list. Kaṇḍā, one of the Twelve Kings, makes no sense in Sinhala culture; it is converted into Baṇḍāra, which of course is generally associated with the traditional collectivity of Twelve Gods. This is not an individual slip of the *kapurāla*, but a "symbolic slip" of the culture. In Pānama (p. 419) the term *kaṇḍāraja* also appears; here also the *kapurāla*s glossed it as "Baṇḍāra." There is no etymological justification for this identity except a phonological resemblance between *baṇḍā* and *kaṇḍā*. But it is significant that when the identity of one of the new Twelve Gods (Kings) is involved, it is made in reference to the old cult of the Twelve Gods (i.e., the Baṇḍāra cult).

In the traditions of the *kapurāla*s of Sīnigama there are several texts that are no longer sung in the *gammaḍuva*. These texts refer to several minor deities like Hañdun Kumāri ("sandalwood princess," one of the Kiri Amma), Ratna Kambili ("golden blanket"?), Kurumbara Dēvatā (one of the Kurumbara), Aiyaṉār (the brother of Skanda, propitiated in the northern dry zone and in the Eastern Province), and Galē Baṇḍāra. It is possible that some of these were part of an older cult of the Twelve Gods; Galē Baṇḍāra ("lord of the rock") is a well-known deity in the Kurunāgala area whose cult has been described by Parker (1909, pp. 177–296).

Finally, there is some very interesting evidence from the traditions of the *gammaḍuva*. In the *gammaḍuva* as it is performed today, Pattini is clearly one of the major deities, on a par with the Gods of the Four Warrants like Viṣṇu and Skanda. But there is an older classification known as the *tunbāge deviyo*, which I gloss as "the gods of the three divisions." These three gods are Pattini, Devol Deviyo, and Dēvatā Baṇḍāra (Däḍimuṇḍa). For example, the *kapurāla* says that the gods of the three divisions are all entitled to the *toraṇa* altar. Devol and Dēvatā Baṇḍāra are clearly not of the major class, though the latter may soon reach that status, owing to his increasing popularity. Furthermore, Dēvatā Baṇḍāra is one of the traditional Twelve Gods in the Hañguraṅketa list and in all three of Gombrich's lists. It seems most likely that these three deities were part of an earlier cluster of Twelve Gods, and because of their importance they were retained but given another numerological classification as "the three gods." Later Pattini rose into the higher category, while the other two retained the lower position. In other words, if my analysis is correct, the cult of the *gammaḍuva* at one time contained a collectivity of Twelve Gods, a part of the operative pantheon. Pattini herself, as well as Dēvatā Baṇḍāra, Devol, and Maṅgara, was part of this collectivity. In this sense Pattini's role was strictly parallel to that of Kiri Amma, the only female deity in the Hañguraṅketa and Mīgala pantheons of the Twelve Gods. These Twelve Gods were pushed aside by the Twelve Kings, and also the major gods like Viṣṇu, Kataragama, and Saman, who in the *gammaḍuva* are part of the operative pantheon, unlike their formal role in Hañguraṅketa. How did this occur?

We can assume that the cult of the Twelve Gods was once also operative in our region. As in Hañguraṅketa and elsewhere, the major gods were probably only formally invoked, at least most of them. Pattini herself was an important deity in village worship, like Kiri Amma, but she was not of the same status as the Gods of the Four Warrants. This role of Pattini would explain why there are no extant bronze sculptures and only a few paintings and iconic representations of Pattini. Neither Kiri Amma nor Maṅgara nor any of the Twelve Gods, in spite of their extreme antiquity, is represented in classical art or poetry or literature. They have remained folk deities, part of a lower tradition. What, then, produced the changes we note in the *gammaḍuva* and in the popular worship of our region? An examination of the historical conditions and literary evidence of the Kōṭṭe period (1410–1544) will provide the answer.

From the fifteenth century onward a series of poems appeared in Sinhala entitled *sandēśa* (messenger or epistle poetry, based on the tradition of Kalidasa's *Meghadūta* ("Cloud Messenger"), with the difference that in the Sinhala traditions the messenger was always a bird carrying an epistle. Most of these poems were of great length, generally more than two hundred four-line stanzas. They described in detail the journey of the bird through various parts of Sri Lanka, particularly in the Southern and Western provinces of our culture area. From these *sandēśa* poems we gain considerable information on religion that is relevant to this book.

In the *sandēśas* written in the Kōṭṭe period (1410–1544) the most important deity mentioned is Upulvan or Viṣṇu. Three extant *sandēśa* poems commence or end the journey of the bird at the great shrine of Viṣṇu in Devundara, in southern Sri Lanka. After Viṣṇu, two other gods receive considerable treatment, Vibhīṣaṇa of Kälaṇiya and Nātha, whose main shrine was Toṭagamuva, in southwestern Sri Lanka, also in our region. Kälaṇiya is near Heyiaṅtuḍuva, site of one of the *gammaḍuva* traditions in this book, and Toṭagamuva is near Sīnigama. Toṭagamuva not only was the center of Nātha worship, it was also a great Buddhist monastery, Vijayabā Pirivena, once presided over by Śrī Rāhula, the author of two great *sandēśa* poems. In Toṭagamuva, Nātha was propitiated along with his consort Tārā. Thus Paranavitana shows clearly that Nātha was none other than the famous Mahāyāna bodhisattva, Avalokiteśvara. Nevertheless it is wrong to assume with Paranavitana that the cult of Nātha and Tārā indicated the existence of Mahāyānism at this period in Sri Lankan history. Mahāyānism may have been in vogue in ancient and medieval Sri Lanka as part of the heterodoxy of the Abhayagiri monastery of Anurādhapura (Paranavitana 1928), but it was not necessarily part of popular Buddhism. Moreover, in the fifteenth century, according to the evidence of the *sandēśas*, Nātha was fast being incorporated into the Theravāda ethos and was treated very much like the other major gods, in the manner discussed in chapter 2. Perhaps owing to his enormous popularity and his Buddhistic nature, he was converted into the very next Buddha-to-be, Maitreya, again in terms of the internal dynamics of the Theravāda pantheon. It is likely that even by this time he was becoming more or less exclusively benevolent and thereby otiose in this region.

Thus, during the period when Kōṭṭe was the capital of Sri Lanka there were three major gods: Nātha, Viṣṇu, and Vibhīṣaṇa. Of these gods Vibhīṣaṇa was probably the guardian of the capital itself and of the sovereignty of the Sinhala kings. The *sandēśa* poems mention two other gods, Kataragama and Saman, though in less detail. It is reasonable to assume that the four guardian gods were chosen from these five major deities. According to one source, the *Nikāya Saṅgraha*, the four guardians of Kōṭṭe were Viṣṇu (Upulvan), Saman, Vibhīṣaṇa, and Skanda (Somaratne 1975, p. 276). But this may not have been an invariant scheme, and one of the other gods may have been substituted for any deity who went out of favor or became otiose.

By the middle of the sixteenth century there was a lull in literary writing; no *sandēśa* poems were written until the Mātara period, 1750–1850. The reason is easy to fathom. By this time the Portuguese were in control of most of this area. They had sacked and destroyed the temple of Vibhīṣaṇa and occupied Kōṭṭe itself. In 1588 they destroyed the great Viṣṇu shrine at Devundara. The area around Toṭagamuva was firmly under Portuguese control, and it probably ceased to be an important religious and cultural center. The destruction of the shrine of Vibhīṣaṇa and the city he protected led to his demise. The Viṣṇu cult, however, moved from Devinuvara (Devundara) to Alutnuvara, at present the shrine of Dēvatā Baṇḍāra. A Portuguese land register (*tombo*) of 1614 refers to Alutnuvara as the shrine of Nārāyaṇa (Pieris 1950, p. 44). Soon after, the Viṣṇu statue at Alutnuvara was transferred to Kandy and installed at its present place, the Mahā Dēvāle (great *dēvāle*) of Kandy. In the late seventeenth century, when there was a reflorescence of *sandēśa* poems in Mātara, southern Sri Lanka, none of these shrines were viable religious centers. Thus *all* Mātara *sandēśa* poetry epistles were taken to the only shrine left intact—the shrine of Kataragama in the remote southeastern corner of the island. By this time, this god had come into prominence as a major intercessionary deity of this region, perhaps second only to the goddess Pattini in public esteem and popularity.

The fifteenth century produced religious conditions in our area that tended to erode the popularity of regional and local deities like the Twelve Gods. The locus of Sinhala civilization moved to this region in the fifteenth century, and concomitantly there were established here the central shrines of all the major gods of the pantheon. These shrines were popular not only with the court and the elite, but also with the masses. This means that the cult of the major gods invaded the rural areas and displaced the older cult of regional and local deities, the Doḷaha Deviyo. The major gods—Viṣṇu, Nātha, Vibhīṣaṇa, Kataragama—became part of the operative pantheon here. The jurisdictional sway of the central gods effectively incorporated the region. This implies a prior sociological and political change. Villages and isolated regions had come under the direct political control of the state. This could occur only after the capital of the Sinhala king moved to the southwest, to Daṁbadeṇiya and later to Kōṭṭe.

Political control of most of the region was easy, since the terrain was not as difficult as in the Kandyan highlands. The *sandēśa* poetry gives us the routes taken by the bird messengers. These routes were not as the bird flies but were well-known land routes and roads. The implication is clear: the whole region was connected by land routes, and the geography of the area was thoroughly familiar to the *sandēśa* poets.

Indirect evidence on pilgrimages leads us to the same conclusion. All the central shrines of the gods were in this region and, except for Kataragama, were accessible. It is likely, then, that pilgrim traffic would also have rendered this area geographically known and accessible to most Sinhala people. In addition to the shrines, the *sandēśa* poetry refers to large monastic schools and temples in this area, for example, at Kälaṇiya, Rayigama, Pānadura, and Toṭagamuva. And above all there was the Śrī Pāda in Sabaragamuva, the sacred mountain where people came to worship the footprint of the Buddha. In addition to pilgrim traffic to worship the *dēva*s, there would have been considerable Buddhist pilgrim traffic also. The implications of the Buddhaization of this region, however, will be discussed later.

The preceding line of argument suggests that after the capital of the Sinhala kings moved to Kōṭṭe in the fifteenth century, the cult of the Twelve Gods was displaced by the state cult of the Gods of the Four Warrants (in reality five for this region). Of the Twelve Gods, the more local ones—that is, those deified local heroes—would more quickly have become eroded, while those with a larger cultural spread (like Dēvaṭā Baṇḍāra, Maṅgara, Kiri Amma, and Daḷa Kumāra, or Garā) would remain, perhaps with diminished importance. This was in fact the case except for the popularity of Dēvatā Baṇḍāra, which I will account for later, and the indispensability of Garā, the remover of *vas*, for Sinhala ritual.

I noted earlier that there is an important convention in Sinhala ritual: the retention of numerology in spite of changes in substance or content. Thus one would not expect the *concept* of the Twelve Gods to have lost its relevance. The obvious solution is to have a new list of Twelve Gods, but how? Again, the logical resolution would be to incorporate the major gods like Viṣṇu and Nātha, who have now come into full prominence, into the cult of the Twelve Gods. This solution has in fact been adopted in some parts of our culture area, but only much later. It is difficult to adopt this solution, since the major gods already constitute a higher-status numerological category of four, and to incorporate them into the category of twelve would be to demote them.

The solution adopted is clear from my texts. The concept of the Twelve Gods was retained, but a new substantive content was poured into it. It was now stated that the Twelve Gods were kings who came to witness the original *gammaḍuva* of Sēraman. These kings were perhaps from the original mythology of the Pattini cult in South India (some could have been Sinhala inventions). Few of the names make much sense in Sinhala culture. Yet several slips in the texts and the ritual performances show survivals of the older cult they displaced. Some of these have been discussed earlier, but let me indicate four such "slips" here.

1. In one stanza (p. 118) the Twelve Gods (Kings), along with Amarāpati, have arrived in the ritual arena. The *kapurāla* told me that Amarāpati ("immortal lady") was the daughter of the king of Soḷī who came with the goddess's anklet to Sri Lanka. Actually Amarāpati is nothing of the sort. She is one of the seven Kiri Amma placated in the traditional cult of the Twelve Gods practiced in other regions of Sri Lanka.

2. Let me refer to another slip, which also constitutes a symbolic statement. On the night of the main ceremony, an elaborate dance in honor of the Twelve Gods (Kings), known as *telmē*, is performed in all the traditions I studied. In Rabalīya the *kapurāla* introduces this ritual dance with the statement: "Ladies and gentlemen, at the time when the original hall [*maḍuva*] was performed by King Sēraman, the Twelve Gods were not pleased. In order to please them the *telmē* was performed." I interpret the meaning of this symbolic statement to indicate the displacement of the older cult of the Twelve Gods by the deities of the *gammaḍuva* as now constituted. The present *maḍuva* was initiated by Sēraman; it displaced the earlier communal ritual (also known as *gammaḍuva*, in all likelihood) that propitiated the Twelve Gods. Therefore "they were not pleased." This statement by the *kapurāla* was not a fortuitous one: he told me his father had employed the exact phraseology.

3. A much more complicated symbolic statement is embodied in the ritual for the Twelve Gods known as *doḷaha peḷapāḷiya*: "spectacle for the Twelve Gods" (pp. 156–64). Here the Twelve Gods (Kings) are offered various spectacles—the pearl umbrella, drum, canopy, and so forth. This is in all probability a continuation of an old tradition. In Haňguraňketa similar but not identical items are performed in honor of their collectivity of Twelve Gods. The striking difference is that the *doḷaha peḷapāḷiya* offers more grandiose items to the Twelve Gods (Kings), in spite of their general lack of importance in our area. The reason again is clear. The traditional cult of the Twelve Gods was a regional one; the gods were Baṇḍāra, or "chiefs," whereas the major gods of the pantheon (the Gods of the Four Warrants) were kings. The spectacles offered to the "chiefs" were a reduced version of the worship of the kings. In the traditions of our area the traditional cult of the Twelve Gods have been converted into that of the Twelve Kings. Hence a more elaborate symbolism is employed—symbols like the sun and moon ensign, and especially the pearl umbrella, the symbol of sovereignty of the *cakravartin*, or world ruler of Buddhist mythology. Yet these kings are unknown in Sinhala culture. They are thus honored with spectacles, as was the traditional custom for kings, then ridiculed or parodied with "fake" objects of ritual service—a phony pearl umbrella, a toy drum, a *vīṇā* made of coconut shell, a ridiculous horn and flute, and so on. Thus the *doḷaha peḷapāḷiya* ritual is a symbolic statement that expresses a certain attitude to the Twelve Kings who usurped the older cult of the Twelve Gods. They are kings, but they are also unknowns in Sinhala culture. They are a parody of kingship. Underlying this ambivalence is a deeper am-

bivalence the Sinhala people feel for kings in general. It is characteristic of the culture to handle these kinds of ambivalence through humor or parody.

4. A similar "symbolic statement" is expressed in the *telmē* ritual. In Sinhala and Indian ritual grammar a clockwise ("right") movement is a propitious one and the counterclockwise ("left") movement is unpropitious. Normally circumambulation of shrines and ritual movement for divinities is a clockwise movement; yet the *telmē* dance in honor of the Twelve Kings is counterclockwise. The twelve *cakravartin* gods are honored with an elaborate dance; yet this is a reverse dance, a parody of real service to divinity.

The Twelve Kings are substituted for the Twelve Gods, and numerology is maintained. Yet it is a poor substitute, a parody. In some areas, particularly highly urbanized towns in our culture area, the notion of the Twelve Gods is even vaguer, and possibly on the way out. In these areas the traditions of the Twelve Kings of the *gammaḍuva* have been forgotten or ignored (owing to their lack of cultural relevance); also, the older tradition of twelve regional gods has become obsolete. In these urban areas the logical solution suggested earlier is adopted: the Twelve Gods are nothing but an association (*samāgama*) of the major gods of the pantheon. Thus Wirz (1954) states that the Twelve Gods, according to his informants, are Devol Deviyo, Pattini, Kataragama, Nātha, Saman, Vibhīṣaṇa, Gini Kurumbara, Vāhala, Däḍimuṇḍa, Mahā Viṣṇu, and Īśvara, a hodgepodge of eleven deities. In the city of Pānadura I met several *kapurālas* who identified the Twelve Gods in a similar fashion: they simply listed the major gods propitiated by them. It was the same in Moraṭuva, another suburb of Colombo. Note that in these urban areas the older tradition of the Twelve Gods as regional deities has been totally forgotten. Thus it is possible to reclassify the major gods (including the Gods of the Four Warrants) into a larger collectivity of twelve, without pejoration or status demotion. Numerology is maintained, and everyone is happy.

Pattini and Kiri Amma

In the previous section I noted two major classifications: the Four Gods and the Twelve Gods. I also noted that not all the Twelve Gods became obsolete; some were retained with diminished status, while others moved upward in the pantheon. It is likely that three of these latter gods were regrouped into a new category: "the gods of the three divisions." These were Pattini, Devol, and Dēvatā Baṇḍāra. But this category, found in some of the ritual texts, is itself a survival, since Pattini has been promoted into the first category. However, nowhere in Sri Lanka is Pattini viewed as one of the Twelve Gods. Pertold (1941) contends that Pattini herself "displaced" a previous indigenous deity, Kiri Amma, who is identified in many traditions as one of the Twelve Gods (in Sinhala the term *deviyo* is a common noun meaning god or goddess). It is very likely that when the Pattini cult was introduced to Sri Lanka from Southern India, the first deity to be "displaced" from the pantheon of the Twelve Gods was Kiri Amma.

Pattini is a mother goddess, and it is plausible that she usurped the place of a preexisting mother goddess. However, a crucial element of the Pattini cult, as against other mother goddess cults in South Asia, is her relationship with Pālañga, her spouse, with whom she cannot have sexual relations. It will be tempting to speculate whether the Pattini-Pālañga relation had a prior parallel in Sri Lankan culture. My view is that such a strict isomorphism between an old and new cult is rarely found. However, there is some similarity between the god Maṅgara, an ancient indigenous deity, and Pālaṅga.

It should be remembered nevertheless that, while Maṅgara is unequivocally a deity, Pālaṅga is not. By contrast Pattini and Kiri Amma are practically isomorphic: the one cult could easily have been displaced, usurped, or invaded by the other.

A word of caution regarding my use of words like "displaced" and "usurped." In the previous section I noted that, although the cult of the Twelve Kings usurped or displaced that of the Twelve Gods, some of the latter continued to exist in the rituals of the *gammaḍuva*. So with Pattini and Kiri Amma. When I speak of Pattini's displacing Kiri Amma, I really mean that the former eroded the latter's sphere of influence. Total displacement of one deity or cult by another does occur in the history of religion; but so does partial displacement. More often we see the latter process reflected in the history of religion, since total displacement is often a long process, and we merely observe one stage in that process. I am, however, certain that Kiri Amma will eventually go *totally* out of vogue in Sinhala culture. In my study of the Pattini cult I will note the erosion of the Kiri Amma cult by the Pattini cult. Yet Kiri Amma continues to be propitiated, almost anachronistically and vestigially in our region.

The worship of Kiri Amma (literally, "milk mother," also "wet nurse" or "grandmother") is found all over Sri Lanka. Kiri Amma, like Pattini, has many functions, but everywhere she is (also like Pattini) associated with infectious diseases and children's diseases and their cure. In our cultural area no rituals for Kiri Amma are performed by professional priests, unlike other areas. Here one Kiri Amma rite still survives; it is known as *kiri ammalāgē dāne*, "almsgiving to the Kiri Amma," and is described by Gombrich (1971b). In general the rite is as follows. When children are sick, generally with infectious diseases (*ammāvarungē leḍa*, "mother's diseases"), seven lactating mothers are invited to the household of the sick child. These mothers are fed with milk rice and oil cakes (*kävun*). At the conclusion of this almsgiving the seven Kiri Amma bless the sick child as they leave the house. In 1956 these rites were still widely practiced in our area, though they are now very scarce.

The resemblance of Kiri Amma to Pattini is very clear: in both the goddess cures children's diseases. In the case of Kiri Amma there is a tradition that she causes children's illnesses. Pattini, being a deity of the higher class, does not have this role, except in Hindu areas of Sri Lanka. She only cures. Pattini, however, has other functions in the rituals of the *gammaḍuva*, whereas very little of Kiri Amma worship survives in our region. Nevertheless, the moment we move from our region to other parts of Sri Lanka the importance of Kiri Amma increases. In Laggala, when children fall ill there is a nightlong ritual where Kiri Amma is propitiated by the *kapurāla*. In Haṅguraṅketa Kiri Amma is one of the most important deities of the pantheon. Not only is she associated with children's diseases, but like Pattini she is a goddess of fertility. Like Pattini, however, Kiri Amma is also paradoxically barren. In Haṅguraṅketa the thanksgiving rituals after harvest (also known as *gammaḍuva*) begin with the ceremonial pounding of the freshly harvested rice offered to the gods. The pounding is done by men dressed in white clothes representing the Kiri Amma. The culminating ritual of Haṅguraṅketa is the boiling of milk, as in the Pattini *gammaḍuva*. But here the *kapurāla*, dressed as Kiri Amma, dances the Kiri Amma dance (*kiri ammā näṭuma*) while the milk boils over. It is clearly Kiri Amma, not Pattini, who is the operative female deity here, as in Laggala and most parts of the country's interior.

Kiri Amma is worshiped generally as a collectivity of seven. However, she is also sometimes worshiped individually in terms of her specific manifestations. The best known of the Kiri Amma are Kukulāpola Kiri Amma (the Kiri Amma of Kukulāpola); and Unapanē Kiri Amma (Kiri Amma of Unapana, a Vädda village). She is also worshiped as Amarāpati, "immortal lady." In the North Western Province, according to Parker, she is the spouse of one of the most important gods of that area, Galē Yakā or Galē Baṇḍāra, one of the Baṇḍāra gods (Parker 1909, pp. 135, 149). This god probably was incorporated into the Sinhala pantheon from the Väddas, since the Sinhala never use the term Yakā to characterize their gods (*yakā* in Sinhala means "demon," whereas for Väddas it could mean "god"). This god is also known as Indigollē Deviyo (the god of Indigollǟve village), and his spouse is Indigollē Kiri Amma. Says Parker:

> The Sinhalese of Indigollaewa and some of the settled Vaeddas near Mahaoya make offerings to Gale Yaka and the Kiriamma, his wife, together; no offerings however are made to her on the hilltops, which are reserved for the Gale Yaka. . . . She is a great provider for the Vaeddas. (Quoted in Seligmann and Seligmann 1911, p. 185)

As Parker indicates, the worship of Kiri Amma extends to the aboriginal Väddas of Sri Lanka. Furthermore, the Kiri Amma cult is part of the operative worship of all sections of Vädda society, from the settled and acculturated to the more primitive wild Väddas studied by the Seligmanns. It is difficult to say whether Kiri Amma worship originated with the Väddas; but the Seligmanns' data clearly show that it has been thoroughly incorporated into Vädda eschatology and worship.

The distinctive features of Vädda worship, when we compare it with Sinhala worship, is that the Väddas have a system of ancestor worship unknown to the Sinhala. Väddas on death become spirits known as *nǟ yakku* ("kin deities") who are propitiated by the living. Spirits of elderly women are known as *mahā yakini* ("great deities," "old deities"), often becoming animistic spirits of natural phenomena (Seligmann and Seligmann 1911, p. 154). The deity who presides over this class of spirits is Mahā Kiri Amma, who, according to the Seligmanns, is more feared than loved.[1] Unapanē Kiri Amma is one of these Mahā Yakini, who brings luck in honey gathering. The Seligmanns say about Kiri Amma: "Although they retain the fondness for children which they felt in their lifetime they not infrequently send sickness, at least among the more sophisticated Veddas" (1911, p. 140).

The Seligmanns describe a ceremony known as *kolamaḍuva* ("leaf-thatch hall") among the acculturated Väddas of Unapana. Here Kiri Amma is seen as a wife of a "regional" deity or Baṇḍāra. Thus Unapanē Kiri Amma is the wife of Unapanē Vanniya, the chief who first brought the paddy fields of Unapana under cultivation. In the invocation uttered in the *kolamaḍuva*, Amarāpati Kiri Amma is also mentioned, but the Seligmanns have little to say about her (1911, pp. 316–17). Amarāpati, or Immortal Lady, is perhaps another term used for Kiri Amma in general. The Seligmanns also say that the idea of Kiri Amma as wife of a deity shows a Sinhala influence. In sum, the Vädda evidence also

1. This Vädda deity Mahā Yakini is incorporated into the rituals at Mahiyaṅgana, where Väddas and Sinhalas meet together in ritual activity. In the annual procession here the god Saman parades the streets with Mahā Dēvi, his sister, and Kalu Dēvatā. Mahā Yakini means "great deity" in Vädda but "great demoness" in Sinhala; therefore she must change into Mahā Dēvi, "great goddess," in Sinhala usage. In low-country exorcistic rituals the demon Kalu Yakā is born out of the womb of Mahā Kalu Kiri Amma. Thus it is very likely that that Mahā Yakini Kalu Dēvatā combination is the same as Mahā Kalu Kiri Amma–Kalu Yakā of low-country exorcisms.

clearly indicates the multiple functions of Kiri Amma—as a deity involved in children's diseases and in gathering honey, as a general provider, and, in Unapana (as in Hañguraṅketa), also associated with agriculture. It is impossible to miss the significance of the name of the deity—Milk Mother—its association on the psychological level with nurturance and, on a further symbolic level, with fertility and the general weal.

In Hañguraṅketa and elsewhere Kiri Amma is generally worshiped as a single person. However, she is also seven, though the only place I have seen a list of seven is in Parker, who quotes Nevill as his authority. These are Mīriyabäddē Kiri Amma, Pusmarāga Kiri Amma, Unapanē Kiri Amma, Kosgama Kiri Amma, Bōvalagedera Kiri Amma, Bālagiri Kiri Amma, and Ginijal Devatāgē Kiri Amma (Parker 1909, p. 137). Of these, Mīriyabäddē Kiri Amma, Bōvalagedera Kiri Amma, and Kosgama Kiri Amma must surely be spouses of three of the Baṇḍāra gods in Sarachchandra's list of the Twelve Gods quoted earlier, namely Mīriyabädde Devi, Bōvala Devi, and Kosgama Devi, respectively (p. 000). In the invocations at Hañguraṅketa the following Kiri Ammas were mentioned: Amarāpati, Kukulāpola, and vague names like Hañdun Kumāri ("sandalwood princess"), Ginijal Kumāri ("princess of the cascades of fire"), Añdun Kumāri ("princess of antinomy or collyrium"). She is also referred to as born of a *mal rēnu*, the flower's filament. Now we know that Pattini is also referred to as Ginijal Pattini ("Pattini of the flames"); she is born also of a flower; and she meditates in the Peak of Antinomy (Añdungiri) before being born in the human world. However, one must be cautious in inferring one-way causality here: it is indeed possible that Pattini also influenced Kiri Amma in those areas where the former was formally propitiated and the latter was the operative female deity. Pattini, after her cult was established, had high formal status, and she could have influenced the indigenous Kiri Amma cult in those remote regions.

One striking feature of the mother goddess cults in Sri Lanka, in contrast to India, is the absence of a multiplicity of goddesses. Basically there are two: Pattini for our culture area and Kiri Amma for the remoter areas. It is true that Kiri Amma is both a deity and a *concept*—that is, a term that could be applied to a local female mother goddess. Nevertheless, the number of Kiri Amma is strictly limited, and most people fuse the concept and the deity into the single term, Kiri Amma. If Kiri Amma was the older deity, as the data indicate, and in reality a pan-Sinhala goddess, it is almost inevitable that it was her cult that was displaced by Pattini. In the *gammaḍuva* of Hañguraṅketa it is Kiri Amma that the *kapurāla* impersonates: milk is boiled in *her* honor. In the Pattini *gammaḍuva* of our region, the *kapurāla* dresses as Pattini, and the boiling of milk is redefined in the context of the Pattini mythology. The conclusion is irresistible: the Pattini cult displaced the Kiri Amma cult. Both cults were embodied in a communal ceremony known as the *gammaḍuva*. Elements of the Kiri Amma cult, like the rite of boiling milk, were incorporated into the Pattini cult. Furthermore, elements of the older *gammaḍuva* in honor of the Twelve Gods were incorporated into the new version of the *gammaḍuva*, as I showed in respect of the *doḷaha peḷapāḷiya* ritual.

Maṅgara: The Risen Lord

Maṅgara also, I noted, had a near pan-Sinhala spread, but his worship spread only as far as acculturated Väddas. Wild Väddas, according to the Seligmanns' account, did not worship Maṅgara. Unfortunately I have not seen Maṅgara rituals, which are scarce nowadays. However, I know that an elaborate ritual for Maṅgara is practiced in parts of Laggala, Panāmure, and Hambegamuva. The latter two places are remote regions in our cultural area. There are rituals for Maṅgara even in areas where the Pattini cult is dominant, such as Sabaragamuva (Ratnapura tradition). In Heyiaṅtuḍuva itself a cousin of the Pattini priest performed rituals for Maṅgara and was given the dubious title of *yak kapurāla* (demon *kapurāla*). I have heard of a specialist of the Maṅgara cult in Horana, within the immediate influence of the Rabalīya tradition.[2] Thus, in spite of the prestige and vast spread of the Pattini cult, the Maṅgara cult also continues to be practiced sporadically in our region. I noted the remnants of the Maṅgara cult in two rituals performed in the *gammaḍuva*, the capture of the elephant and the capture of the buffalo. In Haṅguraṅketa these rituals are for Maṅgara; in Sabaragamuva in our area, they are not performed in the Pattini *gammaḍuva* at all. They are performed *only* in the rituals for Maṅgara. Perhaps the *gammaḍuva* has incorporated an older ritual for Maṅgara, who is in many traditions considered one of the Twelve Gods.

According to the myth, Maṅgaṛa, known as Prince Budusiru, was born in the country of Māyā in Mūladīpa ("original land"), either India or Sri Lanka. When he was born court astrologers predicted that he would be killed by a wild buffalo, owing to his karma from a previous birth, in which he had sucked the milk from the udder of a cow and thus deprived the calf of its milk.

10. The astrologers of that city
    Examined the future events
    "A danger awaits you at nineteen
    From a wild buffalo."

12. "Do not go O Prince
    To the pond of Kadirāva
    There's a buffalo there
    Who'll tear your heart and drink its blood."

The king, his father, was afraid of the son's prowess and banished him. Thus Budusiru sailed the seas with his followers and landed in Usaṅgoḍa, in Ruhuṇa, on the southeast coast of the present Southern Province, between Tangalla and Ambalantoṭa. He got off the ship (a stone raft like that of Devol Deviyo), and sent a cowherd (some accounts say two) to capture a buffalo. Meanwhile Budusiru, or Maṅgara, proceeded toward Kadirāva (another village in this area) with his followers. Soon he saw a large golden *nuga* tree (*Ficus altissima*) surrounded by seven other *nuga* trees, each of a different variety.

37. It could be seen above the forest trees
    Its leaves shone like golden leaves
    In the shade of this pleasant tree
    The lord [Maṅgara] rested.

Soon they heard a thunderous roar and thought there must be a beehive in the *nuga* tree. Sure enough, a swarm of bees shot forth one *yoduna* (about sixteen miles) up the sky. The

2. This information was supplied by Joseph Weeramunda of the Department of Sociology, University of Colombo.

bees were entering the *nuga* tree in three places. Budusiru asked his men to cut the hive so that he could taste its savor. The men put up ladders and climbed the tree; the demon in the tree got angry and said, "The honey in this tree belongs to me, not to you. If you drink it you'll be sorry." The men struck the tree, but their weapons broke; they couldn't even scratch the bark.

47. "The sap of this tree is like blood
The striking axes veer off
There's a demon residing here
So how can we take this hive?"

The mighty god Maṅgara then decided to cut the hive himself. He dealt a blow with his golden ax, and the *nuga* tree opened like a golden door.

50. The opening was like a jewel box
There were golden flutes and curved horns [*kombu*]
Golden bangles twinkling, and shining jewels
There were such divine ornaments.

51. There were golden lassos and goads
There were golden pots and vases
There were golden plows and yokes
There were golden beds and chairs.

52. There were golden *pūnā* pots
There were golden flutes
There were silken shawls
And other golden ornaments.

Maṅgara's followers collected the honey in cupped *nuga* leaves and drank it. They then went on to capture a buffalo. They took a variety of lassos, goads, and weapons and set forth. As they were about to proceed there were three bad omens, the cries of the *kirala* bird, the gecko, and the white monkey; Maṅgara silenced each creature with his will. They went to Kadirāva, and there was the buffalo in the midst of seven lakes. This buffalo was the demon of the tree in a new guise. The men were afraid to approach it, since it was an extraordinary animal. But not Budusiru. The animal waded into the lake, and Budusiru followed it with his golden lasso. The buffalo charged at Maṅgara and killed him; then it killed his followers, all of them.

Meanwhile the cowherd, whom Budusiru had sent earlier, arrived and saw the dead king and his followers. He accosted the deadly animal in the lake and felled it with his spear. (This cowherd was the prototype priest of the Maṅgara cult.)

82. Thereupon he built a hall, dedicated it
Worshiped the gods and asked their leave
He obtained warrant from the gods
To make preparations for boiling milk.

83. The four legs were cut off and skinned
The chest cut off and ribs separated

The flesh was cut and then
Preparations made for boiling milk.

84. The four legs were used for four posts
And the tail cut into four bars
The twelve ribs were used for a stand
The bowels as a pouch for storing firewood[?]

85. The kneecaps were used for hearthstones
The hide stretched into a canopy
The intestines were used as curtains
And the nerves as golden halters.

86. The eyes were used for sapphire lamps
The ears were for fanning the fire
The skull a vessel for boiling milk
The tail cut for an arrow. . . .[3]

Now the cowherd-priest wanted turmeric (for cleansing the arena of pollution?) and went to the goddess Pattini for some. Pattini was angry with them because of the pollution of dead humans and cattle they brought with them. She then went to the *nāga* world accompanied by Prince Cowherd and Prince Milk and got *rat hāl* rice and turmeric from the *nāga* king. Now the "milk boiling" could be performed. When the milk was boiling Pattini sprayed some on Budusiru and his retinue.

93. As if in response to a sudden command
As if emerging from the ambrosia lake
As if awakening from a sleep
The god stood up with his retinue.

They then put the various parts of the buffalo together, and it also came alive with a joyous cry.

Then Maṅgara, the glorious god, with his retinue went and lassoed wild buffalo to capture and tame them. The conclusion of the poem recapitulates the prowess of Maṅgara and invokes his help to dispel illness of the congregation (*ātura*). He is referred to as the god of Ruhuṇa Bintänna—the plains of Ruhuṇa.

There is a close parallel between Maṅgara and Pālaṅga. Maṅgara is slain by the buffalo, and Pālaṅga lies dead under the *kohoṁba* tree. Both are resurrected by Pattini, the former in her role as a goddess who can wake the dead, the latter in her role as *mater dolorosa* and grieving spouse. Maṅgara is a prince, but he is also lord of cowherds; Kōvalan̲ is a merchant, but his name is equivalent to *gopālaka*, in its original Sanskrit, "lord of the cowherd." There is one striking difference, though: Maṅgara's spouse (if he has one) has no active role to play in his resurrection, unlike the Pattini-Pālaṅga relationship. If I were certain that the Maṅgara cult is older than the Pattini cult I could make at least one clear inference—that Maṅgara at one time could have been resurrected only by

3. Even today in Maṅgara rituals this prototype event is symbolically enacted. A life-size image of the bull is constructed and slain at the end of the ritual.

one of the Kiri Amma, since Kiri Amma, as I have shown earlier, was the female goddess who preceded Pattini. In all likelihood the particular deity would be Amarāpati Kiri Amma who, along with Maṅgara is referred to in the *doḷaha peḷapāḷiya* text (p. 167). *Amarā* means literally "undying," but *pati* poses a problem. *Pati* means "lord," or "husband," which does not make sense here, though one could strain the sense and translate it as "lady." Unhappily, I have no evidence yet for the view that Amarāpati, or any of the other Kiri Amma, was involved at one time in Maṅgara's resurrection. There is one stanza, however, in the Rabalīya tradition that identifies Amarāpati with Pattini. It is sung during the consecration of the *gammaḍuva*, in the ritual of merit transfer to the gods (p. 92).

> O goddess Pattini of Madurā
> Her command spreads o'er the whole world
> Today this priest gives you merit of coconut flower offerings
> O goddess Amarāpati accept the merit we give you.

In this stanza, I am virtually certain that Pattini and Amarāpati are identical. In terms of the preceding argument one may plausibly argue that a preexistent cult of Amarāpati Kiri Amma and Maṅgara was displaced by the Pattini-Pālaṅga cult.

Though such an interpretation is plausible, I prefer an alternative one that does not necessarily contradict the preceding argument—that is, that the two cults were parallel, transformations in the sociological sense of a central theme in the history of religion. Let me present the case for this alternative argument.

Unlike the *concept* of Kiri Amma, which is an old cult found even among Väddas, the worship of Maṅgara is found only among the Sinhalas and the more acculturated Väddas. Moreover, the events of the cults take place in Ruhuṇa Bintänna—the plains of Ruhuṇa; the villages referred to in the mythology are in the region between Tangalla and Ambalantoṭa, the flat, jungle dry zone of the Southern Province. This region traditionally practiced little agriculture; it was an interstitial zone, between the older Ruhuṇa civilization, based on agriculture and the tank systems of the region east of Tissa, and the wet zone stretching from Mātara to the west and north. This region of Ruhuṇa Bintänna was sparsely populated by hunters and trappers of buffalo and elephant. Agriculture was at best slash-and-burn or sporadic rice cultivation. Leonard Woolf vividly describes a village in this area in his novel *Village in the Jungle*. Furthermore, the other regions that popularly propitiated Maṅgara—such as Laggala pallēsiya pattu in the dry plains below the Knuckles range in the Central Province, and Hambegamuva and Panāmure in the interior of the east of the Southern Province and the (once) desolate region near Negombo—were similar interstitial zones. Thus my argument: Maṅgara (and Amarāpati) is to the hunting-trapping dry zone what Pālaṅga (and Pattini) is to the agricultural wet zone of the Southern, Western, and Sabaragamuva provinces. The two cults are transformations of a common ritual theme, in two different ecological and occupational zones.

It can easily be demonstrated not only that Maṅgara represents a god who is killed and subsequently resurrected, but that he is the lord of the herd, the hunter and trapper of wild animals. His major "weapons" are the lasso and the goad, used on buffalo and elephants, respectively. In the myth, many weapons and tools emerge from the hive ("womb") of the *nuga* tree, including the yoke and the plow. But the whole content of the Maṅgara myth deals with his killing animals, lassoing buffaloes, and obtaining wild honey, the latter also an important part of the economy of these interstitial regions. Furthermore, a basic opposition exists between the hunting-trapping god Maṅgara and the goddess Pattini, reflective of economic and cultural differences. The cowherd in the myth above kills the buffalo and uses parts of its anatomy to construct ritual altars and decorations. Pattini is repelled by death pollution—that of the slain Maṅgara and his retinue as well as that of the bull. She cleanses this by turmeric obtained from the *nāga* king. Pattini represents the Buddhist ethos of agricultural communities; Maṅgara represents the ethos of hunters and trappers who must, according to all Indian religion, be both sinful and polluted.

What then is the mythic theme that is transformed in the two different ecological-occupational settings? The theme is that of the dying god and the *mater dolorosa* (mother or spouse or both) who resurrects him. As a symbolic system, the rituals and myths that enact this theme are multilayered, significant on the psychological, cultural, and social levels. I shall unravel the psychological meanings of this theme in later chapters. Here let me draw attention to the interpretation of the symbolism on the cultural level advanced by classical scholars like Frazer and Harrison. They have exposed two significant levels of meaning. First, the ritual enactment of the theme in ancient West Asia and the Mediterranean represented the death of the earth in winter and its resurrection in spring. Second, the dying god is the god of grain. The ritual is an enactment of the dying crop after harvest and the later burgeoning of the new grain. Needless to say, the two themes—the seasonal and the vegetational—are interrelated. As far as South Asia is concerned it is the second meaning of the enactment that is relevant, since there is little seasonal variation there.

The level of meaning I am concerned with here is that of depletion and resurgence of fertility, represented by the theme of killing and resurrection. I shall focus on two variations of this theme in the texts at my disposal.

1. Consider the Pattini-Pālaṅga drama enacted in Sri Lanka. Here the enactment is related to a stable agricultural society. In most traditions the ideal (not often put into practice) was to hold the *gammaḍuva* in a harvested rice field (a convention strictly followed in the Haṅguraṅketa *gammaḍuva* for the Twelve Gods). One *kapurāla* told me that when Pālaṅga is killed he is covered with rice straw, but I have not seen this performed. In the enactment here there is extreme concentration on the killing of Pālaṅga, the grief of Pattini, and the resurrection of her consort. The event dealing with the destruction of Madurai is only recited, never enacted. The focus on these three events fits with the agricultural significance of the ritual—the death of the earth and its subsequent regeneration in the new rice.

2. In the Maṅgara ritual, as far as I can reconstruct it from the mythology, the major focus is on the death of the cowherd-god, and also on the wild buffalo that is killed and dismembered. The resurrection theme is there, but no *mater dolorosa*. After the resurrection of Maṅgara there is a graphic description of his shooting buffalo and lassoing them. These transformations once again fit the ethos of hunters and trappers of wild buffalo.

The Bam̆bura: Vädda Elements in the *Gammaḍuva*

The last stanza of the text of merit-giving to the gods that concludes the *gammaḍuva* refers to an enigmatic deity known as Bam̆bura.

Twirling his beard, his sooty face like a demon's
With fierce looks he yells full throated
He'll banish deadly diseases and *dōsa*
Baṁbura will bring full happiness to this village.

This is a clear survival in the Rabalīya tradition, for nowhere else in its ritual traditions is he mentioned. Yet this deity must have been important at one time, since the merit giving ritual concludes with him. From the text it is clear that he is a composite of divine and demonic attributes—like some of the Twelve Gods—and belongs to the *dēvatā* category. Reference to his "twirling his beard" indicates that he appeared onstage at one time in a ritual performance. A comparative study of Baṁbura can help us understand his nature and significance.

Though Baṁbura is a relative unknown in some traditions of the *gammaḍuva* (Rabalīya, Heyiaṁtuduva, Ratnapura), he is known in Mātara and Sīnigama. The ritual drama for Baṁbura performed in Mātara is described later in this work (see pp. 495–99), and the reader is urged to refer to it. Briefly, in Mātara and Sīnigama the Baṁbura dance refers to two comic ritual dramas known as the "shaving" and the "shooting." Both are performed in these areas in lieu of *marā ipäddīma* ("killing and resurrection"), which priests are afraid to perform for fear of *vas*. In the "shaving" Baṁbura, wearing a gross, lascivious mask, appears onstage and with superb comic-mimetic action "shaves" an attendant with a phony razor. In the "shooting" ritual there is obscene dialogue and vulgar action, as Baṁbura shoots his quarry (an attendant) between the legs with a gun. But even in Sīnigama and Mātara no one could say why these dramas are performed or who Baṁbura was. In both traditions, however, these dramas are treated very seriously: in Mātara they are indispensable for any *gammaḍuva*. In both they are recognized as comic substitutes for the "killing and resurrection" drama, as *rāmā märīma* is for the other traditions discussed here.[4]

In Mātara this deity is referred to as Baṁbura, or as Hātabaṁbura. The meaning of *baṁbura* given in Sorata's dictionary is primarily a scavenger or someone who cleans up urine and feces. It also could refer to a hunched person, or even a Berber. Carter's dictionary defines *baṁbura* as "one who has short curled hair." These meanings, I think, are all misleading, at least for interpreting the Baṁbura of our ritual.

References to Baṁburas are found in the "Dove's Message" by Śrī Rāhula, who lived in the reign of Parākramabāhu VI of Kōṭṭe (1410–68). In this poem (stanza 67) the dove is asked to witness the groups of *baṁbura*s in Bēruvala who, intoxicated with toddy, babble and dance, whirling their sticks and "maces" (Säbiheliyan 1967, p. 10). A more elaborate and perhaps more accurate description is found in *Girā Sandēśaya* ("Parrot's Message"), stanza 105, written in the same period, somewhere between A.D. 1450 and 1460, according to Godakumbara (1955, p. 196). The parrot passing through Bēruvala is asked to witness the dance of *baṁbura*s (Piyaratana 1964, p. 19).

Fearsome looking, drunk with opium and ganja
Ears decorated with *attana* and *rat mal* flowers
They shake their maces and *twirl their beards*
Friend [parrot] look at the whirling dances of the *baṁbura*s.

4. Obscenity and humor as an antidote for fear are well recognized in Sri Lanka. For example, if one sees a ghost or fears an imminent spirit attack one shouts obscenities and lifts one's sarong to show one's genitals.

Every edition of these *sandēśa* poems I have seen interprets *baṁbura* to mean Berber. "Berber" in turn has no strict linguistic, cultural, or geographical connotation in Sri Lankan usage. There were communities identified as Berber in literary and historical sources, but it is doubtful whether the term referred to North African Berbers rather than to Africans in general. It is not impossible that Moslem traders from the Middle East who were established on the west coast brought with them North African Berbers, but I doubt they have anything to do with the *baṁbura*s referred to in the texts mentioned above. The *baṁbura*s referred to in the *sandēśa*s have to be interpreted differently.

The *Girā Sandēśaya* reference quoted earlier is to a dance; the *baṁbura*s shake their "maces" (*mugura*), ritual objects also used by deities like Devol Deviyo and Dēvatā Baṇḍāra. They twirl their beards, exactly as in the stanza from the Rabalīya tradition. They look fearsome, as the text and drama of the *Hātabaṁbura* indicate. They wear flowers of *rat mal* (*Ixora coccinea*) and *attana* (*Datura fastuosa*, a hallucinogenic plant), inauspicious flowers in Sinhala belief, often given in demonic offerings. The probability is strong that the reference is to a Dionysian ritual dance where the actors are intoxicated with opium and ganja and with toddy. It is likely that the monks who witnessed these dances were appalled by them, since the Buddhist tradition was ascetic, serene, controlled. In other words, at one time Baṁbura dances such as the ones in Sīnigama and Mātara were practiced by larger numbers of performers in Bēruvala, which again is in our culture area.

The extant Sinhala rituals tell us very little about Baṁbura mythology. But if we extend the range of comparison we can solve the problem. According to the Seligmanns, the Baṁbura Yaka is one of the most important deities of the wild Väddas of Sītala Vanniya. "Bambura Yaka is on the whole not as important as Kande Yaka, though he is certainly not looked upon as so benevolent nor so loved as the latter. . . . Bambura Yaka is a somewhat grim spirit who although he gives yams and helps men to kill pigs, also sends sickness and must be invoked to remove it, and he is also invoked when dogs are lost or taken by shepherds. Because of his giving yams he is sometimes known as Ale (yam) Yaka" (1911, p. 152). The ritual dance for Baṁbura is briefly described by the Seligmanns:

> The dance is pantomimic, and depicts a boar hunt in which Bambura, the boar hunting hero, was aided by a Vedda woman, who killed the pig with the arrow she shot from her husband's bow (1911, p. 237)

The Seligmanns describe at some length this ritual (pp. 238–47), which includes the killing of the boar in pantomime. The conclusion of the rite is humorous:

> Kaira then danced with the *harimitiya* (cane) taking the usual dance steps . . . and he soon became possessed by Bambura Yaka. One of the lads now held the *tadiya* (pingo), then Kaira made a mock search for it for some minutes before he took it from the child. He danced with it over his shoulders with body bent and the *harimitiya* still in his hand. He thus enacted Bambura Yaka returning to the cave with good things in this *tadiya*, and he shouted as every Vedda does within hearing of his home. Seeing the children he seemed to threaten them with his stick, and they ran away laughing. (1911, p. 244)

This is one of the few comic sequences in Vädda ritual, and some of it (Baṁbura bent on his stick) is reminiscent of the "shooting" ritual of Mātara. In the latter Baṁbura goes in search of the quarry and kills it; this is similar to his killing the boar in the Vädda ritual.

The Sinhala ritual, as we now have it, has probably parodied the older Vädda ritual. The significance of the parody will be discussed in chapter 12.

At the time of Seligmanns' fieldwork the wild Väddas were found in small pockets in a 2,400-mile-square area in the northeast part of Sri Lanka. More settled Väddas were found in a larger area, but no Vädda communities are found in any part of our culture area. Yet the historical evidence is clear that they were much more widespread a few centuries ago, probably, according to Nevill, as far north as Puttalam on the west coast and Mātalē in the interior (Seligmann and Seligmann 1911, p. 9, n. 1). The *Parevi Sandēśaya* referred to earlier mentions daughters of Väddas in the area below Samanaḷa Peak, in Sabaragamuva. Even the term Sabaragamuva means the "region of the Sabaras," or hunters, that is, Väddas. The term *sabara*, or hunter, is strikingly reminiscent of the Saoras of Orissa studied by Elwin (1955), and common origins should not be discounted. It is likely that in the fourteenth and fifteenth centuries, and earlier, the Sabaragamuva area were peopled with Väddas, since it was generally isolated and forested. Even after Sinhala civilization was firmly established in the south and west much of this area was remote and inaccessible. Bailey refers to place names in this area that indicate their former existence, like Vädi pangu (Vädda share of land), Vädi kuṁbura (Vädda fields), and Vädivatta (Vädda gardens) (Seligmann and Seligmann 1911, p. 9). Most striking of these names is Väddāgala (Vädda rock), now the location of a Sinhala village I visited in 1961. Habarakaḍa (gateway of the hunters) is also a Sinhala village in Hinidum Pattu, in the Southern Province close to Sabaragamuva. People still say it was a place where Väddas came to barter their produce. My own texts refer to Väddas coming from the direction of Ruhuna as a bad omen (text 42, p. 249).

There is evidence in the rites of the *gammaḍuva*, as in other Sinhala rituals, indicating the existence of Vädda communities in close proximity to Sinhala people in areas that are now exclusively Sinhala. The traditions of Kataragama itself are rooted in Vädda culture, since Valli Amma, Skanda's mistress, is a Vädda woman. The present-day priests of Kataragama, as well as the special female servitors in the Kataragama rituals, claim to be direct descendants of Väddas. This adds considerable plausibility to the Seligmanns' view that the unimposing shrine for Skanda at Kataragama may have originally been a seat of the well-known Vädda deity Kandē Yaka ("god of the mountain"). Kandē Yaka is also worshiped as Kandē Deviyo, one of the Twelve Gods in Haṅguraṅketa, and is clearly distinguished from Skanda. Skanda's Sinhala name Kanda Kumāra (interpreted by Sinhala people to mean "mountain prince") may have promoted the identification of the South Indian deity with the god of the Väddas.[5]

In the *gammaḍuva* itself there is a text known as *vädi pūjāva* (pp. 276–77). This is neither enacted nor sung today, but in all likelihood it was once performed for Väddas who may have wished to participate in the *gammaḍuva*. In the *kohoṁbā kaṅkāriya* ceremony there is also a ritual known as *vädi dāne*, but I have not seen this performed either. However, one text in the *kohoṁbā kaṅkāriya* tradition of *hatara koralē*, known as *väddan aṅḍagāhīma* ("calling the Väddas"), indicates their dispersal in many areas and their geographic and possibly social proximity to Sinhalas. The "roll call" is for Väddas from ninety villages or areas (see Godakumbura 1963, pp. 90–91). Most of the names elude

5. The Sinhala folk etymology for Skanda also indicates this. Skanda is *Is kanda*, "mountain of heads" (see p. 114). This probably indicates the continuity of the idea of Skanda as a mountain deity.

me, but stanzas 35, 36, and 37 of this text deal with areas that are easily identifiable: in and around Kandy, North Central Province, Dumbara valley, and Kotmale valley. Except for the North Central Province these are at present exclusively Sinhala areas.

Perhaps one of the most fascinating references to Väddas in areas that are now Sinhala villages is from Parker (1909). Parker claims to possess a document in which Prince Vijayapāla of Mātalē summoned several Sinhala and Vädda chiefs to help him fight his cousin Rājasiṃha II of Kandy (1634–87). The following Vädda chiefs are mentioned: The Vädda chief of Hulangamuva, named Yahimiput Vädda, Kannila Vädda Pallakanaṅgomuva, Herat Vädda of Nikakoṭuva, Mahā Tampala Vädda of Palāpatvala, Mahā Doṁbā Vädda of Doṁbavala, Valli Vädda of Valli vala (a female chief?), Maha Kuvaḍällā Vädda of Kavuḍupalle, Nayiran Vädda of Nārangomuva, Hērat Baṇḍāra Vädda of Maḍavala, Imiyā Vädda of Kampalla, Makarayā Vädda, Koḍuru Vädda, Räkā Vädda, Mahā Kandē Vädda of Kandapalle, Hēmpeti of Galēvala, Bāju of Udugoḍa, Minimunu of Pallesiya Pattu, Devakriti of Melpitiya, and Kaḍukāra of Bibile (Parker 1909, pp. 101–2). Most of these villages are in the Mātalē District, now inhabited exclusively by Sinhalas. Moreover, just adjacent to these Vädda villages were Sinhala villages, from which the three Sinhala chiefs came—Chandrasekera Mudiyanse of Dubukälē, Kulatunga Mudiyanse of Uḍupihilla, and Vanisekera Mudiyanse of Aluvihāre (Parker 1909, pp. 101–2). And one of the Väddas had the term Baṇḍāra, reserved for Kandyan nobility. Thus it is clear that much of the Mātalē District that is now Sinhala was Vädda in the seventeenth century.

To sum up: It is almost certain that many parts of Sri Lanka were once inhabited by Väddas. Rituals like *vädi pūjāva* of the *gammaḍuva* and *vädi dāne* of the *kohoṁbā kaṅkāriya* probably involved Väddas who were permitted to participate as outsiders in Sinhala ritual. I have described and analyzed elsewhere a similar ceremony in Mahiyaṅgaṇa, where Väddas participate in a ritual known as *vädi perahära* ("Vädda procession"), which defines their role vis-à-vis the larger Sinhala Buddhist community on the national level (Obeyesekere 1963). The *vädi pūjāva* and *vädi dāne* are probably village and local versions of the same phenomenon: Väddas are ritually defined as members of the larger political and socioeconomic structure, and at the same time are excluded from the moral community of Sinhala Buddhists.

Let me make a hypothetical reconstruction of how the Vädda deity Baṁbura came into Sinhala worship, and how his cult then became "transformed" into the *gammaḍuva* traditions of Mātara and Sīnigama as the "shaving" and "shooting" rituals.

One must assume that Baṁbura Yaka of the Väddas of the Seligmanns' day (1911) was also traditionally propitiated in at least the Sabaragamuva Province in our culture area. No direct evidence is available, though we know that some Vädda deities like Kandē Yaka were also propitiated by Sinhala; so were Sinhala deities propitiated by Vädda. Ceremonies like the *kohoṁbā kaṅkāriya* also refer to Vädi Yak (Vädda deity) as a collectivity. There is nothing unusual in the Sinhalas adopting a Vädda deity, but for what reason? Baṁbura was adopted by the Sinhalas in our cultural area for one very good reason: hunting. Sinhala communities, particularly in the forested interior, do hunt, though this activity is devalued by Buddhism. As I showed in the preceding section, these communities are found even today; some practice hunting as a way of life, some use it to supplement rice cultivation. However, when a monastery or temple is established in a village and the people become more Buddhist, the general pattern of hunting as a way of life changes, though *individuals* continue to hunt everywhere in Buddhist Sri Lanka. Now Väddas are the archhunters, and Baṁbura is the hunting god of Väddas. Thus it is reasonable that Baṁbura should be incorporated by Sinhala people who follow a similar occupation. An examination of the "shooting" ritual (pp. 495–99) shows clearly that it is a survival of an earlier hunting ritual, for Baṁbura has a gun (perhaps earlier it would have been a bow and arrow); he searches for his quarry and eventually kills it. The ritual action is reminiscent of the Baṁbura ritual mime of the hunt described by the Seligmanns. Thus at one time Baṁbura had in all probability a similar role in both Vädda and Sinhala hunting communities.

In the fifteenth century Buddhism was firmly established in this region, particularly in the coastal areas, and also in parts of the interior. This would ipso facto have produced a change in hunting as a general pattern of life in many areas under Buddhist influence. Even when hunting existed, it would inevitably have been culturally devalued. Thus Baṁbura himself would be devalued, setting in motion a process of the comic parody of his cult. The cult was transformed at least in Sīnigama and Mātara from a hunting ritual to a comic hunting enactment whose symbolic meaning was based not on sympathetic magic (as in the Vädda ritual hunt), but on much more complex psychological problems. I shall discuss the psychological meaning of the Baṁbura ritual later; here let me simply state what I shall then demonstrate. The Baṁbura rituals deal with castration anxieties, feelings of sexual inadequacy, and fears of impotence. In this ritual the priests act out these anxieties; members of the audience are spectators, at best vicarious participants. The *sandēśa* evidence I quoted earlier shows, I think, that in the fifteenth century this was not the case. Then larger groups of people got together, perhaps consumed intoxicants, and danced the Baṁbura ritual. Castration and impotence anxieties were acted out in a communal ritual dance. There is nothing unusual or culturally alien in this, since similar anxieties were acted out till very recently (and even today in some areas) by groups in a similar Dionysian manner in the *aṅkeḷiya* rituals to be described in part 4 of this book. Here too people dance orgiastically, brandishing sticks (representing the castrated penises of their opponents), and in most areas they are drunk with alcohol (see pp. 387, 406).

External Historical Process: The Foreign Deity, Devol Deviyo

In this section I shall deal with a different aspect of mythic stratigraphy, the way disconcerting external religious influences are handled in the rituals of the *gammaḍuva*, focusing specifically on the rituals associated with Devol Deviyo. In these cases we have no independent historical records to date the events in ritual and myth; nevertheless, we can make certain inferences.

1. As in the previous section, we can make stratigraphic inferences to show which level of beliefs preceded which others, largely through examining symbolic statements.

2. We can specify the type of events that had an impact on the Sinhala culture of this region, these being foreign deities, foreign religious specialists, and, to a lesser extent, foreign traders. By "foreign" I mean South Indian, generally from Orissa, Tamil Nāṭu, Andhra Pradesh, and Kerala. The language they speak is "Tamil" (*demala*), which to Sinhalas meant any southern Indian "foreign" language. The myths and rituals I shall

examine below are "collective" representations" that express the historical processes mentioned earlier.

3. Above all, we can demonstrate how these disturbing alien elements are absorbed into Sinhala culture, especially foreign gods and demons.

The Devol Deviyo myth deals with the earthly life of these gods. They were merchants in a city of Sudduppura (or Kuḍḍhuppura) who came to the Sinhala land to trade. It is impossible to identify Sudduppura; the merchants' home in India is impersonal and generalized. Yet there are details in the myths and rituals of Devol Deviyo that are very specific. As sea traders they load their ships with goods, which are listed; they sail the seas, are shipwrecked, and land in Sri Lanka. In the Ratnapura tradition there are several verses that seem highly realistic descriptions of merchants from abroad coming to Sri Lanka, pitching their tents, and selling their produce.

> The seven people from abroad landed on these shores
> They unloaded here the goods they had brought
> They erected separate shops and stores
> From afar these look like a heavenly city.
>
> In the sands where they unloaded their goods
> They ate and drank heartily seated at table
> They have such pleasing ways when they sell
> "There's no one else like us in the whole world."
>
> They sold their goods to many people
> Now here comes someone to buy some cloth?
> "How much money do you have for buying cloth?"
> "I have money to buy one piece of cloth."

This is an ideal typical description of many discrete events that must have taken place on the west coast of Sri Lanka from very early times. Chinese, Romans, and later Arabs and South Indians brought goods and sold them in the ports of the South and West, which were well established by the ninth century. Sinhalas were not generally seafarers; as settled agriculturists, they must have been profoundly impressed by these merchants. The traders were also a disconcerting presence, since they had alien languages and religions.

The Arab and the South Indian presences were handled in radically different ways. The Arabs, who were involved in active trade before the advent of the Portuguese in 1505, were always an alien group; they were never Sinhalized, nor were their religious beliefs incorporated into Sinhala religion. Arab groups who settled on the coast by and large maintained their ethnic and religious identity, distinct from their Sinhala neighbors. Nevertheless, their presence did have some impact on Sinhala religion: Mecca became well known to Buddhists, and the Buddha himself was given an added cognomen, Makkama Muni, sage of Mecca! It was believed that the Buddha himself planted one of his footprints in the sands of Mecca and the other on Śrī Pāda (Adam's Peak). Furthermore, there was a great *dāgāba*, enshrining the Buddha's relics in Mecca (Makkama Mahā Vehera), according to Sinhala folklore. This notion, I suspect, developed out of the Muslims' disconcerting practice (to the Sinhalas) of praying facing Mecca. From this developed the notion that the Muslim god was subservient to the Buddha; when Muslims worshiped they were in fact also paying homage to the Buddha, recognizing his superiority, for his footprints and relics were enshrined in Mecca. Secondhand descriptions of minarets and domes in Arab cities must have led to the notion of the great *dāgāba* of Mecca. The supremacy of the Buddha in Sri Lanka, his immanent presence in the land of the Dhamma, could not be disputed.

The Muslim habit of worship facing Mecca in turn probably led the Sinhala people in this region to face in the direction of the sacred footprint at Śrī Pāda when uttering the five precepts of Buddhism in their homes. This act constitutes a symbolic statement, in the sense in which I defined it earlier, that in fact the Muslims are doing a similar thing—paying their respects to the Buddha's footprint in Mecca. Thus the words uttered by Devol Deviyo at the commencement of the fire trampling ritual are not idiosyncratic: "I have looked toward Mecca, toward Kälaṇiya, toward the peak of the sacred footprint." All three, according to popular myth were places the Buddha had visited; he had actually set his footmark at Mecca and Śrī Pāda. But note that the old chronicles mention only Kälaṇiya and Śrī Pāda; Mecca is a later invention, prompted by the Muslim presence in Sri Lanka. The Muslims could be tolerated only if their god and their system of worship were, from the Sinhala viewpoint, subsidiary to the Buddha and Buddhism. Not only was Allah worship subsidiary to worship of the Buddha, but the Muslim saints were under the suzerainty of the Sinhala gods. This idea is best expressed at Kataragama in what is probably a much later development. A Muslim saint is buried at Kataragama itself; large numbers of Muslims come to ask favors of this saint. Thus his shrine is under the general jurisdiction of the god Kataragama. Muslims are outside the moral community of Sinhala Buddhists: they, like the Väddas of Mahiyaṅgaṇa (Obeyesekere 1963) are permitted their own system of worship subject to the formal overlordship of Kataragama.

The South Indian presence was treated in a radically different manner. South Indians, particularly Cōḷa invaders, were the traditional enemies of the Sinhala kings. On the other hand, military alliances with South Indian regimes opposed to Cōḷa, as well as marital alliances, were a common feature of Sinhala polity from very early times, but especially after Parākramabāhu I (1153–86). Furthermore, there were South Indian Buddhist regimes such as the Kalabhra rulers, and Buddhist monks and monasteries existed in South India till at least the fourteenth century (see pp. 516–19). South Indian migration therefore lacked the uniform character of the Muslim settlements; there were different types of immigrants—soldiers, merchants, tribesmen, Buddhists, and Hindus, as well as other types of settlers. That they came from different parts of southern India is also clear from Sinhala ritual texts. They could not be isolated, treated separately from the Sinhala Buddhists of this region, or at least not for long. Thus they had to be incorporated into the Sinhala social structure and converted to Sinhala Buddhism. This can easily be demonstrated from later migrations. We know that the *salāgama* caste of the west coast were weavers from South India, probably the Malabar Coast; many of them came in Dutch times. Today most of them are Sinhala-speaking Buddhists. According to Raghavan (1961) the major waves of *karāva* (fishermen) immigration to the west coast occurred after the fifteenth century; today they are, in our region, mostly Sinhala-speaking Buddhists or Catholics. It is therefore very likely that before the fifteenth century South Indian immigrants were also converted into Sinhala Buddhists.

The Devol gods not only are merchants, they are also magicians and religious specialists. The Sīnigama tradition states that one of them, Devol Sāmi, performed magic tricks in Sīnigama, such as changing sand into rice. He married a local lady and had a child.

Here we see reflected the immigration of religious specialists from South India. There are many rituals that depict a similar historical problem. In the Sinhala ritual for countering the effects of sorcery, known as *hūniyan käpilla*, performed in this area there is a ritual drama known as *vaḍiga paṭuna* (the *vaḍiga* chapter). The drama again depicts a group of magicians and exorcists who arrive from *vaḍiga dēsa* (ancient Andhra Pradesh) but, like Devol Deviyo, are made fun of by Sinhalas. I have seen more than a dozen such episodes in Sinhala ritual drama. In Sinhala mythology many magicians and exorcists come from India. Thus, for example, the *gammaḍuva* myth says it was originally performed by Brahmans from India; the archmagician in Sinhala mythology, Malala Rajjuruvo (King of Malala), is from Malaladēsa, which in Sinhala probably meant the hilly region of Malabar. Other sorcerers and magicians came from Oḍḍisi, which is Orissa. In all the ritual dramas I have seen these characters have one common characteristic: they all speak with a Tamil accent. Sometimes they wear the vestment of Tamil religious specialists. They make ludicrous speech errors, resulting in verbal mix-ups. The audience has a great deal of fun at their expense. In the Devol Deviyo drama, as in all others, they make gross mistakes to start with; the drummer corrects them; and soon they begin to understand Sinhala speech. Once again historical process is compressed into symbolic form and depicted in ritual. The ritual drama portrays, in an impersonal symbolic idiom, a process that has occurred continually in history; alien religious specialists come into Sri Lanka, give up their old speech patterns and dress, and become Sinhala speakers. Not only this, these dramas depict a much more important process, the incorporation of the gods of these foreigners into the Sinhala Buddhist pantheon.

The Incorporation of Foreign Deities: Exclusion and Inclusion

Devol Deviyo is a trader and magician; he is also a god. In Sinhala ritual drama the seven Devol gods are depicted as one. Thus the drama of Devol Deviyo is primarily the entry of a foreign deity into Sri Lanka. To enter Sri Lanka it is not sufficient to be Sinhala: it is also necessary to be Buddhist. Alien deities must become Sinhala Buddhist deities. In chapter 2 and elsewhere I have shown how Hindu gods have become Sinhala Buddhist gods: the key mechanism I noted is *varan*, or warrant from the Buddha. In the ritual drama of Devol, as in many others, the historical process whereby an alien deity is incorporated into the Sinhala Buddhist pantheon is presented in symbolic form to the audience as a "cultural performance."

Consider the ritual drama that depicts the coming of Devol Deviyo into Sri Lanka. Devol tries to land, but he is prevented by each of the major gods of Sri Lanka. Devol is the ignorant foreigner: he mocks the gods. Sometimes he is outrageously insulting, as when he calls Kataragama a bastard son of six fathers. However, at each turn the dancer—representing the Sinhala Buddhist audience—corrects him. Devol then recognizes the true power and glory of the Sinhala gods and bursts into a panegyric. Devol's own gods are presented as fatuous beings who can turn "mountains into mountains," unlike the powerful Sinhala gods who convert "plains into mountains" or, like Pattini, resurrect the dead. The alien gods are intimate, pally (they wash your dishes), whereas the Sinhala gods are resplendent and aloof.

In this drama Devol's rod or "mace," the symbol of his power, is sequestered in the *toraṇa*, which is both altar and *vimāna* or abode of the gods. Devol tries to get this, but he is prevented from doing so. Thus Devol the alien god is divested initially of his power. He tries to advance to the abode of the gods but retreats in fear. He comes back and, undeterred, mocks the gods, the Buddha, and the monks. Ultimately he goes up to the *toraṇa*, hands on his head in worship and submission. He now is permitted to take his rod (two instead of one). He has been converted into a Sinhala Buddhist deity, acknowledging the suzerainty of the major gods of the pantheon, guardians of both Buddhism and the secular realm.

In the drama of fire walking there is a similar sequence: Devol utters Tamil gibberish, insults the gods, then, recognizing their worth and might, crosses the barrier and extinguishes the fire. The significance of the barrier comes out clearly in the fire walking drama in the Rabalīya tradition (pp. 144–46) and in practically every other tradition mentioned in this book. The symbolic act is basically simple: a barrier representing the gates of a city (*kaḍavata*) prevents the alien god Devol from crossing over to walk the fire. The whole complex myth of Devol Deviyo trying to land in Sri Lanka is compressed into this symbolism. Devol is an alien god; he cannot cross the barrier without a *sannasa*, or letter of authority from the great Sinhala gods. An assistant reads the *sannasa*, which says that the gods have given him a warrant, and only then does Devol extinguish the flames. In other traditions I have seen a more elaborate dialogue, as in Ratnapura. Devol tries to cross the barrier, but two attendants representing the guardian gods prevent him. Ultimately he pays obeisance to the gods, and they grant him permission. He then reads the *sannasa* giving him warrant. The warrant, or *varan*, is the gods' permission for him both to land in Sri Lanka and also to cross the fire and quell it.

I have discussed the symbolism of the barrier in an earlier paper describing a similar enactment (Obeyesekere 1969a). In this ritual drama the Sanni demons, a collectivity of eighteen demons originally from Kerala, try to land in Sri Lanka. These alien demons are tamed, humanized, made to acknowledge the supremacy of the Buddha and the gods, and finally permitted to cross the barrier. The barrier, then, represents a specific determinate event like Devol Deviyo's being prevented from landing in Sri Lanka; it is also an act of incorporating an alien being into the Sinhala Buddhist pantheon. The symbolism underlying the barrier is identical to what happens in initiation. First, the barrier symbolizes an *exclusion*: the alien being, like a neophyte, is forbidden to cross the barrier. Second, it symbolizes an *inclusion*: the barrier is opened by the gods, or by persons representing Sinhala Buddhist culture, and the alien being crosses over to the other side. The barrier also represents the obstacles that have to be overcome, or tasks performed, before the change of status and is structurally equivalent to ordeals and tests of strength in initiation rites. Translated into cultural terms, the *sannasa* or letter of authority expresses the notion of *varan* or warrant, and crossing the barrier signifies the incorporation of an alien deity into the Sinhala Buddhist pantheon, and his receiving formal status therein.

The alien deity crosses the barrier and is initiated into a new status. Initiation rites, however, also imply changes in moral values concomitant with status change. Thus at puberty the initiate renounces childhood values and learns the values of the adult world. There is a basic value opposition between the contrasted statuses. So it is in this ritual and others of the same type (Obeyesekere 1969a, pp. 207–8). The barrier symbolically separates the mundane, shallow values represented by the alien deity from the ethical values represented by the Buddha and the guardian gods. Thus Devol, standing on the other side of the barrier, tries to bribe the gods, but the dancer says they cannot be bribed, since they are righteous and just, intrinsically moral. Devol's mother-in-law asks him to flout Buddhist values and everyday village morality like respect for elders—but these are the values that are represented on the other side of the barrier.

The significance of the barrier can be better appreciated if we contrast the preceding ritual with one where the barrier is present but is not removed. I refer the reader to my description of a Vädda ritual at Mahiyaṅgaṇa, an important pilgrimage center in eastern Sri Lanka (Obeyesekere 1963).

Väddas (seventy-one in the ritual I witnessed) carrying poles representing spears line up near the shrine of Saman, led by a "chief" carrying a bow and arrow. After circumambulating the shrine three times in a graceful dance, the Väddas suddenly increase the tempo of their dance at a signal from the chief and start hooting, yelling, and brandishing their "spears," frightening the assembled Sinhala spectators. They stage several battles in front of the shrine, during which they "assault" the shrine by striking their spears on its steps. They then run toward the Buddhist temple (*vihāra*) and try to enter the premises of the *dāgäba* where the Buddha relics are enshrined. Here the path is blocked by two "guards" (*murakārayo*), who shout, "You can't approach this place. Go back to the royal altar [*rajavīdiya*, the altar of the guardian deity]." These mock battles are repeated several times and end with the Väddas placing their "spears" gently against the *dāgäba* and worshiping it. They then run toward the monks' residence (*pansala*) and stage a battle, but, as at the *dāgäba*, they end by worshiping the monks gathered there. Then, from the monks' residence back to the shrine where they again "battle," beating their spears against the stone steps of the *dēvāle* until the spears break into small pieces, and finally falling prostrate to worship the gods housed in the shrine. After this they run toward the nearby river ("the ferry crossing of the gods") and bathe and purify themselves. Returning to the shrine calm and self-possessed, they are now permitted to enter the inner sanctum while the *kapurāla* chants an incantation for Saman, Skanda, and the other major deities and blesses the Väddas by lustrating each person with "sandal water." The ritual ends with the Väddas all shouting "*harō-harā*," which in Sri Lanka is the paean of praise for the god Skanda, the great guardian deity of the island and formal overlord of the Vädda pantheon.

The difference in the social functions of the rituals performed by Sinhalas and Väddas is impressive. In the case of the Sinhalas there are no rituals that separate one group from another: all the assembled groups form one moral community participating in common worship. In the case of the Väddas, the rituals define their status in relation to the dominant religion in that they are "prevented" from entering the temple and *dāgäba*. Though they formally acknowledge the supremacy of the Buddha, they are clearly outside the Sinhala Buddhist moral community. Yet they are not total strangers, for both Sinhala and Vädda are united in worship of the guardian deities Saman and Skanda, protectors of the secular and supernatural order of both.

Note the contrasting symbolism. The Väddas are excluded from Buddhist worship and *remain* excluded. They attack the barrier but do not cross over to the other side; instead, their spears break. They recognize the supremacy of Buddhism, but they are outside the Buddhist church. Yet they are not *totally* excluded: after they have purified themselves, they are permitted to enter the shrine of the gods, who are formally suzerain over the Vädda pantheon.

Can the symbolism of the landing of the Devol Deviyo help us further in dating the introduction of his worship into Sri Lanka? All shrines for Devol Deviyo are on the southern and western coasts; it is likely that his worship was introduced to coastal peoples. But there is no hard evidence to identify it with a particular caste group like the *salāgama* or *karāva*, who dominate the coastal regions. We can, however, reasonably infer that the cult of Devol Deviyo came *after* the Pattini cult and that in all probability his shrines at Sīnigama and Vēragoḍa were originally Pattini shrines.

Note the myth of the god. He tries to land in Sri Lanka (i.e., symbolically enter the pantheon), and he is forbidden to do so. He eventually comes to Sīnigama, where the goddess Pattini accosts him. She creates seven mountains of fire that Devol and his assistants trample and extinguish. The myth, as a symbolic statement, indicates that Sīnigama was originally a Pattini shrine. Pattini resists the intrusion of the new cult, but not successfully. I interpret this as a statement indicating that the cult of Devol Deviyo intruded into the Pattini shrine at Sīnigama. We can also get an idea of the nature of the Devol Deviyo cult. It was in all likelihood associated with spectacular fire walking ("mountains of fire"). Furthermore, both Devol and Gini Kurumbara are associated in their mythology with the fire of Basma, the *asura*. Thus it is likely that originally the cult of Devol was associated with spectacular fire trampling rituals, but that these were later reduced in scale, brought in line with Sinhala Buddhist culture, and given medical meaning and significance.

The view that Devol usurped Pattini's place in Sīnigama and Vēragoḍa is given added support when we consider the rituals practiced there. In both places there are images of Devol; both shrines, but specially that at Sīnigama, are associated with ritual cursing and sorcery. Yet the annual ceremonies performed here are not for Devol but for Pattini. Every year a *gammaḍuva* is performed in Vēragoḍa and Sīnigama. The priest of the shrine also considers himself a Pattini priest; indeed, I obtained a set of the *pantis kōlmura*, the thirty-five texts of the Pattini cycle, from his family traditions.

Viṣṇu Alias Upulvan and Dēvatā Baṇḍāra Alias Däḍimuṇḍa

In this section I shall deal with two important deities, once again hoping to throw light on their place both in Sri Lankan history and in the popular pantheon of Sinhala Buddhists of our region. I have not attempted to consider all the major gods, since some of them, like Vibhīṣaṇa and Nātha, are only formally worshiped in the *gammaḍuva* and in Sinhala society today. Regarding Saman I do not have enough ethnological information to add to Paranavitana's historical treatment of his cult (Paranavitana 1958); whatever information I have has been presented earlier. Skanda I have dealt with elsewhere (Obeyesekere 1977, 1978), especially the recent rise of his cult in relation to the decline of the Pattini cult. Viṣṇu is a very important deity in our region and in all of Sri Lanka; he is part of the operative pantheon of the *gammaḍuva*, though he is fast becoming otiose. I also believe that the data in the rituals and myths of the *gammaḍuva* will help us revise Paranavitana's influential thesis on the historical development of Viṣṇu worship in Sri Lanka. Däḍimuṇḍa, or Dēvatā Baṇḍāra, I showed earlier, was at one time part of the pantheon of the Twelve Gods in our region. His recent rise in importance and prominence is related to the historical vicissitudes of the Viṣṇu cult.

In my commentary on the Viṣṇu invocation and in the ritual of the torch of time for Viṣṇu (texts 3, 6, pp. 93–95, 103–6) I discussed two fundamental Sinhala attitudes toward the god. First there are the well-known Hindu attributes of the ten avatars, the *guruḷu* bird, and so forth. In the second text Viṣṇu is incorporated into a Buddhist framework. Viṣṇu tried to show his mastery over the universe by crossing the earth in three steps, but he failed. Thus he is half-Viṣṇu (Aḍa Viṣṇu). He becomes Mūla Viṣṇu, or complete, only when he joins forces with the Buddha in banishing disease from Viśālā, a city associated with Buddhist history and myth. Moreover, a prophecy at birth states that he is destined to protect the Buddha in the Māra war, one of the central episodes of the Buddha legend.

We see here two processes that must have occurred time and again in Sri Lankan history, not only in respect to Viṣṇu but also in relation to other gods introduced from South India, particularly Skanda. The continual influx of South Indian religious specialists would infuse the Viṣṇu or Kataragama cults with Hindu mythic attributes; concomitantly there would be an attempt to deny these or revise them in relation to a dominant Buddhist ethos. This is not to say that there is a Hindu Viṣṇu and a Buddhist Viṣṇu in the Sinhala Buddhist pantheon. Viṣṇu was for at least four centuries, and possibly even much longer (as Upulvan), incorporated into Buddhism, in terms of the mechanisms discussed in chapter 2, such as his conversion into a bodhisattva. Yet the constant influx of Hindu ideas would result in the continuous *accretion* of specific Hindu mythic attributes followed in turn by a Buddhist response. One striking example of this is the Hindu idea of the god's consort mentioned in the *sandēśa* poems and in fifteenth-century inscriptions. This idea cannot be maintained for long in a Theravāda Buddhist ethos; hence it is nonexistent today. In respect to Viṣṇu let me for convenience label the end product of these two processes as two *images* of Viṣṇu, a Hindu one and a Buddhist one, added onto the basic Buddhist conception of Viṣṇu as a bodhisattva and a deity having a warrant (*varan*) from the Buddha. The Buddhist image of Viṣṇu is always linked to the Buddha legend.

My view of the two images of Viṣṇu will, I think, help to clear up Paranavitana's well-known theory regarding Upulvan. Paranavitana states that the term Upulvan, today exclusively associated with Viṣṇu, originally designated a different deity. This deity is referred to in the *Mahāvaṃsa* as being placed in charge of Sri Lanka by the Buddha himself. Upulvan also blessed Vijaya, the founder of the Sinhala race, when he landed in Sri Lanka. According to Paranavitana, Upulvan is none other than the Vedic god Varuṇa. The Sinhala people who colonized Sri Lanka were Indians from northern India who were believers in Upulvan alias Varuṇa. How so? It is very likely, says Paranavitana, that the religious beliefs depicted in the *Rāmāyana* and *Mahābhārata* were those of these original ancestors in their north Indian home. And Varuṇa is an important god in the *Rāmāyana*; therefore it is likely that the original Sinhalas believed in him. The Sanskrit term *varuṇa* became converted into *uppala vaṇṇa* through very complicated phonological changes that he discusses in great detail.

I cannot go into a detailed critique of this influential thesis here except to point out two basic methodological errors. First, the view that the early Sinhala were believers in Varuṇa because they subscribed to the religion of the *Rāmāyana* is preposterous. We know very little about the early settlers in Sri Lanka, least of all whether they were a culturally homogeneous group from a designated region in northern India. If they were, there is still less reason for attributing to them belief in the religious ideology of the *Rāmāyana* and *Mahābhārata*, given the notorious problems involved in dating and contextualizing these texts. Paranavitana himself has his doubts:

> The general opinion among scholars is that the epics, as we have them now, belong to a period between the third century B.C. and the first century A.D., though certain actions *may go back* to a date even earlier. The social and religious conditions they depict, however, *might very well* hold good for the first Aryan colonization of Ceylon, about the fifth century B.C. . . . the stories themselves *could have been known* to the people. (1953, p. 26; my italics)

Thus the major part of these texts, insofar as they refer to conditions after the third century B.C., could simply not apply to immigrants who came to Sri Lanka before the sixth century B.C. Yet Paranavitana ignores these problems. Furthermore, it seems equally plausible, indeed more so, that these immigrants could just as easily have worshiped Viṣṇu himself, either as Kṛiṣṇa or as the dark god of the South Indians, Mayon. In any case Viṣṇu himself was popular by the time of the *Mahābhārata*, and he could well have been incorporated into the *Mahāvaṃsa*, which was written in the fifth century A.D. Thus the first methodological error is to uncritically utilize the *Mahābhārata* and *Rāmāyana* as reflecting the proto-Sinhala religion.

The second methodological criticism is even more serious. The major thrust of Paranavitana's analysis is etymological and phonological. He attempts to trace the history of a cultural complex through shifts in meaning and, more important, through systematic phonological changes. Thus *van* in Upulvan, which Sinhala people have always interpreted to mean *varṇa* or *vaṇṇa*—that is, colored ("lotus-colored")—is, according to Paranavitana, a mistake. The term *van* comes from *vaṇa*, which in turn comes from *varuṇa*. Paranavitana shows the extremely complicated manner in which these changes occurred (1953, p. 24). Most of these alleged phonological changes are highly dubious, at best based on a set of ideal conditions almost never realized in practice. If, for example, Sinhala people were trained philologists, the theory might be justified. Phonological evidence, if it is to be used in cultural analysis, should be predictive, not "postdictive" as in the present case. If Paranavitana worked forward from the term *varuṇa* to *vaṇa* and then *vaṇṇa* in a series of predictive and regular phonological changes, I might be able to accept his argument. But when he traces it backward it is not a predictive process but an ad hoc justification for a conclusion he has already drawn. The change, he says, "must be due to the rendering on to Páli of a name that was in current use in the Sinhalese of his day."

As further "proof" he refers to an old inscription at Mihintale that mentions a princess called Varuṇadata (Varuṇa's gift). "The princess' name shows that her parents must have been devotees of Varuṇa" (1953, p. 24). The absurdity of this kind of analysis can be shown if we take a contemporary example. There are women in Sri Lanka today named "Varuṇi": this means they are Hindu devotees of the Varuṇa cult, according to Paranavitana's kind of analysis. Paranavitana's book is full of similar evidence to "prove" the theory.

One glaring instance of this is the derivation of the first part of the god's name, "Upul." How did this transformation come about? The consensus by Sinhala people that "Upul" meant blue lotus "does not make any sense" (1953, p. 25). The *real* meaning (which, incidentally, has never been actually held by Sinhala people) is based on the fact that

Varuṇa is the "lord of the waters." There are many epithets used to designate this idea in the Sanskrit literature. Other epithets are also appropriate, *even though they are not found in extant literature*! "One such possible epithet is *Uda-pāla*. *Uda* is a synonym of *udaka* and *pāla* can be used with the same meaning as *pati* (lord). . . . As there are no long vowels in ancient Sinhalese, *Udapāla* would have changed to *Udapala*. The loss of the syllable *da* by syncope . . . would also result in *Upala*. It is also conceivable that the vowel in the second syllable of *Udapala* was slurred over in pronunciation, giving rise to *Udpala* and *Uppala*. If the origin of the name is as suggested above the form Upulvan in Sinhalese literature is a natural development from *Upala-vaṇa*" (1953, p. 25). All these changes, it should be noted, are based on an epithet given to Varuṇa by Paranavitana himself, since he admits it is nowhere found in the extant literature. Thus my second criticism: the phonological analysis is methodologically dubious and its practice in this case is blatantly incorrect.

Paranavitana, like other Sinhala scholars before him, adduces evidence from fourteenth- to fifteenth-century literature to show that Viṣṇu and Upulvan were separate deities who by the sixteenth century had coalesced in the form of Viṣṇu. The view that Viṣṇu usurped the position of a preexisting deity is reasonable, since similar processes are often found in the history of religion. What is doubtful, as I suggested earlier, is the identification of this deity, Upulvan, with Varuṇa. However, the sources Paranavitana quotes to show the separate nature of the two deities are by no means clear, particularly in the light of what we know about these deities from the ritual texts. Let us consider these references.

1. The *Tisara Sandēśaya* (verse 18) asserts that Śrī or Lakṣmī (the goddess of prosperity) and Sarasvatī (the goddess of speech), who in mythology are respectively the consorts of Viṣṇu and Brahmā, found Upulvan so irresistible that they deserted their own spouses and lived with him. Paranavitana says that if Upulvan was the same as Viṣṇu this poem would be meaningless, for there is no reason he should grieve when his own spouse remained with him (1953, pp. 20–21).

2. *Kōkila Sandēśaya* (verse 21), in extolling Upulvan, says that he is comparable to Viṣṇu in exceptional powers. If Upulvan is Viṣṇu, this statement, says Paranavitana, also would make no sense.

3. The Lankātilaka rock inscription of King Bhuvenakabāhu IV's reign refers to both Viṣṇu and Upulvan in the same inscription; therefore they must be different gods. "The images of Suyāma, Santuṣita, Śakra, Brahmā, Viṣṇu and Maheśvara, the images of the consorts of these personages, [the images of] the god-king Kihireli-Upulvan, the god kings Sumana, Vibhīṣaṇa-Ganapati, Kanda-Kumāra and others who have assumed the duty of protecting Laṁka" (Paranavitana 1953, p. 21). Kihiräli, incidentally, refers to an eight-century place name in the region of the present-day Viṣṇu shrine.

That Viṣṇu and Upulvan are separately listed need not, I think, warrant the interpretation that Paranavitana and others have held, for, according to Hindu ideas at least, one could have a situation where two distinct gods could on another level become one. For example, any good Hindu could list the following personages separately: Viṣṇu, Kṛiṣṇa, Rāma, Buddha. Though distinct, they are all avatars of one being, Viṣṇu. They are different and at the same time identical. Actually, such listings of the many names of a single deity are commonplace in Hindu worship. If, for example, Upulvan is an early Buddhist image of Viṣṇu and Viṣṇu a later Hindu image, the quotations above would make sense.

Thus the second quotation, which compares Upulvan to Viṣṇu, is no different from a Hindu's comparing Buddha with Kṛiṣṇa in a similar way. In the third quotation note that Viṣṇu is explicitly referred to in a formal Hindu context (Brahmā, Viṣṇu, and Maheśvara), while Upulvan is mentioned in an operative Buddhist context as a guardian of Sri Lanka. Literalism in the interpretation of South Asian religion will not do. Thus we must not be deterred by Paranavitana's view that, since Viṣṇu has four arms and a vehicle, whereas Upulvan has two arms and no vehicle, they are different deities. Even in Hindu iconography Viṣṇu can be depicted in several ways, including having only two arms.

One might argue, however, that the idea of the one and the many is Hindu and is not typical of Buddhism. But consider the following stanza from the texts of the Sīnigama tradition in my possession.

Pulvan surin̆dugana
Rāmaya Uvin̆du samagima
Nāmaya kiyami bätiyena
Van̆din devraja me apa samagina.

Upulvan chief of the host of gods [*sura*]
Along with Rāma and Uvin̆du [Upendra]
With devotion we utter your name[s]
Unitedly we worship these divine kings.

Here Upulvan is Viṣṇu, and so is Rāma, and so is Upendra, which is another term for Viṣṇu as "younger brother of Indra." Another stanza from the same text comes with even a longer list of deities that are separate yet the same.

Uvin̆du Surin̆du Rāmaya Pulvan yana
Devin̆du Viṣṇu ran̆ga Kṛiṣṇa Uvin̆du yana
Meväni nama dasaruvini udārana
Denmata avasara devrada samagina.

Upendra, Rāma chief of *sura*s, and Upulvan
God Viṣṇu, the dancing Kṛiṣṇa and Upendra
Possessed with such noble names and ten shapes
Give me permission, kindly, O king of gods.

The hypothetical examples I quoted earlier have their parallel in current rituals among Sinhala Buddhists. It is also likely that this tendency is an old one, and it may equally well explain the reference to Upulvan and Viṣṇu as separate yet the same in the examples given by Paranavitana and others.

I am advocating the thesis that Upulvan and Viṣṇu are different deities and yet the same. Upulvan in the accepted meaning "blue-lotus-hued" makes more sense that Paranavitana's involved phonological excursus. That the early Sinhala who came from northern India worshiped the popular lotus-colored god of that region is more plausible than their worship of Varuṇa, a deity who never excited the popular imagination. Thus I am inclined to the view that Upulvan was an early Buddhist adaptation of Viṣṇu and was later given the title Upulvan.

Furthermore, when we look at the references to Upulvan in the *gammaḍuva* myth we find that the term Upulvan is in fact a title given to other deities as well. Consider the following references from the Sīnigama texts in my possession.

Dasaratha Pulvan namini udāraya
Tosakara säsakara kimini līlaya
Tosakara Rāvaṇa yudayen genajaya
Nisikara e Saman devińduta väńdajaya

With the noble name of Dasaratha Upulvan
Playful like the moon's form [?]
With joy he was victorious in the Rāvaṇa war
Obtain victory by rightful worship of Saman.

Here Upulvan is also a title for Saman. The reason is clear: Saman was identified, at least later, as Lakṣmaṇa, the brother of Rāma, who in turn is an avatar of Viṣṇu. Thus he is Dasaratha Pulvan; Daśaratha is the father of Rāma and Lakṣmaṇa, and hence Lakṣmaṇa as well as Rāma could be called Dasaratha (U)pulvan.

Däḍimuṇḍa and Upulvan-Viṣṇu

The complexity of the process involved in the historical development of deities can be illustrated with even greater certainty in the relation between Viṣṇu-Upulvan and the god of Alutnuvara, Dēvatā Baṇḍāra alias Däḍimuṇḍa alias Vāhala. I shall demonstrate how attributes of the former were transferred to the latter as a result of historical vicissitudes and, further, how these historical events are expressed in the myths of Däḍimuṇḍa.

Let me start off with two stanzas from the printed version of the Däḍimuṇḍa hǟlla (text 25, pp. 214–20) that show that Däḍimuṇḍa and Upulvan were different deities.

After Däḍimuṇḍa has defended the Buddha in the Māra war he goes to pay homage to Upulvan.

9. Worshiping the Buddha and obtaining his permission
He went to pay respects to King Vessamuni
Who gave him charge over all demons
Then he paid homage to Pulvan the *sura*.

10. He [Upulvan] surveyed the world
And told the great *dēvatā* thus
Descend into Māya country
To build a city there.

The printed version could not have been written before the fifteenth century, since at that time (we know from the *sandēsa* poetry to be quoted later), it was Upulvan (Viṣṇu) and not Däḍimuṇḍa who stood by the Buddha in the Māra war. Moreover, the text is "modern" in language and style; yet it is sufficiently old (or draws upon an older tradition that did not equate Upulvan with Däḍimuṇḍa). However, a verse sung in ongoing operative ritual tradition of Sīnigama seems to make the equation Upulvan = Däḍimuṇḍa.

Pulvan sura purē
Pulvan alut nuvarē
Väjambena häma varē
Vańdin deviyan alutnuvarē.

Upulvan of the city of the gods
Upulvan of Alutnuvara ["new city"]
Who resides there always
Worship the god of Alutnuvara.

This stanza is not in the printed version, but it is found in the texts of today's priests of Sīnigama, for whom the god of Alutnuvara is Däḍimuṇḍa. Thus Upulvan of this verse must be Däḍimuṇḍa, not Viṣṇu. Moreover, the previous stanza of this text refers to Pattini and the very next refers to Devol. The middle reference must be to Däḍimuṇḍa, since these three are often lumped as the *tunbāge deviyo* "the gods of the three divisions." Any possibility of ambiguity is ruled out when we consider the two extra verses sung by the priests of the Rabalīya tradition (*Däḍimuṇḍa hālla*; text 25, pp. 219–20).

Pulvan suriňduta asna sadannē
Malgena suvaňdin yahan tabannē
Avla pahanut niti puda ḍennē
Sellam kara Däḍimuṇḍa vaḍinnē.

Make a throne for Upulvan the *sura*
Offer flowers and scents in his altar
Light lamps and make the right offerings
Playfully arrive here O Däḍimuṇḍa.

Kiyanna aṇasaka melova pasindā
Yakunṭa suriňdek venema kohindā
Budun laňgadi iňda tēva kelendā
Vaḍinna teda äti dēva surindā

Speak of his renown for the world to know
Is there any other god to command demons?
He who stayed near the Buddha and did him service
Arrive O glorious divine *sura* chief.

Upulvan, then, at least according to my texts, is a title given to at least three deities, Viṣṇu himself, Saman-Lakṣmaṇa, and Dēvatā Baṇḍāra or Däḍimuṇḍa, all closely associated with Viṣṇu. The thesis of Sri Lankan scholars that the term Upulvan was later associated with Viṣṇu alone is simply not correct.

That Upulvan is an early Buddhist image of Viṣṇu is of course as impossible to prove as the Varuṇa theory. However, we do know how Upulvan, be he a Buddhist Viṣṇu image or otherwise, was adapted into the Buddha legend in fifteenth- and sixteenth-century texts. According to the *Kōkila Sandēśaya*, Upulvan alone stood by the Buddha and defied the armies of Māra. The incident is also referred to in *Mayura Sandēśaya* (verse 4), which says: "give this message to the god Upulvan of Devundara, who on the occasion of the Buddha's enlightenment [*Buddha maṅgalya*] showed the power of his bow."

None of the extant Buddhist Pāli sources mention this or any event remotely resembling it. According to Ñānavāsa the references to Buddha's battles with the army of Māra as he sat under the bo tree occur only in the Pāli commentaries (Ñānavāsa 1964, pp. 120–22). According to the *Jātaka Nidāna*, the all-powerful gods, including Sakra, ran away leaving the Buddha alone, so frightened were they of Māra's power. Yet Sinhala (probably popular) sources by the fifteenth century have made one exception: Upulvan alone stayed undaunted by the Buddha. This must at one time have been a popular tradition, since one text (no. 6, p. 104) refers to the Buddhist Viṣṇu fighting Māra on Buddha's behalf. Yet all the other ritual texts refer to this event in respect to another Upulvan, Däḍimuṇḍa. One might be tempted to infer that the two Upulvans are the same, in which case the logic of analysis would be as follows. Upulvan (whether he was Viṣṇu or Varuṇa could be ignored) was an old Sinhala deity. In the fourteenth and fifteenth centuries he was associated with the Buddha's battle with Māra as the intrepid god. In the sixteenth century, Upulvan's place was usurped by Viṣṇu; yet he continued to exist as a lower god, Däḍimuṇḍa, the fearless one. Perhaps Däḍimuṇḍa was then identified with Dēvatā Baṇḍāra, one of the Twelve Gods.

I think the preceding explanation is too simplistic and too much like the kind of error I castigated earlier. For example, how does Upulvan as Lakṣmaṇa or Saman come into this? I wish to offer an alternative explanation that is consonant with both the historical and the mythological data.

Upulvan, I submit, was either an indigenous deity or, more likely, an early Sinhala Buddhist adaptation of Viṣṇu, in the manner that Sakra was a Buddhist image of Indra. Once the god is thoroughly Buddhicized and adapted into Sinhala culture he becomes independent of the prototype, as Sakra became independent of Indra. Upulvan was known in the seventh century as Kihiräli-Upulvan, since his great temple was here (Kihiräli), in what is now known as Devinuvara (the city of the god) or Devundara. The *Mahāvaṃsa* reports that Dappula, a prince of the Ruhuṇa in the seventh century, honored this god. The place was very well known in the twelfth century, since Nissanka Malla (1187–96), reigning in Polonnaruva, refers to it as a place of great antiquity (Paranavitana 1953, p. 1).

The *Pärakumbā Sirita* of the fifteenth century states that Dappula installed here a red-sandalwood image of the god that was washed up by the sea. This reference, still current in popular lore, has little historical value and is probably a charter to account for the existence of such an image in the temple in the fifteenth century. By this time the myth had also developed that Upulvan alone stood by the Buddha during his battle with Māra. From the Viṣṇu myth quoted earlier (pp. 103–6) we know that Upulvan obtained *varan* from the Buddha as a protector of Sri Lanka. This, in fact, has been his role from the very founding of the Sinhala race, according to the *Mahāvaṃsa*.

After the fifteenth century there was an influx of Hindu ideas into Sri Lanka. As a result of this there occurred what we see in my *gammaḍuva* texts, a Hindu image of Viṣṇu, which probably existed alongside the worship of Upulvan. It was a matter of time before the two coalesced and Upulvan was identified (once again) with Viṣṇu. This identity was firmly established in the sixteenth century.

In my ritual texts Upulvan is a title: it is given to Viṣṇu himself, to Lakṣmaṇa, and to Däḍimuṇḍa. The generalization from Upulvan to Viṣṇu and from Viṣṇu to Lakṣmaṇa is understandable, since both were sons of Daśaratha (hence "Dasaratha Upulvan"). But where does Däḍimuṇḍa alias Dēvatā Baṇḍāra come into all this? How does *he* get the title Upulvan?

With the coalescing of Viṣṇu and Upulvan, the myth of the Māra battle would inevitably have also been transferred from Upulvan to Viṣṇu. By the time the Portuguese destroyed the god's shrine at Devinuvara in 1588, there was no doubt whatever regarding the identity: Viṣṇu = Upulvan. Furthermore, the descriptions of the temple procession, with its chariots and dance girls, indicated a considerable influx of Hindu ritualism at this central shrine. Then the great Viṣṇu shrine of Devinuvara was razed by the Portuguese; the area itself fell under Portuguese control.

What then happened to Viṣṇu-Upulvan? Let us first consider the historical event and then its later mythologization. Pieris says that after the Portuguese destroyed the shrine of Viṣṇu-Upulvan at Devundara it was transferred to Alutnuvara. Hence the name: the earlier shrine was situated at Devinuvara (Devundara) "the city of the god"; it was now transferred to Alutnuvara "the new city [of the god]." The actual date of the transfer is uncertain, but a Portuguese land register (*tombo*) refers to it in 1614 as the shrine of Nārāyaṇa (i.e., Viṣṇu). Thus it is clear that the transfer was effected almost immediately after the sack of Devinuvara. Pieris goes on to say that during the civil unrest and warfare that followed the deaths of Dharmapāla of Kōṭṭe and Rājasiṃha I of Sītāvaka (1581–93) the gods insignia (*ābharaṇa*) were removed to Kandy, to the present shrine, the Mahā Dēvāle ("great shrine"). When Robert Knox, the famous British prisoner, witnessed the great procession in Kandy during the time of Rājasiṃha II (1635–87), the god was still known as Alutnuvara Deviyo—that is, the memory of Viṣṇu-Upulvan's transfer from Alutnuvara to Kandy was still fresh in the minds of the populace. The date of his installation in Kandy must be after 1614 (the *tombo* reference to Alutnuvara) and before 1679 (the date of Knox's escape.) The reference in Knox also proves conclusively that it was originally Viṣṇu-Upulvan (not Däḍimuṇḍa) who was originally known as the "god of Alutnuvara."

Myth supplies the missing information on how the attributes of Viṣṇu-Upulvan came to be transferred to Däḍimuṇḍa. It also illustrates the "indirect representation" of historical process in mythic terms.

The myth of Däḍimuṇḍa (text 25, pp. 214–20) does several things.

1. The printed (earlier) version has no reference to the destruction of the Devinuvara shrine. It refers only to the continuity of Viṣṇu worship. According to fifteenth-century sources the famous Viṣṇu-Upulvan image was originally washed ashore from somewhere and installed in Devinuvara. This same account is now repeated in text 25; the image is washed ashore and then taken to the Māyāraṭa; and when the king experienced bad omens, a large shrine ("city") was built to house it. This is Alutnuvara, "the new divine city."

2. The text does not say that Däḍimuṇḍa built the city; he only cleaved the rock in order to build the *maluva*, or compound, which is the area where possessions, then and now, took place.

3. The text (25) says that Däḍimuṇḍa obtained permission from Upulvan; thus Däḍimuṇḍa and Viṣṇu-Upulvan are different. However, it is Däḍimuṇḍa, not Viṣṇu, who stood by the Buddha during the Māra war. Yet even the printed version does not state unequivocally that the "sandalwood log" (image) washed ashore was Upulvan-Viṣṇu's; nor does it state that the new "city" built to house it was his. It does not state that they were Däḍimuṇḍa's, either. The vagueness is corrected by the extra stanzas in the ritual traditions. We can reasonably infer that the printed text was written when many of the historical events had been forgotten, probably in the late eighteenth century. By that time Viṣṇu had been firmly established in Kandy, and Däḍimuṇḍa was ensconsed in Alutnuvara. But how did the latter get there?

4. Däḍimuṇḍa is the cognomen given to the deity by the Buddha; his earlier name is Dēvatā Baṇḍāra, one of the gods of the Baṇḍāra cult. He was a provincial deity whose area of authority or *sīmā* was the *hatara kōralē*, the larger district in which Alutnuvara is situated. When Viṣṇu was transferred to Alutnuvara, Däḍimuṇḍa must necessarily have had a role subservient to this great god. Thus we can now explain why Däḍimuṇḍa has another title: Vāhala, or "guardian of the palace"—that is, of the shrine or divine city of Viṣṇu at Alutnuvara. It was also likely, indeed certain, that his traditional role in village society was as a kind of overlord of demons, helping to banish them from the bodies of possessed patients.

5. When Viṣṇu was transferred to Alutnuvara he (Viṣṇu) became *the* god of Alutnuvara. But when he was transferred later to Kandy, Däḍimuṇḍa alone remained there. Since there was then no god there superior to him, Däḍimuṇḍa inevitably became the god of Alutnuvara. As his charisma increased as a vanquisher of demons and a curer of sick (possessed) patients, the myths surrounding Upulvan-Viṣṇu were transferred to him: the attributes of the first god of Alutnuvara (Viṣṇu) were transferred to the second god of Alutnuvara (Däḍimuṇḍa). Thus it was Däḍimuṇḍa who stood by the Buddha in the Māra war; Däḍimuṇḍa has ten apparitions (text 24). Concomitant with the rise of Däḍimuṇḍa there may have been a further elevation of Viṣṇu as an exclusively benevolent deity, which, according to the principles enumerated in chapter 2, must result in the downplaying of Viṣṇu's role as a warlike god and vanquisher of demons. These attributes were taken over by Däḍimuṇḍa, and at least by the end of the nineteenth century his shrine was famous all over the country as a center for demon exorcism.

6. Further changes in the myth of Däḍimuṇḍa have occurred in the operative ritual traditions of Sīnigama and Rabalīya. The ambiguity regarding Upulvan is eliminated: Upulvan is none other than Däḍimuṇḍa himself. Furthermore (probably after the public had forgotten that Alutnuvara was an old Viṣṇu shrine), Däḍimuṇḍa was credited in mythology with a number of accomplishments—he brought into cultivation the paddy lands nearby; it was he who enlisted the help of demons to build *all* the buildings in the divine city. Thus the god who cleaved the rock was also the one who built the city.[6]

6. All my texts indicate that the term Däḍimuṇḍa, the stern or fearless one, is a title given by the Buddha to Dēvatā Baṇḍāra. However, it is possible that this term was originally given to Viṣṇu-Upulvan, since it was he who, in earlier accounts, stood by the Buddha. This fits in with the mythology of Viṣṇu-Upulvan. According to the earlier accounts (e.g., the *Mahāvaṃsa*) Buddha asked Sakra to take charge of protecting Sri Lanka; Sakra in turn delegated this task to Viṣṇu-Upulvan. Viṣṇu-Upulvan thus had warrant from Sakra rather than directly from the Buddha. The later Sinhala myths give him a more powerful legitimation: he stood by the Buddha in the Māra war and obtained warrant (*varan*) from the Buddha himself. In this situation it is likely that the Buddha may have given Viṣṇu-Upulvan another name to commemorate his obtaining a warrant: Däḍimuṇḍa, the fearless one.

If this argument is correct, then Dēvatā Baṇḍara took over both of Viṣṇu's titles—Upulvan and Däḍimuṇḍa. But this issue cannot be resolved without further evidence.

Part Three

Introduction

In chapter 1 I examined the nature of the *pantis kōlmura*, or thirty-five ritual texts. I described them, somewhat arbitrarily, as belonging to three corpora. Corpus 1 deals with the Pattini myths, corpus 2 with the good king of Soḷī (Karikāla) and the bad king of Pāṇḍi (unnamed); corpus 3 is an indigenous one dealing with King Gajabāhu of Sri Lanka and his exploits, especially his terrorizing the king of Soḷī (the son of the good Soḷī of corpus 2), and bringing back to Sri Lanka the anklets (sacra) of the goddess Pattini.

The good king of Soḷī is explicitly viewed as following King Asoka's model of righteous kingship in the text, known as *vitti hata* ("seven exemplary events") presented in chapter 5, while the bad king of Pāṇḍi is his polar opposite, as aspirant to divine pretensions.

The myths and rituals of Soḷī and of Gajabāhu that I shall describe and interpret in chapters 7 and 8 have also been embodied in the chronicles, inscriptions, and popular literature of South India and Sri Lanka. Both Sri Lankan and especially South Indian scholars have interpreted these accounts as reflecting actual historical events. For example, the reign of Karikāla has been culled from these sources and presented in practically every South Indian history text. My own sociological interpretation of the myths and ritual dramas in which these characters appear suggests a radical revision of early South Indian and Sri Lankan history. This analysis also provides a model for examining the historical significance of myth in South Asian culture as well as in other cultures where mythic material is often compounded with history.

7

Cosmic Kingship: The Pataha and Karikāla Myths of Sri Lanka and South India

In the cycle of myths of the *gammaḍuva* there are several texts dealing with the kings of Soḷī and Pāṇḍi that I shall consider in this chapter. These texts are all part of the thirty-five songbooks and were probably enacted traditionally in the form of ritual dramas. However, the myths dealing with the good king of Soḷī are rarely sung today, and I have seen only one ritual drama relating to the myths of the evil king of Pāṇḍi. Yet it was obvious from informant interviews that the Pāṇḍi myths were also enacted in the *gammaḍuva* everywhere till recent times. The demise or decay of these myths is due to their almost total lack of contemporary relevance, but I am fortunate in having the texts of the Soḷī myths and having seen one dramatic performance of the Pāṇḍi myths. It is possible on the basis of these texts and the one performance to interpret these myths sociologically. I believe these two sets of myths deal with two sides of the coin and must be treated in relation to each other: the king of Soḷī represents the good king and the king of Pāṇḍi the "evil" king. The king of Soḷī is in some texts identified with Karikāla, the great South Indian Cōḷa king who lived about the second century A.D., though in the ritual texts he consistently retains a mythical character. At the conclusion of this chapter I will examine the historical versus the mythical nature of this king. I hope such a discussion will throw some light on both Sinhala and early South Indian history.

The Pāṇḍi Myths and Ritual Drama

The five myths of the king of Pāṇḍi that I will consider here are *dan kaṭina* ("offering of robes"), *pāṇḍi naḷuva* ("the beauty of Pāṇḍi"), *amārasaya* ("taste of ambrosia"), *patasa*, or *pataha* ("tank, pond"), and *soḷīpura sāgataya* ("famine in the kingdom of Soḷī"). *Pāṇḍi naḷuva* and *amārasaya* both deal with the birth of Pāṇḍi and his prowess as king as well as with the beauty of the palace of Pāṇḍi. I have seen only one performance of the ritual, performed at Panāmure by Mr. Patināyake, the *kapurāla* of Ūrubokka, Southern

Province, in 1956. Though not enacted dramatically any longer, the myth of the *pataha* is sometimes sung in the *gammaḍuva*. Hugh Nevill (1954, 1:280) says he has one text of the myth from Pānama (Eastern Province) that indicates it was known in that region also. I shall describe the ritual drama of the *pataha* as it was performed by Mr. Patināyake in 1956.

The stage setting for the *pataha* ritual is rather elaborate. Two people dressed in colored robes are seated on chairs set in diagonal corners of the ritual arena. The *kapurāla* enters the arena wearing his dancing kit, his face daubed with white paint. Another dancer (his assistant) accompanying him carries in his hand two "crowns" made of coconut leaves, plantain bark, and cane. The *kapurāla* struts about the arena for a while, then starts singing to the beat of the drums. After singing a few stanzas he utters a prose commentary, explaining to his audience the (rather difficult) verse, filling in parts of the narrative the text is not too clear about, and sometimes, for convenience and to save time, paraphrasing large chunks of verse. For instance, after singing half a dozen verses he introduces himself and the other actors. His prose commentary is interspersed with the conventional "yes" of the drummer.

> *Kapurāla*: Now we've sung a few songs in this assembly here, but it doesn't make too much sense. (yes) Shall I tell you who I am? (yes) I am the chief minister of the Pāṇḍi king, ruler of the eighteen realms. (ah) I am the one who manages all the work of the king. The king gave me this job after great thought. (yes) Because it is necessary for a good minister to know exactly what the king thinks and wants. . . . Such "calculating" ministers are wanted in the king's service.

Then he goes up to the Pāṇḍi king (represented by one of the persons dressed in colorful robes) and places a crown on his head, while an attendant draws an "eye" on the middle of his forehead with red and white paint. He also goes to the other king (later revealed as the king of Soḷī) and places a crown on his head too. The *kapurāla* changes his role as the occasion demands. He sings all the verses, utters the explicatory dialogue, and speaks the lines of the king, the citizens, the minister, and whatever other role is required. Very often his is a plain impersonal running commentary that explains the action being performed in the arena. In the following account I will not attempt to give a verbatim translation of this ritual, but I will quote many verses from the text and often give a paraphrase summary of the narrative. However, at certain interesting points in the drama, I will give the actual words and describe the action. The reader will be able to visualize the arena situation if he remembers the dramatic technique employed—verse, explicatory prose, background action.

The powerful king of Pāṇḍi, with a third eye in his forehead, had a most wonderful city built by the divine architect Viśvakarma himself. It resembled a city of the gods, so large and beautiful was it. Powerful though he was, the king was also a cruel tyrant.

> No kind thought ever ripened in his mind
> His power, however, ripened from day to day
> His mind, like a fearful demon's, "ripened"
> Like warrior-faced Rāvaṇa ripened his strength.
>
> He'd acquired merit by giving alms in a previous birth
> He wore a crown studded with gold and gems

The *cakravartin* Pāṇḍi king with three eyes
Was pleased with the blessed sight of his city.

How did the Pāṇḍi king become such a powerful person, possessed of almost divine attributes? The *pataha* text itself gives very little detail, but the *kapurāla* explains it in retrospect in his prose commentary culled from the poem *dan kaṭina*. Once upon a time, in the city of Kāliṅga in India, there lived a rich merchant who gave six "almshouses" (*dan säl*) consecutively, and on his death was born in heaven as the god Sakra, on account of this meritorious deed. He had a son, who also gave "almshouses" and was born in heaven as the moon. His son too followed his father's footsteps right up to heaven and was the sun god. He in turn had a son named Mātali Divya Putra, Sakra's charioteer, who also obtained a place in heaven. He was followed by his son Pancasika (Pañcaśikha) Divya Putra, the divine musician. Pancasika's son was known as Kaliṅgu Siṭāno, the sixth in line.[1]

Kaliṅgu Siṭāno (merchant of Kāliṅga) was a miserly, avaricious fellow who cared little for the exemplary philanthropy of his ancestors. The five gods in heaven realized that the Siṭāno should be corrected in the interests of his own spiritual well-being. They assumed the guise of beggars, visited the merchant, and begged alms from him. The merchant ordered his servants thus: "Give the beggars stale rice that had been cooked for cattle with curry made of *gon käkiri*" (literally, "bull cucumber," a despised vegetable). The five beggars could hardly eat this disgusting meal; it stuck in their throats; they sprawled on the floor feigning death. When the merchant heard that the beggars were "dead," he thought, "This is a great shame; what will people say?" So he ordered his servants to force rich foods down the lifeless throats of the "beggars." Having done this, he ordered them to inform the king that five starving beggars had come there, and after eating rich food had died. The king sent royal messengers to investigate the cause of death. When the messengers arrived on the scene the "dead" beggars got up and, vomiting out the earlier meal, revealed the shabby deception. They then introduced themselves and, advising the merchant to give alms regularly, departed for heaven once more.

The merchant followed the letter, not the spirit, of the advice. He did give an offering of robes to monks and prayed that he would be born in a thirty-three-story mansion, become ruler of eighteen regions, and possess three eyes. Thus he was born as the king of Pāṇḍi.

He thought deep like the great ocean.
This king, lord of the earth, born of a pure dynasty
Thought: "I am a chief of gods and chief of kings"
He summoned his ministers to the top story of his palace.

Great wise ones of the "court"[2]
Scholars possessed of sharp wisdom

1. The story of the Pāṇḍi king's former birth as Kalingu Siṭāno is directly based on *Sudhā Bhōjana Jātaka*, number 535 in Cowell's translation (1957, 5:202). Kalingu Siṭāno is Maccarīkōsiya, or the millionaire miser. His six ancestors are exactly as listed in the ritual text. However, nowhere in the *Jātaka* is the miser identified with Pāṇḍi. The ritual text clearly attempts to link Pāṇḍi, a protagonist from Hindu South Indian tradition, with the great tradition of Buddhism.

2. I have translated the Sinhala word *maṇḍala* as "court." *Maṇḍala* in the present context refers to the king's court, but it is also a "circle of divine influence."

Brave generals and ministers of the "court"
Bowed before the *daṇḍa*[3] and worshiped the king.

The *kapurāla*, as minister, intersperses the "text" with his own comments and prose summary. The king, he says, wants to know what is lacking in the city. But all his ministers say that it is like a divine city that lacks nothing. However, there is a chief minister–Brahman who was trained to read the king's thoughts. Now the *kapurāla* takes over the role of chief minister. He has just got the permission of the king to "step outside" the king's palace (*vāhala*). The *kapurāla* enacts the "stepping outside" in an unexpected manner. He places his foot on the person of the Pāṇḍi king. Superficially this act may be viewed as one of the typical "comic events" that occur in Sinhala ritual dramas, but such "comic events" have a certain logic that I shall elucidate later.

The king's mind was full of happiness
Like the "infertile" banana tree that always thrives.
"In what respect is our city different from heaven?"
It is a thought that'll bring disaster on him.

The chief minister read the king's mind and replied:

O mighty one, lord of the seven world systems [*sakvaḷa*s]
O warrior powerful as Sakra himself
Like Sakra himself possessing three eyes
Is it your pleasure that we build a pond?

How is it that the minister could read the thoughts of his sovereign so well? The *kapurāla* gives a prose summary of texts like *pāṇḍi naḷuva* and *amārasaya*. The king's capital, he says, is like Sakra's mansion itself. Now Sakra has a city sixty *yodun* in length, a wish-fulfilling tree a hundred *yodun* tall, a pond sixty *yodun* long, and eighty-three "million" (*kelak*) wives and is furthermore a ruler of eighteen regions (*dēsa*). The Pāṇḍi king may not have all these, but he does have hosts of women, is overlord of eighteen regions, too, and also possesses three eyes. Now the next thing the king would desire is obviously a pond to rival Sakra's.

The *kapurāla* says that he as chief minister has read the king's thoughts well, and therefore the king is pleased. In his pleasure the king permits the minister, the *kapurāla* says, to ride the streets of the city on an elephant (a mark of privilege). Now the *kapurāla* performs another bit of horseplay. He pretends the king is the elephant and climbs on the king's back. The "attendant" who is dressed as the Pāṇḍi king is stiff and formal and never loses his look of dignity while this horseplay is going on. The audience, however, is amused. None of these stage directions are, of course, found in the written text.

The king is pleased with the idea and orders his counselors to find an auspicious time for starting on the project.

You who have warrant from Īśvara
You handsome men learned in mathematics
Intelligent as the teachers of the gods themselves
Choose a good moment through your astrology.

3. The *daṇḍa*, or "stick," is the symbol of the king as law enforcer and one who punishes.

At this point again the *kapurāla* stops singing and adopts the role of minister. He goes up to the king and, pretending to be intensely listening to the king's words, "accidentally" places his foot on the king's lap. He says it is impossible to find an auspicious moment on the particular day the king wishes it. For one thing, this is the unfortunate month of December (Uňduvap masa) and also an unlucky day, Tuesday (Aňgaharuvādā), and what is worse the fourth day of the lunar fortnight (Jalavaka riṭṭāva). The ministers inform the king that it would be folly to start a project on the fourth day of the lunar fortnight. But the king isn't interested in all their astrological expatiations.

The great Pāṇḍi king blessed and powerful
Heard what the group of counselors had to say
Like a bull he uttered idiotic words:
"There is no astrology except merit and sin."

He scolds his ministers for their folly and asks them to set out forthwith and look for a suitable place to build the pond. The ministers protest, for building a pond is a hard job and takes time.

O powerful Pāṇḍi king who knows what's right
Five hundred sorrows are involved in cutting a pond
Under the shadows of your command we suffer
O righteous king, one cannot dig a pond in a day.

But the king brushes their protestations aside and orders them to construct a pond "huge in both length and breadth" within seven days.

Messengers are sent forth to summon people to work on the project. In the ritual three boys with toy drums made of coconut shells impersonate the town criers (*aňḍabera kārayō*). They beat the "drums," and the *kapurāla* proclaims the king's message. About ten boys, who play the part of the workers, enter the arena and dig the pit with sticks (representing mamoties).

The next part of the poem is a graphic account of the suffering the people undergo in the construction works. They have to labor from morning till evening, digging the pond and removing the soil.

Within a radius of fifty-five *yodun* in the king's city
They come to dig the Pāṇḍi king's pond
The assembled crowd dig out stumps and roots
They speak to each other about their heads.

He [the king] summoned Brahmans, watchers, and supervisors
To break the laziness in the camp
Young lads were tied up together
And beaten to make them work.

The criticism of the king's conduct is given in lines that suggest that it is the king who is the idler: "The king, who had nothing to do, builds a pond."

The despot comes personally to supervise the work:

Like Sakra his glory spread around
Whirling his gem studded Sakra sword o'er his head

Like Rāvaṇa entering the field of battle
Came the great Pāṇḍi king to the pond one day.

He grabs hold of idlers and beats out their brains
He cuts their bodies and slaughters the lads
He brandishes the powerful sword in his hand
Sparks fly out wherever it strikes.

Workers' heads are cut off without provocation and without formal justice. Things are taking such a turn that one minister overcomes his fear and addresses the king on the suffering of the folk, but to no avail. Meanwhile a wave of discontent runs through the camp. The people complain:

A foolish king, in spite of his broad forehead
To please him we carry large baskets on our heads
We suffer a thousand sorrows and misfortunes
Our heads are bald from carrying these baskets.

The people realize that the project is bound to fail, because the king has ignored astrology and the sanction of custom.

We dig up stones, trees and heap the earth
But, these efforts are worthless, like husking coconuts without kernel.

But they stay on their job, for their fate is determined by the irrevocable law of karma.

People gather to work like a sheaf of reeds
Their mouths were so parched, that they even forgot their suffering
Like bulls they bit their lips and bore it all
Who can escape the sins of past births?

At this point the singing is interspersed with more action. A chair is brought into "mid-arena," where the *pataha* is being dug by the boys (workmen). The king of Pāṇḍi comes up from his seat in the corner of the arena and sits on the chair. The *kapurāla* now takes on the voice of the king—that is, he speaks the lines the king would have spoken. "These are idle workmen, they should be impaled on an *ula* [a pointed iron stake thrust into the anus as punishment in Kandyan times]. No inquiry is necessary." The *kapurāla* quickly changes role and is now simply the narrator: taking a small stick (representing the stake), he places it under the king's chair! The audience thoroughly enjoys the fun.

The ministers now inform the king (after a lengthy extolling of his virtues) that it is impossible to build the pond—the labor force is insufficient. Yet another minister suggests that it could be done—even in one day—if the folk from the eighteen regions were summoned. "Who wouldn't come once they hear your name mentioned?" The king, flattered, agrees with this plan; he writes letters to the various kings of the eighteen regions on golden sheets and seals them. The letters order the kings to come to his capital at once:

We do not doubt that you'd be pleased to pay us a visit
It would be good if you meet us without dallying on the way
The moment you read this letter come to work on our pond
If you don't, our armies will answer you with war.

The kings of the eighteen regions read the letters with utmost respect and decide to obey the dread king's command. In the ritual the kings from various regions are introduced by the *kapurāla*. He throws his right arm round the shoulder of an attendant who impersonates a king and struts with him into the arena. There is a lot of horseplay and high fun as the *kapurāla* introduces each with a song or two. Seventeen kings arrive—the kings of Sēraman Maleviraṭa (Cēra), Telinga (Telegu country), Anga (Bihar region), Vanga (Bengal), Konga (Konku), Kāliṅga (Orissa), Kāsi (Benares), Mangalapura (?), Vaḍiga (Andhra), Laḍa (Gujerat), Gauḍa (near Orissa), Picci (?), Parangi (Portugal), Makkama (Mecca), Ūrumūsi (Ormuz), Bengāla (Bengal), and Kalangu (Kāliṅga?)—with their followers and crowd in on Pāṇḍi city like the Māra hosts. Let me give examples of how the kings are presented onstage.

1. The king of Maleviraṭa is introduced by the *kapurāla*. He says that the Malevi king cannot come near the *prākāra* ("palace wall") of the king of Pāṇḍi. The *kapurāla* himself becomes the king of Malevi and, coming up to the king of Pāṇḍi, places his foot on the latter's buttocks—implying that this protuberance is the *prākāra* of the king!

2. Another king of the eighteen realms is introduced thus: a member of the audience (the king) is grabbed by the *kapurāla*, who puts his arms round the "king" and brings him to Pāṇḍi.

3. The *kapurāla* acts as the king of Ūrumūsi. Since *ūru* is the Sinhala word for pig, the *kapurāla* comes in on all fours, grins showing his teeth like a pig, then approaches Pāṇḍi and goes back. Several attendants cover the head of the king of Pāṇḍi with a white shawl (*piruvaṭa*) so that he does not see this ungainly and unclean sight.

4. The approach of kings and their followers on elephants is imitated by the *kapurāla*. He comes in on all fours like an elephant and jumps on the Pāṇḍi king.

5. The people from the city of Makkama (Mecca) come on horses. This too is imitated, and the *kapurāla* places his foot on the king, shouting "Allah Hullallah!"

Similar acts are performed for other regions—people from Kalaguna Island shout like monkeys and owls. While all this horseplay is going on, to the great amusement of the audience, the king of Pāṇḍi continues to sit on his throne in stiff dignity. While each king is introduced, the *kapurāla* shouts loudly that none of them can approach the *prākāra* of the king.

All these kings are put to work, and they suffer as badly.

> Even the kings who lived in the shade of goodness
> Didn't have a thing to eat the livelong day
> They draw loads of earth and heap them on both sides
> They suffer terribly like rounded-up cattle.

The arena is a bustle of activity, with a dozen boys representing the kings and their followers digging the pond. While this is going on the *kapurāla* continues with his songs, prose commentary, and action. Explaining the songs to the audience, he says there is one part of the pond that is not cut. This is the work allocated to the king of Soḷī, but he has refused to come. King Pāṇḍi is wrathful over this insult. He writes another letter promptly, ordering the king of Soḷī to arrive lest he, Pāṇḍi, like a glowing torch in his anger, wreak fearful reprisal.

If you do not come to work tomorrow
You will be soundly beaten, so be prompt.

He sends a dispatch through a messenger gifted with words. The emissary is a "small boy" who is given the *sannasa* ("letter"), that is, a piece of tender coconut leaf (*gok*). The *kapurāla* carries the boy in his arms and walks to the other end of the arena where the king of Soḷī, dressed in yellow, is seated. He places the boy on his shoulders and sings the songs of the text. Then the *kapurāla* places both boy and *sannasa* on Soḷī's lap. The *kapurāla* continues his singing while Soḷī reads the letter. These songs state how the king of Soḷī, undaunted by the threats of Pāṇḍi, lops off the nose and ear of the emissary and orders that he be fed excrement and urine and sent back to the king of Pāṇḍi. The *kapurāla* carries the child ("emissary") in his arms across to the other side of the arena, where the king of Pāṇḍi sits in his stiff majesty.

The *kapurāla* continues to sing the text, interspersing a prose commentary on the strength and powers and goodness of the king of Soḷī. The examples are conventional stories attributed to just kings in India and kings like the Tamil Eḷāra in Sri Lanka, and also in *Vitti hata* ("seven events," text 43, pp. 273–76). For example, the king of Soḷī gave his own flesh to a cobra in exchange for a frog and, in another instance, a *kobeiya* (dove) it was about to swallow. On another occasion the king's son, while driving a chariot, killed a calf. There had been no injustice in the kingdom for twelve years. Someone rang the "bell of justice." The king went up to inquire and saw a cow at the bell; the cow related the story. The king's son was buried in mud up to his neck and a chariot was driven over him, breaking his neck. The *kapurāla* says that Pāṇḍi is unaware of the powers of Soḷī, who is aided by Sakra. (It is interesting that the *Cilappatikāram* attributes similar virtues to the king of Pāṇḍi also.)

The king of Pāṇḍi, squirming under this insult, marches on the country of Soḷī with a huge force. Meanwhile messengers inform Soḷī that the king of Pāṇḍi is at his gates, but Soḷī, quite undeterred, is determined to vanquish the proud king. He blows a tremendous blast from his conch, and his friend Sakra, hearing this, creates a devastating downpour that lasts seven days.

The rain fell for seven days as if the end of the world were near
Ceaselessly the rain fell, washing away rocks and mountains
The swirling waters engulfed and destroyed the enemy hosts
But the great Pāṇḍi himself managed to escape to Madurā.

Back in his own city the king of Pāṇḍi, deeply chagrined, decides to pay back in kind. He curses the country of Soḷī to be without water for seven years and seven months. His wish is fulfilled. So great is his power that the country of Soḷī is devastated by drought, famine, and pestilence.

Text 46 *Soḷīpura Sāgataya*: Famine in the Kingdom of Soḷī

This is the epilogue to the *pataha* myth. It describes the suffering of the people of Soḷī owing to the curse of the king of Pāṇḍi. The full text in Hevawasam's edition consists of sixty-five stanzas, but in the ritual drama only a few stanzas are sung, along with a prose commentary. The poem is a graphic and realistic description of a natural disaster. The fruits wither on the trees, coconut trees die with the drought, banana trees once blessed with fruit are now dead, crops of yams are burned up. It is as if the king of demons had ravaged the land.

> Without a drop of water they stare
> Without food, the bulls suffer agonies
> Who could even sympathize with them?
> They reach the village borders and drop down.

Pigs dig at water holes for the last stray drops, but to no avail. They nibble the last few blades of paddy. Herds of deer wander in search of water, and turtles are left high and dry in riverbeds. Parrots and elephants die of thirst; the dried-up waters kill the frogs. Fires break out and destroy the orchards of the city, once green and full of fruit. The ravages of the drought increase day by day. Stench from dead animals spreads over the land. The voices of birds fade away.

> Shaking branches about
> With babes under their bellies
> No one e'en to give them alms
> Thus died the monkeys.

The *kapurāla* in his prose commentary says that the gods now realized something had to be done to relieve the sufferings of the kingdom of Soḷī. They begged Sakra to take a hand. Sakra, disguised as an old man, visits Pattini in Aňdungiri Peak and persuades her to come down to earth to break the pride of the king of Pāṇḍi and end the drought in the country of Soḷī.

The *Pataha* Myths and Ritual Drama: An Interpretation

The theme of the myths and ritual drama of the *pataha* can now be stated. Fundamentally it is a presentation of the well-known South and Southeast Asian idea of the divine king living in his "city," which is the representation of the cosmos. Since many scholars such as Heine-Geldern (1942) and Coedes (1968), and more recently Tambiah (1976), have dealt with this theme, I shall not discuss it here. Scholars have described in detail the isomorphism between the divine macrocosm and the human microcosm and the expression of cosmic symbolism in the grand, indeed overpowering, art and architecture of Southeast Asian kingdoms. However, as far as I know there has been no study that tells us what the ordinary people felt about these conceptions, as well as their reaction to the corvée labor that inevitably went to construct these "divine cities." This is not surprising, since the data are lacking; but it is surprising to see scholars treat the material *as if* these conceptions of divinity were uncritically accepted by the masses.

In this section I shall show that the *pataha* ritual is a public reaction and a mode of handling community feelings against the assumption of Hindu ideas of divine kingship and cosmic symbolism by Sinhala kings, who were Buddhists and expected to conform to the Asokan model of the just king. The protest is not one of egalitarianism versus hierarchy but rather is against the king's assumption of divinity. The *pataha* is also a comic parody of cosmic kingship, so that public feelings could be expressed and ventilated through humor. It is also a "protest" against the use of corvée labor for works that did not benefit the public welfare (in the Buddhist sense derived from Asokan kingship), but led to the personal glory and aggrandizement of the king. The king of Pāṇḍi, who usurps the cosmic-divine symbolism, is presented as an evil king; his conceptions of kingship can only bring about a wasteland. In the analysis that follows I shall use evidence from the *pataha* ritual drama described earlier as well as the *pataha* texts. For convenience I shall refer to the Hevawasam edition of these texts, which are fundamentally in agreement with the texts in my possession.

The texts and ritual are explicit in one thing: the king of Pāṇḍi views himself as like Sakra (Indra), the king of the gods himself; his city is a divine city also, like that of Sakra. In his previous birth as Kaliṅgu Siṭāno, Pāṇḍi is genealogically related to Sakra. In both ritual and text, the most conspicuous feature of Pāṇḍi's divinity is his extra forehead eye. If this were Cambodia (or even South India) the significance would be clear at once: the Hindu kings of Angkor viewed themselves as earthly manifestations of Śiva himself, and Śiva is preeminently the god with the middle eye.

However, when Hindu myths are adapted into Sri Lanka, Śiva's attributes are often transferred to Sakra.[4] Thus Sakra (and also the overlord of demons Vessamuni or Vaiṣravaṇa) is viewed as possessing a middle (third) eye. The aim of another ritual—the *am̆ba vidamana* (pp. 227–38, 490–95)—is to blind the king's middle eye and reduce him to human proportions. Thus Pāṇḍi's middle eye represents his power, might, and especially his divinity.[5]

There are three texts that deal with divine cities. *Dan kaṭina* describes Sakra's city, while *pāṇḍi naḷuva* ("the beauty of Pāṇḍi's city") and *amārasaya* ("the taste of ambrosia") describe the city of Pāṇḍi and the king's person. The title of the latter text suggests that Pāṇḍi views himself as immortal and divine like the gods who tasted ambrosia after the churning of the milky ocean. The contrast between Sakra's city and Pāṇḍi's is both explicit and implicit. Let me quote a few stanzas from *dan kaṭina* that describe Sakra's city.

24. Its beauty dazzles the eyes that gaze upon it.
    That divine land [*vimāna*] with its many mansions—
    There lies Sakra's city on the top of Meru
    Ten thousand *yodun* in length and breadth.

26. His diamond palace a thousand *yodun* long
    And five hundred is his hall of justice
    His diamond chariot hundred and fifty *yodun* tall
    And his throne rising to sixty *yodun*.[6]

4. The transfer of Hindu cosmological ideas into popular Buddhist culture sometimes results in "mistakes." The *kapurāla* often says that *anōtatta* is Sakra-Indra's pond, whereas it is one of the seven great lakes of the cosmic Himavat (Himāla). Himavat or Himāla is a cosmic notion not to be confused with the geographic Himalayas.

5. As a psychological symbol the blinding of the middle eye could probably be read as "castration." Translated into the present context, it could refer to the destruction of Pāṇḍi's *śakti*, his source of power.

6. The indigenous terms are as follows: *vijayot pāya*, "diamond palace"; *suddharmā*, "hall of justice"; *vijayot ratha*, "driver and chariot"; and *pañḍupul asna*, "throne made of pale stone." *Yodun*, from the Sanskrit *yojana*, is a distance of roughly sixteen miles.

27. Tied to rafters three hundred *yodun* long
Were golden flags each sixty *yodun* long
Everywhere shone clusters of stars
Above the park Nandana sixty *yodun* long.

28. There was the wish-fulfilling tree a hundred *yodun* tall
Its flowers spread their scents a hundred *yodun* around
And the pond Nandā, also a hundred long
With hundred gateways where gods bathed and sported.

In *pāṇḍi naḷuva*, Sakra himself asks Viśvakarma, the divine architect, to build a city for Pāṇḍi. Viśvakarma's model of the city is described in this text. This model of the ideal city of the king must have been derived from ancient South Indian or Sanskrit texts. As expressed in Sinhala the descriptions do not make much sense. However, the layout of the buildings in the eight directions must have had considerable historical significance, at least in South India (see fig. 8).

The texts refer only to the *vāhala*, either palaces or entrances to the palace, at the eight quarters, but little information is available regarding their nature or purpose. Some of the titles, however, are significant. Thus the southeast "palace" contained the king's courthouse, the west probably referred to a rainmaking area (though the text suggests a harem), and the northwest duplicated Sakra's own palace. The text states that the northwest "palace" contained the royal storehouses where rice, salt, and gifts were stored, while the auspicious northern palace, as the title indicates, housed the Brahman priests and learned minstrels. This description must surely have been based originally on an ideal model of the cosmic city of the divine king. The east is Indra's own direction, and in it is the king's palace, according to verse 168. The palace is the "awesome Rajasiṃha vāsala," and it is none but a replica of Meru.[7] Verse 177 explicitly identifies Pāṇḍi with Puradara (i.e., Indra as "destroyer of the cities") himself.

Carrying the Śrī Kāntā of victory on his chest
And wielding the sword of victory no enemy king dared possess
Wearing his royal ornaments and jeweled crown
Puradara left his heaven and mounted his elephant.

Pāṇḍi naḷuva and *amārasaya* contain other highly elaborate descriptions of the king's person and city. He lives in a thirty-three-story mansion; elsewhere he is depicted as living in the seventh story of his palace. He wears a three-tiered crown resembling Meru. These texts constantly refer to him as *devvap Pāṇḍi*, or *deva devvap Pāṇḍi*, and *bhūpa*. *Dev* is from *deva*, and *vap* is from *bāpa*, "father"—that is, "divine father." *Bhūpa*, means "lord of the earth," a favorite appellation of South Indian (and Sinhala) kings. He is constantly referred to as *sakviti*, that is, *cakravartin*, and symbols of his *cakravartin* status (parasol, scepter, etc.) are described. He is so mighty and distant that the kings of the eighteen

7. Hevawasam's edition describes the king's palace in stanza 168 as follows:
It is bright like the rainbow; the music entraps the ear
The moon palace Meru painted with numerous designs
It is like the great abode of Indra in the direction of Indra (East)
And named the Moon-Meru awesome Rājasiṃha palace.

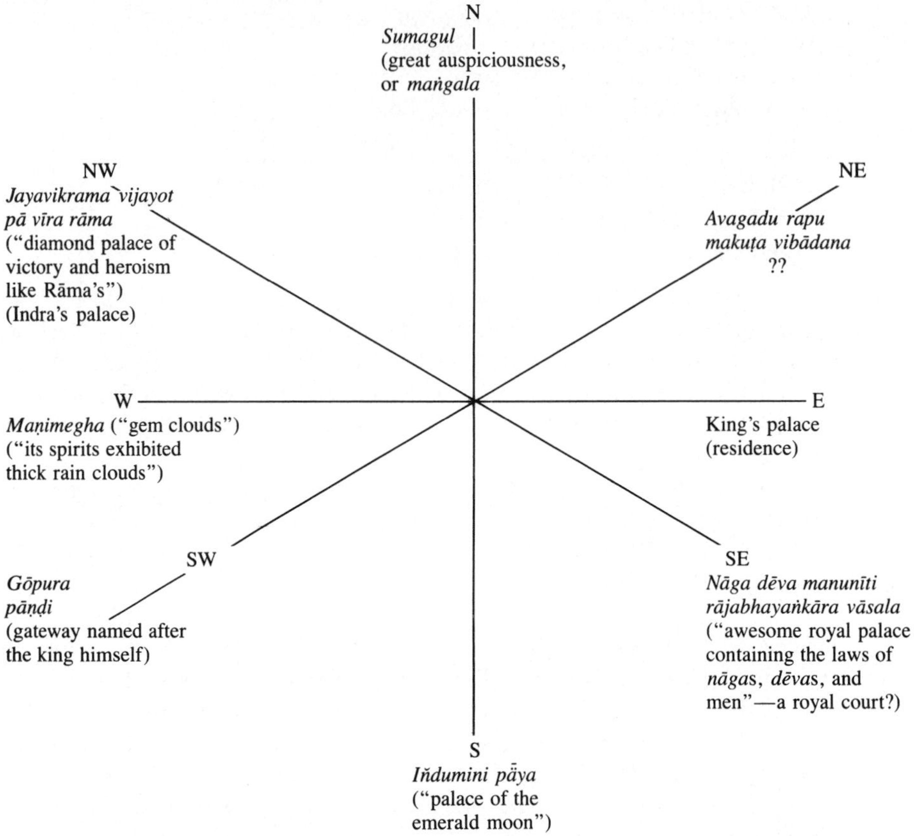

Fig. 8. Viśvakarma's model of the city of Pāṇḍi as described in *pāṇḍi naluva*.

realms cannot even come near the palace wall except on foot. The king's palace with its thirty-three stories is a divine palace, in line with much of Southeast Asian cosmological thinking.

According to both texts and ritual, such aspirations and identifications are clearly wrong. The crisis arrives when Pāṇḍi realizes that his is a divine city except in one respect—it lacks the divine pond, *anōtatta*, situated near Mount Meru, the *axis mundi* of Indian cosmography. In *amārasaya* stanza 69, the king addresses his ministers:

> 69. Gentlemen, our city is the city of the gods
> It also is full of blessedness and seems to lack nothing
> I am lord of the gods, full of blessedness,
> Is there anything lacking in this city?
>
> 72. The king's mind was full of happiness
> Like an infertile banana tree that always thrives
> "In what respect is our city different from heaven?"
> It is a thought that'll bring disaster on him.

The situation here is analogous to the Greek hubris; the criticism of the king is brought out in line 2, with its neat peasant simile. In the *pataha* myth, the king of Pāṇḍi is a "divine king"; but such aspirations are considered heinous and can only result in his downfall.

One of the striking features of the *pataha* ritual is the outrageous lampooning of the divine king and his cosmic city. As a traditional ritual drama the *pataha* must surely have been performed in village communities during the time of the Sinhala kings. The sheer irreverence for divine kingship is almost treasonous, but these communities were probably outside the reach of kingly wrath. Moreover, the ritual drama hid its satiric message in a mythic rather than a historical enactment. Furthermore, while the divine king is irreverently lampooned, a contrasting model of kingship—that of Soḷī—is also presented. It is not kingship that is criticized; only one model of it.[8]

Another major theme in the *pataha* ritual and text is the public reaction to the mustering of corvée labor to construct socially and economically unprofitable works. The focus is specifically on the king's pond, which he hopes will rival Sakra's. The very term used to designate the "pond" is *pataha*, which literally means "pit." The term itself is contemptuous and derogatory, signifying the public attitude to such works. The drama is a public protest against this form of "oriental despotism"—rather than the construction of hydraulic networks for irrigation. It should be noted that mustering labor for the latter task is a legitimate right of sovereignty, called *rājakāriya* ("duty toward the sovereign") in Sinhala kingship. Yet there is a clear protest against corvée in this particular case. "The king who has nothing to do builds a tank." The king is described as a demon, as Rāvaṇa meting out punishment without just inquiry, a tyrant unmindful of the sufferings of his people. The kings of the eighteen realms who owe fealty to Pāṇḍi are also treated like "rounded-up cattle." He wages war against the just king of Soḷī, and in his defeat curses that kingdom with a drought that brings desolation on Soḷīpura (the kingdom of Soḷī). The theme is that of the wasteland, brought about by the curse of an unrighteous monarch. To sum up what I have said so far: the evidence of the *pataha* myth suggests a certain ideology of kingship, a criticism of that ideology in respect to the king of Pāṇḍi, and a protest against the unjust mobilization of labor. Human beings cannot alter these events, for nowhere and at no point does traditional ideology of kingship advocate deposing the king, which would imply the overthrow of legitimate order. Not men but the gods, who are superior to kings, must bring about a new reign of prosperity. This is exactly what happens, when Sakra intercedes on behalf of suffering humanity. Subsequent rituals in the *gammaḍuva* describe the restoration of justice and right and a new era of just kingship.

The values of village communities are opposed to those represented by the king of Pāṇḍi. For example, his ignorance of popular custom and astrology:[9]

8. I believe that a rereading of the Sri Lankan chronicles from an anthropological point of view is necessary to appreciate fully the significance of "historical" events recorded therein.

9. The king of Pāṇḍi's attitude to astrology also had its historical parallel. Pāṇḍi, I noted, speaks like a Buddhist intellectual: "there's no astrology but merit and sin." The *Cūlavaṃsa* records that the Nāyakkar king, Kīrti Śrī Rājasiṃha (A.D. 1741–80), scorned astrology (*Cūlavaṃsa* 1953, part 2, p. 278). The Buddhist monk who compiled the chronicle speaks favorably of the king's attitude, but it is doubtful whether the ordinary villager, who placed great importance on astrology, would have agreed. Incidentally, Kīrti Śrī Rājasiṃha's reign was a period of Buddhist intellectual "revival," and scorn for astrology would be consonant with such an ethos. It is, however, doubtful whether the spirit of the revival permeated the cultural structure of the village.

Like a bull he uttered idiotic words
"There is no astrology but merit and sin."

The ideology of the village comes out clearly in another ritual of the *gammaḍuva*, the *marā ipäddīma* ("killing and resurrection") ritual. Here Pālaṅga, the husband of Pattini, refuses to conform to the conventional court etiquette of obeisance and prostration before the king of Pāṇḍi:

While Pālaṅga was in this wise
When he saw the king of Pāṇḍi
He bowed his head but worshiped not
"Look at this thief's audacity!"

When questioned by a courtier as to the meaning of his unprecedented conduct, Pālaṅga replies:

"Only to the Buddha and the Saṅgha
To my teachers and my parents dear
Even though you call me thief
I'll not worship anyone else."

It is obvious that the audience sympathizes with Pālaṅga and admires his deportment before the "despotic" king. The court etiquette is reprehensible because it demands obeisance over and beyond that given to the Buddha, the Dhamma, and one's parents.

The Historical Background of the *Pataha* Ritual

The corpus of thirty-five ritual texts was, as I noted, composed in the fifteenth and sixteenth centuries. Therefore the *pataha* myths and rituals must obviously relate to this period and after—that is, to the kings of Kōṭṭe and, later, Kandy. Yet the South Indian data to be presented later clearly indicate that these forms of ritual protest existed in southern India much earlier. Thus, while the present version of the *pataha* texts relates to the period after the fifteenth century, it is highly probable that similar enactments existed before this. I shall therefore give a brief resume of the development of kingship in Sri Lanka, focusing especially on the period that my texts unequivocally relate to.

The inquiry is impeded by the fact that historians and archaeologists (with the notable exception of Paranavitana) have not concerned themselves with the layout of the traditional capitals of Sri Lanka in terms of the sort of cosmic kingship that prevailed in other ancient cities, such as those of the ancient Near East, Iran, India, and the Indic states of Southeast Asia. Thus the relative absence of data on cosmic kingship in the great centers of ancient Sinhala civilization, such as Anurādhapura and Polonnaruva, may be interpreted either as the absence of such notions or, more likely, as the absence of directed historical inquiry into the problem. Indeed, we can be almost certain that some cosmological notions (e.g., that of the four quarters) governed the spatial layout of the old cities. Therefore any account of kingship in early and medieval Sri Lanka must be tentative and thoroughly problematic. Fortunately, more reliable historical evidence is available after the fifteenth century.

In the early period of Sri Lanka the rulers were known as *gāmani*, which meant either village leaders (from *gama*, "village," "settlement") or, as Hettiarachchy (1972) surmises, leaders of military bands. If these kings were consecrated it was probably in a simple ceremony without any of the Brahmanic trappings. The critical event is the consecration of Devānampiya Tissa (250–210 B.C.), during whose reign Buddhism was introduced to Sri Lanka by Asokan missionaries. A tenth-century text, the *Vaṃsatthappakāsinī*, says that Sinhala envoys took gifts to Asoka, who asked them about the practice of consecration in Sri Lanka. The envoys replied that no consecration existed outside of the ruler's taking a new staff (*nava yaṭṭhi*). Asoka saw to it that King Devānampiya Tissa was consecrated as king on the Indian model. Hettiarachchy, probably correctly, thinks there was no consecration ritual in Sri Lanka before this event. The consecration of Devānampiya Tissa was "the first of its kind ever performed in Ceylon, and this could be regarded as the beginning of the flow of Indian ideas of kingship into this Island—a flow which was to have far-reaching consequences" (Hettiarachchy 1972, p. 25).

According to the *Vaṃsatthappakāsinī*, the ritual of consecration was as follows. The king sat on a throne of *udumbara* (*Ficus glomerata*) wood, in a specially constructed hall made of the same wood. A *kṣatriya* (royal) maiden poured holy water from the Ganges from a right-spiraled chank, asking the king to protect the "order" of nobles; she was followed by the Brahman court priest (*purōhita*), who performed the rite with a silver shell, and finally by a merchant (*seṭṭhi*), who used a golden shell—each asking the king to rule justly and protect their respective "orders." A curse is also implied, for if the king did not rule justly his head would split into seven pieces (Geiger 1960, pp. 116–17). A Buddhist coloring was given to this essentially Hindu ceremony, for the text says that the clay used to make the vessels in the consecration rituals must be from eight places connected with Buddhism in Sri Lanka (Hettiarachchy 1972, p. 31). This ceremony, or a version of it, apparently continued into Kandyan times.

Paranavitana argues that there were in ancient Sri Lanka two fundamental theories of kingship—the one influenced by Hindu political theory of divine kingship and the other by the Buddhist elective theory; the former probably was fostered by the Brahman priests of the court and the latter by the Theravāda orthodoxy of the *Mahāvihāra*. According to him one of the first kings to espouse the Hindu notion of the king as embodiment of divinity was Vaṭṭagāmanī Abhaya, or Valagambā (89–77 B.C.). Paranavitana shows convincingly that this king was referred to as Pitirāja. The *Mahāvaṃsa* interprets this to mean "father king," because the king adopted his brother's son. But this, argues Paranavitana, is a patent rationalization by the monks who wanted to deny the significance of the title. The adoption of a brother's son is not so extraordinary an event as to justify a new title, particularly since a "brother's son" is addressed and referred to as "son" in Sinhala kinship. His interpretation is that *Pitirāja* is the equivalent of *pitrrāja* (the king of the *pitr*, or ancestors), which is an appellation of Yama, the divine judge (Paranavitana 1958, pp. 62–63). Paranavitana's interpretation is given plausibility by the fact that Vaṭṭagāmanī Abhaya, when he was mobilizing support to fight the Tamil invaders, slew a Sinhala chief who refused to pay obeisance to him. This illustrates that while the king was conscious of his own social distance, the chiefs resisted this idea. The king's action would have ruined his cause but for the intervention of a monk who reconciled the two parties (Paranavitana 1958, pp. 61–67).

An even clearer example is provided four centuries later by King Kassapa I (A.D. 473–91), who had a "remarkable palace built on the summit of Sīgiri rock, so as to identify himself with Kuvera in the paradise of Alakā on the summit of Kailāsa. Such political doctrines were repudiated by the Theravāda school of Buddhism which reigned supreme in Ceylon, but there is no reason why some kings did not attempt to go against orthodoxy and set themselves up as divine rulers" (Paranavitana 1958, p. 63). If Paranavitana is correct, this is the first attempt by a divine king to set up a cosmic city in Sri Lanka. However it is also reasonably clear that conceptions such as that of the divine king, especially the idea of the city modeled on a divine one, were the exception rather than the rule in the Anurādhapura period. An important factor was probably the enormous influence of Theravāda orthodoxy represented by the *Mahāvihāra*. Yet at the end of this period, in the tenth century, the idea prevailed that only a *bodhisattva*, or future Buddha, could be a king of Sri Lanka. It is clear that the Hindu idea of the divinity of the king was now given Buddhist legitimation and significance (Paranavitana 1956, p. 71).

The ideas pertaining to kingship underwent further change after the Cōḷa (Soḷī) conquest in 1017. The continuing influence of Mahayanist and especially Hindu ideas of kingship as embodied in Brahmanic texts combined to produce this change. The title *cakravartin* (universal ruler) was used for the first time in reference to Jayabāhu I (A.D. 1110–11) and became common thereafter. Kings after Vijayabāhu (A.D. 1055–1110) also started systematically espousing South Indian princesses. Rulers began to profess solar and lunar antecedents—the first showing Cōḷa and the second Pāndyan influence. The earliest claim to lunar pretensions on record is by the *Mahādipāda Vīrabāhu* in the reign of Vikramabāhu II (1196). The *Mahādipāda*'s statement runs thus: "We are sprung from the pure dynasty of the Moon, highly esteemed in the world, at the head of all Royal houses" (*Cūlavaṃsa* 1953, part 1, p. 232). Parākramabāhu I (1153–86), the *cakravartin* par excellence of Sri Lankan history, is referred to in the following manner by the chronicler of the *Cūlavaṃsa*: "When the sun, the ancestor of his race, had risen Parākramabāhu who by his singular courage had the whole world under his power" (*Cūlavaṃsa* 1953, part 1, pp. 330–31). The divinity of the king is clearly recognized during this time. "According to Nissankamalla an impartial king was like a Buddha, and though kings appeared in human form, they were to be regarded as gods" (Mendis 1946, p. 99). Details of court ceremonialism are not available, though in all probability it was more elaborate than that of the preceding period. With the increasing social distance between subject and king there must perforce have been an increasing ritualism that symbolized this distance.

Perhaps the first unequivocal example of the cosmic city comes in the twelfth century during the early years of Parākramabāhu I, when he was prince of the *dakkhiṇadēsa*, or southern district. Paranavitana shows in an insightful essay that the ruined city on the present-day Chilaw-Anurādhapura road known as Paṇḍuvas nuvara is in fact Parākramapura, "the city of Parākrama." From my point of view what is most interesting is his description of a special area of the city as representing the cosmos in miniature.

> The site is enclosed by a circular rampart of earth work, which is 66 feet broad at the base, 21 feet at the top, and has an average height of 12 feet. . . . The center of the pavement was occupied not by a stone but by two bricks, on the same level as the surrounding slabs of stone . . . [and] formed the summit of a small brick structure 6½ feet square at the base, rising with irregular sides from a brick pavement which is at a depth of 3 feet 4 inches from the surface of the stone pavement. A cavity, square in section, in the center of this structure had been filled in with layers of quartz nodules alternating with layers of red earth. At the bottom of this cavity was found a terra cotta object, obviously specially prepared, shaped like the frag-

> ment of an egg shell, being a part of the lower half in horizontal section along the long axis.
>
> . . . surrounding the square structure, which was below the ground level, there were several concentric ridges formed of earth faced with brick, mostly fragments. Between these ridges were depressions filled in with whitish clay. . . . In the two inner circles, the white clay was embedded with nodules of quartz. The layer of whitish clay runs beneath the base of the raised ridges. (Paranavitana 1972, pp. 130–31)

Paranavitana's interpretation of this site is as follows:

> The plan reminds one of the manner in which the Universe was conceived by the people of India and Ceylon in ancient times. The square structure corresponds to the mountain Meru, the ridges to the circles of mountains which are said to encompass it, and the depressions to the oceans in between these circles of mountains. Encircling all, it was believed, there was Cakravāla, beyond which the light of the sun and moon does not travel. The central features being buried, the Universe must have been here represented as seen from a point very much above the summit of Meru. In the Ceylon tradition, Mount Meru is the highest, the outer ranges gradually diminishing in height. Here, however, the outer ridges, at least some of them, attain a height greater than that of the Central Mountain. It is not impossible that differences of opinion existed among various sects with regard to the relative heights of the Central Mountain and the Outer Circles of Mountains. The general scheme appears to be broken here and there to represent islands, continents, etc. The object resembling a fragment of egg-shell, probably represented a part of the shell of Brahma's egg (Brahmāṇḍa), fallen down after the cosmos had burnt itself out.
>
> There is thus reason to conclude that the circular site at Pañduvas-nuvara is a representation in miniature of the Universe—the Cakravāla. . . .
>
> . . . But what was its purpose? We know that, during this period, potentates in lands influenced by Indian culture raised models in miniature of the Cosmic Mountain, on the possession of which they based claims to universal dominion. A model of the entire Universe—the Cakravāla—it may be argued, is more efficacious for this purpose than that of the Central Mountain thereof, and a ruler who planned on a grandiose scale could well have thought of making himself the possessor, i.e. the lord, of such a monument. That would have made him a Cakravartin (Universal Monarch) in the eyes of his subjects, according to the belief then prevailing. (Paranavitana 1972, pp. 131–32)

Near the city of Parākrama is a large reservoir (tank) named Panḍāväva, which Paranavitana identifies as the first "sea of Parākrama" referred to in the *Cūlavaṃsa*. Though it is an irrigation work, it is likely that it served another function, as the "milk ocean" of Hindu cosmography, or as *anōtatta*, the cosmic lake of Buddhist mythology. It is likely that the youthful prince, after he became king in his capital at Polonnaruva, had to modify some of his cosmic aspirations to suit the dominant Theravāda orthodoxy. But it is not likely that he abandoned them altogether. Thus the second and massive sea of Parākrama that he constructed in Polonnaruva may have had a deeper cosmic significance than is recognized by contemporary historians. It may have been Parākramabāhu I's unique achievement to have combined cosmic symbolism with the more practical agricultural orientation of his predecessors: a cosmic ocean that is also an irrigation work, thus appeasing Theravāda orthodoxy.

A rereading of the *Cūlavaṃsa* suggests that this interpretation is not as farfetched as it may seem. Chapter 79 of the *Cūlavaṃsa*, entitled "The Laying out of the Gardens and the Like," merits further examination by historians and archaeologists. For example, Parākramabāhu named one park Nandana, which is one of the parks in the Tāvatiṃsa heaven. Indra himself sports there, and *cakravartins* spend time in it after their earthly demise. Another garden was named Mahāmeghavanuyyāna, "the garden of the huge clouds"; yet another was called Rājanārāyana after Viṣṇu, and so forth. The sea of Parākrama, or Parakkamasamudda, had in its midst an island "resplendent with a superb royal palace" (*Cūlavaṃsa* 1953, part 2, pp. 116–18). "The king also had a canal constructed called Gambhīrā (the deep), which started at the flood escape called Makara of the Parakkamasamudda" (*Cūlavaṃsa* 1953, part 2, p. 120). Gambhīrā reminds one of Pāṇḍi's palace, also described as *gambhīrā*, "awesome"; the flood escape of the sea of Parākrama is *makara*, the mythical dragon in Buddhist thought. One of the king's ponds or tanks was named *anōtatta*, the mythic lake that appears in many of our texts and whose waters can resurrect the dead.

With the destruction of Polonnaruva by Māgha in the thirteenth century and the subsequent movement of the capitals to the south and the west, there was an increased rather than decreased South Indian influence on Sinhala kingship, largely owing to the notions introduced in the preceding centuries. That is, conceptions of the king as *cakravartin*, bodhisattva, or Hindu deity (or all three combined), and claims to lunar and solar ancestry introduced a peculiar dilemma into Sinhala politics. It made it hard for a member of Sinhala non-*kṣatriya* aristocracy to become a king without difficult problems of legitimation. This in itself did not deter later Sinhala aristocrats like Konappu Baṇḍāra (Vimala Dharma Sūriya I) and Senerat from becoming kings, but they had to legitimize their claims by marrying South Indian *kṣatriya* princesses with solar or lunar claims. These marriages resulted in Sri Lankan kings having blood ties with South Indian royalty, an early example being Nissanka Malla (1187–96), who had a Kāliṅga ancestry. It is this dilemma, rather than matrilineal inheritance, that paved the way for the Nāyakkars of Madurai to ascend the throne of Kandy in 1739, when the last Sinhala king, Narēndrasiṃha, died without an heir.

There is another factor of considerable significance for our discussion. The movement to the southwest after the thirteenth century was also a movement from the dry to the wet zone, from a hydraulic civilization to one where trade became the major source of revenue. Irrigation reservoirs served no purpose in the wet zone. Hence kings who constructed "ponds" or artificial lakes did so without being able to cover their purpose under the classic guise of an irrigation enterprise. The cosmic symbolism must perforce be laid bare without the traditional rationale or justification for such public works. This is exactly what happened in the wet zone civilization after the fifteenth century.

The Portuguese arrived in Sri Lanka in 1505, and the Kandyan kingdom fell to the British in 1815. The important capitals of the Sinhala kings during this period were Kōṭṭe, Sītāvaka, and Kandy: only the last city survived the attacks of Portuguese and Dutch invaders, and it was the capital of the independent Sinhala kingdom of Kandy until it capitulated to the British in 1815. I shall focus my discussion on the Kandyan kingdom (1474–1815), for which we have considerable evidence, particularly in Dewaraja (1972, pp. 208–21).

Consider Kandyan notions of the person of the king and of court ceremonialism. In Kandyan times the king was clearly a divinity. The traditional notion of the king as a bodhisattva, originating from the tenth century, was linked with the idea that the king was also a *dēva*, a Hindu type of deity. This linkage was perfectly congruent with popular Buddhism, which viewed the *dēva*s as future Buddhas. Rājasiṃha II (1634–89) clearly viewed himself as a deity; Śrī Vijaya Rājasiṃha is described in contemporary sources as an incarnation of the gods, and Kīrti Śrī Rājasiṃha is likened to Sakra himself. The Kuṇḍasāla *sannasa* (copper plate) of 1754 calls the king *parama budhāmkara*, "the most exalted bodhisattva," and the same records compare him to the king of the gods, Sakra himself (Dewaraja 1972, pp. 210–11).

The rituals accorded to the *dēva*s, and known as *tēvāva*, were transferred to the king as a divinity. His person was sacred; to touch him was sacrilege. Knox recorded the gossip that Rājasiṃha II punished with death the courtier who touched him when he was in danger of drowning. "In December 1664 Aṁbanvela Rāla and his confederates conspired to murder Rājasiṃha II. But so imbued were they with the idea of the sanctity of the king's person, that, even when the victim was entrapped, none of the two hundred rebels . . . dared to strike the mortal blow" (Dewaraja 1972, p. 212, also pp. 212–25). We can now appreciate the significance of the vulgar horseplay practiced on the king's person in the *pataha* ritual.

The elaborate court ceremonialism symbolized the social distance between the divine king and the ordinary mortal. Knox gives this account of Rājasiṃha II.

> His pride and affectation of honour is immeasurable. Which appears in his people's manner of Address to him, which he either Commands or allows of. When they come before him they fall flat down on their Faces to the Ground at three several times, and then they sit with their legs under them upon their Knees all the time they are in his presence: And when he bids them to absent they go backwards, until they are out of his sight, or a great distance from him. . . . Nay, He takes on him all the Ceremonies and solemnities of Honour which they show unto their Gods: making his account that he is now their king, so hereafter he shall be one of their Gods. And the people did call him God. (Knox 1681, pp. 60–61)

Dewaraja says that most of court ceremonialism was based on the traditions at Madurai (1972, p. 212). With the Nayakkar accession there was an increasing ceremonialism and a concomitant increase in social distance between king and subject. John Pybus, the British ambassador to the court of Kīrti Śrī Rājasiṃha, describes the abject prostrations he had to undergo in 1762 at the Kandyan court (Raven-Hart 1958). Robert Andrews, another ambassador, gives a graphic account of his presentation to the king (Rājādhi Rājasiṃha) in 1795 and 1796. He says that three curtains were drawn and then:

> the Sovereign of Candia arrived in all his glory seated on a Throne of solid Gold richly studded with precious Stones of various Colors a Crown of Massy Gold adorned his brows enriched with valuable and shining Gems the product of his native Sovereignty the moment he blazed upon our sight Lieutenant Kingston and myself (with the salver on my head) were directed to kneel while the Native Courtiers who attended Us prostrated themselves on the ground. (Lewis 1918, p. 95)

Dewaraja thinks this is a piece of "stage management," which it is not. It is a cultural performance: the king is presented to the representative of another sovereign in his idealized form as a Hindu divinity, and like the latter he is "excluded" behind curtains till the dramatic moment arrives for the devotees to behold him.

Historians have not addressed themselves to the cosmic significance of the city of

Kandy, but there is much indirect evidence available on this subject. That it was a sacred city is clear. There were the shrines for the Four Gods, guardians of the sacred and secular realm, and above all the palace of the tooth relic. The latter was irrevocably associated with the sovereignty and legitimacy of Sinhala kingship. There were other indicators of the sacredness of the city of Kandy. No one except the king was permitted to wear shoes within the city limits, or to ride a horse, elephant, or palanquin. This is exactly the kind of behavior associated even today with sacred premises such as Buddhist temples. But that people resented these ideas is clear from the parody in the *pataha* ritual. Furthermore no one could build a two-story house or use tile roofs or lime plaster, presumably because they would compete with the cosmic symbolism of multistoried structures in the palace premises. The annual procession (*perahära*) of the tooth relic and the Four Gods through the city was, among other things, a public affirmation and legitimation of the city's sacred character (see Seneviratne 1978, pp. 84–88). The king who appeared in the octogonal building, or *pattirippuva*, adjacent to both the palace of the king and the palace of the tooth relic, was probably conceived, on the ideological plane, as a divine being in the center of the eight directions.

But what about cosmic ponds, oceans, and the like and "the city as symbol" in Wheatley's usage (Wheatley 1967)? The statement in the *pataha* that "the king who has nothing to do builds a tank" is almost literally applicable to Rājasiṃha II of Kandy. Says Knox:

> He often employs his People in vast works and that will require years to finish, that he may inure them to Slavery, and prevent them from Plotting against him, as haply they might do if they were at latter leisure. . . . According to the quantity of the work, so he will appoint the People of one Country or two to come in and the Governor of the said Country or Counties to be Overseers of the Work. At such time the soldiers must lay by their Swords, and work among the People. These works are either digging down Hills, and carrying the Earth to fill up Valleys; thus to enlarge his Court, which standeth between two Hills, (a more uneven and unhandsom spot of ground he could not well have found in all his Kingdom); or else making ways for the Water to run into the Pond, and elsewhere for his use in his Palace. Where he hath it running thro in many places unto little Ponds made with Lime and Stone, and full of Fish.
>
> To bring this water to his Palace was no small deal of labour. For not having a more convenient way, they were forced to split a great Mountain in twain to bring the Water thro, and after that to make a Bank cross a Valley for above a Cables length, and in height above four Fathom, with thickness proportionable to maintain it, for the Water to run over the top. Which at first being only Earth, the water would often break down; but now both bottom and sides are paved and wrought up with Stone. After all this, yet it was at least four or five Miles to bring this water in a Ditch; and the Ground all Hills and Valleys, so that they were forced to turn and wind, as the Water would run. Also when they met with Rocks which they could not move, as this Ground is full of them, they made great Fires with wood upon it, until it was soundly hot ; and hereby it became so soft, that they could easily break it with Mawls. . . . Howbeit no love lost between the King and his People. Yet he daily contriveth and buildeth in his Palace like Nebuchadnezzar, wet and dry, day and night, not showing the least sign of Favour to his People. (Knox 1681, pp. 70–72)

Again:

> The People departed with some Satisfaction, and fell to work might and main; and continued at it for near two years together felling Timber, and fetching it out of the

woods, laying Foundations, hewing Stone, till they were almost killed with labour. And being wrought quite tyred, they began to accuse and grumble at one another for having been the occasion of all this toil. After they had laboured thus a long while, they were all discouraged, and the people quiet, the King sent word to them to leave off. And now it lies unfinished, all the Timber brought in, rots upon the place, and the building runs to ruin.

And this is the manner how he employs his People; pulling down and building up again, equalling unequal grounds, making sinks underground for the passage of water thro' his Palace, dragging of great Trees out of the Wood to make Pounds to catch Elephants in his Presence: altho' they could catch them with far less labour, and making houses to keep them in, after they were taken. (Knox 1681, p. 72)

One must not treat Knox's account as historical fact, for it is doubtful whether he was an eyewitness at all (see Goonewardene 1958, pp. 39–53). However, it was undoubtedly popular gossip about Rājasiṃha (and probably other kings too) prevalent in the villages where Knox was "imprisoned." From my point of view such gossip is important, for, irrespective of the historicity of the account, there existed at least a popular characterization of the king that has some parallel to the despotic king of Pāṇḍi of myth. Yet we must probe the significance of Knox's statement further.

The pond Rājasiṃha II built is now filled up; its site is the present Bōgambara Park in Kandy. Clearly Rājasiṃha did not build it for irrigation, since such reservoirs served little purpose in Kandy. The people (in Knox's account) viewed it as a perverse undertaking, but this also seems unlikely in so astute a monarch. Thus it must have been meant either to beautify the city or, more likely, to serve as an earthly replica of a cosmic lake—either Sakra's pond, or *anōtatta*, near Meru in the cosmic Himalaya or the milk ocean. It is important to note that the last king of Kandy, Śrī Vikrama, built a similar pond—the present Kandy Lake, facing the palace of the tooth relic. The people even today call this the "milk ocean" (*kiri muhuda*) and label the wall around it the *ahas paura*, "the ramparts of the sky." Furthermore, the kind of criticism made by the villagers of Rājasiṃha II's time was also made in the popular poetry of the Mātara period regarding Śrī Vikrama's pond: it was built for the king's personal glory, not for the public good.

Rājakāriya, or the service of labor, was required of every citizen and was a privilege of citizenship. But the people were obviously resentful of corvée labor for nonproductive public works. Part of this resentment was caused by the fact that they had another model of just rājakāriya services in the kings of old. They also had another conception of kingship expressed in Buddhist text and tradition, especially pertaining to righteous rule and ceremonial behavior toward social superiors.[10]

Even in Kandyan times the fiction of elective kingship was maintained, specially when the king died without an heir by the anointed queen. The choice of the successor was prearranged (and decided by palace intrigue) by the great chiefs of the kingdom, the *adigar*s, who adopted elaborate public expressions to show that the selected king was in fact the "elect" of the people (Dewaraja 1972, p. 209). The tradition also existed in Kandy that wearing the crown was imitating the gods, and hence coronation was never part of the ceremonies of kingship. Yet we know from the accounts of the ambassadors

10. The paradigmatic case of good kingship is Asoka; in the ritual traditions Soḷī lives up to the Asokan ideal. As for court ceremonialism, the basic principle is clear: the ceremonial attitude toward superiors (divine or earthly) cannot surpass that given the Buddha.

Phybus and Andrews that in fact the king wore a crown on important public occasions—when he had to present himself as a deity. But Davy says the king seldom wore it and substituted a cap instead, owing to "superstitious motives"—no doubt for fear of being struck by *vas* (ritual danger) in imitating the gods. The kings themselves were probably afraid of the role they had to assume (Davy 1821, p. 123).

"Our heads are bald from carrying these baskets," complain the people forced to work on the pond of the Pāṇḍi king of the myth. It is clear that this expression was a popular way of protesting against corvée labor at unpopular public works. Baldeus, the Dutch historian, reports that people complained because Rājasiṃha I of Sītāvaka (1581–92) forced them to carry earth on their heads to build the fortifications of Sītāvaka (Baldeus 1673, p. 7).[11]

It would, however, be wrong to infer from this congruence that the myth refers to a specific king or kings. On the contrary, the myth is nonspecific, general, impersonal. It presents a criticism of a view of divine kingship gone astray, out of touch with the popular notions of righteous kinship and the ideology of village communities. It is also, I believe, a reaction of the provinces against the center. According to Kandyan administration of government, the king instructs the provincial governors (*disāvas*) to supply *rājakāriya* (corvée) services, as Rājasiṃha II did in Knox's account quoted earlier. This is expressed in the *pataha* in the episode where the "kings" of the eighteen realms had to work like slaves.

The Karikāla Myths

An alternative model of kingship—that of the good king—is presented in great detail in the myths relating to Karikāla, the king of Soḷī (Cōḷa). These myths are no longer enacted, but I shall present them in outline from Hevawasam's edition.

Text 47 The Directing of the Waters of the Kāvēri

The gods, including Īśvara and Mahā Brahma, were assembled in heaven to review the affairs of the human world. They then saw that the kingdom of Soḷī was afflicted with a drought, and that only the saint Agastya (or Mā Muni) could end it. Meanwhile Mā Muni himself scanned the world:

4. The great sage Mā Muni scans the world with his divine eye
"If I could get water from the great river [i.e., *anōtatta* lake]
I could end the drought in Soḷīraṭa"
He flew to the Himalayas by his powers.

5. In the golden rock of Himāla
At the foot of a sandalwood tree
Sat the great sage
When a powerful god came up to him.

This divine emissary tells Agastya:

11. My notes have it that a similar complaint was made by the subjects of Jayavarman VII of Cambodia (1181–1200), but I have misplaced the reference.

7. "There's been no thunder or rain
The world's suffered no drought like this
If you go there swiftly now
The world will again bear fruit."

Mā Muni (Agastya) knew he must help to overcome the drought in Soḷī, otherwise the precepts he had assiduously practiced "would suffer as milk in contact with dung," and he would not be able to achieve Nirvāṇa.

11. Thus he preserved his piety [precepts] well
Traversing the Himāla wastes
He flew across the skies, to *anōtatta*
Guided by his divine eye.

But there was no way to enter the lake; there were huge rocks around it, and it was guarded by a fierce cobra whose hood covered the water. This cobra would not let anyone approach it except those who had taken refuge in the Buddha. It could not be tamed by magic or mantras.

The sage stood at the edge of the lake wondering what to do; the gods themselves had assembled there to witness the events. The angry cobra still covered the lake with its sixty coils and would not let the sage take any water. Agastya then decided to take the form of a huge *guruḷu* bird (the mythical eagle, enemy of the cobra and also the vehicle of Viṣṇu). The cobra was frightened and went around the rocks, sixty-eight *yodun* long, that surrounded the lake. Then his anger subsided; he wound up his coils and sank into the earth, making a yawning gap therein.

23. There's no doubt whatever
No cobra was there in the pond
Thus the great Muni
Scooped the waters of *anōtatta*.

24. Growling in lake *anōtatta*
A powerful cobra guarded it
But it's true that as a *guruḷu* bird
The sage Agastya displayed his might.

Now Agastya held up the pot to collect the water when the waters of *anōtatta* rose up sixty *yodun* and gushed into the pot. The pot was only partially filled; yet the lake was dry and the fish were dying. Now Agastya in compassion raised his arms up into the sky, and the rains fell and the lake was full once again. Then he flew away by the powers of levitation.

The gods who had assembled thought that the sage had practiced a deception on them, by emptying the waters of the lake (for his own unknown purposes?). So they went to Īśvara; Īśvara's spouse Umā summoned her son Kaňdapati (Skanda) and "took a little milk from her breast and put a *tilaka* mark on his forehead." Skanda took the form of a beautiful crow and bided his time. Meanwhile Agastya, tired, saw a pond (not *anōtatta*) and decided to have a bath, leaving the pot on the bank. The crow (Skanda) raised the lid of the pot with its beak, hit it with its wings and turned it upside down, then flew away. Thus were the river Kāvēri and the city (Kāvēri paṭuna) formed, since both arose from the pot turned over by the crow (*kā*; from the Tamil *kākam*).

There is a seeming paradox in the myth that could easily be explained in sociological terms. The myth commences with Agastya's own good intentions; he wanted to create a river to bring relief to the country of Soḷī. Yet his intentions become suspect, and (quite without justification) Umā asks Skanda to spill the water from the pot. Thus it is Skanda who in fact created the Kāvēri river. Sociologically the myth does two things: it says that it was Agastya's plan to create the Kāvēri river; and it does not allow the northern sage to complete the task, but brings in the popular god of the Dravidian South to do this. The myth both exemplifies and resolves the tension between the northern Sanskritic and the indigenous southern mythology.

The rest of the poem (stanzas 43–80) is a description of the Kāvēri as it flows through the parched Soḷī land, ending its drought. The fertility of the river swarming with fish of various kinds is described. The various names of the Kāvēri are given: *ahas gaṅga* ("sky river"), *kāla gaṅga* ("river of time"), *bo tutta* ("happy river"), and other names.[12]

Text 48 *Karikāla Upata*: The Origins of Karikāla

At one time the kingdom of Soḷī was ruled by a line of kings belonging to the royal house of the solar dynasty. They were very brave kings. Through this kingdom flowed the captivating river called Kāvēri. The great mass of water that flowed along this river went on its course to the ocean unhindered, and not a single king thought of taming this river by raising its banks. Then a king named Bimba was born. He was a king with very good qualities. This king in his past birth was born into the cultivator caste. Yet from his past births he had acquired a great love for hunting and, and he now went on a hunting expedition with his servants. By this desire he had committed a sin in his heart.

The day he began making preparations to go on the hunting trip he met with bad omens [*bādā*]. That day the king with his men, who were armed with bows, arrows, and spears and carrying rice packets in their hands, went happily to hunt, ignoring the fact that none of these actions were going to give them salvation; they were going to be bound for ever in *saṃsāra*.

9. He [the king] handsome as the flower darter[13]
His sin was also as great
But how and by what chance
Did he commit this heinous sin?

The text explains it. The hunting party came across a deep and large water hole. They gradually filled this with earth so that the fish would be brought up to the surface and could be killed. But, as a result of this sin committed by the king, earth mixed with water fell all over the city. The entire city was covered with mud except the residence of the queen, who, because of her past merit, was unscathed.

14. Owing to her great merit
She stayed in her royal room
Which wasn't covered by that mud
The queen escaped unharmed.

12. The myth of Kāvēri arising from the upturned pot of Agastya is an old one and is referred to in the prologue to the *Maṇimēkalai* (1928, p. 111).

13. "Flower darter," or Malsarā, is an appellation of Anaṅga, the Indian Cupid.

15. Thus she went on
    "I don't know what to do"
    But then all the gods
    Gave her their protection.

She was pregnant and suffered greatly and wept and wailed as she went forth.

18. "Heavy I am with child
    And dead my lord
    My city is mine no more
    Alas! how and where shall I now go?

19. "He who fondled me
    And gave me such love
    My beautiful lord
    Alas! how shall I pass this lonely day?

20. "Shining jeweled torches
    Used to light my way
    But now thick darkness
    How shall I take this trip, alas!"

The queen, however, had committed no sin and came to no harm. Leaving royal comforts, the pregnant queen came to the city of Iňdapet (Indraprastha), and sought shelter in a kind Brahman household. The Brahman woman of the house loved her at once, as if she were her own daughter, and adopted her. The queen asked the Brahman woman to keep her royal background secret. She lived on the seventh floor, well looked after by the Brahman wife. Meanwhile her child (fetus) grew and grew in the womb until the tenth month was reached; ultimately three hundred and sixty days passed.

The queen now experienced labor pains, which grew gradually intense. Tears fell from her eyes. They rubbed oil on her belly (*ikili*, "lap," "groin") to soothe her, while the old Brahman (husband) calculated the auspicious time.

48. The woman had spasms of pain
    The old Brahman consulted omens
    "When two or three hours pass
    There'll be born a *cakravartin*."

49. "This is an astrologically bad moment
    The prince's heart may be affected
    To make the time auspicious for this prince
    Tie the legs and stop the labor now."

50. The beautiful Mount Meru and the Sadat[14] lake danced with joy
    While her legs were bound with a silken shawl
    People impatiently waited
    For the auspicious moment to arrive.

14. *Sadat* is the Sinhala for the Pāli *Caddanta*, the second largest of the seven cosmic lakes in the Himavat.

51. As the great auspicious moment neared
 They were all around her in readiness
 To release the legs tied with silk cloth
 They gently rubbed oil on her belly.

52. Those assembled waited hours not knowing
 That a king with a warrant from Sakra would appear in the world
 When the Brahman with a nod indicated the right time
 They joyously untied the silken shawl.

53. Like the moon that shines in the night
 Or the sun that dispels the dark
 Or the larklike singing of lovely maidens
 The prince emerged from his mother's womb.

The king was born with one hundred and eight auspicious signs that indicated he would be lord of the rose apple continent (India). Flowers rained at every doorstep; celestial damsels appeared in the skies. The day the prince was born the crowned monarchs of the continent fell from their seats—sign that a *cakravartin*, overlord of them all, had been born.

Meanwhile the kingdom of Soḷī had no king. One way of seeking a new king (found in the Buddhist *jātaka*s) was to send the royal elephant around the city, and the elephant would then "pick" the king. Thus the people of Soḷī fed the royal elephant with intoxicants and sent it forth. The angry elephant terrified everybody; it entered the street of the Brahmans ejecting huge balls of dung and tearing off great trees with its trunk. But when it came near the prince (now seven years of age) it became submissive.

68. It made its body rigid; it shook not its tail
 Seeing the prince it stood transfixed
 The prince was calm like a pearl image
 The elephant now knelt before the prince.

69. His auspicious marks were like the moon's spots
 He didn't want to climb the elephant lest he cause it pain
 Yet since he desired the throne of Soḷī city
 He climbed on the "seat" on the elephant's back.

The elephant now got up. The queen mother sensed trouble.

71. Hearing all this commotion
 The mother and Brahman lady knew the elephant would suffer
 In order not to be burdened with this sin
 [They] applied charcoal to the prince's foot.

In the Sinhala text these lines make little sense, but we can supply the missing meaning from the South Indian texts to be presented later. Apparently the animal could not bear the weight of such a powerful prince; thus the mother painted the prince's foot with charcoal because it would (magically) make him light of weight.

The elephant now bore the king triumphantly to the city of Soḷī. He was installed as king and named Karikāla, which in Tamil meant "blackened [charcoal] feet."

Text 49 *Gaṅga Bäṅdīma*: Binding the River

On one level *bäṅdīma* is used in the sense of "building," in this case raising the banks of the Kāvēri river with bunds. But *bäṅdīma* literally means "bind" or "tie" and in Sinhala magic may refer to a magical act for controlling a demon, or evil magic. Sorcery practiced against someone is a *bandana* (see my discussion of *ät bandana*, pp. 172–73). Thus on another level this text may have been associated with a ritual that attempted to control the waters of the Kāvēri through sympathetic magic. Nevertheless, this latter meaning is only peripheral to the main theme of this text.

The river Kāvēri overflowed its banks during the third regnal year of Karikāla, the king of Soḷī raṭa, and wrought a great deal of damage, destroying fields, orchards, and whole villages. The king summoned his ministers and told them that, though his predecessors had left the river untouched, he would control it. He wrote letters to the kings of the eighteen regions and sent each letter with an emissary. The kings read the letters with great respect. The letters commanded each of them to come to Soḷī with a labor force. The arrival of the kings is described very much in the manner of *pataha*.

10. With his retinue decked in gold
    Like a day where *madārā* flowers bloom
    Like ships sailing from Andhra land
    Came the king of Mandarā in haste.

11. Beautiful as a painting on a board
    Possessed of innumerable wealth
    Learning the news the king of Tatta
    Left with many men and gold and silver.

Others come from Kannaḍi (Kannaḍa) and Kuḍa Kāra Ūrumūsi (Ormuz); and then the sultan arrives!

15. On his horse he rode long distances
    An umbrella he held over his head
    Dressed in robes blue and red
    Comes the king sultan in this manner.

16. Came then the king of Anga
    And the noble king of Konga [Konku]
    And the noble famous kings
    Of the lands of Laḍa and Telinga [Telegu].

Six other kings arrive from different lands, and then comes the king of Benares.

28. Spreading his glory like Viṣṇu himself
    Shining like the moon, sweet as sandal
    In fine mien, famous the world o'er
    Comes hastily the king of Benares.

Then come kings from Gauḍi (near Orissa), Aparanga (Indian west coast), Pāṇḍya, Madurā, Aramana (Ramañña, "lower Burma"), Doluvara (Dilvara, east coast), all in great array. They fall at the feet of King Karikāla and worship him. The king graciously entertains them with betel and incense.

34. In order to make them happy
To rest and cool their weariness
He gave resting places
For these who'd traveled from far.

35. In order to please them
That they'd enough to eat and drink
The ministers obeyed the [king's] command
And saw to their needs.

36. They ate and drank and rested
And cooled their weariness,
They chatted among themselves
And so did their followers.

The next morning they went to see the king, who addressed them thus.

38. "Listen to my words, O kings
Don't you know the fact
That the river swirls past
Swiftly through this city.

39. "Therefore O good kings
All of you joyously
Must bind the river to please me
Go now with all your followers."

Unlike the king of Pāṇḍi of the *pataha* text, Karikāla consults astrologers and seeks a propitious time. Initially they raise the bunds with stone, but in a week the waters of the river have destroyed the masonry. Then a bund is built with bricks, but this also comes crumbling down. Ultimately the people decide on a new strategy for building a bund that will surely withstand the water.

49. They sifted potters clay of sticks and stones
Kneaded sesame oil into it
Beautifully thus they "bound" the river
To last a whole *kapa* [*kalpa*].

They raised bunds on both sides of the river in this fashion, using sesame oil to make the sides firm. After the work was completed, tasty food was cooked and served to the royal retinues. Thereafter they all gathered together and celebrated the occasion with water sports.

Text 50 *Diya Keḷi Katāva*: Story of the Water Sports

This is a brief text of forty verses, of which only twenty-eight deal with the water sports; the rest are verses asking Pattini's protection from maleficent planetary influences. The poem deals with the celebration of the completion of the Kāvēri project with water sports in which everyone—citizenry, king, and royalty as well as the deities (Yuvaraja, Yā raja, and Pattini)—participated. It was an occasion of great jubilation and merrymaking.

A series of beautiful stanzas describe the river blooming with lotuses, symbolic of beauty and prosperity.

4. Lotuses floating in the water
White water lilies and lotus blooms
Blue lilies and blue moss
Loitered in the waters.

5. The ripples darted to and fro
Drops of rain gently touched
The blue lilies swaying
And straying in the water.

6. Hurt by the harsh sun
Petals dived underneath
There touching each other
They circled and eddied.

7. The drummers proclaimed the message:
"In order to sport in the river
Come in all your chariots
And decorate your streets."

11. The noble folk that day
Proclaimed the message to the people
Who heard it all
And gaily decked the streets.

15. Smiling without shyness
With high spirits and gay company
Girls frolicked in the river
Carefully avoiding the waves.

21. Then Karikāla noble lord
Stood before the hundred kings
He spoke gentle words to them
And gave them permission to sport.

25. They performed a *telmē* ritual
And the ceremony of head washing [*nānumura*]
They worshiped all the gods
And lit lamps for Giri of the Sea.[15]

The Karikāla Myths and Ritual Drama: An Interpretation

It will be readily apparent that the Karikāla myths are a foil to the *pataha* cluster, presenting the opposed Asokan model of kingship that the people hold as legitimate and morally

15. Giri of the Sea, or Mūdu Giri, is probably a female form of Garā associated with *vas* that strikes people who bathe in open waterways at the "wrong" time.

right.[16] Unhappily the Karikāla myths are no longer acted in the form of a ritual drama. But since the *pataha* was enacted it is also likely that the Karikāla myths were once performed in a similar manner. We can, on the basis of our knowledge of the *pataha* ritual, reconstruct with some plausibility how the Karikāla myths would have been enacted, particularly the myth of the bunding of the Kāvēri. It would be in exactly the manner of the *pataha*—that is, the king of Soḷī (Karikāla) would be onstage, the various feudatory monarchs would assemble; "workers" with "sticks" would come onstage and build the bunds. Right along the *kapurāla* would act as a running commentary, filling the gaps in the narrative, as he did in the *pataha*. The audience would be presented in this way with a picture of the good king (after the ritual drama of the evil king). Indeed, some of the incidents in the Karikāla myths better fit the ethos and context of a ritual drama than of empirical reality. For example, the statement in the myth that potter's clay (*kum̆bal mäṭi*, alternative reading, "clay of nests of potter wasps") mixed with sesame oil was used to build the bunds flouts our sense of reality. However, it fits the ethos and context of a ritual drama very well: the *kapurāla* would have taken some potter's clay, mixed it with sesame oil, and used it in the ritual drama to depict in miniature the building of the bunds. This action may have had a secondary sympathetic magical effect of warding off the flooding of the Kāvēri river by "binding" it, in the magic sense of the term (*bandana*). To sum up, traditionally *two* ritual dramas would have been enacted, one dealing with the evil Pāṇḍi, building a tank to glorify himself, and the other with the good king of Soḷī (Karikāla) raising the banks of the Kāvēri for the public good.

The Karikāla myths are easy to interpret. There is a point-by-point contrast with Pāṇḍi.

1. Karikāla has none of the cosmic divinity of Pāṇḍi—he lacks a third eye, there is no reference to a "divine city," and he treats his subjects courteously and kindly. Further, the Sinhala tradition (infelicitously) tries to make the point that one of Karikāla's ancestors (or Karikāla himself) was a member of the farmer caste (the Sinhala dominant caste) in a previous birth.

2. Karikāla raises the banks of the Kāvēri to prevent floods and foster agriculture, and he constructs rest houses, all for the common weal; by contrast, Pāṇḍi's pond is for his own aggrandizement. Through the vehicle of Karikāla the Sinhala people are upholding and idealizing the Asokan model of kingship that they believed existed in ancient Sri Lanka. These kings of old built artificial lakes and bunded streams to benefit the people, as against another model of kingship that was in force after the fifteenth century. Here kings mobilized corvée labor to build divine palaces, of no use for the public welfare. The model of the good king is Asoka himself, and one text of corpus 1, known as *vitti hata* ("the seven events," text 43), explicitly compares Karikāla with Asoka.

3. The kings from the eighteen realms and their followers suffer badly in Pāṇḍi's camp, whereas they are treated with dignity and courtesy by Soḷī (Karikāla), who holds open house for them.

4. Karikāla consults astrologers and works in accordance with custom, whereas Pāṇḍi flouts them.

5. The people of Soḷī celebrate the completion of the bunding of the Kāvēri with water sports and other festivities, whereas the people of Pāṇḍi suffer greatly under the tyranny of their king. The beautiful description of the water sports with its images of prosperity

16. For an excellent account of the Asokan ideal of kingship, see Tambiah (1976).

and its picture of a joyous populace sporting in a river replete with fish must be contrasted with the previous drought in Soḷī and the depletion of fertility in that kingdom. Thus, underlying the themes sketched earlier is a more widespread universalistic message of the myths: the just king serves the common weal and brings prosperity to the human community, while the actions of the evil king create a wasteland and destroy fertility and prosperity. This is a theme almost everywhere associated with traditional kingship—in Sophoclean drama, in Shakespeare's *Macbeth*, and in all traditional polity. It is expressed as a profound wish in a popular Pāli "prayer" (trans. Hocart 1931, p. 27):

Devo vassatu kālena
Sassa sampatti hetu ca
Pīto bhavatu loko ca
Rājā bhavatu dhammiko

Let the god rain in due time
who promotes the welfare of crops;
and let the world rejoice and
let the king be just.

Karikāla and *Pataha* Myths in South India

The myths and rituals examined in this chapter deal with two personages, Karikāla, the good king of Soḷī, who put people to work bunding the Kāvēri river (a good enterprise), and the evil three-eyed king of Pāṇḍi, who made people work in constructing a pond in order to emulate the gods, a useless enterprise. I have analyzed the various versions of the myth, which all date from after the fifteenth century. Fortunately, we can push the ancestry of these myths still further back into the South Indian origins, thus providing a unique historical record of a tradition of myth and ritual from very ancient times to the present. The preceding analysis of the Karikāla myths and ritual among the Sinhalas may also help us understand the true nature of their South Indian counterparts and thereby throw some light on early South Indian history. The South Indian versions of the Karikāla myths are recorded in Nilakanta Sastri's scholarly work *Studies in Cōḷa History and Administration* (1932), which I shall utilize here.

The earliest references to Karikāla are in the colophons and commentaries to two major Caṅkam works. These Caṅkam poems were composed in the early Christian era, and the colophons deal with the occasion on which they were composed. Some historians argue, with great plausibility, that these colophons were later interpolations, but Nilakanta Sastri thinks most of them were the works of the Caṅkam poets themselves. For the moment let us accept Nilakanta Sastri's view and treat these references as Caṅkam poetry of the early Christian era. Several references to Karikāla are found in the Caṅkam work *Puṟunāṉūṟu* ("Puram Four Hundred"). Several stanzas speak of Karikāla's prowess in war (7, 65), of the suicide of one of his enemies (puram 66), and of the loss the world sustained owing to the death of Karikāla (puram 224) (Nilakanta Sastri 1932, pp. 19–20). Another Caṅkam collection, the *Pattuppāṭṭu* ("Ten Tens") has more detailed references. *Porunarāṟṟuppaṭai*, one of the poems in this collection, mentions Karikāla by name. "He inherited the right to his estate while he was in his mother's womb . . . a statement which the annotator

Naccinārkkiniyar interprets as meaning that Karikāla's birth was delayed by unnatural means, and that he was retained in his mother's womb until the auspicious moment came for his being delivered. The battle of Veṇṇi in which he defeated two great kings (Pāṇḍya and Cēra) on the same field is narrated in some detail" (Nilakantra Sastri 1932, p. 21). The *Paṭṭiṉāppālai*, a poem of 301 lines in the same collection, mentions how Karikāla was imprisoned in his youth but escaped after a fight with the guards and became master of the kingdom. The poem also mentions the tribes he mastered. He also gave up Uraiyur and moved his capital elsewhere. In another part of the poem it says that "Karikāla's sway failed to measure the three worlds but was confined only to this, and his leg suffered from fire, an allusion to the dwarf incarnation of Viṣṇu" (Nilakanta Sastri 1932, p. 22). Nilakanta Sastri concludes that Karikāla's "true" history is contained only in these contemporary poems (1932, p. 70).

I will now present the later developments of the Karikāla myth in South India, selecting the more important references in Nilakanta Sastri's work.

The *Cilappatikāram* has three references to Karikāla. The first (canto 5.2.90–104) refers to Karikāla's having undertaken, at one time, an invasion to the north of India and having obtained presents from the northern kings of Vajra, Magadha, and Avanti. This incident is also referred to in *Maṇimēkalai* (canto 1.1.39). Canto 6.2.159–60 of the *Cilappatikāram* mentions Karikāla's having performed a ceremonial bath or sported in the freshet of the Kāvēri, attended by a large crowd.

> Their multi-coloured clothes and many-sounding tongues resembled the uproar inevitable on the festive occasion when King Karikāla, whose fame reached the celestial world, celebrated the first freshet in the Kāvēri, and came to be mingled with the increasing tumult caused by men and women of the four castes crowding on the narrow place where the great Kāvēri joined the sea. (Dikshitar 1939, pp. 129–30)

This clearly is related to the *diya keḷi katāva* (text 50) in the Sinhala myths of Karikāla. Canto 21.2 describes how the daughter of Karikāla saw her husband being washed away while bathing and miraculously rescued him. There are also references to Karikāla in the commentaries to the *Cilappatikāram*, but these are of little interest.

Nilakanta Sastri does not consider the *Cilappatikāram* a Caṅkam text. The references therein to Karikāla suggest that the events took place in the distant past. Assuming that Karikāla lived about the second century A.D. and that the *Cilappatikāram* was composed at least three centuries later, it seems clear that the myth-making process had taken over by the time the *Cilappatikāram* was written. Here Karikāla is the grandiose hero who quelled the northern monarch, but this improbable event is also credited to the other kings of the Tamil country. Furthermore, if the reference to Karikāla's ceremonial bath in the Kāvēri is similar to the Sinhala *diya keḷi katāva*, then it may well be that the idea of Karikāla as the hero who raised the Kāvēri banks had also developed by this time, for the Sinhala *diya keḷi katāva* celebrates the completion of the Kāvēri floodgates.

There is clear evidence that, by the eighth century at least, Karikāla has become very much like the protatgonist of our myths. Epigraphic sources in Telegu and Tamil, beginning from the eighth century, refer to Karikāla's constructing bunds on the Kāvēri. This of course is the event most often associated with Karikāla, and it is treated by many South Indian historians as a historical occurrence. The earliest clear reference to this event is in the Mālēpādu plates of Puṇyakumāra, where a Telegu family tries to establish its ancestry with Karikāla. "In the family of Karikāla, who was a mandāra tree on the Mandāra mountain, viz. the solar race; who was the worker of many wonders like that of controlling the daughters of Kāvēri, overflowing her banks; who obtained for himself the position of [the headship of the] three kingdoms" (Nilakanta Sastri 1932, p. 27). The Tiruvālangadu plates of Rajendra I (tenth century) and the Leyden grant (eleventh century) also mention the Kāvēri constructions; the former mentions Karikāla as having rebuilt Kāñci. The Kanyākumāri stone inscription, of the same period, adds an interesting detail: "(Karikāla) who was as bright as the sun and who curbed the pride of the insubordinate, controlled the Kāvērī—which, by its excessive floods, caused the earth to be deprived of its produce—by means of a bund formed of earth thrown in baskets carried in hand by (enemy) kings" (Nilakanta Sastri 1932, p. 28). Kings (not necessarily "enemy kings," as Nilakanta Sastri interpolates) working on the bund appear in the Sinhala Karikāla and *pataha* myths also.

These same exploits and further ones are recorded in the Telegu and Tamil popular poetry of a later period. In the *Kaliṅgattupparaṇi*, a probable reference is made to Karikāla, who wiped out the third eye of an enemy, and this reference is explicit in the *ula*s (stanzas) of Oṭṭakkuttaṉ of the twelfth century: "The Cōḷa Karikāla who took the eye of him who did not come to raise the Kāvēri banks which took the earth carried on the heads (of subordinate kings)" (Nilakanta Sastri 1932, pp. 30–31). The same poet in his poem on Kulōttunga II makes it clear that it was the third eye of one Mukhari that was lost (in all probability by an act of imitative magic): "we know of the wiping out of one eye traced on the picture so that the inimical Mukhari lost one of his three eyes" (Nilakanta Sastri 1932, p. 32). The fourteenth-century work the *Navacōlacarita*, a Telegu rendering of a Kannada work, expands this and introduces two further elements—the construction of a tank and a war waged against insubordinate kings. Karikāla decides "that he should raise the banks on either side of the river and dig a tank and earn for himself the religious merit thereof. So he sent for his *samasta*s from the various parts of the realm and all of them came up, with the exception of Bhāskara-Cōḷa and Mukkanti Cōḍa and others who held themselves back on account of their noble birth and other like reasons. The king undertook a *daṇḍayātra* (expedition) against them, and conquered them, and took them captive and compelled them to work on the construction of the banks of the Kāvērī until the task was completed" (Nilakanta Sastri 1932, pp. 35–36). Though this work does not mention the three-eyed king, Telegu epigraphy of the fourteenth century states that the person who lost the third eye was a Pallava king (Trinetra Pallava, "three-eyed Pallava").

The reference to Karikāla's waging war against insubordinate kings is closer to the *pataha* than the Karikāla myths of Sri Lanka. The Sinhala texts also refer to a three-eyed king (Pāṇḍi) who is an enemy of Karikāla. But in the Sinhala myths his eye is wiped out not by Karikāla, but through the intercession of the god Sakra (see the *aṁba vidamana* myth, pp. 227–38). But in both Sinhala and South Indian texts the three-eyed king (irrespective of his name) is the enemy king whose eye is eventually wiped out.

Finally the *Cevvantipurāṇam*, a late seventeenth century work, states that Karikāla, the son of Parantaka, was brought by the state elephant to be enthroned in the Cōḷa kingdom at a time when Uraiyur was destroyed in a sandstorm. The elephant found the boy too heavy, and a saint advised the boy's mother to make a charcoal mark on the soles of his feet to make him lighter. Then the elephant lifted him up on his back and carried him away without difficulty (Nilakanta Sastri 1932, p. 37). This account resembles the Sinhala version in *karikāla upata*, though they are not identical. The rain washing away the mud in the Sinhala version is the sandstorm of the Indian one. It should be noted that the Sinhala texts state that Karikāla's birth was delayed until the auspicious time by binding the legs of the queen; this resembles the annotator's interpretation of the lines in *Pattuppāṭṭu* quoted earlier. Naccinārkkiniyar, the annotator (fourteenth century), says that his birth was delayed by artificial means until the auspicious time came for his being delivered.

The South Indian Myths: An Interpretation

According to Nilakanta Sastri the Karikāla myths have a core of historical truth, particularly those references to him in the colophons of several Caṅkam works. He sums up this historical core as follows:

> He inherited the throne of Cōḷa as a boy; illegitimate attempts were made by his relatives, for a time successfully, to keep him out of his birthright; by his own ingenuity and strength, and with the assistance of friends and partisans from outside, among whom may have been the maternal uncle Irumbiḍarttalai, Karikāla after some years of confinement in a prison, effected his escape from it and succeeded in making himself king. An early accident from fire which maimed him in the leg for life seems to be rather well attested and to furnish the true explanation for his name. (1932, pp. 44–45)

However, much of this so-called historical core also seems legendary, suggesting a variation in the prototypic "myth of the hero" as stated by Otto Rank (1964). The first part of the account above is reminiscent of the Kṛiṣṇa type of myth, while the latter part tantalizingly reminds one of the maimed foot of another hero, Oedipus. Thus it is likely, contra Nilakanta Sastri and practically every historian of South India, that Karikāla is a popular invention serving a mythic purpose, rather than a historical figure.

Probably in the sixth century, and certainly by the eighth, one type of hero is transformed into another: Karikāla becomes the great king who raised the banks of the Kāvēri. I am tempted to speculate that this change was concomitant with changes in South Indian kingship. During this period concepts of divine and cosmic kingship were dominant, and these South Indian ideas were being exported to Southeast Asia. Thus the South Indian Karikāla probably had close resemblance to his Sinhala counterpart—he was held up as the contrasting model of the good king.

Several of the traits associated with the later Karikāla of Telegu and Tamil literature and epigraphy are also found in the Sinhala texts quoted in this chapter, these being:

1. The birth and early life of Karikāla.
2. The bunding of the Kāvēri and/or building a tank near the Kāvēri.
3. The employment of feudatory kings and waging war against insubordinate ones.
4. The existence of a three-eyed enemy king and the eventual destruction of his third eye.

The evidence is strong enough to warrant the conclusion that both the Indian and the Sinhala myths derive from a single body of tradition. Since in Sri Lanka these myths are also associated with ritual and ritual dramas, is it not likely that they were similarly associated in South India? If so, could not the interpretation of the Sinhala myths and rituals help us understand the South Indian ones?

The Indian Karikāla myths deal with two kings, as do the Sinhala versions, thus:

Karikāla, the good king,	*versus*	a three-eyed evil king (known as Trinetra Pallava, Trinetra Navalocana, or Mukhari).

Karikāla does good things that benefit the people. While not much information is available regarding the nature of the three-eyed king, it is likely that he is evil like Pāṇḍi of Sinhala myth, since here also the third eye of the evil king is blinded (though the manner of the blinding in the two cultures is different). Let me first interpret the Indian case.

The Indian sources mention "the wiping of one eye traced on the picture so that the inimical Mukhari lost one of his three eyes." Thus the three-eyed king lost his eye as a result of imitative magic. However, the incident strongly suggests an act performed in the context of a ritual drama. The third eye—like that of Pāṇḍi—represents the evil king's might, his aspiration to be a god. This has to be wiped out. How could the wiping out be enacted in a ritual drama? If, for example, as in the *pataha* ritual, an actor represented the king "onstage," how could the blinding of the eye be enacted? Given Indian and Sinhala cultural beliefs regarding the eye, a direct imitative action would be impossible. No "actor" would tolerate an imitative action directed toward his eye—for fear he will be struck with *vas* (ritual danger) and suffer blindness. The fear of *vas* in reference to eyes is very strong. Not only is one's own eye extremely vulnerable, but rituals of eye laying are hedged with taboos. Eyes are expressive of "life" (*diṣṭi*, "essence"), and eye laying makes a statue "live." Eyes on a statue are laid indirectly—by looking at the statue through a mirror—never directly. If eye laying is performed indirectly, through a mirror, one should expect eye destruction to be performed in a similar indirect way in ritual, in this case by drawing a picture of the victim and erasing his middle eye. Thus it seems to me reasonably clear that the erasing of the eye of the three-eyed king was an act performed in a ritual drama. Note that in the Sinhala myth also the eye of the three-eyed Pāṇḍi is destroyed, but again this is never represented "onstage." In the *aṁba vidamana* ritual ("the shooting of the mango," see pp. 490–94) the *kapurāla*, dressed as Sakra, "shoots" an arrow at a bunch of silver-ornamented mangoes hung at one end of the arena. The juice of the mango falls on the king's middle eye and blinds him. The king never appears onstage; nor is his blinding enacted: this event is simply narrated by the *kapurāla*.

My interpretation, then, is that at least the later Karikāla is a personage of myth, not of history. South Indian historians are wrong when they interpret these mythic events as historical truths. In all probability they were enacted in ritual dramas even in South India. The basic ritual theme in these myths is as follows: there is a good king who works for the public good and an evil king who possesses three eyes in imitation of the gods. There is a grand conflict between these two, culminating in the destruction of the middle eye of the evil king. This basic theme is transformed by adaptation to differing sociopolitical contexts in South India and Sri Lanka.

If my analysis is correct, then some form of ritual protest against the divine king existed all over southern India, among Telegu, Kannada, Tamil, and Malayalam peoples from probably the sixth century till at least the eighteenth. We know only its broad form, not the exact details of such ritual enactments. But through the Sinhala *pataha* and Karikāla rituals and texts we know what the Sinhala adaptation was like. Basically, two models of kingship are offered. At the risk of some oversimplification one can say that they are the Hindu-influenced notion of divine and cosmic kingship and the Buddhist-derived notion of the just king, originally represented in the paradigmatic case of Asoka and embodied in idealized versions of the lives of the old kings of Anurādhapura and Polonnaruva. These ideas do not represent historical reality per se, but rather represent history as filtered through time and through the minds of ordinary people. A continuing dialectic between these opposed modes must have dominated much of popular thinking on kingship in Sri Lanka.

Some contrasts in the Sinhala and South Indian versions illustrate the Buddhist adaptation of the wider generic theme. For example, in the Sinhala texts Karikāla is wholly good and courteous to the subsidiary kings; in some of the South Indian versions he wages war on one or two kings who did not pay him homage or render him service. In another version Karikāla makes subordinate chiefs carry loads of earth—an action only the evil Pāṇḍi practices in the Sinhala texts. This again illustrates what I have stated earlier—in South India the basic theme is clear, but the transformations of this theme in relation to sociopolitical conditions are not. Nevertheless, while we can legitimately speak of the Buddhist adaptation of these myths in Sri Lanka, we cannot deny a similar adaptation in South India. For though it is true that the popularly devalued cosmic model is Hindu derived, it is also true that Hinduism also provided, in the Dharmaśāstras, competing models of just kingship that were similar to the Buddhist models. These problems I believe can now be solved by historians working on the South Indian material through anthropological analysis like that in the preceding pages.

8

Gajabāhu and Ceṅkuṭṭuvaṉ: Culture Heroes and Colonization Myths

In this chapter I shall analyze corpus 3, or the Gajabāhu corpus, of myths that form, as I stated in chapter 1, the indigenous section of the *pantis kōlmura*, the thirty-five ritual texts of the *gammaḍuva*. The reference to Gajabāhu in the *Cilappatikāram* has been used by most scholars to assign a date to that work. My analysis will therefore have two major goals: first to demonstrate the invalidity of the so-called Gajabāhu synchronism, and second to analyze the Gajabāhu myth in sociological terms, as a "colonization myth." I shall show that an analysis of Gajabāhu from an anthropological point of view may help clear up some of the ambiguities and contradictions that center on the historians' view of this figure, both regarding his role in Sinhala culture and history, and also in relation to the *Cilappatikāram*.

The Gajabāhu Synchronism

The problem with Gajabāhu as far as the *Cilappatikāram* is concerned pertains to what is known as the "Gajabāhu synchronism," that is, the attempt to date the *Cilappatikāram* on the basis of its reference to Gajabāhu (Kayavāgu) of Sri Lanka. The Gajabāhu synchronism relates to the reference in the *Cilappatikāram* that Gajabāhu (Kayavāgu) was present at the consecration ceremony of the Pattini temple inaugurated under the patronage of Ceṅkuṭṭuvaṉ. Since Gajabāhu lived in the late second century, according to the *Mahāvaṃsa*, the "Gajabāhu synchronism" has been of crucial importance for South Indian historical and literary chronology. Most scholars of every persuasion, with a few exceptions, are inclined to accept the Gajabāhu synchronism. Scholars of the more patriotic persuasion (for example, Dikshitar), admit it in toto—that is, they are convinced that King Gajabāhu of Sri Lanka not only was present at Ceṅkuṭṭuvaṉ's capital for the ceremony but also introduced the Pattini cult to Sri Lanka, as a commentator's addendum in the *Cilap-*

patikāram states. Several scholars of the tough-minded sort accept it with reservations. They are impressed by the fact that the *Cilappatikāram* refers to Gajabāhu and Ceṅkuṭṭuvaṉ as contemporaries. Though the *Cilappatikāram* was written much later, they believe the reference to the two kings was based on a valid historical tradition.

The importance of the Gajabāhu synchronism for South Indian chronology can be illustrated by a few representative quotations from leading scholars.

> This allusion to the King of Ceylon enables us to fix the date of Imaya Varman. (Kanakasabhhai 1956, p. 6)

> The synchronism of Senguttuvan with Gajabahu I of Ceylon is the sheet anchor of the chronology of early Tamil literature. (Natesan 1959, pp. 206–7)

> Thus the Gajabahu synchronism is explained and the date of the composition of the *Silappadikāram* settled once and for all. (Dikshitar 1939, p. 16)

> It is not unlikely that the legend preserved the memory of a historically correct synchronism. (Nilakanta Sastri 1955, p. 112) [Paranavitana also assents to this view (1959, pp. 184–85).]

In the following pages I shall demonstrate that the Gajabāhu synchronism is worthless for purposes of historical chronology, since the Gajabāhu of the *Cilappatikāram* is a mythical, not a historical, personage. This consideration will also take us to an analysis of the Gajabāhu myth. In the *Cilappatikāram* proper the reference to Gajabāhu of Sri Lanka is as follows:

> The monarch of the world circumambulated the shrine thrice and stood offering his respects. In front of him the Arya Kings released from prison, kings removed from the central jail, the Kongu ruler of Kudagu, the King of Malva and Kayavāgu (Gajabāhu), the King of sea-girt Ceylon, prayed reverentially to the deity thus: "Please grace our countries just as you have done this auspicious day, a fete-day at Imayavaramban's sacrifice." Then a voice from the welkin issued forth: "I have granted the boon." (Dikshitar 1939, pp. 342–43)

It should be noted that this account merely mentions that Gajabāhu was present at the ceremony. The reference to his having introduced the Pattini cult to Sri Lanka occurs in the *Uraiperukaṭṭurai*, a section added to the poem by an early editor (Dikshitar 1939, p. 6). This account actually seems to contradict the former. It states that famine devastated the Pañdyan kingdom after Pattini destroyed Madurai so that the successor to the late king "propitiated the Lady of Chastity by sacrificing a thousand goldsmiths, and celebrated a festival when there was a downpour causing fertility to the land. . . . On hearing this Gajabāhu of Sri Lanka encircled by sea, built a shrine for the Lady of Chastity where daily sacrifices were performed. Thinking that she would remove this distress (of his land), he also instituted annual festivals commencing with the month of Āḍi; then the rains came to stay and increased the fertility of the land so as to produce unfailing crops" (Dikshitar 1939, p. 6).

Thus this part of the story merely states that Gajabāhu instituted the Pattini cult in Sri Lanka. These contradictions, in combination with other reasons, have led Vaiyapuri Pillai to deny the validity of the Gajabāhu synchronism, as well as the account of his presence in the court of Ceṅkuṭṭuvaṉ. He considers these later interpolations (1956, p. 144). Although I agree with Vaiyapuri Pillai, let us submit the Gajabāhu episode to further scrutiny employing an anthropological analysis of the episode.

The arguments advanced by the more dogmatic scholars are briefly as follows: Gajabāhu of Sri Lanka is mentioned in the *Cilappatikāram*; there were two Gajabāhus mentioned in Sri Lankan chronicles, one in the second and the other in the twelfth century; the twelfth century is palpably too late a date; therefore Gajabāhu of the *Cilappatikāram* is Gajabāhu I, who reigned in the second century. That things are much more complicated is apparent from a critical examination of the Sri Lankan chronicles. The earliest reference to Gajabāhu I appears in the *Dīpavaṃsa*, compiled by Sri Lankan monks about the middle of the fourth century. There is a succinct account stating that Gajabāhu was the son of Vaṅkanāsikatissa. "Tissa's son Gajabāhukagāminī caused a great *thūpa* to be built in the delightful Abhayarāma. This royal chief constructed a pond called Gāmini, according to the wish of the mother; this lord ordered the *ārāma* called Rammaka to be built. He ruled twenty-two years over the Island" (*Dīpavaṃsa* 1879, p. 216). The *Mahāvaṃsa*, compiled in the fifth century, is only slightly more detailed. Several references to pious deeds omitted in the earlier account are included here (*Mahāvaṃsa* 1934, pp. 254–55). There are no references here to the Pattini cult or to Gajabāhu's visit to South India. These references are found in the *Rājaratnākara*, a sixteenth-century work, and in the *Rājāvaliya*, probably written in the seventeenth or eighteenth century. Both these are written in Sinhala rather than the Pāli of the early chronicles. The latter text mentions that Gajabāhu went to South India and brought back Buddha relics and the anklets of the goddess Pattini. Before we consider these latter accounts, let us examine the implications of the *Dīpavaṃsa* and *Mahāvaṃsa* accounts of Gajabāhu.

The *Dīpavaṃsa* and *Mahāvaṃsa*, composed as they were in the fourth and fifth centuries, are close to the events of Gajabāhu I's reign. Moreover, the compilers of the two chronicles used preexisting accounts kept by monks in Buddhist temples. It is therefore surprising that Gajabāhu's visit to India is not referred to here. Some writers argue that this incident is omitted because Buddhist compilers did not wish to be associated with a non-Buddhist cult like that of Pattini (Dikshitar 1939). This argument seems to me highly improbable, for both chronicles are replete with references to so-called non-Buddhist practices and beliefs. Actually, according to popular Sinhala tradition, Pattini is not a Hindu but a Buddhist deity and is an aspirant to Buddhahood. Moreover, according to Sinhala tradition embodied in the later accounts, Gajabāhu also brought back with him Buddha relics. It is even more surprising, therefore, that no reference was made to Gajabāhu's visit in the early accounts. Hence I shall draw certain *tentative* generalizations, which I will spell out in detail later.

1. The *Mahāvaṃsa* and *Dīpavaṃsa* make no reference to Gajabāhu's visit to South India because Gajabāhu I of the chronicles made no such visit.

2. The likelihood is that the Pattini cult was not prevalent in Sri Lanka at the time these chronicles were composed. Nowhere in them is there a reference to the goddess Pattini. Since the later Sinhala chronicles do mention Pattini, one could tentatively conclude that the cult was introduced to Sri Lanka sometime after the fifth century but before the sixteenth.

These conclusions will be discussed in more detail in the analysis of the later Sinhala accounts.

Gajabāhu: A Colonization Myth

Let us now consider the sixteenth-and seventeenth-century Sinhala accounts of the Gajabāhu episode. The Sinhala accounts in the two chronicles are basically the same, but since the *Rājāvaliya* is the more detailed I will use it.

> Gajaba, son of king Bapa Vannesi, succeeded to the throne. One night, when walking in the city, he heard a widow weeping because the king of Soli had carried away her children. He said within himself, "Some wrong has been done in this city" and having marked the door of her house with chalk, returned to his palace. In the morning he called his ministers and inquired of them what (they knew of any) acts of justice and injustice in the city. Thereupon they replied, "O great king, it is like a wedding house." The king, being wroth with his ministers, sent for the woman, the door of whose house he had marked with chalk, and asked her (why she wept). The poor woman replied, "I wept because among the 12,000 persons taken captive by the Soli king were my two sons." On hearing these words the king expressed anger against his royal father, and saying "I will go tomorrow to the Soli country," assembled an army and went to Yapapatuna, thinking "I will (myself) bring back the people forcibly carried off by the king of Soli," and having declared it openly, he dismissed the army. Taking the giant Nila with him he went and struck the sea with an iron mace, divided the waters in twain, and going quietly on arrival at the Soli capital, struck terror into the king of Soli, and seated himself on the throne like king Sak; whilst the giant Nila seized the elephants in the city and killed them by striking one against another. The ministers informed the king of Soli of the devastation of the city thus being made. Thereupon he inquired of Gajaba, "Is the Sinhalese host come to destroy this city?" Gajaba replied, "I have a little boy who accompanied me; there is no army," and caused the giant Nila to be brought and made to stand by his side. Thereupon the king of Soli asked "Why has your Majesty come alone without an army?" Gajaba replied, "I have come in order to take back the 12,000 persons whom your royal father brought here as prisoners in the time of my father." To this the king of Soli saying, "A king of our family it was who, in time past, went to the city of the gods and gained victory in the war with the Asuras," refused to send for and deliver the men. Then Gajaba grew wroth and said, "Forthwith restore my 12,000 people, giving 12,000 besides them; else will I destroy this city and reduce it to ashes." Having said thus, he squeezed out water from sand and showed it; squeezed water from his iron mace and showed that. Having in this way intimidated the king of Soli he received the original number supplemented by an equal number of men, as interest, making 24,000 persons in all. He also took away the jewelled anklets of goddess Pattini and the insignia of the gods of the four devalas, and also the bowl-relic which had been carried off in the time of king Valagamba; and admonishing the king not to act thus in future, departed.
>
> On his arrival he landed the captives; sent each captive who owned ancestral property to his inherited estate, and caused the supernumerary captives to be distributed over and to settle in these countries, viz., Alutkuruwa, Sarasiya pattuwa, Yatinuwara, Udunuwara, Tumpane, Hewaheta, Pansiya pattuwa, Egoda Tiha, and Megoda Tiha. This king reigned 24 years, and went to the world of the gods. (*Rājāvaliya* 1900, pp. 40–41)

On reading this version the reader will note that it agrees with the *Cilappatikāram* in only one respect—that Gajabāhu visited South India and was associated with the Pattini cult. It contradicts or omits details given in the *Cilappatikāram*. In the *Rājāvaliya* the reference is to Gajabāhu's having visited Cōḷa (Soḷī), not Cēra, where Ceṅkuṭṭuvaṉ reigned. It is unlikely that he even went to Cēra (assuming for argument's sake that this account has some historicity), for he brought back the anklets of the goddess Pattini *from Cōḷa*. If this is correct the Pattini cult must have been already fully institutionalized in Cōḷa in the second century. Thus the *Cilappatikāram* account that says it was *started* in Cēra by Ceṅkuṭṭuvaṉ is, according to the Sinhala accounts, wrong. Gajabāhu is presented as subservient to Ceṅkuṭṭuvaṉ. In the *Rājaratnākara* and the *Rājāvaliya* he is presented as a grandiose hero. He brings back the insignia of the gods of the four *devāle*s (the Four Gods), the bowl relic of the Buddha, and twelve thousand Tamil prisoners. There is no reference to his having introduced the Pattini cult to Sri Lanka. On the contrary, the assumption in these two accounts is that the Pattini cult was already in existence in Sri Lanka, hence the importance of his bringing back the anklets of that deity. Moreover, as I shall show presently, Sinhala sources generally state that Gajabāhu did *not* introduce the cult. We will therefore have to dismiss the preposterous claims of some scholars who say, like Natesan, that "the introduction of the Pattini cult to Ceylon by Gajabāhu I is confirmed by the *Rājāvaliya*, the Ceylon chronicle" (Natesan 1959, p. 212).

Even a cursory glance at the Gajabāhu story suggests that the account has no historical veracity. The highly improbable ignorance of the king regarding the twelve thousand prisoners taken captive in his father's reign till he is informed of it by an old widow, the cleaving of the ocean in two, and other miraculous events show that this account is hardly historical, though it may be based on some actual event whose nature I am in no position to infer. The account, however, is almost in point-by-point agreement with the Gajabāhu *myth* sung in water cutting rituals. The inference is irresistible: the Gajabāhu story is not a historical episode at all, but a mythic one associated with water cutting (and probably other customs) and incorporated into the two Sinhala chronicles. Thus the reason the earlier *Mahāvaṃsa* account did not mention the episode is that it simply did not take place historically. This is true not only of the Gajabāhu episode but of others as well. Another famous origin myth—that of the Kandyan *kohoṁbā kaṅkāriya*—deals with the illness of King Paṇḍuvāsudēva, Vijaya's nephew. The *Mahāvaṃsa* is singularly silent about this, whereas the *Rājāvaliya* restates almost in toto the mythic version of the episode. Once again the conclusion is that the myth evolved after the fifth century but before the sixteenth and is based on ritual data. But for some scholars these seem incontrovertible historical facts. K. K. Pillay, writing on South Indian colonization of Sri Lanka, asserts: "One of the early references to such settlements is heard of in connection with the reign of Paṇḍuvāsudēva. It is said that for the purpose of curing the illness of the king, certain Brahmins were brought from South India and they were settled in the capital" (Pillay 1963, p. 136).

To sum up what I have said so far. The Gajabāhu episode in the *Rājāvaliya* and *Rājaratnākara* is probably derived from the origin myth of the water cutting ceremony or from similar myths and has nothing to do with the historical Gajabāhu of the *Mahāvaṃsa*, who lived in the second century. The myth, which associates Gajabāhu with the Pattini cult in a manner opposed to the *Cilappatikāram* account, evolved after the fifth century A.D. The *ritual* of water cutting is probably older than the *myth* of origin. For example, even in Sri Lanka water cutting is also associated with festivities involving Skanda (Kataragama); here different myths of origin are involved. The probability is that the Gajabāhu episode was used to explain the origin of water cutting after the Pattini cult became dominant in Sinhala Sri Lanka. The Gajabāhu story itself may have been current before then, that is, before the Pattini cult became dominant. Indeed, Gajabāhu is a typical Sinhala culture hero figure who, like Vijaya, Paṇḍuvāsudēva, and Malala Rajjuruvo of the Sinhala ritual tradition, was the "originator" of various ritual and religious customs and institutions of the Sinhalas. If there was any historicity in these figures, they have been completely transformed in the mythmaking process. Further analysis of the Gajabāhu episode as depicted in the two Sinhala chronicles and in our myths will make this process of mythicization clearer.

An important difference exists between the *Rājāvaliya* account and the myth of Gajabāhu of the water cutting ritual. The *Rājāvaliya* states that the twelve thousand captives brought to Sri Lanka by Gajabāhu were settled in the following regions: Alut Kuruva, Sārasiya Pattuva, Yaṭinuvara, Uḍunuvara, Tumpane, Hevāhäṭa, Pansiya Pattuva, Egoḍa Tiha, and Megoḍa Tiha. The water cutting ritual ignores this detail. A historical literalism in the analysis of the episode would mean that Gajabāhu I, who lived in the second century, waged a war in the Cōḷa country, brought back many prisoners, and settled most of them in certain parts of the Sinhala hill country. By contrast, the king of Cōḷa who lived in Gajabāhu's father's reign put his Sinhala captives to work raising the bunds of the Kāvēri, a useful irrigation enterprise. It was singularly foolish of Gajabāhu not to have used this human labor for similar construction purposes, for the hill country and coastal regions where he settled his captives were, in the second century, remote, inaccessible, and inhospitable. An anthropological analysis treating this episode as a myth yields a different set of conclusions. This version of the Gajabāhu story is what I call a "colonization myth," functionally similar to the Moses myth of the Bible. As an origin myth it explains the existence of South Indian settlers in parts of the Kandyan provinces and coastal regions. These settlers may have come for various reasons—through waves of conquest, peaceful immigration, or being "introduced" by the Sinhala kings themselves. The myth, like other myths of this genre, explains the existence of these groups, probably justifying their "anomalous status," to use Malinowski's words (1955, p. 101), in the Sinhala social structure. Even now there are communities of low subcastes of the *goyigama* (farmer) caste in the Kandyan areas (e.g., near Aṅpiṭiya I have come across one such village) who claim this origin. Their position is slightly inferior to the majority of the *goyigama* caste: their inferiority, as well as their origin, is explained in terms of the identical myth. The myth served as a useful mechanism for incorporating immigrant populations into the Sinhala social structure till recent times.

The earliest reference to Gajabāhu's colonization is in the sixteenth-century *Rājaratnākara*, which states only that the captives were settled in Alut Kuruva, near Negombo. A *kaḍaimpota* (an account of geographical boundaries) quoted by Bell has another account of Gajabāhu's colonization of Alut Kuruva.

> In olden times, after the Rawana War, from Kuru Rata there came to this Island a queen, a royal prince, a rich nobleman, and a learned prime minister, with their retinue, and by order of King Rama dwelt in a place called on that account Kuru Rata. In the year of our great Lord Gautama Buddha, Gajabāhu who came from Kuru Rata, settled people in the (second Kuru Rata), calling it Parana-Kuru-Rata. In another place he sent 1,000 persons, and gave it to them calling it Alut Kuruwa. (Bell 1892, p. 2)

Alut Kuruva is today populated by the *karāva*, or fisher, caste, who in their myths trace their ancestry to the Kauravas (Kuru) of the *Mahābhārata* war. The major waves of *karāva* immigration to Sri Lanka occurred in the fifteenth century and after (Raghavan 1961). The Gajabāhu myth, in its *Rājaratnākara* version, probably explains and justifies the existence of these and similar South Indian groups. The *kaḍaimpota* version has actually converted Gajabāhu to a *karāva* hero, whose home was not Sri Lanka but India. Furthermore, he is a contemporary of the Buddha. No further evidence is required to illustrate the mythic character of Gajabāhu.

The viability of the Gajabāhu myth as a mythical charter for incorporating immigrant groups into the Sinhala social structure continued till recent times. The *demala gattara* (Tamil *gotra*) caste of the Sinhala low country, recent immigrants to Sri Lanka, also trace their ancestry to Gajabāhu's captives. The *salāgama* (*hāli*; originally weavers, later cinnamon peelers), who were earlier immigrants, also have similar mythic charters. The Portuguese historian of Sri Lanka, Father de Queyroz, writing in the seventeenth century about the exploits of the Sinhalas, says: "and once they captured 12,000 foreigners with whom they peopled the country of Dolosdaz-Corla and from these, they say, are descended the Chaleaz who are obliged to get the cinnamon" (De Queyroz 1930, p. 15). Dolosdās Kōrale is in the Mātara district, where once again there are groups of the *salāgama* caste.

Thus the Gajabāhu myth has been a continually viable one, justifying and explaining the existence of South Indian settlers in Sri Lanka. But at what period did this version of the myth arise? Two references in the Sinhala chronicles give us important clues. First, the captives were settled in the Kandyan region and the coastal areas. These regions came into prominence in the fourteenth century and after, particularly with the founding of the Gampola kingdom. The movement to the Kandyan areas was consequent on disastrous invasions by the Cōḷas (tenth century) and later by Māgha of Kāliṅga (thirteenth century), which ruined the magnificent civilizations of Anurādhapura and Polonnaruva. It is most likely that *this version* of the colonization myth evolved after the fourteenth century. It should also be noted that the place names mentioned in these accounts were hardly known in the second century.

There is further evidence that is of some importance. The *Rājaratnākara*, written in the sixteenth century, makes no mention of Gajabāhu's bringing back the anklets of Pattini or the insignia of the Four Gods, but the rest of the episode is recounted. The *Pūjāvaliya*, a thirteenth-century Sinhala text, has even less to say about Gajabāhu:

> Waknaha Tissa's son Gajabāhu "learning that during the reign of his royal father, people were sent from Lanka to work at Kaveri, sent for his ministers, and having made inquiries was highly displeased and took in his hand the iron mace made for him by his royal father. Accompanied by his warriors, with the iron mace in his right hand, to lift which fifty persons were required, circumambulating the sea from left to right, he struck it (with the mace); divided the waters in two by virtue of his meritorious deeds; went to the sea-coast of Soli without wetting his feet; displayed his power; took away twice as many persons as went to work at Kaveri; made a law that henceforth the inhabitants of Lanka shall not go to work at Kaveri; placed guards round the coast; issued a proclamation in Lanka by beat of tom-tom; celebrated his triumph; performed many meritorious deeds; reigned for twenty two years; and went to the divine world." (*Pūjāvaliya* 1895, pp. 21–22)

Table 2
The Evolution of the Gajabāhu Myth

Sri Lankan Chronicles	Cleaves Ocean	Brings Captives	Settles Captives	Brings Buddha Relics	Brings Insignia of Four Gods	Brings Anklets of Pattini	Builds Specific Tanks and Temples
Dīpavaṃsa—fourth century							+
Mahāvaṃsa—fifth century							+
Pūjāvaliya—thirteenth century	+	+					
Rājaratnākara—sixteenth century	+	+	+	+			
Rājāvaliya—seventeenth or eighteenth century	+	+	+	+	+	+	

The *Pūjāvaliya* account makes no mention of his association with the Pattini cult, the Four Gods, or settling captives in specific places, or of the number of captives involved. Moreover nowhere in the *Pūjāvaliya* or in any of the other literature of the thirteenth century, as far as I could gather, is there any reference to the Pattini cult. The evolution of the myth, as it is found in the chronicles, could be presented as in table 2.

Does this mean the cult was not dominant enough to be recorded in the *Mahāvaṃsa* and *Dīpavāṃsa*? There are probably many important incidents in Sri Lanka's history that are not mentioned in the *Mahāvaṃsa* or *Dīpavāṃsa*; thus the absence of reference in the *Mahāvaṃsa* to a certain historical event is no real proof that it did not occur. But note that these two early chronicles do mention Gajabāhu; the "miraculous" exploits of Gajabāhu are not mentioned, however, though these chronicles are full of "miracle," particularly in religious matters. It is therefore reasonable to assume that these works, which contain enough "miracle," would not hesitate to record grandiose events regarding heroic figures if they were current information at the periods when the works were written. There is then a remarkable evolution of the Gajabāhu story from the matter-of-fact historical accounts in the *Dīpavāṃsa* and *Mahāvaṃsa* to the elaborate myth of the *Rājāvaliya*. The mythic elements are present in the thirteenth-century *Pūjāvaliya* and absent in material from the fifth century. The latter three accounts omit factual references to the construction of buildings and tanks. During this period the Gajabāhu of history has been transformed into the Gajabāhu of myth. The *Pūjāvaliya* version commences the mythmaking process by reference to Gajabāhu's cleaving the ocean and bringing back captives.

I noted that the contemporary water cutting ritual celebrated Gajabāhu's cleaving of the ocean and that in all likelihood this origin myth or a similar one was incorporated into the *Rājāvaliya*. It is now obvious that this myth is also included in the earlier *Pūjāvaliya, but without any association with Pattini*. We can derive the following conclusions:

1. The water cutting ritual is even today associated not only with Pattini but also with other deities.

2. In all probability it is a rite antecedent to the Pattini cult.

3. In the Pattini cult in Sri Lanka water cutting is associated with Gajabāhu, but the only substantive connection between the two myths in terms of their content is that Gajabāhu brought back with him the anklets of the deity.

4. The *Pūjāvaliya* account makes no reference to these anklets or to Pattini.

5. It therefore appears that the Gajabāhu myth was the origin myth of water cutting even before the Pattini cult was dominant in Sri Lanka, or that it was independent of the Pattini cult.

As a matter of fact, there is some internal evidence in the *Pūjāvaliya* account to suggest that even this reference has to do with a ritual. Note that Gunasekara, who translated the *Pūjāvaliya*, states that Gajabāhu circumambulated from "right to left" before he split the ocean with his mace. The reference is to South Asian circumambulation where the object of worship is on the right of the person honoring it. The person then moves clockwise in a left-to-right (i.e., rightward) movement. Such circumambulation rites are performed as a prelude to any propitious ritual even today, and it is conceivable that this episode also refers to a ritual. Incidentally, clockwise circumambulation (movement left to right) is viewed as propitious, whereas counterclockwise circumambulation (movement right to left) is unpropitious or inferior. Unhappily, there is some controversy regarding the problem of Gajabāhu's circumambulation of the ocean in Sinhala editions of *Pūjāvaliya*. The word used for circumambulation is *pradakṣinā*, whereas all recent editions of the *Pūjāvaliya* give the word as *dakṣinākoṭa*. *Dakṣina* could best be translated as "gift" or "offering," and *dakṣinākoṭa* could read as "having made a gift or offering." However, Gunasekara, who translated this section of the *Pūjāvaliya* in 1895, also published the Sinhala edition in 1893. His version, which is the result of the collation of several palm-leaf manuscripts, has *pradakṣinākoṭa* "having circumambulated" (Gunasekara 1893, p. 21). Scholars I consulted agreed that *dakṣinākoṭa* is the correct word; the reason they gave was that it was impossible for Gajabāhu to have circumambulated the ocean! My own view is that *pradakṣinākoṭa* ("circumambulated") is the correct interpretation and that *dakṣinākoṭa* is simply a result of a literal interpretation of this episode by editors. The final solution to this problem must await the collation of old palm-leaf manuscripts of the *Pūjāvaliya*.

Thus I state on the basis of the preceding argument that the Gajabāhu myth originated about the thirteenth century and that it was not associated with the Pattini cult. It is probable that this lack of association between the "Gajabāhu cult" and the Pattini cult continued to the fifteenth century, for the *Rājaratnākara* also makes no reference to Pattini. However, according to this account Gajabāhu brought back with him Buddha's alms bowl taken to South India in the time of Valagambā (Vaṭṭagāmanī Abhaya, 89–77 B.C.). What is the mythic significance of this inclusion? According to the *Mahāvaṃsa*, Tamil chiefs from South India captured the revered bowl relic and took it to India (*Mahāvaṃsa* 1934, pp. 232–33). The *Cūlavaṃsa*, which continues the *Mahāvaṃsa* narration, states that in King Upatissa's reign (in A.D. 406) the stone bowl was used by the king himself for a rainmaking ritual (*Cūlavaṃsa* 1953, p. 19). But no reference to the bowl's having been brought back is given in the *Mahāvaṃsa*. A strange lacuna, and not a very comforting one for mass religiosity.

Yet what about the *stone* bowl in Upatissa's reign? The *Mahāvaṃsa* in the early references does not mention that the bowl was made of stone, and it is unlikely that the Buddha used a bowl of this particular substance. The conclusion is again irresistible. The bowl relic was, next to the tooth relic, the major object of mass adoration and also associated with sovereignty. It was taken to South India and lost in Valagambā's reign. Yet mass religiosity cannot brook this loss, and a stone bowl was substituted. (This course of events, incidentally, is identical with the history of the tooth relic, which suffered similar vicissitudes but always managed to get back to Sri Lanka.) But there is a serious gap here, for if the bowl relic was lost in the second century B.C. and yet existed in the fifth century A.D. and thereafter, who recovered it and how? Gajabāhu, of course. By the sixteenth century, when the *Rājaratnākara* was written, Gajabāhu the culture hero was credited with this great achievement. Thus this version of the Gajabāhu myth accounts for the presence of the stone bowl in Sri Lanka.

In the *Rājāvaliya* account of the seventeenth or eighteenth century, two more elements are added to the Gajabāhu myth: Gajabāhu brings back the insignia of the Four Gods and the anklets of the goddess Pattini. What are the Four Dēvāles (shrines), and who are their gods? The *Rājāvaliya* must surely refer to the Four Gods of Kandy, since this was the only kingdom extant at the time the chronicle was written. The Four Gods of Kandy are Nātha, Viṣṇu, Pattini, and Kataragama, all situated near the palace of the tooth relic in Kandy. One of the four gods is Pattini; thus Gajabāhu brings the insignia of Pattini (one of the Four Gods) and her anklets, *which are her insignia*! These contradictions that arise from a literalist interpretation of the episode are resolved if we approach it once again as a myth.

The Four Gods are typically associated with Kandyan kingship, for victory in war and for success in secular undertakings. Kīrti Śrī Rājasiṃha (A.D. 1747–82) inaugurated the procession or *perahära* of the palace of the tooth relic with the Four Gods participating in it (Aluwihare 1964, pp. 2–3). One origin myth of the *perahära* (there are others) states that it was inaugurated to celebrate the victory of Gajabāhu in Cōḷa. Thus the significance of the insignia of the Four Gods is obvious: it is linked to the inauguration of the *perahära* by Gajabāhu. What about the separate reference to Pattini's anklets? The likelihood is that by the time the *Rājāvaliya* was composed the Pattini cult had come into prominence and the water cutting ritual was associated with other rites performed during annual Pattini rituals, as it is even today in some of the collective rituals for Pattini. If so the Gajabāhu myth of water cutting had to be linked with Pattini. This was done through that final version of the myth, which stated that Gajabāhu brought back with him the anklets of the deity.

We are not yet done with the Gajabāhu myth. Gajabāhu, as I noted, is the culture hero to whom are attributed several deeds of cultural significance for the Sinhala people. The earliest extant form of the myth is from the thirteenth century. It was clearly absent in the fifth century. The question is, At what period between the fifth and thirteenth centuries could the myth have evolved? A psychological interpretation of the content of the myth may give us a clue.

Gajabāhu is the hero leading his people from captivity in the Tamil kingdom. He is like Moses of the Bible; he cleaves the river with a rod and parts the seas. Gajabāhu is accompanied by N̄ilamahā Yōdaya, who appears as a demon, Kalu Kumāraya ("the black prince") in other Sinhala myths (Wirz 1954, pp. 34–39). He brings back twelve thousand Cōḷas in addition to the twelve thousand Sinhalas. The number is explained by Spellman in his essay on the ritual significance of the number twelve in Indian culture. Spellman also quotes a Jaina myth, strikingly similar to the Gajabāhu one, in which an ascetic predicting a twelve-year famine led twelve thousand of his people to a more fruitful land (1962, pp. 79–88). Gajabāhu is the great hero, performing miraculous deeds, vanquishing the detested Tamils. The tone and content of the myth are highly "nativistic," though not millenarian. It seems a wish fulfillment rather than a reality, a boost for the self-esteem of a group subject to serious vicissitudes of fortune. The mythic fantasy, I suggest, is the opposite of reality. The question that then arises is, What period between the fifth and thirteenth centuries was conducive to the formation of this myth? The intervening historical events provide the answer.

The low point in Sinhala fortunes came in the late tenth century with systematic South Indian invasions, unlike the more sporadic incursions of the earlier periods. Sri Lanka was a principality of Cōḷa till 1070, when the Sinhala chieftain Kīrti successfully raised the standard of revolt and assumed the crown as Vijayabāhu I (A.D. 1070–1110). After Vijayabāhu there was a temporary resurgence of Sinhala civilization, culminating in the reign of Parākramabāhu the Great. The old capital of Anurādhapura had to be moved to Polonnaruva as a result of the Cōḷa invasions, and under Parākramabāhu I Sinhala civilization reached new heights. But the respite was temporary. In 1214 Māgha of Kāliṅga landed in Sri Lanka with a large army and wrought utter destruction. The *Cūlavaṃsa* gives a detailed account of the havoc caused by Māgha. The *Pūjāvaliya*, written soon after Māgha's invasion, also mentions the tragedy of the Sinhalas. Both accounts mention the number of Kerala troops as twenty-four thousand, a figure that, as I pointed out, cannot be taken literally. The *Rājāvaliya* gives the number as twenty thousand in its brief account of the conquest, quoted below:

> As moral duties were not practised by the inhabitants of Lanka, and the guardian deities of Lanka regarded them not, their sins were visited upon them and unjust deeds became prevalent. The king of Kalinga landed on the island of Lanka with an army of 20,000 able bodied men, fortified himself, took the city of Polonnaruwa, seized king Parakrama Pandi, plucked out his eyes, destroyed the religion and the people, and broke into Ruwanveli and the other dagabas. He caused the Tamils to take and destroy the shrines which resembled the embodied fame of many faithful kings, the pinnacles which were like their crowns, and the precious stones which were as their hearts, and the relics which were like their lives. He wrought confusion in castes by reducing to servitude people of high birth in Lanka, raising people of low birth and holding them in high esteem. He reduced to poverty people of rank; caused the people of Lanka to embrace a false faith; seized those who were observant of morals, and mutilated them, cutting off hands, feet etc., in order to ascertain where they had concealed their wealth; turned Lanka into a house on fire; settled Tamils in every village; and reigned 19 years in the commission of deeds of violence. (*Rājāvaliya* 1900, p. 52)

While Māgha held sway over the old capitals of Anurādhapura and Polonnaruva, Vijayabāhu III established a Sinhala kingdom in Daṁbadeṇiya (the Daṁbadeṇiya dynasty), to the south of the Old Kingdom. He was succeeded by Parākramabāhu II, his son (1236–70). His period was one of intense literary and cultural activity, though he also failed to reunite the whole of Sri Lanka under his dominion. The *Pūjāvaliya*, which gives the first written account of the Gajabāhu episode, was written during this time (in 1266).

The sociohistorical ethos of the time was conducive to the development of a nativistic myth. The late tenth and eleventh centuries saw a serious decline in Sinhala fortunes with the Cōḷa conquest; there was a rapid rise to new heights of glory in the twelfth century; then in the early thirteenth century the Sinhalas sank to their lowest point in the history of the island. If I am right that the fantasy in the myth is the opposite of reality, the period of the depredations of Māgha was probably the time when the myth evolved. I have noted that, while Māgha was ruling in the old kingdom, Vijayabāhu III established the Daṁbadeṇiya dynasty—the myth may have evolved in this region. If so, the *Pūjāvaliya*, composed soon after, merely committed to writing an existing myth.

When we compare the Gajabāhu myth and the Māgha account, we realize again that the former is a myth that is the opposite of the later "reality"; Māgha invades Sri Lanka with twenty-four thousand (or twenty thousand) Kerala troops; Gajabāhu brings back twenty-four thousand. Māgha plunders and terrorizes the Sinhalas, killing their king; Gajabāhu terrorizes the Cōḷas; Māgha populates Sinhala villages with Tamil *conquerors*; Gajabāhu does it with Tamil *captives*. Even more important than these polarities are the social-psychological functions of the myth, which are to boost the self-esteem of people whose "morale" had sunk low in an era of troubles. We note that these heroic exploits are credited to Gajabāhu, who as a result was transformed from a historical into a mythological figure. Unlike millenarian myths, the heroic exploits mentioned are projected into a glorious past rather than a paradisal future. Both types of myths, however, express a "fantasy" that is contrasted with the current reality. If so, the danger in a literalist interpretation of the myth is obvious. As a typical example of such an interpretation I shall quote from one eminent scholar.

> In the reign of the next king a small army of Coḷians invaded Ceylon and carried off much booty and a considerable number of prisoners. This insult was avenged by his son and successor, Gaja-Bāhu (the Elephant-armed), who invaded Tanjore with a large army. The king of Tanjore, intimidated by the sudden attack, acceded to all demands without a single act of hostility. It was the first expedition of the Sinhalas outside their island home, and their success brought about several important and interesting results. Twelve thousand Coḷian prisoners accompanied Gaja-Bāhu on his return home, and they were settled in various parts of the country, where they quite soon became part of the permanent population. Their descendants are scattered in many districts even at the present time, and their language has influenced Sinhala speech in no small measure. A large number of Coḷian words found their way even into the literary dialect of the Sinhalas. The king of Coḷa also presented Gaja-Bahu with the jewelled anklets of the Hindu goddess Pattini and the insignia of four Hindu deities, Viṣṇu, Kartikeya, Nātha and Pattini. The cult of these gods and goddesses was thus introduced into the island; an extensive literature and folklore grew up around these names; special families dedicated themselves to their service, and observances and ceremonies connected with these deities continue to this day. A large number of books dealing with the cult of Pattini are still available. (Malalasekera 1958, p. 50)

What light does the preceding analysis of the Gajabāhu myth throw on the *Cilappatikāram* and the chronology of the early South Indian history? One thing is clear: first, insofar as the Gajabāhu of the Pattini cult is not the historical Gajabāhu who lived in the second century, the "Gajabāhu synchronism" has to be abandoned once and for all. Second, since the Gajabāhu myth probably evolved in the period between the tenth and thirteenth centuries, a late date for the *Cilappatikāram* is more in consonance with the Sinhala evidence. However, there are several problems yet unsolved, for even the most cautious Indian scholars place the *Cilappatikāram* not later than the ninth century.

If so, the Gajabāhu reference, like Iḷaṅkō Aṭikaḷ's kinship with Ceṅkuṭṭuvaṉ, must be a late interpolation, a characteristic feature of early literature. Indian writers have generally used the independent references to Gajabāhu in the *Cilappatikāram* and the Sinhala chronicles as proof of the historical authenticity of the protagonist. For the anthropologist this should prove no problem, since myths have circulated in the Indo-European orbit from the earliest times. The Gajabāhu myth evolved in Sri Lanka and probably diffused to South India, since channels of intercommunication between the two countries existed. When myths are diffused they may be adapted to the sociohistorical context of the recipient nation. Hence we see the difference in attitude to Gajabāhu in the two countries. In Sri Lanka Gajabāhu is the grandiose hero who saved his people from servitude: I noted that the nativism of the myth was conducive to the ethos of the tenth and to the thirteenth centuries, a period when South Indian invasions were most intense. What about the ethos in South India (especially Cōḷa and Kerala, i.e., Cēra) where the invasions sprang from? The reverse of the Sri Lanka situation must surely be true. This factor is given expression in the Indian adaptation of Gajabāhu, for in the *Cilappatikāram* Gajabāhu is not the hero of Sinhala myth. He is subservient to Ceṅkuṭṭuvaṉ, who is the grandiose hero in the Tamil epic, also performing improbable adventures. Thus the two different versions of Gajabāhu are a fascinating example of a mythic figure adapted to suit divergent sociohistorical conditions in two neighboring countries.

We can now easily explain the different roles of Gajabāhu in relation to the Pattini cult. In the Indian version he introduces the cult to Sri Lanka under the patronage of the Cēra king; in the Sinhala version he terrorizes the Cōḷa king and brings back the anklets of the deity, religious objects of great veneration. If we look at the Sinhala versions in toto, Gajabāhu's action here is strictly analogous to his action in respect to the prisoners. The king of Cōḷa captures twelve thousand Sinhala prisoners. Gajabāhu brings them back and in addition takes twelve thousand South Indian prisoners. A Tamil captures the bowl relic in Valagambā's reign; Gajabāhu brings this back *and in addition* brings back the anklets of Pattini and the insignia of the Four Gods. There is method in the organization of the myth, but this cannot be elucidated by a literal examination.

The *Cilappatikāram*, as I have noted, states that Gajabāhu introduced the Pattini cult to Sri Lanka under the patronage of the king of Cēra, Ceṅkuṭṭuvaṉ. The Sinhala Gajabāhu myth does not agree with this. What do the Sinhala *ritual* sources say about the Pattini cult in Sri Lanka? The text of the *maḍu upata*, sung in Pattini rituals, gives us the answer: the Pattini cult was introduced by Sēraman Raju, which literally means "king of Cēra." The term Sēraman ("Cēramān") appears in the Caṅkam literature as a prefix for several South Indian rulers (Vaiyapuri Pillai 1956, pp. 95–99, 110–59). A literalist may now argue on the basis of this that the Pattini cult was introduced by a king of Cēra, probably Ceṅkuṭṭuvaṉ. But this is as farfetched as the Gajabāhu hypothesis, as far as I am concerned. Sēraman Raju, like the kings of Pāṇḍi and Soḷī in other Siṇhala rituals, is a mythical figure. Consider his case as described in the myths. He had a headache because a frog (who carried an enmity toward the king from a previous birth) had entered his nose. He came to Sri Lanka (for some unexplained reason) and had a ritual performed. Divinities like Viśvakarma, the divine architect, and Sakra, the king of the gods, came to his aid. This event occurring in mythical times is a prototype of the present *gammaḍuva* ritual. Thus no historicity can be attributed to this myth. However, while it is true to say that the action of the episode is set in mythic times, the myth, like any other, was composed in historical times. One tentative historical inference we can make is that the Pattini cult may have been introduced by Cēra (Kerala) colonists from Malaladēsa (Malabar).

The Gajabāhu Myth in Social Action

In the preceding pages I have dealt with the following problems: the evolution of Gajabāhu from a historical to a mythic figure and the validity of the Gajabāhu synchronism. In the course of the analysis I have discussed the functions of one version of the Gajabāhu story as a colonization myth used to legitimize the presence and anomalous status of South Indian settlers and to incorporate them into the larger Sinhala society. Let me develop this theme further and illustrate how this myth is actually used by some contemporary social groups.

My first illustration is from the *karāva* fishermen of Negombo. There exist today bilingual fishermen in the area between Chilaw and Negombo, speaking both Sinhala and Tamil. They are "anomalous" in respect to the exclusively Sinhala-speaking fisherfolk south of Negombo and the exclusively Tamil-speaking groups north of Chilaw—a marginal group sandwiched between two exclusive linguistic areas. South of them are predominantly Sinhala-speaking fishermen belonging to three castes—the *karāva*, *durāva*, and *goyigama*. From the point of view of these groups there is a problem. How is it that, while these bilingual fishermen are like themselves in some respects, they are also so different? The Gajabāhu myth is again used to justify the anomalous status of the bilingual groups living in close proximity to the Sinhalas: they are Cōḷa (Soḷī) captives of Gajabāhu that he settled in this region. When recent immigrants from South India become better assimilated into the Sinhala social structure—when they become exclusively Sinhala speaking—the myth has to be refashioned so as to give a higher status to the better assimilated immigrant group. This point could be neatly illustrated in respect to the *karāva* community of Alut Kuruva, south of Negombo. The sixteenth-century *Rājaratnākara* states that Gajabāhu settled his captives in Alut Kuruva. Thus this form of the myth is the one used to refer to present-day bilingual fishermen. It is very likely that at the time the *Rājaratnākara* was written the Alut Kuruva fishermen were also recent immigrants, and hence they were treated as the Cōḷa captives of Gajabāhu rather than the original Sinhalas rescued by him. Today, however, Alut Kuruva is Sinhala speaking and its people have a clear Sinhala identity. The Sinhala *karāva* groups also believe they are descended from the prestigious *kaurava*s mentioned in the *Mahābhārata*. The *kaḍaimpota* version of the colonization of Alut Kuruva quoted by Bell is probably a later version of the myth, adjusted to suit the changed status of the fishermen of Alut Kuruva. In this account Gajabāhu is a contemporary of the Buddha who brought with him settlers from Kururaṭa where the prestigious Kauravas lived.

The Gajabāhu myth, then, is not static but expresses a dialectic between various social groups. A second example from the North Central Province will illustrate this status dialectic carried to an extreme. From the point of view of the higher castes of the region, the blacksmiths of Roṭāväva are inferior. Their inferiority is explained by saying that they are captives that Gajabāhu settled in this region. However, the Väddas of the North Central Province give a different twist to this myth. The Väddas consider themselves the original settlers of Sri Lanka; the blacksmiths of Roṭāväva, as well as the *goyigama* folk (also known as *raṭē minussu*), are all later immigrants and aliens in territory that is rightfully theirs. Thus Väddas state that all groups in the North Central Province except the Väddas are descendants of Gajabāhu's captives. They are no doubt correct, for it is very likely that most, if not all, Sinhala groups in this island were at some period or other immigrants from South India. The Gajabāhu myth is a symbolic way of expressing this sociological fact.

Gajabāhu and Ceṅkuṭṭuvaṉ

What does the preceding analysis of Gajabāhu as a mythic figure rather than a historical personage tell us about Ceṅkuṭṭuvaṉ, the hero-king of part 3 of the *Cilappatikāram*? According to Nilakanta Sastri, Ceṅkuṭṭuvaṉ was an actual historical figure of the third century, and his exploits are described in several Caṅkam works (Nilakanta Sastri 1932). However, his life and exploits as described in the *Cilappatikāram* are of a patently unhistorical and improbable character. Srinivas Iyengar has this to say about Ceṅkuṭṭuvaṉ's expedition to the Himalayas:

> The exploits of Senguttuvan described in the third canto of Silappadikāram are as incredible as those of the hero of Paranar's ode are credible. He marches from the Nilgiris to the banks of the Ganges without any trouble. The poem makes Nurruvar Kannar, whose sway extended from the Nilgiris in the Northern boundary of the Cera country to the Gangetic region offer rather humbly to help Senguttuvan to reach his destination. The phrase Nurruvar Kannar cannot be anything other than a bad translation of Satakani. The Satakani sway extended up to the Ganges region only before 77 A.D., from whence it gradually shrank before the increasing power of the Saka-Pallavas. Canto III then makes Senguttuvan defeat a number of Trans-Gangetic monarchs, for whose existence there is no other evidence, literary or epigraphical, and makes two of the kings carry on their heads the stone which was to represent the deceased Lady Kannaki. All these must be fables, because the transport of an army of the size necessary for the purpose of fighting with the Trans-Gangetic monarchs is a thing that can be imagined only by a Tamil poet ignorant of the geography of India. Indian history affords only one instance of a Tamil army marching up to the banks of the Ganges, and that was the army of Rajendra Coladeva, whose sway already extended to the Mahanadi and from that river to the Ganges it is but a short step. The only other instance of the march of an army from Delhi to Ramesvaram is that of the expedition of Malik Kafur, but right up to the heart of Telingana, i.e. more than half the distance, was already a part of the Delhi Sultanate. We are thus forced to conclude that Senguttuvan's northern expedition was invented by a poet ignorant of Indian geography, and could appear credible only to those ignorant of Indian history. This is another reason why the third canto of Silappadikāram, even though it be conceded to be a genuine part, and not a supplement, of the poem, ought not to be used as a reliable source of ancient South Indian history. (Iyengar 1929, pp. 600–601)

The major exploits of Ceṅkuṭṭuvaṉ are his defeat of the northern kings, his triumphal (and improbable) march up to the Himalayas, and his bringing a stone for carving the image of the goddess. However, the first two exploits are ascribed not only to Ceṅkuṭṭuvaṉ, but also to at least two other South Indian kings who preceded him, according to the *Cilappatikāram*. If one takes these references seriously, as some South Indian scholars do, then one must assume that the conquest of the North must have been a favorite pastime of South Indian kings in the first centuries B.C. or A.D. However, while one may discount their historicity, one must not entirely dismiss their sociological and historical significance. We must assume that the many references to such exploits indicated a widespread *myth* of the northern conquest and the humiliation of the Aryan kings. Myths may not be history in our sense of the term, but they spring from a historical context. As in the case of Gajabāhu, anthropological analysis can perhaps help us understand the historical and cultural signifcance of the Ceṅkuṭṭuvaṉ myth of the northern conquest.

It seems clear that Gajabāhu and Ceṅkuṭṭuvaṉ belong to the same class of mythic hero. Both may have been historical figures, but their cultural and historical significance is in relation to myth. We are dealing with a genre of myth or legend where a hero is credited with deeds of a *seemingly* historical character (e.g., a conquest) that simply could not have occurred in the period concerned. Consider two features of the Gajabāhu myth. First, it is the opposite of the reality; second, it expresses a cultural dialectic going on to this very day—the Sinhala reaction to the constant presence in Sri Lanka of South Indians. I suggest that Ceṅkuṭṭuvaṉ is to southern India vis-à-vis the North as Gajabāhu is to Sri Lanka vis-à-vis South India. Like Gajabāhu with the Cōḷas, Ceṅkuṭṭuvaṉ strikes terror among the Aryans: in a single day he "destroyed the countless armies of the assembled enemies." He transports the image of the goddess on the heads of northern monarchs. Like Gajabāhu ("elephant arm"), he is physically strong; the thickly armored elephants quail in terror as he yokes them (Dikshitar 1939, pp. 168–72).

Ceṅkuṭṭuvaṉ, the grandiose hero (and similar early figures), helps express an ancient cultural dialectic that still continues: a reaction to the claims to military and cultural superiority by the "northern Aryans." As Kamil Zvelebil states, this claimed cultural superiority triumphed in South India by the fifteenth century, when Sanskrit models of literary convention and taste totally overran Tamil literature and Tamil scholars spurned their own earlier works like the *Cilappatikāram* and the Caṅkam literature (Zvelebil 1975, p. 5). In the twentieth century one sees a reaction to the northern cultural dominance and a resurrection of the old dialectic that claimed the superiority of the South. Let us examine the historical conditions in the earlier period of South Indian history that fostered the development of the Ceṅkuṭṭuvaṉ type of myth—the grandiose hero triumphing over the despised Aryans.

If we assume the Gajabāhu/Ceṅkuṭṭuvaṉ parallelism, let us assume further that the events the myths represent also belong to the same class. Thus if the Gajabāhu events are the opposite of the reality, so are the Ceṅkuṭṭuvaṉ events. This implies that my interpretation of Ceṅkuṭṭuvaṉ is diametrically opposed to that of most Tamil scholars, for whom the myth is real history. If Indian invasions, particularly by Māgha of Kāliṅga, were the reality underlying the Gajabāhu myth, what was the reality of the Ceṅkuṭṭuvaṉ events? The myth of the grandiose hero subjugating the despised Aryans of the North was current in South India in the literature of the Caṅkam and post-Caṅkam age. The *reality* of Aryan military superiority is Asoka's conquest in the middle of the third century B.C., which brought Kerala (the home of Ceṅkuṭṭuvaṉ) within his suzerainty. The devastating conquest of Kāliṅga (Orissa) by Asoka must surely have impressed the rulers of the southern kingdoms. Later northern empires like the Gupta, even though they did not conquer the South, must have been a source of fear and threat.

Perhaps even more significant than the military invasions were the Sanskritic, Brahmanic, and Aryan values that were beginning to invade the South in the first two centuries A.D., culminating in the dominance of Nambudiri Brahmans in Kerala by the twelfth century. All this is *denied* in the Ceṅkuṭṭuvaṉ myth. The myth annuls true history and substitutes the society's own view. What is myth to us constitutes actual events that happened to members of the society. Myths like that of Ceṅkuṭṭuvaṉ and Gajabāhu are the people's own view of their history, and hence psychologically more real than the actual events, which, even if they were presented or made available, would be strenuously denied. It is the continuity of the same cultural attitude into modern times that make many South Indian scholars treat these improbable events as if they had actually occurred.

Ceṅkuṭṭuvaṉ, Sēraman, and Gajabāhu

The Gajabāhu myth has multiple functions in Sinhala history, and so does the myth of Ceṅkuṭṭuvaṉ for South India. In addition to conquest, both heroes are credited with institutionalizing the Pattini cult. Consider these references:

1. According to Sinhala myth, Gajabāhu defeats the Cōḷa king and brings back the anklets of the goddess Pattini, which he enshrines in the temple of Navagamuva. He is *not* the culture hero who introduced the cult to Sri Lanka, but in myth he is credited with building the temple of Navagamuva. He gives the cult state patronage.
2. Ceṅkuṭṭuvaṉ defeats the northern kings, who help bring a stone for carving the image of the goddess. He too builds a temple for the goddess and gives the cult state patronage (Dikshitar 1939, pp. 342–43). The likelihood is that the Ceṅkuṭṭuvaṉ myth refers to a popular tradition in South India giving a pedigree for the central shrine of the goddess (probably in Vañci or Koṭunkoḷur), as Gajabāhu does for the central shrine at Navagamuva. A goddess cult that existed at the popular level was later given state patronage and recognition. The Gajabāhu and Ceṅkuṭṭuvaṉ myths are charters that express these sociohistorical events and give them public validation and legitimacy.

Sinhala myth gives Gajabāhu credit for bringing the anklets of the goddess from Cōḷa and, in some traditions of the *gammaḍuva*, with having built the Pattini temple at Navagamuva. He is not credited with having introduced the cult into Sri Lanka. This latter task is attributed to Sēraman (Cēramān), a title given to the ancient kings of Kerala. It is Sēraman who introduced the folk cult—the *gammaḍuva*—at Ruvanvälla, while Gajabāhu built the temple at Navagamuva, a village near Ruvanvälla. The term Sēraman suggests connections with Ceṅkuṭṭuvaṉ, a named Kerala king. What is the relation between them? Probably the tradition was strong in South India that a king of Kerala was responsible for establishing the Pattini cult there. This tradition was carried over to Sri Lanka, so that Sēraman (i.e., king of kerala) introduced the folk version of the cult into Sri Lanka. In southern India the establishment of the state cult was attributed to a specific king of Kerala, the grandiose hero Ceṅkuṭṭuvaṉ. In Sri Lanka this would be impossible, given the Sinhala Buddhist culture; a Sinhala Buddhist king must be credited with establishing the cult on the state level. This is of course Gajabāhu, the hero of Sinhala myth.

Mythicization and Demythicization

The preceding account enables us to highlight twin processes that occur in society and history—mythicization and demythicization. I borrow "mythicization" from Eliade, who used the term to describe the process whereby historical personages and incidents are converted into heroes and episodes in myths (Eliade 1959, pp. 39–46). This process of mythicization is familiar and well documented, but it poses serious problems for scholars who have to unravel myth and history. When the mythicization process is complete, historical material has been totally transformed into myth so that it is almost impossible to abstract the former unless independent evidence from nonmythical sources is available. Raglan (1936) points out these difficulties in his work on the hero, though he overstates his case. Thus we know that the Buddha was a historical personage, and several incidents in his life can be reliably learned from the Buddhist texts. But the *birth* of the Buddha is a historical fact that has been mythicized; hence historical deductions can be made only cautiously and tentatively. When mythicization is complete the anthropologist takes over from the historian, and the story is looked at as a myth, holistically and in toto. Very often viewing the myth *as myth* may give us information about historical processes, as I demonstrated earlier, but such information cannot be gathered by looking at parts of the myth literally, or by abstracting "rational" or commonsense elements from the "nonrational." Thus Gajabāhu is, in the fourth and fifth centuries, a historical personage; by the fourteenth century he has been transformed into a hero of myth who cleaves the ocean and rescues his people from captivity. But even serious scholars have on the basis of this mythic account suggested a prior factual invasion of India by Gajabāhu.

Certain historical personages may be selected in mythmaking for various reasons. In some cases where the mythicization process is not complete, or where the myth and historical evidence coexist independently, it is possible to show these reasons. Thus Lloyd Warner demonstrates how the historical Abraham Lincoln is transformed into the Lincoln of myth. He notes the kinds of mythic transformations that have occurred, the functions of the myth for contemporary Americans, and the somewhat obvious reasons for the choice of Lincoln (Warner 1961, pp. 247–51). In the absence of independent evidence, we cannot say why a particular personage is chosen, though we may be able to relate the genesis of a myth to its psychological or sociocultural background. Thus we do not know why the historical Gajabāhu was chosen as hero for the myth. Perhaps he was traditionally viewed as a strong person; his name literally means "elephant arm," for only a person with giant arm could wield a mace to cleave the ocean and squeeze water out of stone, as Gajabāhu of the myth does. Alternatively it is possible that the historical Gajabāhu took over the name of a preexisting mythic hero.

Though the mythicization of "history" is a well-known process, the "historization" of myth is less well recognized, even when evidence of it is equally clear and abundant. I will use the term "demythicization" to characterize this and related processes whereby old myths are "rationalized" but are used for much the same purposes as traditional myths—as, for example, providing charters for action or to enhance the self-esteem of groups. Demythicization should not be confused with Bultmann's "demythologizing," which denies the literal truth of myth. By contrast, attempts to prove that the resurrection of Christ was an actual event are a case of demythicization. I view demythicization as typically, though not wholly, a modern phenomenon resulting from the impact of rational and scientific thinking on traditional mythology. For traditional societies myths were true events, but these cannot be defended as empirically real within the naturalistic framework of modern rational and scientific thinking. Yet groups and individuals may still need to believe in them, and to permit this myths have to be demythicized. Demythicization may take various forms:

1. Mythic events or beings of central importance for a religious belief system are viewed as empirically verifiable, and we therefore have proofs for the existence of God, or attempts to prove rebirth through hypnotic experiments by contemporary Buddhist "scientists" and philosophers. Very often such "experiments" are simply rationalizations of beliefs accepted a priori.

2. Alternatively, a common form of demythicization is to look upon *some* of the events of myth as expressing historical reality. Thus in Sri Lanka one often hears selectively rationalized versions of the *Rāmāyana*, which depicts the mythic war between Rāvaṇa, the demon king of Lanka, and Rāma of India, the avatar of Viṣṇu. In the *Rāmāyana* there is an elaborate description of the wealth and prosperity of Sri Lanka and an account of how Rāvaṇa flew to India in a "peacock machine." These accounts are rationalized by educated people so that they believe Sri Lanka had a glorious civilization before the Indian colonization of the island in the sixth century B.C., and among the nation's accomplishments is the invention of an aircraft! Though views of this sort are rarely held by serious scholars, they are nevertheless nativistic charters that enhance the self-esteem of people recovering from the demoralizing effects of colonialism. These selectively cognized events have functions similar to those of traditional myths.

3. Finally, I shall draw attention to the situation where the traditional myths are accepted in toto because they are contained in larger religious or secular ideologies that cannot be questioned. The case here is similar to Protestant fundamentalism insofar as the myth is received as fundamentally true, but in fundamentalism there is total acceptance without demythicization. In the type I refer to the myths are accepted, and on the internal evidence of these myths elaborate ("rational") treatises are written regarding their historicity.

To sum up, in all three types a process of demythicization has occurred whereby old myths are given new truth values to suit "rational" attitudes resulting from the impact of science on the contemporary world. The myths are not in Bultmann's sense "demythologized": on the contrary, either they are invested with new truths, or the old truths are given new rationally acceptable proofs, or the old truths are looked upon as true in toto and therefore seen as evidence for historical or scholarly treatises. Yet they also function as mythic charters for contemporary groups. Scholarship, where it is found in such cases, is not true scholarship, since it disregards the logic of evidence and inference and requires a partial or complete suspension of critical thinking and skepticism. "Scholarship" is simply an aspect of the demythicization process, not the goal of inquiry.

My comments on mythicization and demythicization can now be applied to the subject matter of this book. Mythicization is a familiar enough process, and characters like Gajabāhu and Ceṅkuṭṭuvaṉ are historical characters who have been mythicized. What is the relevance of *demythicization* for a discussion of the Pattini cult? My answer is that Pattini is no longer worshiped in India; she has been assimilated into the various *śakti* cults of Brahmanic Hinduism. Yet the Pattini myths are embodied in the Tamil epic the *Cilappatikāram*, and many modern writers on the *Cilappatikāram* have demythicized this epic. Thus Dikshitar, the editor and translator of the *Cilappatikāram*, views the mythic events described there as true (1939, p. 193) and describes the sociocultural background of the period with utter seriousness. Indeed, one writer, Kanakasabhhai, on the basis of evidence in the *Cilappatikāram* and other mythic or epic sources, has written an elaborate social history entitled *The Tamils Eighteen Hundred Years Ago* (Kanakasabhhai 1956). Demythicization of myth, epic, and legend is in general very common in South India (and in Sri Lanka), even among scholars; and as far as the Pattini myths are concerned such demythicization illustrates, paradoxically, their continuing viability for contemporary educated South Indians, even though the cult has lost all its religious significance. The functions of demythicization have to be seen in the context of the language and cultural nationalism of contemporary South Indian politics. Traditional Indological studies have emphasized the Sanskritic civilization of India; the North Indian has been culturally and politically dominant, and recently this has resulted in a strong affirmation of Dravidian values in the South, in both the political and the cultural spheres.

In the political sphere this has led to political action based on regional language nationalism opposed to the Sanskritic and Brahmanic traditions of the North. In the cultural sphere a great deal of scholarly activity has been spent on proving the antiquity and the past glory of Tamil and South Indian civilization. While some of this activity is laudable and reflects good scholarship, a great deal of it is characterized by an incredible jingoism, a narrow fanatical patriotism, and a consistent demythicization of myth. Demythicization, sociologically viewed, provides a new charter for political and social action among South Indian nationalists and, psychologically viewed, functions to enhance their self-esteem and to "overcompensate" those who have felt systematically neglected by the Brahmanic North. Demythicization tries to deny or minimize the influence of Sanskrit on South Indian culture and affirms the antiquity and glory of its own civilization.

Part Four

Introduction

In part 2 I gave a detailed account of the myths and rituals of the *gam-maḍuva* and the cycle of Pattini myths embodied in the thirty-five song-books. I now want to focus on rituals of two types—those that have a serious, controlled, sometimes numinous content and those that are characterized by acting and behavior, often vulgar or obscene. For purely heuristic purposes I shall label the former "ideal representations" and the latter "catharses." Most of the rituals presented in part 2 are ideal representations. Ideal representations consist of myths and rituals sung or performed by a specialist class of priests (*kapurālas*) and presented onstage, as it were, to the assembled audience. I shall single out a special type of ideal representation, a ritual drama that deals with a powerful spiritual theme of central importance to the group. I shall borrow a term from Greek mystery religion and call these numinous performances *dromena*, "things performed." The ritual drama of the "killing and resurrection" is a dromenon par excellence. In ideal representations, and especially in dromena, the psychological problems of the group are brought under fine ego and cognitive controls. Ideal representations also embody cultural, religious, and philosophical values; they are not direct representations, or isomorphic parallels, of the nuclear psychic problems of the group. It is as if these psychological problems were symbolized many times over, brought in line with the higher culture, and given idealistic form. The idea of the sacred, in its numinous sense, is most clearly manifested in these representations. By contrast, there is another group of rituals in the Pattini cult that give more direct expression of the dominant psychological problems and anxieties of the people. The symbolization here is more forthright and easier to unravel. That which is camouflaged in the dromenon is laid bare in the cathartic ritual.

Cathartic rituals are of two types, based on the nature of audience participation. In "cathartic participations" the audience actively participates in the rituals. The *aṅkeḷiya* rituals described in this part of the book are of this type. The congregation moves onto the stage, as it were, and its members temporarily become priests of a sort. In a "cathartic enactment" the audience witnesses a ritual that is staged by priests, but, since the ritual directly taps primary-process material, it permits the audience to *vicariously* participate in the proceedings. Often audience involvement is seen in spontaneous and ribald comments and laughter; by contrast, during dromena the audience is utterly solemn. Ideal representations, especially dromena, are characterized by controlled behavior and seriousness; catharses are characterized by acting-out behavior and generally by levity. Cathartic rituals help the congregation act out their psychic problems, either directly through actual participation or indirectly through identification with the enactment or through vicarious participation. A cathartic ritual is often the obverse of an ideal representation. The ritual drama of the "killing and resurrection" is a dromenon; its humorous parody, the "killing of Rāma," is a cathartic ritual.

In this section I will present four accounts of *aṅkeḷiya* in great detail. I believe that much of the controversy regarding interpretation of ritual is due to inadequate or faulty documentation. *Aṅkeḷiya* has been described by several scholars, among them Yalman (1966), Yocum (1982), and Hiatt (1973), not to mention my own early description and interpretation (Obeyesekere 1958). A large part of these interpretations is wrong simply because these authors (except the last) have not seen these rituals—or have seen only one. Since I shall describe these rituals in detail in chapter 9, the reader can take issue with my interpretations (in part 5) and those of other scholars.

9

The Aṅkeḷiya Rituals

In this chapter I shall describe another set of rituals of the Pattini cult, known as the *aṅkeḷiya*, or "horn game," rituals. The earliest historical reference to *aṅkeḷiya* is from the seventeenth-century descriptions of Knox (1681, p. 99). Informant interviews and the existence all over the country of place names associated with the cult suggest that it was widely prevalent in Sinhala Buddhist and Hindu Sri Lanka except in the North Central and Northern provinces, and perhaps in parts of the North Western Province.

The myths and rituals of *aṅkeḷiya* have no substantive and thematic connections with the main body of Pattini myths sung in the *gammaḍuva* or with the *Cilappatikāraṃ* story. Nevertheless, they are crucial for interpreting the Pattini cult as a "projective" system. In this chapter I shall simply present detailed eyewitness accounts of four *aṅkeḷiya* rituals from different parts of the country: Pānama on the east coast, Malidūva in the Southern Province, Biyanvila in the Western Province near the city of Colombo, and Dunukeula in the Central Province.

Let me first give a brief synthetic account of *aṅkeḷiya* so that the reader will not be confused by the detailed descriptions.

Aṅkeḷiya means "horn game." The theory is that two horns (either sambar horns or wooden hooks representing horns) are interlocked. One horn is tied to a tree generally known as the *aṅ gaha* ("horn tree"); the other is tied to a huge pole that pivots in a hole in the ground. This tree is known as *henakaňda*, or "thunderbolt tree," [1] and two long tug ropes are tied to it. The village divides into two teams—*uḍupila* and *yaṭipila*, which could best be translated as "the team above," or "on top," and "the team below." For easy reference I have used the terms "upper team" and "lower team," but these terms do not imply higher and lower status. The common theory is that lower team (*yaṭipila*) is the team of the goddess Pattini and the upper team (*uḍupila*) that of her consort. The two horns as well as the ropes tied to the thunderbolt tree belong to the two teams. At a signal each team pulls on its rope until one horn snaps. The horn that snaps is the loser; the winning team expresses its jubilation and humiliates the losing team.

1. The belief generally is that a tree struck by lightning should be used for this ritual, but this is not always adhered to in practice. The rainmaking significance of the thunderbolt tree is obvious. In some areas the term *henakaňda* is not used; instead *aṅ kaňda* or *aṅ kanuva* ("horn post") is used.

Aṅkeḷiya at Pānama

The Pānama *aṅkeḷiya* is coordinated with the annual festival for Skanda at Kataragama. It starts as soon as the "water cutting" ritual at Kataragama is over and ends in the full moon of Nikiṇi (August), with the *diya keḷiya* ("water play") ritual. However, these rules may be changed. Since, for example, *aṅkeḷiya* is a ceremony of first fruits, it may be postponed if the harvest is delayed. In general the rituals last for fifteen days of the waxing moon (*pura*). In the first five days the *aṅkeḷiya* is performed by the youths of the village and is known as *kolu aṅ* ("horns for youths"). In the next seven days the game is open to all adult males in the village. On the thirteenth day the ritual known as *valibānava* ("lowering of the tug ropes") is performed. On this day, after 12:00 noon, the temple doors are opened for offerings, and women can enter the temple premises. These activities go on till the next day. On the evening of the fourteenth day the gods are paraded through the village, and on the final day the ritual of water sports (*diya keḷiya*) is performed.

Days	Calendar of Events
1	
2	
3	*kolu aṅkeḷiya* (for youths)
4	
5	
6	
7	
8	
9	*aṅkeḷiya* proper (*maha aṅkeḷiya*)
10	
11	
12	
13	*valibānava*, temple doors open after 12:00 noon
14	Deities taken through village at night
15	*diya keḷiya*, "water play," "water cutting"

The objects used in the *aṅkeḷiya* are very similar to those of other areas:

1. The *aṅ gaha*, or "tree," the post of the upper team.
2. The *henakaňda*, or thunderbolt tree, a large tree trunk about fifteen feet high, ingeniously pivoted in a "channel" six feet long; the post of the lower team.
3. The logs used to hold the thunderbolt tree in position in the socket are called *häpini kaňdan* (*häpini*, "hitting the sides"; *kaňda*, "trunk," "body"; also could mean *häpini*, "female cobra").
4. Attached to each post is a coil of jungle vines known as *pēräs*; attached to these coils are ropes, or *vāran*.
5. The horns are much smaller than the ones used at Biyanvila (see pp. 403–7), but the various parts are similarly named. The short arm of the horn is known as *aňga*

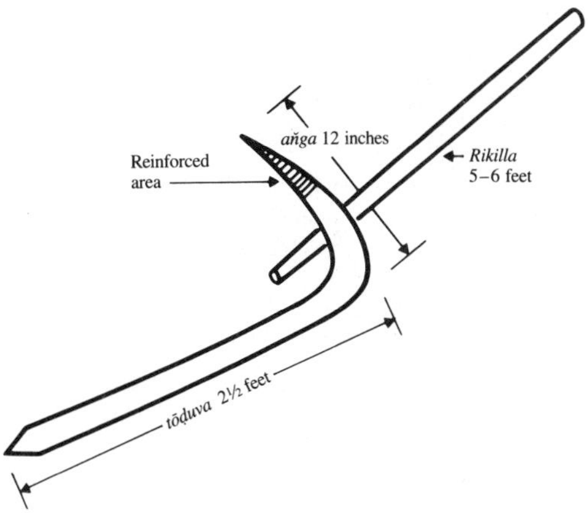

Fig. 9. Drawing of an *aṅkeḷiya* horn from Pānama.

("horn") the long arm is the *tōḍuva* (literally, "ear ornament"). The *rikilla* or *rikili polla* is the long crosspole tied to the *aṅga* and used for controlling the horns during the game.

During the ritual the two horns are hooked together, and each horn is tied to the *pēräs* or coils of its own post with jungle rope. Two tug ropes (*vāran*) are attached to the thunderbolt tree (the post of the lower team), which is sitting in its socket. Each team pulls its own tug rope, causing the thunderbolt tree to move forward in its socket. This causes the interlocked horns to tense, and ultimately one of them snaps. There are experts on each side who control the crosspole (*rikili polla*) to ease the tension on the horns as the teams pull at their tug ropes (see fig. 9).

The *aṅkeḷiya* ritual is performed in the premises of the Pattini shrine (*dēvāle*) about a mile to the west of the village of Pānama. The two brick buildings that house the deities were constructed only about sixty years ago, within the memory of some informants. Before this, the two large tamarind (*siyaṁbalā*) trees served as the shrines for the deities. (Tradition also states that, before this, *aṅkeḷiya* rituals were held in a place called Radälla, five miles from Pānama, actually a part of old Pānama. The residents abandoned the old village and moved to the present site about sixty years ago. There are many paddy fields belonging to Pānama folk near Radälla, and offerings of the first fruits of these fields (*alut sāl dāne*) are given to the gods at that place. However, no *aṅkeḷiya* rituals are now held in Radälla. The two brick buildings house the goddess Pattini and her consort Pālaṅga, here deified as Alut Deviyo ("New Deity"). In addition to these two shrines there are smaller ones for the two guardian gods of the premises, Parakāsa Deviyo of *yaṭipila* and Parakāsa Deviyo of *uḍupila*. These guardians punish those who violate taboos or misbehave within the sacred premises; they also guard the Pattini and Alut Deviyo shrines. The *aṅ gaha* and *henakaňda* are between the two shrines. In general *uḍupila* and *yaṭipila* folk congregate near their respective shrines. During the performance members of one side cannot cross the invisible boundary and walk over to the other side. If one has to cross over for some purpose one must shout and get permission from the other side. This rule is strictly en-

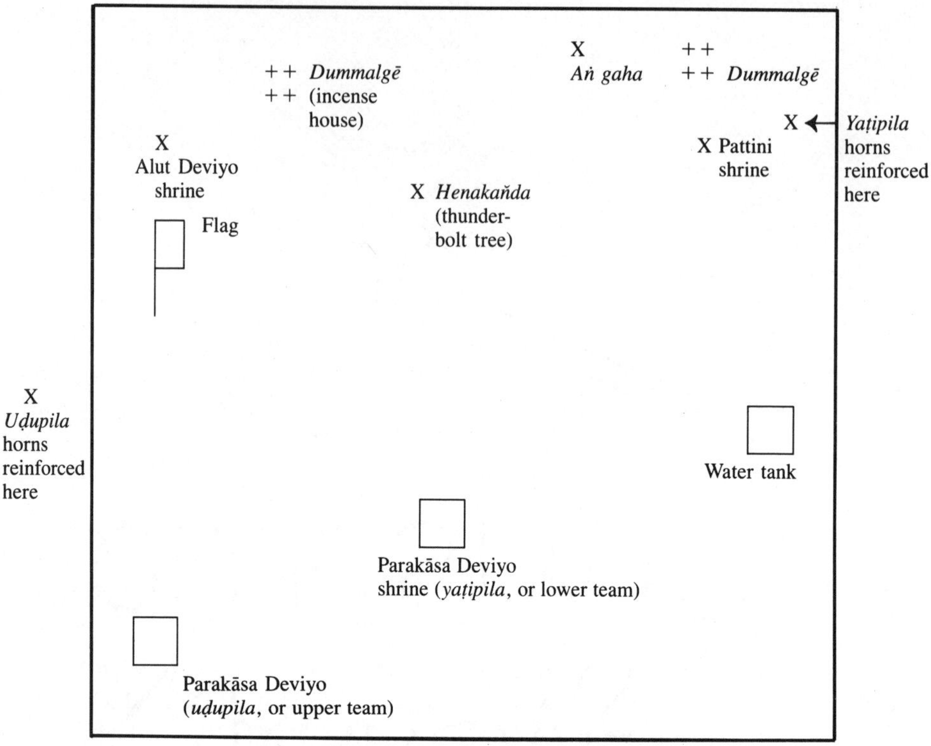

Fig. 10. Layout of the shrine premises at Pānama.

forced. No "modern" lights like kerosene, Petromax, or electric generators are permitted, but only oil lamps using oil extracted from the coconuts the devotees bring to the temple. Figure 10 illustrates the general layout of the sacred area.

The following are the chief officials required for the *aṅkeḷiya*, one for each side: Basnāyaka Nilame (the Tamil term *vaṇṇakar* and the older Sinhala term *betmerāla* were also used), *kapurāla*, and *vaṭṭānḍi*. The Basnāyaka Nilames are the lay heads and managers of the two temples; the *kapurāla* performs the ritual duties associated with each shrine; and the *vaṭṭānḍi* are responsible for organizing and coordinating activities in the shrine premises. All these officials must be free from pollution and conform with norms of purity (*pirisidu*). Indeed, the whole village seems greatly concerned with purity, for during the festival no one is expected to eat meat or fish; only rice and vegetables (especially leaves of trees like *murunga*, *Moringa pterygosperma*) are eaten. Sexual abstinence is also generally practiced, and menstruating women, those likely to menstruate, and those who have just given birth and hence are polluted are sent away to neighboring villages or secluded in menstrual huts (*kuḍiligē*) in the adjacent jungle. Special precautions are required of the officials, specially the *vaṭṭānḍi*. They must take ritual baths daily; they must not eat food from 5:00 P.M., when the rituals commence, till after midnight, when the rituals are over; and they must abstain from sexual intercourse. During the proceedings they cannot leave the temple premises even to answer the call of nature. They must see that everything is ritually pure—that new pots are used and mouth masks are worn by those cooking food for the deities. They eat one meal of rice (*käkuḷuhāl*, "rice from unboiled paddy")[2] with *murunga* leaves per day, and that in small portions. A bit of their food is set aside before they eat for a rite known as *tippāran kavanava*. If the short side of the horn is thin, one can use four splices of wood to reinforce it. This act is euphemistically known as *koṭṭa kavanava*, ("feeding the pillows"). The rice that is kept aside is rubbed into the reinforced horn by the *vaṭṭanḍi*—this is known as *tippāran kavanava* ("feeding the ritual rice").

Vaṭṭānḍi get up at dawn each day to sweep the temple floors and arena grounds and perform their morning ablutions; then they worship the gods in their shrines. At 11:00 A.M. they start cooking rice and vegetable curries in pots. Then they "bathe" their "hands and feet" (*ata paya nānava*) and eat lunch. After this they bathe their hands and feet again and chew betel; this is followed by a short nap. They get up about 2:00 P.M. and prepare themselves for the tasks associated with horn pulling. For this they must wash their heads—*hisanānava*, or "head bathe"—a more serious form of ritual cleansing. Then they arrive at the "horn terminus" (*aṅ handiya*: *aṅ*, "horn"; *handiya*, a place where several roads meet—"junction," "terminus"—the place where the horns are hooked). The special "seat" of the *vaṭṭānḍi* is an umbrellalike structure known as *dummalgē* ("incense house") constructed on the side of each *dēvāle*. Formerly the *vaṭṭānḍi* lived in special huts constructed in the neighboring bush, but this custom died out about 1960. A *vaṭṭānḍi* is viewed as someone who observes *sil* (the Buddhist ten precepts), an almost sacred being. If one team continuously loses it is believed that the *vaṭṭānḍi* is impure, and he is replaced. The two *vaṭṭānḍi* are probably the only persons who refrain from alcohol during this period.

In addition to these officials there are eight *aṅ vaṭṭānḍi* ("horn *vaṭṭānḍi*") on each side. The *aṅ vaṭṭānḍi* have to hook, manipulate, and control the horns during the pull. They are generally strong young men between the ages of twenty and thirty; all of them are thoroughly involved in their team allegiances. Since the injunction on purity does not apply to alcohol, these *aṅ vaṭṭānḍi* are often utterly drunk during the whole course of the festivities. Yet they too observe strictly all the norms of purity along with the other villagers. In addition, they neither shave nor rub oil on their heads for the duration of the ceremonies. If the *vaṭṭānḍi* are perceived as observing *sil* (the precepts) in the Buddhist sense, the *aṅ vaṭṭānḍi* are described as Brahmans (*brahmaṇayo*) by villagers—they must have strong *bhakti*, or devotion. By the term Brahman the villagers refer not to the Indian variety but rather to the unkempt Hindu ascetic *sādhus* they are familiar with at Kataragama. The *aṅ vaṭṭānḍi* are permitted to oil their heads and shave on the thirteenth day, when the shrine doors are ceremonially open for public worship. Thus one of the interesting features of the *aṅkeḷiya* is the alternation of license and restraint—restraint based on pollution taboos, which are widely observed; and license pertaining to alcohol consumption, which is also widely practiced, and to the abuse hurled at the defeated side during the main festivities.

The *aṅkeḷiya* festivities, as I noted, last fifteen days. On the first day the festivities ceremonially open with the *kolu aṅ* ("youth horn") ritual, where only boys under eigh-

2. Normally the unhusked rice or paddy is boiled and then dried in the sun and husked in order to increase the size of the grains.

teen participate. The theory is that there is no conflict or *vādu* (from Sinhala *vāde*, "conflict," "argument," "debate") during *kolu aṅ* This does not mean that the minors who participate in it do not take it seriously. They obviously do, and the victors sing the *hīya*, or paean of exultation. The adults, however, do not take it seriously. Hence adult members of both teams go together into the forest along with *vaṭṭāṇḍi* and *kapurāla*s to cut vines for making the ropes and coils (*pērās*) for the youth horns (*kolu aṅ*). By contrast, on the sixth day each team goes separately to cut vines for the main *aṅkeḷiya* rituals where the adults participate.

These vines are brought back and made into coils for the *uḍupila* post, the horn tree (*aṅ gaha*). While the coils are being looped round the *aṅ gaha* by the *vaṭṭāṇḍi* of the upper team (*pēraha vakkaranava*, "pouring the *pērās*"), the *kapurāla* of the Alut Deviyo shrine becomes possessed (*ārūḍha*) and dances the *alut deviyo näṭuma* ("dance of Alut Deviyo"). In his possessed state he utters *pēna*, or prophecies. The god (resident in the *kapurāla*) asks why he has been called at such an "ungodly hour." An official replies that it is to hold an *aṅkeḷiya* and asks the god to banish (*gasā duru*) all deadly planetary constellations (*maru yōga*) if any exist. The god says he will, and (generally) prophesies that there will be no *varada* ("wrongs," "calamities") for the village, diseases will not arise, and work and jobs (*räkīrakṣāval*) will be plentiful. Then the *pērās* is tied to the *aṅ gaha*. Soon afterward victory is formally given to Pattini (*yaṭipila*) in a ritual that dramatically illustrates the sexual nature of *aṅkeḷiya*. It is performed in the following manner. A miniature "horn" from a thin branch of a *mālittan* (*Wrightia zeylanica*) bush is tied to the coils on the *aṅ gaha*. This is the *uḍupila* horn. Then the "goddess" is hooked to this *uḍupila* horn and the *uḍupila* horn is broken. How is the goddess hooked to the *uḍupila* horn? In Pānama there are no statues of the deities. Rather, the face of the deity is carved on a two-dimensional slab of silver and mounted on the short arm of an old ceremonial horn kept in the inner sanctum of the shrine. Images of both Pattini and Alut Deviyo are mounted on horns in this manner. When victory has to be allocated formally to the *yaṭipila*, the *kapurāla* ceremonially brings this image to the horn terminus and places it (simulating hooking) against the miniature *uḍupila* horn and breaks the latter. This act seems to indicate that hooking and breaking the horns is a symbolic way of representing sexual intercourse.

About 8:00 P.M. the horn of the upper team is tied to the *vāran* ("tug rope") and the lower team horn is hooked onto it for the *kolu aṅ* ritual. The post of the lower team—the thunderbolt tree—is not used for this occasion. Instead, the two long *vāran*, or ropes, are tied to the *yaṭipila* horn, and each team pulls at its rope. Since small "horns" are used, they snap easily. The winning horn is paraded around the arena, to the shouts of "*hī-hai-hō*" by the youths of the village.

Main *Aṅkeḷiya* Rituals (*Mahā Aṅkeḷiya*) at Pānama

The main *aṅkeḷiya* rituals start on the morning of the sixth day and go on for seven days. The proceedings start in much the same manner as with the youth horn ritual. Initially members of both teams go out to cut vines—not together, in concord, as in the youth game, but separately as befits the *vādu*, or conflict, nature of the main *aṅkeḷiya*. Meanwhile the thunderbolt tree of the lower team, which was not used in the minor rites, is ceremonially brought into the horn terminus (*aṅ handiya*). It is covered in white cloth (*piruvaṭa*), and an offering (*aṅ madē*; Tamil *maṭai*) is placed before it. At about 11:00 A.M. the *kapurāla* of the *uḍupila* becomes possessed by Alut Deviyo and utters prophecies like the earlier ones. Then the *henakaňda* is raised and pivoted in the channel. Soon afterward, the umbrellalike structures known as the *dummalgēs* ("incense house"), the "seat" of the *vaṭṭāṇḍi*, are constructed. In each *dummalgē* there is a weak miniature horn, (*deviyannē aňga*, "god's horn," since it is hooked to the deity), to be used for hooking onto the deities later when victory has to be assigned ritually to *one* deity.

Each night, through seven successive nights, as many as four or five horns may be broken. The short arms of the horns are carefully reinforced; then each side measures its horn at the point below the crosspole (*rikili polla*) with a piece of coconut leaf, which it sends by a messenger to the other side to match it with the opposed horn. After the horns are matched in size they are ceremonially brought into the sacred area for hooking. This generally is expected to occur about 6:00 P.M.; however, in the several rituals I witnessed it was done between 9:00 and 10:00 P.M. The *vaṭṭāṇḍi* ceremonially takes the miniature "god horn" (*deiyannē aňga*) to the place where the competition horn is being dressed. Then both horns are "conducted" in procession to the arena. The horn of the lower team is brought first, under a red canopy, on the head of the *vaṭṭāṇḍi*, who wears a mouth mask and has a white shawl (*piruvaṭa*) on his head. Behind him is another man carrying the "god horn"; on one side is a washerman. In front of the canopy a man carrying a *venṭāyama* ("bell cane") leads the procession; behind the canopy trail diverse members of the lower team shouting their paean of exultation: "*hī-hai-hō!*" to the beat of drums, the bursts of firecrackers, and the flare of torches. The procession circumambulates three times *counterclockwise* (i.e., to the left, according to informants) enclosing both *uḍupila* and *yaṭipila* shrines in their rounds. After this the horn is ceremonially placed at the horn terminus (*aṅ handiya*). The procession of the lower team starts soon after in the same manner, except that the horn is carried under a white canopy and they perform a *clockwise* circumambulation (i.e., a rightward movement). This order of precedence is very important and is clearly recognized by the officials, who considered it "the law of this place." Summed up, it means that all proceedings must commence with Alut Deviyo, and Alut Deviyo must go ahead of Pattini in all processional events, because his is the male side (*pirimi pätta*). Yet this principle is "reversed" in the circumambulation rites: the male consort performs a counterclockwise (inferior) movement whereas the goddess moves clockwise, as befits a "superior."

Just before the horns are hooked (*aṅ karalānava*), the *kapurāla* of the upper team once again becomes possessed by Alut Deviyo. Then the horns are hooked. According to theory, the first competition (*vādu*) of the main *aṅkeḷiya* must be won by Alut Deviyo (upper team). If the upper team does not win it is a *kiluṭa* ("impurity") for the village. Furthermore, if the lower team wins several consecutive games, the *kapurāla* of the upper team has to be possessed by Alut Deviyo till the god's side wins. This is in fact what occurred in 1968. On no condition, however, must the main *aṅkeḷiya* rituals extend beyond the seventh day.

Let me now give an example of a typical *aṅkeḷiya* ritual from my notes. When the horns are brought to the "horn terminus" they are again measured for the final checkup, as before, just below the crosspole. Even at this point there is a great deal of argument and mutual recrimination. Every single horn that is to be played that night (generally three or four) has to be measured. If disagreements occur one of three things must be done: a correct size horn must be found and substituted for the oversize horn; the oversize horn must be scraped to size, or the undersize horn must be enlarged with splices (*koṭṭa ka-*

vanava) and rewound. During this preliminary period the obscene language used (e.g., "mother fucker") is phenomenal. After this dialectic is over, the tug ropes are brought out and placed on rock slabs near the two posts by the *vaṭṭāṇḍi*, who pay them obeisance. Then the horns are hooked by the *aṅ vaṭṭāṇḍi* ("horn *vaṭṭāṇḍi*") in a complicated process, and soon afterward participants on both sides pull at their tug ropes. After a few minutes one of the horns breaks.

After the horn is broken the victor horn is covered in red cloth and held aloft, and obscenities of the following sort are performed.

Rank sexual abuse is verbalized, generally pertaining to mother/son and sibling incest.
Obscene gestures pertaining to sexual intercourse are made.
False and obscene (invocations) are made to deities who do not exist in the pantheon, beginning with the phrase "*Ōm namo* . . ."
Prayers to the Buddha are parodied.
Bali are images used in rituals for warding off ill luck and propitiating planetary deities. Here, however, images of the opponents are made and humiliating acts are performed on them.
Nude dances are performed; sarongs are raised and genitals are exposed.
Songs (*baila* and *sivupada*) containing obscenities and imprecations are sung. (See text 52 for some typical obscene songs.)

My general impression was of unbridled enjoyment of obscenities unparalleled in my experience elsewhere in Sri Lanka and rarely equaled in the ethnographic literature. Even people in the temporary teashops outside the shrine premises join in the "fun," hurling insults at various people on the "other side." After the obscenities are over (they may last as much as an hour, sometimes more) the victorious horn—if the upper team has won—is taken in procession counterclockwise round the two shrines, once, with the people singing their paean, "*hī-hai-hō!*" This paean (text 51) asks the goddess to bring prosperity, fertility, and protection to the village.

Then commences the *varadaravanava* ("turning back the wrong") ritual. The meaning of *varadaravanava* (from *varada*, "wrong," and *haravanava*, "turning round," "reversing") is a simple rite, which Yalman has misinterpreted (Yalman 1966, pp. 209–12). In the *aṅkeḷiya* the winning side shouts obscenities and hurls insults at the defeated "kinsmen." These insults are, from the point of view of the conventions that prevail *outside* the ritual situation, utterly "wrong" (*varada*). There is a feeling of "discontent" by the losing side and a possibility, informants rightly say, that people will be offended by the wrong words that have been uttered. The *varadaravanava* ritual corrects these "wrongs," so that the losing side will not take offense. The general procedure is to utter obscene songs then to correct the insults by forgiveness songs; then back again to the obscene songs, and so forth.

The *varadaravanava* ritual is performed in the following manner. After the obscenities and insulting songs are sung, three people on the winning side come in single file to the shrine of the losing side. They all wear white shawls (*piruvaṭa*) on their heads; the person in the middle has a cane with a small "anklet" attached to its head (*venṭāyama* or *vēväla*). These three face the *vaṭṭāṇḍi* of the losing side, who is sitting in the *dummalgē* with other members of his team standing behind him. The man in the middle utters a line of verse, hitting the ground with the *venṭāyama* as he does this, while the other two act as chorus.

The *varadaravanava* ritual is never performed consecutively by any particular team. If, for example, the upper team wins, it may perform *varadaravanava*. But if it wins consecutively it performs no further *varadaravanava*. However, if the lower team wins it (the lower team) can perform *varadaravanava* (see texts 52 and 53).

Valibānava: Lowering of the Ropes

The main *aṅkeḷiya* rituals (*maha aṅkeḷiya*) are over on the twelfth day. On the thirteenth morning women are permitted for the first time to enter the shrine premises. The doors of the shrines, however, are not yet open. The doors can be opened only after the performance of the *valibānava* rituals, either in the late hours of the morning or in early afternoon. *Valibānava* means "pulling of the tug rope" or "lowering of the ropes." The purpose of the ritual is to eliminate the spirit of competition and restore equality of status to the two sides. The ritual is a simple one. Two tough, oversize ceremonial horns kept in the two shrines are brought out into the horn terminus (*aṅ handiya*) and formally hooked. Seven tugs (*vali*) are performed, and no victory is given (or rather both sides are victors), since the horns are not allowed to break. Informants say that the *valibānava* ritual is for females to witness, and true enough this is the first "*aṅkeḷiya*" ritual officially seen by women. The seven tugs (*vali*) probably represent the seven nights of the main *aṅkeḷiya* rituals. Thus *valibānava* is a "fictitious" or "ideal" *aṅkeḷiya* ritual designed for the women to see. Since this is the way men "expect" the women to perceive the "horn play," *valibānava* is rather important to our interpretation. There is no partisan jubilation and dancing associated with *valibānava*.

After the lowering of the ropes the temple doors are opened, and people can come to the shrines of Alut Deviyo and Pattini to fulfill their vows and worship the deities. Most people assemble at the shrine premises on the following morning, except for about twenty-four "nonbelieving" households. Even folk from the villages within a radius of about twenty miles of Pānama—Sinhalas, Hindus, Tamils, and to a lesser extent Tamil-speaking Muslims—come here to fulfill their vows (*bāra*).

As elsewhere in Buddhist and Hindu Sri Lanka, the *bāra* generally consists of images (*rūpa*) and coconut seedlings (representing a "life") offered to the deities ("a life for a life"). In addition, people give the conventional *paṅḍuru* (coins), and they light camphor (*kapuru*) at the steps at the entrance of the shrine. Other offerings include rice, flowers, fruits, oil, and sweetmeats that are later eaten by the officials or distributed among their friends. The only unusual feature of this part of the ceremonies is that people worship the deities in the conventional Sinhala style with folded hands, then cross their hands, touch their ears, and hit two knocks on the head in the Hindu folk style of worship. Hindus who come here always worship in the latter manner.

The Parade of the Deity

On the fourteenth night the goddess is taken in procession with drums, firecrackers, and songs to every household in the village. The traditional practice was for the goddess to be paraded, but not the male deity. However, in 1960 this practice was changed and both deities were paraded. In the procession I witnessed in 1965, the procession broke in two after it entered the village. The Alut Deviyo procession went to households where the husband belonged to the *uḍupila*, and the Pattini procession went to *yaṭipila* households. The explanation generally given was that this was due to the increased size of the village.

This explanation is not entirely satisfactory, and in the ritual I witnessed in 1967 the traditional practice of Pattini alone parading the village was restored after an agreement between the two sides. I describe the 1967 procession below.

The ritual preliminaries begin about 5:00 P.M. with victory given to Pattini. As usual, this commences with the image of Alut Deviyo's being decked ceremonially and brought in an ornamental box, under a canopy. Following the image of the god is the "god's horn" (kept in the "incense house"). A special feature of the procession is the group of *lī keḷiya* ("stick dancers") who head it singing songs from the *marā ipäddīma* ("killing and resurrection"). The Alut Deviyo procession comes in front of the Pattini shrine and waits facing the shrine. Then Pattini is also brought out ceremonially in procession. The two processions, with Alut Deviyo in front, circumambulate the shrines three times (embracing both shrines), counterclockwise (to the left). After this Alut Deviyo is taken into his shrine and ceremonially placed in the inner sanctum. Pattini, however, is placed on the rock slab near the thunderbolt tree (*henakaňda*), ready for the procession into the village. Then Pattini is hooked to the weak "god's horn" (*deviyannē aňga*) of the upper team; the latter is broken, and victory is formally given to Pattini. The Pattini procession circumambulates the Pattini shrine three times clockwise (to the right), and with this the procession to the village commences. Though only the goddess is paraded that night, the *kapurāla*s and the two Basnāyaka Nilames (trustees) of both shrines participate in the procession. The intention here is very clear and is explicitly recognized by the villagers: the competitive games are over, and Pattini is for both sides. Tonight the shrine premises will be desolate, except for two paid watchmen, the two *vaṭṭānḍi*, and the two invisible guardian gods (Parakāsa Deviyo), all of whom protect the sacred premises (*piṭiya rakinava*), and keep Alut Deviyo company, since he cannot be neglected and left alone while Pattini is parading the village.

The parade is headed by *lī keḷiya* ("stick dance") of both teams, singing the *hīya* (paean) mentioned earlier (text 51). At the entrance to the village there is a large stand (*mässa*) with an elaborate *maḍē* (an offering containing rice, flowers, coconut, camphor [*kapuru*], betel, and areca nut) by the *gamarāla* ("village head"). Traditionally the *maḍē* was offered by four *gamarāla*s of the village, but since most of the paddy lands are now owned by a Tamil absentee landlord from Jaffna, his representative acts the *gamarāla* role and offers the *maḍē*. The *kapurāla* lights the camphor and cuts a coconut in two with a knife, symbolizing the consecration of the *maḍē* and its acceptance by the goddess. From this point onward the *lī keḷiya* dancers go in separate groups from house to house, singing secular songs and dancing, utterly drunk. The Pattini procession, headed by drummers followed by the deity and a small group shouting "*hī-hai-hō!*" visit every house in the village. Each household has constructed an altar outside the house containing the following items: a brass pot filled with turmeric water, camphor, betel leaves, flowers, and an oil lamp. Alongside the pot are placed three mango leaves, half of each leaf appearing above the rim of the pot. On top of the pot a husked coconut is placed upright. As the procession nears the house, the residents light firecrackers. One resident of the house pours water from the pot in a long line stretching from the house gate to the altar; the goddess is taken over the wet line by the *kapurāla* of the lower team, who performs most of the "ritual." The wet line is a substitute for the white *pāvaḍa* ("foot cloths") generally laid on the ground for the deity to parade on.

The lower team *kapurāla* takes the coconut from the pot and lays it flat on the altar. He then places the "horn image" (the image of Pattini tied to the *ṛikilla*, i.e., the crosspole used in the ritual) on the altar so that the *rikilla* balances on the coconut. He sprays turmeric water on the altar, incenses the altar, lights camphor, and lays betel leaves and flowers before the image. Meanwhile the *kapurāla* of the upper team, with others in the audience, sings songs of praise on Pattini known as *mal vahada*. The people in the house worship the image and put *pañḍuru* (coins) into the water pot, and the *kapurāla* lustrates the members of the household with sacred water and makes a *tilaka* mark on their foreheads with sandalwood paste.

Then the *kapurāla* of the upper team takes the lighted wick from the oil lamp, holds it under the roof of the house above the altar, extinguishes the wick with turmeric water, and utters a variant of the famous lines describing the quelling of the fires of Madurai:

Hēmē deviyo hēmē mahimā
Hēmē mal väsi vässē mehemā
Madurāvē gini nivvē mehemā.

Thus the gods in all their might
Showered flowery rain from the skies
That's how the fires of Madurā were quenched.

The idea, informants say, is to avoid fires and accidents and in general bring blessings on each household. As one *kapurāla* put it: "May the troubles [*dōsa*] be extinguished [*nivva*], as Pattini quelled the fire in Madurā." The coins (*pañḍuru*) and offerings are taken by the *kapurāla* (by his assistants), while the oil from the lamps and the turmeric water are kept by the household for use as cooling substances (to be drunk or applied to the body).

The procession visits every household in this manner except those that have not constructed altars (indicating some pollution). These activities are over at dawn, and about 6:00 A.M. the goddess is taken back to the sacred premises. However, she is not taken inside the shrine, since the journey into the village may have exposed her to impurities and sources of pollution. She is temporarily placed on the rock slab near the thunderbolt tree (*henakañda*).

Water Sports, or *Diya Keḷiya*: Fifteenth Day

The final and very important ritual of the festival, is the *diya keḷiya* ("water sports"), which commemorates either the incident when Pattini was discovered by the merchant princes as they were sporting in the waters of the Kāvēri or the completion of the Kāvēri project by Karikāla (text 50, pp. 252–53). However, the text known as the *diya keḷiya*, which is part of the low-country "thirty-five songbooks" is not sung at the Pānama water sports ritual. The *diya keḷiya* at Pānama is also sometimes known as the *diya käpīma*, or "water cutting," but the water cutting aspect of the ritual is not emphasized.

The preliminary rites for the *diya keḷiya* start about 6:00 A.M. in the sacred premises. Here, according to informants, another innovation has taken place. These are the *kāvaḍi* dances traditionally performed by Hindus in honor of the god Skanda of Kataragama but now adopted by Buddhists for a similar purpose. Their adoption here has obviously been due to the current vogue of Skanda worship combined with the close proximity of Pānama to the main shrine of Skanda at Kataragama. *Kāvaḍi* dancers wear red—the color of

Skanda—and while they dance they hold above their shoulders the *kāvaḍi*, a wooden arch decked with peacock feathers (real or imitation) representing the peacock vehicle (*vāhana*) of the deity. These dances are generally performed by the young bucks of the village.

The dancers of the upper team, about fifteen of them, arrive first, obtain permission (*avasara*) from officials of both sides, then worship Pattini at her shrine and obtain her permission. They dance before her shrine singing songs from the *marā ipäddīma* in modern *baila* ("swing") and film-music singing styles, to the accompaniment of a European instrument, the harmonium. The main singer is in the middle, surrounded by a circle of dancers. He utters one line, and this is repeated by the others who, while singing, dance round and round in a circle. They then proceed to the Alut Deviyo temple and, after obeisance, perform similar dances. Half an hour later a group of *kāvaḍi* dancers from the lower team performs in a similar fashion, first *inside* the outer sanctum of the Pattini shrine, then outside it, and finally before the Alut Deviyo shrine. While this is going on, the two *vaṭṭānḍi* (from the two sides), wearing mouth masks, bring two pots of turmeric water. They take it to the horn tree or *aṅ gaha* (upper team post) and worship it, after uttering invocations. They repeat the performance at the Pattini shrine. This water will be used to lustrate, purify, and bless the *kāvaḍi* dancers, and others, on both sides.

About 8:00 A.M. Alut Deviyo is given ritual victory in the usual manner—the weak "god's horn" (*deviyannē aňga*) is tied to the thunderbolt tree (*henakaňda*), hooked to the image of the god mounted on the horn, and broken. After this the *kapurāla* of the upper team becomes possessed by Alut Deviyo at their post, the *aṅ gaha*. During the first ten minutes he sings *mal vahada* ("songs of the deity"), then suddenly works himself into a frenzy. He has a billhook (*kätta*) in one hand and holds the *aṅ gaha*, hitting his head on it several times to indicate obeisance and submission. He comes to the post of the lower team and repeats this action, then goes back to his own post. In a brief utterance he predicts fertility and prosperity for the village, an adequate fall of rain for the whole of the Ruhuṇa raṭa (Pānama was part of the old Ruhuṇa raṭa). He then cuts the coils (*pērās*) on both posts (*henakaňda* and *aṅ gaha*) with his knife and falls down in a "faint." Someone lustrates him with water, and he gets up in a few moments. It should be remembered that it is always the *kapurāla* of the upper team who becomes possessed by Alut Deviyo; it is inconceivable that the pure goddess Pattini could possess anyone. Then people assemble to extricate the thunderbolt tree (*henakaňda*) from its socket and logs (*häpini kaňdan*) and cover it in a white cloth (*piruvaṭa*). Later it will be dragged into the neighboring bush and placed alongside a stream that gives water to the Pānama fields, where it will lie till next year's celebration.

After the lowering of the thunderbolt tree (*henakaňda*), the *diya keḷiya* procession is ready to start. Both deities must take part in the procession, and there can be no team conflict (*pilavādu*) here. The procession is headed by two "priests" known as *sāmi*s; each has a stick in his hand for "water cutting." The stick represents the *mugura* ("mace," "rod") probably the prototypical rod of Gajabāhu. They are supposed to be possessed, but "sodden drunk" would be a better characterization of their state. Then follow the *kāvaḍi* dances, consisting of two groups: the adult males mentioned earlier and young schoolgirls wearing white school uniforms with red bands signifying the color of the god Skanda of Kataragama. Then follow the drummers and people with "bell canes" (*venṭāyama*), who sing songs about Pattini. One of the most popular songs describes Pattini and Pālaňga going out in search of the *sapu* tree, but other kinds of flowers bloom on the branches that spring from the different directions of the tree. Ultimately they discover the *sapu* flower, which blooms from the end of the trunk of the *sapu* tree. The content of the myth is the same as that of text 54 from Biyanvila (pp. 419–23).

After this comes the washerman. He is followed by the main image of Alut Deviyo, dressed and mounted on the horn and carried under a canopy in his "box" on the shoulders of one team member. Behind this are other images and (phallic) symbols of the deity such as spears, arrows, and axes carried by various team members. All these people wear mouth masks. Then Pattini follows in a similar manner. At the exit of the premises an offering (*maḍē*) is given to the deities in the manner described earlier. Then the procession proceeds toward the village, and at the village entrance there is once again an offering by the *gamarāla*, the agent of the Tamil landowner. On the way to the beach several offerings are made by various groups of villagers. The *sāmi*s run about in a (drunken) frenzy, and villagers hurl sarcastic and insulting remarks at them, dousing them with large pots of turmeric and margosa water. All along the route people await the procession with offerings or pots of turmeric water (or both); some pour this cleansing water on the images of the deities carried in the procession. The last offering before the procession arrives at the beach is given by the Tamil washermen of Pānama. Then the procession leaves the residential area for the beach, in the dry, scorching sand. The crowd assembles near the beach in a field called *ullēvala* and from there heads to the sea. At the beach the *kapurāla*s present their offerings. The two *sāmi*s then give small margosa branches to each of the assembled men, women, and children. Then the two *sāmi*s jump into the sea carrying the image of Alut Deviyo. Pattini is taken into the sea by another villager, while the *kapurāla* stays on the beach. This is the signal for the assembled people to jump exuberantly into the sea. Some people collect water in small bottles at the point where the deities are immersed. Ideally what *should* have happened was as follows. The two possessed *sāmi*s should jump into the sea with the two sticks (*mugura*, rod) and part the waters as Gajabāhu did. Then two others who carry the images of the deities should plunge them under water at the place where the waters parted. But it is doubtful whether the *sāmi*s in their alcoholic stupor could accomplish what they were expected to do.

After the water sports, the crowd goes back helter-skelter to the shrine premises. Some persons run there and are doused on the way with buckets of cooling turmeric water. They remain in the shrine premises till the *kapurāla*s arrive. The images are also kept outside on the rock slab. When the *kapurāla*s arrive they put the images back into their shrines. The last act is a communal feast given by the village head (*gamarāla*). Two large pots of rice are cooked and consecrated at the two shrines. Then all the assembled people—men, women, children, Tamils, Muslims, Sinhalas, and all the several castes—eat in the same place, of a common meal. This is about 12:00 noon, and the festivities are over.

Aṅkeḷiya at Malidūva, Mātara District

The Ideal Method of Horn Pulling

According to ideal norms prevailing here, the horns should be pulled for seven days. During the first three days the lower team's horn is tied to its post (*henakaṅda*), and the horn of the upper team is tied to the horn tree (*aṅ gaha*); the upper horn should break, and the lower one must therefore win. The lower team's horn (that is, the prospective winner) is consecrated (*pē*), while the upper horn is unconsecrated. All the participants should shout "*hōiya!*" after the horn snaps, and there has to be a circumambulation rite, but no invocation (*puvata*, literally, "proclamation") is uttered. During the next three afternoons the positions are reversed, and the upper team wins the game. But during these three days the "coconut game" (*polkeḷiya*) is performed in the evenings after each *aṅkeḷiya* (see pp. 401–2). At the conclusion of this phase of the *aṅkeḷiya* the earlier procedure is adopted except that the circumambulation of the horn tree (*aṅ gaha*) is followed by circumambulation of the Buddha shrine at the bo tree, culminating in the invocation. No competition should occur during any of these performances, and victory is ensured for the horn that is expected to win by pitting it against a weaker opposing horn. No more than three *aṅkeḷiya* rituals should be held during this phase, though the coconut game (*polkeḷiya*) rituals could go on for many days more. A *pēḷiyāma* (parade or procession ritual) should be performed after the second spell of *aṅkeḷiya* rituals and before the final (seventh) *aṅkeḷiya*. This last *aṅkeḷiya*, which is highly competitive, is performed after the *gammaḍuva* is over but before the communal feast (*dāna*) at noon. Horns of the same size and strength are pitted against each other, but they are never made *pē* ("consecrated"). The two horns are then tied to their respective posts. There is no coconut breaking on this day, and the invocation is not sung. Circumambulation is performed around the horn tree (*aṅ gaha*) as well as the Buddha shrine at the bo tree. Traditionally—though no longer to the same extent—competition was fierce, and the winning side jumped over the shoulders of the losing side, who squatted on the ground in humiliation. Songs insulting the losers were also sung. In the *aṅkeḷiya* rituals at Malidūva only one horn is broken each day.

According to the rules, eighteen villages in the area around Malidūva are involved in the *aṅkeḷiya*. Each family in these villages contributes the following items for the ritual: one measure of rice, two coconuts, one rupee. If rice and coconuts cannot be given, a cash payment is substituted. In addition the organizers of the ritual collect coconut thatch and beams from these villagers for constructing the sheds necessary for the *gammaḍuva*.

Since the *aṅkeḷiya* is held in Malidūva village, the organization of the ritual is in the hands of this village and its neighbor, Bōpiṭiya. "In old times" Malidūva was divided into two physically separate regions; the upper side of the village was allocated to the upper team (*uḍupila*) and the "lower side" to the lower team (*yaṭipila*). If one changes the geographical "side" one also changes the ritual side, according to the chief *vaṭṭāṇḍi* of the upper team. Today this rule no longer operates; allocation to sides is on the basis of "village" affiliation and patrilineal inheritance for males. In general, people of Malidūva belong to the upper team while Bōpiṭiya folk form the lower team. Outsiders and nonvillagers who participate in the ritual generally join the side to which they were affiliated in their villages of origin, or they choose sides on a purely individual basis. Thus the present *grāma sēvaka* ("headman") of Malidūva is a lower team member in his native village twelve miles away and takes the same side in Malidūva. In practice, people could change sides by personal choice even in these two villages, as, for example, if two brothers have fallen out. However, this is rare, and my informants insisted that all members of a family belonged to one side. While wives as females were excluded from the ritual and had to watch it from outside the boundary (*sīmā*), they nevertheless belonged to the same teams as their husbands. Earlier team affiliations, if any, were given up at marriage.

In assessing the statements of the *vaṭṭandi* regarding the "rules," one must recognize that there has been a discontinuity in the performance of *aṅkeḷiya* at Malidūva. The *aṅkeḷiya* ritual I witnessed in 1956 was performed to ward off a serious drought that affected the area. This ritual was held after thirteen years of nonperformance. In 1966, ten years later, I witnessed another *aṅkeḷiya*, performed as a result of a failure of the rice crop, but none had been performed in the intervening period. The 1966 ritual was so successful (partly owing to financial assistance from the anthropologist!) that the villages held another in 1967 to ward off a serious epidemic of chicken pox and crop disease. Thus, except for the last two rituals, there have been major breaks in the continuity of these performances. This discontinuity in tradition was also manifested in the pattern of recruitment of *vaṭṭāṇḍi*. For example in 1966 the *vaṭṭāṇḍi* were as follows:

Uḍupila (upper team)	*Residence*
Malidūva Yaṭiyalagē Ovinis (chief *vaṭṭāṇḍi*)	Malidūva
Brampi Jayasiṃha Don Cārlis Vikramasiṃha	Malidūva
Yaṭipila (lower team)	*Residence*
Malidūva Liyanagē Upānis (chief *vaṭṭāṇḍi*)	Malidūva
Malidūva Liyanagē Gārlis	Bōpiṭiya
Araccige Pīris Hāmi	Bōpiṭiya

First, as far as the *vaṭṭāṇḍi* are concerned the division into villages prevailed except for the chief *vaṭṭāṇḍi* of the lower team, Upānis, who belonged to Malidūva village. Upānis explained the discrepancy in the following manner. The "original" *vaṭṭāṇḍi* of the lower team were Gammāraccigē Baburāla and Gammāraccigē Elias Rāla, both of Kammalgoda, a hamlet belonging to Bōpiṭiya. There were no *vaṭṭāṇḍi* for the upper team, implying that there had been a long discontinuity in tradition. They also could not find any "pupils" to continue the tradition in Bōpiṭiya (lower team) itself, so they trained Malidūva Liyanage Don Dines for the lower team side and Malidūva Yaṭiyalagē Babun for the upper side, both residents of Malidūva. When they died, Don Dines's son Upānis, of Malidūva, took over the lower team leadership and trained the present *vaṭṭāṇḍi*, while Yaṭiyalagē Ovinis, son of Babun, did the same for the upper team. If this account is valid, it is further evidence of a serious discontinuity in tradition.

As elsewhere, the chief actors in this ritual are the *kapurāla* and the *vaṭṭāṇḍi* belonging to the two teams. *Vaṭṭāṇḍi* procure well-tested horns and ropes, supervise the stage setting for the ritual, hook the horns, and shout the slogans and the ritual shouts of joy that the villagers echo. During the festival period the *vaṭṭāṇḍi* have to observe certain prescriptions and proscriptions, as in Pānama—they must observe the norms of purity and pollution, live in special huts, and eat specially cooked foods.

Unlike the situation in Pānama, actual horns are used for hooking in Malidūva—the lower part of the antler and the brow tine of the sambar deer (*Rusa aristotelis*), the former being shortened to about six inches and the latter cut down to two inches. The tougher the horns, the more greatly they are valued. Here also victorious horns are prized heirlooms that have been in certain families for generations. In Malidūva one of the horns used was a champion, always emerging victorious. It was named Vali rāja ("wild king") because of its magnificent strength—a king among horns! Another famous horn was named Vaṅdurukudā ("humped monkey") because a hump on it resembled the anus of a monkey.

Since the Malidūva tradition insists there be no competition on the first six days, it is necessary that a small horn be matched with a larger one. But on the last day, when competition is keen, horns of equal size are matched. Although the lengths of the competing horns may vary, it is essential that the circumference of the two horns at the point where the long arm narrows before meeting the short arm be the same, since this is the most vulnerable area and most liable to snap during the pull.

The dressing of the horns on the last day involves considerable skill and patience, and the *vaṭṭāṇḍi* vie in their efforts to strengthen their respective horns. The long arm of each horn is wrapped tightly with bull hide, all except two inches from the top and an inch or two below. Then a long iron nail is pushed through a hole (already made) in the long arm of the horn just above the reinforced area, jutting out an inch or two on each side. This nail holds in position the coil of ropes (*vāran*) now tied to the end of the horn. Tying these coils is the work of the expert *vaṭṭāṇḍi*. Three people squat in a circle. One places the horn on his thigh and holds it firmly. Two others seated on either side tie the end of the horn with a rope, then take the two ends of the rope round a stake planted a foot or two away, bring the ends back to the arm of the horn, and wind them round the horn. This is done ten times. Then the same procedure is repeated, except that now a knot is tied on the horn. Ten knots (or more) are tied in this manner. After each knot the horn is beaten with a mallet to tighten it. When the requisite number of coils are woven, the stake is removed, leaving a ring of rope and knots (see fig. 11). Then the ring of ropes is tucked together and the horn is covered with a white cloth (*piruvaṭa*, "shawl") and placed in a hollow of the *nuga* or banyan tree (*Ficus altissima*) growing nearby. This hollow is known as the *aṅ peṭṭiya*, or "horn box." The same thing is done to the competing horn.

The ring of rope is necessary to link the horn to the coil of jungle creepers (*pērässa*) attached to the post of each team with a tough ironwood crossbar called the *aṅ polla* ("horn stick") in the Malidūva tradition.

After the horns are dressed, the two horns that are used to break the smaller ones on the first six days are deposited in the "horn box" in the hollow of the banyan (*nuga*) tree and consecrated.

The consecration of the two horns is, of course, an essential item in the ritual, and as always lighting the lamp is the first step. As in most places, a *mal päla*, or altar, of the usual type is erected—in Malidūva in front of the huge banyan tree with its massive foliage and aerial roots. The customary procedure in Malidūva is for the *kapurāla* to place the horns on the altar, sprinkle it with turmeric, and offer a conventional invocation to Pattini. After this the horns are deposited in a hollow among the intertwining aerial roots before they are used for the ritual. The horns that are to be broken are dressed on each day of the ritual.

I shall describe the sixth day of an *aṅkeḷiya* held in Malidūva in 1956, when the upper team (*uḍupila*) has to win, according to theory. In the afternoon (3:30) the *kapurāla* enters the arena to bless the horns. The stage is set for the ceremony. The huge banyan tree serves as the post (*aṅ gaha*, or "horn tree") for the upper team. A few yards away opposite is their opponents' post, the thunderbolt tree, a coconut palm trunk about ten feet high. Its broad end, with the roots cut into a round lump, faces up, and its narrow end is

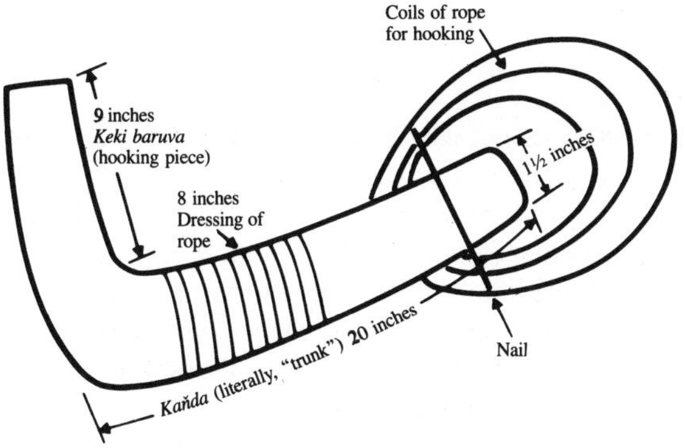

Fig. 11. The *aṅkeḷiya* horn as prepared at Malidūva.

fitted into a groove dug at the bottom of a pit about three feet wide, two feet long, and four feet deep. Stones neatly placed in the groove ensure that the upturned tree moves easily in the socket. A coil of thick jungle creepers (*pērässa*) is wound around each post.

The *kapurāla* lights a clay lamp on the altar. One of the *vaṭṭānḍi* then carries a pot of turmeric water to the bo tree, and after worshiping the tree and the Buddha statue there, he comes back and gives the pot to the *kapurāla*, who incenses the pot with resin and then lustrates himself with turmeric water. While he chants he sprays the arena floor with an areca sprig dipped into the pot of turmeric water as the drummer beats the festival note on his drum. The chant, which is a long, conventional one, invokes the goddess Pattini to hear with her divine ear his complaint, look upon the villagers with her divine eye, and in her great kindness banish all diseases from the villages. The full recital of the plaint (*kannalavva*) takes half an hour. The *kapurāla* lustrates the *vaṭṭānḍi* and then the audience with the turmeric water while he utters the conventional blessing—may you live long—in a slow drawl.

Now it is time for hooking the horns (*aṅ karalānava*). The thunderbolt tree of the lower team (which when not in use is pushed forward toward the post of the upper team) is now strengthened, to the shout of "*hōiya!*" First the horn of the upper team is tied to its post. The *vāran*, or rope rings around the horn, are placed over the *pērässa*, or coils of vines loosely wound round the tree, and a stout pole thrust between the two rings of rope, tightly interlocking them, holding the *vāran* firmly against the *pērässa*. Then the lower team's horn is hooked to the upper team's horn by the *vaṭṭānḍi*, and the rope rings of the lower horn are interlocked with the coils (*pērässa*) on the thunderbolt tree. The *vaṭṭānḍi* cover their respective horns with a white shawl (*piruvaṭa*), and one *vaṭṭānḍi* from each side holds his horn, poised for the fray. The *kapurāla* lustrates the rope as well as the teams with turmeric water and utters "*āyubōvēva*" ("may you live long"). The menfolk of the village hold on to the tug rope—a rope about twenty-five feet long inserted through a hole at the top of the *henakaňda* (*yaṭipila* post). The atmosphere is tense with anticipation and suppressed excitement, and all eyes are on the third *vaṭṭānḍi*, who has to give the lead by uttering the slogan (*valliya*) for heaving the rope.

"*Īnālē, sendirinīlē aiya hōiya addaddā!*" he shouts, and the people at the tug rope shout back "*ho!*" Again the *vaṭṭāṇḍi* yells "*addaddā*" ("heave"), and the villagers shout "*hō!*"

Addaddā! hō!

This goes on until the horn snaps, which generally takes only a few minutes.

Excitement now reigns. The victorious side shouts with glee, while the defeated side appears crestfallen. A *vaṭṭāṇḍi* from the winning side extricates the horn from its trappings and, covering it with a white shawl, places it on his head, also covered with a white cloth (*piruvaṭa*). Four people hold a canopy of white cloth over him, and they all circumambulate the two posts (*aṅ gaha* and *henakaňda*) clockwise three times, with the men and boys of the village following them uttering cries of exultation and ritual shouts of joy while the drums rapidly beat the festival note.

Hōiya! hōiya! . . . hōiya purē hōiya!

Then they run to the bo tree on the farther side of the arena and stop before an altar constructed in front of the tree. With the horn covered in white still on his head, the *vaṭṭāṇḍi* utters the following invocation. No drums are beaten while the invocation is uttered.

Vaṭṭāṇḍi: O great god Viṣṇu [pause] great Viṣṇu
[The villagers, in a loud roar, complete the utterance in a chorus]: God!
Vaṭṭāṇḍi: Come and be present here—Come and be
Chorus: Present here!
Vaṭṭāṇḍi: An invocation, I sing—an invocation
Chorus: I sing.
Vaṭṭāṇḍi: These dances and games, Oh witness—these dances and games
Chorus: Oh witness.
Vaṭṭāṇḍi: The folk on both sides protect—the folk on both sides
Chorus: Protect!
Vaṭṭāṇḍi: *The vaṭṭāṇḍi* oh protect—the *vaṭṭāṇḍi*
Chorus: Oh protect!
Vaṭṭāṇḍi: From misfortune protect us—from misfortune
Chorus: Protect us!
Vaṭṭāṇḍi: Misfortune to come, oh banish—misfortune to come
Chorus: Oh banish!
Vaṭṭāṇḍi: The yield of our crops, increase—the yield of our crops
Chorus: Increase!
Vaṭṭāṇḍi: Our cattle multiply—our cattle
Chorus: Multiply!

After Viṣṇu, other gods—Kataragama (Skanda), the Four Gods, Pasgamanan Deviyo (a local deity, "the God of the Five Villages")—are invoked in the same manner. After this the *vaṭṭāṇḍi* shouts "*Ōhōva!*" to signify the conclusion of the invocation: they all run once more shouting the ritual paean "*hōiya!*" toward the banyan tree, then place the horn in the "horn box." The "box" is then covered with a "curtain" of creamy yellow coconut leaves woven into a mat. The ritual is over at 4:30 P.M.

The technique of the performance had not changed in 1966. One innovation was conspicuous, though. On the third day (when in theory the lower team wins) twenty youths under nineteen years old were given a chance to pull the horns. The horns did not snap in spite of several tries. Then the *kapurāla* lustrated the horns with turmeric water and muttered a "charm" (mantra). The youths pulled again several times, but to no avail. Then twenty additional youths were put to the task. This time the upper team's horn broke, and the unbroken horn was carried under a canopy three times, clockwise, round the thunderbolt tree (*henakan̆da*).

In 1956 as well as in 1966, the last day's performance was the most tense, and more than seventy-five people tugged at the rope. Horns of equal size were matched, and a great deal of bickering and argument occurred among the *vaṭṭānḍi*. However, there were no humiliating songs or insults hurled at the losing side. The winning side expressed their jubilation by prolonged cries of "*hōiya!*"

Several interesting conclusions can be drawn from the preceding account. While the ideal is that both lower and upper teams should win evenly, in fact it is not possible to avoid competition even during the first six days. That the lower horn did not break in the second ritual I have described confirms observations I made every time I witnessed this ritual. This was that, in spite of ideal norms, the *vaṭṭānḍi* on occasion tried to match horns of equal size, and in spite of possible evil consequences sometimes the wrong horn snaps. At other times when the horn does not break, conformity to ideal norms would be achieved by replacing one horn with the required weaker, breakable horn. However, whatever horn snaps, victory is conceded according to the ideal rules. This shows that the spirit of competition threatens to enter even on days when it should not, in theory, exist. Furthermore, the "under nineteen" innovation is an attempt to meet changed conditions in village society, analogous to the "youth horns" (*kolu aṅ*) in Pānama.

In Malidūva, no amount of questioning could elicit whether there was a kinship principle underlying the division into sides, aside from patrilineal inheritance. However, everyone agreed on one thing: that caste was immaterial in team division, so that the same caste will have representatives on both teams. One common formulation was: "There is no *kulabēda* ["caste divisions"] here; we are *eka* ["one"]. All join in pulling the horns and in throwing coconuts." Another feature of the *aṅkeḷiya* in Malidūva was that there was no tradition of Pattini's belonging to the lower team and Pālan̆ga's belonging to the upper. Furthermore, no one had heard of the origin myth of the *aṅkeḷiya* that prevailed elsewhere, neither the villagers nor the *kapurāla*. None of the texts recorded made any reference to these myths either, except that these games (*aṅkeḷiya* and *polkeḷiya*) were originally performed for Vaduru Mādēvi on the instructions of Pattini (see p. 262, stanza 132 of *marā ipäddīma*, text 42). To check whether this was due to the discontinuity in tradition here, I asked the headman, who is an outsider, what the tradition was in his village, twelve miles away. Apparently there was no knowledge of the Pattini/Pālan̆ga opposition, or of the origin myth of *aṅkeḷiya* in his village either. Clearly, therefore, there was no such tradition in villages in this region, in the Mātara district. Furthermore, in Mädagama in the Hinidum Pattu in the Galle district, where I did a field study in 1961 (Obeyesekere 1967), there was a similar ignorance. Mädagama informants stated unequivocally: "Pattini is for both teams."

Polkeḷiya (Coconut Game) at Malidūva

What is striking about the *polkeḷiya*, when contrasted with the *aṅkeḷiya*, is its intense spirit of aggressive competition. The division into two teams is identical with that for the *aṅkeḷiya*, but the game is strictly competitive. There is no attempt, in ideology or in fact, to allocate victory a priori to the two sides, as in the *aṅkeḷiya*. That the competitive spirit has taken over completely is also apparent from the fact that, unlike the *aṅkeḷiya*, there is no fixed number of games to be performed. The coconut game can go on for weeks if the participants so wish. Here individual skill is at a premium, unlike the *aṅkeḷiya*, where at best only the skill of the *vaṭṭāṇḍi* is involved. The coconuts are also not consecrated (*pē*) as are the horns in *aṅkeḷiya*; however, the *kapurāla* lustrates the participants' coconuts with turmeric water. There is also no invocation (*puvata*) or plaint (*kannalavva*).

With the commencement of the game the *aṅpiṭiya* ("horn pitch") is converted to the *polpiṭiya* ("coconut pitch"). The two teams are at the ends of the pitch, about thirty feet apart. In Malidūva the upper team stood by its post (*aṅ gaha*) and the lower team stood at the opposite end near the bo shrine, but this did not seem to have any ritual significance. The game is initiated by the two *vaṭṭāṇḍi* with the toss. The *vaṭṭāṇḍi* of the upper team throws a coconut, and his opponent *vaṭṭāṇḍi* tries to break it with his coconut. The toss is given to the side whose coconut is intact. Then starts the competition proper.

The coconuts that are used are tough, seasoned ones called *porapol* ("fighting coconuts") as against the domestic coconut (*nipol*). The teams face each other, yet any single act involves only two people—the thrower and the person who meets the oncoming coconut with the one in his hand. Let me illustrate the technique involved. X throws a coconut (known as *arina geḍiya*, "nut that is thrown") hard at the opposing team, with the "female" end of the coconut showing (the side containing the germ holes); Y on the other side holds a coconut (known as *ataya*, "thing in the hand") also with the female side pointing forward, and meets the oncoming coconut. If the oncoming coconut breaks, victory is given to Y; but if the *ataya* breaks, the humiliation of Y and his team is very great. When this occurs, the victorious side shouts in jubilation "*hōiya!*" If no coconut breaks, X is given another try. After each throw shouts like *ataya hoṅdai* ("the hand coconut is OK") are heard, and the undamaged coconut is shown to the opposers. The shout "*ataya giya*," "the *ataya* is gone," indicates the reverse. Experienced players attempt to hit the oncoming coconut on the side with the *ataya* in order to break it more easily. In Malidūva victory is determined on a simple basis: the team that breaks the most coconuts wins.

The coconut game not only involves considerable skill, it can be quite dangerous. Hence only experienced and skilled players participate. Bashed hands are not infrequent, and sometimes more serious accidents occur. Even members of the audience can be hurt by coconuts that are thrown so fast as to hit a bystander; or spectators may be hit by flying splinters from the colliding coconuts. The atmosphere is always tense with aggressive excitement, and arguments are frequent. Skilled players brag about their achievements. In the *polkeḷiya* rituals I witnessed in Malidūva the most aggressive, braggadocian players were a man from the washer caste and a *goyigama* man with an amputated leg. Both were excellent players.

Pēḷiyāma: Going in File

The *pēḷiyāma* ritual is performed anytime after the sixth day of horn pulling and before the seventh and final day. *Pēḷiyāma* simply refers to a procession of villagers who go in file past the eighteen villages involved in the Malidūva ritual. Generally the procession takes three days to tour the eighteen villages, but in 1967 it took four days because a new cluster of hamlets in the Galle district—Māgedera—was incorporated into the visitation. This innovation was instituted largely because the *kapurāla* who officiated in the *aṅkeḷiya* celebrations came from Māgedera.

The *pēḷiyāma* starts from Malidūva at 9:00 A.M. The *kapurāla* faces an altar (*mal yahana*) and utters a standard invocation of the *aṅkeḷiya*. After this the demon Garā goes up to a chair on which are lying the *halam̆ba* ("anklets"), covered with a red cloth. The *kapurāla* meanwhile removes the anklets, throws the red shawl around his shoulders, and starts jingling the anklets, one in each hand. He blesses the audience by shaking the anklets in front of them, singing songs on Seven Pattini, then circumambulates the upper post, the horn tree (*aṅ gaha*), three times clockwise, to the accompaniment of four drummers. The procession then commences the journey. In front of the procession is a comically masked drummer—the herald (*an̆ḍabera kārayā*); following him are the four drummers (*davul kārayo*), the *kapurāla* with the anklets in hand, and two (or three) *vaṭṭānḍi* carrying the two horns and the (last) victorious coconut, followed by Garā, continually engaged in *ves pāma* ("shaking his guise"). Following Garā are as many villagers as care to join the procession, carrying torches, flags, and banners. At each village tea, lunch, or refreshments are given to the processionists. At a central spot in the village the *kapurāla* utters an invocation asking the protection and blessings of the deity, while Garā banishes ritual dangers (*vas dōsa*). The villagers gather there and give gifts of coins (*pan̆ḍuru*). Other villagers on the way may join the procession, while some may drop out. After three (or four) days the procession returns to Malidūva.

Aṅkeḷiya at Biyanvila

The following account of *aṅkeḷiya* is from Ihala Biyanvila, a highly urbanized "village" ten miles from Colombo. Most Biyanvila folk are "lower-middle" or "working-class" people who hold jobs in and around Colombo. It was therefore extremely interesting to see the performance of the *aṅkeḷiya* here. When we contrast the Biyanvila *aṅkeḷiya* with Malidūva, one feature stands out conspicuously. In Biyanvila the spirit of competition has triumphed almost completely, so that only lip service is paid to the idea that the goddess's side should win on certain days. The "horns" used are massive tree roots, which sometimes take days to snap.

The layout of the ritual area in Biyanvila is very much like it is in Malidūva (see fig. 12). The *aṅpiṭiya*, or horn pitch, is demarcated with a rope, and no females are allowed within the *sīmā* (sacred area). The lower team's post, unlike the situation in Malidūva and Pānama, is called the *aṅ gaha* or horn tree, but here a jackfruit tree (i.e., "a milk tree") served as the *aṅ gaha*. The post of the upper team was an inverted coconut tree pivoted in the bottom of a pit, but the term given was *aṅ kanuva* ("horn post").

The "horns" used in the Biyanvila *aṅkeḷiya* are not real horns but are made from the roots or branches of trees, generally the *beli* tree (*Aegle marmelos*) or *aṭṭēriya* tree (*Murraya exotica*). I shall omit the descriptions of the complicated manner in which the horns are hooked and instead describe the various parts of the "horn."

The "horn" is composed of a pole about seven feet long, curved in the middle, which is known as *rikilipolla*; attached to the bend of the *rikilipolla* is a slightly curved stick twenty inches long by two inches thick, known as the *toḍuva*. Both are tightly wrapped with bark rope, but a small part of the *toḍuva* top is left jutting out for hooking to the opposing horn with a coil of ropes (*peräs*) and a crossbar (*aṅmōla*).

The rituals are held three times or seven times, one on each Saturday (Kemmura, or auspicious day for rituals for gods) culminating on the last day with a *gammaḍuva*. The

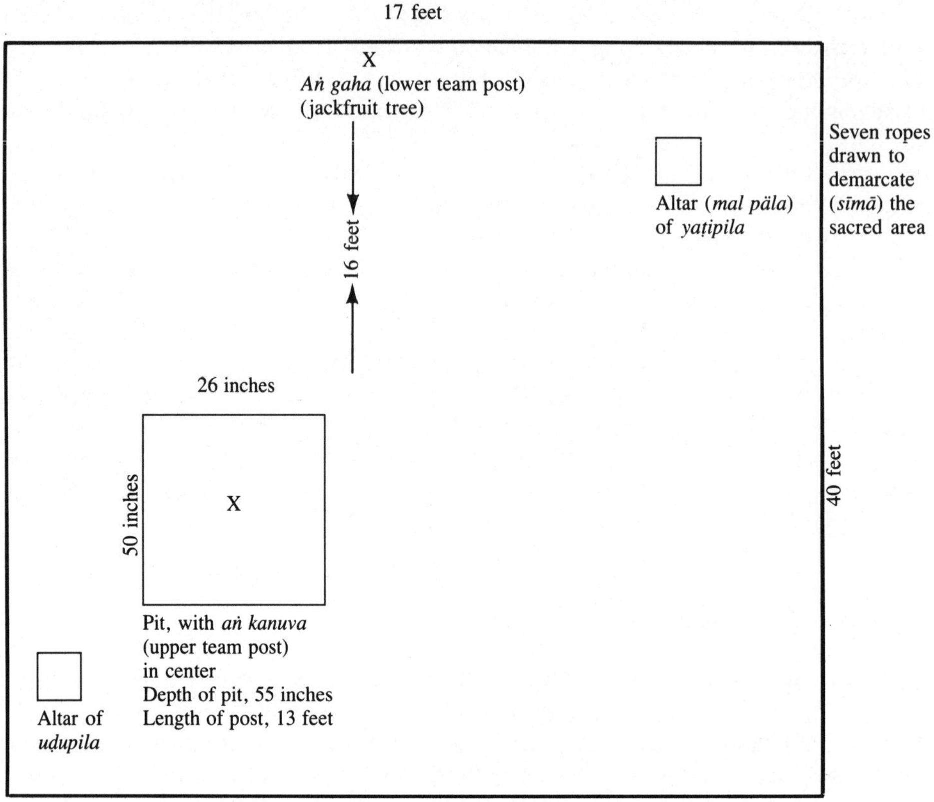

Fig. 12. Layout of the ritual area for the *aṅkeḷiya* at Biyanvila.

start of the series on the first day is a noncompetitive game called the *atgaha keḷiya*. This term does not make much sense taken at face value. A related term, *attagaha mätirīma*, denotes a minor ritual where a charmed branch (*atta*) of a tree (*gaha*), generally lime or mango, is waved before a sick person by a priest. Thus it is almost certain that at one time hooks from small branches (*at*), perhaps of the mango tree, were used in the noncompetitive game (*keḷiya*), very much like the use of forks from the *mālittan* bush in Pānama. In Biyanvila, owing to the near complete takeover of the spirit of competition, two *tōḍu* (plural of *tōḍuva*) of equal size are chosen for the first day's game.

On other days the choice of *tōḍu* is based on their strength, but the protruding uncovered part of the *tōḍuva* must be of the same dimension as that of the opposing one while the reinforced part can be of any size or strength. On the first day, whatever side wins the praises of Pattini are sung; but on other days the games are strictly competitive.

Description of an *Aṅkeḷiya* Performance at Biyanvila

I saw two *aṅkeḷiya* performances in Biyanvila in 1966. On the first occasion no victory was given, since the *tōḍuva* of the upper team broke in the process of hooking. However, a great deal of tension was generated because the *vaṭṭānḍi* of the lower team felt their opponents deliberately picked an oversize *tōḍuva* that would not hook easily.

Since the procedures adopted in both days were identical, I shall give an account of the second contest.

On the night before the *aṅkeḷiya* each group of *vaṭṭānḍi* must tie the *tōḍuva* to the *rikilipolla* and reinforce the "horn" with *beli paṭṭa* (bark of *Aegle marmelos*) and cotton thread (traditionally cowhide supplied by the untouchable beggar [*roḍiya*] caste was used). The process involves great skill, time, and effort. Initially the horns are placed before an altar and an invocation to Pattini is recited. Then comes the reinforcing of the lower team's horn, which takes about seven hours, from 10:00 P.M. to 5:00 A.M. After this is complete, each horn is again placed on a mat or bench in front of an altar. Lights are lit, and the horns are made *pē* (consecrated). After the first day's performance the winning horn is kept inside the shrine (*dēvāle*), while the losing side reinforces another horn in the manner described above and decks it with flowers, garlands, and streamers.

Since the lower team's horn was victorious in the preceding game, it lay decked in the shrine, and the horn of the upper team was kept in the front compound of a house belonging to one of their *vaṭṭānḍi*, before a lighted altar (*mal yahana*). At 2:30 P.M. the *kapurāla* enters the *dēvāle* and utters a conventional invocation, asking the permission, protection, and blessing of the gods for the village. Then the victorious lower team horn is brought out by the *vaṭṭānḍi*, who sing the *aṅkeḷi upata* ("origin of *aṅkeḷiya*" text 54) to the accompaniment of drums. The horn is placed in the veranda of the shrine, and it is there decorated with flowers of various colors, garlands, and gay streamers by some *vaṭṭānḍi*, while others continue their singing and still others rub the *tōḍuva* with yellow turmeric. Another person punctuates the singing with the blowing of the conch; some lovingly fondle and caress the horn. The horn is then covered in pure white cloth (*piruvaṭa*). Then a *vaṭṭānḍi* wearing a white shawl on his head and a mask covering his mouth carries the horn on his head as he walks under a canopy (*uḍuviyan*) in a procession led by the *kapurāla*. The procession proceeds toward the arena. There, to the sound of drums, conches, and singing, the procession circumambulates the *aṅ gaha* three times clockwise while others shout "*sādhu!*" The horn is placed on a mat in front of the *aṅ gaha* and worshiped. The *kapurāla* utters an invocation at the altar, whose purpose is to transfer (*anumōdan kirīma*) merit (*pin*) to the Twelve Gods (Doḷaha Deviyo). Then oil lamps are lit and flowers are placed in the two altars.

Practically the same procedure is adopted in respect to the horn of the upper team. A procession led by the *kapurāla* leaves the *dēvāle* and goes several hundred yards to where the horn is kept. After the invocations are uttered the horn is brought in procession to the arena, and they circumambulate the whole arena (to embrace the posts of both teams). The upper team's horn, which has already been decked, is placed by the side of the lower team's. Now the flowers and decorations of the horns are removed and placed in the two altars.

Arguments during the Hooking of Horns

Tempers are frayed during the hooking of horns, which takes about an hour. There was a complaint that the *tōḍuva* of the upper team was too large, and therefore the excess was scraped so it matched that of their opponents. The hooking process involved many movements that suggested sexual gestures. Often the word *keḷinava* ("play") was used with obscene connotations to suggest intercourse. I managed to note the following incidents in the din of argument and counterargument.

1. "My *massiña*'s [cross-cousin's] son is on the upper team, *ūṭa keḷinna* ["let him play," "screw him!"]," said one man.

2. Father and son, both on the same team, had an argument while attempting to hook the horn. The son left the arena. One informant said, "In this game no *sahōdara* ["brotherliness"]—but everything is all right after the game is over."

3. During hooking the words "*dekama apē*" ("both horns belong to us all") were uttered several times to allay tempers.

4. In general one noted that the members of one's own team were addressed as "*putā*" ("son") and those of the opposite side as "cross-cousin" (*massinā*), as in "*uḍupila massinā*, don't get angry." These are normal extensions of kin terms and do not necessarily imply a division of the two teams on the basis of kinship. It implies, I think, that the kind of solidarity within each team is as if between close patrilateral kin, while the sentiment between the two teams is a kind of joking relationship characteristic of cross-cousins.

5. The word *samāva*, "forgiveness," was constantly used to allay the tempers of offended persons.

As soon as the *tōḍuva* snaps, the fun starts. A leading team member, generally an old man, holds aloft the broken *tōḍuva* for all to see. The winners shout in glee and hurl abuse at the losers. The broken piece of horn is explicitly identified as the broken penises of the defeated team. After the shouting and milling around, some order begins to prevail in the crowd. The winning side assembles, and one person utters a line, while the audience shouts in chorus—"*ahapallā*," "Oh listen ye!" The style of utterance here is very much like the invocation (*puvata*) uttered for the gods in Malidūva or the *hīya* at Pānama, but the excitement in Biyanvila is extraordinarily high, rising practically to a frenzy, as in Pānama. This goes on for about an hour. I quote parts of these utterances from a tape recording.

Leader: Milk will overflow— Chorus: Oh listen ye.
The lower team won.
It's good for the village son—
Not for hatred son—
Diseases will be banished—
Lads of the upper team—
You should be ashamed—
You ran away, cowards—
You upper team bastards—
We are noble ones—
You are mean bastards—
We are meritorious children—
We won a great victory—
We won a good victory—
The children of the upper team—
It isn't nice at all—
You give [sexually] to your mothers—
But lower team children—
Are children of Pattini—

We don't run away—
We of the lower team—
Meritorious are we—
You dogs in the upper team. . . Chorus: Oh listen ye.

After the *tōḍuva* had snapped, about 4:40 P.M. the procession, or *pēḷiyāma*, commences. The procession first goes to the shrine, singing songs on Pattini along the way. If a family has a chair with a white cloth, the procession stops and says anything they wish. Even abuse may be uttered if the people are of the losing team. Fights are not unusual, but none in Biyanvila developed into serious proportions while I was there.

The Basis of Team Division

I could not discover a clear social structural basis for the division into two teams. Informants stated that "in old times" there were definite rules for the division into sides, but "outsiders," then as well as now, could join whichever side they wished. The arrangement today is the same as elsewhere in Sinhala areas—a patrilineal inheritance of one's team membership. Furthermore, all castes can participate in the ritual. Sometimes people change teams. Two brothers belonging to the Jayasūriya Āraccigē *vāsagama* ("patrilineal line") fell out, and one brother joined the lower team. Such instances are rare; generally members of the same *vāsagama* belong to the same team. But a wife may opt to join her husband's side or remain on the side to which she belonged before marriage. One fairly consistent kinship principle seemed to emerge from my interviews—each *vāsagama* belongs to a single side, but this is after all a logical consequence of the patrilineal inheritance of team divsions.

Aṅkeḷiya at Dunukeula

I witnessed a ritual of *aṅkeḷiya* in Dunukeula in the Kotmale district in 1956. I subsequently revisited Dunukeula in 1967 and 1968 to collect more information. The area is interesting because Robert Knox was imprisoned in a village close to Dunukeula. It is therefore likely that the *aṅkeḷiya* ritual that Knox witnessed in the seventeenth century took place in Dunukeula itself or in a village nearby. The ritual I witnessed in Dunukeula was similar to those held in Biyanvila and Pānama, though the scale was much less elaborate. Furthermore, no *gammaḍuva* or any other ancillary ritual was associated with the *aṅkeḷiya* at Dunukeula.

There were no temples or shrines for Pattini or her consort in the village itself. An open area is temporarily converted into a consecrated area sacred to the deity. The village *dēvāle* belonged to the Vali Yakku ("wild demons") and the traditional Twelve Gods (Doḷaha Deviyo), as befits the religious pantheon of "remote" regions (see chap. 5, pp. 285–93). For all matters affecting crops—disease, fertility—they go the Vali Yakku temple or make offerings to Doḷaha Deviyo. The latter helps people with problems pertaining to fields and cattle (*harakā bāna*). For aid regarding "modern" problems like jobs, promotions, passing government examinations, and such, Dunukeula folk visit the Dēvatā Baṇḍāra shrine at Alutnuvara or any Skanda (Kataragama) shrine in the region.

The origin myth of *aṅkeḷiya* is almost the same as in Biyanvila and Pānama. The belief is that Pattini and Pālaṅga climbed the tree to pluck the *sapu* flower; their hooks got entangled and could not be broken. They climbed down, obtained two hooks (*keki*), and thus originated the game of *aṅkeḷiya*. Pattini won the original game. Yet here as elsewhere women are totally excluded from participating in the *aṅkeḷiya*. But the belief exists in Dunukeula that, if a woman pulls at the tug rope or even touches it, the lower team (*yaṭipila*) will win, irrespective of the side to which the woman belongs. This belief is not confined to Dunukeula, for I encountered it in Digalla in the Ūva Province in a ritual I witnessed in March 1956.

In Dunukeula the theory is that the *aṅkeḷiya* should be held in the month of Vesak (May) after the main harvest, or during times of drought and disease. As elsewhere, the view is that its performance banishes drought and infectious diseases and brings fertility to the village. The game is held for seven days (or multiples of seven). Any number of horns may be broken each day, but the number of days must strictly conform with tradition. On the first day two altars (*mässa*) are constructed and two *kapurāla*s from Aṭabāge, a nearby village, are invited to bless the horns and utter invocations. On this day victory is ritually allocated to the lower team (Pattini's side) by pitting a weak upper team horn against a stronger lower team horn. When the lower team wins its members sing paeans of praise on Pattini. The first day's victory, informants say, pleases the deity; moreover, it commemorates the first victory of Pattini with her *hapu kekka* ("forked stick of the *sapu* tree"). On this day the two teams circumambulate their respective posts clockwise while the *kapurāla* utters the *yātikā* ("invocation"). The games that follow thereafter are strictly competitive.

The techniques of pulling and the terminology are very much the same as elsewhere, except that the term *henakaňda* ("thunderbolt tree") is not used. Instead, the post pivoted on the ground is called the *aṅ kaňda* ("horn trunk") and belongs to the lower team. Any tree (except the mango, which is sacred to Pattini) could be used for the upper team. The horns used are the roots of tough trees, generally *mora* (*Nephelium longana*), *damunu* (*Grewia tiliaefolia*), *andara* (*Dichrostachys cinerea*), *nā* (*Mesua ferrea*), or *siyaṁbalā* (*Tamarindus indicus*). The dimensions of the horns are about the same as in Pānama except that the long arms of triumphant horns, kept as heirlooms in Dunukeula, are cut a few inches from the top, a symbolic castration indicating that they are no longer to be used in this fertility ritual. The horns are reinforced with bark strips from the *nuga* tree; traditionally they were reinforced with cowhide. The *roḍiya*s of Kotmalē, whom Dunukeula people say belong to lower team, provided the hide, and they now provide the bark rope, which when wrapped is, as elsewhere, called *vāran*. *Pērās* ("coils") are, as elsewhere, made from tough jungle vines. The whole hook is called *aňga*, but as in both Malidūva and Pānama the long arm is called the *tōḍuva* and the short, reinforced arm the *aňga* (horn), or *aṅ penda*. The ritual is similar to those in Biyanvila and Pānama, and I shall describe only what happens when a horn breaks.

When the horn snaps, the victorious team assembles in the middle of the pitch and shouts paeans of joy while a *vaṭṭānḍi* carries the triumphant horn on his head. In addition to this, victorious "heirloom" horns with such names as *olupäliyāva* ("skull breaker"), *kankoṭavalliya* ("short-eared wild one"), *halaṁba kumāraya* ("prince bracelet") are also taken in procession. The victorious side utters the rankest abuse, makes sexual gestures, parades effigies of members of the defeated team, and sings obscene songs. Knox's description of an *aṅkeḷiya* seen in the mid-seventeenth century in the same area fits exactly with my own eyewitness account.

> There is another Sport, which generally all People used with much delight, being, as they called it, a Sacrifice to one of their Gods; to wit, Potting Dio. And the benefit of it is, that it frees the Country from grief and Diseases. For the beastliness of the Exercise they never celebrated it near any Town, nor in sight of Women, but in a remote place. . . . Upon breaking of the stick, that Party that hath won doth not a little rejoice. Which rejoycing is exprest by Dancing and singing, and uttering such sordid beastly Expressions, together with Postures of their Bodies, as I omit to write them, as being their shame in acting, and would be mine in rehearsing. For he is at that time most renowned that behaves himself most shamelessly and beast-like.
>
> This filthy Solemnity was formerly much in use among them; and even the King himself hath spent time in it, but now lately he hath absolutely forbidden it under penalty of a forfeiture of money. So that now the practice hereof is quite left off.
>
> But tho it is thus gone into dis-use yet out of the great delight that People had in it, they of Gompala would revive it again; and did. (Knox 1681, pp. 157–58)

At the conclusion of the ceremonies, in Dunukeula there is a ceremonial procession called *aṅ väḍamavīma* ("ceremonial procession of the horns"). The winning horns of the respective sides are placed on their *pēräs* (coils) and kept on an altar (*mässa*). Traditional heirloom horns are also brought and placed there. The two *kapurāla*s then utter an invocation known as *aṅ kannalavva* ("horn plaint"). Then they cut the coils, which ritually ends the game. The post of the lower team is also kept aside for next year's use. From here the people go in procession (*perahära*) to the Vali Yakku shrine in the village, which is temporarily "converted" into a Pattini shrine by ceremonially placing the horns there. There, as elsewhere, they offer coins (*pañḍuru*), make vows, utter prayers, and get the blessings of the deity from the *kapurāla*. Thereafter the winning horns and the *raja aṅ* ("king horns," i.e., heirlooms) are taken back to their owners' homes and sequestered there.

The popular views of Pattini and Pālaṅga that do not find expression in the actual myths of either the *aṅkeḷiya* or the *gammaḍuva* show a remarkable consonance with those in other parts of the country. Here too Pālaṅga is called *terunnānse* (term for Buddhist monk). There is agreement with the myths that Pattini was a virgin, but Dunukeula folk elaborate this by saying that this is because Pattini and Pālaṅga tried to have intercourse but failed. This is exactly the view in Malidūva and Sīnigama and is analogous to the view held in the Balangoḍa area that Pattini was a hermaphrodite and did not menstruate.

Division into Teams

In Dunukeula, as elsewhere, the division into teams was on a patrilineal basis, but change of sides was both permitted and practiced. Furthermore, the contemporary teams were also divided by *vāsagama*, so that there seems a firm social structural basis for allocation of sides, very much in the manner of Biyanvila—namely, patrilineal inheritance of sides and clear-cut named patrilineal groups on each side. In fact, however, these contemporary structural alignments are, as in Biyanvila, totally misleading. Most of these *vāsagama*s are not the traditional patrilineal groups associated with an "estate," known as *gedera* in the Kandyan areas and *vāsagama* in the low country. Under the impact of social changes that I have described elsewhere, these groups have lost their corporate character, and new "status lines" with a vague ideology of patrilineal descent have come into being all over Sri Lanka (Obeyesekere 1967, pp. 262–66). In general these new lines adopted high-sounding *paṭabäñdi* ("knighthood titles") of the old Kandyan kingdom. In the Kandyan areas these titles were typically "Mudiyanse," and Pieris records their widespread and indiscriminate adoption for status enhancement in the later Kandyan period (Pieris 1956, p. 173). Thus five of the eight patrilineal groups in the present *aṅkeḷiya* divisions are similar recent Mudiyanse adoptions; none of them have any notion of "exogamy." One group—Allevala Gamage—is a low-country patrilineal *vāsagama* of the type I have recorded (Obeyesekere 1967), and only two have typical Kandyan *gedera* names. It is obvious that Dunukeula village has changed its traditional structure and that new immigrant groups have established themselves in the village. Six *vāsagamas* came originally from Mātara, Ratnapura, Gampola, Galagedara (near Kurunāgala), Pussellāva, and Nuvara Eliya. It is thus clear that serious structural changes have taken place in hamlet structure in Dunukeula similar to those I have described for Mädagama (Obeyesekere 1967), so it seems senseless to talk of the social structure of these Kandyan villages as traditional.

Is there any evidence regarding the original patrilineal groupings in the village of Dunukeula? According to all reliable informants, the original groups were the following:

Pāluvattē gedara (upper team)
Vanahapuvē (subcaste of *goyigama*, upper team)
Pallepaṭṭiyē (inferior subcaste of *goyigama*, lower team)
Piṭiyēgedera (*durā* caste, lower team)

Of the four original groups, two were *gedera* in the Kandyan sense of the term, and two were low subcaste groups of the *goyigama* caste. All these families have emigrated except for Piṭiyēgedera and a few Pallepaṭṭiyē folk. Furthermore, there is clear evidence that the large bulk of the present village lands was originally owned by the Pallepaṭṭiyē (*paṭṭiye* are a subcaste of *goyigama* whose royal duty was looking after the king's cattle). At present most of the village lands are owned by two recent intermarrying status lines—the Illukpiṭiyē Mudiyansē and Vijesiṃha Mudiyansē. They bought these lands from the Pallepaṭṭiyē *gedera* folk. Thus the whole structure of the land tenure system has changed dramatically in Dunukeula.

In addition to these old and new patrilineal groups, past and present residents of the village, there are also two families of the washerman caste who came very recently to Dunukeula. One family came recently from Koṭadeniya near Gelioya and joined the upper team. In their original village there were no team divisions; they simply affiliated themselves with the team of their patrons in the present village. The other family also came from Gelioya, married into the "older" washerman family, but (significantly) adopted the lower team. The older Mudiyansē and Gamagē migrants to the village either continued the affiliations of their villages of origin (e.g., Allevala Gamagē, Illukpiṭiyē Mudiyansē), joined the sides of their spouses, or chose terms on a purely fortuitous basis like patronage.

Almost everywhere in Sri Lanka (except Pānama) in Sinhala and Hindu Tamil areas the theory is that the *aṅkeḷiya* should be held yearly in the month of Vesak, after the main harvest is over. It is therefore a ceremony of first fruits. In Pānama the tradition has changed to September, to fit in with the Skanda ceremonies in nearby Kataragama. In Dunukeula, as in Malidūva and Biyanvila, the continuity of the tradition has totally broken down. The *aṅkeḷiya* rituals were held only in times of excessive drought or infectious diseases. These occasions for the period 1932–69 were as follows: 1934, 1940, 1956, 1959, and 1962 in the village of Aṭabāge, where Dunukeula folk participated. Aṭabāge folk, for their part, participate in the Dunukeula ritual. One reason for this is that in Dunukeula three-fourths of the population belongs to the upper team, whereas in Aṭabāge there are larger numbers on the lower team. *Aṅkeḷiya* is also occasionally held in Pahala Mulgama, which is a *vahumpura* (jaggery-maker caste) village. Five years ago they had a ritual where high-caste Dunukeula people participated on both teams. Thus Dunukeula folk clearly recognize, consciously and overtly, that the caste principle is totally overridden in the *aṅkeḷiya* team division.

Violence and Social Change in *Aṅkeḷiya*

From my descriptions it is apparent that, as a formal enactment, *aṅkeḷiya* is the same everywhere, and this includes the Hindu-Tamil areas of the east coast (pp. 564–69). Nevertheless, in Malidūva, and among the east coast Hindus, the aggressive and cathartic functions of *aṅkeḷiya* are nowadays underplayed—in Malidūva for about three generations, and in the Hindu areas very recently. Does this mean that the Sinhala people of Malidūva and of southern Sri Lanka are less aggressive than their counterparts in, let us say, Pānama? On the contrary, the cultural stereotype of the southerners is quite different: they are considered extremely aggressive. I submit that the relative absence of aggression in *aṅkeḷiya* is related to its decline, which in turn is primarily due to the demographic increase in the villages of Sri Lanka during the past seventy-five years. The influence of the doctrinal traditions of Buddhism and Hinduism, which frown on vulgar, cathartic displays of emotion, is an added cause.

The reason villagers cannot handle their aggressive drives within the confines of the ritual has very little to do with a change in these drives. If at all, greater frustration owing to social change has increased rather than decreased aggression, interpersonal hostility, and suspiciousness. I attribute the demise of *aṅkeḷiya* (or its amendment in the South) to a drastic transformation of the structure and demographic composition of villages. Consider the demographic picture for the island. According to Sarkar, the population per square mile of net land area in 1871 was 113; in 1946 it was 277. Sarkar provides other data (1871–1946) to show that "the population pressure in the peasant sector during the last 75 years has more than doubled" (1957, p. 216). It is very likely that in 1871 *aṅkeḷiya* was being regularly performed; in 1946 it was performed only in the more rural areas; in 1960 it was becoming moribund for the country as a whole.

In other words, *aṅkeḷiya* can function properly only when the population of a village is small, homogeneous, and governed by a stable authority structure. The people of Malidūva can summon enough resources to occasionally hold an *aṅkeḷiya* ritual; however, they have amended the ritual to exclude its cathartic and aggressive elements because, as on the Hindu east coast, it can (and probably did) develop into *real* nonritual violence.

The traditional *aṅkeḷiya* must then be seen in the context of small-scale, stable agricultural communities. The aggression in *aṅkeḷiya* is a model, in exaggerated form, of the pattern of aggression in these communities. For example, I did fieldwork in a remote village of Raṁbadeniya in Laggala district in 1958; in this small community, people have to control their hostile impulses and present a front of formal politeness. Yet I observed that practically every few weeks there occurred what seemed to me a huge flare-up provoked by some trivial stimulus. For example, a child in one family would hit another; the aggrieved mothers would abuse each other; soon male and female kinsmen would take sides, and there would be a vociferous, but entirely verbal, free-for-all of abuse and insults. Then it would subside as dramatically as it started; never have I seen these flare-ups develop into physical violence. This pattern is found in many remote villages, but in the Southern and Western provinces it can, as with *aṅkeḷiya*, lead to physical violence and even murder. *Aṅkeḷiya*, then, is modeled on the pattern of aggression in small villages; yet it is itself a model, in Geertz's sense, for the village to follow, reinforcing that pattern.

Drastic demographic increase is not the only factor, however: there were population migrations from one village to another, altering the traditional kin-based homogeneous character of the village and hamlet social structure, as I demonstrated in an earlier study (Obeyesekere 1967). In the late nineteenth century Pānama probably had about three hundred people; in the 1960s it had more than three thousand. Similar changes have occurred in the other villages mentioned in this chapter. It would have been possible to hold regular *aṅkeḷiya* rituals in the nineteenth century in these villages; in the mid-twentieth century and afterward this would be increasingly difficult for several reasons. First, given the lack of homogeneity in hamlet structure and the breakdown of traditional authority patterns, it would be difficult to muster the resources and enlist the cooperative labor required for large-scale communal enterprises. Second, large numbers competing for scarce resources would have increased interpersonal rivalry and hostility in the village. Third, immigrants from outside coming into the village would not be able to tolerate the insults hurled at them.

The once ubiquitous *aṅkeḷiya* ritual is no longer performed in most parts of Sri Lanka, and one can predict its eventual demise in Malidūva as well as in Pānama. In parts of the Hindu east coast this ritual was performed till very recently. In Karaitivu the performances led to violence spilling over traditional ritual constraints, and several people were hospitalized. Karaitivu informants explained the abolition of *aṅkeḷiya* by saying that the prescribed obscenities and the humiliation of opponents were uncivilized and un-Hindu (chap. 15, p. 564). However, I suspect that the primary reason for the abolition of *aṅkeḷiya* was that people were no longer able to contain their aggression within the confines of the rules of the ritual, and that Hinduism (or Buddhism) was only a secondary cause, or even a rationalization to explain the abolition or nonperformance of these rituals.

The case of Malidūva is instructive in this regard. Here the aggressive shaming behavior is moribund in the *aṅkeḷiya*, yet it surfaces in the *polkeḷiya* ("coconut game," pp. 401–2). But *polkeḷiya* is not an all-village affair like *aṅkeḷiya*. In *polkeḷiya*, selected individuals who are capable of handling aggression participate. The others are organizers and spectators who can intervene if trouble breaks out. This is not possible in *aṅkeḷiya*, where the people assembled in the "horn pitch" are all involved in the team divisions.

RITUAL TEXTS

Text 51 *Hīya*, or Paean, Sung in Pānama

Vaṭṭānḍi: Say the *hīya*
Chorus: *hī-hai-hō*
Not yours: *hī-hai-hō*
Not ours: *hī-hai-hō*
But the Goddess Seven Pattini's: *hī-hai-hō*
Horn procession: *hī-hai-hō*

The play [*keḷiya*] we like: *hī-hai-hō*
The horn we like: *hī-hai-hō*
Let us bring it: *hī-hai-hō*
Let us play [*keḷimu*] here: *hī-hai-hō*
So there be no disease: *hī-hai-hō*
In our village: *hī-hai-hō*
That the paddy crop be as large: *hī-hai-hō*
As the mountains near the fields: *hī-hai-hō*
That the ten farmers [*govi daha dena*]: *hī-hai-hō*
Are protected: *hī-hai-hō*
So that pestilence: *hī-hai-hō*
Is banished: *hī-hai-hō*
So that the village head [*gamarāla*]: *hī-hai-hō*
Is protected: *hī-hai-hō*
That our little ones: *hī-hai-hō*
Are protected: *hī-hai-hō*
So that diseases of the evil eye: *hī-hai-hō*
Are banished; *hī-hai-hō*
That sores and eruptions: *hī-hai-hō*
Are no more: *hī-hai-hō*
The diseases already contracted: *hī-hai-hō*
Be banished.
Even if there's a single man [i.e., if only one person is available for singing the song]: *hī-hai-hō*
Like a demon: *hī-hai-hō*
Run his rounds: *hī-hai-hō*
Ha! Ha! Ha!

Text 52 Obscene Songs Preceding *Varadaravanava* (Turning around of the Wrong)

Baila

Refrain:

1. At the divine palace [*dev mädura*] of the horn pitch go witness [games] in the evening,
   Go witness [games] in the evening.

[Repeat refrain]

2. Here and there are tough guys dripping with saliva [i.e., greedy for sex],
   They strut about the pitch these nervy ones [*nahara kārayin*].

[Repeat refrain]

3. We'll raise their sarongs and hit them with our "stick,"
   Rub oil sediment [on their genitals] and chase them away.

[Repeat refrain]

4. Here and there are *vaṭṭāṇḍi* assembled together, speaking all the time of others' shortcomings;

Having played at horns and lost, they shout these old bears.

[Repeat refrain]

5. These village toughs who create trouble try to lord it in the *aṅkeḷiya*
   Their boss came and pulled horns and ignonimously fell down.

[Repeat refrain]

6. The young bucks who "share" their mothers-in-law and strut about the horn pitch are the people who control the horn
   We'll raise their sarongs and hit them with our stick, rub oil sediment and chase them away.

[Repeat refrain]

7. Having pulled at horns, they've got entangled in them
   They cry in great grief.

[Repeat refrain]

"We go dig for horns [we suffer greatly], and bring them here, but lose badly."
A braggart tells us thus: "O god what happened to us
Let us go into the forest [again], dig for horns, and bring them to the game,
O god help us to pull the horns and beat them, so we too can dance."

8. "The dangerous crosspole is facing me direct, but a big shot is watching from afar
   Aḍō! the long arm (*tōḍuva*) is slipping, shoulder it firmly, but then the hair got entangled in it.
   "Let us go into the forest [again], dig for horns and bring them to the game,
   O god help us to pull the horns and beat them, so we too can dance."

9. "Alas O god what happened to us, why are our people assembled wailing?
   Alas god, what has happened to us, that we lost again this time?"

10. Let us go into the forest. . . ."

Song of the Upper Team

Lads, we are the *keruṅ kārayo* [able ones] of the upper team, we are the able ones—
If we meet these people [i.e., the lower team] on our way, we will thrust cannons up their asses,
If we meet these people on our way we will thrust cannons up their asses.
We will thrust cannons!
We will thrust cannons!

Refrain:

Our pleasures are in the horn pitch
Lads, we are of the upper team, we are the able ones

We are able ones, the clever ones of the upper team
If their chap, a tar barrel, who controls the long arm and the crosspole comes over here
We will rub castor oil, and send into "his" a big injection
[Sinhala *injeṣon*, like "prick" of American slang].

[Repeat refrain]

If their folk come to compete at horn playing
We'll give them their belly's worth of *kōlikuṭṭu* [a banana; the whole line is idiomatic, meaning "we'll give them a physical beating"].
When we pull the tug ropes, it's we who'll win the games
We'll give 'em duck's meat to eat and dumplings [*piṭṭu*] made of chaff,
We'll give 'em duck's meat!
And dumplings made of chaff!

Jōnā and His Mother-in-Law

Chorus: Oh Jōnā, my good Jōnā, you are the partner [*havul kārayā*, i.e., "one who shares"] of your mother-in-law!

I was brought in an unconscious state
Bleeding profusely, when the body energies were moving downward [*bahina kalāva*]
When I regained consciousness and looked around
I was under the bed, *ilavvē!* [alas!]

Chorus: Jōnā, my good Jōnā, you are the partner of your mother-in-law!

When I opened my eyes and looked and saw
Not my *nända* [mother-in-law] but *māma* [father-in-law]
It was a great commotion,
I jumped into the well straight away.

Chorus: Jōnā, my good Jōnā, you are the partner of your mother-in-law!

Then came people from all over
They caught me; what a commotion!
I was in great trouble [pain] at that time
They deposited me in the veranda of the house

Chorus: Jōnā, my good Jōnā, you are the partner of your mother-in-law!

If her daughter wasn't there at that time,
They would've beaten me, *anē*!, so badly,
But for her—owing to their blows—
I would have died on the spot.

Chorus: Jōnā, my good Jōnā, you are the partner of your mother-in-law!

Having seen the calamity that befel me
My mother-in-law was greatly grieved,

She held me, who'd fallen down
And sorrowfully lifted me up.

Chorus: Jōnā, my good Jōnā, you are the partner of your mother-in-law!

My mother-in-law in great grief
Spoke to her daughter who was there,
Held her daughter by the hand,
And gave me in charge of her.

Chorus: Jōnā, do you want your mother-in-law, or your mother-in-law's daughter?
State your wish and I'll see it's fulfilled.
Oh Jōnā don't jump into the well!
Jōnā, my good Jōnā, you are the partner of your mother-in-law.

On Shame: Lower Team Song

Refrain:

People are all around looking at you, aren't you ashamed [*läjja*] to sob for the horn
They are crying, their eyes reddening, and even we onlookers feel like crying.

[Repeat refrain]

Those who say the "truth" [pretend to be virtuous], that is always their side, a bunch of miserable *preta*s [mean ancestral spirits].
Bees and bears, elephants and mongooses and big lizards, all these belong to their side.

[Repeat refrain]

That fellow playing with the crosspole, a greedy-bellied fellow, he's scared stiff to hold the horns;
In trying to hold the crosspole top his penis top swelled to twelve feet.

[Repeat refrain]

They show off to us, though they drink cattle piss and then depart, people of their team;
We shall bend into two and three, get our "poles" all erect, and thrust them up their asses
We shall bend into two and three, get our "poles" all erect, and thrust them up their asses.

[Repeat refrain]

Grandma lady [*ācciamma nōna*], I came looking for you, What are you doing all alone?
I grabbed hold of her hair, put her down on the floor, and there was such a great commotion.

[Repeat refrain]

Traditional Song

Like a cockbird crowing in the garden,
Like a lapwing singing in the park,
Like a fluff of cotton at the end of the branch,
The "mouth lips" of her cunt has "leprosy"!

"Who's the caddish lad who spoke to me, *aḍā*!
In spite of protests [you] grabbed me by the hand
Your mind was bent on fucking [*hukum kävilla*]
Cad, your prick is full of leprosy [*kabara*]."

Two riding gaily in a swing;
While swinging thus, down came their cloths.
Covering "it" with their hands they got off,
The pot-bellied ones tore their cunts off and scrammed.

Friend, we are folk of the upper team,
We've come to the horn pitch with great fun,
Don't you think fish is a tasty food after all,
If you like fish then try eating pricks also.

Isn't it true that cattle lie down in their place of rest
Isn't it true the young girls know best a good fuck [*huk rasa*]
Isn't it true that water flows downstream
Isn't it true that ex-monks [*hīraluva*] fuck at daytime?

"At dawn, in spite of my protests,
The sharp stones and pebbles pricking as I lay on my back
In spite of staring red-faced
A prick, the size of an arm, was thrust into me, up and down."

Dames of the lower team have all sorts of tempting ways,
But their husbands deny that's the case,
They climb talipot palms, with short knives on their waists
They remove talipot husks and put them in their cunts.

Text 53 *Varadaravanava*

Varadaravanava 1: *Yädīma* (Invocation)

In this blessed isle of Lanka laden with plenty
We give various offerings and gifts [to the gods]
To the beautiful and powerful
Prince Skanda, the god
O lord Skanda
O lord Gaṇeśa [Gaṇa Deviňdu]
O goddess Sarasvatī
O Lady of the Earth [Mahikāntā]
We utter this invocation today
Give us blessings and kindness.

The *aṅkeḷiya* performed on the world of humans
Seven times it is performed
If the same is performed correctly
It will light up the whole world.

The adorable and powerful Pattini
Along with her husband, Pālaṅga
Were walking along a path
They saw several ponds [*vil*], and

In the middle of one pond, a *sapu* tree
With *sapu* flowers blooming on it, they saw.
She felt a craving to wear them
And she told Pālaṅga thus:

"Husband, pick them for me."
She felt a terrible grief
She wailed and pleaded
Pattini thus spoke [i.e., the line above].

The loving lass
Left Pālaṅga's side
And climbed up the tree
We will recite how the flower was picked.

Pattini showed her great power,
She ordered forked sticks ["hooks"] to be cut and brought,
She informed him about this,
She informed her husband.

The two of them picked up the two hooks
They put their hooks [to the flower]
And owing to a brisk wind
The two hooks got entangled.

Because they couldn't be extricated
They divided themselves into two sides
The good merchant [caste] husband then
Broke his forked stick [*keki*].

That day they pulled horns [*aṅ vādu*, literally, "conflict or debate with horns"]
Today too we pull horns [*aṅ*]
Thus they gambled
It was designed for the human world.

That day they eagerly played horns,
Today too this present audience
Eagerly divide themselves into two teams
And diseases will by themselves vanish.

Varadaravanava 2

You who bring victory to all beings
Gaṇeśa, and all ye other gods;
Prince Skanda who is guru of all the world
Protect us and give us well-being, O god Skanda.

In the sky above the sun and moon hold sway,
On the earth below the Earth Goddess holds sway,
For the whole world Prince Kaňda holds sway,
For us here Seven Pattini holds sway.

O Pattini full of merit and chaste!
O Prince Skanda guru of the three worlds!
We sing the songs of the *aṅkeḷiya*,
And sing how diseases subside.

Repeatedly sing lovely songs to please the mind,
Invent nice words for the horn-pulling debate,
O you people here don't take offense at wrongs I have done
Forgive us the wrongs and listen to these songs.

a. We of the upper team belong to Kaṇḍāraja [Kaṇḍāraja = Baṇḍāra Raja, i.e., Alut Deviyo]
You of the lower team belong to Seven Pattini,
Don't take to heart any wrong I've done,
Forgive me the wrongs and listen to these songs.

If the lower team wins the following stanza (*b*) is substituted for stanza (*a*).

b. You of the upper team belong to Kaṇḍāraja
We of the lower team belong to Seven Pattini
For the first and last time let us forget all the wrongs
Never again take any wrongs to heart.

O pure gods residing in the *sakvaḷa*s [world systems]
Banish all misfortune [*dōsa*] and protect us all you gods,
With pleasure I sing these songs
Of *aṅkeḷiya* performed in the month of Vesak.

Oleli oleli lola oleli loleiya!
Oli aňga nalavana nuvara loleiya!

Text 54 The Origin of *Aṅkeḷiya* (*Aṅkeḷi Upata*)

O sacred goddess Pattini!
I sing the story of origins;
Banish disaster that's befallen us,
Bring blessings with the *aṅkeḷiya*.

O goddess Nāga Pattini!
Let your *nāga* anklet resound,
Banish disasters that have befallen us,
Bring blessings with the *aṅkeḷiya*.

Goddess Pattini and Prince Pālaṅga
Arrived at a park and were playing [*keḷa-keḷa*]
A blossom from a *sapu* tree was sent there [by Pattini]
This is a trick that Pattini played.

"Dear Lord, let us go look for this flower
Which pond do we seek in our quest for this flower?"
They obtain betel leaves for the first time
And offer betel for the "first god";

They obtain betel leaves for the second time
And offer it to the "second god";
They obtain betel for the third time
And offer it to the "third god."

The same stanza is repeated for the fourth, fifth, sixth, and seventh gods.

They reach the pond [*vila*] where the *nā* tree grows
Round and round the pond they search
But alas, no *sapu* blossoms here, they sorrowfully muse,
"Not here, my lord, let us go farther on."

Sapu: Michelia champaka

They reach the pond where the *väṭakeyi* grows
Round and round the pond they search,
But alas, no *sapu* blossoms here, they sorrowfully muse,
"Not here my lord, let us go farther on."

Väṭakeyi: Pandanus odaratissimus

They reach the pond where the *dunukē* grows,
Round and round the pond they search,
But alas, no *sapu* blossoms here, they sorrowfully muse,
"Not here my lord, let us go farther on."

Dunukē: Pandanus foetidus

They reach the pond where the *sal* tree grows,
Round and round the pond they search,
But, alas, no *sapu* blossoms here, they sorrowfully muse,
"Not here my lord, let us go farther on."

They reach the *savkenda* pond,
Round and round the pond they search,
But, alas, no *sapu* blossoms here, they sorrowfully muse,
"Not here my lord, let us go farther on."

Savkenda: meaning unknown

They reach the pond of *anōtatta* [in Mēru]
Round and round the pond they search
But, alas, no *sapu* blossoms here, they sorrowfully muse,
"Not here my lord, let us go farther on."

They reach the place where four ways meet,
Overjoyed they see the pond where the *sapu* tree grows
Round and round the *sapu* pond they search
But no blossoms in the tree, they sorrowfully muse.

In the *sapu* branch that stretched to the east
No *sapu* flower in that branch did they see,
In the *sapu* branch that stretched from the northeast
No *sapu* flower in that branch did they see.

The same stanza is repeated for the remaining six cardinal points.

In the branch that shot up from the trunk
A beautifully blooming flower they saw;
The goddess Pattini dived into the pond
From under the pond she saw the *sapu* flower.

"After great suffering we saw the flower at last
Now beloved lord how shall we pluck it?"
The gods from above gave them a pole [*daṇḍa*],
The Earth Goddess [Mihikata] gave them a rope.

The god Viṣṇu gave them a golden cutter [*girē*, used for cutting areca nuts]
Pattini tore her shawl into strips
With the *girē* they cut two forked hooks [*keki*, long stick with a "fork" tied at the end].

Pālaṅga climbs the upper side of the trunk,
Pattini climbs the lower side of the tree trunk,
Thus arrived they raise the hooks
And try [to break] the flower with their hooks.

They miss the flower and entangle their hooks,
They pull at their hooks till their hands are red,
"This cannot be done," they cry and descend
And depart to the city.

Pālaṅga finds a thousand males
Pattini a thousand females
The two sides pull their hooks
And Pālaṅga's hook breaks [*biňdenne*, as a vessel is broken].

The women then say thus:
"Pālaṅga you are no male!

"You can't manage [or cope] with us," they say
They abuse and hurl insults in this manner.

Prince Pālaṅga felt a great anger
"Now let us play 'horns,'" he said
They go to Andhra country
They fill eighty bags full of *aṅ dara* ["hornwood"].

The crowd assembled near the paddy field
Doesn't one need a golden rope for the *aṅkeḷiya*?
A golden rope won't do, it isn't strong enough
Give us a solution to this problem.

Get a *roḍiya* [untouchable beggar] of low caste
He will get a rope made of cowhide and buffalo hide
A fathom length from which he makes a rope [*vāran*]
All *dōsa* are banished by that act.

What is the value of the rope for the upper team?
Charge one *panama* [*fanam*, old Portuguese coin] per fathom
What is the value of the rope for the upper team?
Charge one *panama* per fathom

In old times a jackfruit post was planted [at Navagamuva temple]
Without any reason it shot forth branches
The one *kōvila* [Tamil for *dēvāle*] of our Lanka is at Navagamuva
Let us worship goddess Pattini of Navagamuva.

This verse refers to the legend that says the doorposts made of jackfruit wood in the central Pattini shrine at Navagamuva shot forth branches for no explicable reason. This miracle is attributed to Pattini's prowess.

Pattini takes a stick of turmeric in her hand,
Sixty bags of horns she broke with that one yellow stick,
They called Prince Pālaṅga a woman,
"You can't win with us," they shame him.

"Is that the way you play?" they mocked him.
Prince Pālaṅga got very angry
He chased after the goddess Pattini
And Pattini hid behind the tree.

Prince Pālaṅga got stuck there
The goddess Pattini came back [to him]
Having come back she said
"Now husband, do not be angry."

"If chicken pox breaks out—if smallpox breaks out
Plagues, pestilences, such calamities break out
Perform *aṅkeḷiya*—perform *polkeḷiya* [coconut game]
Perform *mal keḷiya* [flower game]—all these are in your charge."

The *aṅkeḷiya* coming from old times,
The *aṅkeḷiya* is here with us today,
The *aṅkeḷiya* that banishes all calamities,
Let us play the *aṅkeḷiya* of Pattini.

Having pulled horns we bring blessings [*set*]
Having played coconuts we bring blessings,
Having played flowers we bring blessings,
The goddess Pattini brings us her blessings.

Part Five

Introduction

In part 5 I shall examine certain important myths and rituals of the Pattini cult as a "projective system," that is, as a symbol system that gives expression to key personality problems or "nuclear psychological constellations" of Hindus and Buddhists. It is impossible to determine how these inferred personality problems are actually distributed in any existing group in India or Sri Lanka. Thus a projective system in my usage is not necessarily related to a "basic personality" or "modal personality." It is related to my hypothetical construction of an "ideal typical" Brahmanic or Buddhist personality. Such ideal types, as Weber pointed out, are never duplicated in reality; only type approximation is possible. Nevertheless, these inferred ideal typical personality traits and motivations must be found in some form or other among actual populations (in unspecifiable and undetermined frequencies) if they are to be used to interpret existing symbolic or projective systems. Yet we simply do not know how these traits are distributed in any sample population. Moreover, I believe that neither psychoanalysis nor psychological anthropology has satisfactorily demonstrated the actual processes whereby "projective systems" are created, changed, or revised and amended through time and among different groups. Is it the work of a number of individuals acting in unison in some special way? Is it the work of special virtuosos, such as priests, shamans, and the like? Are these systems created out of dreams, or the trances of individuals, or some unknown collective consciousness? All I can do here is to relate the inferred ideal typical Hindu and Buddhist deep motivations with the symbolic projective systems. Hence I must plead with the reader to accept the *provisional* nature of the interpretations offered in this part of the book and bear in mind Weber's words:

> It [the ideal type] serves as a harbor until one has learned to navigate safely in the vast sea of empirical facts. The coming of age of science in fact always implies the transcendence of the ideal type, insofar as it was thought of as possessing empirical validity or as a class con-

cept. . . . [Nevertheless] there are sciences to which eternal youth is granted, and the historical disciplines are among them—all those to which the eternally flowing streams of culture perpetually brings new problems. At the very heart of their task lies not only the transiency of *all* ideal types *but* also at the same time the inevitability of *new* ones. (Weber 1949, p. 104)

10

Mother Goddess and Social Structure

Mother goddesses are omnipresent in the regions of southern Asia that have come under the influence of Hinduism. By contrast, Theravāda Buddhism in Southeast Asia has not produced a dominant mother-goddess cult, except for the Pattini cult in Sri Lanka. It is impossible to say why this is so because of the paucity of the empirical data. In this chapter I treat the Sinhala case as a variant of the Hindu scheme, and in the next chapter I will examine some of the critical differences between the two complexes as they are institutionalized in Sri Lanka and India.

This chapter will be concerned with the following problem: How is it that Hindu India developed two fundamental *types* of images of the mother in its projective systems, whereas no such dichotomy appeared in the Sinhala Buddhist pantheon of Sri Lanka? In Hindu India everywhere there are two contrasting images of the mother, first as the cow, passively and unconditionally nurturant, and second as a terrifying mother goddess, vengeful, demonic, and unpredictable, the Kālī image. Both images are consciously recognized as "mothers" and, as I shall explain later, are products of cultural transformations of the infantile experience with actual mothers in the Hindu joint family. Mediating between these two extreme images is a third image—the Pārvatī model—that is neither nurturant nor vengeful, but benevolent. This image is that of the mother as "father's wife," the faithful wife of the great god of the Hindu pantheon (Śiva or Viṣṇu). By contrast, in Buddhist Sri Lanka no such divisions of the maternal image developed. The goddess Pattini can be stern—witness her destruction of Madurai. But in general she is believed to be a benevolent deity, closer to the Pārvatī model on the cultural level but, also on this level, viewed as a mother. Neither the cow nor the goddess Kālī appears in the traditional Sinhala Buddhist pantheon.[1]

I shall spell out the assumptions underlying my analysis of the mother-goddess phenomenon and its variations in India and Sri Lanka.

1. I must qualify this statement with the assertion that Kālī, or a similar type of deity, appears in the lower reaches of the pantheon as a demoness. In other words Sri Lanka had evil demonesses (some of them named Kālī) in the pantheon, but none was elevated to the divine level. These latter beliefs may be termed "occasional," since these demonesses are propitiated only during exorcisms and other rituals for curing afflictions caused by them. There were also no public shrines for these demonesses (until very recently).

1. These goddesses are explicitly referred to as mothers and are addressed as such in the ritual interaction between devotee and deity. Insofar as mother goddesses are representations of human mothers, I shall tentatively view the mother-goddess cult as a "projective system" in the sense that Freud initially discussed in *The Future of an Illusion* (1957), and Kardiner spelled out in more detail later (1945). In the Freud and Kardiner usage, projective systems are culturally constituted representations that permit the expression and channeling of nuclear infantile experiences. Though my view of cultural symbol systems is more complex than Kardiner's, nevertheless I shall provisionally accept the notion of a "projective system" as giving the individual the psychological security to cope with his inner (unconscious) anxieties by projecting them outward into a preexisting cultural belief system. Thus the idea of a projective system is a special way of looking at a religious complex—or, more accurately, at parts of the religious system—that helps canalize the personal projections of members of a group. Any ongoing religion, however, is more than its projective system, since it contains many notions—such as those pertaining to its cosmology and cosmogony or its theories of causation—that may have little to do with the intrapsychic experiences of the individual. Thus the notion of a projective system, as I see it, provides partial understanding: it explains why family images are projected into the cosmos, but it does not explain details of the philosophical speculations woven into these systems through time, and it therefore cannot generate a psychology of knowledge.

2. Mother goddesses will not occur in projective systems if the formal theology or higher doctrinal tradition does not tolerate it and if there exist institutions to compel conformity to the doctrinal ideal. Thus the three great monotheisms—Judaism, Islam, and Protestantism—have no room for the goddess cult. This doctrinal stance is not confined to mother goddesses alone; it is a product of religious rationalization that has little tolerance for *any* forms of popular religiosity.

3. Moreover, there are other cultural conditions that may inhibit or foster the development of projective systems in general. In some cultures, such as the modern industrial states, projective systems may be *diffuse*. Diffuse projective systems involve the projection of, let us say, the maternal image onto a variety of cultural forms, such as film, mass media, popular literature, religion, and politics. Alternatively, it is possible that projection onto a cultural form simply does not occur, in which case the personal projections of an individual remain idiosyncratic and are expressed in noncultural, idiosyncratic media such as dreams and fantasies. Projection onto a coherent cultural structure like religion occurs when two conditions are realized: a general tendency in a particular society to express ideas and feelings in religious terms, which in turn depends on the ego's tolerance of id (fantasy) impulses; and the nature and intensity of the psychological problem that lies at the base of the projections. The latter, when translated into South Asian terms, means that the child's attachment to the mother is extremely intense, and the religious projective system is both a cultural statement and an expression of these intense feelings. The psychoanalytic term *fixation* can be employed to describe the nature of this attachment to the mother. Fixation implies that, psychologically speaking, the umbilical cord has not been cut. Let me add that I do not think fixation, as it occurs in the context of South Asian values, is in itself pathological or abnormal.

4. Ideally we should be able to document the mother-child relationship leading to fixation, with all its regional variations, for the whole of South Asia, but the data are simply lacking. Instead I propose to tackle the problem of the child's relation to the mother in the

following manner. Fixation on the mother is largely dependent on the mother's attitude to the neonate. Basic neonatal attitudes everywhere are biologically determined and could for present purposes be treated as constants; maternal attitudes, by contrast, are culturally influenced. The mother, then, is the major instigator of the relationship that eventually leads to fixation, and her child's psychological development is in great measure based on the feelings she brings to bear on the socialization process. For example, if the mother has a strong need for affect that is not realized by her marriage, she may express that need through her child and thereby promote the child's fixation on her. The latter notion is an inference from the former rather than a product of empirical observation.

Now maternal attitudes can be highly idiosyncratic, and we have to delineate its culturally uniform features to make sense of it. One way of resolving this problem is to say that the recurring and consistent features of the maternal attitude are determined by the female role, its cultural definition, and the social situation in which role playing occurs. For example, we may say that in Indian society a woman's husband and in-laws are aloof; she cannot fulfill her need for love through them; she therefore fulfills it through her child. The social situation, then, is crucial to understanding the mother's attitude to the child. The female role, and the social situation the woman is in, are in turn based on the cultural values of the society, which give meaning to the role and set out the norms for interpersonal interaction. Translated into South Asian terms, the causal nexus is as follows: the values of the society → the female role → mother-child relationship → perception of the deity by the child. It is this causal nexus that I shall spell out in detail in this chapter, focusing explicitly on Hindu India, the locus classicus of the mother goddess.

The Implication of Brahmanic Values for the Female Role and Mother-Child Relation

In social structural terms the major variable in the causal nexus described above is the female role, which is in turn defined by Indian values. However, the term "values" is too vague, since Hindu India is not uniform in its value system. To bring some consistency to the notion of values, let me focus on a major value system that influences many sectors of Hindu society—"the Brahmanic scale of values," or those values enjoined by orthodox Brahmanism. For example, it is likely that there may be a *kṣatriya* (or more specifically Rajput) scale of values that is different from the Brahmanic in relation to both the general life-style (warrior versus scholar) and the female role. There are "*śūdra* values," "tribal values," "Sikh values," and other types of value systems operative in various regions in the Indian subcontinent. My analysis of the mother-goddess cults is applicable only where the Brahmanic values hold sway. The Brahmanic values, however, are not confined to Brahmans; since they constitute the ideal values of Hindu society, they are extraordinarily widespread. Indeed, the process of Sanskritization as described by Srinivas refers to the conversion of non-Brahman caste values into Brahmanic values. Not all Brahmanic values are equally popular, nor does Sanskritization take place at a uniform rate for all values. But one subset within the Brahmanic scale of values has had truly profound effects on an extremely wide range of castes, particularly those occupying the upper to middle ranges in the status hierarchy. These values pertain to the norms of conduct and morality appropriate for females. Thus, in this chapter I am concerned not with the full content of

Brahmanic values, but only with those values that affect the female role, through proscriptions and prescriptions regarding the normative control of drives (particularly sex and aggression), definitions of interpersonal conduct, and moral norms pertaining to marriage and correct living.

While mindful that we are dealing with *ideal typical* situations, let us nevertheless see how the Brahmanic values affect the female role, and how this in turn affects the mother-child relationship. Let us first focus on the woman's role, for this will determine to a great extent her psychological and social relationship with her son.

According to Brahmanic ideology, the goals of marriage are *dharma* ("religious duty"), *prajā* ("progeny"), and *rati* ("pleasure"); thus sex is last in importance, and only a low-caste *śūdra* would marry primarily for pleasure (Kapadia 1955, p. 159). Marriage is a sacrament and generally is performed by a Brahman priest according to orthodox Hindu rites. Since a male heir is necessary to perform funeral rituals that will ensure the individual's salvation, marriage is viewed as absolutely necessary and a religious obligation. Marriage itself is completely irrevocable, and no dissolution is possible. Polygyny is permitted, particularly if no progeny results from the first marriage, but not polyandry. A man can remarry on the death of his wife, but widow marriage is not allowed.

The female ideal, as far as the Brahmanic texts are concerned, is neatly summed up by Srinivas: virginity in brides, chastity in wives, and continence in widows (Srinivas 1956, p. 484). Wifely devotion, known in Sanskrit literature as *pativrata*, is the ideal. *Pativrata* literally means devotion to the husband, an ideal of unquestioning loyalty. Hindu values emphasize unassertiveness in behavior, humility, and submissiveness to the husband (Kapadia 1955, p. 161). Brahmanic texts also enjoin the woman to treat her husband as a deity: the humble wife will eat the remnants from her husband's plate, as devotees eat the remnants (*prasād*) of the food offered to the gods. "Instances are recorded in the Puranic literature where a husband demanded his wife to take him to the house of a prostitute on her shoulder, and the wife willingly did it" (Kapadia 1955, p. 161). To sum up: according to Brahmanic theory the ideal for woman is *pativrata*: its concomitants are virginity at marriage, chastity as the wifely goal, unassertiveness and submissiveness, and unquestioning loyalty to the husband.

Let me quote some of the references to these role norms in the ethnographic literature. Submissiveness:

> it was assumed that a woman deserved no independence; she ought not to do anything on her own responsibility in childhood, or youth, or even in old age. (Dube 1963, p. 187)

> Norms of respectability enjoin almost complete submission on the part of daughters-in-law in particular and women in general. Men can scold their women and even hit them, depending upon their age and kinship status. (Dube 1963, p. 199)

> The mode of greeting for those relations [i.e., in-laws] and for her husband is for the women to bow low to the ground, and place her head on their feet. (Karve 1965, p. 136, on northern zone customs)

Virginity:

> In a large part of Hindu society pre-puberty marriages are regarded as ideal. Virginity is considered to be the most desired quality of a bride. (Dube 1963, p. 181)

> Any sexual lapse by a nubile daughter will bring lasting shame to her natal family. (Madan 1965, p. 77)

Devotion to husband:

Dube mentions the dictum that began to apply as early as A.D. 500.

> The wife ought to revere the husband as a god, even if he were vicious and void of any merit. (Dube 1963, p. 186)

It is thus evident that, according to Brahmanic norms, women are expected to have certain ideal attributes described earlier. The woman who exemplifies these—like Sita in the *Rāmāyana*—represents the ideal female role (see Coomaraswamy 1957, pp. 98–123, for a discussion of this ideal). Insofar as these role ideals are cherished by those caste groups that emulate Brahmanic values, one could presume there would be an attempt to implement them in the actual female role so that the actual measures up to the demands of the ideal. The role ideals must be learned; this is part of a larger process of role learning. Since females' emotional commitment to these ideals must be established, it can be presumed further that they are taught in very early childhood, as part of the socialization of the female child. I shall highlight one major consequence of learning the female role ideals in early childhood and its effect on later role performance. *Since the Hindu female role ideal of pativrata pertains to sex and aggression control, implementing the ideal in the socialization process entails the radical proscription of sexual and aggressive activity, which on the personality level demands the radical and continued repression of sex and aggression drives.* Inhibition of these drives is of course a relative matter, for any society must channel and bring under normative control the imperious drives of sex and aggression. In Hindu society this control as it applies to female role learning is carried to an extreme, and certain psychological problems pertaining to the adult handling of sex and aggression must flow from it. On the personality level certain consequences are expectable; sexual frigidity, somatization of conflicts, propensity to hysteria, and masochistic tendencies owing to the internalization of aggression. These traits are inferred from the effects of role learning; no empirical evidence is available regarding their incidence or distribution in any sample of the population. These are the *expectable* psychological consequences of the implementation of female role norms in the socialization process. Ideal role norms are never fully implemented in any society, and one could, even within India, expect considerable internal cross-societal variation. However, the ideal of aggression and sex control is a value for all Brahmans and for those who emulate them. Gough quite rightly says that the Brahmanic tradition emphasizes the control of libidinal and aggressive drives and that this has consequences later on for the Brahmanic attitude to sex, aggression, and filial piety (Gough 1956, p. 841). It is also likely, indeed inevitable, given the values sketched earlier, that the repression and control of these impulses will be much stronger in females than in males.

The emphasis on virginity in brides has several social consequences, based on the fact that somehow or other virginity at marriage has to be ensured. First, strict precautions must be taken to protect the girl from the possibility of sexual transgression and, even more important, to guard her reputation from any rumor of sexual immodesty, which would severely impair her marriage chances. As the girl nears puberty these precautions are strictly enforced, so that the pubescent girl is never allowed to be out alone but is always in the company of peers or a chaperone, and contact with males, except those of the sibling and parent categories, is restricted. The female grows up in an almost exclusive world of females, which usually results in positive identification with the mother and acceptance of the female role.

The second consequence of the preoccupation with virginity is early marriage, generally child marriage. Virginity at marriage can be ensured if females are married off before they reach puberty or soon afterward. Thus, though child marriages are not enjoined in the older Brahmanic religious texts, they are nevertheless a consequence of parental concern with virginity. Dube briefly traces the development of child marriage in India. He states that by about A.D. 200 marriage became for the woman a substitute for the sacred initiation, or *upanayana*, and was the only sacrament (*samṣkāra*) for the female. Since *upanayana* for boys was performed at the age of nine or ten, this also became the age of marriage for women (Dube 1963, p. 186). During the period A.D. 500–1800 the proper age for marriage was lowered still further, so that a girl had to be married before puberty, the age of eight being regarded as ideal (Dube 1963, p. 188). Because of this, women were denied education and any say whatever in their own marriages.

Third, the girl is given a great deal of protective care to safeguard her virginity. All these factors encourage parents to develop a special attitude toward the female child. *Since the female is viewed by her parents as a temporary status incumbent in the family, her parents show her considerable affection and solicitude and great concern for her welfare; thus the affective needs of the female are largely satisfied in her family of orientation.* Especially significant is the attitude of the father, whose relationship with the girl is not as ambivalent as the mother's. In the Brahmanic situation, as elsewhere, the mother disciplines the daughter and is largely responsible for inculcating in her the female values. The father can be, and is, purely loving and benevolent—an attitude he cannot have toward his son, who must stay in the parental household under paternal control, if not domination. For the girl the father is the ideal; she carries into later life the oedipal fantasy of the handsome and loving father. Moreover, where child marriages occur the girl is still so closely attached to her father that allegiance to her husband becomes especially difficult. The father not only loves his daughter but is also interested in her sexuality. It is imperative that she marry someone he approves; he gives away his daughter as a gift to her future husband—a *kanyā dāna*, "the gift of a virgin." On her part the little satisfaction in marrying an outsider comes from pleasing the father. On his part it is likely that this concern with his daughter's sexuality gives him vicarious, though unrecognized, pleasure. If perchance the daughter elopes or contracts a marriage without parental approval, even if the marriage is within the same caste group, the immediate parental reaction is rage. It is the mother, if anyone, who must allay the father's wrath and eventually effect a reconciliation.

What implications does this proposition about a special parental attitude have for marriage, which—as I pointed out—inevitably comes early? Since the ideal rule of marital residence is patrilocal, the female is transferred from the security of her parents' household into the alien household of her husband's joint family. As Mandelbaum points out, this transfer is traumatic for most young girls, for it involves a radical problem of adjustment from the role of daughter to that of wife and daughter-in-law. Says Karve of the northern zone: "The husband is a shadowy figure, the real people are the parents-in-law and from an indulgent home she has to go to strangers who are ready to find fault with her at the slightest gesture" (Karve 1965, p. 131). Karve notes again:

> Early marriage to a complete stranger out of the native village is a terrible crisis in the girl's life. (Karve 1965, p. 130)
>
> Hundreds of folk songs bear witness to the agony of a girl at parting forever from her parents' home. (1965, p. 131)[2]

In northern India some form of *sapiṇḍa* rule prevails. This rule in its classical form involves "avoiding marriage with somebody who is removed by less than seven degrees from the father and five degrees from the mother" (Karve 1965, p. 117). The consequence of the *sapiṇḍa* rule in northern and central India is that the female is transferred to a group

2. The psychological conflict entailed by early marriage to a complete stranger and by separation from the security of parental care and especially from the father's love is pathetically conveyed in these Pahari folk songs, recorded by Lizelle Reymond, in an eyewitness account of a Brahman wedding:

a. To find a kind husband for his daughter
Her father has searched the four corners of the world!
At last he has found him,
The perfect bridegroom for whom he sought!

The daughter is weeping;
"Father, beloved,
This husband does not please me
His skin is dark as night
But I am pale as the lotus flower!"

"Darling my daughter,
Rama and Krishna are blue as the night
But your husband comes from the country of the light,
Where I went out to seek him!"

But still the child weeps:
"Father, beloved, take pity on me,
Would you give me to this stranger?
You may do with me as you please,
I am a tethered lamb, I have no tongue,
If you will it so he can take me away. . . ."
(Reymond, n.d., p. 114)

b. Today I am like a fledgling on a branch,
But tomorrow I shall fly away.
Father! call for bearers,
Let them prepare my litter,
For I must be gone. . . .
My heart is heavy with grief
For I have become a stranger
In the home where I so often played.
Barriers have arisen between us,
Mountains and rivers already separate us.
Oh! Father! why have you given me away . . .?
(Reymond, n.d., p. 116; see also Lewis 1958, pp. 187–95)

unrelated to her before marriage. In these areas there are customs designed to help women adjust to the new situation at marriage. One technique is to create an *artificial* or fictional set of consanguineal kinsmen from among the women's newly contracted affines, so that these people can, at least in theory, perform the supportive roles incumbent on her true consanguineal kinsmen. Adrian Mayer shows how a woman gets a new fictional father and siblings in her husband's village in the central Indian village of Ramkheri (Mayer 1960, pp. 139–44).

I interpret these customs as designed to provide the female with artificial kinsmen to whom she can turn for succor or help in the situation of kinship alienation that results at marriage. Whether in fact the new kinsmen perform the same roles and provide the same support as the female's actual consanguineal kinsmen probably is empirically variable. The purpose of these customs nevertheless seems clear, though it is doubtful whether they are effective in providing such help, succor, and support.

I noted that at marriage the woman is transferred to the joint family of her husband, initially as a junior female in the new household. Consequently she has now acquired two crucial roles: that of wife and that of daughter-in-law. Let me deal with the wife role first and then consider the role of daughter-in-law.

According to Brahmanic norms the wife is expected to treat her husband as a god. This Brahmanic injunction is not simply a product of the sexism of the Purāṇas and Dharmaśāstras; it is also, I believe, importantly related to the fantasy life of Hindu women. The husband as god is based on the *model* of the man that the woman possesses in her own unconscious, and this in turn is based on her perception of her own father. The extreme idealization of the father occurs at practically every level of Hindu society and extends to Buddhist Sri Lanka. For the Hindu woman her father is *the* model of a man; this model is itself influenced by (and also influences) nonfamilial models of idealized male figures, the guru and the god. It is likely that she would want her husband to fit that model, to be an idealized and loving figure, almost a god. It is very unlikely that any woman consciously believes this parallelism will hold true; but nevertheless I think it is a part of the fantasy life of the Hindu female. In any case the father is the model by which she measures her own husband. Many marriages work or "fail" in terms of this internalized model of the father. In Hindu society the husband-wife tie can be very strong, but this bond is not primarily sexual. The husband can be loved and tolerated only if he is, or rather can be, viewed as a god—that is, an approximation of the woman's model of her father. However, it is likely that in many situations the woman does not take seriously the Hindu ideal of treating the husband as god. Yet among castes who have been most affected by Brahmanic norms there are customs that force the woman to recognize her husband's elevated position—as, for example, her modes of salutation and obeisance to him, and her eating his leftover food. Thus, even if women resist the comparison, it is often forced on them, and this in turn compels them to compare the ideal (the father model) with the reality of the husband. For women in families (especially among Brahman castes) who have been socialized to accepting the husband as a kind of god the reality would be even more difficult to take. To sum up: it is very likely that in a large number of instances the husband can never match his wife's ideal of the male, and often enough the real flesh-and-blood husband is a complete letdown. Hence sensitive females must search elsewhere for loving surrogate male figures, which in Hindu society are the guru and the idealized god (generally Kṛṣṇa in the North and Skanda-Murukaṉ in the South), toward whom a woman can direct her love, her *bhakti*, a combination of eroticism and devotionalism. The loving god and the beloved guru are sublimations of the father imago, and they are transformed many times over in the symbolic universe of Hindu life. For some women it is one way out of the harsh realities of the Hindu joint family. It should be noted that the guru is the only male outside the family with whom the female can interact freely without the taint of suspicion.

The newly married female has a second major role—that of daughter-in-law. As daughter-in-law she comes under the control and authority of her husband's mother. The regime of the mother-in-law is a harsh one, as practically every writer on the joint family has mentioned, particularly in the northern and central zones, where the mother-in-law is a stranger. Mother-in-law/daughter-in-law hostility and jealousy is institutionalized in the Indian joint family and is the subject of gossip, popular idiom, and folktale. These two kinsmen are competitors for the attention and affection of the man.

> The mother-in-law keeps a watchful eye open, and whenever the daughters-in-law make any mistakes they are treated with scornful taunts. (Dube 1963, p. 199)

Karve says that the mother-in-law (or sister-in-law) in the northern zone is especially dreaded. She may "wake up at night and interfere even if the bride goes to her own husband" (Karve 1965, p. 130).

> only when the mother-in-law is old or dead does a woman have freedom of speech or behavior. (Karve 1965, p. 136)

The other roles are not as clearly structured, though according to Karve the relation between a woman and her husband's sister is one of institutionalized hostility, while Madan, writing about Kashmiri Pandits, states that relationships between the in-marrying female spouses consist of constant bickering and jealousy, such that if "sisters-in-law do not have any disputes, the Pandit regard it as rather unusual" (Madan 1965, pp. 170–71).

The female's relations with her husband's younger brothers may be friendly, sometimes a joking relationship (Mandelbaum 1949, p. 102). The husband's father may sometimes be kind, but he is always an aloof figure. In general it can be said that her relations with the males of the household, other than her husband's younger brothers, are distant and aloof. The same aloofness is characteristic of the relations between husband and wife, for two factors militate against any visible display of affection between spouses—the general lack of physical privacy in the joint family household, and a cultural injunction against any such public display. Though overt signs of mutual affection probably do take place at night, the whole Brahmanic cultural tradition, with its evaluation of sex as polluting, of intercourse as physically harmful and morally inferior to abstinence, militates against the sexual bond's developing into a viable sensual relationship. This does not mean that the husband-wife tie is weak. On the contrary, it can be exceptionally strong, but the reinforcers of the marital bond are religious and ideological sentiments rather than those generated from sexual interests, as I noted earlier.

What are the implications of this analysis for the female role? First, *the female's need for love, solicitude, and succor cannot be satisfied in the situation that occurs soon after marriage in the Indian joint family.* Second, *the female retrospectively sentimentalizes the love and affection she received in her own family of orientation before her marriage and contrasts the nurturance of her own mother with the cruelty of her mother-in-law.*

The point of view I have taken involves some qualification regarding an earlier proposition, that the female's need for love is satisfied by her parents while she is living with them. "Satisfaction of the need for love or affect" is a relative matter, for the "satisfaction of affect" here makes sense only in relation to the "starvation of affect" that results from her early sojourn in her husband's joint family, under the regime of her mother-in-law. To meet this psychological problem pertaining to the female role, the Indian joint family everywhere provides one uniform institutional outlet: *it provides means for the female to reestablish kinship ties with her family of orientation during prescribed festival occasions and during life crises, especially sickness and childbirth.* Marriott has described a festival occasion where the daughters return to their parental homes (Marriott 1955, p. 198). More important is the recognition that the woman should return to her own parents during sickness and childbirth. Since these are occasions were regressions occur, the patient requires maximum attention and solicitude. This is obviously not available in her husband's household; the psychological environment for playing the "sick role" is best realized in her parental home. The permissiveness of her own parents is enhanced because the daughter is returning after an absence and because her visit is temporary, so that any negative parental attitudes that may have existed before her marriage are minimized or eliminated in the sentimentality that develops.[3]

According to Brahmanic norms a male heir is indispensable for the salvation of the father. The term for son, *putra*, etymologically means "one who saves the father from going to hell" (Kapadia 1955, p. 158). It is the son who must perform the prescribed Hindu funeral rites that save the father's soul. Thus the absence of a male heir is viewed with dread. These ideological factors affect the female who has just married in two ways: a pervasive fear of barrenness and the fear of not having a male heir (Mandelbaum 1949,

3. Let me quote from the literature references to institutionalized patterns of visiting the parental home during life crises and on ceremonial occasions (a "holiday from life").

> After marriage when she returns to her parental home for brief intervals, she is always treated as a guest and kept free as far as possible from domestic chores. It is realized that she has constantly to work hard at her in-laws, and so the brief sojourns in her parental home are regarded as a period of rest and recreation. (Dube 1963, p. 193; see also p. 199)

Karve, writing about Maharastra (central zone), says:

> It is customary for a girl to come and stay with her parents during her first pregnancy and delivery. A girl and her parents are put to great shame if she has no parental home to go to for her first delivery. (Karve 1965, p. 183)

Also:

> Among most people a woman comes and lives with her parents for each pregnancy and delivery though it is not considered as necessary as at the time of the first delivery. Each feast day brings back the married woman to her father's house. Once a girl comes to her father's house, it is always very difficult to get her back to her husband's house. (Karve 1965, p. 183)

Karve says that the Maharastra pattern is influenced by the customs of the southern area, where the Dravidian kinship system promotes continuation of ties with the parental family. In the northern zone the female almost completely severs connection with her parental family and is more or less fully incorporated into her husband's.

> When she goes back with her husband after the *guana* ceremony, she comes back but rarely on some ceremonial occasions. (Karve 1965, p. 127)

While this may be true of some groups, Madan, writing of the Kashmiri Pandits of the northern zone, says:

> A daughter loses no opportunity of visiting her natal home, in the early years of her married life, to be present at various ritual and ceremonial occasions, such as birthdays and death anniversaries. If taken ill, she may be removed to her natal *chulah* where she feels more relaxed, and hopes to be better looked after. (Madan 1965, p. 126)

p. 103). It is no accident that Indian society is greatly preoccupied with fertility rituals at marriage and has various vows, prayers, and rituals to ward off barrenness. In this kind of situation the birth of a male child is a critical event for every member of the joint family. From the point of view of the female it is a high point in her "moral career" and a realization of her maternal role. From the point of view taken in this chapter the birth of a child, particularly a male child, has further deep emotional meaning for the mother. I noted earlier that the young married woman's "need for love" could not be satisfied in the context of the joint family. *With the birth of the child the female's starved affective needs are realized through her infant, so that she develops an intense symbiotic attachment to her child.* Madan puts this well for the Kashmiri Pandits:

> Not to speak of the father, even gods are said to take the second place, after the mother, in a human being's life. Mythological tales are recounted and actual happenings recalled to stress how love and consideration for one's mother's wishes bring the fulfilment of one's desires. Rather than address the mother as a goddess, the Pandits refer to goddesses, such as Uma, as "the universal mother." The men speak of their women as *bacha parast*, "the devotees of children." The women refer to their children as their "womb" or "entrails," and an "own" child is distinguished from a step-child by being referred to as the child of one's womb or entrails.
>
> The physical intimacy of the mother-child bond is regarded as being without parallel; even the father's role as the begetter is much less stressed and sometimes made the subject of jocular comment in a manner the mother's role never is. Nevertheless, every human being owes his life to both his parents. Moreover, every Pandit man owes his social identity and status to his father. Mother-child relations partake of an emotional intensity which is not often achieved in father-child relations, but the father-son relationship is the very foundation of the Pandit kinship system. (Madan 1965, p. 87)

The growth of the child and his gradual induction into a wider network of kinship relationship puts an end to this "unambiguous" relationship until the birth of the next child repeats it in somewhat diminished form. The most intense relationship, as is expectable, develops between the firstborn male child and his mother, the intensity generally decreasing with the birth of every subsequent child and with the gradual enhancement of the female's status in the joint family as her age and maturity increase and her position becomes more stable.

A beautiful projection of this symbiotic relationship between mother and son is seen in the *Srimad Bhagavatam* (Bhagavat Purāṇa), which deals with one of the most famous of Indian myths, the life of Kṛiṣṇa. I quote the relevant part of the myth in full below. The myth makes psychological sense only in relation to the symbiotic mother-child relationship in the joint family.

> One day, when Krishna was still a little baby, some boys saw him eating mud. When his foster mother, Yasoda, learned of it, she asked the baby to open his mouth. Krishna opened his tiny mouth, and, wonder of wonders! *Yasoda saw the whole universe—the earth, the heaven, the stars, the planets, the sun, and the moon, and innumerable beings—within the mouth of Baby Krishna.* For a moment Yasoda was bewildered, thinking, "Is this a dream or an hallucination? Or is it a real vision, the vision of *my little baby as God himself*?" Soon she composed herself, and prayed thus to the Lord of Love:

"May thou who hast brought us into this world of maya, may thou who hast given me this sense and consciousness that I am Yasoda, queen of Nanda, the mother of Krishna, bestow thy blessings upon us always."

Looking at her baby, she saw him smiling. Then she clasped him to her bosom and kissed him. *Yasoda saw him as her own little baby Krishna*—him verily who was and is worshipped as the Brahman in Vedanta, as the universal Self in yoga, and as the God of Love by devotees; and she found an indescribable joy and happiness in her heart whenever she looked upon him. . . .

Once while Yasoda was holding the baby Krishna on her lap, she set him down suddenly to attend to some milk that was boiling over on the oven. At this the child was much vexed. *In his anger he broke a pot which contained curdled milk and then went to a dark corner of the room, taking some cheese with him.* After eating a part of it himself and getting his little face besmeared with cheese crumbs, he began to feed a monkey. When his mother returned and saw him, she scolded him. *As a punishment, she decided to tie him with a rope to a wooden mortar.* But to her surprise the rope, although long enough, seemed too short. She took more rope, but still it was too short. Then she used all the ropes she could find, but still Krishna could not be tied. This greatly mystified Yasoda. Krishna smiled within himself, but now, seeing that his mother was completely tired out and perplexed, he gently allowed himself to be bound.

He who has neither beginning, nor middle, nor end, who is all-pervading, infinite, and omnipotent, allowed himself to be bound by Yasoda only because of her great love. He is the Lord omnipotent, the Lord of all beings, the controller of all; yet he permits himself to be controlled by those who love him. Not by penance, nor by austerities, nor by study is he attained; but those who love him with whole-souled devotion find him easily, for they are his chosen—they who have pure love in their hearts. Infinite though he is, he may be realized through love. (*Srimad Bhagavatam* 1943, pp. 190–91, my italics)

Those who are familiar with the Kṛiṣṇa legend will know that Yaśodā is Kṛiṣṇa's "foster mother"; yet, as is common in this genre of myth, she is more purely maternal (i.e., loving) than any real mother. She is a "cowherdess," a source of milk, which represents maternal gratification and nurture. From the point of view taken here the most crucial parts of the myth are as follows:

1. Yaśodā sees the universe in the mouth of Kṛiṣṇa. In a sense this statement is true of the mother-son relationship in the joint family, for the whole life of the woman, her universe, is centered on her firstborn son. "Mouth" is highly appropriate, since it is the organ that connects mother with son in early infancy. There is independent evidence that my interpretation of this part of the Kṛiṣṇa myth is correct. If the child is the universe of the mother in this early symbiotic relationship, then the mother is also the universe to the child. This latter idea is excellently conveyed in another well-known Indian myth, that of Skanda and Gaṇeśa. In this myth Umā asks her sons Gaṇeśa and Skanda to circle the universe; while Skanda impetuously circles the physical universe, Gaṇeśa circumambulates his mother, who is *his* universe (see chap. 11 for details).

2. Yaśodā ties the infant Kṛiṣṇa to a mortar. I interpret the mortar to be a womb symbol and the rope the umbilical cord. Tying the infant to the mortar with a rope expresses the symbiotic mother-son relationship on the level of myth. I have no direct evidence from India that the equation "mortar = womb" is correct. Yet in Sri Lanka, which after all has

close cultural similarities with India, the pestle and mortar are used in rituals as male and female generative symbols. Moreover, the mortar contains the seed, which is pounded by the pestle. In many Indian languages seed is the equivalent of semen; the container of the seed (mortar) could easily, on the symbolic level, represent the container of the semen (womb).

3. The cord that ties Kṛiṣṇa to the mortar is always too short. From a literal point of view the umbilical cord, like the cord that binds Kṛiṣṇa, must have a finite length. Psychologically, however, insofar as the cord represents symbiotic maternal love, it is boundless.

4. Kṛiṣṇa lets himself be voluntarily bound by the boundless cord. The significance of this is stated in the text itself: "only because of her great love."

Give the sociological context sketched above, the child's fixation on the mother is perhaps inevitable. However, the intensity of the mother-child relationship is compounded by several factors. First, as psychoanalysts as well as sociologists like Talcott Parsons have pointed out, eroticism is integral to socialization everywhere (Parsons 1954). In the scheme of Brahmanic values eroticism is especially significant, since the female is highly repressed sexually, and some of her repressed feelings must surely receive expression in the intimate context of child rearing. Furthermore, if her sexual needs cannot be fully satisfied in her relationship with her husband, some of these feelings will inevitably be displaced toward the child. If so, the mother-child relationship must take on greater erotic meaning than in many other societies. The mother is a kind of seductress of the child. Mothers, for example, may express these erotic feelings toward the child quite openly, when they unselfconsciously kiss the son's penis (as they do all over South Asia). But this has the effect of enhancing the child's perception of the mother as an erotic object.

Second, this erotic fixation is further compounded by another factor—the mother's repressed hostile rage, which I mentioned earlier. The aggression drive, I noted, is radically proscribed in early childhood, and these repressions are firmly maintained. Furthermore, in northern India in particular child marriages are the norm, and the woman is transferred soon after puberty to the household of her husband's father. She is a physically and psychologically immature girl who has hardly left her childhood behind. At marriage her frustrations are increased as a result of her subservient role in the joint family. Yet there is no outlet for her rage; it cannot be expressed against the frustrating objects (e.g., mother-in-law), nor are symbolic outlets usually provided. Ancient Indian texts mention an "anger room" (*krodhāgāra*) in high-status families where women could act out their rage in isolation, but it is doubtful whether such customs were at any time widespread (Meyer 1952, p. 494). In the absence of such outlets, it is likely that some of this rage will be expressed toward the child, whenever he frustrates the mother, since that is the only object in the sociological landscape toward whom this rage can be directed with impunity. Even if the mother's rage is not expressed in overt physical chastisement, it is likely that the child, involved as he is in symbiotic relation with the mother, subliminally and unconsciously perceives the maternal rage from verbal and nonverbal cues. Furthermore, Carstairs mentions that, while the mother's love is readily available, there are occasions when she is remote and unapproachable—during her menses, where according to Brahmanic values she is polluted and rendered "untouchable." While the remoteness of the mother in this situation is compensated for by surrogate figures within the joint family, it is likely that the image of the untouchable, menstruating (bloody) mother conditions the child's maternal image (Carstairs 1957, p. 158).

These experiences must cause the child to perceive the mother as both loving and hating, close and unapproachable, divine and demonic—all these in extremis. It would be ridiculous to say that all Indian children, even those affected by Brahmanic values, experience the mother in the same manner. For some the maternal rage would be the dominant experience; for others the nurturant, symbiotic relationship; for others a combination of the two; and so forth. Yet these experiences of the mother would occur with sufficient frequency for them to be represented in various ways in the religous projective system.

The mother-child relationship discussed above is, I think, responsible for three images of the mother projected in Indian religious belief and ritual.

1. The sacred cow. If there is anything approaching universality and consistency in the symbiotic mother-child relationship in India, it is the nurturant role of the mother vis-à-vis her child. The mother is the giver of milk and food, which is embedded in the context of nurture and love. This aspect of the maternal image is symbolized in the worship of the cow, the truly universal sacred symbol in India. It is the image of the mother as totally nondemanding, unambiguous, and nurturant and the child as the passive recipient of her love.[4]

2. The Pārvatī image. The benevolent aspect of the maternal image is projected onto Pārvatī or other deities of the same type, like Lakṣmī or Sarasvatī. The relationship of the worshiper with the deity is idealized and loving. The goddess is in general benevolent, beautiful, and helpful to the devoted worshiper. Yet it is probably not the operatively dominant image in Hindu family life, unlike the image of the cow or that of the goddess in her fearsome aspect. On the cultural level this image is that of the mother in her role as "father's wife"; she is the model of Hindu wifely virtues.

3. The Kālī image represents the cruel, unpredictable, smothering, or castrating aspect of the mother, based primarily on the unpredictable (hysterical) nature of maternal rage as perceived by the infant. Like the former, this aspect of the maternal image may be represented by other goddesses of the same class like Durgā or Māriammaṉ or Devī, or the hundreds of mother goddesses of village India. In a sense the images of the cow and of Kālī are opposite extremes or two sides of a larger maternal imago: the totally loving and nurturant mother will smother her child, which then creates for the child the terrifying image of the mother.

The Descent Southward

In the absence of the ethnographic data it is not possible to document with certainty those regions or groups in northern India where the Brahmanic definition of the female role and the worship of these mother deities are absent. I believe all three images of the mother are widespread, though in some regions, such as Bengal, the evil, vengeful aspect of the maternal image represented in Kālī is more prevalent than in others. Kālī, or sometimes Durgā, worship is extremely common and, I think, more important than Pārvatī in the practical religions of ordinary people. It is of course of no consequence to my thesis if these deities were originally Dravidian ones incorporated later on into formal Hinduism.

4. Shulman refers to several cases of the aggressive, violent cow, but this is not the common or dominant Hindu image of the cow (Shulman 1980, pp. 97, 230).

They are omnipresent today, and the manner of their incorporation and widespread acceptance must be seen in relation to the historical development and diffusion of the Brahmanic scale of values. Historically these values spread from the North to the South, where they are also widespread. However, while these norms that define the female role are extremely common even in the South, there are certainly uniquely Dravidian institutional features that mitigate the strain in the female role. The structural situation in which the woman is placed softens some of the harshness of female role norms and promotes her social, if not psychological, adjustment.

What are the sociological or structural factors that help ease the strains of the female role? One of these is the absence of the *sapiṇḍa* rule and the substitution of cross-cousin marriage (or less frequently a man's marriage to his sister's daughter). The consequences of cross-cousin marriage for the female role are far-reaching.

1. Whether a woman marries an immediate or a classificatory cross-cousin, the husband is known, very often a childhood playmate. Indeed, as Yalman points out, since a cross-cousin is a potential husband, the girl can develop very early an erotic-sentimental relationship with him (Yalman 1962, pp. 556–82). (In Sri Lanka folk songs expressing this erotic-sentimental relationship between cross-cousins are quite popular, and I presume this must also be the case in the Dravidian South). Moreover, the girl's mother-in-law is no stranger either, but is her "mother's brother's wife," a positive, affectionate relationship in the southern (Dravidian) kinship systems. At marriage the bride moves into a known household, among familiar kinsmen, generally in a locality not too far from her parental home. Contact with the parents can be continued after marriage much more effectively than in areas where the *sapiṇḍa* rule prevails. Hence we may formulate a general rule: *the closer the kinship tie before marriage, the easier the adjustment to the in-law roles after marriage.*

Thus several of the frustrations that beset the female in the Brahman scale of values are minimized or absent in this case. Since her frustrations are less, I infer that the rage a woman feels is also less here than in the North. It is not absent, since repression of sex and aggression is well established in the personalities of all South Asian women; but the woman is better equipped to handle them.

2. The woman's affective needs are not starved in the virilocal household; she has more objects in the outer environment from whom she receives support and to whom she can give help, nurturance, and succor. Her child is only *one* of these objects, even though the most important one.

3. The Brahmanic values pertaining to sex are the ideal values of the South, but their practical implementation is variable, with high-status families more concerned with their strict implementation than low-status families. However, here also the mother's relation to the child can be erotic, so that she may kiss the child's penis to express her love. Mothers can consciously ignore the erotic component of the relationship, since Indian thought often defines the infant as asexual.

Relative to northern India (but not relative to Southeast Asia), the woman has higher status in the South. Widow remarriage is often permitted, and purdah, or seclusion of women, is nonexistent. Yet several other factors operate in the South. One is early marriage soon after puberty of the sexually inexperienced and immature girl. In general the girl has just left behind a relatively carefree childhood and has to take on the responsibilities of child care. The dramatic shift from childhood to adulthood entails considerable frustration, leading to unpredictable maternal rage that here also can be sensed by the child during the earliest period of mother-child interaction.

My use of the term "Brahmanic scale of values" is a useful heuristic device, but it can be misleading if it implies that other value scales cannot have similar consequences for the female role. In another scale of values one of these maternal images may predominate, given the Indian propensity to canalize personal conflicts through culturally constituted symbol systems. Thus I suspect that the traditional Nāyar (retainer caste) produced definitions and conceptions of the female role different from the Brahmanic in several ways, particularly the syndrome of the "absent husband" and, from the child's viewpoint, the absent father. In the Nāyar situation the mother's brother can of course be a surrogate father, but he is often absent too, serving in the army of the rajas. These factors place a greater onus on the female, so that she has to act as both father and mother (psychologically speaking). This social context then would, I think, conduce to the elaboration of the Kālī type of maternal image as against the nurturant symbol of the cow or the Pārvatī model. Furthermore—and this is most important—the absence of a male figure for positive identification may lead to identification with the (terrifying) mother, much more so than elsewhere in India, at least in enough cases to warrant its objectification in religious symbolism. I refer to the *veḷiccapāṭu* of Kerala, a group of religious specialists who in their trances identify with Kālī and practice head mutilation (see the appendix to chap. 15, pp. 600–602, for details). Clearly this is a difficult performance and, like the mutilations of the *galli*, cannot be practiced by every person who has an identity problem. The *veḷiccapāṭu* therefore not only abreacts his own problems but, as Lévi-Strauss says, becomes a model of the psychological problems of others in the group and abreacts on their behalf (Lévi-Strauss 1963, pp. 167–85).

Social Positioning of the Maternal Images

I shall not discuss here the social position and cultural significance of the nurturant image of the cow, since it is least problematic. The taboo on killing the cow, its veneration, is a near universal feature of Hindu culture and is the symbolic representation of the nurturant mother in the powerful nuclear experience of Hindus. On the cosmic level the same image appears as the heavenly cow (*surabhī dhenu*) who provides freely by fulfilling the wishes of individuals much as the human mother gives freely and unconditionally of her milk. Yet the cow is not a goddess in the pantheon and therefore is not directly relevant here. The cow is an image that reflects a problem of the Hindu experience; it does not help Hindus "reflect" on that experience. The goddesses, insofar as they are manipulated by human agents in ritual and behavior, help human beings express their experiences and in some sense deal with them. However, while the maternal images emerge from intrapsychic and infantile experiences, their cultural expressions as public deities in a pantheon also transcend these experiences and relate, on the conscious level, to other experiential domains. It is the relation of the goddess to these domains, especially the interrelation of the infantile to the sociocultural domains, that I shall now explore.

This discussion must naturally be tentative owing to the paucity of information on practical religion in India. I shall, however, draw on my personal knowledge of the Kālī cult in Hindu Sri Lanka and the excellent description by Babb (1975) of the Hindu pantheon in a village in Madhya Pradesh to push further the line of argument advanced in the preceding pages. The following quotation from Babb, I think, illustrates the general problem of the relation between the two types of deities—the Pārvatī model and the Kālī model. Babb says that the former is implicated in Vedic ritual and family worship while the latter is outside both.

> The goddess as Parvati or Sita appears in popular iconography in a matrimonial context, standing beside and subordinate to her husband. While Lakshmi usually appears alone, she is explicitly understood to be Vishnu's wife. But the goddess as Durga, Mahamaya, Kali, etc. . . . never appears in a matrimonial context, but rather alone, and surrounded with the paraphernalia of killing. (Babb 1975, p. 222)

The Vedic goddesses—the Pārvatī model—are implicated in the family structure, the public status and role system validated by Brahmanic values. According to this scheme, as I noted, the husband is superior and the wife is inferior, submissive. The Vedic deities in myth exemplify this role, and the Vedic rituals are related to the sacramental and life-crisis rituals of the individual vis-à-vis his family and domestic worship. Priestly rituals culminate with the union of the goddess with the god (Pārvatī and Śiva); the divine marriage parallels the human one. The values the goddess represents are those of the wife, as formally enjoined by Brahmanism and institutionalized in the public role. Insofar as goddesses are perceived as mother figures, the Pārvatī model represents the benevolent one, the wife of the god, Śiva, Viṣṇu, or Rāma. The morally sanctioned, predictable aspects of social life are embodied in this divine constellation.

By contrast, the Kālī image represents the wayward, unpredictable dimensions of social experience, outside the family and domestic life. Thus drought, plagues, famine, and pestilence are all due to the wrath of the mother goddess Kālī. When confronted with an unpredictable and uncontrollable disaster like smallpox (or drought), traditional communities must surely have faced a serious cognitive dilemma among other things. How could this disastrous event, which no known technology could cope with, have been caused? A logical explanation in Hindu cultures would be to attribute it to karma or to planetary forces. Another explanation expectable in the culture would be to attribute it to deities, either male or female. Practically all over India (and in the Hindu areas of Sri Lanka) terrible, unforeseen, unpredictable, and uncontrollable events like smallpox or drought are attributed to the rage of a Kālī-type mother goddess. Why? Because this rage is an experienced reality in Hindu infancy and is suited for explaining the wayward, unpredictable nature of the disaster. It is an experientially real and cognitively satisfactory explanation of such events.

It is not only wayward events that are associated with Kālī worship; morally wayward activities are also within her province. Activities that are patently antisocial—particularly sorcery and cursing—are often performed in Kālī shrines, but never in the shrines of any of the Vedic goddesses. Where these features are associated with Kālī worship, her shrines are almost always outside the temple for the Vedic deities. In rituals her marriage is almost never celebrated, but rather its opposite, the abnegation of the male—his surrender, as Carstairs has pointed out (1957, p. 159). The goddess is depicted trampling the male; she is often seen in iconography with the decapitated heads of males. She has to be appeased with animal sacrifices or, where this is not possible, as among the more orthodox, with symbolic substitutes (e.g., a mixture of turmeric and lime to simulate the red color of blood). Here, then, is the reverse of the Vedic rituals: the mother goddess is all-powerful, the male is crushed; he abnegates himself in surrender to the deity. He is, as it were, symbolically castrated. This reflects a dimension of the Hindu experience not recognized on the formal level—that is, the woman as wife, though socially inferior and subordinate to her husband, is on the psychological level a powerful person, as mother. Thus the ontogenetic experience of the terrifying castrating mother is expressed on the cultural level as the goddess minus her consort, who is propitiated to avert the untoward and unpredictable events that beset human beings. The infantile experience of the castrating mother is locked into the public rituals of the non-Vedic mother goddesses.

The Psychological Dimension of Sanskritization

In the preceding pages I have pointed out that not only does Brahmanization or Sanskritization produce a new scale of values, but these values affect certain critical roles, like that of the female, which in turn affect the nature and intensity of the mother-child relationship, thereby entailing the consequences described earlier in this chapter. These consequences constitute the psychological dimension of Sanskritization or Brahmanization. Thus Sanskritization involves not only the changes in values described by Srinivas, or cultural changes like the universalization and parochialization discussed by Marriott (1955), but also changes in family interaction patterns and the socialization of the child, which in turn have a feedback effect on the culture, fostering the commitment to both the nurturant and the Kālī types of maternal image. It must be emphasized, however, that the Brahmanic scale of values is a sufficient but not necessary condition for development of and commitment to these images. It follows from the logic of this argument that if a particular group is low on the Brahmanic value scale, or its functional equivalent, then variations of the maternal image will occur. The Sri Lankan data, both Buddhist and Hindu, will help illustrate these variations.

In Buddhist Sri Lanka the Brahmanic scale of values is supplanted by Buddhist values and different social structural conditions. However, there is nothing in Buddhism that inhibits the development of goddess cults in the practical religion. As I noted earlier, there is one dominant mother goddess here, Pattini, and in the more isolated regions there is an older deity known as Kiri Amma (see pp. 293–96). Basically Pattini is viewed as kind (*karuṇāvayi*), not stern or vindictive. Moreover, and this is another critical difference, infectious diseases are not caused by her—they are generally caused by Vaduru Mādēvi, a demoness. The goddess Pattini *cures* diseases and brings blessings, fertility, and plenty to the land. It is interesting to compare the Sinhala Buddhist with the Hindu (both in Sri Lanka and South India) attitude to the causation of disease and drought.

In *Hindu* Sri Lanka the goddess whose anger causes drought and subsequent illness is Pattini. The prototypical rage and the prototypical drought are seen as the goddess's anger at the unjust death of her husband and her destruction by fire of the city of Madurai. The increase of heat (in the body and in the environment) is due to her anger. This interpretation is rarely given by Sinhala Buddhists: for them the heat is caused by the demoness Vaduru Mādēvi ("the great goddess of plague"), who is never *propitiated* in Sinhala ritual. Vaduru Mādēvi is the Sinhala rendering of the Kālī image, for in many places in India Kālī is simply known as Devī (goddess, queen). The Sinhalas also refer to the demoness of plague as *dēvi*, but she is also recognized as a *yakini* (demoness) in the texts and represented as such in ritual drama (see pp. 261–62). According to Sinhala linguistic usage this demoness should properly be classed as a *yakini*; the name *dēvi* that she is given illustrates her tenuous link (now of no significance) to the Devī of Hinduism.

Pattini, according to Sinhala Buddhists, does not cause diseases but cures them. By contrast, according to Tamil Hindus she both causes them and later cures them when humans propitiate her. These differences in the perception of the deity reflect the values that govern the female role and affect the mother-child relationship in the two cultures. How do these Hindu values discussed earlier in this chapter vary in Buddhist Sri Lanka and affect the mother-child relationship?

First, what I have called "the Brahmanic scale of values" is not, in Buddhist Sri Lanka, anchored to a scheme of religious values as in Hindu India. For example, virginity and chastity in females are not associated with Buddhist ethics or doctrine; one consequence of this is that marriage is a secular affair in Buddhist Sri Lanka, whereas it is a sacrament according to Brahmanic values. Nevertheless, even in Sri Lanka these values are part of a secular ideology; but insofar as these ideals have no religious sanction their practical application shows a great deal of variability. In practical reality they are more the concern of high-status groups than of peasants, though they remain ideals for all.

Second, on the social-structural level Dravidian kinship with cross-cousin marriage prevails, as it does in South India. In addition to the implications this form of kinship has for the female role discussed earlier, the situation in Sri Lanka is rendered even more flexible for several reasons. There is, for example, an absence of joint families; the basic household unit in Sri Lanka is the elementary family, which implies that the female does not come under the immediate authority of a variety of senior kinfolk of the joint family—especially the mother-in-law—as in the neighboring subcontinent. I also suspect that, since there is no religious premium on early marriage, marriages have tended to be later than in southern India. The age of marriage for women is sixteen in Sinhala Buddhist texts, though in reality marriage may have occurred much earlier traditionally. However, prepubertal marriages were rare in Sri Lanka. Nevertheless the mother-child bond was a strong one; yet the need for the mother to act out her inner conflicts through her son would be much less here. In particular I would suspect that the maternal rage would be much less pronounced in this social situation.

The absence of joint families has a consequence for the father's role. Researchers have pointed out the extreme deference a son must pay to the father in the joint family. In some areas the married son cannot assert himself in any way in the household, so that he can hardly speak to his wife in the presence of others or caress or play with his child (Mandelbaum 1949). The absence of an extreme form of patripotestal authority and household structure has important consequences for the Sinhala Buddhist family. The husband can (and must) relate to his wife more directly, and, while the relationship is not necessarily overtly affective, the structural situation need not inhibit the development of affective ties between husband and wife. Father-child relationship tends to be very positive in the first five years of childhood, though later it becomes much more formal and reserved. Thus the mother-child relationship lacks its exclusive character; the child can be inveigled out of the mother's bosom by the father. If the mother's rage and her dependence on the child are less in the Buddhist case, then the child's perception of the mother as a vengeful, smothering being will also be less pronounced. Thus Kālī does not appear in the projective mythology, and Pattini takes her place.

Pattini, however, has *some* of the characteristics of Kālī; she tears out her breast to destroy the city of Madurai. I shall reserve the interpretation of this episode for a later section of this chapter. For the moment let me state that the effect of these conditions is that in Buddhist Sri Lanka the child does not perceive the mother as totally and unconditionally nurturant (cow) or as castrating and fearsome (Kālī). A different image develops, that of a benevolent mother figure, closer to the Pārvatī model than to Kālī—in fact, a different maternal image from the generally operative Indian ones. Further aspects of this image will be presented in the next chapter.

When we move to the Tamil-speaking matrilineal Hindus of the Batticaloa district on the east coast of Sri Lanka, Pattini rather than Kālī is the popular deity. Here also the culture is much less Sanskritized than in the Jaffna district in the extreme North. The Batticaloa *veḷḷāla*s (farmer caste) are organized into matrilineal clans (*kuṭi*), but unlike Nayars they lack the absent-father syndrome. Traditionally they were cut off from the Sanskritized North and were influenced by the Buddhist culture of the Kandyan court. Again we are confronted with the presence and nonpresence of the Pattini cult in relation to the Brahmanic scale of values. Where these values are fully assimilated by the culture (as in the *veḷḷāla*s of the North), Pattini worship as an independent cult simply does not exist; where these values are less firmly established (in the matrilineal *veḷḷāla*s of the east coast), the Pattini cult is widespread. On the east coast one does not come across the Shaivite Hindu temple complexes of the North; only small village temples for the mother goddesses (*ammaṉ*), and small temples for male deities like Gaṇeśa and Aiyanar. Vegetarianism is not widespread in the East, and some east coast Hindus actually eat beef. Nevertheless, east coast *veḷḷāla*s are Hindus and claim to be good ones. One could say that east coast *veḷḷāla*s are less Sanskritized than the northern *veḷḷāla*s; but they are obviously *more* Sanskritized than the Sinhala Buddhists. Rephrasing this in terms of family roles, we might say that the east coast female is less frustrated than her northern counterpart, but more frustrated than her Sinhala counterpart. The implication for socialization is that the child perceives the mother (one aspect of her) as more cruel and unpredictable in the Sanskritized Hindu North, less so in the East, and still less among the Buddhists. In relation to projective systems this means that the Kālī type of maternal image is universally believed in the North, much less accepted in the East, and nonexistent among the Buddhists (at least till very recently).

In terms of cultural projective systems even on the east coast there are striking variations between the Batticaloa matrilineal Hindus and those east coast Hindus farther north near Mulaitivu who have been influenced by orthodox Hinduism and Brahmanism. Both the matrilineal Batticaloa Hindus (*veḷḷāla*s) and those in Mulaitivu propitiate the goddess Pattini, but there are critical differences in these respective projective systems. The myths of Pattini in Mulaitivu described by Nevill (1888, pp. 16–22) view the goddess Pattini as an avatar of Kālī, and in several episodes the goddess behaves with violence and ferocity. By contrast Pattini is not perceived as Kālī in the formal myths of Batticaloa, and she acts with less rage than the Mulaitivu Kālī but more than the Sinhala Buddhist Pattini. Among the Batticaloa Hindus Pattini is the incarnation of the daughter of a Puranic sage, Parācara. However, it is true that nowadays intellectuals try to assimilate Pattini into the Kālī cult and thereby attempt to incorporate her into the Hindu great tradition. The myths sung in the annual festival in May do not make this equation.

Pattini as Kālī: The Mulaitivu (Sanskritized) Version

Let me summarize the main outlines of the Mulaitivu myth of Pattini as recorded by Nevill (1888).

1. The king of Pāṇḍi had issued an edict forbidding the worship of Kālī. He ordered the death of an oil merchant who lit lamps in Kālī's honor. Kālī vowed to destroy the Pāṇḍi king and, to do so, became incarnated as the wife of the oil merchant. The oil merchant was Kōvalan̲, and his wife was Pattini. The birth of Kālī as Pattini is nonexistent in the *Cilappatikāram* as well as the Sinhala Buddhist and Batticaloa Hindu versions.

2. The manner of Kālī's birth is interesting. The god Cokkalinkam (Śiva at Madurai) incarnated Kālī's life in a lime fruit and gave it to Pāṇḍi's queen, Kovilinki. A child was born to her with a golden bangle on her right leg, an amulet on the left, and a garland of flowers round her neck. The royal couple were frightened; they enclosed the child in a coffer and floated it down the river Vaikai. Downstream a merchant prince saw the casket, opened it, and adopted the child. (Note that in effect Pattini later not only destroyed Madurai, but also killed her parents.)

3. The vengeful nature of Pattini is exaggerated in the Mulaitivu version. She constantly curses people and indulges in violence. The following passage is particularly illustrative of her vengeful (though "just") nature.

> She now called the 6000 Pandians outside the Palace, and they obeyed her. She then announced that they were condemned to death, and ordered them to strip off their royal ornaments. . . . Then she forced them to stand upon all fours like cattle, and in degrading posture, and addressed them saying that they had committed three crimes, for each of which they merited death. . . . She now assumed her own divine and terrific aspect, and as Kāli herself, stood before them. She had huge teeth like a lion, protruding eyes like eggs, a trident in one of either hands, right and left, and in the others a garotte, a spear and two knives.
>
> Then she made the Pandians stand in one row, and pierced their bodies with her tridents, and plucking out their bowels, she hung them as garlands on her neck. (Nevill 1888, pp. 21–22)

Elsewhere it is said that "she pierced the belly of Muttumalai with her trident, though she was five months pregnant with child, and garlanded her neck with her bowels," and so forth (Nevill 1888, p. 22).

These bloody accounts are not mentioned in either the *Cilappatikāram* or the Sinhala version, and they are less pronounced in the Batticaloa version. Furthermore, contrast the previous life of Pattini (before her incarnation as Kaṇṇaki) in the three versions. In the Mulaitivu version she is Kālī; in the *Cilappatikāram* she is the wife of a good merchant named Caṅkaman̲; in the Sinhala version she is a saint meditating on Aňdungiri Peak and aspiring to future Buddhahood. The inference is reasonably clear: in Mulaitivu Pattini is gradually being assimilated into the Kālī cult, under the growing influence of the Brahmanic scale of values and its associated socialization experience.

By contrast, consider the Sinhala references to Kālī. I noted that the name of the demoness Vaduru Mādēvi of the Sinhala texts (p. 537) is a Kālī figure given an inferior role in the Sinhala myth. Elsewhere in the Pattini myth an explicit reference to Kālī is found in the ritual drama, *marā ipäddīma* ("killing and resurrection," text 42). Here Pattini's servant is called Kālī; in the ritual drama she is impersonated by an assistant of the *kapurāla*, dressed as a young girl, following her mistress suitcase in hand. The ferocious Kālī of Hindu religion is rendered innocuous and insignificant in Sinhala mythology. To sum up, Sanskritization is not simply a value change entailing the adoption of the Brahmanic scale of values; in the long run these values entail concomitant changes in the female role and in the mother-child relationship, which in turn affect the projective systems of Hinduism, producing in that religion the "cruel" maternal image of the Kālī type. Its relative scarcity historically in parts of South India and in Buddhist Sri Lanka is due to the absence or lack of intensity of these values and their socialization concomitants.

The Emergence of Kālī in Metropolitan Sinhala Religion

My earlier statement that Kālī was nowhere worshiped in Buddhist Sri Lanka requires some qualification, for in the metropolis of Colombo there are recent shrines (*dēvāle*) where Kālī is propitiated, if not as the presiding deity, as one of the major deities in the pantheon. These are not Hindu shrines (*kōvil*) but *dēvāle*s where Buddhists come to worship. This is truly remarkable, for rarely in the traditional regions of Sri Lanka is Kālī propitiated, at least in the Sinhala Buddhist areas of Sri Lanka discussed in this book.

It is difficult to evaluate how widespread the Kālī cult is in the city of Colombo. I have studied in depth one shrine in Colombo where Kālī is worshiped and given a prominent place in the cult proceedings (Obeyesekere 1975b). The city of Colombo has several of these shrines, all recently started, though I have no idea of their number and distribution. In many of them Kālī is one of the major deities, worshiped and propitiated along with other deities including Pattini. These shrines are not confined to any one segment of the city's population and they cut across class lines. Indeed, I have seen highly educated middle-class people, holding important bureaucratic positions in the government, and wealthy members of the elite who have begun to propitiate this deity. What, then, are the antecedent conditions that have brought about these changes—not yet widespread—in the religious pantheon? Does it mean the emergence of the Brahmanic scale of values in Buddhist Sri Lanka?

The answer is that profound value changes, as well as more obvious changes in social organization, have occurred in urban areas in Sri Lanka, specifically in the city of Colombo, which is the center of government and the residential locus of most of Sri Lanka's educated professional and bureaucratic bourgeoisie as well as the city proletariat. These changes in values are an extremely complex problem, and I shall greatly simplify my argument here, since I have discussed some of them in more detail elsewhere (Obeyesekere 1972, 1976, 1977).

Earlier I pointed out that some of the content of the Brahmanic scale of values constituted ideals for Sinhala people, rather than practical ethics. In the nineteenth and twentieth centuries these ethics received reinforcement from an unexpected source, the Protestant Victorian morality introduced by the British during their period of rule, 1815–1948. This morality became the practical ethics for the urban bourgeoisie; the Brahmanic values provided a cultural rationalization of Victorian morals and a mechanism for justifying them as pure indigenous values. Victorian morality was not assimilated in toto; rather, it became intermixed with indigenous values to constitute an ethic for the newly emergent urban bourgeoisie. These values spilled beyond the city and have affected high-status groups in the villages, who emulate city values and want their children to join the ranks of the bourgeoisie. Indeed, I believe the whole nation has reoriented itself to this value system.

These values have drastically affected marriage rules and sexual morality. Traditionally, Sinhalas were basically monogamous, though both polygyny and polyandry were permitted. Sinhala divorce laws were also extremely liberal, mutual consent being all that was required for a valid divorce. By contrast, contemporary laws of marriage and divorce are based on Roman-Dutch and English law. These laws have outlawed polyandry and polygyny and have made divorce extremely difficult to obtain except in the case of adultery, malicious desertion, or incurable impotence at the time of marriage. Underlying these laws is a rigid sexual morality that is not unlike the Brahmanic sexual mores discussed earlier. Women are expected to be submissive and to remain sexually pure until marriage. Parents take care to enforce these ideas, so that females are trained very early to rigidly conform to a pattern of submissiveness and sexual modesty. The effect of these norms on the socialization of the girl is the early and continued employment of repression as a major mechanism of defense for controlling sex and aggression drives. Indeed, I believe the combination of Victorian morality and the Brahmanic (ideal) values has produced a body of repressed females who have surpassed their counterparts in the Victorian Europe of Freud's time and are unparalleled in Sri Lanka's long cultural history.

These sexual mores are complicated by several sociological factors.

1. In village life there are always opportunities for heterosexual contact—in the neighboring bush, sneaking up the backyard, and so on. These contacts are virtually nonexistent in cities, with their nuclear households clustering together and their lack of solidary neighborhoods, or other foci of community consciousness.

2. Cross-cousin marriage with its attendant compensations does not exist in the city. Marriages were arranged till recently, and the husband is an outsider. However, certain compensations are available to the women. Nuclear households are normative in the city, so she does not come under the domination of in-laws. Many households have domestic servants, who help the wife with domestic chores and often serve as scapegoats for her frustrations. Nevertheless, it is likely that sufficiently large numbers of women would tend to express their frustrations through their children, which in turn would result in the child's perceiving the mother as a vengeful and unpredictable person—a Kālī-type maternal image. It should be stressed that Sinhala Buddhist urbanites are highly patriotic, which in Sri Lanka means anti-Hindu. Yet they have taken over a deity who has few roots in the Sinhala Buddhist tradition and whose (despised) South Indian origin they are fully aware of.

3. There is another critical feature of urban social structure that has encouraged this transformation. In urban Sri Lanka parents aspire to white-collar and professional employment for their children, which is radically at variance with the traditional peasant situation. In the latter the son followed the father's footsteps in farming or any other traditional occupation. The father also had the crucial task of training the son in his occupation, leaving the mother to perform a nurturant-expressive rather than an instrumental role. In the urban setup the father is away at work and the mother often has the task of inculcating changed aspirations and the new mores, pushing the child to achieve. This converts the typical traditional Sinhala peasant woman into the "Jewish mother." Given

the cultural propensity toward religious symbolization, the emergent maternal image is expressed through the resurrection of Kālī into urban religion.

The Goddess as Wife and Mother

In the next chapter I shall analyze in detail the nuclear psychological meaning of the goddess Pattini as virgin, wife, and mother in relation to her dying or dead consort Pālañga-Kōvalan̲. Here I shall briefly sketch the social-structural background that may be conducive to the development of the divine image of wife and mother in Sri Lanka.

Let me phrase my argument in the following manner. According to the preceding discussion, the mother-child relationship is a powerful symbiotic bond in Hindu India. On the level of personality this implies that the child will develop strong dependency and nurturant needs; these needs continue to be satisfied in adult life, since the mother is a continuing presence in the joint household. The relationship between a woman's husband and his mother is a continuous one, whereas the husband and wife are strangers recently united in marriage. The mother's continued physical presence in the household implies that she remains the dominant person to her married son. Furthermore, her (jealous) presence thwarts the development of affective and nurturant bonds between the son and his wife. It is the mother, not the wife, who continues to give nurture and love to the son. The wife for her part is sentimentally attached to her own family of orientation and practically tied to her child, who—rather than the husband—becomes her object of nurturance and affection. In this kind of family situation the demand that the wife fulfill her husband's affective and dependency needs can hardly exist. The model wives of the great deities of the Vedic pantheon are not nurturant figures but embodiments of wifely virtue, or *pativrata*, in the Brahmanic value system—it is their loyalty, submissiveness, and devotion to the husband as a deity that are emphasized.

By contrast, in Sri Lanka (and perhaps parts of southern India) the goddess is defined in the culture as wife and mother. Alongside this symbolism there is the associated symbol of the goddess's husband, his death and resurrection. I believe that neither the former nor the latter symbol could fully develop in the structural situation of the Hindu joint family, especially in northern and central India, since the husband-wife roles are totally subordinated to those of the mother, as discussed earlier, and of a father who possesses patripotestal authority. In Sri Lanka the critical difference is that the nuclear household is basic to the family and kinship system. In the nuclear household the mother is a nurturant figure to the son, though less so than among Hindus, but unlike the Hindu case the mother is spatially separated from her son and his wife when he marries. Thus there is at least one critical difference in the two situations—in Sri Lanka the mother is spatially displaced at the marriage of her son. Here also the husband has a strong need for nurturance and support, but this need is not satisfied, and perhaps can never be satisfied, by the wife, given the strength of the bond between mother and son. Furthermore traditional early marriage, even at age sixteen, which is the Buddhist ideal, implies that the wife is incapable of fulfilling these nurturant demands. Indeed, she is herself tied to her own family of orientation and to the strong emotive-erotic attachment to her own father. It is the poignancy of this family situation—the wish for the wife to be a mother, and her inability to fulfill this wish—that is expressed in the special image of the goddess in the Sri Lankan context.

11

Virgin, Wife, and Mother

The Virgin and the Harlot: The South Asian Version

We have several versions of the Pattini myth: that of the *Cilappatikāram*, the Sinhala Pattini myths, and the Tamil Hindu versions from the east coast of Sri Lanka. The major dramatis personae in this story are the goddess Pattini, her husband Pālañga or Kōvalaṉ, and Mādēvi: they represent the theme of the virgin, the harlot, and the fickle husband. The three versions are by no means identical: indeed, there are differences in the three versions. Nevertheless, in all three the central theme of the virgin, the harlot, and the fickle husband is remarkably consistent. Variations of this theme are found in many cultures, as, for example, in contemporary southern Italy and perhaps in all Mediterranean Catholic cultures. However, in Mediterranean cultures the Madonna is virgin and mother, whereas in the Sinhala version she is virgin and wife and mother. If the Madonna is the ideal mother, the goddess Pattini is the ideal wife; nevertheless, she is addressed and propitiated as "mother." The ritual *texts* deal with Pattini in the wife role; but she is mother goddess in the *interaction context* where human beings propitiate her, and in the Hindu areas her shrine is known as the *ammaṉ kōvil* ("mother shrine"). The question I shall address is this: How is it that men perceive Pattini as ideal wife, who is at the same time virgin and mother?

The problem of the virgin and the harlot was dealt with by Freud in two brilliant essays on the psychology of love (1910, 1912). Freud says that some neurotic patients in the society of his period expect certain conditions as a prerequisite for a love relationship. The "object choice" cannot be made unless these conditions are fulfilled. First, a man cannot choose a woman who is unattached; she has to have a husband, betrothed, or near friend. Second, "a virtuous or reputable woman never possesses the charm required to exalt her to an object of love; this attraction is exercised only by one who is more or less sexually discredited, whose fidelity and loyalty admit of doubt." This love relationship with the harlot type absorbs the whole of the mental energy of the man: "such women are the 'only ones it is possible to love,' and the ideal of the lover's own fidelity is invariably set up again, however often it may be shattered in reality" (1910, p. 195).

The source of this feeling is the same as in "normal" love based on the fixation of tenderness and love for the mother. The love for the harlot is *one* of the directions of this fixation, based on excessive libidinal attachment to the mother, unresolved at the oedipal stage and lasting well into puberty. When this happens "maternal characteristics remain stamped on the love objects chosen later—so long that they become easily recognizable mother-surrogates" (Freud 1910, p. 196). According to Freud, the injured third party (husband, betrothed) is none other than the father in the unconscious of these men; and the harlot is the mother.

But why harlot? The harlot, Freud argues, is the very opposite of the mother, who on the conscious level is represented as pure. In the same essay Freud goes on to discuss some of the sociological and psychological factors that assist the association of harlot with mother (1910, p. 200), but the detailed psychodynamics involved are discussed in a later paper entitled "The Most Prevalent Form of Degradation in Erotic Life" (1912).

In this paper Freud is interested in the causes of psychical impotence, defined as "refusal on the part of the sexual organs to execute the sexual act, though both before and after the attempt they can show themselves intact and competent to do so, and although a strong mental inclination to carry out the act is present" (1912, p. 203). In the ideal case the man fails sexually only with certain women. Freud argues that the reason for this peculiarity is that the sexual object is unconsciously associated with a mother or sister and therefore comes under the governance of the incest taboo. Hence the refusal of the sex organ to perform the sexual act, since intercourse is tantamount to incest.

In these cases a healthy (normal) pattern of psychosexual development is not achieved, and there is a disjunction between affection and sensuality. Affection, Freud says, is ontogenetically prior to sensuality and is directed toward family members. Of these the earliest choice of object is the mother. These fixations of the child's affection are maintained throughout childhood, continually absorbing erotic elements, which are thus deflected from their sexual aims. But about puberty the sensual element can no longer be contained. "It never fails, apparently, to pursue the earlier paths and to invest the objects of the primary infantile choice with currents of libido that are now far stronger. But in relation to these objects it is confronted by the obstacle of the incest barrier that has in the meantime been erected" (1912, p. 205). Therefore new objects with whom sex is possible have to be sought, but they are also modeled after the infantile ones, and the tender feelings toward family members are now anchored to the new object choice(s). In a successful marriage tenderness and sensuality are combined in the relationship with one's wife.

This pattern of normal healthy psychosexual development may be disturbed, generally for two reasons. First, the man may not make a correct object choice, because he cannot choose his mate freely. Freud possibly refers here to a sociological factor where the man's mate is chosen for him or where the marriage is one of expediency. In these situations affection and even sexuality cannot be fully realized in the relationship with the wife. More important is the second factor: "the degree of infantile attraction that may be exercised by the infantile objects which should be relinquished, and this is proportionate to the erotic cathexis already attaching to them in childhood" (1912, p. 206). Thus the libido is turned away from reality and becomes firmly fixated on the child's first sexual objects. But naturally this love cannot be realized because of the incest barrier, and so it remains in the unconscious. "In this way it may so happen that the whole current of sensual feeling in the young man may remain attached in the unconscious to incestuous objects, or, to put it in another way, may be fixated to incestuous fantasies" (1912, p. 207). The result is total impotence.

If the fixation on incestuous objects has been less severe, psychosexual development may result in milder forms of impotence. In these cases the sensual feeling is sufficiently strong to be expressed in sexual relationships with others, but such sexual feelings are devoid of tenderness. Thus a restriction is imposed on object choice.

> The sensual feeling that has remained active seeks only objects evoking no reminder of the incestuous persons forbidden to it; the impression made by someone who seems deserving of high estimation leads, not to a sensual excitation, but to feelings of tenderness which remain erotically ineffectual. The erotic life of such people remains dissociated, divided between two channels, the same two that are personified in art as heavenly or earthly (or animal) love. *Where such men love they have no desire and where they desire they cannot love*. (1912, p. 207, my italics)

How do these people resolve their dilemma? They lower the sexual object in their own estimation. "As soon as the sexual object fulfills the condition of being degraded, sensual feeling can have free play, considerable sexual capacity and a high degree of pleasure can be developed" (1912, p. 208). There is a polarity of feeling here: tenderness and affection are exclusively reserved for the incestuous objects and others that represent them (e.g., the wife), and sensuality is reserved for the sexual object (e.g., a mistress). Now Freud can link up this discussion with the theme of the previous paper. "The motives behind the phantasies mentioned in the preceding paper, by which boys degrade the mother to the level of the prostitute, now become intelligible. They represent efforts to bridge the gulf between two currents of erotic feeling, at least in phantasy: by degrading her, to win the mother as an object of sexual desires" (1912, p. 208).

Freud is dealing with a widespread but individualistic problem rather than a sociocultural one. However, Freud's argument can be translated into sociological terms: if fixation on the mother is a consistent feature emerging from the family structure in a particular society, then the consequent conditions mentioned by Freud may also be found in the sociocultural structure. Contextualizing for Sri Lanka, we can say that the family structure there might result in erotic fixation on the mother as a widespread psychological problem. This in turn would lead to certain expectable consequences on the psychological and sociocultural levels.

1. The incestuous feelings for the mother must result in fears of castration as punishment for incestuous wishes, either by the self or by another. In Sri Lanka castration anxiety caused by unconscious incestuous feelings may become complicated by the role of the father. Unlike the situation in Burma (Spiro 1973) and Italy (Parsons 1969), where the father role is weak, in Sri Lanka fatherhood is a positive role. On the projective level it is reflected in the pantheon, where there are gods who are clear-cut father figures, from the stern but loving Skanda to the benevolent Viṣṇu. The psychological consequence of the existence of a strong father role in the context of mother fixation is enhancement of the child's castration fears owing to his incestuous feelings toward the mother. These feelings toward the father as a castrating agent are fostered by an almost universal feature of family sleeping arrangements in Sri Lanka. In general, everywhere in Sri Lanka the son sleeps with the mother on her mat or next to her till he is at least four or five, and in many instances he continues to sleep close to her almost until puberty. The father sleeps on the veranda or porch outside, or in a separate room, and moves in periodically to have sexual intercourse with the mother. In these circumstances the child is an inevitable spectator of

the "primal scene," which reinforces his fear of the father as a castrating agent (and also perhaps is a factor in the formation of the many oedipal myths of father killing in Sri Lanka).

2. As a result of castration anxiety caused by incestuous wishes, one would expect on the psychological level a great deal of anxiety regarding one's sexual potency. I shall label this, for convenience, "impotence anxiety." Impotence anxiety does not mean that actual psychogenic impotence is widespread, only that the *fear* of impotence is extraordinarily common in the society. As is evident from Freud's analysis, what is empirically expectable would not be psychogenic impotence but rather concern with one's sexual adequacy or inadequacy. Impotence anxiety is reinforced by the cultural mores that define sexuality as a necessary but lower form of human activity. In this chapter I am concerned not with the incidence of sexual inadequacy but rather with the almost universal *anxiety* regarding potency, whether or not such anxiety has an objective basis in actual sexual inadequacy. As Masters and Johnson have pointed out, this anxiety regarding sexual inadequacy can come from a variety of sources—for example, from rigid puritan sexual mores, religious beliefs that say sex is evil, and so forth (1970, pp. 137–92). These factors no doubt operate in individual cases in Sri Lanka also, but the one consistent source for sexual anxiety is the psychogenic one of infantile fixation on the mother, which emerges from consistent structural features of the family in Sri Lanka (and of course in India, where the problem is greater).

3. Freud's argument is that the child's erotic fixation on the mother, reaching well into puberty, may result later on in a polarization of affect-tenderness and sensuality, these two being kept apart and expressed in social relationships with two types of female love objects—the "good" woman and the "bad" woman. Both are desirable females, but for different reasons. The first image of the mother is the idealized one: she is pure and undefiled, and therefore virgin. The unconscious equation "wife = mother" can in this case also be consciously recognized, since this female (wife cum mother) is idealized in myth and reverentially treated. It is commonplace for young men and adolescents to state explicitly that they want their prospective wives to be like their mothers, since the latter are idealized. By contrast, the idea of the degraded woman as mother, and to a much less extent as wife, cannot be brought into conscious awareness without producing extreme anxiety and undermining the values of the society. Explicit degradation of the mother does exist, but in special cases and in special ways (see pp. 480–82). In the projective system this leads to a very important "paradox": since the idealized mother is wife and virgin, she cannot bear children and is therefore barren, whereas the harlot (the degraded mistress-mother) is fertile. In the *Cilappatikāram* Pattini is barren, but Mādēvi the courtesan has a child. On the projective level there is therefore a peculiar feature of the mother-goddess cults in all the regions where these cults prevail. Unlike the Venus figurines of Paleolithic Gravettian culture, the childbearing aspects of the "mother" are not emphasized in the mother-goddess cults. Indeed, they are *denied* this, and the mother is generally represented as nonsexual. It is clear that we have here a special representation of the mother as asexual and childless. In the myths Pattini is born from a golden mango fertilized by Sakra, the king of the gods, appearing as a lascivious *senex amans*. But before he fertilizes the golden mango his testicles are pierced in the ritual drama of *aṁba vidamana* (shooting of the mango, pp. 490–95), rendering him sexless and castrated.

In the Pattini cult the goddess is not simply virgin and mother but, most important, is "wife." The wife role of the goddess is central to the myth and the cult; she represents for the congregation the true and ideal wife. This role of the goddess is of course the main contrast between the Virgin Mary cult and the Pattini cult. While the Virgin Mary has occasionally been viewed in the past as the bride of Christ, this notion is not central to Mariolatry, whereas Pattini as wife is crucial to the Sinhala conception. However, in both instances the unconscious equation is "wife = mother"; in the Pattini cult this is explicitly brought to the surface and expressed overtly in the mythology.

The unconscious equation "wife = mother" is again explicable in light of the preceding discussion. The mother is the most important person in the child's early life and becomes a "model" for women in general. This is also true of the father role, which Parsons (1965) points out is extended symbolically to authority figures in general. Similarly, the mother is person, model, and symbol of womanhood, so that a man's relationship to other women is based on the maternal relationship and for most men the ideal wife is modeled on the image of the mother. However, if the incestuous feelings toward the mother are strong, as in the situation of fixation discussed earlier, the "wife = mother" equation is complicated by this incestuous wish, so that "wife" also becomes *unconsciously* governed by the incest taboo. On the psychological level this means that sexual relations with the wife are highly disturbed, governed by feelings of inadequacy. On the projective level in the Pattini cult these feelings are expressed in the idea that Pālaṅga does not have intercourse with his wife, Pattini, who remains a virgin; he has full and unabashed sexual relations with the courtesan Mādēvi. But the courtesan is the sensual aspect of the maternal image, split off from the tender, asexual aspect (which is represented in the goddess).[1]

Is there evidence from the Pattini myths that justifies our psychological inference that Pattini and Mādēvi represent the maternal image, polarized into the good woman and bad woman, and that the psychological conflict here relates to mother-wife and husband-son relations? The Hindu (Mulativu) versions of the Pattini myth from the northeast coast of Sri Lanka (dealing with the former birth of Pattini, Mādēvi, and Kōvalaṉ) say that Pattini was Kālī reincarnated and that Mādēvi was Kōvalaṉ's (Pālaṅga's) wife in their former life. This part of the myth is utterly fascinating, and I shall quote it. The myth states that while awaiting his death at the hands of the executioner Kōvalaṉ prays to the goddess Mīnākṣī, who appears and comforts him. She says: "Why cry, my son? Will not that which is written on the head and in the horoscope come to pass? Ask any boon you wish and it shall be granted."

1. The empirical data for these theoretical inferences are scarce. However, Gough says this of Kumbapetti Brahmans:

> Individual men attempt different solutions to the marital conflict arising from this ambivalence toward women. Several in Kumbapetti seek sensual satisfaction privately with women of the lower tenant castes or of the caste of temple dancing girls. This course appears to arouse much anxiety in them, but enables them to isolate sensuality from the inhibiting influence of the home. Others permit themselves free sensual indulgence with the wife but express guilt on this account and deny the possibility of a tender relationship with women. A few attempt to annihilate sensual desire, to revere the wife, and to confine physical relations to producing children. Each of these varying solutions, though different in form, appears to illustrate an isolation of tender from sensual impulses which is, it seems, an almost inevitable outcome of the childhood and adolescent training of Brahmins. (Gough 1956, p. 842)

Kōvalaṉ replies: "I have only tied the necklet [i.e., *tāli*, symbolizing marriage] on my wife, and *she is still a virgin*." Mīnākṣī replies: "*She is your mother, and you are her son*, and your fate is that you should die in the sixteenth year. *In your former birth you were an oil merchant, and Mātaki* [i.e., Mādēvi] *was your wife*. Kaṇṇaki, however, is no other than Kālī, who has become incarnate to execute vengeance upon the Pāndyan." According to this account Pattini is Kōvalaṉ's wife; she is also a virgin; as an incarnation of Kālī she is his mother, and he is her son. Mādēvi the courtesan was Kōvalaṉ's wife in a previous birth.

Dilemmas, Oppositions, Contradictions

In the preceding section I examined the psychosexual basis for the major theme in the Pattini myth: the virgin and harlot. I also examined the psychological reasons for attributing to the goddess the qualities of virginity, wifehood, and motherhood. These qualities, it should be noted, are expressed in the myths and rituals of the Pattini cult in Buddhist and Hindu Sri Lanka: they are not found in the *Cilappatikāram*, which as a contrived work of art has to "fit" Pattini into the canons of epic literature of the period. In the epic Pattini is depicted as enjoying sex with Kōvalaṉ; but this idea is not mentioned in myth and ritual sources, which are obviously closer to the ideas of ordinary people. This is true not only of Sri Lanka but also of the popular version of the Pattini myths extant in South India, as Beck (1972, p. 25) and Shulman (1980, p. 157) have clearly shown.[2] But these mythical and ritual views of the goddess pose obvious cognitive dilemmas, such as the contradictory attributes of virgin, wife, and mother. Psychological factors are responsible for creating in the projective mythology the notion of a virgin goddess who is also mother cum wife: once created, the cognitive problems these contradictory attributes cause must be resolved on the cultural or individual level. These dilemmas, contradictions, and oppositions are the kind that interest Lévi-Strauss, except that in this case they arise from the psychological factors discussed earlier, rather than being the product of invariant features of the human mind. Let me spell out in detail the culturally defined attributes of the goddess, the cognitive problems they generate, and the attempt to resolve these problems.

Attribute 1

Pattini is a pure being, and the closest female human approximation of this idea is a virgin. In Sri Lanka—among Buddhists and Hindus—everyone emphasizes this attribute; she is pure (*pirisidu*), with no impurity (*kiluṭu*). These are consciously recognized attributes of the goddess. However, in the notion of the goddess's virginity is also embodied

2. Beck, contrasting the *Cilappatikāram* with popular myths, says that in the latter "it is made clear that Kannaki never knew her husband's body and perhaps never even touched him" (Beck 1972, p. 25). Shulman makes a similar comment:

> In popular versions of the *Cilappatikāram*, Kaṇṇaki's special powers derive from the fact that she was never touched by her husband. . . . The *Cilappatikāram* itself, of course, knows nothing of this: Kōvalaṉ and Kaṇṇaki like Kāma and his wife, embrace like serpents intertwined. In the epic, Kaṇṇaki exemplifies the chaste wife devoted to her husband; the folk versions which identify her with the goddess, require her to remain a virgin. (Shulman 1980, p. 157)

the idea of power: virginity bestows power on the female, just as sexual abstinence and withholding of semen are necessary for certain kinds of male power.[3]

Dilemma 1

Pattini is pure, yet she must be born in the human world as a female in order to redeem it. However, ordinary birth, according to South Asian conceptions, is an *impure* process par excellence. Is the pure deity to be conceived in the ordinary fashion, through sexual intercourse, conception in the womb, and birth—all impure processes?

Resolution: Buddhist Sri Lanka

Pattini, to remain pure, must be conceived and born outside the normal manner, unmediated by impure sexual intercourse and semen emission. In Sinhala, births outside of normal bodily processes are known as *opapātika*. Pattini's *opapātika* birth is from a golden mango in the orchard of the king of Pāṇḍi. Sakra, the king of the gods, according to Sinhala myth, shoots the golden mango with an arrow; the juice from the arrow falls on the third eye of the evil king of Pāṇḍi and obliterates it; the terrified king places the mango in a casket and floats it down the river Kāvēri; the merchant prince picks up the casket and opens it after seven days; and lo! he finds a baby girl, whom he adopts as his daughter.

One problem is resolved: Pattini is conceived outside the impure human process, in a golden mango, gold being the purest metal. While Pattini escapes impurity by this mode of conception, we have to explain why conception and the birth process are expressed in that form in the myth. The answer to this question would lead us to a general problem of symbolic representation in myth. Ideas like sexual intercourse, conception, and birth (or any idea) can be stated directly in myth; but sometimes, as in the Pattini myth, this is not possible, for the goddess must not be born in the normal (polluting) manner. When this situation obtains, ideas of procreation and birth must be expressed indirectly, metaphorically, or symbolically, but in a manner consonant with human experience. Now, human beings have experience with sex, birth, and conception in two ways. First, we may experience them directly or get "factual" information regarding these processes. Alternatively, all human beings have experience with these realities indirectly—in dreams. Thus we have two modes of apprehending these (and other related) experiences: a direct or factual mode pertaining to our everyday life and our conscious minds, and an indirect, symbolic mode pertaining to our dream (or fantasy) lives and our unconscious minds. The problem of symbol formation in myth and ritual is often quite simple: when for some reason or other (for logical or psychological reasons) events, ideas, or thoughts cannot be represented in the factual mode, the human mind can fall back on the alternative symbolic mode (of dreams). Thus Pattini cannot be conceived in the ordinary manner: her conception is expressed in the idiom of dreams, which are also part of the psychological experience of the members of the group. This idiom may flout common sense, but it makes

3. Shulman has interesting thoughts regarding virginity and power in South India.

> Virginity is a kind of *tapas*, its loss equivalent to the squandering of accumulated energy. The virgin is invested with innate power (*aṇaṅku*) which, if properly controlled, can be used to great effect; thus in a number of Tamil folk stories a woman's brothers make great efforts to keep her unmarried in order to benefit from her sacred power. For the same reasons, the myths of Kaṉṉiyākumari elect to prevent the union of the goddess with her lord. (Shulman 1980, p. 148)

psychological sense, and people in the society can accept it as true and real. Once these ideas are represented indirectly and symbolically, they are woven into the plot or story of the myth. It should therefore not surprise us that when human beings wish to present in their myths processes of conception and birth that are outside empirical reality, they express these ideas in another, equally familiar symbolic language, that of dreams. In the Pattini myth the symbol of conception is the piercing of the golden mango; mango = vagina; arrow = penis. Even in dreams symbols are not haphazard but, as Hall has convincingly demonstrated, must be organized into the plot or logical structure of the dream (Hall 1966, pp. 2, 7, 20). This is even more imperative in myth, which is essentially a narrative with a plot and a logical sequence of events. The symbolism "arrow pierces mango" has to be cognitively organized into the narrative of the myth. It has to fit into the "story." Thus Sakra comes down to earth in the guise of an old (castrated) man and shoots the mango. It is interesting that *aṁba*, which means mango, can also mean "woman" or "mother." It is also obvious that the priests are aware of the primary meaning of these symbols, for when the myth is enacted in some rituals the *kapurāla* who impersonates Sakra lies on his back, places the bow and arrow below his abdomen, and shoots at the mango (see p. 236). The juice from the mango falls on the middle eye of the king of Pāṇḍi and obliterates it. The king, frightened, places the mango in a casket and floats it down the river, where it is picked up by a merchant prince and his wife. After seven days Pattini is born from the mango. Here again we have the cognitive dilemma: Pattini not only must be conceived but also must be born in the human world. How is she to be thus born and yet avoid the pollution of human childbirth? Since literal childbirth is not possible, the myth has to incorporate a symbolic childbirth, based again on the type of symbolism one encounters in dreams: the casket floating down the river, as Rank points out, is a symbol of birth (Rank 1964; see also Abraham 1909, pp. 22–24).

Pattini, then, is born in a nonhuman manner: her conception is unmediated by sexuality, and her birth is undefiled by the womb's impurities. This idea of the goddess's purity is carried backward into her past lives. Thus in her prior life she was born from the tear of the *nāga* (cobra deity) king, a transparent piece of symbolism. She came down to earth as a young girl to sport in a pond, but a thief stole her clothes. Owing to her sexual shame she was metamorphosed into a blue lotus, a well-known symbol of purity. A Brahman tried to pick the flower, but it dived back into the pond. It is only when the Brahman had observed the Buddhist precepts (presumably the one pertaining to sexual abstinence) that he could pick the flower, which now metamorphosed into a young girl. Thus is Pattini born outside bodily processes. When she grew up the Brahman's wife decided to give her in marriage, but Pattini would not marry a "human thing"; instead, she fled to Aṅdungiri Peak to practice meditation (text 36, p. 230). Similar ideas are implied in accounts of the other lives of Pattini (texts 34 and 35).

Attribute 2

Pattini is virgin, wife, and mother.

Dilemma 2

Pattini is a pure, divine being; yet she is an impure human female. How could she be all these things at the same time?

These ideas have their genesis in the psychological problems discussed earlier; but once established they pose contradictions the group must attempt to resolve. Let me repeat that the purity of Pattini is everywhere stressed by the priests and ordinary folk I have interviewed. No one had the slightest doubt regarding this attribute of the deity, who is flawless and perfect. In Pānama I asked the *kapurāla* of the upper team why Pattini was called Seven Pattini. Instead of giving the conventional answer—that it referred to her seven births—he expressed it in terms of sex and purity. Alut Deviyo (Pālaňga), he said, constantly asks Pattini Deviyo, ever since their marriage, to lie in one bed with him, in order to get her with child. But she says, "I cannot agree; I am pure Pattini. I have no impurity." The *kapurāla* then went on to say that the term "Seven Pattini" refers to the types of abstinence Pattini must practice to maintain her purity. He went on to list six of these, which in turn could be subsumed under the following: Pattini must not have intercourse with her husband; she shall not provide Pālaňga with a son or heir; she has no *kiluṭa* (impurity), and if she has she will drop worms!

Resolution 2A

The two dilemmas are linked in that the purity of the deity is embodied in her virginity, since a virgin is the closest *human* approximation to that condition—unsullied by intercourse and childbirth. The dilemma of virgin cum wife is resolved in the following manner in the formal myths of the Hindus. The east coast Hindus I interviewed resolve it very easily: through child marriage. Pattini was five years old when she married; the marriage could not be consummated because Kōvalan̲ deserted her for the courtesan Mādēvi. Another solution on the east coast is to state that Kōvalan̲ deserted Pattini before they could consummate their marriage, an explanation also found in the South Indian versions of the myth (Beck 1972, p. 25). Thus Pattini can remain virgin and wife.

The introduction of the Mādēvi theme has two functions:

1. It removes the necessity for Pālaňga to have intercourse with Pattini and thereby destroy her virginity and her purity. Pattini can remain pure, while impure sex is confined to Pālaňga and the impure woman Mādēvi.

2. The introduction of the Mādēvi theme is not solely determined by the logical necessity to preserve Pattini's purity, for obviously other themes could be invented to resolve the dilemma. It does this *and in addition* introduces the theme of marital infidelity, which is important to the moral of the myth and also presents the theme of the harlot. The Mādēvi motif links the structural problem of the myth with the moral content of the "story"—that is, marital infidelity.

At age seventeen Pattini (Kaṇṇaki) decides to get her husband back. She does so by various ruses, and soon afterward they set forth to Madurai (see pp. 574–75). Presumably they should have had intercourse during this period, because they meet and remain in each other's company for some time. Yet intercourse, which is the legitimate right of marriage, never takes place, according to east coast informants. In the Mulaitivu version, immediately before his death Kōvalan̲ reaffirms that his wife is a virgin. Thus for some reason they do not or cannot have intercourse: the myths do not give any reason, though the priests, and believers, have their own explanation (which is not incorporated in the myth). Since this explanation is identical with that of Sinhala Buddhists, I shall postpone its discussion.

Resolution 2B

In Buddhist Sri Lanka child marriages simply did not exist and females married post-pubertally, so the Hindu child marriage solution cannot be employed in the Sinhala myth. So how did Pattini escape defloration and sexual intercourse? In the Sinhala myths also, like the Hindu account of Kōvalaṉ's later encounter with his virgin wife, the technique is simply not to mention lovemaking, though of course Kōvalaṉ-Pālaṅga's amours with Mādēvi are recounted in detail. However, Pālaṅga should and could have had intercourse with Pattini, since he had both opportunity and legitimate right.

Though the Pattini myths make no reference to this problem, the priests and practitioners of the cult everywhere in Sri Lanka have an answer. *Pālaṅga-Kōvalaṉ could not have intercourse with Pattini because he was impotent.* The blank space in the myth is filled in by the folk. Pālaṅga-Kōvalaṉ's impotence results in Pattini remaining *virgo intacta.* On the psychological level this is a *projection of the anxieties of people*, else why should they seek this particular solution to the cognitive dilemma of "virgin wife" when many other innocuous solutions are surely possible? The choice of the particular solution indicates a cultural preoccupation with impotence anxiety, which is precisely what I stated, on theoretical grounds, at the beginning of this chapter. It is interesting that, though Pālaṅga-Kōvalaṉ is impotent with Pattini, he manifests no such incapacity with Mādēvi, the courtesan, which again is psychologically expectable in terms of the Freudian explanation discussed earlier.

The cultural projection of Pālaṅga as impotent will help us understand why he is often, in the Sinhala areas, known as *terrunnānse*, the term used for a Buddhist monk. Yalman (1966, p. 214) also notes this but does not explain why Pālaṅga should be called "monk," when obviously he is not one and does not have the qualities of one, being married, nonascetic, and of dubious moral character. The title *terrunnānse*, or "monk," is given to Pālaṅga owing to its symbolic significance: the monk with his shaven head is a sexless—castrated—person, as Leach notes (1958). Now there is added justification for the interpretation of the dead Pālaṅga to be discussed later in this chapter: he is the castrated husband unable to practice intercourse with his virgin wife.

Resolution 2C

Pattini is a hermaphrodite. I encountered this explanation once in Balangoda district of Sri Lanka and nowhere else. At first I was puzzled by this explanation, until I realized that hermaphrodism not only prevents Pattini from having intercourse and bearing children, but also denies her the capacity to menstruate. Of the several explanations given, this one is most effective in that it denies Pattini all female pollution attributes, but in doing so it changes her into a "nonfemale" and does violence to the raison d'être of the whole myth. It is no accident that I encountered this explanation only once, whereas the impotence and castration of Pālaṅga were widespread explanations.

Attribute 3

Pattini is not just virgin and wife; she is also mother.

Dilemma 3

If mother, how could she be virgin; and if childless, how could she be mother?

Resolution 3

There was little overt cultural concern with this dilemma, unlike the previous ones. The answer is simple: Pattini is mother *because* she is goddess, and as goddess she is mother of us all.

The Impotence of Pālaṅga: The Myth of *Aṅkeḷiya*

The formal myths of Pattini in both the Hindu and Buddhist traditions make no mention of Pālaṅga's impotence, as I noted. But this idea is clearly found in the projections of the people and in indirect representation in the ritual drama of the dead Pālaṅga. People may sometimes *directly* speak of Pālaṅga's impotence, but this idea is *indirectly* represented in symbolic form in ritual and myth. The truly indirect and symbolic statement of impotence and failure at intercourse is expressed in the *aṅkeḷiya* myth (see pp. 519–23), which I shall now analyze in detail. The formal myths of Pattini leading to the *marā ipäddīma* ("killing and resurrection") are heroic in content: the *aṅkeḷiya* myth is the other side of the coin.

The *aṅkeḷiya* myth on one level is straightforward: it depicts the origin of *aṅkeḷiya* and gives that ritual, as Malinowski would put it, a *pedigree*. It also helps incorporate the *aṅkeḷiya* rituals with the other rituals of the Pattini cult. On another level the *aṅkeḷiya* myth, I believe, expresses on a wholly symbolic level the idea of intercourse, its failure, and the consequent humiliation felt by the male. As I pointed out earlier, a literal statement of an idea may be impossible in myth for logical or psychological reasons, in which case the idea is represented symbolically in the idiom of dreams and the unconscious. In the present case the reason for indirect representation is psychological: the idea of male impotence is too anxiety provoking to be stated directly. It is therefore indirectly and symbolically stated in the myth.

The origin myth of the *aṅkeḷiya* is found in Dunukeula, Pānama, and Biyanvila; it is totally absent in the Southern Province; in the east coast Tamil area an origin myth totally at variance with those in the Sinhala areas is found (see p. 564). Thus the myth of the *aṅkeḷiya* is not invariably associated with the ritual; the two are separable. Furthermore, the Pānama version of the myth is found in those areas where aggression is most developed, as are also the types of sexual projections I discussed earlier. And, most important, the Pānama myth has on the level of content very little substantive connection with the main body of Pattini myths, found in the thirty-five songbooks, or even the formal myths of Pattini found in the palm-leaf manuscripts in Pānama itself. Everywhere in Sri Lanka the outlines and content of the Pattini story are similar.

What does the *aṅkeḷiya* myth deal with? It deals with how Pattini and her consort tried to "hook" a *sapu* flower (*campaka, Michelia champaca*), and originated the *aṅkeḷiya* ritual. The theme of competition between the two, or that of the *sapu* flower, simply never enters into any of the formal myths of the thirty-five texts. Moreover, the style of the *aṅkeḷiya* myth is less literary and more folksy than that of the formal texts, again suggesting its independence from the main cycle of Pattini myths. The evidence is strong for the following inferences:

1. The *aṅkeḷiya* myth, which is found only in certain regions of Sri Lanka, is a later addition to the Pattini myths.

2. It is clearly absent in the Southern Province, where the team division between the goddess and her consort is nonexistent.

3. The overt purpose of the myth is to explain the origin of the division into two teams of Pālaṅga and Pattini.

4. The myth seems to be associated with those areas where interteam competition is strong and where the expression of sexual abuse and vilification is most developed.

In fact, the origin myth of *aṅkeḷiya* as depicted in Pānama and elsewhere is contradictory to the main body of Pattini myths. The competition between husband and wife that is crucial to the *aṅkeḷiya* myth contradicts the central theme of the Pattini cycle, which is that of *pativrata*, or wifely fidelity. Also, the Pattini myth does have its own references to *aṅkeḷiya* that, even if they do not overtly contradict the Pānama version, hardly lend support to it. One reference is where Pattini quells the demoness of disease, Vaduru Mādēvi, at the *velliye ambalama* and tells her to desist from killing humans and to accept offerings, one of which is the *aṅkeḷiya* (see text 54, pp. 261–62). The other refers to the original performance of the *gammaḍuva* and other rituals by the Brahmans from India to cure the ills of King Sēraman. Among the rituals performed in mythic times was the *aṅkeḷiya* (*aṅ maḍu*) (text 4, pp. 96–99).

The Pānama myth of origin of the *aṅkeḷiya* is one version among differing ones; it is obviously later than the ritual and is an attempt to explain some peculiar features of that ritual not manifest elsewhere—namely, the division into two competitive teams belonging to the goddess and her consort. Since the content of the *aṅkeḷiya* myth is so different from that of the rest of the Pattini cycle, I shall show that it has a symbolic structure that is determined—or overdetermined—by two important problems, a structural one and a psychological one, both of grave concern to the group.

In my previous discussion of the myth of Pattini I showed how certain dilemmas or structural contradictions are resolved on two levels—one on the level of the formal myth itself and another on the level of explanations offered by the ritual practitioners. These latter explanations deal with two basic themes: Pālaṅga could not have intercourse with Pattini because he was impotent; and Pālaṅga is a *terrunnānse*, a monk (i.e., a castrated person), and so cannot have intercourse with her. Since these two "explanations" have no foundation in the main body of myths that are sung in the Pattini cult, and since they are only two out of many logically possible explanations, I inferred that they are used because of the psychological concern Sinhala people have with impotence and castration. I shall now demonstrate that the *aṅkeḷiya* myth—a myth evolved to explain the competitive team division—gives indirect symbolic expression to the structural theme of marriage versus abstinence and to the psychological themes of impotence and castration. In other words, these psychological themes, which are crucial "cultural projections" existing outside the main body of Pattini myths, are now incorporated into a *new* Pattini myth—that of the *aṅkeḷiya*.

In examining how these two themes are enshrined in the myth, we must realize two basic attributes of myth. First, a myth is a story, and these themes must operate within the constraints of a "plot." Second, myth has an overt purpose: in this case we have an "origin myth" to explain the hooking of the horns and the competitive division into two teams. Since I have shown that the myth postdates the ritual, the purpose and plot of the story further require that the goddess should represent one team and her consort the other. The myth, then, moves on two levels: a story level, which has to account for the origin of the *aṅkeḷiya*, and a symbolic level, where major preoccupations of the group—the cognitive problem of legitimate sexual access and the unconscious fantasies of impotence and castration—are expressed. Even the structural theme, I shall show later, has a great deal of psychological meaning and is related on the psychodynamic level to the fear of impotence and castration. All these themes, I suggest, provoke great anxiety and are expressed totally in symbolic form. In the following analysis I will examine not the plot or story of the myth—which is straightforward enough—but rather the underlying symbolic meanings. The reader, it must be repeated, should bear in mind that the symbols operate within the constraints imposed by the formal plot.

Informants in Pānama prefaced the *aṅkeḷiya* myth with another myth that once again expresses the cultural preoccupation with the structural and psychological themes discussed earlier. I present herewith the account given by the *kapurāla* of the upper team (*uḍupila*). His account illustrates the psychological significance of a crucial term employed in *aṅkeḷiya*—*vāddu*, "conflict" or "debate."

> Pattini and Alut Deviyo started from India in two boats, and landed in Sri Lanka at Ōkanda, a village ten miles from Pānama. The boats in which they came got petrified, and even to this day you can see these two large rocks known as *ran oru gala* ["gold boat rock"]. When they landed Pattini made an *adhiṣṭhāna* [wish]: "I have greater power of *adhiṣṭhāna* than Alut Deviyo; if this is so it should rain blood today." Immediately a shower of blood-rain [*lē varṣāva*] fell. Even today you can see the bloodstains [spots] on these two stones, as if it had just rained blood. From here they came to the Gaṇeśa shrine [*gaṇa devi kōvila*]. They placed all their belongings [*baḍu bāhira*] on a rock slab inside the temple and shut the door. Then they came to the two large tamarind trees in the present temple premises. There they *vāddu* ["debated," "argued"]. Pattini climbed one tree [later her shrine] and Alut Deviyo climbed the other, and there they continued their *vāddu*.

Vāddu so far has two references: the conflict between the two teams is known as *vāddu*; the argument between Pattini and Alut Deviyo is also a *vāddu* and represents the prototypical *vāddu*. To the question, "What is the *vāddu* between the two?" the *kapurāla* of the Alut Deviyo shrine (upper team) had this to say: "*Vāddu kiyanne kasāda baṅdina vāddu ne*," "What is meant by *vāddu* is the *vāddu* [debate] about marriage." Requested for further elaboration, the *kapurāla* put it in the following manner: "The *vāddu* is this. When Pattini married Alut Deviyo, she refused to 'give him' [i.e., have sexual intercourse with him], because she must guard [*rakinava*] her virginity and celibacy. That is the reason why there was *vāddu*: she cannot 'give him' [though it is his right of marriage, I may add]. Thus, while the general meaning of the term *vāddu* is "debate" or "conflict," its specific meaning here is a conflict between Pattini and Alut Deviyo (Pālaṅga) because of her refusal to have intercourse with him.

To continue the account:

> Having climbed their respective tamarind trees, they "debate" with songs [*mal vahada*]. But they could not "break" this debate—could not put a stop to it. Then the god Gaṇeśa took two forked sticks [*keki*], hooked them, and having confronted the pair, asked them to establish concord [*sāmadāna*] [by having intercourse]. But Pattini says, "No, I am a Pattini [chaste one] without *kiluṭa* [impurity], hence we can't have concord."

It is clear from the preceding account that "concord" means that which comes from sexual consummation of marriage. If marriage is not consummated there can be only *väddu* ("conflict"), not *sāmadāna* ("concord"). The meaning of the hooked sticks (the text uses the word *keki*, "sticks," not *aṅ*, "horns") also comes out clearly. Gaṇeśa acts as peacemaker and brings out two forked sticks: the implication here is reasonably clear that the forked sticks represent that idea of linking or yoking together in legitimate intercourse. Now the account moves on a *totally* symbolic plane.

> Pattini and Pālaňga continued their *väddu* by entering into a conflict with forked sticks. They pulled at the hooked sticks, but neither could break them. Then Gaṇeśa made a wish [*adhiṣṭhāna*]. He took a pot [*sembu*] of milk in his hands and, accompanied by a Brahman, sought a kind of grass known as *aragum pulla* [which grows in the gardens of Pānama].[4] He put the grass into the bottle of milk. [Presumably this is a kind of fertility magic to make Pālaňga "win."] But Pattini countered this with her own wish [*adhiṣṭhāna*] "I will create a *sapu* tree and at the end of its main trunk [*mudun kaňdē*] I will create a flower. Let Alut Deviyo pick this flower if he can."

Even today, the *kapurāla* added, if you look at a *sapu* tree you will find a flower blossoming at the end of its main trunk. This, in fact, is not true; real *sapu* trees do not show this amazing phenomenon.

The preceding account, then, is a preface to the *aṅkeḷiya* myth sung in the rituals. Then the *kapurāla* added a postscript to the *aṅkeḷiya* myth that is also psychologically revealing.

> The *aṅkeḷiya* story describes the *väddu* between Pattini and Alut Deviyo [Pālaňga]. After the conflict was over they were reconciled [*sāmadāna*], but though reconciled [*sāmadāna*] they cannot have sexual union [*sambandha*].

Now we are in a position to discuss the psychological meaning of the three main symbols in the *aṅkeḷiya* myth—the forked sticks, the *sapu* flower, and tree climbing.

The Forked Sticks (*Keki*)

When Gaṇeśa wanted Pattini and Pālaňga to have sexual intercourse he gave them forked sticks. The idea of sex and marriage as a linking together is well established in Sinhala. Thus *sambandha* (sexual union) means literally "joining together" or "linking"; and in Sinhala marriage the little fingers of the right hands of the bride and groom are joined together with a piece of string by the bride's uncle. Also, there are two terms for marriage in Sinhala that again suggest tying or yoking: *baňdinava*, which means "tying together," and *hirē*, meaning "that which is tightened," "squeezed," "imprisoned." Thus I state that the two forked sticks are a symbolic representation of the idea of intercourse that follows upon marriage.

The *Sapu* Flower

Pattini creates a *sapu* flower in response to Gaṇeśa's magic and says, "Let Alut Deviyo pick this flower if he can." In the context of sex and marriage the *sapu* flower must refer to Pattini's virginity (see also Freud 1961, pp. 373–76, for flower = virginity symbol-

4. This is a corruption of the Tamil *arukkan pillu* (*Andropogon contortus*). The ordinary Sinhala term *ītana* is not used in Pānama, which has been strongly influenced by Tamil culture.

ism). The flower blossoms at the end of the trunk. Now "trunk," *kaňda*, can refer both to the tree trunk and to the human body, as it does in English. I suggest that the flower at the end of the trunk represents the vagina, but specifically *the idea of Pattini's virginity*. Thus Gaṇeśa provides the two forked sticks; the pair hook the sticks, but no one wins. Then Pattini creates the flower, the hooking is successful, and Pattini wins. But this takes us to the main myth, which I will examine presently.

Climbing the Tree

Yalman correctly notes that climbing the tree connotes sex (Yalman 1966, p. 217). Such a view fits in well with the psychoanalytic theory of symbolism, in which climbing stairs, mountains, and such indicates sexual intercourse. If we look at the myth literally, or as reflecting the conventional values of the society, the action of the female deity is singularly indecorous, since climbing trees is viewed as highly improper for females in Sinhala society and is somewhat demeaning even for males. For example, the idiom "tree climber" refers to a man so poor and incompetent that he has no other mode of employment. In one well-known Sinhala myth—that of Sāliya, the son of the famous King Duṭugämuṇu, this tree-climbing theme also appears (Yalman 1966, pp. 215–17). Sāliya, the prince, sees the *roḍiya* girl at the top of a *sal* tree picking flowers (note the symbolism again) and falls in love with her. But it should be noted that the girl belongs to an untouchable beggar caste, and so for her this behavior is not indecorous. But for Pattini it certainly would be.

Thus far I have examined the preface to the *aṅkeḷiya* myth proper and have stated the psychological meaning of three crucial symbols: the forked sticks, the *sapu* flower, and the act of tree climbing. Why is it necessary to express *ideas* in terms of symbols whose meanings are not apparent, on the conscious level at least, to the participants in a culture? I do not subscribe to the view that *all* myths must state ideas indirectly and symbolically; but sometimes myths do so. When they do, we can presume, it is because certain ideas simply cannot be presented *except* symbolically. A literal statement is impossible. For example, in hero myths recorded by Rank the protagonist may be born of human parents, yet the structure of the myth requires that he be reborn through adoptive parents. In these myths the latter rebirth, which cannot occur literally, is made to occur symbolically—as in the symbol of the watery rebirth. In other situations a literal expression of the idea may be psychologically threatening so that, as in dreams, the idea is indirectly or symbolically represented. In the *aṅkeḷiya* myth both these factors operate.

The main structural problem expressed in the *aṅkeḷiya* myth is one of great sociological concern to any social group: the problem of legitimate sexual access at marriage. This is a problem that emerges from the main Pattini myths and is unresolved therein. In those Pattini myths the central problem was the purity of the deity: this had to be reconciled with the fact of being female and impure. There was also a related problem: Pattini is married, but she cannot have intercourse, for that would violate her purity. Yet for any social group sexual access is the legitimate right of marriage. How can this self-evident sociological factor be reconciled with the mythic view that Pattini, who represents the ideal wife, must not have sexual relations with her husband? Clearly the structural theme of the myth violates a crucial behavioral norm.

I noted that two important cultural projections attempt to resolve this dilemma: Pālaňga as being impotent or castrated or both. But these are clearly also projections of anxieties harbored by the group; they also do not receive direct validation from the main corpus of Pattini myths. Furthermore, innocuous "explanations" of why intercourse did not take place between Pattini and Pālaṅga could easily be invented; the *choice* of these two explanations again suggests a cultural preoccupation with the problems of castration and impotence. These threatening ideas have to be expressed indirectly and symbolically in the *aṅkeḷiya* myth.

The major structural problem in the *aṅkeḷiya* myth, then, is to reconcile the legitimate demands of marriage (intercourse) with the demands of Pattini's celibacy and purity (abstention from sex, *brahmacārya*). The problem is impossible to solve literally: Pattini cannot remain pure *and* have intercourse. But, as I shall show later, the problem is of pressing psychological (as well as sociological) importance and demands resolution. If literal resolution is impossible, a symbolic or indirect solution is possible. This is what the *aṅkeḷiya* myth does. At the same time it also weaves into the myth the cultural projections of castration and impotence that I spoke of earlier.

Interpretation of the Myth of *Aṅkeḷiya*

The myth begins with Pattini's creating a *sapu* flower (Pānama) or sending forth a blossom from a *sapu* tree (Biyanvila). In the latter text, which I shall use for analysis, the incident is referred to as a "trick" played by Pattini.

> Goddess Pattini and Prince Pālaṅga
> Arrived at a park and were playing
> A blossom from a *sapu* tree was sent there [by Pattini]
> This is a trick that Pattini played.

From the commonsense point of view all this is absurd, for there is no logical reason for the introduction of the *sapu* flower motif if the purpose of the myth is to explain the origin of *aṅkeḷiya*. Logically the myth has to explain the hooking of the horns and the division into teams; the *sapu* flower is quite unnecessary for this purpose. Indeed, the *sapu* flower never enters into the *ritual* of the *aṅkeḷiya* at all. It seems reasonable to assume that the *sapu* flower is a vehicle for the expression of a different set of ideas. I suggested that the *sapu* flower represents ideas of Pattini's virginity, celibacy, and purity. The structural problem that the *sapu* flower symbol tries to resolve is that, though Pattini is married, she does not let her husband consummate the marriage. Thus Pattini tempts her husband sexually but refuses to be *deflowered*, since this will contradict the fact that she is Pattini, the chaste one. They decide to seek a *vila* (pond, marsh) and look for the *sapu* flower, though *sapu* trees in reality never grow in marshy areas. Thus the pond in which the flower grows is symbolic also: it represents ideas about the female vagina. Note that I do not, in the older psychoanalytic fashion of interpreting symbols, state that *sapu* flower = virginity, or pond = vagina or womb. I emphasise that they are vehicles for expressing *ideas* about virginity and sex, for the symbol does not exist by itself but is manipulated in the narrative or plot of the myth.

Looking for the *sapu* flower and picking it represent two ideas: the idea of Pattini's virginity, and her marriage to Pālaṅga. The myth tries to express and resolve the dilemma that follows from this—How could one marry and yet remain a chaste virgin? The obvious solution is to deny sexual intercourse to the husband, but this involves denial of his legitimate sexual rights. This is one of the major themes expressed indirectly and symbolically in the myth.

The actual quest for the *sapu* flower is "postponed" in the myth, through several techniques.

1. Before they start on their quest the goddess and her consort make offerings to seven gods, identified numerically rather than by name.
2. The pair arrive at six ponds where different kinds of flowers are found, and only at the seventh pond do they discover the *sapu* tree.
3. Even when they discover the *sapu* tree, they see no *sapu* flower at any of the seven cardinal points.

Through these techniques the central action of the story—the discovery of the *sapu* flower—is postponed. Again the repetitive verse technique illustrates the central conflict of the myth—the *sapu* flower has to be picked (Pattini must, according to norms of marriage, give up her virginity), but at the same time it must not be picked (she is *brahmacārya* and cannot have intercourse). Thus the action is postponed and the central conflict avoided. This "avoidance technique" is often found in myth, where a crucial conflicting issue is ignored, avoided, and sidestepped in some manner or other. For example, the biblical genesis myth has to resolve not only the incest of Adam and Eve but also incest in the next generation, for it is obviously through incest that humankind multiplied. The Bible sidesteps this issue, making detailed repetitive references to how one person "begat" the next till the world was populated, but quite ignoring the crucial "begat," namely incest in the second generation (Leach 1969).

After all these circumlocutions, the couple ultimately discovers the *sapu* tree.

> In the branch that shot up from the trunk
> A beautifully blooming flower they saw;
> The goddess Pattini dived into the pond
> From under the pond she saw the *sapu* flower.

The first two lines of the stanza above suggest that the *sapu* flower is not an ordinary one found in nature. Very much the contrary, for the preceding stanzas state that no flowers were found at the seven cardinal points around the trunk where one would *in nature* expect flowers. Rather, the *sapu* flower grows at the end of the main trunk of the tree. I noted that *kaňda*, or "trunk," can mean both tree trunk and the body in Sinhala (as in English); thus the flower that grows at the end of the tree trunk is a superb way of symbolically expressing the idea of *vagina intacta*.

The next two lines, once again, illustrate that analysis of symbolism according to the older psychoanalytic view can be somewhat misleading. From this point of view it makes no sense that Pattini should dive into the pond and see the *sapu* flower. I view the myth as an attempt to resolve the problem of virginity versus wifehood. This cannot be done on the literal level; it is expressed in the symbolic plane of the myth. The problem is expressed through various symbols like that of the *sapu* flower (idea of virginity) and that of the pond (womb). If certain ideas are communicated through these symbols, and if they are means for resolving the central problem confronting the protagonists of the myth, then the myth requires that these protagonists manipulate the symbols in a manner that will not offend the plot structure of myth, for all myths relate a story that has to be cognitively ordered. Thus Pattini's diving into the pond and seeing the *sapu* flower accomplishes two things: it satisfies the story (action) requirement of the myth, and it relates the two sexual symbols, since the *sapu* flower (virginity) is seen from under the pond (womb).

We now reach the critical point of the myth—the *sapu* flower has to be picked (idea of deflowering through intercourse, which is the legitimate right of marriage). The dilemma to be resolved is that intercourse must be had as a right of marriage, yet it must be denied if Pattini is to retain her sexual purity. Various symbolic means could be used to resolve the paradox; its peculiar resolution in this case indicates a special psychological problem faced by members of the society. In the Sinhala (and Indian) cultural context the problem is resolved as follows: *Sexual intercourse is a failure owing to the inadequacy of the male partner*. Thus Pattini can subscribe to the cultural norms of marriage (she is willing to have intercourse), but her consort cannot have successful intercourse with her (though the main myths clearly state he could with Mādēvi the courtesan). *The sexual failure of Pālañga helps preserve Pattini's virginity and her vows of sexual abstinence*. How are these ideas expressed symbolically in the myth? The pair take two hooks, and Pālañga climbs the upper side of the tree trunk while Pattini climbs the lower side. Climbing, as I said, suggests intercourse, in this case the attempt at intercourse. Intercourse, as the psychoanalysts state, can be expressed symbolically in dreams and myths in various ways; its representation as climbing suggests strain involved in the activity. Next the lovers try to pick the flower with their hooks (attempt at deflowering), but they fail.

> They miss the flower and entangle their hooks,
> They pull at their hooks till their hands are red,
> "This cannot be done," they cry and descend
> And depart to the city.

Again the dilemma is unresolved. Intercourse (which is expressed symbolically) has failed; they miss the flower. They leave for their city or village. The myth now, significantly, extends the conflict to include all males and females: the conflict becomes a general one between the sexes.

> Pālañga finds a thousand males
> Pattini a thousand females
> The two sides pull their hooks [*keki*]
> And Pālañga's hook breaks.

The breaking of Pālañga's hook, while Pattini's remains intact, gives expression to the idea of the failure of intercourse and the fear of castration. The next stanza, which contains the abuse by the females, seems to confirm this:

> The women then say thus:
> "Pālañga you are no male
> You can't manage [or cope] with us," they say
> They abuse and hurl insults in this manner.

This idea is repeated later on:

> They called Prince Pālañga a woman [i.e., minus a penis]
> "You can't win with us," they shame him.

Thus far the myth describes the competition between Pattini and Pālaṅga, and later between their teams of men and women. But Pattini's side always wins. The term used for hooks has consistently been *keki*, which signifies a long stick with a fork at the end of it used for picking fruits or flowers from trees. Suddenly toward the very end the word "horn" is used; *keki* is dropped completely from usage from this point onward in the myth.

> Prince Pālaṅga felt a great anger
> Now let us play "horns," he said
> They go to Andhra country
> They fill eighty bags full of *aṅ dara* ["hornwood"].

Aṅdara dēsa (Andhra country)—is a bit of folk etymology, where *aṅ* means "horn" and *dara* means "wood." Thus *Aṅdara dēsa* is the place where "hornwood" (*aṅdara, Dichrostachys cinerea*) is found. The change from *keki* is *aṅ* is significant. It lends further support to my view that the *aṅkeḷiya* ritual antedates the myth; the myth, among other things, attempts to explain the origin of the ritual. But in doing so it also gives symbolic expression to those psychological ideas discussed earlier. In order to do so *keki* (hook) is a more appropriate vehicle than horn (*aṅ*), since *keki* is used in Sinhala society to pick flowers, in this case the *sapu* flower that represents Pattini's virginity. Furthermore, it justifies and validates the use of substitute horns—made of wood (one of which is *aṅdara*)—for the *aṅkeḷiya* ritual.

In the horn game proper recounted at the end of the myth Pālaṅga consistently loses:

> Pattini takes a yellow branch [turmeric] in her hand,
> Sixty bags of horns she broke with that yellow stick . . .
>
> "Is that the way you play?" they mocked him.
> Prince Pālaṅga got very angry.
> He chased after the goddess Pattini
> And Pattini hid behind the tree.

Thus the myth ends with the goddess's side consistently victorious, contradicting, or seeming to contradict, the actual practice of *aṅkeḷiya* in Pānama and Biyanvila, where competition is "open" most of the time.

Let me sum up what has been expressed in the *aṅkeḷiya* myth.

1. The dilemma of legitimate intercourse versus sexual purity is resolved on a totally symbolic level, which is the only level in which it *could* be resolved. Intercourse cannot occur literally between Pattini and Pālaṅga; it is therefore expressed symbolically.

2. Pālaṅga's stick breaks, and he is humiliated. I interpret this as a continuation on the symbolic level of the cultural projection of fears of castration, sexual failure, and impotence.

3. The conflict is generalized to men and women: men lose, and women humiliate them. I suggest that castration and impotence anxiety occurs among significant numbers of men in the population.

In the myth, the precedence of the female deity is clearly established: her side wins. This contradicts or seems to contradict the situation in the ritual, where open competition occurs (except in Malidūva) and winning depends on chance and, to a lesser extent, on skill. It is as if the myth, while recognizing the sociological fact of competition, cannot recognize the precedence of the consort (who is not represented as defiant in the myth) over that of the goddess. How do people in Pānama overcome this difficulty?

Pānama folk have an addendum or postscript to the *aṅkeḷiya* myth. They say, rightly as far as the myth is concerned, that both Pattini and Alut Deviyo (Pālaṅga) want to win. But Pattini wins and Pālaṅga loses. Gaṇeśa (Gaṇa Deviyo) comes to Pālaṅga's aid, because they are both males, informants say. Gaṇeśa (the god with the phallic nose) pleads with Pattini and asks her to permit Alut Deviyo to win. "Alas, sister, even I am ashamed of him [his losing]," and Pattini allows him to win one game for every two that she wins, in the prototypic *aṅkeḷiya* played in mythic times. In the actual contemporary ritual there is once again a justification for Alut Deviyo's victory. The idea is that victory would be impossible for Alut Deviyo's team (*uḍupila*), in spite of all their skill, but for Pattini's gracious willingness to allow them to win. The *kapurāla* of the upper team (*uḍupila*) stated that at the dance of Alut Deviyo (Alut Deviyo *näṭuma*) held at the commencement of the *aṅkeḷiya* festivities, the god gets permission or *avasara* from the goddess Pattini to hold the *aṅkeḷiya* ritual and ensure victory for the upper team. "I am very obedient to you and humble, so please help me," he tells the goddess and worships her. Since she is a woman her mind melts (*hita unuvenava*). She thinks, "a male worships me," and decides to give him victory. I interpret this part of the *aṅkeḷiya* myth as expressing the other side of the coin: sociologically the male is superior, but psychologically he is inferior, because of his failure in intercourse and fears of penile inadequacy.

The Reverse of the Coin: Skanda and Valli Amma

The ritual dramas of the goddess Pattini were universally practiced in the villages of the Western, Southern, and Sabaragamuva provinces, while the *aṅkeḷiya*, as I have noted, was even more widespread in Sri Lanka. Basically the Pattini cult is oriented to males. It is true that the goddess as the curer of infectious diseases and harbinger of fertility is relevant to both males and females, but the psychological dimension of her cult is of critical concern for males. Where these psychological problems are aired in public by villagers, as in the *aṅkeḷiya* at Pānama, women are excluded from the proceedings. The cult nevertheless has considerable psychological meaning to the women also, but of a different order. The dominance and power of women over men in the psychological sense is expressed in the image of the strong, devoted goddess as against the fickle, castrated husband. In the previous chapter we noted that in India these two meanings are expressed in extremis in different symbolic systems and arenas—Pārvatī and Kālī. In the Sinhala ritual the two extreme images are brought together in the middle, so to speak, and thereby made less extreme, then coalesce in the image of Pattini and her consort.

In Sri Lanka the rituals and myths of the Pattini cult emphasized the relationship of the goddess with her consort, the fickle Pālaṅga. Everyone knows the myth of Mādēvi, Pālaṅga's mistress, and reference is made to it in the ritual songs. Several texts about Mādēvi are found in the thirty-five texts, but the ritual dramas do not deal with this aspect of the love relationship. The major focus of the rituals is on the goddess and her consort.

The other side of the relationship—the nuclear constellation of the man and the degraded wife-mother—is expressed in another ritual drama, that of Skanda and Valli Amma, enacted at Kataragama in southeastern Sri Lanka, the great pilgrimage center for Skanda devotees. Today the Skanda cult has almost totally eroded the Pattini cult, for reasons I have discussed elsewhere (Obeyesekere 1977, 1978). Traditionally this ritual enactment was performed only at Kataragama (and perhaps in a few other Kataragama shrines) but nowhere in village collective ceremonies. The Skanda–Valli Amma rituals celebrate the relationship of the god, who has left his legitimate wife Devasena (the daughter of Indra, the king of the gods) for Valli Amma, his mistress, a woman adopted by the aboriginal Väddas. Insofar as this relationship flouts the accepted Sinhala sexual morality as represented by Pattini, it cannot be staged in the collective village rituals in moralistic Theravāda society. Nevertheless, this aspect of the men's relationship with his mistress has great attraction for males, but it must be celebrated outside the village, at the central pilgrimage place at Kataragama. It should be noted that the Skanda–Valli Amma relationship also has great attraction for females, owing to its oedipal significance for them. Let me present the myths and rituals that express this relationship.

> The god Skanda came to Sri Lanka after having fallen out with his brother Gaṅeśa. This was how it occurred: A mango was floating down the stream, and Umā [Pārvatī], the mother, said that whoever rides around the universe first will get the mango. Skanda impulsively got in his golden peacock and went around the universe. But Gaṇeśa, who rode the rat, had more wisdom [cunning?]. He thought: "What could my mother have meant by this?" He then circumambulated his mother, then worshiped her and said, "I have gone round my universe." Since Gaṇeśa was right, his mother gave him the mango. Skanda was furious when he arrived and demanded the mango. But before he could get it Gaṇeśa bit the mango and broke one of his tusks.

Other versions of the myth substitute a golden mango in Umā's possession. Another peasant version is that Umā asked the two sons to go round the circle of salt; Skanda, interpreting this in one way, went round the ocean while Gaṇeśa went round the salt container in his mother's kitchen.

Myths like this one have several levels of meaning. Here also I am interested only in the psychological-erotic symbolism underlying it. Umā, the mother, has a mango (golden mango). The mango is explicitly a vaginal symbol in the Pattini cult, and I suspect in India too (see pp. 235–36). Umā's mango *is* the forbidden fruit. She gives it to Gaṇeśa, who circles his mother, his universe, the center of his life. This is explicit in the myth. Psychologically, Gaṇeśa is the son who is incestuously fixated on the mother. He eats the fruit and his tusk breaks—that is, he is castrated, for this is the consequence of incestuous wishes. Gaṇeśa, it should be noted, is potbellied. In South Asia, as elsewhere, maternal love is often expressed in overfeeding; Gaṇeśa therefore is the pampered son of Umā. Also, he has an elephant head—according to some myths this is because his real head was cut off by his father Śiva. I interpret this as castration by the father, and the substitution of the phallic nose, the elephant head and trunk, is a gross visible sign of his incestuous fixation.

The cruder version of the myth expresses the same symbolism. The mother asks them to go round the circle of salt, which for Skanda is the ocean and for Gaṇeśa is his mother's salt container. I am reminded in this context of James Joyce's characterization of the dead sea in *Ulysses* as "the grey sunken cunt of the world."

Gaṇeśa is one version of the Indian son. He is the oldest male in the (divine) family, and like his earthly counterpart he is pampered by his mother. Incestuously fixated on her, he is sexually crippled, a bachelor god incapable of marrying. In another version of the myth found in the Hindu Northern Province of Sri Lanka (Jaffna) and in South India it is stated that Gaṇeśa does not want to marry, since he wants his wife to be like his mother but none can match this ideal. Thus Gaṇeśa is generally a bachelor god, a rare creature in the Hindu pantheon. Significantly, when Gaṇeśa appears with a consort (*śakti*), as in Tantric forms of Hinduism in Nepal, his tusks are intact. It is also no accident that myths and rituals concerning Gaṇeśa are practically nonexistent in Sri Lanka in the culture area under consideration.[5] The Pālaṅga-Pattini theme better expresses the Sinhala dilemma. In contrast to Gaṇeśa, the younger brother Skanda is a different image of the son. He wants the mango, but he doesn't get it. His erotic fixation is not total. He leaves his mother and brother and comes to Kataragama.

The myth continues:

> Skanda came to Kataragama and there he saw Valli Amma (Mother Valli), a beautiful young girl adopted by the aboriginal hunters. She was picking flowers, and he approached her playing his flute [like another erotic deity, Kṛiṣṇa]. Gods can take many shapes, and so he confronted her in the guise of an old man, still playing the flute. He told Valli: "You are very beautiful. I desire you greatly. Will you marry me?" She said, "Chi! I am not going to marry an old man like you." Said he, "If so I will die," to which she responded: "I couldn't care less." Skanda was sick of life because Valli was so beautiful and she wouldn't have him. But Gaṇeśa saw this with his divine eye and thought of making up with his brother. He appeared as a wild elephant before Valli. She was terrified and asked Skanda to save her. He said, "I will if you marry me." She agreed, but meanwhile the elephant had run into the forest. Then the god revealed himself to her in his handsome form as Murukaṉ and she was happy. However, when she told this to her father he was angry and locked her up in a cave. But Skanda broke open the cave, and ultimately her father agreed to give her to him. The festival at Kataragama is the commemoration of these nuptials.

Let me interpret what I think Skanda represents as against Gaṇeśa. Gaṇeśa is castrated and impotent, a Pālaṅga figure in extremis; Skanda is virile and potent. However, the public celebration of his potency is not with his wife but rather with his mistress, Valli Amma. According to Sinhala beliefs, Skanda left his legitimate spouse Devasena, daughter of the god Indra, for Valli, who is "the secret woman" (*horagǟni*)—that is, the mistress. Valli literally means vine; but Valli Amma is the woman of the forest, the child of aboriginal hunters. Skanda's virility is manifest not in the legitimate wife, but in the mistress. Note that this is identical with one theme of the Pattini rituals—that of the fickle husband's relation with his mistress. At Kataragama, the great pilgrimage center in the jungles of southeastern Sri Lanka, the Skanda–Valli Amma relationship is enacted in great detail.

I noted earlier that it is not possible for village communities to idealize the theme of the "harlot," since it would violate the major moral themes represented by the Pattini myths. Wherever it appears in the Pattini corpus the Mādēvi (harlot) theme is subject to moral

5. Leach says that Gaṇeśa appears with both tusks intact in Pul Eliya, but I have not been able to verify this.

criticism, even though Mādēvi is no ordinary harlot but an accomplished courtesan. The social structure of a pilgrimage center is different from that of the village. When people come to a major pilgrimage center they leave their village identities behind them; the several village communities coalesce into the larger moral community of Sinhala Buddhists (Obeyesekere 1963, pp. 16–20). At the impersonal and egalitarian pilgrimage center of Kataragama the village status system and the moral values that govern it are not in force. Thus the illicit love relationship of the god with his mistress can be joyously celebrated. Its importance for Sinhala culture and personality cannot be overestimated. When Skanda is rejected by his mother (cutting his emotional ties to her) and leaves his legitimate wife, he is fully potent and virile. He joyously celebrates sex with his mistress. I might add that it is only in Buddhist Sri Lanka that this ritual enactment takes place; in Hindu India (and northern Sri Lanka) the Skanda ritual enactments depict his triumph over the *asuras* (titans). Thus the significance of the Skanda–Valli Amma myth and ritual must be seen as a foil to the Pālañga-Pattini rituals enacted on the village level. The dramatic rituals practiced in Kataragama today—fire walking, penances, and extreme forms of body mutilation—are all recent developments (see Obeyesekere 1977, 1978).[6]

The public ritual conducted in Kataragama is one of the fascinating cases in cross-cultural ethnology where a relationship that is illicit and immoral from the standpoint of the people themselves is celebrated joyously without a trace of criticism. Every evening for fifteen days the god is ceremoniously conducted in a magnificent procession to the shrine of Valli Amma, his mistress, situated a few hundred yards away at the end of the "street." It is also interesting that the procession bypasses the shrine of Devasena, his legitimate spouse, without acknowledging her presence. The secret, furtive nature of the journey is expressed in several symbolic sequences. For example, when the procession nears the shrine of Valli Amma, the torches held by attendants are lowered, and the god enters the mistress's chamber in this "dim light." During this whole procession men and women display an extraordinary religious devotion. Hindu women and men follow the caparisoned elephant carrying the god, singing hymns on Murukaṉ, the handsome one. Some weep and others are absorbed in worship while all shout, *"harō! harā!"* which is the halleluljah for Skanda. Few are *consciously* aware that they are publicly celebrating an act that violates some of the most central and cherished moral norms of their society.

The final event in the festival is "water cutting" and water sports.[7] I noted earlier that in its traditional meaning water cutting represented an attempt to control the element of water by magical means. The priests perform this ceremony in a screened-off area up the river. However, like fire walking, water cutting at Kataragama has coalesced with another ritual, that of "water sports." Water sports celebrate the washing of the clothes of the god and his mistress that have been polluted by sexual intercourse, when the god visits her on the final night and stays the whole night in her shrine. A huge concourse of people follows the water cutting procession. As soon as the water is "cut," the assembled throng lets itself go in water sports. A tremendous psychological release has occurred: people jump into the water, splash each other, and give vent to exuberance and joy. The water polluted

6. A Dutch account of 1765, for example, mentions the ritual enactment of the god's visit to his mistress but does not mention fire walking at all (Pieris 1950, pp. 695–701).

7. The water cutting here is different from the simple rite described in chapter 1. It combines two rituals—the actual cutting of the water (*diya käpīma*) and water sports (*diya keḷiya*). This is also true of Pānama. In Kataragama, however, the term generally used is *diya käpīma*, "water cutting."

by the god is pure for them: they drink it and carry it home in bottles. This is something more than "respect pollution" (Harper 1964). They have participated vicariously in the sexual life of the god and his mistress.

As with the Pattini-Pālaṅga dramas, the myths and rituals of Kataragama have significance for females also. The men can identify themselves with the god, who is rejected by his mother and now lives with his mistress after rejecting his wife. To the women, it should be noted, Skanda appears as an old man and only later reveals his handsome form. It is thus possible for females in the society to idealize him as an oedipal father figure, an erotic deity, young and yet old, on whom they can shower their love, as I noted in the previous chapter.

Pattini and the West Asian Mother-Goddess Cults

In this section I shall continue to explore Pattini's relationship with Pālaṅga by comparing it with the ancient West Asian cults of the mother goddess and her dying son Adonis. The classical anthropological treatment of these cults is Frazer's work *Adonis, Attis, Osiris* (Frazer 1914). The various mother-goddess cults that dominated West Asia in ancient times and later diffused to Greece and the far reaches of the Roman Empire have been exhaustively described by classical scholars. James gives an excellent summary of these cults in his book *The Cults of the Mother Goddess* (1959). In a later chapter I shall have more to say about these West Asian cults. Here I shall highlight those features of the cult that help us comprehend its psychodynamics and its relevance for the Pattini cult of Sri Lanka.

The cult of the mother goddess was widespread in western Asia and the whole Mediterranean region from about 500 B.C. and lasted there for three or four centuries after the beginning of the Christian era. The earlier antecedents of the cult need not concern us here, but everywhere in this region the mother goddess was worshiped in one of her forms (as, for example, Hera, Aphrodite, Kybele, Artemis). Associated with her was a young god—Attis, Osiris, Adonis—who was viewed as her husband, lover, and son. The mother goddess was often viewed as both mother and virgin, like her Indian counterpart. Aphrodite, for example, was both mother and virgin (James 1959, p. 149), and Hera renewed her virginity every year by bathing in the Spring of Kanathos at Nauplia (James 1959, p. 147). The cult of the goddess was associated with complex mystery religions whose secrets were accessible only to initiates. One feature of the cult, however, was public, nonesoteric, and extraordinarily widespread in the whole region. It involved a complex ritual drama where the priest impersonated the young god and acted out his death and resurrection. Occasionally the priest may actually have been slain, but more often a ritual mime of the death of the deity was enacted. The most popular of these male gods were Adonis and Attis. Adonis was killed by the boarhound under the yew trees, and so was Attis. Both, according to the popular versions of the myth, are supposed to have castrated themselves. The castration of Attis and his death (*Attis sese mutilans et moriens*) were powerful themes in Greek and Roman art. Attis is depicted as mutilating himself with a stone under a pine or a fir tree (Vermeseren 1966, p. 32). It is interesting that he is often depicted in art and myth lying under a tree, either dead or castrated. Attis's death and his subsequent resurrection were celebrated in Rome in two parts: "the *tristia*, the commemoration of Attis's passion and death, and the *hilaria*, the festivities of his followers who believed that the god comes to life again after a long winter sleep" (Vermeseren 1966, p. 40). Sculpture often depicts Attis as both *tristis* and *hilaris* (Vermeseren 1966, pp. 240–43). James rightly calls these the cults of the "dead god." Thus the cult of the mother goddess in the ancient Mediterranean and West Asian world was often associated with the cult of her son, the "dead god."

Historians of religion generally accept Frazer's interpretation of these rites as a symbolic representation of seasonal change; the death of the earth in winter and the burgeoning of new life in spring. While this interpretation is highly plausible, it nevertheless does not exhaust the symbolic significance of these rites. It also leaves unexplained the significance of the son's castration in the myth and, as I shall show later, the occasional self-castration practiced by the devotees of the cult. I shall speculate how the kinds of psychological problems discussed earlier "overdetermine," in the psychoanalytic sense, the symbolism of these rites.

My assumption is that the necessary sociological condition underlying the mother-goddess cult anywhere is the symbiotic relationship between mother and child, which on the psychological level results in the child's fixation on his mother. This type of mother-child relationship has several psychological consequences.

1. The fixation has an erotic component, so that very often the mother is also, in the unconscious, the lover or bride or wife and the son is husband-lover. This erotic relationship is projected onto the religious system in the symbolism of the goddess and her lover (son).

2. The erotic-symbiotic mother-son relationship that leads to fixation on the mother may lead to the son's psychological identification with her. The frequency and intensity of this identification wish depend on a crucial sociological variable—the presence or absence of a strong father figure. In India generally, patrilineal social organization and patriarchal authority are institutionalized; the father can be a strong, indeed authoritarian, figure. The religious projective system includes not only mother goddesses, but also powerful male deities. The attitude of the worshiper to many of these deities is based on the ideology of filial piety and respect. On the socialization level the existence of the authoritarian father (or father figures like the mother's brother in Kerala) implies that the child would feel afraid of his intense erotic attachment to his mother. One predictable consequence of this fear, according to psychoanalytic theory, would be strong castration anxiety. On the other hand, though the child is attached to the mother in a symbiotic sense, he can also identify himself with a powerful male figure, his father, whom he loves, fears, and hates.

3. If the father is absent, in a psychological or a social sense, the erotic attachment to the mother may be complete. Psychologically this condition may obtain in any society, but especially in the societies of South Asia. Sociologically such a condition is expectable where the father (or a surrogate) is away most of the time, as among seafaring groups or professional military men (e.g., the Nāyars). In either situation one would expect tendencies toward transvestism; alternatively one could expect not castration anxiety, but the wish to self-castrate—to biologically deny one's maleness and become like the mother. This is how I interpret the Australian subincision ritual, which Bettelheim calls vagina

envy (Bettelheim 1962, pp. 31, 53–56). I see it as total psychological identity with the mother, entailing a wish to be like her physiologically. I interpret the self-castration of Adonis and Attis as a projective expression of the same wish. James notes:

> The *galli* of the Syrian goddess Astarte of Hierapolis at the spring festival lacerated their arms and scourged one another to the accompaniment of the beating of drums. . . . Many of the young men were caught up in the frenzy, stripped off their clothes and emasculated themselves, running through the city with the severed organs, and throwing them into any house. In exchange they received female attire and ornaments. (1959, p. 167)

Elsewhere priests castrated themselves or were eunuchs (James 1959, p. 183). James, who in general is averse to psychological interpretations, calls this "sexual mutilation to secure identity with the goddess" (1959, p. 167). It seems most unlikely that this self-castration had to do with the death of the earth in winter and its subsequent regeneration. I am not suggesting that myths like the self-castration of Attis and the actual or displaced self-mutilation of the Galli are an aspect of basic or modal personality of groups among whom these myths and practices are found. Indeed, this is not likely; it only means that the wish to be totally identified with the mother occurred with sufficient frequency in these societies that these motives were objectified in myth and ritual. Perhaps small numbers of people represented in extremis a more widespread and diffuse cultural concern.

If we examine the previous quotation we note that some of the young men lacerated themselves, while others in a greater frenzy castrated themselves. The context makes it clear that laceration and flagellation are a *displacement* of self-castration. There is also a related meaning: I am now a woman and must bleed (menstruate). This has deep implications for our analysis. The wish to be castrated could be expressed directly in several ways or it could be displaced. Alternatively, the priest could castrate himself so that the audience could identify with him. Or the wish could be expressed indirectly or symbolically, as in myths and dreams. It is most unlikely that in general people would actually castrate or mutilate themselves except in the context of religious frenzy like that referred to above. In general one would expect these wishes to be expressed indirectly and symbolically in the religious projective system. And this is how I would interpret the dying god: it is a symbolic and indirect way of expressing the idea of the castrated son cum lover. The narrative statement is: "Attis castrates himself, and later he is killed by the boarhound." Psychologically restated it means, "Attis castrates himself = killed by the boarhound." The second sentence is an indirect restatement of the first. Members of the congregation could now identify with the dead (castrated) son.

The center of the cult of the mother goddess and her dead son was western Asia, including ancient Phrygia, Anatolia, Mesopotamia, and Syria, from where it spread to northern Africa and the whole Mediterranean region. In the first three centuries of the Christian era it was an effective rival to Christianity. It is reasonably clear that the cult of the Virgin Mary was a continuation of the mother-goddess cult. She is, like the others, a virgin and a mother and, at least in ancient times, was sometimes depicted as the bride of Christ. The tendency to deify the Virgin in the early part of the Christian era violated orthodox theology, but it was irresistible, and the Council of Ephesus (A.D. 431) ultimately gave theological sanction to the Marian cultus. While scholars in general recognize, sometimes reluctantly, that the Virgin Mary is a continuance of the mother-goddess tradition, they are unwilling to accept the transformation of Attis and Adonis into the Christ of Roman Catholicism. The dead, bleeding, naked, limp Christ so common in Catholic statuary and symbolism is on the psychological level, though not theologically, the equivalent of Adonis-Attis. It is interesting that in the first four centuries of the Christian era Christ was never represented as dead and bleeding on the cross, for this seemed to contradict the prevailing theological view of him as Christus Victor (Tinsley 1972, p. 26). Tinsley says that "iconographically it takes nearly five centuries before a body of Christ is placed on the cross at all" (1972, p. 26).

> The theological attitudes which delayed this development so long were clearly very powerful, but once realism had been admitted the move to a suffering, bleeding tortured Christ was inevitable . . . it took two centuries from the first appearance of the dead Christ before this treatment became established. (1972, p. 29)

The psychological reasons for this transformation were that under the pressure of widespread motives Christ was being converted into an Attislike deity, and eventually theology had to reconcile itself to this change. Michelangelo's *Pieta* is the finest artistic representation of this idea—the bleeding, dead god (son) in the arms of his mother.

Anne Parsons in her study of the southern Italian family argues that the father role there is weak and so the classical Freudian concept of the oedipal conflict is not applicable. She goes on to say that the child does not identify with the father to introject the paternal value system. She also says that in the religious projective system God the Father is a wholly vague figure, a kind of *deus otiosus*, whereas the Madonna is the key figure the man relates to. He worships the Madonna and identifies with Christ (Parsons 1969). "The man's internalized object in the case of man is a feminine one . . . a matriarchal rather than patriarchal superego" (1969, p. 383). But Parsons says this does not lead to a feminine identification, and here I fail to see her argument. According to my view sketched earlier, this may indeed lead to identification with the mother and a weak male identity, which is expressed on the symbolic plane in the figure of the dead and bleeding (castrated) Christ in the arms of his loving mother. Not only identification but introjection of the "dead god" occurs in the ritual of communion, where the worshiper eats (introjects) the body and blood of Christ.

Now we can see the parallelism between the Pattini cult, the cults of the Asian mother goddesses, and the Marian cultus. Pattini too is a kind of *mater dolorosa* weeping over the body of her dead husband, slain under the margosa tree. The ritual drama of the killing and resurrection (*marā ipäddīma*) represents the southernmost example of the cult of the mother goddess and the "dead god." Yet are we reading too much into the symbolism of the dead Pālaṅga, or is there some independent evidence that the death of Pālaṅga represents a castration symbolism?

There is *some* evidence that is fairly conclusive. Very often in ritual drama the way the actors perform their dramatic roles helps bring out clearly some of the latent meanings of the symbol. For example in the *aṁba vidamana* (shooting of the mango) ritual, the *kapurāla* lies flat on his back, places the bow and arrow on his abdomen, and shoots the golden mango—unmistakably bringing out the sexual meaning of the episode (p. 236). As I noted earlier, a similar thing occurs in the *marā ipäddīma*. Here the demon of death enters the arena and hoots and shrieks around Pālaṅga lying on a mat on the floor. Suddenly he kills Pālaṅga, then thrusts his sword under Pālaṅga's sarong and draws out his "bowels," dripping blood. I interpret this as symbolic (displaced) cutting off of Pālañga's penis. That disembowelment equals castration is clearly recognized in a Tamil myth quoted by Shulman (1980, p. 299).

> Pāvātairāyan̠ once shot an arrow into an anthill by mistake. He took a pickaxe and dug it out, thus unintentionally wounding the goddess who dwelt there. He wished to atone; the goddess asked for food, so he disembowelled himself with a pickaxe and offered her his vitals. . . . The transvestite Pāvātairāyan̠ stands to this day outside the shrines of Ankaḷamman̠; his act of self sacrifice, obviously symbolized by his woman's attire, has won him eternal life as an attendant of the goddess.

The equation of disembowelment with castration, both reduced to the transvestite image of the devotee, is clear from this myth.

In the Hindu northeast-coast (Mulaitivu) version of the myth (which is not dramatically enacted) Kōvalan was buried up to his neck in a pit and an elephant was sent to tear off his head. This failed, so executioners tried to chop his head off, but "the blade refused to cut him and instead there appeared a flower garland around it." According to the psychoanalytic theory of symbolism, chopping the head off is a castration symbol (Freud 1961, pp. 366–67). However, since the "plot" of the myth demands that Kōvalan̠-Pālañga be killed, I would be reluctant to interpret the head-chopping episode as castration except for what follows soon after. According to the myth, the executioners failed to chop Kōvalan̠'s head off, but then he begged them to guard his body until his wife should arrive, and, placing a chopper upon his head, he meditated upon Kaṇṇakai and willed it to pass through his body and cut him in two. In other words, Kōvalan̠ cuts *himself* in two (castrates himself) by thinking of his wife-mother Pattini.

The evidence that fully supports the hypothesis that the bleeding, mutilated Pālañga represents the "castrated son cum husband" comes from the comic ritual drama known as *rāmā märīma* ("killing of Rāma") described earlier (text 45, pp. 277–82). There I noted that *rāmā märīma* is a parody of, and a substitution for, the *marā ipäddīma* ("killing and resurrection"), which priests were reluctant to perform for fear of *vas* (ritual danger). *Rāmā märīma* is a rich, boisterous comedy that has no substantive connection with the Pattini myths. It is an attempt to overcome fear and anxiety by laughing them away, in the way that Sinhala peasants hurl obscenities when they feel they are in the presence of, or pursued by, invisible spirits. In this drama the actors can let themselves go, undaunted by the threat of *vas* (ritual danger).

In *rāmā märīma* the man who is mutilated and killed and subsequently resurrected is Rāma, the servant of a South Indian merchant. Since this ritual is a substitute for *marā ipäddīma*, we can legitimately infer that the mutilation, death, and resurrection of Rāma substitute for the mutilation, death and resurrection of Pālañga. Yet, since Rāma is not Pālañga but only a substitute for him, the actors not only cut up his body and disembowel him, as they did with Pālañga, they conclude the mutilation by chopping off his genitals (p. 000). In the Mātara and Sīnigama traditions another "comic" drama, the Baṁbura ritual, is performed in lieu of the killing and resurrection. Here also, as I shall show in the next chapter, the theme of castration is dominant.

The peasant enactment of Pālañga *mutilans et moriens* finds a striking parallel in the superb sculpture of the grieving Pattini and her dead consort by Sri Lanka's most gifted contemporary sculptor (see p. ii). No traditional artist could have produced anything like it, since the formalism of Sinhala painting and sculpture inhibited the expression of deep psychological motives. Since the modern sculptor does not suffer from the constraints of tradition, he can express in his art the deeper significance of the *mater dolorosa* and the mutilated husband. The spirit of the contemporary sculpture is close to that of the peasant ritual dramas I discussed earlier. It is likely that the modern artist was influenced by Michelangelo's *Pieta*, yet the total effect of the sculpture is different, a unique and powerful rendering of the Sinhala dilemma as expressed in ritual drama. In the *Pieta* the Virgin Mary is *dolorosa*, yet she is composed, even serene, in her grief, with the dead Jesus limp in her arms. By contrast Pattini is contorted with agony, her left breast gouged out, her left hand over her head in the typical Sinhala gesture of despair. Unlike Jesus, whose body is intact, Pālaṅga's body is mutilated, his right leg cut off at the knee and the left at the ankle; his genitals are missing and there are deep gashes at the site. It is fascinating that traditional peasant ritual performers in Sri Lanka and a modern sculptor sensitive to Sinhala culture arrive at a nearly identical portrayal of the *mater dolorosa* and her dead, castrated consort.

There is, I think, further evidence of an indirect sort that the bleeding and dead Pālaṅga represents his castration. This relates to Pattini's reaction to her husband's death, which is the primitive one (in the psychological sense) of *lex talionis*. It is also wildly out of proportion to the provocation, for she destroys a whole city and many of its inhabitants: I do to them a hundredfold what they did to me. If her reaction is one of talion, then it would be plausible to infer that the object (her breast) she used to destroy Madurai is also based on a psychologically motivated talion reaction: my husband is castrated, and I now castrate myself by tearing off my breast. Regarding breast tearing as castration symbolism, Flugel says:

> There is one way in which it is possible to carry out a fairly satisfactory (displaced) castration of the female, which, though not occurring in the mythological material we have considered, is perhaps worth mentioning here; that is, by cutting off the breasts. The breasts constitute an outstanding and vulnerable part of the female reproductive anatomy, corresponding in these two respects to the penis of the male. We know, moreover, that the penis and the breast are often unconsciously identified and that the breast is already for other reasons frequently associated with the earliest development of the castration complex. (Flugel 1924, p. 176)

Starcke (1921) and Lewis (1928, pp. 174ff.) present case material that fully substantiates the view that breast = penis. In the Sinhala case, we must remember, this equation is the product of the fantasy life of males rather than of females. Both Flugel and Starcke also point out that the breast = penis symbolism is overdetermined by the child's infantile rage owing to the weaning trauma (Starcke 1921, p. 183; Flugel 1924, p. 177). This again fits in with the Sinhala experience. In Sri Lanka, as in many other parts of the world, the mother's capacity for childbearing is fully tapped, so that, though the breast is freely offered to the child, it is soon transferred to the next comer. Thus the breasts are a source of both gratification and extreme frustration, Again this psychological experience is the basis for the cultural view, based on the male experience, of the breast as a powerful and dangerous force. Shulman says of South India: "The woman's violent power—sometimes called *aṇaṅku*, and often thought to be concentrated in her breasts—is erotic in character" (1980, p. 140).

To conclude this argument, let me present evidence from myth that suggests that the breast = penis symbolism is valid. In the myth of Vijaya, the founder of the Sinhalas, Kuvēni, the demoness, had three breasts. The middle breast fell off when she met Vijaya, her future lover and husband—that is, she no longer needed the fantasized "penis-breast" (middle breast), since she now had the real thing. A similar belief is recorded by Whitehead for Mīnākṣī of Madurai. Mīnākṣī was a warrior woman who refused to marry anyone; that is, she was a kind of male, and she also had a third breast (substitute for the penis and testicles). But when she met her future husband Śiva the middle breast withered away and she dropped her weapons—she became a normal woman (Whitehead 1921, p. 85).[8] In the Pattini myths it is said that the goddess's breast will be restored when she meets her husband in heaven (text 44, p. 277).

Christ and the Virgin Mary in Sinhala Catholicism

The preceding discussion regarding the psychological similarity between Pattini and the Virgin Mary and between Christ and Pālaṅga leads me to a discussion of the spread of Catholicism in Sri Lanka and some of the psychological factors underlying the diffusion of religions. One of the puzzling features of the religious situation in Sri Lanka is the large number of Christians (9 percent of the population) when their numbers are negligible in the other Theravāda countries of South and Southeast Asia. Buddhism, with its organized monkhood, was one of the few religions that could successfully withstand the Christian missionization. In Sri Lanka Catholics totally outweigh Protestants, who are a politically important but demographically insignificant urban elite. The phenomenon is especially puzzling because Sri Lanka came under the influence of two powerful Protestant colonial powers—the Dutch (1658–1796) and the British (1796–1948)—whereas Portugal was the sole Catholic power (1505–1658), and its sphere of influence was a narrow coastal stretch in the West. There are many reasons for the success of Catholicism, but let me emphasize the one that relates to the subject matter of this book. For Buddhists in practically all of Asia the dead and bleeding (suffering) Christ was utterly revolting and stood in sharp contrast to the Buddha statuary, which emphasized tranquillity, serenity, and the transcendence of suffering. The one exception was Sri Lanka, where there were some startling parallels: the Virgin Mary, who had the attributes of the goddess Pattini, and Pālaṅga who was a Christlike figure (not theologically but in his representation in ritual and myth). According to popular Sinhala beliefs two of the most famous Catholic churches in Sri Lanka—Saint Sebastian's Church near Colombo and the famous shrine of Our Lady of Maḍhu—were originally Pattini shrines. I have interviewed Buddhists who visit the Maḍhu shrine during the annual festival, and they simply believe they are worshiping the goddess Pattini. It is therefore very likely that one reason for the success of Catholicism in Sri Lanka is the affinity between the Catholic and the indigenous deities. Moreover, Catholicism is almost exclusively the religion of the fishermen of the *karāva* and *durāva* castes on the western seaboard. Fishermen are out at sea for most of the time; and many of these are migrant fishermen who move to the east coast when the southwest

8. Shulman mentions another case of the disappearance of the third breast in a woman when she sees the king who is destined to be her husband (Shulman 1980, p. 205).

monsoon hits the west coast and makes fishing hazardous. This kind of sociological situation results in the weak or absent father, fostering in the young child a female identity much like that obtaining in southern Italy. Thus Christ as the bleeding, dead (castrated) son has a great deal of psychological meaning for them. Hence, in spite of the vast *theological* differences between Catholicism and Buddhism, there are powerful *psychological* similarities between the Marian cult and the Pattini cult—which probably promoted the spread of Catholicism among west coast fishermen in Sri Lanka.[9]

The reference to Sinhala Catholicism brings me to the final problem I want to deal with in this chapter—the absence of a harlot in the Catholic projective system. This leads me to make a theoretical point about the nature of projective systems, namely that they are not mere epiphenomena of the personality or social structure but are idea systems that have reference to the cultural and historical experience of a group. Historically Catholicism had a difficult time incorporating the harlot theme into the Marian cult; it would be nearly impossible for orthodox theology to justify a harlot figure in the religious pantheon. Thus there is a lack of fit between the "nuclear psychological constellation" that requires both virgin (the idealized mother) and harlot (the degraded mother) and the orthodox pantheon that provides for the canalization of the idealized mother into the concept of the Virgin Mary but provides no religious object for the canalization of the degraded mother. In this situation two behavioral alternatives are available for the society.

1. Harlot figures may exist in the "diffuse projective systems" of the group—in literature, folklore, gossip, fantasy, or scapegoat figures in the society itself.

2. The mother goddess herself may become the butt of ribald humor in routinized degradations performed by men. Both forms exist in Catholic societies everywhere, the latter being especially conspicuous owing to the two radically contrasted conceptions of the same deity. I have heard Catholic migrant fishermen on the east coast of Sri Lanka, out there alone without their women, haul nets to refrains such as: "Mary, mother of us fuck! fuck! Heave ho!" Induchudan reports a similar phenomenon for the shrine of Kālī at Koṭuṅkoḷūr, near Cochin. During the great festival of the Bharaṇi asterism of the month of Kumpan (February–March) pilgrims from all over Kerala congregate at Koṭuṅkoḷūr (Induchudan 1969, p. 113). Here they sing obscene songs and perform obscene acts and gestures, most of them directed at the goddess herself, deliberately degrading her. I quote a popular saying from Koṭuṅkoḷūr: "If you want to fuck the goddess of Koṭuṅkoḷūr you must have a penis the size of a palmyra tree."[10] These forms of routinized degradation stand in sharp contrast to the Sinhala Buddhist situation, where there are harlot figures such as Mādēvi, Valli Amma, and others, in the projective system. The ritual degradation of the goddess (Kālī or the Virgin Mary) does not occur here, since these feelings can be projected onto culturally constituted objects in the religious belief system. However, even in the Kerala case, and perhaps also for Catholicism, the ritual degradation of the mother

9. A very basic reason for the success of Catholicism in Sri Lanka was that many of the *karāva* fishing communities were recent (i.e., post-sixteenth-century) immigrants from South India and were more vulnerable to Catholic proselytizing. Nevertheless, this factor alone cannot fully explain the success of Catholicism, since *karāva* communities in southern and southwestern Sri Lanka became Buddhist. Several historical and sociological factors were probably operative, the psychological factor of the dying god being only one of them.

10. Induchudan (1969) says that people sing obscene songs but does not mention that they are directed at the goddess. However, the information I gathered in 1974 leaves no doubt regarding this.

occurs *outside* the village, at a famous pilgrimage center where the operative values of the folk society are temporarily suspended.

Nuclear Psychological Constellations and Their Representations

In a preceding argument I referred to Valli Amma as the "degraded" erotic mother, like Mādēvi in the Pattini cult. This must be qualified, for, while the basic psychological problems arising from childhood fixation are as I defined them earlier, they are not directly expressed in ritual and myth. How then are the "nuclear psychological constellations" presented? A mythic tradition is rarely a direct reflex of the unconscious: unconscious primary process material has been worked and reworked in the minds of men through generations and brought in line with other cognitive, conscious, and philosophically profound aspects of the culture. Thus it is not only Pattini who is idealized: Valli Amma and Mādēvi are also idealized in their own way as sensually and erotically desirable images representing a thoroughgoing transformation of the infantile image of the degraded mother-harlot into another picture of the divine. Perhaps this can be further clarified by rephrasing the earlier psychological argument in a sociological manner. How is it that in a society like Sri Lanka women are treated as polluting and socially inferior yet are elevated, on another level, as idealized goddesses—either as Pattini (pure and virginal) or as Valli Amma–Mādēvi (erotic and desirable)? This is because a woman has several roles in society, as wife, as daughter, and as mother. It is the wife who is often viewed as a social inferior; the mother is the reverse; and the daughter is often treated with love. The poignancy of the Sinhala situation is in the man searching for the mother (as pure and undefiled) in his wife and, of course, rarely finding her. The aspect of the degraded mother he may see in the courtesan, harlot, or mistress. Yet what is striking about the Sinhala situation is that the unrealizable quest for the two mothers is resolved in the symbolic plane of myth and religion: the idealized mothers are the goddesses Pattini and Valli Amma. This is true for females also, for whom the god Skanda is what the husband can never be—an erotic, idealized father figure. Contrast this situation with Western romanticism, where one tries to divinize the spouse, an ultimately unrealizable quest since no flesh and blood human can measure up to the ideal. In Sinhala culture idealization can hold full sway untrammeled by the realities of mundane experience.

However, not all mythic representations permit idealization, for oftentimes "ideal representations" are matched with "catharses." In the cathartic rituals the nuclear constellations and primary drives are given freer expression, though also in symbolic form. Thus degradation of the mother is almost never permitted in the "ideal representations" of the priests. It may occur in cathartic rituals like the *aṅkeḷiya* in Sri Lanka or the *bharaṇi* festival of Koṭuṅkoḷūr (Cranganur) in Kerala. Sometimes an "ideal representation" may have a direct cathartic counterpart (the union of the god Skanda with Valli Amma: the water sporting by devotees); at other times a cathartic ritual may develop into an "ideal representation" (*aṅkeḷiya* in Pānama versus Malidūva). But always the cathartic ritual permits what is inhibited in the "ideal representation."

12

Functions of Aṅkeḷiya: Ritual Catharsis and the Collapse of Hierarchy

Restraint and License in the *Aṅkeḷiya*

A conspicuous feature of the competitive *aṅkeḷiya* is the dramatic contrast and alternative swings between the restraints imposed by the observation of taboos and the license permitted by the nonobservation of conventional social prohibitions. Since the word taboo lacks precision, I shall use the general term *interdiction* to characterize forms of conduct that are proscribed on certain occasions. I shall refer to two types of interdictions.

1. Social interdictions apply to everyday interaction. These proscribe acts that threaten to violate the very basic norms of the society, such as those concerned with sex. The incest taboo falls into this class.
2. Ritual interdictions are enjoined by the religion of the group and are strictly enforced on special sacred occasions.

During the period of the *aṅkeḷiya* there is a strict observance of ritual interdictions, especially those pertaining to purity and impurity. The whole village has to be "pure" and free from pollution. Thus menstruating women in Pānama are either sent to kinfolk in other villages or, traditionally at least, banished to specially constructed menstrual huts outside the limits of the village. The whole village must refrain from killing—fishing and hunting—and must totally avoid eating fish and meat in any form. Households that have recently experienced childbirth or death—polluting events—do not participate in any of the activities of the *aṅkeḷiya*. In general people are enjoined to avoid sexual intercourse during this period, and I believe this interdiction is almost universally observed. As I noted elsewhere (pp. 386–87), those directly involved in the ritual—the *vaṭṭāṇḍi*—observe special interdictions such as fasting or eating rice with one herbal dish. It was Durkheim who observed that these types of ritual interdictions, with their emphasis on abstinence, continence, and purity, constitute a kind of asceticism characteristic of even the simplest human societies. Indeed, in Pānama it is explicitly stated that *vaṭṭānḍi* should be like "Brahmans," by which is meant the ascetic *sādhus* who congregate in the main shrine of the god Skanda at nearby Kataragama.

What Durkheim did not correctly observe is that this form of asceticism is in complete contrast to the ascetic role institutionalized in certain historical religions. These ascetic interdictions that preface communal rituals are often a prelude to types of activity that are in a sense the opposite of asceticism—that is, characterized by the very absence of restraint and the suspension of norms of conventional social behavior. This is apparent in the corroboree of the Australian aborigines, as well as in the *aṅkeḷiya* ritual of the Sinhalas. The "asceticism" constituting the system of interdictions—the negative cult, as Durkheim appropriately called it—is not true asceticism, since it is a temporary condition of ritual purity that sets the stage for the relaxation of the conventional social and religious interdictions upon which the well-being of the society depends.

The psychological state of the people as a result of observing ritual interdictions could be characterized as *restraint* and *inhibition*. People are set apart from the gross, mundane world of copulation and food production and consumption. They are in a state of ritual purity that isolates them from the profane world. This psychological setting in which the actors are placed is consonant with the *social* setting of the *aṅkeḷiya* festivities. The ritual of the *aṅkeḷiya* occurs in a specially demarcated area outside the normal bounds or *sīmā* of the village. The ritual area is consecrated and bounded (*sīmā*) as sacred. Females are not permitted within the sacred area, and in Pānama they are not even allowed within sight of the *aṅkeḷiya* area until the competitive festivities are over. So it is in Dunukeula and in many remote areas of Sri Lanka. Let us examine the situation in Pānama, for which I have the best data, since it probably exemplifies the traditional pattern.

The festivities are held at night, and women are excluded. The actors are in a psychological condition of restraint. Yet the ritual itself is a symbolic and vicarious gratification of two of the most dangerous drives—sex and aggression. The exercise of restraint is a prelude to license ritually channeled and expressed according to the rules of the *aṅkeḷiya*. In normal life sex and aggression are normatively defined, controlled and expressed in relation to socially defined goals. But in the ritual there is direct, and also vicarious or indirect, expression through words, gestures, and symbolic actions rather than acts of physical copulation or physical violence. Much of the sexuality and aggression is not goal directed either, but is "free floating"; that is, any form of sex or aggression is permitted verbal and gestural expression within the confines of the *aṅkeḷiya* rules. Thus individuals have an opportunity to "let themselves go" and give expression to deep psychological states, feelings, or needs that simply cannot be expressed, or even consciously recognized, in normal everyday life. Tabooed unconscious and pregenital fixations may therefore receive vicarious expression and gratification during *aṅkeḷiya*.

While free-floating expressions of emotions may be manifest in the *aṅkeḷiya*, this does not mean these are random emotions. *Any* psychological tension, emotion, or need may be expressed by *any* individual; but some of these emotions are expressed in conventional satiric songs that are either traditionally sung during the ceremonies or invented by the two teams before the ritual and sung after each victory. These songs have certain psychological themes that embody those unconscious and taboo emotions that dominate the group as a whole rather than individual team members. It is to these emotions, embodied in song, that we must now turn.

Three major emotional problems are expressed in the *aṅkeḷiya* rituals. Two of these—impotence anxiety and castration anxiety—have been discussed in the previous chapter, and their genesis has been noted. Briefly, impotence anxiety results from prolonged fixation on the mother, reaching into puberty, and castration anxiety is related to the existence of a threatening father figure and defined as "the fear that the genitals will be damaged or destroyed by an external agent, a father figure." Castration anxiety in this sense must be distinguished from self-castration in order to achieve identification with the mother. The former is something dreaded; the latter is something wished for (and symbolically gratified by identifying with the dead god). Since the feared castration is viewed as punishment for the unconscious erotic feelings toward the mother, castration anxiety increases the individual's impotence anxiety. The third proscribed drive expressed in the *aṅkeḷiya* songs is a deep-seated wish for anal intercourse. The genesis of this drive will be discussed presently in the analysis of the *aṅkeḷiya* songs sung at Pānama. The emphasis is on the Pānama data because I have detailed tape recordings and interviews from this village.

Proscribed and Tabooed Drives: Themes of the *Aṅkeḷiya* Songs

Intercourse with the mother-in-law is a major theme in the *aṅkeḷiya* songs. In *aṅkeḷiya* at Pānama the satirical song on Jōna is popular. Jōna is a proper name as well as a term of contempt generally referring to a weakling or fool or a sexually incompetent person. Here Jōna refers to the team that has lost, whose members ipso facto are sexually incompetent. Cross-culturally viewed, the theme of mother-in-law incest seems fairly widespread, and it is likely that in Sri Lanka too it is a displacement of strong incestuous feelings toward one's own mother and a vicarious gratification of these feelings. The reference to sexual intercourse with the grandmother in the song of the upper team (p. 416) probably has the same significance. Direct references to incest with the mother (and sometimes a female sibling) occur all the time in exclamations during the *aṅkeḷiya*, but these are extensions of swearwords employed in everyday life, except of course that their frequency has multiplied greatly and they are used deliberately to humiliate one's opponents. The idealized mother can never be the subject of deliberately constructed obscene songs: but the mother-in-law is a convenient substitute. The mother-in-law (and grandmother) is a mother figure on the harlot model—a degraded sexual object in the Freudian sense. Once she is degraded, it is possible to indulge in obscene sexual humor regarding intercourse with her. The degraded mother also appears as Sakra's wife in the *aṁba vidamana* ritual to be discussed later in this chapter.

Anal Intercourse

Anal intercourse is also one of those proscribed drives that receive vicarious gratification in the obscene songs of the *aṅkeḷiya*, as they indeed do in obscenities in contemporary Western societies. In the *aṅkeḷiya* they have a sadistic and hostile component, as in the song of the upper team.

> If we meet these people [the lower team], we will thrust cannons up their asses
> We will thrust cannons!
> We will thrust cannons!

Or

> We will rub castor oil and send into his a big "injection."

Or in their opponents' song:

> We shall bend into two and three, get our "pole" erect and thrust it up their asses.

It should be noted that anal intercourse here is meant to humiliate or shame the opponent. Culturally it is viewed as a despicable and unnatural thing, but it is obvious that an unconscious wish is being expressed here at the same time.

It is anality rather than the homosexual component that is abhorred in Sinhala society. This attitude has to be seen in the context of Sinhala (and Indian) cultural views regarding pollution. Sex is polluting in general but at the same time is necessary and desirable. While the vagina is desirable sexually, it is also a polluted object, the very source of menstrual pollution and other undesirable excreta. The object that is both *undesirable and polluting* is the anus, as container of feces. It is my view that the revulsive attitude South Asians have toward pollution in general is generalized from the attitude toward feces. In socialization children are trained very early to react to feces with disgust and horror; this is generalized to all forms of dirt and pollution, so that feces becomes a general idiom for the expression of revulsion and disgust. Thus as far as sex is concerned the anal orifice is viewed with horror.

No such attitudes pertain to homosexuality (which in some senses is less polluting than heterosexual intercourse) in its culturally desirable interfemoral form. In fact, premarital or juvenile homosexuality is common and acceptable. The reasons again are based on the fact that male-female companionship outside marriage is virtually absent. Males seek expressive relationships with other males; companionship and friendship are with members of the same sex. Thus it is commonplace to see males holding hands and engaging in forms of affective behavior that in the West are strictly associated with heterosexual relationships. In Sri Lanka such expressions of companionship and warmth would be impossible cross-sexually; they thus receive expression unisexually. This widespread relationship between members of the same sex cannot be viewed as "homosexual" or as an expression of latent homosexuality. It is based on very real human needs for companionship, contact, and mutual succor that cannot be provided by female companionship. The need for companionship, support, nurture, and contact is very strong, since it is stimulated by early and prolonged contact with the mother. But after late childhood these tactile needs cannot be as easily satisfied by the mother or other females. They have to be expressed through relationships with males.

This type of contact between males can lead to homosexual relationships in childhood. Such relationships are not necessarily true homosexuality but are often an expression of sexual needs in the absence of heterosexual outlets. Such homosexuality is between peers among preadolescents, or occurs as pederasty for postadolescents. The young boy, or passive homosexual partner, is viewed as a substitute for a female. In this case the orifice parallel to the female vagina must necessarily be the male anus. But the anus is, as I noted, viewed with horror as a source of pollution. It is desired and abhorred. It is in this context that one must see the problem of sodomy. It is a deep-seated wish that cannot be directly indulged, but is vicariously gratified in the *aṅkeḷiya* ritual (and other rituals also, as we shall see later).

Castration and Impotence Anxiety: Direct Catharsis

The key emotions being expressed in *aṅkeḷiya*, however, are castration and impotence anxieties. In the idealized presentations discussed in chapter 11 there is no direct symbolization or expression of these motivations. The images of the mother-wife goddess and the dead consort are based on these motivations but are not a direct reflection of them. Instead, they are symbolized many times over. Indeed, the function of multiple symbolizations is to avoid confrontation with the sources of motivation, as when the dead and bleeding Pālaṅga represents the idea of the "castrated male." The reason is simple: the killing and resurrection drama not only objectifies deep motivations but also does other things: it expresses the poignancy of the Sinhala family situation, as I noted in chapter 11; it depicts the suffering and loyalty of the wife-mother; on another level it deals with the problem of righteousness and justice in the world; and on yet a different level the superordinate male is made to realize his inner weakness, his fickleness and psychic subordination to the woman. This depth of meaning is paralleled in the beauty of the poetry (poorly captured in my translation) and the somber, stately rituals that enact these themes.

In *aṅkeḷiya* one is in a different world entirely: it reverses the situation of "ideal representations." The deep motivations of castration and impotence anxiety are directly expressed in the abuse uttered during *aṅkeḷiya*. These expressions are consonant, though not wholly so, with the overt cultural purpose of *aṅkeḷiya* as a fertility ritual—the theme of intercourse and expressions of obscenity "fit" the ethos of a fertility ritual.

Nevertheless *aṅkeḷiya* is more. In the previous chapter I noted that the themes of castration and impotence are symbolically expressed in the *aṅkeḷiya* myth. But myth cannot provide catharsis: catharsis must occur either when an audience identifies with a performance or, more effectively, when the audience itself directly participates in the performance. The latter occurs in *aṅkeḷiya*, which is an acting out of the themes of the myth in direct, participatory catharsis.

Everywhere it is performed *aṅkeḷiya* has one consistent feature: horns or their wooden substitutes are hooked, then pulled till one breaks. Now the preface to the *aṅkeḷiya* myth quoted on page 463 makes clear that the hooking of the horns indicates sexual union, or *sambandha* ("linking together"); in Pānama during the preliminary celebrations the images of the male and female deities are mounted on horns and hooked together—once more indicating sexual union. On another level of meaning horns are penises. Note that the horns (whether real or wooden) must, at least ideally, be reinforced with cowhide rope provided by the untouchable *roḍiya* (beggar) caste. This deliberate courting of impurity is a surprising feature of *aṅkeḷiya*, since in general the ritual prescribes strict norms of purity. Moreover, mythology constantly asserts that Pattini is pure and is repelled by impurity; yet the horns are reinforced with cowhide, an extremely impure and defiling material. What the cowhide does, I believe, is to convert the phenomenal object—the horn —into a symbolic object, the penis. Note also that it is men who participate in the pulling: the broken horn represents failure at intercourse and the castrated penis, while the unbroken one suggests successful intercourse and an intact penis. Lester Hiatt, in a sensitive interpretation of *aṅkeḷiya*, says that the hooked horns are the mother and father locked in intercourse, and the "aim of the horn play is to wrench mother and father apart in the act of coitus, breaking the latter's sexual organ in the process . . . a shared fantasy in which the infant emasculates his powerful rival" (Hiatt 1973, p. 244).

My own interpretation is somewhat different, consonant with the views presented in the previous chapters. In Pānama, Dunukeula, and Biyanvila, where team division is strong, the two horns are explicitly viewed as belonging to the goddess and her consort, *not the father*. This is also confirmed by the myths, and it is difficult to get past this fact. In Malidūva the horns belong to the two teams, and neither teams nor horns are associated with the deities. In both instances the symbolism is the same, except that in Malidūva (and the regions around it) the open interpretation of the horns has some clear advantages: the winning horn is the one that has had successful intercourse with the wife-mother, and the broken one is the castrated horn of the opponents (men) who have failed in intercourse. The victory has tremendous psychological value in enhancing the self-esteem of the victors and denying the reality of impotence by attributing it to their dejected opponents. That a similar interpretation holds true for Pānama, Dunukeula, and Biyanvila comes out clearly in what happens soon after the horn is broken: the winning team explicitly associates the broken horn with the castrated penises of the opponents. Furthermore, if the broken horn is the castrated penis, two further crucial projections occur here: the losing team (the horn that breaks) represents castration and failure in intercourse, while the intact horn suggests successful intercourse. Hence the extraordinary triumph displayed at winning and the extreme dejection in losing. These projections dominate the symbolic picture of *aṅkeḷiya* at Biyanvila, Dunukeula, and Pānama. The immense emotional energy invested in the *aṅkeḷiya* by its participants can now be understood. It is not primarily a simple fertility ritual; nor is it, like other rituals of the Pattini cult, a commemorative rite; nor is it a medical ritual to banish disease; it is all these, but it also involves the more powerful unconscious projections that I have discussed. We can now also see the reason for the hypercathexis of the horns both by individuals and by the team as a whole. Horns are decked gaily, caressed, and fondled; the intact horn represents, on the unconscious level, the intact, uncastrated penis. When we look at *aṅkeḷiya* from this perspective we soon realize that a simple symbolic equation is not possible. Perhaps one could characterize *aṅkeḷiya* not as a single symbol, but as a *symbolic field* (Turner 1967, pp. 262–67) where several ideas are being projected—fertility, intercourse, success and failure thereof, castration, feelings of joy or shame. All these constitute the symbolic field of the *aṅkeḷiya*.

Let me now focus on the psychological themes discussed earlier and show how the *aṅkeḷiya* songs give further expression to castration and impotence anxiety.

1. Impotence anxiety, in the sense of penile inadequacy, is manifest in the fantasized size of the penis, which is represented as enormous: the songs refer to penises as "cannons," "poles," or "sticks." In the song of the lower team reference is made to the small penis that swelled to twelve feet, and "traditional song" refers to the penis as the size of an arm.

2. Castration anxiety proper is expressed projectively in the wish to hurt or injure the vagina. Not only do these expressions indicate hostilities and fears regarding heterosexuality, but also, I believe, the wish to hurt the vagina is a displacement of castration fears. References to the "leprous vagina," "tearing cunts off," "putting husks into the vagina" are all expressions of the same motive.

3. Then there are direct references to the penis that is being hurt or damaged in some sense.

We'll raise their sarongs and hit them with our stick.

Or

In trying to hold the *rikilla* top his penis top swelled to twelve feet,

where the reference is to the horn having hit the penis accidentally. References to the "leprous penis" and "eating of pricks" are also of the same type.

In Pānama, and probably in all areas where the competitive aspects of *aṅkeḷiya* are fully developed, opportunity is provided for expressing powerful unconscious sexual motives. It is my view that these motives are not unique to Pānama but are general to Sinhalas (perhaps to Sri Lankan people). In this section I am more concerned with two of these motives—castration and impotence anxiety (and to a lesser extent sodomy)—and their expression in ritual. We may ask, If these motives dominate Sinhala personality in general, shouldn't they receive cathartic expression not only in the competitive *aṅkeḷiya* of Pānama and elsewhere, but also in parts of the Southern and Western provinces where either the *aṅkeḷiya* is not performed or the cathartic mechanisms are not fully developed? In Malidūva (and the Southern Province in general) castration and impotence anxiety are expressed in the breaking of horns, but the overt expressive actions and humiliation of opponents that dominate the Pānama picture are absent. What overt cathartic mechanisms exist in Malidūva and the non-*aṅkeḷiya* regions of Sri Lanka?

The answer to this is simple, but it leads us to a major problem of the human sciences relating to hypothesis testing and predictions. The motives I have discussed—castration and impotence anxiety—are pan-Sinhala and general, but their expression is localized and specific and may take various forms. This is a fundamental issue in any psychological anthropology—the motives may be widespread in a group, but they can be expressed through substantively different customs. Or—and this makes the methodological problem even more complicated—they can be repressed or handled by the individual mechanisms of defense. In other words, there are several major ways of handling motives that dominate the minds of people: through culturally constituted defenses, such as symbolic or projective systems like *aṅkeḷiya*; through role and status resolutions, as where a man's wish to identify with a female may be resolved through a culturally acceptable transvestite role; or through the individual mechanisms of defense. Institutionalized role resolutions cannot deal with motives that are widespread in a population, but these motives can be expressed through either cultural or personal defense mechanisms. This means that the presence of a symbolization for the expression of a motive in one area does not entail its presence in another area; and the absence of such projective mechanisms in one area does not entail the absence of the motive, for that motive could be handled through the individual defense mechanisms, for a variety of reasons. Moreover, these are not either/or choices, since it is likely that in some instances both techniques of psychological conflict resolution may be employed. The task of the anthropologist is to document and analyze the expression of motives through symbol systems; the field of impulse control through individual defenses is the psychologist's domain. Thus everywhere our work must be *interpretation*; testing of hypotheses in the conventional sense is impossible in regard to these symbol systems, and so are rigorous predictions.

The problem of cultural versus individual defenses is relevant, particularly in the context of change and the large-scale dissemination of "bourgeois" values into peasant society. In the Tamil areas of the east coast, it was explicitly recognized that one reason for the contemporary nonperformance of the ritual is that *aṅkeḷiya* (Tamil, *kompu viḷaiyāṭṭu*) is "obscene" and "uncivilized" and should be discouraged. I have heard identical sentiments expressed in the Sinhala areas in respect to *aṅkeḷiya* as well as other "obscene" rituals. In fact, sometimes *kapurāla*s are constrained nowadays to preface a performance of a ritual with an apology asking the audience's forbearance in putting up with "obscenities" that tradition, they say, compels them to perform. These values accelerate the demise of cathartic rituals, and when this occurs the impulses or motives I have discussed may be handled by the individual defense mechanisms.

The problem of how the motives of castration and impotence anxiety are dealt with in the culture therefore is complex. Even in Malidūva, though there is an absence of the more obvious cathartic mechanisms in *aṅkeḷiya* described for Pānama, it is my view that the hooking of the horns expresses an attempt at intercourse and the breaking of the horns symbolizes its failure and castration, as it does elsewhere. Nevertheless, it is indeed true that there is no verbal expression of castration anxiety in the *aṅkeḷiya* at Malidūva, and the expression of aggression is not as great as it is in Pānama. Furthermore, how are these anxieties expressed in those parts of the Western and Southern provinces where *aṅkeḷiya* is not performed at all? While they could be handled individually, one would expect a group ritualization of conflicts, since traditionally Sinhala culture did handle psychological conflicts through ritual—witness the proliferation of exorcistic rituals in Sri Lanka (Wirz 1954). It is indeed my contention that where these motives are inadequately expressed in the *aṅkeḷiya*, or where the *aṅkeḷiya* is not performed, they are expressed in *other* rituals of the Pattini cult. I will now consider some of these rituals.

Cathartic Enactments: *Aṁba Vidamana* and Baṁbura Rituals

In *aṅkeḷiya* the audience directly participates in the ritual action: the catharsis here is most effective since it is most direct. Concomitantly, the symbolization of nuclear motivations either is absent or, if present, is more or less close to the motivational sources. For example, it is obvious for most that the broken horn is the castrated penis of the opponents, whereas the symbolism of the intact horn that is decorated, caressed, and lovingly fondled is not as obvious and probably has significance only the unconscious level. I shall now deal with a different type of cathartic ritual where a ritual drama is enacted, but members of the audience are spectators only. If catharsis occurs it must be *indirect*; not by participating in the action, but by indentifying with it. Cathartic enactments are entirely symbolic performances; primary process motivations are not directly expressed at all but are expressed indirectly in symbol formation. There is also very little philosophic, moral, or numinous content in these cathartic enactments; concomitantly, the symbolization—though real—is still closer to the sources of motivation. Unlike the ideal representations that tend to "cover up" the sources of motivation, the symbolic system here gives them expression, very much in the manner of dream formation from latent to manifest content. Nevertheless, it must be emphasized that these cultural performances have been cognitively reworked through historical time into their present form, unlike the temporary and much more cognitively loose nature of dreams. One feature of cathartic enactments is clear: they may have originally been cathartic *participations* that through time have been converted to *enactments* owing to many reasons such as the operation of values from the orthodox religious doctrines. This is clear from the Baṁbura ritual, which was a participatory performance in the sixteenth century (chap. 6, pp. 305–6) but now is an enactment. Another process can also be observed: the *aṁba vidamana* ("shooting of the mango") ritual may have originally enacted the myth of *aṁba vidamana* faithfully, in which case it would have been a serious, even numinous, representation; nowadays the serious content of the ritual has been played down and cathartic elements dominate the symbolic picture. There may be a variety of reasons for this change, but an important one is the need to give symbolic expression to the deep motivations that trouble the members of a society.

The *aṁba vidamana* (the shooting of the mango, text 36) is a ritual drama that enacts the myth of the birth of the goddess Pattini (see pp. 227–38 for text of the myth) and is performed whenever the *gammaḍuva* is held, except in the Mātara tradition, where the myth is sung without a dramatic performance. This ritual, in my opinion, gives expression to the castration anxiety theme in those areas where the *aṅkeḷiya* is not performed. In theory the *aṁba vidamana* enacts the birth of Pattini. However, a ritual drama is not a literal enactment of a myth (as Frazer thought), so that it is not possible to predict from the extant myth the nature of the dramatic enactment. The drama may add items not found in the myth or may amend or delete items. The *aṁba vidamana* myth describes the mango in the king's orchard, the miracles associated with it, people's futile attempts to pick it, the entry of god Sakra in the guise of an old man who shoots the mango, the blinding of Pāṇḍi's eye by the juice of the mango, and finally how the mango is placed in a casket and floated down the river Kāvēri. In the ritual drama, however, this myth is sung at the beginning and end of the drama; the main emphasis in the drama is totally extraneous to the myth. It emphasizes the entry of the god Sakra and the humorous dialogue he carries on with the drummer. The following is a tape-recorded text from a *gammaḍuva* performance held at Ambalangoḍa in 1967; it is typical of *aṁba vidamana* performances I have seen.

As always in *aṁba vidamana* rituals performed everywhere in Sri Lanka, the *kapurāla* enters the arena wearing an "old man mask," with abdomen protruding, bent double, hobbling with a stick in his hand. This is the standard representation of Sakra and follows the model of the Buddhist *jātaka*s where he comes down to earth in the guise of an old man or a beggar. Sakra enters the arena and comically struts about, feeling the "lump" below his abdomen, while a drummer and an assistant *kapurāla* sing the formal text in the *aṁba vidamana*. This goes on for about ten minutes, after which the following exchange occurs between Sakra, assistant *kapurāla*s, drummers, and sundry members of the audience.

> Sakra: Grandson [*munuburē*]
> [Sakra moans and feigns great pain; he holds the "lump" below his abdomen and collapses on the floor. Members of the audience in feigned solicitude ask concernedly:]
> Oh grandpa [*mutta*]
> Assistant *kapurāla*: *Mutta*, it certainly looks as if you are in great pain [*amāru*, pain, trouble]. I'll send you a helper [*ādāra kāraya*].
> [Sakra now falls on the floor, holding his "lump." Laughter and loud comments from the audience.]
> Sakra: Grandson, *amma* [mother] is going past my groin [*älapata*].

Kapurāla: Not *amma* [mother]—you mean *ämma* [rheumatism].
Sakra: Yes, yes, it is *amma* [mother], you're right.
Kapurāla: *ämma*!
Sakra: All right, *ämma*. Alas grandson, I have the "big disease" [*mahaleḍa*].

A pun, *mahaleḍa*, literally "big disease" referred traditionally to smallpox, but here it refers to the size of the "lump," that is, the testicles.

Kapurāla [Continuing the pun]: That's infectious, and we should not have you anywhere here—we'll send you to the hospital.
Drummer: Now try to sit down properly, grandpa, sit properly.
[Sakra tries to sit properly, but the "lump" gets in his way.]
Drummer: Grandpa has a dangerous disease, I think.
Sakra: Grandson! I have a "big" [*loku*, "large," "big," "serious"] illness.
Drummer: What is the nature of your illness?
Sakra: It is like—like a ball [he blurts out the last word, *bōle vageyi*].
Drummer: *Jam bōle* [large citrus known as *jambōle*]? Or *rubber bole* [rubber ball]?
Members of audience: *bälun bōle da*? [Is it a "balloon ball"?]
[Sakra utters a volley of gibberish.]
Drummer: The disease you've got is not at all good.
Sakra: I've got the *bōle leḍa* ["disease of the balls"].
Drummer: *Jambōle* [large citrus]?
Kapurāla: Here! If you can't tell us plainly what it is, write it down for us, will you?
[Boys in the audience come close to him, and Sakra shouts, "Children don't come here saying *huk! huk!* ("fuck, fuck").]
Sakra: I can't write. Maybe the children here will write it for me.
Drummer: Yes, the kids have written it, and it says *Layanu, abbāyanu, bayanu, labba* [l-a-bb-a, *labba*, i.e., "watermelon"; in vulgar parlance, "testicles"].
Boy: Grandpa can't even write *labba*. What kind of character are you?
[Sakra goes on holding his "lump" and shouting in agony.]
Drummer: I'll tell you how to get this cured quickly.
Sakra: What remedy do you suggest, Grandson!
Drummer: I'll get an Āyurvedic doctor who'll pierce it [*vidinava*].
Sakra: *Vidinava*?
Drummer: Yes, he has *kaṭu* ["thorns", "sharp surgical instruments"] to incise it.
Sakra: Yes, let's get him down, pay him our salutations in the manner customary in this area, and give him gifts. Grandson, how do you set about inviting doctors in your area?
Drummer: We invite them respectfully.
[An assistant, who plays the role of doctor, comes up to Sakra. Sakra salutes him with the conventional greeting *"āyubōvan"* ("may you live long"). Then he pushes out his buttocks and greets the doctor "back first."]
Drummer: Funny way of paying respects.
Sakra: Yes, isn't this a nice way of saluting? In my village we "speak" with our backsides.
[At this point there is a lot of horseplay with the poor doctor, who is bullied, ridiculed, and given false answers. After some time the drummer puts an end to it by speaking firmly and clearly.]
Drummer: This tomfoolery won't do, grandpa. You must not dissemble. Tell us what your problem is exactly and where you are going.

Sakra: Where am I going? I am going forward.

Drummer: What are you here for? What's the news?

Sakra: There are a lot of posters about the place which say: The queen of the king of Pāṇḍi of *āṇḍi* city had an unseasonal mango growing in the royal orchard. Thousands come to shoot it down or cut it. The princes of the eighteen realms also tried to shoot it down but failed. The posters say that anyone who shoots it will be given the king's one and only *gū kumāri* ["shit princess"].

The drummer corrects him: *dū kumāri* (daughter princess).

Sakra: Yes, and also a treasure the weight of an elephant. Thus it was published in the posters.

Drummer: Where did these posters appear?

Sakra: In *āṇḍi nuvara* [the city of *āṇḍi*, "mendicant beggars"].

Drummer: Not *āṇḍi nuvara*, but *pāṇḍi nuvara* [the city of Pāṇḍi]. Thus it happened: in the orchard of the king of Pāṇḍi there grew a mango out of season and the king hath published a message around to say that whoever brings the mango down will get a treasure the weight of an elephant. . . .

Sakra: and the princess his daughter.

Drummer: Yes, these will be given.

Sakra: You know what I did? You know the lady [*hāminē*] in my house?

Drummer: Yes.

Sakra [Shouting loudly]: The *woman* in my house. The woman of ours got the news and told me. "Ah, there's a nice job for you to do," and asked me to do it. She found an auspicious time for the task and said that it is a good omen if I saw a black bull on my way to the orchard. Also, if I stumble on my way that too is fine. She said that the astrologer told her that if I saw a wedding procession it was excellent and I should go ahead.

Drummer: Straightaway, I suppose.

Sakra: You know my wife loves me dearly. Generally when I am about to go somewhere she says, "May you be daubed with cow dung" [an insulting phrase in Buddhist Sri Lanka, in contrast with Hindu India].

Drummer and *kapurāla*: Such love [*ādaraya*]!

Drummer: Why is your head full of holes?

Sakra: Well, once in a while she lets me have it—*tuk! tuk!* [imitating knocks on his head].

Drummer: That again is for love [*ādaraya*].

Sakra: Yes, *āśraya* [Sakra "mistakes" *ādaraya* (love) for *āśraya* (sexual intercourse)]. You know why she wants me to leave our house so often? Because there's a huge *preta* ["mean spirit"] in our house. You know how he comes? He smells nicely of scent and powder and he smokes cigarettes [*pretas* are supposed to emanate a foul odor]. I get a smoke also. This *preta* has a good lineage, so my wife has a good offering for him [*pretas* are in general given mean offerings]. She utters mantras—*kuṭṭu! kuṭṭu!*—and leaves it for him. After which the *preta* eats the stuff.

Drummer: Where are *you* all this time?

Sakra: I am scared to death of this *preta*. I know the "sounds" he makes, and I crawl under a table or bed and sleep.

Drummer: Do the dogs bark when this *preta* arrives?

Sakra: Heavens yes! All the dogs in the neighborhood. Then when I awake I see only footprints, for the *preta* has eaten all the food and left.

Drummer: Do you think this is a *preta*?

Sakra: No?
Drummer: No, it's no *preta*. It's an adulterous visitor.
Sakra: Nonsense, my wife has no visitors.
Drummer: Adulterous visitor, that is.
Sakra: My wife is the showiest woman in the whole place.
Drummer: Now listen, none of this nonsense. Here is the doctor come to cure your disease.
Sakra: Doctor, let me tell you my story. I left home—as I stepped outside I stumbled. That was the first good omen [actually, all the omens he recounts are bad ones]. Then I saw a herd of black cattle and overtook them [one must stop when confronted with a bad omen]. The third good omen of a wedding procession was just perfect. *Aiyo!* There was a nice cane box, and four people were carrying it. There were sounds of music and of flutes and people singing *"Allah, hulallah, maha madulla allah, allah!"*
Drummer: Grandpa, that was a dangerous thing you saw. It's not a *magul* [wedding, auspicious occasion] but a [Muslim] *avamagul* [inauspicious occasion, i.e., funeral].

Then Sakra goes on at great length to prove that it was a wedding—it had a registrar of marriages (i.e., registrar of deaths), a bride dressed in white (the corpse), a wedding throne (the cane coffin), white cloths and blessings (shroud and funeral verses). The drummer admonishes him and tells him not to babble, otherwise he will not get his disease cured.

Drummer: Here is the doctor with his box of surgical [literally, "thorn"] instruments.
Sakra: One thing I must tell the doctor—he must not touch it where it hurts.
[The doctor points a stick (instrument) at the lump. Sakra utters "ah" in feigned agony.]
Sakra: It hurts terribly, terribly, grandson.
Drummer: Surely not, the doctor pierced it nicely.
Sakra: [in pain] *āv! āv!*

The drummer asks Sakra to salute the doctor, but Sakra jumps on him instead. The drummer scolds him and tells him to greet the doctor with *āyubōvan* (may you live long), and Sakra agrees. But at this time the drama is cut short by the (embarrassed) chief *kapurāla*, who tells the actors it is time to finish. Then Sakra comes out with the real reason for his visit and gives a brief summary of the life of Pattini, with special reference to the *pataha* myth and how Sakra asked Pattini to be born from a mango to break the might of the king of Pāṇḍi and relieve the earth of suffering. After this brief recital the drums beat again. A mango branch has been hung in front of the main altar. From this are suspended the silver mangoes belonging to the *kapurāla*. Sakra crouches before the mango branch, bow and arrow in hand; then he dances and sings some lines from the *aṁba vidamana*. After a few minutes he "shoots" the mangoes and leaves the arena. The mangoes are then deposited in the main altar.

The amazing feature about this ritual drama is that it practically ignores the myth it is supposed to enact! The myth is sung at the beginning and end of the ritual. The drama itself revolves around several themes:

1. The unfaithfulness of the wife and the cuckold husband (note the contrast with the myth of Pattini, which emphasizes wifely fidelity). The cuckold husband is a father figure (Sakra), and his wife is the degraded mother.

2. Anal humor, though not sodomy, a characteristic feature of Sinhala ritual dramas. Typical kinds of anal humor are references to feces, greeting persons with the buttocks (see also *pataha* ritual, pp. 328–32), and punning. The kind of anal humor uttered in many comic ritual dramas, "spoonerisms," is not found in this ritual.

3. The two themes mentioned above are really peripheral to the central interest and focus of the ritual drama—that of Sakra himself, with his huge testicles, and the operation performed on these testicles with pointed instruments. This feature of the drama is not a unique invention in Ambalangoḍa but is the dominating feature of most *aṁba vidamana* rituals I have seen. This ritual is extremely humorous, and everyone seems to enjoy it, because no one truly identifies with Sakra, the hump-fronted old man. Castration anxieties are expressed in this manner, but the person who suffers is the old man—the father—rather than the son. If in reality castration anxiety is the fear deriving from the threatening father, this is reversed in the ritual: it is a talion reaction in which the castrating father becomes the ridiculous castrated person, no longer a source of threat to the son.

When the avowed purpose of the drama—the *myth* of *aṁba vidamana*—is ignored and an obscene feature introduced, we must assume that it is due to important motivational factors that demand psychological release and expression. A commonsense explanation will not suffice. For example, Sakra appears in Buddhist *jātaka* folklore as an old man, but the "humped-front" is a Sinhala innovation specific to the ritual. The physiological model for the presentation of god Sakra is that of a person suffering from filariasis of the testicles, but it is unlikely that the Sinhalas are so obsessed with this rare disease, or with the commoner and less dramatic case of hydrocele, that they must depict it in their rituals. The syndrome of a person suffering from enlarged testicles is an expression of the more powerful unconscious motives of castration and impotence anxiety discussed earlier. In *aṁba vidamana* this psychological syndrome deals with the large size of the genitals, as in *aṅkeḷiya*, which depicts anxiety about sexual adequacy; the striking, almost blatant, expression of castration, where the testicles are pricked with pointed instruments, and the expressions of pain by Sakra; sex as painful, which is found in the *aṅkeḷiya* also and is psychologically associated with castration anxiety; Sakra himself presented as a sexually inadequate person, receiving knocks from his wife, who cuckolds him with her paramour.

The Baṁbura Rituals of Malidūva

In the preceding account I demonstrated that castration anxiety is expressed not only in *aṅkeḷiya* but also, in those areas of the Western and Southern and Sabaragamuva provinces where *aṅkeḷiya* is not generally performed, in the *aṁba vidamana* ritual. But what about the Malidūva tradition, where these projections do not overtly occur in *aṅkeḷiya* and where *aṁba vidamana* is also not enacted dramatically? I will now show that these anxieties are in fact depicted in two ritual dramas performed in the Malidūva tradition and in Sīnigama and elsewhere as a substitute for the "killing and resurrection." The reason for the substitution is the widespread belief that even an inadvertent error in performing the "killing and resurrection" drama may result in *vas* (ritual danger)—death, blindness, or impotence to the actors. Since the Baṁbura rituals are obscene cathartic enactments performed in lieu of the serious resurrection drama, one might infer that the motivations that are camouflaged in the dromenon (the serious drama) are laid bare in the comic cathartic performance.

The ritual commences with two *kapurālas* entering the arena to the beat of drums. Each wears a long white beard trailing down to his naked belly, a set of large false teeth made of mother of pearl with two tusks protuding at the ends, a large false nose, and a pair of large bulging eyes. Their heads are covered with black turbans. These grotesque apparitions wonderfully capture the gross carnality and lasciviousness of the *senex amans* type of demon, Baṁbura or Hātabaṁbura. They dance in the arena, shouting and clutching at their stomachs, their dancing bells jingling. Then they start singing and introduce themselves in song—the songs are not so much sung as shouted and are laced with peals of raucous laughter.

> O Hātabaṁbura who has divine warrant
> Change the *dōsa*, send them in another track
> His abode is the stone raft of the god
> To banish *dōsa* the Baṁbura enters the arena.
>
> Lips, teeth, and a beard tied on the face
> Like a wasp, look, he comes running
> Like a wasp he is bent in two
> O Baṁbura bring blessings to last us long.
>
> His head is black, his beard flows down
> Bent in all directions, watch how he enters
> Arrogant as ever, he walks among the gods
> Banish all *dōsa*, O Hātabaṁbura.
>
> He has obtained warrant from Kataragama
> He often snatches money from people
> Alone among gods he is in charge of the four marts
> Protect the *ātura*s often, O Baṁbura.

After further dancing and horseplay one *kapurāla* leaves the arena. An attendant places a chair in midarena and sits on it.

Hātabaṁbura dances around the chair for a few minutes, then goes to work on the poor fellow who is seated. He dances up to the attendant, throws a white cloth around him as the barber does, steps back in a dance to survey his work, then sharpens a "razor" (a strip of banana bark) in superb comic mime, makes "soapsuds" with a brush (another piece of banana bark), and "lathers" the man's face. He steps back to survey his work, dances for a while in the arena, snatches a piece of decorative banana bark from an altar, sharpens this "razor" again, and "shaves" his victim—from his face down to his armpits, then his chest, stopping at his stomach. Next he shaves him from the feet upward, stopping above the knees. Then he trims his victim's beard with two thin strips of banana bark in the same marvelous mime. Now he uses the white cloth as a towel to wipe the attendant's face. Thus done, he replaces the cloth, steps back, dances in the arena, rubbing his palms together as the village barbers do with talcum powder, then dances up to the attendant and "powders" and massages his face. Then he dances in the arena once more, comes back with a "cup of oil" (a cupped leaf), and rubs the attendant's head. Finally he "combs" his hair, removes the cloth, and fans him with it. Then he hauls the man out of the chair, embraces him, and dances with him in midarena, to the embarrassment of his victim. What is impressive is that all the while he performs sodomous and homosexual pranks on his "victim." While shaving, he faces the attendant and thrusts his body forward and backward. While "oiling" the head he performs a sodomous mime. He attempts to fool around with the victim's private parts. The sodomous and homosexual content of the ritual is deliberate and unmistakable.

The Shooting of the Gun

The ritual known as the "shooting of the gun" is again performed by the *kapurāla* dressed as Hātabaṁbura. It is generally performed at about 4:30 A.M., when the audience is feeling drowsy. It is a good antidote to sleep, for the antics of Hātabaṁbura certainly help keep the audience awake. I describe below the essential features of this drama.

> Baṁbura: Well friend, I've come.
> Drummer: You've come?
> Baṁbura: Ha! Ha! friend, I've come, friend, friend.
> Drummer: Then it's time to shoot. . . .
> Baṁbura: Ha friend, I've come to the *nara* [human] world from the *nari* [fox] world.

The word *nari* (fox) is a mistake, and the drummer corrects him, but at the same time the word has a peculiar appropriateness, since the Hātabaṁbura does come from a smelly underworld like the fox.

> Baṁbura: . . . that woman is pestering me—ah friend . . . she says she hasn't eaten for a long time . . . and so she gave me. . . .
> Drummer: What did she give you?
> Baṁbura: A cigar.

Again he confuses his words—he mutilates the words "cigar," "cigarette" and makes them rhyme with "gun."

> Drummer: No, a gun.
> Baṁbura: Ah friend, where is that?

While talking, Hātabaṁbura struts up and down the arena floor. He now sits in front of the gun (made of banana bark) with his legs stretched apart. Hātabaṁbura tells the drummer that his wife, the demoness Sācāpiri, has asked him to come to the human world to make a kill and has given him this gun for the purpose.

> Baṁbura: So I brought this thing along [pointing to the "gun"], but I don't know how to use it. . . .
> Drummer: Have you brought it? You'd better take it up.

Hātabaṁbura looks around him and pretends not to have seen the "gun"; instead, he slowly takes his hand up along his thigh and rests it below his abdomen. More ribald comment soon establishes the connection between the gun and the penis. For instance, he looks for the flintlock in the same manner. The drummer of course corrects him and shows him the "gun."

> Baṁbura: Ah friend, is this my one?
> Drummer: Smell it and you'll find out!

In the same manner he looks for the ramrod, which the drummer says is found at the end of the *kaňda* ("trunk," "thigh," "barrel"). Then once more the drummer has to show him the real "gun" lying on the floor. He takes it and tries to pull out the ramrod—pushing his hand up and down in a masturbatory gesture—but finds the ramrod encrusted with rust through long disuse. No wonder he hasn't "shot" for quite a time and is now impatient to make a kill, he says. However, the ramrod does come out at last, but the drummer has further work for him. He asks Hātabaṁbura to tie a few rags round the ramrod and clean the barrel. This he proceeds to do with the same obscene gestures, by cupping the end of the "barrel" with one hand and continually poking it with the finger of the other hand, imitating intercourse. Gunpowder is rammed in with similar gestures, and then he is asked to put in two bullets.

> Baṁbura: Bullets? Never heard of them. What are they like?
> Drummer: Round balls.
> Baṁbura: Ah, now I remember.

He puts his hand under his buttocks and exclaims: "I've got two, but if I use them up how could I do any more shooting?" But the drummer corrects him, and Hātabaṁbura puts the bullets in with obscene gestures.

> Drummer: Now you will have to . . . pull the trigger.
> Baṁbura: How is that done? . . .

And so it goes on, obscenity piled upon obscenity. Finally Hātabaṁbura has the gun all ready to shoot and tells the drummer, "do something quickly as the gun is about to go off." The matter is taken care of when a man, taking the role of the quarry, lies on a mat. Hātabaṁbura places the gun below his abdomen, a huge extended penis, and struts up and down the arena. Finally he sees the quarry, jumps on him and thrusts the gun between his legs, and falls down in a pretended faint. He wakes up and exclaims that the gun is broken. He then goes looking for the missing parts.

On the face of it there seems no commonsense reason why a ritual depicting a shaving episode and one dealing with a gun should find a place in the ritual cycle of the *gammaḍuva* at Malidūva and Sīnigama. The "shaving" has no reference to a caste ritual of barbers; indeed, it is doubtful whether there was a barber caste in Buddhist Sri Lanka. As far as "shooting the gun" is concerned, there is nothing again in the text to associate it with a fertility or hunting ritual. This may once have been a fertility ritual, but nowadays the Buddhist agriculturists in this area devalue hunting. It is impossible, then, to see this ritual as having some conscious purpose or end like the other rituals of the Pattini cult. Furthermore, informants were completely unable to "explain" the ritual, whereas they could at least state the overt purpose of any other ritual in the Pattini cult. Asked why it is performed, the *kapurāla*s simply assert that it has always been performed in that identical manner, and that it *must* be performed to banish *dōsa*, or misfortune. As Turner says, when there is a total block in indigenous exegesis, one may legitimately infer that the ritual is dealing with unconscious primary process material (Turner 1967, pp. 24, 38).

The unconscious primary process motives that are being expressed are castration and impotence anxieties. The symbolization process here is strictly parallel to that of dreams, and the symbols seem to be of the same order as dream symbols, insofar as they are not incorporated into a higher-level cognitive scheme. It is as if a dream has been "objectified" and represented as a communal ritual. The symbolization is direct and powerful: castration anxiety is represented in the shaving ritual (the symbol of the razor), and impotence fears are expressed in the shooting ritual (the gun symbol). Homosexual sodomy is also acted out in the shaving ritual, though this is not the main drive being expressed.

Like Sakra in the *aṁba vidamana*, the demon Hātabaṁbura is an old person—that is, sexless, "castrated," incapable of functioning sexually. Hātabaṁbura, also like Sakra in the former ritual, is sexually incompetent with his wife, who says she "hasn't eaten for a long time." In the shaving ritual he depicts the public fears of castration anxiety through shaving, which is a symbolic representation of castration. Moreover, all parts of the body are shaved except the genital area, which is deliberately and self-consciously left out. This and the preceding ritual are two clear cases where I am sure the message of the ritual is being communicated to the audience, for, though the ritual is supposed to be funny, the audience responds with anxious, hesitant laughter. It is as if powerful motives that cannot be constrained are being expressed in the ritual. In the *aṁba vidamana* ritual the old man is being castrated by the audience; in the shaving ritual the funny old man is not so funny—he wields the razor and is the castrating father. In the gun ritual impotence anxieties are bared; the elongated, exaggerated penis is strictly parallel to the exaggerated testicles of the old man in *aṁba vidamana* and the phallic objects mentioned in the *aṅkeḷiya* songs of Pānama. Fears regarding potency are expressed in the preoccupation with preparing the gun for shooting, the idea that the gun is about to fire before reaching the quarry, and so forth. Castration fears and the painful, violent nature of intercourse are expressed in the very choice of the symbol—the gun—which breaks into pieces after the shooting is over (like the breaking of the horns in *aṅkeḷiya*), so that Hātabaṁbura has to go look for the missing parts.

A final comment can be made on the three rituals just described—the *aṁba vidamana* and the two Hātabaṁbura rituals. The purpose of the *aṁba vidamana* ritual is the dramatic enactment of the birth of Pattini and the blinding of the king of Pāṇḍi; yet in the ritual drama the overt purpose is relegated to second place and the major emphasis is on Sakra and his castration problems. The two Hātabaṁbura rituals also may have had some overt purpose once (e.g., as a fertility ritual), but this is totally overridden by the symbolic representation of castration and impotence anxiety. The concept of *distortion* is useful in understanding the process going on here: owing to the press of deep-seated psychological motives, the overt purpose of the ritual is distorted and a different symbolic picture, in which these primary process feelings operate, dominates the performance.

The Functions of *Aṅkeḷiya*: On Shame and the Wish to Humiliate

The preceding analyses of *aṅkeḷiya* dealt with its cathartic functions—the expression and ventilation of primary process material. It did not, however, explain the *idiom* in which that material is couched. I shall attempt now to interpret the psychological basis of language and gestural abuse that characterize *aṅkeḷiya*.

The basic dialectic underlying the two teams is simple: the victors are jubilant; they humiliate the defeated and boast about their own greatness. The losers are crestfallen and dejected and passively bear the abuse. There may be a phylogenetic basis for this type of dominance/submission response in our primate heritage. If so, it is almost totally overlaid by two psychological and cultural conditions: the *public shaming* of the defeated and the *public status* (*prestige*) *enhancement* of the victors. The idiom of *aṅkeḷiya* not only is a primary process cathartic mechanism but is also a reflection of, and a mechanism for ventilating, a deep-seated need or drive in Sinhala personality to humiliate others and glorify oneself. These needs arise from the socialization of shame status in Sinhala childhood and culture and have consequences for the individual's "self," in Mead's sense (1934).

There is an extensive psychological literature on "guilt" but very little on "shame," since shame is not the predominant mechanism of control for Western man, at least till very recently. The early anthropological literature, particularly the work of Margaret Mead (1937) and Benedict (1946), spoke of "shame cultures" and "guilt cultures," the former essentially found in non-Western societies and the latter mostly in Western (especially Protestant) nations. Both Mead and Benedict saw shame as an "external sanction" in which conformity to norms is effected through group pressure, whereas "guilt" sanctions are internalized by the individual and constitute that part of the superego known as "conscience." In shame one conforms because one fears social sanctions; in guilt one obeys the internal voice, the censor or the introjected parents, whose punishment acts as a sanction. According to Benedict, Japan is preeminently a shame culture. In shame cultures people are chagrined about acts that Westerners in general would feel guilty about, she says. Shame, unlike guilt, cannot be resolved by confession and atonement. "True shame cultures rely on external sanctions for good behavior, not, as true guilt cultures do, on an internalized conviction of sin. Shame is a reaction to other people's criticism. A man is shamed either by being openly ridiculed or rejected or by fantasizing to himself that he has been made ridiculous. In either case it is a potent sanction. But it requires an audience or at least a man's fantasy of an audience. Guilt does not" (Benedict 1946, p. 223). Both shame and guilt are anchored to morality, but in shame a man "orients himself to the verdict of others" (1946, p. 224).

Several criticisms of this early anthropological view of shame have been made, most notably by Piers and Singer (1933), Lynd (1958), Spiro (1965), and De Vos (1973).

Piers has a complex psychoanalytic argument regarding the genesis of shame, which he views as part of the ego ideal. He says that shame occurs whenever goals and images presented to the ego ideal are not reached. Thus he tends to underplay the anthropological view of shame as an external sanction, though he says that one part of the ego ideal is constituted out of the child's relations with his peers and sibling group (Piers and Singer 1933, p. 16). Singer attempts to give an anthropological extension to Piers's idea. He shows convincingly that the division into shame cultures and guilt cultures is grossly overstated, and that both shame and guilt may coexist in varying degrees even in simple societies. Following Piers, he says that an audience is not necessary for shame sanctions, since shame also can exist as a powerful internalized mechanism of control, acting like guilt in an unconscious manner (Piers and Singer 1933, pp. 51–52). "It too can be regarded as an internalized response to a past threat, but what has been internalized are the ideals of the loving parents and the past threat unconsciously reactivated is abandonment by those loving parents and loss of their love" (1933, p. 52). A serious criticism of this position is that it practically subsumes shame under guilt and ignores the critical importance of the group as a major factor in the socialization of shame.

Spiro in a later reformulation (1965) brings the group back in. He says that moral anxiety is activated by the superego whenever there is an anticipated transgression of moral norms or cultural taboos. He argues for two types of superego, based on the agent of anticipated punishment. In societies where the child is trained by only a few agents of socialization, who themselves administer punishment, one finds individuals who introject the socializing agents and internalize their values. In these situations the introject is the significant other, and the withdrawal of the introject's love constitutes the anticipated punishment. Such societies produce a superego that is "guilt oriented." By contrast, in other societies the child is disciplined by a number of socializing agents, or by trainers who discipline the child by referring to others who will punish him. In these societies individuals internalize the values of the socializing agents, but not the agents themselves. Here it is the withdrawal of the love of others that constitutes the anticipated punishment, and one finds a "shame-oriented" superego (Spiro 1965, pp. 408–9). "However, a person with a shame oriented superego does not suffer shame when he transgresses unless others witness his transgression, for no agent of punishment (the external agent) is present. Instead of experiencing *actual* punishment (shame) he continues to experience *anticipated* punishment (anxiety)" (1965, p. 409).

I shall now spell out my own assumptions regarding the nature of shame, then present an account of how shame is socialized in Sinhala society and discuss the consequences of such socialization for Sinhala personality and culture.

I believe that the classical anthropological dichotomy between guilt cultures and shame cultures must be revised. Guilt itself is constituted of two elements. First there is primary process guilt, which all human beings share as a consequence of being reared in families by human parents. These guilt feelings have been documented in psychoanalysis and pertain to a sense of wrong arising from such things as incest and oedipal conflicts, aggression against parental figures, and sibling rivalries. Then there is secondary guilt, in which these kinds of guilt feelings are anchored to everyday moral norms, so that their anticipated violation activates anxiety in the individual in the form of anticipated punishment by introjected parental figures or the loss of their love. This is the typical Western-Protestant and Jewish type of "guilt," which is deliberately encouraged and inculcated from early childhood. Secondary guilt gets an extra fillip from the breakup of village communities, such as has occurred in the Western world, and from the emergence of atomized nuclear households and neolocal residence patterns. Such a social pattern in extremis leads to what Durkheim labeled egoism—the individual is cut off from traditional social moorings and becomes an object unto himself. Similar social patterns can exist in other societies also, but they stand in sharp contrast to the ideal typical small-scale society that anthropologists study: homogeneous, kin-based, tightly knit, depending for its welfare on limited agricultural (or other) resources. The latter type of social pattern puts a premium on conformity, and often on cooperation. It devalues mobility and high aspiration levels. To bring about this willingness to conform (i.e., create sense of conformity), it is necessary to inculcate a sensitivity to the reaction of others in the socialization process. In these societies *shame* becomes a powerful technique of control, and, as anthropologists have noted, it is based on a special type of sanction—that of the group. In other words, the greater the importance of the real or fantasized "other" (i.e., the group) to the individual and his family, the greater the use of shame as a mechanism of control. Psychoanalytic literature has focused almost exclusively on guilt because its clientele has come from modern industrial societies, not from peasant societies, either in the West or elsewhere. It is very likely that, for example, a European peasant village would employ a great deal more of shame control than a European urban group. When traditional (external) shame controls are no longer operative, then conformity is often effected through another mechanism—guilt. Thus there is a societal necessity for the strong development of internal control, and parents must bring this about in their socialization. The *manner* and *effectiveness* of guilt socialization will in turn vary with the religious and family system and with the role of the parents, especially the father, so that the families in European Jewry and Western Protestantism may be more successful in instilling secondary guilt than, let us say, Catholics. Nevertheless, the manner of effectiveness of guilt controls must be analytically separated from their necessity and the attempt to impose them. It is very unlikely that there exists any society that excludes either shame or (secondary) guilt controls, but the degree and effectiveness of their employment would then vary with the nature of both the society and the socializing agents (i.e., the family).

The necessity and existence of shame must not be confused with the way individuals are socialized to it, which in turn accounts for its varying effectiveness in different cultures. The question whether shame is an external or internal sanction cannot be argued a priori, since this also depends on the technique and manner of shame socialization, as, for example, when shame is anchored to primary guilt. Let me present my argument in the following manner.

1. Classic psychoanalysis, with its emphasis on ego, id, and superego, is not the best model for understanding the psychodynamics of shame. Since shame deals with one's sensitivity to the reactions of others, a different psychological approach may be helpful, at least for presenting the problem. I refer to G. H. Mead's notion of the self, since self in his sense arises out of our relations with others, through taking the "role of the other," "game" and "play" being models of the role-taking process. In "game" the child takes different roles, like that of mother, father, cops and robbers, whereas in the "play" model he takes over the team as an organized whole, "the generalized other." Mead says that the reflexive nature of the self arises out of this type of interaction or role taking. Thus, if our self-concepts are to a great extent constituted of significant others (parents and community), it follows that the reaction of others would affect our sense of self. Insofar as shame represents such an actual or anticipated reaction, it is intrinsically related to our self constructs—self-worth, self-esteem, self-consciousness, self-control—both in a positive sense when we conform and in a negative sense when we violate societal norms. Thus when we change our psychodynamic perspective we can view shame as an *internal* mechanism related to self-concepts of a phenomenological order. These phenomenological self-concepts can of course be assimilated into the analytic framework of psychoanalytic ego psychology through such concepts as ego ideal, ego identity, or ego integrity (Piers and Singer 1933; Erikson 1968, pp. 40–45), but not into the conventional psychoanalytic notions of superego and conscience, which belong to the province of primary- and secondary-process guilt. I am not of course subscribing to the view that self constructs arise from interaction with the group alone, since a person's sense of self-esteem, for ex-

ample, may spring from psychodynamic sources such as infantile narcissism, sense of omnipotence, and object libido, as Erikson says (1968, pp. 70–71). Nevertheless, these self constructs are, in every society, also interlocked with the group in one's relation to it through role taking. Thus Erikson says that "the self-esteem which contributes to a sense of identity is based on the rudiments of skills and social techniques which assume a gradual coincidence of play and skillful performance, of ego ideal and social role" (Erikson 1968, p. 71).

2. Many writers have noted that one consequence of shame is fear of exposure. But this need not be external exposure. Insofar as the self is constituted of others, there may be internal exposure as well as external exposure indicative of an audience. Hence, even when I am alone and commit a wrong I may fear exposure. For example, modern Sinhala women may wear clothes even in the privacy of their bathrooms; even though the door is closed the fantasized other is always present, creating the fear of being exposed.

3. The preceding arguments bring us to another factor in shame, that the reinforcers of shame may sometimes be primary guilt. Erikson, speaking I presume of Western industrial society, stated that "shame is an infantile emotion insufficiently studied because in our civilization it is so early and easily absorbed by guilt" (Erikson 1968, p. 110). The reverse is true for Sri Lanka, as well as many other societies where (secondary) guilt exists but is easily absorbed by shame. For example, De Vos has shown convincingly that Japanese not only are shame-ridden, as Benedict argues, but are also highly guilt-ridden, compounding their social and personal situation (De Vos 1973). In general one would say that in small-scale, face-to-face communities, conformity to everyday social morality and convention is reinforced by shame (the sensitivity to the reaction of "others") without guilt ever entering into it. Yet in some areas of morality and taboo, especially sexuality and aggression control, shame may be reinforced by primary guilt. I think it would be ridiculous to say that in many small-scale societies people would violate the incest taboo if there were no audience. The reinforcers of such taboos are guilt feelings. Thus in Sri Lanka children and young men who masturbate in private are, I found, afraid of discovery (exposure) by "significant others," even though objectively the possibility is nonexistent. Furthermore, this fear, I believe, is reinforced by threat of mutilation (castration) by the father. The razor-wielding old man of the Hātabaṁbura rituals has its parallel in the fantasy life of Sinhalas, but the threat is mitigated by treating him with derision and satire. This derision has other cultural and social concomitants. For example, even the gods and demons of the pantheon are derided and humiliated (see pp. 144, 146–47, 152–55). Again, occasionally in anomic market towns one sees an old beggar or social deviant mercilessly derided and abused by children and adults; the beggar retaliates with abuse and threatens physical violence, which provokes laughter and further derision in a schismogenetic process (Bateson 1958, pp. 175–97). When we compare this phenomenon with the expression of the same idea in ritual drama, we clearly see the social utility of symbolic defenses for fostering social stability by canalizing primary-process needs in a socially nondestructive manner.

4. On the social level, then, shame can be defined as the presence of "others" (i.e., society), actual or fantasized, which acts as a mechanism for social control, fostering conformity to social norms in such a manner that actual or anticipated violation of these norms produces anxiety or fear of "exposure" to the contumely and scorn of others. Shame sanctions can be either external or internal; internal sanctions may sometimes re-

ceive reinforcement from primary-process guilt, but not external sanctions (the outside audience). Internal shame sanctions can best be understood in terms of the symbolic interactionist notion of the "self" and its formation. Such self notions are phenomenal constructs that could be integrated into psychoanalytic ego psychology, as recent psychodynamic theory has attempted to do (e.g., Kohut 1971, 1977).

This definition of shame is useful for comparison, but it does not help us to inquire into deeper and more variable consequences of shame as it is inculcated in different cultures. How do societies build a "sense of shame" into the personalities of their members? As one can in one society speak of a "sense of guilt," one can in another speak of "sense of shame." In socialization the child is taught to react to shame, which may have deep consequences for personality formation. It is here, I think, that shame socialization will show cross-societal variations in both personality and culture, as, for example, between the Mediterranean cultures (Peristiany 1965) and Sri Lanka. I shall spell out the techniques by which a sense of shame is inculcated by early child training in Sri Lanka. I must emphasize that this is a tentative formulation only.

I believe that socialization of shame in Sri Lanka affects the self in such a drastic manner as to leave the individual particularly vulnerable to loss of self-esteem. Often he attempts to bridge this by overcompensation, that is, to glorify his sense of self-worth. This is true of other cultures also, especially Mediterranean cultures. The *degree* to which the self is affected depends on other intrapsychic processes such as the persistence of infantile narcissism. The *idiom* in which the sense of shame and its opposite (attempts at self-glorification) are expressed is also culturally variable. Thus shame (i.e., a sense of shame) is opposed to *honor* in Mediterranean cultures; in Sinhala culture honor in the Mediterranean sense is of little consequence—its equivalent is status and prestige.[1]

I translate the Sinhala term *läjja* as shame; often the term *läjja* is conjoined with *baya* (fear), so that people will speak disapprovingly of someone who has no *läjja-baya*. *Baya* by itself has a variety of uses like the English word "fear." However, when Sinhalas use *baya* in the context of shame they do not mean "cowardly," "fearful," and so forth, for no one approves such behavior. *Baya* when conjoined with *läjja* means "fear of ridicule or social disapproval." Sinhala persons must not only have a sense of shame but also be sensitive to the reaction of others who may shame them. Thus *läjja-baya* refers to shame and the fear of ridicule. There is, it is implied, a minimum dyad in a shame relationship: a person who is shamed and another who causes shame. Ontogenetically speaking, the "shamer" is a parent representing the "generalized others" (i.e., society) who inculcate in the child sensitivity to *läjja-baya*.

In Sinhala society, the higher a family's social position, the greater the preoccupation with *läjja-baya* in socialization, and it reaches its epitome in educated urban people. It is said that low-caste people have little *läjja-baya*; they have no status to lose. It is therefore easiest to see the significance of *läjja-baya* in the socialization practices of high-status people, bearing in mind that they represent in exaggerated form a major preoccupation of Sinhala people.

Läjja-baya is instilled in very early childhood in several ways. Let me focus on verbal

1. I do not wish to overstate the contrast between "honor" and "status," since they are obviously interrelated. In Sri Lanka notions of honor exist, but they are not developed in any systematic way. Written literature also has no references to "codes of honor" such as one finds in Western literature.

instructions given by the socializing agent to the growing child. Bad behavior is corrected in the following manner: "*läjja nädda, mokada minissu kiyanne*," "aren't you ashamed; what'll people say?" When a parent, or other socializing agent, simply says "*läjja nädda*" the rest of the statement is implied, so that the reference to the "others" is contained in it. For females, norms of sexual modesty and proper behavior are inculcated in the same idiom. There is nothing unusual about these practices, which are found in many societies, except for one factor—the failure to conform is associated with ridicule and laughter by the parent, especially the father. Hence, in spite of the cultural view that females should be specially *läjja-baya*, it is the male child who becomes more sensitive to the second part of the verbal set, *baya*, or "fear of ridicule." This is because men have public roles and hence must be more sensitive to the reactions of others. The parent's shaming the child with ridicule has a hostile component that the parent is unaware of, so that the father's oedipal hostility to the son may be expressed in this satiric mode rather than (or in addition to) other kinds of aggressive behavior. The father not only ridicules the child, but he does it before a "public," as is inevitable with shame socialization. The public may be other family members or kinsmen; it can also include outsiders. This is especially true in middle-class households; a father may reveal a child's idiosyncrasies, failures, and "bad habits" to a visiting outsider in the child's presence, and all will laugh, oblivious of the child's sense of humiliation. This mode of socialization is carried on in school also, where shaming through ridicule is the most common method of control employed by teachers, particularly for the control of "brashness," "forwardness," or "impudence." Socialized adults as a consequence have an added "fear" of authority figures; the fear of being ridiculed by them in public for failure. This is reinforced by the authority figures, who like to "pull up" subordinates in the presence of others.

"Fear and shame" are particularly terrifying to some individuals because of their connection with feces in early childhood socialization. Excessive revulsion for feces is inculcated very early. On a purely formal level one might say that Sinhala toilet training is easy and lax, unlike that in Japan or in Western Protestant cultures. But this is misleading, for in human socialization what matters is not so much formal criteria like age and methods of toilet training as the *meaning* with which the socialization agent (the mother) invests the process. In Sri Lanka mothers react hysterically when children play with feces. "*Chi*," the most common expression of revulsion in Sinhala, has its beginnings in the attitude to feces. When children touch mud or dirt the reaction of the mother or nursemaid is "*chi*, don't touch it, feces" (*kakka*). This idiom of revulsion is often extended to the context of shame, so that the term "*chi*" is often associated with *läjja* as "*chi läjjai*," "*chi*, I am ashamed." In middle-class households it is extremely common for the mother or nurse to chastise a child by calling him "*chi*, feces child" (*cī kakka babā*), again lowering the child's sense of self-worth. "To smear someone with shit" is a common idiom for extreme shaming. Occasionally this is actually carried into practice: one may throw human feces or cow dung at an enemy's house, smearing the wall so that the whole world can see his humiliation. In colloquial Sinhala one of the most common words used to describe someone who has been shamed or humiliated by another is *pal vuna*, "stank" (from rotting or stagnant water), ultimately derived from the prototypic source of bad smell—feces.

Here we have one of the real differences between India and Sri Lanka. In Brahmanic Hinduism feces are the vehicle for communicating notions of pollution to the child. The prototypical infantile meaning of feces is pollution; from here it is generalized to all polluting substances, including tabooed food. The revulsion to eating such foods is based on the initial revulsion to feces. I doubt that the imagery of feces is generalized to the self in Hinduism, since in the Brahmanic religious view that self (*ātman*) is immortal and part of the divinity (*Brahman*). The denigration of the self is not possible here, whereas such a denigration is both permissible and apposite in Buddhism, since that religion denies an immortal *ātman* and instead postulates a phenomenal self constituted out of language experience. In Brahmanic Hinduism pollution/purity notions often have the effect of control mechanisms, invading the domain of shame and (secondary) guilt.[2]

Now I can draw certain conclusions regarding the socialization of shame consciousness (a sense of shame) for both Sinhala personality and Sinhala culture.

1. The child's sense of humiliation results in a vulnerable self system. Individuals are susceptible to slights (imagined or real), since they lower self-esteem. Serious insults may result in bursts of rage and uncontrollable violence. Thus informants who have gotten into a violent rage or committed acts of physical violence often identify the immediate stimulus as *nindā* ("insult") or *bāldu* ("loss of status"), which on the psychological level means "loss of self-esteem."

2. There is the reverse of the coin; vulnerability to enhancement of self-esteem. The self requires constant boosting. On the personal level this results in susceptibility to titles, honors, honorifics, and other status symbols that enhance the self, all subtly graded according to social position and role. Direct, unabashed self-glorification, however, is not permitted in everyday intercourse, since it would indicate impudence; but it is permitted in *ritual* contexts such as *aṅkeḷiya*.

3. Since shame is a socially based emotion, Sinhalas are specially sensitive to status precedence, and they fear slights and ridicule especially *in public*. This is clearly seen in public speeches, even parliamentary debates, where ridicule is freely indulged in. In contemporary literary criticism it is almost impossible to carry out an intellectual argument without denigrating the opponent. That is, when an issue becomes public, or an audience is present, psychological problems based on shame become manifest, and personal vilification and abuse inevitably enter the argument. Contemporary English-speaking intellectuals use the English word "hack" to designate this aspect of literary and public debate. "He got hacked" and "hack the bugger" are favorite expressions in the informal idiom of contemporary intellectuals. Even Sinhala-speaking intellectuals have adopted this word: *ūva häk keruva* ("he got hacked"); *hari häk ekak ne maccan* ("helluva hack, no?"). I suspect that the difficulty that public officers of similar or slightly different statuses have in getting along with each other is related to this problem.

4. The continuity in the pattern of shame socialization requires that the son, who in later life becomes a father, must instill the sense of shame in *his* son. Thus a man must become a shamer himself. The wish or need to humiliate becomes a drive in Sinhala personality. It is also a talion reaction to being humiliated by the hostile (castrating) parent: the wish to do unto others what was done to me.

Now let us see how these personality (self) consequences are manifest in Sinhala idiom. Consider ordinary language use. In Sinhala there is no word for guilt or conscience, since

2. It is likely that on the popular level notions of shame are as important as those pertaining to purity and pollution, but they are not articulated with the idiom of feces. Srinivas (1976, pp. 268–73) shows that shame and status are very important in his Mysore village.

these notions are absorbed into a bountiful idiom of shame/status. There are two broad language sets here: one set pertaining to shame/humiliation, that it, loss of self-esteem, and the other to status and enhancement of self-esteem. Some common words and phrases in the first set are as follows: *läjja* (shame), *bāldu* (loss of status), *nindā* (insult), *apahasa* (sarcasm). Consider certain colloquial words: *paṭirōl* (*paṭi* is a silk strap given as an honor in Kandyan times and could be glossed as "medal"; *rōl* is the English word "roll" taken into popular Sinhala). Thus, "the medal has fallen to the ground [dirtied]"—that is, you have lost status. *Pal vuna*, already discussed, means "stank." An extremely degrading phrase is *puka dunna*, "gave him your asshole." The terms in the contrasted set indicate status and enhancement of self-esteem: *tatvaya* (status), *nambu* (prestige), *gavuravaya* (status honor).

Fascinating uses of shame language are found among older generations of English-speaking Sinhalas. Thus: "he bogged his number plate" or "his number plate got bogged" is the English-educated person's version of *paṭirōl*. "Bog" is the turn-of-the-century British public-school euphemism for "feces." It is used as a verb in Sinhala English. "Number plate" is the license plate on one's car (a status symbol) or the brass nameplate outside one's gate. Translated, these sentences mean "You have yourself smeared feces on your nameplate or license plate"—that is, "You have been smeared with feces," indicative of public loss of status and personal humiliation. I have already noted the terms "hack the bugger," or "he got hacked," indicating the hostile as well as anal component in this shame idiom. A common Sinhala-English usage is the conversion of the Sinhala *pal vuna* to the Sinhala-English *pal fied*. Thus "he got palfied," or even "that was a real palfication." "Pug" is another favorite word in common parlance among English-educated children and in the schools. "Pug," of course, is the dog with the ugly face; thus "pug" refers to those who make faces at you when you do something shameful. It also means "humiliation by others." Thus: "he got a pug," "he was pugged." I quote below a ditty I heard sung years ago by young children in an elite private school to humiliate a defeated team or person—an *aṅkeḷiya* performance in miniature!

He got a pug
Rolling in the mud
Hoo! Hoo! Hoo!

"Hoo" is the verbal rendering of the Sinhala "hoot." Traditionally hooting was also used innocuously, for example, to indicate distance ("a hoo distance"; "within hoo shot"). It was also used to deride or boo someone. Nowadays it is used without apparent motive by peer groups in schools and universities, in cinemas, and wherever groups are assembled (political and trade union meetings). An almost indiscriminate use of "hoo" in its derisive form has been a great puzzle to educators, but it makes sense from the point of view adopted in this chapter—the wish to humiliate as a drive. This type of derisive hooting was traditionally expressed in village society in highly structured contexts like *aṅkeḷiya*. In the absence of these structures, derisive hooting is expressed nonritually when groups are gathered and when "others" are available for humiliating. Sometimes any "other" would do to express the drive. At other times "hooting" may be performed without "others" physically present, presumably because even mechanical hooting helps reduce the drive—as, for example, when dormitory students will sporadically hoot at night without any external stimulus.

The *aṅkeḷiya* as a ritual has practically gone out of vogue in Sinhala society. But the *aṅkeḷiya model* of public vilification and abuse is still very dominant. In 1978 I was resident in the guesthouse of the University of Peradeniya revising the final draft of this chapter. It was examination time, and every morning men and women students would walk down the road to the examination hall. Male students in the dormitories bordering the road would assemble in groups and derisively jeer at the students walking down the road, especially at female students. There seemed to be no obvious motive except the wish to humiliate others. This performance had a ceremonial, if not ritual, character. The most common expressions pertained to smell and dirt (prototype feces). "*Aiyo gaňdayi*" ("Alas, you smell bad"); "Did you bathe today?" Similar behavior occurs at public-school cricket matches. The kinds of verbal abuse, pantomiming, and humorous songs of vilification characteristic of *aṅkeḷiya* are performed here also, but intensified and divested of the rules that kept the latter within civil bounds. Thus the *model* of *aṅkeḷiya* is pervasive in Sinhala society: from the socialization in the family to interaction within dyads; from public debates in Parliament to the literary debates of intellectuals; from ditties sung in public schools to university dormitories; from public-school cricket games to, let me add, a lawyer cross-examining a hapless witness.

Thus far I have dealt with the negative components of shame-status socialization: now let us consider its more positive aspects. When the wish to humiliate others is expressed under finer cognitive and ego controls, Sinhala people are superb satirists. Satire is par excellence a literary mode directed at nonconformists and social deviants—be they Tamils with foreign accents, foreign demons and deities, or domestic cuckolds, as in the ritual dramas presented in this book. Furthermore, the socialization of shame has made Sinhalas exceptionally *self-conscious*, in the literal, reflexive sense. They have the capacity to laugh at themselves. Third, humor is endemic in Sinhala society. Everyone delights in verbal play, wit, spoonerisms, and riddles. And finally Sinhalas have, at least traditionally, handled their psychic conflicts through humor, as we have seen in the foregoing presentations, rather than through the extreme forms of ascetic primary process guilt-ridden behavior characteristic of Hindu society.

Part Six

Introduction

In part 5 I made a psychological interpretation of the central theme of the Pattini cult—the relationship of Pattini and her consort Pālaṅga-Kōvalaṉ. There were clear similarities on the psychological level between the Pattini cult and the cults of the famous West Asian mother goddesses. In this section I shall explore the possibility that the Pattini cult diffused from West Asia to the Malabar Coast in India through well-known trade routes.

Initially, in chapter 13, I will examine the sociocultural background of the Pattini cult in the oldest extant sources—the great Tamil epics *Cilappatikāram* and *Maṇimēkalai*. I shall demonstrate that the mythic biography of this goddess is rooted in the heterodox religions of India—Buddhism, Jainism, and Ājīvakaism. The social group that believed in this cult not only was non-Hindu but also belonged to the merchant class that dominated the South Indian foreign trade. With the decline of Buddhism and Jainism in India from the eighth to the thirteenth century, three consequences followed. First, Buddhists were pushed out of South India and settled on Sri Lanka's west coast. They brought with them the Pattini cult, and they translated the texts and adapted the cult to suit the new culture. I shall describe this in the conclusion of chapter 13. Second, in South India itself the original Pattini cult was absorbed into the popular Hindu cults of Kālī, Durgā, or Bhagavatī. These processes of transformation are described in chapter 14. Third, another group of Kerala immigrants settled on the east coast of Sri Lanka and were Hinduized. Their version of the goddess is that of a Hindu deity, but, unlike the situation in South India, the goddess is kept separate from the Kālī cult and retains much of the quality of a folk deity, as in the Sinhala areas. I demonstrate this in chapter 15 and conclude the chapter with the recent Sanskritization of the Pattini cult on the east coast stemming from influences from the orthodox Shaivite North (Jaffna district).

13

The Goddess of the Cilappatikāram and Maṇimēkalai: A Jaina Buddhist Deity

Scholarly opinion in Sri Lanka and South India is practically unanimous that the goddess Pattini is a Hindu deity whose cult originated in southern India and later diffused to Sri Lanka. The direction of diffusion is confirmed by Sinhala ritual texts, which say that King Sēraman (king of Kerala) introduced the cult to Sri Lanka. The South Indian Tamil origin of the cult is reasonably clear from the texts. The reference to their being put into Sinhala verse from original Tamil appears in Hevawasam's edition of the thirty-five ritual texts as well as those in my collection. Consider the following quotations from the Hevawasam edition:

> Having written 700,000 verses in Tamil.
> For seven days read well the signs in the Tamil book.
>
> (Hevawasam 1974, pp. 5, 13)

The existence of Tamil verses interspersed with the Sinhala in one text (*demala sinhala kavi*, *demala sinhala vayinaḍaya*) is additional evidence that these texts may have been translations from the Tamil. The text of the water cutting ritual in Aṅbokke (outside our culture area) says that "Iḷaṅkō the pandit composed [these texts originally] in Tamil verse."

In general scholars as well as laymen tend to assume that everything Indian is Hindu, particularly in religious matters, since except for Islam and pockets of Jews and Christians, Hinduism is practically omnipresent in the subcontinent. Yet Hinduism itself is a vague and ambiguous term, and, historically at least, there have been in the subcontinent other powerful and competing religions. Nevertheless, when we talk of such matters as female deities we tend to associate them exclusively with the Hindu mother goddesses. Yet the *Cilappatikāram* and *Maṇimēkalai*, the great Tamil "epics" that deal with the life of the goddess Pattini, give little support for the view that Kaṇṇaki or Pattini is a Hindu deity. A critical examination of these texts suggests to me an entirely different set of conclusions.

The thesis of this chapter is that Pattini, as she is depicted in the *Cilappatikāram* and *Maṇimēkalai*, is not a Hindu deity but a deity of the heterodox religions—Buddhism, Jainism, and possibly Ājīvakaism. A literalist, nonanthropological reading of the *Cilappatikāram* may give the impression that the cult was a Hindu one, since it was originally institutionalized by Ceṅkuṭṭuvaṉ, who was a Hindu, not a Jaina, monarch. Consider the following quotation, which refers to the installation of the Pattini image:

> To that venerable Lady was dedicated, by the united aid of the *dharmaic* Brahmanas, *purōhitas*, astrologers and export sculptors, a shrine (*Pattinikkōṭṭam*), constructed in all its parts according to the prescribed rules so that it might win the approval of the wise. Therein was planted the image of Pattini, carved with expert handiwork upon the stone brought from the Himalayan slopes, the residences of gods, after prayers to the god (Śiva) on the top of those hills. (Dikshitar 1939, pp. 325–26)

Note that in this account a shrine (*kōṭṭam*) for the goddess was installed by a Shaivite king, Ceṅkuṭṭuvaṉ, by learned Brahmans after worship of Śiva. Does this mean that Pattini was a Hindu deity? Not at all, according to the evidence I shall now present.

1. The shrine for Pattini is a *kōṭṭam*, which, according to Aṭiyārkkunallār, an early commentator on the *Cilappatikāram*, meant a Jaina shrine. Thus Aṭiyārkkunallār says that Iḷaṅkō, the alleged author of the *Cilappatikāram*, resided in Kuṇavāyiṛkōṭṭam, a shrine dedicated to a Jaina deity, Aruhaṉ (Dikshitar 1939, p. 77, n. 2). Dikshitar in his strenuous Hindu patriotism denies this, but we have to take seriously the views of early commentators, who were closer to the period of the poem. If so, the deity referred to in the quotation above may be not Śiva but Aruhaṉ. But even if it was Śiva it does not invalidate my argument.

2. Ceṅkuṭṭuvaṉ is a king often referred to in the earlier Caṅkam (Sangam) literature, which was in fact composed many centuries before the *Cilappatikāram*. An anthropological analysis of this episode as a charter helps us resolve the historical discrepancy. As I noted earlier (p. 377), all this episode implies is that it is an origin myth of a shrine of Pattini in Vañci, the capital of the Cēra kings. Like all origin myths, it gives this shrine (*kōṭṭam*) a pedigree in Malinowski's sense by associating it with the former historical (more likely mythic) king Ceṅkuṭṭuvaṉ. At best the only historicity one can attribute to this event is that this shrine was prominent and received royal patronage. If the myth says it was installed by a Shaivite king, Ceṅkuṭṭuvaṉ, it is reasonable that permission should be obtained from Śiva before the installation ceremonies and, furthermore, that Brahmans of the court should have been involved. Moreover, Hindu kings did, after all, patronize other religions also. According to the *Cilappatikāram*, the king's brother was a Jaina ascetic. Irrespective of the historical validity of this reference, one must at least concede that whoever compiled the epic saw nothing irregular in the Hindu king's having a brother who was a Jaina ascetic. In other words, the reference to Śiva worship and the construction by Ceṅkuṭṭuvaṉ of a Pattini temple do not at all lead to the conclusion that Pattini was a Hindu deity. She may have been one, but this inference is not warranted by the evidence in *Cilappatikāram* and *Maṇimēkalai*, the only two classic Indian texts that provide information on the Pattini cult.

Both poems, as I noted, contain a great many highly improbable events, and one must approach them critically. The authors are not dealing with contemporary events, since such events simply could not have taken place, either for historical reasons (like Ceṅkuṭṭuvaṉ's northern march) or because they violate known laws of nature (like Pattini's burning Madurai with the flames of her breast and Maṇimēkalai's performing miracles). It seems obvious that the authors were dealing with myths. However, one can legitimately assume that the authors' own attitude to the protagonists of these myths will give us a point of view that must surely be significant, and also that these works, like other works of the imagination, must reflect accurately the period in which they were written, such as in descriptions of places and events. For example, there is no reason why factual descriptions of places of worship and religious festivals should be inaccurate.

I contend that the ethos of the *Cilappatikāram* is Jaina, while that of the *Maṇimēkalai* is unequivocally Buddhist. I shall show further that the Pattini cult, as reflected in these two works, is primarily a Jaina-Buddhist, rather than a Hindu cult. This reorientation of perspective will naturally be crucial to understanding the nature of this cult in South India and its later diffusion to Sri Lanka.

The author of the *Cilappatikāram* is Iḷaṅkō Aṭikaḷ (Iḷaṅkōvaṭikaḷ, "prince-ascetic"); *aṭikaḷ* meant Jaina or Buddhist ascetic, in this case Jaina. The author's own treatment of Kaṇṇaki and Kōvalaṉ, the hero and heroine, is also very clear. They are also Jainas. Kōvalaṉ's parents are Buddhists, or possibly Jainas. On the way to Madurai, Kōvalaṉ and Kaṇṇaki meet Kavunti, an ascetic Jaina nun. Kavunti addresses them: "You have attractive features, noble lineage and highly commendable conduct. You appear to be faultlessly observing *dharma* as laid down in the sacred Jaina scriptures" (Dikshitar 1939, p. 158; also Danielou 1965, p. 57). Later on Kaṇṇaki is left in the care of Mātari, a cowherdess. Mātari tells her daughters: "Since this lord (Kōvalaṉ) observes the vows of the Sāvakas, get ready without delay the good vessels," in reference to the Jaina custom of not eating after nightfall (Dikshitar 1939, p. 220; Danielou 1965, pp. 105–6). References are also made to "Jaina temples and other Dharmaic institutions" inside the city (Dikshitar 1939, p. 118; Danielou 1965, p. 23); to Jaina ascetics (Dikshitar 1939, pp. 163, 216–17); to important Jaina deities like Aṟivan (Dikshitar 1939, pp. 158, 171); and to Jaina *yakṣi* cults (Dikshitar 1939, p. 214; Danielou 1965, p. 102). The cowherds who looked after Kaṇṇaki either were Jainas or at least worshiped Jaina deities (Dikshitar 1939, p. 214), and so were the wealthy of the cities who built a pulpit for visiting Jaina ascetics (Dikshitar 1939, p. 157; Danielou 1965, p. 56). These same citizens are referred to as Aryas, either as an honorific or perhaps indicating that they were northerners pushed southward by the expansion of Hinduism (Dikshitar 1939, p. 163; Danielou 1965, p. 61). The only serious religious discourses found in this work are Jaina, such as Kavunti's long sermon to Mātari (Dikshitar 1939, pp. 215–17; Danielou 1965, pp. 103–4) and the philosophical discourse of a wandering Jaina monk (Dikshitar 1939, pp. 164–66; Danielou 1965, p. 62). When Kōvalaṉ and Kaṇṇaki, accompanied by Kavunti, were on their way to Madurai, they met a Brahman who gave them moral and religious advice. Kavunti, speaking on behalf of herself and her companions, replies: "Go your way seeking the feet of the god sacred to you. We go the way suited to us" (Dikshitar 1939, pp. 177–78; Danielou 1965, p. 75). Here the Jaina beliefs of these travelers are held up as a foil to the views of the Brahman priest "versed in the four vedas" (Dikshitar 1939, p. 177; Danielou 1965, p. 75). If, according to the author's conception, Pattini was a Hindu deity, it would indeed be astonishing for her mythobiography to treat her as a Jaina. At least from the author's point of view, she was a Jaina deity (which does not preclude that she may also have been a Hindu deity).

The characters of the Pattini myth are also associated with Buddhism and to a lesser extent with Ājīvakaism. Pattini's own father and mother, according to the *Cilappatikāram*, were Ājīvakas (Dikshitar 1939, p. 308). Ājīvakaism was a religion that was founded by Makkhali Gosāla about the same time as Buddhism and Jainism arose. It was always a minor religion given to an extreme doctrine of predestination and historically related to Jainism (Basham 1951).

Buddhism is as important as Jainism in the Pattini mythobiography. According to the *Cilappatikāram*, Kōvalaṉ's father and mother were Buddhists. The former, on hearing of his son's death, "distributed all his wealth in charity, entered the seven Indra-Vihāras (a Buddhist temple), and began to practice self denial like the three hundred monks who roam the sky, having renounced the world to obtain release from the cycle of births. The wife of him who thus renounced, unable to hear the sorrowful news of the death of her son under such tragic circumstances, died of pity" (Dikshitar 1939, p. 308). Mādēvi (Mātavi), the courtesan, joined a Buddhist nunnery (1939, p. 308), and her daughter Maṇimēkalai later became a Buddhist saint (1939, p. 330). The *Maṇimēkalai*, which deals with the story of Mādēvi's daughter, is outspokenly and polemically Buddhist. According to this poem, one of Kōvalaṉ's ancestors "erected for the Sugata (Buddha) this chaitya of brilliant white stucco with its turrets reaching to the skies" (*Maṇimēkalai* 1928, p. 201). It also states that Kōvalaṉ's father, on hearing of his son's death, renounced lay life and became a Buddhist hermit. The Buddhist author of the *Maṇimēkalai* views the goddess Pattini as a Buddhist deity. In this epic, Maṇimēkalai (Maṇimekhalā) visits the temple in Vañci where the images of Pattini and her husband are installed. The goddess Pattini (i.e., the statue) tells Maṇimēkalai that she and her husband are in heaven now but will one day be reborn in earth "when in the Magadha country of unfailing rain, in the bright city of Kapila, there should appear Buddha of limitless perfection" (*Maṇimēkalai* 1928, p. 188). She continues: "He will there attain to enlightenment under the Bodhi tree and proceed out of mercy to living beings to teach the Four Truths. . . . As a result of our having worshipped at the Seven Vihares of Indra at Kāvēripaṭṭinam, we shall not at the same time be born in a life of suffering, and will then listen to his teaching with attention. The wish to renounce life will then dawn on us. We shall then cease to be reborn on earth" (*Maṇimēkalai* 1928, pp. 188, 201). This makes it very clear that Pattini is seen by the author of the *Maṇimēkalai* as a Buddhist deity aspiring to be born in the dispensation of the next Buddha. She is also viewed as being a Buddhist before her deification, since as a laywoman she worshiped at the Buddhist temple of the Seven Vihāras of Indra at Kāviríppūmpaṭṭiṉam. Thus the evidence of the two classic epics suggests that Pattini was both Jaina *and* Buddhist to the followers of these respective faiths. Hence the Pattini mythobiography seems to be rooted in the heterodox religions of South India—Buddhism, Jainism, and to a lesser extent Ājīvakaism, rather than Vedic Hinduism, Brahmanism, or Dravidian folk religion.

Brahmanism and Dravidian folk religion are referred to in these works, especially in the *Cilappatikāram*. The state cultus was clearly Brahmanic, and the religion of the priests and hill peoples was Dravidian (Dikshitar 1939, pp. 275–91; Danielou 1965, pp. 147–54). However, the evidence is clear that a certain class of people—the merchants to which the characters of the Pattini story belong—were adherents of the heterodox religions. Induchudan puts this well: "they were wealthy merchants. They were a new strata in society not hitherto classified among the people of the five regions, i.e., Mullai, Kurinji, Palai, Murutham and Niythal" (Induchudan 1969, p. 153). Vedic Hinduism was antipathetic to their activities, as, for example, in its ban on travel and contact with foreigners, which would be inimical to the development of the sea trade this class was engaged in. Jainas have traditionally been involved in business and mercantile activity; and Buddhism from its very inception has been supported by a city bourgeoisie.

It makes sociological sense that the merchant classes of South India should opt for the heterodox religions that provided better legitimation of their life-style than orthodox Brahmanism. It should be noted that Kōvalaṉ's family were sea traders and had Maṇimekhalā, the goddess of the sea, as their patron deity (*Maṇimēkalai* 1928, p. 131).

Although Pattini was a Buddhist and Jaina deity, we must remember that her cult was not part of the doctrinal orthodoxy of either Buddhism or Jainism. However, we know from contemporary as well as historical evidence that the harsh doctrinal ethics of these two religions have been mitigated on the popular level. Ramendra Nath Nandi, in a most interesting book, deals with the historical transformation of Jainism that parallels the kind of transformation noted by Weber and confirmed by contemporary social anthropologists for Theravāda Buddhism (Nandi 1973).

Nandi deals with the area north of Tamilnad, the Deccan, and especially the parts of Bangalore and Mysore bordering the Tamil lands. He shows that between the eighth and tenth centuries new Jaina orders, advocating permanent monasteries, had arisen here, as against the doctrinal ideal of wandering mendicant monks. In some sects—the Yāpanīya—the propitiation of planetary deities, occult lore, and demonology and mother-goddess cults were incorporated (Nandi 1973, pp. 41–55). It seems very likely that the Jainism of the *Cilappatikāram* was not that of the early doctrines but was strongly influenced by movements like the Yāpanīya. Thus there seems to be nothing unusual, given the transformations of these religions, in both Buddhism and Jainism worshiping a common set of deities on a popular, subdoctrinal level.

Some of these subdoctrinal views were obviously borrowed from Hinduism and folk religion, as, for example, the Padmāvatī cult, which seems to be a transformation of an ancient Vedic deity Padmā (Nandi 1973, pp. 155–56), and the cult of Jvālāmālinī, which rose to importance in the Karnatak region as early as the seventh century and seems to be based on a Hindu-Dravidian goddess Mahīṣāsuramardinī (Settar 1969).

Furthermore, the worship of the Hindu gods, amply demonstrated in the *Cilappatikāram*, does not by itself indicate that their worship was confined exclusively to Hindus. On the contrary, a great deal of religious eclecticism seems to prevail in the *Cilappatikāram*. For example, Mālatī, a Brahman woman, goes into a Hindu temple and worships Bālarāma, Śiva, and Skanda, then visits the Jaina temple and the temple of the moon (Dikshitar 1939, pp. 151–52; Danielou 1965, p. 52). Similarly, Kōvalaṉ and Kaṇṇaki, who were Jainas, perform marriage rites that were perhaps based on Brahmanism (Dikshitar 1939, pp. 8–9; Danielou 1965, p. 5). There is nothing unusual in all this, since, as I noted, even the heterodox religions had adopted Hindu customs and assimilated Brahmanic deities into their pantheons. These additions are reflected in the *Cilappatikāram* itself. This is clear in the role of Indra as depicted there. He is seen as a Hindu deity but is also worshiped by Buddhists and Jainas. Thus there are constant references in these texts to a famous Buddhist temple known as the sevenfold monastery of Indra. And Kavunti, the Jaina ascetic, recognizes this common heritage when she tells the Vedic Brahman monk that "the literature given by Indra, who lives longer than the Devas, can be found in our holy scriptures" (Dikshitar 1939, p. 177; Danielou 1965, p. 74).

The description of the annual Indra festival in the *Cilappatikāram* indicates that it was patronized by all citizens of Pukār. However, since the city was dominated by merchants, who belonged to the heterodox religions, this festival may have had a Jaina or Buddhist emphasis. Some indirect evidence for this inference is available in the *Maṇimēkalai*. This poem notes that the goddess of the sea destroyed the city of Pukār because it failed to observe the annual Indra festival. Indra was an old Vedic deity, but he was incorporated early into Jainism and Buddhism and became one of the most important gods in these two religions while his importance in Hinduism declined. It is likely that the myth of the destruction of Pukār by the goddess of the sea, the patron deity of traders, owing to the nonperformance of the Indra festival may very well be a rationalization of traders' belonging to the heterodox religions, because of the supercession or suppression of the Indra festival by the Shaivite state cultus.

The internal evidence of the *Cilappatikāram* and *Maṇimēkalai* that Buddhism and Jainism were dominant in the urban merchant classes during the period of these poems is confirmed by historical and archaeological evidence. I assume in accordance with the sober scholarship of Nilakanta Sastri, Basham, Zvelebil, and Vaiyapuri Pillai that these two epics could have been written anywhere between A.D. 500 and 900. This was also the heyday of Buddhism and Jainism in South India.

The action of *Cilappatikāram* and *Maṇimēkalai* takes place in four major cities of the Tamil Nāṭu—Pukár (Kāverippūmpaṭṭiṉam) in Cōḷa, Madurai in Pāṇḍya, Vañci in Kerala—all major ports or mercantile centers—and Kāñci in the Pallava country, where Maṇimēkalai studied Theravāda Buddhism. All four cities were centers of Buddhism and Jainism. Let me document the historical evidence further.

Buddhism and Jainism in South India: The Historical Evidence

In the sixth century, soon after the so-called Caṅkam age, "evil rulers called Kalabhras, had come and upset the established political order which was restored only by the more or less simultaneous emergence of the Pandyas and the Pallavas of the Simhavishnu line" (Nilakanta Sastri 1964, p. 19). The Pāṇḍyans described them as evil, since they upset the traditional Brahmanic sociopolitical order by "confiscating all charitable *devadāna*s and *brahmadeya*s, gifts to gods and Brahmins" (Nilakanta Sastri 1964, p. 19). They were, however, favorable to the Buddhists. "We may perhaps surmise that Kalavar-Kalabhras were a wide-spread tribe whose large scale defection to the heretical faiths resulted in a political and social upset lasting over some generations . . . the Cōḷas disappeared completely in this debacle and do not make significant reappearance till the ninth century" (Nilakanta Sastri 1964, pp. 19–20). Nilakanta Sastri calls this a dark period marked by the ascendancy of Buddhism and perhaps Jainism, but other scholars view it in more optimistic light.

"Buddhaghosa of Magadha, poet, philosopher and commentator and Thera Buddhadatta were patronized by Samghapala, a king of Kanchipuram. The evidence from his works and those of Thera Buddhadatta clearly points out that Kanchipuram, Kaveripattinam and Madurai were three great centers of Pali Buddhism in the fifth century A.D." (Ramachandran 1960, p. 55). The Chinese monk Hiuen Tsang, traveling in South India in 641–42, found Jainism flourishing. He notes that in the Pallava country, which had Kāñci as the capital, there were one hundred Buddhist monasteries and ten thousand monks, but the religion was declining in the Pāṇḍya country. These conditions were perhaps aided by the fact that the enemies of the Pallavas were the natural allies of the Pāṇḍyans, while the rulers of Sri Lanka, as the neighbors of the Pāṇḍyans, were more inclined to be on the side of the Pallavas (Nilakanta Sastri 1964, p. 20).

The heyday of the heterodox religions in South India was probably from the fifth to the eighth century. While all scholars are agreed that Jainism and Buddhism were important religions during this period, there is some difference regarding the weight given them vis-à-vis Brahmanism. In general, Tamil scholars are inclined to think that these were minor religions while Hinduism and Dravidian religion were dominant. Some Malayalam scholars, however, present a different picture. Shreedhara Menon says that before the eighth century Brahmanic Hinduism was simply one of the current religions in South India. "It has been the practice among scholars to refer to the Hindu religious stir of this period in Southern India as a 'revival' or 'renaissance,' but it is a misnomer to call it so . . . (as) Hinduism did not enjoy a position of primacy among the religions of Kerala prior to the Kulasekhara age. It was only one of the religions which held a minor position in the land" (Shreedhara Menon 1967, p. 145). He argues that the period after the eighth century that saw the work of Śaṅkarācārya and the rise of devotional (*bhakti*) religiosity resulted in the spectacular establishment of Hinduism as the dominant religion of the South at the expense of Buddhism and Jainism. Along with this came the rise of the Nambudiri Brahmans as the dominant social group in Kerala and the firm establishment of the *varṇa* system and caste in this region.

Malayalam scholars argue that before this period Jainism and Buddhism were competitors of Hinduism and were probably more popular. The masses probably participated in what may be called Dravidian religion, the operative folk religion of the people. In the literature of the Caṅkam age as well as the *Cilappatikāram* references are made to the goddess Koṟṟavai, who is a proto-Durgā. Besides popular Dravidian religion, Jainism and Buddhism were widespread over the whole Tamil Nāṭu (including Kerala), according to Malayalam scholars. Kunjan Pillai says: "Thus with the advent of the fifth century Jain and Buddhist religions had achieved greater popularity in the Kannada and Tamil countries than the Vedic religion" (Kunjan Pillai 1970, p. 105). There is much archaeological evidence regarding the vitality and importance of Buddhism right down to the ninth century. For example, the Ay king (885–925) in the famous Paliyan copper plate gave extended landed properties in southern Kerala to the Śrī Mūlavāsam Buddhist temple, at one time the most famous center of Buddhist pilgrimages in South India. The same king made gifts to the Jaina temple in the village of Chitaral in the Kanyākumārī district, Tamil Nāṭu.

Although Buddhism was in decline from about the eighth century, it was far from being moribund in South India. "The Chola Theras, Buddhamitra and Mahakasyapa, two scholars from South India, were responsible for the composition of two works *Uttodaya* and *Namarupapariccheda* at Ceylon by Ceylonese monks in the twelfth century A.D. The Talaing records of Kalyani near Pegu of King Dhammazedi gives a list of Buddhist archaryas of South India, Kaccayana, author of the first Pali grammar, Buddhavira and Anuruddha.

. . . In the thirteenth century A.D. Dharmakirti, another celebrated Buddhist scholar, went to Ceylon and organized a conference of Buddhists there" (Ramachandran 1960, p. 57). Buddhism was strongest in urban centers; both Kāñci and Nāgapaṭṭam had considerable Buddhist communities, "and there was frequent intercourse between the Buddhists of Ceylon and their co-religionists at these two places" (Paranavitana 1960a, p. 565). King Parākramabāhu IV (1302–26) appointed a learned monk from Cōḷa to the office of royal teacher (Paranavitana 1960e, p. 773). Gopinatha Rao, the distinguished student of Indian iconography, says on the basis of excavations in Travancore: "The belief among the teachers of history in our schools and colleges is that Buddhism died in the land of its birth not long after its birth, and that the Brahmans killed it and drove away its followers. From what we have said above it would be patent that in Southern India Buddhism flourished till about the end, at least, of the thirteenth century A.D." (Gopinatha Rao 1919, pp. 123–24). Given these continuing contacts between South India and Sri Lanka, it is not surprising to see Tamil taught in the great Buddhist monastery of Toṭagamuva in the fifteenth century.

Jainism in South India showed even greater vitality. Hiuen Tsang, the Chinese Buddhist traveler who visited South India in A.D. 642, mentions some decline in Buddhism but remarks repeatedly that it has yielded to Digambara Jainism (Nilakanta Sastri 1972, p. 427). Srinivasan says that that along with the rise of popular Hinduism of the Nāyanārs and Ālvārs there was considerable Jaina activity in South India and that "almost every village had a considerable Jaina population is attested by the ruins and other extant antiquities and references to Jaina temples and institutions of endowments to them in the hundreds of inscriptions in Tamil, Telegu and Kannada. It is only after 1000 A.D. particularly after the conversion of Hoysala Visnuvardhana from Jainism to Vaisnavism by Ramanuja, and the growth and rise of the Lingayat Saivism, that Jainism weakened in the Kannada and adjoining Telegu areas" (Srinivasan 1975, p. 207). He also documents in detail the systematic conversion of Jaina temples into Śiva temples in many parts of Tamil Nāṭu (1975, pp. 208–9). By contrast, in Kerala the Jaina temples were converted into Bhagavatī shrines by the fourteenth century. This was also true for Buddhist temples, according to Shreedhara Menon (1967, pp. 88–90). That Jaina and Buddhist shrines were converted into shrines of another mother goddess, Bhagavatī, in Kerala suggests very strongly that these religions had their own mother goddesses at least in this region. However, by the end of the fourteenth century Buddhism had practically disappeared from southern India, and Jainism was relegated to a very minor position.

Whether or not the heterodox religions were the major ones in southern India up to the eighth century, it is at least clear that they were important. Hence my argument: if the mythobiography of Pattini is rooted in a Jaina and Buddhist ethos, and if these religions were popular during this period, then it is almost inevitable that the Pattini cult was a Jaina-Buddhist one. It seems very unlikely that Jaina and Buddhist works would narrate a mythobiography that was not part of their current religious heritage.

Scholars have used the late seventh and early eighth centuries A.D. as the starting point of the decline of the heterodox religions in South India for a very good reason—namely, the Hindu "revival" of this period. This "revival" had three major facets. First there was a new philosophical reorientation in traditional Brahmanism, owing largely to the work of Kumārila and Śaṅkara, particularly the latter. Śaṅkara, a Nambudiri Brahman from southern Kerala, "travelled all over India propagating his new philosophy of a rigorously consistent monism and triumphing against all rivals who met him in debate" (Nilakanta Sastri 1966, p. 428). He adopted Buddhist philosophical ideas and also organized Hindu ascetic orders on the lines of the Buddhist *saṅgha*. Second, concomitantly with the former there arose a popular Hindu movement of devotional religiosity, both Shaivite and Vaishnavite, whose followers were known respectively as Nāyanārs and Ālvārs. Gifted saint-poets traversed the countryside, vanquishing in debate Buddhists and Jainas. Hymns, music, and dancing combined with intense devotionalism made it an attractive mass movement. Third, there was a real political change in which Hindu rulers began to patronize Hinduism at the expense of the heterodox religions, and in some cases they persecuted the latter. In Kerala itself there was no real persecution, but elsewhere in South India this indeed occurred. "The conversion of the Pallava and Pandya kings to Hinduism was responsible for the decline of Jainism. This was followed by the massacre of numerous Jain ascetics. Even now the Madura temple celebrates with gaiety the anniversary of the great event of committing to the gallows eight thousand Jains, the majority ascetics" (Kunjan Pillai 1970, p. 108). Nilakanta Sastri does not think this event actually occurred, but it does indicate that there was some persecution of Jainas (and probably Buddhists) during the period of the Hindu revival (Nilakanta Sastri 1966, p. 428). N. Subrahamanian says: "The Buddhists and the Jains were popular and probably enjoyed royal support during the Kalabhra interregnum; and their influence continued in an attenuated form in the following centuries till by about A.D. tenth century they had either died out or had settled down to a low point of public appeal and royal patronage" (1972, p. 383). This is perhaps somewhat exaggerated, since we saw earlier that Jainism enjoyed considerable popularity till at least the eleventh century, though it is very likely that the decline of Buddhism in South India started much earlier. Even so, there were well-known centers of Buddhism in South India till at least the beginning of the fourteenth century.

South India and Sri Lanka: The Jaina and Buddhist Migrations

What are the implications of the decline of Buddhism and Jainism in South India for the Pattini cult in Sri Lanka? Initially let me note that Jainism had considerable vitality in South India till the eleventh and twelfth centuries, and Buddhism, though showing some decline from the sixth century, had adherents in urban centers till at least the same period. Moreover, both the *Cilappatikāram* and the *Maṇimēkalai* refer to Vañci, the capital of the old Cēra kings, as the place where the images of Pattini (and also her consort, according to the *Maṇimēkalai*, were installed). This implies that Vañci, at least, was a center of the cult of the goddess Pattini.

Viewed from an all-India perspective, Buddhism and Jainism were being pushed farther and farther south from the fifth century. With the advent of *bhakti* Hinduism in the South and the espousal of Hinduism by South Indian monarchs, Buddhists and Jainas faced increasing difficulties that were accentuated by the eleventh and twelfth centuries. In the face of these historical forces, Buddhists and Jainas had three alternatives:

1. Move farther and farther south. This they did, witness the Buddhist Śrī Mūlavāsam temple and the Jaina shrines of Chitaral and Kallil in the extreme south of India in the Kanyākumārī district.

2. Assimilate into another Indian religion like Islam or, more likely, Hinduism. This escape route was also probably adopted by the Buddhists and Jainas. The conversion of Buddhist and Jaina temples into Śiva temples (Tamil Nāṭu) and Bhagavatī shrines (Kerala) was probably a strategy adopted by the Buddhists and Jainas themselves as a result of these outside pressures. The Jaina saints of South India, called *aṭikaḷ*s, became, as I shall show later, priests of at least some of the Bhagavatī shrines.

3. Emigrate to other Buddhist nations like Burma, Sri Lanka, Thailand, Cambodia, and Śrī Vijaya. This last alternative was available only to Buddhists, since there were no viable Jaina communities outside India. It is likely that all three escape routes were adopted by the Buddhists. Irrespective of whether there was active persecution of these religions, they were obviously threatened by the new Hindu movements. Thus there was ample motivation for people belonging to the heterodox faiths to migrate as the only viable alternative to being assimilated into Hinduism. Movement into the North would be futile; the closest Buddhist country to South India where continuing cultural contacts between Buddhists existed was, of course, Sri Lanka. Thus Sri Lanka would be the obvious choice, at least for the Buddhists who wanted to migrate. If, then, Buddhism began to decline in India after the eighth century, with near-total demise in the late fourteenth century, this is surely not due entirely to the assimilation of Buddhists into the Hindu fold, or to their persecution; surely there was emigration into the neighboring Buddhist country of Sri Lanka. I have already noted the existence of cultural contacts between Buddhist South India and Sri Lanka, though there is no direct historical evidence for the kind of mass migrations I have inferred. The existence of cultural contacts between monks of the two countries would again have promoted the movement of South Indian Buddhists to Sri Lanka.

The case of the Jainas is much more complicated. Jainism had no real influence outside India, and though it faced similar reactions from Hinduism (indeed, the persecution of Jainas was greater) its capacity for movement was circumscribed. Thus Jainism continued to exist in small pockets, since its populations could not be easily drained off by emigration. Once Jainas began to be pushed out of South India it is likely that they were Hinduized, were eliminated, migrated, or simply stayed on as religious enclaves. The Jainas could go to other Jaina communities farther north, but overseas migration to another Jaina country was impossible since there was no such country. But since the Jainas were being persecuted much more than the Buddhists it is indeed likely that they also migrated to the nearest overseas nation, Sri Lanka. I submit this idea, however, as a possible occurrence, unlike the migration of Buddhists that would have been inevitable.

It should be noted that Jaina migration to Sri Lanka is entirely plausible for other reasons also:

1. Jainism was closer in doctrinal outlook to Buddhism than to Brahmanism. Though Jainism had a harsher doctrinal ethic, its system of *ahiṃsā* (nonviolence), its theory of karma, its conception of the founder, its monk organization (*saṅgha*), its historical derivation from the same region, and its philosophical terminology were strongly akin to Buddhism.

2. While historically Jainism and Buddhism were opposed proselytizing religions, the evidence of the *Cilappatikāram* suggests that they existed side by side in South India.

While the *Maṇimēkalai* shows some anti-Jaina feeling, this is entirely on the level of doctrinal polemic rather than being social or interpersonal. Moreover, both these works show that Jainas could become Buddhists and vice versa.

3. I suggested earlier that on the level of popular subdoctrinal religiosity Jainism and Buddhism shared common beliefs like the Pattini cult. The evidence of the *Cilappatikāram* and *Maṇimēkalai* also clearly indicates that these two religions were at least minimally *shared* by a single group—the merchants—whose class and occupational affiliations may help transcend religious divisions.

If these arguments are correct, one would expect Jainas also to have migrated to Sri Lanka, though in lesser numbers, and eventually to have become assimilated into the dominant Buddhist religion of that country. I must reiterate, however, that this hypothesis of Jaina migration is very tentative. Right through Sri Lanka's history we have had migrations of South Indian Hindus, who were despised and treated antagonistically. Jaina migrations do not seem improbable in this light.

Another indirect piece of evidence comes from a poem written in the Kōṭṭe period (1410–1544) entitled *Vayanti Mālaya* ("the garland of diamonds"), dealing with the Mādēvi story and the seduction of Kōvalan̲. This poem is a secular composition never sung in ritual. It is perhaps derived from a nonritual tradition, since Kōvalan̲ is consistently referred to by that name rather than as Pālañga, which is his name in Sinhala ritual texts. Verse 55 of *Vayanti Mālaya* refers to Kōvalan̲'s sitting in audience with the king of Solī (Cōḷa) and watching Mādēvi dance. Line 3 of verse 55 is the relevant one:

> *bala balā solī raju sabhē siṭi kovalā situ kēvalā.*
>
> gazing [appreciatively] from the Soḷī king's assembly was *kovalā situ kēvalā.*

Kovalā is obviously Kōvalan̲, but *situ kēvalā* is difficult to translate. *Kēvalā* is hermit (Jaina term) and *situ* is "thought"; thus one could gloss this phrase as "Kōvalan̲ the hermit engrossed in thought." That Kōvalan̲ should be called a *kevalin* (an ascetic Jaina monk) is not surprising, since he is also called *terunnānse*, "Buddhist monk," for the psychological reasons discussed in chapter 11. What is striking, however, is the familiarity of the Sinhala author of the fifteenth century with the term for Jaina monk.

Some editions of *Vayanti Mālaya* drop *kēvala* and substitute *kōmala* ("foolish"), presumably because the former word has ceased to make sense in Sinhala. But that the Sinhala clearly used *kēvala* in the sense of Jaina monk comes from another text where Sinhala and Tamil "translations" are given. (Hevawasam 1974; text title, *Sinhala hā demala vayinaḍaya*, p. 347, stanzas 31 and 32). The Sinhala reads thus.
Stanza 31:

> *kasun ruvak sē babalana siri nē*
> *tosin me kī tepulaṭa mana nadinē*
> *dakin e pālañga saramana tadinē*
> *gosin gevan gavu panasak pamanē*

Approximate translation:

> [She was] shining like a golden statue beautifully
> [She said] Listen to my words that please the mind

She saw the monk Pālaṅga
Having traveled about fifty *gavu* [leagues].

The "Tamil translation" of the Sinhala is given in the next stanza.
Stanza 32:

ponnale seyidā pōlē ūlal
kanyaki solḷuni peccile vaḍivil
manmata tapaya kēvala nattil
anpadu kādam unḍō kadayil

This could hardly be called a "translation," but some of the Sinhala words are rendered into Tamil. Thus *ponnale* is the Tamil *ponnāl* "out of gold," and the first line could be reasonably glossed as "she looks like one made of gold." The third line is the critical one: here the Sinhala word *saramana* (Pāli, *śramana*), or "Buddhist monk," is rendered into Tamil as *kēvala*, "Jaina monk." Once again it indicates the Sinhala familiarity with the Jaina term. These two examples do not prove the existence of Jaina migrations: at the very best they indicate Jaina influence in the local Pattini traditions. Thus the question of Jaina migrations into Sri Lanka is plausible but unproved. For the purposes of this book, however, it is the Buddhist migrations that are relevant.

In the heyday of Buddhism in South India we know that Buddhists were migrating to the Indianized states of Southeast Asia. Coedes depicts two early stages of Indianization of Southeast Asia, from the first to the middle of the fourth century, and a second wave of Indianization from the fourth to the mid-sixth century (Coedes 1968, pp. 36–64). Coedes tries to answer the puzzling question of this massive "maritime drive of a people who regarded crossing the 'black water,' and contact with the Mleccha barbarians as bringing defilement and pollution" (1968, p. 19). His view is that trade was the major motive of the Indian colonizers, and that the obstacles to overseas travel were overcome largely through the development of Indian navies, the construction of junks that could carry up to several hundred passengers, and also the development of Buddhism. With Buddhism there arose a more flexible moral attitude toward caste and toward purity/pollution that removed the shackles from maritime trade. "We are thus led to represent the eastward expansion of Indian migration at the beginning of the Christian era as a result, at least, to a considerable degree of commercial enterprise . . . of whom many types are depicted in the ancient Buddhist literature and who seem to have had a particular devotion to the Buddha Dīpaṅkara, 'calmer of the waters'" (Coedes 1968, p. 21).

The Indianization of Southeast Asia was a product of merchant enterprises from various parts of India, but the dominant influence is the South, during the early period of Indianization in particular (Coedes 1968, pp. 31, 32). By the eighth century these movements had subsided, with the establishment of independent Buddhist kingdoms of Southeast Asia, though cultural contact between India and Southeast Asia continued. All these facts have considerable implications for our view of Buddhist emigration to Sri Lanka during its post-eighth-century decline in Southern India.

Movement of Buddhists out of southern India was no new phenomenon. If, then, Buddhists were being pushed out of South India after the eighth century, but more likely about the eleventh century, and if, furthermore, the Southeast Asian routes were no longer so freely available, then it would indeed be extraordinary if they did not migrate to the neighboring Buddhist nation of Sri Lanka. Such migrations must perforce be of a different character from those arising out of mercantile interests in Southeast Asia. Obviously no new states could be founded in Sri Lanka, which was already an established Buddhist nation and also the source for some of the Buddhist influence on Southeast Asia. These movements cannot therefore be those of colonizers, but must be those of immigrants settling down in an established nation.

Peaceful migrations are largely unrecorded in history, particularly if their impact on the dominant political order is minimal. Nevertheless, such movements have profoundly affected the cultural history of nations. In the present case we have no historical record of Jaina and Buddhist migrations: we must therefore infer their occurrence from indirect historical and sociological data. In the preceding pages I have made a strong case for Buddhist migrations from South India. The cultural data in Sri Lanka leaves no doubt that migrations occurred: only their "Buddhist" character is problematical. Ritual texts and folk literature make constant references to South Indian mendicants who come to Sri Lanka. Their arrival is depicted in Sinhala ritual dramas like *vaḍiga paṭuna*, performed in the *hūniyan käpilla* ritual, and in folk plays like Sokari (Sarachchandra 1966, pp. 45–49). Some of these migrants were merchants. I have noted two rituals in the *gammaḍuva* that present detailed dramatic enactments of their arrival in Sri Lanka. In chapter 5 I described the ritual drama that depicts the arrival of the Devol Deviyo, a group of seven merchant princes, in Sri Lanka and their subsequent apotheosis. The other is a ritual drama related to the earlier one and known as *rāmā märīma*, "the killing of Rāma" (text 44). This ritual, as it is performed in Sabaragamuva, deals with the landing of merchants in Sri Lanka. It continues to show how they opened shops and sold their "exotic" wares to the Sinhala villagers. It seems very unlikely that these dramas are figments of the imagination: they probably reflect actual historical processes that occurred in the country.[1]

Kerala and Sri Lanka: The Buddhist Migrations

Earlier in this chapter I suggested that the goddess Pattini was originally a deity of the Jainas and Buddhists of South India, and that, from the evidence of the *Cilappatikāram* and *Maṇimēkalai*, these people were merchants living in urban centers. The Jaina-Buddhist believers of Pattini were largely, but not exclusively, found in Kerala. They were facing opposition from popular resurgent Hinduism from the eighth century, but the strongest reaction came from about the tenth to the twelfth century, when state patronage of these religions practically ceased and active persecution probably occurred. Thus I suggested that large numbers of South Indian Buddhists, especially Kerala Buddhists, were being pushed out of their South Indian homes into Sri Lanka at this time. Let us now consider the independent historically documented evidence for migrations from Kerala to Sri Lanka during this period, especially on the west and south coasts and in the Sabaragamuva region, where the Pattini cult is strongest.

Let me first state my thesis, then document the evidence for substantiating it. I noted in chapter 1 that, after the depredations of Māgha, Sinhala civilization moved to the South

1. My guess is that the so-called Kuṣṭarāja statue at Väligama on the south coast of Sri Lanka was the product of these Buddhist (or even Jaina) migrants from South India.

and West, initially to Daṁbadeṇiya and Kurunāgala (the Daṁbadeṇiya dynasty ending in 1326), and from there to Gampola (near Kandy), whose first king, Bhuvanekabāhu IV, ascended the throne in 1341. Gampola did not exist for long as the capital of the Sinhala kings. Parākramabāhu VI, the last monarch to be given the title "great" in the chronicles, ascended the throne about 1411, initially in Rayigama and then at Kōṭṭe, both in the Western Province. The latter continued to be the capital of the Sinhala kings till 1565. It was in the reign of Parākramabāhu VI that the first unequivocally clear reference to the Pattini cult appears in Sri Lankan history. This is in *Kōkila Sandēśaya*, verse 117, which states that King Parākramabāhu VI built a three-story shrine dedicated to her in the vicinity of his capital in Kōṭṭe (Paranavitana 1960e, p. 766). From the commencement of the Gampola dynasty (1341) and the accession of Parākramabāhu VI in 1411, the politics of the country were dominated by chieftains of "Malabar" (Kerala) descent who originally came from Vañci—the celebrated city of the *Cilappatikāram*, the capital of the ancient Cēra kings, and the city where Ceṅkuṭṭuvaṉ erected the shrine for Pattini.[2]

Formal sovereignty of the Sinhala areas in the middle of the fourteenth century lay in Gampola, initially with Bhuvanekabāhu IV (1341) and later with his brother Parākramabāhu V, both sons of Vijayabāhu V (Paranavitana 1960b, p. 638). Actual power, however, was differently distributed. The North was now dominated by independent Tamil-speaking Shaivite kings, while the Sinhala areas of the western, southern, and central regions were under the effective control of two antagonistic yet intermarrying families, both of whom originally came from Kerala—the Alagakkonāra (Alakeśvara) and the Mehenavara families.[3] The name Alagokkonāra is Tamil or Malayalam, and Alakeśvara is its Sanskrit rendering. An inscription of 1344 at the Kitsirimevan-Kälaṇi vihāra refers to the first Alagakkonāra as the great minister, tenth in succession from Nissanka Alagakkonāra, a great minister who belonged to a noble family of Vañci.[4] The inscription suggests that the present "minister" Alagakkonāra came from a family of "ministers." However, Somaratne says that "the information supplied by a number of contemporary sources apparently reveals that the Alakeśvaras were originally traders who secured a position as court officials in the Sinhalese kingdom" (Somaratne 1975, p. 51). They resided at Rayigama to control the trade of the west coast at the lucrative port of Bēruvala, and they later founded the fortified city of Kōṭṭe to control the port of Colombo. It is probable that the family lived in Sri Lanka for ten generations, which meant from about A.D. 1100. The Mehenavara family also came from Kerala; the family name comes from the Malayalam word *menavan*, "baron" or "minister." They claimed to be descendants of

2. The identification of Vañci is the subject of considerable debate. Some say it is the old port of Musiris or Koṭuṅkoḷūr, while others identify it with the present-day Karur in the Trichinopoly district. Kunjan Pillai (1970) says that many commentators writing after the twelfth century believed Vañci was Koṭuṅkoḷūr, but this may not have been the case in the Caṅkam period. He also says that the Kulasekhara Perumals moved to Koṭuṅkoḷūr after the eighth century and called it Vañci, thus transferring an old name to a new capital.

3. There is some evidence that the two families were related to each other, though the original genealogical connections are difficult to determine.

4. The original inscription reads thus:

Viṣiṣta vañci-paraparen pämini Niṣṣaṃka
Alagakkonāra nam amātyaṣresṭhayānan gē
Paramparaven pävāta ā dasa veni
Alagakkonāra nam amātyottamayānam.

those who came with the bo tree from India in Asoka's time, but Paranavitana says this is an attempt to add distinction to their pedigree, since this family is nowhere mentioned before the Gampola period (Paranavitana 1960b, p. 640). I shall give only a brief account of these families, taken from the more detailed and fascinating account of the politics of this period by Paranavitana (1960b, pp. 636–59) and Somaratne (1975).

When the great Arab traveler Ibn Battuta arrived in Sri Lanka in 1344, the effective control over the Sinhala areas of the present-day Western, Southern, and Sabaragamuva provinces was in the hands of an Alagakkonāra. Ibn Battuta says he possessed the white elephant, the emblem of supreme power. This Alagakkonāra, though not a consecrated sovereign, was an independent ruler who did not owe allegiance to either Bhuvanekabāhu IV of Gampola or his brother Parākramabāhu V of Dädigama. The rival family of the Mehenavara was headed at this time by Sena Laṅkādhikāra, who supported the kings of Gampola and Dädigama. He was married to a sister of Bhuvanekabāhu IV. Ibn Battuta informs us that just before his arrival Alagakkonāra was blinded and deposed by his enemies and his son was installed in his place. If so, this was an irregular succession by the standards of these families, who practiced matrilineal descent. The troubles in the Alagakkonāra family helped Sena Laṅkādhikāra, who began to control areas like Devundara and Väligama in southern Sri Lanka, traditionally under the control of the Alagakkonāras. The latter now had effective control only over the area around Rayigama (near Kalutara, Western Province), their ancestral seat.

The fortunes of the Mehenavara clan soon waned as a result of invasions into Sinhala territory by the ruler of Jaffna, Ārya Cakravarti. Bhuvanekabāhu IV of Gampola had died by then, and his brother Parākramabāhu V took over both Gampola and Dädigama, but soon had to seek refuge in Ruhuṇa. Little is known about subsequent events except that Vikramabahu III, possibly the son of Sena Laṅkādhikāra (Mehenavara), became king through matrilineal succession, since the late king's sister had married Sena Laṅkādhikāra (Paranavitana 1960b, p. 643).

These changes in the fortunes of the Mehenavaras resulted in a dramatic comeback for the Alagakkonāras. Apparently seven members of this family held power one after the other, the first of the new line being Nissanka Alagakkonāra (Somaratne 1975, p. 53). To quote Somaratne:

> According to the contemporary records, Nissanka Alagakkonāra was the person who undertook to liberate the Sinhalese Kingdom from the threatened subjugation by the Aryacakravartis of Jaffna and their South Indian allies, during the reign of Vikramabahu III (A.D. 1357–1374), by building the fortress known as Jayavardhanapura Kōtte. This great warrior and statesman is referred to as *praburaja* in contemporary writings, and became the virtual dictator of the Sinhalese reigning monarch. There are a number of contemporary documents referring to this personage in more laudatory terms than those concerning the reigning monarch. (1975, pp. 53–54)

This same Alagakkonāra was the patron of a convocation of the Buddhist *saṅgha* held in 1369/70 (Somaratne 1975, p. 55). With his construction of the fort at Kōṭṭe and his expulsion of the tax gatherers of the Tamil king of Jaffna, he had total control of the territory and trade of the southern and western regions of Sri Lanka.

On the death of Nissanka Alagakkonāra his son became *prabhurāja*, probably chief minister to the king. Again this violated the norms of matrilineal succession, so that soon afterward Vīra Alakeśvara, his sister's son, became the chief power in the land.[5] But his power was challenged by his younger brother Virābāhu Āpāṇa, who fought at Rayigama, their ancestral seat, and became the de facto ruler of Sri Lanka. He was an intrepid fighter and a patron of letters and was given the title of *yuvaraja* (subking) by the reigning monarch Bhuvanekabāhu V, whose brother-in-law he was (Somaratne 1975, p. 57). At his death his two sons assumed power, but soon afterward his brother Vīra Alakeśvara returned from India and became the chief power in A.D. 1400. Vīra Alakeśvara was captured in Kōṭṭe or Rayigama by an armada led by Cheng Ho, an emissary of the third Ming emperor Cheng Tsu, and taken to the Chinese capital. "The Chinese emperor treated the captives with consideration, set Alagakkonāra and his family free, and ordered those from Ceylon to select 'the most worthy member of their tribe' to be placed on the throne" (Paranavitana 1960b, p. 652). The choice fell, according to Chinese sources, on a person called Yeh-pa-nai-na, which is the Sinhala for *ǟpāṇa*, that is, a person of royal blood. He was accordingly "sent back to Ceylon bearing the seals of office, and was proclaimed king under Chinese suzerainty" (Paranavitana 1960b, p. 652). But this person was apparently murdered in 1414 to give undisputed legitimacy to Parākramabāhu VI of Kōṭṭe (Somaratne 1975, p. 71).

Parākramabāhu was the last king of Sri Lanka to be called "the great," and rightly so. (The father of this monarch was a dignitary with the title *jayamahalana* [Somaratne 1975, p. 63]. Somaratne mentions the historical reference to a person called Bhas Kara Jayamahalana, who was a brother [actual or classificatory] of an Alagakkonāra [1975, p. 83]. Bhaskara is a well-known name in Kerala.) Contemporary sources say that Parākramabāhu VI was also related to the Mehenavara family. He was consecrated king in Rayigama, where he lived for three years, and later made Kōṭṭe his capital. It was this king who erected the three-story shrine for the goddess Pattini in the vicinity of his capital (Paranavitana 1960e, p. 766).

The preceding historical sketch of the period 1341–1415, dominated by Kerala chieftains, is of crucial importance for our study of the Pattini cult and permits us to make some historical and sociological inferences.

1. Consider the background of the Kerala families who effectively controlled the western, southern, and parts of the central provinces of Sri Lanka for more than fifty years. They were originally merchants from Vañci and probably came to Sri Lanka about A.D. 1100. Vañci was a center of the Pattini cult and probably a seat of Jaina and Buddhist merchants. The conclusion is irresistible that these were merchants princes pushed out of India as a result of the post-eighth-century Hindu expansion.

2. It is most unlikely that these two families, particularly the Alagakkonāras, came alone and established themselves as the dominant political power in Sri Lanka. No political leader or group can establish dominance without a power base. In Sri Lanka history there are cases of aliens who were consecrated as kings, but they succeeded only because they had a power base, support either from established Sinhala chiefs or from the army. It would be virtually impossible, sociologically speaking, for an alien merchant family to exercise practical power and mobilize popular support without a power base. In all proba-

5. Somaratne (1975) translated *bǟna* as "brother," which is highly improbable. In common usage *bǟna* is "sister's son," and this fits nicely with the rules of matrilineal succession involved in this case.

bility this power base came from other Kerala and South Indian Buddhist settlers pushed out of their homeland in South India for the same reasons.

3. The vegetation, climate, and ecology of the region dominated by these Kerala chiefs were identical with those of their Kerala homeland. Our hypothesized Kerala immigrants could not have selected a more congenial area to settle, at least from their own point of view.

4. The political conditions of Sri Lanka up to the fourteenth century favored the settlement of Malabar immigrants in the western regions.[6] Up to the thirteenth century Sinhala sovereignty was localized in Anurādhapura and then Polonnaruva. Ruhuṇa had a flourishing civilization, but it was likely that much of the Western and Sabaragamuva provinces were bare, forested country open for immigration. Kerala immigrants, particularly if they were Buddhists, would be welcome.

5. The Alagakkonāras ruled from Rayigama in the Western Province. This was their ancestral home and probably the center of their power base. It is also a region where the Pattini cult is firmly established. The cult was strongest in the Western Province, then in the Southern and Sabaragamuva provinces.[7]

6. The Alagakkonāras and Mehenavaras practiced matrilineal descent, but this was sometimes challenged by patriliny. It is likely that patrilineal descent was the norm of the pre-Kerala Sinhala folk of these areas. And it is likely that patrilineal Malabars also settled in this area, not to mention settlers from Tamil Nāṭu, who were largely patrilineal. However, it is important to note that the Gampola kings came under the influence of the matrilineal Malabars, so that they also practiced matrilineal succession and contracted

6. Later Malabar immigrations are widely documented.

a. The *salāgama* caste were weavers, later cinnamon peelers, from Malabar who were brought to the south coast by the Portuguese. Several of these *salāgamas* have the surname (*vāsagama*) Nambudirige ("of the Nambudiri"). A naive interpretation of this term may lead us to conclude that they were originally Nambudiri Brahmans from Kerala. It is very unlikely that Nambudiri Brahmans ever practiced weaving (an inferior-caste occupation). *Salāgama* (or Chalaiyans) are found in South India to this day as weavers. If so, how did they get the surname Nambudiri?

We have to interpret Sinhala caste dynamics both historically and contextually . The original settlers of the West and South were Sinhala *goyigama* (farmers), some of them originally from Malabar. Much later, in early Portuguese times, there were immigrations of *karāva* (fishermen, *karaiyār* of South India) and *salāgama*. The *karāva* were antagonistic to Sinhala *goyigama*, who were the highest caste in the area. To boost their own status the *karāva* activated the *varṇa* scheme, which was moribund in Sri Lanka. Thus by the *varṇa* scheme *goyigama* are *śūdra*; the *karāva* then pushed their ancestry to the *kuru* (*kaurava*) of the Mahābhārata war, thereby making them *ksatriya*! The *salāgama*, not to be outdone, opposed themselves to the *karāva* (to whom they were traditionally hostile) by claiming Brahman descent, which made them the highest in the *varṇa* scheme! The only Brahmans they knew were the Nambudiris from their original home in Kerala—thus *salāgama* came to be descended from the Nambudiris. Interpretations of caste claims of this sort cannot be taken literally but must be seen as a dialectic of conflict between antagonistic castes.

b. There are many Kerala-derived surnames in low country: Kuruppu (from the Kurups, the masters of Nāyar gymnasiums), Malalasekera (Malala, meaning Kerala), Malalgoda (Kerala village). Other names indicative of Kerala origin are Ilangakoon and perhaps names like Kulasekhera. The study of genealogy of some of these people may give us some clues, but there have been no such studies yet. H. C. P. Bell recorded a tradition in Edandalava in the Kegalle district to two families of Pannikirāla, probably gymnasts of Kerala carrying on their professions here (Bell 1892, p. 50).

7. The first draft of this chapter was written without any reference to the Alagakkonāras and published in Obeyesekere (1980). The Alagakkonāra evidence strikingly corroborates the earlier inferences I made, on purely logical grounds, regarding Kerala migrations into Sri Lanka.

polyandrous unions. This is because the Gampola kings were themselves linked to the Malabar chiefs through marriage alliances. The great king of Kōṭṭe, Parākramabāhu VI, came very much under the Malabar influence like his predecessors. If these Kerala immigrants were Buddhist believers in the Pattini cult, then this deity would inevitably have been popular in the region. Thus Parākramabāhu VI gave state recognition to the cult when he built a shrine in her honor. We can be fairly certain that it was this king, and not Gajabāhu I as myth would have it, who instituted the cult on the state level in his new capital in Kōṭṭe sometime after A.D. 1415. This action would have been especially significant if the king was in fact an Alagakkonāra, which was most likely. The texts of the Pattini cult known as the *pantis kōlmura*, or thirty-five ritual texts, were written down sometime after the ascension of this king, as the literary style of some of them suggests.

I have presented a novel way of looking at medieval Sri Lankan history, which in turn has helped me reinterpret the available historical data in a new light. Clearly, more evidence has to be unearthed before these interpretations can be validated. Novel hypotheses often have this effect: they force us to look for new kinds of evidence and to reorient our perspective on history. I can only present a special point of view: much of the confirmatory evidence must come from later research both in Sri Lanka and in Kerala.

Let me conclude this section by summarizing my argument. Kerala chieftains and very likely other Kerala immigrants were well established in the area of the Western, Southern, and Sabaragamuva provinces by the middle of the fourteenth century. It is difficult to state clearly when they arrived in Sri Lanka. According to the logic of my argument these immigrants were Buddhists pushed out of Kerala and other Buddhist centers in South India after the eighth century, a movement that would have intensified in the tenth and eleventh centuries owing to the accelerated Hinduization of South India and the loss of royal patronage for the heterodox religions. These migrants were soon established in the areas of western and southern Sri Lanka, where they continued their Buddhism and Pattini worship. The cult itself was given state recognition by Parākramabāhu VI, who made Kōṭṭe his capital for the first time in Sri Lankan history. He gave state recognition to the popular goddess of this area, an action politically and culturally intelligible in the context of the Kerala influence on Sri Lankan politics and culture.

The Tamil Epics and the Sinhala Tradition: Continuity in the Buddhist Ethos

The Pattini texts have been summarized or translated in chapter 5. Though these texts vary in style and content from the *Cilappatikāram* and *Maṇimēkalai*, they have an important feature in common—they are all rooted in the heterodox religions, with the Sinhala texts continuing the Buddhist elements of the *Cilappatikāram* and the *Maṇimēkalai*. An examination of some of the Sinhala texts of the Pattini cult may produce further circumstantial evidence regarding Pattini as a Buddhist deity, both in the original Indian context and in the later diffusion of the cult to Sinhala Sri Lanka. Though the Sinhala texts are based on an original Tamil corpus, the goddess herself seems to have no connection whatever with Hinduism or Dravidian folk religion. In the Sinhala texts she is unequivocally presented as a pious Buddhist, lending plausibility to the notion that she may originally have been a South Indian Buddhist deity.

It is interesting to compare her with other major gods incorporated into Buddhism from Hinduism, like Viṣṇu and Skanda. Though these two gods have been divested of some of their Hindu attributes, they also retain some of them. For example, the vehicles they ride (the *garuḍa* bird and the peacock), and their association with the wars against titans (*asuras*) reflect their Hindu mythological origins. Not so with Pattini, who shows no connection with Hinduism. Unlike other gods in the pantheon who had obtained *varan* (warrant) from the Buddha Gautama, Pattini had obtained *vivaraṇa* ("permission," a strictly Buddhist term) from an even earlier Buddha, Kakusaňda, by giving alms to him. This is described in *pattini pätuma* (text 34, pp. 225–26). She was meditating for future Buddhahood on Aňdungiri Peak when the Buddhist god Sakra (the Hindu Indra) asked her to be reborn on earth to quell the might of the Pāṇḍyan king. Several texts are replete with Buddhist moralizing—*pahan gäṁbura*, *tapas gamana* (texts 35, 40)—indicating that the Pattini cult is more suffused in a Buddhist ethos than the cult of any other deity in Sri Lanka. In contemporary Sri Lanka gods like Saman and Viṣṇu and Nātha are viewed as closer to salvation (Nirvāṇa) than Pattini; yet Pattini, as far as the texts are concerned, is more Buddhist than these other deities, indicating again that she may have been a Buddhist deity before her inclusion in the Sinhala pantheon.

One of the texts that is full of Buddhist moralizing is *tapas gamana*, "the voyage to the hermitage." This text deals with the decision of Pālaňga's (Kōvalaṉ's) parents to leave the worldly society of Kāvēri paṭuna (Kāvirippūmpaṭṭiṉam, Pukār) for the life of Buddhist hermits at Kāñci. Let us consider the internal evidence that suggests this text may have been based on a Tamil Buddhist text from South India.

1. The parents of Pālaňga (Kōvalaṉ) have no real significance in the Sinhala belief system. They have no role in the ritual dramas; they are hardly referred to in any other text. The existence of a text containing ninety-eight four-line stanzas on Pālaňga's parents and their renunciation of the world thus seems out of place in Sinhala ritual and mythology.

2. Both the *Cilappatikāram* and the *Maṇimēkalai* assume that Kōvalaṉ's parents were Buddhists; when he heard of Kōvalaṉ's death, his father decided to renounce the world and live in a hermitage. In the Sinhala text both Kōvalaṉ's mother and his father make a similar move and leave for a hermitage in Kāñci. The similarity is striking, suggesting that they come from a common source. The real difference is that in the Sinhala text the couple decides to renounce the world while Pālaňga (Kōvalaṉ) was still alive and married to Pattini. The South Indian tradition of the *Cilappatikāram* and *Maṇimēkalai* makes more sense, since it provides grief as a motivation for the parents of Kōvalaṉ to renounce the world. The Sinhala version seems an attempt to incorporate a South Indian text into the traditions of the thirty-five texts. To have the parents renounce the world *after* the death of Kōvalaṉ would destroy the total conception of the Sinhala rituals. In these rituals the final culminating event is the death of Kōvalaṉ and his resurrection by Pattini, enacted in the ritual drama known as *marā ipäddīma* ("killing and resurrection"). To add a long sequel to this showing the renunciation of the world by Kōvalaṉ's parents (who are of little consequence in the Sinhala myths) would destroy the total conception of the Sinhala ritual cycle of Pattini myths. Hence the renunciation of Kōvalaṉ's parents is placed in the lifetime of Pattini and Kōvalaṉ. But this produces a further problem: no real reason is given for their renunciation of the world.

Finally it should be noted that *tapas gamana* is never sung or enacted in any of the *gammaḍuva* rituals I have seen. Though it is part of the Pattini corpus, priests are ignorant of its content, which again suggests that it is a survival from its South Indian past.

14

The Mater Dolorosa and the Dead God: From West Asia to South India

In the previous chapter I made a case for the goddess Pattini as a Jaina-Buddhist deity. This does not imply that she could not also have been a Hindu deity, though there is little evidence for this in the classic Tamil epics. Furthermore, the central feature of the Sinhala rituals for Pattini is the killing and death of Pālaṅga, Pattini's search for him, her role as *mater dolorosa* weeping over Pālaṅga's corpse, and her resurrection of him. As far as I know the dramatic enactment of the death and resurrection theme is not found anywhere in Hindu ritual, though the theme of the wife resurrecting her husband is found in myth, especially in the well-known myth of Savitri. Thus this central ritual drama is unique in South Asian ritual and was probably confined to the heterodox religions of southern India rather than to Brahmanism, popular Hinduism, or Dravidian folk religion.

While the drama of "death and resurrection" is alien to Hinduism, it is central to the religions of West Asia, probably from very ancient times. This drama also constitutes the classic theme of Frazer's work, and it stimulated much research by later historians of religion. Thus Sri Lanka is the southernmost example of this West Asian theme, and my descriptions of the rituals are the only eyewitness accounts of this great drama. Initially I attributed the parallelism to similar yet independent psychological and social conditions. I am still of the opinion that similar sociocultural and psychological conditions may produce similar symbolic structures and that this is how such parallelisms in geographically unrelated areas occur. Yet, after fieldwork and historical research in Kerala in 1974, I was convinced that the Pattini cult diffused to Kerala (and other parts of South India) from West Asia. Once again I can only open up a new and potentially fruitful area of research in the history and anthropology of religion. The evidence I shall present to substantiate my views must remain tentative and circumstantial.

It is not difficult to establish West Asian contact with India as early as Mohenjodaro and Harappa (e.g., Pigott 1952, pp. 91, 113–31; Basham 1959, pp. 19–21). But in this chapter I want to limit the argument to continuous and intensive contact between West

Asia and Kerala, so as to render plausible the hypothesis of the West Asian origin of the Pattini cult. Some scholars argue that "teak from Kerala was found in buildings erected during the Babylonian era around 600 B.C. at Ur of the Chaldees" (Woodcock 1967, p. 80). However, this is palpably too early a date for my argument, since I am interested in the relation between West Asia and the Jaina-Buddhist merchant communities in southern India. These communities were active in Kerala from at least the beginning of the Christian era and possibly earlier. There is a great deal of evidence for intense and prolonged trade contact between Kerala and West Asia in the first few centuries A.D. I shall focus mainly on one important trade center, Musiris, for two reasons. First, Musiris is probably the modern Koṭuṅkoḷūr (Cranganur), where there is a temple for Kālī that many Kerala historians have identified as an ancient Pattini shrine. Second, it is possible that Vañci, the ancient capital of Kerala and the setting for the third section of the *Cilappatikāram*, was a few miles in the interior from Musiris (Sreedhara Menon 1967, pp. 74–76), though this identification is controversial. It should, however, be remembered that Musiris is only one of the more important ports in Kerala and South India—others like Pukār (Kāvirippūmpaṭṭiṉam) and Tondi, to the north of Musiris, were also important.

The brisk trade between West Asia and India is clear from the work of Strabo, Pliny the Elder, and the anonymous author of *Periplus of the Erythrian Sea*. According to Strabo (A.D. 20) at least 120 ships each year sailed to India from Myos Hormos on the Red Sea (Woodcock 1967, p. 81). This trade dramatically increased when a Greek mariner, Hippolus, discovered in A.D. 45 the pattern of the monsoon winds, which enabled navigators to leave Ocelis near Aden and reach Musiris in forty days (Sreedhara Menon 1967, p. 56). Pliny, writing soon afterward, described the sea voyage from Ocelis to Musiris. *Periplus* (A.D. 77) mentions five ports on the Malabar Coast frequented by Greek traders: "Musiris of the same kingdom (Kerala) abounds in ships sent there with cargoes from Arabia and by the Greeks" (quoted in Nilakanta Sastri 1972, p. 57). In A.D. 125 Pan Long, a Chinese traveler, made a report to his emperor: "from the West Coast it (India) is in communication with Ta-Ts'in (the Roman Province of Syria) and precious objects from Ta-Ts'in are found there" (Nilakanta Sastri 1972, p. 11). There is clear evidence of commercial contact with the Roman Empire right up to the sixth century, for coins belonging to the reigns of Augustus, Tiberius, Caligula, Constantine, and the Byzantine emperors up to Justin I (A.D. 527–65) have been found in various parts of Kerala and South India (see Kunjan Pillai 1970, pp. 393–98, for a discussion of Kerala-Yavana contacts). This trade with the West continued till the sixth century, for Cosmas Indicopleustes, the famous Nestorian traveler from Alexandria, noted that five ports were active in exporting pepper and sandalwood. "Cosmas gave no hint of any state of crisis that might explain the fact that he was the last recorder of the old Alexandrian trade with Kerala, which by now had lasted for at least six centuries. . . . Yet not very long after his visit the great ships of the Greeks ceased for ever their journeys to the harbours of the Malabar Coast" (Woodcock 1967, p. 85). These foreign notices are confirmed by early Tamil Caṅkam (Sangam) literature and the later *Cilappatikāram*, which describes busy ports like Pukār and Musiris. "There appears to have been a Yavana colony on the West Coast, and also a temple of Augustus. The ruins of a Roman factory near Pondicherry have been recently discovered. In the Sangam literature there are many references to wine brought from the Western countries, and also to Yavana girls and men employed by Tamil kings as bodyguards"

(Natesan 1959, p. 214; Woodcock 1966, p. 144). The *Cilappatikāram* has a detailed description of the layout of Pukār (Kāvirippūmpaṭṭiṉam), the city where the parents of Kōvalaṉ and Kaṇṇaki lived. One paragraph is particularly relevant to this discussion:

> The Sun shone over the open terraces, over the warehouses, near the harbours, and over the turrets with airholes looking like the eyes of deer. In different places of Puhār the onlooker's attention was arrested by the sight of Yavanas whose prosperity was never on the wane. On the harbours were to be seen sailors come from distant lands, but for all appearances they lived as one community. . . . In certain places weavers were seen dealing in fine fabrics made of silk, fur and cotton. Whole streets were full of silks, corals, sandal and myrrh, besides a wealth of rare ornaments, perfect pearls, gems and gold, which were beyond reckoning. (Dikshitar 1939, pp. 110–11)

It should be remembered that *yavana*, in Indian languages, had the specific meaning "Greeks" and the more general meaning "foreigners," generally Arabs, Syrians, Jews, and Westerners. However, most of the foreign trade to Malabar and South India during this period was dominated by Alexandria, the great entrepôt of trade in the Greco-Roman world (Woodcock 1966, p. 141). It is likely that some of these *yavana*s mentioned in South Indian literature were Greek-speaking races living in Alexandria and other busy ports of the Levant.

Along with trade, the merchants brought their own religions. Says Woodcock: "But if trade did not follow the flag, religion always followed trade. The Romans started the process with the temple of Augustus which they built in the ancient port of Muziris in the first century A.D." (1967, p. 33). This was followed by Christians and Jews, both claiming an antiquity back to the middle of the first century. Woodcock says that these communities came by the second century at the latest in Greek sailing boats (1967, p. 112). They were firmly established by A.D. 525, for Cosmas refers to them. Then as well as now they were settled in and around Musiris-Koṭuṅkoḷūr. The consensus of Kerala historians is that both communities were well established by the second century. "When we consider the well established trade relations between Kerala and West Asia, there is sufficient ground for the belief that the gospel of Christ might have reached Kerala as early as the first century A.D." (Kunjan Pillai 1970, p. 227).

Consider the implications of the preceding argument. There is evidence that a Roman temple for Augustus existed in Musiris in the first century; Jews, Syrians, and Christians were well established by the sixth century and probably were in Kerala by the second century. Given the importance of Musiris as a trade center, it would indeed be surprising if the Alexandrian and West Asian merchants did not bring with them the more popular religions of the time—the cults of the various mother goddesses and the dead god. Consider also the traditions of the Syrian Christian church of Kerala, according to which Saint Thomas himself came to Koṭuṅkoḷūr (Cranganur) in the first century, converted some of the Brahmans, and established the first indigenous Christian church. Many scholars tend to accept this tradition as having some validity, though it strikes the anthropologist as a myth that validated the antiquity and legitimacy of the Syrian church. Also the view that Saint Thomas initially converted Brahmans seems very much like a later rationalization, since Brahmans were hardly dominant in this period of Kerala history. The more likely explanation is not that Saint Thomas himself established the church in Kerala, but that colonies of Syrian traders existed here from early times and that some of them were

Christians. If this hypothesis is acceptable then it is also likely, indeed inevitable, that some of these Syrians were *not* Christians but followers of the popular religions of West Asia during that time.

It is one thing to introduce an alien religion into a country and another to establish it there. Who were the receivers of the alien religions? Again, the evidence of the Syrian Christians and Jews provides a clue, for when these groups emerge into history they appear as trading and merchant communities. If so, the introduced religions of foreign merchants must have initially been accepted by their counterparts in the busy ports of South and West India. In this regard the *Cilappatikāram* (as well as practically all later versions of the Pattini myths) makes the clear assertion: Pattini and her consort come from an established tradition of seafaring merchants. The parents of Kōvalaṉ and Kaṇṇaki belonged to a wealthy merchant class, owners of ships. They were also a new class, not part of the traditional division of ancient Kerala society. Thus it seems plausible that cults introduced by *foreign* merchants would have taken root among *local* merchant groups later on.

Furthermore, most of these merchants were clearly Buddhists, Jainas, and Ājīvakas. It is likely that the cults of the mother goddess introduced in an early period by foreigners became part of the *popular* religion of the new local entrepreneurs. Since the merchant communities were small, it is also likely that miscegenation and marriage alliances between foreign and local merchants promoted the incorporation of the cults in the local population. Alternatively, one cannot rule out the possibility that the Jaina and Buddhist merchants of the *Cilappatikāram* were, in fact, foreigners who had been Indianized (like the Gandhāra Greeks and the Syrians and Jews later on) and adopted the new non-Dravidian religions like Buddhism and Jainism, but also continued to subscribe to the mystery cults (as Buddhists do even today in regard to "animistic" beliefs).

Once the cult of the mother goddess and the dying god was introduced to South India (not just Kerala), it was obviously the only cult that could take root and be assimilated into the Indian cultural pattern, since the worship of the goddess (if not the dying god) was a preexisting and popular feature of Dravidian folk religion. The introduced deity could be treated as one of the area's own deities. It is interesting that the formally established alien religions like Christianity, Islam, and Judaism were *not* assimilated into the local culture but became instead, *separate religious enclaves*. Thus, not only the social structural situation—the existence of merchant communities—but also the cultural situation favored the assimilation of the cultus.

Syrians, Jews, and Greeks—most of them from Alexandria and other parts of the Levant—were influential in Kerala trade during the first through sixth centuries at least, as I noted. Some of them must obviously have adopted the mother-goddess cults that spread from Anatolia, Lydia (Asia Minor), Phrygia, Egypt, and Syria into the Greco-Roman world from about 500 B.C. The origin and development of these cults in the Roman Empire have been discussed by many scholars. Everywhere in the Roman Empire one of the great mother goddesses was worshiped, with or without her consort, son, or lover (the dead god). Some of the most popular were Kybele, Artemis, and Isis, and their consorts were Attis, Adonis, and Osiris. In chapter 11 I noted one of the central dramas of these goddess cults: the theme of the *mater dolorosa* and the dead god (who is represented as son, lover, or husband, or occasionally as brother of the goddess). This theme was not found in all of the cults, but it was there in some of them. Almost everywhere the goddess was both virgin and mother. "The secret seems to be in the religious thinking of the Mediterranean world as early as the Mycenaean age. The great goddess was revered both as virgin and as mother" (Witt 1971, p. 141). In the Greek pantheon Artemis was the most virginal and maternal. Like Pattini she is mother, yet barren, exhibiting "her absolute freedom from the ties that would have bound her to the male sex" (Witt 1971, p. 142; see also Farnell 1971, 2:442–49).

It is impossible to derive the Pattini cult from any specific goddess cult of West Asia and the Mediterranean. It is equally impossible to specify which community from the West Asian area brought the original form of the Pattini cult. Nevertheless, I shall use the example of the Syrians to show that it was at least possible for them to have introduced the goddess cults of West Asia into India. It was the Syrians who introduced Christianity to India; it is certain that they also had mother-goddess cults. Indeed, Marina Warner says that the earliest Marian liturgy appeared in Syria in A.D. 370, indicating that they had begun to introduce the mother goddess into Christianity very early (Warner 1976, p. 348).

According to Cumont, *Syri negotiatores*, Syrian merchants, had established themselves all over the Latin provinces in the beginning of the Christian era (Cumont 1911, p. 107). In the second century they were on the coast of Asia Minor, on the Piraeus, and in the Archipelago. Some of them went inland into Europe by river routes, up the Danube and the Rhone, into Gaul, and everywhere in the Roman world, "prompted by a lust of gain to defy all dangers" (Cumont 1911, p. 108); they even established themselves in the north of England near Hadrian's Wall (Cumont 1911, p. 112). They exercised a profound influence on the Roman provinces as bankers who monopolized the money business and as traders who sold, among other things, silks and spices (some of which surely came from their colonies in Asia).

They brought their religions along with their trade. These religions were the ecstatic oriental goddess cults, other Semitic religions such as the Baals, and Syrian Christianity. Regarding the first Cumont says: "As soon as the merchants established their places of business in the islands of the Archipelago during the Alexandrian period under the empire, they founded chapels in which they practised their exotic rites. . . . It was easy for the divinities of the Phoenician Coast to cross the seas. Among them were Adonis, whom the women of Byblos mourned; Balmarcodes, 'the lord of the dance' who came from Beirut; Marna the master of the rain, worshiped in Gaza; and Mariema whose nautical holiday was celebrated every spring on the coast near Ostia as well as in the Orient" (Cumont 1911, p. 110). In addition to the half-Hellenized religions, the Syrians introduced deities of purely Semitic character and origin. When Trajan (A.D. 106) extended his dominion as far as the desert over countries that were only superficially Hellenized "and where the native devotions had preserved all the savage fervor," there was a renewed influx of Syrian deities into the Occident (Cumont 1911, p. 111).

One of the most important goddesses introduced to Rome by Syrian slaves and traders was known there as Dea Syria, or more popularly as Diasuria or Iasura (James 1959, p. 183). A graphic description of her cult and that of her consort Hadad (Adad) is given by Lucian in his *De dea Syria*.

> The Syrians give the name Adad to the god they revere as first and greatest of all. They honour him as all powerful, but they associate with him the goddess named *Adargatis*, and assign to these two divinities supreme power over everything, recognizing in them the sun and the earth. Without expressing by numerous names the different aspects of their power, their predominance is implied by the different at-

> tributes assigned to the two divinities. For the statue of *Adad* is encircled by descending rays which indicate that the force of heaven resides in the rays which the sun sends down to earth: the rays of the statue of *Adargatis* rise upwards, a sign that the power of the ascending rays brings to life everything which the earth produces. Below this statue are the figures of lions, emblematic of the earth: for the same reason that the Phrygians so represent the Mother of the gods, that is to say, the earth, borne by lions. (Quoted in James 1959, pp. 184–85)

On the popular level this cult was strikingly similar to the Kybele-Attis cult and entailed self-flagellation and transvestism in order to secure identity with the goddess (James 1959, p. 185). This was one of the many cults introduced by the Syrians to the Greco-Roman world. They had fully established themselves in the Latin provinces from the first to the seventh century (Cumont 1971, p. 107).

In addition to these Syrian and Hellenized goddess cults and Semitic deities, Syrian traders introduced Syrian Christianity. In chapter 11 I noted that it took five centuries before the bleeding Christ was put on the cross. By some accounts it was the Syrians who first started this trend and substituted "reality in all its pathetic horror to a vague symbolism" (Cumont 1911, p. 109). They spread their Christianity to the Malabar Coast, Turkestan, and China. Given the trade and religious activities of this group in other parts of the then-known world, it is inconceivable that they introduced Christianity alone, and not their ecstatic goddess cults, either indigenous Syrian ones or the more controlled Hellenized versions. Clearly, China would hardly have tolerated these goddess cults, which were completely alien to the established culture; but this was not so in India, where there would have been full cultural receptivity. I am not suggesting that the Pattini cult, in its original form, was introduced by Syrian merchants (or soldiers), for other trading groups from the Levant could have introduced it; but the possibility should be borne in mind in future research, particularly in future archaeological excavations in Musiris-Koṭuṅkoḷūr and other areas of the Malabar Coast. As I said earlier, these goddess cults, given the prior existence of mother-goddess cults in India, would inevitably have been assimilated into the Indian religions, unlike great traditions with institutionalized priesthoods and formal doctrines and liturgy, which, owing to their culture-alien nature, must perforce have existed in limited isolation as "enclave religions."

The Pattini Cult in Kerala: the Goddess of Koṭuṅkoḷūr and the Secret Chamber

The hypothesis of the West Asian origins of the Pattini cult is only a plausible speculation. It does, however, highlight the importance of Musiris-Koṭuṅkoḷūr and the region around it, for this was a major center of international commerce, and in the vicinity were, and still are, a large number of Syrian Christians—the only community of Christians surviving from a period before the arrival of the Europeans. In 1431 heavy monsoon rains silted up the port of Koṭuṅkoḷūr and opened up Cochin harbor, which then became the emporium of international trade.

Koṭuṅkoḷūr is also the location of a famous temple of Kālī-Bhagavatī. Hundreds of thousands of pilgrims congregate here during the Bharaṇi festival in February. Many South Indian scholars have argued that the Kālī temple of Koṭuṅkoḷūr was the ancient seat of

Pattini, the very same temple where Ceṅkuṭṭuvan̲ installed her image. The view that this temple was originally built by Ceṅkuṭṭuvan̲ is part of the South Indian scholarly tradition of viewing the Pattini episodes as natural events. While we can discount this view, it is undeniable that a great deal of evidence suggests that Koṭuṅkoḷūr was originally a Pattini shrine. It is also clear that by the fourteenth century it was a Kālī temple, since *Kōkasandēśa*, a fourteenth-century Malayalam poem, refers to it as such. I shall not attempt to marshal the historical and archaeological evidence here, except to refer the reader to the assessment of the relevant date in Induchudan's monograph (1969). I shall only mention some relevant sociological evidence; Induchudan's book supplies further details.

1. The crucial piece of sociological information is that pilgrims who visit Koṭuṅkoḷūr refer to the goddess popularly as Or̲r̲amulacci, "the single-breasted one." Now the main Kālī image in the inner sanctum hasn't this iconographic feature, but it is obviously a popular and well-established usage. The only single-breasted goddess in all of Indian mythology is Pattini.

2. The priests in charge of the temple are called *aṭikaḷ*s. According to the *Tranvancore State Manual*, *aṭikaḷ*s "are said to have been Brahmins originally who underwent social degradation by having officiated as priests in temples dedicated to Bhadrakali and other goddesses that receive offerings of liquor" (1906, p. 335). In the Karnataka area they are engaged in commerce, but in Kerala they officiate as priests in some shrines (Induchudan 1969, p. 118). They are one of the "twice-born" castes, but they appoint Nambudiri Brahmans to perform the regular *pūjā* for the goddess, though they retain full administrative control of the temple. They also have "a limited privilege only to do certain rites on normal days . . . [and] during Bharani," but they refuse to reveal the nature of these rites (Induchudan 1969, p. 119). In the *Cilappatikāram* the term *aṭikaḷ* refers to a Buddhist or Jaina saint, and we know that the traditional author of the *Cilappatikāram* is Iḷaṅkō Aṭikaḷ.

Developing Induchudan's argument, one might speculate that during the heyday of the Pattini cult the *aṭikaḷ*s were priests of the Pattini cult; they were also Buddhist and Jaina saints. With the decay of the Pattini cult, the rise of Brahmanic and Hindu influence after the eighth century, and the extreme rigidity of the caste system that developed concomitantly with Brahmanism, these *aṭikaḷ*s were incorporated as a separate caste. In any case it is striking that they have administrative control of this temple.

That the *aṭikaḷ*s control this temple may explain why normal rituals held in other Kālī temples are not performed in Koṭuṅkoḷūr. "All rituals to Kāli like *Kanamirikkal*, *Aarkal*, *Pana* with planting of *alstonia scholaris* etc. performed as a regular part of *Samghakali* are scrupulously avoided in the Kodungallur temple" (Induchudan 1969, p. 259). This again indicates that Koṭuṅkoḷūr is a special kind of Kālī temple and adds plausibility to the view that it was originally a Pattini shrine.

3. In the western yard of the temple is a small hut built of laterite that houses a deity known as Vasūrimāla. "It is a crude, and vague figure . . . the word means 'garland of small pox.'" (Induchudan 1969, p. 9). This deity is apparently not found anywhere else in Kerala, but she is very popular here. The priestesses of the cult are Nāyar women, and they offer her a red mixture of lime and turmeric (*kuruti*) that represents blood. People come from all over to offer *pūjā*s so she will ward off infectious diseases. Elsewhere in Kerala it is Bhagavatī (Kālī) who is the smallpox diety, but at Koṭuṅkoḷūr Vasūrimāla obviously has that role. A comparison with the Sinhala mythic tradition will help us to

understand this deity. In the myth of the "killing and resurrection," Pattini quells the demon of disease Vadurumāla, which is the exact equivalent of Vasūrimāla, *vaduru* meaning pestilence, especially smallpox. Vadurumāla is sometimes known as Madurumāla, as Vasūrimāla is also known as Masūrimāla. In Sinhala myth she is also known as Vaduru Mādēvi.[1] In Sri Lanka, as in Kerala, this deity is never found in any other ritual or cult. One has to assume that the deity is a *survival* of the ancient form of the Pattini cult as it prevailed in Kerala before its diffusion to Sri Lanka and its incorporation into the Kālī cult.

Whether the temple at Koṭuṅkoḷūr is the original temple built for Kaṇṇaki at Vañci is of no consequence for my thesis. By the fourteenth century it was a Kālī shrine, but much of the stone sculpture there belongs to an earlier period. Perhaps one of the earliest parts of the temple complex is its "secret chamber." Induchudan has assigned it, very rightly, great historical importance. It is also the title of his book. "The eastern-most chamber is a very small one and has no doors or windows, nor any other opening overground. It has no entrance and is shut in all sides. It is a secret chamber" (Induchudan 1969, p. 2). It is made of granite, and there is a stone roof above. Induchudan further says: "There is a door on the western wall of the *sanctum sanctorum* of Kali, which if opened gives you a view of the outside of the western wall of the secret chamber. . . . Some thing terrible and mysterious is presumed to be located in the secret chamber . . . but nobody knows what it is" (1969, p. 13). Sometimes important persons may worship the crimson cloth hung against the western wall of the secret chamber, but there is a taboo on looking inside. According to legend, a carpenter doing repairs on the roof glanced into the chamber and lost his sight. "A very interesting feature of this chamber is that it has a subterranean passage leading out towards the eastern direction and this opens about one hundred yards away to the overground" (1969, p. 13). The mouth of the passage was sealed about a hundred years ago.

The chamber has an east-west orientation, the tunnel opening out toward the east; the secret chamber is at the western end. "According to the Atikal, legends go to say that in olden times they used to enter the passage through the mouth to conduct services in the chamber. When this practice ceased due to the risk of walking through the passage, services came to be done through the eastern door. There were two houses of Atikals called Kunnath madhom and Neelath madhom. One thing that struck me was that both these houses were traditionally located around the mouth of the underground passage" (Induchudan 1969, p. 119).

Induchudan interprets the secret chamber as a megalithic type of structure that housed the remains of Pattini. This is improbable, and I would like to advance an alternative view. During my visit to Koṭuṅkoḷūr I was convinced that the squat enclosed chamber and the underground passage originally had to do with the initiation of priests and devotees of the cult. A neophyte is reborn as a "female" priest or convert of the goddess, thus giving up his male identity for a female one. The squat chamber then would be a symbolic tomb/womb, and the underground tunnel could represent the process of rebirth into a new identity, culminating at the eastern end. Though we can never know the exact nature of the rituals that went on there, we can at least assess the significance of the east-west orienta-

1. In Sinhala tradition Vaduru Mādēvi is identified with Madura Mādēvi, the guardian goddess of Madurai who appears in the *Cilappatikāram*. This is easy to do since the latter has no significance in Sinhala culture.

tion of the chamber and tunnel. The west is the direction of the setting sun (i.e., dying) and the east, the rising sun (i.e., rebirth).

With this interpretation in mind, I inquired whether there were similar structures in Kerala temples. To my great satisfaction, I was told that there is a tunnel (but no chamber) in the Tiruvilvamāmala temple for Śri Rāma in the Palghat district. Again the tunnel is in disuse, but occasionally devotees go through it. What is striking is that the practice of these devotees as well as the tunnel itself is called *punarjani*, "rebirth." I suspect that these tunnels and chambers, which are unusual for Indian religion, are survivals from the Pattini cult in its earliest period in Kerala. But whether they show any West Asian influence is impossible to determine, since Tantrism could have produced a similar phenomenon.[2]

Koṭuṅkoḷūr and Sri Lanka: Pattini's Veil

The evidence of the *Cilappatikāram* suggests that the Pattini cult was strongest in Kerala among urban merchants, since it was here in Vañci, the seat of the ancient Cēra (Kerala) kings, that the cult was given state legitimation. Even if the state legitimation was a "fiction," it meant that the cult was important and that the capital city of Vañci had a central shrine for this deity. Vañci is important to Sri Lanka for another reason: in the previous chapter I noted that the Kerala princes who dominated Sri Lankan politics in the latter half of the fourteenth century originally came from Vañci. If the identification of Vañci with Vañci mutur near the ancient Musiris and present-day Koṭuṅkoḷūr is correct (Shreedhara Menon 1967, p. 76), then this whole region assumes considerable importance for the history of the Pattini cult in both South India and Sri Lanka (as well as for possible antecedents in Syria and West Asia).

There is a curious "survival" that connects the Pattini cult of Sri Lanka with the temple of Koṭuṅkoḷūr (and perhaps even West Asia) but whose significance is difficult to assess. This is the headdress Pattini wears in contemporary Sinhala ritual, a veil that falls back, known as *moṭṭäkkili*. The term *moṭṭäkkili* is used for the ordinary shawl worn over the head by Sinhala women, which is typically found in nineteenth-century Sinhala painting. However, in the ritual the headdress is clearly not a shawl but a veil. This veil is worn by the priest during the very important ritual known as the *salam̆ba sāntiya*, "blessings of the anklet" (see chap. 4, pp. 128–29). In this ritual the priest wears a blouse and a cloth around his waist like a contemporary Sinhala low-country woman (or a Kerala woman). Very tightly covering his head is a veil that falls almost to the hips. A jeweled brooch is stuck on the cloth in the middle of the forehead, so that it looks like a coronet. During the ritual the priest walks before a long line of devotees and blesses them with the sacred anklets. This veil, it must be noted, does not cover the face but falls down at the back. Upham (1829) has a drawing of the goddess wearing something between a shawl and a veil, and he mistakingly called it a *purdah*. There is a strong tradition in Sri Lanka that the priest must wear seven veils when impersonating the goddess. The *kapurāla* of the Mātara tradition says that the god Sakra gave seven shawls to Pattini when he accosted her at

2. I am told that a similar tunnel apparently exists in an old Śiva temple at Sukapuram, where the priest goes through the tunnel into the sanctum, but I have not been able to verify this.

Aṅdungiri Peak, and the *moṭṭäkkili* represents one of these shawls. He himself wears a sari with one veil and a shawl. However the *kapurāla* of Rabalīya in fact wore five veils in several rituals (pp. 118–19, 128–29) and acknowledged that seven was the correct number.

The veil or *moṭṭäkkili* is an ancient and fixed part of Pattini's apparel. In the text known as the *maḍupuraya*, King Sēraman has a dream in which he sees the goddess wearing a *moṭṭäkkili* on her head and anklets on her feet. Thus, anklets and *moṭṭäkkili* are crucial sacred symbols. Although it is an intrinsic part of Pattini's dress, no such headdress is worn by women in any community in Sri Lanka, in the present or the past, as far as I know.

The historical significance of the veil was not apparent to me till I arrived in Kerala. I noticed that Muslim women in Kerala wear a similar headdress, though the color generally is yellow. This headdress replaces the more formal *purdah* found elsewhere in India. It is, of course, inconceivable that the Pattini headdress of the Sinhala people is borrowed from the Muslim women of Kerala. It is possible to argue that originally *moṭṭäkkili* simply meant a shawl, and that the present-day priests simply adopted a veil from their observance of Catholicism. For example, till very recently Buddhist brides in low-country villages occasionally adopted the Christian veil in their wedding ceremonies. A similar custom prevails among the *veḷḷāla* (farmer) caste Hindus of Sri Lanka. Here also the veil—known as *moṭṭākku*—is worn by brides, but this custom, as far as I can gather, is not practiced by Hindus in neighboring South India. Indeed, the veil is nowadays associated with Hindu widowhood and viewed as extremely inauspicious, which makes the wedding custom seem especially remarkable. These customs, I believe, were determined or overdetermined by the very important fact that Pattini, the embodiment of the ideal wife, also wore a veil, according to the rituals and myths of both Buddhists and Hindus in Sri Lanka. In any case, striking confirmation for the veil as an ancient part of Pattini's headdress comes from an unexpected source—once again from some stone sculptures in the Koṭuṅkoḷūr shrine premises.

The relevant stone carvings are found on two pillars on the eastern and southern sides of the secret chamber—two ladies, similarly executed. Each lady has a ball in her right, raised hand; the left seems to be holding her clothes (see plate 25 and Induchudan's description, 1969, p. 297). According to Induchudan (1969, p. 298) these sculptures depict women playing with a wooden ball as described in canto 29 of the *Cilappatikāram* (Dikshitar 1939, pp. 333–34). Be that as it may, the striking feature of the iconography is that both females are wearing veils of exactly the same type as that worn by our contemporary Pattini priests in Sri Lanka. Thus Pattini's veil is no recent innovation but a part of an old, continuing tradition. It adds plausibility to the view that Koṭuṅkoḷūr was originally a Pattini shrine, and it is likely that veils were used in the rituals performed here. Furthermore, since veils were a rare feature of Indian iconography, at least before the Mogul period, we are perhaps justified in linking this item to the West Asian origins of the cult, for there the veil is a well-known feature of the iconography of the mother goddess.[3]

3. Very little can be adduced beyond conjecture till there is a reliable dating of the various sections of the temple of Koṭuṅkoḷūr. For example, the veils on the pillars of Koṭuṅkoḷūr may indicate Mogul influence, but I believe this temple antedates the Mogul invasions.

The Goddess Pattini in Kerala: Transformation into Bhagavatī-Kālī

Several scholars have noted contemporary survivals of the Pattini myth in South India. P. L. Swamy (1971), P. K. Sankara Pillai (1958), and Raghava Iyengar (1964), among others, have documented the transformation of Pattini into Durgā, Kālī, and Draupadī. However, most scholars see the *Cilappatikāram* as the source of the myth and later versions as derivatives, rather than viewing the *Cilappatikāram* itself as part of a long and continuing ritual tradition. One of the most interesting studies is Brenda Beck's paper (1972) in which she compares several versions of the *Cilappatikāram* in order to highlight and explicate stylistic variations of the prototypic myth of Kaṇṇaki and Kōvalaṉ in contemporary Tamil Nāṭu. There is no doubt that the traditions of the Kaṇṇaki-Kōvalaṉ myth have deeply permeated South Indian culture, often to be transformed into something totally different.[4]

It is not in Tamil Nāṭu but in Kerala that the greatest number and variety of survivals of the Pattini cult exist, in ritual practice, in myth, and in bardic traditions. This is to be expected, given the logic of my preceding arguments. The collection and collation of this vast body of material must await the work of Kerala scholars. I can focus on only one theme here: the transformation of the Pattini cult into the Bhagavatī cult as very likely due to the assimilation of a Jaina-Buddhist cult into the Hindu fold. In general this transformation has resulted in converting the ethical and "rational" deity Pattini into the amoral, irrationally destructive Bhagavatī, the dominant mother goddess of Kerala. Concomitantly with this transformation, the *dolorosa* aspect if the goddess fades away and the theme of the resurrection of Kōvalaṉ is either minimized or absent. The stage is totally dominated by Bhagavatī-Kālī.

Here I shall examine only two Kerala myths to show the transformation of Pattini into Kālī, from the near-total assimilation of Pattini into Kālī in myth 1 to their clearly identifiable separate identities in myth 2. These two myth types do not exemplify diachronic stages, since they can exist within the same time span. But they do indicate the processes of change and transformation of one cult into another.

In these myths we can see two interconnections with the Sri Lankan material. First, in both the consort of the goddess is Kōpālakār or Pālakār. It is certain that the Sinhala for Kōvalaṉ, which is Pālaṅga, is a derivative of Pālakār (or Pālakaṉ, as he is sometimes called in Malayalam and Tamil). Second, these myths refer to a north-south division, with the goddess belonging to one and her consort to the other. There is an identical division among the matrilineal Tamil Hindus of the east coast of Sri Lanka, as I shall show in the next chapter. Once again it is certain that this division originated in Kerala, since east

4. For example, I visited a shrine for Cellattammaṉ near Madurai belonging to the Vaṇikar *cettiar* (oil merchants). The main deity of the shrine is Cellattammaṉ, also worshiped by the Cettiar community as Cāmunti Īśvari or Durgā. Beside the bronze image of this goddess is another bronze image with an anklet in the left hand and a taṇṭāyutaṉ (mace, scepter, stick) in the other. There is a middle eye in the forehead. The temple official identified this as Pattini, but it could be any representation of Durgā or Kālī. No worship is directed to this image, the focus of temple ritual being Durgā-Cellattammaṉ. However, the myths recounted by the *pūsāri* indicated their clear affinity to the Kaṇṇaki-Kōvalaṉ myth.

The myth recounted by the *pūsāri* was as follows: In a previous birth Kōvalaṉ was an oilmonger. He wanted to supply lamp oil for the goddess Kālī because of his great devotion for her. The *pūsāri* at that time prevented

coast Tamils came from there. It is likely that this same division, when introduced into the Sinhala areas of Sri Lanka, was either converted into the upper and lower team divisions of their *aṅkeḷiya* or perhaps was rendered redundant by prior team divisions that existed among the Sinhalas.

Though these Kerala influences on the Sri Lankan cult are clear, there are striking differences in the myths of the two areas. The Sri Lankan texts, both among Sinhala Buddhists and among the Tamil Hindus of the east coast, deal entirely with Pattini and her consort, whereas the Kerala texts are thoroughly equivocal in this regard and Pattini is assimilated in various degrees into the Kālī cult. While the Sri Lankan texts are close to the *Cilappatikāram* in their content, the Kerala texts are far removed from it. The likelihood therefore is that the Sri Lankan texts originally came from Kerala, but in a period before the Kerala texts were transformed into Kālī texts. The totality of the evidence marshaled thus far forces us to conclude that Kerala itself had a body of Pattini texts that diffused to Sri Lanka and were of the same type as the extant Sri Lankan myths.

Text 55 Myth 1: The Myth of Dēvi and Conat

The first text I shall quote is from the songs sung during the festivities for Bhagavatī (Kālī), generally from November till about June, when the rains start. These ceremonies are conducted in small Bhagavatī temples known as *kāvu* (literally, "grove"), or in the fields belonging to a particular family or families. Traditionally, the expenditure for this ceremony must be met by a group of families. According to C. Achyuta Menon there are *kāvu*s for the god Aiyappan, for Kālī, and for the snake (*nāga*) deities. In Kerala the most popular are the Bhagavatī *kāvus* (1959, pp. 33–36), though they are not the most numerous, since, according to the *Travancore State Manual*, there were fifteen thousand snake *kāvu*s in the Travancore district alone in 1846 (1906, p. 59). These *kāvu*s, Achyuta Menon rightly says, are part of the older non-Brahmanic cult. Today many of the larger Bhagavatī temples are controlled by Nambudiri Brahmans, though the other castes have their own smaller *kāvu*s.

There are several rituals associated with the festivities of the Bhagavatī cult (see

---

him, because no one but the king could supply oil for the goddess Kālī. He was executed by the king. In his next birth he was born as Kōvalaṉ. Kālī was enraged because of the king's action, and she took the form of Kaṇṇaki, the daughter of a jewel merchant. Kōvalaṉ married Kaṇṇaki, but he did not have intercourse with her or even touch her, since he was human and she was divine.

The rest of the story is as elsewhere. He falls in love with Mātavi and squanders his wealth. He goes to sell Kaṇṇaki's anklet and is betrayed by the goldsmith. Kaṇṇaki goes in search of him and discovers his corpse. She touches his body with a spear, and he comes back to life. He says: "If you are Mātavi, come and sit on my thigh; if you are Kaṇṇaki, go away." This is because she is a goddess and he cannot lust after her. Kaṇṇaki asks him whether he wants a boon. Kōvalaṉ asks her to punish the goldsmith who misguided the king. She agrees and sends Kōvalaṉ up to heaven.

The angry goddess now goes into the house of the goldsmith and disembowels and kills him. Then she goes into the palace and proves her husband's innocence. She then kills the Pāṇḍyan king, sets fire to the city, and, adopting her divine form, ascends to heaven with Īśvara.

According to the *pūcāri* the oilmonger was killed in the present shrine premises. Kōvalaṉ was killed by the king a few miles away at a place called Kōvalaṉ paṭṭal (*paṭṭal*, "place where he fell"). The myth itself is similar to the one held by east coast Tamils of Sri Lanka, who also state that Kōvalaṉ was an oilmonger in his previous birth and was killed by the king of Pāṇḍi. The *Cilappatikāram*, by contrast, has a typical Jaina version of Kōvalaṉ's past birth (see Dikshitar 1939, p. 269).

Achyuta Menon 1959). The one with which we are concerned is the *kālam pāṭṭu* performed by the *vēlan*s and *maṉṉān*s belonging to the *śūdra varṇa*.[5] My informant was a *vēlan*, age forty-nine, literate, having served in the British army in Sri Lanka for two years. His caste is patrilineally organized, unlike most castes in the region, which are matrilineal. *Vēlan*s are below the Nāyar but above agricultural serfs like those in this region (*puḷiyar* and *kaṇakkar*). The latter had their own priests, but my informant claims that he now performs for practically all the castes except the Brahmans within sixty square miles.

The priest performs two types of ceremonies: He may regularly come to a village each year and perform the ceremony, or he may perform occasional ceremonies when households believe that they have been having troubles because of neglect of the goddess (Dēvi). The belief is that performing the ritual will ward off diseases and pestilence (especially smallpox) in the village, that cattle and crops will multiply, and that there will be general prosperity.

In households that have been under the influence of Brahman culture only vegetarian foods will be offered to the deity. Even here blood is symbolically offered to the goddess as *kuruti*, a red mixture of lime and turmeric. In other households the more traditional offerings are also given: the sacrifice of a chicken and toddy. The most important part of the ritual proceedings is the drawing of the multicolored image of the goddess on the floor to the invocation of mantras. Dyes made of the following substances are used: green, *vēṅṅa* (*Pterocarpus marsupium*); yellow, turmeric; red, lime and turmeric; white, rice flour. I quote below one of the mantras uttered while the songs are sung:

> Thou virgin of *cēri* [settlement] of the South who went with Kōpālakār of the northern settlement [*vaṭakkan cēri*]
> Taking with you the dowry of your house
> In a wooden ship of the Arayar [fishermen].

After the drawing of the picture the myths of the goddess are sung for as long as three days. I shall give a brief summary of the myth of the Dēvi as told by my informant. In the myths I shall quote there are elaborate accounts of the birth of the goddess, but my informant's version starts with her marriage.

Dēvi belongs to southern Kollam (Quilon), and her husband Conanata Ponmakan (or Conat Ponmakan) belongs to northern Kollam. The parents of the goddess went north in search of a groom for her; and at the same time, quite independently, the parents of Conat went south in search of a bride for their son. By a strange coincidence they slept in adjacent rooms in an inn one night and overheard each other's conversations. They then came together and negotiated for the marriage of their children. With the help of a maternal uncle who acted as go-between, they settled on a date of marriage.

But Dēvi did not like this marriage proposal, since the man was not her model of a husband. On the day of the wedding she raised all sorts of objections about the garland that was to be put around her neck. Ultimately, she gave the groom one of the garlands she was wearing and ordered him to toss it up. If the garland were to fall around her shoulders

5. According to Thurston, "Velans, like the Pānans, are a caste of devil dancers, sorcerers, and quack doctors, and are, in the northern parts of the state, called Perumannāns or Mannāns (washermen)" (Thurston 1909, 7:342).

it would be a sign that fate had decreed the marriage. Accordingly, Conat threw the garland and it fell around her neck, but its clasp came apart. At that point her maternal uncle, Vāyuputra, pointed out to the groom what had happened, and the groom hooked the clasp back together. But in doing so he touched her (a gross breach of etiquette), and she cursed him—"May you be hanged without being killed for a theft you didn't commit."

The marriage took place, and the bride accepted her fate. However, she came to know that the clasp was promptly hooked as a result of her uncle's warning. So she told her uncle she had something important to say to him, which could not be said at the place of marriage. She invited him to a place called *kotta paṟambu tōṭu*, a rivulet. Dēvi went there with her retinue, accompanied by her uncle. She asked him to come down to the water. When he did she asked him whether he had ever seen stars in the sky at midday. "If you haven't, then look up," she said. When her uncle looked up she cut off his head with her sword. She then gouged out his eyes, and she threw one up with a curse that it might become a star called *eṭṭunāḻika potta* (eighth-hour rising). The other eye also became a star. She made a conch out of her uncle's severed head and placed it in the temple of Aiyappan of the mountain (i.e., at Sabarimāla). She ordered that this conch be sounded at a particular hour when the two stars appeared.

After this she went back to her parents house for the resumption of the marriage arrangements. First there was the ritual of the wife giving milk to the husband, conducted in the bride's house. Then she asked for her dowry (*strīdhanam*) from her father. Her father gave her all her personal belongings. In the detailed list of items she claimed as dowry were various seeds of smallpox. She and her father haggled over several measures of different types of smallpox seeds. They were then given to her, and she in turn gave them to her husband. To test the efficacy of these seeds, she sprayed some on her father's body, and he was at once struck with smallpox. The mother came rushing forward, wailing and weeping. Dēvi then resurrected her father.

Now the father had a minister named Acyutankuṭṭi Metela, who was very strong. He once washed out his mouth and cleaned his face with the ocean's waters, and the ocean became dry. He used to sleep six months of the year. This fellow was asked to carry the goods to the husband's house.[6]

The bride and groom traveled to (northern) Kollam along separate ways. The groom avoided the coast and traveled by the hills because he owed some kind of tax to the goddess of the sea. The bride avoided the hills and went in a ship because she was originally proposed in marriage to Aiyappan of the hills (she didn't like this proposal either). Whoever arrived at Aḻikal (literally, "river mouth") first should wait for the other—this was the arrangement. Dēvi arrived first and grew anxious because her husband was not there, so she created rain, thunder, and whirlwind. These storms uprooted trees that floated down the rivers. Her husband came riding down the river on one of these trees. Thus they found each other at last.

The rest of the journey they traveled together by ship. During this trip Dēvi rubbed the diamond on her wedding ring against a stone to test its quality, and the diamond was displaced from its socket. To repair the ring she summoned a goldsmith (whom she had met while she traveled to Aḻikal without her husband).

After some time they reached the husband's house and settled down. They soon became

6. This character seems to be modeled on that of Kumbhakarṇa of the Rāmāyana.

insolvent because they had no steady source of income and they had spent the dowry. Then Dēvi sent her husband to sell her one remaining anklet. The husband went to the same goldsmith who had previously stolen the anklet belonging to the queen of Pāṇḍi. The goldsmith therefore decided to put the whole blame on Conat. He informed the king that Conat had stolen the queen's anklet. However, the queen did not agree with the goldsmith, and she told the king that it might not really be her anklet. But the king was adamant and issued orders to hang Conat. After he was hanged vultures fed on his body and flew away. When these birds flew over northern Kollam the remnants of his heart and intestines fell near Dēvi's house. She recognized these as her husband's remains. She went to the city of the king of Pāṇḍi with her army (retinue) and resurrected Conat from the dead. She used *darbha* grass (used in ritual, *Poa cynosuroides*) and a shrub, *camata* (*Butea frondosa*), and with these she created the form of her husband. Then she placed on it what remained of his body and revived him. Then she attacked the Pāṇḍyan kingdom with her army. She killed the Pāṇḍyan king and his entire dynasty and also the queen and all the goldsmiths in the city. She then burned the city (with her middle eye?).

Commentary on Myth 1: The Myth of Dēvi and Conat

The preface to the myth clearly indicates that it was originally a Pattini myth, for though the hero is Conat in the main text, the preface refers to him as Kōpālakār (Gopālaka), which is the Sanskritized form of Kōvalaṉ. The goddess is the virgin of the southern settlement, while Kōpālakār belongs to the North. I noted earlier that this division is identical with that prevailing among east coast Hindus of Sri Lanka. The main myth, however, has little substantive connection with the Pattini myths except for the conclusion. Here the connections are clear: there is reference to the consort's selling the anklet, the betrayal by the goldsmith, the queen's goodness and the injustice of the king, and the goddess's vengeance. But the moral significance of the Dēvi myth is entirely different from that of the Pattini myth, for in the former the violence of the goddess's rage is unbounded, and she spares no one, not even the innocent queen. The theme of justice and righteousness that is of such significance in the Pattini myth is totally overridden by the theme of vengeance in the Dēvi myth. As I pointed out in chapter 10, the irrational component is to be expected with the transformation of Pattini into Kālī.

Dēvi's irrationality comes out most clearly in her violent rage against her uncle, her future husband, and her father. How can one explain this terrible reaction? It is because all three are associated with the attempt to deprive her of her virginity. In the myth Dēvi is the reluctant bride, for on the wedding day she made all sorts of objections to the garland (the symbol of wedlock) she must wear. When her future husband threw the garland around her neck the clasp came apart, and it was her uncle who pointed this out. Had the clasp remained open the garland would have fallen and there would have been no wedding. She cursed her husband with death for touching her—she must not be touched, for she must remain pure and undefiled, and therefore her husband must not even touch her. She killed her uncle, and she ravaged her father with smallpox over an argument about her dowry. Again the dowry is a symbol of her wedlock, and her father is responsible for it. In the analysis of the next myth I shall show that the hatred of the goldsmith also has a similar psychological source, for he is the one who makes wedding garlands, rings, and necklaces. The goddess's rage is an infantile psychological reaction totally out of proportion to the provocation.

Text 56 Myth 2: *Torram Pāṭṭu* on Kālī, Kaṇṇi, and Pālakār

Torram pāṭṭu are ritual texts dealing with the life of Bhagavatī. *Torram* means "origin," "birth," or "creation" and is close to the Sinhala word *upata* ("origin," "birth") used to characterize origin myths. These *torram pāṭṭus* are also sung in Kālī temples, very often by members of the *mannān* caste. They are very popular in the Palghat district of central Kerala. The following text is from a palm-leaf manuscript, perhaps belonging to the fourteenth or the fifteenth century, published in the Travancore University Manuscript Series as volume 6, numbers 3 and 4 (1956). An almost identical version has been published by Sankara Pillai (1958).

The first part of the *torram pāṭṭu* deals with Tāruka the demon. The second part deals with the birth of Kaṇṇi (Bhadrakālī) and her conquest of Tāruka. The third part is the birth of Pālakār and his marriage to the goddess. The final section is on the death of Pālakār and the destruction of the Pāṇḍi kingdom. Since this text has been published, I shall focus mainly on the third part, which is most relevant for this analysis.

The first and second parts of the myth are based on the well-known myth of Tāruka and Kālī, and I shall deal with them only briefly.

Tāruka (Dāruka) obtained a boon from Śiva, largely through Pārvatī's intervention, that no man would be able to kill him. Śiva granted him the boon, but Tāruka created chaos. The gods in heaven began to lose their powers, so Śiva decided to create a *woman* who could kill the demon. This was the goddess Kālī.

Śiva created Bhadrakālī from his middle eye. The goddess Bhadrakālī asked Śiva: "O my father, for what purpose have you brought me here?" Śiva replied, "You must kill Tāruka and bring his head to me as a present." The rest of the myth deals with the way Kālī tricked Tāruka into giving her his magic formula and how she waged war against this demon and his followers. Tāruka pleaded with her to spare him, but to no avail. The goddess cut off his head with her lance. She poured his blood into the mouth of her serpent *vētala*. She wrapped his head in the folds of her cloth and gave it to Kanṭa Kāranan, her "brother." The followers of the goddess were given the skin of Tāruka as a cloth and his hands and neck as ornaments; they played with his chest like a ball and used the back of his skull as a ring. The goddess Bhadrakālī cut the body of Tāruka into five pieces and threw them to demons and dogs to eat. She gave his head to Śiva as a present. Śiva was full of admiration for her. "You can go into the forest and live as you like. Please come before me when I want you." She went into the forest, which was full of many flowers.

The third part of the text deals with the story of Pālakār and his marriage to Kaṇṇi, who is a manifestation of Kālī.

There was a king (merchant prince) who lived in northern Kollam (Quilon). He was about sixty-six years old, but he had no children. So he summoned his astrologer, named Dēśavan, and asked him why he was childless. Dēśavan told him this was the result of a curse. The king wanted to know what he could do to overcome the curse (*sāpam*). The astrologer replied, "You must undergo a fast for seven days and visit Parama Śiva with a votive offering of milk."

The king fasted and went to Kailāsa with the vessel. When Śiva became aware of the king's journey, he enlisted Viṣṇu's help and threw the king into hell, since he had not done good deeds.

After seven days of expiation, the king visited Śiva again in Kailāsa. Śiva accepted the king's presents and inquired about his desire. The king replied, "I have no children and so

I have come here." Śiva said, "When you go into the southern region you will see a garden full of bananas. You must pick three from the bunch and come back here." But the king did not see any garden on his way to the southern region, and he was not sure of his way back. While he was aimlessly wandering, he met Viṣṇu in the guise of a beggar. When asked the way, Viṣṇu directed the king back to Kailāsa. There Śiva asked him why he came back without the fruit. "I didn't see any garden with bananas," the king said. Śiva asked, "Who was in your mind when you were there?" The king replied, "I was thinking about my wife." Said Śiva, "You are the most unfaithful man in Kailāsa. If you go there thinking about me you will surely see the garden." The king did so. He found the garden and brought back the fruit to Śiva. Śiva inscribed the future of the king's would-be child on the bananas. According to this inscription the child would grow up to be a merchant. In his seventh year he would engage in business, and at sixteen he would become the head of a household. At eighteen he would become a thief without stealing.

Sure enough, in his seventh year the child went to study. He wore beautiful ornaments, clothes, and rings. The king gave him a golden vessel for drinking and a golden mat to sit on. The king also gave him sandals and gold coins, betel leaves, ornaments, and rice. A servant accompanied him (to school?). Gradually he became a merchant, then head of a family, and finally a thief.

There was a man called Narāyaṇaṉ of southern Kollam. He also had no children. He worshiped Lord Śiva constantly; Śiva was so pleased with him that he summoned him to Kailāsa and gave him a child. It was decided that she should marry the son of the northern king in her seventh year. Accordingly, Narāyaṇaṉ married her to Pālakār in her seventh year. For their marriage Kaṇṇi (the girl) traveled by sea and Pālakār traveled by land. While Kaṇṇi was going north to the marriage festivities she saw a goldsmith bringing the marriage ring. She asked him to give it to her. When the goldsmith was about to give her the ring she pulled her hand back, and the ring fell into the sea. The goldsmith went to the southern side in another ship. Meanwhile Kaṇṇi turned back to retrieve the ring. She plunged the royal sword into the sea and picked up the ring. The goldsmith and his party saw this. He cursed her: "When your husband happens to be a merchant traveling through the ocean, I will call him thief even if he doesn't steal." Then Kaṇṇi replied that she would kill him if that happened.

There are thirty-eight lines in the text that refer to local context. The goddess wanted a ship to sail the seas and asked a *marakkār* (sailor) to find one. He swam underneath the ship and secured it. However, twelve thousand *marakkār*s saw this and, organizing a fleet, surrounded the goddess's ship. But the goddess created a whirlpool that sank the ships, and all the *marakkār*s drowned. She then cursed the *marakkār* women, who turned into stone. This is clearly a localization of the myth and indicates hostility between fishermen and the groups who used this myth in their rituals.

Then she sailed to northern Kollam (Quilon). The merchant prince (king) and his wife had died meanwhile, and Pālakār was heir. He was ruling well and reached his eighteenth year. One day Kaṇṇi asked him to go sell some goods. He lifted up his baggage containing merchandise and was about to commence his journey when the divine girl he had married gave him the two anklets to be sold in the city of the king of Pāṇḍi. Pālakār went to Pāṇḍi city with the two anklets. He reached the area where the goldsmiths lived. The goldsmith of the "Pāṇḍi-Cōḷa king" (Cōlākōṉ-Pāṇṭi) saw the two anklets and invited the merchant home. The goldsmith asked his wife to serve Pālakār with "refreshments" of bread fried in snake oil, rice flakes mixed with the tongues of tigers, and some drinks. But the wife was conscience-stricken. She felt that she could not coldbloodedly kill this handsome merchant, and she expressed these thoughts aloud (to herself). The goldsmith overheard her and, holding her by the hair, hit her with a weapon (*aṭṭaṉampandi*). Frightened, she agreed to make these refreshments for the merchant.

The goldsmith took these refreshments to Pālakār, but the merchant was suspicious. He gave the food to a dog, who ate it and died. Then the goldsmith buried the rest of the food and Pālakār ate some of the food he had brought with him. The goldsmith, who had seen Pālakār's merchandise, said that no one would buy the anklets except Queen Perundēvi herself: "If you give me the anklets I will take them to the queen. If she agrees to buy them, I will take you to see her." Pālakār agreed, and the goldsmith went to the king's (Cōlākōn-Pāṇṭi's) palace.

Apparently Queen Perundēvi had given her own two anklets to the goldsmith for repair, but he had stolen them and blamed it on thieves. He told the queen he had found the thief, and he placed the anklets before her. The queen took the anklets and said: "These are not mine, and if I keep them here danger may befall me." But the king did not believe her. He took her by her hair and threw her into a dry well. Then the king ordered the thief to be brought before him. The goldsmith went to Madurai with soldiers and brought Pālakār before the king. The gallows were prepared, and Pālakār was hanged.

Meanwhile Kaṇṇi dreamed that her husband had been hanged. She locked her house and storerooms and walked a long way. She then had the following encounters.

1. She saw a small dove in a *kūvilam* tree. When she questioned the dove about her husband's whereabouts, it spread its wings and wailed. She gave the dove a boon because of the love it showed for her husband. "May your species live in the abodes of the gods and Śasta (Aiyappan) and eat the food given to the gods."

2. She saw a jackfruit tree and asked the same question of it. The bough of the tree broke, and its sap oozed out. This time her boon was that "the tree should have the privilege to provide a *tirumuṭi* for me to hide and play." (The *tirumuṭi* generally refers to the face of the goddess, often made of silver. It is likely that the reference here is to the altar or the larger structure where her image is kept in collective rituals. This structure must be made of jackfruit wood. In formal usage, however, *tirumuṭi* refers to the crown or matted locks of a deity.)

3. She walked a long way and met a full-grown mango tree. When the tree heard her story it flowered and bloomed. She then cursed the mango tree: "May you be used as firewood to eat [burn] corpses." (Reference here is to the Kerala custom of using the wood of the mango tree for burning corpses.)

4. She met a calf that hung its head carelessly when it heard about the missing man. "When your kind die, their skins will be used for drums that will be beaten before me, so that I may enjoy their sound."

5. After walking a long way she met a Brahman lady who was watering a sugarcane plant. When the lady heard about the goddess's search for her husband she sarcastically remarked that she would rather have spent her time watering plants and earning wages for her effort. Kālī then cursed the Brahman lady: "Let old dying Brahmans marry your kind, and let them die in the very place they married so that you are condemned to live as perpetual widows with shaven heads. You shall not see any other face, nor shall you marry

any other man." (This could in fact occur among the Tamil Brahmans of Kerala, where older men married child brides.) Ultimately she came upon the body of her dead husband, whom she resurrected and took safely to Vembilimode in Vellappanad.[7] She asked two small boys to stand guard over him.

Then she went to the forest of Pūvani and made twelve thousand garlands, which she offered to the Dēva (Śiva?). Thereafter she made seven boxes full of gold. Dēvi (the goddess) then moved to the street of the goldsmiths. She told the goldsmith to make ornaments with the gold. If he completed them in one day he could have half the gold. The goldsmith then asked twelve thousand fellow goldsmiths to do the work. He asked the goddess for the boxes of gold. When she gave him the first box he offered prayers to Gaṇapati (Gaṇeśa); when she gave him the second he prayed to Sarasvatī. However, when he asked for the third box, she refused to give it without their actually starting on the work.

Now Kālī summoned the twelve thousand goldsmiths and assumed her real form. When she looked at them they ran helter-skelter. She looked up at the sky; every weapon she wished for fell into her hands. She wore thirty thousand million cobras on her head; forty thousand million *nāgas* (snakes) on her breast; and seven thousand million *eḷa* snakes wherever there was space in between. She wore an elephant as an ornamental flower, and two elephants as ear ornaments. She descended on the goldsmiths and whirled her discus. She asked the evil goldsmith why he had stolen her goods and anklets and wronged her. The goldsmith wailed: "I committed wrong. Please do not kill me, and I shall give you offerings." But she paid no heed. She seized her divine sword and cut the goldsmith's throat and gouged out his heart. (Thirteen lines are expended in describing how the goldsmith was cut into smaller and smaller pieces.)

She gave the pieces of flesh to demons and went to the city of Pāṇḍi. The king summoned his army of twelve thousand soldiers to fight her. But the mother killed all twelve thousand and drove back the king. She entered the palace, seized the king and cut his throat, and wrapped his head in silk and gave it to the demon Kanṭa Kāranan. Then she went up to Queen Perundēvi and tore out one of the queen's breasts and threw it on the crossroads where the streets of the goldsmiths and merchants (*ceṭṭi*) met; there arose the temple of Mutturāman. Then she tore out the queen's tongue and threw it there: the deity of the Mutturāman temple sprang forth. The goddess appeared before the temple and gave (the temple or the deity?) half a boon. Then she went to Kailāsa (Śiva's abode) and hung the head of the Pāṇḍyan on the left of the head of the demon Tāruka. Finally she went to Koṭuṅkoḷūr (Cranganur), and consecrated her husband (his image) there. She established herself there also.

Commentary on Myth 2: The Myth of Kālī, Kaṇṇi, and Pālakār

Myth 2 is clearly less "integrated" than myth 1. The first part deals with the standard Kerala version of the birth of Kālī as the "daughter" of Śiva and her killing of Tāruka. The second part is substantively a totally different myth, dealing with Kaṇṇi (virgin) and Pālakār. Yet there are also striking similarities between this and the preceding myth.

7. None of my informants could identify these obscure place names. I suspect that Vembilimode is a corruption of the older term *velliambalam* in both the *Cilappatikāram* and Sinhala texts. Vellappanad is probably in the district of Pālkkādu and Tenmalapuram. The Raja of Palghat was called Vellappanātta rāja, according to Gundert's *Malayalam-English Dictionary* (1873, p. 986).

1. Both belong to princely merchant families.
2. The bride is from southern Kollam and the bridegroom from northern Kollam.
3. Her losing the ring at sea and then recovering it is similar to the displaced diamond of myth 1.
4. Kaṇṇi gives the anklets to Pālakār to sell; he is duped by the goldsmith and hanged on the orders of the king.
5. In both versions the wife resurrects her husband's body and destroys Madurai, though these episodes are treated only cursorily. No reference is made in either to the typical Pattini episode of tearing out the breast. In the second myth the protagonist tears off the breast of the Pāṇḍyan queen, a more direct talion reaction.

Nevertheless, several features distinguish the second myth from the first. I have already noted that the first part of myth 2, dealing the Tāruka and Kālī, is substantively different from the second part dealing with Kaṇṇi and Pālakār. Clearly Kaṇṇi and Pālakār are Kaṇṇaki and Kōvalan̲ (Kōpālakār). Unlike Dēvi of the first myth, Kaṇṇi is not a reluctant wife, which brings her close to Pattini-Kaṇṇaki, but in neither of the myths related above is the wife cum goddess a benevolent figure like Pattini. However, Kaṇṇi's rage is less irrational than that of Dēvi in the first myth. Nevertheless, the *lex talionis* reaction at the end, where she destroys even those who are good—like the queen—is more like the wrathful Kālī than the ethical Pattini, who spares the good. Note, for example, Kālī-Kaṇṇi's attitude toward the calf compared with Pattini's in the "killing and resurrection" myth (text 42, pp. 272–73).

Nevertheless, the Kālī-Tāruka part of the myth seems substantively different from the Kaṇṇi part. In the second part of the myth the goddess is Śiva's gift to Narānayṇan̲; she is not explicitly identified as Kālī. Indeed, she is continuously referred to as Kaṇṇi; suddenly, at the end of the myth, she once again becomes Kālī, her truly divine form. The conclusion is inescapable, that the Kaṇṇi part of the myth was originally an independent one later incorporated into the popular Kālī corpus.

The theme of the hatred of the goldsmith is important in this myth, in the previous one, and in the Pattini myths. What is the significance of this theme in Indian culture? I suspect that the social reason for this hatred is the role of goldsmiths in village life in old times. The goldsmiths had access to cash and were perhaps moneylenders and usurers in village India. However, I am also inclined to see deeper and more irrational reasons for this hatred. Consider the references to the goldsmith in some of the myths presented above.

In the Kaṇṇi myth a goldsmith brought the marriage ring for her. She pulled her hand back, and the ring fell into the sea. In the earlier myth the diamond in her ring was displaced from its socket when she met her husband. On one level these references are to Kaṇṇi's or Dēvi's reluctance to get married, for then she might lose her virginity. In the first reference the ring falling into the sea suggests a "psychopathology of everyday life." The displaced diamond is even more interesting. Note one of the problems of these myths: the goddess is a virgin, but she must marry. Dēvi marries Conat (alias Kōpālakār), but my informant, like all others I have interviewed, said that she could not have intercourse. She must remain virgin (*kanyā*). I interpret the ring on the psychological level as a vaginal symbol, and the diamond as representing her virginity. As long as she travels alone the ring is intact, but when her husband joins her something goes wrong; she is still a virgin, but she is married and she is with her husband. The diamond is displaced from its socket.

In this sense the diamond ring is like the anklet, which in the myths also has "diamonds" inside. The hatred of the goldsmith is on one level thoroughly irrational. As I said earlier, the goldsmith makes wedding rings, anklets, and necklaces, thereby being responsible, on the infantile psychological level, for the marriage of the goddess that threatens her virginity.

Muṭippurai in Southern Travancore

In this chapter I have quoted only two myths out of a large number of similar myths found in Kerala, particularly in the central and southern regions. Several Kerala writers have referred to texts that are still closer to the content of the Pattini myths. Śrī Ulloor S. Parameswara Iyer, the author of the well-known *History of Kerala Literature* (1957–65) gives an account of Maṇimaṅka ("gem-virgin") and Pālakār sung by low-caste *maṉṉāns* (washermen) and *marars*, a caste that beat drums for the Nāyar. C. M. S. Chandera (1973) says there are texts known as *kaṇṇaki toṟṟams* that are sung in southern Kerala; this is confirmed by S. Sankara Pillai (1958). As the title implies, these texts explicitly identify the protagonist as Kaṇṇaki (Pattini). Chandera adds that almost identical versions of the myths are found in *nallamah toṟṟams* sung in central Kerala in the Palghat district (Chandera 1973, pp. 38–45). And Anantan Pillai (1968) mentions myths of Kaṇṇaki and Pālakār embodied in texts known as *muṭippurai pāṭṭu* and sung by low-caste groups during annual postharvest festivals in the Travancore district. I shall give below a brief description of these rituals based on Anantan Pillai's account and my own informant interviews.

I have been given several interpretations of the term *muṭippurai pāṭṭu*, one of which means "song of the final story [of the life of the goddess]." However, I am strongly inclined to believe that *muṭippurai* is related to the Sinhala *maḍupuraya* ("hall city"), in which case *muṭi* refers to the crown or silver image of the deity and *purai* is a thatched hut, the *maḍuva*, or "hall," in Sinhala ritual. *Purai* is, I believe, derived originally from the Sanskrit *pura* and in this context means a thatched hut that is also a city (of the gods). Thus *muṭippurai* is the hall (city) where the crown or image of the goddess is installed. The festivities of *muṭippurai*, which is said to last seven days, are held in the Malayalam month of Kumpan or Mīna—that is, about February–March, after the harvest when the fields are dry. The shed is constructed in the fields. This is the ideal, though nowadays it may be held in gardens.

The shed or hut is a large conical structure about twenty feet across and about thirty feet high at the center. There is a crucial north-south orientation here also. The northern side is open, the rest is closed in. Inside the shed at the southern end is the pedestal where two anklets of the deity and sometimes her mounted silver face are installed. These *sacra* are brought ceremonially from a neighboring goddess shrine (*kāvu*) by Brahmans. This temporary shrine is fenced off so that the public is barred. Brahman priests perform daily *pūjās* here for the deity, generally from 6:00 to 7:00 P.M., and *prasād* is offered until 11:00 P.M. for the duration of the seven-day ceremony. Low-caste singers are clustered in the northern end of the shrine on a temporary platform. Sometimes they gather outside the main shed, where they sing the *toṟṟams*, origin myths of Kaṇṇaki. A fenced-off corridor from the open northern end reaches up to the pedestal area so that worshipers can enter to pay homage to the deity and accept *prasād*.

On about the third day comes the *mālapālam* stage of the festival (*māla*, "wedding garland"), which describes the wedding of the goddess and Pālakār. During this recital a lamp is burned in front of the singers and people come forward and make offerings of money. Anantan Pillai, commenting on this stage says: "on the third day the song reaches the marriage scene and then there is that ceremony performed in the temple. The people make themselves merry, singing and dancing" (1968, p. 165). In the Trivandrum area this merrymaking does not take place, though probably at one time it did.

The climax of the festival is a procession where the silver face (*tirumuṭi*) mounted on a wooden stand covered with silk is placed on an elephant with lights and festivities and taken to a nearby temple. Generally, this is a Śasta (Aiyappan) shrine. The belief is that the goddess obtains permission from Śasta before she finally departs to Koṭuṅkoḷūr (the central shrine). During this procession neighboring houses through which the procession passes will be decorated with festoons; bronze lamps and coconut-oil wicks will be lit. Regarding this and the preceding (extinct) part of the ceremony Anantan Pillai says: "Similarly the hero's death is observed with all signs of mourning. Not only in the shrine but in neighboring houses also people observe it. The revival of Pālakan, the hero, is again a day of enjoyment. There is Tālapoli and procession" (1968, p. 165). Lamentation over the death of Pālakār is no longer observed. On the final, seventh day, evil spirits are fed with *kuruti*, a mixture of lime and turmeric representing blood. Originally animals were sacrificed, but this was abolished by the command of the regent in the nineteenth century. On this day the goddess will leave for Koṭuṅkoḷūr. She will stay there for eight to ten days then return to the shrine—not the temporary one, but the Bhagavatī temple where her image is installed. This idea is clearly expressed in a ritual performed on the eighth day after her departure from the *muṭippurai* to Koṭuṅkoḷūr. The anklets and other *sacra* installed in the shed are taken back to their permanent home in the neighboring goddess temple.

The *muṭippurai* ritual cycle of the Travancore district invites comparison with the Sinhala *gammaḍuva* and the rituals of the east coast Tamil Hindus of Sri Lanka to be presented in the next chapter. The physical structure is very much like other temporary structures erected for Bhagavatī-Kālī during postharvest rituals. Yet note that the songs sung in a special area by low-caste groups are on Kaṇṇaki and Pālakār, not on Kālī. It is very likely that this was once a ceremonial complex very much like the *gammaḍuva* but later was taken over and Sanskritized by Brahmans. The earlier ritual texts then become pejorated as a result and relegated to the preserve of low-caste singers.[8]

Anantan Pillai has noted a fascinating aspect of these rituals, either from earlier years or more likely from remoter areas of Travancore. He says that the marriage of Pālakār is celebrated with merrymaking and dancing, while the death of Pālakār is one of lamentation and mourning; the resurrection of Pālakār is once again an occasion for joy. All these expressions of joy or sorrow are not confined to the hall premises but are performed in the "neighboring houses" also (Anantan Pillai 1968, p. 165). It is clear from his account that the marriage scene is not only sung but enacted in the hall, as it is among east coast Tamils

8. P. L. Swamy (1971) has noted a similar process in northern Kerala at the Vīsāri Kāvu *kōvil* at Koyilanti, thirty miles north of Calicut. This is a Bhagavatī shrine, but during the festival period Tamil songs known as *viruttam* containing the Kōvalaṉ-Kaṇṇaki story are sung. The present-day Malayalam-speaking priests do not seem to know the meaning of these verses. This also suggests that the heyday of the Pattini cult in Kerala came before the development of the Malayalam language.

in Sri Lanka today. The death and resurrection of Pālakār was also probably enacted, though Anantan Pillai does not explicitly state it. These expressions of joy or mourning were probably characteristic of Pattini ritual dramas everywhere. On the east coast the marriage of Kaṇṇaki and Kōvalaṉ is celebrated with public joy (see chap. 15, pp. 568–69): in the *gammaḍuva* their marriage is never enacted, and the killing and resurrection of Pālaṅga has practically died out. Yet we know from the comparative data from other cultures that the death and the resurrection of the god was associated with lamentation and joy, as, for example, in the Adonis and Attis rituals. The Romans had technical terms to describe these two phases of the ritual—the *tristia*, "the commemoration of sorrow," and the *hilaria*, "feasts of joy" (Vermeseren 1977, p. 92). These terms excellently describe what probably went on in the grand ritual dramas of the marriage, death, and resurrection of Pālakār-Kōvalaṉ at one time in both Sri Lanka and Kerala and probably elsewhere in southern India.

Pālaṅga: The Guardian of the Cow

The preceding analysis may help us understand the derivation of Pālaṅga, the Sinhala term for Kōvalaṉ. The name Pālaṅga makes no sense in Sinhala. It is clearly a Sinhalization of Pālakār (Pālakaṉ) of the preceding myths. Pālakār (or Pālakaṉ) and Kōvalaṉ are in turn all derived from the Sanskrit *gōpālaka* (Tamil *kōpālakār*) "guardian of the cow." The original significance of the name should also now be clear. The mother goddess, at least in one of her forms, is a cow, a nurturant being. Her consort therefore is the guardian or keeper of the cow—*gōpālaka*. This must be the earliest symbolical meaning of Kōvalaṉ alias Gōpālaka. It certainly does not fit the ethos of the Kālī cult; it fits the Pattini cult better, since here the goddess appears as more kind and benevolent, her nurturance appearing in her final role as *mater dolorosa*. Not only is Kōvalaṉ-Pālaṅga the "guardian of the cow," but the "settlement of cowherders" has an extended symbolic meaning in the Kerala myths and in the *Cilappatikāram*, analogous to similar meanings in Kṛiṣṇa mythology. Cowherds are the ideal community of devotees, who love the deity and are therefore spared from her rage (just or destructive). This symbol has considerable meaning in Hindu culture, but not in Buddhism. Hence when Pālakāṉ was taken over by Sri Lankan Buddhists they Sinhalized his name into Pālaṅga and thereby divested it of its symbolic significance.

15

The Hindu Goddess Pattini

Gajabāhu and the East Coast Tamils

In the previous chapter I noted the transformation of the goddess Pattini into Bhagavatī-Kālī. Nowhere in India today is Pattini worshiped as an autonomous deity, clearly separable from Kālī or Durgā. To observe Pattini not as a Buddhist but as a Hindu deity, one must move to the matrilineal belt of the Batticaloa district of the east coast of Sri Lanka, where there are many shrines dedicated to her as Kaṇṇaki Ammaṉ. If there were any doubts regarding the migration of Kerala people to the west coast of Sri Lanka, there is little doubt regarding their migration to the east. Batticaloa Tamils believe they came originally from Kerala, and furthermore they retain clear features of matriliny, which almost certainly links them to the Malabar Coast. But it is impossible, at this stage of the historical and sociological research of Sri Lanka, to give dates for their immigration.[1]

The east coast Tamils traditionally had many ties with the Sinhalas. In pre-British times their chiefs (rajas) were known as *vanniyar*s and owed feudal obligations to the kings of Kandy. There were also well-established trade routes between Kandy and the east coast. I found several Kandyan art objects in some of these shrines. In addition to trade and feudal links with Kandy, Tamils of the east coast sometimes intermarried with Sinhalas in nearby areas until very recently, when the modern development of Sinhala and Tamil language nationalism put a stop to marriage alliances. Finally, there are many myths that link the people of this region with the Sinhalas, the most important being once again the Gajabāhu myth. Here is one east coast version of this myth:

> In the Tamil country of the Cōḷas Pattini worship was widespread. There were very frequent relations between the Cōḷa kingdom and that of Gajabāhu in Sri Lanka reigning in Kandy! Therefore Gajabāhu went to the Cōḷa kingdom and brought with him the statue of the goddess Pattini depicted with an anklet in her hand, and also a number of priests. The conditions in Gajabāhu's kingdom were so bad that the statue could not be kept or installed there. This was due to a lack of *bhakti* [devotion] on the part of the Kandyan people. The king told his priests to

1. A recent study by Balasundaram (1979, pp. 6–7, 278, 286) highlights some of the sociological and cultural similarities between Kerala and the Batticaloa district.

> take the statue to a place where people were living in piety. It was taken through the whole of Sri Lanka till finally it arrived in the Batticaloa district. The first place the procession touched was Tambiluvil; the last place was Vīramunai.

In all east coast Pattini temples except Karaitivu, the tradition is that the cult was introduced by Gajabāhu. In Karaitivu the tradition is that the matrilineal ancestress of the *kōvilār kuṭi* ("shrine clan") named Devandi, daughter of a Senāpatirāja family reigning in Kerala, brought the cult directly from India.

A more popular folk myth in Karaitivu states that three sisters came to the Batticaloa district from Kerala with a statue of Kaṇṇaki and her anklet. Their first stop was in Vaṭṭapaḷai; next they went southward to Ceṭṭipāḷayam; and finally they reached Karaitivu, where they rested under a margosa tree. After some time they put up a small thatched hut for the goddess; here Petācci, the eldest, settled down. The other two proceeded to Tambiluvil. The descendants of Petācci formed the *kovilār kuṭi*, "the shrine clan," which jointly owns and manages the Karaitivu Kaṇṇaki Ammaṉ temple.

It is difficult to make historical sense of the Gajabāhu myth on the east coast except that it links the Sinhala and Tamil (east coast) worshipers of the cult and justifies the devotional sincerity of the latter. It does, however, indicate the overall importance of the cult in both Sinhala- and Tamil-speaking areas.

Whether or not these mythic sources can tell us much about the date of east coast immigrations, there is circumstantial evidence that does provide a clue. The present-day residents of the east coast speak Tamil; it is possible, therefore, that they migrated into Sri Lanka before the full development of Malayalam in Kerala. One might make the same inference about the migrations to the west and south (Sinhala area) also, since the Sinhala poems are supposed to be derived from Tamil. According to scholars, Malayalam developed out of Kerala Tamil between the tenth and twelfth centuries, though full-fledged literary works in this language first appeared during the thirteenth century. A pattern of migration during the tenth century and after is therefore reasonable and consonant with my analysis of the west coast and south coast migrations in chapter 13. Nevertheless, insofar as there are Tamil speakers even today in southern Kerala, later migrations cannot be ruled out. However, the weight of evidence suggests a post-tenth-century date for both areas.

In this regard let me present a curious cultural survival. The Kaṇṇi myth referred to in chapter 14 mentions a king of Cōḷa-Pāṇḍya. The Sinhalas of the east coast (Pānama), who have been strongly influenced by neighboring Hindus, have texts that refer to "Pāṇḍya that is in Cōḷa"; similar "confusions" appear in the Sinhala texts of the low country, where Kerala is identified as part of Cōḷa (Soḷī) (pp. 102, 188, 190). I soon realized that this was not a confusion of people unacquainted with the history or geography of the region, but on the contrary refers to an important historical reality. Nilakanta Sastri says:

> Rajendra succeeded his father in 1014 and made his son Rajādhirāja I yuvarāja four years later. Rajendra completed the conquest of Ceylon begun by his father; but the Ceylonese never reconciled themselves to this foreign rule and Vikramabāhu I set up rule in South Ceylon from 1029. Pāndya and Kerala became a separate viceroyalty under a prince royal who bore the title Chola-Pāndya and had his headquarters in Madurai. (1964, p. 29)

It is at least clear that the reference to a king of Cōḷa-Pāṇḍya, or "Pāṇḍya that is in Cōḷa" or "the Cōḷa king of Kerala" is a memory of this important historical event. It is remembered in both the Kerala text (the present version probably dates from the fourteenth century) and the Sinhala traditions. While the reference does not prove a hypothesis of immigration during that period, it does indicate that as far as Sri Lanka is concerned the diffusion of the texts (and possibly of peoples) occurred after A.D. 1029.

The Ritual Traditions of East Coast Tamils

While we are almost certain of Kerala migrations to the east coast, there is no evidence that these immigrants were Kerala Buddhists. It is clear, however, that their deity was not a Sanskritic one. It is indeed possible that they were also Buddhists, who were subsequently Hinduized owing to cultural influences stemming from the orthodox North (Jaffna district). In several of the shrine premises I noticed remains of Buddhist pillars and sculptures, and there was a bo tree in one shrine. However, such evidence is not conclusive, since the shrines may have been built on the sites of previous Buddhist temples. Alternatively, the east coast immigrants may have brought with them an already Hinduized cult. While I favor the first interpretation, there is no way of submitting even tentative or circumstantial evidence to justify it. The cult, however, thrives among the Tamil-speaking, matrilineal peoples of this region. Unfortunately, I have not been able to spend much time in this area and have had to work with interpreters for most of the time, so that I did not have full control over the translations and summaries of the texts. I was fortunate enough to see one major annual festival for the goddess in Karaitivu in 1966. Other rituals for the goddess, especially the Tamil version of the horn pulling, or *kompu viḷaiyāṭṭu*, have gone out of vogue in the Eastern Province. Hence most of the ethnographic data in this chapter are presented as ideal-typical descriptive accounts. Such accounts naturally limit the analysis and interpretation of the cult in this region.

The Batticaloa district of the east coast is Sri Lanka's "matrilineal belt." Communities of most castes and religions (Hindu and Muslim) are organized in terms of matrilineal clans, generally known as *kuṭi*. There is considerable information on Hindu and Muslim matrilineal organization in Akkaraipattu (MacGilvray 1974). Hiatt (1973) has a preliminary paper on the *kuṭi* system in Tambiluvil, which is in the region I studied.

My information on the goddess cult comes from the matrilineally organized *veḷḷāla* (cultivator) castes of the Batticaloa district. The *karaiyār* (fisher) castes do not worship Pattini, but rather Kālī or Durgā. The matrilineal *mukkuvār*s (originally fishermen) are cultivators nowadays and worship Pattini-Kaṇṇaki in their own shrines. Even among the matrilineal *veḷḷāla*, Pattini is viewed as an incarnation of Kālī, though she has little of Kālī's malevolence.

Let me focus on the village of Tambiluvil, since sociological data are provided for it by Hiatt (1973). There are five castes in Tambiluvil: the dominant *veḷḷāla* (cultivators) make up 90 percent of the village population, followed by *taṭṭār* (goldsmiths), *kollar* (blacksmiths), *vaṇṇār* (washermen), and *ambaṭṭar* (barbers). *Veḷḷāla* is the Tamil counterpart of the Sinhala *goyigama* caste. Though "farming" is their caste occupation, *veḷḷāla*s and *goyigama*s everywhere have branched into other occupations, in Tambiluvil often as part-time artisans (e.g., carpenters, masons, tailors), excluding caste-associated occupations. Castes tended to be endogamous, but some marriages did occur between *veḷḷāla*s and *mukkuvār*s of neighboring villages (Hiatt 1973, p. 241).

The clan system is confined to the *veḷḷāla*s of Tambiluvil, though some form of matrilineal kinship is found in this area among other groups such as the Muslims and *mukkuvārs*. In Tambiluvil there are twelve named clans (*kuṭi*), differing considerably in size, the two top clans (*kantaṉ* and *kaṭṭapattaṉ*) being the largest. Hiatt could not discover any firm linear ranking of clans, though the prestige rankings placed them on three levels. These prestige rankings are from the perspective of the custodian of the Kaṇṇaki (Pattini) shrine, himself a member of *kaṭṭapattaṉ* clan of class A. Others contested this order of precedence. Hiatt's prestige rank order is presented below:

A. 1. *kantaṉ*, *kaṭṭapattaṉ*
B. 1. *kurukkaḷ* (non-Brahman priest)
C. 1. *ceṭṭi* (former merchants, nowadays cultivators)
2. *kūrakalappaṉ* ("half-mixed")
3. *malavarācan* (inhabitants of Malanad, i.e., the hill country of Kerala)
4. *muṉṉan kaiccavaṭi* ("sixty-hand-bracelet clan"); the women here are expected to wear sixty bangles.
5. *paṇikkār* (elephant trainers)
6. *cariveli* (obscure clan name)
7. *sinkāḷa* (Sinhala)
8. *vaittiyaṉ* (physician)
9. *vēṭar* (Vädda)

The clans, it seems to me, have much of the character of subcastes within the larger *veḷḷāla* caste. In neighboring South India some of these named clans—*ceṭṭi*, *paṇikkār*, *kurukkaḷ*—are named endogamous castes. It is likely that once these castes were exported to the east coast they lost their separate identities and were converted into clans within the *veḷḷāla* caste. In the Sinhala areas a similar phenomenon has occurred among the *heṭṭi* (i.e., *ceṭṭi*), who through time have been assimilated into the *goyigama* caste or subcaste or to a patrilineal line (*vāsagama*) within it, such as *heṭṭige*. The existence of Väddas (*vēṭar*) and Sinhalas as separate clans suggest that they were prior inhabitants who were subsequently incorporated into the overall *kuṭi* organization of the region by later Malabar immigrants.

The ideal is that the two highest clans should intermarry, but in fact this is violated in 50 percent of Hiatt's sample of 141 married couples in Tambiluvil. For the other clans Hiatt was "unable to discover any prescription apart from the rule of exogamy" (1973, p. 238). Endogamy, exogamy, hypergamy, and hypogamy were all practiced, depending perhaps on strategies of marriage, as among the Sinhalas of Mädagama (Obeyesekere 1967).

Vaikāci Caṭaṅku: The Annual Festival for Kaṇṇaki Ammaṉ

Caṭaṅku means "festival" or "celebration"; in Jaffna Tamil parlance it means "marriage celebration," like the term *maṅgalam*. However among the *veḷḷāla*s of the Batticaloa district the reference is to the annual festival at Kaṇṇaki temples. The celebration lasts only seven days in Tambiluvil. In other areas it goes on for eight days, the last day being devoted to *kulirtti*, or the ritual of "cooling." In Tambiluvil *kulirtti* falls on the seventh day, which people here claim is the right tradition. The seventh day must fall on the full moon of the month of Vaikāci (Vesak, May).

The *vaikāci caṭaṅku* commemorates the plea that villagers made to Pattini after she burned the city of Madurai, a plea to put an end to the fire. Pattini agreed and gave the villagers permission to hold a festival in her honor once every year in May.

The overall organization of the festival is in the hands of an official custodian of the Kaṇṇaki temple known as *vaṇṇakār* (Sinhala *basnāyaka*) drawn from the *kāṭṭapattaṉ* clan. The priest or *kappukaṉār* (Sinhala *kapurāla*) is not from the (priest) clan but from the somewhat low-status *malavarācan* clan.[2] The *vattāṇṭi* (Sinhala *vaṭṭāṇḍi*, *vattāḍi*) are drawn from several castes, but their active role is in the *kompu vilaiyāṭṭu* ritual, the Tamil version of the *aṅkeḷiya*. Most important, however, are a set of officials known as the *pākai*, who are the official clan representatives at the festival.

For the horn-pulling and coconut-breaking games the village here as elsewhere is divided into two teams. Unlike the Sinhala areas, here the division is close to the Kerala one (see pp. 544–49), in which the village is divided into a northern settlement (*vaṭaccēri*) and a southern one (*tencēri*). The following are the clans and the clan representatives (*pākai*) within each "settlement." The southern (*tencēri*) is the goddess's side, and its representatives have more important ritual roles than its opponent, the northern side (*vaṭaccēri*).

Tencēri

Clan	Number of Representatives (*pākai*)	Comment
1. *kaṭṭapattaṉ kuṭi*	2	*vaṇṇakār* is from this *kuṭi*
2. *vēṭar kuṭi*	1	
3. *kūrakalappaṉ kuṭi*	1	
4. *sinkāḷa kuṭi*	1	
5. *kurukkaḷ kuṭi*	1	only for *pūjā*, no managerial role
6. *muṉṉan kaiccavaṭi kuṭi*	1	
7. *malavarācan kuṭi*	1	*kappukaṉārs* from this *kuṭi*

The other clans (*kuṭi*) have no official representatives, though they participate in the proceedings.

Vaṭaccēri

Clan
1. *kantaṉ kuṭi*
2. *cariveli kuṭi*
3. *malavarācan kuṭi*
4. *vaittiyan kuṭi*
5. *ceṭṭi kuṭi*
6. *paṇikkār kuṭi*

2. It is likely that the term *kappukaṉār* is derived from the Sinhala *kapurāla* rather than the other way around, since the former term is not found elsewhere among Tamil speakers. I do not know the direction of influence of the other terms common to Sinhalas and east coast Tamils.

In the Kaṇṇaki shrine at Karaitivu the *kappukaṉār* are selected from the *kōvilār kuṭi*, the clan that "owns" the temple.

Though the Kaṇṇaki temple is controlled by the southern side (*tencēri*), the daily *pūjās* are arranged by the clan representatives in consultation with each other. Also, all persons in the village contribute provisions for the *pūjās*.

The festival is announced in a special way. A week before the opening of the doors a barber goes into every street after 7:00 P.M. and shouts out: "Villagers shall meet at such-and-such-day and time at the Ammaṉ temple." With this official announcement the village adopts a series of taboos and ceremonial observances. Till the end of the festival people will adopt a strictly vegetarian diet, keep their houses and compounds clean, and will not fish or slaughter animals or cause pain to any living being. Even fish sellers are not permitted to enter the village. On the prescribed date the villagers will assemble at the *kompuccanti*, (Sinhala *aṅ handiya*, "horn terminus," the area where horns are pulled) presided over by the oldest man in the village.

Before the temple doors are opened one of the clan representatives (*pākai*) will go to the beach and collect seawater in a brass vessel. He then sprinkles the temple premises and the outer shrine area with this. Thereafter the priests or *kappukaṉār* perform the ceremony known as *punyānkam*. They place a *maṭai* ("offering") consisting of raw rice, camphor, bananas, flowers, and incense sticks at the doorway of the temple. In addition to the *maṭai* they also place a brass pot full of water; in the mouth of the pot are some mango leaves, and over them is placed a husked coconut. This is known as *niṟaikuṭam* ("full pot"). Then they collect *pañca kavviyam*—milk, ghee, curd, and urine and feces of the cow—and sprinkle these in the temple premises to the chanting of mantras.

After this the ceremony of *katavu tiṟattal*, ("opening of temple doors") is performed at 7:30 P.M. by the *kappukaṉār*, who chants mantras before putting the key in the keyhole. Mantras must also be chanted while he opens the door and enters. Other officials clean up and light lamps inside the temple for the commencement of the first day's *pūjā*. Note that the *kappukaṉār* cannot open the temple door during the regular year except in special circumstances. When he does he must offer rice and milk (*poṅkal*) to the deity.

As they enter, *maṭai* (offerings) must be laid: a minimum of seven and a maximum of twenty-seven depending on the contributions of people. The order of precedence is as follows:

1. Gaṇeśa: this *maṭai* is essential and can never be omitted.
2. Ammaṉ (literally, "mother," i.e., Kaṇṇaki)
3. Kōvalaṉ
4. Mātavi (Mādēvi)
5. Seven Virgins
6. Wife of the king of Pāṇḍya
7. Sarasvatī (goddess of learning)
8. Māriammaṉ
9. The twelve thousand attendants of Pattini. All the leftover *maṭai* is given to them.

It should be noted that no male deity from the classic pantheon, like Śiva, Viṣṇu, or Murukaṉ, is offered *maṭai* except Gaṇeśa. "Everything must start with Gaṇeśa," a priest told me, which simply reflects the Hindu ritual tradition. Actually no male deity except Gaṇeśa and Kōvalaṉ is offered *maṭai*, and some informants stated that even Kōvalaṉ should not be given *maṭai* in the Pattini temple.

In general a *maṭai* must consist of at least the following placed in a decorated tray (*maṭai taṭṭu*): three betel leaves, three areca nuts, three plantains, flowers, and areca flowers. Gaṇeśa must in addition be given raw rice, coconuts, and a brass full pot with mango leaves.

On either side of the *maṭai* for the goddess are two brass pots containing *apicekakūṭu* ("powder used for anointing"), turmeric, rose water, scents, bananas, areca nuts, betel leaves, flowers, and coins. The outsides of these brass pots, or *pūrṇa kumpam*, are covered with white thread woven in a crisscross pattern. This process involves great skill and patience. The intention is to make the pot pure with a white ("pure") covering. Some areca flowers are also placed within so that their tops show. The mouth of the pot is covered with margosa leaves (*Azadirachta indica*) and the *kappukaṉār* places on this a bronze face of the goddess Pattini (Kaṇṇaki).

The arrangements for the festivities are made with the clan representatives (*pākai*). The first *pūjā* is offered by the *vaṇṇakār* as trustee and head of *kaṭṭapattaṉ* clan. The *pūjā* expenses are borne entirely by him. This *pūjā* will generally be offered after 4:00 P.M., since pots (*kumpam*) and so on have to be made. On other days there are three *pūjā*s each day: the morning *pūjā* is offered at 6:00 A.M., and only flowers are offered; at noon the morning offerings are removed and new offerings are laid; and at 6:00 P.M. the lunch *pūjā* is cleared and the evening offerings are placed on the altars. The ingredients for the noon and evening *pūjā*s are as follows (though the number varies from one shrine to another): five hundred plantains, five hundred areca nuts, five hundred betel leaves, fifteen to twenty drinking coconuts, sugarcane juice, honey, ghee, and fruit juices mixed with unrefined cane sugar (*carkkarai*). After the *pūjā* has been offered to the goddess, the goods are given to the people.

The noon and evening *pūjā*s are offered by the representative of the *sinkāḷa kuṭi* on behalf of his clan. The other representatives collect money from their clans, buy the *pūjā* goods, and bring them into his house. Then these goods are placed in a decorated cart and covered with a white cloth. The cart is taken to the temple in a procession with four drummers making music. The *kappukaṉār* meets the procession at the entrance of the temple. He has a pot of water in one hand and a bunch of margosa leaves in the other. He chants mantras and sprays the goods with margosa leaves dipped in the water.[3] After this the goods can be taken into the temple. During these *pūjā*s a text known as *maḻai kāviyam* ("song of the rain") is sung.

The rest of the schedule for providing the *pūjā* goods is as follows:

Second day: *kurukkaḷ kuṭi*
Third day: *kūrakallapaṉ kuṭi*
Fourth day: *kaṭṭapattaṉ kuṭi*. If this happens to be a Friday the *pūjā* is given by the blacksmiths and goldsmiths of Tambiluvil. This part of the schedule cannot be altered, but the rest is flexible. This custom is not found in other shrines on the east coast.
Fifth day: *muṉṉan kaiccavaṭi kuṭi*
Sixth day: *vēṭar kuṭi*
Seventh day: No *pūjā*, but *poṅkal*, or festivities, start on this day.

3. In Karaitivu it is the three *kappukaṉār*, their mouths covered with masks, who carry the *kumpam*.

The *malavarācan kuṭi* has no special day allocated, since the *kappukaṉār* belongs to that clan. Members of other clans, or any individual, can participate in the *pūjā* by bringing baskets containing offerings (*maṭai peṭṭi*) at any time after the temple doors are opened. There is no fixed quantity, but one essential item is an areca flower. These baskets are made of palmyra leaves; each one is covered with a white cloth and carried on the head. These offerings by the public can be given at any time during the ceremonial period, not necessarily at *pūjā* time. All the items mentioned earlier are used in *pūjā*s. Extra rice is sold at public auction after the festival.

In addition to food, people may bring images of silver or gold, saris, and other clothes as fulfillment of vows. They may bring various objects: for example, for a sick child one may bring coconut or areca-nut seedlings, representing a "child for a child" (*piḷḷaikku-piḷḷai*). Others may bring animals such as goats, calves, or chickens as offerings. All these are accepted in the same manner and auctioned on the last day. Each person carries the basket on his head, takes it around the temple clockwise, and brings it to the hall (outer shrine). The *kappukaṉār* sprinkles the offering with water, and an *atikāri* (officer) of the *kūrakalapaṉ kuṭi* officially accepts it. Sinhalas and Muslims in the area also may bring baskets of offerings.

When an individual offers a *maṭai* (offering), the box is never returned empty by the *kappukaṉār*. He places in it a few betel leaves, areca flowers, plantains, holy ash, and turmeric cream, items that have already been consecrated. In other words, I get part of someone else's offerings, and some of my offerings go to someone else.

Reciting of *Kaṇṇaki Vaḻakkurai*, or Kaṇṇaki's Demand for Justice

As soon as the temple doors are opened the singing of the *Vaḻakkurai* text begins (text 57). Anyone can participate in the singing, but a minimum of two is essential, alternating lines. An important rule is that the recital must be completed on the seventh and final day at the specified time. If the recital approaches the end before that day, as it often does, they must go back to an appropriate place in the text so as to ensure that it will be completed on the seventh day. In Karaitivu the singers must come from the clan that "owns" the temple—that is, the *kōvilār kuṭi*.

Pirakāram, or Procession

From the third day onward a procession goes around the temple premises. On the sixth day the procession (*pirakāram*), which is named *tiruviḻā* (literally, "festival in a temple"), carrying the image of the goddess on a larger *tēr* ("chariot," actually a dome or crownlike structure), goes around the whole village (the consort is never taken in procession). The image taken in the *tiruviḻā* procession is called *eḻuntaruḷiyirunta ammaṉ*, "mother who is taken in procession." A *kumpam* is carried ahead of the goddess, generally by a boy of fifteen to sixteen years. Behind that is the statue, which is dressed and taken in the "chariot" (*tēr*).

On the fifth day a procession consisting of the *kappukaṉār*, the trustees (*vaṇṇakār*), the seven *pākai*, and interested villagers goes to cut the *kalyāṇa kāl* ("wedding post"). The procession is headed by drummers; offerings are carried under an umbrella and a canopy. The marchers select a margosa branch about eight inches around and six feet long from a sturdy tree nearby. Before they cut the branch they offer a *maṭai* at the foot of the tree, utter prayers, and break a coconut. This is, of course, for the tree deity. The first cut in the wood is made by the *kappukaṉār*; then others join in. The branch is covered in white cloth supplied by the washerman and is ceremonially carried back to the temple on the shoulders of two persons. It is washed first in plain water, then in turmeric water and taken into the uncemented back portion of the outer shrine, which is viewed as the third hall.

The *kalyāṇa kāl* is decorated by dipping three fingers in holy ash and smearing the post all over. The *kappukaṉār* then puts in *poṭṭu* (the *tilaka* mark on the forehead) and *kuṅkumam* (red powder). A hole is dug and the following ingredients are put into it: seven grains [paddy, maize, millet, green gram (*muṅ*), black gram, *tiṇai* (small millet), and *eḷḷu* (sesame)] and five metals (gold, silver, brass, copper, steel). Then, at about 5:30 P.M., the margosa post is planted and covered with a white cloth. After this they set up a pot of water with turmeric and put in some flowers. The pot is kept near the foot of the post. Then six posts from the *pūvaracu* (Sinhala *sūriya*, *Thespesia populnea*) tree are planted around the post, and two to five bushels of raw paddy are heaped around the wedding post (*kalyāṇa kāl*). Then a *yantra* is drawn on the paddy in the shape of a six-pointed star with the points connected to the six posts.

People believe the power of Pattini is felt here only after the planting of the wedding post. While planting it they recite the verses relating to the marriage of Kaṇṇaki and Kōvalaṉ, signifying that her greatness was something she earned after marriage.

On the following (sixth) day the post is decorated. They now cover the post with silk saris and hang two coconuts with two areca leaves and margosa leaves and one areca flower. Then a crossbar is tied on the post and a blouse is fitted on this bar, plus fine female jewelry; a mirror is hung from the post.

Kulirtti: The Ritual of Cooling

The *Vaḻakkurai* recital is completed on the seventh morning, a Monday. The Monday-morning *pūjā* cannot be held till the recital is completed. Also, the previous night (Sunday) the goddess is ceremonially taken in procession through the village.

The *kappukaṉār* also goes in the procession. He comes back with the procession early Monday morning and takes the goddess into the temple. He receives (from the officer or *atikāri*) the previous night's *pūjā* food and arranges for the morning *pūjā*. While the *kappukaṉār* is busy arranging the *pūjā*, the reciters continue with *vaḻakkurai*. After the recital is over they tie the palm-leaf (*ōla*) manuscript and give it to the *kappukaṉār*, who puts some flowers on it and places it on the altar with the rest of the offerings. Then the offerings are given to the deities.

The ritual of *kulirtti* and the recital of the text commence immediately after the morning *pūjā* of the seventh day (text 58). The *kappukaṉār* and his assistants lay a white foot cloth twelve feet long in front of the *kalyāṇa kāl*, reaching the door of the shrine. They make a heap of paddy on the cloth and place a mortar on the paddy. They then place a pot containing turmeric water on the mouth of the mortar. The assembled people put coins into the pot. The *kappukaṉār* (who is wearing red female attire) puts two bundles of margosa leaves into the pot, and also the anklets and small round bangles (*ammāṉaikai*) of the goddess. He wears a mouth mask and stands in front of the pot. At this point the singers begin their recital of *kulirtti*, or the "cooling": The *kappukaṉār* takes the anklets and *ammāṉaikai* and shakes them, then puts them back into the pot. Thereafter he takes the bundle of margosa leaves and sprinkles them with the turmeric water from the pot. He then goes into the inner sanctum and brings forth the brass pot used for lustration and sprinkles people with the water. After this is over he serves the people a paste of holy ash, turmeric, and sandalwood. Special food known as *kulirtti pānakam* ("share of cooling foods") is also given to them, after, of course, it is given to the goddess. *Kulirtti pānakam* contains cooling foods such as the following: bananas, mangoes, oranges, sugarcane, pomegranates, unrefined sugar (*carkkarai*), honey, milk, ghee, and other cool substances, to which is added young coconut water. Thereafter the *kappukaṉār* will hand over the seven betel stands to the clan representatives (*pākai*). By 9:00 A.M. on Monday a group of thirty or forty women go into the temple to pound the paddy. They offer a special *maṭai* for the mortars and pestles. Then garlands are put around the mortars and pestles and the women commence pounding and winnowing the paddy. On the same morning, from about 7:00 onward cattle owners will have started bringing in milk from their cows. The officials see to it that the milk is warmed and kept in good condition. While women are pounding paddy and officials are busy with their tasks, another group of people are firing the pots.

The firing of the pots is the culmination of a series of activities that commences on the second day of the ceremony. On that day, about 7:00 A.M., the *kappukaṉār*, trustees (*vaṇṇakār*), and others go in procession, to the beat of drums, to a threshing floor (*kaḷavāyal pūmi*) two miles from the temple to gather the clay for making pots for the festival foods (*poṅkal*) on the seventh day. They carry with them a trayful of *pūjā* goods and coconuts, margosa leaves, areca flowers, and lotus flowers.

The pots are made by women on the seventh day in the temple for making *poṅkal*—rice and milk boiled and offered to the goddess. Initially three pots are made, known as *vināyakar pāṉai*, "Gaṇeśa's pots." These pots are placed on a fire in the main hall of the temple between the *kalyāṇa kāl* and main entrance door (in the outer area). Before the pots are placed on the fire they are placed on a white cloth in front of the temple. The *kappukaṉār* brings a thick thread on which are tied lotus flowers, forming a kind of garland. He chants mantras and winds the garland around the neck of each pot. After this he utters more mantras and lights a fire beside the white cloth. Meanwhile, people shout the praises of the goddess, while the *kappukaṉār* places the pots in the fire about dawn. Cattle owners bring large amounts of milk for this occasion for fear that their animals may be destroyed if they do not comply.

When the milk boils over the *kappukaṉār* takes some from each pot to the goddess's altar. Then the rice is poured into the pots. After the "milk rice" is cooked the pots are taken into the inner shrine and dedicated to the goddess. Twenty-seven *maṭai* are laid, and the rice from the pots is placed on the *maṭai*. These pots are given to members of the congregation. Some informants believe these pots represent the last meal that Pattini cooked for Kōvalaṉ.

Conclusion of the Annual Festival

There are three betel stands (*vaṭṭa*) in the inner shrine. The *kappukaṉār* brings them to the hall and distributes them thus:

1. "This stand is for the village," says the *kappukaṉār*. The practice was for the *vēṭar kuṭi* to take it, but no one now accepts it.

2. The second stand is for the *kurukkaḷ*s (priest clan). Any "priest" except the *kappukaṉār* can receive it. This probably expressed the older ritual right of the *kurukkaḷ* clan for their role as ritual specialists.

3. The third is for the *vaṇṇakārs*, or trustees of the temple. Then food in the twenty-seven *maṭai* is distributed to all the people.

Kulirtti, or Cooling Ritual, in Karaitivu

I present below an account of the *kulirtti* ritual I witnessed in Karaitivu on 30 May 1966 during the annual Pattini festival there. *Kulirtti pūjā* in Karaitivu starts at 4:45 A.M. Officials of the temple and all organizers line up on both sides of the third section (hall) of the temple. In the fourth hall of the temple two persons (generally two trustees or *vaṇṇakārs*) read the *kulirtti* text. One *kappukaṉār* is dressed in a red sari, the others are in white. This red-robed priest utters a mantra and suddenly throws open the curtain covering the altar so that the assembled audience beholds the gorgeously decorated images of the goddess. The effect is dramatic, the audience shouts *harō! harā!* while the temple priests ring handbells.

On the stand in the inner sanctum is a large permanent statue of the goddess; on the left of this are the statues that are normally carried in procession, and on the right is a statue of Piḷḷaiyār (Gaṇeśa). (In 1973 informants denied that a statue of Piḷḷaiyār was kept on the right of the goddess, but my notes are very clear in this regard.) Besides the statues the whole altar is beautifully decorated with flowers of various sorts, mainly lotuses, and lights from different types of oil lamps, giving it an impressive air. Everyone shouts *harō! harā!* while the officials who are lined up utter silent prayers, some with their palms outstretched pleading, others in tears. Meanwhile bells are rung and drums are beaten. The red-robed *kappukaṉār* performs the royal ritual of the Hindu deities—he holds lights from oil lamps, lights from camphor stands, the umbrella (of bronze), a flag and a sun and moon emblem, a yak-tail fan, and so on. This part of the ritual takes about forty-five minutes.

After this is over the officials line up on one side of the fourth hall closer to the audience. This is also the area where the wedding post (*kalyāṇa kāl*) has been planted, and the *kulirtti* proper is performed in the middle of the room in front of the post.

There is a mortar standing upright and covered with a white cloth; a brass pot is placed on this cloth. In the pot is turmeric water, and on top are bundles of margosa leaves with the anklets enmeshed in them. Various offerings (*maṭai*) are also placed near the pot. The red-robed *kappukaṉār* pours water from another pot into the brass pot to the shouts of *haro! hara!* He utters mantras while two persons (*vaṇṇakārs*) continue to recite the *kulirtti* texts. The *kappukaṉār* dips a margosa branch into the pot and lustrates the area in front of him. Women shout *haro! hara!* and perform the *kuravai* (sound made by flapping the tongue against the inside of the mouth). An assistant *kappukaṉār* (in white) periodically lifts two anklets from the pot and jingles them to the sounds of *kuravai* while the texts continue to be recited. During certain intervals the whole pot and its stand are carried by three assistants led by the red-robed *kappukaṉār* clockwise round the *kalyāṇa kāl* and back to the original place.

After about ninety minutes the text recital is over. Then one of the persons reciting the texts utters the *pārvatī mantra* and ceremonially closes his book. The *kappukaṉār* lustrates the officials with the *kulirtti* water, using a margosa branch. Then he goes up to the audience on the two sides of the room and lustrates them also. After this the audience is given the cooked milk rice (*prasād*), which they take home, along with some *kulirtti* water in little bottles.

Kompu Viḷaiyāṭṭu, Horn Game, or *Kompu Murittal*, Breaking of Horns

The origin myth of the horn game among east coast Hindus is radically different from that of Sinhala Buddhists. According to a text known as *kaṇṇaki ammaṉ akaval* (*akaval*, "four-line stanzas"), Pattini was in a rage after burning Madurai, and even the gods were frightened. Viṣṇu thought something should be done to divert her attention, so he took the form of several boys. These boys took turmeric yams shaped like forked sticks and hooked them together. They pulled at these hooks, and when one broke they shouted, "It's a victory for Pattini." Then Pattini forgot her rage. This was all a trick played by Viṣṇu to pacify her.

The actual horn game described below is from informants' accounts of the game as performed in Tambiluvil. It is interesting in that, while the content of the ritual is identical with that in the other Hindu areas in the Eastern Province, the division into teams is different. Tambiluvil is the only place where teams are divided on a matrilineal basis: elsewhere in Sri Lanka, in both Sinhala and Tamil areas, the division is patrilineal, irrespective of the normal rule of descent, which may be patrilineal, matrilineal or bilateral. *Kompu* is generally performed on the following occasions:

1. It can be held independent of the annual festival of *vaikāci caṭaṅku*, which is strictly calendrical. Traditionally, whenever *vaikāci caṭaṅku* is held *kompu* is often performed, but not vice versa.
2. It can be held whenever there is drought or pestilence.
3. It is also regularly held in August to coincide with the beginning of the monsoon. This is known as *kompu tiṭṭam* ("water horn"). If there is any regularity in *kompu*, it is this August ceremony.

Theoretically the *kompu* should be held in Vaikaci (Vesak, May). Traditionally, informants stated, the *kompu* ritual was held yearly, but it has become increasingly difficult to mobilize group resources to hold the ceremony. In 1969 it was decided to scrap the *kompu* entirely owing to a tremendous fight in the village following the utterance of ritual obscenities, which are now viewed by the dominant intelligentsia of Tambiluvil as reprehensible and doctrinally heterodox from the strict Shaivite point of view. (In Karaitivu *kompu* ended in 1955 for the same reason.)

As elsewhere on the east coast, the village divides itself into two "settlements"—the *tencēri* (south settlement), which is the goddess Pattini's side, and the *vaṭaccēri* (north settlement), the side of Sāmi (from the Sanskrit, *svāmi*, "lord"; Sinhala *sāmi*) which is the honoric given to Kōvalaṉ (the Sinhala term Pālaṅga is never used for Pattini's husband on the east coast). The present allocation of clans (*kuṭi*) to the two "settlements" are as indicated on page 557. Some of the traditional clans have dispersed (*paṭṭavali*, "line that has disappeared") and are no longer represented in Tambiluvil. In general the two sides are about equal demographically.

As in the Sinhala areas, there is on the east coast a distinct division of labor between the temple priest and those who organize the *kompu* ritual. The terms are also identical; the Sinhala *kapurāla* is in the Tamil dialect of the east coast *kappukaṉār*; the Sinhala term *vaṭṭāṇḍi* is *vaṭṭaṇṭi* on the east coast. Sometimes *pucāri*, the term common to most of South India, is used instead of *kappukaṉār*. The two *vaṭṭaṇṭi* have taboos similar to those at Pānama. They are strictly vegetarian and remain sexually continent during the festival season. They are not allowed to leave the confines of the sacred area, and they live in a special hut constructed for them. Each *vaṭṭaṇṭi* is paid ninety rupees per month from the temple funds.

The actual ritual is very similar to that held in Pānama. Women are excluded from the sacred area, but unlike the situation in Pānama they are permitted to watch the proceedings "from afar." The "horns" used are in general very small in the initial stage of the game, but larger horns are used later on. The size of the small horn in my possession is about seven by eight inches. The horns of the two settlements are matched in the following manner.

The southern settlement (*tencēri*) picks two horns of identical size and sends them to the northern settlement. They choose one for their use and send the other back for use by the southern settlement. This ensures fairness. Pattini's horn is tied to a tree; the opposing horn of Sāmi is hooked to this, and a long rope is attached to it. There is nothing analogous to the thunderbolt tree (*henakaňda*); people pull the long rope much in the manner of the *kolu aṅ* ("youth horn") ritual of Pānama. As elsewhere, the *vaṭṭaṇṭi* and a few attendants hold the horns and control them while the mass of individuals tug at the rope. The following objects are used: *pilli*, or *pillittaṭi*, the splicers used for reinforcing the horn; *arippu*, a short coil of rope for preventing the horn from slipping; *vaṭakkoṭi* or *vaṭakkayiṟu*, long ropes for pulling the horns.[4] If by any chance the *kompu* do not break, the *vaṭṭaṇṭi* have to remain in the temple premises, without food or sleep (except liquids), till the next day's pull (generally in theory only, since horns almost always break). If Pattini's side is losing continually they must give offerings to the Seven Celestial Virgins; if Sāmi's side loses, offerings are made to the god Aiyaṉār, who goes about naked.

The overriding of the caste principle that is a universal organizational feature of Sinhala rituals is not found in Tambiluvil. In general the *kompu* is performed by all the matrilineal *kuṭi* of the *veḷḷāla* caste. Other named castes like *mukkuvār*, *karaiyār*s (fishermen) are excluded from *kompu* participation. In Tambiluvil an exception was once made. The fifth *kompu* of the *ēṇṭakam* stage (see below) was given to the washermen and barbers at their request. They were allowed to hold the *kompu*, but the actual pulling was by the matrilineal clans (*kuṭi*) of the *veḷḷāla* caste. Furthermore, any member can change sides, but in Tambiluvil this will result in the loss of certain rights of management in the temple. Such a consequence cannot occur in other areas of the east coast, where temple rights are inherited matrilineally but *kompu* teams are patrilineally inherited.

If the community decides to have a *kompu* ritual, they have to make a preliminary vow, which is a promise to the goddess that a *kompu* will be held in her honor within a specified period of time. This vow, which is analogous to the Sinhala *kapa* in the *gammaḍuva*, is performed in the following manner.

The two teams make *kompu* each from freshly cut branches and smear them with tur-

4. The parts of the horn are labeled as follows: the long arm is *mutukumāram*; the short arm, *palvayu*; and the joint of the two arms the *kuccu* (Sinhala *kusa*, "womb").

meric (old victorious *kompus*, unlike the custom in the Sinhala areas, are always kept in the temple and never used a second time). One *kompu* is placed in the Pattini shrine and the other in the Sāmi shrine (in Tambiluvil there is a shrine for Sāmi, but not in Paṭṭimeṭu and Karaitivu) for one to three days, and *pūjās* are offered regularly. After this the horns are ceremonially placed in a central altar constructed in the open area between the two shrines, then they are reinforced and the crosspoles attached. Each *kompu* is covered with margosa leaves and areca flowers. The Pattini (southern side) horn is "dressed," that is, wrapped with silk saris. The horns are not hooked, but they may be kept in state in this manner for a certain time limit that the organizers of the *kompu* must fix beforehand—for example, ten days, one month, or forty days.

This vow is enough to control the drought or pestilence that befell the village, but according to the terms of the vow a full-scale *kompu* ritual has to be held after the termination of the promised period. Thus, when this time limit is up the two parties meet and fix another date for the actual *kompu* ritual.

Pōrtēṅkāi Aṭittal: Coconut-Breaking Contest

The *kompu* rituals must be preceded by a "coconut contest" called *pōrtēṅkāi*, which is identical with the Sinhala term *pora pol* (*pora*, "contest," "fight"; *pol*, "coconut"). However, while the Sinhala coconut game is almost devoid of ritualistic character and has developed in some areas into a totally secular contest, the Tamil *pōrtēṅkāi* is still anchored in ritual and must always be performed before "horn pulling."

The northern settlement (*vaṭaccēri*) and the southern settlement (*tencēri*) jointly collect coconuts from households in the village, generally about a thousand nuts. From these they select about one hundred hard nuts suitable to be used as "breakers," which are evenly divided between the two teams. Any number of members can participate, but in general the numbers are small, about five to nine players on each side. At any particular "throw" there are only two players, one for each team. The two teams face each other at each end of a ridge about fifteen feet long and six inches high, which has been reinforced with mud and water.

The game is simple and does not involve the same skills and hazards as the Sinhala coconut game. The northern settlement (*vaṭaccēri*) man rolls a coconut along the ridge in the direction of the south (*tencēri*). His opponent on the southern team squats on the ground holding a "breaker coconut" with both hands and hits the northern (*vaṭaccēri*) coconut coming along the ridge, trying to break it without damaging the "breaker." All coconuts are believed to have a male and a female side; the female side is the blunt end with three germ holes, and the male side the hard sharp end. The female end of the coconut that is rolled has a pointed tuft of husk covering the female end; the breaker has all the husks removed and the female end exposed. The oncoming coconut is hit with the female end of the breaker. Sometimes a man can get an assistant to move the oncoming nut into a good position for breaking. If the oncoming nut is not broken, it is a victory for that nut's side. This nut is kept aside. If the breaker breaks, then it is also a victory for the other side.

The firm rule is that northern team sends the first nut, and they will continue to roll nuts until they win or lose. Ultimately, the winner is the team with the largest number of unbroken coconuts remaining. After the *pōr* (contest), the winning side shouts, dances, and drums in exultation.

In Tambiluvil the coconut contest is performed in the morning (in the afternoon in Karaitivu), once only, and is never repeated in the course of the ceremonial period. On the evening of the same day there is a ceremonial playing of *kompu* without any element of competition (*kulu kompu*). For this purpose hooks are cut from the *pāvaṭṭai* (*Webera carymbosa*) tree to make two hooks, the larger one for Pattini and the smaller one for Sāmi. These ritual hooks are kept in the altar and used for *pūjā*s and never for "playing." The "horns" used for the contest are never consecrated in this manner. On that first day the two ritual *kompu*s are hooked together, and Sāmi's hook is deliberately broken. A similar performance is enacted on the last day (*taṇṇīr kompu*, "water horn"). These procedures are identical with those in the Sinhala areas.

About three days after the initial formal *kompu*, the "competitive" *kompu* begins. Generally an odd number of *kompu*s have to be broken, one on each day. Most often fifteen *kompu*s are broken during the festivities; the maximum allowable number is twenty-one, but any odd number between fifteen and twenty-one is permitted. The *kompu* is not performed on consecutive days, which is also probably in keeping with the principle of odd numbers. The *kompu*s are broken in three stages; each in ascending order of ritual elaborateness and importance. Assuming that fifteen is the agreed number to be broken, the following are the stages:

Stage one: Three *kompu*s are placed on a *komputtaṭṭu* (a *kompu* "tray" or altar), very much like the *mal yahan*, *mässa*, or *taṭṭu* of Sinhala ritual.

Stage two: Five *kompu*s are placed in a much more elaborate structure called a *kūṭāram* ("throne") about fifteen feet high. (Sometimes *komputtaṭṭu* and *kūṭāram kompu* are played alternatively.)

Stage three: Seven *kompu*s are placed on an *ēṇṭakam*, a seventeen-foot structure with a *tēr* (dome) on top made from the cloths of various colors covering the *ēṇṭakam*. Note again the odd number of horns used in the three stages. If the total number of horns is twenty-one, the number broken during the three stages would be five, seven, and nine. As in Pānama, the victorious side will sing obscene songs humiliating their opponents.

Before the actual play starts the images of Ammaṉ and Sāmi are brought to the *kompu* area. The goddess's image is brought along with a full pot and the *kompu* in the *taṭṭu*. So with Sāmi, both carried in procession. The two processions meet (about 12:30 P.M.) and the priest of the Kaṇṇaki shrine conducts a *pūjā* there. After the *pūjā* both images and *kompu*s are taken back to their shrines. At the shrine the *kompu* is covered up in margosa leaves, areca flowers, and silk cloth. It is later carried on a square plank (not *taṭṭu*), with the same decorations, back to the *kompu* arena.

The two *kompu*s are placed within enclosures made with white cloth by washermen, where they remain till the participants arrive (about 150 players). Soon the *vaṭṭaṇṭi* will arrive after their ritual baths. They carry their respective *kompu*s in the *taṭṭu* to the place where the *kompu*s will be hooked. The hooking place is known as *kompuccanti* ("horn terminus").

Three or five days of *kompu* may be played with the *taṭṭu*; soon a more elaborate structure is made, the *kūṭāram*, or "throne." The *taṭṭu* will now be placed inside the *kūṭaram*.

Ţhe two *kūṭaram*s are not of the same size; the larger *kūṭaram* (and *taṭṭu*) belong to Sāmi. These *kūṭaram*s are elaborately decorated with multicolored cloth. There is also a great deal of competition, with each side trying to outdo the other in constructing a beautiful *kūtaram*. Strict security is maintained so that the other side will not see the *kūtaram* until it is finished.

The third stage of the *kompu*, known as *ēṇṭakam*, follows *kūtaram* after about a week's break. Before the *ēṇṭakam* is fully decorated people stage the *tēr kalyāṇam* ("chariot marriage") anytime during the free week. The southern settlement people go in triumphal procession to the northern settlement shrine complex with a tray containing betel, areca nuts, flowers, plantains, *kuṇkumam*, turmeric, camphor, sandalwood, and holy ash to seek a groom for marriage. An umbrella is held over the tray, and a white canopy is held over the umbrella. As they near the gates of the Sāmi shrine, there is a louder beat of drums, firecrackers are set off, and women joyfully perform the *kuravai* sound. They are met at the entrance by the northern people, who are there with a similar tray, umbrella, and white cloth. The umbrellas and cloths are exchanged. The members of the southern settlement have also brought with them a *vēṭṭi* (white cloth worn by men), a shawl, and a ring, which they give to the north. Northerners apply turmeric cream to the southern people who have arrived there and invite them into the Sāmi temple.

The *vaṭṭaṇṭi* of the northern settlement receive those of the south by offering them betel leaves and inquire about the purpose of their visit. The south replies that it is making a marriage proposal, but the north settlement wants information on dowry, to which the south replies, "land, jewelry, house, and so forth" (as in any conventional proposal). When these discussions are over, the blacksmith comes and throws a silk cloth over the crown of the *ēṇṭakam* (whose framework has been completed), known as *tēr*. Only after this act can the *ēṇṭakam* be decorated.

Two hours after the members of southern settlement have left, the north will reciprocate their visit. They go in a similar procession, but they take female clothes and ornaments: sari, *tāli*, bangles, and jewelry. They are received in the same manner and conducted into the Pattini temple. There they decide on a date for the marriage of *ēṇṭakams*, or *tēr kalyāṇam* (marriage of the chariots).

People can now start decorating the *ēṇṭakam* and complete it with the crown (*tēr*).

Marriage of the Chariots

The marriage of the *ēṇṭakams* also takes place before the *kompu* of the *ēṇṭakam* is played. Houses in the village are decorated, and everywhere there is a sense of joy. The procession of southern settlement come up with their *ēṇṭakam* from their shrine to a position halfway to the *kompuccanti* ("horn terminus"). This is repeated by the north. Each side carries a large white cloth (a sari), which people hold at the four corners. They stay in this position halfway from the shrine to the terminus (*kompuccanti*). Then those holding the two white cloths advance and meet. They tie the two cloths together. Then the two *ēṇṭakams* with a *vaṭṭaṇṭi* on each side also come forward. A southern *vaṭṭaṇṭi* is dressed as the bride and a northern one as the groom. They exchange rings, and the northern man ties a *tāli* around the neck of the southern "female," as in any real marriage ceremony. When the *tāli* tying is over the two *ēṇṭakams* (with the *kompu* in them), which have been brought close together, are purified, and then there is a *pūjā* for the *ēṇṭakams*. Since this is a joyous event the two *ēṇṭakams* are taken in procession to the village with Sāmi's *ēṇṭakam* in front headed by the *vaṭṭaṇṭi* dressed as bridegroom. The southern man dressed as the bride leads that side's own *ēṇṭakam*. They go round the village blessing each household. As they go along the village road one behind the other, people will come out and receive them with pots full of water (*niṟai kuṭam*) and margosa leaves.[5] The two *ēṇṭakams* will stop in front of each house that has a *kumpam* (full pot), and the two will again "join together" there. The *kappukaṉār* burns camphor at every gate, breaks a coconut, pours water from the pot onto the road, and blesses each household, as in Pānama. It is only after the procession is over that the *kompu* breaking is held. (Thus the last stage of the *kompu* is like intercourse following upon marriage.)

The *ēṇṭakam* is a domelike structure about seventeen feet tall, consisting of five steps or shelves. The *kompu* is placed in the second shelf; a *taṭṭu* (tray) is never used for the *ēṇṭakam*. It is decorated profusely with flowers, mirrors, and silk cloths. Immediately after the last *kompu* is broken the tug rope is laid on the ground in a circle. The winning coconuts of both teams are also lined up alongside the tug rope. Then both teams go around in a circle, indicating harmony, singing songs in praise of Pattini known as *ammaṉ paḷḷu*. They go round and round till they have finished singing the twenty stanzas of praise. Then they cut the coconuts with a knife so as to cut the rope also. This ritual is designed to create peace and unity (*campantam*, Sanskrit *sambandha*) between the teams, like the *varadaravanava* ritual of Pānama.

The *kompu* have been placed in the middle of the circle, along with a *maṭai* and a large clay pot containing turmeric water and margosa leaves. Then the water is poured over each team's bundles of *kompu*, after which each carries its own in procession through the village, with Sāmi leading the procession. The *kompus* are tied together in a bundle and carried on the head. The entrance to every household is cleaned and purified, and full pots are placed at each entrance. The householders bathe the people who come there with the water from the pots. Then the procession goes back, and each team keeps its *kompu* in its own temple.

Myths of the East Coast: *Kaṇṇaki Vaḻakkurai*

Text 57 *Kaṇṇaki Vaḻakkurai*

I shall quote below two texts of the Batticaloa Tamils of the east coast. The first text is *kaṇṇaki vaḻakkurai* ("the case for justice as stated by Kaṇṇaki"), referred to earlier, which is sung during the annual festival. Only the barest summary of this text is given; the complete text is available in Pandit V. S. Kandiah's edition (1968). The more important text is the *kaṇṇaki ammaṉ kuḷirtti pāṭal* ("song of the cooling of Kaṇṇaki"), which contains references to the older traditions of the Pattini cult and links the east coast tradition with that of the Sinhalas and the traditions embodied in the *Cilappatikāram*.

The Birth of Kōvalaṉ

During the just and righteous rule of Karikāḷ Valavaṉ (the famous Cōḷa emperor) the Cōḷa kingdom was brimming with prosperity. In its capital, the city of Pūmpukār, there lived a trader named Mācāttuvāṉ, who came from a noble family. He led a happy married life but

5. The full pot used by ordinary people is *niṟai kuṭam*; when priests use the full pot it is called *kumpam*. The latter is sacralized with mantras.

was disappointed in not having a child. Both husband and wife set out on pilgrimage to many temples and performed many charities to obtain a child. Also, they made a vow that they would adorn the pillars of the temples of the city with gold if their desire was granted. One night Mācāttuvāṉ's wife dreamed of obtaining a golden pen by divine grace. When she related this dream to her husband he was elated and performed many *pūjās* to various deities. In due course she gave birth to a male child. Macāttuvāṉ, thrilled, performed the required *pūjās* for the gods and also gave alms to priests and others. In keeping with the custom of the traders, he had a cot specially made and laid the newborn child in it to celebrate the occasion. When this boy was five years old Macāttuvāṉ invited learned priests to initiate the boy in his studies. The boy, named Kōvalaṉ, grew up to be a young man of sixteen years.

The Birth of Ammaṉ

As a result of performing arduous penance, the sage Parācara (a Puranic sage) begot a female child. The god Śiva wanted this child to be a great person and made her take the form of a mango fruit in a tree in the king of Pāṇḍya's orchard at Madurai. There was another reason for Śiva's action. The king had three eyes like the god Śiva himself and was very arrogant about this. Umādevī, wife of Śiva wanted him to change one of the three eyes of the Pāṇḍyan king. Śiva told his wife Umādevī that he had a plan. The daughter of the sage Parācara would take the form of a mango fruit (thus she would be born as the daughter of the Pāṇḍyan king). No sooner would the king receive the mango fruit than he would lose his third eye.

One day the fragrant odor of a sweet, luscious mango filled the air of the king's palace, and his guardsmen informed him about it. The king ordered that the fruit be picked and brought to him. When the guards reached the tree, the fruit had disappeared. When this mystery was related to the king, he personally went to the base of the tree. While he was contemplating picking the fruit a *tāpaci* (a sage who performs penance) passed that way. This *tāpaci* had obtained the history of this mango from the sage Parācara. He offered to help pick it. Accordingly, he fixed an arrow to his bow and shot at the mango. The arrow severed the fruit from the tree, but the mango remained floating in midair above the *tāpaci*'s outstretched hands. The *tāpaci* then went his way. In compliance with what the *tāpaci* said, the Pāṇḍyan king stretched out his hands toward the fruit. The mango fell into the king's hands, but it became a fireball. Shocked, he dropped the fireball and wiped the perspiration from his forehead, thus erasing the eye in the middle of his forehead.

The Pāṇḍyan king was shaken and invited learned priests to find out the causes of the strange event. The priests said the mango did not augur well for his future. They suggested that the mango be given to Pāṇṭimātēvi, the queen. The queen obtained the mango and kept it in a pot of gold. On the third day, in place of the mango she found a baby. In keeping with the instructions given earlier by astrologers, the king placed the child in a casket and put it in the sea.

The casket with the child floated on the sea and drifted toward Kāvirippūmpaṭṭinam. Two traders, Mānākar and Mācāttuvāṉ (or Mācāttāṉ), who were walking along the seashore, sighted it. The first to see the casket was Mānākar. Hence he claimed that what was inside should belong to him. The other trader, Mācāttuvāṉ, claimed the casket.

When the casket reached the shore they opened it and found a charming female child. Mānākar took the child. However, the two traders came to an understanding that when this child grew up she should be given in marriage to Kōvalaṉ, the son of Mācāttuvāṉ. Mānākar took the child to his house in the city and brought her up.

Comment: Thus far the account is very much like the Sinhala text 39 known as *vaňda puvata* ("sins of barrenness") and *kōvil pevīma* ("penance at shrines"). The Sinhala mango birth is here given a more Hindu interpretation. It is difficult to know whether the east coast version of the mango birth was influenced by the Sinhala tradition or whether both derive from an earlier South Indian source.

The Story of the Building of the Ship

Comment: This part of the story incorporates the Pattini myth into local legend and thereby contextualizes it in the conflicts between castes on the east coast of Sri Lanka. Similar localization of the story is also characteristic of the myths I have recorded from Kerala (p. 546).

Arrangements were made for the marriage of Kōvalaṉ and Kaṇṇaki. Goldsmiths were ordered to make jewelry for the bride, especially a gem to be inserted into her golden anklet. Mānākar decided that his daughter should have *nākamaṇi* ("cobra gem") a rare gem possessed by the king of *nāga*s, who lived in Nāgadīpa (the little island off the north coast of Sri Lanka). Since obtaining this was a difficult task, Mānākar, on the advice of priests, entrusted it to Mīkāmān, a chief of the fishing community.

Comment: The references are to the *karaiyār*s (Sinhala *karāva*), who inhabit the coastal regions of South India and Sri Lanka. A large part of the text is devoted to legitimizing the religious orthodoxy of the *karaiyār*s. Their ancestor is genealogically related to Śiva himself, and thus Mīkāmān (literally, "helmsman") is Śiva's kinsman.

Mīkāmān and his friends went in catamarans to visit the king of Eelam (Sri Lanka) to procure timber for building the ship needed to seek the cobra gem. The seaports on the coast of Sri Lanka are mentioned. They then build the ship and set sail for north Sri Lanka.

Comment: At this point another localization of the myth occurs. The *mukkuvār*s are introduced. The *mukkuvār*s are also matrilineal fishermen on the east coast of Sri Lanka, but nowadays they practice agriculture; the northern *mukkuvār*s are patrilineal. *Mukkuvār*s are the traditional enemies of the *karaiyār*s. The *karaiyār/mukkuvār* conflict is now described on a heroic scale like the battle of Rāma and Rāvaṇa, or the Mahābhārata war.

Veṭiyarācaṉ was the chief of the *mukkuvār*s. He sighted Mīkāmān's catamarans and decided to do battle in the sea of Kīrimalai, near Nāgadīpa. Veṭiyarācaṉ was captured by Mīkāmān. One of Veṭiyarācaṉ's men escaped and told the sad news to the queen and to Veṭiyarācaṉ's younger brother Vīranarāṇan. The latter prepared to avenge his brother's defeat. Meanwhile the victorious Mīkāmān arrived in Nāgadīpa and offered the presents sent by Mānākar to the *nāga* king, who was seated in his gem-set throne, effulgent like the sun. Mīkāmān worshiped the *nāga* king. The latter, to test Mīkāmān's heroism, directed many poisonous snakes against him, but Mīkāmān, undaunted, continued to worship the *nāga* king. The king now took the form of an old Brahman and asked Mīkāmān the purpose of his visit. Mīkāmān told him, and the king was pleased. He consulted the *deva*s, sages, and seers around him and then, taking the shape of a red cobra, yielded a bright gem and once again took on the guise of a Brahman. He gave the gem to Mīkāmān, and also gave him a ring as a personal present. Mīkāmān set sail once again, and now he met the fleet of the *mukkuvār* Vīranarāṇan. A battle was fought with neither side victorious. Ultimately Vīranarāṇan challenged Mīkāmān to a duel, and Vīranarāṇan was killed. Now Vīranarāṇan's brother Viḷaṅkutēvaṉ organized a fleet and fought with Mīkāmān. The battle was costly for both sides, but again no one was victorious. Viḷaṅkutēvaṉ wanted a truce, but Mīkāmān insulted him by saying that he wanted both Viḷaṅkutēvaṉ and Veṭiyarācaṉ taken captive to Kāvirippūmpaṭṭinam. Then both agreed to a duel in Veṭiyarācaṉ's presence, but again no victory was won by either side. Then on Veṭiyarācaṉ's pleading the two contenders agreed to stop fighting. Mīkāmān permitted the two brothers to take their men and ships and go home, while Mīkāmān went his way and gave the cobra gem to Mānākar.

Comment: 1. Note that no one wins the war between *karaiyār*s and *mukkuvār*s, but the *karaiyār*s have a slight edge. This text was written from a *veḷḷāla* point of view; it indicates the traditional *mukkvār*/*karaiyār* hostility, but *veḷḷāla*s are outside this conflict as the dominant caste of the region. Their neutrality is expressed by the absence of victory; yet since the *karaiyār*s have a higher caste standing in *veḷḷāla* eyes they are given an edge over the *mukkuvār*s.

2. The Sinhala texts refer to the *nāga* gem in Pattini's anklet. The *nāga salaṁba* is one of her anklets. There are references in Sinhala texts to the anklet's being obtained from the *nāga* king, but no coherent text like that of the *Vaḻakkurai* is extant. The myth that the gem was obtained from the *nāga* king was common to both traditions but not to the *Cilappatikāram*. However, the reference to Mīkāmān and the *karaiyār*/*mukkuvār* conflict is a purely east coast localization of the myth.

The Kōvalaṉ-Kaṇṇaki-Mātavi Triangle

This relationship is very much in line with both the *Cilappatikāram* and the Sinhala texts, and I shall give only the briefest summary. The story of the wedding of Kōvalaṉ and Kaṇṇaki is described at length, yet, unlike the situation in the *Cilappatikāram*, there is no reference to their having consummated their marriage. Instead Kōvalaṉ falls in love with Mātavi (Mādēvi) on the fourth day after the formal wedding. Soon the account shifts to Mātavi, and here it is similar to the Sinhala and *Cilappatikāram* versions.

Ūrvaci was the divine dancer at Indra's court and as a result of a curse by Nārada she was born as Mātavi, the courtesan, daughter of Citrāpati. She was skilled in all the branches of music and drama. Kōvalaṉ was present at her debut at court and fell in love with her. The king gave Mātavi many gifts including a gold chain. He proclaimed that anyone who wished to have Mātavi should pay 1,008 *kalancu* of gold and buy the chain along with her, then give the money to her as a gift.[6] Struck by Kāma's arrow, Kōvalaṉ offered to pay the price. The gold chain was then placed on an elephant's back and paraded in the city streets. Kaṇṇaki, the wife of Kōvalaṉ, also felt very proud and happy. When the elephant passed by her house Kaṇṇaki paid her respects to the gold chain by placing a pot of water at the entrance to her house, lighting camphor, and performing a rite of lights (*āratti*). Later Kōvalaṉ placed the gold chain around Mātavi's neck and followed her to her house, where he made love to her.

Comment: What is striking in this account in contrast to both the *Cilappatikāram* and the Sinhala versions is Kaṇṇaki's (Pattini's) pride in her husband's conquest of Mātavi and her paying homage to the latter's necklace. It signifies her total, unquestioned devotion to

6. *Kalancu* is Sinhala *kalan*: forty grains.

her husband. The tying of the chain signifies that the Kōvalaṉ-Mātavi relationship is permitted and acceptable, yet it is not a legitimate marriage, since the chain is not a *tāli*.

The Story of the Demand for Gold

One day Kōvalaṉ ran short of the gold he was to pay to Mātavi. Mātavi's mother Citrāpati instructed her daughter to collect the entire amount due from Kōvalaṉ. But, Mātavi was reluctant to demand the full amount. She replied, "I have never spoken such words to Kōvalaṉ's face. Hence I shall convey this message through my maid." But her mother insisted that Mātavi herself should demand the gold. Mātavi consented, but she forgot to make the demand while she was with Kōvalaṉ. She asked her mother to be patient and promised to obtain the amount due the following day. Later, while she was spending happy hours with Kōvalaṉ exchanging sentiments of love, she told him what her mother had insisted on. Kōvalaṉ informed Mātavi that his ships were due from foreign lands in a month's time and that he would then pay the full sum. This conversation between Kōvalaṉ and Mātavi was overheard by a woman who repeated it to Kōvalaṉ's wife, Kaṇṇaki. Kaṇṇaki felt sorry for the plight of her husband; tears filled her eyes. Immediately she collected all her jewels and sent them through her maid to be given to Kōvalaṉ. She also sent word to Kōvalaṉ through the same maid that, though she had only her anklet left, it was enough for them to live on comfortably for a hundred years. The box of jewelry was taken to Kōvalaṉ. He opened the box and showed the contents to Mātavi. Kōvalaṉ invited a goldsmith and had the jewelry weighed. The goldsmith melted the jewels, weighed them, and handed over 1,008 *kalancu* of gold to Mātavi's mother, Citrāpati. Citrāpati found there was a small shortage in the weight of the gold and castigated her daughter. Mātavi lost her patience and, in defense of Kōvalaṉ, extolled his great qualities. But Citrāpati was not satisfied. She scolded Mātavi and told her to get rid of Kōvalaṉ. Accordingly, Mātavi persuaded Kōvalaṉ to go with her to watch the beauty of the bountiful waters flowing down the Poṉṉi river. Elaborate arrangements were made and, with a following of several maids, Mātavi and Kōvalaṉ were carried in a palanquin to the banks of the Poṉṉi river. All along the way both Mātavi and Kōvalaṉ were greeted by people with flowers and *āratti* lights. On reaching the riverbank, the maids anointed Mātavi's body with oil, applied *araippu* (a substance used to remove the oil and applied on the head and the body before bathing), and bathed her in the waters of the Kāviri. On finishing her bath, she dried her hair, put on new attire, and in the company of Kōvalaṉ feasted her eyes on the beauty of the Poṉṉi river. She showed Kōvalaṉ the spectacle of the flowing river water, carrying with it various trees such as *pātiri* (*Bigonia chelonoides*), *kētakai* (pandanus) *makiḻ* (*Miumsops elengi*), *cantāṉam* (sandalwood), and *vanni* (*Prospis specigera*) and the carcasses of animals such as tiger, bear, deer, and elephant. After enjoying the scenery of the Poṉṉi river and its natural surroundings, Kōvalaṉ was tormented by a sense of disillusion (which had crept into his mind earlier over the shortage in the gold he had given). It developed into a hatred, which prompted him to leave Mātavi by the riverside and return on foot to the city.

Kōvalaṉ's desertion of Mātavi by the riverside was permanent, and he never returned to her. Mātavi was grief-stricken. She was so weak and overcome by emotion that she had to be helped to her residence in the city by her maid Vayantamālai. Her desire for the love of Kōvalaṉ became unbearable. Her mother Citrāpati tried to console her and reminded her of the qualities expected of the members of her community (*kaṇikayar*). But Mātavi retorted that she was determined not to embrace anyone but Kōvalaṉ. Citrāpati begged her daughter Mātavi to give up her love for Kōvalaṉ. The inconsolable Mātavi bore a child by Kōvalaṉ, named Maṇimēkalai, who was her only comfort.

Mātavi sent Vayantamālai to her lover with a message, reminding him of the good times they had together. It was not her fault, but rather her mother who was angry at the shortage of the gold. She could not bear to suffer separation and begged him to come back. But Kōvalaṉ refused. He felt she had discarded him on the banks of the river.

Comment: Note that in both the Sinhala and the east coast versions Mātavi is in her own way devoted to Kōvalaṉ. Kōvalaṉ, by contrast, is fickle toward both wife and mistress. Also note that Mātavi is no ordinary harlot. Like Aṁbapāli, the courtesan of Vaiśālī in the early Buddhist texts, she is highly regarded by the citizens of the city.

The Reunion with Kaṇṇaki

Repentant, Kōvalaṉ came back to Kaṇṇaki. Kaṇṇaki told him that he could recover his wealth by selling her precious anklet. But he was reluctant to do so, for he said people would shame him for selling his wife's anklet. But she replied that he should sell it to none other than the king of Pāṇḍya himself. Ultimately he agreed, and Kaṇṇaki decided to go with him on the journey. She also advised him on the machinations of evil women, who abounded in Pāṇḍya's kingdom. But Kōvalaṉ professed his repentance. He said he would never have sexual intercourse with anyone save Kaṇṇaki. She cried; he consoled her and took her with him on the journey to Madurai.

The Journey to Madurai on Foot

Comment: In all three accounts the journey of Kaṇṇaki and Kōvalaṉ is mentioned in great detail, but the actual route taken is different in each case. The Sinhala account moves on an impersonal mythic level, whereas the *Cilappatikāram* and east coast accounts are geographically more specific.

Husband and wife left Kāvirippūmpaṭṭinam at sunrise and set out on foot. They passed Tiruvārūr, then toiled through a forest, suffering great hardship, till they reached the temple of Śrī Raṅkam and worshiped the god Raṅkanātaṉ. They rested here awhile and resumed their journey till they reached Uraiyur. Next morning they continued walking until they reached the banks of the Vaikai river, close to Madurai. They then came to a settlement of cowherders, who were kind to them and gave them food (nurturance). A cowherder named Mātari gave them accommodation.

Comment: The first indirect reference to lovemaking is during their stay in the cowherd settlement. There is reference to Kaṇṇaki's giving her husband the ceremonial offering of food before intercourse (Kandiah 1968, p. 280, verse 28). Then Kaṇṇaki eats milk rice, decorates herself, and spreads scented flowers on her bed. Her breasts, which are like young coconuts, swell; she cannot speak coherently; her waist chain becomes loose, and so do her bangles. They enjoy themselves in bed without worry or fear (Kandiah 1968, p. 180, verses 29, 30).

They stayed here a few days, then Kōvalaṉ set out for Madurai by himself. On the way he saw several evil omens (as in the Sinhala text, *bādāvaliya*, or "garland of omens"). He did not proceed to Madurai but came back to the cowherders' settlement. Again he set forth, and once more he saw evil omens. An oracle from the hill tribes practicing rice divination told him his life would be in danger and accurately predicted the events that would take place. Kōvalaṉ ignored this warning and, after propitiating Śiva, proceeded to Madurai.

Comment: 1. It is time to comment on the erotic aspect of the Kōvalaṉ-Kaṇṇaki relationship in the *Vaḻakkurai*. I have noted that the public view everywhere is unequivocal—Kaṇṇaki was never defiled by sexuality. This view is embodied in the Sinhala texts and in South Indian myths noted by Beck and Shulman (see p. 456), but not in the *Cilappatikāram*. There the lovemaking between Kaṇṇaki and Kōvalaṉ is spelled out in great poetic detail. So are the descriptions of Kaṇṇaki's beauty, including her cobra-hood pubis! In the *Vaḻakkurai* the reference to the erotic aspect of their relationship appears in three stages.

a. As I have noted, initially there is no consummation of their marriage. This fits in with popular conceptions of Kaṇṇaki's purity, but not with the conventions of classical poetry.

b. At their reunion Kōvalaṉ promises to have sexual intercourse with Kaṇṇaki and no one else. Yet there is no reference whatever in the text to lovemaking or intercourse.

c. Things are different in the cowherd village (incidentally, the setting for Kṛiṣṇa's eroticism). Though there are no direct references to lovemaking, the implications are very clear—it is implied that they did make love.

What can one make of these references (especially the last) that seem to flout the folk view of Pattini-Kaṇṇaki as undefiled by sexuality? The answer, I think, is that the *Vaḻakkurai* is not an anonymous folk poem but a carefully constructed poem by one Kaṅkēcan, and therefore it must follow accepted poetic conventions, including the prestigious example of the *Cilappatikāram*, which the author was familiar with. At the same time the *ritual* conventions must be maintained, and hence no references to lovemaking are implied till the couple actually reaches the cowherd settlement. Perhaps the author also felt he had to make a concession to the rights of marriage and therefore implies sexual intercourse at that time. Sociologically speaking, the occasion is right for intercourse: the repentant Kōvalaṉ has renounced his mistress and now goes back to his wife, thereby vindicating public morality. Yet this moral stance must meet the ritual stance of ordinary people, who affirm Pattini's purity and freedom from sexual pollution. The *Vaḻakkurai* postpones the socially legitimate sexual intercourse of Kaṇṇaki and Kōvalaṉ till the very end and even then leaves open the possibility for popular interpretation that they in fact did not have intercourse.

2. The cowherd's community is a refuge for Kaṇṇaki and Kōvalaṉ in both the *Cilappatikāram* and the *Vaḻakkurai*. The symbolism here is clear: in many societies cowherders are symbols of nurture and support owing to their association with milk-yielding animals.

3. Several articles in newspapers and popular Tamil journals have attempted to trace Pattini's journey from Kāvirippūmpaṭṭinam to Madurai and, after her apothesis, to the kingdom of Ceṅkuṭṭuvaṉ in Kerala (e.g., *Ananta Vikatan* [a Madras weekly], 27 February 1972, pp. 42–48; K. G. Krishnan in the *Hindu* of 12 February 1972). It was found that the places where Pattini stopped often were sites of abandoned Pattini temples; ergo, Pattini's journey and mythic biography were factual events. It is as if one read an Australian aboriginal myth that said water holes in such and such places were created by ancestors in the dream time. A "scholar" then verifies that in fact there are water holes in the places mentioned in native cosmography; ergo, the Australian myth that ancestors created

the water holes is true (in the naturalistic, demythicized sense). The existence of temple ruins in areas Pattini visited is to be expected, since the myth provides an a posteriori rationale for the existence of these places. The discovery of Troy by archaeologists cannot by itself prove the historical reality of the Trojan war.

The Execution of Kōvalaṉ

Kōvalaṉ went along the streets of Madurai announcing that the anklet was for sale. Failing to sell it, he consulted an astrologer in a school nearby. The astrologer read the position of the planets and told Kōvalaṉ it was a dangerous period for him. The astrologer accurately read Kōvalaṉ's past and predicted that a goldsmith would turn out to be an enemy and that Kōvalaṉ would be taken to the king, accused of theft, and later executed. Kōvalaṉ, in desperation, decided to return home. On the way he met a goldsmith. Kōvalaṉ told the goldsmith the purpose of his visit. The goldsmith said that such a valuable anklet could not be bought by any person save the king. The goldsmith took Kōvalaṉ to the king's palace. While Kōvalaṉ remained outside, the goldsmith went before the king and said: "The [royal] anklet which was lost has now been recovered by me, I have brought along the thief, who came to sell the anklet. Through fear he is waiting at the entrance of the palace." The king immediately ordered Kōvalaṉ to be brought before him. When questioned by the king, Kōvalaṉ gave a true account of his visit. The king told the goldsmith that Kōvalaṉ appeared to be innocent, but the goldsmith said no thief had ever admitted his theft and suggested Kōvalaṉ be killed. The king wanted to inquire further into the matter. He ordered that the anklet be shown to the queen for verification.

The goldsmith himself went to Kōpperuntēvi (Pāṇṭimātēvi), the queen, and addressed her: "Mother! I have brought the anklet that was once stolen from the king's palace, and also the thief. Could you say that this was the anklet that was stolen?" So saying, he showed the anklet. The queen was annoyed and said, "It is not proper to utter falsehoods; this anklet is not ours."

The goldsmith was disappointed. But he returned to the king and told him the anklet was the identical one that had been stolen from the palace. He suggested that it was proper the thief be killed. On hearing these harsh words, Kōvalaṉ was grief-stricken at his fate. He broke into tears. The Pāṇḍyan king, moved by pity, suggested that Kōvalaṉ be set free. But the goldsmith said justice would not prevail in the country if thieves were not killed. The king accepted the goldsmith's statement and ordered Kōvalaṉ's execution. On the orders of the king, Mēkanātaṉ, the best elephant in musth, was drugged and brought before the king, who directed it to kill Kōvalaṉ. Kōvalaṉ surrendered himself to God and stood still, saying, "Let the elephant kill me, if I am guilty." The elephant refused to move toward him in spite of all the efforts by the mahout. Instead it worshiped Kōvalaṉ with its trunk and withdrew. Seeing this, the goldsmith told the king that the elephant could not kill Kōvalaṉ because of his magic powers. Instead Kōvalaṉ should be killed with a battle-ax. The king ordered his messengers to call the executioner, Mālakaṉ.

The messengers went to the abode of Mālakaṉ and conveyed the orders of the king. The executioner asked his wife to bring the battle-ax; while bringing the battle-ax, she sneezed (a bad omen). She feared that some mishap might happen to the king and to the country. But Mālakaṉ ignored his wife's fears and proceeded to the king's palace. However, the evil omens he saw on his way made him to think that some calamity might happen to the city of Madurai. The executioner presented himself before the king. The king ordered

Mālakaṉ to kill Kōvalaṉ with the battle-ax, since he had avoided the elephant by his magic powers. Mālakaṉ, followed by Kōvalaṉ, went to the place of execution, northwest of the king's palace. Mālakaṉ inquired from Kōvalaṉ about the charges leveled against him. Kōvalaṉ mentioned the events that led him to his present fate, and the machinations of the goldsmith. Mālakaṉ realized the blot on the otherwise righteous rule of the Pāṇḍyan king owing to the evil schemes of the goldsmith. He called Kōvalaṉ to his side and told him: "You are not guilty. Hence I will not kill you, but will help you escape from this place. Instead of killing you, I shall kill a young deer with the battle-ax, and show the blood-stained ax to the king." But Kōvalaṉ did not agree. He replied: "I have earned the bad reputation of being a thief. I do not want to remain alive stigmatized as a thief. Hence as the god Tirumal tore up Iraṉiya, you may cut me into two pieces and carry out the orders of the king." Mālakaṉ bade Kōvalaṉ sit under a margosa tree nearby. Kōvalaṉ told Mālakaṉ to do his duty properly and sat down under the tree, with his head bowed and his thoughts on God. After raising the battle-ax thrice, Mālakaṉ executed Kōvalaṉ at the fourth stroke. Kōvalaṉ's body fell to the ground cut into two.

The Dream of Ammaṉ (Kaṇṇaki) and the Revival of Kōvalaṉ

Kaṇṇaki, who was in the house of the cowherdess, inferred from her dreams that some disaster had happened to her husband Kōvalaṉ. She related her dreams to the cowherdess. The cowherdess consoled her, but Kaṇṇaki later dreamed of seeing her husband's body on the funeral pyre. The cowherdess had similar dreams and was certain the Pāṇḍyan king and the city of Madurai were faced with danger. She set out to the city in search of Kōvalaṉ. Nowhere could she find him. In Kaṇṇaki's house the never-fading garland of flowers faded, a bad omen that indicated Kōvalaṉ was in danger. Kaṇṇaki was impatient. She left her house. With a branch of margosa leaves in one hand and her remaining anklet in the other, taking the appearance of Bhadrakālī, she rushed to the city of Madurai (Maturai).

As Kaṇṇaki entered the city of Madurai, she vowed she would send the Pāṇḍyan king to heaven and set Madurai on fire if any calamity had befallen her husband.

Tears flowing from her eyes and with hair disheveled she hurried up and down the streets of Madurai in search of her husband. Her thoughts went back to events in her previous birth. She thought of the evil that had befallen her husband Kōvalaṉ as a result of his association with Mātavi. The sun was about to set. At that time Kaṇṇaki overheard a group of women talking among themselves thus: "The king has ordered a person, accused by the palace goldsmith as a thief, to be killed without a proper inquiry." When she heard these words Kaṇṇaki's fury became worse. In a rage she exclaimed: "The Pāṇḍyan king has killed my husband. I shall devour his life and destroy his city, as Hanuman destroyed by fire Rāvaṇa's city." As she proceeded further, she heard from schoolchildren that the Pāṇḍyan king had ordered a stranger killed with a battle-ax. Kaṇṇaki asked one of the boys to show her the place of execution. The boy told her to follow him and pointed out the place where Kōvalaṉ's body was found. Kaṇṇaki gave the boy a ring. At the sight of Kōvalaṉ's dead body, Kaṇṇaki fell down unconscious. She soon regained her senses and rose up. She joined the two pieces of the body, fell over it, and wept. She looked up to the heavens and stretched out her hands. A beautiful gold needle fell into her hands. She pulled out a thread from the sari she wore. She stitched the two severed pieces together and spoke to her husband's corpse: "Dear, be hungry no longer; let us eat tasty food. Rise up and have your bath. If I were a true woman of chastity, you should live again and rise from the dead. Let us both go to heaven. Rise up." She wept. Kōvalan̲ awoke as if from a deep sleep. He related to Kaṇṇaki what happened in Madurai and the machinations of the goldsmith.

Kaṇṇaki listened to her husband's words and realized that fate was all powerful. She told Kōvalan̲ to go to Tēvakiri ("the abode of the gods") and remain there until she took revenge on the Pāṇḍyan king and set fire to the city of Madurai. As she said these words, Kōvalan̲'s life passed away again. Kaṇṇaki rose up. She praised God, the learned, and the kings and walked toward the city of Madurai.

The Story of the Prosecution

That night Pāṇṭimātēvi ("the Pāṇḍyan queen") awoke from the shock of a bad dream. She told the king she had dreamed of a sweet-voiced woman, with flowing hair and tearful eyes, an anklet in her hand, passing along the streets of Madurai. She had also dreamed that the royal elephant fell down and died; that lightning struck the sky-high *kōpuram* (temple dome), and that the city of Madurai was consumed by fire. The Pāṇḍyan king replied that nothing could be caused by dreams. At that time Kaṇṇaki had arrived at the palace entrance. She asked the guard whether this was the palace of the cruel sinner who called himself a king and had killed Kōvalan̲. The guard at the entrance was shocked at the appearance and words of Kaṇṇaki. He hurried to the king and told him that a woman resembling the goddess Durgā, with tearful eyes and an anklet in one hand and a branch of margosa leaves in the other, was waiting at the entrance. The king said, "Her grievance will be redressed. Let her come into the palace." The guard informed Kaṇṇaki that the king would see her. But Kaṇṇaki threatened to destroy the Pāṇḍyan king, who had killed a trader for the sake of his wealth, and said she would also set fire to Madurai. She wanted the Pāṇḍyan king to come to the entrance and meet her. The guard replied that it was not proper for the king to do so. Kaṇṇaki told the guard that she had in her possession an anklet containing the *nākamani* ("cobra gem"), that her husband had been killed, and that the lustful actions of Mātavi had started to have their repercussions on Madurai. She further said that the king's justice was blemished, since her husband had been executed without a proper inquiry. On hearing these harsh words, the Pāṇḍyan king descended from his throne and came to where Kaṇṇaki stood. He sat on an elevated seat before Kaṇṇaki. The moment he saw Kaṇṇaki, Lakṣmī, goddess of wealth, disappeared from the sight of the Pāṇḍyan king. Kaṇṇaki went before the king. She praised the priests, the royalty, the traders, and the farmers, then asked the king whether he was the person who had killed Kōvalan̲ through listening to the words of the deceitful goldsmith, instead of ruling the country in accordance with the laws of Mānu. The king advised her not to speak disrespectfully, but to state her name, her country, and then her grievance. Kaṇṇaki said she hailed from the land of Cōḷa, which had famous kings noted for their rule of justice and righteousness. She also stated the details of her birth and life and those of her husband Kōvalan̲. She said her anklet contained *nākamani* obtained from Nāgadīpa. She charged that the king had mistaken her anklet for the queen's. She related how they had lost all their wealth and had come to this city to sell one of her anklets. The Pāṇḍyan king, after listening to the charges, replied that persons found stealing had to be destroyed like weeds in a paddy field, irrespective of the community they belonged to. They had to be punished with death; that was justice. As for the disrespectful way Kaṇṇaki addressed him, the king said he forgave her since she was a woman.

Kaṇṇaki worshiped Śiva in her heart and displayed her anklet to the Pāṇḍyan king, saying, "If the queen states that this anklet containing *nākamani* belongs to her, I shall stop pursuing my case and leave this palace. If not, I shall definitely cause this city of Madurai to be consumed by fire." Immediately, the Pāṇḍyan king sent the anklet to the queen through a maid. The maid informed the queen of the argument between Kaṇṇaki and the king over the anklet and advised the queen to say the anklet was hers, since if the king lost the case the entire city of Madurai would be enveloped in flames and the Pāṇḍyan king would lose his life. The queen now realized the folly of having listened to the words of the goldsmith, but she was determined not to lie. She replied that the anklet did not belong to her. The maid went back to the king and said, "The queen swears upon the name of the god Śiva and states that the anklet does not belong to her and that the goldsmith was responsible for this."

The king ordered the messengers to bring the goldsmith, who came trembling in fear. "I relied on your words and had the person who brought this anklet executed. Now this woman, the wife of the dead man, is waiting to take revenge on me." The goldsmith told the king that Kaṇṇaki was a shrew and a thief and possessed magic powers. The Pāṇḍyan king agreed by nodding his head. Meanwhile Kaṇṇaki asked the king what was encased in the queen's anklet. The king replied that the queen's anklet contained pearls. Immediately Kaṇṇaki asked for her anklet. The king was diffident. The ministers, seeing the king's embarrassment, told Kaṇṇaki to get down the anklet herself, if it was indeed hers. Kaṇṇaki thought of God and called for the anklet four times. On the fourth call the anklet descended into her hand. The Pāṇḍyan king said the anklet in her hand contained a different type of gem. He advised Kaṇṇaki to stop arguing her case, since she would lose. Kaṇṇaki dashed the anklet down in the center of the hall. The anklet burst and pieces of the valuable *nākamani* ("gem of the cobra") flew in the face of the Pāṇḍyan king. The king realized he had erred, and, like a person who has taken poison, he fell down dead. Those assembled were overtaken by fear and confusion and prayed to Kaṇṇaki to save their lives. Thereafter she scooped out her left breast and destroyed Madurai by fire.

The Cooling of Kaṇṇaki

After setting fire to Madurai Kaṇṇaki returned to the cowherd's quarter. The cowherdess cooled her breast with ghee and covered it with cotton and prayed to her. She prophesied that the fire would not reach their village. The cowherdesses then purified themselves and cooked a meal of rice and invited Kaṇṇaki to partake of it. But Kaṇṇaki in anger asked them how she could eat when her husband was dead. She then ordered them to go collect the anklet, which was still lying in the king's palace. They then prayed her to cool down and eat the food they offered. This she did. They then asked her to forgive them and create rain so that Madurai would be cooled. She agreed and blessed Madurai with rain, abundance of crops, and prosperity.

Comment: Though there are considerable differences between the east coast version and the Sinhala accounts, the basic plot is the same. However, nowhere on the east coast is the drama of Kōvalaṉ's resurrection enacted. On the east coast the cooling of Kaṇṇaki's (Pattini's) anger is more important than the theme of Kōvalaṉ's resurrection. This fits in with many South Indian folk rituals where the goddess is cooled (e.g., Srinivas 1976, p. 301). On the east coast the invocation of the goddess is in May, the height of the dry season. Thus the cooling rituals make sense here. Among the Sinhalas of the west coast, who have abundant rain, this is not as crucial. They have to ensure a proper balance of rain and sun; hence the water cutting and fire trampling rituals discussed earlier.

Text 58 *Kaṇṇaki Ammaṉ Kulirtti Pātal*, or the Songs on the Cooling of Kaṇṇaki

This is a famous text sung all over the east coast. It clearly illustrates the theme discussed earlier (pp. 43–44), where the goddess's anger is linked to drought and propitiating her cools her anger and brings coolness, rain, and fertility to the earth. The present text is from Tambiluvil, but it is identical with Kandiah's (1968, pp. 432–45) though the numbering of the stanzas is slightly different. The translation is not strictly literal; however, the important verses singled out for comment have been literally translated.

1. There appeared a young woman of godly nature
in the family of traders
and she was destined to marry
a young man named Kōvalaṉ, son of a wealthy trader.

2. This lady married Kōvalaṉ, whose father's name was Mānākar(?)
Because her husband lost all her wealth, by becoming
attached to a dancer Mātavi by name, they had to leave their
home to find their fortunes elsewhere.

3. She left her home and gave her pet parrot
to her friends to look after.

4. They walked a great distance, and during the
middle of their journey, he left Kaṇṇaki in the
care of the ascetic Kavunti.

5. Seated on the bank of the river Vaikai
sorrowfully Kavunti wished that
Kōvalaṉ may have all good luck.

6. Birds like the swans, herons, cranes, and pigeons
kept company with them.
Kōvalaṉ got into a palanquin
and reached the street of the cowherd community.

7. His past karma was responsible for his separation
from his wife; it impelled him to seek his fortune
by trade. Forced by *karma*, he left Kaṇṇaki at
iṭaicēri [the settlement of cowherds] and went
into Madurai for trade.

8. Karma made him offer one of the anklets of Kaṇṇaki
for sale in a merchant's shop. Alas, he did not
even know the real price he should ask for it.

9. The merchants remarked that the price was too much and declined to buy it. So Kōvalaṉ walked to the street where goldsmiths had their shops and offered it for sale.

10. The goldsmiths to whom he showed the anklet asked him to be seated in the shop and, running up to the king, he told to him he had caught the thief who stole the queen's anklet given to him for repairs.

11. The king who was hitherto sinless decided to put Kōvalaṉ to the sword and he had the innocent Kōvalaṉ killed.

12. Kaṇṇaki with a long bunch of hair dreamed of the great tragedy that befell her husband. She at once decided to proceed to Madurai and burn it.

13. Mātari requested Kaṇṇaki to be seated and calm down and said the proposal to burn the capital of Madurai should not be the aim of a lady of great rank and position.

14. So Kaṇṇaki with resignation and sorrow proceeded to the place where her husband was beheaded. She put the severed head back on the body. By the power of her chastity Kōvalaṉ regained his life and told her what had happened to him.

15. The great injustice and sin committed by the Pāṇḍyan king encircled defiled Madurai like a fire; and the plaited one [Kaṇṇaki] fanned the flames by throwing in her breast.

16. The cowherds' wives when they heard of this came running with a hundred vessels full of ghee, and after worshiping at the feet of Kaṇṇaki poured ghee on the fire-emanating breast.

17. Then Cīttalai Cāttaṉ came toward the lady, who had meanwhile cooled down, and said: "O lady of fragrant hair, do not suffer but be gracious."

18. [Kaṇṇaki replied] "O lord I worship your feet; let the settlement of the cowherds be cooled, I will return in the month of Vaikāci [May]," and she treated him with the same courtesy.

19. The companion Mātari and the garlanded lady, who now had become herself, ascended to the heavens so that

the world will prosper, and there she was welcomed by the celestials.

20. She walked slowly toward the holy temple and into the doorway of the inner shrine; she was perfection itself as she walked into the inner shrine of the virgin's own temple.

This reference must be to a central shrine of the goddess, a shrine that was consecrated by her physical presence.

21. Kaṇṇaki with the lush perfumed hair, the one who lost her husband and was separated from him; the ladies decked in their best ornaments danced the *ammāṉai* in her presence.

22. Garlanded and beautiful ladies danced around Kaṇṇaki of the golden hue, whose long hair is like the peahen's; she who was as beautiful as a garland was honored with the *ammāṉai*.

23. With eyes sharp as spears, possessed with the beauty of gold, her presence permeates the world.

24. By destroying with fire the city of the southern king, who was not in his right senses, she came to be praised by all as Pattini; and there she stood and [she also] danced the *ammāṉai*.

25. The world worshiped her as the most virtuous woman when she cooled the city with her songs.

26. She started singing and dancing with her hair loaded with fragrant garlands of flowers and urged the seven worlds to live better. Heavenly beings hearing these songs admired her.

27. Her belly was shaped like a bo tree leaf, her eyes were like lotuses: with her blessings rain started, poured over the earth, to benefit farmers to reap a better harvest.

28. She sang praying that all women may shine in their homes with all her blessings; that poets and learned men may live long in comfort; and that the king may rule the country with justice.

29. She sang to give blessings for women to live in peace and harmony with their husbands and she sang these with the anklet on her head.

30. The peerless [*orumā*] Pattini came so that the seven worlds may flourish and prosper. The great jewellike maiden came so that the whole land may prosper and flourish.

31. She came into this large world, and then she came to this [small] cowherd settlement to save them. She came as a person who loves the cowherds [*pālakār*s]. Yes, indeed she came, the peerless [*orumā*] Pattini.

This is an important verse. It illustrates the idea I mentioned in the previous chapter: the cowherds are the ideal, devoted flock, as in the Kṛiṣṇa myths. It is also clear that the term *pālakār* is not just "lord" or "guardian" but *kōpālakār*, guardian of the cow. All devotees are *pālakār*s in the extended and symbolic sense. In a similar sense the city of the cowherds (stanza 78 below) is any city of the goddess's devotees.

In this text, as in many others sung on the east coast, Kaṇṇaki, after her destruction of Madurai, is referred to as Pattini (unlike Kerala, where the myths no longer employ this term). In one text sung in Tambiluvil (*kaṇṇaki amman kāviam*) the term Pattini is used all the time. It seems clear that the east coast tradition, like the Sinhala, is closer to the older traditions of the cult, as embodied in the *Cilappatikāram*.

32. A courageous and virtuous lady came to the playing grounds to cause the Pāṇḍyan king who fell from justice to die. She came and cut her right breast and threw it at him.

33. O lady who spoke gently, lady who came to raise a fallen [husband]; O lady with the sharp eyes who came to the playing grounds.

34. She came and assembled the severed body of Kōvalan, and questioned him as to what happened.

35. The good lady came to break her anklet, which had the costly gems inside it; she threw it on the floor in front of the king, to prove her case; and she won her case.

36. Lady who is the patron of the whole world; who rules the three worlds; O goddess of the three worlds who dwells in the lotus flower and she who came into the *yādava* [Sanskrit, "cowherd"] settlement that they might prosper.

In this stanza Pattini is identified with Pārvatī, since the above attributes are associated with the latter. In this verse Pattini is referred to as *ātiraiyāl*, which is the feminine of *ātiraiyān*, an appellation of Śiva.

37. This lady came to burn the city of Madurai, the city

renowned in this wide world; and this is the lady who rose up to the heavens with her husband Kōvalaṉ.

38. The lady came to argue her case against the Pāṇḍyan of great majesty, and won the case.

39. With her hair decked in beautiful flowers falling down, she walked through the jungle. With her sharp eyes like the spear she destroyed the wealth and the palace of the Pāṇḍyan whose flag bore the fish as its ensign. O lady please calm and cool down.

40. O lady who came with a mighty anger against the king and destroyed his wealth, calm down, so that the learned may live long; you must come to cool down the seven worlds.

41. O lady with spearlike sharp eyes, you cursed and destroyed the king. You walked behind Kōvalaṉ, disregarding your feet pained by walking through the wild forest, calm and cool down.

42. O lady with unfading flowers on her hair who came to Madurai through the jungle with your maids, who destroyed the richest of kings, calm and cool down.

43. You came to Madurai with burning eyes, radiating flashes of fire, you came with anger against the king and reduced the city of Madurai to ashes, calm and cool down.

44. O lady calm down, you did not even wait to inquire whether it was true that Kōvalaṉ was beheaded, you straightaway killed the king with your anger.

45. O lady who looked like the peacock and walked like that bird, you came in search of the place where your husband was beheaded; your wrath against the king descended from the moon, calm and cool down.

46. O lady of the merchant community who lived at Kāvirippūmpaṭṭinam near the sea, calm and cool down.

47. Please don't be seated in the shade of the young margosa tree, please don't suffer, O lady of great virtue, calm and cool down.

48. O lady who blessed the god of love and urged him to obtain the jewel from the cobra, calm and cool down.

49. O lady of blameless family of very great *nāgas*, O mother who wears the gem of a cobra, calm and cool down.

50. O virgin goddess who forgave and walked behind your husband and thereby lost all your wealth on account of him and when he came repentant you followed him, calm and cool down.

51. O lady you departed from Kāvirippūmpaṭṭinam and then entered a city [Madurai] with flowers, calm and cool down.

52. O lady you entered this garden of flowers with your holy Kavunti, please calm and cool down.

53. O lady who got into a boat and crossing the river Kāviri reached Madurai the rich city which no one can possess, please calm and cool down.

54. O mother when you walked the sweet voice of the birds entered your ears and consoled you, please calm and cool down.

55. O lady you walked through roads where coconut trees shed their fruits, and sweet mango fruits dropped down from the trees, calm and cool down.

56. By following Kōvalaṉ to the city of the Pāṇḍyan you walked in the path of Durgā, please calm and cool down.

57. You entered O beautiful lady into Madurai city in whose tanks fishes sport, calm and cool down.

58. The anklet you wore on your foot, you gave it to Kōvalaṉ for trade and you followed him, calm and cool down.

59. After the murder of Kōvalaṉ, you dreamed of that incident and went forth to make inquiries, calm and cool down.

60. You told the cowherd women of your dream and you became very angry and then proceeded to Madurai, calm and cool down.

61. You went in search of the place of execution where your husband lost his life, and you with your great love and devotion brought him back to life, calm and cool down.

62. You wept saying, "O my husband did you die in the presence of the goldsmith and were you cruelly beheaded?" calm and cool down.

63. You heard all what Kōvalaṉ told you of his execution and then you commanded him to climb the chariot, calm down and cool down.

64. You controlled the rage that came over you when you reached the Pāṇḍyan, you made him shiver with fear and shame, calm and cool down.

65. You went across to palatial gates and you faced the Pāṇḍyan who was frightened to behold you, calm and cool down.

66. "Kōvalaṉ, my husband who knew no evil, why did you get him beheaded? What wrong has he done?" you asked, calm and cool down.

67. You showed him your anklet with gems inside it, and you killed the king without physically injuring him, calm and cool down.

68. You pulled out your right breast out of sorrow and rage, and threw it like a flaming torch to burn the city, calm and cool down.

69. The king ran through seven doors and the breast followed him and killed him by striking his chest.

70. "Kaṇṇaki has killed me because I killed Kōvalaṉ, and I have thereby sinned": thus cried the Pāṇḍyan and threw himself down.

71. O lady you burned the city and burned the goldsmith and the king to ashes, calm and cool down.

72. For the acts against justice, you burned the great city of Madurai and thus you were avenged, and this act is a miracle, calm and cool down.

73. You heard the voice of the goddess of Madurai from the heavens, calm down a little and let your anger cool down.

74. The foolish king who did a great wrong, his city you destroyed, and then you returned to the cowherds' home, calm and cool down.

75. You entered the cowherds' home with the remaining breast and the scar of the other breast.

76. The cowherd women ran inside their homes and brought ghee and applied it to the scar.

77. O beloved of the cowherds, O swanlike lady, please don't burn the cowherds' home, calm and cool down.

78. Whatever cities you may burn, please don't burn this city of the cowherds; as your scarred breast is cooled by the application of butter, let your anger also cool down.

79. O lady who descended down from the great *nāga* race and who wore a serpent gem, calm and cool down.

80. The unthinking king suffered and you burned his city and you ascended to the heavens, calm and cool down.

81. You destroyed the king's city as you had wished, then you ascended to heaven to live in happiness, calm and cool down.

82. You entered the chariot driven by the *deva*s, and you are living with Kōvalaṉ forever, calm and cool down.

83. O pigeons let us pray to the waning moon with folded arms. O you pigeons pronounce the sacred "Oṃ Namaśivāya."

84. O beautiful pigeons bring the betel leaves and let us hope that illnesses and diseases will leave us.

The reference is probably to the Paṭṭimeṭu shrine where the goddess Pattini is worshiped in the form of a golden pigeon. Hence pigeons are sacred creatures in this shrine. Hugh Nevill (1887) has a detailed account of pigeon worship at Paṭṭimeṭu. He says the tradition there is that Pattini worship was introduced from Sītāvaka, the capital of Rājasiṃha I (1581–93). Rājasiṃha also built an impressive *dēvāle* for this goddess.

85. We say let us grow like the bo tree, and let us root in the earth like the *arukam* grass, and like the bamboo let us branch forth and increase in number.

86. May the cattle increase and let there be plenty of milk cows and may all those who live today live forever.

87. Let the cowherds live like pillars of stone, and long live the rice plants.

88. May those who sang these songs live long, and may those who heard these songs live long, and may there be no sickness and disease among those who have heard these songs.

89. Let everyone praise the *Cilappatikāram* whose words are sweet like honey, let them sing those songs daily forever.

90. Today and forever let those who honor this great story live forever and ever.

The Authorship of Texts: Iḷaṅkō Aṭikaḷ and Cīttalai Cāttaṉ

I shall not belabor the differences between the east coast traditions, the Sinhala traditions, and those embodied in the *Cilappatikāram* except to note the local contextualization of the myth and the identification of Pattini with Pārvatī in text 58, verse 36. This is clearly a later interpolation, not warranted by the internal evidence of the texts. I shall focus primarily on text 58, on the cooling of Pattini, since it has references to traditions embodied in the *Cilappatikāram* and thus illustrates the continuity of these traditions into the present.

The *Vāḻakkurai* (text 57) is nevertheless important for understanding the authorship and composition of ritual texts. The author's name is cited as Kaṅkēcan. I noted in chapter 1 that several of the Sinhala texts state the names of their authors. In this kind of situation it is most likely that the authors would adapt preexisting ritual texts to suit the local cultural context. In the Sinhala case it is virtually certain that the authors of the texts adapted Tamil ritual texts to the Sinhala context. On the east coast the author of the *Vāḻakkurai*, Kaṅkēcan, gave the myths of the Pattini cult local contextualization. The tradition of writing down preexisting ritual texts (perhaps from oral tradition) in elegant literary form must have given the authors both social prestige and religious merit. In fact this tradition continues to the present day, since several of my informants have composed verses of praise in honor of Pattini. Kaṅkēcan, the author of the *Vāḻakkurai*, seems to have been aware of the older traditions, particularly those associated with Iḷaṅkō Aṭikaḷ. Stanza 7, on page 144 of Kandiah's edition, reads: "*saranam* [hail!] to sweet Tamil, in which the sage Akastiyar [Agastya] spoke because of the noble deeds of his past life; in this same language I shall tell you one of the stories [or "part of the story"] told by Iḷaṅkō Aṭikaḷ." The tradition is strong that Iḷaṅkō Aṭikaḷ wrote some of these stories. A similar tradition prevails in the water cutting ritual practiced by Sinhalas in Aṅbokke (about fifteen miles north of Mātalē; this ritual is not described in this work). The water cutting text is prefaced with the following:

Ilaṅgō paňḍivarā demalayen kavikarā.

The scholar Ilaṅgō composed these verses in Tamil [originally].

Iḷaṅkō, then, is not simply the author of the *Cilappatikāram*; in popular tradition he is the eponymous author of many Pattini texts. In this regard note that the statement of Iḷaṅkō Aṭikaḷ's authorship of the *Cilappatikāram* does not appear in the body of that epic at all, but rather is cited in one of the prefaces (*patikam*), which in all likelihood was added later. If this is so he is probably not the actual historical author of that work, but a traditional eponymous author of several Pattini texts.

Iḷaṅkō is an *aṭikaḷ*. The *Cilappatikāram* is clear that *aṭikaḷ*s were Jaina and Buddhist ascetics. It is interesting that the stanza referring to Iḷaṅkō quoted earlier begins with the exclamation *saranam*! This term is from the *pāli* of Buddhism and means "refuge." The existence of a Buddhist idiom in a verse that refers to Iḷaṅkō once again suggests a survival from an original Jaina-Buddhist context of the cult.

In the *Cilappatikāram* a poet called Cāttaṉ invites Iḷaṅkō Aṭikaḷ to write a poem on the events of Pattini's life. Cāttaṉ claims to have seen the actual events when Pattini destroyed Madurai (Dikshitar 1939, pp. 77–90). It is striking that the same poet appears in text 58, stanza 17, translated above. Here Cīttalai Cāttaṉ pleads with Pattini and urges her to calm down. She replies: "O lord I worship your feet; let the settlement of the cowherds be cooled, I will return in the month of Vaikāci [May]." And then she went up to heaven. A similar reference is found in the *kaṇṇaki ammaṉ kāviam* ("song of Kaṇṇaki Amman") sung in Tambiluvil (not translated here). According to stanza 17 of this poem Cāttaṉ came to the cowherds' settlement when their womenfolk were cooling Pattini's breasts with butter. Soon afterward (stanza 18) Pattini cooled down, danced the *ammāṉai* (a folk dance), and blessed those assembled. In the next stanza (19) Cīttalai Cāttaṉ asks Pattini when she will appear in the human world again. Pattini replies that she would come every year in May, and then departs to the celestial world. In this stanza Cāttaṉ is referred to as the person "who had a water lily in his head so that when he bent down he would hurt himself."

According to all Tamil scholars Cāttaṉ (Cīttalai Cāttaṉ) is the author of *Maṇimēkalai*, the sequel to the *Cilappatikāram*. But who is he? The preface (*patikam*) to the *Cilappatikāram* says that he belonged to the (sub) caste of corn handlers (*kūlavāṇikaṉ*). Post-fourteenth-century commentators on the *Cilappatikāram* interpret his name "Cīttalai" as "pus head," from the legend that he used to pierce his head with the writing stylus. But this later meaning seems unlikely, though it is uncritically accepted by most scholars. According to the Tamil lexicon, *cāttaṉ* is a term for a Buddhist arhat, or even for the Buddha. The former meaning seems highly apposite, since Cāttaṉ was the supposed author of *Maṇimēkalai*, which has plenty of Buddhist philosophical discourses. Thus I shall tentatively gloss *cāttaṉ* as arhat or, better, "a Buddhist religious specialist." Now the names of the two authors make sense—Iḷaṅkō is an *aṭikaḷ*, a Jaina ascetic, and Cāttan is a Buddhist religious specialist. But what kind of specialist? The author's first name, "Cīttalai," gives us the clue. It is more plausible to derive *cīttalai* from the Sanskrit *sītala*, "cool." Thus, according to my line of thought, Cāttaṉ is not an arhat-type religious specialist but a Buddhist healer. In the east coast text he appears in the context of the *cooling* of the goddess; he intercedes on behalf of the folk and asks her to be gracious (forgiving). It is through him that Pattini informs people that she will return in May (for temple festivities). In the east coast texts Pattini addresses him with great courtesy as "lord." Thus he is also a superior religious specialist—if indeed these myths embody an older tradition—a Buddhist healer who "cools."

But what about the legend of his piercing his head with the stylus? A related tradition exists in the Tambiluvil poems, where his head suffers great pain as a result of a "water lily in his head." Note that both connotations are present here: water lily, representing "coolness," and the pain in the head. I take the tradition of Cāttaṉ's head pain seriously. Piercing the head with pointed objects is found among Sufis in South and Southeast Asia; and also among some contemporary practitioners of the goddess cult in Kerala. These latter, known as *veḷiccapāṭu*, go into a trance state where they identify with the goddess;

then, in this state, they mutilate their heads with a curved sword (see the appendix to this chapter for a description of Kerala *veḷiccapāṭu*). In line with my psychological interpretation in chapter 11, I interpret head piercing or cutting as displaced castration to secure identity with the goddess. If so, it is possible that the term Cāttaṉ does not refer to an actual Buddhist monk or arhat; rather, it may be used in a symbolic sense as a "castrated person," as much as Pālaṅga is referred to as *terrunānse* or *śramaṇa* (both meaning Buddhist monk), which he clearly is not. He is a Buddhist, though not a monk; he was probably a devotee or priest of the mother-goddess cults. It is tempting to speculate that Iḷaṅkō Aṭikaḷ was a similar figure, in which case *some* Jaina *aṭikaḷ*s combined their asceticism with the cult of the mother goddess and had a role similar to the present-day *aṭikaḷ*s of the Kālī shrine at Koṭuṅkoḷūr. It is also certain that Cāttaṉ is metamorphosed into the enigmatic deity Sāta, who appears in several places in the Sinhala texts (see pp. 270–72). Sāta, like Cāttan of the east coast texts, also appears when Pattini is propitiated after the destruction of Madurai. It is doubtful whether he was an actual historical figure at all, and he was no more the author of the *Maṇimēkalai* than Iḷaṅkō Aṭikaḷ was author of the *Cilappatikāram*.

The Sanskritization of the Pattini Cult

The Apotheosis of Pālaṅga

The Pattini cult as institutionalized in the Sinhala areas incorporates little or no Hinduism. Among the east coast Tamils it is also fundamentally a folk cult, except in Tambiluvil and Karaitivu, where Sanskritization is already in full swing. It is true that the entry of Sanskritic elements into folk myth and ritual is inevitable in South Asian religion, but often these elements are not of great significance. For example, Pattini is viewed as an incarnation of Pārvatī or of Kālī, but this becomes manifest only when she destroys Madurai. It is of little significance in the ritual and for most of the myth, except in Mulaitivu (see pp. 447–48).

At the level of folk religion Pālaṅga-Kōvalaṉ poses few problems; he is simply the husband of the goddess. This also poses no problems for a folk religion within a great tradition like Buddhism (or any of the heterodox religions). But not so for Hinduism, where the goddess is an aspect of the male deity, his *śakti*. In such a case a real problem arises in respect to Kōvalaṉ, which must in the long run result in his being deified and incorporated into formal Brahmanic Hinduism. For most villagers there is no such problem until they are confronted with the pressures of Sanskritization. Thus even in parts of Kerala (see pp. 541–50) Kōvalaṉ, or Pālakār, as he is called, is the human consort of Kaṇṇaki rather than a divinity. Among the east-coast Tamils of Sri Lanka too he is not deified, except in Tambiluvil and Karaitivu. True, Kōvalaṉ is called Sāmi, or lord, but it means only that he is the "lord of the goddess"—her spouse. He is not offered special *pūjā*s or treated in any way as a deity in most folk shrines in the Batticaloa district; nor is he housed in a special shrine, except again in Tambiluvil and Karaitivu (and also among the Sinhalas of Pānama).

Pānama constitutes a special case, since it is a bilingual and to a great extent a biracial community. For example, in the same family there can be siblings with Sinhala names like Baṇḍa and Tamil-Hindu names like Subramaniam. Very likely Pānama had both Sinhala-

and Tamil-speaking communities that later became amalgamated through marriage. The rituals of Pānama seem to have been influenced by the east coast Hindus. Thus they seem to have adopted a deified Kōvalan̠ (Sāmi), probably from Tambiluvil, with whom they contract affinal alliances. In Pānama Kōvalan̠ is called Alut Deviyo ("new god"), a category term used in other parts of Sri Lanka as an alias for a newly introduced deity or one recently deified.

While it is true that with Sanskritization there is immediately instigated a process of deification of Pālaṅga, the latter is a poor candidate for divinity. He is a passive, weak, inconstant, "castrated" person. In Sinhala Buddhism he has little chance for promotion, since all its gods have the opposite features: strength, might, glory. In higher Hinduism too, in spite of certain ambiguities in the roles of Śiva and Skanda, the gods are very positive figures, with the exception of Gaṇeśa, whose case I will take up later. Yet in spite of this Kōvalan̠ is deified in some of the traditions of the east coast that have recently been subject to Sanskritization. But given that he is a weak candidate, and given the assimilative character of Hinduism, he must ultimately be replaced altogether or identified as an avatar of a more positive deity.

Often going with Sanskritization is another feature of social change—a move from matriliny to patriliny. Brahmanic Hinduism in general favors a patriarchal ideology, if not always a patrilineal kinship system. The relationship of father and son is, for example, crucial to the formal ideology of filial piety, ritualism, and the ancestor cult of Brahmanic Hinduism, whereas the mother's brother/sister's son relationship has no such significance. In addition to these influences of formal Hinduism on traditional matriliny, there are always the influences stemming from the modern state in recent times and from demographically dominant outside communities that are given to a patriarchal rather than an avuncular ideology, particularly in the realms of authority relations. Thus all over the east coast there is a move toward patriliny, the only exception being the inheritance of temple property and office, which in some villages (e.g., Paṭṭimeṭu) is still on matrilineal lines. Thus the decline of matriliny is, I shall show, related to the elevation of Kōvalan̠ even though he is a poor candidate for divinity in Buddhism and Hinduism.

Basically the relationship between matriliny and the rise and persistence of the Kōvalan̠ cult is not a simple, direct one, but rather is based on a rise in the conception of the male role, patrilineal inheritance of property rights, and a broad-based patriarchal ideology.

It is clear that neither Pattini nor Kōvalan̠ could be characterized as the presiding deity of a matriline, since on the east coast the division of the teams is patrilineal (excepting Tambiluvil). Nevertheless I argue that the deification of the consort has been partially influenced by the challenge to matriliny on the east coast. Or rather the deification process, once started as a result of Sanskritization, gets a fillip from a related process—the patriarchal ideology of Sanskritic Hinduism. I shall use the Sinhala village of Pānama to illustrate these processes rather than the Tamil matrilineal villages, since I have the relevant observational data for the former.

If we examine the formal myths of Pattini as they are sung in both Pānama and the Tamil areas, we note that there is no reference to Alut Deviyo or Sāmi as a god. In this sense all the formal myths of the Pattini cult treat Pālaṅga-Kōvalan̠ simply as the human consort of the goddess. Yet while myth does not give Alut Deviyo divine status, ritual and behavior sometimes do. There is a lag between myth and current ritual and beliefs. Again the inference is that the current attitudes are a product of recent changes that have not been incorporated into formal myth. Furthermore, various degrees of importance and recognition are given to him. For example, in Pānama (Sinhala) and Tambiluvil (Tamil) there are separate shrines for Sāmi or Alut Deviyo, but this is not true in Paṭṭimeṭu and Vīramunai—both Tamil villages—which again suggests that we are dealing with recent changes in ritual organization that have not been institutionally stabilized throughout the region.

Pattini is a female deity, both mother and wife; as wife she is the embodiment of devotion and chastity. The worship of this deity in no way involves the loss of male prestige, since Sinhalas and Tamils also propitiate male deities like Skanda (Kataragama), Gaṇeśa, and Viṣṇu, who take precedence over Pattini in the overall pantheon. However, in the context of the *aṅkeḷiya* ritual itself she is the presiding deity, superior to her consort. What has happened on the east coast is that, owing to changes mentioned earlier, people have found it necessary to emphasize the husband role and the importance of the male line in terms of inheritance and succession, and Alut Deviyo has become the vehicle for expressing and affirming patriliny and for its ritual legitimation. This affirmation received impetus from the ritual context itself, for it fit in with the upper team's motivation to enhance the status of their team. Thus my conclusion: the apotheosis of Kōvalaṉ into Alut Deviyo in Pānama is due to contact with the Sanskritized religion of Tambiluvil, where apotheosis had already occurred as part of a larger Sanskritization process. The new god (Alut Deviyo) then becomes a vehicle for a challenge to matriliny.

Once apotheosis has occurred, fundamental problems of precedence and status must be resolved in the organization of the ritual. Pattini is clearly the presiding deity of the *aṅkeḷiya*; the myths unequivocally affirm her superior status. She also overcame and defeated Pālaṅga in the prototypical game of *aṅkeḷiya*. Yet Alut Deviyo is also a deity and is superior by virtue of being a male. Thus a fundamental problem of precedence arises: in the proceedings of the ritual, who should have precedence, Pattini or Alut Deviyo? This problem is neatly resolved in the Pānama *aṅkeḷiya* in the following manner:

1. In all formal events, like the parade of the deities, Alut Deviyo heads the procession, followed by Pattini. This affirms the higher "social status" of Alut Deviyo as a male. This procedure is also applicable to Tambiluvil and Karaitivu.

2. Yet this is reversed in the circumambulation rites, where the Pattini procession performs clockwise ("left to right") circumambulation, which is superior and propitious, whereas the Alut Deviyo procession performs a counterclockwise ("right to left"), inferior mode of circumambulation (see p. 388). These symbolic actions affirm Pattini's superior "ritual status" in the ongoing proceedings. These acts are of the highest importance and are considered by the officials of Pānama to be the "law of the place." These distinctions are not maintained elsewhere in the Sinhala areas, where all rites of the *aṅkeḷiya*—almost all religious rituals—are performed with clockwise circumambulation.

Pālaṅga's team, I suggested, would attempt to push the claims of the male deity to bolster its own prestige. It was possible for them to do so, since both teams had a general wish to affirm the status of the male deity as a vindication of patriliny. These symbolic actions in ritual are a kind of dialectical expression of social processes. But these processes, if carried too far, can upset the ideology underlying the *aṅkeḷiya*, the ritual superiority of Pattini over her consort. I will discuss how this theologically crucial idea was upset in the period 1960–66 but was restored in 1967.

On the fourteenth day of the *aṅkeḷiya* ritual held in 1967 the goddess Pattini was conducted through the village in procession (see pp. 391–92). This was a revival of the traditional practice that had been abandoned between 1960 and 1966, when an important innovation took place—*both* deities were ceremonially taken in procession through the village. According to the villagers this was due to the sheer fact of demographic increase, which made it impossible for the Pattini procession to visit every household in the village and perform the requisite ritual. Thus both deities paraded the village—the Alut Deviyo procession going to the households of their team members, and Pattini to the lower-team households. I see this innovation as a logical culmination of the processes described earlier. The demographic factor was a convenient rationale for the upper team to get this change accepted. Yet once the change was accepted and implemented several problems were bound to arise.

In accordance with the rules governing precedence, Alut Deviyo had to head the procession into the village. This is a logical step, but it had serious implications. When this occurs within the shrine premises, it is immediately counterbalanced by the circumambulation rites, which affirm the higher ritual status of Pattini. But no such actions are possible in the main procession. The theory underlying the procession is that the deity parades the *sīmā*, the territory over which she has authority. The deity visits every household in the village and blesses each one of them. The principle of heat that causes illness and natural disaster and accident is quelled by the goddess, as the prototypic fire in Madurai was quelled. This idea is given expression in the simple rite where the chief male of the household takes two or three lighted wicks and holds them between two fingers under the thatched roof of the house. The *kapurāla*, on behalf of the goddess, sprays the wicks with turmeric water (heat:cold), extinguishes the fire, and utters the Pānama version of the quelling of the fires of Madurai.

> Thus the gods in all their might
> Showered flowery rain from the skies
> That's how the fires of Madurā were quenched.

It is Pattini, and no other, then, that must bless each household, and it is she who must affirm her suzerainty over the village. This "theology" was upset by the introduction of Alut Deviyo in the procession to the village. A fundamental change of precedence has occurred; he heads the procession, and he also visits the households of the upper team and blesses them. He has taken over Pattini's *ritual* attributes, leading to theological incongruities. For example, it does not make sense for the *kapurāla* of the upper team (Pālaṅga's side) on behalf of Alut Deviyo to utter the prototypic lines of the Madurai fires, since it was Pattini who created the fires and then quelled them.

Thus the action taken in 1960 implied a real change in precedence and status and posed theological difficulties. In addition there was a sociological difficulty, for the lower team was threatened by the status enhancement of the upper team. All these factors resulted in the lower team's insisting on reversion to traditional practice in 1967. There was a big argument, but the traditional procedure was readopted (see pp. 291–92).

Sociologically the problem was compounded by interteam hostility and competition. This meant that the lower team (*yaṭipila*), Pattini's side, is in a sense superior to the upper team (*uḍupila*), that of Alut Deviyo. This problem does not exist in Malidūva, where Pattini is for both teams. In Dunukeula and Biyanvila the problem is slightly more compli-

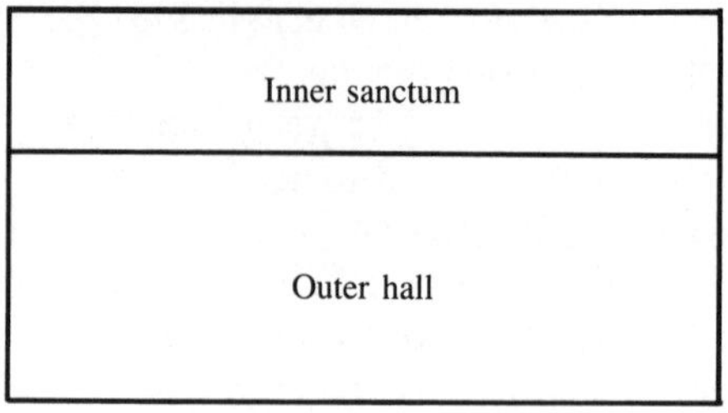

X Stone slab for breaking coconuts and a post for Bhairava (*Vairāvan*)

Fig. 13. Layout of Kaṇṇaki (Pattini) temples on the east coast.

cated because lower and upper represent the prototypic *aṅkeḷiya* between Pattini and her consort Pālaṅga. But in these two places Pālaṅga is not deified as Alut Deviyo, and while there is a great deal of interteam hostility both sides recognize that ultimately Pattini is supreme and is suzerain over both teams. Both teams propitiate her and never her consort, though it is not possible to wholly escape from the taint of ritual inferiority that the upper team suffers. In the rituals, for example, lower-team folk affirm loudly that they belong to the team of pure (*pirisidu*) Pattini. Yet the problem of precedence never arises here, since it is Pattini who is the deity and never her consort.

In Pānama both are deities, and the problem of precedence becomes important. Theologically it is clear that Pattini is superior; nevertheless, in the context of interteam hostility it is not surprising that the upper team should endeavor to raise the prestige of its deity, Alut Deviyo. But when the status of the deity was in fact elevated by consensus during the period 1960–66, this posed not only a theological issue but also a sociological one, for the lower team felt threatened by the elevation of the prestige of the upper team. Thus in 1967 the theological argument was used to resolve these problems and bring reversion to traditional practice.

The Displacement of Kōvalaṉ and the Transformation of Pattini

I noted earlier that Pālaṅga-Kōvalaṉ is a poor candidate for divinity and that Sanskritization must almost by necessity result in his displacement from the pantheon. It is possible to demonstrate this from the east coast Tamil areas where Sanskritization is proceeding rapidly. Let us first consider some of the smaller east coast shrines that have not yet felt the impact of Sanskritization.

The basic physical structure of Kaṇṇaki (Pattini) temples on the east coast is the same as in the Sinhala area (fig. 13). Most of the shrines in the Batticaloa district possess this simple physical structure. This is exactly the structure of Paṭṭimeṭu, a temple corporately owned by the *malavarācan kuṭi*, and managed by the lineage head or *talaivar*, who is also the lay trustee (*vaṇṇakār*) of the shrine. The shrine at Vīramunai has the identical structure.

The position changes remarkably in Tambiluvil and farther north in Karaitivu (near

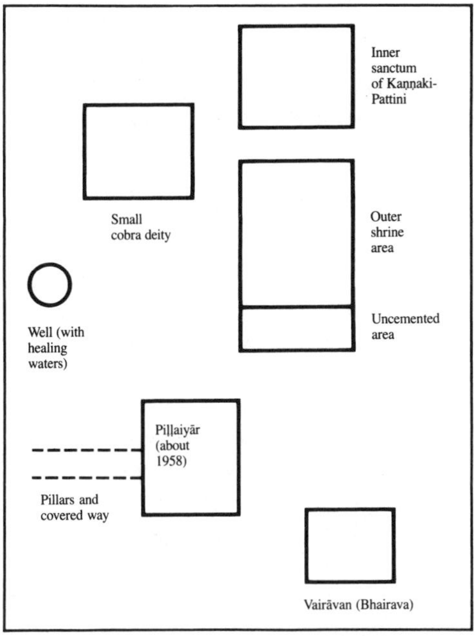

Fig. 14. Layout of the Pattini shrine premises in Tambiluvil. Note that the Kōvalaṉ temple is in a separate area. The cobra deity is very commonly worshiped on the east coast. In the Pattini cult the gem of the *nāga* king was encased in the goddess's anklet.

Kalmunai). Tambiluvil has a highly educated elite—schoolteachers, government officials, and local-level bureaucrats—who have become the agents of "higher" Sanskritic Hinduism. This is even more evident in Karaitivu. In addition, Karaitivu people in particular have official connections with Jaffna, the seat of Shaivite orthodoxy in Sri Lanka. Thus the stage is set for the Sanskritization of the Pattini cult.

First take the case of Tambiluvil. Here there is a shrine for Kōvalaṉ facing the north, constructed in an area separate from that of the main Pattini shrine. The latter area is represented in figure 14.

What is striking when we compare this with the simple form in Paṭṭimeṭu and Viramunai is the Piḷḷaiyār (Gaṇeśa) shrine erected about 1958. The first step in the Sanskritization has taken place—Gaṇeśa has been introduced into the main shrine premises. But why Gaṇeśa and not Skanda, an even more popular deity of the area with a very important shrine of his own at Tirukkovil near Tambiluvil?

In fact the displacement of Kōvalaṉ or Sāmi by Gaṇeśa-Piḷḷaiyār took place much earlier, in 1942. Kōvalaṉ had his shrine beyond the *kompu* arena, as I noted. According to informants it was originally called Kōvalaṉ *kōvil* ("shrine") and later referred to as Sāmi *kōvil*, indicating both the recency of the apotheosis and also the stages involved. In 1942 the people of Tambiluvil replaced this Sāmi shrine with that of Piḷḷaiyār! The rationalization expressed by temple officials was that there was no need for a Sāmi shrine since Pattini was already there, and she was all they needed. There was a further rationalization, which contained considerable truth. People felt there was great tension between persons during *kompu*, including husband and wife. Hence abolishing the Kōvalaṉ-Sāmi shrine would ease *kompu* tensions. The obscenities uttered during *kompu* were anathema to the intelligentsia of Tambiluvil who had initiated Sanskritization. However, the conversion of Sāmi into Piḷḷaiyār in 1942 did not restore amity, since *kompu* was performed for several years more, until serious violence broke out between the two teams and the tradition was terminated. Nevertheless, it is true that *kompu* cannot go on for long if Kōvalaṉ or Sāmi is displaced from the pantheon and from the public belief system.

In Tambiluvil, Sāmi's displacement from the pantheon was not immediately followed by his displacement from the public belief system. *Kompu* continued to be performed, and Sāmi continued to have his role in the annual celebrations in May. But his demotion must perforce result in his eventual displacement from the public belief system also, given the Sanskritization process.

Thus Piḷḷaiyār has come in, in a big way. There are now two shrines for him in Tambiluvil; one is the old Kōvalaṉ shrine, and the other is a shrine built more recently near the Pattini shrine. What factors brought about these changes?

1. Clearly there were strong pressures for Sanskritization in Tambiluvil from its influential and educated elite. Thus the folk deity Kōvalaṉ or Sāmi was displaced by Piḷḷaiyār. But why Piḷḷaiyār?

2. Piḷḷaiyār is a deity popular with ordinary folk in the area. Yet why not Śiva, since Pattini is already viewed as a manifestation of Kālī and Śiva would, as her consort, be the obvious choice if choice was determined by cultural factors alone? Moreover, why not Skanda, whose popularity was very great in the area? Tirukkovil, a famous shrine for Skanda, is only a few miles away from Tambiluvil.

3. My theory is that the vehicle of initial Sanskritization is Piḷḷaiyār because he is psychologically isomorphic with Kōvalaṉ-Sāmi, though culturally and theologically he is radically different. Both Piḷḷaiyār and Kōvalaṉ, as I pointed out earlier, are "castrated" figures, though each in a different way. Hence the psychosocial symbolism stays intact while the cultural system changes dramatically. Sanskritization initiated initially through Piḷḷaiyār can now proceed.

The actual installation of Piḷḷaiyār in the Sāmi shrine in 1942 was performed by South Indian Brahmans who came to Tambiluvil for this purpose. From 1942 to 1955 South Indian Brahmans officiated here, but they had to leave since, according to the version I obtained, it was not a profitable benefice. They preferred to work in the orthodox North. The priestly duties of the Piḷḷaiyār shrine have now been taken over by young priests (*pūcāri*) of the local *kurukkaḷ* (priest) lineage, in spite of the commonly held view that since Brahmans performed the installation rites at a Piḷḷaiyār *kōvil*, only they (Brahmans) could perform the subsequent *pūjā*s for the god. But when the Brahmans left some group had to take their place. The local *kurukkaḷ kuṭi* now affirmed their erstwhile traditional subcaste duty and took over the Piḷḷaiyār *kōvil* in Tambiluvil. Furthermore, they ceased to be folk priests; they were educated and literate young men trained in Tirukesveri under a famous guru.

The processes of Sanskritization discussed above for Tambiluvil had gone at a much faster pace in the northern Pattini shrine of Karaitivu in the Batticaloa district. Figure 15 shows the layout of the shrine premises at Karaitivu, as it was in 1966. In 1925, for exam-

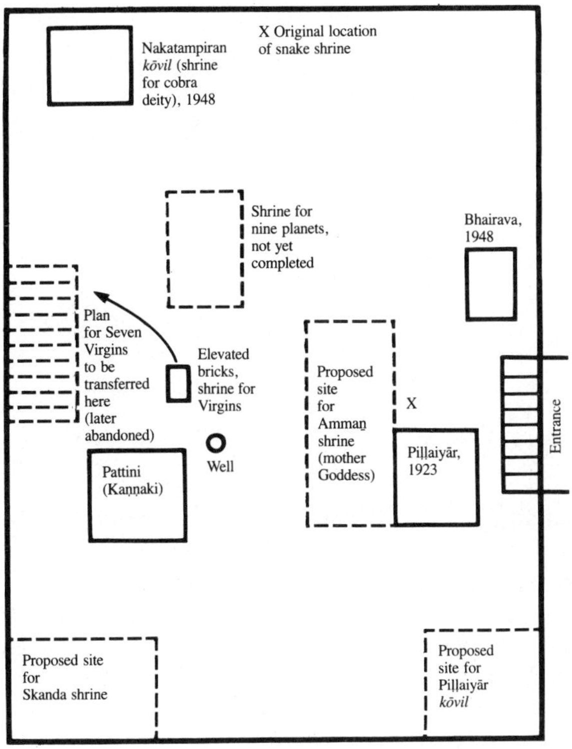

Fig. 15. Premises of the Karaitivu shrine in 1966.

ple, the shrine would have been quite different (fig. 16). In 1925 Karaitivu was very much like Tambiluvil in 1966, and only slightly more elaborate than Paṭṭimeṭu. Note the layout in 1925 of the Piḷḷaiyār *kōvil* and Pattini shrines: they are of the same size and shape, symmetrically placed in relation to each other. Here also the Piḷḷaiyār shrine was originally a Kōvalan̲-Sāmi shrine, on the Tambiluvil model. In 1923 or thereabouts the people of Karaitivu installed a Piḷḷaiyār image there. Thus, as in Tambiluvil, but very much earlier, Kōvalan̲-Sāmi was displaced by Piḷḷaiyār. In fact in the annual celebrations I witnessed in 1966 Piḷḷaiyār took the place of Sāmi in the rituals of the Pattini sanctum, as in figure 17. There are symbolic actions of the type discussed in chapter 5. Piḷḷaiyār has taken Kōvalan̲-Sāmi's place; moreover, Kaṇṇaki herself has become less specific and is referred to more or less exclusively as Amman̲, "mother." What was striking is that the young Brahman priests I interviewed in 1973 *denied* that Piḷḷaiyār was placed next to Pattini in the sanctum, also a kind of symbolic action affirming the separation of Piḷḷaiyār (now physically established) from the folk cult. Moreover, to this day the images of Pattini (Kaṇṇaki) and Piḷḷaiyār are taken in procession through the village. This is unlike the situation in Tambiluvil, where Sāmi still retains this role, but this posture cannot be maintained on the face of encroaching orthodoxy. According to Sanskritic ideas, Piḷḷaiyār is the

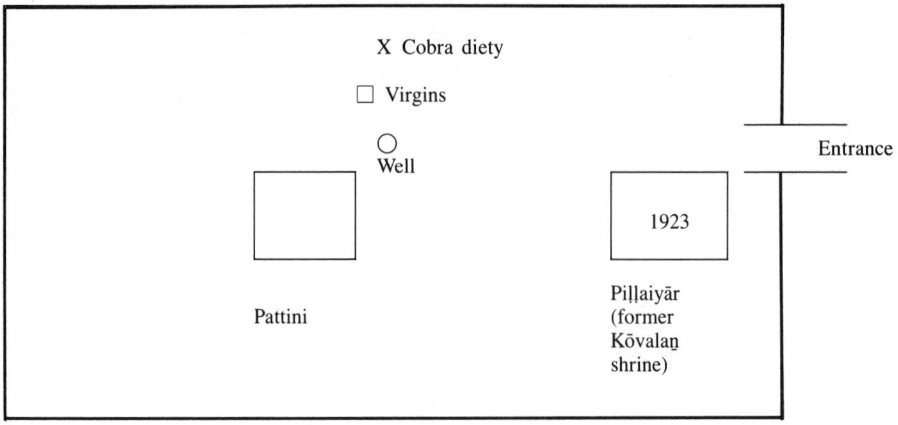

Fig. 16. Premises of the Karaitivu shrine in 1925.

son of Pārvatī and Śiva, whereas Pattini is a manifestation of Kālī and Pārvatī. Bringing the two together in this ceremonial context (implying cohabitation) is tantamount to incest! No wonder the sophisticated priests want to keep Piḷḷaiyār apart from Pattini, whereas the masses must have a figure who is psychologically, if not culturally, the equivalent of Sāmi. This must necessarily be Piḷḷaiyār, since he is the only one in the Sanskritic pantheon who has the right psychological significance.

The following structures were completed in 1967 in Karaitivu: the new Ammaṉ (Kaṇṇaki) shrine; the new Skanda shrine; and the new Piḷḷaiyār shrine. All these innovations were made on the advice of Brahmans and temple masons from the North. These changes were initiated, remember, by the educated elite of Karaitivu, numerically small but politically and socially dominant. One shrine originally planned, however, was subsequently abandoned. This was the shrine for the Seven Virgins, again a part of the folk culture. But why the objection to the Virgins, who after all have a place in higher Hinduism? The reason is once again clear: this is due to the puritanism and notions of propriety of the Karaitivu elite. The Seven Virgins are often propitiated in the traditional temples of the goddess. One ritual is particularly striking. At the start of the annual celebrations of the Pattini temple (e.g., Tambiluvil) a special *pūjā* is offered to the Seven Virgins. *At the same time* a *pūjā* is offered to Aiyaṉār at the Sāmi temple. Aiyaṉār is a naked deity, and so the priest offers the *pūjā* naked. I suspect that the cult of the Virgins was elsewhere also associated with the naked Aiyaṉār and hence was viewed with alarm by the elite.

The elite of Karaitivu wanted to develop the Skanda shrine, but in 1973 this shrine, though completed, was not ceremonially opened. By contrast the *new* Piḷḷaiyār shrine built six months later is functioning well, with Brahman priests officiating. The old Piḷḷaiyār (former Sāmi) shrine is to be demolished soon. When this happens Piḷḷaiyār will be spatially and symbolically further removed from Pattini-Kaṇṇaki. One can ultimately predict the triumph of the Sanskritic myth: Pattini will become Kālī or Pārvatī and Piḷḷaiyār will be her son. The public popularity of Piḷḷaiyār has arisen because he continues to take on the symbolic characteristics of Kōvalaṉ more than any other Sanskritic deity. Now

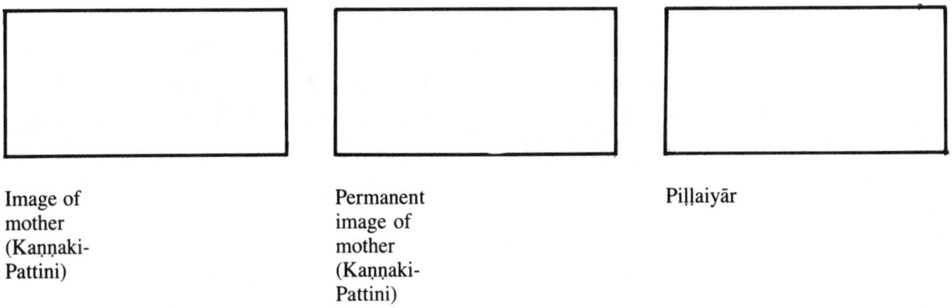

Fig. 17. Displacement of Sāmi by Piḷḷaiyār in the rituals of the Pattini sanctum.

Sanskritization can move ahead: Brahmans officiate at the Piḷḷaiyār shrine, but they do not and cannot officiate at the Kaṇṇaki Ammaṉ shrine. But the local *kappukaṉārs* of the Ammaṉ shrines are also a new breed of priests influenced by the higher Hinduism of the North.

Yet in spite of encroaching Sanskritization the popular cult as of 1973 was that of Ammaṉ and Piḷḷaiyār. The new Kaṇṇaki (Ammaṉ) shrine dominated all the other structures (fig. 18). Although Kaṇṇaki Ammaṉ is still the dominant deity, she is fast losing her identity as a folk goddess. This is seen in the symbolism of the large, impressive curtain that screens off the inner sanctum and hall from the rest of the building in the new shrine. The painting here is not a conventional one of Pattini-Kaṇṇaki but is closer to Durgā. The goddess is represented with four hands in the following manner:

Mango	Anklet
Bare hand	*Triśūla* (trident)

Behind her is a lion. It is clear that the mango and the anklet alone represent iconographically the old Mother (Kaṇṇaki-Pattini); the *triśūla* and lion represent the new Mother (Durgā). The total composition fits the image of Kālī better than that of Pattini-Kaṇṇaki. The priests are unequivocal in this regard: she is Kaṇṇaki, but represented as Durgā and Kālī and the *śakti* of Śiva. It is only a matter of time before shrines like this one become a fully Sanskritized temple complex like the famous Munneśvaram (Śiva) temple complex near Chilaw in northwestern Sri Lanka, which was also originally a shrine for Pattini but now is fully Sanskritized and converted into a Śiva shrine where Brahmans officiate. The goddess is simply Pārvatī, with little resemblance to the Pattini of folk religion.[7]

7. The Hindu "reform" in Sri Lanka was initiated by Āṟumuka Nāvalar in the mid-nineteenth century in Jaffna (northern Sri Lanka). Nāvalar scorned folk religion: "People call themselves Hindu but most of these idiots practise superstitions by worshiping Kādan, Madān, Suḍalayi, Kaṭṭēri, Maturai Viran, Karuppan, . . . Kaṇṇaki and Peycci—all of whom accept animal offerings" (quoted in *Kantapurāṇam Kalāsāram* 1959, p. 82). Note that Kaṇṇaki is equated with semidivine and demonic figures who accept animal sacrifices. As a result of the zeal of the Nāvalar and his compatriots, the processes of Sanskritization noted in this chapter occurred much earlier in the Jaffna district.

Postscript on the Sanskritization of the Pattini Cult

The fateful predictions I made in 1973 were realized recently. In 1978 a *kumpāpicēkam* (literally, "anointing with a full pot") ritual of purification was held in the Kaṇṇaki shrine by the Brahman priests of the Piḷḷaiyār *kōvil* under the auspices of the intelligentsia of Karaitivu. This ritual converted Kaṇṇaki-Pattini into a main goddess of orthodox Śaivism. She is no longer Kaṇṇaki or Pattini or even Kālī or Durgā; she is none other than Pārvatī, the consort of Śiva himself. The *apicēka* (*abhiṣeka*) ritual now permitted Brahmans, traditionally excluded from the Kaṇṇaki shrine, to participate in the ritual proceedings. This will soon result in the Pattini texts' being relegated to nonessential recitals, like the *muṭippurai* texts of southern Travancore described in the previous chapter. Orthodoxy has finally triumphed.

Appendix: The *Veḷiccappāṭu* of Kerala

The Kerala oracles are famous institutions, since practically every major Kālī temple has one attached to it. *Veḷiccapāṭu* belong to one of the non-Brahman castes, ranging from very high to very low. Even where the Kālī temple is under Brahman control, there is a *veḷiccapāṭu* of a high non-Brahman caste attached to it.

The *veḷiccapāṭu* perform two kinds of oracles, one during the annual festivals held at Bhagavatī temples about December or January and the other when they are invited to homes, either by themselves or to perform at the conclusion of other kinds of rituals. I have seen one performance of the latter type, by Tullankara Sankaran (fifty-one years old) of the *puliyār* caste. I shall not describe this performance because the slashing of the head with the sword does not occur here. That occurs in the annual temple performances. The account I have from the high-caste *veḷiccapāṭu* of the Paramakāvu Kālī temple in Trichur agrees substantially with a description of the ritual from 1936 (Kerala Varma Thampuram 1936, pp. 81–85).

My informant tells me that during the temple ritual he places the curved sticklike sword of Kālī against his forehead and hammers at the sword with the anklet of the goddess till he bleeds. Before too much injury can be caused the lineage head of an important Nāyar family takes the anklet away from the oracle "by force" and refuses to give it back to him. The *veḷiccapāṭu* then comes before the audience and utters prophecies—generally standard benedictions indicating prosperity and good fortune during the coming year. My informant told me that in his inspired state he can identify which members of the audience are faithful to the goddess, and he "blesses" only these people.

Then the oracle goes to the inner shrine, falls prostrate on the floor, and worships the goddess. The only medicine he uses is turmeric powder from the offerings given to the deity. Kerala Varma Thampuram says that in "the chronicles of the Nayars, there has never been a case reported of the wound creating complications, or not healing with this process" (1936, p. 83).

In my interviews with two *veḷiccapāṭu*, I was struck that they could not give a rational explanation for the slashing of the forehead. One informant, Parakūṭi Marasiyār, said that the goddess is pleased with the sight of the blood flowing. Neither informant could say why such a sight should be pleasing to the deity. My interpretation is that this action is

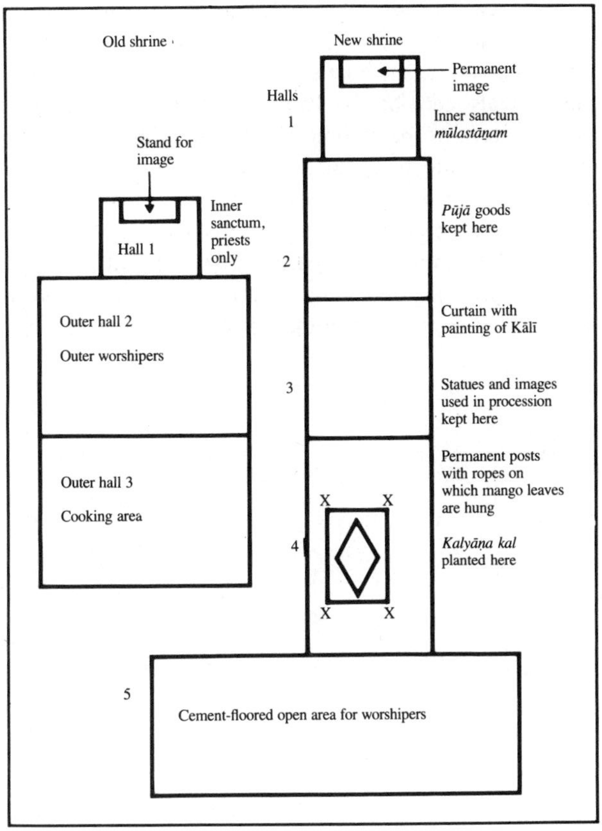

Fig. 18. Kaṇṇaki Ammaṉ shrine in Karaitivu.

significant on the unconscious level and that the goddess is pleased because her servant has "castrated" himself. The *veḷiccapāṭu* dons the clothes worn by Nāyar females; he identifies with the goddess, and his identity is complete only after he slashes his head and forehead. The act following the "castration" is again appropriate to the psychological context: the *veḷiccapāṭu* falls prostrate before the deity in total submission.

The oracles are not an isolated cult group but a firmly established institution in Kerala society. Historically they played a crucial role, often giving religious sanction to social decisions made in the village (Kunjan Pillai 1970, p. 356).

Following Lévi-Strauss (1963), I think it justifiable to state that these oracles act out the group's psychological problems. The *veḷiccapāṭu*, one might say, abreacts on behalf of the group: he represents in extreme the psychological problem of identity with the mother and wanting to be like her physically. It is likely that the selection of oracles favors those individuals who have a strong unconscious female identity and wish to act it out ritually.

The oracle role is not acquired simply by inheritance. When the incumbent oracle dies, resigns, or is deprived of his position (by the temple administration), a close relation (generally affinal) fills his place. My informant Parakūṭi Marasiyār's uncle was the previous oracle in the Paramakāvu temple. Though he had many sisters' sons, the only one who became qualified was Marasiyār, since he showed signs of the "calling," having participated in the temple festivals since he was twelve. Before his initiation at age thirty-two, he underwent forty-one days of meditation in the temple premises. Similarly, my other *puliyār* informant also went into an ecstatic trance while he was worshiping the goddess in the temple and started to shake. In his trance he saw a vision of the forehead of the goddess, then he started to utter prophecies. Since his uncle, who was the previous *veḷiccapāṭu* of the temple, had died three years earlier, he was installed to succeed him. Thus, while relationship to the previous imcumbent is a necessary condition, it is certainly not sufficient to make one a *veḷiccapāṭu*, as in the two cases I have recounted.

Epilogue

It would be impossible to summarize the contents of this book in a few pages, and I shall not attempt to do so. My analysis of the texts and rituals of the Pattini cult has sent tentacles into several social structures and historical periods, into mythic strata from the past, into the workings of Hindu and Buddhist family systems, and into the unconscious motivations of the cult's members and the symbolic systems that nourish their inner lives. We have traversed many historical periods and several lands and seas. Let me come to harbor in this epilogue with a brief summing up of the history of the cult in a coherent chronological sequence and an overview of the implications my findings have for scholarship pertaining to the great epic poem on the goddess Pattini, the *Cilappatikāram.*

The first historically determinate information on the Pattini cult comes from the twin poems the *Cilappatikāram* and the *Maṇimēkalai*. These two texts make it virtually certain that the goddess Pattini was a Jaina and Buddhist (and Ājīvaka) deity and that her cult was rooted in the life of city-dwelling merchant groups practicing these religions. There is no way to precisely determine the date of these two epics, but the scholarly opinion is that they could have been written anytime between the fifth century and the ninth. The events of the poems are from the past; it is therefore likely that the Pattini cult was popular among urban groups subscribing to the "heterodox" religions before the two poems were composed. A crucial event in the *Cilappatikāram* is the construction of a Pattini shrine (*pattinikōṭṭam*) by Ceṅkuṭṭuvaṉ, the famous Cēra king. I interpret this event not as a historical fact but as a charter legitimizing the antiquity and pedigree of a central Pattini shrine existing in Vañci at the time the two poems were written.

The *Cilappatikāram* is a carefully constructed work of art, but we know from current Pattini rituals that the key event in that poem—the killing of Kaṇṇaki-Pattini's consort and his resurrection by her—is a ritual drama performed by priests before an awed audience—a *dromenon*. Since such resurrection dramas are performed nowhere else in South Asia, I speculated that it might have diffused from Western Asia and the Mediterranean region, where such cults were dominant. It would have come via well-known trade routes by merchants and taken root among the merchant groups belonging to the Buddhist, Jaina, and Ājīvaka faiths and living in port cities in southern India. This is not entirely fanciful. We know, for example, that Syrian Christians were well established in Kerala in the early Christian era; if so, it is highly probable that Syrian non-Christian merchant communities who worshiped the mother goddess were also established on the Kerala coast, and perhaps elsewhere in southern India.

The second key piece of determinate information takes us to Sri Lanka, where King Parākramabāhu VI of Kōṭṭe built a shrine for the goddess Pattini in or near the capital city about 1415. There is no historical evidence that any king before him built a shrine for this goddess, but later kings did, such as Rājasiṃha I (A.D. 1581–93), who built an impressive shrine for Pattini at Mädagoḍa. The action of King Parākramabāhu gave royal patronage to a cult that must have existed on the popular level. It elevated the goddess to the status of a major deity, alongside the four established guardian deities of the kingdom: Viṣṇu, Saman, Vibhīṣaṇa, and Kataragama.

The question then is, What motivated this king to establish a shrine for this goddess in his capital city? It was most likely a public gesture as well as a personal act of devotion, a thanksgiving to a deity in whom he believed. I have shown in this work that King Parākramabāhu was a descendant of Malabar (Kerala) chiefs who dominated the politics of the country for about a hundred years from the early fourteenth century. One of these families, the Alakeśvaras, were the de facto rulers of much of the Western Province. They originally came (about A.D. 1100) from Vañci, the site of the famous Pattini shrine (*pattinikōṭṭam*) mentioned in the *Cilappatikāram* and *Maṇimēkalai*. These Kerala families were merchants, like their counterparts in the two epics, and they controlled the lucrative sea trade with Arabs on the west coast. Given these facts, it is virtually certain that these merchants were patrons of the Pattini cult and that King Parākramabāhu simply gave personal thanksgiving and state sanction and patronage to a deity popular with him and his kinsmen who brought him into power.

From here on my argument becomes more speculative, but I think it remains logically consistent and historically plausible. I have argued that the Malabar chiefs could not have established their supremacy without a supporting power base: this support in all likelihood came from other Kerala immigrants in this region. The universality and the popularity of the Pattini cult here are due to their influence. Some of them perhaps were peasants; others were merchants. I have mentioned Sinhala ritual dramas that depict these historical processes. The assimilation of merchants (*heṭṭi, ceṭṭi, seṭṭhi*) into the agrarian structure of Sinhala society is a well-known process, witness *goyigama*-caste surnames like Heṭṭigē, Heṭṭiāracci, and Ladduvaheṭṭi, names that indicate merchant origins.

The important question then is, What made these people move from the cities and perhaps adjacent villages of Kerala (and elsewhere in South India) to Sri Lanka? South Indian historical events provide the answer: the Hindu revival movements commencing after the eighth century pushed Buddhists out of their South Indian homes to seek refuge in a friendly neighboring Buddhist nation. I have argued that at least two major waves of immigration occurred: one went to the west coast, where the immigrants were assimilated into the Sinhala social structure. Here the Tamil Pattini texts were adapted into Sinhala and later formally translated and compiled into a compendium of thirty-five texts, perhaps after the fifteenth century. A second group colonized the east coast of Sri Lanka, retaining their language and texts and also features of matrilineal descent. My work on the east coast convinces me that there was considerable contact between these two groups of people, and this is reflected in their myths and legends. But proof of this must await historical and sociological research by other scholars.

There is a third determinate body of information from primary sources: the contemporary cults of the goddess Pattini in Buddhist and Hindu Sri Lanka and the survivals of this cult in Kerala and elsewhere in South India. My detailed analyses of the myths and rituals of the Pattini cult cannot be summarized here; suffice it to state that I have depicted the historical transformations of the cult in three sociocultural settings. For the Sinhala Buddhist form of the cult I have examined in detail the various historical and cultural strands—mythic stratigraphy—that constitute its ongoing structure.

The notion of *cult* implies that the worship of the goddess is part of the larger institutional setting of Sinhala Buddhism. This larger setting I have discussed in great detail. I have also examined the texts of the cult that are no longer operative and have imaginatively reconstructed their social and cultural significance in the past. This reconstruction made me radically revise the early history of South India and Sri Lanka according to an anthropological analysis of myth and ritual in their appropriate historical setting, rather than letting me see history in myth as historians have hitherto done. My research on the Pattini cult has also made me skeptical of the conventional "empiricist" historiography popular among the very best South Asian scholars. A historiography that relies exclusively on well-documented and incontrovertible historical evidence, such as evidence from inscriptions, must surely be wrong, since it assumes that the *recorded* data must be the *significant* data shaping history and controlling the formation and transformation of the institutions of a people. A more imaginative *interpretation* using a broad variety of sources—from myth, ritual, and popular literature—would correct this narrow perspective. Such interpretations must combine anthropology and history rather than being satisfied with extrapolating history from mythic sources. Such an approach will, I believe, produce new hypotheses that could open up new areas of historical research, and these in turn could be validated by more conventional historical and archaeological methods.

My interpretations of the Pattini cult must also, I believe, lead to a revision of hitherto accepted views of Indian scholars regarding the *Cilappatikāram*. I think I have demolished once and for all the so-called Gajabāhu synchronism. This synchronism can no longer be relied upon as the "sheet anchor" of South Indian historical and literary chronology. The characters in this epic are mythic figures; not only is this true for the protagonists of the tale, but its author, Iḷaṅkō Aṭikaḷ, is the eponymous author of other texts as well. It should be remembered that the reference to him appears only in the preamble (*patikam*) of the *Cilappatikāram*, which was added on to the main story (Zvelebil 1975, p. 112). Cāttaṉ, or Cīttalai Cāttaṉ, to whom the authorship of the *Maṇimēkalai* is attributed, is also a character in myth, associated with the cooling of the goddess's anger.

It seems apparent to me that most South Indian scholars are wrong when they assume that the ritual texts derive from the *Cilappatikāram*; the contrary is truer, that the *Cilappatikāram* is a well-crafted work of art that uses material from a preexistent and coexistent ritual tradition. Insofar as the *Cilappatikāram* was well known and highly regarded, it is likely that it in turn influenced some of the ritual traditions; but the dominant influence, it seems to me, lay in the other direction. This comes out in the preamble to the epic where Cāttaṉ informs Iḷaṅkō Aṭikaḷ about the events he had personally witnessed:

> Holy man, listen! I lay down at midnight in the Velliyambalam of the Manrappodiyil, sacred to Lord Siva who wears the *konrai* flower on His tuft, in the hoary city of Madura of untained fame. I saw the tutelary deity of Madura appearing before the heroic Pattini who was in deep distress and saying: "O lady, who raised furious flames from your breast! Now it is that the action of your previous birth has

> become completed. In your previous birth, the wife of the merchant Sangaman of Singapuram of undying fame laid a curse upon your husband and yourself. O lady of the beautiful tresses of hair! You will see your husband (again) fourteen days from now, not in his human form, but in the divine." This guileless account did I hear. (Dikshitar 1939, p. 78)

I agree with South Indian scholars like Dikshitar who state that Cāttaṉ narrated the events he actually saw (Dikshitar 1939, p. 71), except that I think Cāttaṉ saw not a natural event but a ritual drama!

The words that give a clue to the interpretation of this paragraph are, "Velliyambalam of the Manrappodiyil, sacred to Lord Siva." Dikshitar says, "The term Manrappodiyil shows that the village assembly met in the temple compound where it is natural to suppose that large and shady trees were planted and allowed to grow" (Dikshitar 1939, p. 78, n. 2). Maṉṟappoṭiyil is better elucidated by Srinivas Iyengar thus: "The open place under the tree was called podiyil, podiyam, or poduvil, the public place, also manra or manram. Manram originally meant the village common. . . . The words podiyil or manram also meant the open place under the shade of the tree, generally banyan, where the village elders met to solve village problems" (Iyengar 1929, pp. 180–82). Later on, says Iyengar, a large building was put up so that the term *poṭiyil* could also refer to a town hall. "All these places in the town were in later times used as resting places in processions of the temple gods" (1929, p. 184). The other important word is *veḷḷiyambalam*, from *veḷḷi* meaning "silver" and *ambalam*, a "rest house" or even "temple." Later commentators identified *veḷḷiyambalam* with the great temple of Madurai, but this identification is not valid for the period in which the poem was written. Thus the phrase "Velliyambalam of the Manrappodiyil, sacred to Lord Siva" means something like the following: an open space in a Śiva temple used for public gatherings; a shed or structure constructed in a Śiva temple; a large structure within which was a small hut or shrine; a large tree or open space where rituals were performed. The *Cilappatikāram* states that it was at the *velliyambalam* that Cāttaṉ saw the tutelary goddess of Madurai, known as Madurāpati, appear before the heroic Pattini. In Sinhala tradition Madurāpati is of little significance. She is often identified with Madurumāla (Valurumāla) or Vaduru Mādēvi (Madura Mā), the demoness of pestilence. Vaduru Mādēvi appears before Pattini in the *velliya ambalama* in the Sinhala tradition (pp. 261–64). It is likely that in earlier historical periods Madurāpati would also have appeared at the conclusion of the grand ritual drama of the killing and resurrection as the Sinhala texts seem to suggest (p. 276). There is an interesting survival in the Ūrubokka tradition that further attests to the prior significance of both Madurāpati and *velliya ambalama*. In this tradition there is a special altar for a goddess known as Madura Mādēvi. She is explicitly viewed as a goddess, not as the demoness of pestilence. According to the *kapurāla* she is Pattini herself in a previous birth. He is clearly wrong, for she can be none other than the Madurāpati of the *Cilappatikāram* and of the Sinhala text number 44 (p. 276). Hers is no ordinary altar, but one constructed in the form of a hut and designated *velliya ambalama*! The evidence above strongly suggests that in the *Cilappatikāram* itself *maṉṟappoṭiyil* was an area where the ritual drama of the goddess Pattini was enacted and "*velliyambalam*" perhaps was the hut where Madurāpati appeared before the goddess Pattini and before the audience, including Cāttaṉ. Any Sinhala peasant could make a statement similar to Cāttaṉ's after witnessing a *gammaḍuva* performance; for example: "I saw the goddess Pattini burn the city of Madurā in the *maḍuva*"; "I saw Pattini quell the demoness of disease at the *velliya ambalama*!" Cāttaṉ may have been a mythic character, but the author of the preamble makes him speak like any traditional man who had witnessed a ritual drama, a powerful and moving *dromenon*. The epic is firmly rooted in the popular ritual traditions of the cult of the goddess Pattini.

The epic and the popular ritual and mythic sources are also interrelated in terms of a powerful theme that permeates all versions of the Pattini myth: the notion of the king's justice. This comes out in the Sinhala Buddhist versions of the myth. The rationale for Pattini's birth in the golden mango of the Pāṇḍi king's orchard is to destroy that king's assumption of divinity by blinding his middle eye. The king of Pāṇḍi is evil; opposed to his model of kingship is that of Soḷī (Karikāla), the good king, ruling according to the dictates of royal justice (*dasa rāja dharma*) and emulating the paradigmatic case of Asoka. In the myth and ritual dramas of Pāṇḍi and Soḷī evil triumphs, if only temporarily. This triumph of evil is a realistic appraisal of what must have occurred time and again in the history of South Asian kingdoms—the rule of despotic kings out of touch with popular opinion and with people's conceptions of royal justice. However, the texts of the Pattini cult nowhere uphold the principle of revolt: justice is restored only through the intervention of the goddess Pattini. I have shown in this work that this theme of justice is an ancient one, and versions of it are found in older South Indian literatures. In the Hindu east coast of Sri Lanka also this theme is predominant. The title of the text *Kaṇṇaki Vaḻakkurai*, recited at the annual festival, literally means the case (for justice) as stated by Kaṇṇaki.

One of the fascinating problems that emerge in the historical transformation of the Pattini cult into the Kālī cult is the concomitant transformation of the notion of justice from what one might call righteous or rational justice into a vengeful or "irrational" justice. Thus, according to the *Cilappatikāram*, the Sinhala texts, and the texts of the east coast Hindus, Pattini is an angry deity, but this anger is directed against evil people alone; it spares the good. In all three sources people implore her to calm down, and she listens and heeds their pleas. She even revives the cow that was slaughtered to make a drum for her. By contrast, when the Pattini cult is assimilated into the Kālī cult in South India and in Mulaitivu (northeastern Sri Lanka) the deity becomes irrationally punitive, and vengeance takes the place of rational justice. Furthermore, the seat of Pattini's justice is her breast: in a psychological sense it is the source of both wrath and compassion, and also of love. When Pattini is transformed into Kālī, the breast symbolism also disappears, which means that compassion disappears and wrath reigns supreme. I have shown that one cannot understand these transformations through historical study alone; one must also relate them to conditions in the social structure, to patterns of socialization, and to value changes such as those attendant on Sanskritization. Moreover, the conception of rational justice is not confined to the Pattini cult exclusively but is embodied in the larger religious traditions of Buddhists and Jainas (as well in some Hindu traditions). The *Cilappatikāram* itself has been influenced by these larger traditions, and in spite of its subjection to the accepted conventions of ancient Tamil epic poetry it retains the notion of rational justice as a central theme. The conclusion is once again irresistible: the epic is firmly rooted in the ritual and historical traditions of the cult of the goddess Pattini.

References

Abraham, Karl. 1909. *Dreams and myths: A study in race psychology*, trans. William A. White. *Journal of Nervous and Mental Disease*, Monograph no. 15.

Achyuta Menon, C. 1959. *Kali worship in Kerala*. Madras: Madras University Press.

Aluwihara, B. H. 1964. *The Kandy perahera*. Colombo: Gunasena.

Anantan Pillai, P. 1968. The Kaṇṇaki legend and the *tottam pāṭṭus*. In *Kerala studies: Gopala Menon commemoration volume*, pp. 162–66. Trivandrum.

Ariyapala, M. B. 1956. *Society in medieval Ceylon*. Colombo: Department of Cultural Affairs.

Babb, Lawrence. 1975. *The divine hierarchy*. New York: Columbia University Press.

Balasundaram, E. 1979. *A survey and study of folk songs of the Batticaloa district of Sri Lanka* (Tamil). Madras: Tamil Patippakam.

Baldeus, Philip. 1672 (1958–59). *A true and exact description of the great island of Ceylon*, trans. from the Dutch by Peter Brohier. *Ceylon Historical Journal* 8 (July 1958–April 1959).

Basham, A. L. 1951. *The history and doctrines of the Ājīvakas*. London: Luzac.

———. 1959. *The wonder that was India*. New York: Grove Press.

Bateson, Gregory. 1958. *Naven*. Stanford: Stanford University Press.

Beck, Brenda E. F. 1972. A study of a Tamil epic: Several versions of *Silappadikaram* compared. *Journal of Tamil Studies*, September, pp. 23–38.

Bell, H. C. P. 1892. *Report on the Kegalle district of the Province of Sabaragamuva*. Colombo: Government Press.

Benedict, Ruth. 1946. *The chrysanthemum and the sword*. Boston: Houghton Mifflin.

Bettelheim, Bruno. 1962. *Symbolic wounds: Puberty rites and the envious male*. New York: Collier Books.

Bloomfield, M. 1897 (1964). *Hymns of the Atharvaveda*. Sacred Books of the East, vol. 42, reprint. Delhi: Motilal Banarsidass.

Bogoras, W. 1907. *The Chukchee*. Jessup North Pacific Expedition, vol. 11, Memoirs of the American Museum of Natural History. Leiden.

Boyd, James W. 1975. *Satan and Māra: Christian and Buddhist symbols of evil*. Studies in the History of Religion, supplements to *Numen*, no. 27. Leiden: Brill.

Carstairs, A. Morris. 1957. *The twice born*. London: Hogarth Press.

Chandera, C. M. S. 1973. *Kaṇṇaki Kaṇṇakiyum Cūmakkuvam*. Kottayam: National Book Stall.
Coedes, G. 1968. *The Indianized states of southeast Asia*. Honolulu: East-West Center Press.
Coomaraswamy, A. K. 1957. The status of Indian women. In *The dance of Shiva*. New York: Noonday Press.
Cowell, Edward Byles. 1957. *The jātaka, or stories of the Buddha's former births*, vols. 1–5. London: Luzac for the Pāli Text Society.
Cūlavaṃsa. 1953. *Cūlavaṃsa* (being the more recent part of the *Mahāvaṃsa*), parts 1 and 2, trans. by Wilhelm Geiger, and from the German into English by Mabel Rickmers. Colombo: Government Press.
Cumont, Franz. 1911 (1956). *The Oriental religions in Roman paganism*. New York: Dover Press.
Danielou, Jean. 1965. *The Shilappadikaram* [The ankle bracelet]. New York: New Directions.
Davis, Richard. 1974. Tolerance and ambiguity in northern Thai myth. *Ethnology* 13, no. 1: 1–24.
Davy, John. 1821. *An account of the interior of Ceylon*. London: Longman, Hurst, Rees, Orme, and Brown.
De Queyroz, Father Fernao. 1930. *The temporal and spiritual conquest of Ceylon*, trans. from the Portuguese by S. G. Perera. Colombo: Government Press.
De Vos, George. 1973. The relation of guilt towards parents to achievement and arranged marriage among Japanese. In *Socialization for achievement*. Berkeley: University of California Press.
Dewaraja, Lorna S. 1972. *The Kandyan kingdom, 1707–1760*. Colombo: Lake House Investments.
Dikshitar, V. R. Ramachandra. 1939. *The Silappadikaram*. London: Oxford University Press.
Dīpavaṃsa. 1879. *The Dīpavaṃsa: An ancient Buddhist historical record*. Ed. and trans. Hermann Oldenberg. London: Williams and Norgate.
Dowson, John. 1953. *A classical dictionary of Hindu mythology*. London: Routledge and Kegan Paul.
Dube, S. L. 1963. Men's and women's roles in India: A sociological review. In *Women in the new Asia*, ed. Barbara Ward. Paris: UNESCO.
Durkheim, Emile. 1915. *Elementary forms of the religious life*, trans. from the French by J. W. Swain. Glencoe, Ill.: Free Press.
Eliade, Mircea. 1959. *Cosmos and history*. New York: Harper Torchbooks.
Elwin, Verrier. 1955. *Religion of an Indian tribe*. Bombay: Oxford University Press.
Emeneau, M. B. 1937. Ritual games of the Kotas. *Bulletin of the Sri Rama Varma Research Institute* 5, 2: 114–22.
Erikson, Erik H. 1968. *Identity: Youth and crisis*. New York: Norton.
Farnell, Lewis Richard. 1971. *The cults of the Greek states*, vols. 2 and 3. Chicago: Aegean Press.
Filliozat, J. 1964. *The classical doctrine of Hindu medicine*, trans. Dev Raj Channa. New Delhi: Munshiram Manoharlal.

Flugel, J. C. 1924. Polyphallic symbolism and the castration complex. *International Journal of Psychoanalysis* 5:155–96.

Frazer, Sir James. 1914. *Adonis, Attis, Osiris: Studies in the history of oriental religion*, 3d ed. London: Macmillan.

Freud, Sigmund 1910 (1956). A special type of choice of object made by men. In *Collected Papers*, vol. 4. London: Hogarth Press.

———. 1912 (1956). The most prevalent form of degradation in erotic life. In *Collected Papers*, vol. 4. London: Hogarth Press.

———. 1957. *The future of an illusion*, trans. W. D. Robson-Scott. New York: Doubleday Anchor Books.

———. 1961. *The interpretation of dreams*, trans. James Strachey. New York: Science Editions.

Geiger, W. 1960. *The culture of Ceylon in medieval times*. Weisbaden: Otto Harrassowitz.

Godakumbura, Charles. 1955. *Sinhalese literature*. Colombo: Colombo Apothecaries.

———. 1963. *Kohom̃bā Kaṅkāriya*. Colombo: Government Press.

Gombrich, Richard F. 1966. Consecration of a Buddha image. *Journal of Asian Studies* 26, no. 1:23–26.

———. 1971a. *Precept and practise*. Oxford: Clarendon Press.

———. 1971b. Food for the seven grandmothers: Stages in the universalization of a Sinhalese ritual. *Journal of Asian Studies* 26, no. 1:23–36.

Goonewardene, K. W. 1958. Some comments on Robert Knox and his writings on Ceylon. *University of Ceylon Review* 16:39–52.

Gopinatha Rao, T. A. 1919. *Jaina and Buddhist vestiges in Travancore*. Travancore Archaeological Series, vol. 2, part 2. Trivandrum: Government Press.

Gough, E. Kathleen. 1956. Brahmin kinship in a Tamil village. *American Anthropologist* 58, no. 5:826–53.

Griffith, R. T. H. 1895. *Hymns of the Atharvaveda*, vol. 1. Benares: E. J. Lazarus.

Gunasekara, B., ed. 1893. *The Pūjāvaliya* (Sinhala text). Colombo: Government Press.

Gunasekera, U. Alex. 1953. *Puna maduva*, or the scapegoat idea in Ceylon. *Spolia Zeylanica* 27, no. 1:63–74.

Gundert, Rev. H. 1873. *Malayalam-English dictionary*. C. Stoltz.

Hall, Calvin S. 1966. *The meaning of dreams*. New York: McGraw-Hill.

Halverson, John. 1971. Dynamics of exorcism. *History of Religions* 10, no. 4:334–59.

Harper, Edward B. 1964. Ritual pollution as an integrator of caste and religion. *Journal of Asian Studies* 23:151–97.

Heine-Geldern, Robert. 1942. Conceptions of state and kingship in Southeast Asia. *Far Eastern Quarterly* 11:15–30.

Hettiarachchy, Tilak. 1972. *History of kinship in Ceylon up to the fourth century A.D.* Colombo: Lake House Investments.

Hevawasam, P. B. G. 1974. *Pantis kōlmurakavi*. Colombo: Pradīpa Prakāṣakayō.

Hiatt, L. S. 1973. The Pattini cult of Ceylon: A Tamil perspective. *Social Compass* 20, no. 2:231–50.

Hocart, A. L. 1931. *The temple of the tooth in Kandy*. London: Luzac.

Indrapala, K. 1971. The disintegration of Pollonnaruva. In *The collapse of the Rajarata civilization*. Mimeographed. Peradeniya: Ceylon Studies Seminar.

Induchudan, V. T. 1969. *The secret chamber: A historical, anthropological, and philosophical study of the Kodungallur temple*. Trichur: Cochin Devasom Board.
Iyengar, Srinivas. 1929. *History of the Tamils*. Madras: C. Coomaraswamy Naidu.
James, E. O. 1959. *The cults of the mother goddess: An archaeological and documentary study*. New York: Barnes and Noble.
Kakar, Sudhir. 1978. *The inner world: A psychoanalytic study of childhood and society in India*. Delhi: Oxford University Press.
Kanakasabhhai, V. 1956. *The Tamils eighteen hundred years ago*. Madras: South India Saiva Siddhanta works.
Kandiah, V. S. 1968. *Kaṇṇaki Vaḷakkurai* (Tamil). Jaffna: Dhanalaksmi Book Depot.
Kantapurānam Kalāsāram. 1959. Ed. P. Kanapathypillai. Jaffna: Sri Shansunganatha Press.
Kapadia, K. M. 1955. *Marriage and the family in India*. Oxford: Oxford University Press.
Kardiner, A. 1945. *The psychological frontiers of society*. New York: Columbia University Press.
Karve, I. 1965. *Kinship organization in India*. New Delhi: Asia Publishing House.
Knox, Robert. 1681. *An historical relation of the island of Ceylon in the East Indies*. London: Richard Chiswell.
Kohut, Heinz. 1971. *The analysis of the self*. New York: International Universities Press.
———. 1977. *The restoration of the self*. New York: International Universities Press.
Kunjan Pillai, E. P. N. 1970. *Studies in Kerala history*. Kottayam: National Book Stall.
Leach, E. R. 1958. Magical hair. *Journal of the Royal Anthropological Institute* 88: 147–64.
———. 1969. *Genesis as myth, and other essays*. London: Jonathan Cape.
Lévi-Strauss, Claude. 1963. The sorcerer and his magic. In *Structural Anthropology*. New York: Basic Books.
Lewis, J. P. 1918. Journal of a tour to Candia in the year 1796. *Journal of the Royal Asiatic Society* (Ceylon Branch) 26:6–31.
Lewis, Nolan D. C. 1928. The psychology of the castration reaction. *Psychoanalytic Review* 15:174–77.
Lewis, Oscar. 1958. *Village life in northern India*. Urbana: University of Illinois Press.
Ling, Trevor. 1962. *Buddhism and the mythology of evil*. London: Allen and Unwin.
Lynd, Helen Merrill. 1958. *On shame and the search for identity*. New York: Harcourt Brace.
MacGilvray, Dennis. 1974. *Tamils and Moors: Caste and matriclan structure in eastern Sri Lanka*. Ph.D. diss., University of Chicago.
Madan, T. N. 1965. *Family and kinship: A study of the Pandits of Kashmir*. New Delhi: Asia Publishing House.
Mahāvaṃsa. 1934. *The Mahāvaṃsa* (the great chronicle of Ceylon), trans. Wilhelm Geiger. London: Oxford University Press for the Pāli Text Society.
Malalesekera, G. P. 1938. *Dictionary of Pāli proper names*, vol. 2. London: Pāli Text Society.
———. 1958. *The Pāli literature of Ceylon*. Colombo: M. D. Gunasena.
Malinowski, B. 1955. *Magic, science and religion*. New York: Doubleday Anchor.

Mandelbaum, David G. 1949. The family in India. In *The family: Its function and destiny*, ed. Ruth Nanda Anshen. New York: Harper Brothers.

Maṇimēkalai. 1928. *Manimekhalai in its historical setting*, ed. S. Krishnaswami Aiyangar. London: Luzac.

Marriott, McKim. 1955. Little communities in an indigenous civilization. In *Village India: Studies in the little community*, ed. Robert Redfield and Milton Singer. Chicago: University of Chicago Press.

Masters, W. H., and Johnson, Virginia. 1970. *Human sexual inadequacy*. Boston: Little, Brown.

Mayer, Adrian. 1960. *Caste and kinship in central India*. London: Routledge and Kegan Paul.

Mead, George Herbert. 1934. *Mind, self, and society*. Chicago: University of Chicago Press.

Mead, Margaret. 1937. *Cooperation and competition among primitive peoples*. New York: McGraw-Hill.

Mendis, G. C. 1946. *The early history of Ceylon*. Calcutta: YMCA Publishing House.

Meyer, Jakob. 1952. *Sexual life in ancient India*. London: Routledge and Kegan Paul.

Murphey, Rhoads. 1957. The ruin of ancient Ceylon. *Journal of Asian Studies* 16, no. 2: 181–200.

Ñānavāsa, Hempitigedera. 1964. *The development of the concept of Buddha in Pāli literature*. Ph.D. diss., University of Ceylon (Sri Lanka).

Nandi, Ramendra Nath. 1973. *Religious institutions and cults of the Deccan*. Delhi: Motilal Banarsidass.

Natesan, S. 1959. The Sangam age in Tamilnad. In *History of Ceylon* 1: 206–15. Colombo: Ceylon University Press.

Nevill, Hugh. 1887. Pigeon worship in Ceylon. *Taprobanian* 2, nos. 1: 21–24, 5: 135–36.

———. 1888. The story of Kovalan. *Taprobanian*, February 1888, pp. 16–22.

———. 1954. *Sinhala verse*, vols. 1 and 2, ed. P. E. P. Deraniyagala. Colombo: Government Press.

———. 1955. *Sinhala verse*, vol. 3, ed. P. E. P. Deraniyagala. Colombo: Government Press.

Nilakanta Sastri, K. A. 1932. *Studies in Cōḷa history and administration*. Madras: University of Madras Press.

———. 1955 (1966). *A history of South India*. Madras: Oxford University Press.

———. 1964. *The culture and history of the Tamils*. Calcutta: Firma K. L. Mukhopadhyay.

———. 1972. *Foreign notices of South India from Megasthenes to Ma Huan*. Madras: University of Madras Press.

Obeyesekere, Gananath. 1958. The structure of a Sinhalese ritual. *Ceylon Journal of Historical and Social Studies* 1, no. 2: 192–202.

———. 1963. The Buddhist pantheon in Ceylon and its extensions. In *Anthropological Studies of Theravada Buddhism*, ed. Manning Nash. Cultural Report Series, no. 13. New Haven: Yale University Press.

———. 1966. Theodicy, sin and salvation in a sociology of Buddhism. In *Dialectic in practical religion*, ed. E. R. Leach. Cambridge: Cambridge University Press.

———. 1967. *Land tenure in village Ceylon*. Cambridge: Cambridge University Press.

———. 1969a. The ritual drama of the Sanni demons: Collective representations of disease in Ceylon. *Comparative Studies in Society and History* 11, no. 2:174–216.

———. 1969b. The cultural background of Sinhalese medicine. *Journal of the Anthropological Survey of India* 4:117–39.

———. 1970. The idiom of demonic possession: A case study. *Social Science and Medicine* 4:97–111.

———. 1972. Religious symbolism and political change in Ceylon. In *Two wheels of Dhamma*, ed. Bardwell L. Smith. AAR Monograph 3. Chambersburg, Pa.: American Academy of Religion.

———. 1975a. Sorcery, premeditated murder and the canalization of aggression in Sri Lanka. *Ethnology* 14, no. 1:1–23.

———. 1975b. Psychocultural exegesis of a case of spirit possession in Sri Lanka. *Contributions to Asian Studies* 14:1–23. Reprinted in *Case studies in possession*, ed. Vincent Crapanzano and Vivian Garrison (New York: John Wiley, 1977).

———. 1976. The impact of Ayurvedic ideas on the culture and the individual in Sri Lanka. In *Asian medical systems: A comparative study*, ed. Charles Leslie. Berkeley: University of California Press.

———. 1977. Social change and the deities: The rise of the Kataragama cult in modern Sri Lanka. *Man*, n.s., 12:377–96.

———. 1978. The firewalkers of Kataragama: The rise of *bhakti* religiosity in Buddhist Sri Lanka. *Journal of Asian Studies* 36:457–76.

———. 1980. The goddess Pattini: A Jaina-Buddhist deity. In *Buddhist studies in honour of Walpola Rahula*. London: Gordon Frazer.

———. 1982. The ritual of the leopard's pot: The *pūna yāgaya*. In *E. F. C. Ludowyk Commemoration Volume*, forthcoming.

O'Flaherty, Wendy Doniger. 1973. *Asceticism and eroticism in the mythology of Siva*. London: Oxford University Press.

Paranavitana, S. 1928. Mahayanism in Ceylon. *Ceylon Journal of Science* 2, no. 1: 35–71.

———. 1950. *Sinhalē and the patriots, 1815–1818*. Colombo: Colombo Apothecaries.

———. 1953. *The shrine of Upulvan at Devundara*. Memoirs of the Archaeological Survey of Ceylon, vol. 6. Colombo: Ceylon Government Archaeological Department.

———. 1956. Political and social conditions of medieval Ceylon. In *Sir Paul Pieris felicitation volume*. Colombo: Colombo Apothecaries.

———. 1958. *The god of Adam's Peak*. Ascona (Switzerland): Artibus Asaie Publishers.

———. 1959. Lambakanna dynasty. In *History of Ceylon* ed. H. C. Ray, 1:179–91. Colombo: University of Ceylon Press.

———. 1960a. Civilization of the Pollonnaru period: Religion, literature and art. In *History of Ceylon*, vol. 1, part 2. Colombo: Ceylon University Press.

———. 1960b. Gampola and Rayigama, with an appendix on the pedigree of the Alagokkonars. In *History of Ceylon*, vol. 1, part 2, pp. 636–59. Colombo: University of Ceylon Press.

———. 1960c. The Kotte kingdom up to 1505. In *History of Ceylon*, vol. 1, part 2, pp. 660–83. Colombo: University of Ceylon Press.

———. 1960d. The withdrawal of the Sinhalese from the ancient capitals. In *History of Ceylon*, vol. 1, part 2, pp. 713–20. Colombo: University of Ceylon Press.

———. 1960e. The civilization of the period (Dambadeniya). In *History of Ceylon*, vol. 1, part 2, pp. 713–93. Colombo: University of Ceylon Press.

———. 1972. *Glimpses of Ceylon's past*. Colombo: Lake House.

Parameswara Iyer, Uloor S. 1957–65. *Kēralasāhityacaritram* [History of Kerala literature]. 5 vols. Travancore University Series, no. 30. Trivandrum: Travancore University.

Parker, Henry. 1909. *Ancient Ceylon*. London: Luzac.

Parsons, Anne. 1969. *Belief, magic and anomie: Essays in psychosocial anthropology*. New York: Free Press.

Parsons, Talcott. 1954. The incest taboo in relation to social structure and the socialization of the child. *British Journal of Sociology* 5:101–17.

———. 1965. The father symbol. In *Social structure and personality*. New York: Free Press.

Peristiany, J., ed. 1965. *Honour and shame: The values of Mediterranean society*. London: Weidenfeld and Nicolson.

Pertold, Otaker. 1941. Die ceylonische Gottin Pattini. *Archiv Orientalni* 13:201–26.

Pieris, P. E. 1913. *Ceylon: The Portuguese era*, vol. 1. Colombo: Colombo Apothecaries.

———. 1914. *Ceylon: The Portuguese era*, vol. 2. Colombo: Colombo Apothecaries.

———. 1950. *Sinhale and the patriots, 1815–1818*. Colombo: Colombo Apothecaries.

Pieris, Ralph. 1956. *Sinhalese social organization*. Colombo: University of Ceylon Press.

Piers, Gerhart, and Singer, Milton. 1933. *Shame and guilt: A psychoanalytic and cultural study*. Springfield, Ill.: Charles C. Thomas.

Pigott, Stuart. 1952. *Prehistoric India*. Harmondsworth, England: Penguin.

Pillay, K. K. 1963. *South India and Ceylon*. Madras: University of Madras Press.

Piyaratana Thera, Makuludūve, ed. 1964. *Girā sandēśaya*. Colombo: Gunasena.

Pollard, John. 1965. *Seers, shrines and sirens*. London: George Allen and Unwin.

Powell, Godfrey. 1973. *The Kandyan wars: The British army in Ceylon*. London: Leo Cooper.

Pūjāvaliya. 1895. *The Pūjāvaliya* (a contribution to the history of Ceylon), trans. B. Gunasekara. Colombo: Government Press.

Raby, Namika. 1978. *Bureaucracy, politics and society in a provincial town in Sri Lanka*. Ph.D. diss., University of California, San Diego.

Raghava Iyengar, M. 1964. Pattini dēviyaipparric cila kuruppukal (Tamil, some notes on Pattini worship). *Ārāyceit Tokuti* (Madras).

Raghavan, M. D. 1961. *The karava of Ceylon*. Colombo: K. V. G. de Silva.

Raglan, Lord. 1936. *The hero: A study in tradition myths and drama*. London: Watts.

Rājāvaliya. 1900. *The Rājāvaliya* (a historical narrative of Sinhalese kings from Vijaya to Vimala Dharma Surya II), ed. B. Gunasekara. Colombo: Government Press.

Ramachandran, Sri T. N. 1960. Buddhism in Tamilnad. In *The story of Buddhism with special reference to South India*, ed. A. Aiyappan and P. R. Srinivasan, pp. 52–58. Madras: Government of Madras Press.

Rank, Otto. 1964. *The myth of the birth of the hero*, ed. Philip Freund. New York: Random House.

Raven-Hart, R., ed. 1958. *The Pybus mission to Kandy, 1762*. Colombo: Government Press.

Renou, Louis. 1962. *Hinduism*. New York: George Braziller.

Reymond, Lizelle. n.d. *My life with a Brahmin family*. New York: Roy Publishers.

Reynolds, Frank. 1972. The two wheels of Dhamma: A study in early Buddhism. In *The two wheels of Dhamma*, ed. Bardwell L. Smith. AAR Monograph 3. Chambersburg, Pa.: American Academy of Religion.

Roberts, Michael W. 1971. The ruin of ancient Ceylon and the drift to the southwest. In *The collapse of the Rajarata civilization*, ed. K. Indrapala. Mimeographed. Peradeniya: Ceylon Studies Seminar.

Säbiheliyan, A. 1967. *Parevi sandēśa vivaraṇa*. Colombo: M. D. Gunasena.

Saddharmālaṃkāraya. 1911. Ed. Venerable Kalutara Sārānanda. Sri Lanka: Lankabhinava Viśäta Press.

Saddharmavāda Saṃgrahava. 1909. Ed. Venerable Siddhartha Buddharakṣita. Sri Lanka: Śāstrādhāra Press.

Sankara Pillai, P. K. 1958. *Toṟṟam pāṭṭukal* (Malayalam, a collection of *toṟṟam pāṭṭu*). Kottayam: National Book Stall.

Sarachchandra, E. R. 1953. *The Sinhalese folkplay and the modern stage*. Colombo: Ceylon University Press Board.

———. 1966. *The folk drama of Ceylon*. Colombo: Department of Cultural Affairs.

Sarkar, H. K. 1957. *The demography of Ceylon*. Colombo: Ceylon Government Press.

Seligmann, C. G., and Seligmann, Brenda Z. 1911. *The Veddas*. Cambridge: Cambridge University Press.

Seneviratne, H. L. 1973. L'ordination bouddhiste à Ceylon. *Social Compass* 20:251–58.

———. 1978. *Rituals of the Kandyan state*. Cambridge: Cambridge University Press.

Settar, S. 1969. The cult of Jvālāmālini and the earliest images of Jvālā and Śyāma. *Artibus Asiae* 31, no. 4:309–20.

Shulman, David Dean. 1980. *Tamil temple myths: Sacrifice and divine marriage in the South Indian Śaiva tradition*. Princeton: Princeton University Press.

Somaratne, G. P. V. 1975. *Political history of the kingdom of Kotte*. Nugegoda: Deepanee Printers.

Spellman, John W. 1962. The symbolic significance of the number twelve in ancient India. *Journal of Asian Studies* 22:79–88.

Spiro, Melford E. 1965. *Children of the kibbutz*. New York: Schocken Books.

———. 1966. Buddhism and economic saving in Burma. *American Anthropologist* 68:1163–73.

———. 1973. Symbolism and function in the anthropological study of religion. Paper presented at the International Association of History of Religion, Turku, Finland, 27–31 August 1973.

Sreedhara Menon, A. 1967. *A survey of Kerala history*. Kottayam: National Book Stall. Reprinted 1970.

Srimad Bhagavatam. 1943. *The wisdom of God*, trans. Swami Prabhavananda. Hollywood: Vedanta Press.

Srinivas, M. N. 1956. A note on Sanskritization and Westernization. *Far Eastern Quarterly* 15:481–96.

———. 1976. *Remembered village*. Berkeley and Los Angeles: University of California Press.

Srinivasan, K. R. 1975. South India. In *Jaina art and architecture*, vol. 11, ed. A. Ghosh. New Delhi: Bharatiya Janpith.

Starcke, August. 1921. The castration complex. *International Journal of Psychoanalysis* 2:179–201.

Stevenson, H. N. V. 1954. Status evaluation in the Hindu caste system. *Journal of the Royal Anthropological Institute* 84:45–65.

Subrahamanian, N. 1972. *History of Tamilnad*. Madurai: Koodal Publisher.

Swamy, P. L. 1971. Kaṇṇakiyum bhakavati valipaaṭum (Kannaki and Bhagavati worship). *Ārāycci* 2, no. 4 (Tirunelveli):391–408.

Tambiah, S. J. 1976. *World renouncer and world conqueror*. Cambridge: Cambridge University Press.

Thampuram, Kerala Varma. 1936. Kali cult in Kerala. *Bulletin of the Sri Rama Varma Research Institute* 4:77–97.

Thurston, Edgar, 1909. *Tribes and castes of southern India*, vol. 4. Madras: Madras Government Press.

Tinsley, E. J. 1972. The coming of the dead and naked Christ. *Journal of Religion and Religions* 2:24–36.

Travancore State manual. 1906. Vol. 2. Trivandrum: Travancore Government Press.

Turner, Victor. 1967. *The forest of symbols*. Ithaca: Cornell University Press.

Upham, Edward. 1829. *The history and doctrines of Buddhism*. London: R. Ackerman, Strand.

Vaiyapuri Pillai, S. 1956. *History of Tamil language and literature*. Madras: New Century Book House.

Vermeseren, M. J. 1966. *The legend of Attis in Greek and Roman art*. Leiden: Brill.

———. 1977. *Cybele and Attis: The myth and the cult*. London: Thames and Hudson.

Warner, Marina. 1976. *Alone of all her sex: The myth and cult of the Virgin Mary*. New York: Knopf.

Warner, W. Lloyd. 1961. *The family of God: A symbolic study of Christian life in America*. New Haven: Yale University Press.

Weber, Max. 1949. "Objectivity" in social science. In *The methodology of the social sciences*, trans. and ed. Edward A. Shils and Henry A. Finch, pp. 49–112. New York: Free Press.

———. 1963. *The sociology of religion*, trans. Ephraim Fischoff. Boston: Beacon Press.

Wheatley, Paul. 1967. *The city as symbol*. London: H. K. Lewis.

Whitehead, Henry. 1921. *Village gods of South India*. Calcutta: Oxford University Press.

Wilson, H. H. 1961. *The Vishnu Purana*, trans. from the Sanskrit by H. H. Wilson. Calcutta: Punthi Pustak (reprint).

Wirz, Paul. 1954. *Exorcism and the art of healing in Ceylon*. Leiden: Brill.

Witt, R. E. 1971. *Isis in the Graeco-Roman world*. Ithaca: Cornell University Press.

Woodcock, George. 1966. *The Greeks in India*. London: Faber and Faber.

———. 1967. *Kerala: A portrait of the Malabar Coast*. London: Faber and Faber.

Yalman, Nur. 1962. The structure of the Sinhalese kindred: A reexamination of the Dravidian terminology. *American Anthropologist* 64:548–75.

———. 1964. The structure of Sinhalese healing rituals. *Journal of Asian Studies* 23: 115–50.

———. 1966. Dual organization in Ceylon. In *Anthropological Studies in Theravada Buddhism*, ed. Manning Nash, pp. 197–223. Cultural Report Series, no. 13. New Haven: Yale University Press.

Yocum, Glenn E. 1982. Ankeliya: A literary-historical approach. In *Religious festivals in South India and Sri Lanka*, ed. Guy R. Welbon and Glenn E. Yocum, pp. 313–29. New Delhi: Manohar.

Zvelebil, Kamil. 1975. *Tamil literature*. Leiden: Brill.

Name Index

Subject Index